Dear West Customer:

West Academic Publishing has changed the look of its American Casebook Series®.

In keeping with our efforts to promote sustainability, we have replaced our former covers with book covers that are more environmentally friendly. Our casebooks will now be covered in a 100% renewable natural fiber. In addition, we have migrated to an ink supplier that favors vegetable-based materials, such as soy.

Using soy inks and natural fibers to print our textbooks reduces VOC emissions. Moreover, our primary paper supplier is certified by the Forest Stewardship Council, which is testament to our commitment to conservation and responsible business management.

The new cover design has migrated from the long-standing brown cover to a contemporary charcoal fabric cover with silver-stamped lettering and black accents. Please know that inside the cover, our books continue to provide the same trusted content that you've come to expect from West.

We've retained the ample margins that you have told us you appreciate in our texts while moving to a new, larger font, improving readability. We hope that you will find these books a pleasing addition to your bookshelf.

Another visible change is that you will no longer see the brand name Thomson West on our print products. With the recent merger of Thomson and Reuters, I am pleased to announce that books published under the West Academic Publishing imprint will once again display the West brand.

It will likely be several years before all of our casebooks are published with the new cover and interior design. We ask for your patience as the new covers are rolled out on new and revised books knowing that behind both the new and old covers, you will find the finest in legal education materials for teaching and learning.

Thank you for your continued patronage of the West brand, which is both rooted in history and forward looking towards future innovations in legal education. We invite you to be a part of our next evolution.

Best regards,

Heidi M. Hellekson
Publisher, West Academic Publishing

CASES AND MATERIALS ON
PATENT LAW
Third Edition

■ ■ ■

By
Martin J. Adelman
Theodore and James Pedas Family Professor of
Intellectual Property and Technology Law
George Washington University

Randall R. Rader
Circuit Judge
United States Court of Appeals for the Federal Circuit
Professorial Lecturer in Law
George Washington University

John R. Thomas
Professor of Law
Georgetown University

AMERICAN CASEBOOK SERIES®

WEST®
A Thomson Reuters business

Mat #40713959

American Casebook Series is a trademark registered in the U.S. Patent and Trademark Office.

© West, a Thomson business, 1998, 2003
© 2009 Thomson Reuters

    610 Opperman Drive
    St. Paul, MN 55123
    1–800–313–9378

Printed in the United States of America

ISBN: 978–0–314–19082–6

TEXT IS PRINTED ON 10% POST CONSUMER RECYCLED PAPER

ACKNOWLEDGMENTS

The authors wish to acknowledge that in the writing of this casebook we have been assisted by many colleagues. Special appreciation is due to individuals who, through classroom use or other contributions, helped improve the book. They are Steve Anzalone, Doug Baldwin, Rebecca Eisenberg, Robert Goldman, Mark Janis, Mike Kaminski, Roberta Morris, Gerald Mossinghoff, Kimberly Pace, John Paul, Kathy White and John Witherspoon. The authors gratefully recognize as well the many students at George Washington University, the United States Patent and Trademark Office Juris Masters Program, the University of Virginia, and Wayne State University who have been subjected to evolving versions of this manuscript. Their suggestions and observations have considerably advanced the efforts reflected in this final version of the book, the culmination of seven years of work on a basic patents text.

The authors also give particular thanks to support shown by their respective institutions, and in particular to their Deans, fellow faculty members and administrators. We gratefully acknowledge support offered by the Max Planck Institute for Foreign and Comparative Patent, Copyright and Competition Law of Munich, Germany, and by Finnegan, Henderson, Farabow, Garrett & Dunner, L.L.P., of Washington, D.C. Particular thanks is also due to Mr. Toyomaro Yoshida of the Institute of Intellectual Property in Tokyo, Japan, and to Dr. Paul Tauchner and his colleagues at Vossius & Partner of Munich, Germany.

Any omissions and errors that remain are, of course, the responsibility of the authors. Readers should also note that this project has been a team effort of four very independent members of the patent community, with portions presenting a strongly held view of one author that is not necessarily shared by the others. Although no single author agrees with all of the points made in this book, we felt compelled to include different points of view in order to offer a complete academic presentation.

*

Summary of Contents

Table of Contents

*

TABLE OF CASES

The principal cases are in bold type. Cases cited or discussed in the text
are roman type. References are to pages. Cases cited in principal
cases and within other quoted materials are not included.

CASES AND MATERIALS ON
PATENT LAW
Third Edition

*

CHAPTER ONE

INTRODUCTION

■ ■ ■

Fueled both by its longstanding traditions and the extraordinary dynamism of the modern innovative community, patent law has risen from an obscure station to take a central place within the intellectual property law. Students taking a first look at patents have come at a good time. In recent years the patent law has become a more robust discipline, enriched by increasingly sophisticated legal and economic analysis; recognized as a key determinant of international trade; and marked by an expansion into a array of disciplines that span the entire range of human endeavor.

Now more than ever, patent law is not merely for technicians. The principles underlying this regime of property rights have a broad, humanistic focus that implicate essential societal goals. At heart these goals attempt to strike a balance between the encouragement of the labors that lead to innovation and the dissemination of the fruits of those labors. As you make your way through the materials that follow, consider whether this elusive balance has been achieved.

§ 1.1 OVERVIEW OF THIS CASEBOOK

Any study of patent law must ultimately focus on the current statute, which since 1952 has been codified as Title 35 of the United States Code. The starting point is patent-eligibility as governed by 35 U.S.C.A. § 101. Chapter 2 of this casebook addresses the precise scope of subject matter covered by patents. Section 101 additionally requires that an invention be "useful" to receive patent protection. Chapter 3 considers this requirement.

Perhaps the core requirement of the law is that a patentable invention must be new. If the invention is *precisely* the same as earlier work in the field eligible to be considered, then the inquiry is ended as to the claim in question: it lacks novelty and is denied patent protection by § 102. Chapters 4, 5, and 6 address the often intricate issues surrounding the novelty requirement under United States law.

Even though the invention may go towards novel subject matter, patentability is denied if the claimed invention is "obvious" to "a person

1

having ordinary skill in the art." The § 103 statutory test for obviousness is judged from the viewpoint of the skilled artisan and denies
patentability if the differences between the subject matter and the prior
art would have rendered the subject matter obvious at the time the
invention was made. The nonobviousness standard is addressed in
Chapter 7.

Unlike some other forms of intellectual property, patents do not
arise without the significant involvement of an administrative agency. In
order to obtain protection, inventors must instead undertake the process
of so-called "patent prosecution" at the United States Patent and Trademark Office, also called the "U.S. PTO" or simply the "PTO." Chapters
8 and 9 consider the requirements of patent applications as to both their
"specifications," the often lengthy description of the technical problem
the inventor faced and the invention produced to solve that problem,
and their "claims," the concise delineations of an invention that serve as
the primary source of proprietary rights. Chapter 10 then reviews the
patent acquisition process itself, along with applicant abuses of the
procedure—so-called "inequitable conduct" and "double patenting"—
and their ramifications.

Once the Patent and Trademark Office grants a patent, its proprietor obtains the right to exclude others practicing the invention in the
United States. Those who make or use the invention without the
authority of the patentee commit patent infringement, a topic addressed
in Chapter 11. Beyond those topics already discussed, Chapter 12
considers additional defenses that accused infringers may raise during
suit. Chapter 13 then addresses available remedies under the United
States patent statute. Finally, Chapter 14 considers specialized legislation, known as the Hatch–Waxman Act, that established distinctive rules
for patents on pharmaceuticals and other regulated products.

As you make your way through this casebook, you will note that it is
comparative. Although certainly a tool designed to teach the patent law of
the United States to the exclusion of that of other nations, this text will
constantly refer to aspects of foreign patent systems as well. Where
tribunals from abroad have provided more compelling reasoning to
support a common legal doctrine, or are certain to have foreshadowed
future developments in the United States, this casebook will unhesitat-
ingly stress their reasoning over that of domestic fora. These comparative studies serve as an insightful focus for grasp of domestic doctrines
and stimulate critical thinking about the array of alternatives which exist
under varying statutory regimes.

A second rationale for the comparative approach is far more
prosaic. In the current technological and economic climate, patent
practitioners without an understanding of the international patent system place their clients at a significant disadvantage. It is not an overstatement to say that no patent attorney in the United States truly
practices domestic patent law in our contemporary, globally-oriented

economy. Further, in recent years, reform of United States patent law has largely been motivated by the global international harmonization movement. Lacking a grasp of the relevant issues and actors from without the United States, a would-be patent attorney will not possess the analytical tools to comprehend future changes domestically.

Another focus of the book is on the *historical development* of patent law doctrines. Although certainly presenting the most current law from the United States Supreme Court, Court of Appeals for the Federal Circuit, United States Patent Office, and foreign sources, this casebook does not neglect their antecedents. Patent law is as much a process as a static entity; the ever-quickening reforms of patent systems worldwide render snapshot views extremely inappropriate. Only an appreciation of the contours of earlier statutes and case law allows students to chart the possibilities of future reform and place older, yet frequently cited precedent, in context. In addition, because patent law has a fundamentally *economic* orientation, this casebook will also offer perspectives from law and economics studies to articulate and explain patent law principles.

With these concentrations in mind, the student can find no better introduction to the patent law than through an historical overview.

§ 1.2 FOUNDATIONS OF THE UNITED STATES PATENT SYSTEM

BONITO BOATS, INC. v. THUNDER CRAFT BOATS, INC.

United States Supreme Court, 1989
489 U.S. 141

O'CONNOR, JUSTICE.

II

Article I, § 8, cl. 8, of the Constitution gives Congress the power "[t]o promote the Progress of Science and useful Arts, by securing for limited Times to Authors and Inventors the exclusive Right to their respective Writings and Discoveries." The Patent Clause itself reflects a balance between the need to encourage innovation and the avoidance of monopolies which stifle competition without any concomitant advance in the "Progress of Science and useful Arts." As we have noted in the past, the Clause contains both a grant of power and certain limitations upon the exercise of that power. Congress may not create patent monopolies of unlimited duration, nor may it "authorize the issuance of patents whose effects are to remove existent knowledge from the public domain, or to restrict free access to materials already available." *Graham v. John Deere Co. of Kansas City*, 383 U.S. 1, 6, 86 S.Ct. 684, 688, 15 L.Ed.2d 545 (1966).

From their inception, the federal patent laws have embodied a careful balance between the need to promote innovation and the recognition that imitation and refinement through imitation are both necessary to invention itself and the very lifeblood of a competitive economy. Soon after the adoption of the Constitution, the First Congress enacted the Patent Act of 1790, which allowed the grant of a limited monopoly of 14 years to any applicant that "hath * * * invented or discovered any useful art, manufacture, * * * or device, or any improvement therein not before known or used." 1 Stat. 109, 110. In addition to novelty, the 1790 Act required that the invention be "sufficiently useful and important" to merit the 14–year right of exclusion. Ibid. Section 2 of the Act required that the patentee deposit with the Secretary of State, a specification and if possible a model of the new invention, "which specification shall be so particular, and said models so exact, as not only to distinguish the invention or discovery from other things before known and used, but also to enable a workman or other person skilled in the art or manufacture * * * to make, construct, or use the same, to the end that the public may have the full benefit thereof, after the expiration of the patent term." Ibid.

The first Patent Act established an agency known by self-designation as the "Commissioners for the promotion of Useful Arts," composed of the Secretary of State, the Secretary of the Department of War, and the Attorney General, any two of whom could grant a patent. Thomas Jefferson was the first Secretary of State, and the driving force behind early federal patent policy. For Jefferson, a central tenet of the patent system in a free market economy was that "a machine of which we were possessed, might be applied by every man to any use of which it is susceptible." 13 WRITINGS OF THOMAS JEFFERSON 335 (Memorial ed. 1904). He viewed a grant of patent rights in an idea already disclosed to the public as akin to an ex post facto law, "obstruct[ing] others in the use of what they possessed before." Id., at 326–327. Jefferson also played a large role in the drafting of our Nation's second Patent Act, which became law in 1793. The Patent Act of 1793 carried over the requirement that the subject of a patent application be "not known or used before the application." Ch. 11, 1 Stat. 318, 319. A defense to an infringement action was created where "the thing, thus secured by patent, was not originally discovered by the patentee, but had been in use, or had been described in some public work anterior to the supposed discovery of the patentee." Id., at 322. Thus, from the outset, federal patent law has been about the difficult business "of drawing a line between the things which are worth to the public the embarrassment of an exclusive patent, and those which are not." 13 WRITINGS OF THOMAS JEFFERSON, supra, at 335.

Today's patent statute is remarkably similar to the law as known to Jefferson in 1793. Protection is offered to "[w]hoever invents or discovers any new and useful process, machine, manufacture, or composition of matter, or any new and useful improvement thereof." 35 U.S.C. § 101. Since 1842, Congress has also made protection available for "any new, original and ornamental design for an article of manufacture." 35

U.S.C. § 171. To qualify for protection, a design must present an aesthetically pleasing appearance that is not dictated by function alone, and must satisfy the other criteria of patentability. The novelty requirement of patentability is presently expressed in 35 U.S.C. §§ 102(a) and (b), which provide:

> A person shall be entitled to a patent unless—
>
> (a) the invention was known or used by others in this country, or patented or described in a printed publication in this or a foreign country, before the invention thereof by the applicant for patent, or
>
> (b) the invention was patented or described in a printed publication in this or a foreign country or in public use or on sale in this country more than one year prior to the date of application for patent in the United States * * *.

Sections 102(a) and (b) operate in tandem to exclude from consideration for patent protection knowledge that is already available to the public. They express a congressional determination that the creation of a monopoly in such information would not only serve no socially useful purpose, but would in fact injure the public by removing existing knowledge from public use. From the Patent Act of 1790 to the present day, the public sale of an unpatented article has acted as a complete bar to federal protection of the idea embodied in the article thus placed in public commerce.

In the case of *Pennock v. Dialogue*, 2 Pet. 1, 7 L.Ed. 327 (1829), Justice Story applied these principles under the patent law of 1800. The patentee had developed a new technique for the manufacture of rubber hose for the conveyance of air and fluids. The invention was reduced to practice in 1811, but letters patent were not sought and granted until 1818. In the interval, the patentee had licensed a third party to market the hose, and over 13,000 feet of the new product had been sold in the city of Philadelphia alone. The Court concluded that the patent was invalid due to the prior public sale, indicating that, "if [an inventor] suffers the thing he invented to go into public use, or to be publicly sold for use" "[h]is voluntary act or acquiescence in the public sale and use is an abandonment of his right." *Id.*, 2 Pet., at 23–24. The Court noted that under the common law of England, letters patent were unavailable for the protection of articles in public commerce at the time of the application, id., at 20, and that this same doctrine was immediately embodied in the first patent laws passed in this country. *Id.*, at 21–22.

As the holding of *Pennock* makes clear, the federal patent scheme creates a limited opportunity to obtain a property right in an idea. Once an inventor has decided to lift the veil of secrecy from his work, he must choose the protection of a federal patent or the dedication of his idea to the public at large. As Judge Learned Hand once put it: "[I]t is a condition upon the inventor's right to a patent that he shall not exploit his discovery competitively after it is ready for patenting; he must content himself with either secrecy or legal monopoly." *Metallizing Engineering Co. v. Kenyon Bearing & Auto Parts Co.*, 153 F.2d 516, 520 (CA2), *cert. denied*, 328 U.S. 840, 66 S.Ct. 1016, 90 L.Ed. 1615 (1946).

In addition to the requirements of novelty and utility, the federal patent law has long required that an innovation not be anticipated by the prior art in the field. Even if a particular combination of elements is "novel" in the literal sense of the term, it will not qualify for federal patent protection if its contours are so traced by the existing technology in the field that the "improvement is the work of the skillful mechanic, not that of the inventor." *Hotchkiss v. Greenwood*, 11 How. 248, 267, 13 L.Ed. 683 (1851). In 1952, Congress codified this judicially developed requirement in 35 U.S.C. § 103, which refuses protection to new developments where "the differences between the subject matter sought to be patented and the prior art are such that the subject matter as a whole would have been obvious at the time the invention was made to a person of ordinary skill in the art to which said subject matter pertains." The nonobviousness requirement extends the field of unpatentable material beyond that which is known to the public under § 102, to include that which could readily be deduced from publicly available material by a person of ordinary skill in the pertinent field of endeavor. *See Graham*, 383 U.S., at 15, 86 S.Ct., at 692. Taken together, the novelty and nonobviousness requirements express a congressional determination that the purposes behind the Patent Clause are best served by free competition and exploitation of either that which is already available to the public or that which may be readily discerned from publicly available material. *See Aronson v. Quick Point Pencil Co.*, 440 U.S. 257, 262, 99 S.Ct. 1096, 1099, 59 L.Ed.2d 296 (1979) ("[T]he stringent requirements for patent protection seek to ensure that ideas in the public domain remain there for the use of the public").

The applicant whose invention satisfies the requirements of novelty, nonobviousness, and utility, and who is willing to reveal to the public the substance of his discovery and "the best mode * * * of carrying out his invention," 35 U.S.C. § 112, is granted "the right to exclude others from making, using, or selling the invention throughout the United States," for a period of [20] years. 35 U.S.C. § 154. The federal patent system thus embodies a carefully crafted bargain for encouraging the creation and disclosure of new, useful, and nonobvious advances in technology and design in return for the exclusive right to practice the invention for a period of years. "[The inventor] may keep his invention secret and reap its fruits indefinitely. In consideration of its disclosure and the consequent benefit to the community, the patent is granted. An exclusive enjoyment is guaranteed him for seventeen years, but upon expiration of that period, the knowledge of the invention inures to the people, who are thus enabled without restriction to practice it and profit by its use." *United States v. Dubilier Condenser Corp.*, 289 U.S. 178, 186–187, 53 S.Ct. 554, 557, 77 L.Ed. 1114 (1933).

The attractiveness of such a bargain, and its effectiveness in inducing creative effort and disclosure of the results of that effort, depend almost entirely on a backdrop of free competition in the exploitation of unpatented designs and innovations. The novelty and nonobviousness requirements of patentability embody a congressional understanding, implicit in the Patent Clause itself, that free exploitation of ideas will be the rule, to which the protection of a federal patent is the exception. Moreover, the ultimate goal of the patent system is to bring new designs and technologies into the public domain through disclosure. State law protection for techniques and designs whose disclosure has already been induced by market rewards may conflict with the very purpose of the patent laws by decreasing the range of ideas available as the building blocks of further innovation. The offer of federal protection from competitive exploitation of intellectual property would be rendered meaningless in a world where substantially similar state law protections were readily available. To a limited extent, the federal patent laws must determine not only what is protected, but also what is free for all to use. Cf. *Arkansas Electric Cooperative Corp. v. Arkansas Public Service Comm'n*, 461 U.S. 375, 384, 103 S.Ct. 1905, 1912, 76 L.Ed.2d 1 (1983) ("[A] federal decision to forgo regulation in a given area may imply an authoritative federal determination that the area is best left un regulated, and in that event would have as much pre-emptive force as a decision to regulate").

NOTES

1. The Dual Grant. Scholars who have studied the aforementioned constitutional provision have concluded that it is really two grants of power rolled into one; first, to establish a copyright system and, second, to establish a patent system. Their conclusions have been that the constitutionally-stated purpose of granting patent rights to inventors for their discoveries is the promotion of progress in the "useful Arts," (1979) (Rich, J.), *cert. granted and appeal dismissed, Diamond v. Bergy, aff'd as to related case sub nom Diamond v. Chakrabarty*, 447 U.S. 303 (1980).

2. Substantive Constitutional Patent Law. An argument is sometimes made that there is a "constitutional" standard of "invention" or that it is "unconstitutional" to have a law such as first-to-file or that a particular case should have a certain outcome to meet a "constitutional" standard. As pointed out by Judge Rich in *Bergy*, "the Constitutional clause . . . neither gave to nor preserved in inventors . . . any rights and set no standards for the patentability of individual inventions; it merely empowered Congress, if it elected to do so, to secure to inventors an 'exclusive right' for an unstated 'limited' time for the stated purpose of promoting useful arts."

3. Promoting Progress. Much effort has been devoted towards the study of whether the patent system actually achieves its stated goal of promoting technology. Suppose an economic researcher is actually able to prove that within a given technological field, the patent system actually hinders technological growth. That is, suppose that given the technological patterns within a particular industry—including, for example, product cycle, barriers to market entry, specialized knowledge required to compete—patents actually contributed to market concentration and decreased innovation. Would the grant of patents in that technological field therefore be unconstitutional?

4. Patent Term. As discussed here in Chapter 12, *Prosecution*, the term of a utility patent is 20 years, measured from the date the inventor filed a patent application. Suppose, however, that Congress chooses to extend the term of patents to say, 150 years each. Would such a term run afoul of the Constitution?

5. Inventorship. Under the United States Constitution, which party may obtain a patent? Suppose an inventor is employed by a corporation, and as part of his employment contract he is obliged to assign ownership of all of his inventions, along with any resulting patents, to his employer. However, the parties suffer a falling out and the inventor refuses to apply for any patents. Under the Constitution, does the employer have any redress? Alternatively, suppose the inventor is deceased or otherwise incapacitated. Does the Constitution allow a patent to issue? The legal concept of inventorship is also addressed here in Chapter 12.

§ 1.3 ORIGINS OF THE PATENT SYSTEM

Legal historians have been quick to seize upon venerable antecedents to our contemporary patent law regime. An ancient Greek system of rewarding cooks for excellent recipes, *see* BRUCE BUGBEE, GENESIS OF AMERICAN PATENT AND COPYRIGHT LAW 166 n.5 (1967), exclusive privileges granted for innovations relating to Tyrolean mines in the Fourteenth Century, SEE ERICH KAUFER, THE ECONOMICS OF THE PATENT SYSTEM (1989), and a Florentine patent granted in 1421, *see* M. Frumkin, *The Origin of Patents*, 27 J. PAT. OFF. SOC'Y 166 (1948), have been variously cited as predecessors to the modern patent law. However, most observers consider legislation enacted on March 19, 1474, by the Venetian Republic as the first true patent statute. *See* Giulio Mandich, *Venentian Patents (1450–1550)*, 30 J. PAT. OFF. SOC'Y 166 (1948). With its requirements that the invention be new, useful, and reduced to practice; provision for a ten-year term; and registration and remedial scheme, the Venetian statute bears a remarkable resemblance to the modern law. By the Seventeenth Century, numerous European states had enacted similar legislation. *See* F.D. Prager, *A History of Intellectual Property From 1545 to 1787*, 26 J. PAT. OFF. SOC'Y 711 (1944). For purposes of the common law world, the most significant of these successors was the English Statute of Monopolies, 21 Jac.1 c. 3 (1624), an important commercial statute of the Jacobean era.

§ 1.3[a] THE STATUTE OF MONOPOLIES

By the start of the Seventeenth Century, the English Crown had a long history of awarding importation franchises and other exclusive rights. But this practice had become subject to abuse during the reigns of Elizabeth I and James I, as favored subjects obtained grants of supervision or control over long-established industries. Parliament responded in 1624 by enacting the Statute of Monopolies. *See* Chris R. Kyle, *'But a New Button to an Old Coat': The Enactment of the Statute of Monopolies*, 19 J. LEGAL HISTORY 203 (1998). Although the Statute was principally designed to proscribe monopolistic grants by the Crown, it did authorize the issuance of "letters patent:"

> [B]e it declared and enacted that any declaration before mentioned shall not extend to any letters patent and grants of privilege for the term of fourteen years or under, hereafter to be made of the sole working or making of any manner of new manufactures within this realm, to the true and first inventors of such manufacture....

This exception in section 6 of the Statute of Monopolies is the foundation of patent law in the common law world.

§ 1.3[b] THE U.S. PATENT SYSTEM

The patent tradition established by the Statute of Monopolies continued in many of the New World colonies. For example, a Connecticut statute of 1672 outlawed the award of monopolies except for "such new inventions as shall be judged profitable for the country and for such time as the general court shall judge meet." As well, many colonial governments granted individuals privileges or rewards for their inventions very early in their histories. *See* Edward C. Walterscheid, *The Early Evolution of United States Patent Law: Antecedents (Part I)*, 78 J. PAT. & TRADEMARK OFF. SOC'Y 615 (1996).

§ 1.3[b][1] THE CONSTITUTION AND EARLY PATENT LAWS

By 1787, state grants of patents were at their zenith, and the delegates to the Constitutional Convention apparently realized the possibility of interstate conflicts among competing inventors. James Madison's first draft of the Constitution, introduced as the Virginia Plan, focused on the structure of national government. 1 MAX FARRAND, RECORDS OF THE FEDERAL CONSTITUTION 20–22 (1911). Due to their concentration on these structural concerns, the delegates turned to discussion of many specific national powers late in the Convention. On August 18, 1787, Charles Pinckney proposed the following powers:

> "To grant patents for useful inventions"

> "To secure to Authors exclusive rights for a certain time"

> "To establish public institutions, rewards and immunities for the promotion of agriculture, commerce, trades and manufactures"

FARRAND, Vol. 2 at 322. On the same day, Madison's records of the Convention show that he himself proposed to grant Congress power:

> "To secure to literary authors their copy rights for a limited time"

> "To encourage by premiums & provisions, the advancement of useful knowledge and discoveries"

FARRAND, Vol. 2 at 325. These proposals featured both exclusive rights and outright subsidies for inventive activity. The Convention referred both sets of proposals to the Committee on Detail for incorporation into the next draft of the Constitution. FARRAND, Vol. 2 at 321, 325.

The limited records of the Constitutional Convention of 1787 suggest that Charles Pinckney was the principal source of the national power to grant patents. *See* BRUCE BUGBEE, THE GENESIS OF AMERICAN PATENT AND COPYRIGHT LAW 127 (1967). Pinckney served in the South Carolina legislature in 1784 during creation of one of the more detailed colonial patent statutes. More important, Pinckney served on the Committee on Detail which received his proposal for creation of a national patent power. FARRAND, Vol. 2 at 322.

On September 5, the Committee on Detail recommended to the Convention the intellectual property language now found in the Constitution. FARRAND, Vol. 2 at 509. No doubt the convention's general inclination against direct national involvement in economic affairs inspired the Committee to limit their clause to exclusive rights alone. The Convention unanimously accepted this language. *Id.*

IN RE BERGY

Court of Customs and Patent Appeals, 1979
596 F.2d 952

RICH, JUDGE.

THE CONSTITUTION

The grant of power to Congress to establish a patent system is in these familiar words of Article I, section 8, clauses 8 and 18:

> (The Congress shall have Power) * * * (8) To promote the Progress of Science and useful Arts, by securing for limited Times to Authors and Inventors the exclusive Right to their respective Writings and Discoveries; * * * (And) (18) To make all Laws which shall be necessary and proper for carrying into Execution the foregoing Powers * * *.

Scholars who have studied this provision, its origins, and its subsequent history, have, from time to time, pointed out that it is really two grants of power rolled into one; first, to establish a copyright system and, second, to establish a patent system. See R. DeWolf, An Outline of Copyright Law 15 (1925); K. Lutz, *Patents and Science. A Clarification of the Patent Clause of the Constitution*, 18 Geo.Wash.L.Rev. 50 (1949); P. Federico, *Commentary on the New Patent Act,* 35 U.S.C.A. § 1 to § 110, 1, 3 (1954); G. Rich, *Principles of Patentability,* 28 Geo.Wash.L.Rev. 393 (1960). Their conclusions have been that the constitutionally-stated purpose of granting patent rights to inventors for their discoveries is the promotion of progress in the "useful Arts," rather than in science. In enacting the 1952 Patent Act, both houses of Congress adopted in their reports this construction of the Constitution in identical words, as follows:

> The background, the balanced construction, and the usage current then and later, indicate that the constitutional provision is really two provisions merged into one. The purpose of the first provision is to promote the progress of Science by securing for limited times To authors the exclusive right to their Writings, the word "science" in this connection having the meaning of knowledge in general, which is one of its meanings today. The other provision is that Congress has the power to promote the Progress of useful arts by securing for limited times to inventors the exclusive right to their Discoveries. The first patent law and all patent laws up to a much later period were entitled "Acts to promote the progress of useful arts."

(H.R.Rep.No.1923, 82d Cong., 2d Sess. 4 (1952); S.Rep.No.1979, 82d Cong., 2d Sess. 3 (1952), U.S.Code Cong. & Admin.News 1952, pp. 2394, 2396.)

It is to be observed that the Constitutional clause under consideration neither gave to nor preserved in inventors (or authors) any rights and set no standards for the patentability of individual inventions; it merely empowered Congress, if it elected to do so, to secure to inventors an "exclusive right" for an unstated "limited" time for the stated purpose of promoting useful arts. We have previously pointed out that the present day equivalent of the term "useful arts" employed by the Founding Fathers is "technological arts." *In re Musgrave,* 431 F.2d 882, 893, 57 CCPA 1352, 1367, 167 U.S.P.Q. 280, 289–90 (1970).

§ 1.3[b][2] THE 1790 AND 1793 ACTS

In his State of the Union address to Congress on January 8, 1790, President George Washington addressed intellectual property:

> The advancement of agriculture, commerce, and manufactures, by all proper means, will not, I trust, need recommendation; but I cannot forbear intimating to you the expediency of giving effectual encouragement, as well to the introduction of new and useful inventions from abroad, as to the exertions of skill and genius in producing them at home.

Patent Act of 1790 created Patent Board of review)

ANNALS OF CONGRESS, 1st Cong., 2d Sess., I, 932–33. Spurred by this reminder and numerous petitions from authors and inventors for special national protection, Congress soon enacted the first patent act. Patent Act of 1790, 1 Stat. 109–112 (April 10, 1790). The Act created a board, known as the "Commissioners for the Promotion of the Useful Arts," authorized to determine whether "the invention or discovery [was] sufficiently useful and important" to deserve a patent. The board consisted of the Secretary of State (Thomas Jefferson), Secretary of War (Henry Knox) and the Attorney General (Edmund Randolph). *See* KENNETH W. DOBYNS, THE PATENT OFFICE PONY: A HISTORY OF THE EARLY PATENT OFFICE (1994).

Patent Act of 1793 switched to registration validity left to courts.

This heroic age of patent law proved short lived, as examination duties proved too onerous for the three-member board. Congress responded by enacting the Patent Act of 1793, Act of Feb. 21, 1793, Ch. 11, 2 Stat. 318, which abandoned patent examination in favor of a registration scheme. Under the 1793 Act, the State Department was assigned the wholly administrative task of maintaining a registry of patents. Whether a registered patent was valid and enforceable was left solely to the courts.

§ 1.3[b][3]   THE 1836 AND 1870 ACTS

Act 1836 restored examination Patent Office

1870 Act - define their interest in a drafted claim

Observing that the registration system of the 1793 Act had sometimes encouraged duplicative and fraudulent patents, Congress restored an examination system with the Patent Act of 1836. Act of July 4, 1836, Ch. 357, 5 Stat. 117. The 1836 Act created a Patent Office within the Department of State and provided for the filing and formal examination of patent applications. The 1870 Act largely maintained the provisions of its predecessor, Act of July 8, 1870, Ch. 230, 16 Stat. 198, but at several points stressed that patentees define their proprietary interest in a distinctly drafted claim. Litigation under these two statutes frequently culminated at the Supreme Court, resulting in opinions that established nonobviousness, enablement, experimental use and other fundamental doctrines of contemporary patent law.

§ 1.3[c]   THE PARIS CONVENTION

National treatment - treat foreign patents as national ones

The foundational patent harmonization treaty, the Paris Convention for the Protection of Industrial Property, was formed in 1884. 13 U.S.T. 25. As of April 15, 2002, 163 nations had signed the Paris Convention. The World Intellectual Property Organization (WIPO), a specialized agency located in Geneva, Switzerland, administers this international agreement (and a number of subsequent instruments addressing intellectual property). The Paris Convention commits its signatories to the principle of national treatment, the principle of patent independence, and a system of international priority. Through the national treatment principle, Paris Convention signatories agree to treat foreign inventors no worse than domestic inventors in their patent laws, so long as these foreign inventors are nationals of a Paris Convention signatory state. Paris Convention, Art. 2.

The Paris Convention also calls for the independence of different national patents. Paris Convention, Art. 4bis. Prior to the Paris Convention, many national laws applied a principle of patent dependence against foreign inventors. As a result, domestic patents would expire at the same time any foreign patent covering the same invention lapsed, regardless of the term the patentee was ordinarily due. These provisions sometimes worked a hardship against inventors who had obtained patent protection in many countries, only to discover that marketing the invention was feasible only in some subset of them. Such an inventor would prefer to let some patent rights lapse rather than incur expensive maintenance fees. In a world where patent rights depended on one another, however, allowing one patent to lapse would amount to a global forfeiture of patent rights.

The independence principle established by the Paris Convention put an end to this situation. One significant consequence of the independence of national patents is that they must be enforced individually. Even different national patent instruments with identically drafted descriptions, drawings and claims do not stand or fall together. A competitor who succeeds in invalidating one national patent may face the prospect of repeating the effort within another set of national borders. Similarly, the successful enforcement of a patent in one forum may simply signal the start of patent litigation elsewhere.

The international priority system allows an inventor to file a patent application in one Paris Convention signatory state, which is usually the inventor's home country. Paris Convention, Art. 4. If the inventor subsequently files patent applications in any other Paris Convention signatory state within the next 12 months, overseas patent-granting authorities will treat the application as if it were filed on the first filing date. Critically, information that enters the public domain between the priority date and subsequent filing dates does not prejudice the later applications. Paris Convention priority allows inventors to preserve their original filing dates as they make arrangements to file patent applications overseas. *See generally* G.H.C. BODENHAUSEN, GUIDE TO THE PARIS CONVENTION FOR THE PROTECTION OF INDUSTRIAL PROPERTY (United International Bureau for the Protection of Intellectual Property, Geneva, Switzerland 1968).

§ 1.3[d] PATENTS IN THE TWENTIETH CENTURY

§ 1.3[d][1] U.S. DEVELOPMENTS

The Depression era, with all its sentiments against monopoly, brought with it a vigorous distrust of patents. Although the United States had a statutory patent system more than a century before a statutory antitrust policy, *see*, Sherman Act, 15 U.S.C.A. § 2, 26 Stat. 209 (July 2, 1890), courts often treated patent licensing and enforcement as antitrust violations. *See, e.g., Hensley Equip. Co. v. Esco Corp.*, 383 F.2d 252 (5th Cir.1967) (license restricting licensee to use of only patented product violated Sherman Act). Additionally, federal courts including the Supreme Court created stricter and stricter tests for sufficient "inventiveness" to qualify for a patent. For example, in 1941, the Supreme Court opined: "[T]he new device [a cordless, pop-out cigarette lighter for cars], however useful it may be, must reveal the flash of creative genius." *Cuno Eng. Corp. v. Automatic Devices Corp.*, 314 U.S. 84 (1941); *see also Great Atlantic & Pacific Tea Co. v. Supermarket Equipment Corp.*, 340 U.S. 147 (1950). As a workable rule of law, this standard creates more questions than answers: How much "flash" and how much "genius" suffices to show invention? How does the federal judiciary detect either the flash or the genius? The venerable Judge Learned Hand gave his pithy assessment of this legal test: "[The inventiveness test is] as fugitive, impalpable, wayward, and vague a phantom as exists in the whole paraphernalia of legal concepts." *Harries v. Air King Prod. Co.*, 183 F.2d 158, 162 (2d Cir.1950).

Thus, following the depression and the world wars, these twin foes of intellectual property—misplaced antitrust priorities and subjective inventiveness tests—eroded the incentives of the patent system. The Supreme Court's propensity to strike down patents in this era reached such proportions that Justice Jackson felt compelled to lament in dissent: "[T]he only patent that is valid is one which this Court has not been able to get its hands on." *Jungersen v. Ostby & Barton Co.*, 335 U.S. 560, 571 (1949). Throughout this era, from the advent of its jurisdiction over appeals from the United States Patent Office in 1929, the Court of Customs and Patent Appeals strove to enunciate a more consistent patent policy. Because it had no jurisdiction to hear appeals from infringement actions in the district courts, however, this court could not influence the regional circuits which marched only to the unsteady drumbeat of the Supreme Court.

World War II forced the United States to innovate and experiment. When the war came to a close, the United State found itself in a position of world economic leadership that called for continued incentives for research and development. Market demands for innovation clashed with the confusion in the courts over enforcement of patent policies. This clash produced the first general reform of the patent system since 1870. The centerpiece of the Patent Act of 1952 replaced the subjective invention test with an objective test for nonobviousness. Drawing on the language from an early Supreme Court case, *see Hotchkiss v. Greenwood*, considered here at Chapter 7, the 1952 Act directed courts to determine patentability by an objective comparison of the claimed invention and the prior art at the time of invention. 35 U.S.C.A. § 103. To preclude subjectivity and hindsight analysis, the Act required this comparison to take place from the vantage point of one of ordinary skill in the art. *Id.*

Over a decade later, the Supreme Court finally construed the pivotal language of the 1952 Act. In a trilogy of 1966 cases, reprinted here in Chapter 7, the Supreme Court applied the § 103 obviousness test as the correct test for patentability. These landmark cases should have closed the book on the amorphous invention test. Unfortunately, another Supreme Court opinion (without the careful reasoning of the 1966 trilogy) revived vestiges of the invention test: "A combination of elements may result in an effect greater than the sum of the several effects taken separately. No such synergistic result is argued here." *Anderson's–Black Rock, Inc. v. Pavement Salvage Co.*, 396 U.S. 57, 61 (1969); *see also Sakraida v. Ag Pro, Inc.*, 425 U.S. 273 (1976). Synergism? The Supreme Court's dicta reawakened the ghosts of the invention test and haunted the regional circuits for years.

Two cases in the United States Court of Appeals for the Ninth Circuit present a microcosm of more than a decade of patent law confusion. These two cases, decided within a week of each other in the same circuit, applied vastly different law and reached vastly different results on patentability. In *Reeves Instr. Corp. v. Beckman Instr., Inc.*, the Ninth Circuit applied § 103 as directed by the Supreme Court's 1966 trilogy. The result was a valid patent for an electronic test circuit for analog computers. 444 F.2d 263 (9th Cir.1971). In *Regimbal v. Scymansky*, the same court applied a vague inventiveness test. The result was an invalid patent on a new hops-picking machine. 444 F.2d 333 (9th Cir.1971). This illustration of confusion within a single circuit magnifies as the lens turns to confusion amongst the circuits in this era.

In 1972, Congress created a Commission on Revision of the Federal Court Appellate System, known as the Hruska Commission after its Chairman, Senator Roman L. Hruska (R. Neb.). The Hruska Commission studied primarily the federal judiciary's difficulty in resolving conflicts amongst regional circuit courts. This subject led the Commission to examine patent law. The Commission's patent law consultants concluded:

> Patentees now scramble to get into the 5th, 6th, and 7th circuits since the courts there are not inhospitable to patents whereas infringers scramble to get anywhere but in these circuits.... [Forum shopping of this magnitude] not only increases litigation costs inordinately and decreases one's ability to advise clients, it demeans the entire judicial process and the patent system as well.

Commission on Revision of the Federal Court Appellate System, Structure, and Internal Procedures: Recommendations for Change, 67 F.R.D. 195 (1975) (Conclusions of Commission's consultants, Professor James B. Gambrell and Donald R. Dunner). Despite this condemnation of patent law chaos, the Hruska Commission advised against the central recommendation for reform—a specialized appeals court for patent cases.

As more years passed without resolution of the central patent law conflicts, economic pressure encouraged reconsideration of appellate court reform. By 1978, the Department of Justice had created a new Office for Improvements in the Administration of Justice (OIAJ) headed by Prof. Daniel J. Meador. After considering several models for reform, OIAJ settled on a plan to merge the Court of Claims and the Court of Customs and Patent Appeals into a single appellate court with national jurisdiction over all patent appeals. This proposal sought to resolve the conflicts and forum shopping in patent law by routing all patent appeals to a single court of appeals. This court of appeals would fashion a uniform patent policy, subject to appeal to the Supreme Court.

On March 15, 1979, the Chairman of the Senate Judiciary Committee, Edward M. Kennedy, introduced the OIAJ bill. The bill, S. 1477, passed the Senate before the close of the 96th Congress, but—due to the addition of a controversial amendment unrelated to the court reform proposal—did not pass the House. In the 97th Congress, the legislative process began anew. A few lawmakers expressed concerns that a specialized court might foster legal doctrines out of the mainstream of American jurisprudence or might fall captive to a narrow segment of the bar. This resistance gained little momentum for reasons mentioned in the House Judiciary Committee Report:

> [T]he bill creates a new intermediate appellate court markedly less specialized than either of its predecessors and provides the judges of the new court with a breadth of jurisdiction that rivals in its variety that of the regional circuits.

H.R. Rep. No. 312, 97th Cong., 1st Sess. 19 (1981). Indeed the final version of the organic act for the Federal Circuit provided jurisdiction over more than ten categories of appeals, ranging from patents to customs to taxes to government contracts and more. 28 U.S.C.A. § 1295. Finally, on April 2, 1982, President Ronald Reagan signed into law the Federal Courts Improvements Act of 1982.

Immediately after formation, the Court of Appeals for the Federal Circuit adopted the law of its predecessor courts as binding precedent for its cases as well. *South Corp. v. United States*, 690 F.2d 1368 (Fed.Cir. 1982). Thus the decisions of the Court of Customs and Patent Appeals continued to bind the Federal Circuit. In other respects, however, the advent of the Federal Circuit changed significantly the decisional process for patent policy. For instance, the old Court of Customs and Patent Appeals—a five-judge body—always sat *en banc*. Thus later decisions always controlled any contrary earlier pronouncements. *In re Gosteli*, 872 F.2d 1008, 1011 (Fed.Cir.1989). The Federal Circuit, with up to 12 judges, rarely sits *en banc*. When it does sit *en banc*, of course, it has authority to overrule any prior ruling of the Federal Circuit or its predecessor courts. When sitting, as it customarily does, in three-judge panels, however, the Federal Circuit lacks authority to depart from decisions of earlier panels. The court in *Newell Companies, Inc. v. Kenney Mfg. Co.*, 864 F.2d 757, 765 (Fed.Cir.1988), explained: "This court has adopted the rule that prior decisions of a panel of the court are binding precedent on subsequent panels unless and until overturned in banc. Where there is direct conflict, the precedential decision is the first."

The creation of the Federal Circuit was the first major structural change in the federal appellate system since creation of the regional circuits in 1891. The confusion in patent law reached such proportions in the late 1960s and 1970s that only a structural change of this magnitude would correct the problem. Since its creation, the Federal Circuit has sought to bring uniformity and predictability to patent law. Much of this text tests the success of that venture.

More recently, Congress enacted significant substantive and procedural changes to U.S. patent law via the American Inventors Protection Act of 1999. Pub. L. No. 106–113, 113 Stat. 1501 (Nov. 29, 1999). Among the innovations of the AIPA were the creation of an infringement defense to first inventors of business methods later patented by another; the extension of patent term in the event of processing delays at the PTO; the mandate for publication of certain pending patent applications; and the provision of optional *inter partes* reexamination procedures.

As this book goes to press, discussion of even more dramatic reform continues in the 110th Congress. The proposed Patent Reform Act of 2007 arguably would work the most sweeping reforms to the U.S. patent system since the nineteenth century. Among the more notable of these proposed changes are a shift to a first-inventor-to-file priority system; a requirement that most inventors conduct a prior art search prior to filing a patent application, substantive and procedural modifications to the patent law doctrines of inequitable conduct and willful infringement; amendment of the best mode, venue, and damages statutes; and adoption of post-grant review proceedings. These legislative reform efforts appear likely to continue into the 111th Congress. For more on the ongoing patent reform effort, see John R. Thomas & Wendy H. Schacht, *Patent Reform in the 110th Congress: Innovation Issues*, CRS Report for Congress (Jan. 10, 2008).

§ 1.3[d][2]　WORLD PATENT HARMONIZATION

Following World War II, global changes to the international patent system have proceeded at an accelerated pace. Numerous new treaties followed the Paris Convention now provide inventors with a network of global rights. Among the most significant of these treaties resulted from discussion of a uniform patent system for the then-emerging European Economic Community. Following adoption of a uniform patent classification system, European states agreed to the 1963 Convention on the Unification of Certain Points of Substantive Law on Patents for Inventions. This so-called "Strasbourg Convention" set forth certain common substantive patent law principles, and formed the cornerstone of the European Patent Convention (EPC) to follow a decade later.

In addition to mandating uniform patent-eligibility criteria for member states, the EPC establishes a single patent-granting authority, the European Patent Office. The EPC therefore allows an applicant to file a single patent application at the European Patent Office which may mature into a number of individual national patents. The EPC does not displace individual national patent regimes, but exists alongside them as an alternative route to obtaining intellectual property protection. The regional model of the EPC has been emulated to some degree by contracting states in Africa and the former Soviet Union.

The United States was not entirely idle during this period of European harmonization. As something of a reaction to these efforts, the United States took a leadership position in establishing the Patent Cooperation Treaty (PCT). This treaty was ultimately formed in 1970 by representatives of world patent offices in Washington, D.C., and is open to any country which has joined the Paris Convention. Drafters of the PCT took account for the burden of duplicative patent examination proceedings in many different countries. The PCT allows certain portions of patent acquisition efforts to be completed in a single patent office and applied elsewhere, which should streamline efforts elsewhere.

Subsequently, both the North American Free Trade Agreement (NAFTA) and the Trade–Related Aspects of Intellectual Property of the World Trade Organization (TRIPS Agreement) have provided several further measures of substantive reform. NAFTA sets minimal requirements for a substantive patent law among its signatory nations. The TRIPS Agreement provides even more significant reform, both in the scope of its substantive measures and the breadth of its signatories. The treaty provides uniform legal standards for patentability in every significant aspect of a modern patent system, and further sets forth a patent term of twenty years from the filing date, as well as exclusionary rights conferred to the holder of the patent. Most of these requirements conform with prevailing United States standards.

The TRIPS Agreement is one of the most important commercial treatises in modern history. It revolutionized the treatment of intellectual property in the signatory countries. It requires, for example, that India, a country which has had a weak intellectual property regime essentially since independence, adopt a modern strong system of protection that includes protection for pharmaceutical compounds.

Future multilateral harmonization appears likely at this point, albeit the precise vehicle for achieving this result cannot be named easily. In the early 1990's, the so-called "Patent Law Treaty" or "Basic Proposal" of the World Intellectual Property Organization (WIPO) appeared the most likely prospect for future reform. The Basic Proposal contained numerous substantive provisions regarding patent law reform, although in some aspects this treaty was less comprehensive than the TRIPS Agreement. Unlike the TRIPS Agreement, however, it did contain significant measures with respect to claim interpretation and the doctrine of equivalents. *See* Harold C. Wegner, Patent Harmonization (1993). The shifted emphasis upon the TRIPS Agreement as the primary intellectual property treaty, in combination with a rather abrupt announcement by the United States concerning its continuing support of a first-to-invent system, suspended negotiation at WIPO. Efforts have continued on various WIPO-based international agreements on the patent law.

Recent Free Trade Agreements [FTAs] to which the United States is a signatory have also incorporated increasingly elaborate provisions concerning the patent law. With the Bipartisan Trade Promotion Act of 2002, Pub. L. No. 107–210, 116 Stat. 993 (2002), Congress stated that an overall negotiating objective of such agreements was to encourage our treaty partners to agree to "a standard of [intellectual property] protection similar to that found in United States law." 19 U.S.C. § 3802(b)(4)(A)(i)(II) (2006). In keeping with this mandate, the United States has entered into numerous FTAs that have required their signatories to conform to stipulated standards of patent protection. *See generally Free Trade Agreements: US Strategies and Priorities* (Jeffery J. Schott, ed., 2004). Because the FTAs are drafted in a manner that complies with current U.S. law, their effect is to obligate U.S. treaty partners to amend their patent laws to match or resemble those of the United States.

Another international agreement, exclusively for the states of Europe, consists of the Luxembourg Community Patent Convention (CPC). The CPC provides for a true European patent, in that one administrative agency would issue a single patent effective in every signatory nation. Additionally, patent litigation fora are limited to certain national courts, a Common Appeal Court and the European Court of Justice. The CPC had such a strong start in 1975 that commentators offered varyingly optimistic predictions of the date it would come into effect, all of which have long since passed. Despite several subsequent diplomatic conferences held to promote the treaty, some European nations still have not ratified it, and possibilities for future action are uncertain. *See* Joseph Straus, The Present State of the Patent System in the European Union (1997); Kara M. Bonitatibus, *infra* at p. 902, note 4.

§ 1.4   FORMS OF PATENT PROTECTION

§ 1.4[a]   UTILITY PATENTS

When lay persons use the term "patent," they are most often referring to the intellectual property right more technically known as a "utility patent." Utility patents are the usual sort of patent, pertaining generally to technological products and processes. Utility patents are governed by the Patent Act of 1952, codified in Title 35 of the U.S. Code.

Utility patent rights do not arise automatically. Inventors must prepare and submit applications to the U.S. Patent and Trademark

Office ("PTO") if they wish to obtain utility patent protection. 35 U.S.C. § 111. PTO officials known as examiners then assess whether the application merits the award of a utility patent. 35 U.S.C. § 131.

In deciding whether to approve a utility patent application, a PTO examiner will consider whether the submitted application fully discloses and distinctly claims the invention. 35 U.S.C. § 112. The examiner will also determine whether the invention itself fulfills certain substantive standards set by the Patent Act of 1952. To be patentable, an invention must be useful, novel, and nonobvious. The requirement of usefulness, or utility, is satisfied if the invention is operable and provides a tangible benefit. 35 U.S.C. § 101. To be judged novel, the invention must not be fully anticipated by a prior patent, publication, or other knowledge within the public domain. 35 U.S.C. § 102. A nonobvious invention must not have been readily within the ordinary skills of a competent artisan at the time the invention was made. 35 U.S.C. § 103.

If the PTO allows the utility patent to issue, the proprietor obtains the right to exclude others from making, using, selling, offering to sell, or importing into the United States the patented invention. 35 U.S.C. § 271(a). These rights are not self-enforcing. A patentee bears responsibility for monitoring its competitors to determine whether they are using the patented invention or not. Patent proprietors who wish to compel others to observe their intellectual property rights must usually commence litigation in the federal courts.

The maximum term of utility patent protection is ordinarily set at 20 years from the date the application is filed. 35 U.S.C. § 154(a)(2). The patent applicant gains no enforceable rights until such time as the application is approved for issuance as a granted patent, however. Once the utility patent expires, others may employ the patented invention without compensation to the patentee.

The following example should provide a sense of the modern utility patent instrument. As you review this document, consider the extent to which it provides the following information to members of the technological community:

- A detailed technical description of the invention.
- The extent to which the disclosed technology is regarded as proprietary.
- The basis for the examiner's decision that the patented invention presents a patentable advance over previously known technology.
- The term of the patent.
- An individual who can be contacted for purposes of licensing or obtaining further technical information.

United States Patent [19]

Klumpjan

[11]	Patent Number: **5,190,351**
[45]	Date of Patent: **Mar. 2, 1993**

[54] **WHEELBARROW FOR TRANSPORTING ROCKS AND STONES**

[76] Inventor: **Joe Klumpjan,** 1334 Sunset Dr. Rte. 3, Campbellsport, Wis. 53010

[21] Appl. No.: **825,881**

[22] Filed: **Jan. 27, 1992**

[51] Int. Cl.⁵ B62B 1/24
[52] U.S. Cl. 298/3; 280/47.31
[58] Field of Search 280/47.31, 47.33, 47.23; 298/2, 3

[56] **References Cited**

U.S. PATENT DOCUMENTS

48,101	6/1865	Sanford	298/3
480,670	8/1892	Radley et al.	298/2
642,569	2/1900	Baklund	280/47.31
817,677	4/1906	Smith	280/47.23
845,207	2/1907	Tripp	280/47.3
868,462	10/1907	Lorenzi	280/47.23
1,232,387	7/1917	Parker	298/3
1,305,106	5/1919	Hofer	280/47.23
1,479,223	1/1924	Carroll	280/47.33
1,544,769	7/1925	Nalder	298/3
1,754,835	4/1930	Newton	298/2
2,234,879	3/1941	Shoesmith	298/3
2,608,360	8/1952	Cootware	280/47.3
2,852,304	9/1958	Harrison	298/3
2,889,152	6/1959	Hurst et al.	280/47.31
3,092,418	6/1963	Themascus	298/3

FOREIGN PATENT DOCUMENTS

537556	5/1955	Belgium	298/2
436020	10/1935	United Kingdom	298/3

Primary Examiner—David M. Mitchell
Attorney, Agent, or Firm—Andrus, Sceales, Starke & Sawall

[57] **ABSTRACT**

A wheelbarrow has an enlarged wheel and a low center of gravity for transporting heavy loads. The enlarged wheel and low center of gravity increases the stability of the wheelbarrow. The wheelbarrow includes a payload bucket which is tiltable for dumping the payload. The bucket is mounted such that the dumping operation is behind the wheel of the wheelbarrow, whereby the dumping operation can be completed without substantially altering the center of gravity of the wheelbarrow, further enhancing the stability of the wheelbarrow when transporting heavy loads. The wheelbarrow bucket includes an arcuate or C-shaped bottom facilitating the dumping operation.

3 Claims, 1 Drawing Sheet

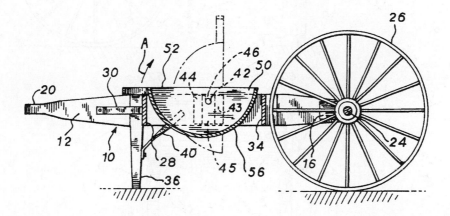

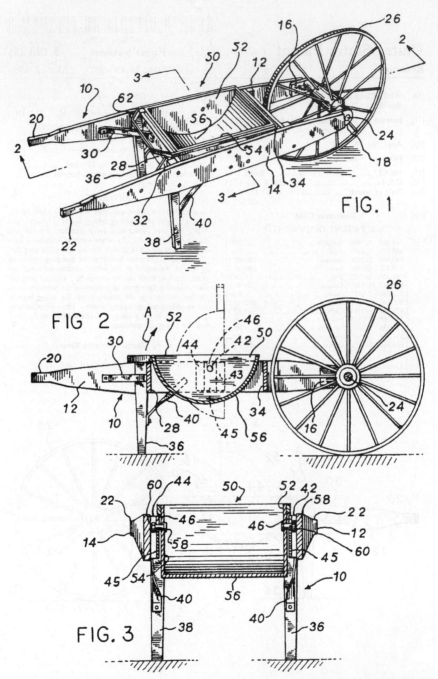

FIG. 1

FIG 2

FIG. 3

5,190,351

1

WHEELBARROW FOR TRANSPORTING ROCKS AND STONES

BACKGROUND OF THE INVENTION

1. Field of the Invention

This invention is generally related to wheelbarrows and is specifically directed to a wheelbarrow for transporting rocks and stones.

2. Description of the Prior Art

Wheelbarrows are well known. However, the wheelbarrows of the prior art are generally designed for general purpose use such as, by way of example, the wheelbarrow disclosed in U.S. Pat. No. 868,462 issued to L. Lorenzi on Oct. 15, 1907. There have also been a number of wheelbarrows designed for specific use such as the wheelbarrow of U.S. Pat. No. 642,569 issued to G. Baklund on Feb. 6, 1900. The Baklund wheelbarrow is specifically designed to carry milk cans and the like.

U.S. Pat. No. 1,479,223 issued to G. Carroll on Jan. 1, 1924 also discloses a wheelbarrow specifically designed for carrying cans but adaptable for general purpose use as well.

U.S. Pat. No. 845,207 issued to C. Tripp on Feb. 26, 1907 discloses a wheelbarrow adapted for carrying unusually large and heavy objects wherein the object such as a barrel is self-leveling and the wheelbarrow has an enlarged wheel to provide better stability.

U.S. Pat. No. 1,754,835 issued to H. B. Newton on Apr. 15, 1930 also discloses a large wheeled wheelbarrow for better distribution of weight when hauling heavy objects.

It is also known to provide dumping wheel barrows as shown, for example, in U.S. Pat. Nos. 1,544,769 issued to G. Nalder on Jul. 7, 1925; 2,234,879 issued to H. Shoesmith on Mar. 11, 1941; 2,852,304 issued to L. E. Harrison on Sep. 16, 1958; and 3,092,418 issued to J. Themascus on Jun. 4, 1963. One of the problems with each of the dumping wheelbarrows of the prior art is the weight is generally distributed above and in substantial vertical alignment with the axis of the wheel, making the wheelbarrow unstable when carrying heavy loads.

U.S. Pat. No. 1,232,387 issued to I. Parker on Jul. 3, 1917 discloses a self-leveling wheelbarrow having a pivotable bucket. However, there is not sufficient clearance between the wheelbarrow and the wheel or other frame members to provide for dumping.

None of the wheelbarrows of the prior art are specifically directed to a transportation device for picking and hauling small stones and rocks from fields which are to be tilled for growing crops. In many regions of the country such as, by way of example, northern New England and Wisconsin and other areas where prehistoric glacier movements deposited large amounts of rubble just beneath the surface and the top soil, small rocks and stones surface with each spring thaw. This provides a continuing problem when preparing fields for planting at the beginning of each growing season. Typically, the rocks and stones must be physically and manually removed from the field before tilling in order to minimize damage to plow shares and the like. Even with the development of modern mechanized equipment for preparing fields, rock and stone removal still remains a substantially manual operation. Often this is accomplished by manually taking a wheelbarrow and a rock fork to the field and physically placing the rocks and stones in the wheelbarrow for transportation to a

2

dump site. However, heretofore there have been no wheelbarrows specifically designed for this purpose. The wheelbarrows are either unstable under heavy load, difficult to manipulate, or are not well designed for the heavy loads and weight distribution generated during the rock picking activity. This requires that the wheelbarrow be used to carry lighter loads, increasing the number of trips and the amount of labor and time required to complete the task.

SUMMARY OF THE INVENTION

The subject invention is specifically directed to a wheelbarrow for picking and removing rocks from tillable fields. The wheelbarrow has a substantially oversized wheel supported on a sturdy frame. The payload bucket is supported on a plane substantially horizontal to the axis of the wheel and is adapted to be pivoted or tilted behind the wheel for dumping the rocks without disturbing the stability of the wheelbarrow. In the preferred embodiment of the invention, the bucket may be removed from the frame by lifting it out of the support channels. The handle for tilting the bucket also serves as the primary support member for supporting the bucket in a normally open, upright position during use. The axle, pivot bucket supports and handles are on a common line, minimizing back strain when lifting large loads.

The wheelbarrow has been found to be particularly well suited for removing rocks and stones from tillable fields. The enlarged wheel provides easy manipulation of the wheelbarrow and increases stability. The low center of gravity of the load increases stability and maneuverability of the wheelbarrow for this task. The low, in-line handles permit easy handling of substantially heavy loads with a minimum of back strain.

It is, therefore, an object and feature of the subject invention to provide for a wheelbarrow which is specifically designed for removing rocks and stones from tillable fields.

It is also an object and feature of the subject invention to provide for a wheelbarrow with a low center of gravity to provide stability in handling heavy loads.

It is a further object and feature of the subject invention to provide for a tiltable wheelbarrow wherein the payload is supported below the axle of the wheel, increasing stability of the wheelbarrow when transporting a heavy payload.

Other objects and features of the invention will be readily apparent from the accompanying drawings and detailed description of the preferred embodiment.

BRIEF DESCRIPTION OF THE DRAWINGS

FIG. 1 is a perspective view of a wheelbarrow made in accordance with the subject invention.

FIG. 2 is a section view of the wheelbarrow taken generally along the line 2—2 of FIG. 1.

FIG. 3 is a section view of the wheelbarrow taken generally along the line 3—3 of FIG. 1.

DETAILED DESCRIPTION OF THE PREFERED EMBODIMENT

The wheelbarrow of the subject invention is shown in FIG. 1 and includes a rigid frame 10 made of wood, steel, or other suitable material. In the preferred embodiment, the frame 10 includes two enlongated side rails 12 and 14 having an axis support such as the brackets 16, 18 at one end of the respective side rails 12, 14

5,190,351

3

and terminating in handles **20, 22** at the opposite end of respective side rails **12, 14**. An axle **24** is supported between the brackets **16** and **18** for rotatably supporting the hubbed wheel **26**. A cross brace **28** secures the side rails **12** and **14** in spaced apart relationship. In the preferred embodiment, a pair of angle brackets **30** and **32** are provided and are suitably secured to the respective side rails **12** and **14** and to the cross brace **28** to increase rigidity of the construction. Also, a second cross brace **34** may be provided just behind the wheel **26** to further increase rigidity of the assembly. In the preferred embodiment, the support legs **36** and **38** are mounted between the cross brace **28** and the respective side rails **12** and **14**. An angle bracket **40** may be attached to each leg **36, 38** and to the respective side rail **12, 14** to further increase the rigidity of the assembly.

In the preferred embodiment of the invention, a pair of support brackets **42** and **44** are secured, one each, to the respective side rails **12** and **14**. As is best shown in FIG. **2**, each support bracket includes a pair of outer base plates **43** and **44** which are secured directly to the respective side rail. The center panel of the bracket includes a raised or spaced plate **45** (see FIG. **3**) which includes a U-shaped channel **46**. The bucket **50** of the wheelbarrow includes a pair of outer side walls **52** and **54**. In the preferred embodiment, the side walls have an arcuate lower edge and a continuous, rounded bottom wall **56** as suitably secured thereto to make an arcuate bucket. Each side wall **52, 54** of the bucket includes a projecting mounting post **58** projecting outwardly from the side wall and having a smooth cylindrical surface adapted to be received in the U-shaped channel **46** of the respective mounting bracket **42, 44** on the side rails **12, 14**. Each mounting post **58** includes an enlarged outer head **60** to assure that the bucket does not inadvertently slip from the mounting brackets. A handle **62** is secured to the rear edge of the bucket **50** and extends toward the wheelbarrow handles **20** and **22**. The handle **62** facilitates in dumping or tilting the bucket, as indicated by arrow A in FIG. **2** and also provides the stop or support member for supporting the bucket in its normal position, by resting on the cross brace **28**.

In the preferred embodiment, the wheel **26** of the wheel barrow is approximately 30 inches in diameter, greatly increasing the stability of the wheelbarrow over the prior art, particularly when carrying substantially heavy loads such as rocks and stones. Also, as can be seen in FIG. **2**, the bucket **50** can be moved to the dump position without substantially altering the center of gravity of the load, further increasing the stability of the wheel barrow during a stone picking and removal operation. In addition, where desired, the bucket may be removed from the frame of the wheelbarrow by simply lifting the bucket and sliding the posts **58** upwardly in the U-shaped channels on the mounting brackets **42, 44**. The arcuate bottom **56** of the bucket greatly facilitates in a dumping operation by permitting the stones to roll

4

or slide out of the bucket without substantially altering the center of gravity during the dumping operation.

The wheelbarrow of the present invention is ideally suited for carrying heavy payloads and is particularly well suited for removing rocks and stones from tillable fields. While specific objects and features of the subject invention have been disclosed in detail herein, it will be readily understood that the invention encompasses all modifications and enhancements within the scope and spirit of the following claims.

I claim:

1. A wheelbarrow for transporting rocks and stones, comprising:

  a. a frame having two elongated, spaced side rails, each with opposite ends, one end of each rail defining a handle and the other end of each rail defining a forward axle support, and at least one cross brace spanning the spaced side rails and securing them in rigid assembly;

  b. an axle mounted in the axle supports;

  c. a wheel mounted on said axle for rotation relative to said frame, wherein the wheel is of a minimum diameter of 30 inches;

  d. a pair of mounting brackets, one each mounted on each side rail intermediately of the opposite ends;

  e. a box having a semicylindrical closed bottom, upstanding side walls having a C-shaped bottom edge and an open top, said box including a pair of axially aligned pivot posts extending from said side walls forwardly of the axis of said semicylindrical bottom to position the center of gravity of said box rearwardly of the axis of said pivot posts, each post adapted to be removably received in one of said brackets for tiltably supporting the box relative to said frame, whereby the box is movable between an upwardly opening filling position with the forward edge of the open top positioned rearwardly of the wheel and a dump position in which the contents of the box are discharged to the rear of the wheel, and wherein said cross brace defines a support for holding the box in the filling position; and

  f. a support secured to and extending downwardly from said frame between the handles and the box for supporting the frame and the box above the ground.

2. The wheelbarrow of claim **1** further including a handle mounted on the continuous member adjacent one end and adapted for engaging the cross-brace when the box is in the normal position.

3. The wheelbarrow of claim **2**, wherein the side rails are substantially parallel and the side walls of the box are substantially parallel to the side rails, each mounting bracket further including a substantially U-shaped channel with an open upper end and wherein each post is of cylindrical cross-section, whereby the post may be rotated relative to the base for moving the box from the normal position to the dump position.

    *   *   *   *   *

§ 1.4[b]   DESIGN PATENTS

Title 35 of the United States Code provides for design patents in a short series of provisions codified at §§ 171–173. Design patents may be awarded for "any new, original and ornamental design for an article of manufacture." 35 U.S.C. § 171. The surface ornamentation, configuration, or shape of an object form the most typical subjects of design patents. The design may be patented only if it is embodied in an article of manufacture, such as furniture, tools, or athletic footwear. The chief limitation on the patentability of designs is that they must be primarily ornamental in character. If the design is dictated by the performance of the article, then it is judged "primarily functional" and ineligible for design patent protection. *See Best Lock Corp. v. Ilco Unican Corp.*, 94 F.3d 1563 (Fed.Cir.1996).

An inventor must file an application at the PTO in order to obtain design patent protection. Design patents are generally subject to all provisions applicable to utility patents, including originality and novelty. The design must also fulfill the requirement of nonobviousness, which is judged from the perspective of "the designer of ordinary capability who designs articles of the type presented in the application." *In re Nalbandian*, 661 F.2d 1214 (CCPA 1981). If the application matures into an issued design patent, the resulting design patent instrument is relatively straightforward. It principally consists of one or more drawings illustrating the proprietary design. The term of a design patent is fourteen years. 35 U.S.C. § 173.

§ 1.4[c]   PLANT PATENTS

The availability of utility patents for plants was for many years the subject of legal uncertainty. Congress responded by enacting the Townsend–Purcell Plant Patent Act. Act of May 23, 1930, 46 Stat. 376. This statute allows a plant patent to issue for distinct and new varieties of plants that have been asexually reproduced. Asexual reproduction results in a plant that is genetically identical to its parent. 35 U.S.C. § 161. Typical asexual reproduction techniques include grafting, budding, the use of cuttings, layering, and other methods. Plants that are produced through seeds, which involves sexual reproduction, are excluded. Also excluded from the Plant Patent Act are tuberpropagated plants or plants found in an uncultivated state. *Id.*

The acquisition and enforcement of plant patents is accomplished in a manner very similar to utility patents. Plant patents are issued by the PTO provided that the novelty and nonobviousness requirements are met. Applicants must submit an application featuring color drawings that disclose all the distinctive characteristics of the plant capable of visual representation. If approved, a plant patent enjoys a term of twenty years from the date of filing. Plant patents are infringed if another asexually reproduces the plant, or uses or sells the plant so reproduced. 35 U.S.C. § 163.

For more details on plant patents, see *J.E.M. AG Supply, Inc. v. Pioneer Hi–Bred International, Inc.,* 534 U.S. 124 (2001); and *Imazio Nursery, Inc. v. Dania Greenhouses,* 69 F.3d 1560 (Fed.Cir.1995).

§ 1.4[d] PATENT–LIKE PLANT VARIETY PROTECTION

Another intellectual property possibility for plants is the Plant Variety Protection Act, or PVPA. This statute may be found in 7 U.S.C. § 2321 and subsequent sections. The PVPA allows the United States to comply with the International Convention for the Protection of New Varieties of Plants, an agreement the United States joined in 1981. The PVPA provides for the issuance of plant variety protection certificates that act similarly to utility and plant patents. Plant variety protection certificates exclusively pertain to sexually reproduced plants, however, including most seed-bearing plants. Fungi and bacteria are ineligible for certification. The plant must be clearly distinguishable from known varieties and stable, in that its distinctive characteristics must breed true with a reasonable degree of reliability. 7 U.S.C. § 2402(a).

A key distinction between the plant patent and plant variety protection regimes is the manner in which the inventor has reproduced the protected plant. Asexual reproduction, which results in a plant genetically identical to its parent, forms the basis of plant patent protection. Certification under the PVPA instead depends upon sexual reproduction, which results in a distinct plant that combines the characteristics of its parents.

Unlike utility and plant patents, which are issued by the PTO, plant variety protection certificates are administered by the Department of Agriculture. To be entitled to a certificate, the plant must be new, distinct, uniform, and stable. If allowed to issue by the Department of Agriculture, the term of a plant variety protection certificate is twenty years (twenty-five years for trees and vines). 7 U.S.C. § 2483(b). The holder of a plant variety certificate obtains the right to "exclude others from selling the variety, or offering it for sale, or reproducing it, importing, or exporting it, or using it in producing (as distinguished from developing) a hybrid or different variety therefrom." 7 U.S.C. § 2483(a).

An important distinction between the utility and plant patents, on one hand, and plant variety protection certificates, on the other, is the availability of two infringement exemptions under the PVPA. The PVPA includes an exemption that broadly states that the "use and reproduction of a protected variety for plant breeding or other bona fide research shall not constitute an infringement." 7 U.S.C. § 2544. In addition, the PVPA grants farmers the right to plant new crops of seeds descended from protected seeds that were legitimately purchased. 7 U.S.C. § 2543. In contrast, neither the utility nor the plant patent statutes contain these exemptions. Such activities may constitute infringements that may expose researchers and farmers to legal liability, including damages and an injunction.

§ 1.5   THE NATURE AND FUNCTION OF THE PATENT SYSTEM

§ 1.5[a]   ECONOMIC RATIONALES

The literature relating the patent system to economic theory is enormous. Perhaps the most complete review of the various theories regarding patents was prepared by Professor Fritz Machlup of Johns Hopkins University and published as Subcomm. on Patents, Trademarks, and Copyrights, & Senate Comm. on the Judiciary, 85th Cong., 2d Sess., An Economic Review of the Patent System (Comm. Print 1958). The following passage comprises a contemporary overview of some of the most current economic theories relating to patents written by Professor Rebecca S. Eisenberg.

§ 1.5[a][1]

SELECTIONS FROM REBECCA S. EISENBERG, PATENTS AND THE PROGRESS OF SCIENCE: EXCLUSIVE RIGHTS AND EXPERIMENTAL USE

56 U. Chi. L. Rev. 1017 (1989)

The United States Constitution posits an instrumental justification for patents, allowing Congress to enact patent legislation for the specific purpose of promoting scientific progress.[1] In analyzing how patents promote scientific progress, the courts have emphasized two mechanisms: first, the prospect of obtaining a patent monopoly provides an incentive to invest in research to make new inventions; and second, the patent system promotes disclosure of new inventions and thereby enlarges the public storehouse of knowledge.[2] Both of these theories have been elaborated and challenged in the economics literature.[3]

---

1.   U.S. Const., Art. I, § 8, cl. 8. This instrumental justification is distinct from moral arguments for patent protection advanced in some European countries, notably France, in the nineteenth century, such as the argument that inventors have a natural property right in their ideas that society is morally obligated to recognize. *See generally* Fritz Machlup and Edith Penrose, *The Patent Controversy in the Nineteenth Century*, 10 J. Econ. Hist. 1, 10–20 (1950). The framers of the United States Constitution rejected the notion that inventors have a natural property right in their inventions. Thus Thomas Jefferson wrote:

Inventions then cannot, in nature, be a subject of property. Society may give an exclusive right to the profits arising from them, as an encouragement to men to pursue ideas which may produce utilities, but this may or may not be done according to the will and convenience of society, without claim or complaint from anybody.

See Walter Hamilton, Investigation of Concentration of Economic Power: Patents & Free Enterprise 21 (TNEC Monograph No. 31) (GPO, 1941) (quoting Thomas Jefferson).

2.   *Kewanee Oil Co. v. Bicron*, 416 U.S. 470, 480–81 (1974).

3.   A third theory, that patents promote "innovation" or investment in the commercial development of inventions, has been advanced by some commentators but has received little attention from the courts.

1. INCENTIVE TO INVENT.

The incentive to invent theory holds that too few inventions will be made in the absence of patent protection because inventions once made are easily appropriated by competitors of the original inventor who have not shared in the costs of invention.[4] If successful inventions are quickly imitated by free riders, competition will drive prices down to a point where the inventor receives no return on the original investment in research and development.[5] As a result, the original inventor may be unable to appropriate enough of the social value of the invention to justify the initial research and development expenditures.[6] The high risk involved in research compounds the likelihood of underinvestment in invention.[7] Thus inventions with potentially great social benefits might never come about, or at least might be significantly delayed, unless private returns to invention were increased above their free market levels. Patents serve to bring the private benefits of inventions in line with their social value by allowing inventors to use their monopoly positions to extract a price that more closely approaches the value that users receive from inventions.[8]

---

4. *See* WARD S. BOWMAN, JR., PATENT AND ANTITRUST LAW 2–3 (Chicago, 1973); FREDERIC M. SCHERER, INDUSTRIAL MARKET STRUCTURE AND ECONOMIC PERFORMANCE 379–99 (Rand McNally, 1970); John S. McGee, *Patent Exploitation: Some Economic and Legal Problems*, 9 J L & ECON 135 (1966); Dan Usher, *The Welfare Economics of Invention*, 31 ECONOMICA 279 (1964); Kenneth J. Arrow, *Economic Welfare and the Allocation of Resources for Invention*, *in* RATE AND DIRECTION OF INVENTIVE ACTIVITY at 609; Richard R. Nelson, *The Economics of Invention: A Survey of the Literature*, 32 J. BUS. 101 (1959); FRITZ MACHLUP, AN ECONOMIC REVIEW OF THE PATENT SYSTEM, Subcomm. on Patents, Trademarks, and Copyrights of the Senate Comm on the Judiciary, Study No. 15, 85th Cong., 2d Sess. (GPO, 1958); Michael Polanyi, *Patent Reform*, 11 REV. OF ECON. STUDIES 61 (1944); Arnold Plant, *The Economic Theory Concerning Patents for Inventions*, 1 ECONOMICA 30 (1934).

5. The costs of research and development leading to a new invention are one-time, "sunk" costs. Once the invention has been made and disclosed, the marginal cost of using more intensively the knowledge gained through prior research is zero. There may still be other variable costs associated with producing goods and services through use of the invention, such as costs for labor and materials, but the invention cost is fixed in the past and need not be incurred again no matter how intensively the invention is used. In a competitive market in which anyone is free to use the invention to produce goods without obligation to the inventor, the cost of the goods sold will be driven down to a price approaching the marginal cost of their production, and thus the selling price will not allow for any return on the sunk cost of the research and development necessary to make the invention in the first place. *See* Machlup, Subcomm. on Patents, Study No 15 at 58–59.

6. *See* SCHERER, INDUSTRIAL MARKET STRUCTURE at 384; William F. Baxter, *Legal Restrictions on Exploitation of the Patent Monopoly: An Economic Analysis*, 76 YALE L. J. 267, 268–69 (1966); Machlup, Subcomm on Patents, Study No. 15 at 57–58.

7. Arrow, Economic Welfare at 614–15; Richard R. Nelson, *The Simple Economics of Basic Scientific Research*, 67 J. POL. ECON. 297 (1959). Arrow suggests that since the output of inventive effort is uncertain, and since there is no adequate market mechanism for shifting this risk, risk aversion can be expected to lead to underinvestment in invention. Arrow, *Economic Welfare* at 611–14, 616. McGee argues that inventors may display risk preference and therefore overinvest in inventive activity. McGee, 9 J. L. ECON. at 136. *See* EDWIN MANSFIELD, ET AL, RESEARCH AND INNOVATION IN THE MODERN CORPORATION 18–63 (Norton, 1971) (finding that firms tend to invest only in R & D projects with high estimated probability of success, but that firms tend to overpredict success).

8. See Baxter, 76 YALE L. J. at 270. An extreme version of this argument (attributed to John Stuart Mill) is that a patent holder can never use the patent monopoly to extract more than the value of the inventor's efforts to society, since consumers will pay the patent holder no more than the invention is worth to them. See Machlup and Penrose, 10 J. ECON. HIST. at 20. This argument rests on the often dubious assumption that the invention would never have been made were it not for the efforts of the inventor who patented it. If instead one assumes that somebody else would eventually have made the same invention, it is no longer clearly appropriate to attribute the full social value of the invention to the efforts of the first inventor. See BOWMAN, PATENT AND ANTITRUST LAW at 17.

Challenges to the incentive to invent justification for patents have taken a variety of forms. The most fundamental objection is that subjecting new inventions to monopoly control restricts their use and thereby reduces the social benefits of patented inventions. It is open to question whether it is necessary to endure the output-restricting effects of patent monopolies in order to stimulate invention.[9] In some cases the head start advantage gained by being first in the market with a new invention may provide a sufficient incentive to promote investment in research.[10] Similarly, the need to keep up with the technological progress of market rivals might stimulate invention without further incentives, or non-patent barriers to market entry may give enough protection from competition to make research and development profitable without patents.[11]

Another objection to the incentive to invent justification is that patent incentives may distort economic activity in ways that undermine efficiency. For example, competing firms hoping to make patentable inventions ahead of their rivals in order to win lucrative patents may spend too much money trying to develop inventions quickly, when the same result could be achieved at less social cost through a less accelerated research effort.[12] The patent system may divert too many resources away from productive activities in which returns are limited by the forces of competition, or it may divert resources from research in fields where patent protection is unavailable to research that is more likely to yield profitable patent monopolies.

Finally, some writers have argued that the patent system may hinder progress through its effects on the research efforts of persons other than the patent holder. The existence of a patent may undermine the incentives of these other persons to make improvements in patented

---

9. Some critics of the patent system have suggested that government could stimulate invention at less social cost by awarding prizes to inventors in lieu of patents. See, for example, Polanyi, 11 Rev. of Econ. Studies at 65. Machlup states that such proposals for alternatives to patents are almost as old as the patent system, and notes that James Madison proposed a system of prizes and bonuses to inventors in lieu of patents at the Constitutional Convention in 1787. Machlup, Subcomm on Patents, Study No. 15 at 15 n. 83; see also Hamilton, Patents and Free Enterprise at 24–25.

Others have argued that inventions arise inevitably with or without government incentives when the state of basic knowledge and other social conditions become favorable. See ABBOTT P. USHER, A HISTORY OF MECHANICAL INVENTIONS 1–31 (McGraw Hill, 1929); S.C. GILFILLAN, THE SOCIOLOGY OF INVENTION 71–78 (Follett, 1935); WILLIAM F. OGBURN, SOCIAL CHANGE 86 (Huebsch, 1923); Machlup, Subcomm on Patents, Study No. 15 at 23 n. 120, 24 n. 127; Alfred E. Kahn, *Fundamental Deficiencies of the American Patent Law*, 30 AM. ECON. REV. 475, 470 81 (1940).

10. SCHERER, INDUSTRIAL MARKET STRUCTURE at 384–87; Machlup, Subcomm on Patents, Study No. 15 at 23 n. 121, 24 n. 128, 38–39 and sources cited therein. *See generally* Jack Hirshleifer, *The Private and Social Value of Information and the Reward to Inventive Activity*, 61 AM. ECON. REV. 561 (1971) (arguing that apart from the profits obtained from patents, innovators may profit by using their advance knowledge, or "foreknowledge," of new technologies to speculate in assets whose value will be affected by the release of the new technology).

11. SCHERER, INDUSTRIAL MARKET STRUCTURE at 387; see Arrow, *Economic Welfare* at 619–22 (arguing that if the problem of appropriability is ignored, firms in a competitive market will have a greater incentive to invent than would a monopolist because the competitive firm's incentive is equal to the full cost reduction on the competitive output, while the monopolist's incentive is diminished by the set-off of preinvention monopoly profits).

12. RICHARD POSNER, ECONOMIC ANALYSIS OF LAW 54 (Little, Brown, 2d ed 1977); Yoram Barzel, *The Optimal Timing of Innovations*, 50 REV. ECON. & STAT. 348 (1968).

technologies.[13] Worse yet, it may force competitors of the patent holder to waste time and effort finding duplicative solutions to technological problems in order to avoid infringement.[14]

2. INCENTIVE TO DISCLOSE.

The incentive to disclose argument, which has been more popular with the courts than with commentators, rests on the premise that in the absence of patent protection inventors would keep their inventions secret in order to prevent competitors from exploiting them.[15] Secrecy prevents the public from gaining the full benefit of new knowledge and leads to wasteful duplicative research.[16]

Economists have questioned whether patents in fact promote disclosure of inventions that would otherwise be kept secret.[17] Secrecy is not

13. SCHERER, INDUSTRIAL MARKET STRUCTURE at 392; Baxter, 76 YALE L. J. at 270; Machlup, Subcomm on Patents, Study No. 15 at 64; Kahn, 30 AM. ECON. REV. at 482; PLANT, 1 ECONOMICA at 46. Edmund Kitch argues that this particular effect of the patent monopoly promotes efficiency in research.

The essence of the argument that patents undermine the incentives of persons other than the patent holders to make improvements in patented inventions is that once an invention is patented, only the patent holder and her licensees are able to reap rewards in the market for research leading to further refinements in the invention, while in the absence of patents competitors would also stand to benefit from such research. This argument overlooks the fact that the value of the improvement to the patent holder and her licensees might still give other researchers an incentive to develop it.

14. Judicial opinions often cite the incentive to invent around patents as a positive benefit of the patent system, reasoning that inventing around patents requires further research and thus stimulates further progress. *See, for example, Yarway Corp. v. Eur–Control U.S.A.,* 775 F.2d 268, 277 (Fed.Cir.1985); *State Indus. v. A.O. Smith Corp.,* 751 F.2d 1226, 1236 (Fed.Cir.1985); *Kimberly-Clark Corp. v. Johnson & Johnson,* 745 F.2d 1437 (Fed.Cir.1984). *See also* John C. Stedman, *Invention and Public Policy,* 12 J. L. & CONTEMP. PROBS 649, 662 (1947).

But some commentators argue that inventing around patents is socially wasteful in that it diverts resources from other productive uses to the task of finding redundant solutions to already solved problems. See, for example, Donald F. Turner, *The Patent System and Competitive Policy,* 44 N.Y.U. L. REV. 449, 455 (1969); Machlup, Subcomm on Patents, Study No 15 at 51. Machlup argues that research to find duplicative solutions to problems is particularly wasteful when done by the holder of the patent on the first solution in order to prevent competitors from inventing around the patent. Id. See BOWMAN, PATENT AND ANTITRUST LAW at 21–22 (arguing that inventing around patents is not necessarily socially wasteful if it leads to the development of superior products or processes, and that it is reasonable to assume that those who incur the costs of inventing around patents foresee inventing superior substitutes); SCHERER, INDUSTRIAL MARKET STRUCTURE at 386–87 (noting that although the pace of technological advance has probably been accelerated in some fields by efforts to invent around patented technologies, resources devoted to circumventing patents might otherwise be allocated to activities with "higher social incremental payoffs"); Martin J. Adelman, *The Supreme Court, Market Structure and Innovation: Chakrabarty, Rohm and Haas,* 27 ANTITRUST BULL. 457, 464 (1982) (arguing that efforts to invent around patent are unlikely to occur unless competitor and patent holder have different views of cost of developing alternative technology and thus are unable to agree on royalty for use of patented technology that makes it uneconomic to develop an alternative).

15. *Universal Oil Prods. Co. v. Globe Oil & Ref. Co.,* 322 U.S. 471, 484 (1944); *Grant v. Raymond,* 31 U.S. 218, 247 (1832); *Sinclair & Carroll Co. v. Interchemical Corp.,* 325 U.S. 327, 331 (1945); *Cross v. Iizuka,* 753 F.2d 1040, 1046 (Fed.Cir.1985); *Flick-Reedy Corp. v. Hydro–Line Mfg. Co.,* 351 F.2d 546, 550–51 (7th Cir.1965); BOWMAN, PATENT AND ANTITRUST LAW at 12–13; S. C. Gilfillan, *The Root of Patents, or Squaring Patents by Their Roots,* 31 J. PAT. OFF. SOC'Y 611, 612 (1949) (deriding "disclosure incentive" as "minor motive" for granting patents and one falling "outside the root of patents").

16. Martin J. Adelman, *Property Rights Theory and Patent–Antitrust: The Role of Compulsory Licensing,* 52 N.Y.U. L. REV. 977, 982 (1977).

17. *See* SCHERER, INDUSTRIAL MARKET STRUCTURE at 381; Machlup, Subcomm on Patents, Study No. 15 at 32–33, 53, 76. *See also* CANADA DEP'T. OF CONSUMER & CORP. AFFAIRS, WORKING PAPER ON PATENT LAW REVISION 40–42 (1976) ("Canada Working Paper").

always a practical strategy for protection,[18] and often secret technologies can eventually be uncovered through reverse engineering.[19] Where long term secrecy is feasible, patent protection for a mere seventeen years might not be an attractive alternative.[20] Moreover, any technology that can be exploited in secrecy by its inventor can probably also be exploited in secrecy by an infringer, making a patent on such an invention difficult to enforce. Finally, some people have questioned whether patent disclosures in fact convey enough information to be useful to the public.[21] The proposition that patents promote disclosure of new inventions by rewarding those who disclose their inventions in patent applications is thus open to doubt on a number of grounds.

Nonetheless, it seems likely that the patent system at least facilitates disclosure by creating rights in inventions that survive disclosure. Secrecy makes it difficult for inventors to sell or license their inventions to others because it is difficult to persuade someone to pay for an idea without disclosing it, yet once the invention is disclosed, the inventor has nothing left to sell. The patent system solves this problem by permitting inventors to disclose their patented inventions to potential users without losing their exclusive rights. If persons receiving disclosure use patented inventions without permission, the patent holders may sue them for infringement.[22]

* * *

There is considerable empirical evidence suggesting that technological change has been an extremely important source of economic growth over time,[23] and that levels of invention are responsive to economic

---

18.   Secrecy is impractical when efficient exploitation of the invention requires communication to a large number of firms. See BOWMAN, PATENT AND ANTITRUST LAW at 13.

19.   Plant, 1 Economica at 44. *See generally Paulik v. Rizkalla*, 760 F.2d 1270, 1276 (Fed.Cir.1985) ("[I]t is a rare invention that cannot be deciphered more readily from its commercial embodiment than from the printed patent").

20.   BOWMAN, PATENT AND ANTITRUST LAW at 13.

21.   Critics of the patent system charge that patent applicants often deliberately withhold important information from patent specifications so that they may continue to protect their "know-how" through trade secrecy. *See, for example, Brenner v. Manson*, 383 U.S. 519, 533–34 (1966). See also Canada Working Paper, at 50–53; Machlup, Subcomm on Patents, Study No. 15 at 32–33; WILLIAM D. NORDHAUS, INVENTION, GROWTH, AND WELFARE: A THEORETICAL TREATMENT OF TECHNOLOGICAL CHANGE 89 (MIT, 1969) ("It is well known that a firm tries not to disclose key parts of the invention in order to reduce the chance of imitation, thereby reducing the effective diffusion of knowledge"); S.C. GILFILLAN, INVENTION AND THE PATENT SYSTEM 61 (GPO, 1064) ("The information disclosed in patents is often not enough, taken by itself, to be of much use to the receiver"); Barkev S. Sanders, Joseph Rossman, and L. James Harris, *Attitudes of Assignees Toward Patented Inventions*, 2 PAT., TRADEMARK & COPYRIGHT J. RES. & EDUC. 463, 467–68 (Dec. 1958) (estimating that about one-half of patented inventions cannot be used without supplementary know-how).

22.   Polanyi, 11 REV. OF ECON. STUDIES at 64. *See also* Edmund W. Kitch, *The Nature and Function of the Patent System*, 20 J. L. & ECON. 265, 277–78 (1977) (asserting that patent law defines a framework of legal relations among firms to facilitate disclosure, licensing, etc.).

23.   See, for example, Moses Abramovitz, *Resource and Output Trends in the U.S. Since 1870*, 46 AM. ECON. REV. 5 (1956) (Amer Econ Assoc Papers and Proceedings); Robert M. Solow, *Technological Change and the Aggregate Production Function*, 39 REV. ECON. & STAT. 312, 320 (1957) (estimating that approximately 80 percent of the growth in nonfarm output per worker in the United States between 1909 and 1949 was attributable to technological change rather than increased capital intensity); EDWARD F. DENISON, THE SOURCES OF ECONOMIC GROWTH IN THE UNITED STATES AND THE ALTERNATIVES BEFORE US 271–72 (Brookings Inst., 1962) (estimating that 36 percent of the rise in

stimuli.[24] But it does not necessarily follow that patent protection is necessary to preserve adequate economic incentives for invention and innovation.

Eric Schiff has compared the historical record of industrial development of countries with and without patent systems during the late nineteenth and early twentieth centuries, finding little evidence that the lack of a patent system hampered industrialization.[25] But the two countries he studied that did not have patent systems—the Netherlands and Switzerland—may have been free riding on domestic and foreign inventions that were stimulated by patent protection abroad.[26] Other studies have attempted to determine, through interviews and questionnaires, the impact of patent incentives on research and development (R & D) decision making in firms. C. T. Taylor and Z. A. Silberston, in their study of the economic impact of the patent system in the United Kingdom, found that the importance of patent protection to the R & D decision making of firms varied across industries.[27] They found that patent protection had a strong influence on the willingness of pharmaceutical firms to invest in research and development, but had no more than a marginal impact on R & D expenditures in the basic chemicals industry.[28] In a similar study of U.S. firms, F. M. Scherer found that

output per worker between 1929 and 1957 was attributable to the advance of scientific and technological knowledge); EDWARD F. DENISON, ACCOUNTING FOR UNITED STATES ECONOMIC GROWTH, 1929–69 128 (Brookings Inst, 1974) (estimating that 27 percent of U.S. economic growth between 1929 and 1969 was attributable to advances in knowledge); Frederic M. Scherer, *Inter–Industry Technology Flows and Productivity Growth*, 64 REV. ECON. & STAT. 627 (1982) (estimating that in the post-War era R & D has added to the rate of growth by about one percentage point per year, or about half of the annual rate of growth in productivity).

24. *See generally* JACOB SCHMOOKLER, INVENTION AND ECONOMIC GROWTH (Harvard, 1966) (finding strong correlation between level of invention as measured by patent statistics and level of investment in capital goods, with peaks and troughs in invention tending to precede rather than to follow peaks and troughs in investment, and concluding that patented inventions are made in response to rising demand in an industry); EDWIN MANSFIELD, ET AL, RESEARCH AND INNOVATION (showing correlation between research and development funds expended and expected success of a research project and profitability of its results, and showing that timing of research and development and innovation are responsive to profit expectations.)

25. ERIC SCHIFF, INDUSTRIALIZATION WITHOUT NATIONAL PATENTS 34–41, 96–106 (Princeton, 1971). Schiff's study focuses on the experiences of the Netherlands, which abolished its patent system in 1869 and did not replace it until 1912, and Switzerland, which did not introduce a comprehensive patent system until 1907.

26. Id. at 23–24, 102–04. During the period under study, citizens of both Switzerland and the Netherlands were eligible for foreign patent protection under the national patent laws of other countries. Id. at 21–23. Schiff found a marked increase in the number of foreign patent applications filed by Dutch citizens after the Netherlands introduced its own patent system, which he interprets as evidence that the availability of patent protection in the Netherlands stimulated an increase in domestic inventive efforts. Id. at 42–51. Scherer suggests a different interpretation of Schiff's data: the passage of a Dutch patent law may have made Dutch citizens more patent-conscious and induced the growth of patent law firms, leading to more patenting abroad of inventions that might have been made with or without patent protection. FREDERIC M. SCHERER, THE ECONOMIC EFFECTS OF COMPULSORY LICENSING 36–37 (N.Y.U., 1977).

27. C. T. TAYLOR AND Z. A. SILBERSTON, THE ECONOMIC IMPACT OF THE PATENT SYSTEM 331–50 (Cambridge, 1973).

28. Attempting to explain this difference, they noted that research expenditures are higher relative to sales volume in the pharmaceutical industry than in the chemical industry, that there are more non-patent barriers to competition in the chemical industry, that patents provide stronger protection in the pharmaceutical field than in the chemical field because of the relative ease of inventing around chemical patents, and that secrecy is not practical in the pharmaceutical industry. Id. at 332–36.

respondents did not consider patents to be particularly important in R & D decision making—except when patent lawyers prepared the responses.[29] Nonetheless, the authors of both studies interpreted their results to suggest that weakening patent protection by providing for compulsory licensing of patented inventions on reasonable terms would lead to greater reliance by firms on secrecy instead of patent protection.

Another empirical approach to determining the adequacy of the current level of patent incentives is to measure the difference between private and social rates of return to investments in research and development. In case studies of seventeen industrial innovations, Edwin Mansfield and his colleagues found that the median estimated social rate of return to investment in R & D was 56 percent, while the median private rate of return was about 25 percent.[30] According to the study, "in about 30% of the cases, the private rate of return was so low that with the benefit of hindsight no firm would have invested in the innovation, but the social rate of return was so high that from society's standpoint the investment was entirely worthwhile."[31] While the authors caution against drawing any inferences about the extent of underinvestment in research and development from their results, the data are certainly consistent with the view that the current level of incentives to make and disclose new inventions is if anything too low. Other studies have tentatively suggested that private rates of return from investments in research and development are significantly higher than returns available on other investments,[32] offering further evidence that firms underinvest in research and development.

* * *

C.   Incentive to Innovate and the Prospect Theory

Although the courts have relied primarily on the incentive to invent and incentive to disclose arguments in support of the patent system,[33] commentators have offered the additional argument that a patent monopoly is necessary to induce firms to invest in "innovation"—i.e., putting existing inventions to practical use. Even after an invention has been made, considerable further investment is often necessary before it is ready for commercial exploitation. Further research and development may be needed to establish the commercial feasibility of the invention

---

29.   SCHERER, COMPULSORY LICENSING at 52–62.

30.   Edwin Mansfield, et al, *Social and Private Rates of Return from Industrial Innovations*, 91 Q J ECON 221, 233–34 (1977).

31.   Id at 235. The gap between social and private rates of return was larger for more important innovations and for innovations that could be imitated at small cost by competitors. Id. at 237.

32.   *See, for example*, EDWIN MANSFIELD, INDUSTRIAL RESEARCH AND TECHNOLOGICAL INNOVATION 65–80 (Norton, 1968).

33.   A rare possible exception is the concurring opinion of Judge Frank in Picard v. United Aircraft Corp., 128 F.2d 632 (2d Cir.1942), in which he states: "The controversy between the defenders and assailants of our patent system may be about a false issue—the stimulus to invention. The real issue may be the stimulus to investment." Id. at 643. This statement suggests a view of the patent system as promoting innovation as well as invention. *See also SCM v. Xerox*, 645 F.2d 1195, 1206 n. 9 (2d Cir.1981).

and to bring it into large scale production. Use of the invention may call for the construction of new plant and equipment. A new product invention may require further refinements to suit the tastes of consumers, as well as promotion and advertising expenditures to persuade consumers to buy it. These additional investments may dwarf the initial research expenditures in making the invention.[34] The protection of a patent monopoly enhances the likelihood that a firm will be willing to undertake these investments.

Like the incentive to invent and incentive to disclose theories, the incentive to innovate theory holds that the patent system achieves its objectives by offering monopoly profits as a lure to promote desired behavior. But it differs from these other theories with respect to the time frame in which the incentive matters. The incentive to invent and incentive to disclose theories are concerned with incentives that operate before a patent issues. These theories assume that the patent monopoly has already served its social function of promoting invention and disclosure as soon as the patent issues, and that enforcement of the patent thereafter is simply the regrettable price that society must pay in order to live up to its end of the bargain.[35] Reducing the strength of existing patents would thus presumably offer short run social benefits by increasing the use of already patented inventions, although in the long run it would reduce incentives to make and disclose new inventions. By contrast, the incentive to innovate theory gives existing patents an ongoing role in preserving the incentives of patent holders to invest in development during the patent term. Reducing the strength of existing patent monopolies might thus have the effect of undermining incentives to put existing technologies into use.[36]

---

34. EDWIN MANSFIELD, ET AL, THE PRODUCTION AND APPLICATION OF NEW INDUSTRIAL TECHNOLOGY (Norton, 1977); Scherer, Industrial Market Structure at 381 (noting that development outlays constitute more than three fourths of all industrial R & D expenditures); JOHN JEWKES, DAVID SAWERS, AND RICHARD STILLERMAN, THE SOURCES OF INVENTION 212–17 (MacMillan, 2d ed 1969). *See also* FREDERIC M. SCHERER, INNOVATION AND GROWTH: SCHUMPETERIAN PERSPECTIVES 3–7 (MIT, 1984) (explaining that firms are more willing to invest large sums in development than in invention because of the unpredictability of initial technical breakthroughs).

35. As Machlup explains:

If one accepts the theory that patent protection has the social function of serving as an incentive for inventive activity, one accepts, by implication, that the beneficial effects of this incentive system must flow, not from existing patents, but from the hope for future profits from future patents; this hope may induce people to undertake certain risky investments and useful activities—to wit, financing and arranging industrial research—which they might not undertake otherwise.... [E]xisting patents impose a burden on society, a burden which it has decided to carry in order to hold out to people the chance of obtaining future profits from future patents on future inventions.

Machlup, Subcomm on Patents, Study No. 15 at 55.

36. While Machlup notes the emergence of "incentive to innovate" arguments and acknowledges that existing patents would play an ongoing role in stimulating post-patent innovation as opposed to pre-patent invention, he does not analyze these arguments beyond stating that they require demonstrating "that innovations based on patentable inventions are socially more desirable than other innovations, and that the free-enterprise system would not, without monopoly incentives, generate investment opportunities to an adequate extent." Id. at 56. He also suggests, without elaboration, that the use of patents to promote innovation rather than invention might not be properly subsumed in the Constitutional goal of promoting "the Progress of Science and useful Arts." Id.

1. THE SCHUMPETERIAN THEORY.

The thesis that monopolies are conducive to innovation is generally associated with the work of Joseph Schumpeter on economic development.[37] While Schumpeter does not focus exclusively on either technological innovations or the patent system, his analysis suggests how patent monopolies might promote technological innovation.[38] He emphatically distinguishes innovation from invention, noting that invention itself produces "no economically relevant effect at all."[39] Innovation, on the other hand, brings about incessant revolutionary changes in the economic system through what Schumpeter calls "a process of creative destruction."[40] In this process, new firms continually arise to carry out new innovations, driving out old firms that provide obsolete goods and services. Competition from new commodities and new technologies is far more significant in this model than price competition among firms offering similar goods and services.

Schumpeter argues that in a dynamic model of the capitalist system, monopoly conditions may promote innovation and growth more effectively than competition. He bases this view primarily on "the tritest common sense," although he also notes as a matter of casual observation that economic advances are more frequently traced to big business than to firms in atomistically competitive industries.[41] He reasons that in the rapidly changing conditions of a capitalist economy, investment in innovation requires some sort of hedge against losses. Protection from competition also allows firms "to gain the time and space for further developments." Finally, and perhaps most important, the prospect of earning more than an ordinary return permits innovators to secure the

---

37. JOSEPH SCHUMPETER, CAPITALISM, SOCIALISM AND DEMOCRACY 81–110 (Harper & Row, 3d ed 1950); JOSEPH SCHUMPETER, 1 BUSINESS CYCLES 84–192 (McGraw Hill, 1939); JOSEPH SCHUMPETER, THE THEORY OF ECONOMIC DEVELOPMENT 61–94 (Transaction reprint, Redvers Opie trans 1983). *See also, generally,* Scherer, Schumpeterian Perspective; Morton I. Kamien and Nancy L. Schwartz, MARKET STRUCTURE AND INNOVATION (Cambridge, 1982); Vernon W. Ruttan, *Usher and Schumpeter on Invention, Innovation, and Technological Change,* 73 Q. J. ECON. 596 (1959); Carolyn S. Solo, *Innovation in the Capitalist Process: A Critique of the Schumpeterian Theory,* 65 Q. J. ECON. 417 (1951).

38. Schumpeter defines innovation broadly to include not only putting new technological inventions into practice, but also carrying out any new combination of productive resources that amounts to "the setting up of a new production function." Schumpeter, 1 Business Cycles at 87. In Schumpeter's usage the term innovation includes the development of new consumer goods, new methods of production, new markets, and new forms of industrial organization. Id. at 84; SCHUMPETER, CAPITALISM, SOCIALISM & DEMOCRACY at 82–83.

39. SCHUMPETER, 1 BUSINESS CYCLES at 84. See also Schumpeter, The Theory of Economic Development at 88–89 ("As long as they are not carried into practice, inventions are economically irrelevant. And to carry any improvement into effect is a task entirely different from the inventing of it.").

40. SCHUMPETER, CAPITALISM, SOCIALISM & DEMOCRACY at 83.

41. Id at 82. For other perspectives, see generally Arrow, Economic Welfare (arguing that incentive to innovate should be greater for competitive firms than for monopolists); Henry Villard, *Competition, Oligopoly and Research,* 66 J POL ECON 483 (1958) (arguing that "competitive oligopoly," characterized by a small number of big firms, promotes research better than either pure competition or monopoly).

Subsequent empirical studies to test Schumpeter's impression that monopoly conditions are more conducive to innovation than competition have been inconclusive. Scherer, Schumpeterian Perspectives at 169–255 and sources cited therein; Kamien and Schwartz, Market Structure at 49–104 and sources cited therein; Scherer, Industrial Market Structure at 363–64 and sources cited therein.

financial backing of capitalists and to bid productive resources away from their current uses. A monopoly position secured through patent protection thus may increase rather than restrict the use of known technologies by facilitating the commercial introduction of such technologies by innovating firms.

2. THE PROSPECT THEORY.

Edmund Kitch offers a more elaborate analysis of the role of patents in post-invention innovation in what he calls the "prospect theory" of patent protection. According to this theory, the patent system promotes efficiency in the allocation of resources to the development of existing inventions by awarding exclusive, publicly recorded ownership in new technological "prospects" shortly after their discovery. The term "prospect theory" highlights an analogy between the functions of patent monopolies and awards of exclusive mineral claims in government owned lands in the American West.[42]

The prospect theory offers a justification for patents that is in keeping with broader theories of property rights elaborated by Harold Demsetz[43] and Richard Posner.[44] These commentators argue that private property rights promote greater efficiency in the use of resources than communal ownership because individuals can be expected to exploit communally owned resources too quickly in order to appropriate the resources for themselves before other community members deplete them. The result will be an exhaustion of resources by individuals in the present, with the costs to be borne by the community as a whole in the future. Private ownership avoids this problem by placing property owners in a position to realize the full costs as well as the benefits of exploitation, thereby internalizing what would be external costs in a system of communal ownership.

The analogy between patents and other types of property[45] is not immediately apparent because inventions that can be used to an unlimited extent without exhaustion do not seem to present the same problems of scarcity and depletion as tangible resources. Kitch clarifies the analogy by noting that while information may be used without exhausting it,

---

42. The analogy between patents and mineral claims was foreshadowed by George Frost in a footnote in a 1946 article. George Frost, *Legal Incidents of Non–Use of Patented Inventions Reconsidered*, 14 GEO. WASH. L. REV. 273, 279 n. 24 (1946) ("An interesting analogy may be drawn between the law relating to patents for inventions and the mining law, an analogy which emphasizes the fact that patents are only one of the many situations where an exclusive grant is provided to encourage effort and capital investment.").

43. Harold Demsetz, *Toward a Theory of Property Rights*, 57 AM. ECON. REV. 347 (1967) (Am Econ Assoc Papers & Proceedings).

44. POSNER, ECONOMIC ANALYSIS OF THE LAW at 27–31.

45. While judicial decisions often speak of patent rights as a species of "property," economists studying the patent system for the most part have not drawn on property rights theory. Indeed, Fritz Machlup argues that the characterization of patents as creating "property rights" in inventions reflects confusion as to the difference between "property" and "monopoly." Machlup, Subcomm on Patents, Study No. 15 at 53–54. Machlup and Penrose trace this confusion to a deliberate "political ruse" advanced by nineteenth century advocates of the patent system in order to claim for their cause the respectable connotations of the word "property" in place of the less favorable connotations of the word "privilege." Machlup and Penrose, 10 J Econ Hist at 16–17.

resources available to use information are scarce, and property rights in inventions can improve the efficiency with which these resources are managed.

Kitch contends that patents promote efficiency in the use of resources to develop patented inventions in part by putting patent owners in a position to coordinate subsequent research and development efforts.[46] Since the owner of a patent has the exclusive right to exploit the technology defined in the patent claims, no one else is likely to invest in developing this technology without first making arrangements with the patent owner; otherwise, the subsequent researchers might ultimately be unable to benefit from their own investment in development for lack of a license to the underlying patented technology. The patent owner is thus in a position to cause researchers to share information and thereby avoid duplicative research efforts. In the absence of a patent, different investigators might try independently to develop the same invention in secrecy, each working without the benefit of the knowledge gained through the efforts of the others. Exclusive rights in technological prospects thus promote efficiency in research after the patent issues by putting the patent holder in a position to monitor and control such research.

Kitch finds support for the thesis that patent rights play a significant role in the ongoing development of patented inventions in two features of the patent system. First, the patent statute authorizes and promotes patent protection at an early stage in the development of new inventions,[47] making it likely that further research will remain to be done in order to develop an invention during the term of the patent. According to Kitch, inventions are commonly patented long before it becomes commercially feasible to exploit them.[48] The inventor who delays filing a patent application while continuing to develop the invention may lose the right to patent protection entirely if in the interim the

---

46. Id. at 276. Kitch also asserts that patents promote efficiency in the development of technological prospects by preserving the incentives of patent holders to develop their inventions without fear that the results of these efforts will be appropriated by competitors and by allowing patent holders to disclose their technological achievements to other firms without losing their exclusive rights, thereby facilitating the transfer of technology among firms and reducing the amount of duplicative research efforts. Id. at 276–79.

47. In order to obtain a patent, an applicant need only show that the invention works—i.e., that it is capable of performing some useful function. The applicant need not show that the invention works better than other means of accomplishing the same purpose, nor even that it works well. All that is necessary is a written disclosure of the invention sufficient to enable someone skilled in the field to reduce the invention to practice—i.e., to make and use it. 35 U.S.C.A. §§ 102(g), 112 (1982). The applicant does not have to describe every possible embodiment of the invention, although § 112 does require disclosure of the "best mode" of practicing the invention known to the inventor at the time the patent application is filed.

48. Empirical evidence contradicts Kitch on this point. Barkev Sanders, in a study of assigned patents issued in 1938, 1948, and 1952, found that of the estimated 10 percent of patented inventions ever put to commercial use, about 40 percent were first put to use before the patent application was filed, about 50 percent were first put to use while the application was pending, and only about 10 percent were first put to use after issuance of the patent. Barkev Sanders, Speedy Entry of Patented Inventions into Commercial Use, 6 Pat, Trademark & Copyright J of Research & Educ 87 (1962). See also Scherer, Compulsory Licensing at 9–10 and sources cited therein (indicating that the making of a patentable invention accompanies or follows commercial development more frequently than it precedes a lengthy period of subsequent development).

inventor makes a public use of the invention[49] or begins to exploit it commercially in secrecy;[50] if the invention is described in the literature or used by others; if intervening progress in the field makes the invention obvious; or if a competitor files an earlier patent application on the same invention.[51]

Second, Kitch asserts that the patent monopoly is generally not limited to the primitive version of the invention described in the patent application, but extends to subsequent refinements as well.[52] Subsequent improved versions of the invention falling within the scope of the patent claims and newly discovered uses for the invention, although the product of further research by others, will still be subject to the control of the patent holder until the patent expires.[53] The patent holder will therefore stand to benefit from subsequent research to improve the invention, while other researchers will have little incentive to pursue further research on a patented invention without first arranging for a license to the underlying patent. Kitch argues that taken together, these features of the patent system tend to promote control over subsequent research on patented inventions by patent holders and their licensees, and that such control promotes efficiency.

§ 1.5[a][2] ADDITIONAL THEORIES

Two other theories relating to the patent law have been discussed in the literature: the "rent dissipation theory" articulated in Mark F. Grady & Jay I. Alexander, *Patent Law and Rent Dissipation*, 78 VA. L. REV. 305 (1992), and the "race to invent" theory set forth in Robert P. Merges & Richard R. Nelson, *On the Complex Economics of Patent Scope*, 90 COLUM. L. REV. 839 (1990). The Merges and Nelson article is part of the burgeoning literature discussing the appropriate way to treat basic and improvement inventions. *See generally* Peter S. Menell, *Intellectual Property: General Theories*, ENCYCLOPEDIA OF LAW & ECONOMICS (2000).

As explained by Professor Eisenberg, one important economic aspect of the patent system that is generally overlooked concerns the

---

49. 35 U.S.C. § 102(b) (1982); Egbert v. Lippmann, 104 U.S. 333 (1881).

50. *See generally Pennock v. Dialogue*, 27 U.S. (2 Pet) 1 (1829); *Metallizing Engineering Co. v. Kenyon Bearing & Auto Parts Co.*, 153 F.2d 516 (2d Cir.1946).

51. Although in the U.S. patent system patent priority is awarded to the first inventor rather than to the first to file a patent application, the date of the patent application is presumed to be the same as the applicant's date of invention unless the inventor is able to prove an earlier invention date. See 35 U.S.C.A. § 102(g) (1982); *Lacotte v. Thomas*, 758 F.2d 611 (Fed.Cir.1985).

52. Kitch, 20 J L & ECON at 268–69. As an empirical matter, this assertion is also subject to doubt. The scope of patent claims will often have to be quite narrow in order to distinguish the patented invention from the prior art. *See generally* Robert P. Merges, *Commercial Success and Patent Standards: Economic Perspectives on Innovation*, 76 CAL. L. REV. 803, 840–41 (1988) and sources cited therein.

53. The subsequent inventor might be entitled to a patent on her improvement or new use of the earlier invention, but would not be able to exploit this patent without the permission of the holder of the patent on the underlying invention. The patent on the improvement or new use would enable the subsequent inventor to prevent the underlying patent holder from using this later invention. Thus no one could use the improvement without the permission of both patent holders. *See, for example, Marconi Wireless Tel. Co. v. DeForest Radio Tel. & Tel. Co.*, 236 F. 942 (S.D.N.Y.1916), *aff'd*, 243 F. 560 (2d Cir.1917).

extensive literature on the relationship between industrial structure and inventive activity. However, while the precise relationship between market structure and innovation is difficult to quantify, a strong patent system should reduce any disparity in incentives to innovate with respect to different market structures. In effect the existence of a patent system makes the industrial structure of a particular industry essentially irrelevant to the innovation process. This may be the most important practical effect of any patent system. *See* Martin J. Adelman, *The Supreme Court, Market Structure and Innovation: Chakrabarty, Rohm and Haas*, 27 ANTITRUST BULL. 457–61 (1982).

§ 1.5[b] PHILOSOPHICAL RATIONALES

In addition to economical studies, legal scholars have frequently, and productively, employed philosophical studies as a prism for critical thinking about the patent laws. In doing so, they have stressed the patent regime as one of property. Certainly the foundational philosophical text for these studies is John Locke's SECOND TREATISE OF GOVERNMENT. *See* JOHN LOCKE, THE SECOND TREATISE OF GOVERNMENT ¶ 27 (1690), in TWO TREATISES OF GOVERNMENT (Peter Laslett ed. 1960). Commentators have turned with less enthusiasm to Georg Wilhelm Friedrich Hegel, who acknowledged intellectual property laws explicitly in his most important political text, THE PHILOSOPHY OF RIGHT. *See* HEGEL'S PHILOSOPHY OF RIGHT (T. M. Knox trans. 1952).

The crux of Locke's celebrated argument concerning property is that divine authority created the world as a universal common, in which all individuals possessed an equal right. An exception to this rule lies in the body of each individual, over which each individual enjoys a property right. Not only is an individual's person his own, but "the labor of his body and the work of his hands, we may say, are properly his," as the immediate extension of his person. A significant condition qualifies this labor-based property right: whenever an individual removes something from the common, there must remain "enough and as good left in the common for others." Applied to the invention of technique and technological artifacts, Locke's theory provides a compelling rationale for the patent system.

In contrast, Hegel reasoned that property results from the expression of individual will. To Hegel, human personality results from the will's continuous effort to impose itself upon the world. Hegel recognized that the interaction of the human will with the external world occurs in part through the occupation and embodiment of external, enduring objects, which society recognizes as property. Importantly for students of the patent law, however, Hegel realized that physical objects need not be the only subject of patent protection; creative expression and the embodiment of ideas are also worthy of protection through a system of exclusive rights. As manifested in intellectual property schemes such as patent protection, Hegelian notions of property provide a suitable mechanism for self-actualization, personal expression, and recognition of the dignity and worth of the individual.

Despite this focus on its place as a species of property, the patent law remains first and foremost a regime of technological evaluation. The writings of those thinkers who have contemplated the nature of technology itself therefore also present a relatively untapped lodestar for those who would assess the patent system. Although the philosophy of technology is a nascent field of study, such seminal figures as John Dewey, Martin Heidegger, and Karl Marx have presented mature thought on technological growth, the ethical context of technique and technological artifacts, and the relationship between man and the made world in which he exists. It is in minds such as these that students can find alternatives to the quantitatively rigid, yet morally ambiguous path of patent law and economics.

Further Reading. Recommended starting points are the scholarly analyses presented in PETER DRAHOS, A PHILOSOPHY OF INTELLECTUAL PROPERTY (1996); Wendy Gordon, *A Property Right in Self–Expression: Equality and Individualism in the Natural Law of Intellectual Property*, 102 YALE L.J. 1533 (1993); and Justin Hughes, *The Philosophy of Intellectual Property*, 77 GEO. L.J. 287 (1988).

§ 1.6 OTHER FORMS OF INTELLECTUAL PROPERTY PROTECTION

Other areas encompassed by the term intellectual property include trademarks, copyrights, semiconductor chip protection and trade secrets. Although a full description of these and related disciplines—including such disparate regimes as industrial design and database registration, anti-counterfeiting measures, and indications of origin—exceeds the scope of this casebook, the following brief review should inform a consideration of the patent law.

§ 1.6[a] TRADEMARKS

The fundamental federal legislation in this field, the Lanham Act, defines a trademark as "any word, name, symbol, or device, or any combination thereof [used] to identify and distinguish his or her goods, including a unique product, from those manufactured or sold by others and to indicate the source of the goods, even if that source is unknown." 15 U.S.C. § 1127. Related concepts include trade names, used to identify a business or vocation, and service marks, used in connection with services, such as those provided by the hotel or restaurant industry. *Id*. Trademark law serves to benefit consumers by allowing them to establish a vocabulary upon which selections among various goods and services can be made.

The determination of whether a mark qualifies for trademark protection depends in part upon its classification as generic, descriptive, suggestive, or arbitrary. *See Abercrombie & Fitch Co. v. Hunting World, Inc.*, 537 F.2d 4 (2d Cir.1976). Generic terms are defined as the ordinary name for that sort of marked product, such as "bread" or "sugar," and can never receive trademark protection. Marks which are ordinarily and naturally used to characterize a product—referred to as descriptive marks—may also not be protected unless they have acquired a certain level of distinctiveness. This distinctiveness, so-called "secondary meaning," refers to an acquired meaning of the mark, typically through exclusive use over a lengthy period, so that it comes to refer to the origin of the goods or services, rather than those goods or services themselves. Thus, terms which merely describe the function of a service, such as "vision center" for optical clinics, or indicate a product's desirable characteristic, such as "honey-baked ham," cannot be valid trademarks absent a further showing of secondary meaning.

Suggestive marks—those which do more than describe, but require some additional thought to indicate the product—are inherently distinctive and therefore subject to protection without the need to prove secondary meaning. Such terms as "Skinvisible" for transparent medical adhesive tape and "Orange Crush" for orange-flavored soft drinks have been held to be suggestive. Arbitrary marks such as "Camel" applied to cigarettes, or coined words like "Kodak" which lack a dictionary meaning, are also considered inherently distinctive.

Importantly when considered in the context of patents, trademark protection can never extend to the functional features of a product. *See Crescent Tool Co. v. Kilborn & Bishop Co.*, 247 F. 299 (2d Cir.1917). Whether a feature is considered functional depends upon its affect upon the cost or quality of the article, as well as the availability of alternative designs. This doctrine is founded on the public interest in preventing a monopoly in useful design features, thereby hindering competitors.

Trademark infringement occurs when another person markets goods bearing a mark sufficiently similar to the trademark that a likelihood of confusion exists as to the source of the goods. 15 U.S.C. § 1125. Factors that inform the likelihood of confusion inquiry include the similarity of appearance of the marks, the strength of the trademark, consumer sophistication, competition between the goods, similarity of sales and distribution channels, the intent of the defendant, and the existence of actual consumer confusion. *See Polaroid Corp. v. Polarad Electronics Corp.*, 287 F.2d 492 (2d Cir.1961).

In contrast to most trademark regimes overseas, the U.S. trademark law allows ownership to result from public use, rather than registration. However, trademarks may be registered with the United States Patent and Trademark Office when they are employed in interstate commerce, providing both evidentiary and substantive advantages in subsequent disputes. 15 U.S.C. § 1051. Trademarks are of potentially perpetual duration but may be extinguished through non-use or loss of distinctiveness. For example, use of the mark may become so widespread that it loses its ability to identify a particular product, becoming generic in the fashion of terms like *aspirin* or *escalator*, or the owner may abandon the mark or license it without the ability to maintain product quality. *See* RESTATEMENT (THIRD) OF UNFAIR COMPETITION §§ 30, 33 (1995).

§ 1.6[b] COPYRIGHTS

Under the Copyright Act of 1976, copyright may extend to any work of authorship. 17 U.S.C. § 102(a). Exemplary of the works of authorship amenable to copyright protection are literary, musical, dramatic, choreographic, graphic, audiovisual, and architectural works, as well as sound recordings. Such works are eligible for copyright protection as soon as they are recorded in a sufficiently stable form, or, in the words of the copyright law, "fixed in any tangible medium of expression." *Id.* No formalities are necessary to secure protection. However, authors that register their works with the Copyright Office, 17 U.S.C. §§ 408–412, and that place a notice of copyright on copies of their works, 17 U.S.C. § § 401–406, are provided certain advantages when enforcing their copyrights.

A work must be original to be protected under the copyright law. 17 U.S.C. § 102(a). The originality requirement is a lenient one, requiring that the work was created by that author and was not copied from another, and that there be a minimal amount of creative authorship. Importantly, copyright protection extends only to the expression of an idea, not the idea itself. 17 U.S.C. § 102(b). For example, no author can obtain copyright protection on the abstract idea of a human changing into an insect. But the expression of that idea in a particular work of authorship with its own characters, plot, mood, and setting—be it Franz Kafka's *The Metamorphosis* or the horror movie *The Fly*—may be accorded copyright protection.

Copyright confers a number of exclusive rights to the author or, in some circumstances, to the employer of the author under the "works made for hire" principle. 17 U.S.C. § 201. The copyright proprietor has the exclusive right to make copies of the protected work and to distribute it to the public. The 1976 Act also awards copyright owners the right to control derivative works, such as translations or screenplay adaptations, that are based upon the protected work. The proprietor further enjoys the exclusive right, with respect to most kinds of works, to display and perform the protected work publicly. 17 U.S.C. § 106.

The exclusive rights of copyright owners are restricted by a number of defenses, the most important of which is the fair use privilege. The fair use privilege allows the unauthorized use of copyrighted works in such contexts as educational activities, literary and social criticism, parody and news reporting. 17 U.S.C. § 107.

Each copyright ordinarily enjoys a term of the life of the author plus seventy years. 17 U.S.C. § 302(a). The copyright proprietor may file a suit in federal court in order to enjoin infringers and obtain monetary remedies. 17 U.S.C. §§ 501–505. Criminal penalties may also apply to copyright infringers. 17 U.S.C. § 506. A copyright, or any of the exclusive rights under a copyright, may be assigned or licensed to others. 17 U.S.C. § 201(d). Individual authors possess the right to terminate such transfers after 35 years, although the transferee may continue to exploit derivative works produced under the transfer prior to its termination. 17 U.S.C. § 203.

[handwritten margin note: cant seek damages enjoinment — criminal penalties too.]

§ 1.6[c]　SEMICONDUCTOR CHIP PROTECTION

Semiconductor chip products, including microprocessors and memories, consist of often vast electronic circuits fabricated onto a single piece of semiconductor substrate. Designers of these products quickly learned that their work were not considered a work of authorship eligible for copyright protection. Similarly, patent protection was largely unavailable due to the nonobviousness requirement—although these products required considerable investment of time and design resources, they were usually the result of ordinary labors of skilled engineers, rather than invention within the meaning of the patent laws. The Semiconductor Chip Protection Act of 1984, Pub. L. 98–620, remedied this situation by allowing designers of new semiconductor chip products to register them at the Copyright Office, obtaining the exclusive right to manufacture and distribute them in the United States for ten years. The Chip Act, which is codified in chapter 9 of title 17 of the U.S. Code, has not been heavily employed and only rarely the subject of litigation. It nonetheless serves as an interesting model of an alternative scheme of protection, with similarities to both patent and copyright law, designed to encompass a new technology.

[handwritten margin note: microprocessor dont fall under copyright or patent. — not nonobvious — 10 yr period.]

§ 1.6[d]　TRADE SECRETS

Trade secret law protects secret, valuable business information from misappropriation by others. Subject matter ranging from marketing data to manufacturing know-how may be protected under the trade secret laws. Trade secret status is not limited to a fixed number of years, but endures so long as the information is valuable and maintained as a secret. *See United States v. Dubilier Condenser Corp.*, 289 U.S. 178, 186 (1933). A trade secret is misappropriated when it has been obtained through the abuse of a confidential relationship or improper means of acquisition. Unlike the Patent Act, trade secret law does not provide a cause of action against an individual who independently developed or reverse engineered the subject matter of the trade secret.

Trade secrecy serves as the chief alternative to the patent system and, as such, is worthy of more detailed review here. An inventor must either maintain a technology as a trade secret, seek patent protection from the PTO, or allow it to enter the public domain. The regime of trade secrets is broader than this, however, for trade secret law may also be used to protect subject matter that is unpatentable. For example, although a list of valued customers does not constitute patent eligible subject matter, it is amenable to protection as a trade secret.

Judicial opinions evince two distinct conceptions of the trade secret law. Some courts focus on trade secrecy as an intellectual property discipline. Under this view, trade secret law creates a proprietary interest just like a copyright, patent, or mark. In deciding whether to grant relief for misappropriation of trade secrets, these courts stress the value and secrecy of the subject matter for which trade secret status is claimed. Other courts have viewed trade secret law as less concerned with creating property than in ensuring proper conduct. In resolving trade secret cases, these courts stress whether the accused misappropriator acquired the information at issue in a fair and ethical manner.

As Judge Posner noted in the leading opinion of *Rockwell Graphic Systems, Inc. v. DEV Industries, Inc.*, 925 F.2d 174 (7th Cir.1991), these conceptions are entirely complementary. The trade secret law encourages industry actors to develop valuable informational resources by protecting them from improper acquisition by others. As well, potential liability for trade secret misappropriation discourages individuals from engaging in activities that do not create wealth, but merely redistribute wealth from one individual to another.

§ 1.6[d][1] SOURCES OF LAW

The modern U.S. law of trade secrets arises from the common law tradition. The English equity courts of the early nineteenth century considered the misappropriation of such secret subject matter as the composition of medical compounds and dyes. Many of these cases involved breaches of confidence between partners, family members, or a master and apprentice. The U.S. courts turned to this early precedent while considering the increasingly complex commercial relationships of an industrial society. Trade secret law continues as an adaptive discipline that has responded to changing technology, increasing employee mobility and heightened entrepreneurial activity.

The American Law Institute's 1939 Restatement of Torts included two sections that defined the subject matter of trade secrets and the misappropriation cause of action. Although this treatment was succinct, these definitions proved influential in the courts. However, trade secrets were not addressed in the 1978 Second Restatement of Torts. The American Law Institute concluded that trade secret law had grown "no more dependent on Tort law than it is on many other general fields of law and upon broad statutory developments," and opted not to house trade secrets there.

The Uniform Trade Secrets Act filled this breach in 1979. 14 U.L.A. 438 (1990). Published by the National Conference of Commissioners on

Uniform State Law, the Uniform Act has been enacted in the majority of *Tort law* states. The Uniform Act generally follows the Restatement of Torts, but *the basis* also relies upon subsequent case law to provide more useful and *of trade secrets* definitive legal standards.

The American Law Institute was not content to rest, however. A distinct Restatement (Third) of Unfair Competition was promulgated in 1993 with a thorough treatment of trade secrets in sections 39–45. The remainder of the work is devoted to trademarks, misappropriation, deceptive marking, the right of publicity, and related doctrines. Like the Restatement of Torts and the Uniform Act, the Restatement of Unfair Competition remains faithful to the case law and does not presume to be an instrument of radical legal reform.

Trade secrets have traditionally been the subject of state law. *traditionally* However, the federal government firmly engaged the law of trade *subject of* secrets in the Economic Espionage Act of 1996. Pub. L. No. 104–294, *state law* §§ 1831–1839, 110 Stat. 3488 (codified at 18 U.S.C. §§ 1831–39). That *Econ Espionage* statute renders the misappropriation of trade secrets a federal crime. *Act 1996* Housed in Title 18 of the United States Code, the Economic Espionage *–Fed Crime* Act provides for substantial fines and imprisonment penalties, as well as criminal forfeiture of property and court order preserving confidentiality of trade secrets. Stiffer penalties are available when trade secrets are misappropriated for the benefit of a foreign government, instrumentality, or agent.

That the common law has been supplemented by these four accounts of trade secrets law may seem to hold tremendous possibility for confusion. However, the substantive law of trade secrets provided in the Restatements, Uniform Act, and Economic Espionage Act is largely consistent. The later sources are marked by more familiar language and a greater level of detail than their predecessors. Although judicial opinions may cite to different authorities, the core precepts of trade secret law remain intact.

§ 1.6[d][2]   ELIGIBLE SUBJECT MATTER

Perhaps due to its origins in the courts of equity, the trade secret law has never overly concerned itself with achieving an exact definition of the sorts of information that may be subjected to trade secret protection. The authorities do agree that there are two principle requirements for maintaining information as a trade secret. First and foremost, the information must have been the subject of reasonable efforts to maintain secrecy. Second, the information must derive commercial value from not being generally known or readily ascertainable by others. RESTATEMENT THIRD, UNFAIR COMPETITION § 39 (1995).

Subject to these overriding requirements of secrecy and value, the Restatements provide that formulae, patterns, devices, or compilations of information may be protected as trade secrets. The case law reveals an enormous variety of information subject to the trade secret laws. This subject matter include lists of customers, marketing data, bid price information, technical designs, manufacturing know-how, computer programs, and chemical formulae. In sum, any distinct, clearly identifiable information may become a trade secret provided that it has value and has been kept secret.

§ 1.6[d][3] SECRECY

The principal gatekeeper to trade secret status is that the information must have been subjected to reasonable efforts to maintain its secrecy. Uniform Trade Secrets Act § 2, 14 U.L.A. 438 (1990). The case law provides no precise standard as to the efforts necessary to qualify the protected subject matter as a trade secret. A would-be trade secret holder need not erect an utterly impenetrable fortress around the information. On the other hand, the owner must make satisfactory efforts to identify the secret subject matter, notify others that it regards the subject matter as proprietary, and protect against reasonably foreseeable intrusions.

In deciding whether reasonable efforts have been made to maintain secrecy, courts will balance the costs of the efforts made against the benefits obtained. *See Rockwell Graphic Sys., Inc. v. DEV Industries, Inc.*, 925 F.2d 174 (7th Cir.1991). The courts do not require costly, burdensome safeguards that would overly disrupt the owner's usual commercial practices. However, if the owner did not engage in prudent precautions that would have yielded security benefits greater than their costs, the case for reasonable secrecy efforts is diminished.

The precautions the holder of commercially valuable information might take to maintain secrecy are legion. For example, employees, visitors, and joint venturers could be required to sign confidentiality agreements. Signs, stamps, and legends may declare that certain subject matter is proprietary. Locked doors, alarms, and guards might deny access to individuals who do not need to know the information. Exit interviews may remind departing employees of their obligations to maintain the protected subject matter in confidence. Pertinent documents and laboratory samples could be destroyed on the premises. Although numerous other measures should be apparent, no absolute rule governs the degree of vigilance that the putative trade secret holder must maintain. Whether a court will find the existence of a trade secret depends upon an overall balancing of the equities of particular cases.

A number of circumstances may negate secrecy. Knowledge that may be readily gained from an inspection of a commercially available product is not secret. Similarly, information that may be found in publicly available journals, texts, or other published materials may not be kept as a trade secret. Issuance of a U.S. patent or publication of a pending patent application also destroys the secrecy of any information claimed within. This result holds even if the published application does not mature into a granted patent, or if the patent is later held invalid. RESTATEMENT THIRD, UNFAIR COMPETITION § 39 cmt. c (1995).

§ 1.6[d][4]　COMMERCIAL VALUE

Information must be sufficiently valuable to provide an actual or potential economic advantage over others to qualify for trade secret protection. RESTATEMENT THIRD, UNFAIR COMPETITION § 39 cmt e (1995). Ordinarily the putative trade secret holder demonstrates value through direct evidence of the significance of the subject matter to its business, or its superiority as compared to public domain alternatives. Courts have also accepted evidence of the cost of developing the information and the extent of the pains taken to protect its secrecy as evidence of value.

Value is seldom a practical issue in trade secret cases. The high cost of enforcing intellectual property rights suggests that plaintiffs will only commence litigation concerning information of considerable value. One decision that did deny a claim for trade secret misappropriation based upon the value requirement was *Religious Technology Center v. Wollersheim*, 796 F.2d 1076 (9th Cir.1986). There, the Church of Scientology accused a former practitioner of misappropriating scriptural materials that addressed a person's spiritual well-being. The Court of Appeals for the Ninth Circuit denied the Church's trade secret claim, concluding that the value of the confidential materials were religious rather than commercial in character.

§ 1.6[d][5]　MISAPPROPRIATION

An enterprise possessing trade secrets will be protected against misappropriation of those trade secrets by others. Some trade secret cases involve parties who initially learn of the trade secret through voluntary disclosure by the trade secret holder, and thereafter either use the secret for their commercial advantage or disclose it to others. Courts will grant relief in this latter class of cases where the defendant violated either an express or implied obligation of confidentiality.

An individual may owe another a duty of confidence through an express promise of confidentiality. Such promises are most typically made by employees, prospective buyers, visitors to a facility, or joint venturers. A duty of confidence may also be implied from the relationship of the parties, even where no express contractual provision exists. If the trade secret holder was reasonable in inferring that the other person consented to an obligation of confidentiality, and the other knew or should have known the disclosure was made in confidence, the court will infer that an obligation of confidentiality existed.

A representative case implying a duty of confidentiality is *Smith v. Dravo Corp.*, 203 F.2d 369 (7th Cir.1953). Smith was in the cargo and freight container business. Dravo expressed an interest in buying Smith's business, and the two entered into negotiations. As part of these discussions Smith showed Dravo secret blueprints and patent applications concerning its innovative cargo containers. The deal fell through and shortly thereafter Dravo began to market freight containers similar to Smith's. Smith sued Dravo for trade secret misappropriation. Although the Court of Appeals for the Seventh Circuit observed that "no express promise of trust was exacted from the defendant," it held that a relationship of trust should be implied from the facts and granted relief.

Other trade secrets cases concern instances where individuals with no relationship to the trade secret holder have acquired the protected subject matter. In those cases, the dispositive legal issue is whether the trade secret was acquired by improper means. A trade secret owner may claim misappropriation if the defendant acquired the trade secret by performing illegal acts. Wiretapping, bribery, fraud, and theft of personal property are exemplary of the industrial espionage condemned under the trade secret law. However, trade secret protection is not limited to acts that are themselves violations of other laws. As demonstrated by the following decision, the courts have also condemned activities that amount to calculated attempts to overcome reasonable efforts to maintain secrecy.

E.I. duPONT deNEMOURS & CO. v. CHRISTOPHER

United States Court of Appeals, Fifth Circuit, 1970
431 F.2d 1012

Before Wisdom, Goldberg, and Ingraham, Circuit Judges.

GOLDBERG, CIRCUIT JUDGE:

This is a case of industrial espionage in which an airplane is the cloak and a camera the dagger. The defendants-appellants, Rolfe and Gary Christopher, are photographers in Beaumont, Texas. The Christophers were hired by an unknown third party to take aerial photographs of new construction at the Beaumont plant of E. I. duPont deNemours & Company, Inc. Sixteen photographs of the DuPont facility were taken from the air on March 19, 1969, and these photographs were later developed and delivered to the third party.

DuPont employees apparently noticed the airplane on March 19 and immediately began an investigation to determine why the craft was circling over the plant. By that afternoon the investigation had disclosed that the craft was involved in a photographic expedition and that the Christophers were the photographers. DuPont contacted the Christophers that same afternoon and asked them to reveal the name of the person or corporation requesting the photographs. The Christophers refused to disclose this information, giving as their reason the client's desire to remain anonymous.

Having reached a dead end in the investigation, DuPont subsequently filed suit against the Christophers, alleging that the Christophers had wrongfully obtained photographs revealing DuPont's trade secrets which they then sold to the undisclosed third party. DuPont contended that it had developed a highly secret but unpatented process for producing methanol, a process which gave DuPont a competitive advantage over other producers. This process, DuPont alleged, was a trade secret developed after much expensive and time-consuming research, and a secret which the company had taken special precautions to safeguard. The area photographed by the Christophers was the plant designed to produce methanol by this secret process, and because the plant was still under construction parts of the process were exposed to view from directly above the construction area. Photographs of that area, DuPont alleged, would enable a skilled person to deduce the secret process for making methanol. DuPont thus contended that the Christophers had wrongfully appropriated DuPont trade secrets by taking the photographs and delivering them to the undisclosed third party. In its suit DuPont asked for damages to cover the loss it had already sustained as a result of the wrongful disclosure of the trade secret and sought temporary and permanent injunctions prohibiting any further circulation of the photographs already taken and prohibiting any additional photographing of the methanol plant.

The Christophers answered with motions to dismiss for lack of jurisdiction and failure to state a claim upon which relief could be granted. Depositions were taken during which the Christophers again refused to disclose the name of the person to whom they had delivered the photographs. DuPont then filed a motion to compel an answer to this question and all related questions.

On June 5, 1969, the trial court held a hearing on all pending motions and an additional motion by the Christophers for summary judgment. The court denied the Christophers' motions to dismiss for want of jurisdiction and failure to state a claim and also denied their motion for summary judgment. The court granted DuPont's motion to compel the Christophers to divulge the name of their client. Having made these rulings, the court then granted the Christophers' motion for an interlocutory appeal under 28 U.S.C.A. § 1292(b) to allow the Christophers to obtain immediate appellate review of the court's finding that DuPont had stated a claim upon which relief could be granted. Agreeing with the trial court's determination that DuPont had stated a valid claim, we affirm the decision of that court.

This is a case of first impression, for the Texas courts have not faced this precise factual issue, and sitting as a diversity court we must sensitize our *Erie* antennae to divine what the Texas courts would do if such a situation were presented to them. The only question involved in this interlocutory appeal is whether DuPont has asserted a claim upon which relief can be granted. The Christophers argued both at trial and before this court that they committed no "actionable wrong" in photographing the DuPont facility and passing these photographs on to their client because they conducted all of their activities in public airspace, violated no government aviation standard, did not breach any confidential relation, and did not engage in any fraudulent or illegal conduct. In short, the Christophers argue that for an appropriation of trade secrets to be wrongful there must be a trespass, other illegal conduct, or breach of a confidential relationship. We disagree.

It is true, as the Christophers assert, that the previous trade secret cases have contained one or more of these elements. However, we do not think that the Texas courts would limit the trade secret protection exclusively to these elements. On the contrary, in *Hyde Corporation v. Huffines*, 1958, 314 S.W.2d 763, the Texas Supreme Court specifically adopted the rule found in the Restatement of Torts which provides:

> "One who discloses or uses another's trade secret, without a privilege to do so, is liable to the other if (a) he discovered the secret by improper means, or (b) his disclosure or use constitutes a breach of confidence reposed in him by the other in disclosing the secret to him * * *."

RESTATEMENT OF TORTS § 757 (1939).

Thus, although the previous cases have dealt with a breach of a confidential relationship, a trespass, or other illegal conduct, the rule is much broader than the cases heretofore encountered. Not limiting itself to specific wrongs, Texas adopted subsection (a) of the Restatement which recognizes a cause of action for the discovery of a trade secret by any 'improper' means.

The defendants, however, read *Furr's Inc. v. United Specialty Advertising Co.*, Tex.Civ.App.1960, 338 S.W.2d 762, as limiting the Texas rule to breach of a confidential relationship. The court in *Furr's* did make the statement that

> "The use of someone else's idea is not automatically a violation of the law. It must be something that meets the requirements of a 'trade secret' and has been obtained through a breach of confidence in order to entitle the injured party to damages and/or injunction."

338 S.W.2d at 766.

We think, however, that the exclusive rule which defendants have extracted from this statement is unwarranted. In the first place, in *Furr's* the court specifically found that there was no trade secret involved because the entire advertising scheme claimed to be the trade secret had been completely divulged to the public. Secondly, the court found that the plaintiff in the course of selling the scheme to the defendant had voluntarily divulged the entire scheme. Thus the court was dealing only with a possible breach of confidence concerning a properly discovered secret; there was never a question of any impropriety in the discovery or any other improper conduct on the part of the defendant. The court merely held that under those circumstances the defendant had not acted improperly if no breach of confidence occurred. We do not read *Furr's* as limiting the trade secret protection to a breach of confidential relationship when the facts of the case do raise the issue of some other wrongful conduct on the part of one discovering the trade secrets of another. If breach of confidence were meant to encompass the entire panoply of commercial improprieties, subsection (a) of the Restatement would be either surplusage or persiflage, an interpretation abhorrent to the traditional precision of the Restatement. We therefore find meaning in subsection (a) and think that the Texas Supreme Court clearly indicated by its adoption that there is a cause of action for the discovery of a trade secret by any "improper means."

The question remaining, therefore, is whether aerial photography of plant construction is an improper means of obtaining another's trade secret. We conclude that it is and that the Texas courts would so hold. The Supreme Court of that state has declared that "the undoubted tendency of the law has been to recognize and enforce higher standards of commercial morality in the business world." *Hyde Corporation v. Huffines, supra* 314 S.W.2d at 773. That court has quoted with approval articles indicating that the proper means of gaining possession of a competitor's secret process is "through inspection and analysis" of the product in order to create a duplicate. *K & G Tool & Service Co. v. G & G Fishing Tool Service,* 1958, 314 S.W.2d 782, 783, 788. Later another Texas court explained:

> "The means by which the discovery is made may be obvious, and the experimentation leading from known factors to presently unknown results may be simple and lying in the public domain. But these facts do not destroy the value of the discovery and will not advantage a competitor who by unfair means obtains the knowledge without paying the price expended by the discoverer."

Brown v. Fowler, Tex.Civ.App.1958, 316 S.W.2d 111, 114.

We think, therefore, that the Texas rule is clear. One may use his competitor's secret process if he discovers the process by reverse engineering applied to the finished product; one may use a competitor's process if he discovers it by his own independent research; but one may not avoid these labors by taking the process from the discoverer without his permission at a time when he is taking reasonable precautions to maintain its secrecy. To obtain knowledge of a process without spending the time and money to discover it independently is improper unless the holder voluntarily discloses it or fails to take reasonable precautions to ensure its secrecy.

In the instant case the Christophers deliberately flew over the Du Pont plant to get pictures of a process which Du Pont had attempted to keep secret. The Christophers delivered their pictures to a third party who was certainly aware of the means by which they had been acquired and who may be planning to use the information contained therein to manufacture methanol by the Du Pont process. The third party has a right to use this process only if he obtains this knowledge through his own research efforts, but thus far all information indicates that the third party has gained this knowledge solely by taking it from Du Pont at a time when Du Pont was making reasonable efforts to preserve its secrecy. In such a situation Du Pont has a valid cause of action to prohibit the Christophers from improperly discovering its trade secret and to prohibit the undisclosed third party from using the improperly obtained information.

We note that this view is in perfect accord with the position taken by the authors of the Restatement. In commenting on improper means of discovery the savants of the Restatement said:

> "f. Improper means of discovery. The discovery of another's trade secret by improper means subjects the actor to liability independently of the harm to the interest in the secret. Thus, if one uses physical force to take a secret formula from another's pocket, or breaks into another's office to steal the formula, his conduct is wrongful and subjects him to liability apart from the rule stated in this Section. Such conduct is also an improper means of procuring the secret under this rule. But means may be improper under this rule even though they do not cause any other harm than that to the interest in the trade secret. Examples of such means are fraudulent misrepresentations to induce disclosure, tapping of telephone wires, eavesdropping or other espionage. A complete catalogue of improper means is not possible. In general they are means which fall below the generally accepted standards of commercial morality and reasonable conduct."

RESTATEMENT OF TORTS § 757, comment f at 10 (1939).

In taking this position we realize that industrial espionage of the sort here perpetrated has become a popular sport in some segments of our industrial community. However, our devotion to free wheeling industrial competition must not force us into accepting the law of the jungle as the standard of morality expected in our commercial relations. Our tolerance of the espionage game must cease when the protections required to prevent another's spying cost so much that the spirit of inventiveness is dampened. Commercial privacy must be protected from espionage which could not have been reasonably anticipated or prevented. We do not mean to imply, however, that everything not in plain view is within the protected vale, nor that all information obtained through every extra optical extension is forbidden. Indeed, for our industrial competition to remain healthy there must be breathing room for observing a competing industrialist. A competitor can and must shop his competition for pricing and examine his products for quality, components, and methods of manufacture. Perhaps ordinary fences and roofs must be built to shut out incursive eyes, but we need not require the discoverer of a trade secret to guard against the unanticipated, the undetectable, or the unpreventable methods of espionage now available.

In the instant case Du Pont was in the midst of constructing a plant. Although after construction the finished plant would have protected much of the process from view, during the period of construction the trade secret was exposed to view from the air. To require Du Pont to put a roof over the unfinished plant to guard its secret would impose an enormous expense to prevent nothing more than a school boy's trick. We introduce here no new or radical ethic since our ethos has never given moral sanction to piracy. The market place must not deviate far from our mores. We should not require a person or corporation to take unreasonable precautions to prevent another from doing that which he ought not do in the first place. Reasonable precautions against predatory eyes we may require, but an impenetrable fortress is an unreasonable requirement, and we are not disposed to burden industrial inventors with such a duty in order to protect the fruits of their efforts. "Improper" will always be a word of many nuances, determined by time, place, and circumstances. We therefore need not proclaim a catalogue of commercial improprieties. Clearly, however, one of its commandments does say "thou shall not appropriate a trade secret through deviousness under circumstances in which countervailing defenses are not reasonably available."

[handwritten margin note: Not requiring unreasonable steps.]

Having concluded that aerial photography, from whatever altitude, is an improper method of discovering the trade secrets exposed during construction of the Du Pont plant, we need not worry about whether the flight pattern chosen by the Christophers violated any federal aviation regulations. Regardless of whether the flight was legal or illegal in that sense, the espionage was an improper means of discovering Du Pont's trade secret.

[handwritten margin note: regardless of whether it was illegal or not it was still improper]

The decision of the trial court is affirmed and the case remanded to that court for proceedings on the merits.

NOTES

1. **Remedies.** An adjudicated trade secret misappropriator may be enjoined and found liable for damages. The modern rule is that injunctions are appropriate only for the period of time that the subject matter of the trade secret would have remained unavailable to the defendant but for the misappropriation. This principle offers a compromise between two more extreme positions established in the case law. Some courts have followed the holding in *Shellmar Products Co. v. Allen–Qualley Co.*, 87 F.2d 104 (7th Cir.1937), and concluded that permanent injunctions were an appropriate remedy for trade secret misappropriation on the ground that trade secrets have no set duration. Other opinions found more favor in Judge Learned Hand's opinion in *Conmar Products Corp. v. Universal Slide Fastener Co.*, 172 F.2d 150 (2d Cir. 1949), to the effect that once a trade secret entered into the public domain, the plaintiff could obtain no injunctive relief whatsoever.

[handwritten margin note: injunction only as long as secret would have remained so. balance between extremes]

Each of these extreme positions is now in disfavor. Contemporary courts have reasoned that the draconian *Shellmar* rule is punitive in character and undermines the public interest in legitimate competition. On the other hand, the *Conmar* rule leads to hard results in cases where the defendant engaged in egregious conduct, particularly where he exposed the trade secret to the public himself. The compromise position of the Uniform Trade Secrets Act states that "an injunction shall be terminated when the trade secret has ceased to exist, but the injunction may be continued for an additional reasonable period of time in order to eliminate commercial advantage that otherwise would be derived from the misappropriation." § 2(a), 14 U.L.A. 438 (1990).

As a result, successful plaintiffs in trade secret proceedings may obtain injunctions limited to the lead time advantage inappropriately gained by the misappropriator. In determining the length of this "head start," courts will weigh evidence as to the amount of time a person of ordinary skill would have required to discover independently or reverse engineer the subject matter of the trade secret. If the misappropriator can demonstrate that the trade secret holder's competitors have legitimately acquired the protected knowledge, then the court will likely decline to award an injunction at all.

Courts have demonstrated flexibility in fashioning monetary remedies for trade secret misappropriation. They will typically award an amount equal to either the loss suffered by the trade secret holder, or the gain realized by misappropriator, whichever is greater. Monetary damages are ordinarily limited to the time that the misappropriated information would not have been available otherwise to the defendant. *See, e.g., Engelhard Industries, Inc. v. Research Instrumental Corp.*, 324 F.2d 347 (9th Cir.1963).

2. Trade Secrets and Patents. Trade secrets and patents coexist in what can be described as an uneasy relationship. A principal purpose of the patent law is the dissemination of knowledge. This goal is realized through the publication of patent instruments that fully disclose the patented invention such that skilled artisans could practice it without undue experimentation. 35 U.S.C. § 112. A law of trade secrets that encourages the withholding of patentable inventions appears fundamentally at odds with this fundamental precept.

This tension results in a patent law that does not favor trade secret holders. One patent law principle that deleteriously impacts trade secret holders is that a later, independent inventor may patent the subject matter of an earlier inventor's trade secret. A first inventor may quickly transition from the status of a trade secret holder to an adjudicated patent infringer. *See* Albert C. Smith & Jared A. Stosberg, *Beware! Trade Secret Software May Be Patented By a Later Inventor*, 7 COMPUTER LAWYER no. 11 at 15 (Nov. 1990). The First Inventor Defense Act of 1999 did soften this traditional principle somewhat, allowing earlier inventors an infringement defense against subsequent patentees of methods of doing business. *See* 35 U.S.C. § 273.

Trade secrets perform a valuable role in the U.S. intellectual property scheme, however. Although patent law is an increasingly capacious regime, its subject matter does not extend to the full array of valuable information that may be the subject of a trade secret. Patent rights too must be affirmatively sought, and their acquisition usually entails significant costs and delays. Some inventors are not well schooled in the rather rarefied patent law regime and may wait overly long before filing a patent application. Even sophisticated enterprises may not recognize the value of an invention until they too have performed acts that defeat its patentability. The trade secret law fills these gaps by providing a modicum of protection for those who take prudent measures to protect valuable information.

Inventors who do not wish to dedicate their technologies to the public domain must choose between maintaining the technology as a trade secret or pursuing patent protection. A number of factors inform this decision. Whether the inventor can keep the technology secret is the most obvious. Many mechanical inventions betray their design upon inspection, while the composition of a chemical compound may be much easier to conceal. The costs associated with acquiring and maintaining patents are another element. A U.S. patent provides rights only within the United States, but discloses its subject matter for anyone in the world to see. Inventors should therefore also consider the expenses of obtaining a patent in each jurisdiction in which he does or wishes to do business.

The product cycle associated with the invention is also of importance. Products with a very short lifespan may be unmarketable by the time a patent issues. Inventors should also consider whether the industry in which they act is patent-intensive. If industry actors tend to invest heavily in maintaining their patent portfolios, then the inventor may well wish to patent for defense purposes or to have a bargaining chip available if he is accused of infringement himself. Legislative enactment of the First Inventor Defense Act of 1999 introduced another element into this calculation. If the invention concerns a "method of doing business" within the meaning of the Act, then the inventor may gain an infringement defense effective against the patents of others the claim that method. 35 U.S.C. § 273.

The publication of a patent application or issuance of a patent will destroy trade secret status for the subject matter that it properly discloses. Nothing prevents a patentee from maintaining an invention as a trade secret until such time, however. This strategy requires the applicant to preserve secrecy until the first of two events: (1) the publication of the application eighteen months following its filing date; or (2) when the PTO issues the patent, for those applications exempted from the publication requirement.

3. Federal Preemption. The tensions between the patent and trade secret laws have sometimes erupted into arguments that the patent statute preempts state trade secret laws. In addition to asserting that trade secrecy discourages disclosure of new inventions, commentators have also observed that the patent law reflects the policy that only new and nonobvious inventions merit proprietary patent rights. Although the requirement that a trade secret not be public knowledge has been equated to the patent law's novelty requirement, the trade secret laws do not demand that the secret subject matter be nonobvious. *See* Gale R. Peterson, *Trade Secrets in an Information Age*, 32 Houston L. Rev. 385 (1995)

[handwritten: trade secrets don't have to be non obvious]

Despite these apparent conflicts, the courts have ruled that trade secret protection may coexist alongside the patent and other intellectual property laws. In *Kewanee Oil Co. v. Bicron Corp.*, 416 U.S. 470 (1974), the Supreme Court observed that trade secret laws also serve a principal purpose of the patent laws, the promotion of innovation. The Court also considered the patent law a far more attractive option for inventors of patentable subject matter and reasoned that most inventors would opt for the patent system. The Court also noted that, as an historical matter, the two bodies of law had been in place since the earliest days of the Republic.

[handwritten: both promote innovation]

Trade Secrets Exercise

You work as a patent attorney in a major metropolitan area. One day, a Mr. Boulanger comes to your office seeking advice. You recognize him as the proprietor of a local bakery shop.

"I need your assistance," Mr. Boulanger says, with obvious concern in his voice. "About two years ago, I developed a formula for low-fat chocolate chip cookies. My products have a homemade taste—that is, they have a crunchy exterior, but a chewy center—but only a fraction of the calories of traditional chocolate chip cookies. I'm selling more cookies than ever before and I want to maintain our unique taste. My trouble is with my former employee, Ms. Cynthia Sisyphus. She left my company a few months ago to start her own bakery shop. Now she has begun to market her own cookies under the trade name 'Infamous Sisyphus.' The cookies taste just like mine! I'm certain that she stole my secret recipe!"

"Once I tasted one of Sisyphus' cookies, I immediately called her." Mr. Boulanger explains. "She claimed that my recipe was simply part of the general knowledge and skills associated with her employment. Her precise words were: 'I'm a baker. My entire set of professional skills consists of knowing various recipes. The only way you would get me to forget how to make chocolate chip cookies would be to perform brain surgery.'"

You ask Mr. Boulanger about the conditions surrounding his cookie recipe. He explains, "Well, I've written the recipe on an index card in my office. The card has the legend TOP SECRET written at the top. I store the index card in my desk, which is ordinarily locked. However, I have other files in my desk, so my accountant, bakers, and other employees need access. Right now I guess about five of my top people have a key to that desk. We're a small company, and I'm usually too busy tinkering with the ovens to stand guard by my desk."

Next, you ask Mr. Boulanger about the terms of the employment contract between his company and Ms. Sisyphus. He responds, "Well, we didn't have a formal contract. I think you lawyers call this arrangement 'employment-at-will' or something like that. But everyone in the bakery business should know that our recipes are confidential. That's how we distinguish ourselves from our competitors. No honest baker would walk out and take a proprietary recipe with him!"

Finally, you inquire as to the details of Mr. Boulanger's secret recipe. After swearing you to secrecy, Mr. Boulanger details a complex set of ingredients and cooking instructions. In essence, he substitutes fructose syrup, polydextrose, guar gum, and various bulking agents for a portion of the more traditional cookie ingredients such as shortening and sugar. These ingredients are then mixed in a precise order and then baked at steadily increasing temperatures until the cookies are complete. "In this way, I can maintain a wonderful taste yet cut the calories and fat by nearly 20%."

"We may seem like a small company now," Mr. Boulanger continues, "but I've got big plans for us. We want to establish retail outlets to sell our cookies domestically and abroad. My market analyst has predicted that our chocolate chip cookies could generate sales of $15 million annually. We could base our entire business on it! Sales of our cookies could continue for ten years or more! Plus ... nobody could ever guess the secret ingredients that make my cookies special! I'm wondering—is this the kind of thing I can get a patent on? And if so, should I try to get a patent on my recipe or keep it as my own secret?"

"But the most important point is my problem with Ms. Sisyphus," Mr. Boulanger concludes. "Will I be able to stop losing a lot of dough to her bakery ... or is that just the way the cookie crumbles?"

How would you advise Mr. Boulanger concerning his chocolate chip cookie recipe?

trade secret — has value and is kept secret
    — yes broke confidence by opening a newshop. (implied)

CHAPTER TWO

PATENT ELIGIBILITY

■ ■ ■

Section 101 of the Patent Act defines the subject matter that may be patented. According to the statute, a person who "invents or discovers any new and useful process, machine, manufacture, or any composition of matter, or any new and useful improvement thereof, may obtain a patent therefore, subject to the conditions and requirements of this title." An invention that falls within one of the four statutory categories—processes, machines, manufactures, and compositions of matter—is eligible to receive a so-called "utility patent" if the other requirements of the Patent Act are met.

The four categories set forth in section 101 refine the term "useful arts," the constitutional expression of the subject matter appropriate for patenting. Historically, the useful arts were contrasted with the liberal and fine arts. The patent system was perceived to be confined to inventions in the field of applied technology. Patentable inventions that employed the natural sciences to manipulate physical forces fell within the useful arts. Innovations that relied upon such things as the social sciences, commercial strategy, or personal skill were often believed to be ineligible for patent protection.

In recent years, however, the patent system has demonstrated an increasing permissiveness towards patent eligible subject matter. In particular, the Court of Appeals for the Federal Circuit has reconsidered earlier case law concerning patent eligibility, ranging from computer software, to printed matter, to methods of doing business. In response to this trend, the Patent and Trademark Office has issued patents involving inventions from a broad range of disciplines, including a golf putt, teaching methods, and techniques of psychological analysis.

The present state of affairs suggests that few, if any restrictions restrict the range of patentable subject matter. Once seemingly limited to natural scientists and engineers, the patent system now appears poised to embrace the broadest reaches of human experience. It is hardly an exaggeration to say that under current law, if you can name it, you can claim it. Much of this chapter will appear of historical significance, with the removal of earlier limitations upon patent eligibility by an increasingly lenient judiciary becoming a familiar pattern. Still, patent eligibility continually proves itself to be an unsettled field. To understand our current state of affairs it is helpful to know how we got here.

Before proceeding further, the reader should note that § 101 twice employs the phrase "new and useful." The section also concludes with the wording, "subject to the conditions and requirements of this title," namely novelty, obviousness, and full disclosure requirements. In light of this wording, the courts have traditionally distinguished patent eligibility from patentability. Thus, the eligibility inquiry into the propriety of property protection for some classes of subject matter is a different matter from determining the newness, nonobviousness, or utility of a particular inventive application. Utility and novelty are addressed in Chapters 3–6 of this casebook.

§ 2.1.   BIOTECHNOLOGY AND PRODUCTS OF NATURE

Since the late 1970s, scientists have been able to cause living organisms to express genetic material from outside their own species, with extraordinary results. New strains of plants produce higher yields, resist viruses and pests, and are productive in formerly inhospitable climates. So-called "transgenic" animals currently produce an array of human pharmaceutical compounds that would otherwise be unavailable due to expense or insufficient sources of supply. Others serve as potent research tools, allowing scientists to explore human diseases for which inadequate, or even no natural animal subjects exist. The prospect of human consumption of superior transgenic livestock, the elimination of certain genetic diseases, and other advances seemingly out of the realm of speculative fiction appear not so distant.

In what may be the only predictable element of this dramatic technical field, applicants quickly sought patent protection for their biotechnology advances. The prospect of patents on "living inventions" ultimately provoked a tremendous outcry, with intense public concern overly a field of law often considered obscure. As you review these materials, consider whether the patent law is itself an appropriate vehicle to resolve the social issues of technical advance.

DIAMOND, COMMISSIONER OF PATENTS AND TRADEMARKS v. CHAKRABARTY

United States Supreme Court, 1980
447 U.S. 303

Dr. Ananda N. Chakrabarty artificially created an oil-eating bacterium and filed a patent application with three sorts of claims. Two of them were in method format—the method of making the bacterium and the method of using the bacterium to consume oil. The third claim category was directed towards the bacterium itself, providing:

7. A bacterium from the genus Pseudomonas containing therein at least two stable energy-generating plasmids, each of said plasmids providing a separate hydrocarbon degradative pathway.

The PTO rejected this latter claim on the ground that the bacterium was a product of nature, or, alternatively, that it was a living thing and therefore outside the purview of Title 35. The Supreme Court ultimately took up the matter and overturned the examiner's rejection in the following opinion.

BURGER, CHIEF JUSTICE.

II

The Constitution grants Congress broad power to legislate to "promote the Progress of Science and useful Arts, by securing for limited Times to Authors and Inventors the exclusive Right to their respective Writings and Discoveries." Art. I, § 8, cl. 8. The patent laws promote this progress by offering inventors exclusive rights for a limited period as an incentive for their inventiveness and research efforts. *Kewanee Oil Co. v. Bicron Corp.*, 416 U.S. 470, 480–481 (1974); *Universal Oil Co. v. Globe Co.*, 322 U.S. 471, 484(1944). The authority of Congress is exercised in the hope that "[t]he productive effort thereby fostered will have a positive effect on society through the introduction of new products and processes of manufacture into the economy, and the emanations by way of increased employment and better lives for our citizens." *Kewanee, supra*, 416 U.S., at 480.

The question before us in this case is a narrow one of statutory interpretation requiring us to construe 35 U.S.C. § 101.... Specifically, we must determine whether respondent's micro-organism constitutes a "manufacture" or "composition of matter" within the meaning of the statute.

III

In cases of statutory construction we begin, of course, with the language of the statute. And "unless otherwise defined, words will be interpreted as taking their ordinary, contemporary common meaning." *Perrin v. United States*, 444 U.S. 37, 42, 100 (1979). We have also cautioned that courts "should not read into the patent laws limitations and conditions which the legislature has not expressed." *United States v. Dubilier Condenser Corp.*, 289 U.S. 178, 199 (1933).

Guided by these canons of construction, this Court has read the term "manufacture" in § 101 in accordance with its dictionary definition to mean "the production of articles for use from raw or prepared materials by giving to these materials new forms, qualities, properties, or combinations, whether by hand-labor or by machinery." *American Fruit Growers, Inc. v. Brogdex Co.*, 283 U.S. 1, 11 (1931). Similarly, "composition of matter" has been construed consistent with its common usage to include "all compositions of two or more substances and ... all composite articles, whether they be the results of chemical union, or of mechanical mixture, or whether they be gases, fluids, powders or solids." *Shell Development Co. v. Watson*, 149 F.Supp. 279, 280 (D.C.1957) (citing 1 A. DELLER, WALKER ON PATENTS § 14, p. 55 (1st ed. 1937)). In choosing such expansive terms as "manufacture" and "composition of matter," modified by the comprehensive "any," Congress plainly contemplated that the patent laws would be given wide scope.

The relevant legislative history also supports a broad construction. The Patent Act of 1793, authored by Thomas Jefferson, defined statutory subject matter as "any new and useful art, machine, manufacture, or composition of matter, or any new or useful improvement [thereof]." Act of Feb. 21, 1793, § 1, 1 Stat. 319. The Act embodied Jefferson's philosophy that "ingenuity should receive a liberal encouragement." 5 WRITINGS OF THOMAS JEFFERSON 75–76 (Washington ed. 1871). See *Graham v. John Deere Co.*, 383 U.S. 1, 7–10 (1966). Subsequent patent statutes in 1836, 1870, and 1874 employed this same broad language. In 1952, when the patent laws were recodified, Congress replaced the word "art" with "process," but otherwise left Jefferson's language intact. The Committee Reports accompanying the 1952 Act inform us that Congress intended statutory subject matter to "include anything under the sun that is made by man." S.Rep.No.1979, 82d Cong., 2d Sess., 5 (1952); H.R.Rep.No.1923, 82d Cong., 2d Sess., 6 (1952).

This is not to suggest that § 101 has no limits or that it embraces every discovery. The laws of nature, physical phenomena, and abstract ideas have been held not patentable. See *Parker v. Flook*, 437 U.S. 584 (1978); *Gottschalk v. Benson*, 409 U.S. 63, 67 (1972); *Funk Brothers Seed Co. v. Kalo Inoculant Co.*, 333 U.S. 127, 130 (1948); *O'Reilly v. Morse*, 15 How. 62, 112–121 (1853); *Le Roy v. Tatham*, 14 How. 156, 175 (1852). Thus, a new mineral discovered in the earth or a new plant found in the wild is not patentable subject matter. Likewise, Einstein could not patent his celebrated law that $E=mc^2$; nor could Newton have patented the law of gravity. Such discoveries are "manifestations of . . . nature, free to all men and reserved exclusively to none." *Funk, supra*, 333 U.S., at 130.

Judged in this light, respondent's micro-organism plainly qualifies as patentable subject matter. His claim is not to a hitherto unknown natural phenomenon, but to a nonnaturally occurring manufacture or composition of matter—a product of human ingenuity "having a distinctive name, character [and] use." *Hartranft v. Wiegmann*, 121 U.S. 609, 615 (1887). The point is underscored dramatically by comparison of the invention here with that in *Funk*. There, the patentee had discovered that there existed in nature certain species of root-nodule bacteria which did not exert a mutually inhibitive effect on each other. He used that discovery to produce a mixed culture capable of inoculating the seeds of leguminous plants. Concluding that the patentee had discovered "only some of the handiwork of nature," the Court ruled the product nonpatentable:

"Each of the species of root-nodule bacteria contained in the package infects the same group of leguminous plants which it always infected. No species acquires a different use. The combination of species produces no new bacteria, no change in the six species of bacteria, and no enlargement of the range of their utility. Each species has the same effect it always had. The bacteria perform in their natural way. Their use in combination does not improve in any way their natural functioning. They serve the ends nature originally provided and act quite independently of any effort of the patentee." 333 U.S., at 131.

Here, by contrast, the patentee has produced a new bacterium with markedly different characteristics from any found in nature and one having the potential for significant utility. His discovery is not nature's handiwork, but his own; accordingly it is patentable subject matter under § 101.

IV

Two contrary arguments are advanced, neither of which we find persuasive.

The petitioner's first argument rests on the enactment of the 1930 Plant Patent Act, which afforded patent protection to certain asexually reproduced plants, and the 1970 Plant Variety Protection Act, which authorized protection for certain sexually reproduced plants but excluded bacteria from its protection. In the petitioner's view, the passage of these Acts evidences congressional understanding that the terms "manufacture" or "composition of matter" do not include living things; if they did, the petitioner argues, neither Act would have been necessary.

We reject this argument. Prior to 1930, two factors were thought to remove plants from patent protection. The first was the belief that plants, even those artificially bred, were products of nature for purposes of the patent law. This position appears to have derived from the decision of the patent office in *Ex parte Latimer*, 1889 Dec.Com.Pat. 123, in which a patent claim for fiber found in the needle of the *Pinus australis* was rejected. The Commissioner reasoned that a contrary result would permit "patents [to] be obtained upon the trees of the forest and the plants of the earth, which of course would be unreasonable and impossible." *Id.*, at 126. The *Latimer* case, it seems, came to "se[t] forth the general stand taken in these matters" that plants were natural products not subject to patent protection. Thorne, *Relation of Patent Law to Natural Products*, 6 J. PAT.OFF.SOC. 23, 24 (1923). The second obstacle to patent protection for plants was the fact that plants were thought not amenable to the "written description" requirement of the patent law. See 35 U.S.C. § 112. Because new plants may differ from old only in color or perfume, differentiation by written description was often impossible. *See* Hearings on H.R.11372 before the House Committee on Patents, 71st Cong., 2d Sess. 7 (1930) (memorandum of Patent Commissioner Robertson).

In enacting the Plant Patent Act, Congress addressed both of these concerns. It explained at length its belief that the work of the plant breeder "in aid of nature" was patentable invention. S.Rep.No.315, 71st Cong., 2d Sess., 6–8 (1930); H.R.Rep.No.1129, 71st Cong., 2d Sess., 7–9 (1930). And it relaxed the written description requirement in favor of "a description . . . as complete as is reasonably possible." 35 U.S.C. § 162. No Committee or Member of Congress, however, expressed the broader view, now urged by the petitioner, that the terms "manufacture" or "composition of matter" exclude living things. The sole support for that position in the legislative history of the 1930 Act is found in the conclusory statement of Secretary of Agriculture Hyde, in a letter to the Chairmen of the House and Senate Committees considering the 1930 Act, that "the patent laws . . . at the present time are understood to cover only inventions or discoveries in the field of inanimate nature." *See* S.Rep.No.315, *supra*, at Appendix A; H.R.Rep.No.1129, *supra*, at Appendix A. Secretary Hyde's opinion, however, is not entitled to controlling weight. His views were solicited on the administration of the new law and not on the scope of patentable subject matter—an area beyond his competence. Moreover, there is language in the House and Senate Committee Reports suggesting that to the extent Congress considered the matter it found the Secretary's dichotomy unpersuasive. The Reports observe:

> "There is a clear and logical distinction *between the discovery of a new variety of plant and of certain inanimate things*, such, for example, as a new and useful natural mineral. The mineral is created wholly by nature unassisted by man. . . . On the other hand, a plant discovery resulting from cultivation is unique, isolated, and is not repeated by nature, nor can it be reproduced by nature unaided by man. . . ." S.Rep.No.315, *supra*, at 6; H.R.Rep.No.1129, *supra*, at 7 (emphasis added).

Congress thus recognized that the relevant distinction was not between living and inanimate things, but between products of nature, whether living or not, and human-made inventions. Here, respondent's microorganism is the result of human ingenuity and research. Hence, the passage of the Plant Patent Act affords the Government no support.

Nor does the passage of the 1970 Plant Variety Protection Act support the Government's position. As the Government acknowledges, sexually reproduced plants were not included under the 1930 Act because new varieties could not be reproduced true-to-type through seedlings. Brief for Petitioner 27, n. 31. By 1970, however, it was generally recognized that true-to-type reproduction was possible and that plant patent protection was therefore appropriate. The 1970 Act extended that protection. There is nothing in its language or history to suggest that it was enacted because § 101 did not include living things.

In particular, we find nothing in the exclusion of bacteria from plant variety protection to support the petitioner's position. The legislative history gives no reason for this exclusion. As the Court of Customs and Patent Appeals suggested, it may simply reflect congressional agreement with the result reached by that court in deciding *In re Arzberger*, 112 F.2d 834 (1940), which held that bacteria were not plants for the purposes of the 1930 Act. Or it may reflect the fact that prior to 1970 the Patent Office had issued patents for bacteria under § 101. In any event, absent some clear indication that Congress "focused on [the] issues ... directly related to the one presently before the Court," *SEC v. Sloan*, 436 U.S. 103, 120–121 (1978), there is no basis for reading into its actions an intent to modify the plain meaning of the words found in § 101.

The petitioner's second argument is that micro-organisms cannot qualify as patentable subject matter until Congress expressly authorizes such protection. His position rests on the fact that genetic technology was unforeseen when Congress enacted § 101. From this it is argued that resolution of the patentability of inventions such as respondent's should be left to Congress. The legislative process, the petitioner argues, is best equipped to weigh the competing economic, social, and scientific considerations involved, and to determine whether living organisms produced by genetic engineering should receive patent protection. In support of this position, the petitioner relies on our recent holding in *Parker v. Flook*, 437 U.S. 584 (1978), and the statement that the judiciary "must proceed cautiously when ... asked to extend patent rights into areas wholly unforeseen by Congress." *Id.*, at 596.

It is, of course, correct that Congress, not the courts, must define the limits of patentability; but it is equally true that once Congress has spoken it is "the province and duty of the judicial department to say what the law is." *Marbury v. Madison*, 1 Cranch 137, 177 (1803). Congress has performed its constitutional role in defining patentable subject matter in § 101; we perform ours in construing the language Congress has employed. In so doing, our obligation is to take statutes as we find them, guided, if ambiguity appears, by the legislative history and statutory purpose. Here, we perceive no ambiguity. The subject-matter provisions of the patent law have been cast in broad terms to fulfill the constitutional and statutory goal of promoting "the Progress of Science and the useful Arts" with all that means for the social and economic benefits envisioned by Jefferson. Broad general language is not necessarily ambiguous when congressional objectives require broad terms.

Nothing in *Flook* is to the contrary. That case applied our prior precedents to determine that a "claim for an improved method of calculation, even when tied to a specific end use, is unpatentable subject matter under § 101." 437 U.S., at 595, n. 18. The Court carefully scrutinized the claim at issue to determine whether it was precluded from patent protection under "the principles underlying the prohibition against patents for 'ideas' or phenomena of nature." *Id.*, at 593. We have done that here. *Flook* did not announce a new principle that inventions in areas not contemplated by Congress when the patent laws were enacted are unpatentable per se.

To read that concept into Flook would frustrate the purposes of the patent law. This Court frequently has observed that a statute is not to be confined to the "particular application[s] ... contemplated by the legislators." *Barr v. United States*, 324 U.S. 83, 90 (1945). This is especially true in the field of patent law. A rule that unanticipated inventions are without protection would conflict with the core concept of the patent law that anticipation undermines patentability. *See Graham v. John Deere Co.*, 383 U.S., at 12–17. Mr. Justice Douglas reminded that the inventions most benefiting mankind are those that "push back the frontiers of chemistry, physics, and the like." *Great A. & P. Tea Co. v. Supermarket Corp.*, 340 U.S. 147, 154 (1950) (concurring opinion). Congress employed broad general language in drafting § 101 precisely because such inventions are often unforeseeable.

To buttress his argument, the petitioner, with the support of amicus, points to grave risks that may be generated by research endeavors such as respondent's. The briefs present a gruesome parade of horribles. Scientists, among them Nobel laureates, are quoted suggesting that genetic research may pose a serious threat to the human race, or, at the very least, that the dangers are far too substantial to permit such research to proceed apace at this time. We are told that genetic research and related technological developments may spread pollution and disease, that it may result in a loss of genetic diversity, and that its practice may tend to depreciate the value of human life. These arguments are forcefully, even passionately, presented; they remind us that, at times, human ingenuity seems unable to control fully the forces it creates—that with Hamlet, it is sometimes better "to bear those ills we have than fly to others that we know not of."

It is argued that this Court should weigh these potential hazards in considering whether respondent's invention is patentable subject matter under § 101. We disagree. The grant or denial of patents on microorganisms is not likely to put an end to genetic research or to its attendant risks. The large amount of research that has already occurred when no researcher had sure knowledge that patent protection would be available suggests that legislative or judicial fiat as to patentability will not deter the scientific mind from probing into the unknown any more than Canute could command the tides. Whether respondent's claims are patentable may determine whether research efforts are accelerated by the hope of reward or slowed by want of incentives, but that is all.

What is more important is that we are without competence to entertain these arguments—either to brush them aside as fantasies generated by fear of the unknown, or to act on them. The choice we are urged to make is a matter of high policy for resolution within the legislative process after the kind of investigation, examination, and study that legislative bodies can provide and courts cannot. That process involves the balancing of competing values and interests, which in our democratic system is the business of elected representatives. Whatever their validity, the contentions now pressed on us should be addressed to the political branches of the Government, the Congress and the Executive, and not to the courts.

We have emphasized in the recent past that "[o]ur individual appraisal of the wisdom or unwisdom of a particular [legislative] course . . . is to be put aside in the process of interpreting a statute." *TVA v. Hill*, 437 U.S., at 194. Our task, rather, is the narrow one of determining what Congress meant by the words it used in the statute; once that is done our powers are exhausted. Congress is free to amend § 101 so as to exclude from patent protection organisms produced by genetic engineering. *Cf.* 42 U.S.C.A. § 2181(a), exempting from patent protection inventions "useful solely in the utilization of special nuclear material or atomic energy in an atomic weapon." Or it may chose to craft a statute specifically designed for such living things. But, until Congress takes such action, this Court must construe the language of § 101 as it is. The language of that section fairly embraces respondent's invention.

NOTES

1. **Questioning *Chakrabarty*.** In *Chakrabarty*, the Supreme Court adopted a definition of the term "composition of matter" to include "all compositions of two or more substances and . . . all composite articles, whether they be the results of chemical union, or of mechanical mixture, or whether they be gases, fluids, powders or solids." If this is so, what role do the terms "machine" and "manufacture" play in § 101?

Consider also the definition of the term "manufacture," which is said to mean "the production of articles for use from raw or prepared materials by giving to these materials new forms, qualities, properties, or combinations, whether by hand-labor or by machinery." Applying these definitions, do you believe a living organism is comfortably described as either a "composition of matter" or "manufacture"? For a different perspective on these questions, see *Harvard College v. Canada*, 4 S.C.R. 34 (Supreme Court of Canada 2002).

2. **Anything Under the Sun.** The *Chakrabarty* Court cites the legislative history of the 1952 Act as stating that patentable subject matter includes "anything under the sun that is made by man." Does § 101 actually incorporate this phrase? Further, observe that the entire sentence from the congressional committee reads:

> A person may have "invented" a machine or a manufacture, which may include anything under the sun that is made by man, but it is not necessarily patentable under section 101 unless the conditions of the title are fulfilled.

Did the Supreme Court's more limited quotation of this language in *Chakrabarty* overlook anything of importance?

3. Isolated and Purified. *Diamond v. Chakrabarty* confirmed the general rule that patents are not available for "products of nature" *per se*. A scientist could therefore not obtain a patent on a previously unknown plant that she discovered in the wild. A patent may be obtained once significant artificial changes are made to that natural substance, however. If a naturally occurring substance is isolated from its source, for example, it may be patented to that extent. The Supreme Court explained in *Diamond v. Chakrabarty* that in such instances, the inventor's "claim is not to hitherto unknown natural phenomenon, but to a nonnaturally occurring manufacture or composition of matter—a product of human ingenuity 'having a distinctive name, character [and] use.'" 447 U.S. at 309–10. Many patents from the biotechnology therefore include the terms "isolated" or "purified" in their claims. *See, e.g.*, U.S. Patent No. 5,955,422 (claiming in part a "pharmaceutical composition comprising a therapeutically effective amount of human erythropoietin and a pharmaceutically acceptable diluent, adjuvant or carrier, wherein said erythropoietin is purified from mammalian cells grown in culture."). *See generally* Eileen M. Kane, *Splitting the Gene: DNA Patents and the Generic Code*, 71 TENN. L. REV. 707 (2004).

4. From *Diamond* to *J.E.M*. Although the *Chakrabarty* was a 5–4 decision, its precedential value has remained steady over the past three decades. Indeed, the Supreme Court took the opportunity to confirm its earlier ruling in 2001. The occasion was *J.E.M. Ag Supply, Inc. v. Pioneer Hi–Bred International*, 534 U.S. 124, 122 S.Ct. 593 (2001). The plaintiff in that litigation, Pioneer, accused Farm Advantage of infringing 17 patents claiming inbred and hybrid corn seed products. Among the defenses of Farm Advantage was that each of the patents was invalid under § 101. Farm Advantage more particularly asserted that Congress had enacted another statute, the Plant Variety Protection Act (PVPA), that was intended to provide the exclusive regime of protection for seed-bearing plants.

In fact, three federal intellectual property regimes potentially establish proprietary rights in plant inventions. The first is the Townsend–Purcell Plant Patent Act of 1930, 46 Stat. 376, which is codified at 35 U.S.C. §§ 161–164. The PTO issues plant patents on distinct and new varieties of plants that have been asexually reproduced, through grafting, budding, or other methods. The second, the PVPA, was enacted by Congress in 1970. Pub. L. No. 91–577, codified at 7 U.S.C. § 2321 *et seq.* The PVPA authorizes the U.S. Department of Agriculture to issue plant variety protection certificates on new, distinct, uniform, and stable sexually reproduced plants, including most seed-bearing plants. Finally, the usual sort of patent, more precisely known as "utility" patents, might also apply to plants depending upon the interpretation of § 101.

In *J.E.M. v. Pioneer*, the Supreme Court concluded that patents might appropriately issue for plants, notwithstanding the existence of the plant-specific statutes. In its 2001 decision, the Supreme Court affirmed the result of the lower courts. Justice Thomas wrote the decision for the majority. He initially observed that § 101 employed broad language, including the words "manufacture" and "composition of matter." These terms readily include artificially generated plants and plant parts, the majority reasoned.

The majority next rejected arguments that congressional enactment of specialized legislation evidenced the congressional intent that living plants could not be the subject of utility patents. Justice Thomas found no specific statement in the legislative history of the utility patent statute or the PVPA suggesting that utility patents could not issue on plants. Instead, he explained, these statutes illustrated only that "Congress *believed* that plants were not patentable under § 101, both because they were living things and because in practice they could not meet the stringent description requirement. Yet these premises were disproved over time." 534 U.S. at 134.

Justice Thomas also observed that a particular legal or property interest is often the subject of multiple statutes. For example, computer software may qualify for protection under both the copyright and patent laws. Justice Thomas concluded that merely because these laws may be of different scope does not suggest that some of them are inapplicable.

5. Patentability in Europe. In contrast to the U.S. statute, the European Patent Convention does not expressly state which sorts of inventions are patent-eligible. The Convention instead defines patent-eligibility in the negative, excluding the following categories of inventions: "(a) discoveries, scientific theories and mathematical methods; (b) aesthetic creations; (c) schemes, rules and methods for performing mental acts, playing games or doing business, and programs for computers; and (d) presentations of information." EPC, Art. 52(2). However, the Convention goes on to state that this subject matter is excluded "only to the extent to which a European patent application or European patent relates to such subject-matter or activities as such." *Id.*, Art. 52(3).

As will be seen, U.S. case law provided, or once did provide, exceptions that are similar to many of those of EPC Article 52. Determination of their precise scope has proven very challenging for a number of reasons. No one discernable purpose unifies these exceptions, at least at any level of precision that is helpful in deciding particular cases. As one example, why did the drafters of the EPC in the same clause prohibit patents on both methods of playing games and programs for computers? Some of the excluded subject matter is subject to other regimes of proprietary rights—for example, copyright applies to aesthetic creations—but others, like scientific theories, are not. And of course, much seems to rest on the enigmatic phrase "as such." For further discussion of these points, see *Aerotel Ltd. v. Telco Holdings Ltd.*, [2007] R.P.C. 7 (Court of Appeal 2006).

6. The TRIPS Agreement. The TRIPS Agreement also weighs in on patent eligibility standards. Article 27 of that agreement defines patentable subject matter as follows:

> 1. Subject to the provisions of paragraphs 2 and 3, patents shall be available for any inventions, whether products or processes, in all fields of technology, provided that they are new, involve an inventive step and are capable of industrial application.[1] Subject to paragraph 4 of Article 65,

---

1. "For the purposes of this Article, the terms 'inventive step' and 'capable of industrial application' may be deemed by a Member to be synonymous with the terms 'non-obvious' and 'useful' respectively."

paragraph 8 of Article 70 and paragraph 3 of this Article, patents shall be available and patent rights enjoyable without discrimination as to the place of invention, the field of technology and whether products are imported or locally produced.

> 2.   Members may exclude from patentability inventions, the prevention within their territory of the commercial exploitation of which is necessary to protect ordre public or morality, including to protect human, animal or plant life or health or to avoid serious prejudice to the environment, provided that such exclusion is not made merely because the exploitation is prohibited by their law.

In paragraph 3, Article 27 of the TRIPS Agreement further provides that members may also exclude from patentability:

> (a) diagnostic, therapeutic and surgical methods for the treatment of humans or animals;

> (b) plants and animals other than micro-organisms, and essentially biological processes for the production of plants or animals other than non-biological and microbiological processes. However, Members shall provide for the protection of plant varieties either by patents or by an effective *sui generis* system or by any combination thereof. The provisions of this subparagraph shall be reviewed four years after the date of entry into force of the WTO Agreement.

The pledge that each WTO member state agreed to allow patents to issue on inventions "in all fields of technology" stands as among the more prominent change to international patent policy wrought by the TRIPS Agreement. Its principal effect was to require the amendment of numerous foreign patent laws that declared pharmaceuticals ineligible for patenting. As the TRIPS Agreement has come to be implemented, both its practical achievability and fairness remain controversial subjects in the international community.

LABORATORY CORPORATION OF AMERICA HOLDINGS v. METABOLITE LABORATORIES, INC.

United States Supreme Court, 2006
548 U.S. 124

Writ of certiorari dismissed as improvidently granted.

JUSTICE BREYER, with whom JUSTICE STEVENS and JUSTICE SOUTER join, dissenting.

This case involves a patent that claims a process for helping to diagnose deficiencies of two vitamins, folate and cobalamin. The process consists of using any test (whether patented or unpatented) to measure the level in a body fluid of an amino acid called homocysteine and then noticing whether its level is elevated above the norm; if so, a vitamin deficiency is likely.

The lower courts held that the patent claim is valid. They also found the petitioner, Laboratory Corporation of America Holdings

(LabCorp), liable for inducing infringement of the claim when it encouraged doctors to order diagnostic tests for measuring homocysteine. The courts assessed damages. And they enjoined LabCorp from using any tests that would lead the doctors it serves to find a vitamin deficiency by taking account of elevated homocysteine levels.

We granted certiorari in this case to determine whether the patent claim is invalid on the ground that it improperly seeks to "claim a monopoly over a basic scientific relationship," namely, the relationship between homocysteine and vitamin deficiency. The Court has dismissed the writ as improvidently granted. In my view, we should not dismiss the writ. The question presented is not unusually difficult. We have the authority to decide it. We said that we would do so. The parties and amici have fully briefed the question. And those who engage in medical research, who practice medicine, and who as patients depend upon proper health care, might well benefit from this Court's authoritative answer.

I

A

The relevant principle of law "[e]xclude[s] from ... patent protection ... laws of nature, natural phenomena, and abstract ideas." *Diamond v. Diehr*, 450 U.S. 175, 185 (1981). This principle finds its roots in both English and American law. See, e.g., *Neilson v. Harford*, Webster's Patent Cases 295, 371 (1841); *Le Roy v. Tatham*, 14 How. 156, 175 (1852); *O'Reilly v. Morse*, 15 How. 62 (1853); *The Telephone Cases*, 126 U.S. 1 (1888). The principle means that Einstein could not have "patent[ed] his celebrated law that $E=mc^2$; nor could Newton have patented the law of gravity." *Diamond v. Chakrabarty*, 447 U.S. 303, 309 (1980). Neither can one patent "a novel and useful mathematical formula," *Parker v. Flook*, 437 U.S. 584, 585 (1978), the motive power of electromagnetism or steam, *Morse, supra*, at 116, "the heat of the sun, electricity, or the qualities of metals," *Funk Brothers Seed Co. v. Kalo Inoculant Co.*, 333 U.S. 127, 130 (1948).

The justification for the principle does not lie in any claim that "laws of nature" are obvious, or that their discovery is easy, or that they are not useful. To the contrary, research into such matters may be costly and time-consuming; monetary incentives may matter; and the fruits of those incentives and that research may prove of great benefit to the human race. Rather, the reason for the exclusion is that sometimes too much patent protection can impede rather than "promote the Progress of Science and useful Arts," the constitutional objective of patent and copyright protection.

The problem arises from the fact that patents do not only encourage research by providing monetary incentives for invention. Sometimes their presence can discourage research by impeding the free exchange of information, for example by forcing researchers to avoid the use of potentially patented ideas, by leading them to conduct costly and time-consuming searches of existing or pending patents, by requiring complex licensing arrangements, and by raising the costs of using the patented information, sometimes prohibitively so.

Patent law seeks to avoid the dangers of overprotection just as surely as it seeks to avoid the diminished incentive to invent that underprotection can threaten. One way in which patent law seeks to sail between these opposing and risky shoals is through rules that bring certain types of invention and discovery within the scope of patentability while excluding others. And scholars have noted that "patent law['s] exclu[sion of] fundamental scientific (including mathematical) and technological principles," (like copyright's exclusion of "ideas") is a rule of the latter variety. W. Landes & R. Posner, *The Economic Structure of Intellectual Property Law* 305 (2003). That rule reflects "both ... the enormous potential for rent seeking that would be created if property rights could be obtained in [those basic principles] and ... the enormous transaction costs that would be imposed on would-be users." *Id.*, at 305–306; *cf. Nichols v. Universal Pictures Corp.*, 45 F.2d 119, 122 (C.A.2 1930) (L. Hand, J.).

Thus, the Court has recognized that "[p]henomena of nature, though just discovered, mental processes, and abstract intellectual concepts are ... the basic tools of scientific and technological work." *Gottschalk v. Benson*, 409 U.S. 63, 67 (1972). It has treated fundamental scientific principles as "part of the storehouse of knowledge" and manifestations of laws of nature as "free to all men and reserved exclusively to none." *Funk Bros., supra*, at 130. And its doing so reflects a basic judgment that protection in such cases, despite its potentially positive incentive effects, would too often severely interfere with, or discourage, development and the further spread of useful knowledge itself.

B

In the 1980s three university doctors, after conducting research into vitamin deficiencies, found a correlation between high levels of homocysteine in the blood and deficiencies of two essential vitamins, folate (folic acid) and cobalamin (vitamin B^{12}). They also developed more accurate methods for testing body fluids for homocysteine, using gas chromatography and mass spectrometry. They published their findings in 1985. They obtained a patent. And that patent eventually found its commercial way into the hands of Competitive Technologies, Inc. (CTI), and its licensee Metabolite Laboratories, Inc. (Metabolite), the respondents here.

The patent contains several claims that cover the researchers' new methods for testing homocysteine levels using gas chromatography and mass spectrometry. In 1991, LabCorp (in fact, a corporate predecessor) took a license from Metabolite permitting it to use the tests described in the patent in return for 27.5% of related revenues. Their agreement permitted LabCorp to terminate the arrangement if "a more cost effective commercial alternative is available that does not infringe a valid and enforceable claim of" the patent.

Until 1998, LabCorp used the patented tests and paid royalties. By that time, however, growing recognition that elevated homocysteine levels might predict risk of heart disease led to increased testing demand. Other companies began to produce alternative testing procedures. And LabCorp decided to use one of these other procedures-a test devised by Abbott Laboratories that LabCorp concluded was "far superior."

LabCorp continued to pay royalties to respondents whenever it used the patented tests. But it concluded that Abbott's test did not fall within the patent's protective scope. And LabCorp consequently refused to pay royalties when it used the Abbott test.

In response, respondents brought this suit against LabCorp for patent infringement and breach of the license agreement. They did not claim that LabCorp's use of the Abbott test infringed the patent's claims describing methods for testing for homocysteine. Instead, respondents relied on a broader claim not limited to those tests, namely claim 13, the sole claim at issue here. That claim-set forth below in its entirety-seeks patent protection for:

> A method for detecting a deficiency of cobalamin or folate in warm-blooded animals comprising the steps of:
>
> assaying a body fluid for an elevated level of total homocysteine; and
>
> correlating an elevated level of total homocysteine in said body fluid with a deficiency of cobalamin or folate.

Claim 13, respondents argued, created a protected monopoly over the process of "correlating" test results and potential vitamin deficiencies. The parties agreed that the words "assaying a body fluid" refer to the use of any test at all, whether patented or not patented, that determines whether a body fluid has an "elevated level of total homocysteine." And at trial, the inventors testified that claim 13's "correlating" step consists simply of a physician's recognizing that a test that shows an elevated homocysteine level-by that very fact-shows the patient likely has a cobalamin or folate deficiency. They added that, because the natural relationship between homocysteine and vitamin deficiency was now well known, such "correlating" would occur automatically in the mind of any competent physician.

On this understanding of the claim, respondents argued, LabCorp was liable for inducing doctors to infringe. More specifically, LabCorp would conduct homocysteine tests and report the results measured in micromoles (millionths of a mole) per liter (symbolized μmol/L). Doctors, because of their training, would know that a normal homocysteine range in blood is between 7 and 22 μmol/L (and in urine between 1 and

20 μmol/L), Supp.App. 14, and would know that an elevated homocysteine level is correlated with a vitamin deficiency. Hence, in reviewing the test results, doctors would look at the μmol/L measure and automatically reach a conclusion about whether or not a person was suffering from a vitamin deficiency. Claim 13 therefore covered every homocysteine test that a doctor reviewed. And since LabCorp had advertised its tests and educated doctors about the correlation, LabCorp should be liable for actively inducing the doctors' infringing acts.

[handwritten margin note: Claim 13 covers all homocysteine tests]

The jury found LabCorp liable on this theory. The District Court calculated damages based on unpaid royalties for some 350,000 homocysteine tests performed by LabCorp using the Abbott method. The court also enjoined LabCorp from performing "any homocysteine-only test, including, without limitation homocysteine-only tests via the Abbott method."

[handwritten margin note: jury found LabCorp liable and enjoined them from performing homocysteine-only tests]

LabCorp appealed. It argued to the Federal Circuit that the trial court was wrong to construe claim 13 so broadly that infringement took place "every time a physician does nothing more than look at a patient's homocysteine level." Indeed, if so construed (rather than construed, say, to cover only patented tests), then claim 13 was "invalid for indefiniteness, lack of written description, non-enablement, anticipation, and obviousness." LabCorp told the Federal Circuit:

[handwritten margin note: LabCorp claims its a basic scientific fact and anyone could patent anything then. Fed Circuit rejected opinion.]

> If the Court were to uphold this vague claim, anyone could obtain a patent on any scientific correlation—that there is a link between fact A and fact B-merely by drafting a patent claiming no more than 'test for fact A and correlate with fact B'. . . . Claim 13 does no more than that. If it is upheld, CTI would improperly gain a monopoly over a basic scientific fact rather than any novel invention of its own. The law is settled that no such claim should be allowed.

The Federal Circuit rejected LabCorp's arguments. . . .

*   *   *

LabCorp filed a petition for certiorari. Question Three of the petition asks "[w]hether a method patent . . . directing a party simply to 'correlate' test results can validly claim a monopoly over a basic scientific relationship . . . such that any doctor necessarily infringes the patent merely by thinking about the relationship after looking at a test result." After calling for and receiving the views of the Solicitor General, we granted the petition, limited to Question Three.

III

I turn to the merits. The researchers who obtained the present patent found that an elevated level of homocysteine in a warm-blooded animal is correlated with folate and cobalamin deficiencies. As construed by the Federal Circuit, claim 13 provides those researchers with control over doctors' efforts to use that correlation to diagnose vitamin deficiencies in a patient. Does the law permit such protection or does claim 13,

[handwritten margin note: Can the law permit such a protection of Claim 13]

in the circumstances, amount to an invalid effort to patent a "phenomenon of nature"?

I concede that the category of non-patentable "phenomena of nature," like the categories of "mental processes," and "abstract intellectual concepts," is not easy to define. After all, many a patentable invention rests upon its inventor's knowledge of natural phenomena; many "process" patents seek to make abstract intellectual concepts workably concrete; and all conscious human action involves a mental process. Nor can one easily use such abstract categories directly to distinguish instances of likely beneficial, from likely harmful, forms of protection.

But this case is not at the boundary. It does not require us to consider the precise scope of the "natural phenomenon" doctrine or any other difficult issue. In my view, claim 13 is invalid no matter how narrowly one reasonably interprets that doctrine.

There can be little doubt that the correlation between homocysteine and vitamin deficiency set forth in claim 13 is a "natural phenomenon."....

* * *

The respondents argue, however, that the correlation is nonetheless patentable because claim 13 packages it in the form of a "process" for detecting vitamin deficiency, with discrete testing and correlating steps. They point to this Court's statements that a "process is not unpatentable simply because it contains a law of nature," *Flook*, 437 U.S., at 590; *see also Gottschalk*, 409 U.S., at 67, and that "an application of a law of nature ... to a known ... process may well be deserving of patent protection." *Diehr*, 450 U.S., at 187. They add that claim 13 is a patentable "application of a law of nature" because, considered as a whole, it (1) "entails a physical transformation of matter," namely, the alteration of a blood sample during whatever test is used, and because it (2) "produces a 'useful, concrete, and tangible result,'" namely, detection of a vitamin deficiency.....

* * *

Even were I to assume (purely for argument's sake) that claim 13 meets certain general definitions of process patentability, however, it still fails the one at issue here: the requirement that it not amount to a simple natural correlation, i.e., a "natural phenomenon."

At most, respondents have simply described the natural law at issue in the abstract patent language of a "process." But they cannot avoid the fact that the process is no more than an instruction to read some numbers in light of medical knowledge. One might, of course, reduce the "process" to a series of steps, e.g., Step 1: gather data; Step 2: read a number; Step 3: compare the number with the norm; Step 4: act accordingly. But one can reduce any process to a series of steps. The question is what those steps embody. And here, aside from the unpatented test, they embody only the correlation between homocysteine and vitamin deficiency that the researchers uncovered. In my view, that correlation is an unpatentable "natural phenomenon," and I can find nothing in claim 13 that adds anything more of significance.

correlation is unpatentable

IV

If I am correct in my conclusion in Part III that the patent is invalid, then special public interest considerations reinforce my view that we should decide this case. To fail to do so threatens to leave the medical profession subject to the restrictions imposed by this individual patent and others of its kind. Those restrictions may inhibit doctors from using their best medical judgment; they may force doctors to spend unnecessary time and energy to enter into license agreements; they may divert resources from the medical task of health care to the legal task of searching patent files for similar simple correlations; they may raise the cost of healthcare while inhibiting its effective delivery.

May force doctors to make bad choices or spend too much money

For these reasons, I respectfully dissent.

NOTES

1. **Digging *LabCorp*.** Although some readers might question the desirability of including a dissent from a dismissal of certiorari as improvidently granted within any casebook, it should be appreciated that three Justices is 60% of a majority, and 75% of the number required to grant certiorari in a future case. Furthermore, these three Justices saw the case as any easy one. For an appreciation of the impact of *Lab. Corp.* upon the Federal Circuit, review the final opinion in this chapter, *In re Bilski*.

2. **Prescription for "*LabCORPSE?*"** With more research, scientists may learn that breast cancer can be detected with near 100% accuracy (and prevented) with knowledge of a "simple natural correlation" between a particular gene and a particular environmental condition. Or maybe scientists will learn that a "simple natural correlation" between two factors in a blood test diagnose ALS in time to prevent it. Thus, patent eligibility in this context poses a difficult question: Does the statute mean to deny protection outright to all research on "simple natural correlations?" If so, of course, investment funds for lab research on those particular "basic scientific relationships" may seek more secure outlets (cosmetics or obesity treatments, unless, of course, they are natural correlations too), leaving labs without resources to find life-saving natural correlations. One way to examine the question of eligibility asks if the public wishes to deny protection for research investments to some fields of scientific endeavor. Is there a substitute for that lab funding without the incentives and protections of the patent system?

3. **Methods of Medical Treatment.** The invention discussed in *LabCorp* brings to mind the special rules pertaining to methods of medical treatment under U.S. patent law. In the mid–1990's, the American Medical Association House of Delegates condemned the patenting of medical and surgical procedures. *See* Brian McCormick, *Just Rewards or Just Plain Wrong? Specter of Royalties*

from Method Patents Stirs Debate, 37 AM. MED. NEWS 3 (1994). The concerns of the AMA and other observers include the threat to public health occasioned by injunctions imposed against the use of patented medical methods; the derogation of the ethical obligations of doctors to disclose medical advances freely; the potential increase to the already extraordinary costs of health care; the interference of the patent system with the ordinary process of peer review of new medical procedures; and the possibility of the invasion of patient privacy in connection with patent enforcement efforts. Are any of these concerns peculiar, or at least peculiarly acute, to the medical profession, as opposed to the class of inventors generally?

In response to this alarm, legislation signed into law on September 30, 1996, created a new 35 U.S.C.A. § 287(c) which deprives patentees of remedies against medical practitioners engaged in infringing "medical activity." The statute defines "medical activity" as "the performance of a medical or surgical procedure on a body." The statute expressly provides that the use of patented machine, machines, or compositions of matter, the practice of a patented use of a composition of matter, and the practice of a patented biotechnology process do not comprise "medical activity." Under § 287(c), injunctions, damages, and attorney fees are unavailable from medical practitioners and related entities. *See* Cynthia M. Ho, *Patents, Patients, and Public Policy: An Incomplete Intersection at 35 U.S.C. § 287(c)*, 33 U.C. DAVIS L. REV. 601 (2000). Does any practical distinction exist between this measure and declaring medical methods not patent eligible under § 101? Does this legislation violate Article 27 of the TRIPS Agreement? *See* generally Gerald J. Mossinghoff, *Remedies Under Patents on Medical and Surgical Procedures*, 78 J. PAT. & TRADEMARK OFF. SOC'Y 789 (1996).

4. Diagnostic Methods. In Europe, the invention involved in the *LabCorp* litigation would be scrutinized to determine whether it could be characterized as a method "of treatment of the human or animal body by surgery or therapy and diagnostic methods practiced on the human or animal body." EPC Art. 53(3). Such methods are expressly barred from patentability under the EPC. However, this exclusionary principle expressly does not apply to "products, in particular substances or compositions, for use in any of these methods." *Id.* It should be appreciated that the chief tribunal of the European Patent Office, the Enlarged Board of Appeal, has interpreted this exception narrowly. See G 1/04 (Dec. 16, 2005). The essence of this interpretation is that a claimed method is deemed an unpatentable "diagnostic method" within the meaning of Article 53(3) only if each of its steps involves the mental activity of attributing particular symptoms to a disease. As a result, claim 13 of Metabolite's patent would seem readily to pass muster even under the EPC.

§ 2.2. COMPUTER–RELATED INVENTIONS AND METHODS OF DOING BUSINESS

Three of the categories of patent-eligible subject matter set forth in 35 U.S.C.A. § 101 refer to physical artifacts themselves: machines, compositions of matter, and articles of manufacture. In themselves, these categories have presented scant difficulties for courts, likely due to their relatively discrete and tangible nature. The fourth possibility, "process," has proven decidedly more difficult. The Patent Act itself is not of considerable assistance in clarifying this term, as it circularly defines process to mean "process, art or method, and includes a new use of a known process, machine, manufacture, composition of matter, or method." 35 U.S.C.A. § 100(b). Following the earlier statutory use of "art," however, the term "process" extends from case law interpreting the British Statute of Monopolies. Although that statute on its face allowed patents only for "new manufactures," the courts soon extended the patent law to embrace technique as well. The primary modern test of the bounds of the broad term process occurred in relation to computer software.

Process more difficult to decide.

process or technique patentable

Computer software, in general terms, is a set of machine-readable instructions capable of performing a particular task. The advent of computer technology strained the Patent Office and the courts to compare patent protection of software with alternatives, such as copyright law. Thus, opponents of eligibility for software argued that computer-related inventions have more in common with abstract principles and mental steps, which do not receive patent protection. On the other hand, computer engineers may design electronic circuits based on theoretical mathematical models, but those computer inventions nonetheless function as machines. The Supreme Court's initial encounter with computer technology came in 1972.

GOTTSCHALK v. BENSON

United States Supreme Court, 1972
409 U.S. 63

MR. JUSTICE DOUGLAS delivered the opinion of the Court.

Respondents filed in the Patent Office an application for an invention which was described as being related 'to the processing of data by program and more particularly to the programmed conversion of numerical information' in general-purpose digital computers. They claimed a method for converting binary-coded decimal (BCD) numerals into pure binary numerals. The claims were not limited to any particular art or technology, to any particular apparatus or machinery, or to any particular end use. They purported to cover any use of the claimed method in a general-purpose digital computer of any type. Claims 8 and 31 were rejected by the Patent Office but sustained by the Court of Customs and Patent Appeals.

The question is whether the method described and claimed is a 'process' within the meaning of the Patent Act. [Claim 8 reads:

The method of converting signals from binary coded decimal form into binary which comprises the steps of

'(1) storing the binary coded decimal signals in a reentrant shift register,

'(2) shifting the signals to the right by at least three places, until there is a binary '1' in the second position of said register,

'(3) masking out said binary '1' in said second position of said register,

'(4) adding a binary '1' to the first position of said register,

'(5) shifting the signals to the left by two positions,

*74 '(6) adding a '1' to said first position, and

'(7) shifting the signals to the right by at least three positions in preparation for a succeeding binary '1' in the second position of said register."]

Here the 'process' claim is so abstract and sweeping as to cover both known and unknown uses of the BCD to pure binary conversion. The end use may (1) vary from the operation of a train to verification of drivers' licenses to researching the law books for precedents and (2) be performed through any existing machinery or future-devised machinery or without any apparatus.

Transformation and reduction of an article 'to a different state or thing' is the clue to the patentability of a process claim that does not include particular machines. So it is that a patent in the process of 'manufacturing fat acids and glycerine from fatty bodies by the action of water at a high temperature and pressure' was sustained in Tilghman v. Proctor, 102 U.S. 707, 721. The Court said, 'The chemical principle or scientific fact upon which it is founded is, that the elements of neutral fat require to be severally united with an atomic equivalent of water in order to separate from each other and become free. This chemical fact was not discovered by Tilghman. He only claims to have invented a particular mode of bringing about the desired chemical union between the fatty elements and water.' Id., at 729.

It is argued that a process patent must either be tied to a particular machine or apparatus or must operate to change articles or materials to a 'different state or thing.' We do not hold that no process patent could ever qualify if it did not meet the requirements of our prior precedents. It is said that the decision precludes a patent for any program servicing a computer. We do not so hold. It is said that we have before us a program for a digital computer but extend our holding to programs for analog computers. We have, however, made clear from the start that we deal with a program only for digital computers. It is said we freeze process patents to old technologies, leaving no room for the revelations of the new, onrushing technology. Such is not our purpose. What we come down to in a nutshell is the following.

It is conceded that one may not patent an idea. But in practical effect that would be the result if the formula for converting BCD numerals to pure binary numerals were patented in this case. The mathematical formula involved here has no substantial practical application except in connection with a digital computer, which means that if the judgment below is affirmed, the patent would wholly pre-empt the mathematical formula and in practical effect would be a patent on the algorithm itself.

If these programs are to be patentable, considerable problems are raised which only committees of Congress can manage, for broad powers of investigation are needed, including hearings which canvass the wide variety of views which those operating in this field entertain. The technological problems tendered in the many briefs before us indicate to us that considered action by the Congress is needed.

Reversed.

NOTES

1. **The Nutshell.** The famous "nutshell" of the *Benson* opinion reasons that the claimed invention was not patent eligible because its only practical application was towards digital computer technology. The nutshell is the paragraph near the end of the majority opinion that begins "It is conceded. . . ." Today that observation strikes a humorous chord. With much of the world economy controlled by digital computers, it seems almost nonsensical to suggest that the invention has no substantial application except in connection with a digital computer. Does some of the Court's problem flow from its inability to project the future usefulness of computer technology? Despite this historical anomaly, would the Court have been more accepting of the invention if it could be applied towards a number of different disciplines? Would the Court have been more accepting if the applicant had specifically identified the invention's end uses in digital computer technology (does it facilitate storage or speed of use)? Consider also the example of a new, high-speed, low-cost electronic circuit designed to be, and only useful as, a computer component. Is such a device patent-eligible under the language of the "nutshell"?

2. **Abstractness?** In *Benson,* Justice Douglas stated at one point:

Here the "process" claim is so abstract and sweeping as to cover both known and unknown uses of the BCD to pure binary conversion.

This allusion to the classic non-statutory, and thus ineligible, category of abstract principles became a key to limiting *Benson* when the Supreme Court changed its direction.

3. **Interchangeable Hardware and Software.** In modern computer technology, hardware and software are fully, and almost instantly, interchangeable. Thus does the act of programming software into a computer's hardware transform the hardware into a new machine? Actually the CCPA had already answered that question:

[I]f a machine is programmed in a certain new and unobvious way, it is physically different from the machine without that program; its memory elements are differently arranged. The fact that these physical changes are invisible to the eye should not tempt us to conclude that the machine has not been changed.

In re Bernhart, 417 F.2d 1395, 1400 (CCPA 1969); *see also In re Prater*, 415 F.2d 1393 (CCPA 1969). Can software escape patent-eligibility problems if claimed in terms of hardware?

DIAMOND v. DIEHR

United States Supreme Court, 1981
450 U.S. 175

James R. Diehr II and Theodore A. Lutton claimed a method of operating molding presses during the production of rubber articles. The inventors asserted that their method ensured that articles remained within the presses for the proper amount of time. Claim 1 of their application provided:

A method of operating a rubber-molding press for precision molded compounds with the aid of a digital computer, comprising:

providing said computer with a data base for said press including at least,

natural logarithm conversion data (ln),

the activation energy constant (c) unique to each batch of said compound being molded, and

a constant (x) dependent upon the geometry of the particular mold of the press,

initiating an interval timer in said computer upon the closure of the press for monitoring the elapsed time of said closure,

constantly determining the temperature (Z) of the mold at a location closely adjacent to the mold cavity in the press during molding,

constantly providing the computer with the temperature (Z),

repetitively calculating in the computer, at frequent intervals during each cure, the Arrhenius equation for reaction time during the cure, which is 'ln v = CZ + x' where v is the total required cure time,

repetitively comparing in the computer at said frequent intervals during the cure each said calculation of the total required cure time calculated with the Arrhenius equation and said elapsed time, and

opening the press automatically when a said comparison indicates equivalence.

The patent examiner rejected the respondents' claims as being drawn to nonstatutory subject matter under 35 U.S.C. § 101. Citing Benson, the examiner considered that the steps of the claimed process implemented in computer software comprised nonstatutory subject matter. The remaining steps—installing rubber in the press and the subsequent closing of the press—were "conventional and necessary to the process and cannot be the basis of patentability." The examiner concluded that the inventors merely claimed a computer program useful towards operating a rubber-molding press.

The Patent and Trademark Office Board of Appeals affirmed the decision of the examiner, but the Court of Customs and Patent Appeals reversed. The CCPA concluded that the claims were not directed to a mathematical algorithm, but rather to an improved process for molding rubber articles. The Commissioner then sought review of the issue before the United States Supreme Court.

JUSTICE REHNQUIST delivered the opinion of the Court.

We granted certiorari to determine whether a process for curing synthetic rubber which includes in several of its steps the use of a mathematical formula and a programmed digital computer is patentable subject matter under 35 U.S.C. § 101.

I

The patent application at issue was filed by the respondents on August 6, 1975. The claimed invention is a process for molding raw, uncured synthetic rubber into cured precision products. The process uses a mold for precisely shaping the uncured material under heat and pressure and then curing the synthetic rubber in the mold so that the product will retain its shape and be functionally operative after the molding is completed.[3]

Respondents claim that their process ensures the production of molded articles which are properly cured. Achieving the perfect cure depends upon several factors including the thickness of the article to be molded, the temperature of the molding process, and the amount of time that the article is allowed to remain in the press. It is possible using well-known time, temperature, and cure relationships to calculate by means of the Arrhenius equation[4] when to open the press and remove the cured product. Nonetheless, according to the respondents, the industry has not been able to obtain uniformly accurate cures because the temperature of the molding press could not be precisely measured, thus making it difficult to do the necessary computations to determine cure time. Because the temperature inside the press has heretofore been viewed as an uncontrollable variable, the conventional industry practice has been to calculate the cure time as the shortest time in which all parts of the product will definitely be cured, assuming a reasonable amount of mold-opening time during loading and unloading. But the shortcoming of this practice is that operating with an uncontrollable variable inevitably led in some instances to overestimating the mold-opening time and overcuring the rubber, and in other instances to underestimating that time and undercuring the product.

---

3. A "cure" is obtained by mixing curing agents into the uncured polymer in advance of molding and then applying heat over a period of time. If the synthetic rubber is cured for the right length of time at the right temperature, it becomes a usable product.

4. The equation is named after its discoverer Svante Arrhenius and has long been used to calculate the cure time in rubber-molding presses. The equation can be expressed as follows:

$$\ln v = CZ + x$$

wherein ln v is the natural logarithm of v, the total required cure time; C is the activation constant, a unique figure for each batch of each compound being molded, determined in accordance with rheometer measurements of each batch; Z is the temperature in the mold; and x is a constant dependent on the geometry of the particular mold in the press. A rheometer is an instrument to measure flow of viscous substances.

Respondents characterize their contribution to the art to reside in the process of constantly measuring the actual temperature inside the mold. These temperature measurements are then automatically fed into a computer which repeatedly recalculates the cure time by use of the Arrhenius equation. When the recalculated time equals the actual time that has elapsed since the press was closed, the computer signals a device to open the press. According to the respondents, the continuous measuring of the temperature inside the mold cavity, the feeding of this information to a digital computer which constantly recalculates the cure time, and the signaling by the computer to open the press, are all new in the art.

II

Last Term in *Diamond v. Chakrabarty*, 447 U.S. 303 (1980), this Court discussed the historical purposes of the patent laws and in particular 35 U.S.C. § 101. As in *Chakrabarty*, we must here construe 35 U.S.C. § 101 which provides: "Whoever, invents or discovers any new and useful process, machine manufacture, or composition of matter, or any new and useful improvement thereof, may obtain a patent therefor, subject to the conditions and requirements of this title."

In cases of statutory construction, we begin with the language of the statute. Unless otherwise defined, "words will be interpreted as taking their ordinary, contemporary, common meaning," and, in dealing with the patent laws, we have more than once cautioned that "courts 'should not read into the patent laws limitations and conditions which the legislature has not expressed.' "

The Patent Act of 1793 defined statutory subject matter as "any new and useful art, machine, manufacture or composition of matter, or any new or useful improvement [thereof]." Act of Feb. 21, 1793, ch. 11, s 1, 1 Stat. 318. Not until the patent laws were recodified in 1952 did Congress replace the word "art" with the word "process." It is that latter word which we confront today, and in order to determine its meaning we may not be unmindful of the Committee Reports accompanying the 1952 Act which inform us that Congress intended statutory subject matter to "include anything under the sun that is made by man." S.Rep.No.1979, 82d Cong., 2d Sess., 5 (1952); H.R.Rep.No.1923, 82d Cong., 2d Sess., 6 (1952).

Although the term "process" was not added to 35 U.S.C. § 101 until 1952 a process has historically enjoyed patent protection because it was considered a form of "art" as that term was used in the 1793 Act.

Analyzing respondents' claims, we think that a physical and chemical process for molding precision synthetic rubber products falls within the § 101 categories of possibly patentable subject matter. That respondents' claims involve the transformation of an article, in this case raw, uncured synthetic rubber, into a different state or thing cannot be disputed. The respondents' claims describe in detail a step-by-step method for accomplishing such, beginning with the loading of a mold with raw, uncured rubber and ending with the eventual opening of the press at the conclusion of the cure. Industrial processes such as this are the types which have historically been eligible to receive the protection of our patent laws.

III

Our conclusion regarding respondents' claims is not altered by the fact that in several steps of the process a mathematical equation and a programmed digital computer are used. This Court has undoubtedly recognized limits to § 101 and every discovery is not embraced within the statutory terms. Excluded from such patent protection are laws of nature, natural phenomena, and abstract ideas. "An idea of itself is not patentable," *Rubber–Tip Pencil Co. v. Howard*, 20 Wall. 498, 507 (1874). "A principle, in the abstract, is a fundamental truth; an original cause; a motive; these cannot be patented, as no one can claim in either of them an exclusive right." *Le Roy v. Tatham*, 14 How. 156, 175 (1852). Only last Term, we explained: "[A] new mineral discovered in the earth or a new plant found in the wild is not patentable subject matter. Likewise, Einstein could not patent his celebrated law that E = mc^2; nor could Newton have patented the law of gravity. Such discoveries are 'manifestations of . . . nature, free to all men and reserved exclusively to none.'" *Diamond v. Chakrabarty*, 447 U.S., at 309, *quoting Funk Bros. Seed Co. v. Kalo Inoculant Co., supra*, at 130.

Our recent holdings in *Gottschalk v. Benson* and *Parker v. Flook*, both of which are computer-related, stand for no more than these long-established principles. In *Benson*, we held unpatentable claims for an algorithm used to convert binary code decimal numbers to equivalent pure binary numbers. The sole practical application of the algorithm was in connection with the programming of a general purpose digital computer. We defined "algorithm" as a "procedure for solving a given type of mathematical problem," and we concluded that such an algorithm, or mathematical formula, is like a law of nature, which cannot be the subject of a patent.[5]

Parker v. Flook presented a similar situation. The claims were drawn to a method for computing an "alarm limit." An "alarm limit" is simply a number and the Court concluded that the application sought to protect a formula for computing this number. Using this formula, the

---

5. The term "algorithm" is subject to a variety of definitions. The petitioner defines the term to mean: "'1. A fixed step-by-step procedure for accomplishing a given result; usually a simplified procedure for solving a complex problem, also a full statement of a finite number of steps. 2. A defined process or set of rules that leads [sic] and assures development of a desired output from a given input. A sequence of formulas and/or algebraic/logical steps to calculate or determine a given task; processing rules.'" Brief for Petitioner in Diamond v. Bradley, O.T. 1980, No. 79–855, p. 6, n. 12, quoting C. SIPPL & R. SIPPL, COMPUTER DICTIONARY AND HANDBOOK 23 (2d ed. 1972). This definition is significantly broader than the definition this Court employed in *Benson* and *Flook*. Our previous decisions regarding the patentability of "algorithms" are necessarily limited to the more narrow definition employed by the Court, and we do not pass judgment on whether processes falling outside the definition previously used by this Court, but within the definition offered by the petitioner, would be patentable subject matter.

updated alarm limit could be calculated if several other variables were known. The application, however, did not purport to explain how these other variables were to be determined, nor did it purport "to contain any disclosure relating to the chemical processes at work, the monitoring of process variables, or the means of setting off an alarm or adjusting an alarm system. All that it provides is a formula for computing an updated alarm limit."

In contrast, the respondents here do not seek to patent a mathematical formula. Instead, they seek patent protection for a process of curing synthetic rubber. Their process admittedly employs a well-known mathematical equation, but they do not seek to pre-empt the use of that equation. Rather, they seek only to foreclose from others the use of that equation in conjunction with all of the other steps in their claimed process. These include installing rubber in a press, closing the mold, constantly determining the temperature of the mold, constantly recalculating the appropriate cure time through the use of the formula and a digital computer, and automatically opening the press at the proper time. Obviously, one does not need a "computer" to cure natural or synthetic rubber, but if the computer use incorporated in the process patent significantly lessens the possibility of "overcuring" or "undercuring," the process as a whole does not thereby become unpatentable subject matter.

Our earlier opinions lend support to our present conclusion that a claim drawn to subject matter otherwise statutory does not become nonstatutory simply because it uses a mathematical formula, computer program, or digital computer. In *Gottschalk v. Benson*, we noted: "It is said that the decision precludes a patent for any program servicing a computer. We do not so hold." 409 U.S., at 71. Similarly, in *Parker v. Flook*, we stated that "a process is not unpatentable simply because it contains a law of nature or a mathematical algorithm." 437 U.S., at 590. It is now commonplace that an application of a law of nature or mathematical formula to a known structure or process may well be deserving of patent protection. As Justice Stone explained four decades ago: "While a scientific truth, or the mathematical expression of it, is not a patentable invention, a novel and useful structure created with the aid of knowledge of scientific truth may be." *Mackay Radio & Telegraph Co. v. Radio of America*, 306 U.S. 86, 94 (1939).

We think this statement in *Mackay* takes us a long way toward the correct answer in this case. Arrhenius' equation is not patentable in isolation, but when a process for curing rubber is devised which incorporates in it a more efficient solution of the equation, that process is at the very least not barred at the threshold by § 101.

In determining the eligibility of respondents' claimed process for patent protection under § 101, their claims must be considered as a whole. It is inappropriate to dissect the claims into old and new elements and then to ignore the presence of the old elements in the analysis. This is particularly true in a process claim because a new combination of steps in a process may be patentable even though all the constituents of the combination were well known and in common use before the combination was made. The "novelty" of any element or steps in a process, or even of the process itself, is of no relevance in determining whether the subject matter of a claim falls within the § 101 categories of possibly patentable subject matter.

It has been urged that novelty is an appropriate consideration under § 101. Presumably, this argument results from the language in § 101 referring to any "new and useful" process, machine, etc. Section 101, however, is a general statement of the type of subject matter that is eligible for patent protection "subject to the conditions and requirements of this title." Specific conditions for patentability follow and § 102 covers in detail the conditions relating to novelty. The question therefore of whether a particular invention is novel is "wholly apart from whether the invention falls into a category of statutory subject matter." *In re Bergy*, 596 F.2d 952, 961 (CCPA 1979).

In this case, it may later be determined that the respondents' process is not deserving of patent protection because it fails to satisfy the statutory conditions of novelty under § 102 or nonobviousness under § 103. A rejection on either of these grounds does not affect the determination that respondents' claims recited subject matter which was eligible for patent protection under § 101.

IV

We have before us today only the question of whether respondents' claims fall within the § 101 categories of possibly patentable subject matter. We view respondents' claims as nothing more than a process for molding rubber products and not as an attempt to patent a mathematical formula. We recognize, of course, that when a claim recites a mathematical formula (or scientific principle or phenomenon of nature), an inquiry must be made into whether the claim is seeking patent protection for that formula in the abstract. A mathematical formula as such is not accorded the protection of our patent laws, *Gottschalk v. Benson*, 409 U.S. 63 (1972), and this principle cannot be circumvented by attempting to limit the use of the formula to a particular technological environment. *Parker v. Flook*, 437 U.S. 584 (1978). Similarly, insignificant post-solution activity will not transform an unpatentable principle into a patentable process. To hold otherwise would allow a competent draftsman to evade the recognized limitations on the type of subject matter eligible for patent protection. On the other hand, when a claim containing a mathematical formula implements or applies that formula in a structure or process which, when considered as a whole, is performing a function which the patent laws were designed to protect (e.g., transforming or reducing an article to a different state or thing), then the claim satisfies the requirements of § 101. Because we do not view respondents' claims as an attempt to patent a mathematical formula, but rather to be drawn to an industrial process for the molding of rubber products, we affirm the judgment of the Court of Customs and Patent Appeals.

NOTES

1. **Physical Steps.** The majority opinion makes much of the physical and chemical processes that accompany the claimed algorithm. Did the invention here pass muster simply because its accompanying application fully described the rubber curing process, as well as claimed the opening of an oven door at its completion? To what extent should this minimal recitation make a difference? Let us suppose, as is most likely the case, that the particular set of equations described in the patent application finds its only use in curing rubber, as compared to, say, baking a cake. Would the supposedly limiting physical processes so heavily relied upon by the Court actually constrain the scope of the invention in any realistic sense, or did they merely present the only valid technical context in which the mathematics would effectively operate?

2. **Something Old; Something New?** The invention in *Diehr* may be seen as the combination of a number of preexisting elements: the Arrhenius equation; integral calculus for constantly calculating the cure time; and such sundry apparatus capable of measuring temperature, opening a press, and performing other tasks. Is this combination of old elements patent eligible subject matter? Does this sort of analysis properly fall within the § 101 inquiry at all, or is this a matter for the novelty requirement (detailed in Chapters 4–6 of this casebook)? What if the inventors had themselves discovered the Arrhenius equation?

3. ***State Street Bank** and **AT&T**.* Following the Supreme Court's opinion in *Diehr*, the Federal Circuit had many occasions to consider patent eligibility principles under § 101. One of the more noteworthy opinions was *State Street Bank & Trust Co. v. Signature Financial Group, Inc.*, 149 F.3d 1368 (Fed. Cir. 1998). That decision addressed U.S. Patent No. 5,193,056, which included the following claim:

State v Signature

data processing to find a stock price for funds

> 1. A data processing system for managing a financial services configuration of a portfolio established as a partnership, each partner being one of a plurality of funds, comprising:
>
> (a) computer processor means for processing data;
>
> (b) storage means for storing data on a storage medium;
>
> (c) first means for initializing the storage medium;
>
> (d) second means for processing data regarding assets in the portfolio and each of the funds from a previous day and data regarding increases or decreases in each of the funds, [sic, funds'] assets and for allocating the percentage share that each fund holds in the portfolio;
>
> (e) third means for processing data regarding daily incremental income, expenses, and net realized gain or loss for the portfolio and for allocating such data among each fund;

(f) fourth means for processing data regarding daily net unrealized gain or loss for the portfolio and for allocating such data among each fund; and

(g) fifth means for processing data regarding aggregate year-end income, expenses, and capital gain or loss for the portfolio and each of the funds.

The Federal Circuit explained that the patent "is generally directed toward a data processing system (the system) for implementing an investment structure which was developed for use in Signature's business as an administrator and accounting agent for mutual funds." *Id.* at 1370. The trial court had held that the claimed invention was not eligible for patenting under § 101:

> In effect, the '056 Patent grants Signature a monopoly on its idea of a multi-tiered partnership portfolio investment structure; patenting an accounting system necessary to carry on a certain type of business is tantamount to a patent on the business itself. Because such abstract ideas are not patentable, either as methods of doing business or as mathematical algorithms, the '056 Patent must fail.

927 F. Supp. 502, 516 (D. Mass. 1996). On appeal, the Federal Circuit rejected each of these lines of reasoning. With respect to assertions that the claimed invention was an abstract mathematical algorithm:

> Today, we hold that the transformation of data, representing discrete dollar amounts, by a machine through a series of mathematical calculations into a final share price, constitutes a practical application of a mathematical algorithm, formula, or calculation, because it produces "a useful, concrete and tangible result"—a final share price momentarily fixed for recording and reporting purposes and even accepted and relied upon by regulatory authorities and in subsequent trades.

149 F.3d at 1373. The Federal Circuit also overturned the rejection of the claim as a method of doing business:

> As an alternative ground for invalidating the '056 patent under § 101, the court relied on the judicially-created, so-called "business method" exception to statutory subject matter. We take this opportunity to lay this ill-conceived exception to rest. Since its inception, the "business method" exception has merely represented the application of some general, but no longer applicable legal principle, perhaps arising out of the "requirement for invention"—which was eliminated by § 103. Since the 1052 Patent Act, business methods have been, and should have been, subject to the same legal requirements for patentability as applied to any other process or method.

149 F.3d at 1375. Shortly after *State Street* issued, the Federal Circuit applied these rules to process claims. *AT&T Corp. v. Excel Communications, Inc.*, 172 F.3d 1352 (Fed.Cir.1999), reviewed the patent eligibility of a method of billing long distance telephone calls. Judge Plager characterized *State Street* as holding that "a mathematical algorithm may be an integral part of patentable subject matter such as a machine or process if the claimed invention as a whole is applied in a 'useful' manner." He further explained for the court:

In the case before us, AT & T did not charge Excel with infringement of its apparatus claims, but limited its infringement charge to the specified method or process claims . . . [W]e consider the scope of section 101 to be the same regardless of the form—machine or process—in which a particular claim is drafted . . . Thus, we are comfortable in applying our reasoning in . . . *State Street* to the method claims at issue in this case.

The invention in *AT&T* went towards a method of inserting data into a long distance call record in order to enable proper billing of the call. Thus, for instance, the data might enable the long distance call company to provide a discount when both the caller and the recipient of the call use the same phone company. This invention solely involved information exchange, not a physical transformation as suggested in some earlier cases, yet the Federal Circuit upheld its patent eligibility as a useful invention.

Many observers viewed the combination of *State Street* and *AT&T* as rendering not just methods of doing business, but virtually any subject matter to be eligible for patenting under § 101. Some commentators believed that these opinions resulted in a "gold rush" mentality where inventors acting within diverse disciplines, including banking, finance, investment, insurance, sales, and taxation, aggressively sought patent protection from the USPTO. The decade following the publication of *State Street* saw considerable debate over the wisdom of patenting processes that some viewed as not being technological in character. The Federal Circuit responded by issuing *In re Bilski*, an *en banc* opinion that may reshape the way innovative firms protect their intellectual property.

IN RE BILSKI

United States Court of Appeals, Federal Circuit, 2008
545 F.3d 943

MICHEL, CHIEF JUDGE.

Bernard L. Bilski and Rand A. Warsaw (collectively, "Applicants") appeal from the final decision of the Board of Patent Appeals and Interferences ("Board") sustaining the rejection of all eleven claims of their U.S. Patent Application Serial No. 08/833,892 (" '892 application"). *See Ex parte Bilski*, 2006 WL 5738364 (B.P.A.I. Sept. 26, 2006). Specifically, Applicants argue that the examiner erroneously rejected the claims as not directed to patent-eligible subject matter under 35 U.S.C. § 101, and that the Board erred in upholding that rejection. We affirm the decision of the Board because we conclude that Applicants' claims are not directed to patent-eligible subject matter, and in doing so, we clarify the standards applicable in determining whether a claimed method constitutes a statutory "process" under § 101.

I.

Applicants filed their patent application on April 10, 1997. The application contains eleven claims, which Applicants argue together here. Claim 1 reads:

A method for managing the consumption risk costs of a commodity sold by a commodity provider at a fixed price comprising the steps of:

(a) initiating a series of transactions between said commodity provider and consumers of said commodity wherein said consumers purchase said commodity at a fixed rate based upon historical averages, said fixed rate corresponding to a risk position of said consumer;

(b) identifying market participants for said commodity having a counter-risk position to said consumers; and

(c) initiating a series of transactions between said commodity provider and said market participants at a second fixed rate such that said series of market participant transactions balances the risk position of said series of consumer transactions.

In essence, the claim is for a method of hedging risk in the field of commodities trading. For example, coal power plants (i.e., "the consumers") purchase coal to produce electricity and are averse to the risk of a spike in demand for coal since such a spike would increase the price and their costs. Conversely, coal mining companies (i.e., the "market participants") are averse to the risk of a sudden drop in demand for coal since such a drop would reduce their sales and depress prices. The claimed method envisions an intermediary, the "commodity provider," that sells coal to the power plants at a fixed price, thus isolating the power plants from the possibility of a spike in demand increasing the price of coal above the fixed price. The same provider buys coal from mining companies at a second fixed price, thereby isolating the mining companies from the possibility that a drop in demand would lower prices below that fixed price. And the provider has thus hedged its risk; if demand and prices skyrocket, it has sold coal at a disadvantageous price but has bought coal at an advantageous price, and vice versa if demand and prices fall. Importantly, however, the claim is not limited to transactions involving actual commodities, and the application discloses that the recited transactions may simply involve options, i.e., rights to purchase or sell the commodity at a particular price within a particular timeframe.

The examiner ultimately rejected claims 1–11 under 35 U.S.C. § 101, stating: "[r]egarding ... claims 1–11, the invention is not implemented on a specific apparatus and merely manipulates [an] abstract idea and solves a purely mathematical problem without any limitation to a practical application, therefore, the invention is not directed to the technological arts." The examiner noted that Applicants had admitted their claims are not limited to operation on a computer, and he concluded that they were not limited by any specific apparatus.

On appeal, the Board held that the examiner erred to the extent he relied on a "technological arts" test because the case law does not support such a test. Further, the Board held that the requirement of a specific apparatus was also erroneous because a claim that does not recite a specific apparatus may still be directed to patent-eligible subject matter "if there is a transformation of physical subject matter from one state to another." Elaborating further, the Board stated: " 'mixing' two elements or compounds to produce a chemical substance or mixture is clearly a statutory transformation although no apparatus is claimed to perform the step and although the step could be performed manually." But the Board concluded that Applicants' claims do not involve any patent-eligible transformation, holding that transformation of "non-physical financial risks and legal liabilities of the commodity provider, the consumer, and the market participants" is not patent-eligible subject matter. The Board also held that Applicants' claims "preempt[ ] any and every possible way of performing the steps of the [claimed process], by human or by any kind of machine or by any combination thereof," and thus concluded that they only claim an abstract idea ineligible for patent protection. Finally, the Board held that Applicants' process as claimed did not produce a "useful, concrete and tangible result," and for this reason as well was not drawn to patent-eligible subject matter. [Applicants appealed.]

II.

Whether a claim is drawn to patent-eligible subject matter under § 101 is a threshold inquiry, and any claim of an application failing the requirements of § 101 must be rejected even if it meets all of the other legal requirements of patentability. *In re Comiskey*, 499 F.3d 1365, 1371 (Fed.Cir.2007) (quoting *Parker v. Flook*, 437 U.S. 584, 593, 98 S.Ct. 2522, 57 L.Ed.2d 451 (1978)); *In re Bergy*, 596 F.2d 952, 960 (CCPA 1979), *vacated as moot sub nom. Diamond v. Chakrabarty*, 444 U.S. 1028, 100 S.Ct. 696, 62 L.Ed.2d 664 (1980). Whether a claim is drawn to patent-eligible subject matter under § 101 is an issue of law that we review de novo. Although claim construction, which we also review de novo, is an important first step in a § 101 analysis, *see State St. Bank & Trust Co. v. Signature Fin. Group*, 149 F.3d 1368, 1370 (Fed.Cir.1998), there is no claim construction dispute in this appeal. We review issues of statutory interpretation such as this one de novo as well.

A.

As this appeal turns on whether Applicants' invention as claimed meets the requirements set forth in § 101, we begin with the words of the statute:

> Whoever invents or discovers any new and useful process, machine, manufacture, or composition of matter, or any new and useful improvement thereof, may obtain a patent therefor, subject to the conditions and requirements of this title.

35 U.S.C. § 101. The statute thus recites four categories of patent-eligible subject matter: processes, machines, manufactures, and compositions of matter. It is undisputed that Applicants' claims are not directed to a machine, manufacture, or composition of matter. Thus, the issue before us involves what the term "process" in § 101 means, and how to

determine whether a given claim—and Applicants' claim 1 in particular—is a "new and useful process."[3]

As several amici have argued, the term "process" is ordinarily broad in meaning, at least in general lay usage. In 1952, at the time Congress amended § 101 to include "process,"[4] the ordinary meaning of the term was: "[a] procedure ... [a] series of actions, motions, or operations definitely conducing to an end, whether voluntary or involuntary." WEBSTER'S NEW INTERNATIONAL DICTIONARY OF THE ENGLISH LANGUAGE 1972 (2d ed.1952). There can be no dispute that Applicants' claim would meet this definition of "process." But the Supreme Court has held that the meaning of "process" as used in § 101 is narrower than its ordinary meaning. *See Flook*, 437 U.S. at 588–89, 98 S.Ct. 2522 ("The holding [in *Benson*] forecloses a purely literal reading of § 101."). Specifically, the Court has held that a claim is not a patent-eligible "process" if it claims "laws of nature, natural phenomena, [or] abstract ideas." *Diamond v. Diehr*, 450 U.S. 175, 185, 101 S.Ct. 1048, 67 L.Ed.2d 155 (1981) (citing *Flook*, 437 U.S. at 589, 98 S.Ct. 2522, and *Gottschalk v. Benson*, 409 U.S. 63, 67, 93 S.Ct. 253, 34 L.Ed.2d 273 (1972)). Such fundamental principles are "part of the storehouse of knowledge of all men ... free to all men and reserved exclusively to none." *Funk Bros. Seed Co. v. Kalo Inoculant Co.*, 333 U.S. 127, 130, 68 S.Ct. 440, 92 L.Ed. 588 (1948); *see also Le Roy v. Tatham*, 55 U.S. (14 How.) 156, 175, 14 L.Ed. 367 (1852) ("A principle, in the abstract, is a fundamental truth; an original cause; a motive; these cannot be patented, as no one can claim in either of them an exclusive right.").

The true issue before us then is whether Applicants are seeking to claim a fundamental principle (such as an abstract idea) or a mental process. And the underlying legal question thus presented is what test or set of criteria governs the determination by the Patent and Trademark Office ("PTO") or courts as to whether a claim to a process is patentable under § 101 or, conversely, is drawn to unpatentable subject matter because it claims only a fundamental principle.

The Supreme Court last addressed this issue in 1981 in *Diehr*, which concerned a patent application seeking to claim a process for producing cured synthetic rubber products. 450 U.S. at 177–79, 101 S.Ct. 1048. The claimed process took temperature readings during cure and used a mathematical algorithm, the Arrhenius equation, to calculate the time when curing would be complete. Noting that a mathematical algorithm alone is unpatentable because mathematical relationships are akin to a

---

3. Congress provided a definition of "process" in 35 U.S.C. § 100(b): "The term 'process' means process, art or method, and includes a new use of a known process, machine, manufacture, composition of matter, or material." However, this provision is unhelpful given that the definition itself uses the term "process."

4. The Patent Act of 1793 originally used the term "art" rather than "process," which remained unchanged until Congress enacted the current version of § 101 in 1952. But the Supreme Court has held that this change did not alter the scope of patent eligibility over processes because "[i]n the language of the patent law, [a process] is an art." *Diamond v. Diehr*, 450 U.S. 175, 182–84, 101 S.Ct. 1048, 67 L.Ed.2d 155 (1981) (quoting *Cochrane v. Deener*, 94 U.S. 780, 787–88, 24 L.Ed. 139 (1877)).

law of nature, the Court nevertheless held that the claimed process was patent-eligible subject matter, stating:

> [The inventors] do not seek to patent a mathematical formula. Instead, they seek patent protection for a process of curing synthetic rubber. Their process admittedly employs a well-known mathematical equation, but they do not seek to pre-empt the use of that equation. Rather, they seek only to foreclose from others the use of that equation in conjunction with all of the other steps in their claimed process.

Id. at 187, 101 S.Ct. 1048. The Court declared that while a claim drawn to a fundamental principle is unpatentable, "an application of a law of nature or mathematical formula to a known structure or process may well be deserving of patent protection." *Id.*; *see also Mackay Radio & Tel. Co. v. Radio Corp. of Am.*, 306 U.S. 86, 94, 59 S.Ct. 427, 83 L.Ed. 506 (1939) ("While a scientific truth, or the mathematical expression of it, is not a patentable invention, a novel and useful structure created with the aid of knowledge of scientific truth may be.").

The Court in *Diehr* thus drew a distinction between those claims that "seek to pre-empt the use of" a fundamental principle, on the one hand, and claims that seek only to foreclose others from using a particular "application" of that fundamental principle, on the other. 450 U.S. at 187, 101 S.Ct. 1048. Patents, by definition, grant the power to exclude others from practicing that which the patent claims. *Diehr* can be understood to suggest that whether a claim is drawn only to a fundamental principle is essentially an inquiry into the scope of that exclusion; i.e., whether the effect of allowing the claim would be to allow the patentee to pre-empt substantially all uses of that fundamental principle. If so, the claim is not drawn to patent-eligible subject matter.

In *Diehr*, the Court held that the claims at issue did not pre-empt all uses of the Arrhenius equation but rather claimed only "a process for curing rubber ... which incorporates in it a more efficient solution of the equation." 450 U.S. at 188, 101 S.Ct. 1048. The process as claimed included several specific steps to control the curing of rubber more precisely: "These include installing rubber in a press, closing the mold, constantly determining the temperature of the mold, constantly recalculating the appropriate cure time through the use of the formula and a digital computer, and automatically opening the press at the proper time." *Id.* at 187, 101 S.Ct. 1048. Thus, one would still be able to use the Arrhenius equation in any process not involving curing rubber, and more importantly, even in any process to cure rubber that did not include performing "all of the other steps in their claimed process." *See id.; see also Tilghman v. Proctor*, 102 U.S. 707, 729, 26 L.Ed. 279 (1880) (holding patentable a process of breaking down fat molecules into fatty acids and glycerine in water specifically requiring both high heat and high pressure since other processes, known or as yet unknown, using the reaction of water and fat molecules were not claimed).

In contrast to *Diehr*, the earlier *Benson* case presented the Court with claims drawn to a process of converting data in binary-coded decimal ("BCD") format to pure binary format via an algorithm programmed onto a digital computer. *Benson*, 409 U.S. at 65, 93 S.Ct. 253. The Court held the claims to be drawn to unpatentable subject matter:

> It is conceded that one may not patent an idea. But in practical effect that would be the result if the formula for converting BCD numerals to pure binary numerals were patented in this case. The mathematical formula involved here has no substantial practical application except in connection with a digital computer, which means that if the judgment below is affirmed, the patent would wholly pre-empt the mathematical formula and in practical effect would be a patent on the algorithm itself.

Id. at 71–72, 93 S.Ct. 253. Because the algorithm had no uses other than those that would be covered by the claims (i.e., any conversion of BCD to pure binary on a digital computer), the claims pre-empted all uses of the algorithm and thus they were effectively drawn to the algorithm itself. *See also O'Reilly v. Morse*, 56 U.S. (15 How.) 62, 113, 14 L.Ed. 601 (1853) (holding ineligible a claim pre-empting all uses of electromagnetism to print characters at a distance).

The question before us then is whether Applicants' claim recites a fundamental principle and, if so, whether it would pre-empt substantially all uses of that fundamental principle if allowed. Unfortunately, this inquiry is hardly straightforward. How does one determine whether a given claim would pre-empt all uses of a fundamental principle? Analogizing to the facts of *Diehr* or *Benson* is of limited usefulness because the more challenging process claims of the twenty-first century are seldom so clearly limited in scope as the highly specific, plainly corporeal industrial manufacturing process of *Diehr*; nor are they typically as broadly claimed or purely abstract and mathematical as the algorithm of *Benson*.

The Supreme Court, however, has enunciated a definitive test to determine whether a process claim is tailored narrowly enough to encompass only a particular application of a fundamental principle rather than to pre-empt the principle itself. A claimed process is surely patent-eligible under § 101 if: (1) it is tied to a particular machine or apparatus, or (2) it transforms a particular article into a different state or thing. *See Benson*, 409 U.S. at 70, 93 S.Ct. 253 ("Transformation and reduction of an article 'to a different state or thing' is the clue to the patentability of a process claim that does not include particular machines."); *Diehr*, 450 U.S. at 192, 101 S.Ct. 1048 (holding that use of mathematical formula in process transforming or reducing an article to a different state or thing constitutes patent-eligible subject matter); *see also Flook*, 437 U.S. at 589 n. 9, 98 S.Ct. 2522 ("An argument can be made [that the Supreme] Court has only recognized a process as within the statutory definition when it either was tied to a particular apparatus or operated to change materials to a 'different state or thing' "); *Cochrane v. Deener*, 94 U.S. 780, 788, 24 L.Ed. 139 (1876) ("A process is . . . an act, or a series of acts, performed upon the subject-matter to be transformed and reduced to a different state or thing."). A claimed process involving a fundamental principle that uses a particular machine or apparatus would not pre-empt uses of the principle that do not also use the specified machine or apparatus in the manner claimed. And a claimed process that transforms a particular article to a specified different state or thing by applying a fundamental principle would not pre-empt the use of the principle to transform any other article, to transform the same article but in a manner not covered by the claim, or to do anything other than transform the specified article.

The process claimed in *Diehr*, for example, clearly met both criteria. The process operated on a computerized rubber curing apparatus and transformed raw, uncured rubber into molded, cured rubber products. The claim at issue in *Flook*, in contrast, was directed to using a particular mathematical formula to calculate an "alarm limit"—a value that would indicate an abnormal condition during an unspecified chemical reaction. The Court rejected the claim as drawn to the formula itself because the claim did not include any limitations specifying "how to select the appropriate margin of safety, the weighting factor, or any of the other variables . . . the chemical processes at work, the [mechanism for] monitoring of process variables, or the means of setting off an alarm or adjusting an alarm system." The claim thus was not limited to any particular chemical (or other) transformation; nor was it tied to any specific machine or apparatus for any of its process steps, such as the selection or monitoring of variables or the setting off or adjusting of the alarm.[8]

A canvas of earlier Supreme Court cases reveals that the results of those decisions were also consistent with the machine-or-transformation test later articulated in *Benson* and reaffirmed in *Diehr*. *See Tilghman*, 102 U.S. at 729 (particular process of transforming fats into constituent compounds held patentable); *Cochrane*, 94 U.S. at 785–88 (process transforming grain meal into purified flour held patentable); *Morse*, 56 U.S. (15 How.) at 113 (process of using electromagnetism to print characters at a distance that was not transformative or tied to any particular apparatus held unpatentable). Interestingly, *Benson* presents a difficult case under its own test in that the claimed process operated on a machine, a digital computer, but was still held to be ineligible subject matter.[9] However, in *Benson*, the limitations tying the process to a

---

8. To the extent it may be argued that *Flook* did not explicitly follow the machine-or-transformation test first articulated in *Benson*, we note that the more recent decision in *Diehr* reaffirmed the machine-or-transformation test. *See Diehr*, 450 U.S. at 191–92, 101 S.Ct. 1048. Moreover, the *Diehr* Court explained that *Flook* "presented a similar situation" to Benson and considered it consistent with the holdings of *Diehr* and *Benson*. *Diehr* at 186–87, 189, 191–92, 101 S.Ct. 1048. We thus follow the *Diehr* Court's understanding of *Flook*.

9. We acknowledge that the Supreme Court in *Benson* stated that the claims at issue "were not limited . . . to any particular apparatus or machinery." 409 U.S. at 64, 93 S.Ct. 253. However, the Court immediately thereafter stated: "[The claims] purported to cover any use of the claimed

computer were not actually limiting because the fundamental principle at issue, a particular algorithm, had no utility other than operating on a digital computer. *Benson*, 409 U.S. at 71–72, 93 S.Ct. 253. Thus, the claim's tie to a digital computer did not reduce the pre-emptive footprint of the claim since all uses of the algorithm were still covered by the claim.

B.

Applicants and several amici have argued that the Supreme Court did not intend the machine-or-transformation test to be the sole test governing § 101 analyses. As already noted, however, the Court explicitly stated in *Benson* that "[t]ransformation and reduction of an article 'to a different state or thing' is the clue to the patentability of a process claim that does not include particular machines."[11] 409 U.S. at 70, 93 S.Ct. 253. And the Court itself later noted in *Flook* that at least so far it had "only recognized a process as within the statutory definition when it either was tied to a particular apparatus or operated to change materials to a 'different state or thing.'" 437 U.S. at 589 n. 9, 98 S.Ct. 2522. Finally, the Court in *Diehr* once again applied the machine-or-transformation test in its most recent decision regarding the patentability of processes under § 101.

We recognize, however, that the Court was initially equivocal in first putting forward this test in *Benson*. As the Applicants and several amici point out, the Court there stated:

> It is argued that a process patent must either be tied to a particular machine or apparatus or must operate to change articles or materials to a 'different state or thing.' We do not hold that no process patent could ever qualify if it did not meet the requirements of our prior precedents.

Benson, 409 U.S. at 71, 93 S.Ct. 253. In *Flook*, the Court took note that this statement had been made in *Benson* but merely stated: "As in *Benson*, we assume that a valid process patent may issue even if it does not meet [the machine-or-transformation test]." 437 U.S. at 589 n. 9, 98 S.Ct. 2522 (emphasis added). And this caveat was not repeated in *Diehr* when the Court reaffirmed the machine-or-transformation test. *See Diehr*, 450 U.S. at 184, 101 S.Ct. 1048 (quoting *Benson*, 409 U.S. at 70, 93 S.Ct. 253) ("Transformation and reduction of an article 'to a different state or thing' is the clue to the patentability of a process claim that does

---

method in a general-purpose digital computer of any type." *Id.* And, as discussed herein, the Court relied for its holding on its understanding that the claimed process pre-empted all uses of the recited algorithm because its only possible use was on a digital computer. Id. at 71–72, 93 S.Ct. 253. The *Diehr* Court, in discussing *Benson*, relied only on this latter understanding of the *Benson* claims. *See Diehr*, 450 U.S. at 185–87, 101 S.Ct. 1048. We must do the same.

11. We believe that the Supreme Court spoke of the machine-or-transformation test as the "clue" to patent-eligibility because the test is the tool used to determine whether a claim is drawn to a statutory "process"—the statute does not itself explicitly mention machine implementation or transformation. We do not consider the word "clue" to indicate that the machine-or-implementation test is optional or merely advisory. Rather, the Court described it as the clue, not merely "a" clue. *See Benson*, 409 U.S. at 70, 93 S.Ct. 253.

not include particular machines."). Therefore, we believe our reliance on the Supreme Court's machine-or-transformation test as the applicable test for § 101 analyses of process claims is sound.

Nevertheless, we agree that future developments in technology and the sciences may present difficult challenges to the machine-or-transformation test, just as the widespread use of computers and the advent of the Internet has begun to challenge it in the past decade. Thus, we recognize that the Supreme Court may ultimately decide to alter or perhaps even set aside this test to accommodate emerging technologies. And we certainly do not rule out the possibility that this court may in the future refine or augment the test or how it is applied. At present, however, and certainly for the present case, we see no need for such a departure and reaffirm that the machine-or-transformation test, properly applied, is the governing test for determining patent eligibility of a process under § 101.

C.

As a corollary, the *Diehr* Court also held that mere field-of-use limitations are generally insufficient to render an otherwise ineligible process claim patent-eligible. *See* 450 U.S. at 191–92, 101 S.Ct. 1048 (noting that ineligibility under § 101 "cannot be circumvented by attempting to limit the use of the formula to a particular technological environment"). We recognize that tension may be seen between this consideration and the Court's overall goal of preventing the wholesale pre-emption of fundamental principles. Why not permit patentees to avoid overbroad pre-emption by limiting claim scope to particular fields of use? This tension is resolved, however, by recalling the purpose behind the Supreme Court's discussion of pre-emption, namely that pre-emption is merely an indication that a claim seeks to cover a fundamental principle itself rather than only a specific application of that principle. Pre-emption of all uses of a fundamental principle in all fields and pre-emption of all uses of the principle in only one field both indicate that the claim is not limited to a particular application of the principle. *See Diehr*, 450 U.S. at 193 n. 14, 101 S.Ct. 1048 ("A mathematical formula in the abstract is nonstatutory subject matter regardless of whether the patent is intended to cover all uses of the formula or only limited uses."). In contrast, a claim that is tied to a particular machine or brings about a particular transformation of a particular article does not pre-empt all uses of a fundamental principle in any field but rather is limited to a particular use, a specific application. Therefore, it is not drawn to the principle in the abstract.

The *Diehr* Court also reaffirmed a second corollary to the machine-or-transformation test by stating that "insignificant postsolution activity will not transform an unpatentable principle into a patentable process." *Id.* at 191–92, 101 S.Ct. 1048; *see also Flook*, 437 U.S. at 590, 98 S.Ct. 2522 ("The notion that post-solution activity, no matter how conventional or obvious in itself, can transform an unpatentable principle into a patentable process exalts form over substance."). The Court in *Flook* reasoned:

> A competent draftsman could attach some form of post-solution activity to almost any mathematical formula; the Pythagorean theorem would not have been patentable, or partially patentable, because a patent application contained a final step indicating that the formula, when solved, could be usefully applied to existing surveying techniques.

437 U.S. at 590, 98 S.Ct. 2522.[13] Therefore, even if a claim recites a specific machine or a particular transformation of a specific article, the recited machine or transformation must not constitute mere "insignificant postsolution activity."[14]

D.

We discern two other important aspects of the Supreme Court's § 101 jurisprudence. First, the Court has held that whether a claimed process is novel or non-obvious is irrelevant to the § 101 analysis. *Diehr*, 450 U.S. at 188–91, 101 S.Ct. 1048. Rather, such considerations are governed by 35 U.S.C. § 102 (novelty) and § 103 (non-obviousness). Although § 101 refers to "new and useful" processes, it is overall "a general statement of the type of subject matter that is eligible for patent protection 'subject to the conditions and requirements of this title.'" *Diehr*, 450 U.S. at 189, 101 S.Ct. 1048 (quoting § 101). As the legislative history of § 101 indicates, Congress did not intend the "new and useful" language of § 101 to constitute an independent requirement of novelty or non-obviousness distinct from the more specific and detailed requirements of §§ 102 and 103, respectively. *Diehr*, 450 U.S. at 190–91, 101 S.Ct. 1048.[15] So here, it is irrelevant to the § 101 analysis whether Applicants' claimed process is novel or non-obvious.

Second, the Court has made clear that it is inappropriate to determine the patent-eligibility of a claim as a whole based on whether selected limitations constitute patent-eligible subject matter. *Flook*, 437 U.S. at 594, 98 S.Ct. 2522 ("Our approach to respondent's application is, however, not at all inconsistent with the view that a patent claim must be considered as a whole."); *Diehr*, 450 U.S. at 188, 101 S.Ct. 1048 ("It is inappropriate to dissect the claims into old and new elements and then to ignore the presence of the old elements in the analysis."). After all, even though a fundamental principle itself is not patent-eligible, processes incorporating a fundamental principle may be patent-eligible.

---

13. The example of the Pythagorean theorem applied to surveying techniques could also be considered an example of a mere field-of-use limitation.

14. Although the Court spoke of "postsolution" activity, we have recognized that the Court's reasoning is equally applicable to any insignificant extra-solution activity regardless of where and when it appears in the claimed process.

15. By the same token, considerations of adequate written description, enablement, best mode, etc., are also irrelevant to the § 101 analysis because they, too, are governed by other provisions of the Patent Act. Section 101 does, however, allow for patents only on useful inventions. *Brenner v. Manson*, 383 U.S. 519, 532–35, 86 S.Ct. 1033, 16 L.Ed.2d 69 (1966).

Thus, it is irrelevant that any individual step or limitation of such processes by itself would be unpatentable under § 101.

III.

In the years following the Supreme Court's decisions in *Benson*, *Flook*, and *Diehr*, our predecessor court and this court have reviewed numerous cases presenting a wide variety of process claims, some in technology areas unimaginable when those seminal Supreme Court cases were heard. Looking to these precedents, we find a wealth of detailed guidance and helpful examples on how to determine the patent-eligibility of process claims.

A.

Before we turn to our precedents, however, we first address the issue of whether several other purported articulations of § 101 tests are valid and useful. The first of these is known as the *Freeman-Walter-Abele* test after the three decisions of our predecessor court that formulated and then refined the test: *In re Freeman*, 573 F.2d 1237 (CCPA 1978); *In re Walter*, 618 F.2d 758 (CCPA 1980); and *In re Abele*, 684 F.2d 902 (CCPA 1982). This test, in its final form, had two steps: (1) determining whether the claim recites an "algorithm" within the meaning of *Benson*, then (2) determining whether that algorithm is "applied in any manner to physical elements or process steps." *Abele*, 684 F.2d at 905–07.

Some may question the continued viability of this test, arguing that it appears to conflict with the Supreme Court's proscription against dissecting a claim and evaluating patent-eligibility on the basis of individual limitations. *See Flook*, 437 U.S. at 594, 98 S.Ct. 2522 (requiring analysis of claim as a whole in § 101 analysis). In light of the present opinion, we conclude that the *Freeman-Walter-Abele* test is inadequate. Indeed, we have already recognized that a claim failing that test may nonetheless be patent-eligible. *See In re Grams*, 888 F.2d 835, 838–39 (Fed.Cir.1989). Rather, the machine-or-transformation test is the applicable test for patent-eligible subject matter.

The second articulation we now revisit is the "useful, concrete, and tangible result" language associated with *State Street*, although first set forth in *Alappat State St.*, 149 F.3d at 1373 ("Today, we hold that the transformation of data, representing discrete dollar amounts, by a machine through a series of mathematical calculations into a final share price, constitutes a [patent-eligible invention] because it produces 'a useful, concrete and tangible result'...."); *Alappat*, 33 F.3d at 1544 ("This is not a disembodied mathematical concept which may be characterized as an 'abstract idea,' but rather a specific machine to produce a useful, concrete, and tangible result."). The basis for this language in *State Street* and *Alappat* was that the Supreme Court has explained that "certain types of mathematical subject matter, standing alone, represent nothing more than abstract ideas until reduced to some type of practical application." *Alappat*, 33 F.3d at 1543; *see also State St.*, 149 F.3d at 1373.

To be sure, a process tied to a particular machine, or transforming or reducing a particular article into a different state or thing, will generally produce a "concrete" and "tangible" result as those terms were used in our prior decisions. But while looking for "a useful, concrete and tangible result" may in many instances provide useful indications of whether a claim is drawn to a fundamental principle or a practical application of such a principle, that inquiry is insufficient to determine whether a claim is patent-eligible under § 101. And it was certainly never intended to supplant the Supreme Court's test. Therefore, we also conclude that the "useful, concrete and tangible result" inquiry is inadequate and reaffirm that the machine-or-transformation test outlined by the Supreme Court is the proper test to apply.

We next turn to the so-called "technological arts test" that some amici urge us to adopt. We perceive that the contours of such a test, however, would be unclear because the meanings of the terms "technological arts" and "technology" are both ambiguous and ever-changing. And no such test has ever been explicitly adopted by the Supreme Court, this court, or our predecessor court, as the Board correctly observed here. Therefore, we decline to do so and continue to rely on the machine-or-transformation test as articulated by the Supreme Court.

We further reject calls for categorical exclusions beyond those for fundamental principles already identified by the Supreme Court. We rejected just such an exclusion in *State Street*, noting that the so-called "business method exception" was unlawful and that business method claims (and indeed all process claims) are "subject to the same legal requirements for patentability as applied to any other process or method." 149 F.3d at 1375–76. We reaffirm this conclusion.

B.

With these preliminary issues resolved, we now turn to how our case law elaborates on the § 101 analysis set forth by the Supreme Court. To the extent that some of the reasoning in these decisions relied on considerations or tests, such as "useful, concrete and tangible result," that are no longer valid as explained above, those aspects of the decisions should no longer be relied on. Thus, we reexamine the facts of certain cases under the correct test to glean greater guidance as to how to perform the § 101 analysis using the machine-or-transformation test.

The machine-or-transformation test is a two-branched inquiry; an applicant may show that a process claim satisfies § 101 either by showing that his claim is tied to a particular machine, or by showing that his claim transforms an article. *See Benson*, 409 U.S. at 70, 93 S.Ct. 253. Certain considerations are applicable to analysis under either branch. First, as illustrated by *Benson* and discussed below, the use of a specific machine or transformation of an article must impose meaningful limits on the claim's scope to impart patent-eligibility. *See Benson*, 409 U.S. at 71–72, 93 S.Ct. 253. Second, the involvement of the machine or transformation in the claimed process must not merely be insignificant extra-solution activity. *See Flook*, 437 U.S. at 590, 98 S.Ct. 2522.

As to machine implementation, Applicants themselves admit that the language of claim 1 does not limit any process step to any specific machine or apparatus. As a result, issues specific to the machine implementation part of the test are not before us today. We leave to future cases the elaboration of the precise contours of machine implementation, as well as the answers to particular questions, such as whether or when recitation of a computer suffices to tie a process claim to a particular machine.

We will, however, consider some of our past cases to gain insight into the transformation part of the test. A claimed process is patent-eligible if it transforms an article into a different state or thing. This transformation must be central to the purpose of the claimed process. But the main aspect of the transformation test that requires clarification here is what sorts of things constitute "articles" such that their transformation is sufficient to impart patent-eligibility under § 101. It is virtually self-evident that a process for a chemical or physical transformation of physical objects or substances is patent-eligible subject matter. As the Supreme Court stated in *Benson*:

> [T]he arts of tanning, dyeing, making waterproof cloth, vulcanizing India rubber, smelting ores ... are instances, however, where the use of chemical substances or physical acts, such as temperature control, changes articles or materials. The chemical process or the physical acts which transform the raw material are, however, sufficiently definite to confine the patent monopoly within rather definite bounds.

409 U.S. at 70, 93 S.Ct. 253 (quoting *Corning v. Burden*, 56 U.S. (15 How.) 252, 267–68, 14 L.Ed. 683 (1854)); *see also Diehr*, 450 U.S. at 184, 101 S.Ct. 1048 (process of curing rubber); *Tilghman*, 102 U.S. at 729 (process of reducing fats into constituent acids and glycerine).

The raw materials of many information-age processes, however, are electronic signals and electronically-manipulated data. And some so-called business methods, such as that claimed in the present case, involve the manipulation of even more abstract constructs such as legal obligations, organizational relationships, and business risks. Which, if any, of these processes qualify as a transformation or reduction of an article into a different state or thing constituting patent-eligible subject matter?

Our case law has taken a measured approach to this question, and we see no reason here to expand the boundaries of what constitutes patent-eligible transformations of articles.

Our predecessor court's mixed result in *Abele* illustrates this point. There, we held unpatentable a broad independent claim reciting a process of graphically displaying variances of data from average values. *Abele*, 684 F.2d at 909. That claim did not specify any particular type or nature of data; nor did it specify how or from where the data was obtained or what the data represented. *Id.; see also In re Meyer*, 688 F.2d 789, 792–93 (CCPA 1982) (process claim involving undefined "complex system" and indeterminate "factors" drawn from unspecified "testing" not patent-eligible). In contrast, we held one of Abele's dependent claims to be drawn to patent-eligible subject matter where it specified that "said data is X-ray attenuation data produced in a two dimensional field by a computed tomography scanner." *Abele*, 684 F.2d at 908–09. This data clearly represented physical and tangible objects, namely the structure of bones, organs, and other body tissues. Thus, the transformation of that raw data into a particular visual depiction of a physical object on a display was sufficient to render that more narrowly-claimed process patent-eligible.

We further note for clarity that the electronic transformation of the data itself into a visual depiction in *Abele* was sufficient; the claim was not required to involve any transformation of the underlying physical object that the data represented. We believe this is faithful to the concern the Supreme Court articulated as the basis for the machine-or-transformation test, namely the prevention of pre-emption of fundamental principles. So long as the claimed process is limited to a practical application of a fundamental principle to transform specific data, and the claim is limited to a visual depiction that represents specific physical objects or substances, there is no danger that the scope of the claim would wholly pre-empt all uses of the principle.

This court and our predecessor court have frequently stated that adding a data-gathering step to an algorithm is insufficient to convert that algorithm into a patent-eligible process. *E.g., Grams*, 888 F.2d at 840 (step of "deriv[ing] data for the algorithm will not render the claim statutory"); *Meyer*, 688 F.2d at 794 ("[data-gathering] step[s] cannot make an otherwise nonstatutory claim statutory"). For example, in *Grams* we held unpatentable a process of performing a clinical test and, based on the data from that test, determining if an abnormality existed and possible causes of any abnormality. We rejected the claim because it was merely an algorithm combined with a data-gathering step. We note that, at least in most cases, gathering data would not constitute a transformation of any article. A requirement simply that data inputs be gathered—without specifying how—is a meaningless limit on a claim to an algorithm because every algorithm inherently requires the gathering of data inputs. Further, the inherent step of gathering data can also fairly be characterized as insignificant extra-solution activity. *See Flook*, 437 U.S. at 590, 98 S.Ct. 2522.

Similarly, *In re Schrader* presented claims directed to a method of conducting an auction of multiple items in which the winning bids were selected in a manner that maximized the total price of all the items (rather than to the highest individual bid for each item separately). 22 F.3d 290, 291 (Fed.Cir.1994). We held the claims to be drawn to unpatentable subject matter, namely a mathematical optimization algorithm. No specific machine or apparatus was recited. The claimed method did require a step of recording the bids on each item, though no particular manner of recording (e.g., on paper, on a computer) was specified. But, relying on *Flook*, we held that this step constituted insignificant extra-solution activity.

IV.

We now turn to the facts of this case. As outlined above, the operative question before this court is whether Applicants' claim 1 satisfies the transformation branch of the machine-or-transformation test.

We hold that the Applicants' process as claimed does not transform any article to a different state or thing. Purported transformations or manipulations simply of public or private legal obligations or relationships, business risks, or other such abstractions cannot meet the test because they are not physical objects or substances, and they are not representative of physical objects or substances. Applicants' process at most incorporates only such ineligible transformations. *See* Appellants' Br. at 11 ("[The claimed process] transforms the relationships between the commodity provider, the consumers and market participants. . . .") As discussed earlier, the process as claimed encompasses the exchange of only options, which are simply legal rights to purchase some commodity at a given price in a given time period. The claim only refers to "transactions" involving the exchange of these legal rights at a "fixed rate corresponding to a risk position." Thus, claim 1 does not involve the transformation of any physical object or substance, or an electronic signal representative of any physical object or substance. Given its admitted failure to meet the machine implementation part of the test as well, the claim entirely fails the machine-or-transformation test and is not drawn to patent-eligible subject matter.

Applicants' arguments are unavailing because they rely on incorrect or insufficient considerations and do not address their claim's failure to meet the requirements of the Supreme Court's machine-or-transformation test. First, they argue that claim 1 produces "useful, concrete and tangible results." But as already discussed, this is insufficient to establish patent-eligibility under § 101. Applicants also argue that their claimed process does not comprise only "steps that are totally or substantially practiced in the mind but clearly require physical activity which have [sic] a tangible result." But as previously discussed, the correct analysis is whether the claim meets the machine-or-transformation test, not whether it recites "physical steps." Even if it is true that Applicant's claim "can only be practiced by a series of physical acts" as they argue, its clear failure to satisfy the machine-or-transformation test is fatal. Thus, while we agree with Applicants that the only limit to patent-eligibility imposed by Congress is that the invention fall within one of the four categories enumerated in § 101, we must apply the Supreme Court's test to determine whether a claim to a process is drawn to a statutory "process" within the meaning of § 101. Applied here, Applicants' claim fails that test so it is not drawn to a "process" under § 101 as that term has been interpreted.

On the other hand, while we agree with the PTO that the machine-or-transformation test is the correct test to apply in determining whether a process claim is patent-eligible under § 101, we do not agree, as discussed earlier, that this amounts to a "technological arts" test. Neither the PTO nor the courts may pay short shrift to the machine-or-transformation test by using purported equivalents or shortcuts such as a "technological arts" requirement. Rather, the machine-or-transformation test is the only applicable test and must be applied, in light of the guidance provided by the Supreme Court and this court, when evaluating the patent-eligibility of process claims. When we do so here, however, we must conclude, as the PTO did, that Applicants' claim fails the test.

Applicants here seek to claim a non-transformative process that encompasses a purely mental process of performing requisite mathematical calculations without the aid of a computer or any other device, mentally identifying those transactions that the calculations have revealed would hedge each other's risks, and performing the post-solution step of consummating those transactions. Therefore, claim 1 would effectively pre-empt any application of the fundamental concept of hedging and mathematical calculations inherent in hedging (not even limited to any particular mathematical formula). And while Applicants argue that the scope of this pre-emption is limited to hedging as applied in the area of consumable commodities, the Supreme Court's reasoning has made clear that effective pre-emption of all applications of hedging even just within the area of consumable commodities is impermissible. *See Diehr*, 450 U.S. at 191–92, 101 S.Ct. 1048 (holding that field-of-use limitations are insufficient to impart patent-eligibility to otherwise unpatentable claims drawn to fundamental principles). Moreover, while the claimed process contains physical steps (initiating, identifying), it does not involve transforming an article into a different state or thing. Therefore, Applicants' claim is not drawn to patent-eligible subject matter under § 101.

CONCLUSION

Because the applicable test to determine whether a claim is drawn to a patent-eligible process under § 101 is the machine-or-transformation test set forth by the Supreme Court and clarified herein, and Applicants' claim here plainly fails that test, the decision of the Board is AFFIRMED.

NEWMAN, CIRCUIT JUDGE, dissenting.

The court today acts en banc to impose a new and far-reaching restriction on the kinds of inventions that are eligible to participate in the patent system. The court achieves this result by redefining the word "process" in the patent statute, to exclude all processes that do not transform physical matter or that are not performed by machines. The court thus excludes many of the kinds of inventions that apply today's electronic and photonic technologies, as well as other processes that handle data and information in novel ways. Such processes have long been patent eligible, and contribute to the vigor and variety of today's Information Age. This exclusion of process inventions is contrary to statute, contrary to precedent, and a negation of the constitutional mandate. Its impact on the future, as well as on the thousands of patents already granted, is unknown.

This exclusion is imposed at the threshold, before it is determined whether the excluded process is new, non-obvious, enabled, described, particularly claimed, etc.; that is, before the new process is examined for patentability. For example, we do not know whether the Bilski process would be found patentable under the statutory criteria, for they were never applied.

The innovations of the "knowledge economy"—of "digital prosperity"—have been dominant contributors to today's economic growth and societal change. Revision of the commercial structure affecting major aspects of today's industry should be approached with care, for there has been significant reliance on the law as it has existed, as many amici curiae pointed out. Indeed, the full reach of today's change of law is not clear, and the majority opinion states that many existing situations may require reassessment under the new criteria.

Uncertainty is the enemy of innovation. These new uncertainties not only diminish the incentives available to new enterprise, but disrupt the settled expectations of those who relied on the law as it existed. I respectfully dissent.

This court now rejects its own CCPA and Federal Circuit precedent

The majority opinion holds that there is a Supreme Court restriction on process patents, "enunciated" in *Benson*, *Flook*, and *Diehr*; and that this restriction was improperly ignored by the Federal Circuit and the Court of Customs and Patent Appeals, leading us into error which we must now correct. Thus this court announces that our prior decisions may no longer be relied upon. The effect on the patents and businesses that did rely on them is not considered.

The now-discarded criterion of a "useful, concrete, and tangible result" has proved to be of ready and comprehensible applicability in a large variety of processes of the information and digital ages. The court in *State Street Bank* reinforced the thesis that there is no reason, in statute or policy, to exclude computer-implemented and information-based inventions from access to patentability. The holdings and reasoning of *Alappat* and *State Street Bank* guided the inventions of the electronic age into the patent system, while remaining faithful to the *Diehr* distinction between abstract ideas such as mathematical formulae and their application in a particular process for a specified purpose. And patentability has always required compliance with all of the requirements of the statute, including novelty, non-obviousness, utility, and the provisions of Section 112.

The public has relied on the rulings of this court and of the Supreme Court

The decisions in *Alappat* and *State Street Bank* confirmed the patent eligibility of many evolving areas of commerce, as inventors and investors explored new technological capabilities. The public and the economy have experienced extraordinary advances in information-based and computer-managed processes, supported by an enlarging patent base. The PTO reports that in Class 705, the examination classification associated with "business methods" and most likely to receive inventions that may not use machinery or transform physical matter, there were almost 10,000 patent applications filed in FY 2006 alone, and over 40,000 applications filed since FY 98 when State Street Bank was decided. An amicus in the present case reports that over 15,000 patents classified in Class 705 have issued. The industries identified with information-based and data-handling processes, as several amici curiae explain and illustrate, include fields as diverse as banking and finance, insurance, data processing, industrial engineering, and medicine.

Stable law, on which industry can rely, is a foundation of commercial advance into new products and processes. Inventiveness in the computer and information services fields has placed the United States in a position of technological and commercial preeminence. The information technology industry is reported to be "the key factor responsible for reversing the 20–year productivity slow-down from the mid–1970s to the mid–1990s and in driving today's robust productivity growth." R.D. Atkinson & A.S. McKay, *Digital Prosperity: Understanding the Economic Benefits of the Information Technology Revolution* 10 (Info. Tech. & Innovation Found.2007), available at http://www.itif.org/files/digital_prosperity. pdf. By revenue estimates, in 2005 the software and information sectors constituted the fourth largest industry in the United States, with significantly faster growth than the overall U.S. economy. Software & Info. Indus. Ass'n, *Software and Information: Driving the Knowledge Economy* 7–8 (2008), http://www.siia.net/estore/globecon-08.pdf. A Congressional Report in 2006 stated:

> As recently as 1978, intangible assets, such as intellectual property, accounted for 20 percent of corporate assets with the vast majority of value (80 percent) attributed to tangible assets such as facilities and equipment. By 1997, the trend reversed; 73 percent of corporate assets were intangible and only 27 percent were tangible.

H.R.Rep. No. 109–673 (accompanying a bill concerning judicial resources).

This powerful economic move toward "intangibles" is a challenge to the backward-looking change of this court's ruling today. Until the shift represented by today's decision, statute and precedent have provided stability in the rapidly moving and commercially vibrant fields of the Information Age. Despite the economic importance of these interests, the consequences of our decision have not been considered. I don't know how much human creativity and commercial activity will be devalued by today's change in law; but neither do my colleagues.

The Section 101 interpretation that is now uprooted has the authority of years of reliance, and ought not be disturbed absent the most compelling reasons.

Uncertain guidance for the future

Not only past expectations, but future hopes, are disrupted by uncertainty as to application of the new restrictions on patent eligibility. For example, the court states that even if a process is "tied to" a machine or transforms matter, the machine or transformation must impose "meaningful limits" and cannot constitute "insignificant extra-solution activity". We are advised that transformation must be "central to the purpose of the claimed process," id., although we are not told what kinds of transformations may qualify. These concepts raise new conflicts with precedent.

This court and the Supreme Court have stated that "there is no legally recognizable or protected 'essential' element, 'gist' or 'heart' of the invention in a combination patent." *Allen Eng'g Corp. v. Bartell Industries, Inc.*, 299 F.3d 1336, 1345 (Fed.Cir.2002) (quoting Aro *Mfg. Co. v. Convertible Top Replacement Co.*, 365 U.S. 336, 345, 81 S.Ct. 599, 5 L.Ed.2d 592 (1961)). This rule applies with equal force to process patents, *see W.L. Gore & Associates, Inc. v. Garlock, Inc.*, 721 F.2d 1540, 1548 (Fed.Cir.1983) (there is no gist of the invention rule for process patents), and is in accord with the rule that the invention must be considered as a whole, rather than "dissected," in assessing its patent eligibility under Section 101, *see Diehr*, 450 U.S. at 188, 101 S.Ct. 1048. It is difficult to predict an adjudicator's view of the "invention as a whole," now that patent examiners and judges are instructed to weigh the different process components for their "centrality" and the "significance" of their "extra-solution activity" in a Section 101 inquiry.

As for whether machine implementation will impose "meaningful limits in a particular case," the "meaningfulness" of computer usage in the great variety of technical and informational subject matter that is computer-facilitated is apparently now a flexible parameter of Section 101. Each patent examination center, each trial court, each panel of this court, will have a blank slate on which to uphold or invalidate claims based on whether there are sufficient "meaningful limits", or whether a transformation is adequately "central," or the "significance" of process steps. These qualifiers, appended to a novel test which itself is neither suggested nor supported by statutory text, legislative history, or judicial precedent, raise more questions than they answer. These new standards add delay, uncertainty, and cost, but do not add confidence in reliable standards for Section 101.

Other aspects of the changes of law also contribute uncertainty. We aren't told when, or if, software instructions implemented on a general purpose computer are deemed "tied" to a "particular machine," for if *Alappat*'s guidance that software converts a general purpose computer into a special purpose machine remains applicable, there is no need for the present ruling. For the thousands of inventors who obtained patents under the court's now-discarded criteria, their property rights are now vulnerable.

Although this uncertainty may invite some to try their luck in court, the wider effect will be a disincentive to innovation-based commerce. For inventors, investors, competitors, and the public, the most grievous consequence is the effect on inventions not made or not developed because of uncertainty as to patent protection. Only the successes need the patent right.

CONCLUSION

In sum, the text of Section 101, its statutory history, its interpretation by the Supreme Court, and its application by the courts, contravene this court's redefinition of the statutory term "process." The court's decision affects present and future rights and incentives, and usurps the legislative role. The judicial role is to support stability and predictability in the law, with fidelity to statute and precedent, and respect for the principles of stare decisis.

Patents provide an incentive to invest in and work in new directions. In *United States v. Line Material Co.*, 333 U.S. 287, 332, 68 S.Ct. 550, 92 L.Ed. 701 (1948), Justice Burton, joined by Chief Justice Vinson and Justice Frankfurter, remarked that "the frontiers of science have expanded until civilization now depends largely upon discoveries on those frontiers to meet the infinite needs of the future. The United States, thus far, has taken a leading part in making those discoveries and in putting them to use." This remains true today. It is antithetical to this incentive to restrict eligibility for patenting to what has been done in the past, and to foreclose what might be done in the future.

MAYER, CIRCUIT JUDGE, dissenting.

The *en banc* order in this case asked: "Whether it is appropriate to reconsider *State Street Bank & Trust Co. v. Signature Financial Group, Inc.*, 149 F.3d 1368 (Fed.Cir.1998), and *AT & T Corp. v. Excel Communications, Inc.*, 172 F.3d 1352 (Fed.Cir.1999), in this case and, if so, whether those cases should be overruled in any respect?" I would answer that question with an emphatic "yes." The patent system is intended to protect and promote advances in science and technology, not ideas about how to structure commercial transactions. Claim 1 of the application of Bilski is not eligible for patent protection because it is directed to a method of conducting business. Affording patent protection to business methods lacks constitutional and statutory support, serves to hinder rather than promote innovation and usurps that which rightfully belongs in the public domain. *State Street* and *AT & T* should be overruled.

I.

In discussing the scope of copyright protection, the Supreme Court has noted that " 'a page of history is worth a volume of logic.' " *Eldred v. Ashcroft*, 537 U.S. 186, 200, 123 S.Ct. 769, 154 L.Ed.2d 683 (2003) (quoting *New York Trust Co. v. Eisner*, 256 U.S. 345, 349, 41 S.Ct. 506, 65 L.Ed. 963 (1921)). The same holds true with respect to patent protection. From a historical perspective, it is highly unlikely that the framers of the Constitution's intellectual property clause intended to grant patent protection to methods of conducting business. To the contrary, "those who formulated the Constitution were familiar with the long struggle over monopolies so prominent in English history, where exclusive rights to engage even in ordinary business activities were granted so frequently by the Crown for the financial benefits accruing to the Crown only." *In re Yuan*, 38 C.C.P.A. 967, 188 F.2d 377, 380 (1951). The Statute of Monopolies, enacted in 1624, curtailed the Crown's ability to grant "monopolies to court favorites in goods or businesses which had long before been enjoyed by the public." *Graham v. John Deere Co.*, 383 U.S. 1, 5, 86 S.Ct. 684, 15 L.Ed.2d 545 (1966). When drafting the Constitution, the framers were well aware of the abuses that led to the English Statute of Monopolies and therefore "consciously acted to bar Congress from granting letters patent in particular types of business." *In re Comiskey*, 499 F.3d 1365, 1375 (Fed.Cir.2007).

There is nothing in the early patent statutes to indicate that Congress intended business methods to constitute patentable subject matter. As early as 1869, the Commissioner of Patents said that "[i]t is contrary . . . to the spirit of the law, as construed by the office for many years, to grant patents for methods of book-keeping," *Ex parte Abraham*, 1869 Dec. Comm'r Pat. 59, 59 (1869), and by 1893 the courts had concluded that "a method of transacting common business . . . does not seem to be patentable as an art," *United States Credit Sys. Co. v. Am. Credit Indem. Co.*, 53 F. 818, 819 (C.C.S.D.N.Y.1893), aff'd on other grounds, 59 F. 139 (2d Cir.1893). By 1952, when Congress enacted the current Patent Act, it was widely acknowledged that methods of doing business were ineligible for patent protection. *See, e.g., Loew's Drive–In Theatres, Inc. v. Park–In Theatres, Inc.*, 174 F.2d 547, 552 (1st Cir.1949) ("[A] system for the transaction of business . . . however novel, useful, or commercially successful is not patentable apart from the means for making the system practically useful, or carrying it out."); *In re Patton*, 29 C.C.P.A. 982, 127 F.2d 324 (1942) (noting that "a system of transacting business, apart from the means for carrying out such system" is not patentable); *Hotel Sec. Checking Co. v. Lorraine Co.*, 160 F. 467, 469 (2d Cir.1908) ("A system of transacting business disconnected from the means for carrying out the system is not, within the most liberal interpretation of the term, an art."); *In re Moeser*, 27 App. D.C. 307, 310

(1906) (holding that a system for burial insurance contracts was not patentable because "contracts or proposals for contracts, devised or adopted as a method of transacting a particular class of . . . business, [are] not patentable as an art"); see also 145 Cong. Rec. H6,947 (Aug. 3, 1999) (statement of Rep. Manzullo) ("Before the *State Street Bank and Trust* case . . . it was universally thought that methods of doing or conducting business were not patentable items.").

In passing the 1952 Act, Congress re-enacted statutory language that had long existed, thus signaling its intent to carry forward the body of case law that had developed under prior versions of the statute. Because there is nothing in the language of the 1952 Act, or its legislative history, to indicate that Congress intended to modify the rule against patenting business methods, we must presume that no change in the rule was intended. If Congress had wished to change the established practice of disallowing patents on business methods, it was quite capable of doing so explicitly. *See Parker v. Flook*, 437 U.S. 584, 596, 98 S.Ct. 2522, 57 L.Ed.2d 451 (1978) (stressing that courts "must proceed cautiously when . . . asked to extend patent rights into areas wholly unforeseen by Congress").

State Street's decision to jettison the prohibition against patenting methods of doing business contravenes congressional intent. Because (1) "the framers consciously acted to bar Congress from granting letters patent in particular types of business," *Comiskey*, 499 F.3d at 1375, and (2) Congress evidenced no intent to modify the long-established rule against business method patents when it enacted the 1952 Patent Act, it is hard to fathom how the issuance of patents on business methods can be supported.

II.

Business method patents have been justified, in significant measure, by a misapprehension of the legislative history of the 1952 Patent Act. In particular, proponents of such patents have asserted that the Act's legislative history states that Congress intended statutory subject matter to "include anything under the sun that is made by man." *AT&T*, 172 F.3d at 1355 (Fed.Cir.1999) (citations and internal quotation marks omitted); *see also Diamond v. Chakrabarty*, 447 U.S. 303, 309, 100 S.Ct. 2204, 65 L.Ed.2d 144 (1980). Read in context, however, the legislative history says no such thing. The full statement from the committee report reads: "A person may have 'invented' a machine or a manufacture, which may include anything under the sun that is made by man, but it is not necessarily patentable under section 101 unless the conditions of the title are fulfilled." S.Rep. No.1979, 82d Cong., 2d Sess. 5 (1952), U.S.CODE CONG. & ADMIN.NEWS 1952, pp. 2394, 2399 (emphasis added); H.R.Rep. No.1923, 82d Cong., 2d Sess. 6 (1952) (emphasis added).

This statement does not support the contention that Congress intended "anything under the sun" to be patentable. To the contrary, the language supports the opposite view: a person may have "invented" anything under the sun, but it is "not necessarily patentable" unless the statutory requirements for patentability have been satisfied. Thus, the legislative history oft-cited to support business method patents under-cuts, rather than supports, the notion that Congress intended to extend the scope of section 101 to encompass such methods.

Moreover, the cited legislative history is not discussing process claims at all. The quoted language is discussing "machines" and "manu-factures;" it is therefore surprising that it has been thought a fit basis for allowing patents on business processes.

III.

The Constitution does not grant Congress unfettered authority to issue patents. See U.S. Const. art. I, § 8. Instead, the patent power is a "qualified authority . . . [which] is limited to the promotion of advances in the 'useful arts.' " *Graham*, 383 U.S. at 5, 86 S.Ct. 684. What the framers described as "useful arts," we in modern times call "technology." *Paulik v. Rizkalla*, 760 F.2d 1270, 1276 (Fed.Cir.1985) (en banc). Therefore, by mandating that patents advance the useful arts, "[t]he Constitution explicitly limited patentability to . . . 'the process today called technological innovation.' " *Comiskey*, 499 F.3d at 1375 (quoting *Paulik*, 760 F.2d at 1276).

Before *State Street* led us down the wrong path, this court had rightly concluded that patents were designed to protect technological innovations, not ideas about the best way to run a business. We had thus rejected as unpatentable a method for coordinating firefighting efforts, *Patton*, 127 F.2d at 326–27, a method for deciding how salesmen should best handle customers, *In re Maucorps*, 609 F.2d 481 (CCPA 1979), and a computerized method for aiding a neurologist in diagnosing patients, *In re Meyer*, 688 F.2d 789 (CCPA 1982). We stated that patentable processes must "be in the technological arts so as to be in consonance with the Constitutional purpose to promote the progress of 'useful arts.' " *In re Musgrave*, 57 C.C.P.A. 1352, 431 F.2d 882, 893 (CCPA 1970) (emphasis added).

Business method patents do not promote the "useful arts" because they are not directed to any technological or scientific innovation. Although business method applications may use technology—such as computers—to accomplish desired results, the innovative aspect of the claimed method is an entrepreneurial rather than a technological one. Thus, although Bilski's claimed hedging method could theoretically be implemented on a computer, that alone does not render it patentable. *See Diehr*, 450 U.S. at 192 n. 14, 101 S.Ct. 1048 (Patentability cannot be established by the "token" use of technology.); *Gottschalk v. Benson*, 409 U.S. 63, 64–66, 93 S.Ct. 253, 34 L.Ed.2d 273 (1972) (finding unpatentable a method of programming a general purpose digital computer to convert signals from binary-coded decimal to pure binary form). Where a claimed business method simply uses a known machine to do what it was designed to do, such as using a computer to gather data or perform calculations, use of that machine will not bring otherwise unpatentable subject matter within the ambit of section 101. *See Benson*, 409 U.S. at 67, 93 S.Ct. 253 (finding a process unpatentable where "[t]he mathematical procedures [could] be carried out in existing computers long in use, no new machinery being necessary").

IV.

State Street has launched a legal tsunami, inundating the patent office with applications seeking protection for common business practices. Applications for Class 705 (business method) patents increased from fewer than 1,000 applications in 1997 to more than 11,000 applications in 2007. See United States Patent and Trademark Office, *Class 705 Application Filings and Patents Issued Data*, available at http://www.uspto.gov/web/menu/pbmethod/applicationfiling.htm (information available as of Jan. 2008).

Patents granted in the wake of *State Street* have ranged from the somewhat ridiculous to the truly absurd. See, e.g., U.S. Patent No. 5,851,117 (method of training janitors to dust and vacuum using video displays); U.S. Patent No. 5,862,223 (method for selling expert advice); U.S. Patent No. 6,014,643 (method for trading securities); U.S. Patent No. 6,119,099 (method of enticing customers to order additional food at a fast food restaurant); U.S. Patent No. 6,329,919 (system for toilet reservations); U.S. Patent No. 7,255,277 (method of using color-coded bracelets to designate dating status in order to limit "the embarrassment of rejection"). There has even been a patent issued on a method for obtaining a patent. *See* U.S. Patent No. 6,049,811. Not surprisingly, *State Street* and its progeny have generated a thundering chorus of criticism.

There are a host of difficulties associated with allowing patents to issue on methods of conducting business. Not only do such patents tend to impede rather than promote innovation, they are frequently of poor quality. Most fundamentally, they raise significant First Amendment concerns by imposing broad restrictions on speech and the free flow of ideas.

A.

"[T]he underlying policy of the patent system [is] that 'the things which are worth to the public the embarrassment of an exclusive patent,' . . . must outweigh the restrictive effect of the limited patent monopoly." *Graham*, 383 U.S. at 10–11, 86 S.Ct. 684 (quoting letter from Thomas Jefferson to Isaac McPherson (Aug. 1813)). Thus, Congress may not expand the scope of "the patent monopoly without regard to the . . . advancement or social benefit gained thereby." *Id.* at 6, 86 S.Ct. 684.

Patents should be granted to those inventions "which would not be disclosed or devised but for the inducement of a patent." Id. at 11, 86 S.Ct. 684. Methods of doing business have existed since the earliest days of the Patent Act and have flourished even in the absence of patent protection. Commentators have argued that "the broad grant of patent protection for methods of doing business is something of a square peg in a sinkhole of uncertain dimensions" since "[n]owhere in the substantial literature on innovation is there a statement that the United States economy suffers from a lack of innovation in methods of doing business." [Leo J. Raskind, *The Bad Business of Unlimited Patent Protection for Methods of Doing Business*, 10 FORDHAM INTELL. PROP. MEDIA & ENT. L.J. 61, 92–93 (1999). Instead, "the long history of U.S. business is one of innovation, emulation, and innovation again. It also is a history of remarkable creativity and success, all without business method patents until the past few years." [Nicholas A. Smith, *Business Method Patents and Their Limits: Justifications, History, and the Emergence of a Claim Construction Jurisprudence*, 9 MICH. TELECOMM. & TECH. L. REV. 177, 178 (2002)].

B.

"[S]ometimes *too much* patent protection can impede rather than 'promote the Progress of Science and useful Arts,' the constitutional objective of patent and copyright protection." *Lab. Corp. of Am. Holdings v. Metabolite Labs., Inc.*, 548 U.S. 124, 126, 126 S.Ct. 2921, 165 L.Ed.2d 399 (2006) (Breyer, J., joined by Stevens and Souter, JJ., dissenting from dismissal of writ of certiorari) (emphasis in original). This is particularly true in the context of patents on methods of conducting business. Instead of providing incentives to competitors to develop improved business techniques, business method patents remove building blocks of commercial innovation from the public domain. Because they restrict competitors from using and improving upon patented business methods, such patents stifle innovation. When "we grant rights to exclude unnecessarily, we . . . limit competition with no quid pro quo. Retarding competition retards further development." [Malla Pollack, *The Multiple Unconstitutionality of Business Method Patents*, 28 RUTGERS COMPUTER & TECH. L.J. 61, 76 (2002)]. "Think how the airline industry might now be structured if the first company to offer frequent flyer miles had enjoyed the sole right to award them or how differently mergers and acquisitions would be financed . . . if the use of junk bonds had been protected by a patent." [Rochelle Cooper, *Are Business Method Patents Bad for Business?*, 16 SANTA CLARA COMPUTER & HIGH TECH. L.J. 264, 264 (2000).] By affording patent protection to business practices, "the government distorts the operation of the free market system and reduces the gains from the operation of the market." [James S. Sfekas, *Controlling Business Method Patents: How the Japanese Standard for Patenting Software Could Bring Limitations to Business Method Patents in the United States*, 16 Pac. Rim L. & Pol'y J. 197, 214 (2007)].

C.

Another significant problem that plagues business method patents is that they tend to be of poor overall quality. *See eBay Inc. v. MercExchange, L.L.C.*, 547 U.S. 388, 397, 126 S.Ct. 1837, 164 L.Ed.2d 641 (2006) (Kennedy, J., joined by Stevens, Souter, and Breyer, JJ., concurring) (noting the "potential vagueness and suspect validity" of some of "the burgeoning number of patents over business methods"). Commentators have lamented "the frequency with which the Patent Office issues patents on shockingly mundane business inventions." Dreyfuss, *supra* at 268. One reason for the poor quality of business method patents is the lack of readily accessible prior art references. Because business methods were not patentable prior to *State Street*, "there is very little patent-related prior art readily at hand to the examiner corps." Dreyfuss, *supra* at 269.

Furthermore, information about methods of conducting business, unlike information about technological endeavors, is often not documented or published in scholarly journals. The fact that examiners lack the resources to weed out undeserving applications "has led to the improper approval of a large number of patents, leaving private parties to clean up the mess through litigation." [William Krause, *Sweeping the E–Commerce Minefield: The Need for a Workable Business Method Exception*, 24 SEATTLE U. L. REV. 79, 97 (2000)].

Allowing patents to issue on business methods shifts critical resources away from promoting and protecting truly useful technological advances. As discussed previously, the patent office has been deluged with business method applications in recent years. Time spent on such applications is time not spent on applications which claim true innovations. When already overburdened examiners are forced to devote significant time to reviewing large numbers of business method applications, the public's access to new and beneficial technologies is unjustifiably delayed.

D.

Patenting business methods allows private parties to claim exclusive ownership of ideas and practices which rightfully belong in the public domain. "It is a matter of public interest that [economic] decisions, in the aggregate, be intelligent and well informed. To this end, the free flow of commercial information is indispensable." *Virginia State Bd. of Pharmacy v. Virginia Citizens Consumer Council, Inc.*, 425 U.S. 748, 765, 96 S.Ct. 1817, 48 L.Ed.2d 346 (1976). Thus, "the stringent requirements for patent protection seek to assure that ideas in the public domain remain there for the free use of the public." *Aronson v. Quick Point Pencil Co.*, 440 U.S. 257, 262, 99 S.Ct. 1096, 59 L.Ed.2d 296 (1979).

Bilski's claimed method consists essentially of two conversations. The first conversation is between a commodity provider and a commodity consumer, while the second conversation is between the provider and "market participants" who have "a counter-risk position to . . . consumers." His claims provide almost no details as to the contents of these conversations.

Like many business method applications, Bilski's application is very broadly drafted. It covers a wide range of means for "hedging" in commodity transactions. If his application were allowed, anyone who discussed ways to balance market risks in any sort of commodity could face potential infringement liability. By adopting overly expansive standards for patentability, the government enables private parties to impose broad and unwarranted burdens on speech and the free flow of ideas.

To the extent that business methods are deemed patentable, individuals can face unexpected potential infringement liability for everyday conversations and commercial interactions. "[I]mplicit in the Patent Clause itself [is the understanding] that free exploitation of ideas will be the rule, to which the protection of a federal patent is the exception." *Bonito Boats, Inc. v. Thunder Craft Boats, Inc.*, 489 U.S. 141, 151, 109 S.Ct. 971, 103 L.Ed.2d 118 (1989). In the wake of *State Street*, too many patent holders have been allowed to claim exclusive ownership of subject matter that rightfully belongs in the public domain.

V.

The majority's proposed "machine-or-transformation test" for patentability will do little to stem the growth of patents on non-technological methods and ideas. Quite simply, in the context of business method patent applications, the majority's proposed standard can be too easily circumvented. Through clever draftsmanship, nearly every process claim can be rewritten to include a physical transformation. Bilski, for example, could simply add a requirement that a commodity consumer install a meter to record commodity consumption. He could then argue that installation of this meter was a "physical transformation," sufficient to satisfy the majority's proposed patentability test.

Even as written, Bilski's claim arguably involves a physical transformation. Prior to utilizing Bilski's method, commodity providers and commodity consumers are not involved in transactions to buy and sell a commodity at a fixed rate. By using Bilski's claimed method, however, providers and consumers enter into a series of transactions allowing them to buy and sell a particular commodity at a particular price. Entering into a transaction is a physical process: telephone calls are made, meetings are held, and market participants must physically execute contracts. Market participants go from a state of not being in a commodity transaction to a state of being in such a transaction. The majority, however, fails to explain how this sort of physical transformation is insufficient to satisfy its proposed patent eligibility standard.

The majority suggests that a technological arts test is nothing more that a "shortcut" for its machine-or-transformation test. To the contrary, however, the two tests are fundamentally different. Consider U.S. Patent No. 7,261,652, which is directed to a method of putting a golf ball, U.S. Patent No. 6,368,227, which is directed to a method of swinging on a swing suspended on a tree branch, and U.S. Patent No. 5,443,036, which is directed to a method of "inducing cats to exercise." Each of these "inventions" involves a physical transformation that is central to the claimed method: the golfer's stroke is changed, a person on a swing starts swinging, and the sedentary cat becomes a fit feline. Thus, under the majority's approach, each of these inventions is patent eligible. Under a technological arts test, however, none of these inventions is eligible for patent protection because none involves any advance in science or technology.

Regardless of whether a claimed process involves a "physical transformation," it should not be patent eligible unless it is directed to an advance in science or technology. *See Benson*, 409 U.S. at 64–71, 93 S.Ct. 253 (finding a process unpatentable even though it "transformed" binary-coded decimals into pure binary numbers using a general purpose computer). Although the Supreme Court has stated that a patentable process will usually involve a transformation of physical matter, *see id.* at 70, 93 S.Ct. 253, it has never found a process patent eligible which did not involve a scientific or technological innovation.

The majority refuses to inject a technology requirement into the section 101 analysis because it believes that the terms "technological arts" and "technology" are "ambiguous." To the contrary, however, the meaning of these terms is not particularly difficult to grasp. As discussed more fully in section III, a claimed process is technological to the extent it applies laws of nature to new ends. By contrast, a process is non-technological where its inventive concept is the application of principles drawn not from the natural sciences but from disciplines such as business, law, sociology, or psychology. The inventive aspect of Bilski's claimed process is the application of business principles, not laws of nature; it is therefore non-technological and ineligible for patent protection.

Unlike a technological standard for patentability, the majority's proposed test will be exceedingly difficult to apply. The standard that the majority proposes for inclusion in the patentability lexicon—"transformation of any physical object or substance, or an electronic signal representative of any physical object or substance,"—is unnecessarily complex and will only lead to further uncertainty regarding the scope of patentable subject matter. As noted in *In re Nuijten*, 500 F.3d 1346, 1353 (Fed.Cir.2007), defining the term "physical" can be an "esoteric and metaphysical" inquiry. Indeed, although this court has struggled for years to set out what constitutes sufficient physical transformation to render a process patentable, we have yet to provide a consistent or satisfactory resolution of this issue.

We took this case en banc in a long-overdue effort to resolve primal questions on the metes and bounds of statutory subject matter. The patent system has run amok, and the USPTO, as well as the larger patent community, has actively sought guidance from this court in making sense of our section 101 jurisprudence. The majority, however, fails to enlighten three of the thorniest issues in the patentability thicket: (1) the continued viability of business method patents, (2) what constitutes sufficient physical transformation or machine-implementation to render a process patentable, and (3) the extent to which computer software and computer-implemented processes constitute statutory subject matter. The majority's "measured approach" to the section 101 analysis, will do little to restore public confidence in the patent system or stem the growth of patents on business methods and other non-technological ideas.

VI.

Where the advance over the prior art on which the applicant relies to make his invention patentable is an advance in a field of endeavor such as law (like the arbitration method in *Comiskey*), business (like the method claimed by *Bilski*) or other liberal—as opposed to technological—arts, the application falls outside the ambit of patentable subject matter. The time is ripe to repudiate *State Street* and to recalibrate the standards for patent eligibility, thereby ensuring that the patent system can fulfill its constitutional mandate to protect and promote truly useful innovations in science and technology. I dissent from the majority's failure to do so.

RADER, CIRCUIT JUDGE, dissenting.

This court labors for page after page, paragraph after paragraph, explanation after explanation to say what could have been said in a single sentence: "Because Bilski claims merely an abstract idea, this court affirms the Board's rejection." If the only problem of this vast judicial tome were its circuitous path, I would not dissent, but this venture also disrupts settled and wise principles of law.

Much of the court's difficulty lies in its reliance on dicta taken out of context from numerous Supreme Court opinions dealing with the technology of the past. In other words, as innovators seek the path to the next tech no-revolution, this court ties our patent system to dicta from an industrial age decades removed from the bleeding edge. A direct reading of the Supreme Court's principles and cases on patent eligibility would yield the one-sentence resolution suggested above. Because this court, however, links patent eligibility to the age of iron and steel at a time of subatomic particles and terabytes, I must respectfully dissent.

I

The Patent Law of the United States has always embodied the philosophy that "ingenuity should receive a liberal encouragement." Writings of Thomas Jefferson 75–76 (Washington ed. 1871); *see also Diamond v. Chakrabarty*, 447 U.S. 303, 308–09, 100 S.Ct. 2204, 65 L.Ed.2d 144 (1980). True to this principle, the original Act made "any new and useful art, machine, manufacture or composition of matter" patent eligible. Act of Feb. 21, 1793, ch. 11, § 1, 1 Stat. 318 (emphasis supplied). Even as the laws have evolved, that bedrock principle remains at their foundation. Thus, the Patent Act from its inception focused patentability on the specific characteristics of the claimed invention—its novelty and utility—not on its particular subject matter category.

The modern incarnation of section 101 holds fast to that principle, setting forth the broad categories of patent eligible subject matter, and conditioning patentability on the characteristics, not the category, of the claimed invention[.] As I have suggested, the Supreme Court requires this court to rely on the "ordinary, contemporary, common meaning" of these words. *Diamond v. Diehr*, 450 U.S. 175, 182, 101 S.Ct. 1048, 67 L.Ed.2d 155 (1981). If this court would follow that Supreme Court rule, it would afford broad patent protection to new and useful inventions that fall within the enumerated categories and satisfy the other conditions of patentability. That is, after all, precisely what the statute says.

In *Diehr*, the Supreme Court adopted a very useful algorithm for determining patentable subject matter, namely, follow the Patent Act itself. After setting forth the procedural history of that case, the Supreme Court stated: "In cases of statutory construction, we begin with the language of the statute." *Diehr*, 450 U.S. at 182, 101 S.Ct. 1048. With an eye to the *Benson* language (so central to this court's reasoning) that "[t]ransformation and reduction of an article 'to a different state or thing' is the clue to the patentability of a process claim that does not include particular machines," *Gottschalk v. Benson*, 409 U.S. 63, 72, 93 S.Ct. 253, 34 L.Ed.2d 273 (1972), the Court then noted:

> [I]n dealing with the patent laws, we have more than once cautioned that "courts 'should not read into the patent laws limitations and conditions which the legislature has not expressed.' "

Diehr, 450 U.S. at 182, 101 S.Ct. 1048 (citations omitted). Indeed section 101's term "process" contains no hint of an exclusion for certain types of methods. This court today nonetheless holds that a process is eligible only if it falls within certain subsets of "process." Ironically the Patent Act itself specifically defines "process" without any of these judicial innovations. 35 U.S.C. § 100(b). Therefore, as *Diehr* commands, this court should refrain from creating new circuitous judge-made tests.

II

With all of its legal sophistry, the court's new test for eligibility today does not answer the most fundamental question of all: why would the expansive language of section 101 preclude protection of innovation simply because it is not transformational or properly linked to a machine (whatever that means)? Stated even more simply, why should some categories of invention deserve no protection?

This court, which reads the fine print of Supreme Court decisions from the Industrial Age with admirable precision, misses the real import of those decisions. The Supreme Court has answered the fundamental question above many times. The Supreme Court has counseled that the only limits on eligibility are inventions that embrace natural laws, natural phenomena, and abstract ideas. *See, e.g., Diehr*, 450 U.S. at 185,

101 S.Ct. 1048 ("This Court has undoubtedly recognized limits to § 101 and every discovery is not embraced within the statutory terms. Excluded from such patent protection are laws of nature, natural phenomena, and abstract ideas."). In *Diehr*, the Supreme Court's last pronouncement on eligibility for "processes," the Court said directly that its only exclusions from the statutory language are these three common law exclusions: "Our recent holdings . . . stand for no more than these long-established principles." *Id.* at 185, 101 S.Ct. 1048.

When considering the eligibility of "processes," this court should focus on the potential for an abstract claim. Such an abstract claim would appear in a form that is not even susceptible to examination against prior art under the traditional tests for patentability. Thus this court would wish to ensure that the claim supplied some concrete, tangible technology for examination. Indeed the hedging claim at stake in this appeal is a classic example of abstractness. Bilski's method for hedging risk in commodities trading is either a vague economic concept or obvious on its face. Hedging is a fundamental economic practice long prevalent in our system of commerce and taught in any introductory finance class. In any event, this facially abstract claim does not warrant the creation of new eligibility exclusions.

IV

In sum, this court today invents several circuitous and unnecessary tests. It should have merely noted that Bilski attempts to patent an abstract idea. Nothing more was needed. Instead this opinion propagates unanswerable questions: What form or amount of "transformation" suffices? When is a "representative" of a physical object sufficiently linked to that object to satisfy the transformation test? (e.g., Does only vital sign data taken directly from a patient qualify, or can population data derived in part from statistics and extrapolation be used?) What link to a machine is sufficient to invoke the "or machine" prong? Are the "specific" machines of *Benson* required, or can a general purpose computer qualify? What constitutes "extra-solution activity?" If a process may meet eligibility muster as a "machine," why does the Act "require" a machine link for a "process" to show eligibility? Does the rule against redundancy itself suggest an inadequacy in this complex spider web of tests supposedly "required" by the language of section 101?

One final point, reading section 101 as it is written will not permit a flurry of frivolous and useless inventions. Even beyond the exclusion for abstractness, the final clause of section 101—"subject to the conditions and requirements of this title"—ensures that a claimed invention must still satisfy the "conditions and requirements" set forth in the remainder title 35. Id. These statutory conditions and requirements better serve the function of screening out unpatentable inventions than some vague "transformation" or "proper machine link" test.

In simple terms, the statute does not mention "transformations" or any of the other Industrial Age descriptions of subject matter categories that this court endows with inordinate importance today. The Act has not empowered the courts to impose limitations on patent eligible subject matter beyond the broad and ordinary meaning of the terms process, machine, manufacture, and composition of matter. It has instead preserved the promise of patent protection for still unknown fields of invention.

Innovation has moved beyond the brick and mortar world. Even this court's test, with its caveats and winding explanations seems to recognize this. Today's software transforms our lives without physical anchors. This court's test not only risks hobbling these advances, but precluding patent protection for tomorrow's technologies. "We still do not know one thousandth of one percent of what nature has revealed to us." Attributed to Albert Einstein. If this court has its way, the Patent Act may not incentivize, but complicate, our search for the vast secrets of nature. When all else fails, consult the statute.

NOTES

1. **The *Bilski* Opinions.** Readers should note that your casebook editors have significantly trimmed the original text of the *Bilski* opinions. Review of the original texts of these opinions will prove instructive for those with particular interest in § 101 jurisprudence. More specifically, the edited version of *Bilski* omits the concurring opinion of Judge Dyk (joined by Judge Linn), as well as Judge Newman's reaction to that opinion. Judge Dyk fully supported the majority, but offered some responses to the dissenting opinions of Judges Newman and Rader (the opinions of both Judge Mayer and Judge Rader are styled as dissents but in reality both concur in the result of finding the claims ineligible for patenting). Judge Dyk analyzed the history of the English and U.S. patent jurisprudence commencing with the Statute of Monopolies and the Act of 1793, respectively. He concluded that "the history of § 101 fully supports the majority's holding that Bilski's claim does not recite patentable subject matter" and that the majority decision reflected "careful and respectful adherence to the Congressional purpose" in enacting patent legislation. Despite the legitimate questions of applying eighteenth and nineteenth century legal and technological precedents to modern problems, Judge Dyk found that history enlightening for the age of quantum mechanics. Judge Newman responded to Judge Dyk's concurrence by observing distinctions between English and U.S. law, and by further asserting that its "selective" historical treatment might "propagate misunderstanding."

2. **Back to the Future.** The *Bilski* "transformation or machine" test is not novel and innovative. In fact, various iterations of these same tests prevailed up until *State Street Bank* in 1998. The venerable Circuit Judge Rich drafted *State Street* for the express purpose of putting an end to the *Freeman–Walter–Abele* test and other judicial efforts to determine "how much transformation is transformative" or "how much linkage and to what kind of machine serves the transcend abstractness." In a sense, *Bilski's* "contribution" is to return the law of patent eligibility to the uncertainty that prevailed a few days before the *en banc*

opinion in *In re Alappat*, 33 F.3d 1526 (Fed. Cir. 1994). Ultimately, after struggling through the eighties and the early nineties with eligibility cases, the Federal Circuit abandoned the task of defining degrees of transformation and machine linkage. Will it find those tests more illuminating on this trip into the past?

3. Field Restrictions. Is it wise categorically to exclude certain areas of inventive activity from the possibility of patent protection? Doing so may limit intellectual property rights in any number of inventions—for example, a way to reduce the cost or distribution of certain product—where the key innovation is not technological, but rather intangible. This step may also cause clever patent attorneys to draft more convoluted claim language to bypass these restrictions, so that a method of financing student loans suddenly is presented to the PTO as a financial calculator or specially programmed computer. On the other hand, does this step represent an antitrust-like *per se* rule that patent protection is some fields of endeavor is not necessary to promote innovation, would not improve social welfare overall, or would conflict with some other policy goal?

4. Tax Strategy Patents. With the rise of the patented business method came tax strategy patents—proprietary techniques that individuals and enterprises might use in order to reduce their tax obligations. Among the patents in this line were a "Method and apparatus for tax efficient investment management," U.S. Patent No. 7,031,937; "Use tax optimization process and system," U.S. Patent No. 6,298,333; and "Computerized system and method for optimizing after-tax proceeds," U.S. Patent No. 6,115,697. Yet the most famous instrument within this category remains the so-called SOGRAT patent, titled "[e]stablishing and managing grantor retained annuity trusts funded by nonqualified stock options." The abstract of U.S. Patent No. 6,567,790 explains that it concerns:

> An estate planning method for minimizing transfer tax liability with respect to the transfer of the value of stock options from a holder of stock options to a family member of the holder. The method comprises establishing a Grantor Retained Annuity Trust (GRAT) funded with nonqualified stock options. The method maximizes the transfer of wealth from the grantor of the GRAT to a family member by minimizing the amount of estate and gift taxes paid. By placing the options outside the grantor's estate, the method takes advantage of the appreciation of the options in said GRAT.

On January 6, 2006, the proprietor of the SOGRAT patent, Wealth Transfer Group L.L.C., brought charges of infringement against John W. Rowe, the former executive chairman of Aetna Inc. Wealth Transfer Group reportedly asserted that Rowe had infringed the SOGRAT patent by establishing one or more GRATs that were funded by nonqualified stock options from Aetna. Because the parties to the litigation reached a confidential settlement on March 12, 2007, the courts did not have the opportunity to address the validity and infringement of the SOGRAT patent specifically, nor the concept of tax strategy patents more generally.

Tax strategy patents have been the subject of a spirited debate. Some observers believe that such patents negatively impact social welfare. According to some observers, tax strategy patents may limit the ability of taxpayers to utilize provisions of the tax code, interfering with congressional intent and leading to distortions in tax obligations. Others assert that tax strategy patents potentially complicate legal compliance by tax professionals and taxpayers alike. Still others believe that the patent system should not provide incentives for individuals to develop new ways to reduce their tax liability. See generally William A. Drennan, *The Patented Loophole: How Should Congress Respond to this Judicial Invention?*, 59 FLORIDA L. REV. 229 (2007).

Other experts believe that these concerns are overstated, and also make the affirmative case that tax strategy patents may provide positive social benefits. They explain that patents on "business methods" have been obtained and enforced for many years. They also observe that the grant of a patent does not imply government approval of the practice of the patented invention, and that professionals in many spheres of endeavor have long had to account for the patent system during their decision-making process. They also believe that the availability of tax strategy patents may promote innovation in a field of endeavor that is demonstrably valuable. Further, such patents might promote public disclosure of tax strategies to tax professionals, taxpayers, and responsible government officials alike. *See generally* Stephen T. Schreiner and George Y. Wang, *Discussions on Tax Patents Have Lost Focus*, IP LAW 360 at 1–3 (July 21, 2006).

As this book goes to press, the 111th Congress is currently considering legislative reforms that would ban such patents outright, or limit the remedies associated with tax strategy patents. Is such legislation necessary in the wake of *Bilski*?

5. Software and Business Methods in Europe. Article 52(2) of the European Patent Convention explicitly places "programs for computers," "mathematical methods," and "presentations of information" without the scope of patent eligibility. But despite these seeming prohibitions, the European Patent Office has granted patents to a wide variety of computer-related inventions. The appropriate scope of coverage for such inventions under the Convention has been the subject of considerable debate and arguably conflicting decisions from national courts of Europe and the tribunals of the European Patent Office.

6. Software and Business Methods in Japan. Japanese patent law is generally permissive of patents upon software. Unless they can be successfully characterized as computer programs, however, business methods have fared less well. General notions of patent eligibility are founded in Article 2(1) of the Japanese Patent Act, which defines "invention" as the "highly advanced creation of technical ideas by which a law of nature is utilized." A patent application which claims a natural law itself will thus be rejected as nonstatutory. Within the computer arts, inventions which control hardware processes or process information based upon the physical or technical qualities of an object may receive patent protection; patent ineligible inventions are those which perform "information processing . . . based on mathematical methods, schemes, rules or methods for doing business or performing mental activities." *See* *generally Examination Guidelines for Patent and Utility Model in Japan* (AIPPI Japan).

Statutory Subject Matter Exercises

Are any of the following inventions patent eligible under U.S. law? Does the result differ under the laws of Japan or Europe?

1.   A three-dimensional cube-shaped puzzle. Each face of the puzzle consists of eight smaller cubelets of differing colors. The user attempts to solve the puzzle by rotating rows of cubelets around one of several internal axes until a preselected pattern is obtained.

2.   A technique for counting playing cards that supposedly makes its user an unbeatable blackjack player.

3.   As the menu at a local restaurant proudly proclaims, "Every dish comes with a wonderful complement, our patented banana hollandaise sauce."

4.   A method of lifting heavy weights through a modified "clean-and-jerk" technique, suitable for use by Olympic athletes.

5.   A new perfume, cologne or scent.

6.   A method of preventing repetitive stress injuries during computer keyboard usage by holding one's hand, wrists and forearms in a straight and fluid line.

7.   A character assessment method comprising (1) instructing the person to produce a drawing which includes a pictorial representation of a hand, eye, flower, star, half-circle and other objects; and (2) subjecting the drawing to a psychological interpretation.

8.   A method of remodeling a building, comprising (1) presenting design ideas to a client; (2) allowing the client to select her favorite design; (3) taking a photograph of the building; and (4) preparing a drawing of the proposed remodeled building employing the photograph and the preferred design.

9.   The "Human Wave" commonly performed by spectators at sporting events.

Chapter Three

Utility

■ ■ ■

In addition to setting forth the categories of patent eligible subject matter, 35 U.S.C.A. § 101 requires that an invention be "useful" in order to receive patent protection. At first blush, this requirement may appear rather trivial: determining whether particular subject matter may be put towards some useful purpose would not seem to be overly difficult. The costs associated with patent acquisition and enforcement further suggest that the inventor of something useless would likely not bother to obtain a patent, nor would there be a large number of potential infringers against which to invoke a proprietary right. This intuition is largely correct: the utility requirement is one that is rarely invoked, either by patent examiners considering an application or by accused infringers seeking to strike down an issued patent.

Nonetheless, even this seemingly straightforward provision brings forth a host of policy issues. One is the measuring stick: should the claimed invention merely be useful for some practical purpose in and of itself, or should it be superior to known technologies? Is the demonstration that an invention may lead to a further invention by itself sufficient to provide patentable utility? And should an assessment of such factors as the invention's social, economic, or environmental impact accompany the decision to allow a patent to issue?

In making your way through the cases that follow, note that what amounts to a rejection of a patent under § 101 may alternatively be couched in the statutory language of 35 U.S.C.A. § 112, ¶ 1. This provision, which this casebook considers in more detail in Chapter 11, requires that patent applications include a description of how to use the invention disclosed within an application. As one may suspect, an applicant who is unaware of a use for an invention has scant ability to elaborate on this use in the patent instrument itself.

The first opinion of the chapter comes from a hand that will be frequently encountered by any student of United States patent law. Joseph Story, Associate Justice of the United States Supreme Court and Dane Professor at Harvard Law School, is best known for such opinions as *Martin v. Hunter's Lessee* and *Swift v. Tyson*, as well as a dozen volumes of legal commentary. But while riding circuit in New England, Story also built a foundation of judicial precedent which continue to shape

United States patent law. Among these is *Lowell v. Lewis*, a succinct jury charge that set forth the contours of the utility requirement which persist today.

§ 3.1 GENERAL PRINCIPLES

LOWELL v. LEWIS

Circuit Court, D. Massachusetts, 1817
15 F.Cas. 1018

STORY, CIRCUIT JUSTICE.

To entitle the plaintiff to a verdict, he must establish, that his machine is a new and useful invention; and of these facts his patent is to be considered merely prima facie evidence of a very slight nature. He must, in the first place, establish it to be a useful invention; for the law will not allow the plaintiff to recover, if the invention be of a mischievous or injurious tendency. The defendant, however, has asserted a much more broad and sweeping doctrine; and one, which I feel myself called upon to negative in the most explicit manner. He contends, that it is necessary for the plaintiff to prove, that his invention is of general utility; so that in fact, for the ordinary purposes of life, it must supersede the pumps in common use. In short, that it must be, for the public, a better pump than the common pump; and that unless the plaintiff can establish this position, the law will not give him the benefit of a patent, even though in some peculiar cases his invention might be applied with advantage. I do not so understand the law. The patent act (Act Feb. 21, 1793, c. 11 [1 Stat. 318]) uses the phrase "useful invention" mere incidentally; it occurs only in the first section, and there it seems merely descriptive of the subject matter of the application, or of the conviction of the applicant. The language is, "when any person or persons shall allege, that he or they have invented any new and useful art, machine," & c., he or they may, on pursuing the directions of the act, obtain a patent. * * * All that the law requires is, that the invention should not be frivolous or injurious to the well-being, good policy, or sound morals of society. The word "useful," therefore, is incorporated into the act in contradistinction to mischievous or immoral. For instance, a new invention to poison people, or to promote debauchery, or to facilitate private assassination, is not a patentable invention. But if the invention steers wide of these objections, whether it be more or less useful is a circumstance very material to the interests of the patentee, but of no importance to the public. If it be not extensively useful, it will silently sink into contempt and disregard.

NOTES

1. **Storied Remarks.** Justice Story added in a Note published at 3 Wheat App. xiii, 1818, that: "By *useful* invention, in the patent act, is meant an invention which may be applied to a beneficial use in society, in contradistinc-

tion to an invention injurious to the morals, health or good order of society, or frivolous and insignificant." *See also Bedford v. Hunt*, 3 Fed. Cas. 37 (C.C.Mass. 1817). This definition was substantially echoed in the noted patent law treatise written by Professor William Robinson at the close of the nineteenth century. According to Professor Robinson, to satisfy the utility requirement an invention must simply be more than "a mere curiosity, a scientific process exciting wonder yet not producing physical results, or [a] frivolous or trifling article not aiding in the progress nor increasing the possession of the human race." 1 W. ROBINSON, TREATISE ON THE LAW OF PATENTS FOR USEFUL INVENTIONS 463 (1890).

2. **Practical Utility.** Courts, as well as the Patent and Trademark Office, have also employed the utility requirement to deny patentability to wholly inoperable inventions. *See, e.g., In re Speas*, 273 Fed.Appx. 945 (Fed. Cir. 2008) (devices and systems that violate the second law of thermodynamics); *Newman v. Quigg*, 877 F.2d 1575 (Fed.Cir.1989) (perpetual motion machine); *In re Perrigo*, 48 F.2d 965 (CCPA 1931) (method and apparatus for accumulating and transforming ether electric energy); *Ex parte Heicklen*, 16 U.S.P.Q.2d 1463 (BPAI 1989) (method to retard the aging process). This sense of "practical" or "beneficial" utility is an all-or-nothing proposition: Either the claimed invention possesses utility or it does not.

3. **Modern Advertising.** How many advertisements have you seen or heard trumpeting the fact that the advertised product has been patented? Now that you know more about the utility requirement, what do you think of them?

4. **Examination of Useless Inventions.** During the period Justice Story authored these statements, the U.S. patent system did not include a professional examining corps providing a rigorous substantive review process that it does today. Given this change, does Justice Story's assertion that no harm befalls the public if a patented invention possesses limited utility remain correct? Doesn't the public suffer the burden of lengthened examination times when notoriously overworked patent examiners must allocate scarce resources towards the extended consideration of worthless technologies?

5. **Modern Perspectives on the Utility Requirement.** Justice Story's remarks in *Lowell v. Lewis* should drive home the fact that the patent system is not necessarily looking for something better; just something different. This latter goal is met through the patent law's novelty and nonobviousness requirements. For most inventions outside the fields of chemistry and biotechnology—which are taken up shortly—utility plays only a minor role as a requisite to patentability at the Patent and Trademark Office or as a defense to patent infringement in the courts.

One class of patentable subject matter has persistently been scrutinized via the utility requirement, however. Accused infringers have often invoked the utility requirement where the sole use of a patented invention is to further fraudulent or immoral conduct. The following decision presents the latest thinking on the role of the utility requirement in such cases.

JUICY WHIP, INC. v. ORANGE BANG, INC.

United States Court of Appeals, Federal Circuit, 1999
185 F.3d 1364

BRYSON, CIRCUIT JUDGE.

[handwritten margin note: district court patent invalid lack of utility]

The district court in this case held a patent invalid for lack of utility on the ground that the patented invention was designed to deceive customers by imitating another product and thereby increasing sales of a particular good. We reverse and remand.

I

Juicy Whip, Inc., is the assignee of United States Patent No. 5,575,405, which is entitled "Post–Mix Beverage Dispenser With an Associated Simulated Display of Beverage." A "post-mix" beverage dispenser stores beverage syrup concentrate and water in separate locations until the beverage is ready to be dispensed. The syrup and water are mixed together immediately before the beverage is dispensed, which is usually after the consumer requests the beverage. In contrast, in a "pre-mix" beverage dispenser, the syrup concentrate and water are pre-mixed and the beverage is stored in a display reservoir bowl until it is ready to be dispensed. The display bowl is said to stimulate impulse buying by providing the consumer with a visual beverage display. A pre-mix display bowl, however, has a limited capacity and is subject to contamination by bacteria. It therefore must be refilled and cleaned frequently.

[handwritten margin note: Post MIX Dispenser w/ fake premix dispenser to promote impulse buying]

The invention claimed in the '405 patent is a post-mix beverage dispenser that is designed to look like a pre-mix beverage dispenser. The claims require the post-mix dispenser to have a transparent bowl that is filled with a fluid that simulates the appearance of the dispensed beverage and is resistant to bacterial growth. The claims also require that the dispenser create the visual impression that the bowl is the principal source of the dispensed beverage, although in fact the beverage is mixed immediately before it is dispensed, as in conventional post-mix dispensers.

[handwritten margin note: just designed to look like pre-mix machine]

Claim 1 is representative of the claims at issue. It reads as follows:

In a post-mix beverage dispenser of the type having an outlet for discharging beverage components in predetermined proportions to provide a serving of dispensed beverage, the improvement which comprises:

a transparent bowl having no fluid connection with the outlet and visibly containing a quantity of fluid;

said fluid being resistant to organic growth and simulating the appearance of the dispensed beverage;

said bowl being positioned relative to the outlet to create the visual impression that said bowl is the reservoir and principal source of the dispensed beverage from the outlet; and

[handwritten margin note: Steps to building it]

said bowl and said quantity of fluid visible within said bowl cooperating to create the visual impression that multiple servings of the dispensed beverage are stored within said bowl.

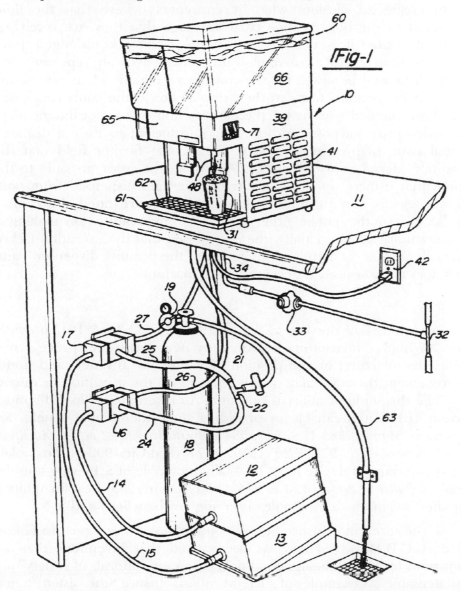

Juicy Whip sued defendants Orange Bang, Inc., and Unique Beverage Dispensers, Inc., (collectively, "Orange Bang") in the United States District Court for the Central District of California, alleging that they were infringing the claims of the '405 patent. Orange Bang moved for summary judgment of invalidity, and the district court granted Orange Bang's motion on the ground that the invention lacked utility and thus was unpatentable under 35 U.S.C. § 101.

The court concluded that the invention lacked utility because its purpose was to increase sales by deception, *i.e.*, through imitation of another product. The court explained that the purpose of the invention "is to create an illusion, whereby customers believe that the fluid contained in the bowl is the actual beverage that they are receiving, when of course it is not." Although the court acknowledged Juicy Whip's argument that the invention provides an accurate representation of the dispensed beverage for the consumer's benefit while eliminating the need for retailers to clean their display bowls, the court concluded that those claimed reasons for the patent's utility "are not independent of its deceptive purpose, and are thus insufficient to raise a disputed factual issue to present to a jury." The court further held that the invention lacked utility because it "improves the prior art only to the extent that it increases the salability of beverages dispensed from post-mix dispensers"; an invention lacks utility, the court stated, if it confers no benefit to the public other than the opportunity for making a product more salable. Finally, the court ruled that the invention lacked utility because it "is merely an imitation of the pre-mix dispenser," and thus does not constitute a new and useful machine.

II

Section 101 of the Patent Act of 1952, 35 U.S.C. § 101, provides that "[w]hoever invents or discovers any new and useful process, machine, manufacture, or composition of matter, or any new and useful improvement thereof," may obtain a patent on the invention or discovery. The threshold of utility is not high: An invention is "useful" under section 101 if it is capable of providing some identifiable benefit. *See Brenner v. Manson*, 383 U.S. 519, 534 (1966); *Brooktree Corp. v. Advanced Micro Devices, Inc.*, 977 F.2d 1555, 1571 (Fed.Cir.1992) ("To violate § 101 the claimed device must be totally incapable of achieving a useful result"); *Fuller v. Berger*, 120 F. 274, 275 (7th Cir.1903) (test for utility is whether invention "is incapable of serving any beneficial end").

To be sure, since Justice Story's opinion in *Lowell v. Lewis*, 15 F. Cas. 1018 (C.C.D.Mass.1817), it has been stated that inventions that are "injurious to the well-being, good policy, or sound morals of society" are unpatentable. As examples of such inventions, Justice Story listed "a new invention to poison people, or to promote debauchery, or to facilitate private assassination." *Id.* at 1019. Courts have continued to recite Justice Story's formulation, *see Tol–O–Matic, Inc. v. Proma Produkt–Und Marketing Gesellschaft m.b.H.*, 945 F.2d 1546, 1552–53 (Fed.Cir.1991); *In re Nelson*, 280 F.2d 172, 178–79 (CCPA 1960), but the principle that inventions are invalid if they are principally designed to serve immoral or illegal purposes has not been applied broadly in recent years. For example, years ago courts invalidated patents on gambling devices on the ground that they were immoral, *see e.g.*, *Brewer v. Lichtenstein*, 278 F. 512 (7th Cir.1922); *Schultze v. Holtz*, 82 F. 448 (N.D.Cal.1897); *National*

Automatic Device Co. v. Lloyd, 40 F. 89 (N.D.Ill.1889), but that is no longer the law, *see In re Murphy,* 200 USPQ 801 (PTO Bd.App.1977).

In holding the patent in this case invalid for lack of utility, the district court relied on two Second Circuit cases dating from the early years of this century, *Rickard v. Du Bon,* 103 F. 868 (2d Cir.1900), and *Scott & Williams v. Aristo Hosiery Co.,* 7 F.2d 1003 (2d Cir.1925). In the *Rickard* case, the court held invalid a patent on a process for treating tobacco plants to make their leaves appear spotted. At the time of the invention, according to the court, cigar smokers considered cigars with spotted wrappers to be of superior quality, and the invention was designed to make unspotted tobacco leaves appear to be of the spotted—and thus more desirable—type. The court noted that the invention did not promote the burning quality of the leaf or improve its quality in any way; "the only effect, if not the only object, of such treatment, is to spot the tobacco, and counterfeit the leaf spotted by natural causes."

The *Aristo Hosiery* case concerned a patent claiming a seamless stocking with a structure on the back of the stocking that imitated a seamed stocking. The imitation was commercially useful because at the time of the invention many consumers regarded seams in stockings as an indication of higher quality. The court noted that the imitation seam did not "change or improve the structure or the utility of the article," and that the record in the case justified the conclusion that true seamed stockings were superior to the seamless stockings that were the subject of the patent. *See Aristo Hosiery,* 7 F.2d at 1004. "At best," the court stated, "the seamless stocking has imitation marks for the purposes of deception, and the idea prevails that with such imitation the article is more salable." That was not enough, the court concluded, to render the invention patentable.

We decline to follow *Rickard* and *Aristo Hosiery,* as we do not regard them as representing the correct view of the doctrine of utility under the Patent Act of 1952. The fact that one product can be altered to make it look like another is in itself a specific benefit sufficient to satisfy the statutory requirement of utility.

It is not at all unusual for a product to be designed to appear to viewers to be something it is not. For example, cubic zirconium is designed to simulate a diamond, imitation gold leaf is designed to imitate real gold leaf, synthetic fabrics are designed to simulate expensive natural fabrics, and imitation leather is designed to look like real leather. In each case, the invention of the product or process that makes such imitation possible has "utility" within the meaning of the patent statute, and indeed there are numerous patents directed toward making one product imitate another. *See, e.g.,* U.S. Pat. No. 5,762,968 (method for producing imitation grill marks on food without using heat); U.S. Pat. No. 5,899,038 (laminated flooring imitating wood); U.S. Pat. No. 5,571,545 (imitation hamburger). Much of the value of such products resides in the fact that they appear to be something they are not. Thus,

in this case the claimed post-mix dispenser meets the statutory requirement of utility by embodying the features of a post-mix dispenser while
imitating the visual appearance of a pre-mix dispenser.

The fact that customers may believe they are receiving fluid directly
from the display tank does not deprive the invention of utility. Orange
Bang has not argued that it is unlawful to display a representation of the
beverage in the manner that fluid is displayed in the reservoir of the
invention, even though the fluid is not what the customer will actually
receive. Moreover, even if the use of a reservoir containing fluid that is
not dispensed is considered deceptive, that is not by itself sufficient to
render the invention unpatentable. The requirement of "utility" in
patent law is not a directive to the Patent and Trademark Office or the
courts to serve as arbiters of deceptive trade practices. Other agencies,
such as the Federal Trade Commission and the Food and Drug Administration, are assigned the task of protecting consumers from fraud and
deception in the sale of food products. *Cf. In re Watson,* 517 F.2d 465,
474–76 (CCPA 1975) (stating that it is not the province of the Patent
Office to determine, under section 101, whether drugs are safe). As the
Supreme Court put the point more generally, "Congress never intended
that the patent laws should displace the police powers of the States,
meaning by that term those powers by which the health, good order,
peace and general welfare of the community are promoted." *Webber v.
Virginia,* 103 U.S. (13 Otto) 344, 347–48 (1880).

Of course, Congress is free to declare particular types of inventions
unpatentable for a variety of reasons, including deceptiveness. *Cf.* 42
U.S.C. § 2181(a) (exempting from patent protection inventions useful
solely in connection with special nuclear material or atomic weapons).
Until such time as Congress does so, however, we find no basis in
section 101 to hold that inventions can be ruled unpatentable for lack of
utility simply because they have the capacity to fool some members of
the public. The district court therefore erred in holding that the
invention of the '405 patent lacks utility because it deceives the public
through imitation in a manner that is designed to increase product sales.

REVERSED AND REMANDED.

NOTES

1. **Moral Utility.** Arguments based upon "moral utility" are seldom raised
in the modern patent system. Why is it troubling that an accused infringer
would raise an invalidity defense based upon moral utility? In addition, if the
accused infringer prevails, what is the result in terms of public use of the
immoral invention?

2. **Utility and Technology Assessment.** Should the patent system remain
oblivious to the social, economic, and environmental impacts of the technologies it embraces, remaining instead a "narrowly focused celebration of technical
skill"? John R. Thomas, *The Question Concerning Patent Law and Pioneer Inven-*

tions, 10 HIGH TECH. L.J. 35, 102 (1995). Or would we "be wise to question patent grants for inventions such as handguns, machines for processing chewing tobacco, and ozone-depleting spray canisters"? *Id.*

3. Moral Utility and Biotechnology. Margo Bagley has directed pointed criticism towards the decline of the moral utility standard in U.S. patent law. She recognizes that a "combination of the demise of the moral utility doctrine, along with expansive judicial interpretations of the scope of patent-eligible subject matter, has resulted in virtually no basis on which the USPTO or courts can deny patent protection to morally controversial, but otherwise patentable, subject matter." Margo A. Bagley, *Patent First, Ask Questions Later: Morality and Biotechnology in Patent Law*, 45 WM. & MARY L. REV. (2003). She further observes:

> Biotechnology is an area in which many morally controversial inventions are generated. Controversial patented biotech inventions include: isolated genes, sequenced DNA, medical procedures, embryonic stem cells, genetically modified transgenic animals, and methods of cloning mammals. The moral controversies surrounding these and other biotech inventions stem from several concerns including those arising from the mixing of human and animal species, the denigration of human dignity, the destruction of potential human life, and the ownership of humans. The availability of government imprimatur granting exclusive rights over morally controversial inventions is especially problematic in the area of biotechnology because no one should "own" and the government should not encourage certain inventions.

Id. at 475–76. Of course, patent system provides only the right to exclude, 35 U.S.C. § 271, and not the affirmative right to do. Stated differently, the issuance of a patent does not confer the government's approval actually to practice the patented invention. Do you agree with Professor Bagley's concerns over the lack of a moral utility assessment in the discipline of biotechnology?

4. Ordre Public. Many foreign patent statutes, including the European Patent Convention, allow patent offices and courts to exclude inventions that offend notions of morality from patenting. This common requirement is reflected in Article 27, paragraph 2 of the TRIPS Agreement, which provides:

> Members may exclude from patentability inventions, the prevention within their territory of the commercial exploitation of which is necessary to protect *ordre public* or morality, including to protect human, animal or plant life or health or to avoid serious prejudice to the environment, provided that such exclusion is not made merely because the exploitation is prohibited by their law.

This morality notion has often multiplied the cost of obtaining patents on biotechnology in Europe. Animal rights activists and other moral campaigners can challenge or oppose patents on living organisms. Does this have the effect of giving international corporations an additional incentive to seek protection for biotechnology first in the United States where morality is not a factor?

§ 3.2 THE UTILITY REQUIREMENT IN CHEMISTRY AND BIOTECHNOLOGY

Outside the chemical and biotechnological arts, utility is a scarcely questioned component of the vast majority of claimed inventions. Utility matters in these fields largely due to the distinct technological environment in which some of these inventions arise. Rather than constructing a device directed towards a specific application, as say, an electrical engineer does while designing a new circuit, chemists and biotechnicians may synthesize new compounds without a preexisting knowledge of their precise use. They may generate the compounds based on the behavior of related ones, or may wish to explore a class of compounds for which some technical application may develop in the future. In such cases the inventor may have little more than an educated guess about what the newly created compound actually does.

The invention discussed in the Supreme Court's *Brenner v. Manson* decision arose in this fashion. The compound at issue there was a steroid. Steroids can be viewed as a "backbone" carbon rings with a variety of uses depending upon the other atoms which are joined with them. Certain contraceptives, muscle growth stimulants, and tumor inhibitors employ steroids. Chemists of the 1950's needed methods for synthesizing steroids. Yet when they sought patent protection on their results, they discover that the ordinarily dormant utility requirement posed considerable obstacles.

The incredible life story of George Rosenkranz is portrayed in "Mexico's Pill Pioneer" by Gerald S. Cohen (available at http://www.paho.org/english/DPI/Number13_article4_7.htm). It describes his work at Syntex, a tiny bit of which is involved in the famous case that follows. Andrew John Manson worked for Sterling Drug. It was his burden to show that he had made his process invention before the Mexican filing date of Howard Ringold and George Rosenkranz in order to provoke an interference with their issued United States patent, a patent that disclosed and claimed the process which Manson was trying to patent and which said that "[T]he products of the process of the present invention have a useful high anabolic-androgenic ratio and are especially valuable for treatment of those ailments where an anabolic or antiestrogenic effect together with a lesser androgenic effect is desired."

BRENNER, COMMISSIONER OF PATENTS v. MANSON

United States Supreme Court, 1966
383 U.S. 519

MR. JUSTICE FORTAS delivered the opinion of the Court.

In December 1957, Howard Ringold and George Rosenkranz applied for a patent on an allegedly novel process for making certain known steroids. They claimed priority as of December 17, 1956, the date on which they had filed for a Mexican patent. United States Patent No. 2,908,693 issued late in 1959.

In January 1960, respondent Manson, a chemist engaged in steroid research, filed an application to patent precisely the same process described by Ringold and Rosenkranz. He asserted that it was he who had discovered the process, and that he had done so before December 17, 1956. Accordingly, he requested that an "interference" be declared in order to try out the issue of priority between his claim and that of Ringold and Rosenkranz.

A Patent Office examiner denied Manson's application, and the denial was affirmed by the Board of Appeals within the Patent Office. The ground for rejection was the failure "to disclose any utility for" the chemical compound produced by the process. Letter of Examiner, dated May 24, 1960. This omission was not cured, in the opinion of the Patent Office, by Manson's reference to an article in the November 1956 issue of the Journal of Organic Chemistry, 21 J. ORG. CHEM. 1333–1335, which revealed that steroids of a class which included the compound in question were undergoing screening for possible tumor-inhibiting effects in mice, and that a homologue[3] adjacent to Manson's steroid had proven effective in that role. Said the Board of Appeals, "It is our view that the statutory requirement of usefulness of a product cannot be presumed merely because it happens to be closely related to another compound which is known to be useful."

The Court of Customs and Patent Appeals (hereinafter CCPA) reversed, Chief Judge Worley dissenting. The court held that Manson was entitled to a declaration of interference since 'where a claimed process produces a known product it is not necessary to show utility for the product,' so long as the product 'is not alleged to be detrimental to the public interest.' Certiorari was granted to resolve this running dispute over what constitutes 'utility' in chemical process claims....

II

Our starting point is the proposition, neither disputed nor disputable, that one may patent only that which is "useful." Suffice it to say that the concept of utility has maintained a central place in all of our patent legislation, beginning with the first patent law in 1790 and culminating in the present law's provision that

> "Whoever invents or discovers any new and useful process, machine, manufacture, or composition of matter, or any new and useful improvement thereof, may obtain a patent therefor, subject to the conditions and requirements of this title."

As is so often the case, however, a simple, everyday word can be pregnant with ambiguity when applied to the facts of life. That this is so is demonstrated by the present conflict between the Patent Office and the CCPA over how the test is to be applied to a chemical process which

---

3. "A homologous series is a family of chemically related compounds, the composition of which varies from member to member by CH_2 (one atom of carbon and two atoms of hydrogen)..... Chemists knowing the properties of one member of a series would in general know what to expect in adjacent members." *Application of Henze*, 181 F.2d 196, 200–01 (CCPA 1950).

yields an already known product whose utility, other than as a possible object of scientific inquiry, has not yet been evidenced. It was not long ago that agency and court seemed of one mind on the question. In *[In re] Bremner*, 182 F.2d 216, 217, the court affirmed rejection by the Patent Office of both process and product claims. It noted that "no use for the products claimed to be developed by the processes had been shown in the specification." It held that "It was never intended that a patent be granted upon a product, or a process producing a product, unless such product be useful." Nor was this new doctrine in the court.

The Patent Office has remained stead-fast in this view. The CCPA, however, has moved sharply away from Bremner. The trend began in *[In re] Nelson*, 280 F.2d 172, 47 C.C.P.A. (Pat.) 1031. There, the court reversed the Patent Office's rejection of a claim on a process yielding chemical intermediates "useful to chemists doing research on steroids," despite the absence of evidence that any of the steroids thus ultimately produced were themselves "useful." The trend has accelerated, culminating in the present case where the court held it sufficient that a process produces the result intended and is not "detrimental to the public interest." 333 F.2d at 238.

It is not remarkable that differences arise as to how the test of usefulness is to be applied to chemical processes. Even if we knew precisely what Congress meant in 1790 when it devised the "new and useful" phraseology and in subsequent re-enactments of the test, we should have difficulty in applying it in the context of contemporary chemistry where research is as comprehensive as man's grasp and where little or nothing is wholly beyond the pale of "utility"—if that word is given its broadest reach.

Respondent does not—at least in the first instance—rest upon the extreme proposition, advanced by the court below, that a novel chemical process is patentable so long as it yields the intended product and so long as the product is not itself "detrimental." Nor does he commit the outcome of his claim to the slightly more conventional proposition that any process is "useful" within the meaning of § 101 if it produces a compound whose potential usefulness is under investigation by serious scientific researchers, although he urges this position, too, as an alternative basis for affirming the decision of the CCPA. Rather, he begins with the much more orthodox argument that his process has a specific utility which would entitle him to a declaration of interference even under the Patent Office's reading of § 101. The claim is that the supporting affidavits filed pursuant to Rule 204(b), by reference to Ringold's 1956 article, reveal that an adjacent homologue of the steroid yielded by his process has been demonstrated to have tumor-inhibiting effects in mice, and that this discloses the requisite utility. We do not accept any of these theories as an adequate basis for overriding the determination of the Patent Office that the "utility" requirement has not been met.

Even on the assumption that the process would be patentable were respondent to show that the steroid produced had a tumor-inhibiting effect in mice, we would not overrule the Patent Office finding that respondent has not made such a showing. The Patent Office held that, despite the reference to the adjacent homologue, respondent's papers did not disclose a sufficient likelihood that the steroid yielded by his process would have similar tumor-inhibiting characteristics. Indeed, respondent himself recognized that the presumption that adjacent homologues have the same utility has been challenged in the steroid field because of "a greater known unpredictability of compounds in that field." In these circumstances and in this technical area, we would not overturn the finding of the Primary Examiner, affirmed by the Board of Appeals and not challenged by the CCPA.

The second and third points of respondent's argument present issues of much importance. Is a chemical process "useful" within the meaning of § 101 either (1) because it works, i.e., produces the intended product? or (2) because the compound yielded belongs to a class of compounds now the subject of serious scientific investigation? These contentions present the basic problem for our adjudication. Since we find no specific assistance in the legislative materials underlying § 101, we are remitted to an analysis of the problem in light of the general intent of Congress, the purposes of the patent system, and the implications of a decision one way or the other.

In support of his plea that we attenuate the requirement of "utility," respondent relies upon Justice Story's well-known statement that a "useful" invention is one "which may be applied to a beneficial use in society, in contradistinction to an invention injurious to the morals, health, or good order of society, or frivolous and insignificant" and upon the assertion that to do so would encourage inventors of new processes to publicize the event for the benefit of the entire scientific community, thus widening the search for uses and increasing the fund of scientific knowledge. Justice Story's language sheds little light on our subject. Narrowly read, it does no more than compel us to decide whether the invention in question is "frivolous and insignificant"—a query no easier of application than the one built into the statute. Read more broadly, so as to allow the patenting of any invention not positively harmful to society, it places such a special meaning on the word "useful" that we cannot accept it in the absence of evidence that Congress so intended. There are, after all, many things in this world which may not be considered "useful" but which, nevertheless are totally without a capacity for harm.

It is true, of course, that one of the purposes of the patent system is to encourage dissemination of information concerning discoveries and inventions. And it may be that inability to patent a process to some extent discourages disclosure and leads to greater secrecy than would otherwise be the case. The inventor of the process, or the corporate organization by which he is employed, has some incentive to keep the invention secret while uses for the product are searched out. However, in light of the highly developed art of drafting patent claims so that they disclose as little useful information as possible—while broadening the scope of the claim as widely as possible—the argument based upon the virtue of disclosure must be warily evaluated. Moreover, the pressure for secrecy is easily exaggerated, for if the inventor of a process cannot himself ascertain a "use" for that which his process yields, he has every incentive to make his invention known to those able to do so. Finally, how likely is disclosure of a patented process to spur research by others into the uses to which the product may be put? To the extent that the patentee has power to enforce his patent, there is little incentive for others to undertake a search for uses.

Whatever weight is attached to the value of encouraging disclosure and of inhibiting secrecy, we believe a more compelling consideration is that a process patent in the chemical field, which has not been developed and pointed to the degree of specific utility, creates a monopoly of knowledge which should be granted only if clearly commanded by the statute. Until the process claim has been reduced to production of a product shown to be useful, the metes and bounds of that monopoly are not capable of precise delineation. It may engross a vast, unknown, and perhaps unknowable area. Such a patent may confer power to block off whole areas of scientific development, without compensating benefit to the public. The basic quid pro quo contemplated by the Constitution and the Congress for granting a patent monopoly is the benefit derived by the public from an invention with substantial utility. Unless and until a process is refined and developed to this point—where specific benefit exists in currently available form—there is insufficient justification for permitting an applicant to engross what may prove to be a broad field.

These arguments for and against the patentability of a process which either has no known use or is useful only in the sense that it may be an object of scientific research would apply equally to the patenting of the product produced by the process. Respondent appears to concede that with respect to a product, as opposed to a process, Congress has struck the balance on the side of nonpatentability unless "utility" is shown. Indeed, the decisions of the CCPA are in accord with the view that a product may not be patented absent a showing of utility greater than any adduced in the present case. We find absolutely no warrant for the proposition that although Congress intended that no patent be granted on a chemical compound whose sole "utility" consists of its potential role as an object of use-testing, a different set of rules was meant to apply to the process which yielded the unpatentable product. That proposition seems to us little more than an attempt to evade the impact of the rules which concededly govern patentability of the product itself.

This is not to say that we mean to disparage the importance of contributions to the fund of scientific information short of the invention of something "useful," or that we are blind to the prospect that what now seems without "use" may tomorrow command the grateful attention of the public. But a patent is not a hunting license. It is not a reward for the search, but compensation for its successful conclusion. "[A] patent system must be related to the world of commerce rather than to the realm of philosophy."

MR. JUSTICE DOUGLAS * * * dissents on the merits of the controversy for substantially the reasons stated by MR. JUSTICE HARLAN.

MR. JUSTICE HARLAN, concurring in part and dissenting in part.

I cannot agree with [the Court's] resolution of the important question of patentability.

Respondent has contended that a workable chemical process, which is both new and sufficiently nonobvious to satisfy the patent statute, is by its existence alone a contribution to chemistry and "useful" as the statute employs that term. Certainly this reading of "useful" in the statute is within the scope of the constitutional grant, which states only that "[t]o promote the Progress of Science and useful Arts," the exclusive right to "Writings and Discoveries" may be secured for limited times to those who produce them. Art. I, § 8. Yet the patent statute is somewhat differently worded and is on its face open both to respondent's construction and to the contrary reading given it by the Court. In the absence of legislative history on this issue, we are thrown back on policy and practice. Because I believe that the Court's policy arguments are not convincing and that past practice favors the respondent, I would reject the narrow definition of "useful" and uphold the judgment of the Court of Customs and Patent Appeals (hereafter CCPA).

The Court's opinion sets out about half a dozen reasons in support of its interpretation. Several of these arguments seem to me to have almost no force. For instance, it is suggested that "[u]ntil the process claim has been reduced to production of a product shown to be useful, the metes and bounds of that monopoly are not capable of precise delineation" and "[i]t may engross a vast, unknown, and perhaps unknowable area". I fail to see the relevance of these assertions; process claims are not disallowed because the products they produce may be of "vast" importance nor, in any event, does advance knowledge of a specific product use provide much safeguard on this score or fix "metes and bounds" precisely since a hundred more uses may be found after a patent is granted and greatly enhance its value.

The further argument that an established product use is part of "(t)he basic quid pro quo" for the patent or is the requisite "successful conclusion" of the inventor's search appears to beg the very question whether the process is "useful" simply because it facilitates further research into possible product uses. The same infirmity seems to inhere in the Court's argument that chemical products lacking immediate utility cannot be distinguished for present purposes from the processes which create them, that respondent appears to concede and the CCPA holds that the products are nonpatentable, and that therefore the processes are nonpatentable. Assuming that the two classes cannot be distinguished, a point not adequately considered in the briefs, and assuming further that the CCPA has firmly held such products nonpatentable, this permits us to conclude only that the CCPA is wrong either as to the products or as to the processes and affords no basis for deciding whether both or neither should be patentable absent a specific product use.

More to the point, I think, are the Court's remaining, prudential arguments against patentability: namely, that disclosure induced by allowing a patent is partly undercut by patent-application drafting techniques, that disclosure may occur without granting a patent, and that a patent will discourage others from inventing uses for the product. How far opaque drafting may lessen the public benefits resulting from the issuance of a patent is not shown by any evidence in this case but, more important, the argument operates against all patents and gives no reason for singling out the class involved here. The thought that these inventions may be more likely than most to be disclosed even if patents are not allowed may have more force; but while empirical study of the industry might reveal that chemical researchers would behave in this fashion, the abstractly logical choice for them seems to me to maintain secrecy until a product use can be discovered. As to discouraging the search by others for product uses, there is no doubt this risk exists but the price paid for any patent is that research on other uses or improvements may be hampered because the original patentee will reap much of the reward. From the standpoint of the public interest the Constitution seems to have resolved that choice in favor of patentability.

What I find most troubling about the result reached by the Court is the impact it may have on chemical research. Chemistry is a highly interrelated field and a tangible benefit for society may be the outcome of a number of different discoveries, one discovery building upon the next. To encourage one chemist or research facility to invent and disseminate new processes and products may be vital to progress, although the product or process be without "utility" as the Court defines the term, because that discovery permits someone else to take a further but perhaps less difficult step leading to a commercially useful item. In my view, our awareness in this age of the importance of achieving and publicizing basic research should lead this Court to resolve uncertainties in its favor and uphold the respondent's position in this case.

This position is strengthened, I think, by what appears to have been the practice of the Patent Office during most of this century. While available proof is not conclusive, the commentators seem to be in agreement that until [In re] Bremner, 182 F.2d 216, in 1950, chemical patent applications were commonly granted although no resulting end use was stated or the statement was in extremely broad terms. Taking this to be true, Bremner represented a deviation from established practice which the CCPA has now sought to remedy in part only to find that the

Patent Office does not want to return to the beaten track. If usefulness was typically regarded as inherent during a long and prolific period of chemical research and development in this country, surely this is added reason why the Court's result should not be adopted until Congress expressly mandates it, presumably on the basis of empirical data which this Court does not possess.

Court should let Congress decide

Fully recognizing that there is ample room for disagreement on this problem when, as here, it is reviewed in the abstract, I believe the decision below should be affirmed.

NOTES

1. **The Heightened Utility Standard of *Brenner v. Manson*.** The Supreme Court's holding provided a particularly hard result, as a utility for the claimed chemical compound had been disclosed to the public following the application's filing date. Manson did not know of the utility at the time the application was submitted to the Patent and Trademark Office, however. Of course, any chemical compound inherently possesses any useful properties that it may possess at the moment of its creation; does § 101 provide that an invention must be "useful" or that it must be "known to be useful"? Alternatively, is *Brenner v. Manson* less about the utility requirement itself (§ 101) than disclosure of that utility in a patent application (§ 112, ¶ 1)? Suppose Manson's application had indicated that, at least when present in sufficient quantities, the claimed steroid compound served as a handy paper weight? Consider also the critical remarks of Justice Fortas regarding the patent bar and claim drafting—how does this commentary have anything to do with utility?

2. **"No–Brenner" Questions.** What if at the time of Manson's invention, several thousand research groups all sought to buy steroids made by his process. Would Justice Fortas still claim that Manson's process was not useful? Also, under *Brenner v. Manson*, may an inventor obtain a patent on a new research telescope?

3. **Patenting at the Lab Bench.** Historical experience demonstrates that inventors have frequently uncovered additional valuable uses of known chemical compounds. For example, iodine, originally used in the photographic and dye-making industries, and the explosive nitroglycerin found further uses in medicine, as an antiseptic and heart medication, respectively. Which way should this insight cut with respect to the utility requirement? Should courts and the Patent and Trademark Office recognize that the utility of a chemical intermediate is often a moving target? Or, should the patent law strictly uphold the utility requirement?

4. **Is Usefulness Effectiveness?** When *Brenner v. Manson* speaks of usefulness in terms of a "benefit derived by the public from an invention with substantial utility," it raises questions about inventions which do not literally advance the art because they are less effective than existing technology. Is effectiveness in this sense part of the test for utility? The Federal Circuit, speaking through Judge Edward Smith, encountered a simple invention for mud flaps on automobiles. The Circuit stated:

Finding that an invention is an "improvement" is not a prerequisite to patentability. It is possible for an invention to be less effective than existing devices but nevertheless meet the statutory criteria for patentability.

Custom Accessories v. Jeffrey–Allan Indus., 807 F.2d 955, 960 n. 12 (Fed. Cir.1986).

5. Comparative Approaches. Foreign patent systems typically do not mandate that patented inventions be useful, but instead impose a parallel requirement termed "industrial applicability." Article 52(1) EPC. Article 57 EPC provides that "[a]n invention shall be considered susceptible of industrial application if it can be made or used in any kind of industry, including agriculture." The European Patent Office Guidelines indicate that the term "industry" "should be understood in its broad sense as including any physical activity of 'technical character,' i.e., an activity which belongs to the useful or practical arts as distinct from the aesthetic arts." Part C at 40. The Japanese patent law has similar standards in place. *See* Art. 29(1). Would *Brenner v. Manson* have been decided differently in Europe and Japan?

§ 3.3 THE UTILITY REQUIREMENT AT THE FEDERAL CIRCUIT

IN RE FISHER

United States Court of Appeals, Federal Circuit, 2005
421 F.3d 1365

Before Michel, Chief Judge, Rader and Bryson, Circuit Judges.

Michel, Chief Judge.

Dane K. Fisher and Raghunath Lalgudi (collectively "Fisher") appeal from the decision of the U.S. Patent and Trademark Office ("PTO") Board of Patent Appeals and Interferences ("Board") affirming the examiner's final rejection of the only pending claim of application Serial No. 09/619,643 (the "'643 application"), entitled "Nucleic Acid Molecules and Other Molecules Associated with Plants," as unpatentable for lack of utility under 35 U.S.C. § 101.... Because we conclude that substantial evidence supports the Board's findings that the claimed invention lacks a specific and substantial utility and that the '643 application does not enable one of ordinary skill in the art to use the invention, we affirm.

I. Background

A. Molecular Genetics and ESTs

The claimed invention relates to five purified nucleic acid sequences that encode proteins and protein fragments in maize plants. The claimed sequences are commonly referred to as "expressed sequence tags" or "ESTs." Before delving into the specifics of this case, it is important to understand more about the basic principles of molecular genetics and the role of ESTs.

Genes are located on chromosomes in the nucleus of a cell and are made of deoxyribonucleic acid ("DNA"). DNA is composed of two strands of nucleotides in double helix formation. The nucleotides contain one of four bases, adenine ("A"), guanine ("G"), cytosine ("C"), and thymine ("T"), that are linked by hydrogen bonds to form complementary base pairs (*i.e.*, A–T and G–C).

When a gene is expressed in a cell, the relevant double-stranded DNA sequence is transcribed into a single strand of messenger ribonucleic acid ("mRNA"). Messenger RNA contains three of the same bases as DNA (A, G, and C), but contains uracil ("U") instead of thymine. mRNA is released from the nucleus of a cell and used by ribosomes found in the cytoplasm to produce proteins.

Complementary DNA ("cDNA") is produced synthetically by reverse transcribing mRNA. cDNA, like naturally occurring DNA, is composed of nucleotides containing the four nitrogenous bases, A, T, G, and C. Scientists routinely compile cDNA into libraries to study the kinds of genes expressed in a certain tissue at a particular point in time. One of the goals of this research is to learn what genes and downstream proteins are expressed in a cell so as to regulate gene expression and control protein synthesis.

An EST is a short nucleotide sequence that represents a fragment of a cDNA clone. It is typically generated by isolating a cDNA clone and sequencing a small number of nucleotides located at the end of one of the two cDNA strands. When an EST is introduced into a sample containing a mixture of DNA, the EST may hybridize with a portion of DNA. Such binding shows that the gene corresponding to the EST was being expressed at the time of mRNA extraction.

Claim 1 of the '643 application recites:

> A substantially purified nucleic acid molecule that encodes a maize protein or fragment thereof comprising a nucleic acid sequence selected from the group consisting of SEQ ID NO: 1 through SEQ ID NO: 5.

The ESTs set forth in SEQ ID NO: 1 through SEQ ID NO: 5 are obtained from cDNA library LIB3115, which was generated from pooled leaf tissue harvested from maize plants (RX601, Asgrow Seed Company, Des Moines, Iowa, U.S.A.) grown in the fields at Asgrow research stations. SEQ ID NO:1 through SEQ ID NO:5 consist of 429, 423, 365, 411, and 331 nucleotides, respectively. When Fisher filed the '643 application, he claimed ESTs corresponding to genes expressed from the maize pooled leaf tissue at the time of anthesis. Nevertheless, Fisher did not know the precise structure or function of either the genes or the proteins encoded for by those genes.

The '643 application generally discloses that the five claimed ESTs may be used in a variety of ways, including: (1) serving as a molecular marker for mapping the entire maize genome, which consists of ten chromosomes that collectively encompass roughly 50,000 genes; (2)

measuring the level of mRNA in a tissue sample via microarray technology to provide information about gene expression; (3) providing a source for primers for use in the polymerase chain reaction ("PCR") process to enable rapid and inexpensive duplication of specific genes; (4) identifying the presence or absence of a polymorphism; (5) isolating promoters via chromosome walking; (6) controlling protein expression; and (7) locating genetic molecules of other plants and organisms.

B.   Final Rejection

In a final rejection, dated September 6, 2001, the examiner rejected claim 1 for lack of utility under § 101. The examiner found that the claimed ESTs were not supported by a specific and substantial utility. She concluded that the disclosed uses were not specific to the claimed ESTs, but instead were generally applicable to any EST. For example, the examiner noted that any EST may serve as a molecular tag to isolate genetic regions. She also concluded that the claimed ESTs lacked a substantial utility because there was no known use for the proteins produced as final products resulting from processes involving the claimed ESTs. The examiner stated: "Utilities that require or constitute carrying out further research to identify or reasonably confirm a 'real world' context of use are not substantial utilities." [Fisher appealed to the PTO Board.]

C.   Board Proceedings

The Board considered each of Fisher's seven potential uses but noted that Fisher focused its appeal on only two: (1) use for the identification of polymorphisms; and (2) use as probes or as a source for primers. As to the first, the Board found that the application failed to explain why the claimed ESTs would be useful in detecting polymorphisms in maize plants. The Board reasoned that "[w]ithout knowing any further information in regard to the gene represented by an EST, as here, detection of the presence or absence of a polymorphism provides the barest information in regard to genetic heritage." Thus, the Board concluded that Fisher's asserted uses for the claimed ESTs tended to the "insubstantial use" end of the spectrum between a substantial and an insubstantial utility.

The Board also concluded that using the claimed ESTs to isolate nucleic acid molecules of other plants and organisms, which themselves had no known utility, is not a substantial utility. Specifically, the Board noted that Fisher argued that the "claimed ESTs may be useful in searching for promoters that are only active in leaves at the time of anthesis." The Board found, however, that the application failed to show that the claimed ESTs would be expressed only during anthesis or that they would be capable of isolating a promoter active in maize leaves at the time of anthesis.

Additionally, the Board addressed the remaining asserted utilities, highlighting in particular the use of the claimed ESTs to monitor gene expression by measuring the level of mRNA through microarray technology and to serve as molecular markers. The Board found that using the claimed ESTs in screens does not provide a specific benefit because the application fails to provide any teaching regarding how to use the data relating to gene expression. The Board analogized the facts to those in *Brenner v. Manson*, 383 U.S. 519 (1966), in which an applicant claimed a process of making a compound having no known use. In that case, the Supreme Court affirmed the rejection of the application on § 101 grounds. Here, the Board reasoned: "Just as the process in *Brenner* lacked utility because the specification did not disclose how to use the end-product, the products claimed here lack utility, because even if used in gene expression assays, the specification does not disclose how to use SEQ ID NO: 1–5 specific gene expression data." The Board offered a similar rationale for the use of the claimed ESTs as molecular markers. Accordingly, the Board affirmed the examiner's rejection of the '643 application for lack of utility under § 101. The Board also affirmed the examiner's rejection of the '643 application for lack of enablement under § 112, first paragraph, since the enablement rejection was made as a corollary to the utility rejection.

Fisher timely appealed.

II. Discussion

Whether an application discloses a utility for a claimed invention is a question of fact. We consequently review the Board's determination that the '643 application failed to satisfy the utility requirement of § 101 for substantial evidence.

Fisher asserts that the Board unilaterally applied a heightened standard for utility in the case of ESTs, conditioning patentability upon "some undefined 'spectrum' of knowledge concerning the corresponding gene function." Fisher contends that the standard is not so high and that Congress intended the language of § 101 to be given broad construction. In particular, Fisher contends that § 101 requires only that the claimed invention "not be frivolous, or injurious to the well-being, good policy, or good morals of society," essentially adopting Justice Story's view of a useful invention from *Lowell v. Lewis*, 15 F.Cas. 1018, 1019 (No. 8568) (C.C.D.Mass.1817). Under the correct application of the law, Fisher argues, the record shows that the claimed ESTs provide seven specific and substantial uses, regardless whether the functions of the genes corresponding to the claimed ESTs are known. Fisher claims that the Board's attempt to equate the claimed ESTs with the chemical compositions in Brenner was misplaced. . . . Fisher likewise argues that the general commercial success of ESTs in the marketplace confirms the utility of the claimed ESTs. Hence, Fisher avers that the Board's decision was not supported by substantial evidence and should be reversed.

The government agrees with Fisher that the utility threshold is not high, but disagrees with Fisher's allegation that the Board applied a heightened utility standard. The government contends that a patent applicant need disclose only a single specific and substantial utility pursuant to *Brenner,* the very standard articulated in the PTO's "Utility Examination Guidelines" ("Utility Guidelines") and followed here when examining the '643 application. It argues that Fisher failed to meet that standard because Fisher's alleged uses are so general as to be meaningless. What is more, the government asserts that the same generic uses could apply not only to the five claimed ESTs but also to any EST derived from any organism. It thus argues that the seven utilities alleged by Fisher are merely starting points for further research, not the end point of any research effort. It further disputes the importance of the commercial success of ESTs in the marketplace, pointing out that Fisher's evidence involved only databases, clone sets, and microarrays, not the five claimed ESTs. Therefore, the government contends that we should affirm the Board's decision.

Several academic institutions and biotechnology and pharmaceutical companies write as amici curiae in support of the government. Like the government, they assert that Fisher's claimed uses are nothing more than a "laundry list" of research plans, each general and speculative, none providing a specific and substantial benefit in currently available form. The amici also advocate that the claimed ESTs are the objects of further research aimed at identifying what genes of unknown function are expressed during anthesis and what proteins of unknown function are encoded for by those genes. Until the corresponding genes and proteins have a known function, the amici argue, the claimed ESTs lack utility under § 101 and are not patentable.

We agree with both the government and the amici that none of Fisher's seven asserted uses meets the utility requirement of § 101. Section 101 provides: "Whoever invents . . . any new and *useful* . . . composition of matter . . . may obtain a patent therefor. . . ." (Emphasis added). In *Brenner,* the Supreme Court explained what is required to establish the usefulness of a new invention, noting at the outset that "a simple, everyday word ["useful," as found in § 101] can be pregnant with ambiguity when applied to the facts of life." 383 U.S. at 529. Contrary to Fisher's argument that § 101 only requires an invention that is not "frivolous, injurious to the well-being, good policy, or good morals of society," the Supreme Court appeared to reject Justice Story's de minimis view of utility. The Supreme Court observed that Justice Story's definition "sheds little light on our subject," on the one hand framing the relevant inquiry as "whether the invention in question is 'frivolous and insignificant'" if narrowly read, while on the other hand "allowing the patenting of any invention not positively harmful to society" if more broadly read. In its place, the Supreme Court announced a more rigorous test, stating:

> The basic *quid pro quo* contemplated by the Constitution and the Congress for granting a patent monopoly is the benefit derived by the public from an invention with *substantial utility.* Unless and until

a process is refined and developed to this point-where *specific benefit exists in currently available form*-there is insufficient justification for permitting an applicant to engross what may prove to be a broad field.

Following *Brenner,* our predecessor court, the Court of Customs and Patent Appeals, and this court have required a claimed invention to have a specific and substantial utility to satisfy § 101. *See, e.g., Fujikawa v. Wattanasin,* 93 F.3d 1559, 1563 (Fed.Cir.1996) ("Consequently, it is well established that a patent may not be granted to an invention unless substantial or practical utility for the invention has been discovered and disclosed.").

The Supreme Court has not defined what the terms "specific" and "substantial" mean per se. Nevertheless, together with the Court of Customs and Patent Appeals, we have offered guidance as to the uses which would meet the utility standard of § 101. From this, we can discern the kind of disclosure an application must contain to establish a specific and substantial utility for the claimed invention.

Courts have used the labels "practical utility" and "real world" utility interchangeably in determining whether an invention offers a "substantial" utility. Indeed, the Court of Customs and Patent Appeals stated that " '[p]ractical utility' is a shorthand way of attributing 'real-world' value to claimed subject matter. In other words, one skilled in the art can use a claimed discovery in a manner which provides some *immediate benefit to the public.*" [*Nelson v. Bowler,* 626 F.2d 853, 856 (CCPA 1980)] (emphasis added). It thus is clear that an application must show that an invention is useful to the public as disclosed in its current form, not that it may prove useful at some future date after further research. Simply put, to satisfy the "substantial" utility requirement, an asserted use must show that that claimed invention has a significant and present-ly available benefit to the public.

Turning to the "specific" utility requirement, an application must disclose a use which is not so vague as to be meaningless. Indeed, one of our predecessor courts has observed "that the nebulous expressions 'biological activity' or 'biological properties' appearing in the specifica-tion convey no more explicit indication of the usefulness of the com-pounds and how to use them than did the equally obscure expression 'useful for technical and pharmaceutical purposes' unsuccessfully relied upon by the appellant in *In re Diedrich* [318 F.2d 946 (1963)]." *In re Kirk,* 376 F.2d 936, 941 (1967). Thus, in addition to providing a "substantial" utility, an asserted use must also show that that claimed invention can be used to provide a well-defined and particular benefit to the public.

In 2001, partially in response to questions about the patentability of ESTs, the PTO issued Utility Guidelines governing its internal practice for determining whether a claimed invention satisfies § 101. *See* Utility Examination Guidelines, 66 FED.REG. 1092 (Jan. 5, 2001). The PTO incorporated these guidelines into the Manual of Patent Examining

Procedure ("MPEP"). The MPEP and Guidelines "are not binding on this court, but may be given judicial notice to the extent they do not conflict with the statute." *Enzo Biochem v. Gen–Probe*, 323 F.3d 956, 964 (Fed.Cir.2002) (citing *Molins PLC v. Textron, Inc.*, 48 F.3d 1172, 1180 n. 10 (Fed.Cir.1995)). According to the Utility Guidelines, a specific utility is particular to the subject matter claimed and would not be applicable to a broad class of invention. MPEP § 2107.01. The Utility Guidelines also explain that a substantial utility defines a "real world" use. In particular, "[u]tilities that require or constitute carrying out further research to identify or reasonably confirm a 'real world' context of use are not substantial utilities." *Id.* Further, the Utility Guidelines discuss "research tools," a term often given to inventions used to conduct research. The PTO particularly cautions that

> [a]n assessment that focuses on whether an invention is useful only in a research setting thus does not address whether the invention is in fact "useful" in a patent sense. [The PTO] must distinguish between inventions that have a specifically identified substantial utility and inventions whose asserted utility requires further research to identify or reasonably confirm.

Id. The PTO's standards for assessing whether a claimed invention has a specific and substantial utility comport with this court's interpretation of the utility requirement of § 101.

Turning to the parties' arguments, Fisher first raises a legal issue, charging that the Board applied a heightened standard for utility in the case of ESTs. Fisher apparently bases this argument on statements made by the Board in connection with its discussion of whether the claimed ESTs can be used to identify a polymorphism. In that context, the Board stated:

> Somewhere between having no knowledge (the present circumstances) and having complete knowledge of the gene and its role in the plant's development lies the line between 'utility' and 'substantial utility.' We need not draw the line or further define it in this case because the facts in this case represent the lowest end of the *spectrum, i.e.*, an insubstantial use.

Fisher reads the word "spectrum" out of context, claiming that the word somehow implies the application of a higher standard for utility than required by § 101. We conclude, however, that the Board did not apply an incorrect legal standard. In its decision, the Board made reference to a "spectrum" to differentiate between a substantial utility, which satisfies the utility requirement of § 101, and an insubstantial utility, which fails to satisfy § 101. The Board plainly did not announce or apply a new test for assessing the utility of ESTs. It simply followed the Utility Guidelines and MPEP, which mandate the specific and substantial utility test set forth in *Brenner*. Indeed, we note that Example 9 of the PTO's "Revised Interim Utility Guidelines Training Materials" is applicable to the facts here. *See* U.S. Pat. & Trademark Off., Revised Interim Utility Guidelines

Training Materials 50–53 (1999), *available at* www.uspto.gov/web/menu/utility.pdf. In that example, a cDNA fragment disclosed as being useful as a probe to obtain the full length gene corresponding to a cDNA fragment was deemed to lack a specific and substantial utility. Additionally, the MPEP particularly explains that a claim directed to a polynucleotide disclosed to be useful as a "gene probe" or "chromosome marker," as is the case here, fails to satisfy the specific utility requirement unless a specific DNA target is also disclosed. MPEP § 2107.01.

Regarding the seven uses asserted by Fisher, we observe that each claimed EST uniquely corresponds to the single gene from which it was transcribed ("underlying gene"). As of the filing date of the '643 application, Fisher admits that the underlying genes have no known functions. Fisher, nevertheless, claims that this fact is irrelevant because the seven asserted uses are not related to the functions of the underlying genes. We are not convinced by this contention. Essentially, the claimed ESTs act as no more than research intermediates that may help scientists to isolate the particular underlying protein-encoding genes and conduct further experimentation on those genes. The overall goal of such experimentation is presumably to understand the maize genome—the functions of the underlying genes, the identity of the encoded proteins, the role those proteins play during anthesis, whether polymorphisms exist, the identity of promoters that trigger protein expression, whether protein expression may be controlled, etc. Accordingly, the claimed ESTs are, in words of the Supreme Court, mere "object[s] of use-testing," to wit, objects upon which scientific research could be performed with no assurance that anything useful will be discovered in the end. *Brenner*, 383 U.S. at 535.

Fisher compares the claimed ESTs to certain other patentable research tools, such as a microscope. Although this comparison may, on first blush, be appealing in that both a microscope and one of the claimed ESTs can be used to generate scientific data about a sample having unknown properties, Fisher's analogy is flawed. As the government points out, a microscope has the specific benefit of optically magnifying an object to immediately reveal its structure. One of the claimed ESTs, by contrast, can only be used to detect the presence of genetic material having the same structure as the EST itself. It is unable to provide any information about the overall structure let alone the function of the underlying gene. Accordingly, while a microscope can offer an immediate, real world benefit in a variety of applications, the same cannot be said for the claimed ESTs. Fisher's proposed analogy is thus inapt. Hence, we conclude that Fisher's asserted uses are insufficient to meet the standard for a "substantial" utility under § 101.

Moreover, all of Fisher's asserted uses represent merely hypothetical possibilities, objectives which the claimed ESTs, or any EST for that matter, *could* possibly achieve, but none for which they have been used in the real world. Focusing on the two uses emphasized by Fisher at oral argument, Fisher maintains that the claimed ESTs could be used to identify polymorphisms or to isolate promoters. Nevertheless, in the face of a utility rejection, Fisher has not presented any evidence, as the Board well noted, showing that the claimed ESTs have been used in either way. That is, Fisher does not present either a single polymorphism or a single promoter, assuming at least one of each exists, actually identified by using the claimed ESTs. Further, Fisher has not shown that a polymorphism or promoter so identified would have a "specific and substantial" use. The Board, in fact, correctly recognized this very deficiency and cited it as one of the reasons for upholding the examiner's final rejection.

With respect to the remaining asserted uses, there is no disclosure in the specification showing that any of the claimed ESTs were used as a molecular marker on a map of the maize genome. There also is no disclosure establishing that any of the claimed ESTs were used or, for that matter, could be used to control or provide information about gene expression. Significantly, despite the fact that maize leaves produce over two thousand different proteins during anthesis, Fisher failed to show that one of the claimed ESTs translates into a portion of one of those proteins. Fisher likewise did not provide any evidence showing that the claimed ESTs were used to locate genetic molecules in other plants and organisms. What is more, Fisher has not proffered any evidence showing that any such generic molecules would themselves have a specific and substantial utility. Consequently, because Fisher failed to prove that its claimed ESTs can be successfully used in the seven ways disclosed in the '643 application, we have no choice but to conclude that the claimed ESTs do not have a "substantial" utility under § 101.

Furthermore, Fisher's seven asserted uses are plainly not "specific." Any EST transcribed from any gene in the maize genome has the potential to perform any one of the alleged uses. That is, any EST transcribed from any gene in the maize genome may be a molecular marker or a source for primers. Likewise, any EST transcribed from any gene in the maize genome may be used to measure the level of mRNA in a tissue sample, identify the presence or absence of a polymorphism, isolate promoters, control protein expression, or locate genetic molecules of other plants and organisms. Nothing about Fisher's seven alleged uses set the five claimed ESTs apart from the more than 32,000 ESTs disclosed in the '643 application or indeed from any EST derived from any organism. Accordingly, we conclude that Fisher has only disclosed general uses for its claimed ESTs, not specific ones that satisfy § 101.

We agree with the Board that the facts here are similar to those in *Brenner*. There, as noted above, the applicant claimed a process for preparing compounds of unknown use. Similarly, Fisher filed an application claiming five particular ESTs which are capable of hybridizing with underlying genes of unknown function found in the maize genome. The *Brenner* court held that the claimed process lacked a utility because it could be used only to produce a compound of unknown use. The

Brenner court stated: "We find absolutely no warrant for the proposition that although Congress intended that no patent be granted on a chemical compound whose sole 'utility' consists of its potential role as an object of use-testing, a different set of rules was meant to apply to the process which yielded the unpatentable product." 383 U.S. at 535, 86 S.Ct. 1033. Applying that same logic here, we conclude that the claimed ESTs, which do not correlate to an underlying gene of known function, fail to meet the standard for utility intended by Congress.

Here, granting a patent to Fisher for its five claimed ESTs would amount to a hunting license because the claimed ESTs can be used only to gain further information about the underlying genes and the proteins encoded for by those genes. The claimed ESTs themselves are not an end of Fisher's research effort, but only tools to be used along the way in the search for a practical utility. Thus, while Fisher's claimed ESTs may add a noteworthy contribution to biotechnology research, our precedent dictates that the '643 application does not meet the utility requirement of § 101 because Fisher does not identify the function for the underlying protein-encoding genes. Absent such identification, we hold that the claimed ESTs have not been researched and understood to the point of providing an immediate, well-defined, real world benefit to the public meriting the grant of a patent.

As a final matter, we observe that the government and its amici express concern that allowing EST patents without proof of utility would discourage research, delay scientific discovery, and thwart progress in the "useful Arts" and "Science." *See* U.S. CONST. art. I, § 8, cl. 8. The government and its amici point out that allowing EST claims like Fisher's would give rise to multiple patents, likely owned by several different companies, relating to the same underlying gene and expressed protein. Such a situation, the government and amici predict, would result in an unnecessarily convoluted licensing environment for those interested in researching that gene and/or protein.

The concerns of the government and amici, which may or may not be valid, are not ones that should be considered in deciding whether the application for the claimed ESTs meets the utility requirement of § 101. The same may be said for the resource and managerial problems that the PTO potentially would face if applicants present the PTO with an onslaught of patent applications directed to particular ESTs. Congress did not intend for these practical implications to affect the determination of whether an invention satisfies the requirements set forth in 35 U.S.C. §§ 101, 102, 103, and 112. They are public policy considerations which are more appropriately directed to Congress as the legislative branch of government, rather than this court as a judicial body responsible simply for interpreting and applying statutory law. Under Title 35, an applicant is entitled to a patent if his invention is new, useful, nonobvious, and his application adequately describes the claimed invention, teaches others how to make and use the claimed invention, and discloses the best mode for practicing the claimed invention. What is more, when Congress enacted § 101, it indicated that "anything under the sun that is made by man" constitutes potential subject matter for a patent. S.Rep. No. 82–1979, at 7 (1952), U.S.Code Cong. & Admin.News at 2394, 2399. Policy reasons aside, because we conclude that the utility requirement of § 101 is not met, we hold that Fisher is not entitled to a patent for the five claimed ESTs.

AFFIRMED.

RADER, CIRCUIT JUDGE, dissenting.

This court today determines that expressed sequence tags (ESTs) do not satisfy 35 U.S.C. § 101 unless there is a known use for the genes from which each EST is transcribed. While I agree that an invention must demonstrate utility to satisfy § 101, these claimed ESTs have such a utility, at least as research tools in isolating and studying other molecules. Therefore, I respectfully dissent.

Several, if not all, of Fisher's asserted utilities claim that ESTs function to study other molecules. In simple terms, ESTs are research tools. Admittedly ESTs have use only in a research setting. However, the value and utility of research tools generally is beyond question, even though limited to a laboratory setting. *See* MPEP § 2107.01 at 2100–33 (8th ed. 2001, rev. Feb.2003) ("Many research tools such as gas chromatographs, screening assays, and nucleotide sequencing techniques have a clear, specific and unquestionable utility (e.g., they are useful in analyzing compounds)."). Thus, if the claimed ESTs qualify as research tools, then they have a "specific" and "substantial" utility sufficient for § 101. If these ESTs do not enhance research, then *Brenner v. Manson*, 383 U.S. 519 (1966) (involving the patentability of methods for producing compounds having no known use) controls and erects a § 101 bar for lack of utility. For the following reasons, these claimed ESTs are more akin to patentable research tools than to the unpatentable methods in *Brenner*.

In *Brenner*, the Court confronted a growing conflict between this court's predecessor, the Court of Customs and Patent Appeals (CCPA), and the Patent Office over the patentability of methods of producing compounds with no known use . . . . . This case is very different. Unlike the methods and compounds in *Brenner . . .*, Fisher's claimed EST's *are* beneficial to society. As an example, these research tools "may help scientists to isolate the particular underlying protein-encoding genes . . . [with the] overall goal of such experimentation . . . presumably [being] to understand the maize genome[.]" *Majority Opinion*, at 1373. They also can serve as a probe introduced into a sample tissue to confirm "that the gene corresponding to the EST was being expressed in the sample tissue at the time of mRNA extraction." *Id.* at 1367.

These research tools are similar to a microscope; both take a researcher one step closer to identifying and understanding a previously unknown and invisible structure. Both supply information about a molecular structure. Both advance research and bring scientists closer to unlocking the secrets of the corn genome to provide better food production for the hungry world. If a microscope has § 101 utility, so too do these ESTs.

The Board and this court acknowledge that the ESTs perform a function, that they have a utility, but proceed quickly to a value judgment that the utility would not produce enough valuable information. The Board instead complains that the information these ESTs supply is too "insubstantial" to merit protection. Yet this conclusion denies the very nature of scientific advance. Science always advances in small incremental steps. While acknowledging the patentability of research tools generally (and microscopes as one example thereof), this court concludes with little scientific foundation that these ESTs do not qualify as research tools because they do not "offer an immediate, real world benefit" because further research is required to understand the underlying gene. This court further faults the EST research for lacking any "assurance that anything useful will be discovered in the end." These criticisms would foreclose much scientific research and many vital research tools. Often scientists embark on research with no assurance of success and knowing that even success will demand "significant additional research."

Nonetheless, this court, oblivious to the challenges of complex research, discounts these ESTs because it concludes (without scientific evidence) that they do not supply enough information. This court reasons that a research tool has a "specific" and "substantial" utility *only* if the studied object is readily understandable using the claimed tool— that no further research is required. Surely this cannot be the law. Otherwise, only the final step of a lengthy incremental research inquiry gets protection.

Even with a microscope, significant additional research is often required to ascertain the particular function of a "revealed" structure. To illustrate, a cancerous growth, magnified with a patented microscope, can be identified and distinguished from other healthy cells by a properly trained doctor or researcher. But even today, the scientific community still does not fully grasp the reasons that cancerous growths increase in mass and spread throughout the body, or the nature of compounds that interact with them, or the interactions of environmental or genetic conditions that contribute to developing cancer. Significant additional research is required to answer these questions. Even with answers to these questions, the cure for cancer will remain in the distance. Yet the microscope still has "utility" under § 101. Why? Because it takes the researcher one step closer to answering these questions. Each step, even if small in isolation, is nonetheless a benefit to society sufficient to give a viable research tool "utility" under § 101. In fact, experiments that fail still serve to eliminate some possibilities and provide information to the research process.

The United States Patent Office, above all, should recognize the incremental nature of scientific endeavor. Yet, in the interest of easing its administrative load, the Patent Office will eliminate some research tools as providing "insubstantial" advances. How does the Patent Office know which "insubstantial" research step will contribute to a substantial breakthrough in genomic study? Quite simply, it does not.

In addition, this court faults Fisher for not presenting evidence of utility showing that the claimed ESTs "have been used in the real world." To the contrary, this court misapprehended the proper procedure. Fisher asserted seven different utilities. The Board rejected two of these assertions outright as "insubstantial." This summary dismissal deprived Fisher of any chance to proffer evidence. Rather than fault Fisher for not presenting evidence it was prevented from offering, this court should instead observe that the Board did not satisfy its burden of challenging Fisher's presumptively correct assertion that the ESTs were *capable* of performing those functions.

Abandoning the proper legal procedure, the Board reasoned that the molecules studied with these ESTs showed no particular use, therefore the ESTs themselves also lacked a utility. In so ruling, the Board did not reject Fisher's utilities on the basis that the ESTs were *unable to perform* the purported utilities. Thus, the Board did not establish a prima facie challenge to the ESTs' ability to perform these two utilities. Without anything to rebut, Fisher had no obligation or opportunity to provide evidence in rebuttal. Thus, I respectfully disagree with this court's conclusion that the Board's decision can be affirmed on the basis that Fisher did not supply evidence of the ESTs' ability to perform the asserted utilities.

In truth, I have some sympathy with the Patent Office's dilemma. The Office needs some tool to reject inventions that may advance the "useful arts" but not sufficiently to warrant the valuable exclusive right of a patent. The Patent Office has seized upon this utility requirement to reject these research tools as contributing "insubstantially" to the advance of the useful arts. The utility requirement is ill suited to that task, however, because it lacks any standard for assessing the state of the prior art and the contributions of the claimed advance. The proper tool for assessing sufficient contribution to the useful arts is the obviousness requirement of 35 U.S.C. § 103. Unfortunately this court has deprived the Patent Office of the obviousness requirement for genomic inventions. See In re Deuel, 51 F.3d 1552 (Fed.Cir.1995); Philippe Ducor, *The Federal Circuit and In re Deuel: Does § 103 apply to Naturally Occurring DNA?*, 77 J. PAT. & TRADEMARK OFF. SOC'Y 871, 883 (Nov.1995) ("The Court of Appeals for the Federal Circuit could have formulated its opinion in only one sentence: '35 U.S.C. § 103 does not apply to newly retrieved natural DNA sequences.' "); see also over fifty additional articles critical of Deuel in the "Citing References" tab for Deuel on Westlaw. Nonetheless, rather than distort the utility test, the Patent Office should seek ways to apply the correct test, the test used world wide for such assessments (other than in the United States), namely inventive step or obviousness.

Thus, for the foregoing reasons, I would find that Fisher's asserted utilities qualify the claimed ESTs as research tools useful in the study of other molecules. Because research tools provide a cognizable benefit to society, much like a microscope, the ESTs claimed here have "utility" under § 101.

ESTs have utility

NOTES

1. Utility as a Research Tool. Should the current utility standard be revised, at least when an invention fairly qualifies as a research tool? One student commentator thinks so. Lilian Ewing, In re Fisher: *Denial of Patents for ESTs Signals Deeper Problems in the Utility Prong for Patentability*, 8 MINN. J. L. SCI. & TECH. 645 (2007), proposes that patent law's utility doctrine should account for an invention's "real world" uses in a research and laboratory setting, even if the invention does not result in immediate public benefits. The author identifies the following National Institutes of Health guidelines, which consider whether a particular resource qualifies as a research tool, as providing a helpful first step:

> 1. The primary usefulness of the resource has as a tool for discovery rather than an FDA-approved product or integral component of such a product;

> 2. Whether the resource is a broad, enabling invention that will be useful to many scientists . . . rather than a project or product-specific resource; and

> 3. Whether the resource is readily useable or distributable as a tool rather than the situation where private sector involvement is necessary or the most expedient means for developing or distributing the resource.

Id. at 670 (quoting NIH Principles and Guidelines, 64 FED. REG. 72,090, 72,094 (Dec. 23, 1999)).

2. Alternative Protection Regimes? Following *Fisher*, patents appear to be unavailable for ESTs that attempt to claim entire genes or proteins based only upon the EST, or are not directed to either a known target or known gene. What options remain for biotechnology firms? One is to maintain ESTs as a trade secret, and indeed numerous proprietary EST databases have been created. *See* William F. Lee, *et al.*, *Limits on Patentability In Life Sciences: Claims Covering Expressed Sequence Tags*, 6 SEDONA CONF. J. 95, 114 (2005). For a proposed alternative regime of intellectual property protection, see Molly A. Holman & Stephen R. Munzer, *Intellectual Property Rights in Genes and Gene Fragments: A Registration Solution for Expressed Sequence Tags*, 85 IOWA L. REV. 735 (2000).

Utility Exercise

On December 18, 1997, Stuart Newman, a professor of cell biology and anatomy at New York Medical College, and Jeremy Rifkin, president of the Foundation on Economic Trends, jointly filed a patent application claiming a technique for combining human and animal embryo cells to produce a single animal-human embryo. This embryo could then be implanted in a surrogate mother to produce a "chimera," or mixture of the two species. Combinations reportedly described in the Newman–Rifkin application include mouse-human, baboon-human, chimpanzee-human, and pig-human chimera. Newman and Rifkin have stated that they have no intention of producing such hybrids. They instead filed the application in order to provoke debate about the ethics of patenting life forms.

The Patent and Trademark Office responded by releasing a "media advisory" titled "Facts on Patenting Life Forms Having a Relationship to Humans." This document cited case law, including *Lowell v. Lewis*, interpreting the utility requirement as excluding patents on inventions "injurious to the well-being, good policy or sound morals of society." It further stated "that inventions directed to human/non-human chimera could, under certain circumstances, not be patentable because, among other things, they would fail to meet the public policy and morality aspects of the utility requirement." During a subsequent interview, then Patent and Trademark Office Commissioner Bruce Lehman reportedly stated that "there will be no patents on monsters, at least not while I'm commissioner."

Do you believe that the Patent and Trademark Office position accurately reflects the latest thinking on the utility requirement? For more information on this episode, see Cynthia M. Ho, *Splicing Morality and Patent Law: Issues Arising from Mixing Mice and Men*, 2 Wash. Univ. J. L. & Policy 247 (2000); Thomas A. Magnani, Note, *The Patentability of Human–Animal Chimeras*, 14 Berkeley Tech. L.J. 443 (1999).

No. morals are for Congress not the PTO

CHAPTER FOUR

ANTICIPATION

■ ■ ■

Broadly stated, patent-eligible subject matter is patentable if the claimed subject matter possesses *utility*, and is both *novel* under 35 U.S.C.A. § 102 and *nonobvious* under 35 U.S.C.A. § 103. Of these four general requirements, novelty is perhaps the patent system's central value: to become eligible for the reward of a patent, an inventor must accomplish something new. Although simply expressed, the statutory basis for novelty and other patent-defeating events, including forfeitures, is among the more complex in patent law. 35 U.S.C.A. § 102 provides:

A person shall be entitled to a patent unless—

(a) the invention was known or used by others in this country, or patented or described in a printed publication in this or a foreign country, before the invention thereof by the applicant for patent, or

(b) the invention was patented or described in a printed publication in this or a foreign country or in public use or on sale in this country, more than one year prior to the date of the application for patent in the United States, or

(c) he has abandoned the invention, or

(d) the invention was first patented or caused to be patented, or was the subject of an inventor's certificate, by the applicant or his legal representatives or assigns in a foreign country prior to the date of the application for patent in this country on an application for patent or inventor's certificate filed more than twelve months before the filing of the application in the United States, or

(e) The invention was described in—

(1) an application for patent, published under section 122(b), by another filed in the United States before the invention by the applicant for patent or

(2) a patent granted on an application for patent by another filed in the United States before the invention by the applicant for patent, except that an international application filed under the treaty defined in section 351(a) shall have the effects for the purposes of this subsection of an application filed in the United

States only if the international application designated the United States and was published under Article 21(2) of such treaty in the English language; or

(f) he did not himself invent the subject matter sought to be patented, or

(g)(1) during the course of an interference conducted under section 135 or section 291, another inventor involved therein establishes, to the extent permitted in section 104, that before such person's invention thereof the invention was made by such other inventor and not abandoned, suppressed, or concealed, or

(2) before such person's invention thereof, the invention was made in this country by another inventor who had not abandoned, suppressed, or concealed it. In determining priority of invention under this subsection, there shall be considered not only the respective dates of conception and reduction to practice of the invention, but also the reasonable diligence of one who was first to conceive and last to reduce to practice, from a time prior to conception by the other.

Section 102 embraces a host of issues, of which two are central: the requirement of novelty, expressed in §§ 102(a), (e) and (g), and the so-called "statutory bars" of §§ 102(b) and (d). A key distinction between them is the time at which patent-defeating activity occurs. Novelty is keyed to the time the inventor completed the invention—the "invention date." The statutory bars are keyed to the day on which the inventor submitted an application to the U.S. Patent and Trademark Office—the "filing date."

The novelty sections mandate that only the first inventor of a technology can obtain a patent, regardless of whether a later inventor filed an earlier application on the same technology. These provisions are the basis of the "first to invent" priority system unique to the United States. When multiple persons claim the right to a patent on a given technology, this system allows inventors who were not the first to reach the Patent Office to establish their right to the patent by demonstrating inventive acts prior to those of their competitors.

Every other patent-issuing state currently sponsors a "race to the Patent Office" recordation system similar to that of domestic real property law. Under this "first to file" regime, the inventor who first files a patent application obtains the patent, even if another actually invented the technology first. The disparity between the United States "first to invent" system and the "first to file" regimes in the rest of the world remains of crucial importance, particularly for applicants seeking patent protection in many nations.

The statutory bars of § 102(b) are tied to the filing of a patent application. The point in time one year prior to the filing date is termed the "critical date," and statutorily specified activities such as publications or sales act to bar, or prevent, the applicant from obtaining a patent if they occur before the critical date. Section 102(b) thus produces a one-year "grace period" which allows an inventor to determine whether patent protection is desirable, and, if so, to prepare an application. If, for example, the inventor publishes an article in a scientific journal on a given date, he knows that he has one year in which to file an application. Note that the inventor has a broader range of concerns than merely his own behavior, because uses, sales, and other technical disclosures by third parties will also start the one-year clock running. Chapter 5 discusses statutory bars in more detail.

Beyond §§ 102(a) and (b), the remaining paragraphs of § 102 provide for additional patent-defeating events. Abandonment of an invention to the public amounts to a forfeiture of patent rights under § 102(c). Section 102(d) creates a statutory bar if the United States application has not been filed within one year of a foreign application on the same invention that ultimately ripened into a foreign patent right. Section 102(f) addresses the issue of derivation, denying a patent to those who have taken their technological ideas from the true inventor.

A determination of novelty requires two distinct inquiries. Section 102 requires that the current state of knowledge known to the art must be assessed as a basis for comparison. This step requires a determination of which sources from the universe of available knowledge are pertinent to the novelty inquiry. The Patent Act defines the materials—usually called "references"—that may be used to judge the novelty of the claimed invention in § 102. Typical references under § 102 include such documentary materials as patents and publications, as well as the fact of actual uses or sales of a technology within the United States. The sum of these references is denominated the "prior art."

Once we have identified all possible references that might give rise to novelty or statutory bar issues, section 102 also requires that we ask whether any one of those references fully anticipates a claim. The standard of anticipation is a strict one. Each and every element of the claimed invention must be disclosed in a single, enabling reference. This casebook takes up this standard next.

TITANIUM METALS CORP. OF AMERICA v. BANNER

United States Court of Appeals, Federal Circuit, 1985
778 F.2d 775

Before Rich, Circuit Judge, Nichols, Senior Circuit Judge, and Newman, Circuit Judge.

Rich, Circuit Judge. This appeal is from an Order of the United States District Court for the District of Columbia in a civil action brought pursuant to 35 U.S.C. § 145 against Donald W. Banner as Commissioner of Patents and Trademarks authorizing the Commissioner to issue to appellee a patent containing claims 1, 2, and 3 of patent application serial No. 598,935 for "TITANIUM ALLOY." The Commissioner has appealed. We reverse.

The inventors, Loren C. Covington and Howard R. Palmer, employees of appellee to whom they have assigned their invention and the application thereon, filed an application on March 29, 1974, serial No. 455,964, to patent an alloy they developed. The application involved on this appeal is a continuation-in-part thereof, filed July 25, 1975, containing the three claims on appeal. The alloy is made primarily of titanium (Ti) and contains small amounts of nickel (Ni) and molybdenum (Mo) as alloying ingredients to give the alloy certain desirable properties, particularly corrosion resistance in hot brine solutions, while retaining workability so that articles such as tubing can be fabricated from it by rolling, welding and other techniques. The inventors apparently also found that iron content should be limited, iron being an undesired impurity rather than an alloying ingredient. They determined the permissible ranges of the components, above and below which the desired properties were not obtained. A precise definition of the invention sought to be patented is found in the claims, set forth below, claim 3 representing the preferred composition, it being understood, however, that no iron at all would be even more preferred. 1. A titanium base alloy consisting essentially by weight of about 0.6% to 0.9% nickel, 0.2% to 0.4% molybdenum, up to 0.2% maximum iron, balance titanium, said alloy being characterized by good corrosion resistance in hot brine environments. 2. A titanium base alloy as set forth in Claim 1 having up to 0.1% iron, balance titanium. 3. A titanium base alloy as set forth in Claim 1 having 0.8% nickel, 0.3% molybdenum, up to 0.1% maximum iron, balance titanium.

The examiner's final rejection, repeated in his Answer on appeal to the Patent and Trademark Office (PTO) Board of Appeals (board), was on the grounds that claims 1 and 2 are anticipated (fully met) by, and claim 3 would have been obvious from, an article by Kalabukhova and Mikheyew, Investigation of the Mechanical Properties of Ti–Mo–Ni Alloys, Russian Metallurgy (Metally) No. 3, pages 130–133 (1970) (in the court below and hereinafter called "the Russian article") under 35 U.S.C. §§ 102 and 103, respectively. The board affirmed the examiner's rejection. However, it mistakenly proceeded on the assumption that all three claims had been rejected as anticipated under § 102 by the Russian article and ignored the obviousness rejection. On this appeal the PTO says it does not pursue the § 103 rejection further. Appellee proceeds on the basis that only the § 102 rejection is before us.

The Russian article is short (3 pages), highly technical, and contains 10 graphs as part of the discussion. As its title indicates, it relates to ternary Ti–Mo–Ni alloys, the subject of the application at bar. The examiner and the board both found that it would disclose to one skilled in the art an alloy on which at least claims 1 and 2 read, so that those claims would not be allowable under the statute because of lack of novelty of their subject matter. Since the article does not specifically disclose such an alloy in words, a little thinking is required about what it would disclose to one knowledgeable about Ti–Ni–Mo alloys. The PTO did that thinking as follows: Figure lc [a graph] shows data for the ternary titanium alloy which contains Mo and Ni in the ratio of 1:3. Amongst the actual points on the graph is one at 1% Mo + Ni. At this point, the amounts of Mo and Ni would be 0.25% and 0.75% respectively. A similar point appears on the graph shown in Figure 2 of the article.... Appellants do not deny that the data points are disclosed in the reference. In fact, the Hall affidavit indicates at least two specific points (at 1% and 1.25% Mo + Ni) which would represent a description of alloys falling within the scope of the instant claims.

Appellants dont deny the data points are disclosed in the reference

Fig. 1. Effect of Alloy
          Composition on the
          Ultimate Strength,
          Yield Point and
          Elongation of Ti-Mo-Ni
          Alloys for Mo:Ri Ratios
          of 3:1, 1:1 and 1:3
          (a, b and c respectively)
          and for Binary Ti-Ni
          Alloys (d).

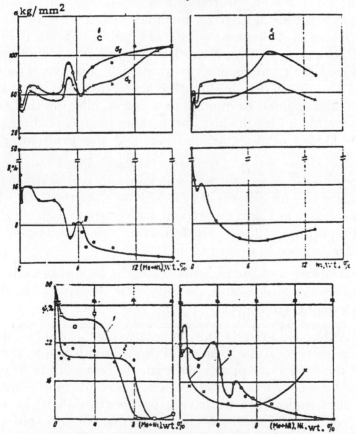

Fig. 2. Variation of the Reduction in Area of Ti-Mo-Ni Alloys
          (1, 2, 3 - Alloys of Series I, II and III Respectively) and of
          Ti-Ni Alloys (4) with the (Mo+Ni) Content (1-3) and the Ni
          Content (4).

On that basis, the board found that the claimed alloys were not new, because they were disclosed in the prior art. It having been argued that the Russian article contains no disclosure of corrosion-resistant properties of any of the alloys, the board held: The fact that a particular property or the end use for this alloy as contemplated by appellants was not recognized in the article is of no consequence. It therefore held the Russian article to be an anticipation, noting that although the article does not discuss corrosion resistance, it does disclose other properties such as strength and ductility. The PTO further points out that the authors of the reference must have made the alloys to obtain the data points.

Being dissatisfied with the decision of the board, Titanium Metals Corporation of America, as assignee of the Covington and Palmer application, then brought an action in the District Court for the District of Columbia against the Commissioner pursuant to 35 U.S.C. § 145, its complaint alleging that the board's decision "was erroneous and contrary to law," and making profert of a certified copy of the application and all papers in the file thereof, together with a copy of the Russian article which was the sole basis of the PTO refusal to allow the claims. It prayed that the court adjudge it entitled to a patent containing claims 1–3 and authorize the Commissioner to grant such a patent. The Commissioner filed an answer denying that the applicants were the first inventors of the alloys claimed or entitled to a patent, alleging that the claims are not patentable under the law, and making profert of the Examiner's Answer, the Board of Appeals' decision, and the prior art reference.

The case came on for trial on January 24, 1980, before the Honorable John G. Penn and was concluded in two and a half hours. The testimony of one witness was heard by the court, Dr. James C. Williams, professor at Carnegie–Mellon University in Pittsburgh and an expert in titanium metallurgy. His testimony was about equally divided between direct and cross examination.

At the conclusion of the plaintiff's case, the following exchange took place between the judge and the Associate Solicitor for the PTO:

THE COURT: All right. Mr. Tarring?

MR. TARRING: Your Honor, generally the position of the Patent Office is we rely on the position of the tribunals below, the examiner and the Board of Appeals and their decisions are both present in the exhibit which I submitted earlier. I was not quite sure whether you would prefer that we have a post-trial brief in the matter. If that's your preference we could do that or I could make an argument on the basis of the law right now. I don't know what your preference would be. Otherwise, I'm not going to call any witnesses.

THE COURT: You are not going to what?

MR. TARRING: I have no intention of calling any witnesses so it's really a matter of argument at this point, I think.

THE COURT: Of course, I have received your pre-trial briefs.

After further discussion, it was settled that both parties would file further briefs after the hearing transcript had been prepared. They were filed in April and May, 1980. On November 16, 1984, the District Court entered the Order appealed from followed on November 28 by a supporting memorandum opinion. January 10, 1985, the PTO filed its Notice of Appeal. This court has heard oral argument and received briefs.

THE DISTRICT COURT OPINION

We are left in no doubt that the court was impressed by the totality of the evidence that the applicants for patent had discovered or invented and disclosed knowledge which is not to be found in the reference, nor do we have any doubt about that ourselves. But those facts are beside the point. The patent law imposes certain fundamental conditions for patentability, paramount among them being the condition that what is sought to be patented, as determined by the claims, be new. The basic provision of Title 35 applicable here is § 101, providing in relevant part: "Whoever invents or discovers any new . . . composition of matter, or any new . . . improvement thereof, may obtain a patent therefor, subject to the conditions and requirements of this title." The title of the application here involved is "Titanium Alloy," a composition of matter. Surprisingly, in all of the evidence, nobody discussed the key issue of whether the alloy was new, which is the essence of the anticipation issue, including the expert Dr. Williams. Plaintiff's counsel, bringing Dr. Williams' testimony to its climax, after he had explained the nature of the ingredients, the alloys made therefrom, and their superior corrosion resistance in hot brine, etc., repetitively asked him such questions as "Does the [Russian] article direct you as one skilled in the art to a titanium alloy having nickel present in an amount between .6 and .9 percent molybdenum in an amount between .2 and .4 percent?" (emphasis ours) followed by "Is there anything mentioned in the article about corrosion resistance?" Of course, the answers were emphatically negative. But this and like testimony does not deal with the critical question: do claims 1 and 2, to which the questions obviously relate, read on or encompass an alloy which was already known by reason of the disclosure of the Russian article?

Section 102, the usual basis for rejection for lack of novelty or anticipation, lays down certain principles for determining the novelty required by § 101, among which are the provisions in § 102(a) and (b) that the claimed invention has not been "described in a printed publication in this or a foreign country," either (a) before the invention by the applicant or (b) more than one year before the application date to which he is entitled (strictly a "loss of right" provision similar to novelty). Either provision applies in this case, the Russian article having a date some 5 years prior to the filing date and its status as "prior art" not being questioned. The PTO was never specific as to what part of § 102 applies, merely rejecting on § 102. The question, therefore, is whether claims 1 and 2 encompass and, if allowed, would enable plaintiff-appellee to exclude others from making, using, or selling an alloy described in the Russian article. *See* 35 U.S.C. § 154.

To answer the question we need only turn to the affidavit of James A. Hall, a metallurgist employed by appellee's TIMET Division, who undertook to analyze the Russian article disclosure by calculating the ingredient percentages shown in the graph data points, which he presented in tabular form. There are 15 items in his table. The second item shows a titanium base alloy containing 0.25% by weight Mo and 0.75% Ni and this is squarely within the ranges of 0.2–0.4% Mo and 0.6–0.9% Ni of claims 1 and 2. As to that disclosed alloy of the prior art, there can be no question that claims 1 and 2 read on it and would be infringed by anyone making, using, or selling it. Therefore, the statute prohibits a patent containing them. This seems to be a case either of not adequately considering the novelty requirement of the statute, the true meaning of the correlative term "anticipation," or the meaning of the claims. By reason of the court's quotations from cases holding that a reference is not an anticipation which does not enable one skilled in the art to practice the claimed invention, it appears that the trial court thought there was some deficiency in the Russian article on that score. Enablement in this case involves only being able to make the alloy, given the ingredients and their proportions without more. The evidence here, however, clearly answers that question in two ways. Appellee's own patent application does not undertake to tell anyone how to make the alloy it describes and seeks to patent. It assumes that those skilled in the art would know how. Secondly, appellee's expert, Dr. Williams, testified on cross examination that given the alloy information in the Russian article, he would know how to prepare the alloys "by at least three techniques." Enablement is not a problem in this case.

As we read the situation, the court was misled by the arguments and evidence to the effect that the inventors here found out and disclosed in their application many things that one cannot learn from reading the Russian article and that this was sufficient in law to justify granting them a patent for their contributions—such things as what good corrosion resistance the claimed alloys have against hot brine, which possibly was not known, and the range limits of the Ni and Mo content, outside of which that resistance diminishes, which are teachings of very useful information. These things the applicants teach the art and the Russian article does not. Indeed, appellee's counsel argued in his opening statement to the trial court that the PTO's refusal of a patent was "directly contrary to the requirement of Article I, Section 8, of the Constitution," which authorizes Congress to create a patent law. But throughout the trial counsel never came to grips with the real issues: (1) what do the claims cover and (2) is what they cover new? Under the laws Congress wrote, they must be considered. Congress has not seen fit to permit the patenting of an old alloy, known to others through a printed publication, by one who has discovered its corrosion resistance or other useful properties, or has found out to what extent one can modify the composition of the alloy without losing such properties.

It is also an elementary principle of patent law that when, as by a recitation of ranges or otherwise, a claim covers several compositions, the claim is "anticipated" if one of them is in the prior art.

For all of the foregoing reasons, the court below committed clear error and legal error in authorizing the issuance of a patent on claims 1 and 2 since, properly construed, they are anticipated under § 102 by the Russian article which admittedly discloses an alloy on which these claims read.

[handwritten margin notes: If covering several ranges if one is known claim fits — wrong to issue patent on claims 1 and 2.]

NOTES

1. **A Four Corners Defense.** It may be convenient to consider anticipation as a "four corners" doctrine. *Dewey & Almy Chem. Co. v. Mimex Co.*, 124 F.2d 986 (2d Cir.1942). If the claimed invention can be found within the ambit of a single prior art reference, then the invention has been anticipated. References may not be combined during this inquiry, nor may elements that are analogous to the disclosure of a reference be considered.

Some earlier cases adopted a broader view of anticipation. In *Straussler v. United States*, 339 F.2d 670, 671 (Ct.Cl.1964) (emphasis added), the Court of Claims indicated:

> The test for determining if a reference anticipates a claim of a patent is whether the reference contains within its four corners adequate directions for the practice of the patent claim invalidated. . . . Stated another way, the reference must disclose all the elements of the claimed combination, *or their mechanical equivalents*, functioning in substantially the same way to produce substantially the same result.

Contemporary case law does not look beyond the reference itself when addressing § 102 issues. A prior art rejection may still occur based upon the proximity of a single piece of prior art to a claimed invention, but this inquiry is cast in terms of § 103 and nonobviousness.

The European view of novelty is also strict; equivalent embodiments of the disclosure of a prior art reference do not impact a novelty determination under the European Patent Convention. *See* "Fuel Injector Valve," T 167/48 (OJ EPO 1987, 369). In contrast, Japanese patent law tends to adopt a more liberal view of novelty. Its "substantial identity" test lies somewhere between the modern United States approach and what both systems refer to as "obviousness" or "inventive step." *See* Toshiko Takenaka, *The Substantial Identity Rule Under the Japanese Novelty Standard*, 9 UCLA PAC. BASIN L.J. 220 (1991).

2. **Genus/Species Cases.** A particular problem with respect to the identity requirement of anticipation occurs when the inventor has claimed some subset of a known broader range. The inventor may have chosen a lesser number of chemical compounds, or perhaps a smaller numerical range of temperature, voltage, or some other physical quantity, than that known to the art. The patent

bar often refers to the applicant's selection as a "species" chosen from out of the prior art "genus." What is the effect of such a selection upon the novelty of the applicant's claim? As suggested by *In re Kalm*, 378 F.2d 959 (CCPA 1967), the applicant must demonstrate that the claimed species has improved or distinct properties over other members of the prior art genus. In holding that the applicant before it had in fact claimed a novel compound, the *Kalm* court indicated that:

> When one speaks of a "genus" in the chemical arts, one ordinarily speaks of a group of compounds closely related both in structure and in properties. Appellant has found a group of chemical compounds which possess properties diametrically opposite to the properties disclosed by Siemer [the prior art reference] for his compounds. It is quite evident that Siemer never made the present compounds; of if he did, he never tested them to determine what effect they would have on the central nervous system, since, if he had, he could not logically have failed to report the seemingly anomalous result appellant has discovered.

> While it is not necessary that a reference disclose every property or attribute of a composition of matter to be a valid anticipation, appellant has found properties for his claimed compounds which are totally incompatible and inconsistent with, not merely complementary or in addition to, those attributed by Siemer to his compounds. It is our view that [the earlier inventor] never intended to, nor does he, disclose compounds within the scope of appellant's claims.

378 F.2d at 963. The determination of whether a prior art genus anticipates a claimed species is necessarily case-by-case. 1 MARTIN J. ADELMAN, PATENT LAW PERSPECTIVES, § 2.2[4] at n.67 (2d ed. 1996) provides a list of factors which the courts have considered within the chemical arts:

> (1) The number of compounds embraced by the most specific prior art description;

> (2) The degree of structural similarity between the compounds of that group;

> (3) The number of properties shared by compounds of that group;

> (4) Whether the properties of the claimed compounds are the same as, consistent with or diametrically opposite to the properties disclosed in the prior art;

> (5) The number of parameters that can be varied among the most specifically described group of prior art compounds; and

> (6) Whether the claimed materials are physical mixtures or the product of chemical reactions.

What about the reverse situation, where the prior art discloses a narrow range and the claimed invention is to a broader, encompassing range? *Titanium Metals* provides the answer: "It is an elementary principle of patent law that when, as by a recitation of ranges or otherwise, a claim covers several compositions, the claim is 'anticipated' if *one* of them is in the prior art."

The European patent system addresses the novelty of genus/species inventions similarly to that of the United States. The Guidelines for Examination in the European Patent Office indicate at Part C, Chapter IV, § 7.4 that:

> In considering novelty it should be borne in mind that a generic disclosure does not usually take away the novelty of any specific example falling within the terms of that disclosure, but that a specific disclosure does take away the novelty of a generic claim embracing that disclosure, e.g., a disclosure of copper takes away the novelty of metal as a generic concept, but not the novelty of any metal other than copper, and one of the rivets takes away the novelty of fastening rivets as a generic concept, but not the novelty of any fastening other than rivets.

3. More on the Enablement Requirement. To fulfill the enablement requirement of anticipation, does a prior art reference also need to disclose a use for a claimed compound? The Federal Circuit stated that it does not in *In re Schoenwald*, 964 F.2d 1122 (Fed.Cir.1992). There, Schoenwald claimed the compound N–cyclohexyl–N–methyl–2–phenylethylamine as well as its pharmaceutical use. The Patent and Trademark Office rejected a claim to the compound as anticipated under § 102(b) by a JOURNAL OF ORGANIC CHEMISTRY article. That article specifically described the claimed compound but did not provide any use for it. Judge Mayer affirmed the PTO decision, stating that:

> So it is beyond argument that no utility need be disclosed for a reference to be anticipatory of a claim to an old compound. The compound appellants are attempting to patent is not new—the use they discovered is, and they received a method patent for that. Their complaint that this is insufficient because their reward should be consistent with the full extent of their contribution is hollow. Their contribution was finding a use for the compound, not discovering the compound itself. Therefore they are being rewarded fully for their contribution; any more would be a gratuity.

4. Comparative Approaches to Enablement. A European Patent Office Board of Appeal has interpreted Article 54 of the European Patent Convention

> in the sense that anything comprised in the state of the art can only be regarded as having been made available to the public in so far as the information given to the person skilled in the art is sufficient to enable him to practise the technical teaching which is the subject of the disclosure, taking into account the general knowledge in the field to be expected of him.

T 26/85 (OJ EPO 1990, 22, 27). Consider a reference containing technical information stored only on a microchip. The information is not readily accessible, although it could be obtained following a time-consuming, costly analysis of the microchip. Would the United States and European patent systems consider the reference enabling and thus part of the prior art? *See* T 461/88 (OJ EPO 1993, 295).

While the enablement requirement might seem self-evident to you and, indeed, is now the general rule worldwide, many English judges did not impose such a requirement. The issue of whether English patent law required an enabling disclosure was not settled until the House of Lords decided *Asahi Kasei Kogyo KK's Application,* [1991] R.P.C. 485 (H.L.), which imposed this stricture. Can you think of an argument that would support the overruled English judges?

5. Inherency. A frequently occurring fact pattern involves a prior art reference that intrinsically, rather than explicitly, discloses a subsequently claimed invention. Whether this reference should be considered patent-defeating under § 102 is addressed by the doctrine of inherency, considered in the next decision.

SCHERING CORP. v. GENEVA PHARMACEUTICALS, INC.

Court of Appeals for the Federal Circuit, 2003
339 F.3d 1373

Before Rader, Circuit Judge, Plager, Senior Circuit Judge, and Bryson, Circuit Judge.

RADER, CIRCUIT JUDGE.

On summary judgment, the United States District Court for the District of New Jersey determined that claims 1 and 3 of U.S. Patent No. 4,659,716 (the '716 patent) are invalid. Because the district court correctly found that U.S. Patent No. 4,282,233 (the '233 patent) inherently anticipates claims 1 and 3 of the '716 patent, this court affirms.

I.

Schering Corporation (Schering) owns the '233 and '716 patents on antihistamines. Antihistamines inhibit the histamines that cause allergic symptoms.

The prior art '233 patent covers the antihistamine loratadine, the active component of a pharmaceutical that Schering markets as CLARITIN™. Unlike conventional antihistamines when CLARITIN™ was launched, loratadine does not cause drowsiness.

The more recent '716 patent at issue in this case covers a metabolite of loratadine called descarboethoxyloratadine (DCL). A metabolite is the compound formed in the patient's body upon ingestion of a pharmaceutical. The ingested pharmaceutical undergoes a chemical conversion in the digestion process to form a new metabolite compound. The metabolite DCL is also a non-drowsy antihistamine. The '716 patent issued in April 1987 and will expire in April 2004 (the '233 patent issued in 1981 and has since expired).

Structurally, loratadine and its metabolite DCL differ only in that loratadine has a carboethoxy group (i.e.,-COOEt) on a ring nitrogen, while DCL has a hydrogen atom on that ring nitrogen:

Loratadine ('233 patent)   DCL ('716 patent)

Claim 1 of the '716 patent covers DCL (for X = Cl), its fluorine analog, and their salts; claim 3 covers only DCL and its salts:

1. A compound of the formula

or a pharmaceutically acceptable salt thereof, wherein X represents Cl or F.

3. A compound having the structural formula

or a pharmaceutically acceptable salt thereof.

The '233 patent issued on August 4, 1981, over one year before the earliest priority date of the '716 patent, February 15, 1984. The '233 patent is thus prior art to the '716 patent. *See* 35 U.S.C. § 102(b) (2000) ("A person shall be entitled to a patent unless . . . the invention was patented . . . in this or a foreign country . . . more than one year prior to the date of the application for patent in the United States."). The '233 patent discloses a class of compounds including loratadine. The '233 patent claims loratadine in claim 7. The '233 patent claims four other compounds in claims 8–11. . . . The '233 patent does not expressly disclose DCL and does not refer to metabolites of loratadine.

Schering filed suit for infringement [against numerous defendants who sought to market generic versions of lortadine]. The district court concluded that the '233 patent anticipated claims 1 and 3 of the '716 patent under 35 U.S.C. § 102(b). The district court therefore granted the appellees' motions for summary judgment of invalidity. Schering timely appealed to this court. . . .

II.

A.

A patent is invalid for anticipation if a single prior art reference discloses each and every limitation of the claimed invention. *Lewmar Marine, Inc. v. Barient, Inc.*, 827 F.2d 744, 747 (Fed. Cir. 1987). Moreover, a prior art reference may anticipate without disclosing a feature of the claimed invention if that missing characteristic is necessarily present, or inherent, in the single anticipating reference. *Continental Can Co. v. Monsanto Co.*, 948 F.2d 1264, 1268 (Fed. Cir. 1991).

At the outset, this court rejects the contention that inherent anticipation requires recognition in the prior art. Other precedents of this court have held that inherent anticipation does not require that a person of ordinary skill in the art at the time would have recognized the inherent disclosure. *E.g., In re Cruciferous Sprout Litig.*, 301 F.3d 1343, 1351 (Fed. Cir. 2002); *MEHL/Biophile Int'l Corp. v. Milgraum*, 192 F.3d 1362, 1366 (Fed. Cir. 1999) ("Where ... the result is a necessary consequence of what was deliberately intended, it is of no import that the article's authors did not appreciate the results."); *Atlas Powder Co. v. Ireco, Inc.*, 190 F.3d at 1342, 1348–49 (Fed. Cir. 1999) ("Because 'sufficient aeration' was inherent in the prior art, it is irrelevant that the prior art did not recognize the key aspect of [the] invention.... An inherent structure, composition, or function is not necessarily known."). Thus, recognition by a person of ordinary skill in the art before the critical date of the '716 patent is not required to show anticipation by inherency. The district court therefore did not err in allowing for later recognition of the inherent characteristics of the prior art '233 patent.

Contrary to Schering's contention, *Continental Can* does not stand for the proposition that an inherent feature of a prior art reference must be perceived as such by a person of ordinary skill in the art before the critical date. In *Continental Can*, this court vacated summary judgment of anticipation of claims reciting a plastic bottle with hollow ribs over a prior art reference disclosing a plastic bottle. The record contained conflicting expert testimony about whether the ribs of the prior art plastic bottle were solid. The accused infringer's expert testified that the prior art plastic bottle was made by blow molding, a process that would inherently produce hollow ribs. The patentee's experts testified that the prior art plastic bottle had solid ribs. The patentee disputed whether the blow molding inherently produced hollow ribs. Given the disputed material fact, this court vacated the summary judgment as improper. *Continental Can* makes no reference to whether the inherent feature, hollow ribs, was recognized before or after the critical date of the patent at issue. Read in context, *Continental Can* stands for the proposition that inherency, like anticipation itself, requires a determination of the meaning of the prior art. Thus, a court may consult artisans of ordinary skill to ascertain their understanding about subject matter disclosed by the prior art, including features inherent in the prior art. A court may resolve factual questions about the subject matter in the prior art by examining the reference through the eyes of a person of ordinary skill in the art, among other sources of evidence about the meaning of the prior art. Thus, in *Continental Can*, this court did not require past recognition of the inherent feature, but only allowed recourse to opinions of skilled artisans to determine the scope of the prior art reference.

Cases dealing with "accidental, unwitting, and unappreciated" anticipation also do not show that inherency requires recognition. *See Eibel Process Co. v. Minn. & Ontario Paper Co.*, 261 U.S. 45 (1923); *Tilghman v. Proctor*, 102 U.S. 707 (1880). In contrast to the present case, the record in *Eibel* and *Tilghman* did not show that the prior art produced the claimed subject matter. The patent at issue in *Tilghman* claimed a method of forming free fatty acids and glycerine by heating fats with water at high pressure. In *Tilghman*, the record did not show conclusively that the claimed process occurred in the prior art. In reviewing the prior art, the Court referred hypothetically to possible disclosure of the claimed process. For example, the Court stated "[w]e do not regard the accidental formation of fat acid in Perkins's steam cylinder . . . (if the scum which rose on the water issuing from the ejection pipe was fat acid) as of any consequence in this inquiry." *Tilghman*, 102 U.S. at 711. In *Eibel*, the Court found no evidence of the claimed subject matter in the prior art. *Eibel*, 261 U.S. at 66 ("[W]e find no evidence that any pitch of the wire . . . had brought about such a result . . . and . . . if it had done so under unusual conditions, accidental results, not intended and not appreciated, do not constitute anticipation.").

In the context of accidental anticipation, DCL is not formed accidentally or under unusual conditions when loratadine is ingested. The record shows that DCL necessarily and inevitably forms from loratadine under normal conditions. DCL is a necessary consequence of administering loratadine to patients. The record also shows that DCL provides a useful result, because it serves as an active non-drowsy antihistamine. In sum, this court's precedent does not require a skilled artisan to recognize the inherent characteristic in the prior art that anticipates the claimed invention.

B.

This court recognizes that this may be a case of first impression, because the prior art supplies no express description of any part of the claimed subject matter. The prior art '233 patent does not disclose any compound that is identifiable as DCL. In this court's prior inherency cases, a single prior art reference generally contained an incomplete description of the anticipatory subject matter, i.e., a partial description missing certain aspects. Inherency supplied the missing aspect of the description. Upon proof that the missing description is inherent in the prior art, that single prior art reference placed the claimed subject matter in the public domain. This case does not present the issue of a missing feature of the claimed invention. Rather, the new structure in this case, DCL, is not described by the prior '233 patent.

Patent law nonetheless establishes that a prior art reference which expressly or inherently contains each and every limitation of the claimed subject matter anticipates and invalidates. *See, e.g., EMI Group N. Am., Inc., v. Cypress Semiconductor Corp.*, 268 F.3d 1342, 1350 (Fed. Cir. 2001) ("A prior art reference anticipates a patent claim if the reference discloses, either expressly or inherently, all of the limitations of the claim."); *Verdegaal Bros., Inc. v. Union Oil Co. of Cal.*, 814 F.2d 628, 631 (Fed. Cir. 1987) ("A claim is anticipated only if each and every element as set forth in the claim is found, either expressly or inherently described, in a single prior art reference."). In these prior cases, however, inherency was only necessary to supply a single missing limitation that was not expressly disclosed in the prior art. This case, as explained before, asks this court to find anticipation when the entire structure of the claimed subject matter is inherent in the prior art.

Because inherency places subject matter in the public domain as well as an express disclosure, the inherent disclosure of the entire claimed subject matter anticipates as well as inherent disclosure of a single feature of the claimed subject matter. The extent of the inherent disclosure does not limit its anticipatory effect. In general, a limitation or the entire invention is inherent and in the public domain if it is the "natural result flowing from" the explicit disclosure of the prior art.

In reaching this conclusion, this court is aware of *In re Seaborg*, 328 F.2d 996 (CCPA 1964). In that case, this court's predecessor considered claims drawn to an isotope of americium made by nuclear reaction in light of a prior art patent disclosing a similar nuclear reaction process but with no disclosure of the claimed isotope. The court reversed a United States Patent and Trademark Office rejection of the claims for lack of novelty. This court's predecessor found that the prior art process did not anticipate the claims because the process would have produced at most one billionth of a gram of the isotope in forty tons of radioactive material, i.e., the isotope would have been undetectable. *Id.* at 998–99 ("[T]he claimed product, if it was produced in the Fermi process, was produced in such minuscule amounts and under such conditions that its presence was undetectable."). In this case, DCL forms in readily detectable amounts as shown by the extensive record evidence of testing done on humans to verify the formation of DCL upon ingestion of loratadine.

This court sees no reason to modify the general rule for inherent anticipation in a case where inherency supplies the entire anticipatory subject matter. The patent law principle "that which would literally infringe if later in time anticipates if earlier," *Bristol–Myers Squibb Co. v. Ben Venue Labs., Inc.*, 246 F.3d 1368, 1378 (Fed. Cir. 2001), bolsters this conclusion. Similarly, "if granting patent protection on the disputed claim would allow the patentee to exclude the public from practicing the prior art, then that claim is anticipated." *Atlas Powder*, 190 F.3d at 1346. "The public remains free to make, use, or sell prior art compositions or processes, regardless of whether or not they understand their complete makeup or the underlying scientific principles which allow them to operate. The doctrine of anticipation by inherency, among other doctrines, enforces that basic principle." *Id.* at 1348. Thus, inherency operates to anticipate entire inventions as well as single limitations within an invention.

Turning to this case, the use of loratadine would infringe claims 1 and 3 of the '716 patent covering the metabolite DCL. This court has recognized that a person may infringe a claim to a metabolite if the person ingests a compound that metabolizes to form the metabolite. *See Hoechst–Roussel Pharms., Inc. v. Lehman*, 109 F.3d 756, 759 (Fed. Cir. 1997) ("[T]he right to exclude may arise from the fact that when administered, [the accused product] metabolizes into another product

... which Hoechst has claimed."); *see also Zenith Labs., Inc. v. Bristol–Myers Squibb Co.*, 19 F.3d 1418, 1421–22 (Fed. Cir. 1994) (stating that a compound claim could cover a compound formed upon ingestion). An identical metabolite must then anticipate if earlier in time than the claimed compound.

The record shows that the metabolite of the prior art loratadine is the same compound as the claimed invention. Claims 1 and 3 are compound claims in which individual compounds are claimed in the alternative in Markush format. DCL is within the scope of claims 1 and 3. Because the prior art metabolite inherently disclosed DCL, claims 1 and 3 are anticipated and invalid. In other words, the record shows that a patient ingesting loratadine would necessarily metabolize that compound to DCL. That later act would thus infringe claims 1 and 3. Thus, a prior art reference showing administration of loratadine to a patient anticipates claims 1 and 3.

C.

This court next examines whether Schering's secret tests of loratadine before the critical date placed DCL in the public domain. Before the critical date, Schering only tested loratadine in secret. Thus, according to Schering, "DCL was not publicly used, or described in any printed publication, until after February 15, 1983, the critical date for the '716 patent under 35 U.S.C. § 102(b)." Schering thus argues that DCL did not "exist" in the public domain such that DCL could be prior art against the '716 patent.

Anticipation does not require the actual creation or reduction to practice of the prior art subject matter; anticipation requires only an enabling disclosure. *In re Donohue*, 766 F.2d 531, 533 (Fed. Cir. 1985). Thus, actual administration of loratadine to patients before the critical date of the '716 patent is irrelevant. The '233 patent suffices as an anticipatory prior art reference if it discloses in an enabling manner the administration of loratadine to patients.

Thus, this court examines whether the '233 patent contains an enabling disclosure of DCL. A reference may enable one of skill in the art to make and use a compound even if the author or inventor did not actually make or reduce to practice that subject matter. *Bristol–Myers*, 246 F.3d at 1379; *see also In re Donohue*, 766 F.2d at 533 (sustaining an anticipation rejection over a reference disclosing a compound and other references disclosing sufficient information to make that compound). Indeed, information arising after the critical date may show that the claimed subject matter, as disclosed in a prior art reference, "was in the public's possession." *Bristol–Myers*, 246 F.3d at 1379.

An anticipatory reference need only enable subject matter that falls within the scope of the claims at issue, nothing more. To qualify as an enabled reference, the '233 patent need not describe how to make DCL in its isolated form. The '233 patent need only describe how to make

DCL in any form encompassed by a compound claim covering DCL, e.g., DCL as a metabolite in a patient's body. The '233 patent discloses administering loratadine to a patient. A person of ordinary skill in the art could practice the '233 patent without undue experimentation. The inherent result of administering loratadine to a patient is the formation of DCL. The '233 patent thus provides an enabling disclosure for making DCL.

D.

Finally, this court's conclusion on inherent anticipation in this case does not preclude patent protection for metabolites of known drugs. With proper claiming, patent protection is available for metabolites of known drugs. *Cf. In re Kratz,* 592 F.2d 1169, 1174 (CCPA 1979) (stating that a naturally occurring strawberry constituent compound does not anticipate claims to the substantially pure compound); *In re Bergstrom,* 427 F.2d 1394, 1401–02 (CCPA 1970) (stating that a material occurring in nature in less pure form does not anticipate claims to the pure material).

But those metabolites may not receive protection via compound claims. In this case, for instance, claims 1 and 3 broadly encompass compounds defined by structure only. Such bare compound claims include within their scope the recited compounds as chemical species in any surroundings, including within the human body as metabolites of a drug. As this case holds, these broad compound claims are inherently anticipated by a prior art disclosure of a drug that metabolizes into the claimed compound.

A skilled patent drafter, however, might fashion a claim to cover the metabolite in a way that avoids anticipation. For example, the metabolite may be claimed in its pure and isolated form, as in *Kratz* and *Bergstrom,* or as a pharmaceutical composition (e.g., with a pharmaceutically acceptable carrier). The patent drafter could also claim a method of administering the metabolite or the corresponding pharmaceutical composition. The '233 patent would not provide an enabling disclosure to anticipate such claims because, for instance, the '233 patent does not disclose isolation of DCL.

The '716 patent contains claims 5–13 covering pharmaceutical compositions and claims 14–16 covering methods of treating allergic reactions by administering compounds that include DCL. These claims were not found anticipated by the '233 patent.

Editor's Note: *Following a petition, the Federal Circuit decided not to rehear* Schering v. Genenva *en banc. The opinions of two of the judges who dissented from rehearing are reproduced in part below.*

PAULINE NEWMAN, CIRCUIT JUDGE, dissenting from denial of rehearing en banc.

I write to state my concern for the panel's departure from the established law of anticipation. The court holds "anticipated" a novel chemical compound (descarbethoxyloratidine or DCL), a compound not known to the prior art and that did not previously exist. The Schering inventor discovered it *in vivo* as a degradation product of loratidine, isolated it, determined its structure, and found its biologic properties. The panel nonetheless holds that this new compound is unpatentable on the ground of "inherent anticipation."

The law is that a product is "anticipated" if it is not new. Conversely, it is not anticipated if it is new. A new product may of course be unpatentable based on obviousness, but it is not subject to unpatentability for lack of novelty. No precedent supports the position that a product whose existence was not previously known and is not in the prior art is always unpatentable on the ground that it existed undiscovered. If the law is to be changed in this direction it must be done *en banc*.

The panel appears to have reached the correct result of no liability for infringement, but for the wrong reason. According to the briefs, the defendants are doing only what was claimed in the expired loratidine patent, not in suit. However, instead of simply ruling that Schering cannot prevent the practice of the expired patent in accordance with its teachings, the panel strains to hold that this newly discovered, previously unknown product cannot be validly patented. That is not the law. I also point out that the issue here is validity, not infringement.

Note the word "discovery" in the patent statute. "The term 'invention' means invention or discovery." 35 U.S.C. § 100(a). It was and is well understood that an inventor may discover something that already existed. That the thing was there, undiscovered, does not render it "inherently anticipated." The panel's proposed rule may have particular impact on the discovery of biological products. Does the panel intend that no newly discovered product found in an organism can be patented? Such a ruling does not comport with either the patent statute or the incentive purposes of the patent system.

Precedent concerning "anticipation" has dealt with diverse factual situations, applying the common thread that novel subject matter may or may not be patentable, depending on whether it is also unobvious, while subject matter that is not novel cannot be patented. A newly discovered attribute or property of something that was already known is patentable only as a method-of-use, but does not impart patentability to the known product. However, a previously unknown product does not become unpatentable simply because it existed before it was discovered. Precedent deals primarily with application of the law to situations where (1) a single prior art reference teaches all the elements of a product as claimed; in such case, the discovery of a new use or function does not render the product itself patentable; and (2) a single prior art reference does not teach all of the claimed elements; in such case the factual question arises of whether the omitted element is shown elsewhere (in which event the issue is obviousness) or whether the omitted element would have been known to be present in the reference subject matter, in which case the issue is <u>anticipation</u>. For example, in *In re Schreiber*, 128 F.3d 1473 (Fed. Cir. 1997) the applicant sought to patent a conical spout to dispense popped popcorn; the same conical spout was shown in the prior art as an oil dispenser. The product itself was thus held unpatentable as anticipated. In *MEHL/Biophile International Corp. v. Milgraum*, 192 F.3d 1362 (Fed. Cir. 1999) the prior art showed all of the claimed steps of laser irradiation of hair follicles, but did not mention hair removal; the court held that this effect was inherent in the prior art process, and that the same process steps could not be claimed, the court stating that "nothing in the claim limits the method's reach to human skin." *Id.* at 1366. In *Titanium Metals Corp. v. Banner*, 778 F.2d 775 (Fed. Cir. 1985) the court held that the discovery of the property of corrosion resistance of a known alloy did not impart patentability to the known alloy, for the property was inherent in the alloy.

In all applications of the law of <u>anticipation, the initial consideration is whether the thing that is claimed was disclosed in a single prior art reference</u>. When all of the elements of the claim are not shown in the prior art, <u>precedent requires that the missing element was nonetheless known to be present in the subject matter of the reference, and that the claim is directed to the known subject matter.</u> Although the panel now purports to disavow this precedent, such a change of law requires *en banc* action of the court. See, for example, the precedent represented by and cited in such cases as *Continental Can Co. USA v. Monsanto Co.*, 948 F.2d 1264 (Fed. Cir. 1991), where the law of "inherency" is applied to subject matter wherein all of the elements of the claim are not shown in the prior art:

> To serve as an anticipation when the reference is silent about the asserted inherent characteristic, such gap in the reference may be filled with recourse to extrinsic evidence. Such evidence must make clear that the missing descriptive matter is necessarily present in the thing described in the reference, and that it would be so recognized by persons of ordinary skill. . . .

> This modest flexibility in the rule that "anticipation" requires that every element of the claims appear in a single reference accommodates situations where the common knowledge of technologists is not recorded in the reference; that is, where technological facts are known to those in the field of the invention, albeit not known to judges.

Id. at 1269–70. The analytic tool of "inherency" allows determination of whether subject matter that is not taught in the single reference was nonetheless known in the field of the invention. This was acknowledged in *EMI Group North America, Inc. v. Cypress Semiconductor Corp.*, 268 F.3d 1342 (Fed. Cir. 2001):

> This requirement, that a person of ordinary skill in the art must recognize that the missing descriptive matter is necessarily present in the reference, may be sensible for claims that recite limitations of

structure, compositions of matter, and method steps which could be inherently found in the prior art. Such recognition by one of ordinary skill may be important for establishing that the descriptive matter would inherently exist for every combination of a claim's limitation.

Id. at 1350–51. The panel now contradicts this body of precedent, stating that it "rejects the contention that inherent anticipation requires recognition in the prior art." A rejection of precedent requires *en banc* action, not panel disruption.

No reference shows the claimed descarbethoxyloratidine, or that a person of ordinary skill would have known that DCL is formed *in vivo* upon ingestion of loratidine. Precedent is directly contrary to the panel's holding that although no one knew of the existence of DCL, it is unpatentable because it in fact existed.

Whether it is desirable new policy to bar the patentability of products that have not yet been discovered is a result I seriously doubt. The court should speak with one voice on this important question. Thus I must, respectfully, dissent from the court's refusal to review this case *en banc*.

NOTES

1. **Infringement by Digestion?** For medical reasons, sound drug development accounts for the creation and behavior of metabolites. However, identification of metabolites also holds significant intellectual property implications. In a patenting strategy that the *Wall Street Journal* dubbed the "metabolite defense," Gardiner Harris & Chris Adams, *The 'Metabolite Defense,'* WALL STREET J. A1 (July 12, 2001), brand-name drug companies would procure patent protection upon metabolites. Even if first-generation patents on the parent drug had expired, generic competitors could be sued on the grounds that they sought to induce infringement of the metabolite patent by encouraging patients to ingest the pill, and therefore internally generate the metabolite. This technique is among many that patent proprietors sometimes term "lifecycle management," while critics prefer the phrase "evergreening of patent protection" instead.

Although some observers view the holding of *Schering v. Geneva* as stretching the inherency doctrine to its limits, the opinion placed significant limitations upon a practice some public health advocates viewed as abusive. One potential critique of the opinion is that it creates uncertainties regarding any compound with pharmacological properties. Under *Schering v. Geneva*, a patent directed towards a previously unknown compound may be considered anticipated if the compound is later discovered to be a metabolite of a compound known to the prior art.

2. **Benefit versus Recognition?** Under the *Schering v. Geneva* holding, an inventor cannot obtain a patent in circumstances where members of the public have already benefited from the invention, even if they don't know precisely how that benefit was conferred. The jurists who dissented from the denial of

rehearing *en banc* instead asserted that public recognition of the invention is required for inherent anticipation to occur. The patent law encounters this problem of hidden information in other contexts. For example, you will learn in the next chapter of this casebook that a trade secret does not qualify as "prior art" under § 102(a) or (b). As a result, if (1) inventor A invents a new technology but maintains it as a trade secret, (2) inventor B independently invents the same technology at a later time, but files a patent application, the outcome is that inventor B obtains the patent and may charge inventor A with infringement. Does that settled patent law doctrine support the majority or the dissenters in *Schering v. Geneva?* For further discussion of the inherency doctrine in patent law, see Dan L. Burk & Mark A. Lemley, *Inherency*, 47 WM. & MARY L. REV. 371 (2005).

3. Is the Skilled Artisan Always Relevant to Inherency? In *Continental Can,* the Federal Circuit stated that anticipation by inherency requires "that the missing descriptive matter is necessarily present in the thing described in the reference, and that it would be so recognized by persons of ordinary skill." At another point, the Circuit emphasized that inherency accommodates "the common knowledge of technologists . . . not recorded in the reference." In a later case, *EMI Group of N. Am. Inc. v. Cypress Semiconductor Corp.*, 268 F.3d 1342, 1350–51 (Fed.Cir.2001), the Federal Circuit clarified these references:

> This requirement, that a person of ordinary skill in the art must recognize that the missing descriptive matter is necessarily present in the reference, may be sensible for claims that recite limitations of structure, compositions of matter, and method steps which could be inherently found in the prior art. . . . Theoretical mechanisms or rules of natural law that are recited in a claim, that themselves are not patentable, however, do not need to be recognized by one of ordinary skill in the art for a finding of inherency. A person of ordinary skill does not need to recognize that a method or structure behaves according to a law of nature in order to fully and effectively practice the method or structure.

A hypothetical example clarifies this principle. Humans lit fires for thousands of years before realizing that oxygen is necessary to create and maintain a flame. The first person to discover the necessity of oxygen certainly could not have obtained a valid patent claim for "a method of making a fire by lighting a flame in the presence of oxygen." Even if prior art on lighting fires did not disclose the importance of oxygen and one of ordinary skill in the art did not know about the importance of oxygen, understanding this law of nature would not give the discoverer a right to exclude others from practicing the prior art of making fires.

4. Comparative Approaches. In litigation in Germany, England, and the United States over a patent relating to the anti-histamine drug terfenadine, commonly known as Seldane, the question of whether the basic patent covering terfenadine inherently disclosed the patented metabolite was raised. In Germany and in the United States the courts avoided the issue by narrowly interpreting the claims, but this route was not taken by the House of Lords in *Merrell*

Dow Pharmaceuticals Inc. v. H.N. Norton & Co. Ltd., [1996] R.P.C. 76. Instead the House dealt directly with the issue of inherent anticipation.

Merrell Dow patented terfenadine in many countries in the 1970s. Subsequently, Merrell Dow did further work on how terfenadine functioned in humans. It discovered that it was 99.5% metabolized in the liver and then isolated the key metabolite formed in the liver, the patented acid metabolite. Merrell Dow then asserted the patent on the acid metabolite against Norton. It charged that Norton, who was selling terfenadine to people who, when they ingested terfenadine, created in their livers the patented acid metabolite. Thus, according to Merrell Dow, those who ingested terfenadine were direct infringers and Norton a contributory infringer. The House of Lords held that the acid metabolite was inherently described in the original terfenadine patent because it teaches that the ingestion of terfenadine will produce a chemical reaction in the body. Hence, it was made as a direct consequence of ingesting terfenadine. Lord Hoffmann's speech to the House of Lords included the following explanation:

> In this case, knowledge of the acid metabolite was in my view made available to the public by the terfenadine specification under the description "a part of the chemical reaction in the human body produced by the ingestion of terfenadine and having an anti-histamine effect." Was this description sufficient to make the product part of the state of the art? For many purposes, obviously not. It would not enable anyone to work the invention in the form of isolating or synthesizing the acid metabolite. But for the purpose of working the invention by making the acid metabolite in the body by ingesting terfenadine, I think it plainly was. It enabled the public to work the invention by making the acid metabolite in their livers. The fact that they would not have been able to describe the chemical reaction in these terms does not mean that they were not working the invention. Whether or not a person is working a product invention is an objective fact independent of what he knows or thinks about what he is doing.

Anticipation Exercise

You are a prior art searcher working for a private firm, Skillful Searchers, Inc., located in Crystal City, Virginia. On June 1, 2009, you receive a call from Eve Klayton, a patent attorney who is a frequent client. She requests that you search through prior patents and technical literature for a description of a toothbrush with two key features:

>   (1) bristles fabricated from an artificial fiber, known in the trade as NYLANON, which supposedly is particularly effective at removing plaque; and

>   (2) a specially-shaped handle which is easy to grip.

Klayton explains that she is trying to cite references against the '123 patent, which was filed on January 19, 2008. Klayton ideally seeks an anticipating reference, and in particular one under § 102(b).

Your searches through patents and printed publication are unavailing. However, while surfing on the Internet one evening, you discover a home page entitled "Fiendish Fluoridators." The home page appears to comprise a collection of various textual files relating to the study of dental instruments, including toothbrushes. One of the files on the "Fiendish Fluoridators" home page contains the following passage:

> Beyond education on the proper use of a toothbrush, one can improve the effectiveness of brushing through improved toothbrush design. Experiments have demonstrated that plaque removal rates are greatly increased where toothbrush bristles are fabricated from an artificial fiber called "NYLANON." Additionally, certain **toothbrush handle designs** have increased toothbrush effectiveness.

You recognize that the highlighted words comprise an invitation to employ "hypertext"; by clicking on your mouse, you can retrieve further information on the selected item. Intrigued, you move your cursor to the highlighted words and click on your mouse. Immediately, a second file appears on your computer screen. The second file originates from a different home page, which is entitled "Healthy Smiles." The second file provides diagrams and a detailed textual discussion of the precise handle design claimed in the '123 patent.

Further research indicates that "The DDS Catalog" home page was created on June 7, 2004, while the "Healthy Smiles" home page was created on May 10, 2005. Neither home page has since been modified, meaning that the files you accessed were undisputably available on the Internet as of those respective dates. You also learn that "The DDS Catalog" home page is based on a computer system in Davis, California, while the "Healthy Smiles" home page originates from a computer in Toronto, Canada.

Do your findings on the Internet constitute an anticipating reference under § 102(b)?

CHAPTER FIVE

STATUTORY BARS

■ ■ ■

The previous chapter of this casebook discussed the patent system's core value: novelty. Embedded in the statutory provision defining novelty and prior art for obviousness, 35 U.S.C.A. § 102, is a provision that creates statutory bars, namely subsection (b). This provision defeats any patent if the invention therein was "in public use or on sale in this country, more than one year prior to the filing date." Although simply stated, the policy rationales behind § 102(b) bear some discussion at the outset.

The reason for the statutory bars becomes apparent by comparing the "first to invent" patent system of the United States with the "first to file" patent systems in the rest of the world. This book discusses that contrast in more detail later, but at this juncture it suffices to note that every patent system in the world outside the United States sponsors a "race to the Patent Office" recordation system similar to that of domestic real property law. Under these "first to file" regimes, the inventor who first files a patent application obtains the patent, even if another actually invented the technology first. The United States, on the other hand, promises a patent to the first inventor, regardless of whether someone else files an application earlier claiming the same invention. In the United States, only the first inventor gets a patent, not someone who filed earlier.

With that understanding, the reason for 102(b) becomes clear by considering a hypothetical. Assume that you invent a new pill that corrects cartilage deterioration by growing new cartilage. Of course, your invention has its problems. For instance, it is expensive to make and has side effects like protruding noses and drooping ear lobes. What would you do? In a pure "first to invent" system, the answer is simple. You would wait. You would let others independently create the same invention, develop the expensive manufacturing and marketing capabilities, and solve the side effects problems. Then you would step in, claim your exclusive right as the first inventor, and demand a sizeable share of the new pharmaceutical enterprise. A "pure" first to invent system could also foster another unsavory strategy. In the same cartilage pill hypothetical, the inventor could bring the product to market and begin to reap a profit only to file for a patent many years later when competition

180

arises. In the meantime, the inventor has prolonged indefinitely the limited time of the exclusive right. Under a pure "first to invent" system, nothing would forbid either strategy.

Because of the § 102 (b) statutory bars, the United States patent system is not a "pure" first to file regime. Instead these bars encourage timely filing and disclosure of inventive activity. Under section 102 (b), an inventor must file within a year of any public use or offer to sell the invention. Thus, the natural drive to use and profit from an invention also promotes timely patent filing. As this chapter shows, anyone, including individuals unknown to the inventor, can defeat the patent by placing the invention in public use or on sale. Thus, due to section 102 (b), inventors risk loss of their exclusive right if they attempt to adopt a waiting strategy.

Section 102(b) is not entirely prohibitory. The statute also provides a distinct advantage to inventors. The language of § 102(b) keys the patent defeating events to the filing date. The point in time one year before the filing date is termed the "critical date." Therefore, statutorily barred activities, like publishing the invention in a scientific article or offering it for sale, even a day before that critical date, defeat the patent. This effect sounds onerous, but in practice § 102(b) provides a one-year "grace period." This grace period permits the inventor to weigh the advantages of patent protection, to perfect the invention, and to draft a patent application. Moreover, the inventor, in most instances, controls the outset of that grace period. From the time the inventor publicizes or commercializes the invention, he knows that he has one year in which to file an application. Of course, the inventor must remember that third party activities will also start the one-year clock running.

Besides setting a novelty standard, § 102 as a whole also defines the categories of prior art for obviousness determinations. With that in mind, the statutory bars of § 102 (b) correct one other defect in first-to-invent systems. This correction is described in 1 MARTIN J. ADELMAN, PATENT LAW PERSPECTIVES, § 2.3[7.§ 6] at n.36 (2d ed. 1992):

> Commentators often remark that the United States has a first-to-invent rather than a first-to-file system. However, a pure first-to-invent system makes it difficult if not impossible for a member of the public to determine the prior art against which the claimed advance must be judged at least with respect to activities within a few years of the filing date. Section 102(b) dramatically changes this situation. Thus, in reality the United States has a modified first-to-file system in that it affixes prior art status to specific activities dated more than one year before the effective United States filing date irrespective of the invention date. Of course, additional prior art may be generated by activities within the one-year period that occur before the invention date and come within the definition of 35 U.S.C.A. § 102(a). In addition, 35 U.S.C.A. §§ 102(e), (f) and (g) also generate prior art. Nevertheless, a basic and large class of prior

[margin note: 102(b) creates prior art]

art is created by Section 102(b) that cannot be challenged by the inventor based on his date of invention.

As you study § 102(b) ask yourself whether this is the unspoken basis for the expansive interpretation that the courts have given to this section.

[margin note: Pennock v Dialogue]

As a matter of history, the first U.S. Patent Act to contain a statutory bar was the 1836 Act. The 1836 provision, however, was actually codification of the famous case of *Pennock v. Dialogue*, 27 U.S. (2 Pet.) 1 (1829). In this case, the most renowned Supreme Court Justice in matters of patent law, Joseph Story, recognized that a first-to-invent patent system has the inherent flaws discussed above. Justice Story stated the problem in these terms:

[margin note: Story explains problem w/o statutory bars]

> If an inventor should be permitted to hold back from the knowledge of the public the secrets of his invention; if he should for a long period of years retain the monopoly, and make, and sell his invention publicly, and thus gather the whole profits of it, relying upon his superior skill and knowledge of the structure; and then, and then only, when the danger of competition should force him to secure the exclusive right, he should be allowed to take out a patent, and thus exclude the public from any farther use than what should be derived under it during his fourteen years; it would materially retard the progress of science and the useful arts, and give a premium to those who should be least prompt to communicate their discoveries.

[margin note: Story enacting a statutory bars]

With this recognition, Justice Story also proscribed the solution to this problem:

> [I]f he [the inventor] shall put [the invention] into public use, or sell it for public use before he applies for a patent, ... this should furnish another bar to his claim.

[margin note: original 2 year grace period]

With this famous case as the foundation, the 1836 law enacted a statutory bar. The 1839 Act clarified that a third party, unknown to the inventor, may place an invention into public use or on sale and also ameliorated the bar by enacting a 2–year grace period.

[margin note: Europe and Japan – no grace periods]

[margin note: Canada – 1 year.]

Although this introduction has emphasized the corrective function of the bars in a first to file regime, foreign systems also have statutory bars with the filing date as the trigger. These "first to file" systems, however, offer a grace period, if at all, under more limited circumstances. Due to the beneficial aspects of section 102 (b), a United States inventor can sell a commercial embodiment of his invention as long as he files an application within one year. In Europe and Japan, such a sale before filing ordinarily defeats the patent. Canada has the most enlightened grace period in a first-to-file patent system. Under the Canadian system, disclosure of an invention to the public by an applicant or by a person who obtained knowledge of the invention, directly or indirectly, from the applicant, is not patent defeating if done within a year of the filing date. See William Lesser, *Grace Periods in First-to-File Countries*, 3 EUR. INTELL. PROP. REV. 81 (1987).

The "public use or on sale" statutory bars of § 102(b) divide into two sorts: those activities performed by the applicant, and those by third parties. This Chapter approaches the cases in that order. This Chapter will then turn to the "patented" and "printed publication" bars, as well as consider the territorial limitations set out in § 102(b).

Beyond § 102(b), the remaining paragraphs of § 102 provide for additional patent-defeating events. Abandonment of an invention to the public amounts to a forfeiture of patent rights under § 102(c). Section 102(d) creates a statutory bar if the United States application has not been filed within one year of a foreign application on the same invention that ultimately ripened into a foreign patent right.

§ 5.1   APPLICANT ACTIVITIES § 102(b)

§ 5.1[a]   "PUBLIC USE"

EGBERT v. LIPPMANN

United States Supreme Court, 1881
104 U.S. (14 Otto) 333

MR. JUSTICE WOODS delivered the opinion of the court.

This suit was brought for an alleged infringement of the complainant's reissued letters-patent, No. 5216, dated Jan. 7, 1873, for an improvement in corset-springs.

The original letters bear date July 17, 1866, and were issued to Samuel H. Barnes. The reissue was made to the complainant, under her then name, Frances Lee Barnes, executrix of the original patentee.

The specification for the reissue declares:

"This invention consists in forming the springs of corsets of two or more metallic plates, placed one upon another, and so connected as to prevent them from sliding off each other laterally or edgewise, and at the same time admit of their playing or sliding upon each other, in the direction of their length or longitudinally, whereby their flexibility and elasticity are greatly increased, while at the same time much strength is obtained."

The second claim is as follows:

"A pair of corset-springs, each member of the pair being composed or two or more metallic plates, placed one on another, and fastened together at their centres, and so connected at or near each end that they can move or play on each other in the direction of their length."

The bill alleges that Barnes was the original and first inventor of the improvement covered by the reissued letters-patent, and that it had not, at the time of his application for the original letters, been for more than two years in public use or on sale, with his consent or allowance.

The answer takes issue on this averment and also denies infringement. On a final hearing the court dismissed the bill, and the complainant appealed.

We have, therefore, to consider whether the defense that the patented invention had, with the consent of the inventor, been publicly used for more than two years prior to his application for the original letters, is sustained by the testimony in the record.

The sixth, seventh, and fifteenth sections of the act of July 4, 1836, c. 357 (5 Stat. 117), as qualified by the seventh section of the act of March 8, 1839, c. 88 (id. 353), were in force at the date of his application. Their effect is to render letters-patent invalid if the invention which they cover was in public use, with the consent and allowance of the inventor, for more than two years prior to his application. Since the passage of the act of 1839 it has been strenuously contended that the public use of an invention for more than two years before such application, even without his consent and allowance, renders the letters-patent therefor void.

It is unnecessary in this case to decide this question, for the alleged use of the invention covered by the letters-patent to Barnes is conceded to have been with his express consent.

The evidence on which the defendants rely to establish a prior public use of the invention consists mainly of the testimony of the complainant.

She testifies that Barnes invented the improvement covered by his patent between January and May, 1855; that between the dates named the witness and her friend Miss Cugier were complaining of the breaking of their corset-steels. Barnes, who was present, and was an intimate friend of the witness, said he thought he could make her a pair that would not break. At their next interview he presented her with a pair of corset-steels which he himself had made. The witness wore these steels a long time. In 1858 Barnes made and presented to her another pair, which she also wore a long time. When the corsets in which these steels were used wore out, the witness ripped them open and took out the steels and put them in new corsets. This was done several times.

It is admitted, and, in fact, is asserted, by complainant, that these steels embodied the invention afterwards patented by Barnes and covered by the reissued letters-patent on which this suit is brought.

Joseph H. Sturgis, another witness for complainant, testifies that in 1863 Barnes spoke to him about two inventions made by himself, one of which was a corset-steel, and that he went to the house of Barnes to see them. Before this time, and after the transactions testified to by the complainant, Barnes and she had intermarried. Barnes said his wife had a pair of steels made according to his invention in the corsets which she was then wearing, and if she would take them off he would show them to witness. Mrs. Barnes went out, and returned with a pair of corsets and a pair of scissors, and ripped the corsets open and took out the steels. Barnes then explained to witness how they were made and used.

The question for our decision is, whether this testimony shows a public use within the meaning of the statute.

We observe, in the first place, that to constitute the public use of an invention it is not necessary that more than one of the patented articles should be publicly used. The use of a great number may tend to strengthen the proof, but one well-defined case of such use is just as effectual to annul the patent as many. *McClurg v. Kingsland*, 1 How. 202; *Consolidated Fruit–Jar Co. v. Wright*, 94 U.S. 92; *Pitts v. Hall*, 2 Blatchf. 229. For instance, if the inventor of a mower, a printing-press, or a railway-car makes and sells only one of the articles invented by him, and allows the vendee to use it for two years, without restriction or limitation, the use is just as public as if he had sold and allowed the use of a great number.

We remark, secondly, that, whether the use of an invention is public or private does not necessarily depend upon the number of persons to whom its use is known. If an inventor, having made his device, gives or sells it to another, to be used by the donee or vendee, without limitation or restriction, or injunction of secrecy, and it is so used, such use is public, even though the use and knowledge of the use may be confined to one person.

We say, thirdly, that some inventions are by their very character only capable of being used where they cannot be seen or observed by the public eye. An invention may consist of a lever or spring, hidden in the running gear of a watch, or of a rachet, shaft, or cog-wheel covered from view in the recesses of a machine for spinning or weaving. Nevertheless, if its inventor sells a machine of which his invention forms a part, and allows it to be used without restriction of any kind, the use is a public one. So, on the other hand, a use necessarily open to public view, if made in good faith solely to test the qualities of the invention, and for the purpose of experiment, is not a public use within the meaning of the statute. *Elizabeth v. Pavement Company*, 97 U.S. 126; *Shaw v. Cooper*, 7 Pet. 292.

Tested by these principles, we think the evidence of the complainant herself shows that for more than two years before the application for the original letters there was, by the consent and allowance of Barnes, a public use of the invention, covered by them. He made and gave to her two pairs of corset-steels, constructed according to his device, one in 1855 and one in 1858. They were presented to her for use. He imposed no obligation of secrecy, nor any condition or restriction whatever. They were not presented for the purpose of experiment, nor to test their qualities. No such claim is set up in her testimony. The invention was at the time complete, and there is no evidence that it was afterwards changed or improved. The donee of the steels used them for years for the purpose and in the manner designed by the inventor. They were not capable of any other use. She might have exhibited them to any person, or made other steels of the same kind, and used or sold them without violating any condition or restriction imposed on her by the inventor.

According to the testimony of the complainant, the invention was completed and put into use in 1855. The inventor slept on his rights for eleven years. Letters-patent were not applied for till March, 1866. In the mean time, the invention had found its way into general, and almost universal, use. A great part of the record is taken up with the testimony of the manufacturers and venders of corset-steels, showing that before he applied for letters the principle of his device was almost universally used in the manufacture of corset-steels. It is fair to presume that having learned from this general use that there was some value in his invention, he attempted to resume, by his application, what by his acts he had clearly dedicated to the public.

"An abandonment of an invention to the public may be evinced by the conduct of the inventor at any time, even within the two years named in the law. The effect of the law is that no such consequence will necessarily follow from the invention being in public use or on sale, with the inventor's consent and allowance, at any time within the two years before his application; but that, if the invention is in public use or on sale prior to that time, it will be conclusive evidence of abandonment, and the patent will be void." *Elizabeth v. Pavement Company, supra*.

We are of opinion that the defense of two years' public use, by the consent and allowance of the inventor, before he made application for letters-patent, is satisfactorily established by the evidence.

Mr. Justice Miller dissenting.

A private use with consent, which could lead to no copy or reproduction of the machine, which taught the nature of the invention to no one but the party to whom such consent was given, which left the public at large as ignorant of this as it was before the author's discovery, was no abandonment to the public, and did not defeat his claim for a patent. If the little steep spring inserted in a single pair of corsets, and used by only one woman, covered by her outer-clothing, and in a position always withheld from public observation, is a public use of that piece of steel, I am at a loss to know the line between a private and a public use.

The opinion argues that the use was public, because, with the consent of the inventor to its use, no limitation was imposed in regard to its use in public. It may be well imagined that a prohibition to the party so permitted against exposing her use of the steel spring to public observation would have been supposed to be a piece of irony. An objection quite the opposite of this suggested by the opinion is, that the invention was incapable of a public use. That is to say, that while the statute says the right to the patent can only be defeated by a use which is public, it is equally fatal to the claim, when it is permitted to be used at all, that the article can never be used in public.

I cannot on such reasoning as this eliminate from the statute the word public, and disregard its obvious importance in connection with the remainder of the act, for the purpose of defeating a patent otherwise meritorious.

NOTES

1.   The Meaning of "Public." In what sense was the use by Ms. Barnes a public one? Was this use truly "public," or simply not secret, i.e., a "non-informing" use? How can a use be "public" if only a few members of the community know about it? Consider elements that might be relevant: the number of observers, the intent of the inventor, the number of uses of the invention, and the extent to which observers understand the disclosed technology. Why should a non-commercial, non-informing use be patent defeating?

2.   Dissecting Disclosure. Beyond the ordinary meaning of the term "public," how does *Egbert* impact a fundamental goal of the patent system, the disclosure of technological advance? If an inventor's earlier use reveals a given technology to only an exceedingly small subset of the public that is technologically unsophisticated, and yet this public use results in the unavailability of patent protection, how will the technology be disclosed to an appreciative public in any sense? Note that a non-informing use is not patent defeating in either Europe or Japan.

3.   Confidentiality Restrictions? What Form? At several points in *Egbert*, the Supreme Court noted that the invention entered use "without limitation or restriction, or injunction of secrecy...." In the first place, would the results of this case have changed if the inventor had requested confidentiality of Ms. Barnes? What form would that confidentiality agreement need to take?

In a modern public use case, the inventor of a famous cube puzzle built models of his invention as early as 1957 and used them personally. In 1968, he built a working prototype of his puzzle. He brought it to work where his boss and a few close colleagues saw it and used it. The boss liked the puzzle. In March of 1969, Nichols, the inventor, sold to his employer, Moleculon, all rights in the puzzle in exchange for a share of any proceeds. On March 3, 1970, Nichols filed a patent application on behalf of Moleculon. The patent issued two years later. In a later infringement suit, the defendant defended on the basis of public use. The Federal Circuit, speaking through Judge Baldwin, distinguished *Egbert*:

> The district court distinguished *Egbert* because here Nichols had not given over the invention for free and unrestricted use by another person. Based on the personal relationships and surrounding circumstances, the court found that Nichols at all times retained control over the puzzle's use and the distribution of information concerning it. The court characterized Nichol's use as private and for his own enjoyment. We see neither legal error in the analysis nor clear error in the findings.

> As for [the boss's] brief use of the puzzle, the court found that Nichols retained control even though he and [the boss] had not entered into any

express confidentiality agreement. The court held, and we agree, that the presence or absence of such an agreement is not determinative of the public use issue.

Moleculon Research Corp. v. CBS, Inc., 793 F.2d 1261, 1266 (Fed.Cir.1986). Is a confidentiality agreement as important as *Egbert* seemed to say? If close personal relationships can substitute for a confidentiality agreement, why did Egbert lose? After all, Ms. Barnes was the inventor's "intimate friend," whom he later married.

4. The Equities. Could the Court's decision have been motivated by the eleven-year delay between the filing date and the time the inventor knew of Ms. Barnes' use? Suppose a subsequent inventor of corset steels attempted to obtain a patent on the technology; would the same equities apply? Issues of third party activities are taken up in § 5.2 of this text.

METALLIZING ENGINEERING CO. v. KENYON BEARING & AUTO PARTS

Circuit Court of Appeals, Second Circuit, 1946
153 F.2d 516

Before L. Hand, Augustus N. Hand, and Clark, Circuit Judges.

L. Hand, Circuit Judge.

The defendants appeal from the usual decree holding valid and infringed all but three of the claims of a reissued patent, issued to the plaintiff's assignor, Meduna; the original patent issued on May 25, 1943, upon an application filed on August 6, 1942. The patent is for the process of "so conditioning a metal surface that the same is, as a rule, capable of bonding thereto applied spray metal to a higher degree than is normally procurable with hitherto known practices." It is primarily useful for building up the worn metal parts of a machine.

The only question which we find necessary to decide is as to Meduna's public use of the patented process more than one year before August 6, 1942. The district judge made findings about this, which are supported by the testimony and which we accept.... The kernel of them is the following: "the inventor's main purpose in his use of the process prior to August 6, 1941, and especially in respect to all jobs for owners not known to him, was commercial, and * * * an experimental purpose in connection with such use was subordinate only." Upon this finding he concluded as matter of law that, since the use before the critical date—August 6, 1941—was not primarily for the purposes of experiment, the use was not excused for that reason. Moreover, he also concluded that the use was not public but secret, and for that reason that its predominantly commercial character did prevent it from invalidating the patent. For the last he relied upon our decisions in *Peerless Roll Leaf Co. v. Griffin & Sons,* 29 F.2d 646, and *Gillman v. Stern,* 114 F.2d 28. We think that his analysis of *Peerless Roll Leaf Co. v. Griffin & Sons,* was altogether correct, and that he had no alternative but to follow that decision; on the other hand, we now think that we were then wrong and that the decision must be overruled for reasons we shall state. *Gillman v. Stern*, supra, was, however, rightly decided.

Section one of the first and second Patent Acts, 1 Stat. 109 and 318, declared that the petition for a patent must state that the subject matter had not been "before known or used." Section six of the Act of 1836, 5 Stat. 117, changed this by providing in addition that the invention must not at the time of the application for a patent have been "in public use or on sale" with the inventor's "consent or allowance"; and Sec. 7 of the Act of 1839, 5 Stat. 353, provided that "no patent shall be held to be invalid by reason of such purchase, sale, or use prior to the application for a patent * * * except on proof of abandonment of such invention to the public; or that such purchase, sale, or prior use has been for more than two years prior to such application * * *." Section 4886 of the Revised Statutes made it a condition upon patentability that the invention shall not have been "in public use or on sale for more than two years prior to his application," and that it shall not have been "proved to have been abandoned." This is in substance the same as the Act of 1839, and is precisely the same as Sec. 31 of Title 35, U.S.C.A. except that the prior use is now limited to the United States, and to one year before the application. Sec. 1, Chap. 391, 29 Stat. 692; Sec. 1, Chap. 450, 53 Stat. 1212, 35 U.S.C.A. § 31. So far as we can find, the first case which dealt with the effect of prior use by the patentee was *Pennock v. Dialogue*, 2 Pet. 1, 4, 7 L.Ed. 327, in which the invention had been completed in 1811, and the patent granted in 1818 for a process of making hose by which the sections were joined together in such a way that the joints resisted pressure as well as the other parts. It did not appear that the joints in any way disclosed the process; but the patentee, between the discovery of the invention and the grant of the patent, had sold 13,000 feet of hose; and as to this the judge charged: "If the public, with the knowledge and tacit consent of the inventor, be permitted to use the invention, without opposition, it is a fraud on the public afterwards to take out a patent." The Supreme Court affirmed a judgment for the defendant, on the ground that the invention had been "known or used before the application." "If an inventor should be permitted to hold back from the knowledge of the public the secrets of his invention; if he should * * * make and sell his invention publicly, and thus gather the whole profits, * * * it would materially retard the progress of science and the useful arts" to allow him fourteen years of legal monopoly "when the danger of competition should force him to secure the exclusive right" 2 Pet. at page 19, 7 L.Ed. 327. In *Shaw v. Cooper*, 7 Pet. 292, 8 L.Ed. 689, the public use was not by the inventory, but he had neglected to prevent it after he had learned of it, and this defeated the patent. "Whatever may be the intention of the inventor, if he suffers his invention to go into public use, through any means whatsoever, without an immediate assertion of his right, he is not entitled to a patent" 7 Pet. at page 323, 8 L.Ed. 689. In *Kendall v. Winsor*, 21 How. 322, 16 L.Ed. 165, the inventor had kept the machine secret, but had sold the harness which it produced, so that the facts presented the same situation as here. Since the jury brought in a verdict for the defendant on the issue of abandonment, the case adds nothing except for the dicta on page 328 of 21 How., 16 L.Ed. 165: "the inventor who designedly, and with the view of applying it indefinitely and exclusively for his own profit, withholds his invention for the public, comes not within the policy or objects of the Constitution or acts of Congress." In *Egbert v. Lippmann*, 104 U.S. 333, 26 L.Ed. 755, although the patent was for the product which was sold, nothing could be learned about it without taking it apart, yet it was a public use within the statute. In *Hall v. Macneale*, 107 U.S. 90, 2 S.Ct. 73, 27 L.Ed. 367, the situation was the same.

In the lower courts we may begin with the often cited decision in *Macbeth-Evans Glass Co. v. General Electric Co.*, 6 Cir., 246 F. 695, which concerned a process patent for making illuminating glass. The patentee had kept the process as secret as possible, but for ten years had sold the glass, although this did not, so far as appears, disclose the process. The court held the patent invalid for two reasons, as we understand them: the first was that the delay either indicated an intention to abandon, or was of itself a forfeiture, because of the inconsistency of a practical monopoly by means of secrecy and of a later legal monopoly by means of a patent. So far, it was not an interpretation of "prior use" in the statute; but, beginning on page 702 of 246 F. 695 Judge Warrington seems to have been construing that phrase and to hold that the sales were such a use. In *Allinson Manufacturing Co. v. Ideal Filter Co.*, 8 Cir., 21 F.2d 22, the patent was for a machine for purifying gasoline: the machine was kept secret, but the gasoline had been sold for a period of six years before the application was filed. As in *Macbeth-Evans Glass Co. v. General Electric Co.*, *supra*, 6 Cir., 246 F. 695, the court apparently invalidated the patent on two grounds: one was that the inventor had abandoned the right to a patent, or had forfeited it by his long delay. We are disposed however to read the latter part—pages 27 and 28 of 21 F.2d—as holding that the sale of gasoline was a "prior use" of the machine, notwithstanding its concealment. Certainly, the following quotation from *Pitts v. Hall*, Fed. Cas. No. 11,192, 2 Blatchf. 229, was not otherwise apposite; a patentee "is not allowed to derive any benefit from the sale or use of his machine, without forfeiting his right, except within two years prior to the time he makes his application." On the other hand in *Stresau v. Ipsen*, 77 F.2d 937, 22 C.C.P.A. (Patents) 1352, the Court of Customs and Patent Appeals did indeed decide that a process claim might be valid when the inventor had kept the process secret but had sold the product.

Coming now to our own decisions (the opinions in all of which I wrote), the first was *Grasselli Chemical Co. v. National Aniline & Chemical Co.*, 2 Cir., 26 F.2d 305, in which the patent was for a process which had been kept secret, but the product had been sold upon the market for more than two years. We held that, although the process could not have been discovered from the product, the sales constituted a "prior use," relying upon *Egbert v. Lippmann, supra,* 104 U.S. 333, 26 L.Ed. 755, and *Hall v. Macneale, supra,* 107 U.S. 90, 2 S.Ct. 73, 27 L.Ed. 367. There was nothing in this inconsistent with what we are now holding. But in *Peerless Roll Leaf Co. v. Griffin & Sons, supra,* 2 Cir., 29 F.2d 646, where the patent was for a machine, which had been kept secret, but whose output had been freely sold on the market, we sustained the patent on the ground that "the sale of the product was irrelevant, since no knowledge could possibly be acquired of the machine in that way. In this respect the machine differs from a process * * * or from any other invention necessarily contained in a product" 29 F.2d at page 649. So far as we can now find, there is nothing to support this distinction in the authorities, and we shall try to show that we misapprehended the theory on which the prior use by an inventor forfeits his right to a patent. In *Aerovox Corp. v. Polymet Manufacturing Corp., supra,* 2 Cir., 67 F.2d 860, the patent was also for a process, the use of which we held not to have been experimental, though not secret. Thus our decision sustaining the patent was right; but apparently we were by implication reverting to the doctrine of the Peerless case when we added that it was doubtful whether the process could be detected from the product, although we cited only *Hall v. Macneale, supra,* 107 U.S. 90, 2 S.Ct. 73, 27 L.Ed. 367, and *Grasselli Chemical Co. v. National Aniline Co., supra* (2 Cir., 26 F.2d 305). In *Gillman v. Stern, supra,* 2 Cir., 114 F.2d 28, it was not the inventor, but a third person who used the machine secretly and sold the product openly, and there was therefore no question either of abandonment or forfeiture by the inventor. The only issue was whether a prior use which did not disclose the invention to the art was within the statute; and it is well settled that it is not. As in the case of any other anticipation, the issue of invention must then be determined by how much the inventor has contributed any new information to the art. * * *

From the foregoing it appears that in *Peerless Roll Leaf Co. v. Griffin & Sons, supra,* 2 Cir., 29 F.2d 646, we confused two separate doctrines: (1) The effect upon his right to a patent of the inventor's competitive exploitation of his machine or of his process; (2) the contribution which a prior use by another person makes to the art. Both do indeed come within the phrase, "prior use"; but the first is a defence for quite different reasons from the second. It had its origin—at least in this country—in the passage we have quoted from *Pennock v. Dialogue, supra,* 2 Pet. 1, 7 L.Ed. 327; i.e., that it is a condition upon an inventor's right to a patent that he shall not exploit his discovery competitively after it is ready for patenting; he must content himself with either secrecy, or legal monopoly. It is true that for the limited period of two years he was allowed to do so, possibly in order to give him time to prepare an application; and even that has been recently cut down by half. But if he goes beyond that period of probation, he forfeits his right regardless of how little the public may have learned about the invention; just as he can forfeit it by too long concealment, even without exploiting the invention at all. *Woodbridge v. United States*, 263 U.S. 50, 44 S.Ct. 45, 68 L.Ed. 159; *Macbeth-Evans Glass Co. v. General Electric Co., supra*, 6 Cir., 246 F. 695. Such a forfeiture has nothing to do with abandonment, which presupposes a deliberate, though not necessarily an express, surrender of any right to a patent. Although the evidence of both may at times overlap, each comes from a quite different legal source: one, from the fact that by renouncing the right the inventor irrevocably surrenders it; the other, from the fiat of Congress that it is part of the consideration for a patent that the public shall as soon as possible begin to enjoy the disclosure.

It is indeed true that an inventor may continue for more than a year to practice his invention for his private purposes of his own enjoyment and later patent it. But that is, properly considered, not an exception to the doctrine, for he is not then making use of his secret to gain a competitive advantage over others; he does not thereby extend the period of his monopoly. Besides, as we have seen, even that privilege has its limits, for he may conceal it so long that he will lose his right to a patent even though he does not use it at all. With that question we have not however any concern here.

Judgment reversed; complaint dismissed.

NOTES

1. **Heavy Metal.** *Metallizing Engineering* is a dense piece of text that can make for difficult reading. Although one can succinctly state its holding—that secret commercial exploitation of an invention by the inventor constitutes a "public use" under § 102(b)—concise explanations of this rule of patent law seem more difficult to come by. Are you satisfied with the attempt in *D.L. Auld Co. v. Chroma Graphics Corp.*, 714 F.2d 1144 (Fed.Cir.1983), providing: "The 'forfeiture' theory expressed in *Metallizing* parallels the statutory scheme of 35 U.S.C.A. § 102(b), the intent of which is to preclude the attempts by the inventor or his assignee to profit from commercial use of an invention for more than a year before an application for patent is filed." Is Judge Hand's holding a matter fairly grounded in § 102(b); the abandonment provision of § 102(c), considered later in this Chapter; or, even worse, naked public policy? Given that § 102(b) itself draws no distinction between applicants and third parties when it provides for bars based upon "public use," what policies did Judge Hand animate here?

2. **"Public" = "Secret."** Why was it so important to prevent an inventor from secretly using his invention commercially for more than a year prior to filing for a patent that Judge Hand was willing to torture the English language and hold that the word "public" really meant "secret" when modifying "use?"

3. **Federal Circuit Adoption.** The Court of Appeals for the Federal Circuit approved of Judge Learned Hand's reasoning early in its history. As discussed in *D.L. Auld Co. v. Chroma Graphics Corp.*, 714 F.2d 1144 (Fed.Cir. 1983):

Where a method is kept secret, and remains secret after a sale of the product of the method, that sale will not, of course, bar another inventor from the grant of a patent on that method. The situation is different where, as here, that sale is made by the applicant for patent or his assignee. Though the magistrate referred to § 102(b), he did so in recognizing that the "activity" of [the inventor] here was that which the statute "attempts to limit to one year." In so doing, the magistrate correctly applied the concept explicated in *Metallizing*, i.e., that a party's placing of the product of a method invention on sale more than a year before that party's application filing date must act as a forfeiture of any right to the grant of a valid patent on the method to that party if circumvention of the policy animating § 102(b) is to be avoided in respect of patents on method inventions.

5.1[b] EXPERIMENTAL USE

CITY OF ELIZABETH v. AMERICAN NICHOLSON PAVEMENT CO.

United States Supreme Court, 1877
97 U.S. (7 Otto) 126

This suit was brought by the American Nicholson Pavement Company against the city of Elizabeth, N. J., George W. Tubbs, and the New Jersey Wood–Paving Company, a corporation of New Jersey, upon a patent issued to Samuel Nicholson, dated Aug. 20, 1867, for a new and improved wooden pavement, being a second reissue of a patent issued to said Nicholson Aug. 8, 1854. The reissued patent was extended in 1868 for a further term of seven years. A copy of it is appended to the bill; and, in the specification, it is declared that the nature and object of the invention consists in providing a process or mode of constructing wooden block pavements upon a foundation along a street or roadway with facility, cheapness, and accuracy, and also in the creation and construction of such a wooden pavement as shall be comparatively permanent and durable, by so uniting and combining all its parts, both superstructure and foundation, as to provide against the slipping of the horses' feet, against noise, against unequal wear, and against rot and consequent sinking away from below. Two plans of making this pavement are specified. Both require a proper foundation on which to lay the blocks, consisting of tarred-paper or hydraulic cement covering the surface of the road-bed to the depth of about two inches, or of a flooring of boards or plank, also covered with tar, or other preventive of moisture. On this foundation, one plan is to set square blocks on end arranged like a checker-board, the alternate rows being shorter than the others, so as to leave narrow grooves or channel-ways to be filled with small broken stone or gravel, and then pouring over the whole melted tar or pitch, whereby the cavities are all filled and cemented together. The other plan is, to arrange the blocks in rows transversely across the street, separated a small space (of about an inch) by strips of board at the bottom, which serve to keep the blocks at a uniform distance apart, and then filling these spaces with the same material as before. The blocks forming the pavement are about eight inches high. The alternate rows of short blocks in the first plan and the strips of board in the second plan should not be higher than four inches.

The bill charges that the defendants infringed this patent by laying down wooden pavements in the city of Elizabeth, N. J., constructed in substantial conformity with the process patented, and prays an account of profits, and an injunction.

The defendants answered in due course. They also averred that the alleged invention of Nicholson was in public use, with his consent and allowance, for six years before he applied for a patent, on a certain avenue in Boston called the Mill-dam; and contended that said public use worked an abandonment of the pretended invention.

The question to be considered is, whether Nicholson's invention was in public use or on sale, with his consent and allowance, for more than two years prior to his application for a patent, within the meaning of the sixth, seventh, and fifteenth sections of the act of 1836, as qualified by the seventh section of the act of 1839, which were the acts in force in 1854, when he obtained his patent. It is contended by the appellants that the pavement which Nicholson put down by way of experiment, on Mill-dam Avenue in Boston, in 1848, was publicly used for the space of six years before his application for a patent, and that this was a public use within the meaning of the law.

To determine this question, it is necessary to examine the circumstances under which this pavement was put down, and the object and purpose that Nicholson had in view. It is perfectly clear from the evidence that he did not intend to abandon his right to a patent. He had filed a caveat in August, 1847, and he constructed the pavement in question by way of experiment, for the purpose of testing its qualities. The road in which it was put down, though a public road, belonged to the Boston and Roxbury Mill Corporation, which received toll for its use; and Nicholson was a stockholder and treasurer of the corporation. The pavement in question was about seventy-five feet in length, and was laid adjoining to the toll-gate and in front of the toll-house. It was constructed by Nicholson at his own expense, and was placed by him where it was, in order to see the effect upon it of heavily loaded wagons, and of varied and constant use; and also to ascertain its durability, and liability to decay. Joseph L. Lang, who was toll-collector for many years, commencing in 1849, familiar with the road before that time, and with this pavement from the time of its origin, testified as follows:

> "Mr. Nicholson was there almost daily, and when he came he would examine the pavement, would often walk over it, cane in hand, striking it with his cane, and making particular examination of its condition. He asked me very often how people liked it, and asked me a great many questions about it. I have heard him say a number of times that this was his first experiment with this pave-

ment, and he thought that it was wearing very well. The circumstances that made this locality desirable for the purpose of obtaining a satisfactory test of the durability and value of the pavement were: that there would be a better chance to lay it there; he would have more room and a better chance than in the city; and, besides, it was a place where most everybody went over it, rich and poor. It was a great thoroughfare out of Boston. It was frequently travelled by teams having a load of five or six tons, and some larger. As these teams usually stopped at the toll-house, and started again, the stopping and starting would make as severe a trial to the pavement as it could be put to."

This evidence is corroborated by that of several other witnesses in the cause; the result of the whole being that Nicholson merely intended this piece of pavement as an experiment, to test its usefulness and durability. Was this a public use, within the meaning of the law?

An abandonment of an invention to the public may be evinced by the conduct of the inventor at any time, even within the two years named in the law. The effect of the law is, that no such consequence will necessarily follow from the invention being in public use or on sale, with the inventor's consent and allowance, at any time within two years before his application; but that, if the invention is in public use or on sale prior to that time, it will be conclusive evidence of abandonment, and the patent will be void.

But, in this case, it becomes important to inquire what is such a public use as will have the effect referred to. That the use of the pavement in question was public in one sense cannot be disputed. But can it be said that the invention was in public use? The use of an invention by the inventor himself, or of any other person under his direction, by way of experiment, and in order to bring the invention to perfection, has never been regarded as such a use. CURTIS, PATENTS, sect. 381; *Shaw v. Cooper*, 7 Pet. 292.

Now, the nature of a street pavement is such that it cannot be experimented upon satisfactorily except on a highway, which is always public.

When the subject of invention is a machine, it may be tested and tried in a building, either with or without closed doors. In either case, such use is not a public use, within the meaning of the statute, so long as the inventor is engaged, in good faith, in testing its operation. He may see cause to alter it and improve it, or not. His experiments will reveal the fact whether any and what alterations may be necessary. If durability is one of the qualities to be attained, a long period, perhaps years, may be necessary to enable the inventor to discover whether his purpose is accomplished. And though, during all that period, he may not find that any changes are necessary, yet he may be justly said to be using his machine only by way of experiment; and no one would say that such a use, pursued with a bona fide intent of testing the qualities of the machine, would be a public use, within the meaning of the statute. So long as he does not voluntarily allow others to make it and use it, and so long as it is not on sale for general use, he keeps the invention under his own control, and does not lose his title to a patent.

It would not be necessary, in such a case, that the machine should be put up and used only in the inventor's own shop or premises. He may have it put up and used in the premises of another, and the use may inure to the benefit of the owner of the establishment. Still, if used under the surveillance of the inventor, and for the purpose of enabling him to test the machine, and ascertain whether it will answer the purpose intended, and make such alterations and improvements as experience demonstrates to be necessary, it will still be a mere experimental use, and not a public use, within the meaning of the statute.

Whilst the supposed machine is in such experimental use, the public may be incidentally deriving a benefit from it. If it be a grist-mill, or a carding-machine, customers from the surrounding country may enjoy the use of it by having their grain made into flour, or their wool into rolls, and still it will not be in public use, within the meaning of the law.

But if the inventor allows his machine to be used by other persons generally, either with or without compensation, or if it is, with his consent, put on sale for such use, then it will be in public use and on public sale, within the meaning of the law.

If, now, we apply the same principles to this case, the analogy will be seen at once. Nicholson wished to experiment on his pavement. He believed it to be a good thing, but he was not sure; and the only mode in which he could test it was to place a specimen of it in a public roadway. He did this at his own expense, and with the consent of the owners of the road. Durability was one of the qualities to be attained. He wanted to know whether his pavement would stand, and whether it would resist decay. Its character for durability could not be ascertained without its being subjected to use for a considerable time. He subjected it to such use, in good faith, for the simple purpose of ascertaining whether it was what he claimed it to be. Did he do any thing more than the inventor of the supposed machine might do, in testing his invention? The public had the incidental use of the pavement, it is true; but was the invention in public use, within the meaning of the statute? We think not. The proprietors of the road alone used the invention, and used it at Nicholson's request, by way of experiment. The only way in which they could use it was by allowing the public to pass over the pavement.

Had the city of Boston, or other parties, used the invention, by laying down the pavement in other streets and places, with Nicholson's consent and allowance, then, indeed, the invention itself would have been in public use, within the meaning of the law; but this was not the case. Nicholson did not sell it, nor allow others to use it or sell it. He did not let it go beyond his control. He did nothing that indicated any intent to do so. He kept it under his own eyes, and never for a moment abandoned the intent to obtain a patent for it.

In this connection, it is proper to make another remark. It is not a public knowledge of his invention that precludes the inventor from obtaining a patent for it, but a public use or sale of it. In England, formerly, as well as under our Patent Act of 1793, if an inventor did not keep his invention secret, if a knowledge of it became public before his application for a patent, he could not obtain one. To be patentable, an invention must not have been known or used before the application; but this has not been the law of this country since the passage of the act of 1836, and it has been very much qualified in England. *Lewis v. Marling*, 10 B. & C. 22. Therefore, if it were true that during the whole period in which the pavement was used, the public knew how it was constructed, it would make no difference in the result.

It is sometimes said that an inventor acquires an undue advantage over the public by delaying to take out a patent, inasmuch as he thereby preserves the monopoly to himself for a longer period than is allowed by the policy of the law; but this cannot be said with justice when the delay is occasioned by a bona fide effort to bring his invention to perfection, or to ascertain whether it will answer the purpose intended. His monopoly only continues for the allotted period, in any event; and it is the interest of the public, as well as himself, that the invention should be perfect and properly tested, before a patent is granted for it. Any attempt to use it for a profit, and not by way of experiment, for a longer period than two years before the application, would deprive the inventor of his right to a patent.

NOTES

1. **Comparison to *Egbert*.** Justice Story strove in *Pennock* to encourage early filing of an invention. Does *City of Elizabeth* undercut the policies of *Pennock*? What did Nicholson do differently from Egbert, the corset springs inventor? What evidence could Nicholson muster that Egbert could not?

2. **The Experimental Use Negation.** What statutory language dictates the result in *City of Elizabeth*? Is experimentation a "use" within the meaning of "public use" in § 102(b)? Is experimentation an exception to the public use and on sale statutory bars *or* a recognition that experimentation on an invention cannot be a public use nor an offer for sale of the invention?

A Federal Circuit opinion answers these questions. The invention was a novel orthodontic appliance for which the inventor filed a patent application on February 19, 1962. Before the critical date, the inventor used the dental device on three patients. In 1958, 1959, and 1960, the inventor used the device on one patient, but kept only "scanty records." The inventor made no commercial sales of the device until 1966. The trial court "placed a heavy burden of proof on the patent owner to prove that the inventor's use had been experimental." Judge Nies explained the district court's error:

[marginalia: public use under 102(b)]

[I]t is incorrect to impose on the patent owner, as the trial court in this case did, the burden of proving that a "public use" was "experimental." These are not two separable issues. It is incorrect to ask: "Was it a public use?" and then, "Was it experimental?" Rather, the court is faced with a single issue: Was it public use under section 102(b)?

Turning to the instant case, we note first that disclosure of the seating device to patients could not be avoided in any testing. . . . In any event, a pledge of confidentiality is indicative of the inventor's continued control which here is established inherently by the dentist-patient relationship of the parties. . . . Yet no [inventions] were offered competing orthodontists despite the fact this was one facet of the inventor's total business activity.

TP Laboratories, Inc. v. Professional Positioners, Inc., 724 F.2d 965, 971–73 (Fed.Cir.1984). Does the distinction between an experimental use "exception" and a "negation" really mean anything beyond semantics? Who has the burden to prove a patent invalid and why? You will revisit this issue in connection with *Lough v. Brunswick, infra.*

3.   Experimenting on the Claimed Invention or on its General Purposes? As a general rule, an experimental use only negates a statutory bar when the inventor was testing claimed features of the invention. *In re Theis*, 610 F.2d 786, 793 (CCPA 1979) ("It is settled law that . . . experimental sale . . . does not apply to experiments performed with respect to non-claimed features of an invention."); *LaBounty Mfg. Inc. v. United States Int'l Trade Comm'n*, 958 F.2d 1066, 1074 (Fed.Cir.1992); *In re Brigance*, 792 F.2d 1103, 1109 (Fed.Cir.1986). In some instances, however, the Federal Circuit has allowed an experimental use to negate a § 102 (b) bar when the testing did not focus on a claimed feature. In *Grain Processing Corp. v. American Maize–Products Co.*, 840 F.2d 902 (Fed.Cir.1988), a patentee sent samples of its food additive to manufacturers for testing. The Federal Circuit noted that the minimal testing was to check for adverse interactions with other food products. *Id.* at 906. The claims in *Grain Processing*, however, do not recite "food interactions" as a claimed feature. Can this result be justified as reasonable testing of the product's utility or is this a conflict in Federal Circuit application of the experimental use negation?

For another example, consider the *Manville Sales* case discussed in the next note. The inventor tested the luminaire assembly for durability in the severe winter environment, but the claims do not refer to severe conditions or durability. *See* 917 F.2d at 550. Some of the difficulty may arise from the need to test an invention for utility, i.e., to show that it works for its intended purpose. *Scott v. Finney*, 34 F.3d 1058, 1061 (Fed.Cir.1994). An inventor may test for the general workability of an invention and its suitability for the marketplace, for example, avoiding food interactions or durability in winter, without claiming those features which are necessary for general workability and marketability. Are utility testing and experimental use testing the same thing? If the answer is "no" because experimental use testing is more strictly confined to claimed features, does the potential overlap of utility testing and testing the claimed features explain the Federal Circuit's decision to relax the experimental use testing requirements in *Manville Sales* and *Grain Processing*?

4. Modern Experimental Use. In a modern case, the invention was an improvement in the design of lights along highways. The invention facilitated repair and maintenance of the luminaires at the top of the 150–foot pole which supported the lights. The inventor needed to test the invention in difficult weather conditions. In November, 1971, the inventor sold a prototype of his design to the State of Wyoming for installation at a rest area near Rawlins which was not yet open to the public. In March 1972, the inventor inspected the invention and determined it had survived the winter. He then authorized sales of his device. In June, 1972, the rest area opened to the public. The inventor filed for patent protection on February 3, 1973. Judge Michel delivered the decision of the Federal Circuit:

> In order to determine whether an invention was on sale or in public use, we must consider how the totality of the circumstances comports with the policies underlying the on sale and public use bars.

> First, Manville did nothing to lead the public to believe that its iris arm invention was in "the public domain." On the contrary, Manville conveyed to a Wyoming official that its use of the invention on one pole at one site in Wyoming was experimental. Although Manville did not advise anyone else that its use was experimental and was not intended to release its invention into the public domain, the particular circumstances made such efforts unnecessary. Manville marked its design drawing with a confidentiality notice before disclosing it to a Wyoming official, and Wyoming law prohibited officials from disclosing confidential information.

> Second, Manville did not attempt to extend the patent term by commercially exploiting its invention more than one year before it filed a patent application. Manville retained ownership of the lowering device and did not notify its sales personnel about the invention, or initiate a sales campaign to market the iris arm design until March of 1972, after it first determined, based on inspecting the Fort Steele device, that the iris arms worked for their intended purpose.

> Moreover, although Manville eventually received compensation for the iris arm device in fulfillment of its original contract with Wyoming, a sale that is primarily for experimental purposes, as opposed to commercial exploitation, does not raise an on sale bar. *See Baker Oil Tools, Inc. v. Geo Vann, Inc.*, 828 F.2d 1558, 1563 (Fed.Cir.1987).

> Finally, Manville's actions are entirely consistent with the policy "favoring prompt and widespread disclosure of 'inventions.'" The iris arm device was specifically designed to withstand year around weather. Prior to its testing in the winter environment, there really was no basis for confidence by the inventor that the invention would perform as intended, and hence no proven invention to disclose.

Manville Sales Corp. v. Paramount Systems, Inc., 917 F.2d 544, 549–550 (Fed.Cir. 1990). How important was the site chosen for this experiment—a rest area in Wyoming not yet open to the public? How about the fact that the invention was situated at the top of a 150–foot pole throughout the experimentation?

Manville also introduces the close relationship between reduction to practice, the test for completion of an invention, and the public use and on-sale bars. *UMC Electronics* gives this question a different analysis.

5. Market Testing as Experimentation? In *In re Smith*, 714 F.2d 1127, 1135 (Fed.Cir.1983), the Federal Circuit dealt with the question of whether market testing for consumer satisfaction qualified as an experimental use. The inventor tested the invention—a carpet deodorizer—with consumers more than a year before the application. After showing a video presentation about the product and giving several consumers samples to try in their homes, the inventor asked them about the pricing of the product, the believability of its qualities, and their purchase intent. The Federal Circuit upheld a public use bar:

> The experimental use exception, however, does not include market testing where the inventor is attempting to gauge consumer demand for his claimed invention. The purpose of such activities is commercial exploitation and not experimentation.

In re Smith, 714 F.2d at 1135. Judge Nichols dissented, noting that the line between testing the market and testing the product may be difficult to discern. Do the policies underlying the public use bar support this result? Note as well that the Federal Circuit referred loosely to the experimental use doctrine as an "exception" to public use. Is experimental use technically an "exception" or a "negation?"

§ 5.1[c]   "ON SALE"

PFAFF v. WELLS ELECTRONICS, INC.

Supreme Court of the United States, 1998
525 U.S. 55

Justice Stevens delivered the opinion for a unanimous court:

Section 102(b) of the Patent Act of 1952 provides that no person is entitled to patent an "invention" that has been "on sale" more than one year before filing a patent application. We granted certiorari to determine whether the commercial marketing of a newly invented product may mark the beginning of the 1–year period even though the invention has not yet been reduced to practice.

I

On April 19, 1982, petitioner, Wayne Pfaff, filed an application for a patent on a computer chip socket. Therefore, April 19, 1981, constitutes the critical date for purposes of the on-sale bar of 35 U.S.C. § 102(b); if the 1–year period began to run before that date, Pfaff lost his right to patent his invention.

Pfaff commenced work on the socket in November 1980, when representatives of Texas Instruments asked him to develop a new device for mounting and removing semiconductor chip carriers. In response to this request, he prepared detailed engineering drawings that described the design, the dimensions, and the materials to be used in making the socket. Pfaff sent those drawings to a manufacturer in February or March 1981.

Prior to March 17, 1981, Pfaff showed a sketch of his concept to representatives of Texas Instruments. On April 8, 1981, they provided Pfaff with a written confirmation of a previously placed oral purchase order for 30,100 of his new sockets for a total price of $91,155. In accord with his normal practice, Pfaff did not make and test a prototype of the new device before offering to sell it in commercial quantities.

The manufacturer took several months to develop the customized tooling necessary to produce the device, and Pfaff did not fill the order until July 1981. The evidence therefore indicates that Pfaff first reduced his invention to practice in the summer of 1981. The socket achieved substantial commercial success before Patent No. 4,491,377 ('377 patent) issued to Pfaff on January 1, 1985.

After the patent issued, petitioner brought an infringement action against respondent, Wells Electronics, Inc., the manufacturer of a competing socket. Wells prevailed on the basis of a finding of no infringement. When respondent began to market a modified device, petitioner brought this suit, alleging that the modifications infringed six of the claims in the '377 patent.

After a full evidentiary hearing before a Special Master, the District Court held that two of those claims (1 and 6) were invalid because they had been anticipated in the prior art. Nevertheless, the court concluded that four other claims (7, 10, 11, and 19) were valid and three (7, 10, and 11) were infringed by various models of respondent's sockets. Adopting the Special Master's findings, the District Court rejected respondent's § 102(b) defense because Pfaff had filed the application for the '377 patent less than a year after reducing the invention to practice.

The Court of Appeals reversed, finding all six claims invalid. 124 F.3d 1429 (C.A.Fed.1997). Four of the claims (1, 6, 7, and 10) described the socket that Pfaff had sold to Texas Instruments prior to April 8, 1981. Because that device had been offered for sale on a commercial basis more than one year before the patent application was filed on April 19, 1982, the court concluded that those claims were invalid under § 102(b). That conclusion rested on the court's view that as long as the invention was "substantially complete at the time of sale," the 1–year period began to run, even though the invention had not yet been reduced to practice. Id., at 1434. The other two claims (11 and 19) described a feature that had not been included in Pfaff's initial design, but the Court of Appeals concluded as a matter of law that the additional feature was not itself patentable because it was an obvious addition to the prior art. Given the court's § 102(b) holding, the prior art included Pfaff's first four claims.

Because other courts have held or assumed that an invention cannot be "on sale" within the meaning of § 102(b) unless and until it has been reduced to practice, *see, e.g., Timely Products Corp. v. Arron*, 523 F.2d 288, 299–302 (C.A.2 1975), and because the text of § 102(b) makes no reference to "substantial completion" of an invention, we granted certiorari. 523 U.S. 1003, 118 S.Ct. 1183, 140 L.Ed.2d 315 (1998).

II

The primary meaning of the word "invention" in the Patent Act unquestionably refers to the inventor's conception rather than to a physical embodiment of that idea. The statute does not contain any express requirement that an invention must be reduced to practice before it can be patented. Neither the statutory definition of the term in § 100 nor the basic conditions for obtaining a patent set forth in § 101 make any mention of "reduction to practice." The statute's only specific reference to that term is found in § 102(g), which sets forth the standard for resolving priority contests between two competing claimants to a patent. That subsection provides:

> "In determining priority of invention there shall be considered not only the respective dates of conception and reduction to practice of the invention, but also the reasonable diligence of one who was first to conceive and last to reduce to practice, from a time prior to conception by the other."

Thus, assuming diligence on the part of the applicant, it is normally the first inventor to conceive, rather than the first to reduce to practice, who establishes the right to the patent.

It is well settled that an invention may be patented before it is reduced to practice. In 1888, this Court upheld a patent issued to Alexander Graham Bell even though he had filed his application before constructing a working telephone. Chief Justice Waite's reasoning in that case merits quoting at length:

> "It is quite true that when Bell applied for his patent he had never actually transmitted telegraphically spoken words so that they could be distinctly heard and understood at the receiving end of his line, but in his specification he did describe accurately and with admirable clearness his process, that is to say, the exact electrical condition that must be created to accomplish his purpose, and he also described, with sufficient precision to enable one of ordinary skill in such matters to make it, a form of apparatus which, if used in the way pointed out, would produce the required effect, receive the words, and carry them to and deliver them at the appointed place. The particular instrument which he had, and which he used in his experiments, did not, under the circumstances in which it was tried, reproduce the words spoken, so that they could be clearly understood, but the proof is abundant and of the most convincing character, that other instruments, carefully constructed and made exactly in accordance with the specification, without any additions whatever, have operated and will operate successfully. A good

mechanic of proper skill in matters of the kind can take the patent and, by following the specification strictly, can, without more, construct an apparatus which, when used in the way pointed out, will do all that it is claimed the method or process will do...."

"The law does not require that a discoverer or inventor, in order to get a patent for a process, must have succeeded in bringing his art to the highest degree of perfection. It is enough if he describes his method with sufficient clearness and precision to enable those skilled in the matter to understand what the process is, and if he points out some practicable way of putting it into operation." *The Telephone Cases*, 126 U.S. 1, 535–536, 8 S.Ct. 778, 31 L.Ed. 863 (1888).

When we apply the reasoning of *The Telephone Cases* to the facts of the case before us today, it is evident that Pfaff could have obtained a patent on his novel socket when he accepted the purchase order from Texas Instruments for 30,100 units. At that time he provided the manufacturer with a description and drawings that had "sufficient clearness and precision to enable those skilled in the matter" to produce the device. The parties agree that the sockets manufactured to fill that order embody Pfaff's conception as set forth in claims 1, 6, 7, and 10 of the '377 patent. We can find no basis in the text of § 102(b) or in the facts of this case for concluding that Pfaff's invention was not "on sale" within the meaning of the statute until after it had been reduced to practice.

III

Pfaff nevertheless argues that longstanding precedent, buttressed by the strong interest in providing inventors with a clear standard identifying the onset of the 1–year period, justifies a special interpretation of the word "invention" as used in § 102(b). We are persuaded that this nontextual argument should be rejected.

As we have often explained, most recently in *Bonito Boats, Inc. v. Thunder Craft Boats, Inc.*, 489 U.S. 141, 151, 109 S.Ct. 971(1989), the patent system represents a carefully crafted bargain that encourages both the creation and the public disclosure of new and useful advances in technology, in return for an exclusive monopoly for a limited period of time. The balance between the interest in motivating innovation and enlightenment by rewarding invention with patent protection on the one hand, and the interest in avoiding monopolies that unnecessarily stifle competition on the other, has been a feature of the federal patent laws since their inception.

Consistent with these ends, § 102 of the Patent Act serves as a limiting provision, both excluding ideas that are in the public domain from patent protection and confining the duration of the monopoly to the statutory term. *See, e.g., Frantz Mfg. Co. v. Phenix Mfg. Co.*, 457 F.2d 314, 320 (C.A.7 1972).

Don't like to remove items already in the public

↓

but inventors allowed to test products in public if for experimental.

Act of 1836 added "on sale" limit.

↓

2 years to make sure inventor filed patent

1939 shortened to one year.

π claims "substantially complete" too vague

Fed Circuit "totality of circumstances" too vague

We originally held that an inventor loses his right to a patent if he puts his invention into public use before filing a patent application. "His voluntary act or acquiescence in the public sale and use is an abandonment of his right." *Pennock v. Dialogue*, 2 Pet. 1, 24, 7 L.Ed. 327 (1829) (Story, J.). A similar reluctance to allow an inventor to remove existing knowledge from public use undergirds the on-sale bar.

Nevertheless, an inventor who seeks to perfect his discovery may conduct extensive testing without losing his right to obtain a patent for his invention—even if such testing occurs in the public eye. The law has long recognized the distinction between inventions put to experimental use and products sold commercially. *Elizabeth v. American Nicholson Pavement Co.*, 97 U.S. 126, 137 (1877).

The patent laws therefore seek both to protect the public's right to retain knowledge already in the public domain and the inventor's right to control whether and when he may patent his invention. The Patent Act of 1836, 5 Stat. 117, was the first statute that expressly included an on-sale bar to the issuance of a patent. Like the earlier holding in *Pennock*, that provision precluded patentability if the invention had been placed on sale at any time before the patent application was filed. In 1839, Congress ameliorated that requirement by enacting a 2–year grace period in which the inventor could file an application. 5 Stat. 353.

In *Andrews v. Hovey*, 123 U.S. 267, 274, 8 S.Ct. 101 (1887), we noted that the purpose of that amendment was "to fix a period of limitation which should be certain"; it required the inventor to make sure that a patent application was filed "within two years from the completion of his invention," *ibid*. In 1939, Congress reduced the grace period from two years to one year. 53 Stat. 1212.

Petitioner correctly argues that these provisions identify an interest in providing inventors with a definite standard for determining when a patent application must be filed. A rule that makes the timeliness of an application depend on the date when an invention is "substantially complete" seriously undermines the interest in certainty. Moreover, such a rule finds no support in the text of the statute. Thus, petitioner's argument calls into question the standard applied by the Court of Appeals, but it does not persuade us that it is necessary to engraft a reduction to practice element into the meaning of the term "invention" as used in § 102(b). The Federal Circuit has developed a multifactor, "totality of the circumstances" test to determine the trigger for the on-sale bar. *See, e.g., Micro Chemical, Inc. v. Great Plains Chemical Co.*, 103 F.3d 1538, 1544 (C.A.Fed.1997). As the Federal Circuit itself has noted, this test "has been criticized as unnecessarily vague." *Seal-Flex, Inc. v. Athletic Track & Court Construction*, 98 F.3d 1318, 1323, n. 2 (C.A.Fed. 1996).

The word "invention" must refer to a concept that is complete, rather than merely one that is "substantially complete." It is true that reduction to practice ordinarily provides the best evidence that an invention is complete. But just because reduction to practice is sufficient evidence of completion, it does not follow that proof of reduction to practice is necessary in every case. Indeed, both the facts of *The Telephone Cases* and the facts of this case demonstrate that one can prove that an invention is complete and ready for patenting before it has actually been reduced to practice.

We conclude, therefore, that the on-sale bar applies when two conditions are satisfied before the critical date. First, the product must be the subject of a commercial offer for sale. An inventor can both understand and control the timing of the first commercial marketing of his invention. The experimental use doctrine, for example, has not generated concerns about indefiniteness, and we perceive no reason why unmanageable uncertainty should attend a rule that measures the application of the on-sale bar of § 102(b) against the date when an invention that is ready for patenting is first marketed commercially. In this case the acceptance of the purchase order prior to April 8, 1981, makes it clear that such an offer had been made, and there is no question that the sale was commercial rather than experimental in character.

Second, the invention must be ready for patenting. That condition may be satisfied in at least two ways: by proof of reduction to practice before the critical date; or by proof that prior to the critical date the inventor had prepared drawings or other descriptions of the invention that were sufficiently specific to enable a person skilled in the art to practice the invention. In this case the second condition of the on-sale bar is satisfied because the drawings Pfaff sent to the manufacturer before the critical date fully disclosed the invention.

The evidence in this case thus fulfills the two essential conditions of the on-sale bar. As succinctly stated by Learned Hand:

> "[I]t is a condition upon an inventor's right to a patent that he shall not exploit his discovery competitively after it is ready for patenting; he must content himself with either secrecy, or legal monopoly." *Metallizing Engineering Co. v. Kenyon Bearing & Auto Parts Co.*, 153 F.2d 516, 520 (C.A.2 1946).

The judgment of the Court of Appeals finds support not only in the text of the statute but also in the basic policies underlying the statutory scheme, including § 102(b). When Pfaff accepted the purchase order for his new sockets prior to April 8, 1981, his invention was ready for patenting. The fact that the manufacturer was able to produce the socket using his detailed drawings and specifications demonstrates this fact. Furthermore, those sockets contained all the elements of the invention claimed in the '377 patent. Therefore, Pfaff's '377 patent is invalid because the invention had been on sale for more than one year in this country before he filed his patent application. Accordingly, the judgment of the Court of Appeals is affirmed.

NOTES

1. **The Problem Solved by *Pfaff*.** *Pfaff* does not address at length the problem that it solved. The inventive process, of course, generally occurs in increments. As the inventor progresses slowly day by day toward solution of a problem, events may often transpire that place the emerging technology in public use or on sale. Perhaps the marketing department works independent of the engineering department. This poses a difficult question: At what point is the invention sufficiently complete to have been in public use or on sale? Despite some earlier case law suggesting a reduction to practice standard for invention completeness (invention in existence and proven to operate for its intended purpose), *Timely Prods. Corp. v. Arron,* 523 F.2d 288 (2d Cir.1975), the Federal Circuit set a confusing standard from the outset. *UMC Electronics Co. v. U.S.,* 816 F.2d 647 (Fed.Cir.1987). In *UMC,* a government contractor offered to sell the U.S. a sophisticated device for Navy aircraft. At the time of this offer to sell, the contractor had not yet completed this new device. In finding sufficient completeness to impose a bar, the Federal Circuit declined to apply the reduction to practice standard and instead invoked a confusing standard: "[T]he challenger has the burden of proving . . . that the subject matter of the sale or offer to sell fully anticipated the claimed invention or would have rendered the claimed invention obvious by its addition to the prior art." Aside from the question of how an invention becomes "prior art" against itself, this formulation offered almost no clear rule for the completeness problem. Sometimes the Federal Circuit would attempt to apply this confusing rule. *See, e.g., Envirotech Corp. v. Westech Eng'g, Inc.,* 904 F.2d 1571 (Fed.Cir.1990). Other times the Federal Circuit declined to apply the *UMC* rule in favor of other tests. *See, e.g., Micro Chem., Inc. v. Great Plains Chem. Co., Inc.* 103 F.3d 1538 (Fed.Cir.1997)(substantially completed invention with reason to expect that it would work for its intended purpose upon completion). Did the Supreme Court's decision alleviate this competition of standards?

2. **The Federal Circuit's Application of the Supreme Court's Answer.** As discussed above, before *Pfaff,* the bar would operate if the claimed invention was merely obvious in light of what was offered for sale. In *Scaltech, Inc. v. Retec/Tetra, LLC,* 156 F.3d 1193 1998), a case initially decided before *Pfaff,* Judge Rich relied on *UMC*'s obviousness test to determine if an invention was obvious in light of the process offered for sale. When *Pfaff* issued, Judge Rich granted a petition for rehearing and revised the opinion:

> If the process that was offered for sale inherently possessed each of the claim limitations, then the process was on sale.

Inherency, of course, is a principle of anticipation requiring a showing that the process offered for sale necessarily included (though not necessarily recognized to include) each of the claim limitations. Was this reading faithful to the "ready for patenting" test?

Another case is a nearly inexplicable return to the *UMC* standard. In *Tec Air Inc. v. Denso Mfg. Michigan Inc.,* 192 F.3d 1353 (Fed.Cir.1999), Chief Judge Mayer stated:

Denso stresses that the August 1974 drawing shows that the invention was ready for patenting, thus satisfying the second prong of *Pfaff*. However, because the offer for sale did not involve subject matter that either anticipates the invention or would have rendered it obvious, *Pfaff*'s second prong is irrelevant. *Pfaff* did not remove the requirement that the subject matter of the commercial offer for sale be something within the scope of the claim.

Fortunately, the Federal Circuit has not persisted in this apparent rejection of *Pfaff*'s second prong. In more recent cases, the Federal Circuit has faithfully applied the enablement standard in *Pfaff*'s ready-for-patenting test. *Robotic Vision Sys. v. View Eng. Inc.*, 249 F.3d 1307 (Fed.Cir.2001):

[T]he [trial] court [correctly] concluded that the invention was ready for patenting because the inventor's disclosure was also an enabling disclosure, *i.e.*, one that was sufficiently specific to enable his co-worker, who was a person skilled in the art, to practice the invention.

3. Sale of Patent Rights. Suppose that an inventor sells all right, title, and interest in an invention—in other words, any prospective patent rights themselves—prior to the critical date. Should this offer run afoul of the statutory bar of § 102(b)? *See Moleculon Research Corp. v. CBS, Inc.*, 793 F.2d 1261 (Fed.Cir. 1986). As you answer this question, consider the policies underlying the statutory bar, the business realities facing the employed inventor, and the practical difficulty of distinguishing sales of an embodiment of an invention from sales of the invention itself.

4. Sales to Related Parties. The courts have sometimes struggled with the commercial environment of technology-related industry, as transactions between joint ventures and commonly controlled corporations strain the boundaries of the § 102(b) bar. In *Ferag AG v. Quipp Inc.*, 45 F.3d 1562 (Fed.Cir. 1995), the court noted that: "A section 102(b) sale or offer must involve separate entities. Where, as in this case, the parties to an alleged sale are related, it is more difficult to determine whether the inventor is attempting to commercialize his invention; accordingly, in such cases whether there is a statutory bar depends on whether the seller so controls the purchaser that the invention remains out of the public's hands." In *Ferag*, Judge Mayer considered a patentee's sale to its exclusive U.S. distributor, of which it retained only 50% ownership, and concluded: "Because Ferag could not control Ferag, Inc.'s marketing of the invention, the two companies were separate entities for section 102(b) purposes and the transaction between them gives rise to a statutory bar."

Continental Can Co. v. Monsanto Co., 948 F.2d 1264 (Fed.Cir.1991), went the other way when considering a confidential manufacturer-customer development project between a third party, Admiral Plastics, and the Coca–Cola Company. Under the terms of an agreement, Admiral produced various plastic bottles and supplied them to Coca–Cola for testing; the project was ultimately terminated because the bottles failed to fulfill certain contractually specified mechanical performance requirements. The court noted that

[T]he "on sale" bar of § 102(b) does not arise simply because the intended customer was participating in development and testing. In *Baker Oil Tools,*

Inc. v. Geo Vann, Inc., 828 F.2d 1558, 1563–65 (Fed.Cir.1987), this court summarized various factors pertinent to the "on sale" bar when there is an issue concerning the relationship between the patentee and the customer: for example, whether there was a need for testing by other than the patentee; the amount of control exercised; the stage of development of the invention; whether payments were made and the basis thereof; whether confidentiality was required; and whether technological changes were made. All of the circumstances attending the relationship must be considered in light of the public policy underlying § 102(b).

On the facts of the case, the Federal Circuit concluded that the "Marcus bottle was part of a terminated development project that never bore fruit commercially and was cloaked in confidentiality. While the line is not always bright between development and being on sale, see generally *UMC Electronics,* in this case the line was not crossed."

5. Reduction to Practice and Experimental Use. The *Pfaff* rule could conflict with a great deal of prior case law on application of the experimental use negation. As a negation, experimental use is not an independent test, but an application of the standard statutory bar test of *Pfaff* in a setting that does not suggest that a public use or offer for sale was commercial. Under a pure ready for patenting test, however, the point of assessing application of the bar moves back along the inventive continuum to the point where the inventor enables the invention. Does this leave much room for experimenting? Experimenting is usually associated with reducing the invention to practice. Thus, does the new test swallow the experimental use negation? The Federal Circuit confronted that question in *EZ Dock v. Schafer Sys. Inc.,* 276 F.3d 1347 (Fed.Cir.2002):

> In *Pfaff,* the Supreme Court expressly preserved the experimental use or sale negation of the section 102 bars: "Nevertheless, an inventor who seeks to perfect his discovery may conduct extensive testing without losing his right to obtain a patent for his invention—even if such testing occurs in the public eye. The law has long recognized the distinction between inventions put to experimental use and products sold commercially." *Pfaff,* 525 U.S. at 64. Indeed in *Pfaff,* the Supreme Court reiterated its guidance in *City of Elizabeth v. American Nicholson Pavement Co.,* 97 U.S. 126, 137 (1877), that an inventor does not inappropriately delay filing "by a bona fide effort to bring his invention to perfection, or to ascertain whether it will answer the purpose intended." Thus, the Supreme Court and this court apply the experimental use negation without conflict with the "ready for patenting" prong of the new on-sale bar test. Indeed as noted earlier, the Supreme Court acknowledged that a litigant may show readiness for patenting with evidence of reduction to practice. Like evidence of experimentation sufficient to negate a bar, reduction to practice involves proof that an invention will work for its intended purpose. Even beyond this overlap of the experimental use negation and the ready for patenting standard, however, the Supreme Court explicitly preserved proof of experimentation as a negation of statutory bars.

Judge Linn authored a thoughtful concurrence sustaining the result in *EZ Dock*, but reading the relationship between experimenting and *Pfaff* differently:

> Because nothing in *Pfaff* altered the transitional significance of reduction to practice for experimental use negation, the heretofore complementary nature of the two tests and the symmetry that such congruence brought to the analytical framework disappeared. Traversing this new landscape now demands in each case a careful examination of the purpose of the use contemplated in a potentially barring sale, not merely that the invention then may be in an experimental stage, and signals a shift in focus from the second prong to the first in evaluating experimental use negation.

Experimental use survives *Pfaff*, but apparently on a somewhat different footing. Incidentally, the facts of *EZ Dock* are very similar to the facts of *Lough*, but the result is different. To what do you attribute the difference?

6. The "Ready for Patenting" Standard in Canada. The next chapter in this book considers the rules of determining when an invention is made for the purposes of deciding who is the first inventor or other priority questions. These rules are far more complicated than the "ready for patenting" test in *Pfaff*. The Canadian patent system had used the "ready for patenting" rule for over 100 years to determine priority questions. As you proceed to chapter 6, consider whether the Canadian (*Pfaff*) approach would serve as a better mechanism for determining priority than the approach developed in the United States?

§ 5.2　THIRD PARTY ACTIVITIES § 102(b)

Section 102 states simply: "A person shall be entitled to a patent unless . . . (b) the invention was . . . in public use or on sale in this country, more than one year prior to the date of the application for patent in the United States." The statutory language says nothing about how the invention is put into public use or on sale. In the cases up to this point in this Chapter, the inventors themselves took some action that arguably exploited or disclosed their invention before the critical date. The next inquiry is different: What are the implications of someone other than the inventor putting the invention into public use or on sale before the critical date?

Intuition may tell you that an inventor should not be allowed to obtain patent protection for a technology that someone else has already placed into the public domain. The other individual's open public use should dissuade any would-be inventor from seeking exclusive rights in that technology. But suppose that the other individual's use of the invention could not be readily discerned by an observer? Alternatively, suppose that an individual had maintained a technology as a secret; should such a use suffice to bar an inventor a patent even though she brought the invention into public knowledge? This casebook considers these issues by dividing third party activities into three categories: uses which themselves inform others about the invention, uses which by their nature do not inform others about the invention, and secret uses.

§ 5.2[a]   INFORMING USES

ELECTRIC STORAGE BATTERY CO. v. SHIMADZU

United States Supreme Court, 1939
307 U.S. 5

MR. JUSTICE ROBERTS delivered the opinion of the Court.

The courts below have held valid and infringed certain claims of three patents granted to Genzo Shimadzu, a citizen and resident of Japan. The earliest is for a method of forming a finely divided and, consequently, more chemically reactive, lead powder. The second is for a method or process of manufacturing a fine powder composed of lead suboxide and metallic lead and for the product of the process. The third is for an apparatus for the continuous production of lead oxides in the form of a dry fine powder. Such powder is useful in the manufacture of plates for storage batteries.

The inventions which are the basis of the patents were conceived by Shimadzu and reduced to practise in Japan not later than August 1919. He did not disclose the inventions to anyone in the United States before he applied for United States patents. Application was presented for No. 1,584,149 on January 30, 1922; for No. 1,584,150 on July 14, 1923; and for No. 1,896,020 on April 27, 1926. The inventions were not patented or described in a printed publication in this or any foreign country prior to the filing of the applications. The petitioner, without knowledge of Shimadzu's inventions, began the use of a machine, which involved both the method and the apparatus of the patents, at Philadelphia, Pennsylvania, early in 1921 and attained commercial production in June 1921. Over the objection of the petitioner the respondents were permitted by testimony, and by the introduction of contemporaneous drawings and note books, to carry the date of invention back to August 1919, and the courts below fixed that as the date of invention and reduction to practise in Japan.

If a valid patent is to issue, the invention must not have been in public use in this country for more than two years prior to the filing of the application. Such public use is an affirmative defense to be pleaded and proved. The respondents insist that the findings respecting the defense, on which the petitioner relies, are unsupported by the evidence. We cannot agree with either position. * * *

In the present case the evidence is that the petitioner, since June 1921, has continuously employed the alleged infringing machine and process for the production of lead oxide powder used in the manufacture of plates for storage batteries which have been sold in quantity. There is no finding, and we think none would have been justified, to the effect that the machine, process, and product were not well known to the employes in the plant, or that efforts were made to conceal them from anyone who had a legitimate interest in understanding them. This use, begun more than two years before Shimadzu applied for patents 1,584,150 and 1,896,020, invalidated the claims in suit.

[handwritten margin note: Two patents No good.]

NOTES

1. Informing Use. The technology in *Electric Storage Battery* was buried in a battery. On what basis did the Supreme Court decide that this technology was in "public" use? This result, of course, is consistent with *Egbert*. Thus, this public use adequately informed the public of the presence in the public domain of the invention. Does the rule change when the invention does not inform the public of invention?

2. The Statutory Bar Period. In 1939, Congress shortened the two-year statutory bar period discussed in *Electric Storage Battery* to its present length of one year. The Senate Report offers an explanation:

> In 1839, when the period of 2 years was first adopted, it may have been a proper length of time for an inventor to make up his mind whether or not to file a patent application for patent. Under present conditions 2 years appears unduly long and operates as a handicap to industry. Reduction of the period would serve to bring the date of patenting closer to the time when the invention is made, and would expedite applications, not only in their filing but also in their process through the Patent Office. One year is believed to be a very fair period for all concerned.

How does a reduction in the bar period possibly bring the date of patenting close to the time the invention was made? At any rate, are you impressed with the quantitative nature of the congressional determination of the optimal grace period? Have contemporary artifacts sufficiently changed industrial conditions such that the statutory bar period should be shortened again?

§ 5.2[b]   NON-INFORMING USES

ABBOTT LABORATORIES v. GENEVA PHARMACEUTICALS, INC.

United States Court of Appeals for the Federal Circuit, 1999
182 F.3d 1315

Before Plager, Lourie, and Bryson, Circuit Judges.

LOURIE, CIRCUIT JUDGE.

Abbott Laboratories appeals from the summary judgment of the United States District Court for the Northern District of Illinois holding claim 4 of its United States Patent 5,504,207 invalid under the on-sale provision of 35 U.S.C. § 102(b) (1994). *See Abbott Labs. v. Geneva Pharms., Inc.* (N.D.Ill. Sept. 1, 1998). Because we conclude that the district court properly granted summary judgment of invalidity, we affirm.

[handwritten margin note: Abbott appeals summary judgment of invalid claim of patent on sale]

[handwritten margin note: Court affirms]

BACKGROUND

Terazosin hydrochloride is a pharmaceutical compound used for the treatment of hypertension and benign prostatic hyperplasia. Abbott

Laboratories has marketed it exclusively under the trademark Hytrin since 1987. Abbott's Hytrin tablets contain the dihydrate crystalline form of terazosin hydrochloride. Terazosin hydrochloride also exists in four anhydrous crystalline forms, and claim 4 of the '207 patent specifically claims the Form IV anhydrate. Claim 4 reads as follows: "4. The anhydrous Form IV crystalline modification of 1–(4–amino–6, 7–dimethoxy–2–quinazolinyl)–4–(2–tetrahydrofuroyl)piperazine hydrochloride characterized by principal peaks in the powder X-ray diffraction pattern at values of. . . ." The particular peaks are not important to the resolution of this case.

Abbott sued Geneva Pharmaceuticals, Inc., Novopharm Limited, and Invamed, Inc. for infringement of the '207 patent after each of them filed an Abbreviated New Drug Application (ANDA) at the United States Food and Drug Administration seeking approval to market a generic version of Hytrin containing the Form IV anhydrate. It is an act of patent infringement under certain circumstances to file an ANDA seeking approval to commercially manufacture, use, or sell a drug claimed in a patent before the expiration date of such patent. *See* 35 U.S.C. § 271(e)(2)(A) (1994). It is undisputed that such circumstances apply here. The cases were consolidated in the United States District Court for the Northern District of Illinois. The defendants each raised the affirmative defense of patent invalidity under the on-sale bar of 35 U.S.C. § 102(b), asserting that Form IV was anticipated because it was sold in the United States more than one year before the '207 patent's filing date, October 18, 1994.

It is undisputed on appeal that a company not party to this law suit, Byron Chemical Company, Inc., made at least three sales of Form IV terazosin hydrochloride anhydrate in the United States more than one year before the October 18, 1994 filing date. Byron sold a five-kilogram lot of anhydrous terazosin hydrochloride during the 1989–90 period and another lot in 1991 to defendant Geneva. Byron sold a third lot to Warner Chilcott Laboratories in 1992. Byron did not manufacture the compound itself; it bought it from two foreign manufacturers—Imhausen–Chemie GMBH in Germany and Yogodawa Pharmaceutical Company in Japan. None of these sales transactions specified which crystalline form of the anhydrous compound was being sold. Thus, at the time of the sales, the parties to the United States transactions did not know the identity of the particular crystalline form with which they were dealing. It was not until after the United States sales transactions were completed that Abbott and Geneva each tested samples from these lots and determined that the Form IV anhydrate crystal was what had been sold. Specifically, Abbott in 1995, and Geneva in 1996, each performed x-ray diffraction analyses on samples from these lots and found that the samples exhibited the pattern of principal peaks at the particular values disclosed in claim 4 that characterize the Form IV anhydrate crystal.

On defendants' motions for summary judgment, the district court held that the United States sales invalidated claim 4 under the on-sale bar. The court reasoned that Form IV was in the public domain, that buyers had come to rely on it being freely available, and that it was immaterial that the parties were unaware of the nature of that particular crystal form. Abbott timely appealed to this court.

DISCUSSION

The ultimate determination whether an invention was on sale within the meaning of § 102(b) is a question of law which we review de novo. *See Manville Sales Corp. v. Paramount Sys., Inc.*, 917 F.2d 544, 549 (Fed.Cir.1990). A patent is invalid under § 102(b) if "the invention was ... on sale in this country, more than one year prior to the date of the application for patent in the United States...." Because Abbott filed the application for the '207 patent on October 18, 1994, the critical date for purposes of the on-sale bar is October 18, 1993. As the parties challenging the validity of a presumptively valid patent, see 35 U.S.C. § 282 (1994), the defendants bore the burden of proving the existence of an on-sale bar by clear and convincing evidence. In this case, there are no facts in dispute, leaving only the legal issue whether the § 102(b) on-sale bar invalidates the patent.

Abbott argues that claim 4 is not invalid under the on-sale bar because the "invention" was not on sale. For an "invention" to be on sale, Abbott submits, the parties must "conceive," or know precisely, the nature of the subject matter with which they are dealing. Since the parties did not know that they were dealing with Form IV, Abbott reasons, they did not "conceive" the subject matter sold and therefore there was no "invention" on sale. The defendants respond that we need only apply the two-part test for the on-sale bar recently set forth by the Supreme Court in *Pfaff v. Wells Electronics, Inc.*, and that, under this test, it is irrelevant that the parties to the sales did not know that they were dealing with Form IV rather than with another anhydrous terazosin hydrochloride crystalline form.

We agree with defendants that claim 4 is invalid and that the parties' ignorance that they were dealing with Form IV is irrelevant. The Supreme Court has recently stated a two-part test for determining when the on-sale bar applies. Before the critical date, the invention must both be the subject of a commercial sale or offer for sale and be "ready for patenting." *See Pfaff* (rejecting the "totality of the circumstances" test for determining whether an invention was on sale before the critical date). An invention may be shown to be "ready for patenting," *inter alia*, by "proof of reduction to practice before the critical date." *Id.*

The invention at issue in this case clearly meets the *Pfaff* test. Even though the parties did not know it at the time, it is undisputed that Form IV was the subject matter of at least three commercial sales in the United States before the critical date. It is also clear that the invention was "ready for patenting" because at least two foreign manufacturers had already reduced it to practice. Furthermore, the statutory on-sale bar is not subject to exceptions for sales made by third parties either innocently or fraudulently. *See Evans Cooling Sys., Inc. v. General Motors Corp.*, 125 F.3d 1448, 1453–54 (Fed.Cir.1997). The fact that these sales were not made by Abbott is therefore irrelevant.

Abbott insists that there can be no on-sale bar unless conception of the invention has been proved, and that the lack of knowledge of the exact crystalline nature of the material that was sold precludes there having been a conception. We disagree that proof of conception was required. The fact that the claimed material was sold under circumstances in which no question existed that it was useful means that it was reduced to practice. In any event, this is not a priority dispute in which conception is a critical issue. The sale of the material in question obviates any need for inquiry into conception.

Abbott cites cases holding that the accidental, unintended, and unappreciated production of the product or process in question does not constitute anticipation. *See, e.g., Tilghman v. Proctor*, 102 U.S. 707, 711–12, (1881) (an accidental and incidental production of fatty acids by means not understood or appreciated did not anticipate a patented process for separating fatty bodies into fatty acids and glycerin. Those cases are all off the point because they involved the issue whether the claimed inventions were anticipated by earlier work that produced no useful or appreciated result. In contrast, the material here, having been sold, was decidedly useful and appreciated.)

Abbott argues that the invention was not on sale because those who sold the claimed product did not know all of its characteristics. We disagree. It is well settled in the law that there is no requirement that a sales offer specifically identify all the characteristics of an invention offered for sale or that the parties recognize the significance of all of these characteristics at the time of the offer. See *Scaltech Inc. v. Retec/Tetra, L.L.C.*, 178 F.3d 1378, 1384 (Fed.Cir.1999). If a product that is offered for sale inherently possesses each of the limitations of the claims, then the invention is on sale, whether or not the parties to the transaction recognize that the product possesses the claimed characteristics. *See id.; J.A. LaPorte, Inc. v. Norfolk Dredging Co.*, 787 F.2d 1577, 1582–83 (Fed.Cir.1986) ("[T]he question is not whether the sale, even a third party sale, 'discloses' the invention at the time of the sale, but whether the sale relates to a device that embodies the invention.") (emphasis in original). In this case, it is undisputed that Form IV falls within the scope of claim 4. The fact that the parties to the sales transactions did not know they were dealing in Form IV at the time of the sales is therefore irrelevant to the question whether it was "on sale" before the critical date.

One of the primary purposes of the on-sale bar is to prohibit the withdrawal of inventions that have been placed into the public domain through commercialization. *See, e.g., King Instrument Corp. v. Otari Corp.*, 767 F.2d 853, 860 (Fed.Cir.1985) (the discovery of a new property of an old compound does not make claims to that compound patentable). For these reasons, we affirm the district court's judgment holding claim 4 of the '207 patent invalid.

Notes

1. **Another View of Non–Informing Uses.** In another case authored by Judge Lourie, *Baxter Int'l v. Cobe Labs., Inc.*, 88 F.3d 1054 (Fed.Cir.1996), the Federal Circuit upheld a statutory bar on an inventive centrifuge device that did not damage blood platelets. The facts disclosed that an NIH laboratory had used such a centrifuge at its closed campus in Bethesda, Maryland. Judge Newman dissented:

> This new rule of law, that unpublished laboratory use after a reduction to practice is a public use, creates a new and mischievous category of "secret" prior art. I respectfully dissent from the court's ruling, for it is contrary to, and misapplies, the law of 35 U.S.C. § 102 ... the patent statute and precedent do not elevate private laboratory use after a reduction to practice to "public use" under § 102(b). When the public use is unknown and unknowable information in the possession of third persons, 35 U.S.C. § 102 accommodates such "secret prior art" only in the limited circumstances of § 102(e). This new category of internal laboratory use is immune to the most painstaking documentary search. The court thus produces a perpetual cloud on any issued patent, defeating the objective standards and policy considerations embodied in the § 102 definitions of prior art. It is incorrect to interpret 35 U.S.C. § 102(b) to mean that laboratory use after a reduction to practice is a "public use," and thus a bar against any patent application filed, by anyone, more than a year thereafter. Section 102(b) was not intended to add to the bars based on information not published or publicly known or otherwise within the definition of prior art.

Even Judge Newman would be constrained to agree that an obscure foreign publication describing the Suaudeau centrifuge would fall within § 102(b); does such a scenario mark a substantially greater degree of dissemination than use in a private laboratory that was open at least to lab personnel? Consider as well the economics of searching for existing technology as opposed to the economics of reinventing that technology. Are there situations where the law should encourage an investigation to determine whether a particular technology exists, as opposed to the reinvention of that technology?

2. **Theft as Prior Use.** Suppose an unscrupulous individual steals an inventor's ideas and makes a commercial, informing use of them prior to the critical date. Should such activity constitute a "public use" under § 102(b)? The court in *Lorenz v. Colgate–Palmolive Peet Co.*, 167 F.2d 423 (3d Cir.1948), reached a seemingly hard result on this issue:

> The prior-public-use proviso ... was enacted by Congress in the public interest. It contains no qualification or exception which limits the nature of the public use. We think that Congress intended that if an inventor does not protect his discovery by an application for a patent within the period prescribed by the Act, and an intervening public use arises from any source whatsoever, the inventor must be barred from a

patent or from the fruits of his monopoly, if a patent has issued to him. There is not a single word in the statute which would tend to put an inventor, whose disclosures have been pirated, in any different position from one who has permitted the use of his process.

What do you think of this reasoning? Does any word of the statute distinguish between applicant and third party uses? Or would a contrary result provide open ground for collusion and ignore the reality that the inventor remains in control of her own destiny in such situations?

§ 5.2[c] SECRET USES

W. L. GORE & ASSOCIATES v. GARLOCK, INC.

United States Court of Appeals, Federal Circuit, 1983
721 F.2d 1540

Before Markey, Chief Judge, and Davis and Miller, Circuit Judges.

MARKEY, CHIEF JUDGE.

Appeal from a judgment of the District Court for the Northern District of Ohio holding U.S. Patents 3,953,566 ('566) and 4,187,390 ('390) invalid. We affirm in part, reverse in part, and remand for a determination of the infringement issue.

BACKGROUND

Tape of unsintered polytetrafluorethylene (PTFE) (known by the trademark TEFLON of E.I. du Pont de Nemours, Inc.) had been stretched in small increments. W.L. Gore & Associates, Inc. (Gore), assignee of the patents in suit, experienced a tape breakage problem in the operation of its "401" tape stretching machine. Dr. Robert Gore, Vice President of Gore, developed the invention disclosed and claimed in the '566 and '390 patents in the course of his effort to solve that problem. The 401 machine was disclosed and claimed in Gore's U.S. Patent 3,664,915 ('915) and was the invention of Wilbert L. Gore, Dr. Gore's father. PTFE tape had been sold as thread seal tape, i.e., tape used to keep pipe joints from leaking. The '915 patent, the application for which was filed on October 3, 1969, makes no reference to stretch rate, at 10% per second or otherwise, or to matrix tensile strength in excess of 7,300 psi.

Dr. Gore experimented with heating and stretching of highly crystalline PTFE rods. Despite slow, careful stretching, the rods broke when stretched a relatively small amount. Conventional wisdom in the art taught that breakage could be avoided only by slowing the stretch rate or by decreasing the crystallinity. In late October, 1969, Dr. Gore discovered, contrary to that teaching, that stretching the rods as fast as possible enabled him to stretch them to more than ten times their original length with no breakage. Further, though the rod was thus greatly lengthened, its diameter remained virtually unchanged throughout its length. The rapid stretching also transformed the hard, shiny rods into rods of a soft, flexible material.

Gore developed several PTFE products by rapidly stretching highly crystalline PTFE, including: (1) porous film for filters and laminates; (2) fabric laminates of PTFE film bonded to fabric to produce a remarkable material having the contradictory properties of impermeability to liquid water and permeability to water vapor, the material being used to make "breathable" rainwear and filters; (3) porous yarn for weaving or braiding into other products, like space suits and pump packing; (4) tubes used as replacements for human arteries and veins; and (5) insulation for high performance electric cables.

On May 21, 1970, Gore filed the patent application that resulted in the patents in suit. The '566 patent has 24 claims directed to processes for stretching highly crystalline, unsintered, PTFE. The processes, inter alia, include the steps of stretching PTFE at a rate above 10% per second and at a temperature between about 35 degrees C and the crystalline melt point of PTFE. The '390 patent has 77 claims directed to various products obtained by processes of the '566 patent.

SECTION 102(B) AND THE CROPPER MACHINE

In 1966 John W. Cropper (Cropper) of New Zealand developed and constructed a machine for producing stretched and unstretched PTFE thread seal tape. In 1967, Cropper sent a letter to a company in Massachusetts, offering to sell his machine, describing its operation, and enclosing a photo. Nothing came of that letter. There is no evidence and no finding that the present inventions thereby became known or used in this country.

In 1968, Cropper sold his machine to Budd, which at some point thereafter used it to produce and sell PTFE threat seal tape. The sales agreement between Cropper and Budd provided:

ARTICLE "E"—PROTECTION OF TRADE SECRETS ETC.

1. BUDD agrees that while this agreement is in force it will not reproduce any copies of the said apparatus without the express written permission of Cropper nor will it divulge to any person or persons other than its own employees or employees of its affiliated corporations any of the said known-how or any details whatsoever relating to the apparatus. 2. BUDD agrees to take all proper steps to ensure that its employees observe the terms of Article "E" 1 and further agrees that whenever it is proper to do so it will take legal action in a Court of competent jurisdiction to enforce any one or more of the legal or equitable remedies available to a trade secret plaintiff. Budd told its employees the Cropper machine was confidential and required them to sign confidentiality agreements. Budd otherwise treated the Cropper machine like its other manufacturing equipment.

A former Budd employee said Budd made no effort to keep the secret. That Budd did not keep the machine hidden from employees legally bound to keep their knowledge confidential does not evidence a failure to maintain the secret. Similarly, that du Pont employees were shown the machine to see if they could help increase its speed does not itself establish a breach of the secrecy agreement. There is no evidence of when that viewing occurred. There is no evidence that a viewer of the machine could thereby learn anything of which process, among all possible processes, the machine is being used to practice. As Cropper testified, looking at the machine in operation does not reveal whether it is stretching, and if so, at what speed. Nor does looking disclose whether the crystallinity and temperature elements of the invention set forth in the claims are involved. There is no evidence that Budd's secret use of the Cropper machine made knowledge of the claimed process accessible to the public.

The district court held all claims of the '566 patent invalid under 102(b), supra, note 3, because "the invention" was "in public use [and] on sale" by Budd more than one year before Gore's application for patent. Beyond a failure to consider each of the claims independently, 35 U.S.C. § 282, and a failure of proof that the claimed inventions as a whole were practiced by Budd before the critical May 21, 1969 date, it was error to hold that Budd's activity with the Cropper machine, as above indicated, was a "public" use of the processes claimed in the '566 patent, that activity having been secret, not public.

Assuming, arguendo, that Budd sold tape produced on the Cropper machine before October 1969, and that that tape was made by a process set forth in a claim of the '566 patent, the issue under § 102(b) is whether that sale would defeat Dr. Gore's right to a patent on the process inventions set forth in the claims.

If Budd offered and sold anything, it was only tape, not whatever process was used in producing it. Neither party contends, and there was no evidence, that the public could learn the claimed process by examining the tape. If Budd and Cropper commercialized the tape, that could result in a forfeiture of a patent granted them for their process on an application filed by them more than a year later. *D.L. Auld Co. v. Chroma Graphics Corp.*, 714 F.2d 1144, at 1147–48 (Fed.Cir.1983); *See Metallizing Engineering Co. v. Kenyon Bearing & Auto Parts Co.*, 153 F.2d 516 (2d Cir.1946). There is no reason or statutory basis, however, on which Budd's and Cropper's secret commercialization of a process, if established, could be held a bar to the grant of a patent to Gore on that process.

Early public disclosure is a linchpin of the patent system. As between a prior inventor who benefits from a process by selling its product but suppresses, conceals, or otherwise keeps the process from the public, and a later inventor who promptly files a patent application from which the public will gain a disclosure of the process, the law

law favors disclosure over trade secrets.

favors the latter. The district court therefore erred as a matter of law in applying the statute and in its determination that Budd's secret use of the Cropper machine and sale of tape rendered all process claims of the '566 patent invalid under § 102(b).

APPENDIX

Claims of the '566 patent discussed at trial:

1. A process for the production of a porous article of manufacture of a polymer of tetrafluoroethylene which process comprises expanding a shaped article consisting essentially of highly crystalline poly (tetrafluoroethylene) made by a paste-forming extrusion technique, after removal of lubricant, by stretching said unsintered shaped article at a rate exceeding about 10% per second and maintaining said shaped article at a temperature between about 35 degrees C. and the crystalline melt point of said tetrafluoroethylene polymer during said stretching.

3. The process of claim 1 in which the rate of stretch is about 100% per second.

17. The process of claim 1 in which the shaped article is expanded such that its final length in the direction of expansion is greater than about twice the original length.

19. The process of claim 17 in which said final length is greater than about five times the original length.

NOTES

1. *Gore* **as a § 102(g) Case.** This material is so difficult that even a patent expert of Chief Judge Markey's caliber seems to have confused § 102(a) and (b). See 1 MARTIN J. ADELMAN, PATENT LAW PERSPECTIVES, § 2.3[8.–4] at n.41 (2d ed. 1992). Once you have had the opportunity to take up § 102(g) in the next chapter, consider whether the discussion of § 102(b) in *Gore* might more properly relate to that paragraph. For example, does the court draw attention to the invention date or the critical date? Does the court's description of the facts instead convince you that Budd and Cropper, the third-party inventors, concealed their invention? A further consideration of concealment under § 102(g) is taken up in this text at Chapter 5.

2. **A Potent Process?** What significance attaches to the fact that process claims were involved in *Gore v. Garlock*? Suppose the asserted claims had been to the PTFE tape itself: should the result differ?

3. **A Question of Perspective?** The facts of this case adequately show the problem with making a secret use a bar, namely Budd would get both use of the trade secret and the ability to bar Gore from attaining a patent after extensive investments to develop the technology independently. Of course, Budd could respond that as first inventor, and as such he should have the option to acquire a patent or retain his new technology as a trade secret. Gore in turn would respond that he should not be barred when Budd elected to forego patenting in favor of trade secret protection. Does this sound familiar?

Budd's argument in favor of first inventor's choice is simply a restatement of problem with first-to-invent systems that Justice Story confronted in *Pennock*. Thus, this case really brings the statutory bar question full circle.

§ 5.3   ABANDONMENT § 102(c)

Review of the statutory predecessors to § 102(c) does much to explain the true impact of this provision. The Act of 1836 indicated that no patent could issue to an inventor if the claimed invention was "in public use or on sale, with his consent or allowance." Three years later, Congress changed this language by mandating that "no patent shall be held to be invalid by reason of such purchase, sale or prior use to the application of the patent ... except on proof [1] of abandonment of such invention to the public or [2] that such purchase, sale or prior use has been for more than two years prior to such application for a patent." In 1870, language similar to that of the current statute was introduced. The grant of a patent was then permissible if the invention was "not in public use or on sale for more than two years prior to such application for a patent."

102(c)
- surrender
of an
invention to
the public.

As such, the current language referring to abandonment of the invention should not be read literally. Section 102(c) does not refer to the relinquishment of the invention itself; it instead refers to the surrender of an invention *to the public*. In other words, § 102(c) provides that appropriate conduct by the inventor can lead to the forfeiture of the right to obtain a patent on the invention. For instance, in an early case, *Kendall v. Winsor*, 62 U.S. (21 How.) 322 (1858), the Supreme Court explained the meaning of abandonment. In this case, Winsor patented a harness-making machine. One of his employees, Aldridge left his service and began making copies of the patented machine in another state. Winsor sued for patent infringement. The defendants argued that Winsor had repeatedly stated that he preferred not to obtain a patent, but rather to maintain his technology as a trade secret and rely on the difficulty of reverse engineering the complex machine. Although Winsor later changed his mind and obtained a patent, the defendants still asserted that his statements amounted to an abandonment. The Supreme Court upheld the jury's finding of infringement. In the process it commented on abandonment:

> It is the unquestionable right of every inventor to confer gratuitously the benefits of his ingenuity upon the public, and this he may do either by express declaration or by conduct equally significant with language-such, for instance, as an acquiescence with full knowledge in the use of his invention by others; or he may forfeit his rights as an inventor by a wilful or negligent postponement of his claims, or by an attempt to withhold the benefit of his improvement from the public until a similar or the same improvement should have been made and introduced by others ... But there may be cases in which the knowledge of the invention many

be surreptitiously obtained, and communicated to the public, that do not affect the right of the inventor. Under such circumstances, no presumption can arise in favor of an abandonment of the right to the inventor to the public, though an acquiescence on his part will lay the foundation for such a presumption.

Contemporary decisions rarely rely upon abandonment under § 102(c) as a basis for defeating a patent right. They instead turn to § 102(b), which provides more specified details on when the patent right is lost. In some sense, if the conditions of § 102(b) are fulfilled, then the law deems the inventor to have abandoned the right to obtain patent protection.

[handwritten: 102(b) used mostly today]

§ 5.4　DELAYED UNITED STATES FILING § 102(d)

Section 102(d) bars a U.S. patent when (1) an inventor files a foreign patent application more than twelve months before filing the U.S. application, and (2) a foreign patent results from that application prior to the U.S. filing date. The requirements are conjunctive: both requirements must be met in order to trigger § 102(d) and bar the issuance of a patent. By encouraging prompt filing in the United States, § 102(d) ensures that the term of U.S. patents will not appreciably extend past the expiration date of parallel foreign patents.

[handwritten: 102(d) - bars US, patent if you file for a foreign patent more than 12 months before filing US patent. and you get the foreign patent]

An example illustrates the application of § 102(d). Suppose that Orlanth, the inventor of an electric trolling motor, files an application at the Swedish Patent Office on May 25, 2008. The Swedish application matures into a granted Swedish patent on August 1, 2009. If Orlanth has not filed his U.S. patent application at the PTO as of August 1, 2009, the date of the Swedish patent grant, the § 102(d) bar would be triggered.

Commentators have often approached § 102(d) with some distaste. Because inventors may choose to file a patent application only in the United States, the policy goal of assuring that the U.S. market will become patent-free contemporaneously with foreign markets seems poorly served via the § 102(d) bar. More telling is that § 102(d) almost exclusively works against foreign inventors. Individuals based in the United States seldom encounter problems with § 102(d), for inventors the world over tend to file applications in their home patent offices first. And while this statute comports with the letter of Article 27 of the TRIPS Agreement, which requires that "patents shall be available ... without discrimination as to the place of the invention," § 102(d) in practice derogates from the principle of national treatment of foreign inventors.

[handwritten: harsh against foreign inventors who file in there own country first.]

Until a decade ago, the best that could be said about § 102(d) is that it was seldom employed. Because patent prosecution almost always requires more than one year to complete, and because most foreign patent applications are published more than twelve months before their grant, the published application itself might be available as "printed publication" under § 102(b). However, a Federal Circuit opinion interpreting § 102(d), *In re Kathawala*, 9 F.3d 942 (Fed.Cir.1993), appears to have breathed new life into the statute.

Kathawala, inventor of cholesterol-inhibiting compounds, filed patent applications in the United States, Greece, and Spain. The three applications included substantially the same specifications but contained differing claims. The Greek patent claimed compounds, pharmaceutical compositions, methods of use, and methods of making. The U.S. patent contained all but the latter sort of claims. The Spanish patent claimed only the method of making the compound. Not only was the U.S. application filed more than one year after the Greek and Spanish applications were filed, each of these foreign applications actually led to granted patents before the U.S. filing date.

Appealing the PTO's imposition of a § 102(d) bar before the Federal Circuit, Kathawala offered two arguments worthy of note here. First, Kathawala asserted that because the Spanish patent contained only method of making claims, which were not claimed in the U.S. application, the invention claimed in the United States had not been previously "patented" in a foreign country within the meaning of § 102(d). Kathawala also urged that the claims of the Greek patent were invalid because, at the time the patent issued, the Greek patent law actually disallowed patents directed to pharmaceuticals.

The Federal Circuit had little trouble dispensing with these arguments. According to Judge Lourie, § 102(d) should not be given a constrained reading. It was enough that Kathawala's Spanish application disclosed and provided the opportunity to claim all aspects of his invention, including the compounds themselves. Allowing dilatory inventors to obtain U.S. patents on others aspect of the same "invention" patented too long ago abroad would frustrate the policy of the statute, according to the court. The court also dismissed Kathawala's arguments regarding the Greek patent, declining to speculate on the patent eligibility law of Greece. Both Greek and U.S. patents included claims towards the same subject matter because Kathawala had put them there, and their validity was irrelevant to whether the subject matter was "patented" in accordance with § 102(d).

Not only was the *Kathawala* court's unwillingness to consider Greek patent law surprising, its generous view of patented subject matter seems questionable. Few members of the patent community would say that disclosed but unclaimed subject matter is patented, for the claims are the measure of patentee rights. Perhaps *Kathawala* should have been an obviousness case. But given the robust holding in *Kathawala*, applicants should be particularly wary of foreign patent registration regimes. Under these systems, foreign patent offices do not fully examine applications for compliance with the patent law, leading to short processing times and prompt issuances of foreign patents.

STATUTORY BAR EXERCISES

Dr. Martha Bjorn works for the research and development arm of Unstrung Incorporated, a premium sports equipment manufacturer located entirely within the United States. On July 4, 2006, she invents a new process for producing tennis rackets which fulfill the standards set forth by the dominant professional tennis organization. The process results in tennis rackets identical to those made by prior art processes, but does so more quickly and cheaply. As Unstrung's patent attorney has quite a backlog of other patent applications, a United States application claiming the Bjorn process is not filed until November 14, 2007.

[margin: invents July 4 2006]

[margin: Filed Nov 14, 2007]

Would any of the following activities bar the issue of a patent to the Bjorn invention under § 102?

[margin: Aug 1, 2006 date-experiment]

1. Unstrung Incorporated begins development efforts to adopt Bjorn's process to the realities of the factory production line on August 1, 2006. After modifying its existing manufacturing processes to fit the Bjorn process and working out the bugs, Unstrung judges these efforts to be successful by November 19, 2006. At that point, Unstrung then begins commercial production.

[margin: good critical date Nov 14,]

[margin: Aug started retooling factory. Nov. 19 2006 begin commercialization]

2. A few days after completing her invention, Bjorn writes an article about the process and submits it to a technical journal. The article is published on December 15, 2006.

[margin: good after critical date]

[margin: Publishes art Dec 15 2006]

3. Unstrung Incorporated begins shipping tennis rackets produced by the Bjorn process to distributors on February 1, 2007. Retailers makes the first sales of Bjorn-produced rackets to consumers by February 10, 2007.

[margin: good in grace per rod.]

[margin: Feb 1 shipped Feb 10 2007 sold]

4. An unrelated party located in the United States, Swish Limited, had developed a similar process to that invented by Bjorn. Swish perfected the process on October 7, 2006, and produced several dozen rackets. Ultimately, however, they decided not to employ the process on a larger scale for financial reasons. Swish maintained the process documentation and resulting rackets under lock and key, and the Swish employee-inventors maintained the pledge of confidentiality they had agreed to in their employment contracts.

[margin: good secret use]

[margin: Another company creates but doesn't sell. keeps under lock and key]

5. During his September 15, 2003, retirement luncheon in Campos, Brazil, the senior engineer of a local sporting goods maker offers some advice on ways to improve the production of tennis racquets. The steps he proposes are quite similar to those ultimately suggested by Bjorn. The remarks are in Portuguese and go unrecorded.

[margin: good only oral word in Europe]

[margin: Just oral remarks good 102(f) rejection if Bjorn in attendance.]

6. Mr. Forehand is the president, chief executive officer, and sole shareholder of Unstrung Incorporated. Forehand is presented with the "Sports Manufacturing Person of the Year Award" at an elaborate industry-sponsored dinner on August 27, 2006. In a fit of largess

following this acknowledgment by his peers, Forehand fully describes the Bjorn process during his acceptance speech. He then declares that "I believe this invention will transform the world of tennis and feel that all of us should participate in this dramatic possibility. I hereby dedicate our new invention to the public." The next morning, Forehand has second thoughts and orders the filing of a patent application as above.

7. Unstrung Incorporated's patent attorney contacts two foreign associates and asks them to file patent applications claiming the Bjorn process in Sweden and Germany, respectively. The Swedish application is filed on July 15, 2006, and issues on October 13, 2007. The German application is filed on August 17, 2006, and issues as a granted patent on January 15, 2008.

CHAPTER SIX

NOVELTY: PRIOR INVENTION

■ ■ ■

This Chapter turns to the second strand of issues running through the paragraphs of § 102. Section 102(a) straightforwardly states the essential first-to-invent rule which dominates United States novelty analysis. It does so by supplying a basis for rejecting patent applications which describe an invention "known or used in this country, or patented or described in a printed publication in this or a foreign country, before the invention thereof by the applicant for a patent." Section 102(a) requires some form of public knowledge of the first inventor's invention before the second inventor forms the subject matter of his patent application or patent. Section 102(e) deals with a special category of secret knowledge of a first inventor's work: a patent application, filed prior to the invention date, which has actually matured into a published application or granted patent, but which does not claim the invention.

Section 102(g) is a general provision covering secret work by a first inventor that becomes known to the public after the invention by the second inventor. Section 102(g) serves as the basis for a so-called "interference"—an intricate administrative proceeding between two or more inventors, each asserting that it was the first inventor and therefore should obtain the award of a patent. Section 102(g) has another, more humble use: simply as another category of prior art which may be used as the basis of a rejection for anticipation or nonobviousness. In this case, the party asserting the statute is not claiming the invention for itself, but arguing that the issued patent is invalid. This effort usually involves the identification of a third party which invented first. In this sense, § 102(g) acts similarly to § 102(a). But, as we shall see, § 102(g) does not embrace a first inventor whose work was secret when the second inventor/applicant made his invention.

Section 102(f) prevents a patent from issuing to an applicant who "did not himself invent the subject matter sought to be patented." If the applicant derived the invention from another, then no patent can result from his application. Although the derivation requirement could well be considered, as distinct from the prior art generating provisions of §§ 102(a), (e), and (g), it sufficiently buttresses the novelty requirement to be considered with them.

In contrast to Chapter 5, *Statutory Bars*, the novelty issues addressed in this Chapter should not be considered as fundamental to the world's patent systems. In fact, they are entirely unique to the first-to-invent system of the United States. If the United States ever adopts a first-to-file system, this Chapter could be cleanly excised from the book. As you make your way through this Chapter, consider those values which the first-to-invent system purports to foster, the extent to which it actually meets these ends, and whether the United States patent community can long afford to maintain the inherent uncertainties, high transaction costs, and legal isolation of its unique novelty regime.

§ 6.1   PRIOR INVENTION UNDER § 102(a)

WOODCOCK v. PARKER

Circuit Court, District of Massachusetts, 1813
30 Fed.Cas. 491

STORY, CIRCUIT JUSTICE, in summing up the cause, directed the jury as follows: The first inventor is entitled to the benefit of his invention, if he reduce it to practice and obtain a patent therefor, and a subsequent inventor cannot, by obtaining a patent therefor, oust the first inventor of his right, or maintain an action against him for the use of his own invention. In the present case, as the defendants claim their right to use the machine in controversy by a good derivative title from Samuel Parker, if the jury are satisfied that said Parker was the first and original inventor of the machine, the plaintiff cannot, under all the circumstances, maintain his action; notwithstanding he may have been a subsequent inventor, without any knowledge of the prior existence of the machine, or communication with the first inventor. It is not necessary to consider, whether if the first inventor should wholly abandon his invention and never reduce it to practice, so as to produce useful effects, a second inventor might not be entitled to the benefit of the statute patent: because here there is not the slightest evidence of such abandonment. Parker is proved to have put his machine in operation; it produced useful effects, and he followed up his invention by obtaining a patent from the department of state.

NOTES

1.   **The "First and Original" Inventor.** Although the Statute of Monopolies indicated that patents could issue to the "true and first inventor," *An Act Concerning Monopolies and Dispensations with Penal Laws, and the Forfeitures Thereof*, 21 JAC. 1, ch. 3, § 6 (1623), it did not specify whether this "first" individual was the first applicant or the first inventor in fact. Justice Story's statement in *Woodcock* is among the earliest explaining a key concept of a first-to-invent system: that potentially novelty-destroying technology is measured from the date of invention, not the filing date. The Patent Act of 1836 was the first statute explicitly to embody the concept that "known or used" applied to acts before the invention date and not the filing date:

That any person or persons having discovered or invented any new or useful art, machine, manufacture, or composition of matter, or any new and useful improvement on any art, machine, manufacture, or composition of matter, not known or used by others before his or their discovery or invention thereof, and not, at the time of his application for a patent, in public use or on sale, with his consent or allowance, as the inventor or discoverer; and shall desire to obtain an exclusive property therein, may make application in writing to the Commissioner of Patents, expressing such desire, and the Commissioner, on due proceedings had, may grant a patent therefor.

In its modern incarnation, this rule is expressed in § 102(a) as follows:

A person shall be entitled to a patent unless—

(a) the invention was known or used by others in this country, or patented or described in a printed publication in this or a foreign country, before the invention thereof by the applicant for patent. . . .

See generally FRANK E. ROBBINS, THE DEFENSE OF PRIOR INVENTION: PATENT INFRINGEMENT LITIGATION (1977).

2. Disclosure of Invention Date. It may surprise you to learn that despite the primacy of the invention date in the United States patent statute, inventors have never been required to provide their dates of invention when they file applications with the United States Patent and Trademark Office. Instead, applicants' dates of inventive activity are revealed on an *ad hoc* basis in response to references cited by the examiner via so-called "Rule 131 affidavits," discussed later in this Chapter. Why does the United States patent system act so peculiarly with regard to invention date?

3. The Meaning of "Known or Used." This casebook has already considered the impact of the territorial limitations of § 102(a), as well as the meaning of its use of the phrase "patented or described in a printed publication," in Chapter 4. Section 102(a) employs a new term, however: the invention must be "known or used by others."

This phrase should be contrasted with the "public use" requirement of § 102(b). Chapter 4 of this casebook dealt at length with the sorts of public uses that could create a statutory bar under § 102(b). As you may suspect, the same issues arise under § 102(a) as well. Here, of course, no distinction can be drawn between the applicant and a third party—the issue is always whether a third party's use suffices to render him the prior inventor in terms of the patent law. But the question of whether secret and noninforming uses pass muster under § 102(a) remains.

GILLMAN v. STERN
Circuit Court of Appeals, Second Circuit, 1940
114 F.2d 28

Before L. Hand, Augustus N. Hand, and Chase, Circuit Judges.

L. HAND, CIRCUIT JUDGE.

Both the plaintiffs and the defendant appeal from the judgment in this action. The plaintiffs filed the usual complaint, asking an injunction for the infringement of Patent No. 1,919,674, issued on July 25, 1933, to the Sterling Airbrush Co., assignee of Laszlo Wenczel, for a pneumatic 'puffing machine.' The defendant set up a number of defenses: [including] that there had been a prior use of it by one Haas, at least as early as 1930 (the application was filed on January 21, 1931).... The judge held the patent invalid because anticipated by the prior use of Haas....

The patent was for a pneumatic machine for quilting; i.e., it blew thread or yarn "into packets formed in the fabric to stuff the same to impart a raised or embossed design".

[U]pon the issue of invalidity the defendant relies ... upon the prior use by Haas. Haas at some time undoubtedly did invent a "puffing machine" designed to perform the same work as plaintiff's machine. Further, his first "puffer" was substantially the same as the plaintiff's; and, if it had been properly proved, it might be hard to support the patent. However, not only was there no evidence as to the date of it except the work of Haas and his wife—who knew incidentally nothing of its construction—but again and again, Haas spoke of it as an unsatisfactory temporary device which he had discarded before he began to do any business. It must certainly be considered an abandoned experiment and is therefore immaterial. Haas also testified that in the autumn of 1929 he invented another "puffer" in general structure like the first, except that there was no means—as in Wenczel's machine—to vary the air pressure by changing the position of any member like the "tube, 40." The plaintiff insists that for this reason it cannot anticipate, and literally that is true; but possibly, if it could be deemed a part of the prior art, the step between it and Wenczel's disclosure would not justify a monopoly. Besides, claim one does not incorporate the "regulating valve," i.e., the "tube 40." We need not, however, pass upon this question, or indeed whether the evidence of its date of production satisfied the exacting standard set by the *Barbed Wire Patent Case*, 143 U.S. 275, 12 S.Ct. 443, 450, 36 L.Ed. 154 for it is clear that it was never in prior "public use," and that Haas was not a "first inventor." It was always kept as strictly secret as was possible, consistently with its exploitation. In general, everybody was carefully kept out of Haas' shop where the four machines were used. He testified that "no one was allowed to enter but my employees," girls he had had "for years"; and that he "had instructed my girls that if anybody should ask to get any kind of information simply tell them you don't know. In fact I have my shop door so arranged that it could only be opened from the inside." He also enjoined secrecy on his wife who testified "no one ever got into the place and no one ever saw the machine. He made everything himself." Indeed, as a condition upon even testifying in the case at bar Haas insisted, and the judge ordered, that the lawyers should be sworn to keep secret all he said about the construction of the "puffer," and that it should not be printed in the record, but typed and sealed for the inspection of the judges alone. It does not appear that the "girls" knew how the machines which they used were made, or how they operated.

The only exception to this was a disclosure, such as it was, to two members of a firm going by the name of the Bona Fide Embroidery Co.—Custer and Kadison. In the same autumn of 1929 they and Haas testified that they had seen some of his quilting and were anxious to get the whole of his output. They went to his shop to satisfy themselves; Custer said that "it was very vital at that time that I should know the workings of the machine for my production of the proper designs." (By "workings he could only have meant how it performed for he never learned its construction.") After this visit the two agreed that Haas should give them his whole production and that they should sell it; they even talked about taking out a patent, but did not have the necessary money. Thus, Haas kept his machine absolutely secret from the outside world except to secure selling agents for its product, and then it was only its performance, not its construction that even they learned. Moreover, Custer and Kadison had the same motive to suppress whatever information they got that Haas had, for without a patent the secret was all that protected their market.

Such a use is clearly not a "public" one, and such an inventor is not a "first inventor." In *Gayler v. Wilder*, 10 How. 477, 481, 497, 13 L.Ed. 504, the question was whether the condition—which has always been in the statute—that the patentee must be the "first and original inventor" was defeated by anyone who had earlier conceived the same invention, or only by one who had also in some way made public his results. A majority of the court held that only the second would defeat a patent on the ground that what had not in fact enriched the art, should not count; and the doctrine is now well fixed. *Alexander Milburn Co. v. Davis–Bournonville Co.*, 270 U.S. 390, 46 S.Ct. 324, 70 L.Ed. 651. Just as a secret use is not a "public use," so a secret inventor is not a "first inventor." *Acme Flexible Clasp Co. v. Cary Mfg. Co.*, C.C., 96 F. 344; *Diamond Patent Co. v. S. E. Carr Co.*, 9 Cir., 217 F. 400, 404; *A. Schrader's Sons v. Wein Sales Corp.*, 2 Cir., 9 F.2d 306; *Peerless Roll Leaf Co. v. H. Griffin & Sons Co.*, 2 Cir., 29 F.2d 646. Haas' user was one where "the machine, process, and product were not well known to the employes in the plant," and where "efforts were made to conceal them from anyone who had a legitimate interest in understanding them," if by "legitimate interest" one means something more than curiosity or mischief. *Electric Battery Co. v. Shimadzu*, 307 U.S. 5, 20, 59 S.Ct. 675, 684, 83 L.Ed. 1071. In *E. W. Bliss Co. v. Southern Can Co.*, D.C., 251 F. 903, 908, 909, *affirmed* 4 Cir., 265 F. 1018, although people were kept out of the factory, the exclusion was not, as in Haas' case, directed to the secrecy of the supposed anticipation.

We are to distinguish between a public user which does not inform the art (*Hall v. Macneale*, 107 U.S. 90, 97, 2 S.Ct. 73, 27 L.Ed. 367) and a secret user; some confusion has resulted from the failure to do so. It is true that in each case the fund of common knowledge is not enriched, and that might indeed have been good reason originally for throwing out each as anticipations. But when the statute made any "public use" fatal to a patent, and when thereafter the court held that it was equally fatal, whether or not the patentee had consented to it, there was no escape from holding—contrary to the underlying theory of the law—that it was irrelevant whether the use informed the public so that they could profit by it. Nevertheless, it was still true that secret uses were not public uses, whether or not public uses might on occasion have no public value. Perhaps it was originally open to argument that the statute merely meant to confine prior "public uses" to the prospective patentee and to be evidence of abandonment, and that "first inventor" meant to include anyone who first conceived the thing in tangible enough form to be persuasive. But, rightly or wrongly, the law did not develop so, and it is now too late to change. Hence the anomaly that by secreting a machine one may keep it from becoming an anticipation, even though its public use would really have told nobody anything about it.

NOTES

1. **§ 102(a) vs. § 102(b).** Although Judge Learned Hand's choice of words is sometimes dated, his conclusion that secret uses do not comprise prior art under § 102(a) remains good law. What does Judge Hand say about noninforming uses? Does a comparison of third party noninforming and secret uses under § 102(a) and § 102(b) reveal consistent conclusions by the courts?

2. ***Gillman* After *Metallizing*.** Recall that in his later opinion in *Metallizing Engineering*, reprinted here in Chapter 4, Judge Hand conceded some prior confusion in his earlier decisions. Nonetheless, he insisted that he had properly decided *Gillman*. Given *Gillman*'s citation of statutory bar cases such as *Electric Storage Battery v. Shimadzu*, also provided in Chapter 4, are you convinced? Do § 102(a) and § 102(b) necessarily fulfill the same policies in this regard?

3. **Later Holdings.** Numerous subsequent cases follow *Gillman*'s insertion of the word "public" into § 102(a). *Levi Strauss & Co. v. Golden Trade, S.r.L.*, 1995 WL 710822 (S.D.N.Y.1995) provides an apt summary:

> Under section 102(a), even though the text only requires that the prior invention be "known or used," the challenger must show public knowledge or use, where the "public" means those skilled in the art. This does not require actual knowledge or use by the public, just that the prior invention was publicly accessible. Accessibility may be satisfied by work done in the open "and in the ordinary course of the activities of the employer." This public accessibility requirement is consistent with the policy that the patent system will not grant a patent for something previously done; thus the inventor is required to disclose known prior art.

National Tractor Pullers Ass'n v. Watkins, 205 U.S.P.Q. 892 (N.D.Ill.1980), presents one of the more unusual factual circumstances in which this rule was applied. There, the declaratory judgment plaintiff asserted that a patented device useful in tractor pulling contests was invalid under § 102(a). The plaintiff pointed to drawings made by a third party on the underside of a tablecloth in his mother's kitchen. The drawings had never been printed prior to their destruction, nor had the depicted device been commercialized. The court concluded that these drawings did not comprise prior art: "Prior knowledge as set forth in 35 U.S.C.A. § 102(a) must be prior public knowledge, that is knowledge which is reasonably accessible to the public."

4. **The First Inventor Defense.** One of the titles of the American Inventors Protection Act of 1999, the First Inventor Defense Act, created an infringement defense for an earlier inventor of a method of doing or conducting business that was later patented by another. *See* 35 U.S.C.A. § 273. The defendant must have reduced the infringing subject matter to practice one year before the effective filing date of the patent and made commercial use of that subject matter in the United States before the effective filing date. Congress enacted this legislation in response to the Federal Circuit's holding in *State Street Bank*—reprinted here in Chapter Two—and out of awareness of the prior art status of trade secrets. For more on the First Inventor Defense Act, see § 16.3 of this casebook.

5. **Northern Exposure.** Relative to the United States, the Canadian system was a more "pure" first-to-invent system; potentially novelty destroying technology would be that invented anywhere in the world whether secret or public prior to the invention date of the applicant. The decision of the Privy Council reaching this conclusion, *Christiana v. Rice,*[1931] A.C. 770, remains one of the great cases in patent law. *Christiana* traces the history of the Canadian patent law to the landmark 1836 Act in the United States. However, it then holds that a second inventor may not obtain a patent regardless of the circumstances surrounding the first invention. Thus, contrary to the law in the United States, *Christiana* held that a first inventor who maintains his invention in secret in a foreign country has engaged in patent defeating activity in Canada. This pure first-to-file approach was too much for the Canadian Parliament. In 1935 Parliament limited patent defeating activity to secret activity that ultimately resorted in the filing a patent application in Canada or where the information was made available to the public before the second inventor filed for his patent, *Patent Act*. R.S., c. P–4, § 61. All of this is now history since Canada abandoned the first-to-invent approach to patent law in 1989, 35–36 Elizabeth II, Chapter 41.

6. **Rule 131 Practice.** An important aspect of Patent Office practice is the use of Rule 131. This Rule allows applicants to declare an invention date prior to the date of a prior art reference. The need for Rule 131 arises because inventors need not attest to their date of inventive activity when they file patent applications. Instead, they reveal their invention date on an *ad hoc* basis when the examiner produces a pertinent prior art reference. Use of Rule 131 is informally known as "swearing behind" or "antedating" a reference. Rule 131 itself provides:

Code of Federal Regulations Title 37

§ 1.131　Affidavit or declaration of prior invention to overcome cited patent or publication.

(a)(1) When any claim of an application or a patent under reexamination is rejected under 35 U.S.C.A. 102(a) or (e), or 35 U.S.C.A. 103 based on a

U.S. patent to another which is prior art under 35 U.S.C.A. 102(a) or (e) and which substantially shows or describes but does not claim the same patentable invention, as defined in 37 C.F.R.§ 1.601(n), or on reference to a foreign patent or to a printed publication, the inventor of the subject matter of the rejected claim, the owner of the patent under reexamination, or the party qualified under 37 C.F.R. § 1.42, 1.43 or 1.47, may submit an appropriate oath or declaration to overcome the patent or publication. The oath or declaration must include facts showing a completion of the invention in this country or in a NAFTA or WTO member country before the filing date of the application on which the U.S. patent issued, or before the date of the foreign patent, or before the date of the printed publication. When an appropriate oath or declaration is made, the patent or publication cited shall not bar the grant of a patent to the inventor or the confirmation of the patentability of the claims of the patent, unless the date of such patent or printed publication is more than one year prior to the date on which the inventor's or patent owner's application was filed in this country.

(2) A date of completion of the invention may not be established under this section before December 8, 1993, in a NAFTA country, or before January 1, 1996, in a WTO Member country other than a NAFTA country.

(b) The showing of facts shall be such, in character and weight, as to establish reduction to practice prior to the effective date of the reference, or conception of the invention prior to the effective date of the reference coupled with due diligence from prior to said date to a subsequent reduction to practice or to the filing of the application. Original exhibits of drawings or records, or photocopies thereof, must accompany and form part of the affidavit or declaration of their absence satisfactorily explained.

* * *

Rule 131 has no applicability to statutory bars such as § 102(b), which are keyed to the filing date of the patent application. Further, the use of Rule 131 should not be confused with a true interference proceeding under § 102(g). As explained in *In re Zletz*, 893 F.2d 319 (Fed.Cir.1989):

> Rule 131 provides an *ex parte* mechanism whereby a patent applicant may antedate subject matter in a reference, even if the reference describes the same invention that is claimed by the applicant, provided that the same invention is not claimed in the reference when the reference is a United States patent. As explained in *In re McKellin*, 529 F.2d 1324, 1329, 188 U.S.P.Q. 428, 434 (CCPA 1976), the disclosure in a reference United States patent does not fall under 35 U.S.C.A. § 102(g) but under 35 U.S.C.A. § 102(e), and thus can be antedated in accordance with Rule 131. But when the subject matter sought to be antedated is claimed in the reference patent, Rule 131 is not available and an interference must be had to determine priority.

§ 6.2 THE ELEMENTS OF "INVENTION" UNDER § 102(g)

Section 102(g) consists of two sub-paragraphs, serving two principal purposes in the patent law. Section 102(g)(1) provides a mechanism for resolving disputes relating to so-called "priority of invention." In this class of cases, one party seeks more than merely the denial of another's entitlement to patent rights on a particular technology. It also seeks to obtain patent rights for itself.

The need to determine priority of invention should be clear. As rivals across the globe compete to develop valuable technologies, they will often develop similar or identical inventions at approximately the same time. In such circumstances, the U.S. patent system has adopted a winner-take-all policy. Only the person or persons that first developed a particular technology will be awarded a patent. This policy is implemented through the rules set forth in § 102(g), which determine which actor will be judged the first inventor in terms of the patent law. The administrative procedure through which these substantive rules are effected, a so-called "interference," is described below.

The second sub-paragraph, § 102(g)(2), expressly states the general rule of priority: "A person shall be entitled to a patent unless . . . before the applicant's invention thereof the invention was made in this country by another. . . ." Section 102(g)(2) then states an important exception to this rule. If the first inventor has "abandoned, suppressed or concealed" the technology at issue, then he has essentially forfeited his special status in accordance with § 102(g)(2). Section 102(g)(2) goes on to instruct that "[i]n determining priority of invention there shall be considered not only the respective dates of conception and reduction to practice of the invention, but also the reasonable diligence of one who was first to conceive and last to reduce to practice, from a time prior to conception by the other."

Like most of the other paragraphs of § 102, § 102(g)(2) provides a source of prior art that may be used as the basis of a rejection for anticipation or nonobviousness. In these circumstances, the party asserting a § 102(g) reference is not claiming the invention for itself, but arguing that the issued patent is invalid. This effort usually involves the identification of a third party that allegedly invented first. In this sense, then, § 102(g) functions similarly to § 102(a).

§ 6.2[a] PATENT INTERFERENCES

As noted above, § 102(g) serves not only as a category of prior art, but also as the fountainhead of patent interference law. An overview of this complex proceeding, as set forth in more detail in § 135 and the Patent Office Regulations (Title 37 of the Code of Federal Regulations), should assist your understanding of the § 102(g) cases that follow.

Interferences may occur between two pending applications, or between a pending application and an issued, unexpired patent. The Patent Office will call for an interference when "an application is made for a patent which ... would interfere with any pending application, or with any unexpired patent...." 35 U.S.C.A. § 135. An examiner may declare an interference upon learning of two conflicting applications without any activity by the applicants. Alternatively, an applicant may initiate an interference upon discovering a newly issued United States patent that claims the same invention.

Patent interference procedures typically involve some particular terminology. Many cases will refer to so-called "senior" and "junior" parties: "A senior party is the party with the earliest effective filing date.... A junior party is any other party." 37 C.F.R. § 1.601(m). Interferences also make use of a concept called a "count," which corresponds to a claim which the interfering parties share. The counts of an interference define what the dispute is about; this is the subject matter which each of the parties asserts that it invented first.

The court in *Hahn v. Wong*, 892 F.2d 1028 (Fed.Cir.1989), described the opening phases of an interference as follows:

> Both the patent statute and the regulations of the Patent and Trademark Office authorize an interference between an application for a patent and an issued patent. 35 U.S.C.A. § 135(a) (Supp. V 1987) and 37 C.F.R. § 1.606 (1988). If the effective filing date of the application is more than three months after the effective filing date of the patent, the applicant is required to file evidence demonstrating that the "applicant is prima facie entitled to a judgment relative to the patentee," and "an explanation stating with particularity" why he "is prima facie entitled to the judgment." 37 C.F.R. § 1.608(b) (1988).

> When an application for an interference is filed, a primary examiner makes a preliminary determination "whether a basis upon which the applicant would be entitled to a judgment relative to the patentee is alleged and, if a basis is alleged, an interference may be declared." 37 C.F.R. § 1.608(b). As the Commissioner of Patents and Trademarks explained in his brief amicus curiae in this case, the "one and only one, purpose" of the primary examiner's examination of the application is "to determine whether the applicant alleges a date of invention prior to the effective date of the patent" (emphasis in original). See also M.P.E.P. § 2308.02, last paragraph.

> If the primary examiner makes a preliminary determination that the application meets that requirement, the application is referred to an examiner-in-chief to determine whether an interference should go forward. See 37 C.F.R. §§ 1.609 & 1.610(a) (1988). If the examiner-in-chief determines that a prima facie case for priority has been established, the interference proceeds. 37 C.F.R. § 1.617(a) (1988). If however, the examiner-in-chief concludes that

a prima facie case has not been shown, the examiner-in-chief declares an interference but "enter[s] an order stating the reasons for the opinion and directing the applicant, within a time set in the order, to show cause why summary judgment should not be entered against the applicant." Id. If such an order to show cause issues, the applicant "may file a response to the order and state any reasons why summary judgment should not be entered." 37 C.F.R. § 1.617(b). The rule states, however,

> Additional evidence shall not be presented by the applicant or considered by the Board unless the applicant shows good cause why any additional evidence was not initially presented with the evidence filed under § 1.608(b). Id.

A panel of the Board then determines whether (1) summary judgment should be entered against the applicant or (2) the interference should proceed. 37 C.F.R. § 1.617(g).

If the interference continues, next comes the filing of applicant preliminary statements. These statements contain allegations of the dates of various inventive activities the parties believe they can establish during an interference. After preliminary statements have been filed, the parties may submit various motions to the Board of Patent Appeals and Interferences, raising issues that will be contested during the interference. 37 C.F.R. § 1.633. These motions may address topics strictly unrelated to the interference. For example, a motion might contend that a party to the interference derived the invention from the moving party. If granted, the Patent Office would deny the nonmovant a patent under § 102(f) and dissolve the interference.

The trial phase of the interference follows. The parties are given the opportunity to present affidavits, declarations, and exhibits such as laboratory notebooks and publications. After the trial comes a final hearing before a three-member panel of the Board of Patent Appeals and Interferences, consisting solely of oral argument by the parties. The Board then issues its decision, typically awarding priority of invention to one of the interfering parties.

Interferences may be resolved in other ways, however. One party may assert ordinary grounds for patent invalidity, for example, that the patent claims subject matter ineligible for patenting. This effort tends to be rather uncommon, as often a defense which invalidates one application or patent will be effective for them all; but sometimes the result that no one obtains a patent is a satisfactory solution to one of the parties to the interference. Settlement between the parties is another option, although Congress has recognized the possibility of collusive arrangements with anticompetitive effects. The result is 35 U.S.C.A. § 135(c), which requires that the parties file copies of agreements reached in contemplation of termination of an interference. The filed agreements are available for public inspection.

Sometimes the Patent Office and applicants do not become aware of interfering applications, with the result that two patents directed towards the same inventive concept issue. Section 291 of the Patent Act, entitled "Interfering Patents," addresses these hopefully rare circumstances. Owners of interfering patents may have their respective rights determined by a federal district court following the filing of a civil suit.

For more details on interference practice, the venerable multi-volume treatise CHARLES W. RIVISE & A.D. CAESAR, INTERFERENCE LAW AND PRACTICE (1940) remains the best starting point. *See also* BRUCE M. COLLINS, CURRENT PATENT INTERFERENCE PRACTICE (1992); MAURICE H. KLITZMAN, PATENT INTERFERENCE LAW AND PRACTICE (1984).

§ 6.2[b] THE RULE OF PRIORITY

With this overview of interference practice complete, we next consider the workings of the United States priority regime. In *Christie v. Seybold*, 55 F. 69, 76 (6th Cir.1893), Judge (later President, later Chief Justice) Taft set forth the following statement:

It is obvious from the foregoing that the man who first reduces an invention to practice is prima facie the first and true inventor, but that the man who first conceives, and, in a mental sense, first invents, a machine, art, or composition of matter, may date his patentable invention back to the time of its conception, if he connects the conception with its reduction to practice by reasonable diligence on his part, so that they are substantially one continuous act. The burden is on the second reducer to practice to show the prior conception, and to establish the connection between that conception and his reduction to practice by proof of due diligence. It has sometimes been held, in the decisions in the patent office, that the necessity for diligence on the part of the first conceiver does not arise until the date of the second conception; but this, we think, cannot be supported on principle. The diligence of the first reducer to practice is necessarily immaterial. It is not a race of diligence between the two inventors in the sense that the right to the patent is to be determined by comparing the diligence of the two, because the first reducer to practice, no matter what his diligence or want of it, is prior in right unless the first conceiver was using reasonable diligence at the time of the second conception and the first reduction to practice. The language of the statute, (section 4920,) in the use of the imperfect tense, "was using reasonable diligence," shows the legislative intent to confer a prior right on a first conceiver in a case where, after his mental act of invention, and pending his diligent reduction to practice, another inventor enters the field and perfects the invention before his rival. The reasonable diligence of the first conceiver must be pending at the time of the second conception, and must therefore be prior to it. Reasonable diligence by the first conceiver, beginning when his rival enters the field, could only carry his invention back to the date of the second conception, and in the race from that time the second conceiver must win because of his first reduction to practice.

Section 102(g) today states the general rule: the first inventor to reduce an invention to practice wins the priority contest. But if the inventor who is first to conceive the invention, but second to reduce the invention to practice, can show diligence from the time prior to the conception date of the first to reduce to practice, he will displace the first to reduce the invention to practice as the first inventor at law. The remaining portions of § 5.2 of this text consider the details of each of the requirements noted in § 102(g): conception, reduction to practice, and diligence.

[handwritten margin notes: Today / First to reduce to practice wins unless first inventor can show diligence.]

§ 6.2[c]　CONCEPTION

OKA v. YOUSSEFYEH

United States Court of Appeals, Federal Circuit, 1988
849 F.2d 581

Before Markey, Chief Judge, Rich, Circuit Judge, and Miller, Senior Circuit Judge.

MARKEY, CHIEF JUDGE.

The Patent and Trademark Office Board of Patent Appeals and Interferences (board), in Interference No. 101,111, awarded priority of invention to junior party Youssefyeh et al. over senior party Oka et al., who relied on their October 31, 1980 Japanese filing date under 35 U.S.C. § 119. We reverse.

[handwritten margin notes: PTO and Appeals board award to junior party / This court reverses]

BACKGROUND

The sole generic count in the interference is directed to compounds possessing angiotensin converting enzyme inhibition activity, and is set forth as follows:

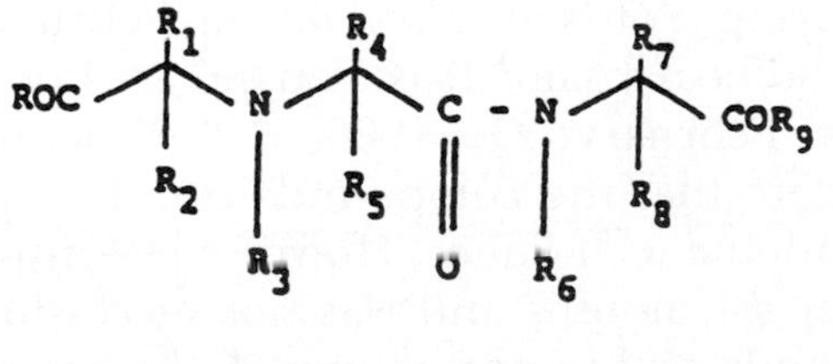

[handwritten margin notes: I count / Same compound]

wherein: R and R sub9 are independently hydroxy or lower alkoxy; R sub1 is hydrogen, lower alkyl or aryl lower alkyl; R sub2, R sub3, R sub4, R sub5, R sub7 and R sub8 are hydrogen or lower alkyl; R sub6 is indanyl; and their pharmaceutically acceptable salts.

The compounds can be described as optionally esterified carboxyalkyl substituted dipeptides that contain two amino acid groups, one of which, typically a glycine, bears a group R sub6, defined as an "indanyl group". The indanyl glycine of the count may be a Cycloaliphatically-bonded Indanyl, typically a 2–indanyl group, or an Aromatically-bonded Indanyl, typically a 5–indanyl group.

On February 27, 1980, one of Youssefyeh's co-inventors, Suh, recorded in his notebook this structural formula, encompassing billions of compounds within the class of 2–Indanyl Glycines:

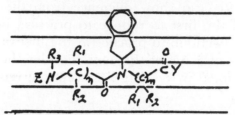

OPINION

Conception requires (1) the idea of the structure of the chemical compound, and (2) possession of an operative method of making it. Youssefyeh quotes from *Townsend v. Smith*, 36 F.2d 292, 295, 4 U.S.P.Q. 269, 271 (CCPA 1929): Conception may conveniently be considered as consisting of two parts. The first part is "the directing conception" and may be defined as the idea or conception that a certain desired result may be obtained by following a particular general plan. The directing conception is often referred to as the inventive concept, thought or idea. The second part of conception is "the selection of the means for effectively carrying out the directing conception."

When, as is often the case, a method of making a compound with conventional techniques is a matter of routine knowledge among those skilled in the art, a compound has been deemed to have been conceived when it was described, and the question of whether the conceiver was in possession of a method of making it is simply not raised. In the present case, the board itself recognized that conception required both a description, i.e., the idea, of a compound and possession of a method for making it. In denying Youssefyeh's claim of February 27, 1980, as its conception date, the board said: It is Youssefyeh's position that conception occurred on February 27, 1980, * * * because the inventors believed on that date that the compounds could be prepared in accordance with conventional techniques. However, Bernstein, a skilled Ph.D. chemist, spent over six months and was not successful in preparing the 2–indanyl compounds within the scope of the count, a circumstance which indicates that the inventors did not contemplate an operative invention, e.g., an operative method for making the compounds as of February 27, 1980.

The board made these not clearly erroneous findings: (1) because Youssefyeh had only the idea of a 2–indanyl class of compounds on February 27, 1980, it did not establish conception on that date; (2) Youssefyeh was in possession of a method of making a compound outside the scope of the interference count on October 10, 1980; (3) during the last week of October 1980, co-applicant Suh directed his assistant to use the October 10, 1980 method to prepare a species of a 5–indanyl class of compounds within the scope of the interference count; (4) the assistant successfully did so in December 1980; (5) Youssefyeh reduced the invention to practice on January 9, 1981.[1] Based on findings (2), (3), and (4), the board found that "an operative procedure was realized for preparing the 5–indanyl compound" as of October 10, 1980. That finding was clearly erroneous.

The board correctly noted that conception of a species within a genus may constitute conception of the genus. However, as Youssefyeh acknowledges, 2–indanyl compounds and 5–indanyl compounds are different species within the generic interference count. Youssefyeh did not conceive of the 2–indanyl compound as an operative invention on February 27, 1980 because it lacked at that time (and on this record never acquired) possession of a method for making it. Youssefyeh did not conceive of the 5–indanyl compound as an operative invention on October 10, 1980 because it lacked at that time the idea of the 5–indanyl compound, and the method it then possessed was a method for making something else. Thus Youssefyeh did not establish conception of either species before Oka's filing date.

That the October 10 method was found in December, after Oka's filing date, to be an effective method of making the 5–indanyl compound did not serve to move the date on which Youssefyeh had the idea of the 5–indanyl compound back to October 10, 1980. There is no evidence that that method could be used to make the 2–indanyl compound, and, given the difference between aromatically-bonded and cycloaliphatically-bonded indanyl glycines, there is no basis for a view that a description or method of making one is applicable to the other. The board made no finding that Youssefyeh had the idea of a 5–indanyl compound before the last week of October 1980. Youssefyeh does not argue, and no one testified, that it did have that idea before that time. The record would not in any event support such a finding. The board therefore erred in determining that Youssefyeh had established conception as of October 10, 1980.

Because Oka is the senior party, Youssefyeh was required to establish reduction to practice before Oka's filing date, or conception before that date coupled with reasonable diligence from just before that date to Youssefyeh's filing date. 35 U.S.C. § 102(g). The board's finding that Youssefyeh initiated preparation of a 5–indanyl compound "in the last week of October 1980" supports the conclusion that Youssefyeh failed to establish conception, much less a reduction to practice, of that class of compounds earlier than October 31, 1980. In dealing with a reduction

---

1. In view of our determination respecting conception, we need not and do not reach the parties' arguments on diligence and reduction to practice, except to note that neither party argues that the dual requirement for conception of an operative invention (idea plus method of making) equates conception with reduction to practice. The latter in this case would involve verification of the compound's utility as a hypotensive agent.

to practice, the court in *Haultain v. DeWindt*, 254 F.2d 141 (CCPA 1958), stated, "Further, where testimony merely places the acts within a stated time period, the inventor has not established a date for his activities earlier than the last day of the period." Id. at 142. That rule is equally appropriate in establishing a date of conception, nor does Youssefyeh dispute Oka's position that "the last week in October" means October 31.

If conception and filing date a tie, winner is senior.

Thus Youssefyeh's conception and Oka's filing date are the same, i.e., October 31, 1980. Oka, as the senior party, is presumptively entitled to an award of priority, and Youssefyeh, as the junior party in an interference between pending applications, must overcome that presumption with a preponderance of the evidence. In the event of a tie, therefore, priority must be awarded to the senior party. Because Youssefyeh, the junior party, failed to show a conception date earlier than Oka's filing date, Oka is entitled to priority. We reverse the board's award of priority to Youssefyeh.

REVERSED.

NOTES

1. And a Tie Goes to ... Do you agree with Chief Judge Markey's conversion of the procedural assignment of the burden of proof to the junior party into a substantive rule of priority? Note that current U.S. Patent and Trademark Office practice places the burden on the junior party only to overcome the senior party's filing date in order to provoke the interference. *See* 37 C.F.R. § 1.657 (1996). The junior party need not win the entire interference at first blush, nor is the senior party's inventive activity prior to its filing date even relevant at that point. Further, once the junior party has fulfilled this burden, then any presumption should vanish under the "bursting bubble" theory of presumptions endorsed by the *en banc* Federal Circuit in *A.C. Aukerman Co. v. R.L. Chaides Construction Co*, 960 F.2d 1020 (Fed.Cir.1992).

defining conception

2. Rule of Conception. To show conception, an inventor must present proof showing possession or knowledge of each feature of the count and communicated to a corroborating witness in sufficient detail to enable one of skill in the art to replicate the invention. *See Coleman v. Dines*, 754 F.2d 353, 359 (Fed.Cir.1985). The Federal Circuit confronted a situation where proof of conception was an exchange of letters between two individuals. One of them, Coleman, claimed that the letters show his prior conception. The Federal Circuit disagreed:

> The difficulty here is that initial formation in Coleman's mind must be, but was not, firmly established. The evidence did not show that Coleman's "completed thought" was disclosed to others. [cite deleted] What was shown here, at best, was that the ideas were "intermingled," and not that Coleman was the "spark."

Id. at 360. Could the letters have sufficed to show conception if they showed that Coleman was the "spark?" How should an individual inventor demonstrate her "sparkness" when more than one person contributes to the inventive process?

3. Comparative Approaches. The difficulty of determining which of several parties with identical priority dates should receive the patent grant is not unique to first-to-invent systems like that of the United States. In a first-to-file regime, ties of this sort could also occur when multiple inventors simply file patent applications addressing the same invention on the same day. Article 39(2) of the Japanese Patent Act provides for this situation as follows:

> Where two or more patent applications relating to the same invention are filed on the same date, only one such applicant, agreed upon after mutual consultation among all the applicants, may obtain a patent for the invention. If no agreement is reached or no consultation is possible, none of the applicants shall obtain a patent for the invention.

Compare this approach with that set out by Article 54 of the European Patent Convention, which provides:

> (1) An invention shall be considered to be new if does not form part of the state of the art.

> (2) The state of the art shall be held to comprising everything made available to the public by means of a written or oral description, by use, or in any other way, before the date of filing of the European patent application.

> (3) Additionally, the content of European patent applications as filed, of which the dates of filing are prior to the date referred to in paragraph 2 and which were published under Article 93 on or after that date, shall be considered as comprised in the state of the art.

How does this language impact several inventors, or their assignees, who file applications to the same invention on the same day? Of the three approaches, which do you favor?

§ 6.2[d]   REDUCTION TO PRACTICE

An inventor may reduce an invention to practice in two ways: constructively, by filing a patent application, and actually, by building and testing a physical embodiment of the invention. If the reduction to practice is to be constructive, the filed application must fully disclose the invention. As noted in *Travis v. Baker*, 137 F.2d 109 (CCPA 1943), an application "must be for the same invention as that defined in the count in an interference, and it must contain a disclosure of the invention sufficiently adequate to enable one skilled in the art to practice the invention defined by the count, with all the limitations contained in the count, without the exercise of inventive facilities." As the next case indicates, the doctrine of actual reduction to practice imposes similar requirements.

[handwritten margin notes: Can get reduction to practice in two ways ① filing a patent ② actually building the invention. if by filing must give details how to make]

SCOTT v. FINNEY

United States Court of Appeals, Federal Circuit, 1994
34 F.3d 1058

Before Lourie, Rader, and Schall, Circuit Judges.

RADER, CIRCUIT JUDGE.

The Board of Patent Appeals and Interferences awarded priority in Interference No. 102,429 to the senior party, Dr. Roy P. Finney. The Board held that the junior party, Dr. F. Brantley Scott and John H. Burton, did not show a reduction to practice before Dr. Finney's date of invention. Because the Board imposed an overly strict requirement for testing to show reduction to practice, this court reverses and remands.

BACKGROUND

This interference involves Dr. Finney's United States Patent No. 4,791,917, which was accorded the benefit of its May 15, 1980 parent application, and the Scott and Burton application, Serial No. 07/241,-826, which was accorded the benefit of its parent application Serial No. 06/264,202, filed May 15, 1981. Although the Scott and Burton application claims a joint invention of both applicants, Dr. Scott is the sole inventor of the subject matter in interference No. 102,429.

The invention is a penile implant for men unable to obtain or maintain an erection. The prosthetic device is a self-contained unit that permits the patient to simulate an erection. The implant contains two reservoirs connected through a valve. The invention operates by shifting the inflating liquid between the two reservoirs. When the penis is flaccid, the invention maintains inflating liquid in a reservoir at the base of the penis. A simulated erection occurs when the liquid shifts through the valve into the elongated reservoir implanted in the forward section of the penis.

Prior art devices fell into two categories: flexible rods and inflatable devices. Flexible rods had the disadvantage of making the penis permanently erect. The prior inflatable devices relied on fluid from a source and pump external to the body to inflate tubes implanted in the penis. These devices also had several disadvantages.

The Interference Count at issue states:

An implantable penile prosthesis for implanting completely within a patient's penis comprising at least one elongated member having a flexible distal forward section for implantation within the pendulous penis, said forward section being constructed to rigidize upon being filled with pressuring fluid; a proximal, rearward section adapted to be implanted within the root end of the penis, said rearward section containing a fluid reservoir chamber, externally operable pump means in said member for transferring fluid under pressure to said flexible distal forward section of said member for achieving an erection; and valve means positioned within said member which open when said pump is operated so that fluid is forced from said pump through said valve means into said flexible distal forward section of said chamber.

The parties to this interference had contested related subject matter in an earlier interference, No. 101,149. The count of 101,149 was a species of the generic count in this interference. Dr. Scott won that earlier interference.

In this interference, No. 102,429, Dr. Finney's application has an earlier filing date than Scott's application. Dr. Scott still has, however, an earlier conception date. Dr. Scott did not present evidence of diligence after conception of his invention. Rather, Dr. Scott opted to show an actual reduction to practice before Dr. Finney's date of invention.

Before the Board, Dr. Scott's primary evidence of actual reduction to practice was a videotape. The videotape showed an operation where the surgeon inserted Dr. Scott's prototype device into the penis of an anesthetized patient. The videotape showed the surgeon manipulating the implanted device. Several times the device simulated an erection when the surgeon manipulated the valve. Several times the fluid filled the forward reservoir. Several times the surgeon returned the penis to a flaccid condition by draining the fluid back into the rear reservoir. The Board found:

> It is uncontested that the penile implant used in the in-and-out procedure did rigidify the penis by pressurization of the rear chamber and did produce an erection. After the device was actuated to form the erection, the valve mechanism was manipulated to allow the device to become flaccid. . . .

Although not part of the count, the parties agree that the invention envisions implantation of two devices—one on either side of the penis. In the videotaped demonstration, the surgeon implanted only a single prosthesis into the patient. Although using only a single prosthesis, the videotape showed a penis with enough rigidity to produce an erection. After manipulating the implanted device through the skin to simulate having and losing an erection, the surgeon removed Dr. Scott's prototype and inserted a prior art external pump mechanism.

Dr. Scott supplied other evidence as well. He presented evidence of testing for leakage, disclosed that the fabrication material was common in implanted devices, and supplied the testimony of Dr. Drogo K. Montague, an expert in the field. Dr. Montague personally handled the device at issue and viewed the videotape. He testified that the video showed, even with only a single tube, sufficient rigidity for intercourse.

In opposition, Dr. Finney testified personally about the difficulty of determining sufficient rigidity for intercourse on the basis of insertion in an anesthetized patient. Both Drs. Finney and Montague agreed that insertion of two tubes would greatly enhance rigidity.

Board finds not enough evidence to show reduction to practice & Appealled.

The Board discerned insufficient evidence to show reduction to practice. Specifically, the Board determined that Dr. Scott had not shown utility, i.e., that the device would successfully operate under actual use conditions for a reasonable length of time. Thus, the Board required "testing of an implantable medical device under actual use conditions or testing under conditions that closely simulate actual use conditions for an appropriate period of time."

Because Dr. Scott had not tested his device in actual intercourse or in similar conditions to intercourse for a proper period of time, the Board determined that Dr. Scott had not reduced his invention to practice. The Board awarded the count to Dr. Finney. This appeal followed.

DISCUSSION

Review de novo reduction to practice

The issue of reduction to practice is a question of law which this court reviews de novo. This court reviews the Board's factual findings under the clearly erroneous standard.

Scott - junior party has to show reduction to practice before senior party or conception before and reasonable diligence

The Scott and Burton application was copending with that of Dr. Finney. Consequently, as the junior party in this interference, Dr. Scott had the burden to show prior invention by a preponderance of evidence. To show prior invention, the junior party must show reduction to practice of the invention before the senior party, or, if the junior party reduced to practice later, conception before the senior party followed by reasonable diligence in reducing it to practice.

Scott chose reduction to practice - did he show invention suitable for its intended purpose

To show reduction to practice, the junior party must demonstrate that the invention is "suitable for its intended purpose." *Steinberg v. Seitz*, 517 F.2d 1359, 1363 (CCPA 1975). When testing is necessary to show proof of actual reduction to practice, the embodiment relied upon as evidence of priority must actually work for its intended purpose. Because Dr. Scott relied on such testing, this court must examine the quality and quantity of testing asserted to show a reduction to practice.

Simple devices need no testing to prove reduction to practice

Testing sufficient to show a reduction to practice has often been at issue in interference proceedings. *Newkirk*, 825 F.2d at 1582 ("proof of actual reduction to practice requires demonstration that the embodiment relied upon as evidence of priority actually worked for its intended purpose"); *see also Kimberly–Clark Corp. v. Johnson & Johnson*, 745 F.2d 1437, 1445 (Fed.Cir.1984) (same); *Wiesner v. Weigert*, 666 F.2d 582, 588 (CCPA 1981) (same). By the same token, this court has also indicated "that '[s]ome devices are so simple and their purpose and efficacy so obvious that their complete construction is sufficient to demonstrate workability.'" *King Instrument Corp. v. Otari Corp.*, 767 F.2d 853, 861 (Fed.Cir.1985) (quoting *Eastern Rotorcraft Corp. v. United States*, 384 F.2d 429, 431 (Ct.Cl.1967)). Indeed, the Supreme Court, in a case featuring evidence of testing, cited approvingly three decisions of the United States Court of Appeals for the District of Columbia which stated that simple devices need no testing to show reduction to practice.

In cases requiring testing, this court's predecessor addressed many times the nature of testing necessary to show reduction to practice. Several important principles emerge from these cases. For instance, the testing requirement depends on the particular facts of each case, with the court guided by a common sense approach in weighing the sufficiency of the testing. Reduction to practice does not require "that the invention, when tested, be in a commercially satisfactory stage of development." Testing need not show utility beyond a possibility of failure, but only utility beyond a probability of failure. When reviewing the sufficiency of evidence of reduction to practice, this court applies a reasonableness standard.

Complex inventions and problems in some cases require laboratory tests that "accurately duplicate actual working conditions in practical use." *Elmore v. Schmitt*, 278 F.2d 510, 513 (CCPA 1960); *accord Koval v. Bodenschatz*, 463 F.2d 442, 447 (CCPA 1972) (testing of electrical circuit breaker did not test higher voltages); *Anderson v. Scinta*, 372 F.2d 523, 527 (CCPA 1967) (testing of windshield wiper blades did not simulate effect of wind on windshield); *but cf. Paivinen v. Sands*, 339 F.2d 217, 225–26 (CCPA 1964) (oscilloscope testing of magnetic switching circuit necessarily involved high speed switching). In *Elmore*, the Court of Customs and Patent Appeals noted that the various tests on a binary counter for sophisticated radar and video equipment did not account for "the resistance and character of load, nature of pulses, including voltage, duration and amplitude, and amount of capacitance used." *Elmore*, 278 F.2d at 512. The court also noted that the tests did not "reproduce[ ] the conditions of temperature, vibration, or sustained operation which would usually be encountered in a specific use." *Id. Elmore* demanded closer correlation between testing conditions and actual use conditions because the presence of many variables in that precision electronics field would otherwise raise doubts about the invention's actual capacity to solve the problem.

Less complex inventions and problems do not demand such stringent testing. In *Sellner v. Solloway*, 267 F.2d 321(CCPA 1959), for example, the inventor presented his invention, an exercise chair, at a birthday party. Because "the device involved and manner in which it is intended to operate are comparatively simple," *id.* at 323, the court sustained the sufficiency of this rudimentary testing by individuals without particular skills.

This court's predecessor well summarized many of these principles:

> A certain amount of "common sense" must be applied in determining the extent of testing required. Depending on its nature, the invention may be tested under actual conditions of use, or may be tested under "bench" or laboratory conditions which fully duplicate each and every condition of actual use, or in some cases, may be tested under laboratory conditions which do not duplicate all of the conditions of actual use. In instances where the invention

is sufficiently simple, mere construction or synthesis of the subject matter may be sufficient to show that it will operate satisfactorily.

Gordon, 347 F.2d at 1006. This statement captures the underlying principle that governs the nature of testing necessary to show reduction to practice—the character of the testing varies with the character of the invention and the problem it solves.

Another predecessor to this court summarized, "the inquiry is not what kind of test was conducted, but whether the test conducted showed that the invention would work as intended in its contemplated use." *Eastern Rotorcraft Corp. v. United States*, 384 F.2d 429, 431 (Ct.Cl.1967). Thus, the Court of Claims focused on the workability of the invention in the context of the problem it solved. The nature and complexity of the problem necessarily influence the nature and sufficiency of the testing necessary to show a reduction to practice. In any event, the testing should demonstrate "the soundness of the principles of operation of the invention." *Wolter v. Belicka*, 409 F.2d 255, 263 (CCPA 1969) (Rich, J., dissenting). The inventor need show only that the invention is "suitable" for its intended use.

All cases deciding the sufficiency of testing to show reduction to practice share a common theme. In each case, the court examined the record to discern whether the testing in fact demonstrated a solution to the problem intended to be solved by the invention. *See, e.g., Farrand Optical Co. v. United States*, 325 F.2d 328, 333 (2d Cir.1963) ("The essential inquiry here is whether the advance in the art represented by the invention . . . was embodied in a workable device that demonstrated that it could do what it was claimed to be capable of doing.") (emphasis added). In tests showing the invention's solution of a problem, the courts have not required commercial perfection nor absolute replication of the circumstances of the invention's ultimate use. Rather, they have instead adopted a common sense assessment. This common sense approach prescribes more scrupulous testing under circumstances approaching actual use conditions when the problem includes many uncertainties. On the other hand, when the problem to be solved does not present myriad variables, common sense similarly permits little or no testing to show the soundness of the principles of operation of the invention.

In the prosthetic implants field, polyurethane materials and inflatable penile prostheses were old in the art. They were tested extensively. Only the insertion and hydraulics of a manipulable valve separating two implanted reservoirs were new. Thus, Dr. Scott had the burden to show that his novel valve and dual reservoir system would simulate an erection for sexual intercourse when manipulated through the skin. Consequently, the problem presented to Dr. Scott, when viewed from the vantage point of earlier proven aspects of penile implant technology, was relatively uncomplicated.

In the videotape presentation, Dr. Scott demonstrated sufficiently the workability of his invention to solve the problems of a wholly internal penile implant. The videotaped operation showed both rigidity for intercourse and operability of the valve to inflate and deflate the device through the skin. The use of materials previously shown to work in prosthetic implants over a reasonable period of time also showed the durability of the invention for its intended purpose. In sum, Dr. Scott showed sufficient testing to establish a reasonable expectation that his invention would work under normal conditions for its intended purpose, beyond a probability of failure.

The Board erred by setting the reduction to practice standard too high. The Board erroneously suggested that a showing of reduction to practice requires human testing in actual use circumstances for a period of time. See *Engelhardt v. Judd*, 369 F.2d 408, 410–11 (CCPA 1966) (human testing of antihistamine and antiserotonin unnecessary in light of tests on laboratory animals). Reduction to practice, however, does not require actual use, but only a reasonable showing that the invention will work to overcome the problem it addresses. The videotape showed the rigidity and manipulability of the valve through the skin necessary for actual use. Experts testified to the invention's suitability for actual use. In the context of this art and this problem, Dr. Scott made that reasonable showing.

The Board rejected these proofs because the device was not actually used during intercourse. In this instance of a solution to a relatively simple problem, the Board required more testing than necessary to show that the device would work for its intended purpose. Even accepting the Board's conclusion that the intended purpose is to facilitate normal sexual intercourse, prior art prosthetic devices had fully tested the workability of most features of Dr. Scott's invention. Dr. Scott used the same tested and workable materials and designs of prior art implants. Only the hydraulics of a fully self-contained internal prosthesis remained to be tested for workability. Dr. Scott adequately showed the workability of these features.

Testing for the full safety and effectiveness of a prosthetic device is more properly left to the Food and Drug Administration (FDA). Title 35 does not demand that such human testing occur within the confines of Patent and Trademark Office (PTO) proceedings.

The Board's holding that Dr. Scott did not reduce his invention to practice before the May 15, 1980 filing date of Dr. Finney is reversed. Dr. Finney asserted that Dr. Scott abandoned, suppressed, or concealed the invention embodied by the count within the meaning of 35 U.S.C. § 102(g) (1988). The Board did not reach this issue in light of its holding that no reduction to practice occurred. Because the Board has not considered this issue, this court remands for a determination of whether Dr. Scott abandoned, suppressed, or concealed the invention within the meaning of § 102(g).

REVERSED AND REMANDED.

NOTES

1. Constructive Reduction to Practice. Given the patent law's emphasis on tangible, material inventions, what do you think of the doctrine of constructive reduction to practice? Does it tend to confuse events which occurred in the patent office, as compared to acts in the field? In the absence of the constructive reduction to practice doctrine, one who failed to actually reduce his invention to practice before his filing date could not get an invention date earlier than his filing date. Would it be better law to give one who actually built something the opportunity to obtain an earlier filing date?

2. Continued Prosecution Required. An applicant must continue to prosecute a patent for that instrument to constitute a constructive reduction to practice. If an application is abandoned, its filing date may be used as evidence of conception of the invention. *See In re Costello*, 717 F.2d 1346 (Fed.Cir.1983).

3. Standard for Proof of Actual Reduction to Practice. *Newkirk* states the classic test for reduction to practice: Does the embodiment relied upon for proof of reduction to practice actually work for its intended purpose? However, the Federal Circuit has indicated that this requirement is not always necessary:

> Our predecessor court has recognized that the invention must have been "sufficiently tested to demonstrate that it will work for its intended purpose." ... Moreover, the district court might have considered that "[s]ome devices are so simple and their purpose and efficacy so obvious that the complete construction is sufficient to demonstrate their workability." *Eastern Rotorcraft Corp. v. United States*, 384 F.2d 429, 431 (Ct.Cl. 1967).... Accordingly, the district court did not err in inferring that the '358 invention embodied in an existing machine was sufficiently tested to constitute a reduction to practice.

King Instr. Corp. v. Otari Corp., 767 F.2d 853, 861 (Fed.Cir.1985). How did *Scott v. Finney* reconcile this apparent inconsistency?

4. Simultaneous Conception and Reduction to Practice. In *Amgen, Inc. v. Chugai Pharmaceutical Co.*, 927 F.2d 1200 (Fed.Cir.1991), the court discussed circumstances in which conception and reduction to practice can occur simultaneously. The case concerned U.S. Patent 4,703,008, entitled "DNA Sequences Encoding Erythropoietin," which issued on October 27, 1987, to Amgen assignee Dr. Fu–Kuen Lin. The patent claimed purified and isolated DNA sequences encoding erythropoietin, as well as host cells transformed or transfected with a DNA sequence. Among the asserted claims was claim 2, which provided for: "A purified and isolated DNA sequence consisting essentially of a DNA sequence encoding human erythropoietin." Following Amgen's successful infringement suit against Chugai Pharmaceutical Co., Chugai appealed to the Federal Circuit, asserting that the '008 patent was invalid under § 102(g). The court explained:

> In some instances, an inventor is unable to establish a conception until he has reduced the invention to practice through a successful experiment.

This situation results in a simultaneous conception and reduction to practice. See 3 D. CHISUM, PATENTS § 10.04[5] (1990). We agree with the district court that that is what occurred in this case.

The invention recited in claim 2 is a "purified and isolated DNA sequence" encoding human EPO. The structure of this DNA sequence was unknown until 1983, when the gene was cloned by Lin; Fritsch was unaware of it until 1984. As Dr. Sadler, an expert for Genetics Institute, testified in his deposition: "You have to clone it first to get the sequence." In order to design a set of degenerate probes, one of which will hybridize with a particular gene, the amino acid sequence, or a portion thereof, of the protein of interest must be known. Prior to 1983, the amino acid sequence for EPO was uncertain, and in some positions the sequence envisioned was incorrect. Thus, until Fritsch had a complete mental conception of a purified and isolated DNA sequence encoding EPO and a method for its preparation, in which the precise identity of the sequence is envisioned, or in terms of other characteristics sufficient to distinguish it from other genes, all he had was an objective to make an invention which he could not then adequately describe or define.

A gene is a chemical compound, albeit a complex one, and it is well established in our law that conception of a chemical compound requires that the inventor be able to define it so as to distinguish it from other materials, and to describe how to obtain it. Conception does not occur unless one has a mental picture of the structure of the chemical, or is able to define it by its method of preparation, its physical or chemical properties, or whatever characteristics sufficiently distinguish it. It is not sufficient to define it solely by its principal biological property, e.g., encoding human erythropoietin, because an alleged conception having no more specificity than that is simply a wish to know the identity of any material with that biological property. We hold that when an inventor is unable to envision the detailed constitution of a gene so as to distinguish it from other materials, as well as a method for obtaining it, conception has not been achieved until reduction to practice has occurred, i.e., until after the gene has been isolated.

§ 6.2[e]   DILIGENCE

GOULD v. SCHAWLOW

United States Court of Customs and Patent Appeals, 1966
363 F.2d 908

Before Worley, Chief Judge, and Rich, Martin, Smith and Almond, Judges.

WORLEY, CHIEF JUDGE.

Gould appeals from the decision of the Board of Patent Interferences which awarded priority of invention of the subject matter set forth in four counts to the senior party, Schawlow and Townes (Schawlow). After reviewing a voluminous record in light of appellant's allegations of reversible error, but finding none, we affirm that decision.

The invention relates to an apparatus for light amplification by stimulated emission of radiation, better known by the acronym 'laser.'

It appears that amplification of electromagnetic radiation by stimulated emission of radiation was first realized on a practical basis by devices operating in the microwave frequency range. The laser is described in the record as an extension of the maser principle to optical wavelengths, i.e. infrared, visible and ultraviolet light. No matter in what portion of the electromagnetic spectrum it is designed to operate, it appears that the heart of a maser-like device is a working medium, generally a gas or solid, containing atoms or molecules which have one or more sets of energy levels. Unlike the situation ordinarily prevailing in a volume of matter at equilibrium, where the lower energy states of the material will be more heavily populated with atoms or molecules than the higher energy levels, the laser working medium contains material in which a higher energy level is populated by a significantly greater number of atoms than is a lower energy level of the material. A working medium in such a non-equilibrium condition is said to have an "inverted population" or "negative temperature." The means used to excite or "pump" the working medium to create an inverted population of atoms or molecules may comprise a source of electromagnetic energy, for example, a strong light of suitable wavelength directed at the working medium.

The record also shows that a medium in which a population inversion exists may be stimulated to emit its stored energy by wave energy (microwave energy in a "maser" and light energy in a "laser") of the frequency corresponding to the energy separation of the inverted pair of energy levels, thus amplifying the stimulating signal. In marked contrast to white light from the sun or an electric light bulb, which consists of a whole spectrum of colors and which is emitted in a random, non-directional manner when excited atoms spontaneously return to a lower energy level, the light radiation emerging from the laser device here under conditions of stimulated emission is both "temporally coherent" (a term used to describe the monochromatic nature of the emitted light) and "spatially coherent" (a term used to describe the tendency of the emergent light to undergo little divergence or spreading).

The counts of the interference relate to a laser comprising an active medium with the requisite energy level characteristics, means for pumping that medium, and a cavity resonator to enhance the laser operation. The cavity employed in microwave masers which characteristically has dimensions of the order of one wavelength, e.g. 1–100 centimeters, cannot be conveniently employed in light amplifiers because of the shortness (10–(5)—10–(2) cm) of light wavelengths. Rather, a cavity is utilized which has dimensions on the order of thousands or more of light wavelengths. Typically, the cavity defined by the counts is formed by a pair of spaced, plane, parallel optical reflectors, at least one of which is partially transparent, and side members through which pumping energy is admitted and some of the spontaneous and undesired stimulated emission, deviating in its travel from an axis perpendicular to the reflecting end plates, is allowed to escape. The laser employing a pair of opposed reflectors is now termed a Fabry–Perot laser, since the structure involved is reminiscent of the so-called Fabry–Perot interferometer used by physicists for a number of years. The desired output beam of the laser is built up or amplified by repeated passes back and forth along the axis perpendicular to the reflecting end plates, ultimately passing out of the cavity through the partially transparent end reflecting member in coherent form.

Fabry–Perot laser bounces around inside until amped then shot out

With the advent of devices capable of amplifying radiation other than microwaves, the term "maser" has assumed a more general meaning—molecular amplification by stimulated emission of radiation. The Schawlow patent uses the expression "optical maser" to denote an apparatus performing the function of the "laser." As a consequence, the counts employ the expression "maser." Count 1, to which we have added numerals keyed to Fig. 2 of the Schawlow patent reproduced below, is representative:

maser – molecular amp by stimulated emission of radiation

Count 1 of Schawlow

1. A maser generator comprising a chamber (14) having end reflective parallel members (16, 17) and side members (15), a negative temperature medium disposed within said chamber, and means (20) arranged about said chamber for pumping said medium, said side members being transparent to the pumping energy and transparent to or absorptive of other energy radiated thereat.

What it entails

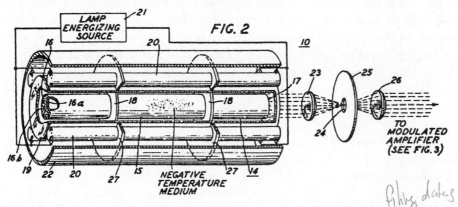

FIG. 2

Both Schawlow and Gould rely on their filing dates of July 30, 1958, and April 6, 1959, respectively, for constructive reduction to practice of the subject matter in interference, neither party alleging an actual reduction to practice prior to those dates. Under such circumstances it is, of course, well established interference law that the junior party, here Gould, must prove by a preponderance of the evidence reasonable diligence in reducing it to practice commencing from a time just prior to July 30, 1958, to his filing date of April 6, 1959. 35 U.S.C. 102(g).

Schawlow July 30 1958

Gould Apr. 6 1959

filing dates for reduction to practice

So junior party must show reasonable diligence in reducing to practice

before July 30, 1958 to Apr 6 1959

Diligence

To establish reasonable diligence during the critical period from just prior to July 30, 1958, to April 6, 1959, Gould relies principally on his own testimony; that of his wife, Ruth; Exhibit 9, a notebook said to represent a 'distillation' of his efforts from November 1957 to December 1958; and the testimony of his patent attorney relating to their joint activities from December 1958 to April 1959.

Little or no question has been raised by either the board or Schawlow concerning Gould's diligence from December 1958 to his filing date of April 6, 1959. The record shows that during that time Gould's attorney prepared the present application while concurrently engaged in a 40-day patent infringement trial in Utica, New York. Under the circumstances, we do not think further discussion of the activities of Gould or his attorney during that period of time is necessary.

It appears from Gould's testimony that, shortly after recording his alleged conception in Exhibit 1, he became cognizant of the potential high cost of building his proposed device, and also became "aware of the considerable experimental difficulties in dealing with the alkali elements," the material he proposed as a working medium in that notebook. He began to consider "other possibilities that might be easier * * * to build," stating that "I was more interested in seeing it (the laser) built than trying to protect myself in my patent interests." He testified that he worked on such theoretical considerations evenings and weekends at home and in libraries, studying "a large amount of background material" and making "rough calculations in connection with that background material." As an example of some of the things he did during that period Gould stated he "conceived of a number of other pumping mechanisms besides optical pumping," and spent "maybe a hundred hours" searching the "M.I.T. wave length tables" for coincidences between strong spectral lines to find "elements that could be optically pumped." He also described the laser invention "briefly" to his patent attorney in January 1958, and was advised at that time that Columbia University would have no patent rights in that invention. The motivation for that visit to his attorney, Gould stated, was that he realized "more and more what an important development" the laser would be, having, written the notebook constituting Exhibit 1 and having made a further study of the background material.

In the belief he would not be able to do experimental work on the laser at Columbia University until he had completed his thesis, Gould simultaneously sought to locate a research facility where experimental laser work could be done. To that end he visited Stevens Institute of Technology sometime between November 1957 and February 1958, where Professor Bostick told Gould that there were insufficient funds available at Stevens to support work in the laser field. Gould stated he described the laser "in great detail" in March 1958 to his friend, Dr.

Alan Berman, an individual "knowledgeable in the area of masers, generally," upon seeking employment to work on the laser at Hudson Laboratories, where Dr. Berman was associate director.

In late March 1958, Gould left Columbia University without completing his Ph.D. degree requirements, and joined the staff at TRG, Inc. According to Gould, his reason for leaving Columbia and joining TRG was to have an opportunity to do experimental work on the laser, having understood from his interviews with Dr. Daly of that company that he would have such an opportunity after completing his initial assignment on a research contract relating to a rubidium gas frequency standard, a project which occupied Gould's working time until the end of May 1958. While on that project, he disclosed his laser concept to co-worker Newstein. His next project was to write a proposal to build a rubidium maser which occupied his time until June 13; in the ensuing months through October, Gould apparently was engaged in experimental work on the rubidium maser.

During his free time from March to June 1958, Gould stated he "was busy formulating and writing down in a notebook the principles of the laser." The notebook referred to apparently is Exhibit 9, about which we will have more to say later. Gould testified he took 6 ½ days off from work at TRG in July, telling Dr. Goldmuntz, TRG's president, that he wished to finish writing his thesis. Actually, Gould stated, the real purpose of taking time off was "to get this laser notebook written," since he believed he would never finish it in a reasonable time by working on it only on weekends and evenings. Gould testified he took off two days in August, three days in September, 13 ½ days in October and 12 days in November for the same purpose. In August, Gould again talked to Dr. Berman concerning the laser, explaining, "how it worked and what its applications would be."

Toward the end of September 1958, Gould first informed Dr. Goldmuntz of his ideas concerning the laser, and was subsequently assigned to write, on company time, a proposal describing the device and methods of building it. By the middle of December 1958, the proposal was completed and submitted to various government agencies and Aerojet General Corporation for evaluation. The Advanced Research Projects Agency subsequently awarded TRG a research contract totaling nearly a million dollars for development of the subject matter of the proposal.

Summarizing his activities over the period November 1957 to December 1958, Gould estimated he spent "approximately a thousand hours" acquiring the knowledge which enabled him to devise the ideas expressed in Exhibit 9, and that there were no months or weeks during that period in which he did not "work on the laser."

In commenting on Gould's evidence of diligence, the board stated:

    * * * we do not find that a sufficient account has been made of the critical period so that we can assure ourselves that no unexplained lapse appears therein. Occurrences such as Gould's failure to participate in the reconditioning of his boat in the spring of 1958, and conversations such as those with co-worker Newstein at TRG, Inc. and with Dr. Alan Berman at beach parties in May and August, 1958 do not corroborate specific significant acts directly related to giving the invention a physical embodiment. Such evidence is far too fragmentary, and leaves to mere inference that Gould was actively engaged in reducing the invention to practice during this crucial period. We are not prepared to make this inference.

Nor are we. Even were we to disregard for the moment the necessity for corroboration and thus give Gould's testimony the full weight to which properly corroborated testimony in an interference is entitled, we find the testimony in and of itself insufficient to adequately establish what Gould did and when he did it. Little attempt has been made to identify particular activity with particular times during the critical period of concern—July to December 1958 and especially July, August and September 1958—or to establish how such activity related to reducing to practice the subject matter of the counts. In our view, Gould's testimony taken as a whole does not set forth adequate facts to support a finding of that continuity of activity which constitutes reasonable diligence. Merely stating that there were no weeks or months that he "did not work on the laser" is not enough, absent supporting facts showing specifically what that "work" consisted of and when it was performed.

Much of Gould's more detailed testimony, as summarized above, relates to the period November 1957 to March 1958. Apart form his general assertions that there were no weeks or months in 1958 that he did not work on the laser, we find the only relevant activities from July to September 1958 referred to by Gould are his acts of taking off from work at TRG in those months and his discussion with Dr. Berman in August. Gould asserts the board erred in basing its decision as to the question of diligence in part on the extent to which Gould took days off from TRG to record his ideas in Exhibit 9. While reasonable diligence does not require that one abandon his means of livelihood to further his reduction to practice, it was incumbent upon Gould, if he intends to rely on the taking of time from his normal employment as acts of diligence, to establish what was done and when it was done. Merely stating, for example, that he took off 6 ½ days in July, 2 days in August, and 3 days in September does not enable us to ascertain the extent of time gaps in his activity. The months of July and August, bracketing Schawlow's entry into the field, are critical to Gould's case, and a lapse of nearly two months would result if 6 ½ days were taken at the start of that period and the 2 days at the end. The party chargeable with diligence must account for the entire period during which diligence is required. Gould has not done so here. As in *Ireland v. Smith*, 97 F.2d 95:

We may surmise that appellant was probably diligent * * * but mere surmise cannot take the place of proof * * *.

Finally, Gould contends that the board has taken a "formalistic approach" to the doctrine of reasonable diligence in its statement:

> * * * we are not convinced that he was proceeding with due diligence in reducing the subject matter of the counts to practice during that portion of the critical period just prior to and after July 30, 1958, the record date of the senior party's entry into the field.

Whatever due diligence may be, Gould asserts, it would appear to reflect a particularly high standard, more than the "reasonable diligence" required by statute, and may not properly be required to establish priority. The effect of the board's holding, Gould contends, is to deny him the benefit of the principle that

> * * * An inventor who is the first to conceive an invention can prevail, no matter how limited his resources may be, and no matter how long it should take him to complete the invention, if he devotes those resources at his command with reasonable and continuous diligence toward the actual reduction to practice of the invention.

Similar arguments have been made over the years, but the fact remains that the presence or absence of reasonable diligence must necessarily be determined by the evidence adduced in each case. Here the board held, and properly so, that Gould had failed to provide sufficient evidence to discharge his burden of proving reasonable diligence in reducing the invention to practice.

Gould would have us believe that his alleged efforts to construct a simpler and less expensive embodiment of his conception are penalized, rather than rewarded, by the patent statutes—statutes which have contributed mightily to the unprecedented advances of this country in so many fields. But such is not the case. Congress has wisely provided the same opportunity for the inventor whose attic is his laboratory as for the giants of modern industry to file a patent application and obtain the protection thereby afforded. We are aware of no valid reason why Gould could not have taken advantage of his opportunity to timely file his application and obtain the benefits of a constructive reduction to practice as did Schawlow.

Clearly it was the intent of Congress to assure the first inventor who had completed the mental act of invention that he should not be deprived of his reward by reason of delays which he could not reasonably avoid in giving his invention to the public. But we must bear in mind that it was not alone to reward the inventor that the patent monopoly was granted. The public was to get its reward and have the advantage of the inventor's discovery as early as was reasonably possible. * * * Our review of the record with due regard for Gould's arguments convinces us that the board did not err in awarding Schawlow and Townes priority of invention.

The decision is affirmed.

NOTES

1. **Diligence Policy.** Why does United States patent law feature a diligence requirement? Perhaps because it recognizes that anyone can have a good idea without needing considerable funding. In contrast, reduction to practice typically requires that an inventor marshal significant resources, either to construct a working prototype or to engage the services of a patent attorney. So long as the inventor remains diligent in working towards either sort of reduction to practice, § 102(g) will preserve the privileged first inventor status. The statute may thus be seen as promoting an equality of opportunity between actors in the technological community with different levels of financial means. But is equality of opportunity worth the added complexity of a first-to-invent system?

2. **Dispelling Diligence Misconceptions.** The following points are often troublesome to students of § 102(g).

Diligence is only apposite where one party claims an earlier conception date, but a later reduction to practice date. The inventor who is both first to conceive and first to reduce an invention to practice wins the priority contest without having to show diligence. Once again, though, a holding of abandonment is possible if the inventor waits too long before filing a patent application.

Only one party's diligence is relevant in a priority contest. Section 102(g) is concerned with the diligence only of the inventor who was first to conceive, but second to reduce to practice. Competing inventors do not engage in any sort of diligence race. If the first inventor to reduce the invention to practice overly delays in bringing the invention forth, however, that delay may well be considered an abandonment.

The required period of diligence for the inventor who was first to conceive, but last to reduce to practice, begins at the time "prior to the conception by the other" and ends when the inventor who was first to conceive reduces the invention to practice. No amount of diligence which begins after the other's conception date, or occurs after reduction to practice has taken place, bears upon the priority contest.

3. **Diligence and Constructive Reduction to Practice.** How does an inventor prove diligence when relying on a constructive reduction to practice—that is, when the inventor hires a patent attorney to file an application claiming the invention? Cases have recognized that other demands upon a patent attorney's workload may excuse delay in filing a particular application. In general, if the attorney takes the application up within a reasonable time, such as in the order it was received, then the inventor will be found diligent. In another case involving Gordon Gould, the court reasoned that: "The fact that Gould's patent attorney, Mr. Keegan, was able to prepare and file a 132–page patent application with 56 claims while simultaneously involved in a long infringement trial establishes diligence from at least as early as December, 1958 through the filing in April, 1959." *Gould v. General Photonics Corp.*, 534 F.Supp.

399, 404 (N.D.Cal.1982). The court in *Mendenhall v. Astec Industries, Inc.*, 13 U.S.P.Q.2d 1913 (E.D.Tenn.1988), *aff'd*, 887 F.2d 1094 (Fed.Cir.1989), was less sympathetic towards a junior practitioner. It held that diligence was not established where the patent attorney worked on client matters received following his hiring by the inventor, sat for a state bar examination, and took a vacation following that examination.

4. *Gould*: The Rest of the Story. Gould lost this interference, but still acquired numerous patents on basic laser technology. *See Gould v. Quigg*, 822 F.2d 1074 (Fed.Cir.1987); *Gould v. Control Laser Corp.*, 705 F.2d 1340 (Fed.Cir. 1983); *In re Gould*, 673 F.2d 1385 (CCPA 1982); *Gould v. Hellwarth*, 472 F.2d 1383 (CCPA 1973).

§ 6.2[f]   CORROBORATION

An inventor may make use of the various inventive activities— conception, reduction to practice, and diligence—only if they have been corroborated.

WOODLAND TRUST v. FLOWERTREE NURSERY, INC.

United States Court of Appeals, Federal Circuit, 1998
148 F.3d 1368

Before Newman, Michel, and Clevenger, Circuit Judges.

PAULINE NEWMAN, CIRCUIT JUDGE.

Woodland Trust appeals the judgment of the United States District Court for the Middle District of Florida, holding United States Patent 4,763,440 (the '440 patent) invalid based on prior knowledge and use by others. Because uncorroborated oral testimony, particularly that of interested persons recalling long-past events, does not, of itself, provide the clear and convincing evidence required to invalidate a patent on this ground, the judgment is reversed.

BACKGROUND

The '440 patent, inventor Gregory James, is assigned to Woodland Trust. The invention is a method and apparatus for protecting a plot of foliage plants from freezing, by establishing an insulating covering of ice over ground level watering. It is described as particularly applicable to ferns grown in Florida for floral use. Claim 1 is illustrative, and describes the patented method:

1. A method for protecting a ground plot of foliage plants from freezing, said method comprising the steps of:

(a) providing ground-level sprinklers throughout said plot;

(b) covering said plot and said ground-level sprinklers with a covering of the type having openings therein;

(c) providing elevated sprinklers above said covering;

[handwritten margin notes: long past events recalled by persons not enough for prior use and knowledge]

[handwritten margin notes: Invention protects plants from freezing by insulating them w/ ice. applies to ferns]

(d) sprinkling said plot with water through said ground-level sprinklers; and

(e) sprinkling said covering with water through said elevated sprinklers as the ambient temperature drops to about 32F., whereby the water from said elevated sprinklers freezes in the openings of said covering and holds heat released during operation of said ground-level sprinklers under said covering.

The patent application was filed on July 1, 1983; the patent issued on August 16, 1988. In response to Woodland's suit for patent infringement, filed in 1993, Flowertree Nursery pled several defenses, including patent invalidity under 35 U.S.C. § 102(a), § 102(b), and § 103. Under § 102(a), Flowertree stated that the method was previously known and used by each of Joseph Burke and William Hawkins (an owner of Flowertree) in the 1960s and 1970s at their nurseries in Florida, and was then discontinued by these users in 1976 and 1978. The district court found that Hawkins' system at Flowertree was reconstructed in 1988.

Four witnesses testified in support of the defense of prior knowledge and use: Mark Hawkins, Joseph Burke, Charles Hudson, and John Kaufmann. Mark Hawkins is the son of William Hawkins; he testified that his father's system, on which he worked as a child, was destroyed by a tornado in 1978, and was not reconstructed until 1988. Joseph Burke is a nursery owner who has known William Hawkins since the 1960s; he testified that he used the same system as shown in the patent, but tore it down in 1976 and did not rebuild it. Charles Hudson is a nursery owner who had worked for Joseph Burke, and John Kaufmann is a life-long friend of William Hawkins; they testified that they observed the patented system at the Burke or Hawkins nursery, before its use was discontinued. Woodland provided conflicting testimony; a witness named Marcus Crosby explained that he described the patented system to William Hawkins, his employer at Flowertree in 1988, after learning about it during his prior employment with Gregory James.

The district court credited the statements of all of the Flowertree witnesses, holding that "to discredit those witnesses in this case the court would be obliged to conclude that all four were deliberate perjurers." On the basis of this testimony the district court found that the apparatus claims of the '440 patent were anticipated under 35 U.S.C. § 102(a) by the Hawkins and Burke systems "which constitute prior art that was known publicly for many years before the filing date of the application for patent," and that the method claims of the '440 patent were anticipated under § 102(a) by the Burke method which was "openly and publicly used in the ordinary course of business" such that "the methods claimed in the patent were 'known' and 'used' by others more than one year before the filing date of the original application for the patent." The district court held the patent invalid, and did not discuss other defenses raised by Flowertree.

DISCUSSION

A

35 U.S.C. § 102(a) provides:

§ 102. A person shall be entitled to a patent unless—

(a) the invention was known or used by others in this country, or patented or described in a printed publication in this or a foreign country, before the invention thereof by the applicant for patent. . . .

Section 102(a) establishes that a person can not patent what was already known to others. If the invention was known to or used by others in this country before the date of the patentee's invention, the later inventor has not contributed to the store of knowledge, and has no entitlement to a patent. Accordingly, in order to invalidate a patent based on prior knowledge or use, that knowledge or use must have been available to the public. *See Carella v. Starlight Archery*, 804 F.2d 135, 139, 231 U.S.P.Q. 644, 646 (Fed.Cir.1986) (the § 102(a) language "known or used by others in this country" means knowledge or use which is accessible to the public); 35 U.S.C. § 102(a) reviser's note (1952) (noting that " 'known' has been held to mean 'publicly known' " and that "no change in the language is made at this time"); P.J. Federico, *Commentary on the New Patent Act* (1954) *reprinted in* 75 J. PAT. TRADEMARK OFF. SOC'Y 161, 178 (1993) ("interpretation [of § 102(a)] by the courts excludes various kinds of private knowledge not known to the public"; these "narrowing interpretations are not changed").

Therefore, notwithstanding abandonment of the prior use—which may preclude a challenge under § 102(g)—prior knowledge or use by others may invalidate a patent under § 102(a) if the prior knowledge or use was accessible to the public.

The district court also referred to the criteria of § 102(b), which establishes a one year grace period based on publication or public use or sale, after which an inventor is barred from access to the patent system. Section 102(b), unlike § 102(a), is primarily concerned with the policy that encourages an inventor to enter the patent system promptly, while recognizing a one year period of public knowledge or use or commercial exploitation before the patent application must be filed. Thus an inventor's own prior commercial use, albeit kept secret, may constitute a public use or sale under § 102(b), barring him from obtaining a patent. *See Egbert v. Lippmann*, 104 U.S. 333, 336, 26 L.Ed. 755 (1881) (inventor's unobservable prior use was a "public use").

However, when an asserted prior use is not that of the applicant, § 102(b) is not a bar when that prior use or knowledge is not available to the public. *See W.L. Gore & Assocs., Inc. v. Garlock, Inc.*, 721 F.2d 1540, 1550 (Fed.Cir.1983) (third party secret commercial activity, more than one year before the patent application of another, is not a § 102(b) bar).

B

Woodland argues that the uncorroborated oral testimony of persons related to or associated with the defendant can not provide the clear and convincing evidence that precedent requires to establish prior knowledge and use, particularly in view of the many years of asserted commercial use, the passage of time after the asserted use, and the acknowledged abandonment of the system by both asserted prior users. Flowertree responds that the district court's finding of prior use turned entirely on credibility, and that the credibility assessment of the trier of fact is entitled to great respect and should not be overturned on appeal.

Although an appellate court is indeed in a poor position to assess credibility, there is a very heavy burden to be met by one challenging validity when the only evidence is the oral testimony of interested persons and their friends, particularly as to long-past events. Corroboration of oral evidence of prior invention is the general rule in patent disputes. "Throughout the history of the determination of patent rights, oral testimony by an alleged inventor asserting priority over a patentee's rights is regarded with skepticism, and as a result, such inventor testimony must be supported by some type of corroborating evidence." *Price v. Symsek*, 988 F.2d 1187, 1194 (Fed.Cir.1993). In assessing corroboration, this court has endorsed the following criteria, as compiled in *In re Reuter*, 670 F.2d 1015, 1021 n. 9 (Cust. & Pat.App.1981):

(1) the relationship between the corroborating witness and the alleged prior user,

(2) the time period between the event and trial,

(3) the interest of the corroborating witness in the subject matter in suit,

(4) contradiction or impeachment of the witness' testimony,

(5) the extent and details of the corroborating testimony,

(6) the witness' familiarity with the subject matter of the patented invention and the prior use,

(7) probability that a prior use could occur considering the state of the art at the time,

(8) impact of the invention on the industry, and the commercial value of its practice.

Price, 988 F.2d at 1195 n. 3. Such an analysis can be described as application of a "rule of reason" to the corroboration requirement. *See Mahurkar v. C.R. Bard, Inc.*, 79 F.3d 1572, 1577 (Fed.Cir.1996) (citing *Barbed Wire Patent Case*, 143 U.S. 275, 12 S.Ct. 443, 36 L.Ed. 154 (1892) and explaining that the corroboration requirement "arose out of a concern that inventors testifying in patent infringement cases would be tempted to remember facts favorable to their case by the lure of protecting their patent or defeating another's patent").

The *Barbed Wire Patent Case* litigation concerned a patent that was granted in 1874 for a barbed wire fence. Some twenty-four witnesses appeared on behalf of the accused infringers, all testifying that they had seen the same barbed wire fence exhibited by a Mr. Morley at the Delhi county fair in 1858. Witnesses testified to various events, one to having helped Morley put up the fence, another to hitching a horse to the fence and later finding the horse's nose bloodied by the barbs, another to having received a sample of Morley barbed wire which he produced at the trial, another that a boy was thrown against the Morley fence and that scars were still visible from the barbs, and others that they were attracted to the fence and paid close attention to its construction. The patentee, in turn, presented witnesses who testified that they had attended the Delhi fair but had seen "nothing of the Morley fence," in the district court's words. The son of the witness who produced a sample of barbed wire contradicted his father's testimony. The district court deemed it extremely unlikely that all of the defendants' witnesses were lying, and held the patent invalid. *Washburn & Moen Mfg. Co. v. Beat Em All Barb–Wire Co.*, 33 F. 261 (C.C.N.D.Iowa 1888), *rev'd, Barbed Wire Patent Case*, 143 U.S. 275, 12 S.Ct. 443, 36 L.Ed. 154 (1892). The Supreme Court, reversing, discussed the unreliability of testimony as to long-past events:

> In view of the unsatisfactory character of testimony, arising from the forgetfulness of witnesses, their liability to mistakes, their proneness to recollect things as the party calling them would have them recollect them, aside from the temptation to actual perjury, courts have not only imposed upon defendants the burden of proving such devices, but have required that the proof shall be clear, satisfactory, and beyond a reasonable doubt.

143 U.S. at 284, 12 S.Ct. 443. The Court concluded that:

> Witnesses whose memories are prodded by the eagerness of interested parties to elicit testimony favorable to themselves are not usually to be depended upon for accurate information.

Id. The Court thus required proof of prior knowledge and use that is "clear, satisfactory, and beyond a reasonable doubt." Discussing this standard, Professor Chisum observes:

> As to the exact standard of the burden of persuasion on prior use, Justice Brown in the *Barbed Wire Patent Case* did at one point refer to proof "beyond a reasonable doubt," the extremely stringent standard of criminal law. But in later cases, the Court seemed to construe the burden as one of "clear and convincing evidence," a test used in a number of areas of patent law.

1 DONALD S. CHISUM, PATENTS § 3.05[2] at 3–86 (Rel. May 1988).

In *Eibel Process Co. v. Minnesota & Ontario Paper Co.*, 261 U.S. 45, 43 S.Ct. 322, 67 L.Ed. 523 (1923) the Court cited its decision in *Barbed Wire Patent Case* as standing for the requirement of "clear and satisfactory" evidence when considering the probative value of oral evidence of prior knowledge and use of a patented invention:

> The oral evidence on this point falls far short of being enough to overcome the presumption of novelty from the granting of the patent. The temptation to remember in such cases and the ease with which honest witnesses can convince themselves after many years of having had a conception at the basis of a valuable patent, are well known in this branch of law, and have properly led to a rule that evidence to prove prior discovery must be clear and satisfactory

Eibel, 261 U.S. at 60, 43 S.Ct. 322. In that case the standard of "clear and satisfactory" evidence was held not met by the oral evidence of interested persons.

In *Radio Corp. v. Radio Engineering Laboratories*, 293 U.S. 1, 55 S.Ct. 928, 79 L.Ed. 163 (1934), the Court again discussed the issue, citing *inter alia* the *Barbed Wire Patent Case* and its criterion of "beyond a reasonable doubt." The Court explained that this was guidance, not prescription, while stressing that the burden of persuasion is heavy on an infringer who asserts that he created and used the same invention before the patentee:

> The context suggests that in these and like phrases the courts were not defining a standard in terms of scientific accuracy or literal precision, but were offering counsel and suggestion to guide the course of judgment. Through all the verbal variances, however, there runs this common core of thought and truth, that one otherwise an infringer who assails the validity of a patent fair upon its face bears a heavy burden of persuasion, and fails unless his evidence has more than a dubious preponderance.

293 U.S. at 8, 55 S.Ct. 928. This guidance, applied to this case, reinforces the heavy burden when establishing prior public knowledge and use based on long-past events. The Supreme Court's view of human nature as well as human recollection, whether deemed cynical or realistic, retains its cogency. This view is reinforced, in modern times, by the ubiquitous paper trail of virtually all commercial activity. It is rare indeed that some physical record (*e.g.*, a written document such as notes, letters, invoices, notebooks, or a sketch or drawing or photograph showing the device, a model, or some other contemporaneous record) does not exist.

In this case, despite the asserted many years of commercial and public use, we take note of the absence of any physical record to support the oral evidence. *Cf. Eibel*, 261 U.S. at 60, 43 S.Ct. 322 ("not a single written record, letter, or specification of prior date"). The asserted prior knowledge and use by Hawkins and Burke was said to have begun approximately thirty years ago and to have continued for about a decade. Hawkins testified that his prior use was terminated in 1978, and the district court found that Hawkins' system was not reconstructed until

1988. The relationship of the witnesses and the fact that the asserted prior uses ended twenty years before the trial, and were abandoned until the defendant reportedly learned of the patentee's practices, underscore the failure of this oral evidence to provide clear and convincing evidence of prior knowledge and use. The district court did not rely on the two undated photographs, and indeed their lack of detail and clarity can not have provided documentary support.

[handwritten margin notes: abandoned until learned another was using it; two undated photos no good.]

With the guidance of precedent, whose cautions stressed the frailty of memory of things long past and the temptation to remember facts favorable to the cause of one's relative or friend, we conclude that this oral evidence, standing alone, did not provide the clear and convincing evidence necessary to invalidate a patent on the ground of prior knowledge and use under § 102(a).

[handwritten margin notes: oral evidence standing alone not enough.]

The judgment of invalidity on this ground is reversed. The case is remanded for further proceedings.

REVERSED AND REMANDED.

NOTES

1. **The Shopbook Rule.** Federal Rules of Evidence 803(6) provides that:

> The following are not excluded by the hearsay rule, even though the declarant is available as a witness. A memorandum, report, record, or data compilation, in any form, of acts, events, conditions, opinions, or diagnoses, made at or near the time by, or from the information transmitted by, a person with knowledge, if kept in the course of a regularly conducted business activity, and if it was the regular practice of that business activity to make the memorandum, report, record, or data compilation, all as shown by the testimony of the custodian or other qualified witness, unless the source of information or the method or circumstances of preparation indicate lack of trustworthiness. The term "business" as used in this paragraph includes business, institution, association, profession, occupation, and calling of every kind, whether or not conducted for profit.

This provision has been held not to apply to prove dates of inventive activity. As indicated in *Horton v. Stevens*, 7 U.S.P.Q.2d 1245, 1248–49 (Bd. Pat. App. & Int'f 1988):

> The so-called Shop–Book rule does not apply to reports of scientific work in an interference proceeding. Such reports generally cannot be relied upon to prove the facts asserted therein, and therefore cannot be relied on to establish reduction to practice, since they are self-serving and not an independent corroboration of an inventor's testimony.

2. **Corroboration and the Rule of Reason.** The requirement of corroboration is an important restraint on claims of prior invention. In short, the rule prevents fraud. The requirement of corroboration can be very stringent. In this case, for instance, a witness testified that he had read and understood a notebook entry on a date which ensured prior reduction to practice. Senior Judge Friedman rejected this proof of corroboration:

Those affiants' statements that by a certain date they had "read and understood" specified pages of Stephen Hahn's laboratory notebooks did not corroborate a reduction to practice. They established only that those pages existed on a certain date; they did not independently corroborate the statements made on those pages.

Hahn v. Wong, 892 F.2d 1028, 1033 (Fed.Cir.1989). In another instance, the Federal Circuit upheld an inventor's offer of his laboratory notebook showing his practice of the claimed invention. As corroboration, the Federal Circuit allowed (1) testimony of a co-worker that the inventor had acquired the supplies for the inventive method, (2) testimony of another co-worker that he had seen the product produced by the claimed method, and (3) general evidence that the company followed a program to record inventive activity. *Lacotte v. Thomas*, 758 F.2d 611 (Fed.Cir.1985).

To ease the requirement of corroboration, *Coleman v. Dines*, 754 F.2d at 360, the Federal Circuit employs a rule of reason. This rule counsels the reasonable consideration of all evidence when weighing claims of inventorship. In one application of this rule, the Board of Patent Appeals and Interferences had rejected corroborating evidence because the inventor did not present the testimony of the laboratory technicians who actually observed the test results showing reduction to practice. The Federal Circuit, reversed:

> Under the rule of reason, this court cannot ignore the realities of technical operations in modern day research laboratories. [cite deleted] Recognizing these realities, a junior technician performing perfunctory tasks under the supervision of a senior scientist is not generally necessary to verify the reliability of evidence about scientific methods or data. In the absence of indicia calling into question the trustworthiness of the senior scientist's testimony, the rule of reason permits the Board to rely on the trained supervisor's testimony to ascertain scientific methods or results.

Holmwood v. Sugavanam, 948 F.2d 1236, 1239 (Fed.Cir.1991).

§ 6.3 PATENT AWARD TO THE SECOND INVENTOR

Section 102(g) further provides that first inventors can lose that special status through their own conduct: namely, where they "abandoned, suppressed, or concealed" the invention. The following decision presents the latest thinking on this forfeiture provision.

APOTEX USA, INC. v. MERCK & CO., INC.

United States Court of Appeals, Federal Circuit, 2001
254 F.3d 1031

Before Lourie, Clevenger, and Linn, Circuit Judges.

Lourie, Circuit Judge.

Apotex USA, Inc. appeals from the decision of the United States District Court for the Northern District of Illinois granting Merck & Co.,

Inc.'s motion for summary judgment that the claims of U.S. Patents 5,573,780 and 5,690,962 are invalid under 35 U.S.C. § 102(g). Because the district court did not err in granting summary judgment that the '780 and '962 patents are invalid under 35 U.S.C. § 102(g), we affirm.

BACKGROUND

Apotex is the assignee of the '780 and '962 patents, which relate to a process for making a stable solid formulation of enalapril sodium for use in the treatment of high blood pressure. Claim 1 of the '780 patent, which is representative of the claims at issue, reads as follows:

1. A process of manufacture of a pharmaceutical solid composition comprising enalapril sodium, which process comprises the steps of:

i) a) mixing enalapril maleate with an alkaline sodium compound and at least one other excipient, adding water sufficient to moisten, and mixing to achieve a wet mass, or

b) mixing enalapril maleate with at least one excipient other than an alkaline sodium compound, adding a solution of an alkaline sodium compound in water, sufficient to moisten and mixing to achieve a wet mass; thereby to achieve a reaction without converting the enalapril maleate to a clear solution of enalapril sodium and maleic acid sodium salt in water,

ii) drying the wet mass, and

iii) further processing the dried material into tablets.

The claims of the '962 patent, which is a continuation of the application that led to the '780 patent, are identical to those found in the '780 patent except that they are not restricted to tablet form, but rather encompass any solid pharmaceutical dosage form of enalapril sodium. This distinction is not material to the resolution of this appeal.

Merck manufactures enalapril sodium under the trade name Vasotec®, and has been continuously manufacturing and commercially selling Vasotec® tablets since 1983. Merck owns both U.S. and Canadian patents covering the enalapril sodium compound, but does not own a patent covering its process of manufacturing Vasotec®. However, in 1992, Merck disclosed the ingredients utilized in its Vasotec® manufacturing process in a Canadian product monograph, and more than 30,000 copies of the monograph were distributed in 1993 alone .. Merck also disclosed the ingredients used in manufacturing Renitec® (the trademark used for its enalapril sodium product sold in various foreign countries) in the 1988 edition of the DICTIONNAIRE VIDAL, a French pharmaceutical dictionary.

In 1991, Merck and its Canadian subsidiary, Merck Frosst Canada, Inc., sued Apotex's Canadian affiliate, Apotex Canada, for infringement of Merck's Canadian patent covering the enalapril sodium compound. During the 1994 trial ("the Canadian trial"), Brian McLeod, Merck's then-vice president of marketing, performed a step-by-step narration of a videotape demonstrating Merck's process of manufacturing Vasotec®. Within days of hearing this testimony, Dr. Bernard Sherman, an Apotex official, allegedly conceived the patented process at issue.

Apotex filed the present action against Merck, alleging that Merck's process of manufacturing Vasotec® infringes all of the claims of both the '780 and '962 patents. Both parties filed cross-motions for summary judgment on the issue of infringement, and Merck cross-moved for summary judgment of invalidity under § 102(g). The district court granted Apotex's motion for summary judgment of infringement, but also granted Merck's cross-motion for summary judgment of invalidity because it found that Merck invented the process claimed in the '780 and '962 patents within the United States before Apotex, and did not abandon, suppress, or conceal that invention within the meaning of § 102(g).

Apotex thereafter filed a motion asking the court to reconsider its grant of summary judgment of invalidity, which the district court denied. Apotex appeals from the district court's grant of summary judgment of invalidity.

DISCUSSION

Summary judgment is appropriate "if the pleadings, depositions, answers to interrogatories, and admissions on file, together with the affidavits, if any, show that there is no genuine issue as to any material fact and that the moving party is entitled to a judgment as a matter of law." FED.R.CIV.P. 56(c). For purposes of the motion, "[t]he evidence of the nonmovant is to be believed, and all justifiable inferences are to be drawn in his favor." *Anderson v. Liberty Lobby, Inc.*, 477 U.S. 242, 255, 106 S.Ct. 2505, 91 L.Ed.2d 202 (1986). We review a district court's grant of a motion for summary judgment *de novo*. *Ethicon Endo–Surgery, Inc. v. United States Surgical Corp.*, 149 F.3d 1309, 1315 (Fed.Cir.1998).

Apotex argues that the district court improperly invalidated the '780 and '962 patents because Merck failed to prove by clear and convincing evidence that it did not suppress or conceal the patented process. Apotex contends that proof of invalidity under § 102(g) requires Merck to prove that it did not suppress or conceal the process of manufacturing Vasotec® Tablets based on its activities within the United States, and that Merck's foreign disclosures therefore cannot be used to satisfy its burden of proof. Apotex also contends that, in any event, Merck's foreign disclosures fail to prove that it did not suppress or conceal the process because nothing in the testimony from the Canadian trial, the product monograph, or the French dictionary disclosed the use of water, the occurrence of an acid-base chemical reaction between enalapril maleate and sodium bicarbonate, or the resultant enalapril sodium product. Finally, Apotex argues that the evidence demonstrates that Merck in fact suppressed, or concealed its invention by failing to file a patent application on the process, by submitting misleading information in its New Drug Application ("NDA") that only disclosed the starting ingredients used to make Vasotec®, and by preventing the details of its process from circulating outside of the company.

Merck responds that § 102(g) only requires proof that the prior invention was made in the United States, and that evidence of lack of suppression or concealment can be proven by both foreign and domestic activities. Merck further argues that it did not suppress or conceal the process because it used it commercially, disclosed it in open court directly to its competitor, and published the ingredients used to make Vasotec® tablets in both the product monograph and the French dictionary. Merck also argues that the submissions it made with respect to its NDA were proper and in any event could not constitute suppression or concealment because it was the Food and Drug Administration that never made those submissions public. Finally, Merck contends that the process was not suppressed or concealed because it was obvious and Dr. Sherman admitted that Vasotec® tablets could be reverse-engineered to reveal the details of the process.

Section 102(g) operates to ensure that a patent is awarded only to the "first" inventor in law. In addition to governing priority determinations in interference proceedings in the United States Patent and Trademark Office, § 102(g) may be asserted as a basis for invalidating a patent in defense to an infringement suit. *New Idea Farm Equip. Corp. v. Sperry Corp.*, 916 F.2d 1561, 1566 (Fed.Cir.1990) (citation omitted). That section provides in relevant part that: "A person shall be entitled to a patent unless ... before such person's invention thereof, the invention was made in this country by another inventor who had not abandoned, suppressed, or concealed it." 35 U.S.C.A. § 102(g) (West Supp.2000). Therefore, if a patentee's invention has been made by another, prior inventor who has not abandoned, suppressed, or concealed the invention, § 102(g) will invalidate that patent.

Apotex does not dispute that Merck invented the patented process in the United States well before Dr. Sherman's alleged date of conception. Apotex also concedes that Merck did not abandon its process of manufacturing Vasotec® tablets as shown by its continuous commercial use of the process since 1983. The sole issue on appeal, therefore, is whether Merck "suppressed" or "concealed" the process within the meaning of § 102(g). Whether suppression or concealment has occurred is a question of law, which we review *de novo*.

As an initial matter, we disagree with Apotex's interpretation of § 102(g) as requiring proof negating suppression or concealment to arise from activities occurring within the United States. The plain language of § 102(g) clearly requires that the prior invention be made "in this country." However, in light of the grammatical structure of § 102(g), it would be a strained reading of that provision to interpret the language "in this country" to also modify the requirement that the prior invention was "not ... abandoned, suppressed, or concealed." A more reasonable interpretation is that it only modifies the antecedent verb "made," but not the "abandoned, suppressed, or concealed" clause that follows it. Had Congress intended the phrase "in this country" to modify "abandoned, suppressed, or concealed," it would have inserted language to that effect.

Indeed, if there were any doubt, the legislative history of § 102(g) demonstrates that Congress contemplated that precise modification, as it applied to another clause in § 102(g), and failed to adopt it. An earlier version of that provision considered in the House read as follows:

> [B]efore the applicant's invention thereof the invention was in fact made *in this country* by another who had not abandoned it and who was using reasonable diligence *in this country* in reducing it to practice or had reduced it to practice.

H.R. 3760, 82nd Cong. (1951) (emphasis added). The fact that the drafters found it desirable to emphasize that the language "in this country" applies to "using reasonable diligence" as well as to the word "made" supports the conclusion that it only modifies the verb that precedes it and not any subordinate clause that follows it. Accordingly, based upon the plain language of § 102(g) and the relevant legislative history of that provision, we conclude that the language "in this country" only applies to the country where "the invention was made," and that proof negating suppression or concealment is not limited to activities occurring within the United States.

We next turn to an issue that has not been squarely addressed by this court in considering suppression or concealment as negating prior invention in a defense to an infringement suit under § 102(g)—the burdens of proof governing such a determination. Section 282 of the Patent Act provides that "[a] patent shall be presumed valid." 35 U.S.C.A. § 282 (West Supp.2000). In order to overcome the presumption of validity, the party challenging a patent must prove facts supporting a determination of invalidity by clear and convincing evidence. *Am. Hoist & Derrick Co. v. Sowa & Sons, Inc.*, 725 F.2d 1350, 1360 (Fed.Cir. 1984). Section 282 applies with full force to a § 102(g) defense, and thus a party asserting invalidity under § 102(g) must prove facts by clear and convincing evidence establishing a prior invention that was not abandoned, suppressed, or concealed.

In *Young v. Dworkin,* one of our predecessor courts set forth the relevant burdens of proof governing a determination whether a prior invention was suppressed or concealed, in the context of an interference between co-pending applications, as follows:

> The sole remaining question is whether the board correctly held that junior party-appellant suppressed or concealed his invention within the meaning of 35 U.S.C. § 102(g). Here, the senior party-appellee bears the burden of proof by a preponderance of the evidence, notwithstanding junior party-appellant's burden on the issue of priority of invention which he has sustained.

Young v. Dworkin, 489 F.2d 1277, 1279 (CCPA 1974). Thus, under § 102(g) interference law involving co-pending applications, once the first party to invent has established priority of invention, the second party to conceive and reduce the invention to practice has the burden of proving that the first party suppressed or concealed the invention. In such an interference, the first party to invent does not bear any burden of proof regarding suppression or concealment once it has established an earlier date of invention.

A § 102(g) prior invention defense is governed by the identical "suppressed or concealed" language applicable to priority determinations in interference proceedings. We must therefore interpret the § 102(g) defense provision consistently with established interference law. However, infringement actions implicating a § 102(g) defense differ from interferences in that a patent has been granted on the invention at issue, and therefore the presumption of validity under § 282 applies. Because the patentee (analogous to the second-to-invent in the interference context) has the benefit of the presumption of validity, that party should only be held to bear a burden of producing evidence indicating that the prior inventor may have suppressed or concealed the invention once the challenger (analogous to the first-to-invent in the interference context) has established prior invention by clear and convincing evidence. That burden bears a rough similarity to placing the burden of proving suppression or concealment on the second-to-invent under interference law, but at the same time is appropriately limited to one of production, not persuasion, giving due regard to the presumption of validity.

We therefore interpret § 102(g) as requiring that once a challenger of a patent has proven by clear and convincing evidence that "the invention was made in this country by another inventor," the burden of production shifts to the patentee to produce evidence sufficient to create a genuine issue of material fact as to whether the prior inventor has suppressed or concealed the invention. However, in accordance with the statutory presumption in 35 U.S.C. § 282, the ultimate burden of persuasion remains with the party challenging the validity of the patent. Once the patentee has satisfied its burden of production, the party alleging invalidity under § 102(g) must rebut any alleged suppression or concealment with clear and convincing evidence to the contrary.

Our case law distinguishes between two types of suppression or concealment. The first is implicated in a situation in which an inventor actively suppresses or conceals his invention from the public. *Fujikawa v. Wattanasin*, 93 F.3d 1559, 1567 (Fed.Cir.1996) (citing *Kendall v. Winsor*, 62 U.S. (21 How.) 322, 328, 16 L.Ed. 165 (1858)). The second involves a legal inference of suppression or concealment based upon an unreasonable delay in filing a patent application.[2] *Peeler v. Miller*, 535 F.2d 647,

---

2. A subset of the category of "inferred" suppression or concealment arises in a situation in which the first inventor is "spurred" into filing a patent application by another application, *Mason v.*

655 (1976) (holding that a four-year delay in filing a patent application after the invention was perfected was unreasonably long); *Shindelar v. Holdeman*, 628 F.2d 1337, 1342 (1980) (finding suppression or concealment because no reasonable explanation was given for the two-year and five-month delay between reduction to practice and the filing of a patent application). The latter type is involved here.

Although a prior inventor implicated in a § 102(g) infringement defense may not have filed a patent application, in contrast to an interference contestant, that party's delay in otherwise bringing the knowledge of the invention to the public may nevertheless raise a similar inference of suppression or concealment. *See Int'l Glass Co. v. United States*, 408 F.2d 395, 403 (Ct.Cl.1969) (holding that the prior invention of a process did not invalidate a patent on the same process under § 102(g) because the prior inventor did nothing to make the invention known to the public). Even though there is no explicit disclosure requirement in § 102(g), the spirit and policy of the patent laws encourage an inventor to take steps to ensure that "the public has gained knowledge of the invention which will insure its preservation in the public domain" or else run the risk of being dominated by the patent of another. *Palmer v. Dudzik*, 481 F.2d 1377, 1387 (CCPA 1973). Absent a satisfactory explanation for the delay or the presence of other mitigating facts, a prior invention will therefore be deemed suppressed or concealed within the meaning of § 102(g) "if, within a reasonable time after completion, no steps are taken to make the invention publicly known." *Int'l Glass*, 408 F.2d at 403.

In the case at hand, we find that Apotex has satisfied its burden of producing evidence sufficient to create a genuine issue of material fact that Merck suppressed or concealed its process of manufacturing enalapril sodium tablets. We emphasize at the outset that although § 102(g) prior art must be somehow made available to the public in order to defeat another patent, a § 102(g) prior inventor is under no obligation to file a patent application. Thus, while Merck's failure to file a patent application may be relevant to a determination whether it suppressed or concealed its process, especially if there were evidence that such failure was based on a decision to retain the invention as a trade secret, that failure alone does not satisfy the patentee's burden of producing evidence sufficient to create a genuine issue of material fact of suppression or concealment.

However, Apotex did allege that Merck failed to make its invention publicly known. Merck perfected its process and began commercially using the process to manufacture Vasotec® tablets no later than 1983. Although Merck argues that its process was disclosed to the public because its Vasotec® tablets could have been reverse-engineered, that argument is based on the admissions of Dr. Sherman, who drew upon the information provided in Merck's subsequent disclosures to deter-

Hepburn, 13 App.D.C. 86 (D.C.Cir.1898), or by the commercial activity of another, *Woofter v. Carlson*, 367 F.2d 436, 445–446 (CCPA 1966). This case does not involve "spurring."

mine the details of the process.[3] Thus, it appears that Merck took no steps to make the invention publicly known for nearly five years, when it first published the ingredients used in its process in the 1988 edition of the DICTIONNAIRE VIDAL. We find that such a delay raises an inference that Merck suppressed or concealed its invention. Accordingly, because Apotex has successfully discharged its burden of going forward with evidence creating a genuine issue of material fact of suppression or concealment, the burden shifts to Merck to rebut that showing by clear and convincing evidence to the contrary.

We conclude that Merck has succeeded in rebutting the inference of suppression or concealment created by its period of inactivity by clear and convincing evidence. In *Paulik v. Rizkalla*, we stated the rule that "the first inventor will not be barred from relying on later, resumed activity antedating an opponent's entry into the field, merely because the work done before the delay was sufficient to amount to a reduction to practice." 760 F.2d 1270, 1275 (Fed.Cir.1985) (holding that the inference of suppression or concealment from a four-year delay between reduction to practice and the filing of a patent application was overcome by the first inventor's resumption of activity before the second inventor's date of conception). Thus, even though Merck may have suppressed or concealed the process for a period of time after it reduced it to practice in 1983, as long as it "resumed activity" (*i.e.*, made the benefits of its invention known to the public) before Apotex's entry into the field, it cannot be deemed to have suppressed or concealed the invention within the meaning of § 102(g).

Merck made several disclosures following its period of suppression or concealment that made the invention publicly known, all of which took place before Apotex's entry into the field (here, Dr. Sherman's alleged conception in April of 1994). First, Merck disclosed the ingredients used in manufacturing Vasotec® tablets in the 1988 edition of the Dictionnaire Vidal. It also widely distributed the product monograph in Canada from October 1992 through 1994, which similarly disclosed the ingredients it used in its manufacturing process. Merck also provided a step-by-step description of the process through the testimony given by Brian McLeod at the Canadian trial on March 28, 1994.

Apotex argues that these disclosures inadequately described Merck's process of manufacturing Vasotec® tablets, and therefore that the public never received the benefit of the invention. However, Dr. Sherman admitted both in his deposition in this case and in his 1994 Statement of Facts prepared for the Canadian trial that his inspection of the Vasotec® tablets that Merck sold commercially revealed that they were made using a wet granulation process. He also admitted that, after learning of the

---

3. It is worth noting that if it were clear that Merck's process could be reverse-engineered by one of ordinary skill through an inspection of Vasotec® tablets, Apotex could not benefit from the inference of suppression or concealment because Merck could not be said to have delayed in making the benefits of its invention known to the public. *See Palmer*, 481 F.2d at 1386–87 (stating that a commercial use of an invention will preclude a finding of suppression or concealment only when such use enables the public to learn of the invention).

disclosed starting ingredients from the Canadian product monograph (which included sodium bicarbonate), it "immediately occurred" to him and was "obvious to any knowledgeable formulator or chemist" that the final enalapril sodium product in the Vasotec® tablets was the result of an acid-base chemical reaction between enalapril maleate and sodium bicarbonate in water. Merck's various disclosures, in conjunction with Apotex's admissions, therefore clearly and convincingly prove that Merck made the knowledge of its invention available to the public, thereby satisfying its burden of rebutting Apotex's evidence of suppression or concealment.

Moreover, Apotex's argument that Merck suppressed or concealed the process by submitting misleading information to the FDA in 1983 is irrelevant because any suppression that was implicated was overcome by Merck's subsequent activity. We therefore conclude that the district court did not err in granting summary judgment that the '780 and '962 patents are invalid under § 102(g).

NOTES

1. **Is this Diligence?** As a technical matter, diligence plays no role in determining abandonment, suppression, or concealment. Diligence is limited to instances when an inventor is second to reduce to practice, but relies instead on proof of prior conception to show prior inventorship. Nonetheless, the acts and intentions of an applicant accused of 102(g) abandonment—sometimes referred to loosely as "diligence"—often determine the outcome of a priority issue.

2. **May I Abandon my Abandonment?** In *Paulik v. Rizkalla*, 760 F.2d 1270 (Fed.Cir.1985), Rizkalla was the senior party in an interference, having filed a patent application on March 10, 1975. Paulik had actually reduced the invention to practice as early as November 1970 and filed an invention disclosure form with his employer's patent department at that time. The patent department initially opted not to pursue patent protection on the invention, but began to draft an application in January or February 1975. Paulik's application was filed on June 30, 1975. The PTO Board awarded priority of invention to Rizkalla. According to the Board, Paulik's conduct fell within the language of § 102(g) denying priority of inventorship to those who have "abandoned, suppressed or concealed" the invention.

Following Paulik's appeal to the Federal Circuit, the *en banc* court reversed. The majority of the court held that an inventor, after taking no action for years, could renew inventive activities and recover from a charge of abandonment. Paulik could obtain priority if, on remand, he could "demonstrate that he had renewed activity on the invention and that he proceeded diligently to file his patent application, starting before the earliest date to which Rizkalla is entitled." Writing for the majority, Judge Newman reasoned that a contrary result would discourage inventors "from working on projects that had been 'too long' set aside, because of the impossibility of relying, in a priority contest, on either their original work or their renewed work."

A vigorous dissent authored by Judge Friedman urged that the majority's view could not be squared with the plain language of § 102(g). According to the dissent, the statute provided only that one who has abandoned, suppressed, or concealed an invention has forfeited priority, with no opportunity for redemption. The dissent also questioned whether Paulik, whose deliberate suppression of the invention caused it to be the junior party, was truly deserving of priority over Rizkalla. Finally, the dissent charged the majority with adding an additional complexity to interference proceedings.

§ 6.4   DISCLOSURE IN UNITED STATES PATENT APPLICATIONS—§ 102(e)

ALEXANDER MILBURN CO. v. DAVIS–BOURNONVILLE CO.

United States Supreme Court, 1926
270 U.S. 390

MR. JUSTICE HOLMES delivered the opinion of the Court.

This is a suit for the infringement of the plaintiff's patent for an improvement in welding and cutting apparatus alleged to have been the invention of one Whitford. The suit embraced other matters but this is the only one material here. The defence is that Whitford was not the first inventor of the thing patented, and the answer gives notice that to prove the invalidity of the patent evidence will be offered that one Clifford invented the thing, his patent being referred to and identified. The application for the plaintiff's patent was filed on March 4, 1911, and the patent was issued on June 4, 1912. There was no evidence carrying Whitford's invention further back. Clifford's application was filed on January 31, 1911, before Whitford's, and his patent was issued on February 6, 1912. It is not disputed that this application gave a complete and adequate description of the thing patented to Whitford, but it did not claim it. The District Court gave the plaintiff a decree, holding that while Clifford might have added this claim to his application, yet as he did not, he was not a prior inventor. The decree was affirmed by the Circuit Court of Appeals. There is a conflict between this decision and those of other Circuit Courts of Appeal, especially the sixth. Therefore a writ of certiorari was granted by this Court.

The patent law authorizes a person who has invented an improvement like the present, "not known or used by others in this country, before his invention," etc., to obtain a patent for it. Rev. Sts. § 4886, amended by Act March 3, 1897, c. 391, § 1, 29 Stat. 692 (Comp. St. § 9430). Among the defences to a suit for infringement the fourth specified by the statute is that the patentee 'was not the original and first inventor or discoverer of any material and substantial part of the thing patented.' Rev. Sts. § 4920, amended by Act March 3, 1897, c. 391, § 2, 29 Stat. 692 (Comp. St. § 9466). Taking these words in their natural sense as they would be read by the common man, obviously one is not the first inventor if, as was the case here, somebody else has made a complete and adequate description of the thing claimed before the earliest moment to which the alleged inventor can carry his invention back. But the words cannot be taken quite so simply. In view of the gain to the public that the patent laws mean to secure we assume for purposes of decision that it would have been no bar to Whitford's patent if Clifford had written out his prior description and kept it in his portfolio uncommunicated to anyone. More than that, since the decision in the case of the Cornplanter Patent, 23 Wall. 181, it is said, at all events for many years, the Patent Office has made no search among abandoned patent applications, and by the words of the statute a previous foreign invention does not invalidate a patent granted here if it has not been patented or described in a printed publication. Rev. Sts. § 4923 (Comp. St. § 9469). *See Westinghouse Machine Co. v. General Electric Co.*, 207 F. 75, 126 C. C. A. 575. These analogies prevailed in the minds of the courts below.

On the other hand publication in a periodical is a bar. This as it seems to us is more than an arbitrary enactment, and illustrates, as does the rule concerning previous public use, the principle that, subject to the exceptions mentioned, one really must be the first inventor in order to be entitled to a patent. *Coffin v. Ogden*, 18 Wall. 120, 21 L. Ed. 821. We understand the Circuit Court of Appeals to admit that if Whitford had not applied for his patent until after the issue to Clifford, the disclosure by the latter would have had the same effect as the publication of the same words in a periodical, although not made the basis of a claim. The invention is made public property as much in the one case as in the other. But if this be true, as we think that it is, it seems to us that a sound distinction cannot be taken between that case and a patent applied for before but not granted until after a second patent is sought. The delays of the patent office ought not to cut down the effect of what has been done. The description shows that Whitford was not the first inventor. Clifford had done all that he could do to make his description public. He had taken steps that would make it public as soon as the Patent Office did its work, although, of course, amendments might be required of him before the end could be reached. We see no reason in the words or policy of the law for allowing Whitford to profit by the delay and make himself out to be the first inventor when he was not so in fact, when Clifford had shown knowledge inconsistent with the allowance of Whitford's claim, *(Webster) Loom Co. v. Higgins*, 105 U. S. 580, 26 L. Ed. 1177, and when otherwise the publication of his patent would abandon the thing described to the public unless it already was old, *McClain v. Ortmayer*, 12 S. Ct. 76, 141 U. S. 419, 424, 35 L. Ed. 800. *Underwood v. Gerber*, 13 S. Ct. 854, 149 U. S. 224, 230, 37 L. Ed. 710.

The question is not whether Clifford showed himself by the description to be the first inventor. By putting it in that form it is comparatively easy to take the next step and say that he is not an inventor in the sense of the statute unless he makes a claim. The question is whether Clifford's disclosure made it impossible for Whitford to claim the invention at a later date. The disclosure would have had the same effect as at present if Clifford had added to his description a statement that he did not claim the thing described because he abandoned it or because he believed it to be old. It is not necessary to show who did invent the thing in order to show that Whitford did not.

even if Clifford claimed be abandoned it it would make no difference.

It is said that without a claim the thing described is not reduced to practice. But this seems to us to rest on a false theory helped out by the fiction that by a claim it is reduced to practice. A new application and a claim may be based on the original description within two years, and the original priority established notwithstanding intervening claims. *Chapman v. Wintroath*, 40 S. Ct. 234, 252 U. S. 126, 137, 64 L. Ed. 491. A description that would bar a patent if printed in a periodical or in an issued patent is equally effective in an application so far as reduction to practice goes.

description in a patent app some as if printed

As to the analogies relied upon below, the disregard of abandoned patent applications however explained cannot be taken to establish a principle beyond the rule as actually applied. As an empirical rule it no doubt is convenient if not necessary to the Patent Office, and we are not disposed to disturb it, although we infer that originally the practice of the Office was different. The policy of the statute as to foreign inventions obviously stands on its own footing and cannot be applied to domestic affairs. The fundamental rule we repeat is that the patentee must be the first inventor. The qualifications in aid of a wish to encourage improvements or to avoid laborious investigations do not prevent the rule from applying here.

patentee must be first to invent.

Decree reversed.

NOTES

1. **Statutory Codification.** The holding in *Alexander Milburn* was subsequently codified as § 102(e). As amended by the American Inventors Protection Act of 1999, § 102(e) consists of two sub-paragraphs. Section 102(e)(1) provides that a published patent application that discloses, but does not claim the invention constitutes prior art as of its filing date. Section 102(e)(2) works similarly. an issued patent that discloses, but does not claim the invention, constitutes prior art as of its filing date.

In approaching § 102(e) for the first time, one should remember procedures followed at the PTO. The PTO's current practice is to publish some of the pending patent applications eighteen months following the filing date. Not all applications are published, however. Specifically, where an applicant certifies that he will not seek foreign patent rights pertaining to that invention, the PTO will not publish the U.S. application. As a result, some patent applications are published approximately 18 months after they are filed. Other patent applications are never published at all, and their contents become publicly accessible only if the PTO allows them to issue as granted patents.

The purpose of § 102(e) is to define the point at which these published applications and issued patents serve as prior art against others. Our previous discussion of § 102(a) and (b) has shown that the patent law usually does not allow references that are not available to the public, such as trade secrets, to have patent-defeating effect. The most appropriate date for a published application or issued patent to have prior art effect might seem to be the date it actually issues from the PTO. Are you persuaded by the different conclusion of *Alexander Milburn*: that the disclosures of the patent instrument should have the status of the prior art as of their filing date?

2. The Disclosed Invention. What significance attaches to the fact that Clifford disclosed but did not claim the invention in Whitford's application?

3. The Patent Cooperation Treaty. In alluding to § 351(a) of the Patent Act, both sub-paragraphs of § 102(e) rather obliquely refer to the provisions of the Patent Cooperation Treaty (PCT). Section 102(e)(1) provides that PCT international applications designating the United States and published in the English language will have prior art effect as of their filing date. Section 102(e)(2) indicates that *Alexander Milburn* does not apply to so-called "international applications" under the PCT. Neither of these provisions changes the basic *Alexander Milburn* rule with respect to non-PCT applications filed in the United States. The PCT is discussed in greater detail in this casebook at Chapter 14.

4. Comparative Approaches. The European Patent Convention follows the same rule espoused in § 102(e), as noted in Article 54(3):

> Additionally, the content of the European patent applications as filed of which the dates of filing are prior to [the filing date] and which were published . . . on or after that date, shall be considered as comprised in the state of the art.

Only the withdrawal of the prior application prior to publication excludes that application from the prior art. What are the merits of such a rule? What should be the effect upon novelty if the EPO accidentally publishes a withdrawn application? *See* European Patent Office Examination Guidelines C–IV, 6.1a; decision J 5/81, OJ EPO 1982, 115. Japan follows a similar rule to that in Europe. *See* Japanese Patent Act § 29bis.

The modern European approach replaced the earlier so-called "prior claim" approach that was employed by, among others, the English courts. A good explanation of the advantages of the whole contents approach over the prior claim approach is found in the Banks Report (THE BRITISH PATENT SYSTEM, REPORT OF THE COMMITTEE TO EXAMINE THE PATENT SYSTEM AND PATENT LAW) 87–97 (1970) (Cmnd 4407), a report that led to the Patent Act 1977. The Report at pages 87–88 describes the difference between these approaches as follows:

> There are two basic approaches to the problem. The first, which for convenience we shall refer to as the "prior claim" approach, depends upon a comparison of the *claims* of the later application with the *claims* of the earlier. The second, which we refer to as the "whole contents" approach depends upon a comparison of the *claims* of the later application with the *disclosure* or contends of the earlier one.

The philosophical approach is different in the two cases. The prior claim approach is based upon the premise that the Crown cannot grant the same monopoly twice and since the monopoly is delineated by the claims it should be the claims of the two conflict applications which are compared, and then only when a patent has been granted on the earlier application. With this approach it does not matter that the invention claimed in the later claim has already been disclosed, but not claimed, in the earlier application.

The philosophy behind the whole contents approach is not only that the Crown should not grant the same monopoly twice but also that it is against the public interest to grant a patent for subject matter which has already been publicly disclosed in an earlier application, notwithstanding that the disclosure was not public until after the priority date of the later application or that no patent may be finally granted on it. In other words, only the first person to take steps to disclose such subject matter to the public by means of a patent application has the right to a monopoly for it.

§ 6.5   DERIVATION—THEFT FROM A PRIOR INVENTOR—§ 102(f)

Unsurprisingly, the patent law seeks not only the first, but the actual inventor. If the applicant in fact derived the invention from another, then no patent can issue. Section 102(f) thus bars a patent to an applicant who "did not himself invent the subject matter sought to be patented."

AGAWAM WOOLEN CO. v. JORDAN

United States Supreme Court, 1868
74 U.S. (7 Wall.) 583

Mr. Justice Clifford delivered the opinion of the court.

The settled rule of law is, that whoever first perfects a machine is entitled to the patent, and is the real inventor, although others may have previously had the idea and made some experiments towards putting it in practice. He is the inventor and is entitled to the patent who first brought the machine to perfection and made it capable of useful operation.

No one is entitled to a patent for that which he did not invent unless he can show a legal title to the same from the inventor or by operation of law; but where a person has discovered an improved principle in a machine, manufacture, or composition of matter, and employs other persons to assist him in carrying out that principle, and they, in the course of experiments arising from that employment, make valuable discoveries ancillary to the plan and preconceived design of the employer, such suggested improvements are in general to be regarded as the property of the party who discovered the original improved principle, and may be embodied in his patent as a part of his invention.

Suggestions from another, made during the progress of such experiments, in order that they may be sufficient to defeat a patent subsequently issued, must have embraced the plan of the improvement, and must have furnished such information to the person to whom the communication was made that it would have enabled an ordinary mechanic, without the exercise of any ingenuity and special skill on his part, to construct and put the improvement in successful operation.

Persons employed, as much as employers, are entitled to their own independent inventions, but where the employer has conceived the plan of an invention and is engaged in experiments to perfect it, no suggestions from an employee, not amounting to a new method or arrangement, which, in itself is a complete invention, is sufficient to deprive the employer of the exclusive property in the perfected improvement. But where the suggestions go to make up a complete and perfect machine, embracing the substance of all that is embodied in the patent subsequently issued to the party to whom the suggestions were made, the patent is invalid, because the real invention or discovery belonged to another.

Guided by this well-established principles, the first inquiry is, what was actually done by the person who, as alleged by the respondents, was the real inventor of what is described in the reissued letters patent? They do not pretend that he invented or even suggested the entire invention, nor all of the several elements embraced in any one of the separate combinations, as expressed in the claims of the patent; and if they did, it could not for a moment be sustained, as it finds no support whatever in the evidence. None of the devices described in the specifications are new, but the claims of the patent are for the several combinations of the described elements arranged in the manner set forth, and for the purpose of working out the described results.

Regarded in that light, it is clear that the concession that the person named did not invent nor suggest the entire invention, nor any one of the separate combinations, is equivalent to an abandonment of the proposition under consideration, as it is clear to a demonstration that nothing short of that averment can be a valid defence. Respondents do not allege in the answer that the person named was a joint inventor with the original patentee, but the allegation is that he made the invention, and they deny that the assignor of the complainant ever bestowed any ingenuity upon what is described in the letters patent as his improvement. Such a defence cannot be successful unless it is proved, as common justice would forbid that any partial aid rendered under such circumstances, during the progress of experiments in perfecting the improvement, should enable the person rendering the aid to appropriate to himself the entire result of the ingenuity and toil of the originator, or put it in the power of any subsequent infringer to defeat the patent under the plea that the invention was made by the assistant and not by the originator of the plan.

The evidence shows that the original patentee was born in 1793, and that he commenced working on machinery in his youth, while he was with his father, and that, as early as the year 1812, he went into the employment of certain machinists, residing at Worcester, Massachusetts, who were engaged in constructing machinery for the manufacture of wool and cotton. While in their employment, he began experiments in woolen machinery. Those experiments were directed to the object of improving the billy, for the purpose of drawing out the carriage more accurately, and thereby making better work. Several years were spent in that business, but, in 1820, he went to Halifax, in that State, and, while there, he made numerous experiments to get rid of the billy entirely, and to dispense with short rolls, and substitute long rolls in their place. He remained there three years, and, during that time, he was constantly engaged in experiments to accomplish those objects. In the spring of 1823 he moved to Dedham, in the same State, and there hired a mill, and engaged in the manufacture of broadcloth, and also carried on the machine business, and the witness also states that he then prosecuted his experiments on a large scale.

Cans were used as a receptacle for the rovings, delivered from the doffers, before the drawing-off and winding apparatus, described in the patent, was invented. Rovings, before that invention, were spun from cans, instead of being wound upon, and spun from, spools or bobbins. Considerable importance is attached to the new method, as it was largely by that means that the use of the endless roving was made practical, and that the difficulty produced by the kinking of the roving, incident to the use of the cans, was overcome.

Theory of the respondents is, that the new method of accomplishing that function was invented by Edward Winslow, but their witness, John D. Cooper, only testifies that he made or suggested the spool and drum, which are not the only elements of that apparatus. Unaccompanied by the traverser, they would, perhaps, be better than the cans, but it is clear that the apparatus would be incomplete without that device, as it is by that means that the bobbins are evenly wound with the roving.

Testimony of that witness is, that he first suggested to Winslow that the roving must be would on a spool, else they never could make good yarn, and he proceeds to state that they procured some pasteboard, and that Winslow made a pattern for a spool and drum from that material. Explanations, in detail, are given by the witness, of the several steps taken by them in accomplishing the change in the apparatus, and the witness states that the original patentee never saw the spool and drum until he came into the mill and saw those devices in the machine. Argument for the respondents is, that the spool and drum were invented by that party while he was in the employment of the original patentee, but the complainant denies the theory of fact involved in the proposition, and insists that the statement of the witness are untrue, and that he is not entitled to credit. Further statement of the witness is, that the improvement, as soon as it was perfected, was applied to all the carding and spinning machines in the mill, and that the mills, so adjusted as to embrace that improvement, were put in successful operation during the summer and autumn of that year.

Two answers are made by the complainant to the defence founded on that testimony, both of which are sustained by the court. 1. Suppose the testimony of the witness to be all true, the complainant contends that it is not sufficiently comprehensive to support the allegations of the answer, nor even to support the proposition presented in the brief of the respondents. Taken in the strongest view for the respondents, the testimony merely shows that Winslow, or the witness Cooper, or both together, after the originator of the plan had nearly completed his great and valuable improvement, and while he was still prosecuting his experiments with the utmost diligence, suggested the spool and drum as substitutes for the cans, and that Winslow actually made those devices, and, with the aid of witness, put them into one of the machines as an experiment. When their employer first examined the arrangement, rude as it was, he expressed great satisfaction with it, but upon seeing it tried he pronounced it of no value. Neither of those opinions, however, turned out to be quite correct, as, upon further trial, when better adjusted, and by adding the traverser, so that the contrivance would wind the roving evenly on the spool, it proved to be a useful auxiliary part of the invention.

Valuable though it was and is, as aiding in the accomplishment of the desired result, it is nevertheless a great error to regard it as the invention described in the subsequent patent, or as such a material part of the same that it confers any right upon the party who made the suggestion to claim to be the inventor, or a joint inventor, of the improvement, or to suppose that the proof of what was done by that party can constitute any defence, as against the owner of the patent, to the charge of infringement.

Second answer to the defence founded on that testimony is, that the testimony is unreliable, because the witness is not entitled to credit. Hundreds of pages of the transcript are filled with proof, introduced either to assail or support the credit of that witness; but the court is of the opinion that it is not necessary to enter into those details, as the decision must be in favor of the appellee, even if every word stated by that witness is taken to be true. Entirely satisfied with our conclusion upon the merits, we are the less inclined to enter into those details, as a full analysis of the proofs within reasonable limits would be impracticable; but it is proper to say that the proofs have been carefully examined, and it is the opinion of the court that the letters patent in this case cannot be held to be invalid upon such testimony.

NOTES

1. Derivation at the Federal Circuit. In 1997, the Federal Circuit had occasion to clarify a point of confusion that had crept into its case law. That court had earlier held that: "To invalidate a patent for derivation of invention, a party must demonstrate that the named inventor in the patent acquired knowledge of the claimed invention from another, or at least so much of the claimed invention as would have made it obvious to one of ordinary skill in the art." *New England Braiding Co. v. A.W. Chesterton Co.*, 970 F.2d 878, 883 (Fed.Cir.1992) (citing *Agawam*). That statement raised the issue of whether § 102(f) went only towards strict anticipations, or to obvious variants as will be discussed in Chapter 8 of this casebook. In *Gambro Lundia AB v. Baxter Healthcare Corp.*, 110 F.3d 1573 (Fed.Cir.1997), the Federal Circuit noted:

> Citing *New England Braiding Co. v. A.W. Chesterton Co.*, 970 F.2d 878 (Fed.Cir.1992), the district court concluded that Baxter did not need to prove communication of the entire conception, but rather only so much of the invention "as would have made it obvious to one of ordinary skill in the art." Based on this reasoning, the district court applied the obviousness standard in 35 U.S.C.A. § 103 (1994) to determine that the named inventors received enough information to make the invention obvious to one skilled in the dialysis art. This reasoning, however, misconstrues the dictum in *New England Braiding* and introduces incorrectly an obviousness analysis into the test for derivation.

> The Supreme Court announced the standard for finding communication of a prior conception over 125 years ago in *Agawam Woolen v. Jordan*, 74 U.S. (7 Wall.) 583, 19 L.Ed. 177 (1868). The Court required a showing that the communication "enabled an ordinary mechanic, without the exercise of any ingenuity and special skill on his part, to construct and put the improvement in successful operation." This court's predecessor consistently applied this Supreme Court standard.

> This court recognizes that the district court's incorrect derivation standard springs from dictum in this court's *New England Braiding* decision. In that case, this court noted: "To invalidate a patent for derivation of invention, a party must demonstrate that the named inventor in the patent acquired knowledge of the claimed invention from another, or at least so much of the claimed invention as would have made it obvious to one of ordinary skill in the art." *New England Braiding*, 970 F.2d at 883. This dictum did not in fact incorporate a determination of obviousness into a Section 102(f) analysis. Indeed, this court in *New England Braiding* did not apply such a test.... Thus, *New England Braiding* did not incorporate an obviousness test into the § 102(f) analysis.

For consideration of § 102(f) as a source of prior art for nonobviousness determinations under § 103, see Chapter 8. For another example where the Federal Circuit arguably discounted the distinction between novelty and nonobviousness, recall *In re Kathawala*'s discussion of § 102(d), reviewed here in Chapter 5.

2. Derivation and Inventorship. Derivation issues sometimes arise in the context of an interference. Under these circumstances, one party to the interference asserts that the other party actually acquired the idea of the invention from him. "To prove derivation in an interference proceeding, the person attacking the patent must establish prior conception of the claimed subject matter and communication of the conception to the adverse claimant." *Price v. Symsek*, 988 F.2d 1187 (Fed.Cir.1993). *See also Sewall v. Walters*, 21 F.3d 411 (Fed.Cir.1994).

3. Patents of Importation. Early English law did not bar one who derived from a foreign inventor from obtaining a so-called "patent of importation" in England. *Edgeberry v. Stephens*, ENGLISH PATENT CASES 8 (King's Bench 1691). This possibility has since been eliminated from all modern patent regimes, although the right of the first importer to obtain an English patent remained a part of the law until the Patents Act 1977, *Easycase Inc. v. Bryan Lawrence & Co.*, [1995] F.S.R. 597 (Patents Court). Nonetheless, under contemporary United States law, consider the role that § 104 might play with regard to § 102(f). Are acts performed in countries which are not signatories to NAFTA or members of the WTO admissible as evidence of derivation? *See Hedgewick v. Akers*, 497 F.2d 905 (CCPA 1974).

§ 6.6   A NOTE ON FIRST–TO–FILE VERSUS FIRST–TO–INVENT

The following excerpt from THE ADVISORY COMMISSION ON PATENT LAW REFORM, A REPORT TO THE SECRETARY OF COMMERCE 43–45 (1992), presents a thoughtful commentary on the factors guiding the adoption of a first-to-file system in the United States.

In the United States, when more than one patent application is filed claiming the same invention, the patent will be awarded to the applicant who establishes the earliest acts of invention in the United States and who has not thereafter suppressed, abandoned or concealed the invention ("first-to-invent" system). Applicants are permitted to establish a date of invention that is prior to the filing date in an interference proceeding conducted in the U.S. Patent and Trademark Office (USPTO). In contrast, in nearly every other country which provides patent protection, priority of invention is established by the earliest effective filing date of a patent application disclosing and claiming the invention ("first-to-file").

A long-standing issue in discussions on patent law reform has been whether the United States should change its patent system to conform with the manner of awarding priority of invention in other countries. The question is again a dominant issue in discussion regarding patent law reform due to negotiations designed to achieve global harmonization of the intellectual property laws....

The principal objections raised to first-to-file by members of the public included:

• small entities might be placed at a disadvantage in the "race to the Patent Office" because of limited resources to prepare and file patent applications;

- a first-to-file system might tend to foster premature and sketchy disclosures in hastily-filed patent applications;

- the possibility of theft of an invention from the true inventor could be increased in a first-to-file system;

- the opportunity to explore commercialization possibilities prior to filing would be reduced because of the importance of early filing;

- the USPTO could be burdened with an increased volume of patent applications filed for defensive purposes.

Those members of the public responding in favor of adopting a first-to-file system raised the following points:

- most of U.S. industry is acting now on a first-to-file basis, even in the United States, to avoid forfeiture of patent rights abroad, and the first-to-invent system could be hurting the competitiveness of U.S. industry;

- a U.S. first-to-file system would encourage early filing worldwide, so that patent rights are not forfeited, and would promote the early public disclosure of inventions;

- an agreement by the United States to a harmonization treaty requiring a change to first-to-file could bring dramatic improvements in the patent systems of foreign countries for U.S. applicants seeking patents abroad;

- a first-to-file system could greatly decrease the complexity, length and expense associated with current USPTO interference procedures; and

- the first-to-file rule would provide a definite, readily determinable and legally-fixed date of priority of invention, would eliminate uncertainties associated with interferences and would provide greater reliability for U.S. patents.

From a purely statistical viewpoint there would seem to be little difference in result between a first-to-invent patent system and a first-to-file patent system. More than 99.9% of the U.S. patent applications now being filed raise no dispute as to the identity of the first inventor. Even when such disputes arise, the inventor who filed first ("senior party") is procedurally favored in the highly complex interference proceeding that follows—the senior party prevails in a significant majority of such interferences. The actual effect of a switch to a first-to-file system of priority, thus, is likely to have little or no actual significance in terms of inventors losing priority of invention to other inventors, based upon these statistical findings.

However, patents vary widely in terms of commercial importance. The public comments, as well as the experience of many Commission members, suggest that applications involved in interferences are almost always drawn to those inventions that are very important commercially. Because such inventions are often developed to answer needs in very competitive markets, the high stakes in such situations drive parties to engage in hard-fought priority contests.

The Commission feels that their recommendation to convert the U.S. system to one that measures priority based upon the first-to-file, as a whole, represents a favorable change for U.S. applicants, both large and small, in terms of ease of filing, clarification of rights, and, importantly, international competitiveness.

A short history of the development of these two systems of priority is found in P.J. Federico, *Patent Interferences in the United States Patent Office*, 2 INT'L REV. INDUS. PROP. & COPYRIGHT L. 21, 22–24 (1971). The early English practice that allowed for the possibility that the law officers of the Crown could conduct an investigation into rival claims of inventorship is described in the leading English patent treatise of its day, W.M. HINDMARCH, A TREATISE ON THE LAW RELATIVE TO PATENT PRIVILEGES 503–46 (1846).

A recent patent law reform bill, H.R. 1908, that passed the House of Representatives in the 110th Congress included a provision to convert the U.S. patent law to a "first inventor to file" rule. If enacted at some future point, this provision would represent a significant step towards harmonizing the U.S. patent system with the rest of the world.

Novelty Exercises

While working in her United States laboratory, Andrea conceives of the idea of using a certain compound as a semiconductor dopant on January 10, 2006. She writes the idea down in her notebook under the heading "Dopant X Project," but immediately puts it aside in favor of completing some other projects of a personal and professional nature. Eventually, she turns again to "Dopant X," and after some intermittent efforts she fabricates a working semiconductor chip on August 14, 2006. She immediately notifies her patent attorney of the invention, and an application is filed on October 1, 2006. During this entire process, she maintains the invention in secrecy.

Based upon the different additional facts provided below, will Andrea be awarded priority of invention? Unless otherwise noted, assume that all activity occurred within the United States.

1.   Benkei, an electrical engineer based in Japan, had described the use of Dopant X in a Japanese electronics journal published on November 3, 2006.

2.   Chelsea conceived of Dopant X on June 15, 2006, and by working continuously on the project was able to produce the chip on September 1, 2006.

3.   Diane developed the idea of using Dopant X on September 3, 2005. She did nothing more with the project until the start of the new year, but then worked on a full-time, daily basis beginning January 3,

2001. She was at last able to construct a working chip on November 20, 2006.

4.   Edward conceived of the invention on January 15, 2006, and continued work on the project for the next two months. After several false starts, he halts work on the project entirely on March 21, 2006. After spending some spare moments reflecting on his earlier work in the early summer months, he then renews his efforts on the project in late July. He successfully builds the semiconductor on August 7, 2006.

conceived Jan 15, 2006
stops March 21, 2006
starts in July
reduce → Aug?
No patent

5.   Felicia conceives of the a new transistor on June 20, 2005, and immediately informs her patent agent. A patent application claiming the transistor on December 1, 2005. Along with several other doping agents described as useful in implementing the transistor through semiconductor materials, the application's specification suggests the use of Dopant X. Felicia then constructs the transistor using a known dopant on June 4, 2007. Her patent is granted on April 23, 2008.

patent of Andrea in Felicia's patent as a claim
– no patent.

CHAPTER SEVEN

NONOBVIOUSNESS

■ ■ ■

Beyond novelty and utility, an invention must also sufficiently advance the useful arts in order to warrant the award of an exclusive right. The doctrine of obviousness compares the claimed invention with the state of the prior art to make that assessment. Novelty, the other patent doctrine that examines prior art, primarily protects the public domain by precluding patent protection if an invention is already available to the public. Obviousness, in contrast, does not apply if each and every feature of the claimed invention already appears in the public domain.

Patent law recognizes that invention is generally the conception of a new combination of several old elements. Such a combination may or may not sufficiently advance the useful arts to merit the award of a proprietary interest, however. In terms of obviousness, the new combination does not warrant a patent if, from the vantage point of one of ordinary skill in the art at the time of invention, this new combination would have been obvious.

Section 103 (a) of the Patent Act sets forth the precise parameters of the obviousness requirement:

> A patent may not be obtained though the invention is not identically disclosed or described as set forth in section 102 of this title, if the differences between the subject matter sought to be patented and the prior art are such that the subject matter as a whole would have been obvious at the time the invention was made to a person having ordinary skill in the art to which the subject matter pertains. Patentability shall not be negatived by the manner in which the invention is made.

Because obviousness is the most significant gatekeeper to patentability, this section deserves some further dissection.

At the outset, section 103 refers to inventions that are "not identically disclosed or described as set forth in section 102." This phrase distinguishes obviousness from novelty. A novelty assessment is almost quantitative. If a single prior art reference describes each feature of the claimed invention, a relatively rare occurrence, then the invention is not novel. Obviousness, on the other hand, requires a series of factual assessments culminating in an often-difficult qualitative judgment of the creative achievement involved in the invention.

Section 103 next begins to set forth the methodology of the obviousness test. Specifically, it refers to "the differences between the subject matter sought to be patented and the prior art." The "subject matter sought to be patented" is a lengthy term for the inventor's claims. The "prior art," though not expressly defined, generally refers to the references stipulated in section 102—patents, printed publications, and so forth. Thus, the same information that can defeat the novelty of a claimed invention under section 102 will, generally speaking, constitute the prior art base for evaluation under section 103. Thus, section 103 requires an assessment of the differences between the claimed invention and the entire body of prior art.

In making this assessment of differences, section 103 specifically requires consideration of the claimed invention "as a whole." As already noted, inventions are often new combinations. The "as a whole" instruction prevents evaluation of the invention part by part. Without this important requirement, an assessment might break an invention into its component parts (A + B + C), then find a prior art reference containing A, another containing B, and another containing C and on that basis alone declare the invention obvious. An analysis of this character would discount the value of combining the various elements in a new way to achieve a new result—often the central creative feature.

To avoid undervaluing the combination, section 103 requires the obviousness assessment to compare the invention as a whole to the prior art. An actual invention illustrates this principle. In the early 1980s, some scientists at 3M Corporation combined an old adhesive (seemingly useless because it did not permanently stick) with note-sized paper to create Post–It® notes. The invention replaced bulky paper clips and staples as the best way to attach a note to a page. The invention became almost instantly a worldwide commercial success. This invention, however, was merely the combination of a known glue (element A) with note-sized paper (element B). Both elements were clearly available in the prior art. Evaluating the invention part by part might have rendered this patentable invention obvious. Evaluating it "as a whole" shows that this new combination warranted an exclusive right.

Section 103 next sets forth the test for patentability. Specifically patentability depends on whether the claimed invention "would have been obvious." To understand the meaning of "obvious" in this context requires vast experience and skill in applying this legal test. Indeed many synonyms have attempted to capture the meaning of "obvious," including terms like "inventiveness," "inventive intellectual product," and, particularly overseas, "inventive step." A decision rendered over a century ago by Lindley, L.J., in *Gadd & Mason v. The Mayor of Manchester*, 9 R.P.C. 516, 524, 67 L.T. 569, 9 T.L.R. 42 (1892) provides some insight into the term:

The difficulty of saying where invention sufficient to support a patent exists and where it does not, is well known to all persons conversant with patent law.... If, practically speaking, there are no difficulties to be overcome in adapting an old contrivance to a new purpose, there can be no ingenuity in overcoming them, [and] there will be no invention.... The same rule will, I apprehend, also apply to cases in which the mode of overcoming the so-called difficulties is so obvious to every one of ordinary intelligence and acquaintance with the subject matter of the patent, as to present no difficulty to any such person. Such cases present no real difficulty to people conversant with the matter in hand, and admit of no sufficient ingenuity to support a patent. If, in these two classes of cases, patents could be supported, they would be intolerable nuisances, and would seriously impede all improvements in the practical application of common knowledge.

In sum, "obviousness" is the standard that prevents trivial advances in the useful arts from winning patent protection. Section 103 thus creates a "patent-free" zone around the state of the art, allowing skilled technicians to complete routine work such as the straightforward substitution of materials, the ordinary streamlining of parts and technical processes, and the usual marginal improvements which occur as a technology matures. Only where a claimed invention surpasses this ordinary, continuous flow of technical progress will it surmount the "obviousness" requirement.

Next, and of vital importance, section 103 makes the relevant time for assessment of obviousness "the time the invention was made." While absolutely essential to an objective assessment of obviousness, this requirement makes the legal test very difficult to implement. To apply the obviousness test properly, a patent examiner or court must enter a state of "self-induced amnesia." In literal terms, the examiner or court must forget the claimed invention and evaluate its differences from the prior art at a time before its creation. This exercise sounds easy, but is not. Inventions often change the way we view an entire problem. Consider again the Post–It® note example. In hindsight, it seems easy to combine the tacky but non-adhesive glue with note-sized paper. Indeed, in retrospect, "anyone could do it." In fact, however, the non-adhesive glue existed for many years without a use until some creative mind conceived of the new and incredibly useful combination. Much of the case law and methodology of the obviousness requirement is designed to prevent hindsight—using the invention itself as a road map to select prior art and to evaluate the differences between the invention and the prior art.

Finally, section 103 sets the objective standard for the obviousness determination. The statute specifies that patent examiners and courts do not evaluate the invention according to their own skill and intellect. The test is not whether the invention elicits a "Gee Whiz" reaction from the examiner or court. Instead the examiner or court must make the determination from the vantage point of "a person having ordinary skill in the art." The perspective of this skilled artisan becomes the lens through which the examiner observes all the facts and makes the final judgment. Usually patent examiners and courts acquire this perspective by immersion in the prior art that provides the skilled artisan with their peculiar knowledge and understanding.

The result of this standard is that PTO examiners and judges decide whether an inventor's work product constitutes a sufficient technical advance over the state of the art to receive a patent. This determination is one of the more challenging legal feats in all of common law jurisprudence. The difficulty of framing this concept is demonstrated by the fact that the initial codification of a "novelty plus" requirement is of recent statutory vintage. Section 103 only became part of the Patent Act in 1952. The history leading up to its enactment illustrates the long-standing difficulty of finding a suitable test to measure "inventiveness."

§ 7.1   THE HISTORICAL STANDARD OF INVENTION

The development of a third significant standard of patentability alongside the novelty and utility requirements has an extraordinary history. Although early U.S. patent statutes allowed a patent to issue if the invention was deemed "sufficiently . . . important," *see* Patent Act of 1790, § 1, 1 Statutes at Large 109, *reprinted in* P.J. Federico, *The First Patent Act*, 14 J. PAT. OFF. SOC'Y 237, 250 (1932), scant legal consequences appeared to attach to this requirement. Indeed, as noted, the 1952 Act provided the first statutory requirement for patentability beyond novelty and utility. Before 1952, the courts and early patent administrators developed certain "negative rules" for patentability determinations. *See* HANNS ULRICH, STANDARDS OF PATENTABILITY FOR EUROPEAN INVENTIONS 60–62. For instance, mere changes in material, proportion, or form over existing technology or mere combinations of known mechanisms would not warrant a patent. *See* P.J. Federico, *Operation of the Patent Act of 1790*, 18 J. PAT. OFF. SOC'Y 237 (1936). The doctrinal moorings of these accepted conventions remained uncertain, however, until the Supreme Court issued its opinion in *Hotchkiss v. Greenwood*. This 1851 case began the progress toward section 103. In this case, for the first time, the Court stated that only "inventions" were patentable, and that in order to constitute an invention, a new technology must transcend the everyday efforts of a skilled mechanic.

HOTCHKISS v. GREENWOOD
United States Supreme Court, 1850
52 U.S.(11 How.) 248

MR. JUSTICE NELSON delivered the opinion of the court.

This is a writ of error to the Circuit Court of the United States for the District of Ohio.

The suit was brought against the defendants for the alleged infringement of a patent for a new and useful improvement in making door and other knobs of all kinds of clay used in pottery, and of porcelain.

The improvement consists in making the knobs of clay or porcelain, and in fitting them for their application to doors, locks, and furniture, and various other uses to which they may be adapted; but more especially in this, that of having the cavity in the knob in which the screw or shank is inserted, and by which it is fastened, largest at the bottom and in the form of dovetail, or wedge reversed, and a screw formed therein by pouring in metal in a fused state; and, after referring to drawings of the article thus made, the patentees conclude as follows:

> "What we claim as our invention, and desire to secure by letters patent, is the manufacturing of knobs, as stated in the foregoing specifications, of potter's clay, or any kind of clay used in pottery, and shaped and finished by moulding, turning, burning, and glazing; and also of porcelain."

The court charged the jury that, if knobs of the same form and for the same purposes as that claimed by the patentees, made of metal or other material, had been before known and used; and if the spindle and shank, in the form used by them, had been before known and used, and had been attached to the metallic knob by means of a cavity in the form of dovetail and infusion of melted metal, the same as the mode claimed by the patentees, in the attachment of the shank and spindle to their knob; and the knob of clay was simply the substitution of one material for another, the spindle and shank being the same as before in common use, and also the mode of connecting them by dovetail to the knob the same as before in common use, and no more ingenuity or skill required to construct the knob in this way than that possessed by an ordinary mechanic acquainted with the business, the patent was invalid, and the plaintiffs were not entitled to a verdict.

This instruction, it is claimed, is erroneous, and one for which a new trial should be granted.

The instruction assumes, and, as was admitted on the argument, properly assumes, that knobs of metal, wood, & c., connected with a shank and spindle, in the mode and by the means used by the patentees in their manufacture, had been before known, and were in public use at the date of the patent; and hence the only novelty which could be claimed on their part was the adaptation of this old contrivance to knobs of potter's clay or porcelain; in other words, the novelty consisted in the substitution of the clay knob in the place of one made of metal or wood, as the case might be. And in order to appreciate still more clearly the extent of the novelty claimed, it is proper to add, that this knob of potter's clay is not new, and therefore constitutes no part of the discovery. If it was, a very different question would arise; as it might very well be urged, and successfully urged, that a knob of a new composition of matter, to which this old contrivance had been applied, and which resulted in a new and useful article, was the proper subject of a patent.

The novelty would consist in the new composition made practically useful for the purposes of life, by the means and contrivances mentioned. It would be a new manufacture, and none the less so, within the meaning of the patent law, because the means employed to adapt the new composition to a useful purpose was old, or well known.

But in the case before us, the knob is not new, nor the metallic shank and spindle, nor the dovetail form of the cavity in the knob, nor the means by which the metallic shank is securely fastened therein. All these were well known, and in common use; and the only thing new is the substitution of a knob of a different material from that heretofore used in connection with this arrangement.

Now it may very well be, that, by connecting the clay or porcelain knob with the metallic shank in this well-known mode, an article is produced better and cheaper than in the case of the metallic or wood knob; but this does not result from any new mechanical device or contrivance, but from the fact, that the material of which the knob is composed happens to be better adapted to the purpose for which it is made. The improvement consists in the superiority of the material, and which is not new, over that previously employed in making the knob.

But this, of itself, can never be the subject of a patent. No one will pretend that a machine, made, in whole or in part, of materials better adapted to the purpose for which it is used than the materials of which the old one is constructed, and for that reason better and cheaper, can be distinguished from the old one; or, in the sense of the patent law, can entitle the manufacturer to a patent.

The difference is formal, and destitute of ingenuity or invention. It may afford evidence of judgment and skill in the selection and adaptation of the materials in the manufacture of the instrument for the purposes intended, but nothing more.

It seemed to be supposed, on the argument, that this mode of fastening the shank to the clay knob produced a new and peculiar effect upon the article, beyond that produced when applied to the metallic knob, inasmuch as the fused metal by which the shank was fastened to the knob prevented the shank from acting immediately upon the knob, it being inclosed and firmly held by the metal; that for this reason the clay or porcelain knob was not so liable to crack or be broken, but was made firm and strong, and more durable.

This is doubtless true. But the peculiar effect thus referred to is not distinguishable from that which would exist in the case of the wood knob, or one of bone or ivory, or of other materials that might be mentioned.

here work is of a skillful mechanic, not that of the inventor

Now if the foregoing view of the improvement claimed in this patent be correct, it is quite apparent that there was no error in the submission of the questions presented at the trial to the jury; for unless more ingenuity and skill in applying the old method of fastening the shank and the knob were required in the application of it to the clay or porcelain knob than were possessed by an ordinary mechanic acquainted with the business, there was an absence of that degree of skill and ingenuity which constitute essential elements of every invention. In other words, the improvement is the work of the skilful mechanic, not that of the inventor.

We think, therefore, that the judgment is, and must be, affirmed.

NOTES

1. The Post–*Hotchkiss* Era. The *Hotchkiss* case has often been read as presenting the initial presentation of an additional inventiveness standard beyond that of utility and novelty. *See Graham v. John Deere Co.*, 383 U.S. 1, 3–4, 86 S.Ct. 684, 686, 15 L.Ed.2d 545 (1966) (Clark, J.) ("the 1952 [Patent] Act was intended to codify judicial precedents embracing the principle long ago announced by this Court in *Hotchkiss v. Greenwood*, 11 How. 248, 13 L.Ed. 683 (1851) * * *."); *Roanwell Corp. v. Plantronics, Inc.*, 429 U.S. 1004, 1005, 97 S.Ct. 538, 539, 50 L.Ed.2d 617 (1976) (White, J., dissenting from denial of certiorari) ("This Court long ago established that the sine qua non of patentability is 'invention' and that the protection of the patent law does not extend to an 'improvement [that] is the work of the skilled mechanic, not that of the inventor.' *Hotchkiss v. Greenwood*, 52 U.S. (11 How.) 248, 267, 13 L.Ed. 683 (1850)."); *Lee v. Runge*, 404 U.S. 887, 891, 92 S.Ct. 197, 199, 30 L.Ed.2d 169 (1971) (Douglas, J., dissenting from denial of certiorari).

The Supreme Court's articulation in *Hotchkiss* was not itself a pioneering invention, but a combination of pre-existing legal art. Many courts since the early nineteenth century had examined differences between the invention and the prior art. *See, e.g., Knight v. Baltimore & O. R. Co.*, 14 F.Cas. 758, No. 7882 (C.C.Md.1840) ("[i]f, before his first patent * * *, the same principle, in the same combination, which he describes as his improvement, was in public use, in ordinary carriages, upon common roads, the plaintiff was not entitled to a patent for applying the same thing to railway carriages, unless the improvement he claims contain something new *and material*, either in principle, in combination, or in the mode of operation, in order to adapt it to its new use."). *Cf. Earle v. Sawyer*, 8 F.Cas. 254, 4 Mason 1, 1 Robb.Pat.Cas. 490 (C.C.Mass. 1825) (No. 4247) (Story, J.).

In any event, *Hotchkiss* articulated a doctrine that focused on the "inventiveness" of the invention. Sadly the vague and highly abstract nature of the Supreme Court's invention test caused wildly varying results and interpretations. In the Supreme Court alone, the standard for sufficient "inventiveness" took the form of "inventive effort," *Smith v. Goodyear Dental Vulcanite Co.*, 93 U.S. 486, 497 (1876); "a substantial invention or discovery," *Atlantic Works v. Brady*, 107 U.S. 192, 200 (1883); "the creative work in the inventive faculty,"

Hollister v. Benedict & Burnham Mfg. Co., 113 U.S. 59, 73 (1885); "that impalpable something," *McClain v. Ortmayer*, 141 U.S. 419, 427 (1891); and "inventive skill," *Ansonia Brass & Copper Co. v. Electrical Supply Co.*, 144 U.S. 11, 18 (1892). One court went so far as to demand "something new, unexpected and exciting," which the disgruntled patentee protested on appeal with the comment that "there is nothing very exciting about automobile transmissions." *Thurber Corp. v. Fairchild Motor Corp.*, 269 F.2d 841, 849 (5th Cir.1959). As Judge Learned Hand noted, the invention standard was "as fugitive, impalpable, wayward and vague a phantom as exists in the whole paraphernalia of legal concepts." *Harries v. Air King Prods.*, 183 F.2d 158 (2d Cir.1950).

In parallel with the rise of the antitrust movement, the standard of invention became increasingly difficult to satisfy, particularly at the Supreme Court. The Court's predilection for striking down patents led Justice Jackson to state "that the only patent that is valid is one which this Court has not been able to get its hands on." *Jungersen v. Ostby and Barton Co.*, 335 U.S. 560, 572 (1949). His observation had been proceeded by the standard set in *Cuno Engineering Corp. v. Automatic Devices Corp.*, 314 U.S. 84, 90 (1941), where the Court had elaborated upon the invention standard:

> We may concede that the functions performed by Mead's combination were new and useful. But that does not necessarily make the device patentable. Under the statute ... the device must not only be "new and useful," it must also be an "invention" or discovery. " ... It has been recognized that if an improvement is to obtain the privileged position of a patent more ingenuity must be involved than the work of a mechanic skilled in the art.... That is to say, the new device, *however useful it may be, must reveal the flash of creative genius, not merely the skill of the calling*. If it fails, it has not established its right to a private grant in the public domain."

The patent community considered this "flash of genius" standard as a literal declaration of war against the patent system. But the high water mark of this "war on patents" was perhaps the following decision.

   2. Development of Inventive Step Abroad. A mandatory feature of contemporary patent systems, the origin of the inventive step requirement has been traced to the U.S. Supreme Court opinion in *Hotchkiss v. Greenwood*. See Friedrich–Karl Beier, *The Inventive Step in Its Historical Development*, 17 INT'L. REV. INDUS. PROP. & COPYRIGHT L. 301 (1986). Development of this requirement in Germany took some unusual turns in that civil law regime. Although the first patent statute for the unified German Empire, the 1877 Act, did not include a requirement of technical advance or inventive step, by the turn of the century the Imperial Patent Office began imposing patentability requirements extending past novelty. *Id.* Observers of the British system follow the modern requirement of inventive step to at least as early as Lord Herschell's opinion for the House of Lords in *Vickers v. Sidell*, 7 R.P.C. 292 (1890), which intoned a standard of obviousness and, prophetically, counseled against the use of hindsight when judging inventions. France was quite a latecomer in requiring inventive step: the French Patent Law of 1844 stated only the requirements of novelty and industrial application, a situation that was not changed until the

Patent Law of January 2, 1968. *See* Joanna Schmidt–Szalewski, *Nonobviousness as a Requirement of Patentability in French Law*, 23 Int'l Rev. Indus. Prop. & Copyright L. 725 (1992).

GREAT A. & P. TEA CO. v. SUPERMARKET EQUIPMENT CORP.

United States Supreme Court, 1950
340 U.S. 147

Mr. Justice Jackson delivered the opinion of the Court.

Two courts below have concurred in holding three patent claims to be valid, and it is stipulated that, if valid, they have been infringed. The issue, for the resolution of which we granted certiorari, is whether they applied correct criteria of invention. We hold that they have not, and that by standards appropriate for a combination patent these claims are invalid.

Stated without artifice, the claims assert invention of a cashier's counter equipped with a three-sided frame, or rack, with no top or bottom, which, which pushed or pulled, will move groceries deposited within it by a customer to the checking clerk and leave them there when it is pushed back to repeat the operation. It is kept on the counter by guides. That the resultant device words as claimed, speeds the customer on his way, reduces checking costs for the merchant, has been widely adopted and successfully used, appear beyond dispute.

The District Court explicitly found that each element in this device was known to prior art. "However," it found, "the conception of a counter with an extension to receive a bottomless self-unloading tray with which to push the contents of the tray in front of the cashier was a decidedly novel feature and constitutes a new and useful combination." The Court of Appeals regarded this finding of invention as one of fact, sustained by substantial evidence, and affirmed it as not clearly erroneous. It identified no other new or different element to constitute invention and overcame its doubts by consideration of the need for some such device and evidence of commercial success of this one.

While this Court has sustained combination patents, it never has ventured to give a precise and comprehensive definition of the test to be applied in such cases. The voluminous literature which the subject has excited discloses no such test. It is agreed that the key to patentability of a mechanical device that brings old factors into cooperation is presence or lack of invention. In course of time the profession came to employ the term "combination" to imply its presence and the term "aggregation" to signify its absence, thus making antonyms in legal art of words which in ordinary speech are more nearly synonyms. However useful as words of art to denote in short form that an assembly of units has failed or has met the examination for invention, their employment as tests to determine invention results in nothing but confusion. The concept of invention is inherently elusive when applied to combination of old elements. This, together with the imprecision of our language, have counseled courts and text writers to be cautious in affirmative definitions or rules on the subject.

The negative rule accrued from many litigations was condensed about as precisely as the subject permits in *Lincoln Engineering Co. of Illinois v. Stewart–Warner Corp.*, 303 U.S. 545, 549, 549, 58 S.Ct. 662, 664, 82 L.Ed. 1008: "The mere aggregation of a number of old parts or elements which, in the aggregation, perform or produce no new or different function or operation than that theretofore performed or produced by them, is not patentable invention." The conjunction or concert of known elements must contribute something; only when the whole in some way exceeds the sum of its parts is the accumulation of old devices patentable. Elements may, of course, especially in chemistry or electronics, take on some new quality or function from being brought into concert, but this is not a usual result of uniting elements old in mechanics. This case is wanting in any unusual or surprising consequences from the unification of the elements here concerned, and there is nothing to indicate that the lower courts scrutinized the claims in the light of this rather severe test.

Neither court below has made any finding that old elements which made up this device perform any additional or different function in the combination than they perform out of it. This counter does what a store counter always has done—it supports merchandise at a convenient height while the customer makes his purchases and the merchant his sales. The three-sided rack will draw or push goods put within it from one place to another—just what any such a rack would do on any smooth surface—and the guide rails keep it from falling or sliding off from the counter, as guide rails have ever done. Two and two have been added together, and still they make only four.

Courts should scrutinize combination patent claims with a care proportioned to the difficulty and improbability of finding invention in an assembly of old elements. The function of a patent is to add to the sum of useful knowledge. Patents cannot be sustained when, on the contrary, their effect is to subtract from former resources freely available to skilled artisans. A patent for a combination which only unites old elements with no change in their respective functions, such as is presented here, obviously withdraws what already is known into the field of its monopoly and diminishes the resources available to skillful men. This patentee has added nothing to the total stock of knowledge, but has merely brought together segments of prior art and claims them in congregation as a monopoly.

Reversed.

MR. JUSTICE DOUGLAS, with whom MR. JUSTICE BLACK agrees, concurring.

It is worth emphasis that every patent case involving validity presents a question which requires reference to a standard written into the

Constitution. Article I, § 8, contains a grant to the Congress of the power to permit patents to be issued. But unlike most of the specific powers which Congress is given, that grant is qualified. The Congress does not have free reign, for example, to decide that patents should be easily or freely given. The Congress acts under the restraint imposed by the statement of purpose in Art. I, § 8. The purpose is 'To promote the Progress of Science and useful Arts'. The means for achievement of that end is the grant for a limited time to inventors of the exclusive right to their inventions.

Every patent is the grant of a privilege of exacting tolls from the public. The Framers plainly did not want those monopolies freely granted. The invention, to justify a patent, had to serve the ends of science—to push back the frontiers of chemistry, physics, and the like; to make a distinctive contribution to scientific knowledge. That is why through the years the opinions of the Court commonly have taken "inventive genius" as the test. It is not enough that an article is new and useful. The Constitution never sanctioned the patenting of gadgets. Patents serve a higher end—the advancement of science. An invention need not be as startling as an atomic bomb to be patentable. But is has to be of such quality and distinction that masters of the scientific field in which it falls will recognize it as an advance. Mr. Justice Bradley stated in *Atlantic Works v. Brady*, 107 U.S. 192, 200, 2 S.Ct. 225, 231, 27 L.Ed. 438, the consequences of a looser standard: "It was never the object of those laws to grant a monopoly for every trifling device, every shadow of a shade of an idea, which would naturally and spontaneously occur to any skilled mechanic or operator in the ordinary progress of manufactures. Such an indiscriminate creation of exclusive privileges tends rather to obstruct than to stimulate invention. It creates a class of speculative schemers who make it their business to watch the advancing wave of improvement, and gather its foam in the form of patented monopolies, which enable them to lay a heavy tax upon the industry of the country, without contributing anything to the real advancement of the arts. It embarrasses the honest pursuit of business with fears and apprehensions of concealed liens and unknown liabilities to lawsuits and vexatious accountings for profits made in good faith."

The standard of patentability is a constitutional standard; and the question of validity of a patent is a question of law.

The attempts through the years to get a broader, looser conception of patents than the Constitution contemplates have been persistent. The Patent Office, like most administrative agencies, has looked with favor on the opportunity which the exercise of discretion affords to expand its own jurisdiction. And so it has placed a host of gadgets under the armour of patents—gadgets that obviously have had no place in the constitutional scheme of advancing scientific knowledge.

The patent involved in the present case belongs to this list of incredible patents which the Patent Office has spawned. The fact that a patent as flimsy and as spurious as this one has to be brought all the way to this Court to be declared invalid dramatically illustrates how far our patent system frequently departs from the constitutional standards which are supposed to govern.

[handwritten marginalia: Patent system here has strayed from Constitutional Standard.]

NOTE

Dissatisfaction with the Supreme Court's increasingly onerous standard of invention was among the reasons leading to the articulation of a statutory basis for the invention standard in the Patent Act of 1952. An individual intimately involved with the creation of the 1952 Act, the Honorable Giles S. Rich, noted the intended impact of the drafters of § 103 as follows:

1. *It put the* [invention] *requirement into the statutes for the first time, in section 103.* ... Though one may call section 103 "codification" it took a case law doctrine, expressed in hundreds of different ways, and put it into statutory language in a single form approved by Congress. In such form it became law superior to that which may be derived from any prior court opinion.

2. *The Patent Act of 1952 expresses the prerequisite to patentability without any reference to "invention" as a legal requirement.* Nowhere in the entire act is there a reference to any requirement of "invention" and the drafters did this deliberately in an effort to free the law and lawyers from bondage to that old and meaningless term. The word "invention" is used in the statute only to refer to the thing invented. That is why the requirement of "invention" should be referred to, it at all, only with respect to that which is dead.

3. *The act sets as the standard of patentability the unobviousness of the invention, at the time it was made, to person having ordinary skill in the art.* Therefore, what we have today, and have had since January 1, 1953, is a requirement of *unobviousness*, rather than a requirement of "invention."

Giles S. Rich, *The Principles of Patentability*, 42 J. PAT. OFF. SOC'Y 75, 89 (1960). Following the enactment of section 103, attention turned to the way the Supreme Court would interpret the statute. Unfortunately the Supreme Court was not swift to answer. Thirteen years after the effective date of the 1952 Act, the Court finally took up its pen in three cases—*Graham v. John Deere*, *Cook Chemical*, and *Adams*—of such importance to the patent bar that they became known merely as "The Trilogy." These decisions are probably still the most important patent cases in modern history. Certainly they are the most important cases relative to the nonobviousness requirement.

§ 7.2 THE MODERN STANDARD OF NONOBVIOUSNESS

§ 7.2[a] THE TRILOGY

GRAHAM v. JOHN DEERE CO.

United States Supreme Court, 1966
383 U.S. 1

MR. JUSTICE CLARK delivered the opinion of the Court.

After a lapse of 15 years, the Court again focuses its attention on the patentability of inventions under the standard of Art. I, § 8, cl. 8, of the Constitution and under the conditions prescribed by the laws of the United States. Since our last expression on patent validity, *Great A. & P. Tea Co. v. Supermarket Equipment Corp.*, 340 U.S. 147, 71 S.Ct. 127, 95 L.Ed. 162 (1950), the Congress has for the first time expressly added a third statutory dimension to the two requirements of novelty and utility that had been the sole statutory test since the Patent Act of 1793. This is the test of obviousness, i.e., whether "the subject matter sought to be patented and the prior art are such that the subject matter as a whole would have been obvious at the time the invention was made to a person having ordinary skill in the art to which said subject matter pertains. Patentability shall not be negatived by the manner in which the invention was made." § 103 of the Patent Act of 1952, 35 U.S.C. § 103 (1964 ed.).

We have concluded that the 1952 Act was intended to codify judicial precedents embracing the principle long ago announced by this Court in *Hotchkiss v. Greenwood*, 11 How. 248, 13 L.Ed. 683 (1851), and that, while the clear language of § 103 places emphasis on an inquiry into obviousness, the general level of innovation necessary to sustain patentability remains the same.

Graham v. John Deere Co., an infringement suit by petitioners, presents a conflict between two Circuits over the validity of a single patent on a "Clamp for vibrating Shank Plows." The invention, a combination of old mechanical elements, involves a device designed to absorb shock from plow shanks as they plow through rocky soil and thus to prevent damage to the plow. In 1955, the Fifth Circuit had held the patent valid under its rule that when a combination produces an "old result in a cheaper and otherwise more advantageous way," it is patentable. *Jeoffroy Mfg., Inc. v. Graham*, 219 F.2d 511, *cert. denied*, 350 U.S. 826, 76 S.Ct. 55, 100 L.Ed. 738. In 1964, the Eighth Circuit held, in the case at bar, that there was no new result in the patented combination and that the patent was, therefore, not valid. 333 F.2d 529, *reversing* D.C., 216 F.Supp. 272. We granted *certiorari*, 379 U.S. 956, 85 S.Ct. 652, 13 L.Ed.2d 553. Although we have determined that neither Circuit applied the correct test, we conclude that the patent is invalid under § 103 and, therefore, we affirm the judgment of the Eighth Circuit.

II.

Congress quickly responded to the bidding of the Constitution by enacting the Patent Act of 1790 during the second session of the First Congress. It created an agency in the Department of State headed by the Secretary of State, the Secretary of the Department of War and the Attorney General, any two of whom could issue a patent for a period not exceeding 14 years to any petitioner that "hath * * * invented or discovered any useful art, manufacture, * * * or device, or any improvement therein not before known or used" if the board found that "the invention or discovery (was) sufficiently useful and important * * *." 1 Stat. 110. This group, whose members administered the patent system along with their other public duties, was known by its own designation as "Commissioners for the Promotion of Useful Arts."

Thomas Jefferson, who as Secretary of State was a member of the group, was its moving spirit and might well be called the "first administrator of our patent system." See Federico, *Operation of the Patent Act of 1790*, 18 J.Pat.Off.Soc. 237, 238 (1936). He was not only an administrator of the patent system under the 1790 Act, but was also the author of the 1793 Patent Act. In addition, Jefferson was himself an inventor of great note. His unpatented improvements on plows, to mention but one line of his inventions, won acclaim and recognition on both sides of the Atlantic. Because of his active interest and influence in the early development of the patent system, Jefferson's views on the general nature of the limited patent monopoly under the Constitution, as well as his conclusions as to conditions for patentability under the statutory scheme, are worthy of note.

Jefferson's philosophy on the nature and purpose of the patent monopoly is expressed in a letter to Isaac McPherson (Aug. 1813), a portion of which we set out in the margin. He rejected a natural-rights theory in intellectual property rights and clearly recognized the social and economic rationale of the patent system. The patent monopoly was not designed to secure to the inventor his natural right in his discoveries. Rather, it was a reward, an inducement, to bring forth new knowledge. The grant of an exclusive right to an invention was the creation of society—at odds with the inherent free nature of disclosed ideas—and was not to be freely given. Only inventions and discoveries which furthered human knowledge, and were new and useful, justified the special inducement of a limited private monopoly. Jefferson did not believe in granting patents for small details, obvious improvements, or frivolous devices. His writings evidence his insistence upon a high level of patentability.

As a member of the patent board for several years, Jefferson saw clearly the difficulty in "drawing a line between the things which are worth to the public the embarrassment of an exclusive patent, and those which are not." The board on which he served sought to draw such a line and formulated several rules which are preserved in Jefferson's

[handwritten margin note: turned it over to the courts]

correspondence.[12] Despite the board's efforts, Jefferson saw "with what slow progress a system of general rules could be matured." Because of the "abundance" of cases and the fact that the investigations occupied "more time of the members of the board than they could spare from higher duties, the whole was turned over to the judiciary, to be matured into a system, under which every one might know when his actions were safe and lawful." Letter to McPherson, supra, at 181, 182. Apparently Congress agreed with Jefferson and the board that the courts should develop additional conditions for patentability. Although the Patent Act was amended, revised or codified some 50 times between 1790 and 1950, Congress steered clear of a statutory set of requirements other than the bare novelty and utility tests reformulated in Jefferson's draft of the 1793 Patent Act.

[handwritten margin note: no statutory requirements other than novelty and utility]

III.

[handwritten margin note: hard to draw a line on balancing act between patent and no patent]

The difficulty of formulating conditions for patentability was heightened by the generality of the constitutional grant and the statutes implementing it, together with the underlying policy of the patent system that "the things which are worth to the public the embarrassment of an exclusive patent," as Jefferson put it, must outweigh the restrictive effect of the limited patent monopoly. The inherent problem was to develop some means of weeding out those inventions which would not be disclosed or devised but for the inducement of a patent.

This Court formulated a general condition of patentability in 1851 in *Hotchkiss v. Greenwood*, 11 How. 248, 13 L.Ed. 683. The patent involved a mere substitution of materials—porcelain or clay for wood or metal in doorknobs—and the Court condemned it, holding:

[handwritten margin note: Hotchkiss standard]

> "(U)nless more ingenuity and skill * * * were required * * * than were possessed by an ordinary mechanic acquainted with the business, there was an absence of that degree of skill and ingenuity which constitute essential elements of every invention. In other words, the improvement is the work of the skilful mechanic, not that of the inventor." At p. 267.

Hotchkiss, by positing the condition that a patentable invention evidence more ingenuity and skill than that possessed by an ordinary mechanic acquainted with the business, merely distinguished between new and useful innovations that were capable of sustaining a patent and those that were not. The *Hotchkiss* test laid the cornerstone of the judicial evolution suggested by Jefferson and left to the courts by Congress. The language in the case, and in those which followed, gave birth to

---

12. "(A) machine of which we are possessed, might be applied by every man to any use of which it is susceptible." Letter to Isaac McPherson, supra, at 181. "(A) change of material should not give title to a patent. As the making a ploughshare of cast rather than of wrought iron; a comb of iron instead of horn or of ivory * * *." Ibid. "(A) mere change of form should give no right to a patent, as a high-quartered shoe instead of a low one; a round hat instead of a three-square; or a square bucket instead of a round one." Id., at 181–182. "(A combined use of old implements.) A man has a right to use a saw, an axe, a plane separately; may he not combine their uses on the same piece of wood?" Letter to Oliver Evans, (Jan. 1814), VI WRITINGS OF THOMAS JEFFERSON, at 298 (Washington ed.).

"invention" as a word of legal art signifying patentable inventions. Yet, as this Court has observed, "(t)he truth is, the word ('invention') cannot be defined in such manner as to afford any substantial aid in determining whether a particular device involves an exercise of the inventive faculty or not." *McClain v. Ortmayer*, 141 U.S. 419, 427, 12 S.Ct. 76, 78, 35 L.Ed. 800 (1891); *Great A. & P. Tea Co. v. Supermarket Equipment Corp., supra*, 340 U.S., at 151, 71 S.Ct. at 129. Its use as a label brought about a large variety of opinions as to its meaning both in the Patent Office, in the courts, and at the bar. The *Hotchkiss* formulation, however, lies not in any label, but in its functional approach to questions of patentability. In practice, *Hotchkiss* has required a comparison between the subject matter of the patent, or patent application, and the background skill of the calling. It has been from this comparison that patentability was in each case determined.

IV.

THE 1952 PATENT ACT.

[Section 103] is cast in relatively unambiguous terms. Patentability is to depend, in addition to novelty and utility, upon the "non-obvious" nature of the "subject matter sought to be patented" to a person having ordinary skill in the pertinent art.

The first sentence of this section is strongly reminiscent of the language in *Hotchkiss*. Both formulations place emphasis on the pertinent are existing at the time the invention was made and both are implicitly tied to advances in that art. The major distinction is that Congress has emphasized "nonobviousness" as the operative test of the section, rather than the less definite "invention" language of *Hotchkiss* that Congress thought had led to "a large variety" of expressions in decisions and writings. In the title itself the Congress used the phrase "Conditions for patentability; non-obvious subject matter", thus focusing upon "nonobviousness" rather than "invention." The Senate and House Reports, S.Rep. No. 1979, 82d Cong., 2d Sess. (1952); H.R.Rep. No. 1923, 82d Cong., 2d Sess. (1952), U.S.Code Congressional and Administrative News 1952, p. 2394, reflect this emphasis in these terms:

> "Section 103 states this requirement in the title. It refers to the difference between the subject matter sought to be patented and the prior art, meaning what was known before as described in section 102. If this difference is such that the subject matter as a whole would have been obvious at the time to a person skilled in the art, then the subject matter cannot be patented. 'That provision paraphrases language which has often been used in decisions of the courts, and the section is added to the statute for uniformity and definiteness. This section should have a stabilizing effect and minimize great departures which have appeared in some cases.'"
> H.R.Rep., supra, at 7; S.Rep., supra, at 6.

It is undisputed that this section was, for the first time, a statutory expression of an additional requirement for patentability, originally expressed in *Hotchkiss*. It also seems apparent that Congress intended by the last sentence of § 103 to abolish the test it believed this Court announced in the controversial phrase "flash of creative genius," used in *Cuno Engineering Corp. v. Automatic Devices Corp.*, 314 U.S. 84, 62 S.Ct. 37, 86 L.Ed. 58 (1941).

It is contended, however, by some of the parties and by several of the amici that the first sentence of § 103 was intended to sweep away judicial precedents and to lower the level of patentability.... We believe that this legislative history, as well as other sources, shows that the revision was not intended by Congress to change the general level of patentable invention. We conclude that the section was intended merely as a codification of judicial precedents embracing the Hotchkiss condition, with congressional directions that inquiries into the obviousness of the subject matter sought to be patented are a prerequisite to patentability.

V.

Approached in this light, the § 103 additional condition, when followed realistically, will permit a more practical test of patentability. The emphasis on non-obviousness is one of inquiry, not quality, and, as such, comports with the constitutional strictures.

While the ultimate question of patent validity is one of law, *Great A. & P. Tea Co. v. Supermarket Equipment Corp., supra*, 340 U.S. at 155, 71 S.Ct. at 131, the § 103 condition, which is but one of three conditions, each of which must be satisfied, lends itself to several basic factual inquiries. Under § 103, the scope and content of the prior art are to be determined; differences between the prior art and the claims at issue are to be ascertained; and the level of ordinary skill in the pertinent art resolved. Against this background, the obviousness or nonobviousness of the subject matter is determined. Such secondary considerations as commercial success, long felt but unsolved needs, failure of others, etc., might be utilized to give light to the circumstances surrounding the origin of the subject matter sought to be patented. As indicia of obviousness or nonobviousness, these inquiries may have relevancy. See Note, *Subtests of "Nonobviousness": A Nontechnical Approach to Patent Validity*, 112 U.PA.L.REV. 1169 (1964) .....

Although we conclude here that the inquiry which the Patent Office and the courts must make as to patentability must be beamed with greater intensity on the requirements of § 103, it bears repeating that we find no change in the general strictness with which the overall test is to be applied. We have been urged to find in § 103 a relaxed standard, supposedly a congressional reaction to the "increased standard" applied by this Court in its decisions over the last 20 or 30 years. The standard has remained invariable in this Court. Technology, however, has advanced—and with remarkable rapidity in the last 50 years. Moreover, the ambit of applicable art in given fields of science has widened by disciplines unheard of a half century ago. It is but an evenhanded application to require that those persons granted the benefit of a patent monopoly be charged with an awareness of these changed conditions. The same is true of the less technical, but still useful arts. He who seeks to build a better mousetrap today has a long path to tread before reaching the Patent Office.

VI.

This patent, No. 2,627,798 (hereinafter called the '798 patent) relates to a spring clamp which permits plow shanks to be pushed upward when they hit obstructions in the soil, and then springs the shanks back into normal position when the obstruction is passed over. The device, which we show diagrammatically in the accompanying sketches (Appendix, Fig. 1), is fixed to the plow frame as a unit. The mechanism around which the controversy center is basically a hinge. The top half of it, known as the upper plate (marked 1 in the sketches), is a heavy metal piece clamped to the plow frame (2) and is stationary relative to the plow frame. The lower half of the hinge, known as the hinge plate (3), is connected to the rear of the upper plate by a hinge pin (4) and rotates downward with respect to it. The shank (5), which is bolted to the forward end of the hinge plate (at 6), runs beneath the plate and parallel to it for about nine inches, passes through a stirrup (7), and then continues backward for several feet curving down toward the ground. The chisel (8), which does the actual plowing, is attached to the rear end of the shank. As the plow frame is pulled forward, the chisel rips through the soil, thereby plowing it. In the normal position, the hinge plate and the shank are kept tight against the upper plate by a spring (9), which is atop the upper plate. A rod (10) runs through the center of the spring, extending down through holes in both plates and the shank. Its upper end is bolted to the top of the spring while its lower end is hooked against the underside of the shank.

When the chisel hits a rock or other obstruction in the soil, the obstruction forces the chisel and the rear portion of the shank to move upward. The shank is pivoted (at 11) against the rear of the hinge plate and pries open the hinge against the closing tendency of the spring. (See sketch labeled "Open Position," Appendix, Fig. 1.) This closing tendency is caused by the fact that, as the hinge is opened, the connecting rod is pulled downward and the spring is compressed. When the obstruction is passed over, the upward force on the chisel disappears and the spring pulls the shank and hinge plate back into their original position. The lower, rear portion of the hinge plate is constructed in the form of a stirrup (7) which brackets the shank, passing around and beneath it. The shank fits loosely into the stirrup (permitting a slight up and down play). The stirrup is designed to prevent the shank from recoiling away from the hinge plate, and thus prevents excessive strain on the shank near its bolted connection. The stirrup also girds the shank, preventing it from fishtailing from side to side.

In practical use, a number of spring-hinge-shank combinations are clamped to a plow frame, forming a set of ground-working chisels capable of withstanding the shock of rocks and other obstructions in the soil without breaking the shanks. . . .

THE PRIOR ART.

We confine our discussion to the prior patent of Graham, '811, and to the Glencoe clamp device, both among the references asserted by respondents. The Graham '811 and '798 patent devices are similar in all elements, save two: (1) the stirrup and the bolted connection of the shank to the hinge plate do not appear in '811; and (2) the position of the shank is reversed, being placed in patent '811 above the hinge plate, sandwiched between it and the upper plate. The shank is held in place by the spring rod which is hooked against the bottom of the hinge plate passing through a slot in the shank. Other differences are of no consequence to our examination. In practice the '811 patent arrangement permitted the shank to wobble or fishtail because it was not rigidly fixed to the hinge plate; moreover, as the hinge plate was below the shank, the latter caused wear on the upper plate, a member difficult to repair or replace. . . .

Graham did not urge before the Patent Office the greater "flexing" qualities of the '798 patent arrangement which he so heavily relied on in the courts. The sole element in patent '798 which petitioners argue before us is the interchanging of the shank and hinge plate and the consequences flowing from this arrangement. The contention is that this arrangement—which petitioners claim is not disclosed in the prior art—permits the shank to flex under stress for its entire length. As we have sketched (see sketch, "Graham '798 Patent" in Appendix, Fig. 2), when the chisel hits an obstruction the resultant force (A) pushes the rear of the shank upward and the shank pivots against the rear of the hinge plate at (C). The natural tendency is for that portion of the shank between the pivot point and the bolted connection (i.e., between C and D) to bow downward and away from the hinge plate. The maximum distance (B) that the shank moves away from the plate is slight—for emphasis, greatly exaggerated in the sketches. . . .

THE OBVIOUSNESS OF THE DIFFERENCES.

We cannot agree with petitioners. We assume that the prior art does not disclose such an arrangement as petitioners claim in patent '798. Still we do not believe that the argument on which petitioners' contention is bottomed supports the validity of the patent. The tendency of the shank to flex is the same in all cases. If free-flexing, as petitioners now argue, is the crucial difference above the prior art, then it appears evident that the desired result would be obtainable by not boxing the shank within the confines of the hinge. The only other effective place available in the arrangement was to attach it below the hinge plate and run it through a stirrup or bracket that would not disturb its flexing qualities. Certainly a person having ordinary skill in the prior art, given the fact that the flex in the shank could be utilized more effectively if allowed to run the entire length of the shank, would immediately see that the thing to do was what Graham did, i.e., invert the shank and the hinge plate.

Petitioners' argument basing validity on the free-flex theory raised for the first time on appeal is reminiscent of *Lincoln Engineering Co. of Illinois v. Stewart–Warner Corp.*, 303 U.S. 545, 58 S.Ct. 662, 82 L.Ed. 1008 (1938), where the Court called such an effort "an afterthought. No such function * * * is hinted at in the specifications of the patent. If this were so vital an element in the functioning of the apparatus, it is strange that all mention of it was omitted." At p. 550, 58 S.Ct. at p. 665. No "flexing" argument was raised in the Patent Office. Indeed, the trial judge specifically found that "flexing is not a claim of the patent in suit * * *" and would not permit interrogation as to flexing in the accused devices. Moreover, the clear testimony of petitioners' experts shows that the flexing advantages flowing from the '798 arrangement are not, in fact, a significant feature in the patent.

We find no nonobvious facets in the '798 arrangement. The wear and repair claims were sufficient to overcome the patent examiner's original conclusions as to the validity of the patent. However, some of the prior art, notably Glencoe, was not before him. There the hinge plate is below the shank but, as the courts below found, all of the elements in the '798 patent are present in the Glencoe structure. Furthermore, even though the position of the shank and hinge plate appears reversed in Glencoe, the mechanical operation is identical. The shank there pivots about the underside of the stirrup, which in Glencoe is above the shank. In other words, the stirrup in Glencoe serves exactly the same function as the heel of the hinge plate in '798. The mere shifting of the wear point to the heel of the '798 hinge plate from the stirrup of Glencoe—itself a part of the hinge plate—presents no operative mechanical distinctions, much less nonobvious differences.

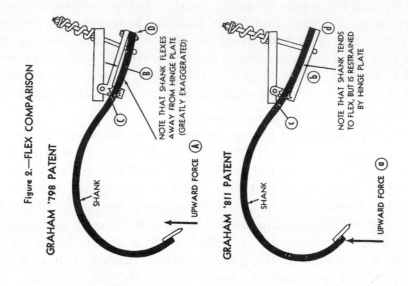

Figure 2.—FLEX COMPARISON

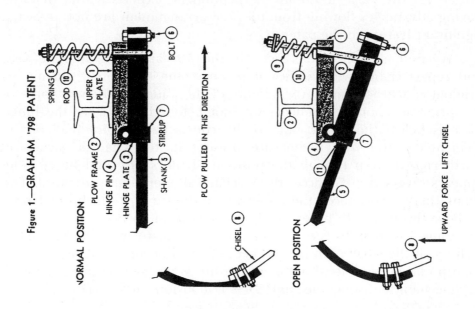

Figure 1.—GRAHAM '798 PATENT

NOTES

1. Questions of Law and Fact. The *Graham* court indicated that nonobviousness presents a mixed question of fact and law: although the ultimate conclusion of validity is a legal question, the underlying inquires are factual in nature. *See also, e.g., Minnesota Mining & Manufacturing Co. v. Johnson & Johnson Orthopaedics, Inc.,* 976 F.2d 1559 (Fed.Cir.1992); *In re Vaeck,* 947 F.2d 488 (Fed.Cir.1991). How does the categorization of nonobviousness as law or fact impact the role of jury involvement in this decision? How about the standard of review before the Federal Circuit?

2. The Level of Skill in the Art. Determination of the appropriate level of skill in the art often proves a difficult inquiry. In *Environmental Designs, Ltd. v. Union Oil Co.*, 713 F.2d 693, 696 (Fed.Cir.1983), the court provided the following list of factors to be considered in determining the level of ordinary skill in the art:

(1) the educational level of the inventor;

(2) type of problems encountered in the art;

(3) prior art solutions to those problems;

(4) rapidity with which inventions are made;

(5) sophistication of the technology;

(6) educational level of active workers in the field.

Litigation experience shows that the accused infringer will seek to prove a high level of skill in the art; the patent holder, a low level of skill in the art. Why? Perhaps the ultimate example of this trend is demonstrated by the opinion of the European Patent Office Board of Appeal in T 60/89 (OJ 1992, 268), which rejected the argument that the person of skill in the art should be considered a Nobel Prize recipient. The Board concluded that:

> It is the opinion of the Board that the skilled person in the field of genetic engineering in 1978 is not to be defined as a Nobel Prize laureate, even if a number of scientists working in this field at that time were actually awarded the Nobel Prize. Rather, it is understood that the skilled person was to be seen as a graduate scientist or a team of scientists of that skill, working in laboratories which developed from molecular genetics to genetic engineering techniques at that time.

3. How the Invention Was Made. The first sentence of § 103(a) indicates that "patentability shall not be negatived by the manner in which the invention was made." This language was meant to place on a level footing inventions inspired by a "flash of genius" with those created through the plodding path of exhaustive research and development. Thus, the patent statute offers its awards to accidental or lucky inventors, even though such incentives had nothing to do with the development of the invention. Why should patents be awarded to those technologists who were not inspired to invent by the patent system itself? Ironically, then, did pre-Trilogy courts have the matter precisely backwards? For an argument that the nonobviousness requirement stands as a proxy for such inquiries, see Edmund Kitch, *Graham v. John Deere Co.: New Standards for Patents*, 1966 SUP. CT. REV. 293, a portion of which is reprinted later in this chapter.

4. Further Reading. For reflections by Justice Clark's law clerk on the circumstances leading to The Trilogy, see Charles D. Reed, *Some Reflections on* Graham v. John Deere Co., *in* NONOBVIOUSNESS-THE ULTIMATE CONDITION OF PATENTABILITY 2:301 (John F. Witherspoon ed. 1978). A transcript of the oral argument in *United States v. Adams* is set forth as an Appendix to that text. A fine historical analysis of the requirement of inventive step in the English-speaking world is JOHN BOCHNOVIC, THE INVENTIVE STEP (1982) (IIC Studies Vol. 5).

5. Teaching, Suggestion, Motivation. Following the enactment of the Federal Courts Improvement Act of 1982, the Federal Circuit became the chief judicial steward of the nonobviousness requirement. In its effort to develop a fair and objective standard that avoided the problem of hindsight, the Court of Appeals seized upon a concept developed by one of its predecessor courts, the CCPA. Under this notion, some teaching, suggestion, or motivation must have provided a person of ordinary skill in the art cause to combine the references to produce the claimed invention with a reasonable probability of success. In *Pro–Mold & Tool Co. v. Great Lakes Plastics, Inc.*, 75 F.3d 1568 (Fed.Cir.1996), the Federal Circuit explained that the reason to produce the claimed invention may come from one of three sources:

(1) the references themselves,

(2) knowledge of those skilled in the art, or

(3) the nature of the problem to be solved, leading inventors to look to references relating to possible solutions to that problem.

Note, however, that the reason to develop the claimed invention need not have been explicit–an implicit suggestion may be enough. As the Federal Circuit put it, there is "no requirement that the prior art contain an express suggestion to combine known elements to achieve the claimed invention." *Motorola, Inc. v. Interdigital Tech. Corp.*, 121 F.3d 1461, 1472 (Fed. Cir. 1997).

Some observers believed that the "TSM" standard increasingly came to dominate the law of obviousness. Ultimately the Supreme Court joined the discussion, for the first time in a generation issuing its first opinion on the most significant requirement for patenting.

KSR INTERNATIONAL CO. v. TELEFLEX INC.

Supreme Court of the United States, 2007
550 U.S. 398

KENNEDY, J., delivered the opinion for a unanimous Court.

Teleflex Incorporated and its subsidiary Technology Holding Company—both referred to here as Teleflex—sued KSR International Company for patent infringement. The patent at issue, United States Patent No. 6,237,565 B1, is entitled "Adjustable Pedal Assembly With Electronic Throttle Control." The patentee is Steven J. Engelgau, and the patent is referred to as "the Engelgau patent." Teleflex holds the exclusive license to the patent.

Claim 4 of the Engelgau patent describes a mechanism for combining an electronic sensor with an adjustable automobile pedal so the pedal's position can be transmitted to a computer that controls the throttle in the vehicle's engine. When Teleflex accused KSR of infringing the Engelgau patent by adding an electronic sensor to one of KSR's previously designed pedals, KSR countered that claim 4 was invalid under the Patent Act, 35 U.S.C. § 103, because its subject matter was obvious. [The following figure from the Engelgau patent shows the claimed invention:]

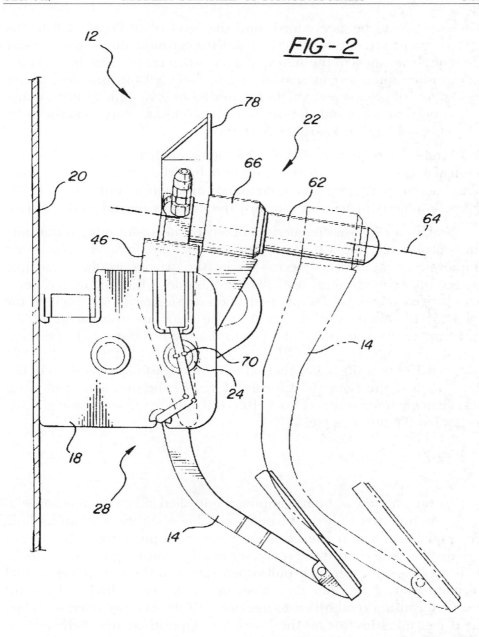

FIG - 2

Section 103 forbids issuance of a patent when "the differences between the subject matter sought to be patented and the prior art are such that the subject matter as a whole would have been obvious at the time the invention was made to a person having ordinary skill in the art to which said subject matter pertains."

In *Graham v. John Deere Co.*, the Court set out a framework for applying the statutory language of § 103, language itself based on the logic of the earlier decision in *Hotchkiss v. Greenwood,* and its progeny. The analysis is objective:

"Under § 103, the scope and content of the prior art are to be determined; differences between the prior art and the claims at issue are to be ascertained; and the level of ordinary skill in the pertinent art resolved. Against this background the obviousness or nonobviousness of the subject matter is determined. Such secondary considerations as commercial success, long felt but unsolved needs, failure of others, etc., might be utilized to give light to the circumstances surrounding the origin of the subject matter sought to be patented." *Id.*, at 17–18, 86 S.Ct. 684.

While the sequence of these questions might be reordered in any particular case, the factors continue to define the inquiry that controls. If a court, or patent examiner, conducts this analysis and concludes the claimed subject matter was obvious, the claim is invalid under § 103.

Seeking to resolve the question of obviousness with more uniformity and consistency, the Court of Appeals for the Federal Circuit has employed an approach referred to by the parties as the "teaching, suggestion, or motivation" test (TSM test), under which a patent claim is only proved obvious if "some motivation or suggestion to combine the prior art teachings" can be found in the prior art, the nature of the problem, or the knowledge of a person having ordinary skill in the art. See, *e.g.*, *Al–Site Corp. v. VSI Int'l, Inc.*, 174 F.3d 1308, 1323–1324 (C.A.Fed.1999). KSR challenges that test, or at least its application in this case. Because the Court of Appeals addressed the question of obviousness in a manner contrary to § 103 and our precedents, we granted certiorari. We now reverse.

I

A

In car engines without computer-controlled throttles, the accelerator pedal interacts with the throttle via cable or other mechanical link. The pedal arm acts as a lever rotating around a pivot point. In a cable-actuated throttle control the rotation caused by pushing down the pedal pulls a cable, which in turn pulls open valves in the carburetor or fuel injection unit. The wider the valves open, the more fuel and air are released, causing combustion to increase and the car to accelerate. When the driver takes his foot off the pedal, the opposite occurs as the cable is released and the valves slide closed.

In the 1990's it became more common to install computers in cars to control engine operation. Computer-controlled throttles open and close valves in response to electronic signals, not through force transferred from the pedal by a mechanical link. Constant, delicate adjustments of air and fuel mixture are possible. The computer's rapid processing of factors beyond the pedal's position improves fuel efficiency and engine performance.

For a computer-controlled throttle to respond to a driver's operation of the car, the computer must know what is happening with the pedal. A cable or mechanical link does not suffice for this purpose; at some point, an electronic sensor is necessary to translate the mechanical operation into digital data the computer can understand.

Before discussing sensors further we turn to the mechanical design of the pedal itself. In the traditional design a pedal can be pushed down or released but cannot have its position in the footwell adjusted by sliding the pedal forward or back. As a result, a driver who wishes to be closer or farther from the pedal must either reposition himself in the driver's seat or move the seat in some way. In cars with deep footwells these are imperfect solutions for drivers of smaller stature. To solve the problem, inventors, beginning in the 1970's, designed pedals that could be adjusted to change their location in the footwell. Important for this case are two adjustable pedals disclosed in U.S. Patent Nos. 5,010,782 (filed July 28, 1989) (Asano) and 5,460,061 (filed Sept. 17, 1993) (Redding). The Asano patent reveals a support structure that houses the pedal so that even when the pedal location is adjusted relative to the driver, one of the pedal's pivot points stays fixed. The pedal is also designed so that the force necessary to push the pedal down is the same regardless of adjustments to its location. [The following figure shows the Asano prior art reference:]

[Handwritten margin notes:] traditional pedals had no adjustment · had to move seat · 1970 inventors solved this problem · Asano Patent July 28 1989 · Redding Sept 17, 1993 · Asano – pivot point remained in place whole time

FIG. 5

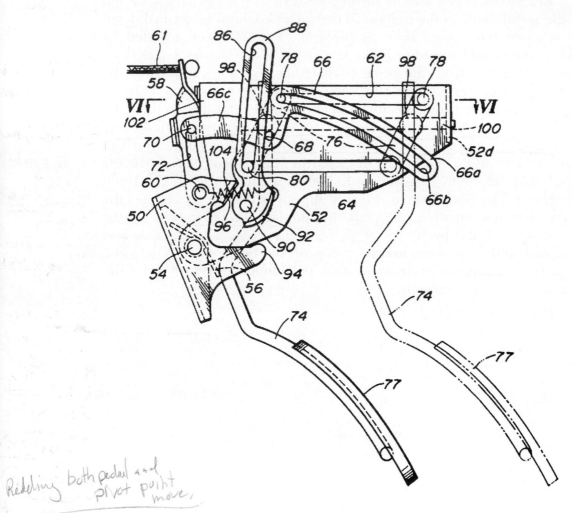

Reddling both pedal and pivot point move.

electronic senor patents

936 Sept 1991

- detect pedals position in pedal assembly not engine. Senor on pivot point.

811 - moved the senor to fixed port to prevent damage.

The Redding patent reveals a different, sliding mechanism where both the pedal and the pivot point are adjusted.

We return to sensors. Well before Engelgau applied for his challenged patent, some inventors had obtained patents involving electronic pedal sensors for computer-controlled throttles. These inventions, such as the device disclosed in U.S. Patent No. 5,241,936 (filed Sept. 9, 1991) ('936), taught that it was preferable to detect the pedal's position in the pedal assembly, not in the engine. The '936 patent disclosed a pedal with an electronic sensor on a pivot point in the pedal assembly. U.S. Patent No. 5,063,811 (filed July 9, 1990) (Smith) taught that to prevent the wires connecting the sensor to the computer from chafing and wearing out, and to avoid grime and damage from the driver's foot, the sensor should be put on a fixed part of the pedal assembly rather than in or on the pedal's footpad.

In addition to patents for pedals with integrated sensors inventors obtained patents for self-contained modular sensors. A modular sensor is designed independently of a given pedal so that it can be taken off the shelf and attached to mechanical pedals of various sorts, enabling the pedals to be used in automobiles with computer-controlled throttles. One such sensor was disclosed in U.S. Patent No. 5,385,068 (filed Dec. 18, 1992) ('068). In 1994, Chevrolet manufactured a line of trucks using modular sensors "attached to the pedal support bracket, adjacent to the pedal and engaged with the pivot shaft about which the pedal rotates in operation." 298 F.Supp.2d 581, 589 (E.D.Mich.2003).

The prior art contained patents involving the placement of sensors on adjustable pedals as well. For example, U.S. Patent No. 5,819,593 (filed Aug. 17, 1995) (Rixon) discloses an adjustable pedal assembly with an electronic sensor for detecting the pedal's position. In the Rixon pedal the sensor is located in the pedal footpad. The Rixon pedal was known to suffer from wire chafing when the pedal was depressed and released.

This short account of pedal and sensor technology leads to the instant case.

B

KSR, a Canadian company, manufactures and supplies auto parts, including pedal systems. Ford Motor Company hired KSR in 1998 to supply an adjustable pedal system for various lines of automobiles with cable-actuated throttle controls. KSR developed an adjustable mechanical pedal for Ford and obtained U.S. Patent No. 6,151,976 (filed July 16, 1999) ('976) for the design. In 2000, KSR was chosen by General Motors Corporation (GMC or GM) to supply adjustable pedal systems for Chevrolet and GMC light trucks that used engines with computer-controlled throttles. To make the '976 pedal compatible with the trucks, KSR merely took that design and added a modular sensor.

Teleflex is a rival to KSR in the design and manufacture of adjustable pedals. As noted, it is the exclusive licensee of the Engelgau patent. Engelgau filed the patent application on August 22, 2000 as a continuation of a previous application for U.S. Patent No. 6,109,241, which was filed on January 26, 1999. He has sworn he invented the patent's subject matter on February 14, 1998. The Engelgau patent discloses an adjustable electronic pedal described in the specification as a "simplified vehicle control pedal assembly that is less expensive, and which uses fewer parts and is easier to package within the vehicle." Engelgau, col. 2, lines 2–5, Supplemental App. 6. Claim 4 of the patent, at issue here, describes:

"A vehicle control pedal apparatus comprising:

a support adapted to be mounted to a vehicle structure;

an adjustable pedal assembly having a pedal arm moveable in for[e] and aft directions with respect to said support;

a pivot for pivotally supporting said adjustable pedal assembly with respect to said support and defining a pivot axis; and

an electronic control attached to said support for controlling a vehicle system;

said apparatus characterized by said electronic control being responsive to said pivot for providing a signal that corresponds to pedal arm position as said pedal arm pivots about said pivot axis between rest and applied positions wherein the position of said pivot remains constant while said pedal arm moves in fore and aft directions with respect to said pivot." *Id.*, col. 6, lines 17–36, Supplemental App. 8 (diagram numbers omitted).

We agree with the District Court that the claim discloses "a position-adjustable pedal assembly with an electronic pedal position sensor attached to the support member of the pedal assembly. Attaching the sensor to the support member allows the sensor to remain in a fixed position while the driver adjusts the pedal." 298 F.Supp.2d, at 586–587.

Before issuing the Engelgau patent the U.S. Patent and Trademark Office (PTO) rejected one of the patent claims that was similar to, but broader than, the present claim 4. The claim did not include the requirement that the sensor be placed on a fixed pivot point. The PTO concluded the claim was an obvious combination of the prior art disclosed in Redding and Smith, explaining:

" 'Since the prior ar[t] references are from the field of endeavor, the purpose disclosed . . . would have been recognized in the pertinent art of Redding. Therefore it would have been obvious . . . to provide the device of Redding with the . . . means attached to a support member as taught by Smith.' " *Id.*, at 595.

In other words Redding provided an example of an adjustable pedal and Smith explained how to mount a sensor on a pedal's support structure, and the rejected patent claim merely put these two teachings together.

Although the broader claim was rejected, claim 4 was later allowed because it included the limitation of a fixed pivot point, which distinguished the design from Redding's. *Ibid.* Engelgau had not included Asano among the prior art references, and Asano was not mentioned in the patent's prosecution. Thus, the PTO did not have before it an adjustable pedal with a fixed pivot point. The patent issued on May 29, 2001 and was assigned to Teleflex.

Upon learning of KSR's design for GM, Teleflex sent a warning letter informing KSR that its proposal would violate the Engelgau patent. " 'Teleflex believes that any supplier of a product that combines an adjustable pedal with an electronic throttle control necessarily employs technology covered by one or more' " of Teleflex's patents. *Id.*, at 585. KSR refused to enter a royalty arrangement with Teleflex; so Teleflex sued for infringement, asserting KSR's pedal infringed the

Engelgau patent and two other patents. *Ibid.* Teleflex later abandoned its claims regarding the other patents and dedicated the patents to the public. The remaining contention was that KSR's pedal system for GM infringed claim 4 of the Engelgau patent. Teleflex has not argued that the other three claims of the patent are infringed by KSR's pedal, nor has Teleflex argued that the mechanical adjustable pedal designed by KSR for Ford infringed any of its patents.

C

The District Court granted summary judgment in KSR's favor. After reviewing the pertinent history of pedal design, the scope of the Engelgau patent, and the relevant prior art, the court considered the validity of the contested claim. By direction of 35 U.S.C. § 282, an issued patent is presumed valid. The District Court applied *Graham's* framework to determine whether under summary-judgment standards KSR had overcome the presumption and demonstrated that claim 4 was obvious in light of the prior art in existence when the claimed subject matter was invented. See § 102(a).

The District Court determined, in light of the expert testimony and the parties' stipulations, that the level of ordinary skill in pedal design was " 'an undergraduate degree in mechanical engineering (or an equivalent amount of industry experience) [and] familiarity with pedal control systems for vehicles.' " The court then set forth the relevant prior art, including the patents and pedal designs described above.

Following *Graham's* direction, the court compared the teachings of the prior art to the claims of Engelgau. It found "little difference." Asano taught everything contained in claim 4 except the use of a sensor to detect the pedal's position and transmit it to the computer controlling the throttle. That additional aspect was revealed in sources such as the '068 patent and the sensors used by Chevrolet.

Under the controlling cases from the Court of Appeals for the Federal Circuit, however, the District Court was not permitted to stop there. The court was required also to apply the TSM test. The District Court held KSR had satisfied the test. It reasoned (1) the state of the industry would lead inevitably to combinations of electronic sensors and adjustable pedals, (2) Rixon provided the basis for these developments, and (3) Smith taught a solution to the wire chafing problems in Rixon, namely locating the sensor on the fixed structure of the pedal. This could lead to the combination of Asano, or a pedal like it, with a pedal position sensor.

The conclusion that the Engelgau design was obvious was supported, in the District Court's view, by the PTO's rejection of the broader version of claim 4. Had Engelgau included Asano in his patent application, it reasoned, the PTO would have found claim 4 to be an obvious combination of Asano and Smith, as it had found the broader version an obvious combination of Redding and Smith. As a final matter, the District Court held that the secondary factor of Teleflex's commercial success with pedals based on Engelgau's design did not alter its conclusion. The District Court granted summary judgment for KSR.

With principal reliance on the TSM test, the Court of Appeals reversed. It ruled the District Court had not been strict enough in applying the test, having failed to make " 'finding[s] as to the specific understanding or principle within the knowledge of a skilled artisan that would have motivated one with no knowledge of [the] invention'... to attach an electronic control to the support bracket of the Asano assembly." The Court of Appeals held that the District Court was incorrect that the nature of the problem to be solved satisfied this requirement because unless the "prior art references address[ed] the precise problem that the patentee was trying to solve," the problem would not motivate an inventor to look at those references.

Here, the Court of Appeals found, the Asano pedal was designed to solve the " 'constant ratio problem' "—that is, to ensure that the force required to depress the pedal is the same no matter how the pedal is adjusted—whereas Engelgau sought to provide a simpler, smaller, cheaper adjustable electronic pedal. *Ibid.* As for Rixon, the court explained, that pedal suffered from the problem of wire chafing but was not designed to solve it. In the court's view Rixon did not teach anything helpful to Engelgau's purpose. Smith, in turn, did not relate to adjustable pedals and did not "necessarily go to the issue of motivation to attach the electronic control on the support bracket of the pedal assembly." *Ibid.* When the patents were interpreted in this way, the Court of Appeals held, they would not have led a person of ordinary skill to put a sensor on the sort of pedal described in Asano.

That it might have been obvious to try the combination of Asano and a sensor was likewise irrelevant, in the court's view, because " ' "[o]bvious to try" has long been held not to constitute obviousness.' "

The Court of Appeals also faulted the District Court's consideration of the PTO's rejection of the broader version of claim 4. The District Court's role, the Court of Appeals explained, was not to speculate regarding what the PTO might have done had the Engelgau patent mentioned Asano. Rather, the court held, the District Court was obliged first to presume that the issued patent was valid and then to render its own independent judgment of obviousness based on a review of the prior art. The fact that the PTO had rejected the broader version of claim 4, the Court of Appeals said, had no place in that analysis.

The Court of Appeals further held that genuine issues of material fact precluded summary judgment. Teleflex had proffered statements from one expert that claim 4 " 'was a simple, elegant, and novel combination of features,' " compared to Rixon, and from another expert that claim 4 was nonobvious because, unlike in Rixon, the sensor was mounted on the support bracket rather than the pedal itself. This evidence, the court concluded, sufficed to require a trial.

II

A

We begin by rejecting the rigid approach of the Court of Appeals. Throughout this Court's engagement with the question of obviousness, our cases have set forth an expansive and flexible approach inconsistent with the way the Court of Appeals applied its TSM test here. To be sure, *Graham* recognized the need for "uniformity and definiteness." Yet the principles laid down in *Graham* reaffirmed the "functional approach" of *Hotchkiss*. To this end, *Graham* set forth a broad inquiry and invited courts, where appropriate, to look at any secondary considerations that would prove instructive.

Neither the enactment of § 103 nor the analysis in *Graham* disturbed this Court's earlier instructions concerning the need for caution in granting a patent based on the combination of elements found in the prior art. For over a half century, the Court has held that a "patent for a combination which only unites old elements with no change in their respective functions . . . obviously withdraws what is already known into the field of its monopoly and diminishes the resources available to skillful men." *Great Atlantic & Pacific Tea Co. v. Supermarket Equipment Corp.*, 340 U.S. 147, 152, 71 S.Ct. 127, 95 L.Ed. 162 (1950). This is a principal reason for declining to allow patents for what is obvious. The combination of familiar elements according to known methods is likely to be obvious when it does no more than yield predictable results. Three cases decided after *Graham* illustrate the application of this doctrine.

In *United States v. Adams*, 383 U.S. 39, 40, 86 S.Ct. 708, 15 L.Ed.2d 572 (1966), a companion case to *Graham*, the Court considered the obviousness of a "wet battery" that varied from prior designs in two ways: It contained water, rather than the acids conventionally employed in storage batteries; and its electrodes were magnesium and cuprous chloride, rather than zinc and silver chloride. The Court recognized that when a patent claims a structure already known in the prior art that is altered by the mere substitution of one element for another known in the field, the combination must do more than yield a predictable result. It nevertheless rejected the Government's claim that Adams's battery was obvious. The Court relied upon the corollary principle that when the prior art teaches away from combining certain known elements, discovery of a successful means of combining them is more likely to be nonobvious. When Adams designed his battery, the prior art warned that risks were involved in using the types of electrodes he employed. The fact that the elements worked together in an unexpected and fruitful manner supported the conclusion that Adams's design was not obvious to those skilled in the art.

In *Anderson's–Black Rock, Inc. v. Pavement Salvage Co.*, 396 U.S. 57, 90 S.Ct. 305, 24 L.Ed.2d 258 (1969), the Court elaborated on this approach. The subject matter of the patent before the Court was a device combining two pre-existing elements: a radiant-heat burner and

[handwritten margin notes: Anderson — radiant heat burner and paving machine. Both acted as they should. Useful - but obvious. Failed 103. Sakraida — if old elements preform same function than combo obvious]

a paving machine. The device, the Court concluded, did not create some new synergy: The radiant-heat burner functioned just as a burner was expected to function; and the paving machine did the same. The two in combination did no more than they would in separate, sequential operation. In those circumstances, "while the combination of old elements performed a useful function, it added nothing to the nature and quality of the radiant-heat burner already patented," and the patent failed under § 103.

Finally, in *Sakraida v. Ag Pro, Inc.*, 425 U.S. 273, 96 S.Ct. 1532, 47 L.Ed.2d 784 (1976), the Court derived from the precedents the conclusion that when a patent "simply arranges old elements with each performing the same function it had been known to perform" and yields no more than one would expect from such an arrangement, the combination is obvious.

[handwritten margin note: is improvement more than the predictable use of prior art elements according to their estab. functions]

The principles underlying these cases are instructive when the question is whether a patent claiming the combination of elements of prior art is obvious. When a work is available in one field of endeavor, design incentives and other market forces can prompt variations of it, either in the same field or a different one. If a person of ordinary skill can implement a predictable variation, § 103 likely bars its patentability. For the same reason, if a technique has been used to improve one device, and a person of ordinary skill in the art would recognize that it would improve similar devices in the same way, using the technique is obvious unless its actual application is beyond his or her skill. *Sakraida* and *Anderson's–Black Rock* are illustrative—a court must ask whether the improvement is more than the predictable use of prior art elements according to their established functions.

[handwritten margin note: Do not need precise teachings directed to the specific subject matter of the challenged claim.]

Following these principles may be more difficult in other cases than it is here because the claimed subject matter may involve more than the simple substitution of one known element for another or the mere application of a known technique to a piece of prior art ready for the improvement. Often, it will be necessary for a court to look to interrelated teachings of multiple patents; the effects of demands known to the design community or present in the marketplace; and the background knowledge possessed by a person having ordinary skill in the art, all in order to determine whether there was an apparent reason to combine the known elements in the fashion claimed by the patent at issue. To facilitate review, this analysis should be made explicit. Our precedents make clear, however, the analysis need not seek out precise teachings directed to the specific subject matter of the challenged claim, for a court can take account of the inferences and creative steps that a person of ordinary skill in the art would employ.

B

When it first established the requirement of demonstrating a teaching, suggestion, or motivation to combine known elements in order to show that the combination is obvious, the Court of Customs and Patent

Appeals captured a helpful insight. As is clear from cases such as *Adams*, a patent composed of several elements is not proved obvious merely by demonstrating that each of its elements was, independently, known in the prior art. Although common sense directs one to look with care at a patent application that claims as innovation the combination of two known devices according to their established functions, it can be important to identify a reason that would have prompted a person of ordinary skill in the relevant field to combine the elements in the way the claimed new invention does. This is so because inventions in most, if not all, instances rely upon building blocks long since uncovered, and claimed discoveries almost of necessity will be combinations of what, in some sense, is already known.

Helpful insights, however, need not become rigid and mandatory formulas; and when it is so applied, the TSM test is incompatible with our precedents. The obviousness analysis cannot be confined by a formalistic conception of the words teaching, suggestion, and motivation, or by overemphasis on the importance of published articles and the explicit content of issued patents. The diversity of inventive pursuits and of modern technology counsels against limiting the analysis in this way. In many fields it may be that there is little discussion of obvious techniques or combinations, and it often may be the case that market demand, rather than scientific literature, will drive design trends. Granting patent protection to advances that would occur in the ordinary course without real innovation retards progress and may, in the case of patents combining previously known elements, deprive prior inventions of their value or utility.

In the years since the Court of Customs and Patent Appeals set forth the essence of the TSM test, the Court of Appeals no doubt has applied the test in accord with these principles in many cases. There is no necessary inconsistency between the idea underlying the TSM test and the *Graham* analysis. But when a court transforms the general principle into a rigid rule that limits the obviousness inquiry, as the Court of Appeals did here, it errs.

C

The flaws in the analysis of the Court of Appeals relate for the most part to the court's narrow conception of the obviousness inquiry reflected in its application of the TSM test. In determining whether the subject matter of a patent claim is obvious, neither the particular motivation nor the avowed purpose of the patentee controls. What matters is the objective reach of the claim. If the claim extends to what is obvious, it is invalid under § 103. One of the ways in which a patent's subject matter can be proved obvious is by noting that there existed at the time of invention a known problem for which there was an obvious solution encompassed by the patent's claims.

The first error of the Court of Appeals in this case was to foreclose this reasoning by holding that courts and patent examiners should look only to the problem the patentee was trying to solve. The Court of Appeals failed to recognize that the problem motivating the patentee may be only one of many addressed by the patent's subject matter. The question is not whether the combination was obvious to the patentee but whether the combination was obvious to a person with ordinary skill in the art. Under the correct analysis, any need or problem known in the field of endeavor at the time of invention and addressed by the patent can provide a reason for combining the elements in the manner claimed.

The second error of the Court of Appeals lay in its assumption that a person of ordinary skill attempting to solve a problem will be led only to those elements of prior art designed to solve the same problem. The primary purpose of Asano was solving the constant ratio problem; so, the court concluded, an inventor considering how to put a sensor on an adjustable pedal would have no reason to consider putting it on the Asano pedal. *Ibid.* Common sense teaches, however, that familiar items may have obvious uses beyond their primary purposes, and in many cases a person of ordinary skill will be able to fit the teachings of multiple patents together like pieces of a puzzle. Regardless of Asano's primary purpose, the design provided an obvious example of an adjustable pedal with a fixed pivot point; and the prior art was replete with patents indicating that a fixed pivot point was an ideal mount for a sensor. The idea that a designer hoping to make an adjustable electronic pedal would ignore Asano because Asano was designed to solve the constant ratio problem makes little sense. A person of ordinary skill is also a person of ordinary creativity, not an automaton.

The same constricted analysis led the Court of Appeals to conclude, in error, that a patent claim cannot be proved obvious merely by showing that the combination of elements was "obvious to try." When there is a design need or market pressure to solve a problem and there are a finite number of identified, predictable solutions, a person of ordinary skill has good reason to pursue the known options within his or her technical grasp. If this leads to the anticipated success, it is likely the product not of innovation but of ordinary skill and common sense. In that instance the fact that a combination was obvious to try might show that it was obvious under § 103.

The Court of Appeals, finally, drew the wrong conclusion from the risk of courts and patent examiners falling prey to hindsight bias. A factfinder should be aware, of course, of the distortion caused by hindsight bias and must be cautious of arguments reliant upon *ex post* reasoning. Rigid preventative rules that deny factfinders recourse to common sense, however, are neither necessary under our case law nor consistent with it.

III

When we apply the standards we have explained to the instant facts, claim 4 must be found obvious. We agree with and adopt the District

Court's recitation of the relevant prior art and its determination of the level of ordinary skill in the field. As did the District Court, we see little difference between the teachings of Asano and Smith and the adjustable electronic pedal disclosed in claim 4 of the Engelgau patent. A person having ordinary skill in the art could have combined Asano with a pedal position sensor in a fashion encompassed by claim 4, and would have seen the benefits of doing so.

The District Court was correct to conclude that, as of the time Engelgau designed the subject matter in claim 4, it was obvious to a person of ordinary skill to combine Asano with a pivot-mounted pedal position sensor. There then existed a marketplace that created a strong incentive to convert mechanical pedals to electronic pedals, and the prior art taught a number of methods for achieving this advance. The Court of Appeals considered the issue too narrowly by, in effect, asking whether a pedal designer writing on a blank slate would have chosen both Asano and a modular sensor similar to the ones used in the Chevrolet truckline and disclosed in the '068 patent. The District Court employed this narrow inquiry as well, though it reached the correct result nevertheless. The proper question to have asked was whether a pedal designer of ordinary skill, facing the wide range of needs created by developments in the field of endeavor, would have seen a benefit to upgrading Asano with a sensor.

In automotive design, as in many other fields, the interaction of multiple components means that changing one component often requires the others to be modified as well. Technological developments made it clear that engines using computer-controlled throttles would become standard. As a result, designers might have decided to design new pedals from scratch; but they also would have had reason to make pre-existing pedals work with the new engines. Indeed, upgrading its own pre-existing model led KSR to design the pedal now accused of infringing the Engelgau patent.

For a designer starting with Asano, the question was where to attach the sensor. The consequent legal question, then, is whether a pedal designer of ordinary skill starting with Asano would have found it obvious to put the sensor on a fixed pivot point. The prior art discussed above leads us to the conclusion that attaching the sensor where both KSR and Engelgau put it would have been obvious to a person of ordinary skill.

The '936 patent taught the utility of putting the sensor on the pedal device, not in the engine. Smith, in turn, explained to put the sensor not on the pedal's footpad but instead on its support structure. And from the known wire-chafing problems of Rixon, and Smith's teaching that "the pedal assemblies must not precipitate any motion in the connecting wires," the designer would know to place the sensor on a nonmoving part of the pedal structure. The most obvious nonmoving point on the structure from which a sensor can easily detect the pedal's position is a pivot point. The designer, accordingly, would follow Smith in mounting the sensor on a pivot, thereby designing an adjustable electronic pedal covered by claim 4.

Just as it was possible to begin with the objective to upgrade Asano to work with a computer-controlled throttle, so too was it possible to take an adjustable electronic pedal like Rixon and seek an improvement that would avoid the wire-chafing problem. Following similar steps to those just explained, a designer would learn from Smith to avoid sensor movement and would come, thereby, to Asano because Asano disclosed an adjustable pedal with a fixed pivot.

Teleflex indirectly argues that the prior art taught away from attaching a sensor to Asano because Asano in its view is bulky, complex, and expensive. The only evidence Teleflex marshals in support of this argument, however, is the Radcliffe declaration, which merely indicates that Asano would not have solved Engelgau's goal of making a small, simple, and inexpensive pedal. What the declaration does not indicate is that Asano was somehow so flawed that there was no reason to upgrade it, or pedals like it, to be compatible with modern engines. Indeed, Teleflex's own declarations refute this conclusion. Dr. Radcliffe states that Rixon suffered from the same bulk and complexity as did Asano. See *id.*, at 206. Teleflex's other expert, however, explained that Rixon was itself designed by adding a sensor to a pre-existing mechanical pedal. See *id.*, at 209. If Rixon's base pedal was not too flawed to upgrade, then Dr. Radcliffe's declaration does not show Asano was either. Teleflex may have made a plausible argument that Asano is inefficient as compared to Engelgau's preferred embodiment, but to judge Asano against Engelgau would be to engage in the very hindsight bias Teleflex rightly urges must be avoided. Accordingly, Teleflex has not shown anything in the prior art that taught away from the use of Asano.

Like the District Court, finally, we conclude Teleflex has shown no secondary factors to dislodge the determination that claim 4 is obvious. Proper application of *Graham* and our other precedents to these facts therefore leads to the conclusion that claim 4 encompassed obvious subject matter. As a result, the claim fails to meet the requirement of § 103.

We need not reach the question whether the failure to disclose Asano during the prosecution of Engelgau voids the presumption of validity given to issued patents, for claim 4 is obvious despite the presumption. We nevertheless think it appropriate to note that the rationale underlying the presumption—that the PTO, in its expertise, has approved the claim—seems much diminished here.

IV

A separate ground the Court of Appeals gave for reversing the order for summary judgment was the existence of a dispute over an issue of material fact. We disagree with the Court of Appeals on this point as well. To the extent the court understood the *Graham* approach to exclude the possibility of summary judgment when an expert provides a conclusory affidavit addressing the question of obviousness, it misunderstood the role expert testimony plays in the analysis. In considering summary judgment on that question the district court can and should take into account expert testimony, which may resolve or keep open certain questions of fact. That is not the end of the issue, however. The ultimate judgment of obviousness is a legal determination. Where, as here, the content of the prior art, the scope of the patent claim, and the level of ordinary skill in the art are not in material dispute, and the obviousness of the claim is apparent in light of these factors, summary judgment is appropriate. Nothing in the declarations proffered by Teleflex prevented the District Court from reaching the careful conclusions underlying its order for summary judgment in this case.

* * *

We build and create by bringing to the tangible and palpable reality around us new works based on instinct, simple logic, ordinary inferences, extraordinary ideas, and sometimes even genius. These advances, once part of our shared knowledge, define a new threshold from which innovation starts once more. And as progress beginning from higher levels of achievement is expected in the normal course, the results of ordinary innovation are not the subject of exclusive rights under the patent laws. Were it otherwise patents might stifle, rather than promote, the progress of useful arts. See U.S. Const., Art. I, § 8, cl. 8. These premises led to the bar on patents claiming obvious subject matter established in *Hotchkiss* and codified in § 103. Application of the bar must not be confined within a test or formulation too constrained to serve its purpose.

KSR provided convincing evidence that mounting a modular sensor on a fixed pivot point of the Asano pedal was a design step well within the grasp of a person of ordinary skill in the relevant art. Its arguments, and the record, demonstrate that claim 4 of the Engelgau patent is obvious. In rejecting the District Court's rulings, the Court of Appeals analyzed the issue in a narrow, rigid manner inconsistent with § 103 and our precedents. The judgment of the Court of Appeals is reversed, and the case remanded for further proceedings consistent with this opinion.

It is so ordered.

NOTES

1. What Was Old Is New Again. Other than addressing the TSM standard, the Court all but ignored a quarter-century of nonobviousness jurisprudence developed by the Federal Circuit. The Court instead relied upon a number of its older opinions on the subject. As a result, terms like "combination inventions" and "synergy" appear to have once more entered the playing field, even though the Federal Circuit early on viewed them as discarded relics of nonobviousness doctrine. *See, e.g., Chore–Time Equip., Inc. v. Cumberland Corp.*, 713 F.2d 774, 781 (Fed.Cir.1983) ("A requirement that an invention reflect 'synergism' or achieve a 'synergistic result,' before it may be held patentable appears nowhere in the statute, 35 U.S.C. . . . References to synergism as a patentability requirement are, therefore, unnecessary and confusing."); *Medtronic, Inc. v. Cardiac Pacemakers, Inc.*, 721 F.2d 1563, 1566 (Fed.Cir.1983) ("There is neither a statutory distinction between 'combination patents' and some other, never defined type of patent, nor a reason to treat the conditions for patentability differently with respect to 'combination patents.' "). Of course, the Federal Circuit's concern over synergy was that it invited a comparison of the invention with the prior art—by definition a hindsight analysis. Any new synergy analysis cannot compare the invention after its creation to the prior art because the Supreme Court also warned against "the distortion caused by hindsight bias . . . and *ex post* reasoning."

Some commentators have also seen the *KSR* opinion as directly repudiating several tenets of nonobviousness doctrine developed by the Federal Circuit. For example, the Court of Appeals had disapproved reference to "common sense" in the nonobviousness analysis, *see In re Lee*, 277 F.3d 1338, 1344–45 (Fed. Cir. 2002), yet the Supreme Court expressly allowed factfinders to rely upon such understandings. The Federal Circuit viewed the commercial success of the claimed invention as evidence of nonobviousness, a topic this casebook considers next, yet the Supreme Court instead saw "market forces" as suggesting that an invention would have been obvious. The Court further disagreed both with the Federal Circuit's rejection of the "obvious to try" standard for obviousness and with the focus of the Court of Appeals upon the problem the inventor was trying to solve as the starting point for further analysis.

The view that *KSR* was a groundbreaking event is not shared by all members of the patent community, however. For another perspective, see the next note.

2. *KSR* Didn't Change Anything. On the other hand, some observers believe that *KSR* did little to change the law of nonobviousness at the Federal Circuit and elsewhere. The Court did not completely banish the TSM test from nonobviousness jurisprudence so long as the standard is used flexibly. The Supreme Court, like the Federal Circuit, also expressed a preference for an explicit, articulated analysis of the obviousness of a claimed invention. And the Court followed *Graham v. John Deere* by characterizing nonobviousness as a question of law. For all practical purposes, this classification reserves the issue for the Federal Circuit. As several jurists of the Federal Circuit have stated in public presentations, *KSR* may therefore have scant impact upon judicial interpretation of § 103 in days yet to come. For a masterful discussion of both perspectives upon *KSR*, see Rebecca S. Eisenberg, *Pharma's Nonobvious Problem*, 12 LEWIS & CLARK L. REV. 375 (2008).

Of course, the view of KSR that matters most of all is the perspective of the Federal Circuit. The next case in this chapter will give some hints about the Federal Circuit's approach to *KSR*.

3.   The Problem–Solution Approach. The European Patent Office uses a "problem-solution" approach, which descends from the mandate of European Patent Convention Rule 27(1)(c) that European applications "disclose the invention, as claimed, in such terms that the technical problem (even if not expressly stated as such) and its solution can be understood. . . ." The Guidelines for Examination in the European Patent Office, Part C at 50 (Dec. 1994), offer the following description:

> In the problem and solution approach there are three main stages:
>
> 1.   determining the closest prior art,
>
> 2.   establishing the technical problem to be solved, and
>
> 3.   determining whether or not the claimed invention, starting from the closest prior art and the technical problem, would have been obvious to the skilled person.

This test is designed to lead to an objective assessment of inventive step which allows no room for consideration of the features of the claimed invention itself. To some extent, however, European practice may simply shift the difficulty from defining the standard of invention to framing the appropriate technical problem that the invention is supposed to solve. Moreover, what if the inventive step is realizing or identifying the problem?

The Technical Board of Appeal considered this problem in *Etching Process*, T 229/85 3.3.1, [1987] Offic. J. Eur. Pat. Off. 237, which involved a claimed process for etching metal surfaces useful in the production of printed circuits. Metals such as copper can be etched using solutions containing, for example, sulphuric acid and hydrogen peroxide. A practical difficulty in employing this etching solution is that metal ions released during the etching process catalyze the decomposition of hydrogen peroxide. The prior art, including a United States patent, added a negative catalyst to the solution in order to inhibit the undesired decomposition of hydrogen peroxide. The claimed process tried a new approach: it added hydrogen peroxide to the etching solution directly before the etching was to occur, and only in such small amounts that would, as a practical matter, be entirely consumed during the etching process. The Examining Division rejected the claim as lacking inventive step, but the Board disagreed, stating:

> The disputed decision states that because of the problem set the solution proposed in the application would have been obvious by simply reasoning to a person skilled in the art having knowledge of [the United States patent]. The problem is seen as to prevent the decomposition of hydrogen peroxide without using negative catalysts (stabilisers). This definition of the problem, possibly influenced by the information contained in the present application . . . , inadmissibly incorporates part of the solution offered by the invention. The idea of doing away with stabilisers is an

essential part of the teaching of the invention as reflected in the solution given above and ultimately consisting in regulating the amount of hydrogen peroxide added to the solution and its timing. However, the technical problem addressed by an invention must be so formulated as not to contain pointers to the solution, since including part of a solution offered by an invention in the statement of the problem must, when the state of the art is assessed in terms of that problem, necessarily result in an ex post facto view being taken of inventive activity. For this reason alone the decision of the Examining Division cannot stand.

The Board preferred a statement of the problem as "to devise an etching process ... involving as low a consumption of hydrogen peroxide as possible and which permits the spent etching solution to be regenerated without difficulty...." Which version of the "problem" do you prefer? For further discussion, see George S.A. Szabo, *The Problem and Solution Approach in the European Patent Office*, 26 INT'L REV. INDUS. PROP. & COPYRIGHT L. 457 (1995).

    4. Inventive Step in Japan. Another leading patent-granting state, Japan, sets forth its inventive step requirement in section 29(2) of the Japanese Patent Law. That statute provides:

> Where an invention could easily have been made, prior to the filing of a patent application, by a person having ordinary skill in the art to which the invention pertains ... a patent shall not be granted for such an invention....

The Japanese Examination Guidelines provide that "a person having ordinary skill in the art" is a hypothetical person:

> who has the common general knowledge in the art to which the invention pertains at the time of filing of an application, and has ability to use ordinary technical means for research and development;

> who has ability to exercise ordinary creative ability in selecting materials and changing designs; and

> who is able to comprehend as his own knowledge all technical matters in the state of the art in the field to which an invention pertains at the time of filing of a patent application.

> In addition, a person skilled in the art is deemed to be able to comprehend as his own knowledge all technical matters in the field of technology relevant to a problem to be solved by an invention.

Is the standard of "easily made" the same as "would have been obvious"? See David J. Abraham, *Shinpo–Sei: Japanese Inventive Step Meets U.S. Non–Obviousness*, 77 J. PAT. & TRADEMARK OFF. SOC'Y 528 (1995). The Guidelines go on to indicate that "a person skilled in the art could have been able to easily arrive at a claimed invention by exercising ordinary creativity" on the basis of the prior art.

IN RE TRANSLOGIC TECHNOLOGY, INC.

United States Court of Appeals, Federal Circuit (2007)
504 F.3d 1249

RADER, CIRCUIT JUDGE.

The United States Patent and Trademark Office's Board of Patent Appeals and Interferences ("Board") upheld the examiner's rejection of U.S. Patent No. 5,162,666 ("the 666 patent") in a reexamination proceeding, Appeal No.2005–1050. Because the 666 patent would have been obvious at the time of invention, this court affirms.

I

The United States Patent and Trademark Office issued the 666 patent, entitled "Transmission Gate Series Multiplexer", on November 10, 1992 from an application filed on March 15, 1991. In addition to this appeal from the Board's decision, the 666 patent is the subject of a patent infringement litigation between Translogic Technology, Inc. ("Translogic") and Hitachi, Ltd. et al. ("Hitachi") in the United States District Court for the District of Oregon. The district court case began on March 24, 1999. Thereafter, on June 4, 1999 and ending on September 27, 2002, Hitachi filed five third-party requests for reexamination of the 666 patent. The Patent Office merged the various requests into a single proceeding. On March 8, 2004, the merged reexamination resulted in the rejection of claims 16, 17, 39–45, 47 and 48 under 35 U.S.C. § 103(a) because they would have been obvious at the time of invention. The Patent Office found the claims obvious in light of the references Gorai … in view of Weste. During the reexamination proceedings, Translogic cancelled original claims 1–15 and 18–27, and newly added claims 28–38 and 46. Translogic then appealed to the Board. On July 14, 2005, the Board affirmed the rejection. The Board denied Translogic's request for reconsideration. Translogic then appealed the Board's decision to this court.

During this entire reexamination process, the district court infringement case proceeded in parallel. In October 2003, a jury upheld the patent as valid. In February 2005, the district court granted summary judgment of infringement with respect to some, but not all, of Hitachi's accused products. In May 2005, a jury found Hitachi had induced infringement and held Hitachi liable for $86.5 million in damages. The district court entered a permanent injunction, which, after Hitachi's interlocutory appeal, this court stayed.

After post-trial briefing, the district court entered final judgment against Hitachi in December 2005. Hitachi appealed to this court. This court consolidated the interlocutory appeal with the appeal from the final judgment and added Translogic's reexamination appeal from the Board to the same panel. This opinion only addresses Translogic's reexamination appeal from the Board.

The 666 patent deals with multiplexers. A multiplexer is a type of electrical circuit. A multiplexer has multiple inputs, one or more control lines, and one output. The signals on the control lines select one of the various inputs to be passed to the output. In a 2:1 multiplexer, a single output value is selected from two inputs. Similarly, in 4:1 and 8:1 multiplexers, a single output is selected from among four or eight inputs, respectively. Thus, the invention selects one of the multiple inputs to pass to the output.

The number of control lines (x) for a conventional multiplexer depends on the number of inputs to the multiplexer. Generally, a given number of control lines (x) can select one output from among a maximum of 2 inputs. In a 4:1 multiplexer, two control lines (x = 2) are used to select among ... 4 inputs, and in an 8:1 multiplexer, three control lines (x = 3) can select between ... 8 inputs....

The 666 patent describes a multiplexer that couples together multiple stages of 2:1 multiplexers in series. The 666 patent specifically uses a transmission gate multiplexer ("TGM") as each 2:1 multiplexer. Figure 3 of the 666 patent (see below) illustrates a 4:1 series multiplexer that connects three TGMs (i.e., A, B and C) in series. [On a basic level, the invention claims a cascading multiplexer configuration, shown in the prior art by the Gorai reference. The invention combined that configuration with TGM circuits, shown in the prior art by the Weste reference. The following figure from the patent shows this arrangement:]

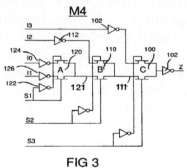

FIG 3

In the figure above, lines S1, S2, and S3 are control lines and lines I0, I1, I2, and I3 are input lines. The series multiplexer operates in cascade by passing the selected input to the output in a series of selections.... The claims on appeal specify multiplexers with multiple 2:1 TGMs connected in series.... [The issue of obviousness essentially asks if one of skill in the art would have considered it obvious at the time of invention to combine the prior art Gorai cascading multiplexer configuration with the TGM circuits found in Weste prior art.]

During the reexamination, Translogic agreed that all of the claims on appeal stood or fell with claims 47 and 48:

47. A multiplexer circuit comprising:

a first stage TGM circuit having first and second signal input terminals, a control input terminal and an output terminal;

the first and second signal input terminals coupled to receive first and second input variables, respectively;

the control input coupled to receive a first control signal;

a second stage TGM circuit having first and second signal input terminals, a control input terminal and an output terminal;

one of the second stage input terminals coupled to the first stage output terminal; the other one of the second stage signal input terminals coupled to receive a third input variable;

the second stage control input terminal coupled to receive a second control signal;

a third stage TGM circuit having first and second signal input terminals, a control input terminal and an output terminal;

one of the third stage input terminals coupled to the second stage output terminal;

the other one of the third stage input terminals coupled to receive a fourth input variable;

and the third stage control input variable coupled to receive a third control signal whereby the circuit forms a 4:1 multiplexer....

The Board affirmed the rejection of claims 47 and 48 as obvious under § 103(a). In applying the obviousness test, the Board relied on Gorai combined with Weste.... The Gorai reference [is a] technical article; the Weste reference is a textbook. The Board found that Fig. 3 of Gorai (see below) discloses a three-stage multiplexer circuit with four inputs (hp, gp, hp–1, h1) and three control inputs (xp, xp–1 and x1).

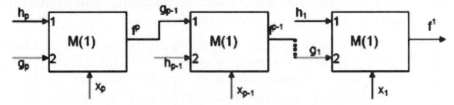

Fig. 3 A cascade network of p-stages of M(1)s

The Board found that Gorai does not disclose use of TGMs for each multiplexer stage (i.e., M(1)) in Fig. 3. The Board, however, found that Weste taught a 2:1 TGM circuit to transfer a logic 0 or a logic 1 between the input and output. The Weste reference discloses and teaches a TGM . . .

The Board thus found that a person of ordinary skill in the art would have been motivated to use a TGM circuit as taught in Weste for the multiplexer stages in Gorai....

II

Section 103 within title 35 of the U.S.Code "forbids issuance of a patent when 'the differences between the subject matter sought to be patented and the prior art are such that the subject matter as a whole would have been obvious at the time the invention was made to a person having ordinary skill in the art to which said subject matter pertains.' " KSR Int'l Co. v. Teleflex Inc., 550 U.S. ___, 127 S.Ct. 1727, 1734, 167 L.Ed.2d 705 (2007); (quoting 35 U.S.C. § 103). "Determination of obviousness under 35 U.S.C. § 103 is a legal conclusion based on underlying facts." In re Kumar, 418 F.3d 1361, 1365 (Fed.Cir.2005). This court reviews "the Board's ultimate determination of obviousness de novo." In re Kotzab, 217 F.3d 1365, 1369 (Fed.Cir.2000).

III

An invention is unpatentable as obvious if the differences between the patented subject matter and the prior art would have been obvious at the time of invention to a person of ordinary skill in the art. In re Gartside, 203 F.3d 1305, 1319 (Fed.Cir.2000). In a recent case, the Supreme Court reiterated the basic principles for an obviousness inquiry. KSR Int'l Co. v. Teleflex Inc., 550 U.S. ___, 127 S.Ct. 1727, 167 L.Ed.2d 705 (2007). KSR featured rather simple technology-an adjustable throttle pedal for an automobile, the Engelgau patent (U.S. Pat. No. 6,237,565 ("the 565 patent")). Adjustable pedal technology accommodates an automobile throttle to drivers of different heights. This patented technology combined an adjustable pedal with an electronic sensor to measure the pedal depression. Both of these features were in the prior art. An Asano patent claimed an adjustable pedal like Engelgau; a Rixon patent (as modified by a Smith reference) disclosed electronic calibration features like Engelgau. The PTO had not considered the Asano reference during the prosecution of the Engelgau patent.

When Teleflex sued KSR for infringement, the district court invalidated the 565 patent on summary judgment. This court reversed because the trial court had not made specific findings to show a teaching, suggestion, or motivation to combine ("TSM test"). The Supreme Court, in turn, reversed: "A person having ordinary skill in the art could have combined Asano with a pedal position sensor in a fashion encompassed by claim 4, and would have seen the benefits of doing so." KSR Int'l Co., 550 U.S. at ___, 127 S.Ct. at 1743.

On one level, KSR corrected a rather straightforward error. The error appears right before footnote 3 in this court's opinion:

> In this case, the Asano patent does not address the same problem as the 565 patent. The objective of the 565 patent was to design a smaller, less complex, and less expensive electronic pedal assembly. The Asano patent, on the other hand, was directed at solving the "constant ratio problem."

Teleflex, Inc. v. KSR Int'l, Co., 119 Fed.Appx. 282, 288 (Fed.Cir.2005). This passage overlooks the fundamental proposition that obvious variants of prior art references are themselves part of the public domain. See KSR Int'l Co., 550 U.S. at ___; DyStar Textilfarben GmbH & Co. Deutschland KG v. C.H. Patrick Co., 464 F.3d 1356, 1361 (Fed.Cir. 2006). In context of KSR, the Asano teachings and its obvious variants were relevant prior art, even if that patent did address a different problem (the constant ratio problem). The Supreme Court highlighted that error in its opinion:

> The primary purpose of Asano was solving the constant ratio problem; so, the court concluded, an inventor considering how to put a sensor on an adjustable pedal would have no reason to consider putting it on the Asano pedal. Common sense teaches, however, that familiar items may have obvious uses beyond their primary purposes, and in many cases a person of ordinary skill will be able to fit the teachings of multiple patents together like pieces of a puzzle. Regardless of Asano's primary purpose, the design provided an obvious example of an adjustable pedal with a fixed pivot point; and the prior art was replete with patents indicating that a fixed pivot point was an ideal mount for a sensor. The idea that a designer hoping to make an adjustable electronic pedal would ignore Asano because Asano was designed to solve the constant ratio problem makes little sense.

KSR Int'l Co., 550 U.S. at ___.

The Supreme Court also criticized this court's "rigid and mandatory" application of the motivation to combine test: "The obviousness analysis cannot be confined by a formalistic conception of the words teaching, suggestion, and motivation, or by overemphasis on the importance of published articles and the explicit content of issued patents." Id. at 1741. Instead, the Supreme Court advised that "common sense" would extend the use of customary knowledge in the obviousness equation: "A person of ordinary skill is also a person of ordinary creativity, not an automaton." Id. at 1742. Thus, the Supreme Court set aside any "rigid" application of the TSM test and ensured use of customary knowledge as an ingredient in that equation.

The Supreme Court observed that this court had also "elaborated a broader conception of the TSM test than was applied in [KSR]." Id. at 1743. Specifically the Court referred to DyStar Textilfarben GmbH & Co. v. C.H. Patrick Co., wherein this court noted: "Our suggestion test is in actuality quite flexible and not only permits, but requires, consideration of common knowledge and common sense." 464 F.3d 1356, 1367 (Fed.Cir.2006) (emphasis original). The Court suggested that this formulation would be more consistent with the Supreme Court's restatement of the TSM test. KSR Int'l Co., 127 S.Ct. at 1739. In any event, as the Supreme Court suggests, a flexible approach to the TSM test prevents hindsight and focuses on evidence before the time of invention, without unduly constraining the breadth of knowledge available to one of ordinary skill in the art during the obviousness analysis.

This court finds that the claims of the 666 patent were unpatentable under 35 U.S.C. § 103(a). Gorai is within the scope of the relevant prior art because it both predates the 666 patent filing date of March 15, 1991 and discloses series 2–input multiplexer circuits. See Stratoflex, Inc. v. Aeroquip Corp., 713 F.2d 1530, 1535 (Fed.Cir.1983). Moreover a person of ordinary skill in the art would have a thorough understanding of electrical switching systems and knowledge of actual electrical implementations of multiplexers such as the TGMs in Weste.

In this appeal, Translogic proffers two arguments to attempt to show that the Gorai reference is not prior art with respect to the 666 patent. Initially, Translogic contends that neither the Gorai algorithm nor its circuit realizations provide a multiplexer function. In fact, since the entire point of Gorai's article revolves around logic, not multiplexing, with series connectivity among M(1) circuits, Translogic contends that Gorai teaches away from multiplexers. Next, Translogic contends that the Gorai reference discloses an algorithm capable of providing designs for a large number of circuits, while the inventor of the 666 patent was modifying one circuit, a multiplexer, with utmost regard for its performance. In other words, while Gorai discloses an algorithm to design logic circuits based on functional parameters, the 666 patent improves a known circuit. In sum, Translogic's argument tries to state that the Gorai reference is not relevant prior art because the reference does not specifically disclose a N:1 series multiplexer but only discloses an algorithm to realize logic functions by using 2:1 multiplexers connected in series.

In its prior art argument, Translogic is making the same error corrected by the Supreme Court in KSR. Translogic mistakenly argues that variants of a circuit connecting 2:1 multiplexers in series are not relevant prior art with respect to the 666 patent because these variants do not address the same problem, namely an improved multiplexer circuit. However, this argument overlooks the fundamental proposition that the series circuits in Gorai are prior art within the public domain and the common knowledge of a person of ordinary skill in the art. Thus, the Gorai reference is a relevant prior art reference with respect to the 666 patent and clearly discloses a series 2:1 multiplexer circuit. . . .

Translogic contends that Gorai does not teach or suggest the use of TGMs for each M(1) stage (i.e., 2:1 multiplexer). Translogic admits that the Weste reference does disclose a TGM circuit; however, Translogic argues that Weste provides no specific teaching, suggestion or motivation to use TGMs in a series circuit such as shown in Gorai Fig. 3. Furthermore, Translogic notes that Weste discloses a TGM used for a single multiplexer but does not include any reference to coupled TGMs in series. Thus, according to Translogic, the Weste reference does not provide the necessary teaching, suggestion or motivation to combine the use of TGMs with the Gorai reference.

As articulated by the Supreme Court in KSR, an obviousness analysis "need not seek out precise teachings directed to the specific subject matter of the challenged claim, for a court can take account of the inferences and creative steps that a person of ordinary skill in the art would employ." 550 U.S. at ___, 127 S.Ct. at 1741. In this case, a person of ordinary skill in the art at the time of the invention would have recognized the value of using a known element, a 2:1 TGM, as taught by Weste, for the 2:1 multiplexers in the series arrangement of multiplexers in Gorai. A person of ordinary skill in the art would have appreciated that any conventional multiplexer circuit could be utilized to implement the 2:1 multiplexer circuits in Gorai. After all, TGMs were well-known multiplexer circuits as evidenced by the Weste 1985 textbook. In other words, in looking for a multiplexer circuit for the individual 2:1 multiplexers disclosed in Gorai, a person of ordinary skill in the art would have solved this design need by "pursu[ing] known options within his or her technical grasp." Id. at 1742. Thus, this court agrees with the Board's determination. The Board based its decision on sound reasoning that a person of ordinary skill in the art would select a specific circuit based on the need for a 2:1 multiplexer circuit for the individual multiplexers shown in Gorai. Specifically, a person of ordinary skill in the art at the time of the invention would have been able to choose TGMs as an option. While other circuits could have been used to implement the 2:1 multiplexers, TGMs were a well-known circuit as shown by the explanation of TGM circuits in the 1985 textbook by Weste. This court finds that substantial evidence in the record supports the Board's finding that a person of ordinary skill in the art would have used TGMs in the N:1 circuit configuration shown in Gorai. In sum, this court agrees with the Board's conclusion that the 666 patent is unpatentable under 35 U.S.C. § 103(a) over Gorai in view of Weste.

AFFIRMED

NOTES

1. Did TSM survive KSR? In the *Translogic* opinion above, the Federal Circuit uses a TSM analysis to find that the '666 patent would have been obvious to one of skill in the art at the time of invention. The Federal Circuit in another case has stated directly that TSM, flexibly applied, remains an important part of the obviousness analysis:

> The Supreme Court explained its reason for castigating a "rigid" TSM test: "The obviousness analysis cannot be confined by a formalistic conception of the words teaching, suggestion, and motivation, or by overemphasis on the importance of published articles and the explicit content of issued patents." Indeed a rigid requirement of reliance on written prior art or patent references would, as the Supreme Court noted, unduly confine the use of

the knowledge and creativity within the grasp of an ordinarily skilled artisan. S. Ct. at 1742.

As this court has explained, however, a flexible TSM test remains the primary guarantor against a non-statutory hindsight analysis such as occurred in this case. [citing *Translogic*]. The TSM test, flexibly applied, merely assures that the obviousness test proceeds on the basis of evidence—teachings, suggestions (a tellingly broad term), or motivations (an equally broad term)—that arise before the time of invention as the statute requires. As KSR requires, those teachings, suggestions, or motivations need not always be written references but may be found within the knowledge and creativity of ordinarily skilled artisans.

Ortho–McNeil Pharm. v. Mylan Labs., 520 F.3d 1358, 1364–65 (Fed. Cir. 2008). In *Ortho–McNeil*, the Federal Circuit upheld the patent under the flexible TSM analysis. What is the real difference between a "rigid" and "flexible" application of the TSM test? If the Federal Circuit is correct as it said in *Dystar* that its TSM test was already flexible, then what will be the lasting legacy of KSR? Actually the answer may appear in the biotechnology field.

The *Ortho–McNeil* decision also suggests that the TSM test is really not a creation of the Federal Circuit, but a statutory mandate. Where does the TSM test appear in § 103? If the TSM test is just another way of saying that the party challenging a patent must provide evidence—any kind of evidence—even a "suggestion" or "motivation" within the common sense of an ordinarily skilled artisan—from a time before the date of invention, is TSM anything more than a restatement of the obviousness test itself?

2. Did the Supreme Court just correct a "rather straightforward error?" At one point in *Tranlogic*, the Federal Circuit goes out of its way to confess its error in dismissing the Asano reference. By the way, a clue about that error appears in the citation to the Federal Circuit *Teleflex v. KSR* case. That case does not appear in WEST's Federal 3d reporter because it was a nonprecedential opinion. Due to Federal Circuit procedure, a nonprecedential opinion may have been reviewed by only the 3 judges on the panel, not the entire court (as occurs with all opinions in the Federal 3d reporter).

§ 7.2[b]   THE OBJECTIVE TESTS

Although jurists and patent examiners cannot literally go back in time to perform experiments and acquire the experience of persons of ordinary skill in the art, they can look to actual occurrences for insights into the question of nonobviousness. In the *Graham v. Deere* case, the Supreme Court made direct reference to these objective indicia or "secondary considerations" of nonobviousness: "Such secondary considerations as commercial success, long felt but unsolved needs, failure of others, etc., might be utilized to give light to the circumstances surrounding the origins of the subject matter sought to be patented. As indicia of obviousness or nonobviousness, these inquiries may have relevancy." 383 U.S. at 17–18. The Federal Circuit has struck the "may" from the last sentence of the Supreme Court's advice. These objective indicia are no longer merely "secondary," but are essential to the obviousness inquiry. Indeed a new invention is often better measured in the marketplace than in the courtroom.

There is one catch, however, to use of objective indicia of nonobviousness. The applicant or patentee must show a nexus between the claimed invention and the objective evidence. In the case of commercial success, for instance, the applicant or patentee must show that the success is the result of the innovative claims, not merely the result of effective marketing strategies or general popularity of like products in the prior art.

ORMCO CORP. v. ALIGN TECHNOLOGY, INC.

Court of Appeals for the Federal Circuit, 2006
463 F.3d 1299

Before Schall, Gajarsa, and Dyk, Circuit Judges.

DYK, CIRCUIT JUDGE.

Ormco Corporation and its subsidiary, Allesee Orthodontic Appliances, Inc. (collectively "Ormco"), appeal from the judgment of the United States District Court for the Central District of California finding, *inter alia*, that claims 1–3 and 7 of Align Corporation's ("Align's") U.S. Patent No. 6,554,611 (the '611 patent) ... are infringed by Ormco's "Red, White & Blue" ("RW & B") orthodontic product [and] that those claims are not invalid. We reverse the district court's grant of summary judgment that the patents are not invalid, and hold that all six claims would have been obvious under 35 U.S.C. § 103(a) (2000). We therefore need not reach the district court's finding of infringement.

BACKGROUND

Align is the holder of the '611 and '548 patents, which disclose systems of orthodontic devices for moving teeth from an initial configuration to a final configuration. The patents disclose a series of retainers. The first retainer is designed to move a patient's teeth from an initial position to an intermediate position. Once the teeth have reached the intermediate position, the patient discards the first retainer and inserts the next retainer in the series, which moves the teeth an additional amount. The patents disclose at least three retainers in a series. When the patient finishes using the last retainer, the course is complete and the patient's teeth have achieved the final configuration.

Independent claim 1 of the '611 patent is an apparatus claim that recites:

1. A system for repositioning teeth from an initial tooth arrangement to a final tooth arrangement, said system comprising a plurality of dental incremental position adjustment appliances including:

a first appliance having a geometry selected to reposition the teeth from the initial tooth arrangement to a first intermediate arrangement;

one or more intermediate appliances having geometries selected to progressively reposition the teeth from the first intermediate arrangement to successive intermediate arrangements;

a final appliance having a geometry selected to progressively reposition the teeth from the last intermediate arrangement to the final tooth arrangement;

and *instructions* which set forth that the patient is to wear the individual appliances in a predetermined order which will progressively move the patient's teeth toward the final arrangement, *a package, said package containing said first appliance, said one more [sic] intermediate appliances and said final appliance, wherein the appliances are provided in a single package to the patient.*

Claim 1 of the '611 patent essentially requires (a) three or more appliances with geometries selected to progressively reposition teeth; (b) instructions regarding order of use; and (c) provision of the appliances in a single package to the patient.

II

Two prior art references are potentially pertinent, both of which disclose the use of orthodontic systems by doctors and their patients.

Dr. Truax, an orthodontist, practiced an orthodontic technique that involved taking a single mold of a patient's teeth, repositioning the "tooth cavities" on the mold to their desired positions, then at the same time making three appliances from the repositioned mold, each with a different thickness. A thinner appliance, which applied less force, was to be used before a thicker appliance. Dr. Truax gave each patient one appliance at a time, providing the next appliance in the series after reviewing the patient's progress. The parties dispute whether Dr. Truax provided instructions to the patients regarding order of use of the appliances.

A second orthodontist, Dr. Rains, practiced a similar technique. Dr. Rains also used a series of three plastic retainers to incrementally adjust patient's teeth. Unlike Dr. Truax, Dr. Rains generally made the appliances one at a time. During each patient visit, Dr. Rains would take a mold of the patient's teeth and then create an appliance based on that mold with the appropriate geometry.

DISCUSSION

Ormco contends that claims 1–3 and 7 of the '611 patent ... are invalid because they would have been obvious or are anticipated under 35 U.S.C. §§ 102(a) (2000) and 103(a). Align does not challenge the district court's determination that other claims of the '548 patent are invalid. We review the district court's grant of summary judgment without deference.

"Prior art" in the obviousness context includes the material identified in section 102(a). *See Riverwood Int'l Corp. v. R.A. Jones & Co.,* 324 F.3d 1346, 1354 (Fed.Cir.2003). Section 102(a) provides that a person is not entitled to a patent if "the invention was known or used by others in this country, or patented or described in a printed publication in this or a foreign country, before the invention thereof by the applicant for patent." 35 U.S.C. § 102(a). Art that is not accessible to the public is generally not recognized as prior art. *See Minn. Mining & Mfg. Co. v. Chemque, Inc.,* 303 F.3d 1294, 1301 (Fed.Cir.2002); *OddzOn Prods., Inc. v. Just Toys, Inc.,* 122 F.3d 1396, 1402 (Fed.Cir.1997). Pertinent to this appeal, Ormco relies on Dr. Truax's orthodontic practice, and an instruction sheet he distributed to orthodontists, in order to establish the obviousness of the disputed claims. Thus, Ormco relies on "knowledge or use by others" that is corroborated by documentary evidence. Align claims that the Truax reference was not part of the prior art because it was not publicly accessible. However, we conclude that Dr. Truax's practice and his instruction sheet were sufficiently publicly accessible to qualify as prior art. It is undisputed that Dr. Truax promoted his system to other orthodontists through seminars and clinics and distributed his instruction sheet at those clinics. *See Baxter Int'l, Inc. v. Cobe Labs., Inc.,* 88 F.3d 1054, 1058 (Fed.Cir.1996) (defining "public use" in 102(b) context as including "any use of [the claimed] invention by a person other than the inventor who is under no limitation, restriction or obligation of secrecy to the inventor") (quoting *In re Smith,* 714 F.2d 1127, 1134 (Fed.Cir.1983)); 1–3 Chisum on Patents § 3.05 (2006) ("[A]t most the publicity requirement in Section 102(a) means the absence of affirmative steps to conceal.").

I

We first address Ormco's argument that claim 1 of the '611 patent would have been obvious in view of the Truax reference and regulations of the Food and Drug Administration ("FDA") that generally require the provision of instructions with medical devices. Under 35 U.S.C. § 103(a), a claimed invention is unpatentable if the differences between it and the prior art are such that the subject matter as a whole would have been obvious at the time the invention was made to a person having ordinary skill in the pertinent art. 35 U.S.C. § 103(a) (2000); *Graham v. John Deere Co.,* 383 U.S. 1, 13–14, 86 S.Ct. 684, 15 L.Ed.2d 545 (1966). Obviousness is a legal question where, as here, the relevant underlying facts are undisputed. *Iron Grip Barbell Co. v. USA Sports, Inc.,* 392 F.3d 1317, 1323 (Fed.Cir.2004).

Claim 1 of the '611 patent requires (a) three or more appliances with geometries selected to progressively reposition teeth, (b) instructions regarding order of use, and (c) a single package for provision of the appliances to the patient.

It is undisputed that Dr. Truax's orthodontic system used several clear plastic appliances that fit over the patient's teeth, each appliance composed of plastic of a different thickness (the thicknesses typically varied from 0.015 to 0.030 inches). A thinner device exerted less force on the teeth than a thicker device, and a thinner device was thus used before the next thicker device. The district court held that Dr. Truax's practice does not meet the "geometry" limitation of claim 1 because the claim requires three or more appliances with "different geometries." In the district court's view, the different thicknesses of Dr. Truax's devices do not qualify as different geometries.

In keeping with the district court's claim construction, Align contends that appliances have different geometries only if the positions of the tooth cavities change from one appliance to another. We disagree. We first look to the specification for guidance as to the meaning of claim language, *Phillips v. AWH Corp.*, 415 F.3d 1303, 1315–16 (Fed.Cir.2005) (en banc). Here the specification does not define the term "geometry," though Align points out that it discloses only appliances with different tooth positions. Thus, the specification's language does no more than describe preferred embodiments, and "we have repeatedly warned against confining the claims to [the disclosed] embodiments." *Phillips*, 415 F.3d at 1323. Under these circumstances we appropriately look to dictionary definitions. The parties agree that resort to dictionaries is useful to determine the meaning of the term "geometry." As the district court correctly stated, "[t]he ordinary meaning of 'geometry' in the context of the claims is a figure characterized by points, lines, or planes." *Ormco Corp. v. Align Tech., Inc.*, No. SA–CV–03–16–GLT, slip op. at 3 (C.D.Cal. Feb. 24, 2005) (citing *Webster's New World Dictionary Third College Edition* 564 (1988)). In other words, geometry means "configuration" or "shape." Unlike the district court, we think that objects of different thicknesses plainly have different "configurations" or "shapes." Furthermore, the specification indicates that "[i]n a broadest sense, the methods of the present invention can employ any of the known positioners, retainers, or other removable appliances which are known for finishing and maintaining teeth positions in connection with conventional orthodontic treatment." Thus, we conclude that the Truax devices satisfy the "geometries" limitation of claim 1.

We also disagree with the district court's construction of claim 1 in one other respect. We reject the district court's conclusion that the "single package" limitation of claim 1 of the '611 patent merely requires that devices be "capable of" being provided to the patient in a single package. Here, the claims are written to require that the devices actually be in a single "package." In similar contexts, our cases have rejected claim constructions that would merely require that infringing devices be capable of being modified to conform to a specified claim limitation. With these constructions of claim 1's limitations, we turn to the question of whether the Truax devices rendered claim 1 obvious.

Even though Dr. Truax created several appliances at one time, with the required geometries, Align contends that Dr. Truax never provided his patients with all these appliances in a single package, and that it would not have been obvious to vary Truax in this respect.

A claim can be obvious even where all of the claimed features are not found in specific prior art references, where "there is a showing of a suggestion or motivation to modify the teachings of [the prior art] to the claimed invention." *SIBIA Neurosciences, Inc. v. Cadus Pharm. Corp.*, 225 F.3d 1349, 1356 (Fed.Cir.2000) (concluding that patent would have been obvious in light of teachings in prior art which provided motivation and suggestion to modify existing techniques to arrive at method in question). "A suggestion, teaching, or motivation to combine the relevant prior art teachings does not have to be found explicitly in the prior art, as 'the teaching, motivation, or suggestion may be implicit from the prior art as a whole, rather than expressly stated in the references.... The test for an implicit showing is what the combined teachings, knowledge of one of ordinary skill in the art, and the nature of the problem to be solved as a whole would have suggested to those of ordinary skill in the art.'" *In re Kahn*, 441 F.3d 977, 987–88 (Fed.Cir. 2006).

However, a reference that "teaches away" from a given combination may negate a motivation to modify the prior art to meet the claimed invention. *See, e.g., Medichem, S.A. v. Rolabo, S.L.*, 437 F.3d 1157, 1165 (Fed.Cir.2006). "A reference may be said to teach away when a person of ordinary skill, upon reading the reference, would be discouraged from following the path set out in the reference, or would be led in a direction divergent from the path that was taken by the applicant." *In re Kahn*, 441 F.3d at 990.

Align points out that Dr. Truax examined each patient's progress before giving that patient a new appliance, and that the Truax reference thus does not provide a motivation or suggestion to provide the appliances at one time. Indeed, Align contends, the Truax reference teaches away from providing all appliances at one time. When Dr. Truax was asked whether he ever gave patients more than one appliance at a time, he replied, "No, because we want to manage it.... [I]t would be ridiculous" to expect the patient to replace appliances on his own. He explained that he provided patients with one appliance at a time because in his view "[s]omeone that knows what they're doing [i.e., the orthodontist] ... can see the [tooth] movements [and determine when to change appliances based on those tooth movements] ...," so as to prevent the patient from moving too quickly through appliances. *Id.* In other words, Truax taught that the treatment was more effective if the orthodontist determined when to change appliances, rather than providing several appliances to the patient and allowing the patient to change from one appliance to the next. Under these circumstances, argues Align, it would not have been obvious to provide all appliances to a patient in a single package.

Understanding the parties' contentions requires a brief description of the prior art to which the patented invention and Truax were both directed. As the '611 patent describes, traditional orthodontic work involved providing the patient with a single device that was adjusted periodically by the dentist. Traditional braces utilized a force-inducing component called an "archwire" to move the patient's teeth. The archwire "is attached to ["brackets" that have been cemented to the patient's teeth] "by way of slots in the brackets. After the archwire has been installed, "periodic meetings with the orthodontist are required, during which the patient's braces will be adjusted by installing a different archwire . . . or by replacing or tightening existing [wires]." Thus, "the use of braces is unsightly [and] uncomfortable. . . ."

The patented device here (and Truax) avoided the necessity for adjustment by the dentist by the use of multiple appliances that were changed periodically. Align asserts that there is an important difference between the patented device and Truax in that the patented device avoids a visit to the dentist in order to determine when substitution of the new device is appropriate. But there is nothing in the claim language that requires the devices be substitutable by the patient. In other words, the claims do not require that the device be capable of replacement by the patient rather than the dentist, or preclude visits to the dentist during the treatment regimen. Indeed, the specification makes quite clear that the patient may periodically visit the dentist during treatment.[10] The claim does not preclude returning to the dentist to determine the appropriate time to replace appliances, just as Truax taught.

Under these circumstances, we do not think that the single package limitation makes the device of the '611 patent claims patentably distinct. Providing the devices to the patient in one package, as opposed to two packages or three packages is not a novel or patentable feature in the light of the well-known practice of packaging items in the manner most convenient to the purchaser.

We also think that adding the instructions limitation does not render claim 1 of the '611 patent non-obvious. The parties dispute whether Dr. Truax provided instructions to his patients regarding the order of use of the appliances. However, Align conceded at oral argu-

---

10. As the specification explains in the "Brief Summary of the Invention,"

Unlike braces, the patient need not visit the treating professional every time an adjustment in the treatment is made. *While the patients will usually want to visit their treating professionals periodically to assure that treatment is going according to the original plan,* eliminating the need to visit the treating professional each time an adjustment is to be made allows the treatment to be carried out in many more, but smaller, successive steps while still reducing the time spent by the treating professional with the individual patient.

The specification states that the orthodontist may, during a patient visit, choose to adjust the treatment schedule:

In general, the transition to the next appliance can be based on a number of factors [and may not occur on a predetermined schedule]. . . . [A]ctual patient response can be taken into account. . . . In some cases, for patients whose teeth are responding very quickly, it may be possible for a treating professional to decide to skip one or more intermediate appliances. . . .

ment that the general practice of providing instructions on how to use a medical device would have been obvious. Furthermore, statutes and regulations promulgated under the Food, Drug, and Cosmetic Act ("FDCA") generally require instructions for medical devices.[11] Whether or not these regulations apply to the specific orthodontic devices involved here, they supply ample evidence of a motivation to provide instructions as to how to use the devices.

[The Federal Circuit further concluded that dependent claims 2, 3, and 7 also would have been obvious in view of the prior art and were therefore invalid.]

IV

Finally, we consider Align's contention that secondary considerations support the district court's finding of nonobviousness of the claims.

In *Graham,* the Supreme Court held that "[s]econdary considerations [such] as commercial success, long felt but unsolved needs, failure of others, etc., might be utilized to give light to the circumstances surrounding the origin of the subject matter sought to be patented" and "may have relevancy" as indicia of obviousness. 383 U.S. at 17–18, 86 S.Ct. 684. A nonmovant may rebut a prima facie showing of obviousness with objective indicia of nonobviousness. *WMS Gaming, Inc. v. Int'l Game Tech.,* 184 F.3d 1339, 1359 (Fed.Cir.1999).

Align urges (and the district court agreed) that the novelty of these claims is established by the commercial success of the Invisalign product, by long-felt but unresolved needs satisfied by the claimed features, and by the fact that others had tried and failed to meet the same needs.

Evidence of commercial success, or other secondary considerations, is only significant if there is a nexus between the claimed invention and the commercial success. As we explained in *J.T. Eaton & Co. v. Atlantic Paste & Glue Co.,* 106 F.3d 1563 (Fed.Cir.1997), "[w]hen a patentee can demonstrate commercial success, usually shown by significant sales in a relevant market, and that the successful product is the invention disclosed and claimed in the patent, it is presumed that the commercial success is due to the patented invention." *Id.* at 1571; *see also Brown & Williamson,* 229 F.3d at 1130 (stating the presumption that commercial success is due to the patented invention applies "if the marketed product embodies the claimed features, and is coextensive with them."). Thus, if the commercial success is due to an unclaimed feature of the device, the commercial success is irrelevant. So too if the feature that

---

11. *See, e.g.,*21 U.S.C. § 352 (2000) ("A drug or device shall be deemed to be misbranded ... [u]nless its labeling bears ... adequate directions for use."); 21 U.S.C. § 321 (2000) (defining "device" for purposes of the FDCA as "an ... apparatus ... which is ... intended to affect the structure or any function of the body of man...."); 21 C.F.R. § 801.5 (2005) (defining "adequate directions for use").

creates the commercial success was known in the prior art, the success is not pertinent.[14]

Here, it is undisputed that Align's Invisalign product is commercially successful. However, the evidence clearly rebuts the presumption that Invisalign's success was due to the claimed and novel features. Align relies on testimony and an expert report of Dr. Covell, and testimony of Align's own CEO, Thomas Prescott. In large part these witnesses testified that commercial success was due to unclaimed or non-novel features of the device—the aesthetic appeal and improved comfort of transparent devices without brackets and wire, and the computerized design and manufacture of the appliances.[15] Indeed, Align itself only argues that the commercial success is due "partially" to claimed features.

Nonetheless, Align argues that the commercial success was due at least in part to claimed and novel features. Thus, Align's witnesses also suggested that the commercial success was due to reduction in time spent in the dentist's chair, a reduction resulting from the provision of multiple appliances to the patient at one time.[16] But, as we have noted above, to the extent that such a time savings was the result of the use of multiple appliances (rather than a single device requiring individual adjustment), that feature was not new; Truax had already accomplished this. And to the extent that the time savings resulted from the patient's

---

14. *See J.T. Eaton,* 106 F.3d at 1571 ("[T]he asserted commercial success of the product must be due to the merits of the claimed invention beyond what was readily available in the prior art."); *Richdel, Inc. v. Sunspool Corp.,* 714 F.2d 1573, 1580 (Fed.Cir.1983) (holding claims obvious despite purported showing of commercial success when patentee failed to show that "such commercial success as its marketed system enjoyed was due to anything disclosed in the patent in suit which was not readily available in the prior art").

15. J.A. at 3200 (Invisalign resolved "aesthetic concerns associated with braces"); J.A. at 3019 (listing benefit of "[e]limination of abrasive discomfort associated with wires and braces"); J.A. at 3199 (Align's CEO stating that Invisalign was successful because it "reduce[d] the pain of orthodontic treatment, h[e]ld some teeth without moving them (unlike with braces, where all teeth move) and ... better promote[d] the health of the teeth through ease of brushing and flossing [because they are removable]."); J.A. at 3201 ("[T]he success of Invisalign aligners also results in part from the computerized design and manufacture of the aligners."); J.A. at 3022 ("Because of the 3D graphical imaging and precise computer manipulation of 'virtual' models, more precise tooth movements involving a greater number of teeth are possible with the Invisalign System.") (internal quotations omitted).

The multitude of contemporaneous newspaper articles that Dr. Covell cites, which reviewed the Invisalign system shortly after its introduction, confirm that Invisilign's invisibility, computerized design and manufacturing process, and the absence of metal braces were primary factors that brought about its success. See J.A. at 3023 (listing article titles: "Straight teeth without the suit of armor," "Bracing for a change; INVISALIGN helps correct dental, vanity problems for adults," "Going wireless; Invisalign braces offer a clear alternative to traditional 'railroad tracks,' ...", "Seen up close, Invisalign's Smile Isn't Perfect; the 'Invisible' Braces Are Pricey and Not Right for Everyone But They Can Make Dentists Rich," "So long metal mouth;" "nearly invisible dental braces taking big bite of orthodontic market.", "Orthodontics via Silicon Valley; A Start–Up Uses Computer Modeling And Venture Capital to Reach Patients," "A Stealth Substitute for Braces, Designed Only for Adults," "Do Those Invisible Braces Live Up to All the Hype?", "Health News, No More Metal Mouth," "Setting the record straight on those invisible braces," "Some orthodontists grit teeth over popular invisible braces.").

16. J.A. at 3027 ("[T]he use of a series of clear appliances that are designed to be delivered to the patient in one appointment (which must be marked to indicate the order of their use), rather than braces that must be periodically adjusted, contributed to the success of the Invisalign system."); J.A. at 3201 (Align's CEO stated that the success of Invisalign was due at least in part to the fact that patients and orthodontists had a need for less patient time in the orthodontic chair, and "the fact that [the Invisalign product] can be supplied in a single package to the patient, with instructions to the patient regarding order of use, reduces the chair time required.").

substitution of a new device without visiting the dentist, that feature was not claimed. Finally, to the extent that these witnesses testified that the aesthetic appeal resulted from changing the devices every two weeks and avoiding the use of dirty and worn devices,[17] this feature was also not new; it had been accomplished by Truax.

We conclude that the evidence does not show that the commercial success was the result of claimed and novel features. Nor has Align submitted probative evidence that claimed and novel features met a long-felt but unresolved need.

With respect to "failures of others," Align has submitted evidence that, prior to the introduction of the successful Invisalign and RW & B products, other orthodontists had tried and failed to develop a functional, invisible orthodontic system. Again, the evidence does not suggest that these prior attempts failed because the devices lacked the claimed features.

We therefore conclude that the evidence of secondary considerations is inadequate to raise any doubt as to the obviousness of claims 1–3 and 7 of the '611 patent and claims 10 and 17 of the '548 patent.

CONCLUSION

For the foregoing reasons, we hold that claims 1–3 and 7 of the '611 patent ... are invalid as obvious. We therefore reverse the district court's finding that the claims are valid. In light of this holding, we need not reach the district court's finding of infringement.

REVERSED.

NOTES

1. **Secondary considerations in the wake of *KSR*.** Unfortunately the facts of *KSR* did not give the Supreme Court a chance to discuss the objective criteria directly. The Court's references to common sense and market forces, however, suggest that the Court perceived a wider role for the secondary considerations in the obviousness analysis. Indeed the Federal Circuit seems to have picked up those hints and emphasized secondary considerations in the wake of *KSR*:

> Specifically, the record shows powerful unexpected results (anticonvulsive activity) for topiramate. The record also shows skepticism of experts and copying—other respected sources of objective evidence of nonobviousness—as well as commercial success. As this court has repeatedly explained, this evidence is not just a cumulative or confirmatory part of the obviousness calculus but constitutes independent evidence of nonobviousness. *Catalina Lighting, Inc. v. Lamps Plus, Inc.*, 295 F.3d 1277, 1288 (Fed.Cir. 2002) ("Objective indicia may often be the most probative and cogent evidence of nonobviousness in the record.").

17. J.A. at 3201 (Align's CEO stated that "[t]he use of the Invisalign aligners for 2 weeks at a time also enables the patients to move often to a new appliance, which is naturally more aesthetically pleasing than older appliances that necessarily become dirty and worn.")

Ortho–McNeil Pharm. v. Mylan Labs., 520 F.3d 1358, 1365 (Fed. Cir. 2008).

    2. Commentary on the Objective Tests. Edmund Kitch, Graham v. John Deere Co.: *New Standards for Patents*, 1966 SUPREME COURT REV. 293 (reprinted in 49 J. PAT. OFF. SOC'Y 237, 282–85), criticized the objective tests of nonobviousness as follows:

> But how is commercial success relevant to non-obviousness? The argument for commercial success is set out in a law review note cited with apparent approval by the [Supreme] Court in [the *Cook Chemical* cases]:

>> The possibility of market success attendant upon the solution of an existing problem may induce innovators to attempt a solution. If in fact a product attains a high degree of commercial success, there is a basis for inferring that such attempts have been made and failed. Thus the rationale is similar to that of longfelt demand and is for the same reasons a legitimate test of invention.

> [*Subtests of "Nonobviousness": A Nontechnical Approach to Patent Validity*, 112 U. PA. L. REV. 1169, 1175 (1964).] This argument involves four inferences. First, that the commercial success is due to the innovation. Second, that if an improvement has in fact become commercially successful, it is likely that this potential commercial success was perceived before its development. Third, the potential commercial success having been perceived, it is likely that efforts were made to develop the improvement. Fourth, the efforts having been made by men of skill in the art, they failed because the patentee was the first to reduce his development to practice. Since men of skill in the art tried but failed, the improvement is clearly non-obvious.

> Each inference is weak. The commercial success might not be due to the innovation but rather . . . to "sales promotion ability, manufacturing technique, ready access to markets, consumer appeal design factors, and advertising budget." But given the commercial success of the innovation, why is it likely that the commercial potential was perceived in advance? And why is it likely that because the commercial potential was perceived, men of skill began to work on the problems of that innovation as opposed to other potential improvements? And if men of skill start to work on the improvement, why does the fact that the patentee was first to perfect the improvement mean that others failed? Perhaps they were only a little slower. This seems a fragile thread on which to hang a conclusion of non-obviousness, particularly in a case where the patentee shows only commercial success but does not show that the commercial potential was perceived or that attempts actually were made but failed. How, then, does commercial success constitute a helping hand? The Court said that "there legal inferences or subtests do focus attention on economic and motivational rather than technical issues and are, therefore, more susceptible of judicial treatment than are the highly technical facts often present in patent litigation." Perhaps commercial success is a familiar distraction for judges confused by the facts.

> It is not difficult to see why lawyers for patent owners are eager to introduce evidence of commercial success. By introducing evidence of

commercial success the lawyer is telling the judge that his client's patent is very valuable and that if the judge holds the patent invalid he is destroying expectations of great value. . . . Since it is unlikely that patents that are not commercially successful will be brought to litigation, this amounts to a suggestion that borderline cases be decided in favor of patentees. In fact, if one is willing to infer from the litigation itself that the patent is valuable because it is worth litigating, and that since it is valuable it must be commercially successful, one ends up with the rule that all patents that are litigated should be held valid.

If commercial success is a relevant "economic issue," then one can argue that it should be a factor weighing against patentability in borderline cases. Commercially successful patents are the ones that truly impose a monopoly tax on the market, and therefore courts should be even more cautious in holding them valid. Furthermore, it is in the area of innovations that quickly meet consumer acceptance that the innovator has the best chance of recovering his special costs without a patent monopoly. The chances of doing this in any particular case depend, of course, on the good-will advantages of being the first and the speed with which potential competitors can enter. But the more quickly a substantial market can be developed and its profit returns enjoyed, the greater (as a general rule) would seem to be the advantages accruing to the innovator who enters the market first. He will not need extensive market development that will alert potential competitors before the profits begin. Thus, in the area of commercially successful improvement quickly recognized by the market, a patent is less likely to be necessary to evoke the improvement. The argument assumes, of course, that the commercial potential is perceived in advance by the innovator so that it can affect his decision to develop the innovation. This is not necessarily so, but the same assumption is made by the traditional argument for commercial success as a factor favoring a finding of invention. At the very least, these two arguments should cancel each other and leave commercial success with no role to play in a nonobviousness inquiry.

For quite the opposite view, see Jochen Pagenberg, *The Evaluation of "Inventive Step" in the European Patent System—More Objective Standards Needed*, 9 INT'L REV. INDUS. PROP. & COPYRIGHT L. 1, 121 (1978), urging that secondary considerations are more reliable indicia of nonobviousness and should hold a dominant position in inventive step determinations.

3. Copying. Copying, particularly when the accused infringer did not copy any other prior art, can be strong evidence of nonobviousness. *Specialty Composites v. Cabot Corp.*, 845 F.2d 981 (Fed.Cir.1988). Copying, too, must be given weight according to its context. Copying is not persuasive, for instance, when the accused product is not identical to the claimed invention and the accused infringer vigorously denies infringement. *Pentec Inc. v. Graphic Controls Corp.*, 776 F.2d 309 (Fed.Cir.1985). Copying is a high form of flattery but could also occur because the copyist is confident that the invention is not patentable.

4. Prior Failures. Prior failures by other inventors has been called "virtually irrefutable" evidence of nonobviousness. *Panduit Corp. v. Dennison Mfg. Co.*, 774 F.2d 1082 (Fed.Cir.1985), *vacated on other grounds*, 475 U.S. 809 (1986). However, once again, prior failures are not viewed uncritically. Evidence of prior failure is not persuasive if the person who failed had only scant knowledge of the prior art or, more important, was not motivated to succeed due to satisfaction with the status quo. *In re Sneed*, 710 F.2d 1544 (Fed.Cir. 1983). Moreover evidence of other failures very rarely relates to exactly the same problem that the invention solved. Therefore, the use of this evidence must assure that the failures sought the answer to the same problem.

5. Licenses. Evidence of extensive licensing may be persuasive of industry respect for the invention—strong evidence of nonobviousness. On the other hand, a long period of no infringement may show that the licenses are in fact motivated by a desire to avoid litigation, rather than by respect for the strength of the invention. *Pentec Inc. v. Graphic Controls Corp.*, 776 F.2d 309 (Fed.Cir. 1985); *EWP Corp. v. Reliance Universal Inc.*, 755 F.2d 898 (Fed.Cir.1985). Moreover in a healthy market, many licenses are part of a larger cross-licensing arrangement that undermines the nexus between a particular license in a large package and the claimed features it licenses.

6. Long–Felt Need. The nature of the problem is certainly relevant to the obviousness inquiry. *Northern Telecom Inc. v. Datapoint Corp.*, 908 F.2d 931 (Fed.Cir.1990). Moreover, an invention need not solve some long-standing problem, but can instead create a new want or need and still be nonobvious. *Leinoff v. Louis Milona & Sons*, 726 F.2d 734 (Fed.Cir.1984). On the other hand, the nexus requirement will place a burden on the applicant or patentee to show that the felt need correlates with the problem solved by the invention.

7. Unexpected Results. Does this sound like a recycled version of the "synergism" test? Remember that the "synergism" test *required* some superior or unexpected result to qualify for patent protection. In this case, this objective criterion acknowledges the common sense observation that surprise and commendation by experts at the time of learning of the invention buttresses a case for nonobviousness. *Specialty Composites v. Cabot Corp.*, 845 F.2d 981 (Fed.Cir. 1988); *Burlington Indus. Inc. v. Quigg*, 822 F.2d 1581 (Fed.Cir.1987). On the other hand, this evidence can suffer from the hindsight problem. This evidence necessarily appears after the invention has changed expectations. Because expectations are by nature subjective, another danger is that litigation itself can alter the nature and intensity of expectations.

8. Skepticism. The skepticism of an expert, expressed before the inventor proved it wrong, bolsters the case for nonobviousness. *In re O'Farrell*, 853 F.2d 894 (Fed.Cir.1988). Because this evidence arises before the invention, it has particular persuasiveness. Sadly it is also among the rarest forms of objective evidence of nonobviousness. Skilled artisans rarely pronounce categorical judgments of doom on a technology that later revises all thinking in the field.

9. Commercial Success: Whose? Courts have sometimes counted the sales of infringers, as well as those of the patentee, in order to determine whether an invention enjoyed commercial success. "Commercial success of an invention is measured by the sales of the infringers as well as the sales of [the patentee]." *Syntex (U.S.A.) Inc. v. Paragon Optical Inc.*, 7 U.S.P.Q.2d 1001 (D.Ariz.1987). As noted in one dissent: "Now, as a matter of common sense, the way one proves commercial success of a patented invention is, first, to demonstrate the success of the patentee or one or more licensees. Second, once an infringer is sued and proved to be an infringer, its sales are appropriately proved and added to the others." *Truswal Sys. Corp. v. Hydro–Air Eng'g, Inc.*, 813 F.2d 1207 (Fed.Cir.1987) (Rich, J., dissenting). What difficulties does this approach create for discovery and the presentation of evidence during an infringement trial, particularly where the accused infringer contends that the claimed invention would have been obvious?

Depending on market factors, upon which no two economists agree, this evidence can be relevant to nonobviousness. Because easy to acquire, however, this type of evidence appears often in nonobviousness cases.

10. Independent Development. Evidence of contemporaneous independent invention is objective evidence that may not benefit the applicant or patentee. If actually contemporaneous and not based on derivation from the purported inventor, this type of evidence may show that others could easily achieve the same invention. *See, Monarch Knitting Mach. Corp. v. Sulzer Morat GmbH,* 139 F.3d 877 (Fed.Cir.1998).

11. The Prima Facie Case of Nonobviousness. Patent Office procedures places considerable emphasis on a so-called "prima facie case" of nonobviousness. In *In re Oetiker*, 977 F.2d 1443 (Fed.Cir.1992), the Federal Circuit noted:

> The prima facie case is a procedural tool of patent examination, allocating the burdens of going forward as between examiner and applicant. The term "prima facie case" refers only to the initial examination step. As discussed in *In re Piasecki*, 745 F.2d 1468, 1472 (Fed.Cir.1984), the examiner bears the initial burden, on review of the prior art or on any other ground, of presenting a *prima facie* case of unpatentability. If that burden is met, the burden of coming forward with evidence or argument shifts to the applicant. After evidence or argument is submitted by the applicant in response, patentability is determined on the totality of the record, by a preponderance of evidence with due consideration to persuasiveness of argument.

> If examination at the initial stage does not produce a prima facie case of unpatentability, then without more the applicant is entitled to grant of the patent.

> In reviewing the examiner's decision on appeal, the Board must necessarily weigh all of the evidence and argument. An observation by the Board that the examiner made a prima facie case is not improper, as long as the ultimate determination of patentability is made on the entire record.

In practice this *prima facie* practice often means that the examiner will enter an initial rejection based on a comparison of the claimed invention with the prior art. At that stage of the prosecution process, the applicant is not likely to have submitted any objective evidence of nonobviousness. Upon receipt of the rejection, the burden shifts to the applicant to rebut the prima facie case of obviousness. At that point, the applicant my supply objective evidence along with the rest of its case for nonobviousness.

§ 7.3 OBVIOUSNESS IN CHEMISTRY AND BIOTECHNOLOGY

With characteristic conclusiveness, the Federal Circuit noted: "[T]he requirement of unobviousness in the case of chemical inventions is the same as for other types of inventions." *In re Johnson*, 747 F.2d 1456, 1460 (Fed.Cir.1984). To the contrary, obviousness as applied to the landscape of chemical technologies has presented a distinct set of issues for the patent law. The search for a coherent nonobviousness doctrine in biotechnology has also proven elusive, as demonstrated by the enactment of § 103(b), a complex standard of nonobviousness for certain biotechnologies. An introduction to the considerable body of precedent concerning obviousness in chemistry and biotechnology follows.

§ 7.3[a] COMPOSITION CLAIMS

Patenting in the chemical and biotechnology areas focuses first and foremost on claiming "new entities," shorter new molecules constituting "new chemical entities" and the longer chains from recombinant biotechnology. Unlike mechanical patenting where the "thing" to be patented can be accurately pictured in three dimensions through a plurality of drawings, the chemical entity is rarely if ever pictured as a three dimensional structure that in the end gives rise to its properties. Rather, chemists use a two-dimensional representation—the structural formula—to *identify* the structure.

For literally six decades in the patenting of chemical entities, the bar focused so intensely upon the "label," the structural formula, that for the patent profession the label became the reality. Thus, like a tic-tac-toe game of "X" and "O" marks on a two-dimensional surface, the battleground for patenting chemical entities was a determination whether the *label* for a claimed compound was or was not "obvious" from the *label* for a prior art compound. If the labels were very close, then the claimed compound was "structurally obvious." This conclusion closed the book on patenting the compound, per se. Instead, if the claimed compound possessed an unexpected property vis-a-vis the prior art compound, the inventor was encouraged to claim a method of use of the compound (as opposed to a claim to the compound *per se*).

Numerous cases over a period of more than sixty years established a basis for denial of a claim to new chemical entity based upon "structural obviousness," dating back to at least *Bender v. Hoffmann*, 1898 C.D. 262, and sustained through *In re Henze*, 181 F.2d 196 (CCPA 1950), and *In re Hass*, 141 F.2d 122 (CCPA 1944). The primary thread throughout this line of cases was whether a certain change from an old compound was sufficiently removed so that it could not be considered "structurally obvious": This was the starting and end point of the investigation. *See generally* Harold C. Wegner, *Prima Facie Obviousness of Chemical Compounds*, 6 AM. PAT. L. ASS'N Q.J. 271 (1978).

Although the CCPA had earlier suggested in dictum that applicants could overcome a prima facie case of obviousness through a showing regarding the compound's properties, the court had not squarely applied these concepts until its seminal decision in *In re Papesch*.

IN RE PAPESCH

United States Court of Customs and Patent Appeals, 1963
315 F.2d 381

The applicant claimed a family of compounds including representative compound 2,4,6–triethylpyrazolo(4,3–d)–4,5,6,7–tetrahydropyrimidine–5,7–dione (ethyl = CH_3-CH_2-), that was admittedly "structurally obvious" in light of a compound dislcosed by Robbins, 2,4,6–trimethylpyrazolo(4,3–d)–4,5,6,7–tetrahydropyrimidine–5,7–dione (methyl = CH_3-). The applicant stated in his specification that "[t]he tri[ethyl] compound[] . . . ha[s] been found to possess unexpectedly potent anti-inflammatory activity in contrast to the [prior art] trimethyl compound." A researcher's affidavit reported comparative tests of the Robins et al. trimethyl compound and the applicant's triethyl compound which show that the latter is an active anti-inflammatory agent while the prior art compound is completely inactive for that utility.

Worley, Chief Judge and Rich, Martin, Arthur M. Smith and Almond, Associate Judges.

RICH, ASSOCIATE JUDGE.

[C]omparing the specific compound of claim 2 with the prior art, the compounds differ only in that where [Papesch] has three ethyl groups the [Robbins] prior art has three methyl groups, a total difference of three-CH_2 groups.

The claims are rejected only on the ground that they are [obvious] over a single reference which discloses . . . a lower homolog of the claimcd compounds . . . and proof has been given showing that the compound of claim 2 . . . possesses an advantageous pharmacological property shown not to be possessed by the prior art compound.

From the standpoint of patent law, a compound and all of its properties are inseparable; they are one and the same thing. The graphic formulae, the chemical nomenclature, the systems of classification and study such as the concepts of homology, isomerism, etc., are mere symbols by which compounds can be identified, classified, and compared. But a formula is not a compound and while it may serve in a claim to identify what is being patented, as the metes and bounds of a deed identify a plot of land, the thing that is patented is not the formula but the compound identified by it. And the patentability of the thing does not depend on the similarity of its formula to that of another compound but of the similarity of the former compound to the latter.

There is no basis in law for ignoring any property in making such a comparison. An assumed similarity based on a comparison of formulae must give way to evidence that the assumption is erroneous.

The argument has been made that patentability is here being asserted only on the basis of one property, the anti-inflammatory activity, and that the compounds claimed and the compound of the prior art presumably have many properties in common. Presumably they do, but presumption is all we have here. The same is true of all of the compounds of the above cases which were held patentable over compounds of the prior art, many of which must have had more in common by way of properties than the compounds here because the relationships, structurally, were even closer than here.

As to the examiner's view that in a case such as this the applicant should claim his invention as a process utilizing the newly discovered property, the board appears to have ignored it, properly we think. It is contrary to practically all of the above decisions wherein no fault was found with granting product claims. Such claims have well-recognized advantages to those in the business of making and selling compounds, in contrast to process-of-use claims, because competitors in the sale of compounds are not generally users.

As should be apparent from the foregoing, we regard the board's opinion and decision as contrary to well established law. We see no reason to change that law. The decision is therefore reversed.

WORLEY, CHIEF JUDGE, concurred in the result.

* * *

NOTES

1. *Papesch* **at the Federal Circuit:** An early Federal Circuit case confirmed the role of *Papesch* and displayed its continued doctrinal development. In *In re Lalu*, 747 F.2d 703 (Fed.Cir.1984), Judge Baldwin overturned the Board's finding of *prima facie* obviousness:

> Ultimately our analysis of the obviousness or nonobviousness of appellants' claimed compounds requires inquiry as to whether there is anything in the Oesterling reference which would suggest the expected properties of the claimed compounds or whether Oesterling discloses any utility for the intermediate sulfonyl chlorides which would support an expectation that the claimed compounds would have similar properties.

> There is no disclosure that the Oesterling compounds would have any properties in common with those of appellants' compounds, as those properties of the former relate to the use of the compounds for base neutralization, catalysis, metal cleaning, and fuel. The mere fact that Oesterling's sulfonyl chlorides can be used as intermediates in the production of the corresponding sulfonic acids does not provide adequate motivation for one of ordinary skill in the art to stop the Oesterling synthesis and

investigate the intermediate sulfonyl chlorides with an expectation of arriving at appellants' claimed sulfonyl halides for use as corrosion inhibiting agents, surface active agents, or leveling agents.

2. Balancing New and Old Uses. In the next case the full court took up the question of chemical obviousness where the closest prior art compounds had the same essential structure as the compounds claimed by the applicant, but the existence of an important property of both the prior art compounds and the claimed compounds was discovered by the applicant.

IN RE DILLON

United States Court of Appeals, Federal Circuit, 1990
919 F.2d 688

The applicant claimed compositions containing tetra-orthoesters useful as fuel additives to reduce soot emissions. The tetra-orthoesters were "structurally obvious" from tri-orthoesters that were also disclosed in the prior art as fuel additives, but in order to obtain a different benefit: dewatering. The PTO Board affirmed the examiner's rejection, holding that there was a "reasonable expectation" that the tri-and tetra-orthoesther fuel compositions would have similar properties, based on "close structural and chemical similarity" between them and the fact that both the applicant and the prior art noted their use as fuel additives. According to the Board, the applicant could have traversed the obviousness rejection by showing an unexpected advantage or superiority of her claimed tetra-orthoesters as compared with the tri-orthoesthers, but had not done so.

A three-judge panel of the Federal Circuit reversed the rejection, stating that "a prima facie case of obviousness is not deemed made unless both (1) the new compound or composition is structurally similar to the reference compound or composition and (2) there is some suggestion or expectation in the prior art that the new compound or composition will have the same or a similar utility as that discovered by the applicant." In re Dillon, 892 F.2d 1554, 1560 (Fed.Cir.1989) (withdrawn panel opinion). From a petition for hearing en banc, this proceeding followed.

Nies, Chief Judge, Rich, Circuit Judge, Cowen, Senior Circuit Judge, Markey (who sat as chief judge during argument) Pauline Newman, Archer, Mayer, Michel, Plager, Lourie, Clevenger, and Rader, Circuit Judges.

LOURIE, CIRCUIT JUDGE.

THE ISSUE

The issue before this court is whether the Board erred in rejecting as obvious under 35 U.S.C. § 103 claims to Dillon's new compositions and to the new method of reducing particulate emissions, when the additives in the new compositions are structurally similar to additives in known compositions, having a different use, but the new method of reducing particulate emissions is neither taught nor suggested by the prior art.

The Board found that the claims to compositions of a hydrocarbon fuel and a tetra-orthoester were *prima facie* obvious over Sweeney '417 and '267 in view of Elliott and Howk. We agree. Appellant argues that none of these references discloses or suggests the new use which she has discovered. That is, of course, true, but the composition claims are not limited to this new use; *i.e.*, they are not physically or structurally distinguishable over the prior art compositions except with respect to the orthoester component. We believe that the PTO has established, through its combination of references, that there is a sufficiently close relationship between the tri-orthoesters and tetra-orthoesters (see the cited Elliott and Howk references) in the fuel oil art to create an expectation that hydrocarbon fuel compositions containing the tetra-esters would have similar properties, including water scavenging, to like compositions containing the tri-esters, and to provide the motivation to make such new compositions. Howk teaches use of both tri-and tetra-orthoesters in a similar type of chemical reaction. Elliott teaches their equivalence for a particular practical use.

Our case law well establishes that such a fact situation gives rise to a *prima facie* case of obviousness.

This court, in reconsidering this case *in banc*, reaffirms that structural similarity between claimed and prior art subject matter, proved by combining references or otherwise, where the prior art gives reason or motivation to make the claimed compositions, creates a *prima facie* case of obviousness, and that the burden (and opportunity) then falls on an applicant to rebut that *prima facie* case. Such rebuttal or argument can consist of a comparison of test data showing that the claimed compositions possess unexpectedly improved properties or properties that the prior art does not have (*In re Albrecht*, 514 F.2d 1389, 1396 (CCPA 1975); *Murch*, 464 F.2d at 1056, 175 U.S.P.Q. at 92), that the prior art is so deficient that there is no motivation to make what might otherwise appear to be obvious changes (*Albrecht*, 514 F.2d at 1396; *In re Stemniski*, 444 F.2d 581 (CCPA 1971); *In re Ruschig*, 343 F.2d 965 (CCPA 1965)), or any other argument or presentation of evidence that is pertinent. There is no question that all evidence of the properties of the claimed compositions and the prior art must be considered in determining the ultimate question of patentability, but it is also clear that the discovery that a claimed composition possesses a property not disclosed for the prior art subject matter, does not by itself defeat a *prima facie* case. *Shetty*, 566 F.2d at 86. Each situation must be considered on its own facts, but it is not necessary in order to establish a *prima facie* case of obviousness that both a structural similarity between a claimed and prior art compound (or a key component of a composition) be shown and that there be a suggestion in or expectation from *the prior art* that the claimed compound or composition will have the same or a similar utility *as one newly discovered by applicant*. To the extent that [*In re Wright*, 848 F.2d 1216 (Fed.Cir.1988)] suggests or holds to the contrary, it is hereby overruled. In particular, the statement that a *prima facie* obviousness rejection is not supported if no reference shows or suggests the newly-discovered properties and results of a claimed structure is not the law.

Under the facts ... we have concluded that a *prima facie* case has been established. The art provided the motivation to make the claimed compositions in the expectation that they would have similar properties. Appellant had the opportunity to rebut the *prima facie* case. She did not present any showing of data to the effect that her compositions had properties not possessed by the prior art compositions or that they possessed them to an unexpectedly greater degree. She attempted to refute the significance of the teachings of the prior art references. She did not succeed and we do not believe the PTO was in error in its decision.

While [the prior art] Sweeney [reference] does not suggest appellant's use, her composition claims are not limited to that use; the claims merely recite compositions analogous to those in the Sweeney patents, and appellant has made no showing overcoming the *prima facie* presumption of similar properties for those analogous compositions. The mention in the appealed claims that the amount of orthoester must be sufficient to reduce particulate emissions is not a distinguishing limitation of the claims, unless that amount is different from the prior art and critical to the use of the claimed composition. *See In re Reni*, 419 F.2d 922, 925 (CCPA 1970). That is not the case here. The amount of ester recited in the dependent claims can be from 0.05–49%, a very broad range; a preferred range is .05–9%, compared with a percentage in Sweeney '417 approximately equimolar to the amounts of water in the fuel which the ester is intended to remove (.01–5%).

Appellant urges that the Board erred in not considering the unexpected results produced by her invention and in not considering the claimed invention as a whole. The Board found, on the other hand, that no showing was made of unexpected results for the claimed compositions compared with the compositions of Sweeney. We agree. Clearly, in determining patentability the Board was obligated to consider all the evidence of the properties of the claimed invention as a whole, compared with those of the prior art. However, after the PTO made a showing that the prior art compositions suggested the claimed compositions, the burden was on the applicant to overcome the presumption of obviousness that was created, and that was not done. For example, she produced no evidence that her compositions possessed properties not possessed by the prior art compositions. Nor did she show that the prior art compositions and use were so lacking in significance that there was no motivation for others to make obvious variants. There was no attempt to argue the relative importance of the claimed compositions compared with the prior art.

[T]he cases [cited in the dissent] establish that if an examiner considers that he has found prior art close enough to the claimed invention to give one skilled in the relevant chemical art the motivation to make close relatives (homologs, analogs, isomers, etc.) of the prior art compound(s), then there arises what has been called a presumption of obviousness or a *prima facie* case of obviousness. *In re Henze*, 181 F.2d 196 (CCPA 1950); *In re Hass*, 141 F.2d 122, 127, 130 (CCPA 1944). The burden then shifts to the applicant, who then can present arguments and/or data to show that what appears to be obvious, is not in fact that, when the invention is looked at as a whole. *In re Papesch*, 315 F.2d 381 (CCPA 1963). The cases of *Hass* and *Henze* established the rule that, unless an applicant showed that the prior art compound lacked the property or advantage asserted for the claimed compound, the presumption of unpatentability was not overcome.

Exactly what facts constituted a *prima facie* case varied from case to case, but it was not the law that, where an applicant asserted that an invention possessed properties not known to be possessed by the prior art, no *prima facie* case was established unless the reference also showed the novel activity. There are cases, cited in the dissent, in which a *prima facie* case was not established based on lack of structural similarity. Some of the cited cases also contained language suggesting that the fact that the claimed and the prior art compounds possessed the same activity were added factors in the establishment of the *prima facie* case. Those cases did not say, however, as the dissent asserts, that, in the absence of the similarity of activities, there would have been no *prima facie* case.

Stemniski . . . overruled *[In re] Henze*[, 181 F.2d 196 (CCPA 1950),] and *In re Riden*, 318 F.2d 761 (CCPA 1963) (a case similar to *Henze*), "to the extent that [they] are inconsistent with the views expressed herein." 444 F.2d at 587. The views that were expressed therein were that:

> [w]here the prior art reference neither discloses nor suggests a utility for certain described compounds, why should it be said that a reference makes obvious to one of ordinary skill in the art an isomer, homolog or analog or related structure, when that mythical, but intensely practical, person knows of no "practical" reason to make the reference compounds, much less any structurally related compounds?

Id. at 586. Thus, *Stemniski*, rather than destroying the established practice of rejecting closely-related compounds as *prima facie* obvious, qualified it by holding that a presumption is not created when the reference compound is so lacking in any utility that there is no motivation to make close relatives.

Properties . . . *are* relevant to the creation of a *prima facie* case in the sense of affecting the motivation of a researcher to make compounds closely related to or suggested by a prior art compound, but it is not required, as stated in the dissent, that the prior art disclose or suggest the properties newly-discovered by an applicant in order for there to be a *prima facie* case of obviousness.

The dissent cites the seminal case of *Papesch*, suggesting that it rejected the principle that we now "adopt," thereby implying that we are weakening *Papesch*. We are doing nothing of the sort. *Papesch* indeed stated that a compound and all of its properties are inseparable and must be considered in the determination of obviousness. We heartily agree and intend not to retreat from *Papesch* one inch. *Papesch*, however, did not deal with the requirements for establishing a *prima facie* case, but whether the examiner had to consider the properties of an invention at all, when there was a presumption of obviousness. 315 F.2d at 391. The reference disclosed a lower homolog of the claimed compounds, so it was clear that impliedly a *prima facie* case existed; the question was whether, under those circumstances, the biological data were admissible at all. The court ruled that they were, *id.* at 391, and we agree with that result. The dissent quotes the brief passage at the end of the *Papesch* opinion to the effect that the prior art must "at least to a degree" disclose the applicant's desired property, *id.* at 392, but this brief mention was not central to the decision in that case and did not refer to the requirements of a *prima facie* case. *Papesch* is irrelevant to the question of the requirements for a *prima facie* case, which is the question we have here.

The dissent mentions positions advanced by the Commissioner, including the *In re Mod*, 408 F.2d 1055 (CCPA 1969), and *In re De Montmollin*, 344 F.2d 976 (CCPA 1965) decisions. [W]e note that neither *Mod* nor *De Montmollin* dealt with the requirements of a *prima facie* case. They concerned the question whether the existence of a new property for claimed compounds in addition to a property common to both the claimed and related prior art compounds rendered the claimed compounds unobvious. We are not faced with that question today.

Other cases, e.g., *In re Gyurik*, 596 F.2d 1012, 1018 (CCPA 1979) ("[n]o common-properties presumption rises from the mere occurrence of a claimed compound at an intermediate point in a conventional reaction yielding a specifically named prior art compound"), have qualified the original rule of the Hass–Henze cases, but it is clear that they have not enunciated a rule that, in order to make a *prima facie* case of obviousness, the examiner must show that the prior art suggests a new property discovered by applicant. In not accepting that principle today, as urged in the dissent, we are therefore not retreating from the recent trend of case law development or changing the law.

Another example of the lack of direct pertinence of a case quoted in the dissent is *May*, which the dissent cites as an example of the consistent line of decisions to the effect that "both structure and properties must be suggested in the prior art before a *prima facie* case of obviousness was deemed made." This case does not state that both structure and properties "must" be suggested. The claimed and prior art compositions were both disclosed as having analgesic activity; it was conceded that a *prima facie* case was made out, but the court concluded that applicants had rebutted the presumed expectation that structurally similar compounds have similar properties with a showing of an actual unexpected difference of properties between the claimed compound and the prior art.

574 F.2d at 1095. The applicant in that case thus made a showing that Dillon did not make in this case.

Properties must be considered in the overall evaluation of obviousness, and the lack of any disclosure of useful properties for a prior art compound may indicate a lack of motivation to make related compounds, thereby precluding a *prima facie* case, but it is not correct that similarity of structure and a suggestion of *the activity of an applicant's compounds* in the prior art are necessary before a *prima facie* case is established.

NOTES

1. **Chemical obviousness in the wake of *KSR*.** In *Takeda Chemical Indus. v. Alphapharm*, 492 F.3d 1350, 1356–57 (Fed. Cir. 2007), the Federal Circuit speaking through Judge Lourie, who also authored *Dillon*, advised that the standard prima facie obviousness standard for chemical compounds would remain the same after *KSR*:

> That test for prima facie obviousness for chemical compounds is consistent with the legal principles enunciated in KSR. While the KSR Court rejected a rigid application of the teaching, suggestion, or motivation ("TSM") test in an obviousness inquiry, the Court acknowledged the importance of identifying "a reason that would have prompted a person of ordinary skill in the relevant field to combine the elements in the way the claimed new invention does" in an obviousness determination. KSR, 127 S.Ct. at 1731. Moreover, the Court indicated that there is "no necessary inconsistency between the idea underlying the TSM test and the Graham analysis." Id. As long as the test is not applied as a "rigid and mandatory" formula, that test can provide "helpful insight" to an obviousness inquiry. Id. Thus, in cases involving new chemical compounds, it remains necessary to identify some reason that would have led a chemist to modify a known compound in a particular manner to establish prima facie obviousness of a new claimed compound.

2. **But what about "obvious to try?"** The Federal Circuit and its predecessor criticized incomplete obviousness analyses for stopping at the "obvious to try" stage. Thus, in pre-*KSR* patent parlance, "obvious to try" was synonomous with "nonobvious." For instance, in *In re O'Farrell*, 853 F.2d 894, 903 (Fed. Cir. 1988), Judge Rich explained:

> In some cases, what would have been "obvious to try" would have been to vary all parameters or try each of numerous possible choices until one possibly arrived at a successful result, where the prior art gave either no indication of which parameters were critical or no direction as to which of many possible choices is likely to be successful.

KSR suggests, however, that precluding an "obvious to try" analysis might be one of the flaws in the Federal Circuit's "narrow" obviousness practice. 127 S. Ct. at 1732. In an effort to reconcile *KSR* with established patent law doctrine, the Federal Circuit examined the *KSR* case in detail:

In *KSR*, the Supreme Court noted that an invention may have been obvious "[w]hen there [was] . . . a design need or market pressure to solve a problem and there [were] . . . a finite number of identified, predictable solutions." 127 S.Ct. at 1742. The Supreme Court's analysis in *KSR* thus relies on several assumptions about the prior art landscape. First, *KSR* assumes a starting reference point or points in the art, prior to the time of invention, from which a skilled artisan might identify a problem and pursue potential solutions. Second, *KSR* presupposes that the record up to the time of invention would give some reasons, available within the knowledge of one of skill in the art, to make particular modifications to achieve the claimed compound. See *Takeda*, 492 F.3d at 1357. Third, the Supreme Court's analysis in *KSR* presumes that the record before the time of invention would supply some reasons for narrowing the prior art universe to a "finite number of identified, predictable solutions," 127 S.Ct. at 1742. In *Ortho–McNeil*, (Fed.Cir.2008), this court further explained that this "easily traversed, small and finite number of alternatives . . . might support an inference of obviousness." To the extent an art is unpredictable, as the chemical arts often are, *KSR*'s focus on these "identified, predictable solutions" may present a difficult hurdle because potential solutions are less likely to be genuinely predictable.

Esai Co. Ltd. v. Dr. Reddy's, 2008 WL 279 1884 (July 21, 2008). Thus the Federal Circuit appears to adhere to the basic concept that an invention from a prior art landscape with numerous possible choices and no parameters to narrow the search will still weigh heavily on the nonobviousness side of the scale.

    3. Methods of Making. Consider the situation of a "structurally obvious" variation where the prior art discloses a use for the prior art compound, but no operative method to make a claimed variation. Hence, because the prior art supplies no operative method known or obvious to a worker skilled in the art to make the claimed compound, this situation would compel a conclusion of nonobviousness. *See, In re Hoeksema*, 399 F.2d 269 (CCPA 1968) (N-methyl "homolog" of known amine established by affidavit as requiring inventive synthesis); see also *In re Grose*, 592 F.2d 1161 (CCPA 1979) ("the absence of a known or obvious process for making the claimed compounds overcomes a presumption that the compounds are obvious"). Should the patentability of a product be predicated on the nonobviousness of the process of making the product? If not, why not? *See* 2 MARTIN J. ADELMAN, PATENT LAW PERSPECTIVES, § 2.6[10] at notes 93, 94, and 142 (2d ed. 1991 and 2008) for a general discussion of the applicability of this rule to certain biotechnology inventions.

    4. New Uses. If a chemist invents a new chemical compound that is prima facie obvious (due to a prior art compound that teaches use of a closely related compound), should this inventor be able to overcome the obviousness problem by arguing that he discovered a new use for his compound that is far more important than the one known in the art? What if the closely related prior art compound, in fact, has the same newly discovered property? Why can't the inventor overcome the obviousness objection based on the newly discovered use? Is it proper to use unknown properties of prior art compounds to reject a claim of overcoming a prima facie obviousness rejection? Consider the following controversial analysis while thinking about these questions:

In discussing patent policy concerning product claims for chemical compositions, it is helpful to begin by remembering that there are two kinds of claims known to patent law, a claim to a physical entity (e.g., product, apparatus) and a claim to a physical activity (e.g., method, process, use). If available, an applicant, if required to make a choice, normally would want a patent on the product for which he has discovered a use rather than on a method of use because of ease of enforcement and because the product patent will cover additional uses discovered by others. In other words a product claim is easier to enforce and of greater scope. Still, the law does not require an election since both types of claims may be obtained based on the same invention, provided that the invention is one that justifies the grant of a product claim. Thus, patent law informed by policy must set standards for deciding when the discovery of a use should entitle the inventor to both a use and a product claim.

One who discovers a use for a chemical composition may not have made it for the first time. Arguably, one who discovers the first practical use for a known composition should have a good claim to a patent covering it. The public, before the inventor came along, lacked a use for it and arguably should reward the discoverer of that use with control over the composition. Yet, the law is clear that one who discovers this first use, but is not the first to create it, may not receive a product patent covering the existing product. This principle is rooted in the idea that one cannot patent what is already in existence, but it creates no barrier to a patent on a product that is structurally obvious. Such a product would be expected to have the same utility, but it is not in existence since it neither exists physically nor is it described in an enabling publication. Thus there is no legal bar to granting a patent on such a composition. The inventor has both brought the composition into existence and discovered a utility for it. Of course, the actual making of the composition may have been the routine application of well-known chemical principles, but since it did not formally exist, the question of granting a product claim to it can and should be decided based on patent policy. Here there is general agreement that granting a product patent to one who both formally brings the invention into existence and discovers a practical use for it, is sound policy for it provides considerable encouragement for the act of bringing forth and discovering a practical use of a product. This added incentive counterbalances the discouragement to third-party discovery of other uses.

The same reasoning supports permitting the discoverer of a new use for a new composition to patent that composition so long as the use discovered is, on balance, more important than the use known to the art. This would provide an added incentive to those seeking to discover new properties and at the same time, protect the public from having to pay for the known uses unless the new discovery is sufficiently important on balance to justify that imposition. The discoverer of that use should not lose his patent merely because his discovery is so broad that it embraces compositions existing in the prior art. Thus, sound public policy would have permitted Dillon, if she had chosen to do so, to overcome the *prima facie* case against her by showing that her discovery of soot reduction was far more important, both technically and commercially, that the known dewatering use.

2 MARTIN J. ADELMAN, PATENT LAW PERSPECTIVES, § 2.6[7.–3–2] at n.132 (2d ed. 1996).

§ 7.3[b] OBVIOUSNESS FOR BIOTECHNOLOGY

As already discussed, chemical arts are already a novel art field that receives somewhat novel treatment in U.S. obviousness case law. The doctrine of obviousness has placed great emphasis on structure for chemical inventions. As a matter of science, chemistry's emphasis on structure does not have the same significance for genetic engineering in the biotechnology field. Unlike chemistry with over a hundred elements and countless isotopes bonded in infinite ways, genetic engineering uses only four building blocks (the nucleotide bases, Adenine, Guanine, Cytocine, and Thymine)—always linked in two pairs. In some ways, this aspect of biotechnology more resembles computer technology—1s and 0s constantly repeating to carry a code—than chemistry. In other words, biotechnology often features code breaking skills more often than chemical structure skills. Libraries of past codes (cDNA sequences) and known cloning methods (which design a probe that will bind or hybridize with the desired cDNA sequence) are the tools of biotechnology. Chemistry's emphasis on structure, therefore, may have limitations in its application to biotechnology just as it would have limitations in application to computer technology where the "structure" of a computer program can morph from hardware structure to software code with the touch of a button.

With this cursory introduction to differences between chemistry and biotechnology, the Federal Circuit's application of chemical standards for obviousness to biotechnological inventions takes on some context.

IN RE DEUEL

United States Court of Appeals, Federal Circuit, 1995
51 F.3d 1552

Before Archer, Chief Judge, Nies and Lourie, Circuit Judges.

LOURIE, CIRCUIT JUDGE.

Thomas F. Deuel, Yue–Sheng Li, Ned R. Siegel, and Peter G. Milner (collectively "Deuel") appeal from the November 30, 1993 decision of the U.S. Patent and Trademark Office Board of Patent Appeals and Interferences affirming the examiner's final rejection of claims 4–7 of application Serial No. 07/542,232, entitled "Heparin–Binding Growth

Factor," as unpatentable on the ground of obviousness under 35 U.S.C. § 103 (1988). Because the Board erred in concluding that Deuel's claims 5 and 7 directed to specific cDNA molecules would have been obvious in light of the applied references, and no other basis exists in the record to support the rejection with respect to claims 4 and 6 generically covering all possible DNA molecules coding for the disclosed proteins, we reverse.

Background

The claimed invention relates to isolated and purified DNA and cDNA molecules encoding heparin-binding growth factors ("HBGFs"). HBGFs are proteins that stimulate mitogenic activity (cell division) and thus facilitate the repair or replacement of damaged or diseased tissue. DNA (deoxyribonucleic acid) is a generic term which encompasses an enormous number of complex macromolecules made up of nucleotide units. DNAs consist of four different nucleotides containing the nitrogenous bases adenine, guanine, cytosine, and thymine. A sequential grouping of three such nucleotides (a "codon") codes for one amino acid. A DNA's sequence of codons thus determines the sequence of amino acids assembled during protein synthesis. Since there are 64 possible codons, but only 20 natural amino acids, most amino acids are coded for by more than one codon. This is referred to as the "redundancy" or "degeneracy" of the genetic code.

DNA functions as a blueprint of an organism's genetic information. It is the major component of genes, which are located on chromosomes in the cell nucleus. Only a small part of chromosomal DNA encodes functional proteins. Messenger ribonucleic acid ("mRNA") is a similar molecule that is made or transcribed from DNA as part of the process of protein synthesis. Complementary DNA ("cDNA") is a complementary copy ("clone") of mRNA, made in the laboratory by reverse transcription of mRNA. Like mRNA, cDNA contains only the protein-encoding regions of DNA. Thus, once a cDNA's nucleotide sequence is known, the amino acid sequence of the protein for which it codes may be predicted using the genetic code relationship between codons and amino acids. The reverse is not true, however, due to the degeneracy of the code. Many other DNAs may code for a particular protein. The functional relationships between DNA, mRNA, cDNA, and a protein may conveniently be expressed as follows:

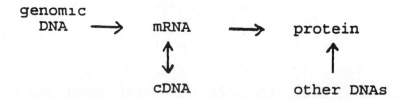

Collections ("libraries") of DNA and cDNA molecules derived from various species may be constructed in the laboratory or obtained from

commercial sources. Complementary DNA libraries contain a mixture of cDNA clones reverse-transcribed from the mRNAs found in a specific tissue source. Complementary DNA libraries are tissue-specific because proteins and their corresponding mRNAs are only made ("expressed") in specific tissues, depending upon the protein. Genomic DNA ("gDNA") libraries, by contrast, theoretically contain all of a species' chromosomal DNA. The molecules present in cDNA and DNA libraries may be of unknown function and chemical structure, and the proteins which they encode may be unknown. However, one may attempt to retrieve molecules of interest from cDNA or gDNA libraries by screening such libraries with a gene probe, which is a synthetic radiolabelled nucleic acid sequence designed to bond ("hybridize") with a target complementary base sequence. Such "gene cloning" techniques thus exploit the fact that the bases in DNA always hybridize in complementary pairs: adenine bonds with thymine and guanine bonds with cytosine. A gene probe for potentially isolating DNA or cDNA encoding a protein may be designed once the protein's amino acid sequence, or a portion thereof, is known.

As disclosed in Deuel's patent application, Deuel isolated and purified HBGF from bovine uterine tissue, found that it exhibited mitogenic activity, and determined the first 25 amino acids of the protein's N-terminal sequence. Deuel then isolated a cDNA molecule encoding bovine uterine HBGF by screening a bovine uterine cDNA library with an oligonucleotide probe designed using the experimentally determined N-terminal sequence of the HBGF. Deuel purified and sequenced the cDNA molecule, which was found to consist of a sequence of 1196 nucleotide base pairs. From the cDNA's nucleotide sequence, Deuel then predicted the complete amino acid sequence of bovine uterine HBGF disclosed in Deuel's application.

Deuel also isolated a cDNA molecule encoding human placental HBGF by screening a human placental cDNA library using the isolated bovine uterine cDNA clone as a probe. Deuel purified and sequenced the human placental cDNA clone, which was found to consist of a sequence of 961 nucleotide base pairs. From the nucleotide sequence of the cDNA molecule encoding human placental HBGF, Deuel predicted the complete amino acid sequence of human placental HBGF disclosed in Deuel's application. The predicted human placental and bovine uterine HBGFs each have 168 amino acids and calculated molecular weights of 18.9 kD. Of the 168 amino acids present in the two HBGFs discovered by Deuel, 163 are identical. Deuel's application does not describe the chemical structure of, or state how to isolate and purify, any DNA or cDNA molecule except the disclosed human placental and bovine uterine cDNAs, which are the subject of claims 5 and 7.

Claims 4–7 on appeal are all independent claims and read, in relevant part, as follows:

4. A purified and isolated DNA sequence consisting of a sequence encoding human heparin binding growth factor of 168 amino acids having the following amino acid sequence: Met Gln Ala . . . [remainder of 168 amino acid sequence].

5. The purified and isolated cDNA of human heparin-binding growth factor having the following nucleotide sequence: GTCAAAGGCA . . . [remainder of 961 nucleotide sequence].

6. A purified and isolated DNA sequence consisting of a sequence encoding bovine heparin binding growth factor of 168 amino acids having the following amino acid sequence: Met Gln Thr . . . [remainder of 168 amino acid sequence].

7. The purified and isolated cDNA of bovine heparin-binding growth factor having the following nucleotide sequence: GA-GTGGAGAG . . . [remainder of 1196 nucleotide sequence].

Claims 4 and 6 generically encompass all isolated/purified DNA sequences (natural and synthetic) encoding human and bovine HBGFs, despite the fact that Deuel's application does not describe the chemical structure of, or tell how to obtain, any DNA or cDNA except the two disclosed cDNA molecules. Because of the redundancy of the genetic code, claims 4 and 6 each encompass an enormous number of DNA molecules, including the isolated/purified chromosomal DNAs encoding the human and bovine proteins. Claims 5 and 7, on the other hand, are directed to the specifically disclosed cDNA molecules encoding human and bovine HBGFs, respectively.

During prosecution, the examiner rejected claims 4–7 under 35 U.S.C. § 103 as unpatentable over the combined teachings of Bohlen and Maniatis. The Bohlen reference discloses a group of protein growth factors designated as heparin-binding brain mitogens ("HBBMs") useful in treating burns and promoting the formation, maintenance, and repair of tissue, particularly neural tissue. Bohlen isolated three such HBBMs from human and bovine brain tissue. These proteins have respective molecular weights of 15 kD, 16 kD, and 18 kD. Bohlen determined the first 19 amino acids of the proteins' N-terminal sequences, which were found to be identical for human and bovine HBBMs. Bohlen teaches that HBBMs are brain-specific, and suggests that the proteins may be homologous between species. The reference provides no teachings concerning DNA or cDNA coding for HBBMs.

Maniatis describes a method of isolating DNAs or cDNAs by screening a DNA or cDNA library with a gene probe. The reference outlines a general technique for cloning a gene; it does not describe how to isolate a particular DNA or cDNA molecule. Maniatis does not discuss certain steps necessary to isolate a target cDNA, e.g., selecting a tissue-specific cDNA library containing a target cDNA and designing an oligonucleotide probe that will hybridize with the target cDNA.

The examiner asserted that, given Bohlen's disclosure of a heparin-binding protein and its N-terminal sequence and Maniatis's gene cloning method, it would have been prima facie obvious to one of ordinary skill in the art at the time of the invention to clone a gene for HBGF. According to the examiner, Bohlen's published N-terminal sequence would have motivated a person of ordinary skill in the art to clone such a gene because cloning the gene would allow recombinant production of HBGF, a useful protein. The examiner reasoned that a person of ordinary skill in the art could have designed a gene probe based on Bohlen's disclosed N-terminal sequence, then screened a DNA library in accordance with Maniatis's gene cloning method to isolate a gene encoding an HBGF. The examiner did not distinguish between claims 4 and 6 generically directed to all DNA sequences encoding human and bovine HBGFs and claims 5 and 7 reciting particular cDNAs.

In reply, Deuel argued, inter alia, that Bohlen teaches away from the claimed cDNA molecules because Bohlen suggests that HBBMs are brain-specific and, thus, a person of ordinary skill in the art would not have tried to isolate corresponding cDNA clones from human placental and bovine uterine cDNA libraries. The examiner made the rejection final, however, asserting that

> [t]he starting materials are not relevant in this case, because it was well known in the art at the time the invention was made that proteins, especially the general class of heparin binding proteins, are highly homologous between species and tissue type. It would have been entirely obvious to attempt to isolate a known protein from different tissue types and even different species.

No prior art was cited to support the proposition that it would have been obvious to screen human placental and bovine uterine cDNA libraries for the claimed cDNA clones. Presumably, the examiner was relying on Bohlen's suggestion that HBBMs may be homologous between species, although the examiner did not explain how homology between species suggests homology between tissue types.

The Board affirmed the examiner's final rejection. In its opening remarks, the Board noted that it is "constantly advised by the patent examiners, who are highly skilled in this art, that cloning procedures are routine in the art." According to the Board, "the examiners urge that when the sequence of a protein is placed into the public domain, the gene is also placed into the public domain because of the routine nature of cloning techniques." Addressing the rejection at issue, the Board determined that Bohlen's disclosure of the existence and isolation of HBBM, a functional protein, would also advise a person of ordinary skill in the art that a gene exists encoding HBBM. The Board found that a person of ordinary skill in the art would have been motivated to isolate such a gene because the protein has useful mitogenic properties, and isolating the gene for HBBM would permit large quantities of the protein to be produced for study and possible commercial use. Like the examiner, the Board asserted, without explanation, that HBBMs are the same as HBGFs and that the genes encoding these proteins are identical. The Board concluded that "the Bohlen reference would have suggested to those of ordinary skill in this art that they should make the gene, and the Maniatis reference would have taught a technique for 'making' the gene with a reasonable expectation of success." Responding to Deuel's argument that the claimed cDNA clones were isolated from human placental and bovine uterine cDNA libraries, whereas the combined teachings of Bohlen and Maniatis would only have suggested screening a brain tissue cDNA library, the Board stated that "the claims before us are directed to the product and not the method of isolation. Appellants have not shown that the claimed DNA was not present in and could not have been readily isolated from the brain tissue utilized by Bohlen." Deuel now appeals.

DISCUSSION

On appeal, Deuel challenges the Board's determination that the applied references establish a prima facie case of obviousness. In response, the PTO maintains that the claimed invention would have been prima facie obvious over the combined teachings of Bohlen and Maniatis. Thus, the appeal raises the important question whether the combination of a prior art reference teaching a method of gene cloning, together with a reference disclosing a partial amino acid sequence of a protein, may render DNA and cDNA molecules encoding the protein prima facie obvious under § 103.

Deuel argues that the PTO failed to follow the proper legal standard in determining that the claimed cDNA molecules would have been prima facie obvious despite the lack of structurally similar compounds in the prior art. Deuel argues that the PTO has not cited a reference teaching cDNA molecules, but instead has improperly rejected the claims based on the alleged obviousness of a method of making the molecules. We agree.

Because Deuel claims new chemical entities in structural terms, a prima facie case of unpatentability requires that the teachings of the prior art suggest the claimed compounds to a person of ordinary skill in the art. Normally a prima facie case of obviousness is based upon structural similarity, i.e., an established structural relationship between a prior art compound and the claimed compound. Structural relationships may provide the requisite motivation or suggestion to modify known compounds to obtain new compounds. For example, a prior art compound may suggest its homologs because homologs often have similar properties and therefore chemists of ordinary skill would ordinarily contemplate making them to try to obtain compounds with improved properties. Similarly, a known compound may suggest its analogs or isomers, either geometric isomers (cis v. trans) or position isomers (e.g., ortho v. para).

In all of these cases, however, the prior art teaches a specific, structurally-definable compound and the question becomes whether the prior art would have suggested making the specific molecular modifications necessary to achieve the claimed invention.

Here, the prior art does not disclose any relevant cDNA molecules, let alone close relatives of the specific, structurally-defined cDNA molecules of claims 5 and 7 that might render them obvious. Maniatis suggests an allegedly obvious process for trying to isolate cDNA molecules, but that, as we will indicate below, does not fill the gap regarding the subject matter of claims 5 and 7. Further, while the general idea of the claimed molecules, their function, and their general chemical nature may have been obvious from Bohlen's teachings, and the knowledge that some gene existed may have been clear, the precise cDNA molecules of claims 5 and 7 would not have been obvious over the Bohlen reference because Bohlen teaches proteins, not the claimed or closely related cDNA molecules. The redundancy of the genetic code precluded contemplation of or focus on the specific cDNA molecules of claims 5 and 7. Thus, one could not have conceived the subject matter of claims 5 and 7 based on the teachings in the cited prior art because, until the claimed molecules were actually isolated and purified, it would have been highly unlikely for one of ordinary skill in the art to contemplate what was ultimately obtained. What cannot be contemplated or conceived cannot be obvious.

The PTO's theory that one might have been motivated to try to do what Deuel in fact accomplished amounts to speculation and an impermissible hindsight reconstruction of the claimed invention. It also ignores the fact that claims 5 and 7 are limited to specific compounds, and any motivation that existed was a general one, to try to obtain a gene that was yet undefined and may have constituted many forms. A general motivation to search for some gene that exists does not necessarily make obvious a specifically-defined gene that is subsequently obtained as a result of that search. More is needed and it is not found here.

The genetic code relationship between proteins and nucleic acids does not overcome the deficiencies of the cited references. A prior art disclosure of the amino acid sequence of a protein does not necessarily render particular DNA molecules encoding the protein obvious because the redundancy of the genetic code permits one to hypothesize an enormous number of DNA sequences coding for the protein. No particular one of these DNAs can be obvious unless there is something in the prior art to lead to the particular DNA and indicate that it should be prepared. We recently held in *In re Baird*, 16 F.3d 380 (Fed.Cir.1994), that a broad genus does not necessarily render obvious each compound within its scope. Similarly, knowledge of a protein does not give one a conception of a particular DNA encoding it. Thus, a fortiori, Bohlen's disclosure of the N-terminal portion of a protein, which the PTO urges is the same as HBGF, would not have suggested the particular cDNA molecules defined by claims 5 and 7. This is so even though one skilled in the art knew that some DNA, albeit not in purified and isolated form, did exist. The compounds of claims 5 and 7 are specific compounds not suggested by the prior art. A different result might pertain, however, if there were prior art, e.g., a protein of sufficiently small size and simplicity, so that lacking redundancy, each possible DNA would be obvious over the protein. See *In re Petering*, 301 F.2d 676 (CCPA 1962) (prior art reference disclosing limited genus of 20 compounds rendered every species within the genus unpatentable). That is not the case here.

The PTO's focus on known methods for potentially isolating the claimed DNA molecules is also misplaced because the claims at issue define compounds, not methods. See *In re Bell*, 991 F.2d 781, 785 (Fed.Cir.1993). In *Bell*, the PTO asserted a rejection based upon the combination of a primary reference disclosing a protein (and its complete amino acid sequence) with a secondary reference describing a general method of gene cloning. We reversed the rejection, holding in part that "[t]he PTO's focus on Bell's method is misplaced. Bell does not claim a method. Bell claims compositions, and the issue is the obviousness of the claimed compositions, not of the method by which they are made." Id.

We today reaffirm the principle, stated in *Bell*, that the existence of a general method of isolating cDNA or DNA molecules is essentially irrelevant to the question whether the specific molecules themselves would have been obvious, in the absence of other prior art that suggests the claimed DNAs. A prior art disclosure of a process reciting a particular compound or obvious variant thereof as a product of the process is, of course, another matter, raising issues of anticipation under 35 U.S.C. § 102 as well as obviousness under § 103. Moreover, where there is prior art that suggests a claimed compound, the existence, or lack thereof, of an enabling process for making that compound is surely a factor in any patentability determination. See *In re Brown*, 329 F.2d 1006 (CCPA 1964) (reversing rejection for lack of an enabling method of making the claimed compound). There must, however, still be prior art that suggests the claimed compound in order for a prima facie case of obviousness to be made out; as we have already indicated, that prior art was lacking here with respect to claims 5 and 7. Thus, even if, as the examiner stated, the existence of general cloning techniques, coupled with knowledge of a protein's structure, might have provided motivation to prepare a cDNA or made it obvious to prepare a cDNA, that does not necessarily make obvious a particular claimed cDNA. "Obvious to try" has long been held not to constitute obviousness. *In re O'Farrell*, 853 F.2d 894, 903 (Fed.Cir.1988). A general incentive does not make obvious a particular result, nor does the existence of techniques by which those efforts can be carried out. Thus, Maniatis's teachings, even in combination with Bohlen, fail to suggest the claimed invention.

The PTO argues that a compound may be defined by its process of preparation and therefore that a conceived process for making or isolating it provides a definition for it and can render it obvious. It cites *Amgen, Inc. v. Chugai Pharmaceutical Co.*, 927 F.2d 1200 (Fed.Cir.1991), for that proposition. We disagree. The fact that one can conceive a general process in advance for preparing an undefined compound does not mean that a claimed specific compound was precisely envisioned and therefore obvious. A substance may indeed be defined by its process of preparation. That occurs, however, when it has already been prepared by that process and one therefore knows that the result of that process is the stated compound. The process is part of the definition of the compound. But that is not possible in advance, especially when the hypothetical process is only a general one. Thus, a conceived method of preparing some undefined DNA does not define it with the precision necessary to render it obvious over the protein it encodes. We did not state otherwise in *Amgen*. See *Amgen*, 927 F.2d at 1206–09 (isolated/purified human gene held nonobvious; no conception of gene without envisioning its precise identity despite conception of general process of preparation).

We conclude that, because the applied references do not teach or suggest the claimed cDNA molecules, the final rejection of claims 5 and 7 must be reversed. See also *Bell*, 991 F.2d at 784–85(human DNA sequences encoding IGF proteins nonobvious over asserted combination of references showing gene cloning method and complete amino acid sequences of IGFs).

Claims 4 and 6 are of a different scope than claims 5 and 7. As is conceded by Deuel, they generically encompass all DNA sequences encoding human and bovine HBGFs. Written in such a result-oriented form, claims 4 and 6 are thus tantamount to the general idea of all genes encoding the protein, all solutions to the problem. Such an idea might have been obvious from the complete amino acid sequence of the protein, coupled with knowledge of the genetic code, because this information may have enabled a person of ordinary skill in the art to envision the idea of, and, perhaps with the aid of a computer, even identify all members of the claimed genus. The Bohlen reference, however, only discloses a partial amino acid sequence, and thus it appears that, based on the above analysis, the claimed genus would not have been obvious over this prior art disclosure. We will therefore also reverse the final rejection of claims 4 and 6 because neither the Board nor the patent examiner articulated any separate reasons for holding these claims unpatentable apart from the grounds discussed above.

The Board's decision affirming the final rejection of claims 4–7 is reversed.

REVERSED.

NOTES

1. **What is the Obviousness Standard After *Deuel*?** What exactly did the inventor Deuel contribute to the art that supported the grant of a patent? Would you agree with the proposition that the Federal Circuit in *Deuel* eliminated the need to consider § 103 where the claim is directed to a gene

coding for a protein? If so, is there any public policy that you would assert supports this elimination of the obviousness requirement? In view of the redundancy of the genetic code, is a patent on the actual gene used in nature of any practical value?

Did *Deuel* overlook a prior and better test for obviousness in a biotech setting, namely *In re O'Farrell*, 853 F.2d 894 (Fed.Cir.1988). In *O'Farrell*, Judge Rich stated: "[A]ll that is required [for obviousness] is a reasonable expectation of success." 853 F.2d at 903–04. The *O'Farrell* court then acknowledged the processes that produce biotechnological inventions rather than deeming them "irrelevant" as in *Deuel*. On what basis can the Federal Circuit deem "a general method of isolating cDNA or DNA molecules ... essentially irrelevant to the question of whether the specific molecules themselves would have been obvious?" What would a biotechnologist use other than the methods and tools of biotechnology to obtain the claimed molecules? In any event, the *Deuel* rule is unique to the United States.

2. Dueling Views About *Deuel* and *KSR*. Is *Deuel* still good law after *KSR*? The USPTO Board has called this holding into doubt:

> To the extent *Deuel* is considered relevant to this case, we note the Supreme Court recently cast doubt on the viability of *Deuel* to the extent the Federal Circuit rejected an "obvious to try" test. Under *KSR*, it's now apparent "obvious to try" may be an appropriate test in more situations than we previously contemplated.

Ex parte Kubin, 83 U.S.P.Q.2d 1410, 1414 (Bd. Pat. App. & Int'f 2007). Yet the Federal Circuit has held that *Deuel* "is consistent with the legal principles enunciated in *KSR*." *Takeda Chem. Indus., Ltd. v. Alphapharm Pty., Ltd.*, 492 F.3d 1350, 1356 (Fed. Cir. 2007). Which entity has the better of this argument?

3. More About Product Claims Supported by a Nonobvious Method. In Note 3 after *In re Dillon*, a question is raised regarding the appropriateness of basing the patentability of chemical compounds on their method of manufacture. Assume you agree that *In re Hoeksema* was wrongly decided, does it follow that one should not be able to argue that a gene is nonobvious based on the fact that the method for discovering it was itself nonobvious. For an argument that genes are a special case see 2 MARTIN J. ADELMAN, PATENT LAW PERSPECTIVES, § 2.6[7.–2] at n.183 (2d ed. 1993) where the author states:

> The essential differences between discovering genes and discovering obviously desirable products arises because ordinarily one must practice the unobvious process to make the obviously desirable product. Take, for example, a claim to a purified protein made by an unobvious purification process. To make more of the protein, this process must be used. However, once one isolates a gene by an unobvious method, the gene can be used and cloned without limit without infringing a claim to the process of isolating the gene. Therefore, to give meaningful protection to this unobvious discovery product protection is required.

§ 7.4 PRIOR ART FOR OBVIOUSNESS

Conveniently for the student who has just considered novelty, discussion of whether a particular prior art reference is eligible to destroy the nonobviousness of a claimed invention is also framed within the categories set forth in § 102. Thus, the question courts have posed is whether technology described within, say, § 102(b), applies not only to a novelty analysis but also towards nonobviousness under § 103(a). Even more pleasantly, the case law has developed a general answer: with one significant qualification, art that applies to the novelty determination also applies for nonobviousness. So, it is often possible to take the same group of references relevant for novelty, and by combining them or looking past the contents of a single reference, undertake the nonobviousness inquiry.

Although this issue is now more settled for the dominant prior art categories, study of the contours of the prior art for § 103(a) remains interesting for some additional reasons. First, the cases have carved out a few narrowly defined exceptions where art that applies for novelty purposes does not apply for nonobviousness. Second, as an historical matter, the United States patent system has not always embraced each of the § 102 categories in the context of nonobviousness. The case law instead includes crucial points of departure that map the policy debate regarding the proper "scope and content of the prior art" of § 103(a). Finally, patent systems abroad have not always made the same choices as the United States when resolving issues pertaining to inventive step. An understanding of these differences is both worthwhile as a practical matter and an acknowledgment of the difficulties future harmonization efforts must face.

The significant qualification noted above relates to the additional requirement that a reference spring from a so-called "analogous" art in order to be considered pertinent for nonobviousness. Thus, the availability of a technology under § 102 is a necessary, but not sufficient condition for it to apply to an analysis under § 103(a). The technology must also issue from a technical discipline that is relevant to the claimed invention. The determination of whether an art is analogous to that of the claimed invention, and therefore a potential source of prior art for purposes of nonobviousness, is taken up later in this Chapter.

To set the stage for the next judicial opinion, consider the following hypothetical. Suppose that an inventor files an application at the PTO on June 1, 2009. The USPTO rejects the application, reasoning that the claimed invention would have been obvious in view of a journal article published on May 1, 2008—a reference that plainly qualifies as prior art under § 102(b). The applicant responds by demonstrating a date of invention of April 1, 2008, and by observing that § 103(a) calls for the obviousness analysis to occur "at the time the invention was made...." Because the journal article was published subsequent to the date of invention, the applicant contends, it should not qualify as prior art for purpose of obviousness. Who has the better of the argument? The CCPA answered that question in its *Foster* opinion.

§ 7.4[a] PRIOR ART UNDER SECTION 102

IN RE FOSTER

Court of Customs and Patent Appeals, 1965
343 F.2d 980

Before Worley, Chief Judge, and Rich, Martin, Smith and Almond, Judges.

ALMOND, JUDGE.

This is an appeal from the decision of the Board of Appeals affirming the rejection of the claims in appellant's patent application.

Because of the importance of the question to the law of patents, we have deemed it desirable to reconsider what is the statutory basis of this "unpatentable over" or obviousness type of rejection, such as we have here and had before us in [*In re Palmquist*, 319 F.2d 547 (CCPA 1963),] under the circumstance that the reference or references have effective dates more than one year prior to the filing date of the applicant. More specifically, we have reconsidered the result again urged on us here, as allegedly authorized by section 103, that a reference having a date more than a year prior to the filing date may be disposed of by showing an invention date prior to the reference date, contrary to the express provision in Patent Office Rule 131.

[Section 102(b)] presents a sort of statute of limitations, formerly two years, now one year, within which an inventor, even though he has made a patentable invention, must act on penalty of loss of his right to patent. What starts the period running is clearly the availability of the invention to the public through the categories of disclosure enumerated in 102(b), which include "a printed publication" anywhere describing the invention. There appears to be no dispute about the operation of this statute in "complete anticipation" situations but the contention seems to be that 102(b) has no applicability where the invention is not completely disclosed in a single patent or publication, that is to say where the rejection involves the addition to the disclosure of the reference of the ordinary skill of the art or the disclosure of another reference which indicates what those of ordinary skill in the art are presumed to know, and to have known for more than a year before the application was filed. Upon a complete reexamination of this matter, we are convinced that the contention is contrary to the policy consideration which motivated the enactment by Congress of a statutory bar. On logic and principle we think this contention is unsound, and we also believe it is contrary to the patent law as it has actually existed since at least 1898.

First, as to principle, since the purpose of the statute has always been to require filing of the application within the prescribed period after the time the public came into possession of the invention, we cannot see that it makes any difference how it came into such possession, whether by a public use, a sale, a single patent or publication, or by combinations of one or more of the foregoing. In considering this principle we assume, of course, that by these means the invention has become obvious to that segment of the "public" having ordinary skill in the art. Once this has happened, the purpose of the law is to give the inventor only a year within which to file and this would seem to be liberal treatment. Whenever an applicant undertakes, under Rule 131, to swear back of a reference having an effective date more than a year before his filing date, he is automatically conceding that he made his invention more than a year before he filed. If the reference contains enough disclosure to make his invention obvious, the principle of the statute would seem to require denial of a patent to him. The same is true where a combination of two publications or patents makes the invention obvious and they both have dates more than a year before the filing date.

As to dealing with the express language of 102(b), for example, "described in a printed publication," technically, we see no reason to so read the words of the statute as to preclude the use of more than one reference; nor do we find in the context anything to show that "a printed publication" cannot include two or more printed publications. We do not have two publications here, but we did in *Palmquist*, and it is a common situation.

As to what the law has been, more particularly what it was prior to 1953, when the new patent act and its section 103 became effective, there is a paucity of direct precedents on the precise problem. We think there is a reason for this. Under the old law (R.S. § 4886, where 102(b) finds its origin) patents were refused or invalidated on references dated more than a year before the filing date because the invention was anticipated or, if they were not, then because there was no "invention," the latter rejection being based either on (a) a single nonanticipatory reference plus the skill of the art or (b) on a plurality of references. There was no need to seek out the precise statutory basis because it was R.S. § 4886 in any event, read in the light of the Supreme Court's interpretation of the law that there must always be "invention." This issue was determined on the disclosures of the references relied on and if they had dates more than one year before the filing date, it was assumed they could be relied on to establish a "statutory bar." There was an express prohibition in Rule 131 and in its predecessor Rule 75 against antedating a reference having a date more than a year prior to the filing date and there was no basis on which to contest it. The accepted state of law is exemplified by the following sentences in MCCRADY'S PATENT OFFICE PRACTICE, 4th ed. (1959), Sec. 127, p. 176:

"Prior art specified by 35 USC 102, which has an effective date more than one year prior to the effective filing date of an application, constitutes a bar under the language of that statute. Until 1940 the period was two years."

"Procedurally, the significance of the statutory bar lies in the fact that it cannot be antedated by evidence of applicant's earlier invention, as by affidavits under Rule 131, or by evidence presented in an infringement suit."

Our decision in *Palmquist* appears to have been the first to hold otherwise.

It would seem that the practical operation of the prior law was that references having effective dates more than a year before applicant's filing date were always considered to be effective as references, regardless of the applicant's date of invention, and that rejections were then predicated thereon for "lack of invention" without making the distinction which we now seem to see as implicit in sections 102 and 103, "anticipation" or no novelty situations under 102 and "obviousness" situations under 103. But on further reflection, we now feel bound to point out that of equal importance is the question of loss of right predicated on a one-year time-bar which, it seems clear to us, has never been limited to "anticipation" situations, involving only a single reference, but has included as well "no invention" (now "obviousness") situations. It follows that where the time-bar is involved, the actual date of invention becomes irrelevant and that it is not in accordance with either the letter or the principle of the law, or its past interpretation over a very long period, to permit an applicant to dispose of a reference having a date more than one year prior to his filing date by proving his actual date of invention.

Such a result was permitted by our decision in *Palmquist* and to the extent that it permitted a reference, having a publication date more than one year prior to the United States filing date to which the applicant was entitled, to be disposed of by proof of a date of invention earlier than the date of the reference, that decision is hereby overruled.

NOTES

1. **Extending the Impact of § 102(b).** As a stepdaughter of the first-to-invent regime, § 102(b) works to spur inventors to file patent applications. If an inventor places a technology within the public domain, or observes that his invention is publicly available, then he is charged with a prompt application to preserve his patent rights. Why should this purpose impact § 103(a) art at all? Should inventors be charged with making their own nonobviousness determinations when deciding whether to apply for patent rights or not? Does this case support the view that § 102(b)'s primary function is to remedy a defect in the first-to-invent system by creating certain prior art that does not depend on when the patented invention was made?

2. **The Other Prior Art Categories.** The courts have never questioned that subject matter qualifying as prior art under § 102(a) may be considered for

purposes of the obviousness analysis. By extension, prior art under §§ 102(f) and (g) has also been deemed appropriate to consider under § 103(a). *See OddzOn Products, Inc. v. Just Toys, Inc.*, 122 F.3d 1396 (Fed. Cir. 1997). The Supreme Court has concluded that § 102(e) art may be used in the obviousness analysis as well. *See Hazeltine Research, Inc. v. Brenner*, 382 U.S. 252 (1965).

Prior art under § 102(d) rarely impacts the nonobviousness determination under § 103(a). International circumstances already result in infrequent resort to § 102(d); additionally, circumstances where an inventor files a United States application sufficiently different from an earlier foreign application to raise obviousness questions would be relatively rare. *See* Gerald Sobel, *Prior Art and Obviousness*, 47 J. Pat. Off. Soc'y 79, 84 (1965). However, the policy underpinnings of the § 102(b)—the encouragement of prompt filing—also largely inform § 102(d). Does *Foster*'s treatment of § 102(b) therefore allow any inferences to be drawn about the prior art effect of § 102(d) for obviousness determinations? Compare the dicta in the CCPA decision in *In re Bass, infra,* with the view of the Patent Office in *Ex Parte Appeal No. 242–47*, 196 U.S.P.Q. 828 (Pat. & Tr. Bd.App.1976).

3. *In re Bass* and § 103(c). The rather complex provision codified at § 103(c) originated as a congressional response to *In re Bass*, 474 F.2d 1276 (CCPA 1973). There, co-inventors Bass, Jenkins, and Horvat had applied for a patent on an air control system for carding machines. Their effective filing date was October 11, 1965. The PTO rejected their claims on the ground of nonobviousness, and following an appeal the CCPA affirmed. Among the references cited were two patents: a patent granted to Bass and Horvat, which had matured from an application filed on August 23, 1965; and a patent issued to Jenkins, based on an October 13, 1964, application.

The correspondence of inventor surnames between the application and the prior art patents was not a coincidence. In fact, the PTO and CCPA cited the earlier work of Bass, Jenkins and Horvat against them. They did so following the traditional patent law principle that each new combination of joint inventors constitutes a distinct inventive entity. This principle holds even where these combinations share individual inventors. For example, the joint inventors Bass, Jenkins and Horvat were considered a different inventive entity than the team of Bass and Horvat. Each group of natural persons essentially acquires its own legal identity; they, as a whole, constitute "the inventor" of that technology.

In re Bass demonstrated that the setting of contemporary technology development may lead to harsh results when corporations file patent applications. Where one corporation employs numerous experts to engage in collaborative research and development efforts, the shifting composition of inventive teams can result in rather strained holdings of nonobviousness. Ordinarily, the patent statute establishes that an inventor's own prior inventive efforts may not anticipate a subsequent patent application. For example, in § 102(g), the invention must be made by "another" to serve as prior art. But since legally distinct inventors result from different inventive entities, an anticipation rejection is possible even if only a slight change in personnel occurs. In a particularly fertile and interactive corporate research department, inventors could find themselves unable to obtain patents due to "in-house" rejections for obviousness based upon efforts by their peers, and even in part by themselves!

Congress enacted § 103(c)(1) to solve the problem highlighted in *In re Bass*. As amended in 1999, this provision read:

> Subject matter developed by another person, which qualifies as prior art only under subsection (e), (f) or (g) of section 102 of this title, shall not preclude patentability under this section where the subject matter and the claimed invention were, at the time the invention was made, owned by the same person or subject to an obligation of assignment to the same person.

The workings of § 103(c)(1) can prove elusive, but an example should lend some clarity to its provisions. Suppose that two inventors, Ryu and Yuko, each work for the Yoshida Corporation. As part of their employment contracts, Ryu and Yuko have agreed to assign inventions that they develop to the Yoshida Corporation. Ryu conceives of a new ultrasonic diagnosing apparatus on December 15, 2008. He immediately informs Yuko about his idea. Working diligently in his laboratory, Ryu reduces the invention to practice on January 31, 2009. The Yoshida Corporation files a patent application on Ryu's behalf on March 1, 2001. The Ryu patent issues on October 23, 2010.

On March 17, 2009, Yuko realizes that she can improve upon Ryu's ultrasonic diagnosing apparatus. Because of her workload, she does not start on the project until April 7, 2009. Without further consulting Ryu, she ultimately completes her ultrasonic diagnosing apparatus on May 20, 2009. Although Yuko's invention represents an improvement over Ryu's ultrasonic diagnosing apparatus, it would have been obvious in light of the Ryu apparatus. The Yoshida Corporation files a patent application on behalf of Yuko on October 1, 2009.

Under these facts, the Ryu patent cannot serve as prior art against Yuko. The statutory bars of § 102(b) and (d) are not triggered here. There is also no indication that Ryu's invention was "known or used by others" within the meaning of § 102(a), given the judicial requirement of a public knowledge or use. If § 103(c) were not available, the Ryu patent would constitute prior art under § 102(e) because Yuko's invention date occurred after the Ryu application was filed. Absent § 103(c), the Ryu patent would also serve as prior art under § 102(f) because Yuko derived a obvious variation of her invention from Ryu. Further, without § 103(c) Ryu's work would be available under § 102(g), Ryu both conceived and reduced his invention to practice prior to Yuko's conception date. However, because § 103(c) exempts § 102(e), (f) and (g) art from the nonobviousness inquiry where the inventions were subject to an common obligation of assignment, the Yoshida Corporation may obtain patents on both the Ryu and Yuko inventions.

Section 103(c)(1) is a narrowly worded provision. If a reference is otherwise available as prior art, such as under § 102(a) or (b), then it remains pertinent to § 103(a). Also recall that § 103(c)(1) solely concerns nonobviousness. It does not affect the availability of prior art for purposes of anticipation.

Congress established § 103(c)(2) via the Cooperative Research and Technology Enhancement Act of 2004, more commonly known as the CREATE Act.

That provision acts similarly to § 103(c)(1), allowing a patent applicant or proprietor to disqualify subject matter arising from collaborative research ventures as prior art if that subject matter qualifies solely under § 102(e), (f), or (g). In particular, a claimed invention and subject matter developed by a another person are deemed to be jointly owned if (A) the claimed invention was made by or on behalf of parties to a joint research agreement that was in effect on or before the date the claimed invention was made; (B) the claimed invention was made as a result of activities undertaken within the scope of the joint research agreement; and (C) the application for patent for the claimed invention discloses or is amended to disclose the names of the parties to the joint research agreement.

§ 7.4[b]   ANALOGOUS ARTS

Simply because a technology is available under § 102 is not enough to render it applicable to the nonobviousness determination. The technology must also issue from an "analogous art"—a technical area judged sufficiently germane to that of the claimed invention. Thus, although a person of skill in a given technical area is presumed to have access to all of the technical knowledge comprising the state of the art, this knowledge can only be employed within the constraints of the abilities and expertise of practitioners within that field. The next decision considers the standard of pertinence for prior art in the obviousness equation.

IN RE CLAY

United States Court of Appeals, Federal Circuit, 1992
966 F.2d 656

Before Plager, Lourie, and Clevenger, Circuit Judges.

Lourie, Circuit Judge.

Carl D. Clay appeals the decision of the United States Patent and Trademark Office, Board of Patent Appeals and Interferences, Appeal No. 90–2262, affirming the rejection of claims 1–11 and 13 as being unpatentable under 35 U.S.C. § 103. These are all the remaining claims in application Serial No. 245,083, filed April 28, 1987, entitled "Storage of a Refined Liquid Hydrocarbon Product." We reverse.

[handwritten margin notes:] Appeal of PTO and Board of Patent Appeals

Appeal reversed.

Filed April 28 1987

Storage of Refined Liquid Hydrocarbon Product.

BACKGROUND

Fig. 1

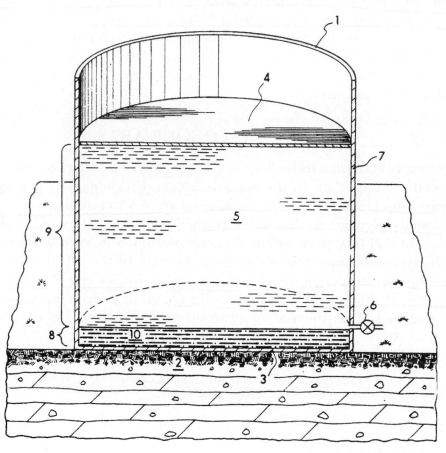

Clay's invention, assigned to Marathon Oil Company, is a process for storing refined liquid hydrocarbon product in a storage tank having a dead volume between the tank bottom and its outlet port. The process involves preparing a gelation solution which gels after it is placed in the tank's dead volume; the gel can easily be removed by adding to the tank a gel-degrading agent such as hydrogen peroxide.

Two prior art references were applied against the claims on appeal. They were U.S. Patent 4,664,294 (Hetherington), which discloses an apparatus for displacing dead space liquid using impervious bladders, or large bags, formed with flexible membranes; and U.S. Patent 4,683,949 (Sydansk), also assigned to Clay's assignee, Marathon Oil Company, which discloses a process for reducing the permeability of hydrocarbon-bearing formations and thus improving oil production, using a gel similar to that in Clay's invention.

[handwritten margin notes: Clay assigned to Marathon Oil Company process for storing refined liquid hydrocarbon product in a storage tank; two prior arts; liquid bladders and process to reduce permeability of oil using a gel; why gel to remove dead space]

The Board agreed with the examiner that, although neither reference alone describes Clay's invention, Hetherington and Sydansk combined support a conclusion of obviousness. It held that one skilled in the art would glean from Hetherington that Clay's invention "was appreciated in the prior art and solutions to that problem generally involved filling the dead space with something."

The Board also held that Sydansk would have provided one skilled in the art with information that a gelation system would have been impervious to hydrocarbons once the system gelled. The Board combined the references, finding that the "cavities" filled by Sydansk are sufficiently similar to the "volume or void space" being filled by Hetherington for one of ordinary skill to have recognized the applicability of the gel to Hetherington.

DISCUSSION

The issue presented in this appeal is whether the Board's conclusion was correct that Clay's invention would have been obvious from the combined teachings of Hetherington and Sydansk. Although this conclusion is one of law, such determinations are made against a background of several factual inquiries, one of which is the scope and content of the prior art.

A prerequisite to making this finding is determining what is "prior art," in order to consider whether "the differences between the subject matter sought to be patented and the prior art are such that the subject matter as a whole would have been obvious at the time the invention was made to a person having ordinary skill in the art." 35 U.S.C. § 103. Although § 103 does not, by its terms, define the "art to which [the] subject matter [sought to be patented] pertains," this determination is frequently couched in terms of whether the art is analogous or not, i.e., whether the art is "too remote to be treated as prior art." *In re Sovish*, 769 F.2d 738, 741 (Fed.Cir.1985).

Clay argues that the claims at issue were improperly rejected over Hetherington and Sydansk, because Sydansk is nonanalogous art. Whether a reference in the prior art is "analogous" is a fact question. Thus, we review the Board's decision on this point under the clearly erroneous standard.

Two criteria have evolved for determining whether prior art is analogous: (1) whether the art is from the same field of endeavor, regardless of the problem addressed, and (2) if the reference is not within the field of the inventor's endeavor, whether the reference still is reasonably pertinent to the particular problem with which the inventor is involved.

The Board found Sydansk to be within the field of Clay's endeavor because, as the Examiner stated, "one of ordinary skill in the art would certainly glean from [Sydansk] that the rigid gel as taught therein would have a number of applications within the manipulation of the storage and processing of hydrocarbon liquids ... [and that] the gel as taught in Sydansk would be expected to function in a similar manner as the bladders in the Hetherington patent." These findings are clearly erroneous.

The PTO argues that Sydansk and Clay's inventions are part of a common endeavor—"maximizing withdrawal of petroleum stored in petroleum reservoirs." However, Sydansk cannot be considered to be within Clay's field of endeavor merely because both relate to the petroleum industry. Sydansk teaches the use of a gel in unconfined and irregular volumes within generally underground natural oil-bearing formations to channel flow in a desired direction; Clay teaches the introduction of gel to the confined dead volume of a man-made storage tank. The Sydansk process operates in extreme conditions, with petroleum formation temperatures as high as 115 degrees C and at significant well bore pressures; Clay's process apparently operates at ambient temperature and atmospheric pressure. Clay's field of endeavor is the storage of refined liquid hydrocarbons. The field of endeavor of Sydansk's invention, on the other hand, is the extraction of crude petroleum. The Board clearly erred in considering Sydansk to be within the same field of endeavor as Clay's.

Even though the art disclosed in Sydansk is not within Clay's field of endeavor, the reference may still properly be combined with Hetherington if it is reasonably pertinent to the problem Clay attempts to solve. A reference is reasonably pertinent if, even though it may be in a different field from that of the inventor's endeavor, it is one which, because of the matter with which it deals, logically would have commended itself to an inventor's attention in considering his problem. Thus, the purposes of both the invention and the prior art are important in determining whether the reference is reasonably pertinent to the problem the invention attempts to solve. If a reference disclosure has the same purpose as the claimed invention, the reference relates to the same problem, and that fact supports use of that reference in an obviousness rejection. An inventor may well have been motivated to consider the reference when making his invention. If it is directed to a different purpose, the inventor would accordingly have had less motivation or occasion to consider it.

Sydansk's gel treatment of underground formations functions to fill anomalies so as to improve flow profiles and sweep efficiencies of injection and production fluids through a formation, while Clay's gel functions to displace liquid product from the dead volume of a storage tank. Sydansk is concerned with plugging formation anomalies so that fluid is subsequently diverted by the gel into the formation matrix, thereby forcing bypassed oil contained in the matrix toward a production well. Sydansk is faced with the problem of recovering oil from rock, i.e., from a matrix which is porous, permeable sedimentary rock of a subterranean formation where water has channeled through formation anomalies and bypassed oil present in the matrix. Such a problem is not reasonably pertinent to the particular problem with which Clay was involved—preventing loss of stored product to tank dead volume while preventing contamination of such product. Moreover, the subterranean formation of Sydansk is not structurally similar to, does not operate under the same temperature and pressure as, and does not function like Clay's storage tanks. *See In re Ellis*, 476 F.2d 1370, 1372 (CCPA 1973) ("the similarities and differences in structure and function of the invention disclosed in the references ... carry far greater weight [in determining analogy]").

A person having ordinary skill in the art would not reasonably have expected to solve the problem of dead volume in tanks for storing refined petroleum by considering a reference dealing with plugging underground formation anomalies. The Board's finding to the contrary is clearly erroneous. Since Sydansk is non-analogous art, the rejection over Hetherington in view of Sydansk cannot be sustained.

NOTES

1. **Pertinent Prior Art.** Why need the patent law go to these lengths to distinguish analogous technical fields from nonpertinent prior art? Recall that novelty determination has no test of relevance; novelty-defeating technology can come from a technical fields very distant from that of the claimed invention. Why should nonobviousness differ from novelty in this respect?

2. **The Patent Office Classification Scheme.** The United States Patent and Trademark Office maintains a patent classification system to assist examiners in their searches of the prior art. Should this regime carry weight in determining whether prior art is analogous or not to the claimed invention? Most courts lend the PTO system some credence in this determination, but do not make it conclusive. As noted in *In re Mlot–Fijalkowski*, 676 F.2d 666 (CCPA 1982): "Such evidence is inherently weak ... because considerations in forming a classification system differ from those relating to a person of ordinary skill seeking solution for a particular problem."

3. **Analogous Simple Mechanical Arts.** The breadth of knowledge embraced within the simple mechanical arts often leads to surprising results in patent cases. In *Sage Products Inc. v. Devon Industries Inc.*, 880 F.Supp. 718 (C.D.Cal.1994), the court held that a 1891 patent on a "simple and secure street letter-box" formed analogous art to a disposal container for hazardous medical waste. According to the court, the patent on the letter-box "was concerned with a container which could receive deposits, yet prevent persons from reaching inside," exactly the task to which the disposal container was directed. Another decision, *In re Paulsen*, 30 F.3d 1475 (Fed.Cir.1994), held that references "directed to hinges and latches as used in a desktop telephone directory, a piano lid, a kitchen cabinet, a washing machine cabinet, a wooden furniture cabinet, or a two-part housing for storing stereo cassettes" were analogous art to a claim for a portable computer. The court reasoned:

> The problems encountered by the inventors of the [patented portable computer] were problems that were not unique to portable computers.

They concerned how to connect and secure the computer's display housing to the computer while meeting certain size constraints and functional requirements. The prior art cited by the examiner discloses various means of connecting a cover (or lid) to a device so that the cover is free to swing radially along the connection axis, as well as means of securing the cover in an open or closed position. We agree with the Board that given the nature of the problem confronted by the inventors, one of ordinary skill in the art "would have consulted the mechanical arts for housings, hinges, latches, springs, etc." Thus, the cited references are "reasonably pertinent" and we therefore conclude that the Board's findings that the references are analogous was not clearly erroneous.

Does the application of such diverse and venerable art strike you as fair? What other approaches could the patent law adopt?

4. Comparative Approaches. Numerous decisions from the Boards of Appeal of the European Patent Office establish that, for purposes of a determination of "inventive step," the person of ordinary skill in the art will refer to the state of the art in neighboring fields as well as to general technical knowledge. That the determination of whether a field borders upon the subject matter of the invention is often a fine one is demonstrated by "Pencil Sharpener/Moebius," European Patent Office, Technical Board of Appeal 3.2.1, [1986] Off. J. Eur. Pat. Off. 50, where the Board reasoned that:

5.3   . . . The Examining Division arrived at its conclusion because it was of the opinion that a person skilled in the art wishing to improve the sharpener according to the German application (Auslegeschrift) 1 003 093 could also be expected to take into account also the field of securing mechanisms for savings-box slots. Such securing mechanisms represented a neighbouring field because both pencil sharpeners and savings boxes belonged to the "broader field of the closing of containers." The Board is unable to share this view.

5.3.1   While it is indeed perfectly reasonable to expect a person skilled in the art if need be, i.e., in the absence of useful suggestions in the relevant field as to how a given problem might be solved, to look for suitable parallels in neighboring fields, the question of what is a neighbouring field is one of fact and the solution depends, in the opinion of the Board, on whether the fields are so closely related that the person skilled in the art seeking a solution to a given problem would take into account developments in the neighbouring field. It is furthermore quite reasonable to expect a skilled person to refer to the state of the art in the general field of technology in which the same problem or problems similar to those in the special field of the application extensively arise and of which a person skilled in the art must be expected to be aware.

5.3.2   In the present case, even adopting the same premise as the Examining Division that the person skilled in the art by abstracting the problem would eventually, in his search for suggestions as to how he might solve the problem underlying the application, turn to the broader, that is to say general field of container closing, while he would then have entered what the Examining Division considers to be the generic field, he would not have reached the field of securing mechanisms for savings-box slots. In view of the technological differences between the two fields—storage of coins in a container as opposed to sharpening of pencils with provision for collection of shavings—there is no reason why it should occur to a skilled person to refer to his specific area—which the Examining Division considers to be part of the same broader field—to see how similar problems are solved there. . . .

5.3.4 The field of such securing mechanisms is therefore not one of the neighbouring fields to which a skilled person concerned with the development of pencil sharpeners would also refer, should the need arise, in search of appropriate solutions to his problem.

Another example of this approach is provided by an application describing a carpet with fiber-optic cables woven into its pile. When exposed to a light source, the carpet produced decorative effects. The Examining Division rejected the application based upon a United States patent describing a wig which also featured fiber-optic cables, but the Mechanical Board of Appeal 3.2.3 reversed based upon the problems solved by the products and the demands made upon the products during use. T 767/89 (Apr. 16, 1991). Do you agree with the Board's distinction, or would you consider it instead mere hairsplitting?

Nonobviousness Exercise

Your client has is concerned over the possibility that a competitor may assert United States Patent No. 5,291,976 against it. The '976 patent describes an improved wheeled suitcase and luggage support structure which includes:

(1) a rectangular frame with two horizontal and two vertical members;

(2) wheels on the lower horizontal members;

(3) a pull-up handle connected to the rectangular frame; and

(4) a wedging member, preferably frustroconical in shape, frictionally received in a bore which keeps the pull-up handle in a fully extended position.

According to the '976 patent, the suitcase can be attached to the rectangular frame either permanently, by rivets or other means, or temporarily, through use of an elastic cord or similar mechanism. The '976 patent indicates that the claimed design provides several advantages, including one-handed operation of the handle, no lost space in the suitcase due to the placement of the wheels and handle on the frame, and ease of manufacture. Claim 1 of the '976 patent provides:

1. A suitcase comprising: a luggage member, and a support structure attached to the luggage member, the support structure comprising a first horizontal member having two wheels thereon to facilitate towing on the ground, a second horizontal member, two tubular members

coupling the first and second horizontal members, thereby forming a rectangular frame; a shaft in extensible slidable engagement in each of said tubular members, the shafts being connected by a first handle, the shafts being extensible between a collapsed portion in the tubular members and a fully extended portion to enable towing of the luggage member on the wheels, at least one of the shafts including a wedging member slidable within the respective tubular member which is received frictionally in a first bore provided at an end of the respective tubular member adjacent the second horizontal member to maintain the shafts in a fully extended position.

Figure 1 of the '976 patent shows a perspective view of the suitcase; Figure 2 illustrates the wedging and tubular members.

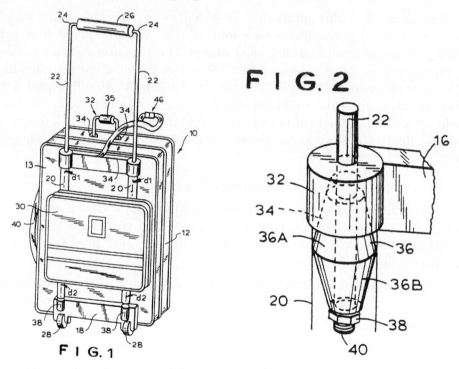

A prior art search has revealed three other U.S. patents, all of which serve as prior art to the '976 patent. None of these references was before the examiner during the prosecution of the '976 patent. The first, U.S. Patent No. 5,024,455, is entitled "Luggage Cart" and was filed by Schrecongost. The Schrecongost patent covers an external rectangular frame with two horizontal structures, two vertical members, wheels attached to an axle on the base of the frame, and a telescopically extendable U-shaped handle. The locking mechanism for the handle uses spring-loaded detents to encourage either of two pairs of notches in the U-shaped handle to hold the handle in either the extended or the collapsed position. Luggage may be attached permanently or temporarily to the frame via brackets. Figure 3 shows a front perspective view from the Schrecongost patent.

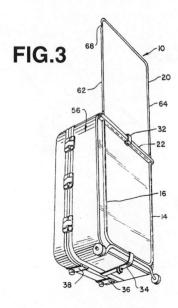

FIG.3

U.S. Patent No. 4,995,487, claiming a "Wheeled Suitcase and Luggage Support," lists one Plath as the inventor. The Plath patent describes a suitcase with built-in wheels and a retractable, friction-locking handle. Plath's locking mechanism differs somewhat from that of the '976 patent, however. When the handle has reached its maximum extension, offset guide means wedge the lower end segment of the handle road against its sleeve and brushing means, binding the handle frictionally in position. To retract the handle, the user must apply downward pressure to the gripping means to overcome the friction force of the rod against the inner through-bore of the brushing means and sleeve. Users may operate the locking mechanism with one hand. Figure 4 depicts a rear perspective view from the Plath patent; Figure 5 shows a partial elevational view of the suitcase showing the handle assembly in extended position.

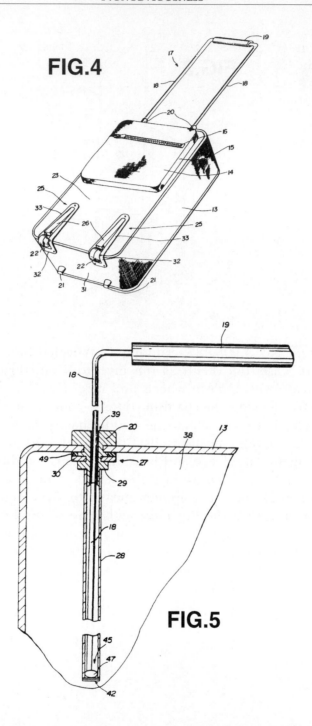

FIG.4

FIG.5

U.S. Patent No. 3,998,476 describes a "Portable Luggage Carrier with Telescoping Handle" invented by Kazmark. Kazmark discusses the use of a cart which is intended to be attached externally to a piece of luggage. The cart includes telescopically related tubes connected by a gripping handle. The tubes may be locked into their fully extended position by the use of a pair of locking mechanisms, which consist of spring-loaded button-shaped elements which are forced through a matching hole when the tubes are extended. The cart also includes wheels attached to an axle at the base of the cart. Figure 6 illustrates a perspective view from the Kazmark patent.

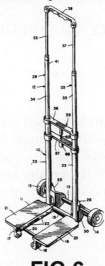

FIG.6

How would you advise your client regarding the validity of the '976 patent?

CHAPTER EIGHT

THE PATENT SPECIFICATION

■ ■ ■

Analogized to the contract law, the Patent Act permits the formation of binding agreements between inventors and the public. Under these agreements, inventors receive exclusive rights in exchange for full disclosure of their inventions. To ensure that the public gets its share of the bargain, the Patent Act includes provisions to ensure adequate disclosure of inventions. The U.S. patent statute sets forth these provisions at § 112 ¶ 1:

> The specification shall contain a written description of the invention, and of the manner and process of making and using it, in such full, clear, concise, and exact terms as to enable any person skilled in the art to which it pertains, or with which it is most nearly connected, to make and use the same, and shall set forth the best mode contemplated by the inventor of carrying out his invention.

This important section requires both that the applicant disclose "how to make" and "how to use" the claimed invention. Section 112 ¶ 1 further requires disclosure of the "best mode contemplated by the inventor," a unique aspect of United States law taken up in Chapter 10.

The central doctrine to ensure adequate disclosure—the "how to make and use" requirements—is referred to as "enablement." Enablement is potentially at issue for every claim in every patent. As the essential bargain for the exclusive right of the patent, the patentee must teach the public to make and use the invention. In other words, the patent instrument itself must "enable" other skilled artisans to practice the disclosed technology. The first U.S. patent statute, the Patent Act of 1790, expressed this policy as follows:

> [W]hich specification shall be so particular as * * * to enable a workman or other person skilled in the art of manufacture, whereof it is a branch, or wherewith it may be the nearest connected, to make, construct or use the same, to the end that the public may have the full benefit thereof, after the expiration of the patent term. . . .

Enablement accomplishes more in the Patent Act than just requiring adequate disclosure of inventive details. As already noted, patent claims stake the outer boundaries of the right to exclude. Those claims, however, often use abstract and indeterminate terms to define the extent of those boundaries. Without a clear test to tie the claim disclosure to the extent of the inventor's contribution to the useful arts, those claims could expand to encompass more than the inventor actually invented. The enablement requirement serves to delimit the boundaries of patent protection by ensuring that the scope of a patent claim accords with the extent of the inventor's technical contribution.

Section 112 ¶ 1 also refers to a "written description," a reference upon which the case law has constructed a separate doctrine. The so-called "written description" doctrine ordinarily operates to police priority when inventors amend their disclosures. The Patent Act allows inventors to amend their applications during the application process and after their original filing date. When an applicant adds new claims or new subject matter to existing claims after the original filing date, the "written description" test requires that the original specification support the new matter. The written description requirement thus ensures that inventors may not improperly amend their patents by including subsequent technical advances in a previously filed application.

In addition to setting out the wholly objective requirements, section 112 further provides that the specification "shall set forth the best mode contemplated by the inventor of carrying out his invention." This provision requires disclosure in the patent specification of any specific instrumentalities or techniques that the inventor recognized at the time of filing as the best way of carrying out the invention. Thus, beyond enabling one of skill in the art to make and use the claimed invention, the specification must also disclose the inventor's trade secrets for practicing the invention.

§ 8.1   ENABLEMENT

The "how to make" requirement of 35 U.S.C.A. § 112, ¶ 1, provides that "[t]he specification shall contain * * * the manner and process of making * * * [the invention], in such full, clear, concise, and exact terms as to enable any person skilled in the art to which it pertains, or with which it is most nearly connected, to make * * * the [invention]." The specification ideally provides a cookbook recipe showing a person of skill in the art "how to make" the invention. Starting with the state of technology in the prior art, enablement requires the specification to teach how to make the claimed invention.

GOULD v. HELLWARTH
United States Court of Customs and Patent Appeals, 1973
472 F.2d 1383

Before Markey, Chief Judge, and Rich, Almond, Baldwin, and Lane, Associate Judges.

LANE, JUDGE.

This appeal is from the decision of the Board of Patent Interferences awarding Hellwarth, the junior party, priority of invention as to two counts to a so-called "Q-switched" or "Giant Pulse" laser. Hellwarth is involved on his application serial No. 128,458 filed August 1, 1961. The appellant, Gould, is involved on his application serial No. 804,540 filed April 6, 1959. The determinative issue is whether the disclosure of the Gould application was adequate to enable a person skilled in the art to make an operable device (35 U.S.C. 112). We agree with the board that it was not and affirm its decision.

THE SUBJECT MATTER

The laser is a device which provides light amplification by stimulated emission of radiation. Amplification of electronic radiation by stimulated emission of radiation was first attained by devices operating in the microwave frequency range and known by the acronym "maser." The laser, also known as an "optical maser," resulted subsequently when such amplification was achieved at light or optical frequencies. The basic requirement of a maser or laser is a working medium, usually a gas or a solid, containing atoms or molecules having one or more sets of energy levels. Unlike the condition at equilibrium, where lower energy states of a material are more heavily populated than the higher energy states, material constituting a laser working medium must have a higher energy level populated by a significantly greater number of atoms or molecules than a lower level. A medium in such nonequilibrium condition is said to have an "inverted population" or "negative temperature." The medium may be excited or "pumped" to provide the inverted population by means of a source of electromagnetic energy, such as a strong light of suitable wavelength. Laser activity results from the medium in a state of population inversion emitting wave energy of a frequency corresponding to the separation of the inverted pair of energy levels.

The two counts define an "optical maser" comprising basic laser elements—a laser material, means for pumping the material to a condition of stimulated emission, and reflecting means defining a radiation path in the material for repeatedly reflecting the stimulated emission energy radiated by the material between the reflecting means. Additionally, they call for the combination with those elements of means intermediate the reflecting means in the path of the radiated energy for altering the amount of stimulated energy reflected by the reflecting means. The altering means permits impeding the reflections to prevent emissions from the laser for certain periods to allow build-up of the amount of population inversion so that "giant pulses" of greatly enhanced energy concentration are emitted when the impediment is removed. The name "Q-switched" is applied to the modified laser because the altering means controls or varies the electrical quality or "Q" of the "cavity" in which the working material is confined.

Count 3 is representative of the involved counts and reads as follows:

> 3. Apparatus for controlling the stimulated emission energy output of an optical maser comprising an optical maser material, means for pumping said material to a condition of stimulated emission, means for abstracting energy from said maser, reflecting means defining a radiation path including said maser material for repeatedly reflecting the stimulated emission energy radiated by said material between said reflecting means, [and] means in the path of said radiated energy for altering the amount of stimulated energy reflected between said reflecting means.

THE PROCEEDINGS BELOW

Hellwarth asserted no date of invention prior to Gould's filing date. No priority evidence was submitted by either party and both parties rely on their filing dates. On motion by Hellwarth, final hearing was set to consider the sufficiency of the Gould application, and Hellwarth was granted permission to take testimony of Dr. Bela Lengyel on that question. Appellant took testimony of Dr. Arnold Bloom, Dr. Grant Fowles and Paul Rabinowitz in rebuttal. Lengyel had worked at Hughes Aircraft when the first operable laser was built there by Dr. Theodore H. Maiman in 1960. Lengyel was chairman of a college physics department at the time of testifying and had done extensive writing in the laser field. Bloom and Grant did extensive work in the laser field beginning in 1961 and 1962, respectively. Rabinowitz was employed by TRG, Inc. on laser projects which began in 1959. As the board recognized, all four witnesses were highly qualified in the laser field at the time they testified.

The Gould application includes a lengthy disclosure directed to obtaining laser action. It also suggests certain uses and refinements for an operable laser, including means for Q-switching such a laser. It is not questioned that the disclosure of the Q-switching feature would be adequate if the application adequately disclosed an operable laser in which the feature could be incorporated. Rather, appellee charged, and the board agreed, that the disclosure was insufficient as of its filing date to enable a person skilled in the art to make an operable laser.

Lengyel's testimony was summarized by the board as follows (with reference to the record omitted):

> The testimony of Lengyel is to the effect that as of 1959 the Gould disclosure did not have sufficient information for one skilled in the art to construct an operative laser of any kind and noted that the Schawlow–Townes paper included most of the information that was available but an operable laser was not made until 1960 by Maiman. According to Lengyel, in order to construct an operable laser one skilled in quantum electronics would have to know the physical parameters of the material, e.g., its temperature or temper-

ature range; if gas filled, the pressure and approximate size or some relationship between the possible dimensions of the device. The minimum radiation necessary for its excitation if optically excited should be known. If excited by discharge, then the condition of operation of that discharge should be known. The basic properties of the cavity such as reflectivity and curvature of the mirrors should be known. The relation between the various parameters would have to be known quite precisely in order to obtain an operable laser.

Lengyel in his testimony reviewed the Gould disclosure and pointed out that although details are disclosed with respect to various lasers, the application does not disclose a complete set of operating parameters for any laser.

The board reviewed the testimony of appellant's witnesses at length, noting particularly that Bloom and Fowles expressed the opinion that the Gould application gave sufficient information as of 1959 to build a laser. However, it stated:

> The testimony of all the witnesses is fairly consistent in recognizing that the Gould application does disclose various working mediums, dimensions and theories but there is no information which is complete enough for one skilled in the art to build an operative laser particularly at a time when one "skilled in the art of lasers" was virtually non-existent.

The board also stated:

> The testimony of the witnesses has been helpful to the extent of indicating what knowledge is necessary to construct an operative laser. However, this knowledge, as evidenced by documents entered in evidence ... is the summation of the work of many men spending considerable time experimenting. For the witnesses or any other men skilled in the art to state with certainty what they would have done with the Gould disclosure, coupled with whatever prior knowledge was available in 1959, even with an intense desire for success, is pure speculation.

In reaching the ultimate conclusion that "Gould had inadequate disclosure as of 1959 to build an operative laser," the board stated:

> The Gould specification has much disclosure but much work had to be done subsequent to the filing of the application before an operative laser was made. The patent statutes do not contemplate grant of patents for such a disclosure, which is merely a fertile field for experimentation.

OPINION

Appellant emphasizes that the counts are not drawn to a laser per se but to a laser modified by means for permitting Q-switched or pulsed operation. He also argues that Hellwarth derived the laser per se on which he imposes Q-switching from the ruby laser successfully operated by his then co-worker at Hughes Aircraft Company, Maiman, before the Hellwarth application was filed. It is apparent, however, that such circumstances are common, if not usual, with respect to improvement inventions like that involved here, and they have no bearing on the outcome. As in any priority dispute, Gould can prevail only if his application meets the requirements set out in the first paragraph of 35 U.S.C. 112. The application must include a disclosure of the invention "in such terms as to enable any person skilled in the art to which it pertains, or with which it is most nearly connected, to make and use the same."

As recognized by Gould in his application, the problem faced by one seeking to make an operable laser in 1959 was that of successfully applying the principle of amplification by stimulated emission of radiation, which had been successfully applied to microwaves in the maser, to optical or light radiation. Cavities or resonators used to confine the working medium in masers, which characteristically had dimensions in the order of one wavelength, e.g. 1–100 centimeters, could not be used in light amplification because of the comparatively short wavelength of light. As Gould points out in his brief:

> Masers operate at microwave frequencies so that their wavelengths differ by a factor of a thousand or more from those of lasers and thus make the maser microwave resonator technology inadaptable to lasers.

While all the difficulties faced in making an operable laser need not be enumerated, it is clear from events that followed that the transition from microwave to light wavelengths proved no easy task.

Dr. Townes, in cooperation with Dr. A. Schawlow of Bell Laboratories, suggested the possibility of making the extension from masers to light wavelengths in a paper published in 1958. Gould, who had been a graduate student at Columbia University where Townes taught, had begun a literature search in the field. He gained employment with TRG and prepared for it a proposal for research work to build a laser, based largely on the same material as his application. That proposal resulted in a contract with Advanced Research Projects Agency, a Government agency, for research and development work in the amount of nearly one million dollars. The resulting project was assigned a secret security classification. Gould continued to work for TRG but was excluded from the project for inability to obtain security clearance. TRG spent the nearly one million dollar sum in the year following Gould's filling date (May 1959 to May 1960) is attempting to build a laser, but its efforts resulted in failure.

In the meantime, other scientists were also seeking to produce a laser. Maiman achieved the first operable laser in a pink ruby medium in April of 1960. Appellee, a co-worker of Maiman at Hughes Aircraft, disclosed the Q-switched laser in conjunction with such a ruby laser in his application here. After Maiman's success, his ruby laser was promptly duplicated in other laboratories. Soon thereafter laser activity was achieved in other media by other experimenters. As an example, Javan, Bennett and Herriott of Bell Laboratories announced success with a helium-cesium laser at the end of 1960. Gould and others at TRG arrived at an optically pumped helium-cesium laser in 1961 or 1962.

This brief history of the attainment of the final operating lasers gives firm support to the board's conclusion that the Gould application was insufficient to teach a person skilled in the art how to make a laser. Whether the "person skilled in the art" is viewed in terms of the laser art, even though an operable laser had not yet been made, or with regard to the art to which the laser "is most nearly connected" (35 U.S.C. 112) is not material. The board, as well as the witnesses, considered the case in light of what would be taught to a highly trained person knowledgeable in the fields of microwave masers, spectroscopy, atomic physics and aware of published proposals for making a laser, and we do the same.

The testimony of appellant's witnesses was generally in agreement with Lengyel's view that the application does not disclose a complete set of parameters for a laser as well as his observations as to what knowledge was necessary to produce an operable laser. Opinions of Bloom and Fowles contrary to the board on the ultimate question of whether the Gould disclosure was adequate to enable a person skilled in the art to make an operable laser are incompatible with their testimony as well as that of Lengyel and the other evidence.

In arguing that he does disclose the parameters necessary for a particular laser, appellant states that "[p]erhaps the best example of a complete description of a specific embodiment in the Gould application" is a portion which suggests use of "a gaseous atmosphere comprising a mixture of sodium and mercury" as the working medium. However, both Lengyel, in 1967, and Bloom, in 1968, testified that no sodium-mercury laser had been known to operate. In view of the widespread efforts to obtain laser action in different media, which the record shows followed Maiman's initial success in 1960, no basis is seen for accepting this alleged "complete description" as teaching how to make an operable laser.

Appellant also refers to TRG's having constructed an operable helium-cesium laser "after the restrictions on Gould were relaxed enough to permit him to make significant contributions to the development." However, it is plain from the application and the testimony that neither physical dimensions nor particular operating conditions for such a laser are given in the Gould application. Also it was not until between January and April of 1962 that TRG's optically pumped helium-cesium laser was operated. By that time, the state of the art had been advanced by the successful operation of the ruby laser by Maiman and the helium-cesium laser by Javan and his associates. Additionally, a nearly confocal arrangement of mirrors, based on a proposal made by Bell Laboratories in 1961 and not on the Gould disclosure, was used. These circumstances are inconsistent with any claim that the Gould application adequately disclosed how to make an operable helium-cesium laser.

Nor does a claim by appellant that his application "discloses the ruby laser" find any factual support. The application merely lists ruby as a possible alternative medium with the suggestion that it be a single crystal. Information as to the type, size or orientation of the crystal and exactly how it is to be excited is not given. While ruby, in certain forms, was a known maser material, reports of TRG work made of record show that its workers considered it as a laser material in early 1960 but rejected it. Maiman made extensive investigation before finding that a particular ruby material, a pink ruby, would provide an operative laser under particular conditions.

We conclude that the Gould application involved herein does not provide an enabling disclosure of how to make the subject matter of the counts. The decision of the board awarding priority of invention to Hellwarth is accordingly affirmed.

NOTES

1. **Gould and the Laser Patent.** Assume that once workers in the field learn how to make a laser, the disclosure in the '540 application would enable them to construct a Q-switched laser. How then could it be fair to hold that the claims of the '540 application were invalid because they were not enabled by that disclosure?

Consider also that Gould's predicament in this case may be seen as a matter of timing. Had Gould filed or re-filed his application prior to Hellwarth's conception of his Q-switch, but subsequent to the publication of Maiman's successful ruby laser, Gould would have won the interference and become the proprietor of U.S. Pat. No. 3,928,815. Why should the patent laws reward late filing, particularly where an application discloses an improvement over an earlier and non-enabled invention, but which becomes enabled during the pendency of the application?

Gordon Gould's 1959 patent application spawned an impressive amount of litigation, of which the above case is merely one example. This case should not convey the incorrect impression that Gould lost all rights to obtain a patent on a laser. Creative patent attorneys later drafted claims to an optical amplifier based on Gould's original specification. In cases such as *Gould v. Control Laser Corp.*, 866 F.2d 1391 (Fed.Cir.1989), a jury held that laser devices infringed these claims. As a result, Gould later collected considerable royalties from the application.

2. **The Specification as a Production Document.** It is difficult to state concisely the precise level of detail required for a patent specification to satisfy the enablement requirement. The Federal Circuit in *Christianson v. Colt Industries Operating Corp.*, 822 F.2d 1544 (Fed. Cir. 1987) addressed this problem:

Dont need to show how to mass-produce.

Patents are not production documents, and nothing in the patent law requires that a patentee must disclose data on how to mass-produce the invented product.... [T]he law has never required that a patentee who elects to manufacture its claimed invention must disclose in its patents the dimensions, tolerances, drawings and other parameters of mass production not necessary to enable one skilled in the art to practice (as distinguished from mass-produce) the invention. Nor it is an objective of the patent system to supply, free of charge, production data and production drawings to competing manufacturers.

3.   The Germ of an Idea. In *Genentech, Inc. v. Novo Nordisk*, 108 F.3d 1361 (Fed. Cir. 1997), the court struck down a patent directed towards a method for producing a protein of hGH amino acids including the step of cleaving a conjugate protein to produce the desired protein, part of a process commonly called "cleavable fusion expression." The defendant, Novo, urged that the patent did not provide an enabling disclosure with a mere statement of the possibility of cleavable fusion expression, along with disclosure of the DNA sequence encoding hGH, a single enzyme for cleaving undisclosed conjugate proteins, and a statement of that enzyme's cleavage sites as being potential amino acid extensions conjugated to hGH. The patentee, Genentech, instead argued that those skilled in the art of recombinant protein expression and purification at the time of filing, July 5, 1979, would have been able to use cleavable fusion expression to produce hGH without undue experimentation. The Federal Circuit concluded:

> There is no dispute that the portion of the specification chiefly relied upon by Genentech and by the district court, does not describe in any detail whatsoever how to make hGH using cleavable fusion expression. For example, no reaction conditions for the steps needed to produce hGH are provided; no description of any specific cleavable conjugate protein appears. The relevant portion of the specification merely describes three (or perhaps four) applications for which cleavable fusion expression is generally well-suited and then names an enzyme that might be used as a cleavage agent (trypsin), along with sites at which it cleaves ("arg-arg or lys-lys, etc."). Thus, the specification does not describe a specific material to be cleaved or any reaction conditions under which cleavable fusion expression would work....

> Genentech's arguments, focused almost exclusively on the level of skill in the art, ignore the essence of the enablement requirement. Patent protection is granted in return for an enabling disclosure of an invention, not for vague intimations of general ideas that may or may not be workable. Tossing out the mere germ of an idea does not constitute enabling disclosure. While every aspect of a generic claim certainly need not have been carried out by an inventor, or exemplified in the specification, reasonable detail must be provided in order to enable members of the public to understand and carry out the invention. That requirement has not been met in this specification with respect to the cleavable fusion expression of hGH.

... However, when there is no disclosure of any specific starting material or of any of the conditions under which a process can be carried out, undue experimentation is required; there is a failure to meet the enablement requirement that cannot be rectified by asserting that all the disclosure related to the process is within the skill of the art. It is the specification, not the knowledge of one skilled in the art, that must supply the novel aspects of an invention in order to constitute adequate enablement.

[handwritten margin note: things needed to meet the ↑enablement requirement]

What is the border between a "mere germ of an idea" and an enabled invention? This opinion at least gives some parameters for biotechnology— starting materials, conditions for a process, and disclosure of the process itself. Further discussion of the enablement requirement in the context of biotechnology follows later in this Chapter.

4. **Enabling Edison?** An old Supreme Court case presented an interesting historical setting for the enablement doctrine. Sawyer and Mann sued the Edison Electric Light Company for infringement of a patent claiming "[a]n incandescing conductor for an electric lamp, of carbonized fibrous or textile material...." Edison had independently discovered that a particular strain of bamboo, when carbonized, served best as a filament. The Supreme Court invalidated the Sawyer and Mann patent with the following reasoning:

> Is the complainant entitled to a monopoly of all fibrous and textile materials for incandescent conductors? If the patentees had discovered in fibrous and textile substances a quality common to them all, or to them generally, as distinguishing them from other materials, such as minerals, etc., and such quality or characteristic adapted them peculiarly to incandescent conductors, such claim might not be too broad.... Instead of confining themselves to carbonized paper, as they might properly have done, and in fact did in their third claim, they made a broad claim for every fibrous or textile material, when in fact an examination of over 6,000 vegetable growths showed that none of them possessed the peculiar qualities that fitted them for that purpose. Was everybody, then, precluded by this broad claim from making further investigation? We think not.

> * * *

> The question really is whether the imperfectly successful experiments of Sawyer and Mann, with carbonized paper and wood carbon, conceding all that is claimed for them, authorize them to put under tribute the results of the brilliant discoveries made by others.

> * * *

> If the description be so vague and uncertain that no one can tell, except by independent experiments, how to construct the patented device, the patent is void.

[handwritten margin note: old S.C. on enablement]

Consolidated Elec. Light Co. v. McKeesport, 159 U.S. 465 (1895). The Supreme Court was apparently impressed with "the brilliant discoveries made by [Edison]" in competition with Sawyer and Man. This case illustrates a further purpose of enablement—delimiting the bounds of an invention to leave adequate room for further improvements. Thus, enablement draws the line between initial inventions and patentable improvements. Does the Supreme Court suggest how Sawyer and Man might have enabled their broad claims? Due to Sawyer's and Man's failure to enable the scope of their claims, is the Supreme Court justified in invalidating the patent? How does this result promote invention and innovation?

5. The Deposit Requirement. The advent of biotechnology placed new strains upon the enablement requirement. Some inventions cannot be enabled by a written explanation. The way to enable such inventions is to provide a sample. Major patent offices therefore adopted a procedure whereby inventors of novel microorganisms could fulfill statutory enablement requirements by depositing a sample of the organism in a facility open to the public. *E.g.*, *Bäckerhefe* ("Baker's Yeast"), 1975 GRUR 430 (German Federal Supreme Court); *American Cyanamid Co. (Dann's) Patent*, [1971] RPC 425, [1970] FSR 443 (House of Lords); *In re Lundak*, 773 F.2d 1216 (Fed.Cir.1985); *see also* Aiji Watanabe, *The Current Status and Problems in the Deposit of Patented Mircoorganisms in Japan*, in 4 IIP BULLETIN 32 (1995). The inventor of a novel microorganism subsequently faced two significant problems when attempting to obtain patent protection in many different countries. First, with needless expense and repetition, the inventor had to deposit a sample of an organism in each country where patent protection was sought. Second, the inventor had to ensure that each depository would maintain a policy of public access for the duration of the patent.

The Budapest Treaty on the International Recognition of Deposits of Microorganisms for the Purposes of Patent Protection addressed these problems with duplicative deposit requirements. The Budapest Treaty establishes an international certification process for depository organizations that store, catalog, and maintain samples of microorganisms. Treaty signatories have agreed that use of any single International Depository Authority (IDA) will fulfill the deposit requirement of their patent law. Thus, a deposit in one repository will operate as a deposit in each nation. The treaty is largely a procedural one, however; it does not address the extent of the disclosure requirements established by individual national patent laws.

Does the deposit concept have application outside the field of biotechnology? It bears similarity to the former requirement of United States patent law that applicants submit a model or exhibit along with their applications. Now, the U.S. Patent and Trademark Office only very rarely requires models along with applications, usually where the applicant claims a perpetual motion machine or apparatus of that nature. *See* 35 U.S.C. § 114; *Manual of Patent Examining Procedure* § 608.03. For discussion and sketches of the old U.S. Patent Office Model Room, as well as an enjoyable depiction of life in the Patent Office from its founding to the mid-twentieth century, see KENNETH W. DOBYNS, THE PATENT OFFICE PONY: A HISTORY OF THE EARLY PATENT OFFICE (1994).

6. Enablement and Repetition. Suppose the successful implementation of an invention as disclosed depends on chance and is to some extent unrepeatable. A biotechnology application might involve a microbiological process involving mutations, where success in replicating the invention may not be certainly and reliably achieved. In contrast, an application in the electrical arts might concern the production of magnetic cores, where the limitations of current manufacturing techniques will render some portion of them inoperable. Are there any differences between these circumstances that should influence the decision whether or not to consider the disclosure enabling.

7. Enablement and Scientific Truths. What if the inventor is unaware or actually misinformed about the scientific principles that form the basis of the technical advance? Consider Niels Anton Christiansen's patent on the O-ring, U.S. Patent No. 2,180,795 (1939), "which ranks with the safety pin, paper clip, and zipper on the short list of humankind's simplest, most useful, most ubiquitous, and most elegant inventions." George Wise, *Inventors and Corporations in the Maturing Electrical Industry, 1890–1940*, in INVENTIVE MINDS: CREATIVITY IN TECHNOLOGY 291 (Robert J. Weber & David N. Perkins, eds. 1992). The term "O-ring" describes a hard rubber donut in a square-sided groove with length greater than, and width slightly less than, the ring's cross-section diameter. The O-ring most commonly serves as a piston seal in devices ranging from fountain pens to hydraulic presses, allowing pistons to slide readily without blocking fluid flow. In 1986, design flaws concerning O-rings on the space shuttle *Challenger* focused national interest upon this common technology.

An examination of Christiansen's '795 patent indicates that the inventor did not possess an accurate knowledge of why a rubber ring arranged in this way did not suffer the wear and leaking of its predecessors. The patent's specification asserted that the O-ring was "continuously kneaded or worked to enhance its life," much as if the rubber donut were a sort of muscle continuously being flexed. Later experimentation revealed that the rubber ring in fact undergoes a brief rolling motion during usage, allowing the piston's hydraulic fluid to lubricate the ring. This lubrication increases the ring's life and reduces wear.

If later scientific advances reveal that earlier understandings regarding the operation of a particular invention were incorrect, should the patent be invalidated as nonenabling? *See Diamond Rubber Co. v. Consolidated Rubber Tire Co.*, 220 U.S. 428, 435–36 (1911).

8. Comparative Note. The patent laws of the United States, Europe, and Japan are substantially harmonized on the point of how-to-make enablement. Article 83 of the European Patent Convention provides that: "The European patent application must disclose the invention in a manner sufficiently clear and complete for it to be carried out by a person skilled in the art."

In Japan, section 36(4) notes that: "The detailed explanation of the invention . . . shall state the purpose, constitution and effect of the invention in such a manner that it may be easily carried out by a person having ordinary skill in the art to which the invention pertains." The Tokyo High Court has recognized that the specification need not "disclose also the matters known at the technical level contemporary to the filing date (or priority date) and self-evident to those skilled in the art. Such matters could be understood to those skilled in the art who read the specification, without explicit explanation." (gyoke) No. 199/1975 (the "sodium aluminate" case); *see* TETSU TANABE & HAROLD C. WEGNER, JAPANESE PATENT PRACTICE 120 (1986).

ATLAS POWDER CO. v. E.I. DU PONT DE NEMOURS & CO.

United States Court of Appeals, Federal Circuit, 1984
750 F.2d 1569

Before Markey, Chief Judge, and Baldwin and Miller, Circuit Judges.

BALDWIN, CIRCUIT JUDGE.

This is an appeal by E.I. du Pont De Nemours & Co. and its customer Alamo Explosives Co., Inc. (collectively, "Du Pont"). The appeal is from a final judgment of the United States District Court for the Northern District of Texas holding product claims 1–5, 7, 12–14, and 16–17 of U.S. Patent No. 3,447,978 ('978 patent), issued to Harold Bluhm on June 3, 1969 and assigned to the Atlas Powder Co. ("Atlas"), not invalid under 35 U.S.C. §§ 102, 103, and 112, not fraudulently procured, and infringed. We affirm.

BACKGROUND

Briefly, the '978 patent relates to blasting agents, i.e., chemical mixtures that are relatively insensitive to normal modes of detonation but can be made to detonate with a high strength explosive primer. By the mid–1960's, blasting agents consisted of two major types: "ANFO" and "water-containing".

An "ANFO" blasting agent comprised a mixture of particulate ammonium nitrate, usually in the form of small round aggregates known as "prills", and fuel oil (e.g., diesel fuel). They were widely used in mining and construction because of their low cost, ease of handling, and ability to be mixed at the blast site rather than prepackaged at the plant. However, to work properly they could be used only in "dry" holes (without water) because water desensitized the mixture, rendering it nondetonable.

A "water-containing" blasting agent, which was water resistant, generally comprised a slurry of particulate ammonium nitrate (or other oxidizing salt), a solid or liquid fuel, at least 5 percent water, and, as a sensitizer to increase explosive power, either a high explosive such as TNT or a chemical such as nitric acid. Often, a gelling agent was added, particularly in the chemical sensitized slurries, to prevent the separation of sensitizers from slurry by forming a gel (a colloid in which the disperse phase has combined with the continuous phase to produce a viscous, jelly-like product). The use of sensitizers in water-containing blasting agents made preparation and handling more difficult and dangerous and, hence, more costly.

Before the '978 invention, Atlas manufactured a gelled slurry blasting agent called Aquanite, based on U.S. Patent No. 3,164,503, issued to Gehrig and assigned to Atlas. Aquanite used as a sensitizer nitric acid, which was highly caustic to skin and clothing and tended to separate out of the product even in the presence of a gelling agent, thereby reducing the product's stability and shelf life. Also, Aquanite was "hypergolic", i.e., it ignited wood, coal and various chemicals upon contact, which was suspected of causing the blasting agent to detonate prematurely.

THE INVENTION

In 1965, Atlas assigned Harold Bluhm to investigate stabilizing its Aquanite gel. Bluhm experimented with various "emulsions" that did not contain nitric acid or a gelling agent. (An emulsion is a stable mixture of two immiscible liquids; a "water-in-oil" emulsion has a continuous oil and discontinuous aqueous phase; an "oil-in-water" emulsion is the reverse.) In early 1966, Bluhm formulated an intimately mixed water-in-oil, water resistant emulsion blasting agent. The product was sensitized with entrapped air rather than high explosives or chemicals and is the subject matter of the claims at issue. Representative is Claim 1:

　　1.　　An emulsion blasting agent consisting essentially of:

　　　　an aqueous solution of ammonium nitrate forming a discontinuous emulsion phase;

　　　　a carbonaceous fuel forming a continuous emulsion phase;

　　　　an occluded gas dispersed within said emulsion and comprising at least 4% by volume, thereof at 70 degrees F. and atmospheric pressure;

　　　　and a water-in-oil type emulsifying agent;

　　　　said carbonaceous fuel having a consistency such that said occluded gas is held in said emulsion at a temperature of 70 degrees F.

Claim 1 is the only independent claim in suit. The other, dependent claims describe various ingredients, such as microspheres for the occluded gas, additional fuels (e.g., aluminum), specific ranges of ingredients, and various properties of the blasting agent.

Du Pont's Activities

Du Pont sold a gelled slurry blasting agent until the latter part of the 1970's. In 1976, Du Pont formed a team to study the feasibility of an emulsion blasting agent. The team succeeded in making a water-in-oil emulsion blasting agent which Du Pont began making and selling in August 1978. Atlas sued for infringement in December 1979.

The District Court Proceedings

A non-jury trial was held between January 28 and February 2, 1982. The district court [held] that ... the claims were not invalid for the patent's failure to comply with the "best mode", enablement, and "overclaiming" requirements of 35 U.S.C. § 112.... On appeal, Du Pont contests those holdings, except for the one on best mode.

Issue

Whether the district court erred in holding the patent claims at issue not invalid because of nonenablement.

OPINION

The district court rejected Du Pont's arguments of "overly broad", "overclaiming", and "non-enablement", and its argument that the broad scope of the claims is not supported by the limited disclosure present. In essence, those arguments are one: the '978 disclosure does not enable one of ordinary skill in the art to make and use the claimed invention, and hence, the claimed invention is invalid under 35 U.S.C. § 112, ¶ 1.

To be enabling under § 112, a patent must contain a description that enables one skilled in the art to make and use the claimed invention. *Raytheon Co. v. Roper Corp.*, 724 F.2d at 960. That some experimentation is necessary does not preclude enablement; the amount of experimentation, however, must not be unduly extensive. Determining enablement is a question of law.

Du Pont argues that the patent disclosure lists numerous salts, fuels, and emulsifiers that could form thousands of emulsions but there is no commensurate teaching as to which combination would work. The disclosure, according to Du Pont, is nothing more than "a list of candidate ingredients" from which one skilled in the art would have to select and experiment unduly to find an operable emulsion.

The district court held it would have been impossible for Bluhm to list all operable emulsions and exclude the inoperable ones. Further, it found such list unnecessary, because one skilled in the art would know how to select a salt and fuel and then apply "Bancroft's Rule" to determine the proper emulsifier. Bancroft's Rule was found by the district court to be a "basic principle of emulsion chemistry," and Du Pont has not shown that finding to be clearly erroneous.

We agree with the district court's conclusion on enablement. Even if some of the claimed combinations were inoperative, the claims are not necessarily invalid. "It is not a function of the claims to specifically exclude ... possible inoperative substances...." *In re Dinh–Nguyen*, 492 F.2d 856, 858–59 (CCPA 1974). Of course, if the number of inoperative combinations becomes significant, and in effect forces one of ordinary skill in the art to experiment unduly in order to practice the claimed invention, the claims might indeed be invalid. That, however, has not been shown to be the case here.

Du Pont contends that, because the '978 examples are "merely prophetic", they do not aid one skilled in the art in making the invention.[1] Because they are prophetic, argues Du Pont, there can be no guarantee that the examples would actually work.

Use of prophetic examples, however, does not automatically make a patent non-enabling. The burden is on one challenging validity to show by clear and convincing evidence that the prophetic examples together with other parts of the specification are not enabling. Du Pont did not meet that burden here. To the contrary, the district court found that the "prophetic" examples of the specification were based on actual experiments that were slightly modified in the patent to reflect what the inventor believed to be optimum, and hence, they would be helpful in enabling someone to make the invention.

Du Pont argues that of some 300 experiments performed by Atlas before the filing of the '978 patent application, Atlas' records indicated that 40 percent failed "for some reason or another". The district court agreed that Atlas' records showed 40 percent "failed", but found that Atlas' listing of an experiment as a "failure" or "unsatisfactory" was misleading. Experiments were designated "failures", the district court found, in essence because they were not optimal under all conditions, but such optimality is not required for a valid patent. The district court also found that one skilled in the art would know how to modify slightly many of those "failures" to form a better emulsion. Du Pont has not persuaded us that the district court was clearly erroneous in those findings.

Du Pont asserts that Atlas was able to produce suitable emulsions with only two emulsifiers, "Atmos 300" and "Span 80", and therefore, the disclosure should be construed to read upon only those two emulsifiers. However, Du Pont did not prove that the other disclosed emulsifiers were inoperable. The district court credited testimony by Atlas' expert, Dr. Fowkes, to the effect that he had successfully formed a number of detonable emulsions using a variety of emulsifiers specified in the '978 patent. Further, the district court found that one skilled in the art would know which emulsifiers would work in a given system. Indeed, the district court found that Du Pont's own researchers had little difficulty in making satisfactory emulsions with the emulsifying agents, salts, and fuels listed in the '978 patent. Those findings have not been shown to be clearly erroneous.

In sum, we conclude that Du Pont has failed to show that the district court erred in determining enablement.

---

1. The PTO Manual of Patent Examining Procedure (MPEP) § 608.01(p)(D) (5th ed. 1983), states: Simulated or predicted test results and prophetical examples (paper examples) are permitted in patent applications. Working examples correspond to work actually performed and may describe tests which have actually been conducted and results that were achieved. Paper examples describe the manner and process of making an embodiment of the invention which has not actually been conducted. Paper examples should not be represented as work actually done. Paper examples should not be described using the past tense.

NOTES

1. **Prophetic Examples.** Does this case suggest to patent practitioners that it is OK to guess, so long as the guess turns out to be right? At least in Canada the answer is no according to the Supreme Court of Canada, *Apotex Inc. v. Wellcome Foundation Ltd.*, 2002 SCC 77.

2. **Inoperative Embodiments.** If the patent law is directed towards applied technology, why does it allow patents to describe, and even claim, embodiments that are inoperative? Should the burden fall on the applicant to claim a working invention or members of the public who must attempt to piece together the invention for themselves? How many inoperative combinations should suffice to render the patent invalid for lack of enablement?

3. **Enablement and Claim Scope.** In modern patent law, the enablement doctrine also operates to delimit the appropriate scope of patent claims. Specifically, enablement links the protection afforded by the claims to the extent of the inventor's contribution to the useful arts. The following two decisions explore this aspect of the enablement doctrine.

IN RE WRIGHT

United States Court of Appeals, Federal Circuit, 1993
999 F.2d 1557

Before Rich, Newman, and Rader, Circuit Judges.

RICH, J.

Dr. Stephen E. Wright appeals from the January 16, 1992 decision of the Board of Patent Appeals and Interferences (Board) of the United States Patent and Trademark Office (PTO) sustaining the Examiner's rejection of claims 1–23, 15–42, and 45–48 of application Serial No. 06/914,620 under 35 USC Section 112, first paragraph, as unsupported by an enabling disclosure. We affirm.

I.   BACKGROUND

A.   The Invention

The claims on appeal are directed to processes for producing live, non-pathogenic vaccines against pathogenic RNA viruses (claims 1–10, 22–37, 40, 45, and 46), vaccines produced by these processes (claims 11, 12, 15–21, 38, and 39), and methods of using certain of these claimed vaccines to protect living organisms against RNA viruses (claims 41 and 42). Wright's specification provides a general description of these processes, vaccines, and methods of use, but only a single working example.

In this example, Wright describes the production of a recombinant vaccine which confers immunity in chickens against the RNA tumor virus known as Prague Avian Sarcoma Virus (PrASV), a member of the Rous Associated Virus (RAV) family. To produce this vaccine, Wright first identified the antigenic gene region of the genome of PrASV as being in the envelope A (env A) gene region of this virus, and then isolated and cloned a large quantity of this antigenic gene region.

Following cloning, Wright introduced by transfection the cloned env A genes into C/O cells, a particular chicken embryo cell line. The C/O cells were then infected with the endogenous, non-oncogenic, O-type Rous Associated Virus (RAV–O) and incubated. Genetic recombination and viral replication occurred during incubation, resulting in an impure vaccine containing particles of the recombinant virus referred to as RAV–O Acn, or RAV_O–A. Wright then purified this vaccine to obtain a vaccine containing only genetic recombinant RAV–Acn virus particles. The Examiner ultimately allowed claims 13, 14, 43, and 44, which are specific to the particular process and vaccine disclosed in this example.

Wright seeks allowance, however, of claims which would provide, in varying degrees, a much broader scope of protection than the allowed claims. For example, independent process claim 1 reads:

A process for producing a live non-pathogenic vaccine for a pathogenic RNA virus, comprising the steps of identifying the antigenic and pathogenic gene regions of said virus; performing gene alteration to produce a genome which codes for the antigenicity of the virus, but does not have its pathogenicity; and obtaining an expression of the gene.

Dependent claims 2–10, 22–35, and 40 recite additional limitations to this process. Independent claims 36 and 45 and claims 37 and 46 dependent therefrom, respectively, are also directed to processes for producing vaccines.

Independent product claim 11 reads:

A live, non-pathogenic vaccine for a pathogenic RNA virus, comprising an immunologically effective amount of a viral antigenic, genomic expression having an antigenic determinant region of the RNA virus, but no pathogenic properties.

Dependent claims 15–21 recite additional limitations to this vaccine. Independent claims 38 and 47 and claims 39 and 48 dependent therefrom, respectively, are also directed to vaccines.

Dependent claims 41 and 42 recite methods of protecting living organisms against RNA viruses, which comprise introducing into a host an immunologically effective amount of the vaccine of claims 11 and 38, respectively.

B.　The Rejection

The Examiner took the position in her Examiner's Answer that the claims presently on appeal are not supported by an enabling disclosure because one of ordinary skill in the art would have had to engage in undue experimentation in February of 1983 (the effective filing date of Wright's application) to practice the subject matter of these claims, given their breadth, the unpredictability in the art, and the limited guidance Wright provides in his application. The Examiner noted that many of Wright's claims read on vaccines against all pathogenic RNA viruses, even though RNA viruses are a very diverse and genetically complex group of viruses which include, among others, acquired immunodeficiency syndrome (AIDS) viruses, leukemia viruses, and sarcoma viruses. The Examiner argued that Wright's single working example merely evidenced that Wright had obtained successfully a particular recombinant virus vaccine, and that this single success did not provide "sufficient likelihood" that other recombinant RNA viruses could be constructed without undue experimentation, or if they were constructed, that they would be useful in the design of like viral vaccines. The Examiner noted the inability of the scientific community to develop an efficacious AIDS virus vaccine for humans despite devoting a considerable amount of time and money to do so.

The Examiner further argued that, even though retroviruses as a class may exhibit similar gene order and possess envelope proteins, this alone does not support a general conclusion that all RNA virus envelope proteins will confer protection against the corresponding virus. The Examiner asserted that this held true even among avian RNA tumor viruses. At page 11 of her Answer, the Examiner stated that "one envelope gene's immunogenicity cannot be extrapolated to another envelope gene. The efficacy of each should be ascertained individually."

To support the foregoing, the Examiner relied upon an article by Thomas J. Matthews et al., *Prospects for Development of a Vaccine Against HIV, in Human Retroviruses, Cancer, and AIDS: Approaches to Prevention and Therapy* 313–25 (1988). This article indicates that AIDS retroviruses, which represent only a subset of all RNA viruses, were known even as late as 1988 to show great genetic diversity, including divergent virus envelopes. It further indicates that, although AIDS retroviruses elicited strong immune responses in goats and chimps in 1988, the resulting antibodies did not prevent retrovirus infectivity. Moreover, this article also recognizes at page 321 that, as of 1988, animal models for HIV infection and disease were likely to be imperfect, and therefore testing of primary vaccine candidates in man was necessary to determine safety, immunogenicity and efficacy.

Finally, the Examiner also argued that, irrespective of immunogenicity and vaccine considerations, the methods of identification, isolation, cloning, and recombination which Wright describes in his application in only a very general manner were not so developed in 1983 as to enable, without undue experimentation, the design and production of recombinant virus vaccines against any and all RNA viruses. The Examiner also asserted that the considerable amount of time and effort that it took Wright to construct the particular avian recombinant virus described in his single working example and to establish its efficacy as a vaccinating agent illustrates the amount of undue experimentation that would have been required in February of 1983 to practice Wright's invention, especially given that the efficacy of the developed virus could not be extrapolated with any certainty to other recombinant viruses at that time.

C. The Board Decision

In its January 16, 1992 decision, the Board held that the Examiner did not err in questioning the enablement of the physiological activity required by the appealed claims, given the breadth of these claims and the fact that a vaccine must by definition provoke an immunoprotective response upon administration. The Board further held that the record did not support Wright's arguments that this single working example enables some of his dependent claims which are closer in scope to the allowed claims than to independent claims 1 and 11. The Board found that, even if Wright was correct in stating that it was generally known that an "immune response" is assured by use of an antigenic envelope protein, the record did not establish that such an "immune response" would have been an immunoprotective one, or moreover, that one skilled in this art would have expected such a result in February of 1983. The Board relied upon the Matthews et al. article as evidencing that "the mere use of an envelope protein gene in the present invention is not seen to necessarily result in the obtention of successful vaccines throughout the scope of even these more limited claims."

II. DISCUSSION

In the present case, the PTO set forth a reasonable basis for finding that the scope of the appealed claims is not enabled by the general description and the single working example in the specification. Consequently, the burden shifted to Wright to present persuasive arguments, supported by suitable proofs where necessary, that the appealed claims are truly enabled. Wright failed to meet this burden.

Both the Examiner and the Board correctly pointed out that Wright's appealed claims are directed to vaccines, and methods of making and using these vaccines, which must by definition trigger an immunoprotective response in the host vaccinated; mere antigenic response is not enough. Both also correctly pointed out that Wright attempts to claim in many of the appealed claims any and all live, non-pathogenic vaccines, and processes for making such vaccines, which elicit immunoprotective activity in any animal toward any RNA virus. In addition, both properly stressed that many of the appealed claims encompass vaccines against AIDS viruses and that, because of the high degree of genetic, antigenic variations in such viruses, no one has yet, years after his invention, developed a generally successful AIDS virus vaccine.

The Matthews et al. article, published approximately 5 years after the effective filing date of Wright's application, adequately supports the Examiner's and the Board's position that, in February of 1983, the physiological activity of RNA viruses was sufficiently unpredictable that Wright's success in developing his specific avian recombinant virus vaccine would not have led one of ordinary skill in the art to believe reasonably that all living organisms could be immunized against infection by any pathogenic RNA virus by inoculating them with a live virus containing the antigenic code but not the pathogenic code of the RNA virus. The general description and the single example in Wright's specification, directed to a uniquely tailored in vitro method of producing in chicken C/O cells a vaccine against the PrASV avian tumor virus containing live RAV–Acn virus particles, did nothing more in February of 1983 than invite experimentation to determine whether other vaccines having in vivo immunoprotective activity could be constructed for other RNA viruses.

Wright argues that he has constructed successfully an env C recombinant vaccine according to the present invention and that certain recombinant AIDS virus vaccines carrying SIV (simian immunodeficiency virus) and HIV (human immunodeficiency virus) envelope genes have been produced which confer protective immunity in the animal models where they have been tested, and that these developments illustrate that the art is not so unpredictable as to require undue experimentation. However, all of these developments occurred after the effective filing date of Wright's application and are of no significance regarding what one skilled in the art believed as of that date. Furthermore, the fact that a few vaccines have been developed since the filing of Wright's application certainly does not by itself rebut the PTO's assertions regarding undue experimentation. Moreover, whether a few AIDS virus vaccines have been developed which confer immunity in some animal models is not the issue. The Examiner made reference to the difficulty that the scientific community is having in developing generally successful AIDS virus vaccines merely to illustrate that the art is not even today as predictable as Wright has suggested that it was back in 1983.

Wright also argues that several affidavits of record, namely, an October 22, 1984 declaration by Wright, an October 23, 1984 affidavit by O'Neill, and October 28, 1988 affidavits by Bennett and Burnett, successfully rebut the Board's and the Examiner's assertions regarding undue experimentation. However, Wright did not set forth in his brief to the Board any specific arguments regarding these affidavits, as required by 37 CFR 1.192(a), and therefore we are not required to address the arguments that Wright presents in this appeal regarding these affidavits.

Nevertheless, we note that each of these affidavits fails in its purpose because each merely contains unsupported conclusory statements as to the ultimate legal question. Furthermore, Burnett and Bennett do not even indicate in their affidavits that they actually reviewed the specification of Wright's application. In addition, although Wright states in his declaration that the individual steps making up his claimed process were "well within the skill of the art" at the time that he filed his application and makes reference to a list of publications that he contends supports this conclusory statement, a list which Wright also makes reference to in his arguments to this court, Wright fails to point out with any particularity in this declaration, or in his arguments to this court, how the listed documents evidence that a skilled artisan in

February of 1983 would have been able to carry out, without undue experimentation, the identification, isolation, cloning, recombination, and efficacy testing steps required to practice the full scope of the appealed claims.

Wright further argues that, even if those claims which provide a broad scope of protection are not enabled, this is not the case as to those claims restricted to vaccines against avian tumor viruses. Wright maintains that there is no doubt that it was known in 1983 that the technique of producing a live vaccine proven effective for one particular strain of avian RNA viruses would be effective as to other strains of avian RNA viruses. Wright argues that the scientific literature supports the position that the art was predictable at least with respect to avian RNA viruses, because gene function and order are similar among all avian RNA viruses.

We are not persuaded. Wright has failed to establish by evidence or arguments that, in February of 1983, a skilled scientist would have believed reasonably that Wright's success with a particular strain of an avian RNA virus could be extrapolated with a reasonable expectation of success to other avian RNA viruses. Indeed, Wright has failed to point out with any particularity the scientific literature existing in February of 1983 that supports his position. Furthermore, Wright's May 17, 1989 declaration indicates that Wright himself believed during the relevant time period that in vivo testing was necessary to determine the efficacy of vaccines. In this declaration, Wright stated in pertinent part:

> Preparation of a patent application following conception of the invention awaited such time as there was a reasonable expectation that the results of innoculation [sic] would be successful. This became apparent only by reason of survival of the chickens that had been innoculated [sic].

Wright now argues that all he meant by the foregoing was that in vivo efficacy testing was necessary for the first avian RNA viruses vaccine that he developed in order to prove his hypothesis. Wright asserts that, once his hypothesis had been proven, a skilled artisan would have expected that similar in vivo results could be obtained for vaccines developed for other avian retroviruses. However, a paper that Wright co-authored with David Bennett, titled "Avian Retroviral Recombinant Expressing Foreign Envelope Delays Tumor Formation of ASV–A–Induced Sarcoma," which was attached to a declaration by Wright dated November 19, 1985, suggests that, even as late as 1985, the genetic diversity existing among chickens alone required efficacy testing even among the members of this narrow group.

Accordingly, we see no error in the Board's finding that one skilled in the art would not have believed as early as February of 1983 that the success of Wright's one example could be extrapolated with a reasonable expectation of success to all avian RNA viruses.

NOTES

1. The Wright Result? How much patent protection do you believe Wright should have obtained based upon his single working example? If Wright was first to discover this method, why should he not have a right to exclude anyone who made a vaccine using as an antigen the antigenic section of that virus' genes? Or should his alternative argument, that he could obtain the right to exclude others from avian RNA viruses, have been accepted? Similarly, in regard to the *Enzo* case, discussed in the next note, what protection should Masayori Inouye have received for the idea of antisense and its successful application to three genes in E. Coli?

2. Making Sense of Antisense. In *Enzo Biochem, Inc., v. Calgene, Inc.,* 188 F.3d 1362 (Fed. Cir. 1999), the Federal Circuit considered a claim that essentially covered the use of antisense technology in all types of cells—based on a disclosure that taught how to use antitsense technology with respect to three genes in one organism (*E. coli*). As explained by Judge Lourie:

> Antisense technology aims to control the expression of a particular gene by blocking the translation of the mRNA produced by the transcription of that gene. Translation is blocked by incorporation of a specially designed DNA construct into the cell of interest; this construct contains part or all of the nucleotide sequence of the gene to be blocked, except that the sequence is inverted relative to its natural conformation.... The antisense DNA constructs typically resemble their native counterparts in that the inverted gene sequence is preceded by a promoter sequence ... and followed by a termination sequence.... The inverted gene sequence is transcribed by an RNA polymerase as if it were the gene sequence in its proper orientation, thereby generating an RNA strand which is complementary to, and thereby able to bind to, the mRNA transcript of the native gene. This RNA strand is known as messenger interfering complementary RNA ("micRNA"), because when it binds the native mRNA, that mRNA cannot be translated. Consequently, the protein for which that gene codes can no longer be produced, and gene expression is thereby blocked.

188 F.3d at 1366–67. After concluding the Antisense technology is very unpredictable, the court remarked:

> The district court found that the amount of direction presented and the number of working examples provided in the specifications were "very narrow," despite the wide breadth of the claims at issue, the unpredictability of antisense technology, and the high quantity of experimentation necessary to practice antisense in cells outside of *E. coli*.... Outside of the three genes regulated in *E. coli*, virtually no guidance, direction, or working examples were provided for practicing the invention in eukaryotes, or even any prokaryote other than *E. coli*. In addressing a similar case involving limited disclosure, we observed that:
>
> > It is well settled that patent applicants are not required to disclose every species encompassed by their claims, even in an unpredictable

art. However, there must be sufficient disclosure, either through illustrative examples or terminology, to teach those of ordinary skill how to make and use the invention as broadly as it is claimed.

Here, however, the teachings set forth in the specifications provide no more than a "plan" or "invitation" for those of skill in the art to experiment practicing antisense in eukaryotic cells; they do not provide sufficient guidance or specificity as to how to execute that plan....

Tossing out the mere germ of an idea does not constitute enabling disclosure. While every aspect of a generic claim certainly need not have been carried out by an inventor, or exemplified in the specification, reasonable detail must be provided in order to enable members of the public to understand and carry out the invention.

188 F.3d at 1374.

PHARMACEUTICAL RESOURCES, INC. v. ROXANE LABORATORIES, INC.

United States Court of Appeals for the Federal Circuit, 2007
253 Fed. Appx. 26

Before Michel, Chief Judge, Moore, Circuit Judge, and Cote, District Judge.

Moore, Circuit Judge.

Pharmaceutical Resources, Inc. and Par Pharmaceuticals, Inc. (Par, collectively) appeal the district court's grant of summary judgment of invalidity of the asserted claims in U.S. Patent Nos. 6,593,318 (the '318 patent) and 6,593,320 (the '320 patent) in favor of defendant Roxane Laboratories, Inc. (Roxane). *Pharm. Res., Inc. v. Roxane Labs., Inc.*, 2006 WL 3231427 (D.N.J. Nov. 8, 2006). Because the district court properly determined that the asserted claims of the '318 and '320 patents are invalid as a matter of law under 35 U.S.C. § 112, first paragraph, for lack of enablement, we *affirm* the judgment.

BACKGROUND

The '320 patent [and] '318 patent ... share a common specification, which was first filed as Serial No. 09/063,241 ("the 241 application," now U.S. Patent No. 6,028,065). The '318 and '320 patents relate to stable flocculated suspensions of megestrol acetate and methods for making such suspensions.

Bristol–Myers Squibb (BMS) was the first company to develop and patent a liquid pharmaceutical composition of megestrol acetate. BMS' U.S. Patent No. 5,338,732 (the Atzinger patent) teaches that stable suspensions of megestrol acetate can be created but that the type and concentration of the surfactant in solution is critical to creating a stable flocculated suspension. The Atzinger patent discloses only one stable flocculated suspension composition, combining megestrol acetate with polyethylene glycol as a wetting agent and polysorbate 80 as a surfactant.

When Par formulated a generic version of BMS's patented product, it sought to design around the Atzinger patent claims by utilizing other surfactants and wetting agents. In developing its own product, Par discovered that flocculated suspensions of megestrol acetate could be formed using a much wider range of ingredients and concentrations than taught in the Atzinger patent, including other surfactants and wetting agents. Through those efforts, Par received a series of patents on its flocculated suspensions, including the '318 and '320 patents.

Par brought the present suit in 2003, asserting that Roxane infringes certain claims in the '318 and '320 patents. Roxane denies infringement and asserts that the claims of the '318 and '320 patents are invalid and unenforceable. After the district court issued a *Markman* order, Roxane moved for summary judgment of invalidity, arguing, *inter alia*, that the asserted claims in the '318 and '320 patents are invalid for lack of enablement. At issue are independent claims 19 and 41 of the '318 patent (and claims 20, 25–27, 32, 34, 42, 47, and 53 dependent thereon) and independent claim 1 from the '320 patent (and claims 2 and 6 dependent thereon). Claim 19 of '318 patent recites:

> Claim 19. An oral pharmaceutical composition in the form of a stable flocculated suspension in water comprising: (a) megestrol acetate; (b) at least two compounds selected from the group consisting of polyethylene glycol, propylene glycol, glycerol, and sorbitol; and (c) a surfactant.

The district court granted Roxane's motion for summary judgment, concluding that "as a matter of law Par is not entitled to the broad claims it asserts in this action."

Par appeals the district court's grant of summary judgment of invalidity.

ANALYSIS

We review a district court's grant of summary judgment de novo, reapplying the standard applicable at the district court. *See Rhodia Chimie v. PPG Indus., Inc.*, 402 F.3d 1371, 1376 (Fed.Cir.2005). Although a patent claim is presumed enabled unless proven otherwise by clear and convincing evidence, *Ormco Corp. v. Align Tech., Inc.*, 498 F.3d 1307, 1317–18 (Fed.Cir.2007), to defeat Roxane's motion for summary judgment Par must put forth evidence that does "more than simply raise some doubt regarding enablement: 'If the evidence is merely colorable, or is not significantly probative, summary judgment may be granted.'" *Johns Hopkins Univ. v. CellPro, Inc.*, 152 F.3d 1342, 1359 (Fed.Cir.1998) (quoting *Anderson v. Liberty Lobby, Inc.* 477 U.S. 242, 249–50 (1986)).

Whether the subject matter of a patent claim satisfies the enablement requirement under 35 U.S.C. § 112, first paragraph, is a question of law, reviewed de novo, based on underlying facts, reviewed for clear error. *AK Steel Corp. v. Sollac & Ugine*, 344 F.3d 1234, 1238–39 (Fed.Cir. 2003). In *In re Wands*, 858 F.2d 731, 737 (Fed.Cir.1988), this court set forth eight factors relevant to the enablement analysis:

> (1) the quantity of experimentation necessary, (2) the amount of direction or guidance presented, (3) the presence or absence of working examples, (4) the nature of the invention, (5) the state of the prior art, (6) the relative skill of those in the art, (7) the predictability or unpredictability of the art, and (8) the breadth of the claims.

In this case, Par sought extremely broad claims in a field of art that it acknowledged was highly unpredictable, therefore, Par has set a high burden that its patent disclosure must meet to satisfy the requisite *quid pro quo* of patent enablement. *See Liebel–Flarsheim Co. v. Medrad, Inc.*, 481 F.3d 1371, 1380 (Fed.Cir.2007) ("The motto, 'beware of what one asks for,' might be applicable here."). The scintilla of evidence put forward by Par to suggest that the claims are enabled, most of which actually conflicts with the intrinsic evidence in this case, does not raise a genuine issue of material fact.

A. *Unpredictability of the Art*

In this case, *all* of the record evidence establishes that the art of making stable flocculated suspensions of megestrol acetate is highly unpredictable. The common disclosure of the '318 and '320 patents discusses this unpredictability:

> The surfactants in a stable flocculated suspension need to be selected carefully and be used within a critical concentration range because even minor changes can have an effect on the properties of such a stable formulation. This is particularly true for megestrol acetate because predictability based on prior art teachings does not apply in this case, as noted hereinabove.

Par also stressed the unpredictability of this particular pharmaceutical formulation field during prosecution of the 241 application:

> [B]ased on the uncertainty of results once any modification in types of ingredients or amounts is made, as discussed in the prior art including Atzinger at al. [sic] ..., a person skilled in the art would not have any reasonable expectation of success in maintaining a stable flocculated suspension of megestrol acetate once a change in the type or amount of surfactant or wetting agent is made.

The extrinsic evidence also supports the conclusion that the relevant field is unpredictable. During its previous litigation with BMS, for instance, Par relied in part on the unpredictability of this art field. Par's technical expert opined on the nature of the art, stating:

> Formulating a flocculated suspension is, in my view, one of the most delicate formulation efforts in terms of balancing the excipients, and it is also very difficult to predict in terms of what its properties will

be or what the effect of different excipients will be. There is no known method in the art to predict whether a change in inactive ingredients will produce a stable suspension.

In the current litigation, Par's technical expert, Dr. Klibanov, explained that "megestrol acetate is sufficiently unique as a compound [such] that prior art references teaching how to wet other insoluble compounds provide absolutely no guidance with regard to wetting megestrol acetate." Similarly, Dr. Chao, a named inventor of the '318 and '320 patents, testified that predictions could not be made regarding whether or not particular combinations of ingredients including megestrol acetate would form a stable flocculated compound, but rather, this required actual experimentation.

B.   Breadth of the Claims

In addition, the district court concluded that claims 19 and 41 of the '318 patent and claim 1 of the '320 patent "have an extraordinarily broad scope."

Par argued that the claims at issue are not as broad as suggested by the district court because the hypothetical pharmaceutical formulator would start experimenting with the twenty-two surfactants that the United States Pharmacopoeia and National Formulary (USP–NF) has recognized and approved for use in oral pharmaceuticals in order to practice the invention. In addition, Par argues that the district court erred in assuming that the claims covered use of a surfactant in *any* concentration.

The claims allow the choice of *any* surfactant in *any* concentration (with the exception that claim 1 of the '320 patent does not permit polysorbate as the surfactant if polyethylene glycol is the chosen wetting agent). The language of the claims and the specification both suggest that the claims encompass hundreds of possible surfactants. Par admitted as much in oral argument. Further, the disclosure of the '318 and '320 patents list dozens of "suitable" surfactant genera beyond those listed by the USP–NF.

Moreover, nothing in the language of the claims limits the concentration of surfactant. The specification gives a preferred concentration range for only one surfactant, docusate sodium. To the extent that Par now suggests that an ordinarily skilled artisan would know that surfactant concentrations over 0.030% weight-per-volume would not work, it follows that a large part of the asserted claims' scope is directed toward inoperative embodiments. The number of inoperative combinations is significant when assessing the experimentation that an ordinarily skilled artisan would need to practice the claimed invention. *Atlas Powder Co. v. E.I. du Pont De Nemours & Co.*, 750 F.2d 1569, 1576 (Fed. Cir. 1984).

We thus conclude that the district court properly determined that the claims at issue "have an extraordinarily broad scope." The district court also correctly noted in its analysis that our case law requires that the full scope of the claims be enabled. *See Liebel–Flarsheim Co.*, 481 F.3d at 1379; *AK Steel*, 344 F.3d at 1241.

C. Enablement of the Asserted Claims

Taking into account the broad scope of the claims and the highly unpredictable nature of the art, Par's evidence regarding enablement fails to establish a genuine issue of material fact as to whether or not the claims are enabled and therefore fails to defeat summary judgment.

Par's specification discloses only three working examples, utilizing only one new surfactant. Given the highly unpredictable nature of the invention and the extremely broad scope of the claims, these three working examples do not provide an enabling disclosure commensurate with the entire scope of the claims.

Additionally, the two declarations from Par's expert witnesses on the issue of enablement are conclusory and lack evidentiary support or specifics as to the experimentation that would be needed to practice the entire scope of the claims. Accordingly, these declarations are legally insufficient to raise a genuine issue of material fact as to whether the claims are enabled. *See, e.g., Automotive Tech. Int'l v. BMW of N. Am., Inc.*, 501 F.3d 1274, 1284–85 (Fed.Cir.2007) ("[H]aving failed to provide any detail regarding why no experimentation was necessary, the declaration does not create a genuine issue of material fact as to enablement.").

Finally, Par argues that its own experiments with megestrol acetate solutions, to which the inventor, Dr. Femia, testified, are sufficient to create a genuine issue of material fact regarding enablement of the asserted claims. The district court determined that this evidence supports a conclusion of lack of enablement because it evidences numerous unsuccessful attempts by Par to practice subject matter within the scope of the claims.

Interpreting Dr. Femia's testimony in the light most favorable to Par, that Dr. Femia was successful in formulating the claimed composition with seven surfactants, gives rise to "merely colorable" evidence, and fails to create a genuine issue of material fact as to enablement of the full scope of the claims. It is highly relevant that the intrinsic evidence stresses the criticality of the choice of surfactant and concentration. Given this fact, the extraordinarily broad scope of the claims, which encompasses hundreds of surfactants, the high degree of unpredictability of the art, and the minimal guidance provided by the three working examples in the specification, the mere fact that Par's inventors were able to create successfully a stable flocculated megestrol acetate suspension with seven surfactants does not create a genuine issue of material fact regarding enablement.

Based on the foregoing, we conclude as a matter of law that each of the asserted claims of the '318 and '320 patents is invalid under 35 U.S.C. § 112, first paragraph, for lack of enablement. Accordingly, we affirm.

NOTES

1. **Striking a Balance.** Balancing the scope of patent protection and the extent of the inventor's contribution is a difficult task. If courts strictly limit the scope of patent protection to the specific examples disclosed in the specification, competitors could readily circumvent the patent through minor changes in design. But if the protection is advanced too liberally, then the patentee could obtain a windfall that strangles future technical advance. The Supreme Court's wariness of the latter was demonstrated when it encountered Samuel Morse's telegraphy patent. The final claim of that patent provided:

> Eighth. I do not propose to limit myself to the specific machinery, or parts of machinery, described in the foregoing specifications and claims; the essence of my invention being the use of the motive power of the electric or falvanic current, which I call electro-magnetism, however developed, for making or printing intelligible characters, letters, or signs, at any distances, being a new application of that power, of which I claim to be the first inventor or discoverer.

See O'Reilly v. Morse, 56 U.S. (15 How.) 62, 86 (1853). The Court held the claim invalid:

> Indeed, if the eighth claim of the patentee can be maintained, there was no necessity for any specification, further than to say that he had discovered that, by using the motive power of electro-magnetism, he could print intelligible characters at any distance. We presume it will be admitted on all hands, that no patent could have issued on such a specification. Yet this claim can derive no aid from the specification filed. It is outside of it, and the patentee claims beyond it.

This rejection would today be cast in terms of enablement: Morse had simply claimed far more than he had invented. A more recent decision *In re Cook*, 439 F.2d 730 (CCPA 1971), covers much the same ground.

2. **Enablement, claim scope, and improvement inventions.** It is axiomatic that an invention that improves on a basic innovation is not enabled by the disclosure of the basic innovation because the improvement must show a non-obvious advance to get a patent. These, improvement inventions—sometimes referred to as dependent inventions—are common. An improvement, however, cannot act to invalidate basic inventions on the theory that an embodiment within the scope of the claims (the improvement) was not enabled by the specification of the original basic invention.

In *Liebel-Flarsheim Co. v. Medrad, Inc.*, 481 F.3d 1371 (Fed. Cir. 2007), the Federal Circuit considered patents on a front-loading fluid injector with a replaceable syringe for delivering a contrast agent to a patient. Because the syringe can withstand high pressures, the disclosure showed an embodiment that includes a pressure jacket. In fact, every embodiment in the patent includes such a jacket. The claims in the originally filed application explicitly recited a pressure jacket in front of the opening for the syringe. The claims before the Federal Circuit did not, however, recite a pressure jacket. The accused fluid injectors did not use a pressure jacket. The Federal Circuit concluded that the claims that did not expressly require a pressure jacket were invalid because the specification did not enable any injector without a pressure jacket. The Federal Circuit reasoned that one of ordinary skill in the art would have to experiment unduly to make an injector without a pressure jacket. In other words, those claims were overbroad.

From another vantage point, the accused product without the pressure jacket was probably simply an improved embodiment of the invention. This improvement would not need to show enablement. The Federal Circuit did not discuss this prospect. Do you think the Federal Circuit simply overlooked the fundamental proposition of patent law that improvement inventions are by definition not enabled? Alternatively, maybe the Circuit considered it obvious the same injectors without a pressure jacket was a different embodiment entirely rather than an improvement on the disclosed injector invention?

§ 8.2 "WRITTEN DESCRIPTION"— PROSCRIPTION ON NEW MATTER

The written description requirement is a substitute for a different statutory provision. In 35 U.S.C.A. § 132, the Patent Act states: "No amendment shall introduce new matter into the disclosure of the invention." Thus, the Patent Act forbids any new claim, claim amendment, or addition to the specification after the filing date from introducing new matter into the disclosure. This requirement prevents an applicant from continually updating his application or adding new inventive ideas that actually came after the original filing date. Thus, this new matter prohibition polices the priority dates of inventive ideas. Thus, to amend a claim or add a new claim without encountering the new matter proscription, an applicant must show that the original application disclosed or contained the subject matter included in the amendment. In other words, any claims amended after the filing date or new claims filed after the filing date must contain the same invention as the original disclosure. The new claims or amendment cannot contain new matter.

In the United States, case law changed the legal basis for a new matter rejection to a written description rejection under 35 U.S.C.A. § 112. *In re Rasmussen,* 650 F.2d 1212 (CCPA 1981). Written description, however, performs the same priority policing function. Therefore, although the written description requirement ordinarily serves a different purpose than enablement, the next case demonstrates that distinguishing the two doctrines and their statutory bases may prove more elusive. Moreover, as later cases will show, changing the legal basis of the new matter rejection in the United States has opened the door to unusual applications of the written description requirement.

VAS–CATH INC. v. MAHURKAR

United States Court of Appeals, Federal Circuit, 1991
935 F.2d 1555

Before Rich, Michel and Plager, Circuit Judges.

RICH, CIRCUIT JUDGE.

Sakharam D. Mahurkar and Quinton Instruments Company (collectively Mahurkar) appeal from the partial final judgment of the United States District Court for the Northern District of Illinois, Easterbrook, J., sitting by designation. Granting partial summary judgment to Vas–Cath Incorporated and its licensee Gambro, Inc. (collectively Vas–Cath), the district court declared Mahurkar's two United States utility patents Nos. 4,568,329 ('329 patent) and 4,692,141 ('141 patent), titled "Double Lumen Catheter," invalid as anticipated under 35 U.S.C. § 102(b). In reaching its decision, the district court concluded that none of the twenty-one claims of the two utility patents was entitled, under 35 U.S.C. § 120, to the benefit of the filing date of Mahurkar's earlier-filed United States design patent application Serial No. 356,081 ('081 design application), which comprised the same drawings as the utility patents, because the design application did not provide a "written description of the invention" as required by 35 U.S.C. § 112, first paragraph. We reverse the grant of summary judgment with respect to all claims.

BACKGROUND

Sakharam Mahurkar filed the '081 design application, also titled "Double Lumen Catheter," on March 8, 1982. The application was abandoned on November 30, 1984. Figures 1–6 of the '081 design application are reproduced below.

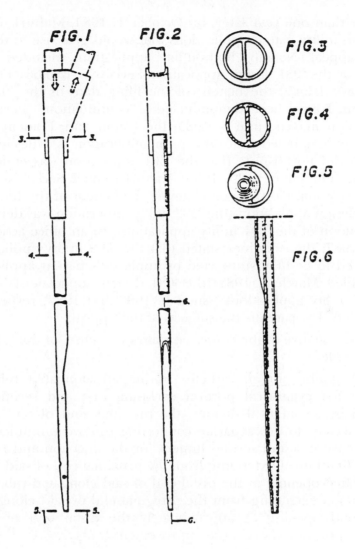

FIG.1   FIG.2   FIG.3

FIG.4

FIG.5

FIG.6

As shown, Mahurkar's catheter comprises a pair of tubes (lumens) designed to allow blood to be removed from an artery, processed in an apparatus that removes impurities, and returned close to the place of removal. Prior art catheters utilized concentric circular lumens, while Mahurkar's employs joined semi-circular tubes that come to a single tapered tip. Advantageously, the puncture area of Mahurkar's semicircular catheter is 42% less than that of a coaxial catheter carrying the same quantity of blood, and its conical tip yields low rates of injury to the blood. The prior art coaxial catheters are now obsolete; Mahurkar's catheters appear to represent more than half of the world's sales.

After filing the '081 design application, Mahurkar also filed a Canadian Industrial Design application comprising the same drawings plus additional textual description. On August 9, 1982, Canadian Industrial Design 50,089 (Canadian '089) issued on that application.

More than one year later, on October 1, 1984, Mahurkar filed the first of two utility patent applications that would give rise to the patents now on appeal. Notably, both utility applications included the same drawings as the '081 design application. Serial No. 656,601 ('601 utility application) claimed the benefit of the filing date of the '081 design application, having been denominated a "continuation" thereof. In an Office Action mailed June 6, 1985, the Patent and Trademark Office (PTO) examiner noted that "the prior application is a design application," but did not dispute that the '601 application was entitled to its filing date. On January 29, 1986, Mahurkar filed Serial No. 823,592 ('592 utility application), again claiming the benefit of the filing date of the '081 design application (the '592 utility application was denominated a continuation of the '601 utility application). In an office action mailed April 1, 1987, the examiner stated that the '592 utility application was "considered to be fully supported by applicant's parent application SN 356,081 filed March 8, 1982 [the '081 design application]." The '601 and '592 utility applications issued in 1986 and 1987, respectively, as the '329 and '141 patents, the subjects of this appeal.

[Representative of the contested claims is claim 7 of the '329 patent, which provided:

7. A double lumen catheter having an elongated tube with a proximal first cylindrical portion enclosing first and second lumens separated by an internal divider, the proximal end of said elongated tube connecting to two separate connecting tubes communicating with the respective first and second lumens for the injection and removal of fluid, the first lumen extending from the proximal end of said elongated tube to a first opening at the distal end of said elongated tube, and the second lumen extending from the proximal end of said elongated tube to a second opening at approximately the distal end of said first cylindrical portion, wherein the improvement comprises:

> said elongated tube having at its distal end a smooth conical tapered tip that smoothly merges with a second cylindrical portion of said elongated tube,

> and said second cylindrical portion enclosing the first lumen from the conical tapered tip to approximately the location of said second opening, said second cylindrical portion having a diameter substantially greater than one-half but substantially less than a full diameter of said first cylindrical portion,

> said divider in said first cylindrical portion being planar,

> the lumens being "D" shaped in cross-section in said first cylindrical portion,

> the elongated tube being provided with a plurality of holes in the region of the conical tapered tip, and

> said first cylindrical portion of the elongated tube smoothly merging with said second cylindrical portion of the elongated tube.]

Vas–Cath sued Mahurkar in June 1988, seeking a declaratory judgment that the catheters it manufactured did not infringe Mahurkar's '329 and '141 utility patents. Vas–Cath's complaint alleged, inter alia, that the '329 and '141 patents were both invalid as anticipated under 35 U.S.C. § 102(b) by Canadian '089. Vas–Cath's anticipation theory was premised on the argument that the '329 and '141 patents were not entitled under 35 U.S.C. § 120 to the filing date of the '081 design application because its drawings did not provide an adequate "written description" of the claimed invention as required by 35 U.S.C. § 112, first paragraph.

Mahurkar counterclaimed, alleging infringement. Both parties moved for summary judgment on certain issues, including validity. For purposes of the summary judgment motion, Mahurkar conceded that, if he could not antedate it, Canadian '089 would represent an enabling and thus anticipating § 102(b) reference against the claims of his '329 and '141 utility patents. Vas–Cath conceded that the '081 design drawings enabled one skilled in the art to practice the claimed invention within the meaning of 35 U.S.C. § 112, first paragraph. Thus, the question before the district court was whether the disclosure of the '081 design application, namely, the drawings without more, adequately meets the "written description" requirement also contained in § 112, first paragraph, so as to entitle Mahurkar to the benefit of the 1982 filing date of the '081 design application for his two utility patents and thereby antedates Canadian '089.

Concluding that the drawings do not do so, and that therefore the utility patents are anticipated by Canadian '089, the district court held the '329 and '141 patents wholly invalid under 35 U.S.C. § 102(b).... This appeal followed.

DISCUSSION

The issue before us is whether the district court erred in concluding, on summary judgment, that the disclosure of the '081 design application does not provide a § 112, first paragraph "written description" adequate to support each of the claims of the '329 and '141 patents. If the court so erred as to any of the 21 claims at issue, the admittedly anticipatory disclosure of Canadian '089 will have been antedated (and the basis for the court's grant of summary judgment nullified) as to those claims.

THE "WRITTEN DESCRIPTION" REQUIREMENT OF § 112

Application of the "written description" requirement ... is central to resolution of this appeal. The district court, having reviewed this court's decisions on the subject, remarked that "[u]nfortunately, it is not so easy to tell what the law of the Federal Circuit is." Perhaps that is so, and, therefore, before proceeding to the merits, we review the case law development of the "written description" requirement with a view to improving the situation.

The cases indicate that the "written description" requirement most often comes into play where claims not presented in the application when filed are presented thereafter. Alternatively, patent applicants often seek the benefit of the filing date of an earlier-filed foreign or United States application under 35 U.S.C. § 119 or 35 U.S.C. § 120, respectively, for claims of a later-filed application. The question raised by these situations is most often phrased as whether the application provides "adequate support" for the claim(s) at issue; it has also been analyzed in terms of "new matter" under 35 U.S.C. § 132. The "written description" question similarly arises in the interference context, where the issue is whether the specification of one party to the interference can support the claim(s) corresponding to the count(s) at issue, i.e., whether that party "can make the claim" corresponding to the interference count.

To the uninitiated, it may seem anomalous that the first paragraph of 35 U.S.C. § 112 has been interpreted as requiring a separate "description of the invention," when the invention is, necessarily, the subject matter defined in the claims under consideration. One may wonder what purpose a separate "written description" requirement serves, when the second paragraph of § 112 expressly requires that the applicant conclude his specification "with one or more claims particularly pointing out and distinctly claiming the subject matter which the applicant regards as his invention."

One explanation is historical: the "written description" requirement was a part of the patent statutes at a time before claims were required. A case in point is *Evans v. Eaton*, 20 U.S. (7 Wheat.) 356 (1822), in which the Supreme Court affirmed the circuit court's decision that the plaintiff's patent was "deficient," and that the plaintiff could not recover for infringement thereunder. The patent laws then in effect, namely the Patent Act of 1793, did not require claims, but did require, in its 3d section, that the patent applicant "deliver a written description of his invention, and of the manner of using, or process of compounding, the same, in such full, clear and exact terms, as to distinguish the same from all things before known, and to enable any person skilled in the art or science of which it is a branch, or with which it is most nearly connected, to make, compound and use the same. . . ." In view of this language, the Court concluded that the specification of a patent had two objects, the first of which was "to enable artisans to make and use [the invention]. . . ." The second object of the specification was to put the public in possession of what the party claims as his own invention, so as to ascertain if he claims anything that is in common use, or is already known, and to guard against prejudice or injury from the use of an invention which the party may otherwise innocently suppose not to be patented. It is, therefore, for the purpose of warning an innocent purchaser, or other person using a machine, of his infringement of the patent; and at the same time, of taking from the inventor the means of practising upon the credulity or the fears of other persons, by pretending that his invention is more than what it really is, or different from its ostensible objects, that the patentee is required to distinguish his invention in his specification. *Id.* at 434.

A second, policy-based rationale for the inclusion in § 112 of both the first paragraph "written description" and the second paragraph "definiteness" requirements was set forth in *Rengo Co. v. Molins Mach. Co.*, 657 F.2d 535, 551 (3d Cir.), *cert. denied*, 454 U.S. 1055 (1981):

> [T]here is a subtle relationship between the policies underlying the description and definiteness requirements, as the two standards, while complementary, approach a similar problem from different directions. Adequate description of the invention guards against the inventor's overreaching by insisting that he recount his invention in such detail that his future claims can be determined to be encompassed within his original creation. The definiteness requirement shapes the future conduct of persons other than the inventor, by insisting that they receive notice of the scope of the patented device.

[handwritten margin note: written description guards against inventor's overreaching by describing invention in such detail that you can tell if future claims are included or not]

With respect to the first paragraph of § 112 the severability of its "written description" provision from its enablement ("make and use") provision was recognized by this court's predecessor, the Court of Customs and Patent Appeals, as early as *In re Ruschig*, 379 F.2d 990 (CCPA 1967). Although the appellants in that case had presumed that the rejection appealed from was based on the enablement requirement of § 112, the court disagreed:

> [The question is not whether [one skilled in the art] would be so enabled but whether the specification discloses the compound to him, specifically, as something appellants actually invented.... If [the rejection is] based on section 112, it is on the requirement thereof that "The specification shall contain a written description of the invention * * *."

The issue, as the court saw it, was one of fact: "Does the specification convey clearly to those skilled in the art, to whom it is addressed, in any way, the information that appellants invented that specific compound [claimed]?"

In a 1971 case again involving chemical subject matter, the court expressly stated that "it is possible for a specification to enable the practice of an invention as broadly as it is claimed, and still not describe that invention." *In re DiLeone*, 436 F.2d 1404, 1405 (CCPA 1971). As an example, the court posited the situation "where the specification discusses only compound A and contains no broadening language of any kind. This might very well enable one skilled in the art to make and use compounds B and C; yet the class consisting of A, B and C has not been described."

[handwritten margin note: specs may enable one to create claims not described in written description]

Since its inception, the Court of Appeals for the Federal Circuit has frequently addressed the "written description" requirement of § 112. A fairly uniform standard for determining compliance with the "written description" requirement has been maintained throughout: "Although [the applicant] does not have to describe exactly the subject matter claimed, ... the description must clearly allow persons of ordinary skill in the art to recognize that [he or she] invented what is claimed." *In re Gosteli*, 872 F.2d 1008, 1012 (Fed.Cir.1989) (citations omitted). "[T]he test for sufficiency of support in a parent application is whether the disclosure of the application relied upon 'reasonably conveys to the artisan that the inventor had possession at that time of the later claimed subject matter.'" *Ralston Purina Co. v. Far–Mar–Co, Inc.*, 772 F.2d 1570, 1575 (Fed.Cir.1985). Our cases also provide that compliance with the "written description" requirement of § 112 is a question of fact, to be reviewed under the clearly erroneous standard.

The purpose of the "written description" requirement is broader than to merely explain how to "make and use"; the applicant must also convey with reasonable clarity to those skilled in the art that, as of the filing date sought, he or she was in possession of the invention. The invention is, for purposes of the "written description" inquiry, whatever is now claimed.

THE DISTRICT COURT'S ANALYSIS

We agree with the district court's conclusion that drawings alone may be sufficient to provide the "written description of the invention" required by § 112, first paragraph.

Whether the drawings are those of a design application or a utility application is not determinative, although in most cases the latter are much more detailed. In the instant case, however, the design drawings are substantially identical to the utility application drawings.

Although we join with the district court in concluding that drawings may suffice to satisfy the "written description" requirement of § 112, we can not agree with the legal standard that the court imposed for "written description" compliance, nor with the court's conclusion that no genuine issues of material fact were in dispute.

With respect to the former, the district court stated that although the '081 design drawings in question "allowed practice" [i.e., enabled], they did not necessarily show what the invention is, when "the invention" could be a subset or a superset of the features shown. Is the invention the semi-circular lumens? The conical tip? The ratio at which the tip tapers? The shape, size, and placement of the inlets and outlets? You can measure all of these things from the diagrams in serial '081 and so can practice the device, but you cannot tell, because serial '081 does not say, what combination of these things is "the invention", and what range of variation is allowed without exceeding the scope of the claims. To show one example of an invention, even a working model, is not to describe what is novel or important.

We find the district court's concern with "what the invention is" misplaced, and its requirement that the '081 drawings "describe what is novel or important" legal error. There is "no legally recognizable or protected 'essential' element, 'gist' or 'heart' of the invention in a combination patent." *Aro Mfg. Co. v. Convertible Top Replacement Co.*, 365 U.S. 336, 345 (1961). "The invention" is defined by the claims on appeal. The instant claims do not recite only a pair of semi-circular lumens, or a conical tip, or a ratio at which the tip tapers, or the shape, size, and placement of the inlets and outlets; they claim a double lumen catheter having a combination of those features. That combination invention is what the '081 drawings show. As the district court itself recognized, "what Mahurkar eventually patented is exactly what the pictures in serial '081 show."

We find the "range of variation" question, much emphasized by the parties, more troublesome. The district court stated that "although Mahurkar's patents use the same diagrams, [the claims] contain limitations that did not follow ineluctably [i.e., inevitably] from the diagrams." As an example, the court stated (presumably with respect to independent claims 1 and 7 of the '329 patent) that the utility patents claim a return lumen that is "substantially greater than one-half but substantially less than a full diameter" after it makes the transition from semi-circular to circular cross-section, and the drawings of serial '081 fall in this range. But until the utility application was filed, nothing established that they had to—for that matter that the utility patent would claim anything other than the precise ratio in the diagrams....". Mahurkar argues that one of ordinary skill in this art, looking at the '081 drawings, would be able to derive the claimed range.

The declaration of Dr. Stephen Ash, submitted by Mahurkar, is directed to these concerns. Dr. Ash, a physician specializing in nephrology (the study of the kidney and its diseases) and chairman of a corporation that develops and manufactures biomedical devices including catheters, explains why one of skill in the art of catheter design and manufacture, studying the drawings of the '081 application in early 1982, would have understood from them that the return lumen must have a diameter within the range recited by independent claims 1 and 7 of the '329 patent. Dr. Ash explains in detail that a return (longer) lumen of diameter less than half that of the two lumens combined would produce too great a pressure increase, while a return lumen of diameter equal or larger than that of the two lumens combined would result in too great a pressure drop. "Ordinary experience with the flow of blood in catheters would lead directly away from any such arrangement," Ash states.

Although the district court found this reasoning "logical," it noted that later patents issued to Mahurkar disclose diameter ratios closer to 1.0 (U.S. Patent No. 4,584,968) and exactly 0.5 (U.S. Des. Patent No. 272,651). If these other ratios were desirable, the district court queried, "how does serial '081 necessarily exclude the[m]?"

The district court erred in taking Mahurkar's other patents into account. Mahurkar's later patenting of inventions involving different range limitations is irrelevant to the issue at hand. Application sufficiency under § 112, first paragraph, must be judged as of the filing date.

081 drawing dont have to exclude all ranges other than those claimed

The court further erred in applying a legal standard that essentially required the drawings of the '081 design application to necessarily exclude all diameters other than those within the claimed range. We question whether any drawing could ever do so. At least with respect to independent claims 1 and 7 of the '329 patent and claims depending therefrom, the proper test is whether the drawings conveyed with reasonable clarity to those of ordinary skill that Mahurkar had in fact invented the catheter recited in those claims, having (among several other limitations) a return lumen diameter substantially less than 1.0 but substantially greater than 0.5 times the diameter of the combined lumens. Consideration of what the drawings conveyed to persons of ordinary skill is essential.

CONCLUSION

Reversed Remanded.

The district court's grant of summary judgment, holding all claims of the '329 and '141 patents invalid under 35 U.S.C. § 102(b), is hereby reversed as to all claims, and the case remanded for further proceedings consistent herewith.

REVERSED and REMANDED.

NOTES

1. Description by Design? Was the district court so far off in its analysis of the effect of the design patent application? This original design application showed just one embodiment of the invention that was later claimed in the utility patent application. The inventor essentially argued that the other claimed embodiments were readily apparent from the design patent application drawings. But doesn't the fact that the inventor filed a design patent application rather than a utility application suggest that he believed he had only developed a new design, and that the other embodiments were developed later? The inventor had previously testified that he was an independent researcher at the time he developed the double lumen catheter. He further testified the he filed the design patent application because it was significantly less expensive to prosecute than a utility patent application. Should this make a difference?

2. On Remand. Judge Easterbrook concluded on remand that, in light of the Federal Circuit's opinion in Vas–Cath:

    I must decide whether such a person would understand the drawings of the design application as showing that Mahurkar was in possession, when he filed the design application, of the features claimed in the utility application. The answer to that question must be "yes." The drawings accompanying the design and utility applications are identical (except for the addition of arrows and numbers to the utility drawings). The utility application simply lays out the details of what the design drawings show—to be precise, the utility claims narrate what features of the drawings are important, without adding anything. I find that Mahurkar was in possession of the whole invention when he filed the design applications, and the drawings in the design application would have enabled a person of ordinary skill in the art to draft the written claims that appeared in the design application.

In re Mahurkar Patent Litigation, 831 F.Supp. 1354 (N.D. Ill. 1993), *aff'd*, 71 F.3d 1573 (Fed. Cir. 1995). A third Federal Circuit opinion addressing the double lumen catheter patent may be found in *Mahurkar v. C.R. Bard, Inc.*, 79 F.3d 1572 (Fed. Cir.1 996).

3. The Amendment of Patent Claims. Why should the patent law allow applicants to amend patent claims at all? Don't third parties have an interest in learning the extent of the protected technology as soon as possible? Or is the ultimate scope of protection best determined after a comprehensive examination by expert patent office examiners, rather than preliminarily by the applicant? See Rudolf Krasser, Possibilities of Amendment of Patent Claims During the Examination Procedure, 23 INT'L REV. INDUS. PROP. & COPYRIGHT L. 467 (1992).

4. The Future of the Written Description Rejection. Although the United States once set its patent term as seventeen years from the issuance date, it now grants a patent term of twenty years from the filing date. Do you believe this shift will result in any changes in the frequency with which the written description requirement is the subject of litigation?

5. Written Description and Genus/Species Problems. Courts and the Patent Office sometimes confront thorny written description issues when considering cases involving initial genus and subsequent species claims. To what extent should the initial disclosure of a broad genus allow the applicant to claim subsequently a narrow species? Although various tribunals addressing this issue have vacillated in their responses to this issue, see *In re Smith*, 458 F.2d 1389 (CCPA 1972), the current answer was well stated in *Ex parte Westphal*, 26 U.S.P.Q.2d 1858 (Bd. Pat. App. & Int'f):

> It has specifically been held that the disclosure of a genus and a species of a subgenus within that genus is not sufficient description of the subgenus to comply with the description requirement . . . unless there are specific facts which lead to a determination that a subgenus is implicitly described.

6. A Thought on Specification vs. Claims. From *In re Dossel*, 115 F.3d 942 (Fed.Cir.1997):

> Modern usage does not always conform to that statutory structure. For example, when discussing the process of claim construction, it is not uncommon for the process to be described as requiring an examination of the claims, the specification, and the prosecution history, treating them as distinct entities. . . . The emphasis in today's law on the centrality of claims has made this a natural enough construct, and the same point might be made, in the terms of the statute, by saying: "To ascertain the meaning of claims, we consider three sources: the claims, the written description, and the prosecution history."

To make the point even clearer, and without changing the terms of the statute, it might be written in the following manner:

§ 112   Specification

(1) Written description. The specification shall contain a written description . . . as to enable any person skilled in the art . . .

(2) Claims. The written description shall be followed by one or more claims.

(a) A claim shall particularly point out and distinctly claim the subject matter

. . . .

(b) A claim may be written in independent or dependent form. . . .

(c) A claim in dependent form shall contain. . . .

(d) A claim in multiple dependent form shall contain. . . .

(e) An element in a claim for a combination may be expressed as a means or step for performing a specified function . . .

7. Comparative Note. The European Patent Convention indicates at Article 123(2) that: "A European patent application or a European patent may not be amended in such a way that it contains subject matter which extends beyond the content of the application as filed." The Japanese patent statute includes a similar standard.

THE GENTRY GALLERY, INC. v. THE BERKLINE CORP.

United States Court of Appeals, Federal Circuit, 1998
134 F.3d 1473

LOURIE, CIRCUIT JUDGE.

The Gentry Gallery appeals from the judgment of the United States District Court for the District of Massachusetts holding that the Berkline Corporation does not infringe U.S. Patent 5,064,244. . . . *See Gentry Gallery, Inc. v. Berkline Corp.*, 30 USPQ2d 1132 (D. Mass. 1994)(*Gentry I*). Berkline cross-appeals from the decision that the patent was not shown to be invalid. [B]ecause the court clearly erred in finding that the written description portion of the specification supported certain of the broader claims asserted by Gentry, we reverse the decision that those claims are not invalid under 35 U.S.C. § 112, ¶ 1.

BACKGROUND

Gentry owns the '244 patent, which is directed to a unit of a sectional sofa in which two independent reclining seats ("recliners") face in the same direction. Sectional sofas are typically organized in an L-shape with "arms" at the exposed ends of the linear sections. According to the patent specification, because recliners usually have had adjustment controls on their arms, sectional sofas were able to contain two recliners only if they were located at the exposed ends of the linear sections. Due to the typical L-shaped configuration of sectional sofas, the recliners therefore faced in different directions. Such an arrangement was "not usually comfortable when the occupants are watching television because one or both occupants must turn their heads to watch the same [television] set. Furthermore, the separation of the two reclining seats at opposite ends of a sectional sofa is not comfortable or conducive to intimate conversation."

The invention of the patent solved this supposed dilemma by, *inter alia,* placing a "console" between two recliners which face in the same direction. This console "accommodates the controls for both reclining seats," thus eliminating the need to position each recliner at an exposed end of a linear section. Accordingly, both recliners can then be located on the same linear section allowing two people to recline while watching television and facing in the same direction. Claim 1, which is the broadest claim of the patent, reads in relevant part:

> A sectional sofa comprising:
>
> a pair of reclining seats disposed in parallel relationship with one another in a double reclining seat sectional sofa section being without an arm at one end . . . ,
>
> each of said reclining seats having a backrest and seat cushions and movable between upright and reclined positions . . . ,
>
> a *fixed console* disposed in the double reclining seat sofa section between the pair of reclining seats and with the console and reclining seats together comprising a unitary structure,
>
> said console including an armrest portion for each of the reclining seats; said arm rests remaining fixed when the reclining seats move from one to another of their positions,
>
> and *a pair of control means,* one for each reclining seat; *mounted on the double reclining seat sofa section* . . . .

Claims 9, 10, 12–15, and 19–21 are directed to a sectional sofa in which the control means are specifically located on the console.

In 1991, Gentry filed suit . . . alleging that Berkline infringed the patent by manufacturing and selling sectional sofas having two recliners facing in the same direction. In the allegedly infringing sofas, the recliners were separated by a seat which has a back cushion that may be pivoted down onto the seat, so that the seat back may serve as a tabletop between the recliners. . . . The district court granted Berkline's motion for summary judgment of non-infringement, but denied its motions for summary judgment of invalidity and unenforceability. [The district court held that the '244 patent was not invalid and enforceable.]

DISCUSSION

Berkline . . . argues that claims 1–8, 11, and 16–18 are invalid because they are directed to sectional sofas in which the location of the recliner controls is not limited to the console. According to Berkline, because the patent only describes sofas having controls on the console and an object of the invention is to provide a sectional sofa "with a console ... that accommodates the controls for both the reclining seats," '244 patent, col. 1, ll. 35–37, the claimed sofas are not described within the meaning of § 112, ¶ 1. Berkline also relies on Sproule's [the inventor's] testimony that "locating the controls on the console is definitely the way we solved it [the problem of building sectional sofa with parallel recliners] on the original group [of sofas]." Gentry responds that the disclosure represents only Sproule's preferred embodiment, in which the controls are on the console, and therefore supports claims directed to a sofa in which the controls may be located elsewhere. Gentry relies on *Ethicon Endo–Surgery, Inc. v. United States Surgical Corp.*, 93 F.3d 1572, 1582 n. 7 (Fed.Cir.1996), and *In re Rasmussen*, 650 F.2d 1212, 1214 (CCPA 1981), for the proposition that an applicant need not describe more than one embodiment of a broad claim to adequately support that claim.

We agree with Berkline that the patent's disclosure does not support claims in which the location of the recliner controls is other than on the console. Whether a specification complies with the written description requirement of § 112, ¶ 1, is a question of fact, which we review for clear error on appeal from a bench trial. *See Vas–Cath Inc. v. Mahurkar*, 935 F.2d 1555, 1563 (Fed.Cir.1991). To fulfill the written description requirement, the patent specification "must clearly allow persons of ordinary skill in the art to recognize that [the inventor] invented what is claimed." *In re Gosteli*, 872 F.2d 1008, 1012 (Fed.Cir.1989). An applicant complies with the written description requirement "by describing *the invention,* with all its claimed limitations." *Lockwood v. American Airlines, Inc.*, 107 F.3d 1565, 1572 (1997).

It is a truism that a claim need not be limited to a preferred embodiment. However, in a given case, the scope of the right to exclude may be limited by a narrow disclosure. For example, as we have recently held, a disclosure of a television set with a keypad, connected to a central computer with a video disk player did not support claims directed to "an individual terminal containing a video disk player." *See id.*(stating that claims directed to a "distinct invention from that disclosed in the specification" do not satisfy the written description requirement); *see also Regents of the Univ. of Cal. v. Eli Lilly & Co.*, 119 F.3d 1559, 1568 (Fed.Cir.1997) (stating that the case law does "not compel the conclusion that a description of a species always constitutes a description of a genus of which it is a part").

In this case, the original disclosure clearly identifies the console as the only possible location for the controls. It provides for only the most minor variation in the location of the controls, noting that the control "may be mounted on top or side surfaces of the console rather than on the front wall ... without departing from this invention." '244 patent, col. 2, line 68 to col. 3, line 3. No similar variation beyond the console is even suggested. Additionally, the only discernible purpose for the console is to house the controls. As the disclosure states, identifying the only purpose relevant to the console, "[a]nother object of the present invention is to provide . . . a console positioned between [the reclining seats] that accommodates the controls for both of the reclining seats." *Id.* at col. 1, ll. 33–37. Thus, locating the controls anywhere but on the console is outside the stated purpose of the invention. Moreover, consistent with this disclosure, Sproule's broadest original claim was directed to a sofa comprising, *inter alia,* "control means located upon the center console to enable each of the pair of reclining seats to move separately between the reclined and upright positions." Finally, although not dispositive, because one can add claims to a pending application directed to adequately described subject matter, Sproule admitted at trial that he did not consider placing the controls outside the console until he became aware that some of Gentry's competitors were so locating the recliner controls. Accordingly, when viewed in its entirety, the disclosure is limited to sofas in which the recliner control is located on the console.

Gentry's reliance on *Ethicon* is misplaced. It is true, as Gentry observes, that we noted that "an applicant . . . is generally allowed claims, when the art permits, which cover more than the specific embodiment shown." *Ethicon,* 93 F.3d at 1582 n. 7 (quoting *In re Vickers,* 141 F.2d 522, 525 (CCPA 1944)). However, we were also careful to point out in that opinion that the applicant "was free to draft claim[s] broadly (within the limits imposed by the prior art) to exclude the lockout's exact location as a limitation of the claimed invention" only because he "did not consider the precise location of the lockout to be an element of his invention." *Id.* Here, as indicated above, it is clear that Sproule considered the location of the recliner controls on the console to be an essential element of his invention. Accordingly, his original disclosure serves to limit the permissible breadth of his later-drafted claims.

Similarly, *In re Rasmussen* does not support Gentry's position. In that case, our predecessor court restated the uncontroversial proposition that "a claim may be broader than the specific embodiment disclosed in a specification." 650 F.2d at 1215. However, the court also made clear that "[a]n applicant is entitled to claims as broad as the prior art *and his disclosure* will allow." *Id.* at 1214 (emphasis added). The claims at issue in *Rasmussen,* which were limited to the generic step of "adheringly applying" one layer to an adjacent layer, satisfied the written description requirement only because "one skilled in the art who read [the] specification would understand that it is unimportant how the layers are adhered, so long as they are adhered." Here, on the contrary, one skilled in the art would clearly understand that it was not only important, but essential to Sproule's invention, for the controls to be on the console.

In sum, the cases on which Gentry relies do not stand for the proposition that an applicant can broaden his claims to the extent that they are effectively bounded only by the prior art. Rather, they make clear that claims may be no broader than the supporting disclosure, and therefore that a narrow disclosure will limit claim breadth. Here, Sproule's disclosure unambiguously limited the location of the controls to the console. Accordingly, the district court clearly erred in finding that he was entitled to claims in which the recliner controls are not located on the console. We therefore reverse the judgment that claims 1–8, 11, and 16–18, were not shown to be invalid. [Reversed in relevant part.]

NOTES

1. **Written Description Policy.** The policy undergirding the written description requirement is that patent proprietors should not be allowed to gain proprietary rights in inventions they had not thought of at the time they filed their applications. This reasoning at times conflicts with the law and policy of the enablement requirement, which allows patent coverage to extend to manifestations of the claimed invention that were enabled at the time the application was filed. No wonder, then, that critics of the written description requirement have viewed it as an "enablement plus" standard that defeats sound patent policy (see the dissenting opinions in *Enzo Biochem* below). The Federal Circuit has yet to reconcile these competing strands of § 112, ¶ 1, if indeed they can be reconciled at all.

2. **A Question of Fact?** The Federal Circuit has explained that such issues as enablement and the construction of patent claims present questions of law. *See Markman v. Westview Instruments, Inc.*, 52 F.3d 967, 978 (Fed. Cir. 1995), aff'd, 417 U.S. 370 (1996) ("The reason that the courts construe patent claims as a matter of law and should not give such task to the jury as a factual matter is straightforward: It has long been and continues to be a fundamental principle of American law that 'the construction of a written evidence is exclusively with the court.'") (citation omitted). Yet the Court of Appeals deems observance of the written description requirement to be a question of fact. *See Union Oil Co. v. Atlantic Richfield Co.*, 208 F.3d 989, 996 (Fed. Cir. 2000). One consequence of this ruling is that the Federal Circuit reviews a jury's determinations regarding the written description requirement under the "substantial evidence" standard. *Id.* Is this dichotomy sensible?

3. **The Decline of the Recliner Case?** *Gentry Gallery* has been subject to considerable critical commentary, *see, e.g.,* Harris A. Pitlick, *The Mutation on the Description Requirement Gene*, 80 J. PAT. & TRADEMARK OFF. SOC'Y 209 (1998), although supporters can be found as well, *see, e.g.,* Matthew L. Goska, *Of Omitted Elements and Overreaching Inventions: The Principle of Gentry Gallery Should Not Be Discarded*, 29 AM. INTELL. PROP. L. ASS'N Q.J. 471 (2001). Subsequent Federal Circuit opinions have arguably stepped back a bit from some of the more sweeping statements in the "couch case." In *Cooper Cameron Corp. v. Kvaerner Oilfield Products, Inc.*, 291 F.3d 1317, 1323 (Fed. Cir. 2002) (citations omitted), Judge Lourie explained:

> In *Gentry*, the original disclosure identified the console of a sectional sofa as the only possible location for the controls. We held that the asserted claims

were invalid because the location of the recliner controls in the claims was not limited to the console. In reaching that conclusion, we stated: "[I]t is clear that [the inventor] considered the location of the recliner controls on the console to be an essential element of his invention. Accordingly, his original disclosure serves to limit the permissible breadth of his after-drafted claims." In so stating, we did not announce a new "essential element" test mandating an inquiry into what an inventor considers to be essential to his invention and requiring that the claims incorporate those elements. Use of particular language explaining a decision does not necessarily create a new legal test. Rather, in *Gentry,* we applied and merely expounded upon the unremarkable proposition that a broad claim is invalid when the entirety of the specification clearly indicates that the invention is of a much narrower scope There was no description or support whatever in the *Gentry* patent of the controls being other than on the console.

Viewing *Gentry Gallery* as involving an unusual set of circumstances limits the impact of this holding, and it also holds lessons for patent drafters. What language might you avoid when you draft a patent specification with an eye toward circumventing written description concerns?

§ 8.3 "WRITTEN DESCRIPTION"—PRO-SCRIPTION APPLIED TO CLAIMS WITHOUT PRIORITY ISSUES

In a remarkable decision with little, if any, apparent support in the statute or case law, the Federal Circuit held in the case that follows that the specification did not adequately describe originally filed subject matter. This quixotic rule calls into question the seemly fundamental point that the claims are part of the specification and disclosure. While the case involved several issues, the focus for students is whether an originally filed claim in the application that led to U.S. Patent 4,652,525 ('525) is invalid for failure to satisfy the written description requirement.

REGENTS OF THE UNIVERSITY OF CALIFORNIA v. ELI LILLY & CO.

United States Court of Appeals, Federal Circuit, 1997
119 F.3d 1559

Before Newman, Lourie, and Bryson, Circuit Judges.

LOURIE, CIRCUIT JUDGE.

* * *

The patents in suit relate to recombinant DNA technology and, more specifically, to recombinant plasmids and microorganisms that producehuman insulin, a protein involved in the regulation of sugar metabolism. A person unable to produce insulin is afflicted with diabetes. Prior to the development of recombinant techniques for the production of human insulin, diabetic patients were treated with injections of animal insulin, which often caused allergic reactions. Human insulin produced by recombinant methods is less likely to produce such reactions. It consists of two separate amino acid chains, a 21–amino acid A chain and a 30–amino acid B chain, which are linked only by disulfide bonds. Healthy people produce insulin in vivo via the terminal enzymatic cleavage of preproinsulin (PPI) to yield proinsulin (PI), a single amino acid chain consisting of the A and B chains, linked by a sequence of additional amino acids that positions the A and B chains so that the disulfide bonds are readily formed. The PI is then further cleaved to liberate the linking sequence and yield insulin.

The '525 patent, the application for which was filed in May 1977, was based upon the determination of the PI and PPI cDNA sequences found in rats. Claim 1 of that patent reads as follows: "A recombinant plasmid replicable in procaryotic host containing within its nucleotide sequence a subsequence having the structure of the reverse transcript of an mRNA of a vertebrate, which mRNA encodes insulin." Claim 2 relates to a recombinant procaryotic microorganism containing vertebrate insulin-encoding cDNA. Claims 4 and 5 depend from claim 2, and are limited, respectively, to mammalian and human insulin cDNA. Claim 6 depends from claim 1 and requires that the plasmid contain "at least one genetic determinant of the plasmid col E1." Claim 7 depends from claim 2 and requires that the microorganism be of a particular strain.

* * *

The district court ruled that all of the claims of the '525 patent that UC asserted against Lilly, viz., claims 1, 2, and 4–7, are invalid under § 112, ¶ 1, because the specification, although it provided an adequate written description of rat cDNA, did not provide an adequate written description of the cDNA required by the asserted claims. 39 USPQ2d at 1239–41.

Whether a specification complies with the written description requirement of § 112, ¶ 1, is a question of fact, which we review for clear error on appeal from a bench trial. *Vas-Cath Inc. v. Mahurkar*, 935 F.2d 1555, 1563 (Fed. Cir. 1991); *Ralston Purina Co. v. Far–Mar–Co, Inc.*, 772 F.2d 1570, 1575 (Fed. Cir. 1985). To fulfill the written description requirement, a patent specification must describe an invention and do so in sufficient detail that one skilled in the art can clearly conclude that "the inventor invented the claimed invention." *Lockwood v. American Airlines, Inc.*, 107 F.3d 1565, 1572 (Fed. Cir. 1997); *In re Gosteli*, 872 F.2d 1008, 1012 (Fed. Cir. 1989) ("[T]he description must clearly allow persons of ordinary skill in the art to recognize that [the inventor] invented what is claimed."). Thus, an applicant complies with the written description requirement "by describing the invention, with all its claimed limitations, not that which makes it obvious," and by using "such descriptive means as words, structures, figures, diagrams, formulas, etc., that set forth the claimed invention." *Lockwood*, 107 F.3d at 1572.

An adequate written description of a DNA, such as the cDNA of the recombinant plasmids and microorganisms of the '525 patent, "requires a precise definition, such as by structure, formula, chemical name, or physical properties," not a mere wish or plan for obtaining the claimed chemical invention. *Fiers v. Revel*, 984 F.2d 1164, 1171 (Fed. Cir. 1993). Accordingly, "an adequate written description of a DNA requires more than a mere statement that it is part of the invention and reference to a potential method for isolating it; what is required is a description of the DNA itself." *Id*. at 1170.

We first consider claim 5, which is specific to a microorganism containing a human insulin cDNA. UC argues that the district court clearly erred in finding that claim 5 is invalid under § 112, ¶ 1. Specifically, UC argues that a constructive or prophetic example in the '525 specification describes in sufficient detail how to prepare the claimed organism. Lilly responds that the district court properly applied the written description requirement, as this court applied it in *Fiers*, 984 F.2d at 1170–71, and thus did not clearly err in finding that the cDNA encoding human insulin required by claim 5 is not adequately described in the '525 patent.

Claim 5 is directed to a recombinant procaryotic microorganism modified so that it contains "a nucleotide sequence having the structure of the reverse transcript of an mRNA of a [human], which mRNA encodes insulin." Thus, the definition of the claimed microorganism is one that requires human insulin-encoding cDNA. The patent describes a method of obtaining this cDNA by means of a constructive example, Example 6. This example, however, provides only a general method for obtaining the human cDNA (it incorporates by reference the method used to obtain the rat cDNA) along with the amino acid sequences of human insulin A and B chains. Whether or not it provides an enabling disclosure, it does not provide a written description of the cDNA encoding human insulin, which is necessary to provide a written description of the subject matter of claim 5. The name cDNA is not itself a written description of that DNA; it conveys no distinguishing information concerning its identity. While the example provides a process for obtaining human insulin-encoding cDNA, there is no further information in the patent pertaining to that cDNA's relevant structural or physical characteristics; in other words, it thus does not describe human insulin cDNA. Describing a method of preparing a cDNA or even describing the protein that the cDNA encodes, as the example does, does not necessarily describe the cDNA itself. No sequence information indicating which nucleotides constitute human cDNA appears in the patent, as appears for rat cDNA in Example 5 of the patent. Accordingly, the specification does not provide a written description of the invention of claim 5.

As indicated, Example 6 provides the amino acid sequence of the human insulin A and B chains, but that disclosure also fails to describe the cDNA. Recently, we held that a description which renders obvious a claimed invention is not sufficient to satisfy the written description requirement of that invention. *Lockwood*, 107 F.3d at 1572. We had previously held that a claim to a specific DNA is not made obvious by mere knowledge of a desired protein sequence and methods for generating the DNA that encodes that protein. *See, e.g., In re Deuel*, 51 F.3d 1552, 1558 (1995) ("A prior art disclosure of the amino acid sequence of a protein does not necessarily render particular DNA molecules encoding the protein obvious because the redundancy of the genetic code permits one to hypothesize an enormous number of DNA sequences coding for the protein."); *In re Bell*, 991 F.2d 781, 785 (Fed. Cir. 1993). Thus, a fortiori, a description that does not render a claimed invention obvious does not sufficiently describe that invention for purposes of § 112, ¶ 1. Because the '525 specification provides only a general method of producing human insulin cDNA and a description of the human insulin A and B chain amino acid sequences that cDNA encodes, it does not provide a written description of human insulin cDNA. Accordingly, the district court did not err in concluding that claim 5 is invalid for failure to provide an adequate written description.

UC also argues that the district court erred in holding claims 1 and 2, which generically recite cDNA encoding vertebrate insulin, and claim 4, which is directed generically to cDNA encoding mammalian insulin, invalid. Dependent claims 6 and 7 similarly recite cDNA encoding vertebrate insulin. In support of this argument, UC cites the disclosure of a species (the rat insulin-encoding cDNA) within the scope of those generic claims. UC argues, citing *In re Angstadt*, 537 F.2d 498 (CCPA 1976) and *Utter v. Hiraga*, 845 F.2d 993 (Fed. Cir. 1988), that because the '525 specification meets the requirements of § 112, ¶ 1, for a species within both of these genera, the specification necessarily also describes these genera. Lilly responds that the district court did not clearly err in finding that cDNA encoding mammalian and vertebrate insulin were not adequately described in the '525 patent, because description of one species of a genus is not necessarily a description of the genus.

We agree with Lilly that the claims are invalid. Contrary to UC's argument, a description of rat insulin cDNA is not a description of the broad classes of vertebrate or mammalian insulin cDNA. A written description of an invention involving a chemical genus, like a description of a chemical species, "requires a precise definition, such as by structure, formula, [or] chemical name," of the claimed subject matter sufficient to distinguish it from other materials. *Fiers*, 984 F.2d at 1171; *In re Smythe*, 480 F.2d 1376, 1383 (CCPA 1973) ("In other cases, particularly but not necessarily, chemical cases, where there is unpredictability in performance of certain species or subcombinations other than those specifically enumerated, one skilled in the art may be found not to have been placed in possession of a genus. . . .").

The cases UC cites in support of its argument do not lead to the result it seeks. These cases do not compel the conclusion that a description of a species always constitutes a description of a genus of which it is a part. These cases only establish that every species in a genus need not be described in order that a genus meet the written description requirement. *See Utter*, 845 F.2d at 998–99 ("A specification may, within the meaning of § 112 ¶ 1, contain a written description of a broadly claimed invention without describing all species that claim encompasses.") (affirming board's finding that an application that "describes in detail the geometry and components that make its internal pivot embodiment work" also sufficiently describes an interference count that is "silent as to the location of the pivot"). In addition, Angstadt is an enablement case and Utter involves machinery of limited scope bearing no relation to the complex biochemical claims before us.

In claims involving chemical materials, generic formulae usually indicate with specificity what the generic claims encompass. One skilled in the art can distinguish such a formula from others and can identify many of the species that the claims encompass. Accordingly, such a formula is normally an adequate description of the claimed genus. In claims to genetic material, however, a generic statement such as "vertebrate insulin cDNA" or "mammalian insulin cDNA," without more, is not an adequate written description of the genus because it does not distinguish the claimed genus from others, except by function. It does not specifically define any of the genes that fall within its definition. It does not define any structural features commonly possessed by members of the genus that distinguish them from others. One skilled in the art therefore cannot, as one can do with a fully described genus, visualize or recognize the identity of the members of the genus. A definition by function, as we have previously indicated, does not suffice to define the genus because it is only an indication of what the gene does, rather than what it is. *See Fiers*, 984 F.2d at 1169–71 (discussing *Amgen*). It is only a definition of a useful result rather than a definition of what achieves that result. Many such genes may achieve that result. The description requirement of the patent statute requires a description of an invention, not an indication of a result that one might achieve if one made that invention. *See In re Wilder*, 736 F.2d 1516, 1521 (Fed. Cir. 1984) (affirming rejection because the specification does "little more than outlin[e] goals appellants hope the claimed invention achieves and the problems the invention will hopefully ameliorate."). Accordingly, naming a type of material generally known to exist, in the absence of knowledge as to what that material consists of, is not a description of that material.

Thus, as we have previously held, a cDNA is not defined or described by the mere name "cDNA," even if accompanied by the name of the protein that it encodes, but requires a kind of specificity usually achieved by means of the recitation of the sequence of nucleotides that make up the cDNA. *See Fiers*, 984 F.2d at 1171. A description of a genus of cDNAs may be achieved by means of a recitation of a representative number of cDNAs, defined by nucleotide sequence, falling within the scope of the genus or of a recitation of structural features common to the members of the genus, which features constitute a substantial portion of the genus. This is analogous to enablement of a genus under § 112, ¶ 1, by showing the enablement of a representative number of species within the genus. *See Angstadt*, 537 F.2d at 502–03 (deciding that applicants "are not required to disclose every species encompassed by their claims even in an unpredictable art" and that the disclosure of forty working examples sufficiently described subject matter of claims directed to a generic process); *In re Robins*, 429 F.2d 452, 456–57 (CCPA 1970) ("Mention of representative compounds encompassed by generic claim language clearly is not required by § 112 or any other provision of the statute. But, where no explicit description of a generic invention is to be found in the specification ... mention of representative compounds may provide an implicit description upon which to base generic claim language."); *Cf. Gosteli*, 872 F.2d at 1012 (determining that the disclosure of two chemical compounds within a subgenus did not describe that subgenus); *In re Grimme*, 274 F.2d 949, 952 (CCPA 1960) ("[I]t has been consistently held that the naming of one member of such a group is not, in itself, a proper basis for a claim to the entire group. However, it may not be necessary to enumerate a plurality of species if a genus is sufficiently identified in an application by 'other appropriate language.' ") (citations omitted). We will not speculate in what other ways a broad genus of genetic material may be properly described, but it is clear to us, as it was to the district court, that the claimed genera of vertebrate and mammal cDNA are not described by the general language of the '525 patent's written description supported only by the specific nucleotide sequence of rat insulin.

Accordingly, we reject UC's argument that the district court clearly erred in finding claims 1, 2, 4, 6, and 7 invalid for failure to provide an adequate written description. Because we affirm the district court's ruling that all of the claims of the '525 patent asserted against Lilly are invalid, we need not consider whether Lilly infringed those claims. *See B.F. Goodrich Co. v. Aircraft Braking Sys. Corp.*, 72 F.3d 1577, 1583 (Fed. Cir. 1996).

NOTES

1. Assume Enablement. If the specification taught how to obtain cDNA coding for human insulin without undue experimentation, why did the Federal Circuit determine that the inventor must actually derive the human insulin and then obtain and disclose its nucleotide-by-nucleotide sequence? Do you believe that actually characterizing the cDNA should be a requirement of patentability assuming all other requirements of the law are met?

2. *Lilly* **Description and** *In re Deuel.* Both the description doctrine set out in *Lilly* and the obviousness test for biotechnological inventions set forth in

Deuel set U.S. patent law at odds with most of the world's patent laws. Of course, obviousness carries the role of preventing the public from bearing the costs of a patent for technological advances that produce only negligible gain in valuable scientific knowledge. *Deuel* left almost no obviousness bar to miniscule advances in biotech inventions. Does *Lilly* (wittingly or unwittingly) try to use the description doctrine to fill the gap left by *Deuel*? Can a description doctrine perform that function? Does this description doctrine render invalid technology worthy of patentability for lack of a technical disclosure and also admit technology that an operative obviousness test might exclude?

3. Does Chemical Structure Properly Describe the Inventive Features of Genetic Engineering? *Lilly*, with its emphasis on disclosure of a structure, formula, or chemical name, uses chemical structure as the legal analogue to evaluate inventions in the field of genetic engineering. The chemical arts are already a novel art field which receives somewhat novel treatment in the case law of patents. As a matter of science, does chemistry's emphasis on structure properly reflect the inventive feature of many genetic engineering inventions? Consider again some of the differences between chemical arts and the art of genetic engineering. Unlike chemistry with over a hundred elements and countless isotopes bonded in infinite ways, genetic engineering uses only a few nucleic acids as building blocks and for DNA the nucleic acids are used in pairs. Would it be proper to say that genetic engineering more resembles computer technology—1s and 0s constantly repeating to carry a code—than chemistry? In other words, genetic engineering features code breaking skills more than chemical structure skills. Indeed libraries of past codes (cDNA sequences) and known cloning methods (which design a probe that will bind or hybridize with the desired cDNA sequence) are everyday tools. In sum, chemical compounds are synthesized; proteins created through the methods of genetic engineering are analyzed. While the structure of a chemical compound depends on the electrical and physical relationship of those elements to each other, the structure of a protein created by genetic engineering is the result of a sequence code expressed in nucleic acids. In short, is chemical structure the proper standard to evaluate full description of a genetic engineering invention when that art does not appear to be a structure-based art?

4. Debate at the Federal Circuit. In the case that follows four judges of the Federal Circuit voted to consider *Lilly en banc* (and another indicated publicly his willingness to reconsider *Lilly* when another case arises). While the court's opinion is itself interesting, the most informative opinions are the dissent of Judge Rader joined by Judges Gajarsa and Linn to the denial of a hearing *en banc* and Judge Lourie's considered response joined in by Judge Newman.

ENZO BIOCHEM, INC. v. GEN–PROBE INC.

United States Court of Appeals for the Federal Circuit, 2002
323 F.3d 956

Rader, Circuit Judge, with whom Gajarsa and Linn, Circuit Judges, join, dissenting from the court's decision not to hear the case *en banc*.

Because the greater mistake in this case is misapplication of this court's written description case law, this opinion devotes only a few paragraphs to the statutory interpretation question. The United States' brief as *amicus curiae* in support of rehearing *en banc* states concisely this Enzo opinion's disregard for the statute:

> A straightforward reading of the text of section 112 suggests that the test for an adequate written description is whether it provides enough written information for others to make and use the invention. The statute provides that the "specification shall contain a written description of the invention … in such full, clear, concise, and exact terms as to enable any person skilled in the art … to make and use the same." 35 U.S.C. § 112 ¶ 1. Thus, an adequate written description assures that others can "make and use" the invention.

If it is possible to characterize disregard of statutory text as a secondary mistake, this case fits that classification. The more important problem is disregard for the case law that originated the written description requirement and applied it for over thirty years.

ORIGIN AND HISTORY OF THE WRITTEN DESCRIPTION REQUIREMENT

The words "written description" first appeared in the Patent Act of 1793. At that time, of course, patents did not require claims but only a written description sufficient "to distinguish [the invention] from all other things before known or used." In *Evans v. Eaton*, 20 U.S. 356 (1822), the Supreme Court construed the description language to require applicants to enable their inventions and to provide the notice function of claims:

> [After enablement,] [t]he other object of the specification is to put the public in possession of what the party claims as his own invention, so as to ascertain if he claims any thing that is in common use, or is already known …

Id. at 433. In later enactments, this notice function was assigned to claims, leaving enablement as the only purpose of the "written description" language. As noted in the United States' brief, the modern descendant of the 1793 phrase still requires only a written description "in such … terms as to enable [the invention]." 35 U.S.C. § 112. In *J.E.M. AG Supply*, 122 S.Ct. 593, 604 (2001), the Supreme Court … found no general disclosure requirement in title 35 other than enablement.

Before 1967, this court's predecessor, the United States Court of Customs and Patent … wrote in detail about section 112, paragraph 1, and found only two requirements—enablement (the A requirement under Judge Rich's terminology) and best mode (the B requirement). *In re Gay*, 309 F.2d 769, 772 (CCPA, 1962).

In 1967, the Court of Customs and Patent Appeals first separated a new written description (WD) requirement from the enablement requirement of § 112. The reason for this new judge-made doctrine needs some explanation. Every patent system must have some provision to prevent applicants from using the amendment process to update their disclosures (claims or specifications) during their pendency before the patent office. Otherwise applicants could add new matter to their disclosures and date them back to their original filing date, thus defeating an accurate accounting of the priority of invention. Priority—always a vital issue in patent prosecution procedures—often determines entitlement to an invention. Before 1967, the United States Patent Office and the Court of Customs and Patent Appeals used a "new matter" rejection to ensure that applicants did not update their disclosures after the original filing date of the application. This "new matter" rejection had a statutory basis: "No amendment shall introduce new matter into the disclosure of the invention." 35 U.S.C. § 132.

In 1967, in *In re Ruschig*, 379 F.2d 990 (CCPA 1967), this court's predecessor created for the first time a new WD doctrine to enforce priority. . . . To deal with new matter in the claims, the court calved a new WD doctrine out of the § 112 enablement requirement. As long as the new WD doctrine applied according to its original purpose as an identical twin of the § 132 new matter doctrine, these technical distinctions were of little practical consequence.

In any event, the WD doctrine, at its inception had a very clear function preventing new matter from creeping into claim amendments. Judge Rich, the author of *Ruschig*, often reiterated the purpose of WD. For instance in the case of *In re Wertheim*, 541 F .2d 257 (CCPA 1976), the Court of Customs and Patent Appeals confronted a priority issue:

> The dispositive issue under this heading is whether appellants' parent and Swiss applications comply with 35 U.S.C. § 112, first paragraph, including the description requirement, as to the subject matter of these claims. If they do, these claims are entitled to the filing dates of the *parent* application. . . . [A] right of foreign *priority* in appellants' Swiss application will antedate Pfluger 1966 and remove it as prior art against the claims.

Id. at 261 (emphasis added).

In 1981, the Court of Customs and Patent Appeals noted that the two rejections were interchangeable: "This court, ha[s] said that a rejection of an amended claim under § 132 is *equivalent* to a rejection under § 112, first paragraph." *In re Rasmussen*, 650 F.2d 1212, 1214 (CCPA, 1981) (emphasis added). To avoid confusion between new matter rejections and objections, the court chose to eliminate the § 132/ § 112 rejections and to use § 112 for new matter rejections (claims): "The proper basis for rejection of a claim amended to recite elements thought to be without support in the original disclosure, therefore, is § 112, first paragraph, not § 132." Id. The purpose of the doctrine did not change. As the sentence above states explicitly, the § 112 doctrine, like its corollary § 132, policed priority, nothing more.

The Federal Circuit continued to follow this binding precedent. See, e.g., *Vas–Cath*, 935 F.2d at 1560 ("The question raised by these situations is most often phrased as whether the application provides 'adequate support' for the claim(s) at issue; it has also been analyzed in terms of 'new matter' under 35 U.S.C. § 132."); *In re Wright*, 866 F.2d 422, 424 (Fed.Cir.1989); *In re Kaslow*, 707 F.2d 1366 (Fed. Cir. 1983). In fact, this Circuit's test for written description required assessment of the specification to check "later claimed subject matter." Id. at 1375 [T]his Circuit did not apply WD to claims without priority problems because the doctrine had no purpose beyond policing priority.

THE DEVIATION FROM THIRTY YEARS OF PRECEDENT

In 1997, for the first time, this court purported to apply WD as a general disclosure doctrine in place of enablement, rather than as a priority doctrine. *Regents of the Univ. of Cal. v. Eli Lilly and Co.*, 119 F.3d 1559 (Fed. Cir. 1997). In *Lilly*, this court found that the '525 patent specification does not provide a WD of human insulin cDNA despite the disclosure of a general method of producing human insulin cDNA and a description of the human insulin A and B chain amino acid sequences that cDNA encodes. 119 F.3d at 1567. In the words of the court, "a description that does not render a claimed invention obvious does not sufficiently describe that invention for purposes of § 112, ¶ 1." Id. At another point, the court stated: "An adequate written description of a DNA ... 'requires a precise definition, such as by structure, formula, chemical name, or physical properties....' " Id. at 1566. In sum, the *Lilly* opinion does not test a later claim amendment against the specification for priority, but asserts a new free-standing disclosure requirement in place of the statutory standard of enablement....

Under the correct written description test, one of skill in the art would have recognized that the '525 patent in *Lilly* had no new matter or priority problems. In terms of the statutory test for adequacy of disclosure, the patent disclosure undoubtedly warranted rejection for lack of enablement. Under the *Wands* test for enablement, 858 F.2d 731 (Fed.Cir.1988), the inventor certainly did not show one of skill in the art how to make human insulin cDNA. U.S. Pat. No. 4,652,525, the patent at issue in Lilly, was filed in 1983, but claimed priority to a parent filed in 1977. In 1977, biotechnology was still in its infancy. In fact, the Maxam and Gilbert method of sequencing DNA was just published in 1977. Cloning in that era was, at a minimum, unpredictable and would have required vast amounts of experimentation to accomplish. Therefore, the patent's prophetic disclosure of human insulin cDNA hardly enabled its production as claimed. Instead of pursuing this obvious avenue of rejection, the Federal Circuit reached out beyond the statute and the case law to create a new general disclosure. As noted, from its creation through thirty years of application, WD had never been a free-standing substitute for enablement.

* * *

WHY DOES THIS MATTER?

As both *Lilly* and this case show, the aberrant form of WD requires far more specific disclosure than enablement. ... Thus, the new breed of WD evident in *Lilly* and this case threatens to further disrupt the patent system by replacing enablement the statutory test for adequate disclosure. *See*, Rai, Arti, *"Intellectual Property Rights in Biotechnology: Addressing New Technology"* 34 Wake Forest L.Rev. 827, 834–35 (Fall, 1999) ("Thus in [*Lilly*] ... the CAFC broke new ground by applying the written description requirement not only to later-filed claims but also to claims filed in the original patent.... T]he *Lilly* court used the written description requirement as a type of elevated enablement requirement."); Mueller, Janice M., *"The Evolving Application of the Written Description Requirement to Biotechnological Inventions"* 13 Berkeley Tech. L.J. 615, 617 (Spring 1998) ("The Lilly decision establishes uniquely rigorous rules for the description of biotechnological subject matter that significantly contort written description doctrine away from its historic origins and policy grounding. The *Lilly* court elevate[s] written description to an effective 'super enablement' standard....").

* * *

For biotech inventions, according to the *Lilly* standard, § 112, ¶ 1 requires a precise listing of the DNA sequence nucleotide-by-nucleotide. Enablement, on the other hand, requires that the specification show one of skill in the art how to acquire that sequence on their own. As a test for biotech claims without priority issues, WD may well jeopardize a sizeable percentage of claims filed before the Lilly departure in 1997. These patents had no notice of a change in the statutory standard for disclosure.

* * *

[This dissent then includes an appendix with every written description case of the Federal Circuit or the CCPA from 1967 to the present showing that each of them, with the exception of *Lilly* applied the written description test only to police priority.]

LOURIE, CIRCUIT JUDGE, with whom NEWMAN, CIRCUIT JUDGE, joins, concurring in the court's decision not to hear the case *en banc*.

The dissenters believe that the written description requirement is simply a requirement for enablement. With all due respect, that is incorrect. The complete statutory provision is as follows:

The specification shall contain a written description of the invention, and of the manner and process of making and using it, in such full, clear, concise, and exact terms as to enable any person skilled in the art to which it pertains or with which it is most nearly connected, to make and use the same, and shall set forth the best mode contemplated by the inventor of carrying out his invention.

35 U.S.C. § 112, ¶ 1 (1994) (emphasis added). I read the statute so as to give effect to its language. The statute states that the invention must be described. That is basic patent law, the *quid pro quo* for the grant of a patent. Judge Rader notes that historically the written description requirement served a purpose when claims were not required. While that may be correct, when the statute began requiring claims, it was not amended to delete the requirement; note the comma between the description requirement and the enablement provision, and the "and" that follows the comma. Judge Rich, whom Judge Rader cites, was in fact one of the earliest interpreters of the statute as having separate enablement and written description requirements. *In re Ruschig*, 379 F.2d 990, 995–996 (C.C.P.A.1967); *Vas–Cath Inc. v. Mahurkar*, 935 F.2d 1555, 1563 (Fed.Cir.1991).

* * *

It is said that applying the written description requirement outside of the priority context was novel until several years ago. Maybe so, maybe not; certainly such a holding was not precluded by statute or precedent. New interpretations of old statutes in light of new fact situations occur all the time. I believe these issues have arisen in recent years for the same reason that more doctrine of equivalents issues are in the courts, viz., because perceptions that patents are stronger tempt patent owners to try to assert their patents beyond the original intentions of the inventors and their attorney. That is why the issues are being raised and that is why we have to decide them. Claims are now being asserted to cover what was not reasonably described in the patent.

Moreover, the dissenters would limit the requirement, to the extent that they credit the written description portion of the statute as being a separate requirement at all, to priority issues. The statute does not say "a written description of the invention for purposes of policing priority." While it has arisen primarily in cases involving priority issues, Congress has not so limited the statute, and we have failed to so limit it as well. As for the lack of earlier cases on this issue, it regularly happens in adjudication that issues do not arise until counsel raise them, and, when that occurs, courts are then required to decide them. Even now, a written description issue should not arise unless a patentee seeks to have his claims interpreted to include subject matter that he has not adequately disclosed in his patent. Although it is true that the written description requirement has been applied rigorously in some recent cases, I do not believe that any of those cases were decided wrongly. * * * Interpretation of written description as this court has done furthers the goal of the law to have claims commensurate in scope with what has been disclosed to the public.

* * *

Moreover, even if written description is related to and overlaps with "new matter," so what? One can fail to meet the requirements of the statute in more than one manner, and in any event the case cited as equating those two requirements in fact distinguishes § § 112 and 132 as concerning: (1) claims not supported by the disclosure; and (2) the prohibition of new matter to the disclosure, respectively. *In re Rasmussen*, 650 F.2d 1212, 1214–15 (CCPA 1981). *Rasmussen* states that "[t]he proper basis for rejection of a claim amended to recite elements thought to be without support in the original disclosure, therefore, is § 112, first paragraph, not § 132." Id.

In addition, we do not "elevate 'possession' to the posture of a statutory test of patentability." Rather, the opinion refines the "possession" test for circumstances such as these in which the inventors showed possession of a species of the invention by reference to a deposit, but may not have described what else within the scope of the claims they had possession of. While "possession" is a relevant factor in determining whether an invention is described, it is only a criterion for satisfying the statutory written description requirement. Showing possession is not necessarily equivalent to providing a written description.

* * *

In sum, we have evolved a consistent body of law over a number of years, based on the statute and basic principles of patent law. I see no reason to hear this case *en banc* and rewrite the statute.

NOTES

1. **Biotechnology and Written Description.** As applied to originally filed claims, the written description requirement has achieved its greatest notoriety in the field of biotechnology. *See* Arti Rai, *Intellectual Property Rights in Biotechnology: Addressing New Technology*, 34 WAKE FOREST L. REV. 827 (1999). On this front it has been subject to particular criticism as a "super enablement" standard unique to biotechnology. Janice M. Mueller, *The Evolving Application of the Written Description Requirement to Biotechnological Inventions*, 13 BERKELEY TECH. L.J. 615, 617 (1998) ("The *Lilly* decision establishes uniquely rigorous rules for the description of biotechnological subject matter that significantly contort written description doctrine away from its historic origins and policy grounding."). Others have defended this posture:

> [T]he holding in *Lilly* actually avoided a disaster that would have crippled the biotechnology industry. The enormous amount of time and money companies spend to study DNA and protein variants, to clone homologous genes and protein family members, and to mine databases would no longer be justified had the court found the written description in [the asserted patent] adequate.
>
> Through application of the written description requirement, courts can distinguish between claims to technologies that are too broad or basic to justify patent protection, and those dealing with other types of technologies that are more predictable and may justify broader protection. Thus, the Federal Circuit has decided that the uniqueness of biotechnology inventions claiming DNA sequences requires the application of a stringent

written description requirement to protect the public from inventors seeking to slow the pace of research by preempting future developments before they arrive.

Mark J. Stewart, Note, *The Written Description Requirement of 35 U.S.C. § 112 ¶ 1: The Standard After* Regents of the University of California v. Eli Lilly & Co., 32 IND. L. REV. 537, 563–64 (1999). On the other hand, the written description requirement has also been applied to originally filed claims in patents claiming such technologies as alkaline batteries, *see Energizer Holdings, Inc. v. ITC*, 2008 WL 1791980 (Fed. Cir. 2008), digital image technology, *see LizardTech, Inc. v. Earth Resource Mapping, Inc.*, 424 F.3d 1336 (Fed. Cir. 2005), and, as we have seen, household furniture, *see Gentry Gallery, Inc. v. Berkline Corp.*, 134 F.3d 1473 (Fed. Cir. 1998).

   2. PTO Guidelines and Training Materials. The PTO has issued guidelines in order to assist the examining corps in applying the written description requirement. *See* USPTO, *Guidelines for Examination of Patent Applications Under the 35 U.S.C. 112, ¶ 1, "Written Description" Requirement*, 66 FED. REG. 1099 (Jan. 5, 2001). As framed by the USPTO, in order to "satisfy the written description requirement, the patent specification must describe the claimed invention in sufficient detail that one skilled in the art can reasonably concluded that the inventor had possession of the invention." *Id.* at 1104. More recently, the USPTO issued a helpful set of guidelines that incorporates a number of examples that largely follow the facts described in specific Federal Circuit written description opinions. USPTO, WRITTEN DESCRIPTION TRAINING MATERIALS (Mar. 25, 2008). The USPTO deemed the following factors to be relevant to the "possession" inquiry:

   a. Actual reduction to practice

   b. Disclosure of drawings or structural chemical formulas

   c. Sufficient relevant identifying characteristics, such as:

      i. Complete structure

      ii. Partial structure

      iii. Physical and/or chemical properties

      iv. Functional characteristics when coupled with a known or disclosed correlation between function and structure

   d. Method of making the claimed invention

   e. Level of skill and knowledge in the art

   f. Predictability in the art.

Id. at 1. With respect to a claimed genus, examiners are instructed to "consider each of the above factors to determine whether there is disclosure of a representative number of species which would lead one skilled in the art to conclude that the applicant was in possession of the claimed invention." The number of species required to represent a genus will vary, depending on the level of skill and knowledge in the art and the variability among the claimed genus. For instance, fewer species will be required where the skill and knowledge in the art is high, and more species will be required where the claimed genus is highly variable" *Id.* at 1–2.

§ 8.4   BEST MODE

CHEMCAST CORP. v. ARCO INDUSTRIES CORP.

United States Court of Appeals, Federal Circuit, 1990
913 F.2d 923

Before Archer and Mayer, Circuit Judges, and George, District Judge.

MAYER, CIRCUIT JUDGE.

Chemcast Corporation appeals the judgment of the United States District Court for the Eastern District of Michigan that Claim 6 of United States Patent No. 4,081,879 ('879 patent), the only claim in suit, is invalid because of the inventor's failure to disclose the best mode as required by 35 U.S.C. § 112. We affirm.

BACKGROUND

The '879 patent claims a sealing member in the form of a grommet or plug button that is designed to seal an opening in, for example, a sheet metal panel. Claim 6, the only claim in suit, depends from Claim 1.

> 1. A grommet for sealing an opening in a panel, said grommet comprising an annular base portion having a continuous circumferential and axial extending sealing band surface, an annular locking portion having a continuous circumferential and axial extending ridge portion approximately the same diameter as said sealing band surface, said sealing band surface constituting an axial extending continuation of said ridge portion, said locking portion and said base portion being in contact with each other and integrally bonded together, said base portion comprising an elastomeric material and said locking portion being more rigid than said base portion, whereby when the grommet is installed in a panel opening, the locking portion is inserted through the opening to a position on the opposite side of the panel from the base portion locking the grommet in place, and said sealing band surface forms a complete seal continuously around the entire inner periphery of the panel opening.

> 6. The grommet as defined in claim 1 wherein the material forming said base portion has a durometer hardness reading of less than 60 Shore A and the material forming said locking portion has a durometer hardness reading of more than 70 Shore A.

The grommet of Claim 6 is referred to as a dual durometer grommet because it may be composed either of two materials that differ in hardness or of a single material that varies in hardness. In either case, the different hardnesses can be, and for a sufficiently large hardness differential must be, measured with different durometers: Shore A for the softer base portion and Shore D for the harder locking portion. The harder locking portion of the grommet is the focus of this case.

Chemcast and its competitor Arco Industries Corporation are both engaged in the manufacture and sale of sealing members such as grommets, gaskets, and plug buttons. Both sell their products primarily to the automobile industry. Ex–Arco employee Phillip L. Rubright founded Chemcast in 1973 and subsequently conceived of and designed specifically for Oldsmobile, a Chemcast customer, the dual durometer '879 grommet. He filed a patent application together with an assignment of invention to Chemcast in January of 1976; the '879 patent issued in April of 1978.

Chemcast subsequently sued Arco for infringement of Claim 6 of the '879 patent. Arco counterclaimed that the patent was invalid on several grounds, including Rubright's failure to comply with 35 U.S.C. § 112.

[The district court invalidated the patent for failure to satisfy the best mode requirement.] According to the court, the principal shortcomings of the disclosure were its failure to specify (1) the particular type, (2) the hardness, and (3) the supplier and trade name, of the material used to make the locking portion of the grommet. Therefore, it held that the application as filed failed adequately to disclose the best mode of practicing the invention contemplated by Rubright. Chemcast appeals.

DISCUSSION

A.

The first paragraph of 35 U.S.C. § 112 (1982) provides: "The specification [A] shall contain a written description of the invention, and of the manner and process of making and using it, in such full, clear, concise, and exact terms as to enable any person skilled in the art to which it pertains, or with which it is most nearly connected, to make and use the same, and [B] shall set forth the best mode contemplated by the inventor of carrying out his invention." We long ago drew and often have focused upon the critical distinction between requirement [A], "enablement," and requirement [B], "best mode." The essence of portion [A] is that a specification shall disclose an invention in such a manner as will enable one skilled in the art to make and utilize it. Separate and distinct from portion [A] is portion [B], the essence of which requires an inventor to disclose the best mode contemplated by him, as of the time he executes the application, of carrying out his invention. Manifestly, the sole purpose of this latter requirement is to restrain inventors from applying for patents while at the same time concealing from the public preferred embodiments of their inventions which they have in fact conceived.

The best mode inquiry focuses on the inventor's state of mind as of the time he filed his application—a subjective, factual question. But this focus is not exclusive. Our statements that "there is no objective standard by which to judge the adequacy of a best mode disclosure," and that "only evidence of concealment (accidental or intentional) is to be considered," *In re Sherwood*, 613 F.2d 809, 816 (CCPA 1980), quoted in *DeGeorge v. Bernier*, 768 F.2d 1318, 1324 (Fed.Cir.1985), assumed that both the level of skill in the art and the scope of the claimed invention were additional, objective metes and bounds of a best mode disclosure.

Of necessity, the disclosure required by section 112 is directed to those skilled in the art. Therefore, one must consider the level of skill in the relevant art in determining whether a specification discloses the best mode. We have consistently recognized that whether a best mode disclosure is adequate, that is, whether the inventor concealed a better mode of practicing his invention than he disclosed, is a function of not only what the inventor knew but also how one skilled in the art would have understood his disclosure.

The other objective limitation on the extent of the disclosure required to comply with the best mode requirement is, of course, the scope of the claimed invention. "It is concealment of the best mode of practicing the claimed invention that section 112 ¶ 1 is designed to prohibit." *Randomex Inc. v. Scopus Corp.*, 849 F.2d at 585, 588 (Fed.Cir. 1988); see *Christianson v. Colt Indus. Oper. Corp.*, 870 F.2d 1292, 1301 (7th Cir.1989) ("Again, the focus of the best mode requirement, as it was with the enablement requirement, is on the claimed invention. Thus, before determining whether there is evidence of concealment, the scope of the invention must be delimited."). Thus, in *Randomex*, the inventor's deliberate concealment of his cleaning fluid formula did not violate the best mode requirement because his "invention neither added nor claimed to add anything to the prior art respecting cleaning fluid." 849 F.2d at 590. Similarly, in *Christianson*, the inventor's failure to disclose information that would have enabled the claimed rifle parts to be interchangeable with all M–16 rifle parts did not invalidate his patents because "the best mode for making and using and carrying out the claimed inventions [did] not entail or involve either the M–16 rifle or interchangeability." 870 F.2d at 1302. Finally, in *DeGeorge* we reversed a finding that an inventor's nondisclosure of unclaimed circuitry with which his claimed circuitry interfaced violated the best mode requirement: "Because the properly construed count does not include a word processor, failure to meet the best mode requirement here should not arise from an absence of information on the word processor."

In short, a proper best mode analysis has two components. The first is whether, at the time the inventor filed his patent application, he knew of a mode of practicing his claimed invention that he considered to be better than any other. This part of the inquiry is wholly subjective, and resolves whether the inventor must disclose any facts in addition to those sufficient for enablement. If the inventor in fact contemplated such a preferred mode, the second part of the analysis compares what he knew with what he disclosed—is the disclosure adequate to enable one skilled in the art to practice the best mode or, in other words, has the inventor "concealed" his preferred mode from the "public"? Assessing the adequacy of the disclosure, as opposed to its necessity, is largely an objective inquiry that depends upon the scope of the claimed invention and the level of skill in the art.

Notwithstanding the mixed nature of the best mode inquiry, and perhaps because of our routine focus on its subjective portion, we have consistently treated the question as a whole as factual. "Compliance with the best mode requirement, because it depends on the applicant's state of mind, is a question of fact subject to the clearly erroneous standard of review." [*Spectra–Physics, Inc. v. Coherent, Inc.*, 827 F.2d 1524, 1535 (Fed.Cir.1987).] We adhere to that standard here, and review the district court's best mode determination accordingly.

B.

Chemcast alleges that the trial court erred in its best mode analysis by failing to focus, as required, on the claimed invention and on whether the inventor, Rubright, concealed a better mode than he disclosed. Neither allegation has any merit.

Chemcast first argues that, because the '879 patent does not claim any specific material for making the locking portion of the grommet, Rubright's failure to disclose the particular material that he thought worked the best does not violate the best mode requirement. This argument confuses best mode and enablement. A patent applicant must disclose the best mode of carrying out his claimed invention, not merely a mode of making and using what is claimed. A specification can be enabling yet fail to disclose an applicant's contemplated best mode. See *Spectra-Physics*, 827 F.2d at 1537. Indeed, most of the cases in which we have said that the best mode requirement was violated addressed situations where an inventor failed to disclose non-claimed elements that were nevertheless necessary to practice the best mode of carrying out the claimed invention. See, e.g., *Spectra-Physics*, 827 F.2d at 1536 (failure to disclose specific braze cycle constituting preferred means of attachment violated best mode even though no particular attachment means claimed).

Moreover, Chemcast is mistaken in its claim interpretation. While the critical limitation of Claim 6 is a hardness differential of 10 points on the Shore A scale between the grommet base and locking portions, and not a particular material type, some material meeting both this limitation and that of Claim 1, that "said base portion compris[e] an elastomeric material and said locking portion be[ ] more rigid than said base portion," is claimed. That the claim is broad is no reason to excuse noncompliance with the best mode requirement. Here, the information the applicant is accused of concealing is not merely necessary to practice the claimed invention, as in *Dana* fluoride surface treatment was "necessary to satisfactory performance" of the claimed valve stem seal; it also describes the preferred embodiment of a claimed element, as in *Spectra–Physics* the undisclosed braze cycle was the preferred "means for attaching" and "securing" claimed in the patents at issue.

Chemcast's second argument is equally misplaced. The court devoted no fewer than 13 factual findings to what the inventor Rubright knew as of the filing date of the '879 application. Those findings focus, as did the parties, on the type, hardness, and supplier of the material used to make the locking portion of the grommet. The court found that Rubright selected the material for the locking portion, a rigid polyvinyl chloride (PVC) plastisol composition; knew that the preferred hardness of this material was 75 +/− 5 Shore D; and purchased all of the grommet material under the trade name R–4467 from Reynosol Corporation (Reynosol), which had spent 750 man-hours developing the compound specifically for Chemcast. Furthermore, the court found that at the time the '879 application was filed, the only embodiment of the claimed invention known to Rubright was a grommet composed of R–4467, a rigid PVC plastisol composition with a locking portion hardness of 75 +/− 5 Shore D. Id. at 2006.

In light of what Rubright knew, the specification, as issued, was manifestly deficient. It disclosed the following: The annular locking portion [ ] of the sealing member [ ] is preferably comprised of a rigid castable material, such as a castable resinous material, either a thermoplastic or thermosetting resin, or any mixtures thereof, for example, polyurethane or polyvinyl chloride. The [locking] portion [ ] also should be made of a material that is sufficiently hard and rigid so that it cannot be radially compressed, such as when it is inserted in the opening [ ] in the panel [ ]. Materials having a durometer hardness reading of 70 Shore A or harder are suitable in this regard. Col. 4, 11.53–63. The material hardness (75 Shore D) and supplier/trade name (Reynosol compound R–4467) are not explicitly disclosed here or anywhere else in the specification.

Nor, in light of the level of skill in the art, are they implicitly disclosed. Given the specification, one skilled in the art simply could not divine Rubright's preferred material hardness. The court found that "the specification of the open-ended range of materials of '70 Shore A or harder' conceals the best mode 75 Shore D material in part because materials of Shore A and Shore D hardnesses are recognized as different types of materials with different classes of physical properties." As for the specific supplier and trade name designation of the preferred material, the court found that disclosing a list of generic potential materials was "not an adequate disclosure of the best mode PVC Re[y]nosol Compound R–4467."

We agree. That "at least eight other PVC composition suppliers [ ] could have formulated satisfactory materials for the dual durometer grommet," 5 U.S.P.Q.2d at 1235, does not, as Chemcast urges, excuse

Rubright's concealment of his preferred material, and the only one of which he was aware. Again Chemcast confuses enablement and best mode. The question is not whether those skilled in the art could make or use the '879 grommet without knowledge of Reynosol compound R–4467; it is whether they could practice Rubright's contemplated best mode which, the court found, included specifically the Reynosol compound. Rubright knew that Reynosol had developed R–4467 specifically for Chemcast and had expended several months and many hundred man-hours in doing so. Because Chemcast used only R–4467, because certain characteristics of the grommet material were claimed elements of the '879 invention, and because Rubright himself did not know the formula, composition, or method of manufacture of R–4467, section 112 obligated Rubright to disclose the specific supplier and trade name of his preferred material.

Other facts Chemcast points to as obviating the need for Rubright's disclosure of "Reynosol R–4467" are simply irrelevant. That Reynosol considered the formulation of R–4467 a trade secret and that it offered the compound only to Chemcast, id., do not bear on the state of Rubright's knowledge or the quality of his disclosure. First, it is undisputed that Rubright did not know either the precise formulation or method of manufacture of R–4467; he knew only that it was a rigid PVC plastisol composition denominated "R–4467" by Reynosol. Whatever the scope of Reynosol's asserted trade secret, to the extent it includes information known by Rubright that he considered part of his preferred mode, section 112 requires that he divulge it. Second, whether and to whom Reynosol chooses to sell its products cannot control the extent to which Rubright must disclose his best mode. Were this the law, inventors like Rubright could readily circumvent the best mode requirement by concluding sole-user agreements with the suppliers of their preferred materials.

Nor does the fact that Rubright developed his preferred mode with the requirements of a particular customer in mind excuse its concealment; compliance with section 112 does not turn on why or for whom an inventor develops his invention. An inventor need not disclose manufacturing data or the requirements of a particular customer if that information is not part of the best mode of practicing the claimed invention, see *Christianson*, 870 F.2d at 1302 (citing *Christianson*, 822 F.2d at 1563), but the converse also is true. Whether characterizable as "manufacturing data," "customer requirements," or even "trade secrets," information necessary to practice the best mode simply must be disclosed.

Given the specification and the level of skill or understanding in the art, skilled practitioners could neither have known what Rubright's contemplated best mode was nor have carried it out. Indeed, on these facts, they would not even have known where to look. This is not a case, like Randomex, where the inventor indiscriminately disclosed his preferred mode along with other possible modes. *See* 849 F.2d at 589.

Rubright did not disclose his preferred mode at all. His preferred material hardness, 75 Shore D, is three hardness scales removed from the 70 Shore A hardness mentioned in the specification. Neither his preferred source, Reynosol Compound R–4467, nor any other is disclosed.

In this situation and on these facts, where the inventor has failed to disclose the only mode he ever contemplated of carrying out his invention, the best mode requirement is violated.

Accordingly, the judgment of the district court is affirmed.

failed best mode of 112

NOTES

1. **Best Mode Policy.** The best mode requirement appears to be based on the idea that the public is entitled to have access to the patentee's best mode from the patent instrument itself. Isn't it better to ask whether the public needs access to the best mode at all? Consider a hypothetical where an inventor contemporaneously submits an article to a leading technical publication including the best mode and files a patent application without this information. By the time the application matures into an issued patent, the published article has been in the public domain for several years. In this situation, does it make any sense to strike down the patent for failure to disclose the best mode?

2. **Burying the Best Mode.** In *Randomex Inc. v. Scopus Corp.*, 849 F.2d 585 (Fed.Cir.1988), the court considered the possibility of "burying" the best mode by concealing it among a large number of less favored alternatives. Here, the majority opinion held that the patentee did not violate § 112 through the "indiscriminate disclosure in this instance of the preferred cleaning fluid along with one other possible cleaning fluid . . . ." Judge Mayer dissented:

> [The inventor] only named [the preferred embodiment] as one among many possible solutions, and then only by its trade name, not generically. He did not disclose which of the suggested modes was the "best mode contemplated by him" for practicing the invention. His disclosure does not satisfy section 112 because he buried his best mode in a list of less satisfactory ones.

849 F.2d at 592. Note that although some drafters explicitly identify one embodiment as the best mode, no statute or rule mandates how the patent instrument should set forth the best mode. In fact Judge Bissell, who wrote for the court in *Randomex* gave an example of best mode disclosure:

> For example, if one should invent a new and improved internal combustion engine, the best mode requirement would require a patentee to divulge the fuel on which it would run best. The patentee, however, would not be required to disclose the formula for refining gasoline or any other petroleum product. Every requirement is met if the patentee truthfully stated that the engine ran smoothly and powerfully on Brand X super-premium lead free "or equal."

849 F.2d at 590 n. *. Is Judge Bissel correct that a claim to an engine requires disclosure of a preferred fuel? The inventor did not invent a fuel, why would a

fuel be a best mode? This question gets more coverage in the next case in this chapter.

3.   Burying the Best Mode II. One of the more unusual fact patterns in Federal Circuit history involved burying (literally) the best mode. *See Shearing v. Iolab Corp.*, 975 F.2d 1541 (Fed.Cir.1992). Dr. Shearing acquired a process patent, U.S. Patent No. 4,159,546, for an improved method of implanting an artificial optic lens into the posterior chamber of the eye. Before Dr. Shearing's innovation, physicians would implant a J-loop artificial lens in front of the iris, a process that often tore delicate eye tissue. Dr. Shearing sued Iolab for infringement. Iolab countered that a Dr. Simcoe had practiced the method before Dr. Shearing and that Dr. Shearing did not disclose his best mode, namely compressing both loops on the artificial lens to fit it past the small opening in the pupil. To resolve the issue, the patentee actually exhumed the body of one of Dr. Simcoe's patients. Upon exhumation of the body, an examination showed Dr. Simcoe had not implanted a J-loop artificial lens at all. The Federal Circuit also sustained the jury's conclusion that Dr. Shearing had not concealed a best mode:

> The jury also heard testimony refuting any concealment by Dr. Shearing of superior loop compression. In addition to the language about "directing" the second strand, at least two references in the '546 specification suggest superior loop compression:
>
>> Thus, since full compression of at least one of the strands during implantation is essential according to the procedure described herein....
>
> U.S. Patent No. 4,159,546, col. 5, lines 18–20. This statement suggests compression of more than just one strand or loop. The specification also states:
>
>> directing said second strand against the ciliary body opposite said first strand....

Id. at col. 6, lines 8–9. This statement would also teach one skilled in the art to compress both strands.

975 F.2d at 1545–46. In addition to teaching the rewards of full discovery, this case teaches that the best mode need only be disclosed in terms sufficient to inform one of skill in the practice of the invention.

4.   Best Mode Abroad. Section 4 of the now-superseded British Patent Act of 1949 mandated that applicants "shall disclose the best method of performing the invention which is known to the applicant and for which he is entitled to claim protection." An earlier Canadian statute tracked the "best mode" language of the United States statute more closely; as explained in IMMANUEL GOLDSMITH, PATENTS OF INVENTION § 177 (1981), the Canadian patent law required that the inventor "put the public in possession of the invention in as full and ample a manner as he himself possesses it and give to them the opportunity of deriving benefits therefrom equal to the benefits accruing to him." However, some jurisdictions have since abrogated requirements that parallel the United States "best mode" requirement.

Even when foreign patent systems do not impose a best mode requirement, foreign applicants often include this information in their applications as well. In no small part they do so because they contemplate the possibility of filing an application in the United States under the Paris Convention. Because the applicant may not augment her initial disclosure when later filing in the United States, but must fulfill disclosure requirements such as best mode, inclusion of the best mode is often prudent. Similarly, the following passage, directed towards Japanese law, explains why American applicants seldom delete the best mode from their foreign applications that are based on a United States priority date.

> The United States patent law requires under the first paragraph of 35 U.S.C.A. § 112 that the inventor set forth the "best mode contemplated" for carrying out the invention as of the filing date. This is *recommended* by the Japanese Patent Office, but it is not a basis for a ground of rejection of the application or of invalidity of the patent.
>
> It would seem unwarranted to *delete* the best mode known to the applicant from the American text serving as the draft for the Japanese application. Presumably, the best mode will be published in the form of an American patent, and it would be naive to presume that Japanese industry is not aware of the American patent literature.
>
> Assume that the best mode of the American text is taken out of the Japanese case, and that eventually a copier of the best mode is sued for infringement in a District Court in Japan. If the wording of the claims and the specification make the generic coverage unclear, it is possible that the judge may well ... leav[e] the best mode outside the scope of protection.

TETSU TANABE & HAROLD C. WEGNER, JAPANESE PATENT LAW § 422 (1979).

5. "The inventor" Means "The Inventor." In *Glaxo Inc. v. Novopharm Ltd.*, 52 F.3d 1043 (Fed.Cir.1995), the Federal Circuit confronted the question of who is the inventor for purposes of best mode enforcement. In a case involving the anti-ulcer medication Zantac®, Glaxo's patent counsel learned that Glaxo had a secret process that made the invention easier to put into pharmaceutical compositions. In sum, Glaxo's attorney and others within the corporation knew of a best mode. The inventor, Dr. Crookes, did not know that Glaxo had developed the best mode. The Federal Circuit determined that only the inventor's knowledge is relevant to the best mode inquiry:

> The statutory language could not be clearer. The best mode of carrying out an invention, indeed if there is one, to be disclosed is that "contemplated by the inventor." ... There is simply no evidence in the record before us that the inventor of the '431 patent knew of and concealed the azeotroping process when his application was filed.

52 F.3d at 1049. Even though Glaxo apparently screened Crookes from any knowledge of the best mode, the Federal Circuit refused to invalidate the patent. Judge Mayer dissented:

> With this case, the court blesses corporate shell games resulting from organizational gerrymandering and willful ignorance by which one can

secure the monopoly of a patent while hiding the best mode of practicing the invention the law expects to be made public in return for its protection.

52 F.3d at 1053. As the director of a corporate research and development department, what advice would you give to the inventors in your division after *Glaxo*? Why do you think the Federal Circuit takes such a literal approach to enforcing the best mode requirement? The next case again offers some hints about an answer.

6.   *Chemcast* recast: In *Chemcast*, Judge Mayer opined that "most of the cases in which we have said that the best mode requirement was violated addressed situations where the inventor failed to disclose non-claimed elements that were nevertheless necessary to practice the best mode." *Chemcast*, 913 F.2d at 927. This statement seems to defy the standard rule that the best mode requirement only extends to claimed elements of the invention. This statement prompted an explanation in Judge Rader's concurrence in *Bayer*, the next case in this chapter:

> Despite its language about "non-claimed elements," the *Chemcast* claim recited a "locking portion . . . more rigid than said base portion." *Id.* at 925. Thus, the best mode violation in that case—a grommet of specified rigidity—was within the scope of the claims. *Chemcast*'s comment about "non-claimed elements" was purely dicta. Contrary to the *Chemcast* dicta, an undisclosed feature only becomes a "best mode" candidate—by statutory definition—if it arises within the scope of the claimed invention.
>
> In *Chemcast*, the inventor's specification disclosed a grommet of "rigid castable resinous material . . . for example, polyurethane or polyvinyl chloride . . . [with] a durometer hardness reading of 70 Shore A or harder." Chemcast, 913 F.2d at 929. No doubt the inventor thought that this disclosure was sufficient. After all, the inventor disclosed a preferred embodiment. Moreover, Chemcast Corporation's actual product, R–4467, was indeed PVC with a hardness reading above Shore A 70—consistent with that disclosure.
>
> The Federal Circuit, however, perceived concealment—the second prong of the best mode requirement. This court noted that R–4467 had a material hardness of 75 on the Shore D scale—"three hardness scales removed from the 70 Shore A hardness mentioned in the specification." *Id.* at 930. This circuit further stressed that the inventors had "expended several months and many hundred man-hours" developing R 4467. *Id.* at 929. Chemcast is a concealment case, indeed an enthusiastic application of the concealment standard. In its zeal to reach the concealment issue, the Federal Circuit stretched its purported definition of best modes to encompass "unclaimed features," but that certainly does not override prior binding case law.

Bayer AG v. Schein Pharm., 301 F.3d 1306 at n. 6 (Fed.Cir.2002) (Rader J., concurring). The best mode requirement has two prongs—"contemplation" and "concealment." Although a violation requires satisfaction of both prongs, can a strong case of "concealment" strengthen a weak case of "contemplation"?

7. Best Mode and Continuing Applications. In *Transco Products Inc. v. Performance Contracting, Inc.*, 38 F.3d 551 (Fed.Cir.1994), Judge Rich concluded that so-called continuing applications, considered here at Chapter 12, need not be updated with the inventor's most recent best mode. One commentator noted the countervailing policies as follows:

> If there is a strong policy reason for the best mode requirement, and there is not, then if one sought the special benefits of the continuation procedure, one of the costs of that benefit might fairly be an updated disclosure. After all, other patent systems do not give an applicant the right to continue prosecution simply through the mechanism of paying a fee in return for the right to file a continuation application. Hence, it would not be unreasonable to assert that in addition to paying an additional fee, an applicant may file a continuation application, but to do so requires that he update his best mode disclosure.

3 MARTIN J. ADELMAN, PATENT LAW PERSPECTIVES § 2.9 [2.4–1] (1996).

8. Comparison with Inequitable Conduct. Contrast an applicant's failure to disclose the best mode with inequitable conduct, a topic this casebook takes up at Chapter 12. Is failure to include the best mode something of a "lesser included offense" relevant to inequitable conduct? Do you observe a significant difference between the penalties/invalidity as compared with unenforceability for violation of these standards? Keep in mind that the best mode requirement applies to each claim individually while inequitable conduct as to one claim invalidates all claims in the patent.

9. Is Best Mode a "self enforcing" "trap for the unwary?" A 2002 opinion explained the Federal Circuit's general practice of construing the best mode requirement very narrowly:

> In most instances, the best mode requirement is self-enforcing. If an inventor does not disclose a critical trade secret within the best mode requirement, that nondisclosure puts the value of the entire patented invention at risk-a risk beyond the requirements of § 112. Competitors in the same technology can, and invariably will, discover the undisclosed trade secret and claim it in a separate patent application. When that application ripens into a patent, the competitor will have a blocking patent that could compromise much of the value of the original patent. Therefore, an informed patent applicant will never withhold a genuine best mode. Informed patent applicants will always either disclose the best mode in the original patent's specification (often as a dependent claim) or, if the trade secret is not part of the claimed invention (as in this case), file a separate patent application on the separate innovation (also as in this case). Because informed patent applicants know to avoid best mode problems, this § 112 requirement is invariably little more than a trap for the uninformed applicant—usually a university or independent inventor without corporate legal resources. Because the best mode requirement is a trap for the unwary, the Federal Circuit has wisely followed the statutory "scope of the claimed invention" rule to confine the reach of this snare.

Bayer AG v. Schein Pharm., 301 F.3d 1306, 1325 (Fed. Cir. 2002)(Rader, J., concurring).

10. The Advisory Commission Report. Consider the following paragraphs from the 1992 Advisory Commission on Patent Law Reform.

The Commission recommends elimination of the best mode requirement. First, the best mode requirement is not necessary to ensure "full and fair" disclosures of patented inventions. The objective requirement of enablement ensures that the public is put in possession of at least one operable embodiment of a patented invention. . . .

Second, aside from the positive requirement for adequate disclosure imposed by the enablement requirement, there are substantive deterrents to concealment of useful or material information in patent documents. Active concealment by a patent applicant of a material element of his invention renders the entire patent unenforceable, through the inequitable conduct doctrine. Concealment of non-material information, but "significant" embodiments of a patented invention places a "concealment-oriented" patent applicant at risk from later innovators who discover and then patent the significantly superior improvement. . . .

Third, the best mode requirement does not effectively compel higher quality disclosures. This is due to the substantive and non-mandatory nature of the requirement. The best mode requirement does not require disclosure of an objectively superior method; it only requires disclosure of what the applicant perceives to be the best mode at the time the patent application was filed. . . . If, at the time the patent application was filed, the applicant does not view one mode as being superior to others, there is no best mode to disclose. Thus, the requirement will have not direct effect on compelling a higher quality disclosure.

Fourth, in rapidly evolving technologies, such as biotechnology or computer-program related inventions, the "best mode" of an invention at the time the patent application is filed may differ dramatically, and is likely to be inferior to the "best mode" at the time the patent is granted. . . .

Finally, the best mode requirement as we know it has been an element of the U.S. patent system only since the 1952 Patent Act. . . . Thus, the best mode requirement is not the long-standing and integral element of the patent system some perceive it to be.

THE ADVISORY COMMISSION ON PATENT LAW REFORM, A REPORT TO THE SECRETARY OF COMMERCE 102–03 (1992). At least one defender of the best mode requirement found these comments misplaced. Jerry R. Selinger, *In Defense of "Best Mode": Preserving the Benefit of the Bargain for the Public*, 43 CATHOLIC U. L. REV. 1071, 1104–05 (1994), traces the best mode requirement to the earliest U.S. patent statutes and offers the following counterarguments to the Advisory Commission:

Best mode serves two purposes that complement enablement: (1) to ensure the public receives not merely a disclosure of the invention, but the best way contemplated by the inventor of carrying out the invention; and

(2) to allow the public to compete fairly with the patentee after the patent expires. Clearly, if the statutory best mode obligation is repealed, the public will no longer receive the benefit of the additional disclosure compelled by best mode. There are several cases in which patentees have satisfied the enabling obligation, while still concealing relevant information. Even with the present statutory best mode disclosure requirement, applicants sometimes withhold important technical details to which the public is entitled. Inventors realistically will not disclose more than they are absolutely required to divulge. Without a best mode obligation, enablement will establish both the upper and lower boundaries of disclosure. The Advisory Commission's reasons for eliminating best mode and the supposed benefits to be derived therefrom must be weighed against the definable, if not quantifiable, loss of information that the public will suffer. . . .

Seeking to justify its premise, the Advisory Commission suggests that "there are substantive deterrents to concealment of useful or material information in patent documents." One such deterrent is said to be the doctrine of inequitable conduct. Inequitable conduct relates to how the inventor and patent counsel conduct themselves during negotiations with the Patent Office, normally after the application has been filed. A finding of inequitable conduct requires a misrepresentation that is material to the examination process. While a material misrepresentation is an essential element of inequitable conduct, the essence of non-compliance with best mode is concealment rather than overt misrepresentation. Inequitable conduct would not inhibit an inventor from disclosing a second-best mode. Consequently, reliance on inequitable conduct has not—and will not—protect the important public policies embodied in the best mode requirement.

Enablement also differs from best mode in that compliance with enablement inherently does not compel disclosure of the best mode. For an enablement analysis, a court makes an objective determination as to whether a hypothetical person skilled in the art could practice the invention. A factfinder need not consider whether the inventor intended to deceive or mislead, so long as the patent specification is enabling. Invalidity for failure to provide an enabling disclosure is not an effective alternative either.

11. Patent Reform Proposal. Legislation introduced in the 109th Congress proposed the elimination of the best mode requirement. However, in the 110th Congress, H.R. 1908 took a different approach. The Patent Reform Act of 2007, which passed the House of Representatives, the best mode requirement continues to apply to all patents, but it no longer forms the basis for a defense to a charge of patent infringement during enforcement litigation or post-grant review proceedings. Compliance with the best mode requirement would remain subject to review by USPTO examiners during the initial prosecution of a patent. Is this an apt compromise between detractors and supporters of the best mode requirement?

Exercise

Rameau is an inventor and licensed United States patent agent. Late in the evening on December 31, 1997, he conceives of the idea of an improved champagne corkscrew. He subsequently prepares a sales brochure with a detailed and complete description of the new corkscrew for distribution at the wine festival at a regional wine festival held in Napa, California, on September 10, 1998.

Two days before the festival, Rameau considers whether he should file a patent application on the corkscrew. Although 35 U.S.C. § 102(b) provides him with a one-year grace period in the United States, he recalls that most foreign patent systems are absolute novelty regimes. Distribution of the sales brochures could thus be fatal to Rameau's potential patent rights elsewhere. Rameau hastily drafts an application that evening and files it at the United States Patent and Trademark Office the next day, on September 9, 1998.

At the festival, Rameau distributes over 1500 brochures to prospective customers. A few days later, Rameau reviews his patent application and realizes that he did not describe grasping arms which seize the champagne stopper, a key feature of the invention that the sales brochure detailed. Rameau very much doubts that skilled workers in the field could make or use his invention without this additional information.

How may Rameau modify his patent specification in order to meet § 112, first paragraph? Does Rameau possess any other options in order to fulfill the requirements of § 112, first paragraph?

CHAPTER NINE

CLAIMS

■ ■ ■

The essence of the patent right is the right to exclude others from making, using, selling, or offering to sell the claimed invention. The claims define the bounds of that right to exclude. Accordingly, the claims are the most significant part of the entire patent instrument. As such, they are the principal focus of the dialogue the patent drafter will have with an inventor, of the entire prosecution process, and ultimately of any licensing activity or infringement suit to enforce patent rights.

Claims are, without doubt, the most difficult legal instrument to draft. Claims are both legal and technical instruments. As legal instruments, they must precisely define entitlements for worldwide markets and industries. As technical documents, they must inform other scientists and skilled artisans of the technical advance. In performing these two functions, claims must accurately reflect and distinguish all prior art—a retrospective challenge. Claims must also envision prospectively the direction of subsequent research to ensure improvements within the scope of the invention cannot evade the property rights. Finally, of course, the claims must capture the entirety of the inventive advance.

The starting point for patent claims is the statute, 35 U.S.C.A. § 112, that sets forth formal and substantive requirements for drafting and interpreting claims. With the paragraphs numbered for convenience, § 112 provides:

§ 112. Specification

* * *

[¶ 2]   The specification shall conclude with one or more claims particularly pointing out and distinctly claiming the subject matter which the applicant regards as his invention.

[¶ 3]   A claim may be written in independent or, if the nature of the case admits, in dependent or multiple dependent form.

[¶ 4]   Subject to the following paragraph, a claim in dependent form shall contain a reference to a claim previously set forth and then specify a further limitation of the subject matter claimed. A claim in dependent form shall be construed to incorporate by reference all the limitations of the claim to which it refers.

[¶ 5] A claim in multiple dependent form shall contain a reference, in the alternative only, to more than one claim previously set forth and then specify a further limitation of the subject matter claimed. A multiple dependent claim shall not serve as a basis for any other multiple dependent claim. A multiple dependent claim shall be construed to incorporate by reference all the limitations of the particular claim in relation to which it is being considered.

[¶ 6] An element in a claim for a combination may be expressed as a means or step for performing a specified function without the recital of structure, material, or acts in support thereof, and such claim shall be construed to cover the corresponding structure, material, or acts described in the specification and equivalents thereof.

The core provision, paragraph 2, instructs patent drafters to set forth distinctly the bounds of the invention. Patent claims must give a clear indication to others of the limits of the property right. The remaining paragraphs address specific claim formats: paragraphs 3–5 govern so-called "dependent" claims, while the sixth paragraph of § 112 provides for "means-plus-function" claims.

This introduction to the nature of claims and a couple notable claim formats is just that—an introduction. Proper drafting and prosecution of claims is a legal and technical skill worthy of a lifetime of study. That study would necessarily embrace much more than the statutory requirements. United States patent claiming practice is largely driven by Patent Office policies, past judicial treatment of claim terms and formats, and well-established traditions of the patent bar. This chapter will introduce some of the directives of the Patent Act as well as the significant extra-statutory law that governs the art of claim drafting. Perhaps the best service of this chapter is to caution future practitioners that claim drafting requires considerable experience and skill.

§ 9.1 UNITED STATES PERIPHERAL CLAIMING TECHNIQUE

EX PARTE FRESSOLA

U.S. Patent and Trademark Office Board of Patent Appeals and Interferences, 1993
27 U.S.P.Q.2d 1608

Before Serota, Chairman, Lovel, McCandlish, Hairston, and Cardillo, Examiners-in-Chief.

SEROTA, CHAIRMAN.

This is an appeal from the examiner's final rejection of claim 42. The disclosed invention is described by appellant as follows:

The invention includes a method and system of producing stereographic images of celestial objects which use distance information to offset one of two images produced on a display device. A digital computer under program control is used in combination with a user input device, such as keyboard, and a display device, such as a computer monitor and/or a printer.

Claim 42 reads:

> 42.   A system for the display of stereographic three-dimensional images of celestial objects as disclosed in the specification and drawings herein.

The appealed claim 42 stands rejected under 35 U.S.C. Section 112 ¶ 2 as failing to particularly point out and distinctly claim the subject matter which applicant regards as his invention. We affirm.

OPINION

35 U.S.C. Section 112 ¶ 2

The claims measure the scope of the protected patent right and "must comply accurately and precisely with the statutory requirements." *United Carbon Co. v. Binney & Smith Co.*, 317 U.S. 228, 232, 55 U.S.P.Q. 381, 383–84 (1942). Claims in utility applications[1] that define the invention entirely by reference to the specification and/or drawings, so-called "omnibus" or "formal" claims, while perhaps once accepted in American patent practice, are properly rejected under Section 112 ¶ 2 as failing to particularly point out and distinctly claim the invention.

The written description and the claims are separate statutory requirements. Modern claim practice requires that the claims stand alone to define the invention. Incorporation into the claims by express reference to the specification and/or drawings is not permitted except in very limited circumstances.

Early claim forms were significantly different in style and content from modern claims. *See Pennwalt Corporation v. Durand–Wayland, Inc.*, 833 F.2d 931, 957–59, 4 U.S.P.Q.2d 1737, 1758–1760 (Fed.Cir.1987), *cert. denied*, 485 U.S. 961 (1988) (NEWMAN, J., commentary) (evolution of claim form); DELLER, Sections 1–11. The original method of claiming in this country was based on the central definition where the claims named the broad features of the invention (often just an enumeration of the elements and the reference characters of the drawings) together with a phrase such as "substantially as set forth." These claims were construed to "incorporate by reference the description in the specification and equivalents thereof." *Pennwalt*, 833 F.2d at 959, 4 U.S.P.Q.2d at 1759. During this early period, "[t]he drawings and description were the main thing, the claims merely an adjunct thereto." DELLER, Section 4.

Beginning with the Patent Act of 1870, the claims took on more importance. As described in DELLER, Section 7:

---

1.   This analysis is limited to claims in utility applications. Plant patent claims are defined "in formal terms to the plant shown and described." 35 U.S.C. Section 162. Claims in design patents are recited in formal terms to the ornamental design "as shown" or, where there is a properly included special description of the design, the ornamental design "as shown and described." MPEP Section 1503.01.

They became much more self-sufficient in that they gave the cooperative relationship of the elements enumerated, instead of a mere catalog of elements followed by some such phrase as "constructed and adapted to operate substantially as set forth."

The method of claiming shifted from the central definition to the peripheral definition. As described in DELLER, Section 5:

> Central definition involves the drafting of a narrow claim setting forth a typical embodiment coupled with broad interpretation by the courts to include all equivalent constructions. Peripheral definition involves marking out the periphery or boundary of the area covered by the claim and holding as infringements only such constructions as lie within that area.

The conversion from the central definition to the peripheral definition was due to the more rigorous requirements for the claim to stand alone to define the invention and the refusal of the courts to expand the scope of the claims beyond their literal terms. Modern claim interpretation is based on the peripheral system where the scope of the claim is not expanded. *See Wilson Sporting Goods Co. v. David Geoffrey & Assoc.*, 904 F.2d 677, 684 (Fed.Cir.1990) (doctrine of equivalents does not expand claims, it only expands right to exclude to "equivalents"). Modern claim interpretation requires that the claims particularly point out and distinctly claim the invention without reading in limitations from the specification.

Phrases in claims referring back to the description and drawing such as "substantially as described" or "as herein shown and described" were once customary in claims in the days of the central definition. Deller, Section 25. Expressions referring back to the disclosure are sometimes referred to by patent authors as "backfiring" expressions. The "substantially as described" expressions were generally used as an addendum to the elements of the claim. Insofar as we have been able to determine, claims consisting entirely of a reference to the specification and/or drawings were held to be indefinite very early in the period of transition toward increased definiteness in claiming. As stated in *Ex parte Rice*, 1874 Dec. Comm'r Pat. 44, 45 (Comm'r Pat. 1874):

> In this case the applicant puts in but a single claim, reading as following:
>
> > *As a new article of manufacture, mats made of corn-husks, substantially in the manner described.*

The examiner ought to have objected to this claim, for the reason that it does not properly comply with the requirements of section 26 of the patent act, which, after setting forth what shall be the character of a specification, says, "and he shall particularly point out and distinctly claim the part, improvement, or combination which he claims as his invention or discovery." The mere reference to the body of the specification by the terms "substantially in the manner described" is not "particularly" pointing out and "distinctly" claiming the alleged invention, and therefore does not comply with the requirements of the statute.

In *National Tube Co. v. Mark*, 216 F. 507, 515–22 (6th Cir.1914), the court reviewed the authorities and held that phrases such as "substantially as described" should be given no interpretative importance. To the extent that such phrases require the claim to be read in light of the specification, they add nothing to the claim. The court in *National Tube* did not review any cases where the claim was entirely a reference to the specification, probably because it, like us, was unable to find any. The *National Tube* case marks the beginning of the end of the use of expressions referring back to the specification and drawings. *See* Jessup, *The Doctrine of Equivalents*, 54 J. PAT. OFF. SOC'Y 248 (1972). The Patent Office has consistently refused to afford weight to "substantially as described" and similar expressions. . . .

ANALYSIS AND DECISION

We agree with the examiner's conclusion that claim 42 is indefinite and fails to particularly point out and distinctly claim what applicant regards as his invention as required by Section 112 ¶ 2. First, claim 42 does not comply with the requirement of Section 112 ¶ 2 that the claims particularly point out and distinctly describe the invention because it relies entirely on incorporation by reference of the specification and drawings. The written description and the claims are separate statutory requirements. As stated long ago in *Ex parte Holt*, 1884 Dec. Comm'r Pat. 43, 62–63 (Comm'r Pat. 1884):

> The aim, end, and purpose of the specification, under the present statute, is to describe the invention sought to be covered by the patent, and the manner of making, constructing, and using the same. The aim, the end, the purpose of the claim is to point out particularly and distinctly define the invention to be secured to the individual. The claim is the measure of the patent, and the day has passed when the courts will search the specification for information which it is the very office of the claim to impart.

A claim which refers to the specification defeats the purpose of a claim. The limited exceptions which permit incorporation by reference do not apply because the system can be described in words without reference to the specification and drawings. . . .

Second, the history of phrases which incorporate by reference to the specification and/or drawings shows the difficulty and inconsistency in interpreting such phrases, which have no fixed legal meaning. Claim 42 is indefinite because it is impossible to determine how much of the disclosure is incorporated by reference into claim 42, or to what extent claim 42 would be interpreted to cover equivalents. The phrase "as disclosed in the specification and drawings herein" in claim 42 is interpreted to read on the whole or any part of the disclosure.

Third, assuming, arguendo, that incorporation by reference were a permissible mode of claiming, claim 42 is indefinite because the specification and drawings to which it refers do not particularly point out and distinctly define what invention is intended to be circumscribed by claim 42. Instead of succinctly enumerating the elements and limitations which constitute the boundary of the invention, claim 42 requires that the limitations be gleaned from an analysis of 19 figures of drawings and 147 pages of specification, including 28 pages of description of the background prior art and the method, 45 pages of program listing in Table 1, 73 pages of data in Table 2, and additional disclosed commercial Turbo Graphix (Registered) procedures. As has been held by our former reviewing court in the case of *In re Clemens*, 622 F.2d 1029, 206 U.S.P.Q. 289 (CCPA 1980), the specification in order to comply with the requirements of the first paragraph of 35 U.S.C. 112, frequently includes matter which is not the invention of the applicant. The description includes large quantities of extraneous matter such as example images, descriptions of prior art, alternative features (inverse display, marking arrow, stereo versus non-stereo display, etc.), which obscures the system claim boundaries; it does not particularly point out and distinctly claim the invention. The fact that the specification is directed primarily at the method for displaying, while claim 42 is for a system, further contributes to making claim 42 indefinite. The specification is also indefinite because of the following statements in the specification:

> Although described in part by a computer program written in Turbo Pascal (Registered) for use on an IBM PC (Registered) or compatible personal computer, it is apparent that the concepts described can be readily adapted to other computer languages and computer systems.

Appellant apparently wants to protect the underlying process steps of the program source code in Table 1 as performed by the computer, not the source code itself which does not run on the computer. However, instead of reciting the steps performed by the program in terms of English language descriptions, the specification requires extraction of the steps embedded in the program code written in Pascal programming language; this does not particularly point out or distinctly claim the invention. The following statement at the end of the specification also renders the scope of claim 42 indefinite (page 29):

> [S]ince changes may be made in carrying out the methodology of the invention, including the computer program or other instructions used, it is intended that all matter contained in the above description or shown in the accompanying drawings shall be interpreted as illustrative, and not in a limiting sense.

In view of this statement, it is impossible to tell what parts of the specification are and are not intended to be limiting, or what modifications would fall within the scope of claim 42.

We turn now to appellant's arguments. It is argued:

Because Congress has placed no limitations on how an applicant claims his invention, applicant respectfully argues that claim 42, a so-called "omnibus" claim, specifically references the specification and, therefore, particularly points out and distinctly claims the subject matter which the applicant regards as his invention.

Aside from the formal single sentence claim requirement, there are few restrictions on how an invention must be claimed as long as the claim satisfies Section 112 ¶ 2. However, the omnibus claim does not satisfy Section 112 § 2 because the claim does not itself define the invention, but relies on external material.

It is argued that claim 42 is, in effect, a "picture claim" which is limited to the exact structure of the invention as shown in specification and figures:

> [A] claim which merely recites the specification and the drawings is most limited in scope and protects only the device shown and described.

This is only appellant's interpretation of claim 42. Claim 42 can be interpreted to incorporate all or only part of the disclosure. In addition, it is not certain that claim 42 is limited to the exact description in the specification and drawings in view of the statements made at page 29 of the specification discussed, supra. It is argued that claim 42 provides the requisite notice to the public of what will infringe:

> [T]he rejected claim 42 is quite clear and would be understandable to one of ordinary skill in the art as such person would simply examine the specification and the corresponding figures and would know exactly what the invention is. In fact, a person of ordinary skill in the art would be provided with more specific notice because if his product was not specifically described and shown in the specification and the figures, he would be sure that he was not infringing the patent.

As discussed, supra, we do not agree that the specification and drawings, assuming they could be incorporated by reference into claim 42, particularly point out and distinctly claim the invention. The claims define the boundary of the invention. The metes and bounds of what the Appellant regards as his invention must be clearly set forth in order that the public at a time after the patent is granted may evaluate what is infringed, and what would be dominated by or within the patented claims.

Appellant notes that omnibus-style claims are accepted in the United Kingdom and that the United Kingdom's patent law regarding claim requirements is substantially similar to Section 112 ¶ 2. The only issue is United States law. We decline to speculate on the reasons why foreign countries allow or require omnibus-style claims.

CONCLUSION

The rejection of claim 42 for failing to particularly point out and distinctly claim the invention under 35 U.S.C. Section 112 ¶ 2 is affirmed.

AFFIRMED.

NOTES

1. Claims and the Specification. Although the United States patent system rejects omnibus claims in utility patents, one should not take this ruling as denying any interplay between a patent's claims and the remainder of its specification. In fact, courts interpret claims in light of the specification. *Markman v. Westview Instruments, Inc.*, 52 F.3d 967 (Fed.Cir.1995), *aff'd*, 517 U.S. 370 (1996). Further, in instances where the drafter invokes § 112 ¶ 6, the statute directs that the structure in the specification (corresponding to the claimed function) will govern the literal meaning of the functional element. *See* § 11.2[c], *infra*. Chapter 15, *Infringement*, considers further the relationship between claims and the remainder of the specification.

2. The One–Sentence Rule. The United States Patent and Trademark Office additionally mandates that a patent claim be composed as a single English sentence. This rule was challenged in *Fressola v. Manbeck*, 36 U.S.P.Q.2d 1211 (D.D.C.1995), on the basis of the Administrative Procedure Act. The court replied:

> The Plaintiff here contends that the one-sentence requirement bears no reasonable relationship to the language of and policies behind 35 U.S.C. Section 112. As noted above, this statute requires patent applications to conclude with "one or more claims particularly pointing out and distinctly claiming the subject matter which the applicant regards as his invention."
>
> The Plaintiff first argues that no reasonable relationship links the one-sentence rule to the statutory requirement that the claim "particularly point[ ] out" and "distinctly claim [ ]" the invention. Id. The Court, however, discerns no tension between this statutory language and the application of the one-sentence rule. Although this portion of the statute undoubtedly seeks to protect the inventor and the public from the uncertainty that would arise from unclear claims, the record in this case supports the Defendant's expert judgment that the one-sentence rule has no impact on the clarity of claims and has fostered the efficient processing of several million patent applications. Through simple changes in punctuation, an applicant could transform any multiple-sentence claim into a single-sentence claim. Indeed, the Court believes the one-sentence rule may even advance these statutory goals by encouraging claims that are generally more succinct than multiple-sentence claims of the same scope.
>
> The Plaintiff also argues that, because the one-sentence rule limits the manner in which an applicant can claim his discovery, it does not reasonably relate to the statute's dictate that the claim describe "the subject matter which the applicant regards as his invention." Once again, the Court finds that the one-sentence rule does not conflict with this portion of the statute. While the statutory language may give the applicant ultimate control over the substance of his claim, it does not appear to speak to matters of pure form, such as the number of sentences allowed per claim; in other words, since an applicant can (as described above) make exactly

the same claim in one sentence as he could in multiple sentences, the uniform format prescribed by the one-sentence rule does not interfere with his ability to claim whatever he "regards as his invention."

3. The Art of Claim Drafting. Claims drafting is, without doubt, the most difficult form of technical writing, requiring considerable analytic and research skills, as well as scientific and technical competence. Claims must reduce sophisticated technical concepts to a single sentence, and yet present an accurate description of the invention. They must also reflect a keen awareness of the technical field in which the invention lies. Often only a few carefully chosen words of limitation mark a patentable distinction between the claimed invention and prior technical knowledge.

Claims drafters also operate within the true "multiple claim" system long in effect in the United States. Each patent may have multiple claims. Moreover a patentee may assert each and every claim of a patent, either alone or in combination, against an accused infringer. Each claim is important. The result of this system is that claims drafters typically craft a series of claims in each application, forming a "reverse pyramid" of successively narrower claims. The first claim of the patent is very broad and abstract. The narrowest claim usually describes a product the inventor would actually consider putting into commercial practice. Intermediate claims are set to varying levels of abstraction, each taking a place on the spectrum of technologies surrounding the narrowly focused commercial embodiment of the invention.

Why? Because the patentee wishes to enforce the narrowest possible claim against an accused infringer; the narrower the claim, the greater the likelihood that such a claim will withstand a defense of invalidity. As the number of limitations in a claim rises, the likelihood that prior art will render that claim anticipated (35 U.S.C.A. § 102) or obvious (35 U.S.C.A.§ 103) falls. Importantly, experienced claim drafters recognize that pertinent prior art may well emerge after patent issuance. Thus, they must foresee the possibility of new prior art references arising when the claims are tested in court. Also, the narrower the claim, the greater the difficulty an accused infringer will have in making an attack based upon enablement (35 U.S.C.A. § 112).

On the other hand, the patentee also wants the broadest claim possible in order to have the possibility of reaching as many competitors as possible. Therefore a skillful claims drafter seeks to write the broadest claim the PTO will allow to acquire enforceable protection in each patent instrument.

§ 9.2 PATENT CLAIM FORMAT

Although patent applicants enjoy relatively free hands in setting forth the substance of a claim, years of Patent Office interpretation and judicial precedent have resulted in relatively standardized claim formatting. The United States Patent and Trademark Office requires a three-part claim: the preamble, the transition phrase, and the body. As assisted by the courts, the Patent and Trademark Office has also developed rules regarding the meaning and effect of each of these portions of a claim.

Further, a discrete number of well-known claim formats have arisen over decades of patent practice. Most claims that patent practitioners will read or draft fall into the categories of apparatus, article of manufacture, composition of matter, or method claims. In other words, claims to the categories of statutory subject matter set forth in § 101. But in addition, some specialized claim formats, with particularized meanings in the art, have emerged to accommodate the demands of technical subject matter. This section further explores four of these: product-by-process, functional, Jepson, and Markush claim styles.

§ 9.2[a]   ELEMENTAL CLAIM STRUCTURE

§ 9.2[a][1]   THE PREAMBLE

A claim begins with the object of the sentence, e.g., *"A method of making coffee...."* The preamble generally states the general use or purpose of the invention. It thus helps to show the broad area of technology to which the invention belongs and may help the PTO assign the invention to an examining group.

A primary question in patent enforcement that arises again and again is whether the preamble recitation serves to limit the scope of the claims. The rule for this question is not easy to state. Depending on its importance to give meaning to the claim, the introduction ("preamble") may or may not constitute a limitation on the scope of the claim. In somewhat colloquial (and admittedly illogical) terms, when it matters, the preamble will serve as a limitation on the claimed subject matter. Stated more elegantly, a preamble has the import that the claim as a whole assigns to it. *Bell Comm. Research, Inc. v. Vitalink Comm. Corp.*, 55 F.3d 615 (Fed.Cir.1995). Of course, the colloquial overstatement of the rule at least serves to warn claim drafters to anticipate that unnecessary verbiage in the preamble can reduce the scope of patent coverage. A recent Federal Circuit case explores the factors determining when a preamble limits and the implications of that limitation.

**CATALINA MARKETING INTERNATIONAL
v. COOLSAVINGS.COM, INC.**

United States Court of Appeals, Federal Circuit, 2002
289 F.3d 801

Before Mayer, Chief Judge, and Rader, and Prost, Circuit Judges.

RADER, CIRCUIT JUDGE.

On summary judgment, the United States District Court for the Northern District of Illinois held that Coolsavings.com, Inc. (Coolsavings) did not infringe, either literally or by equivalents, the claims of Catalina Marketing International, Inc.'s (Catalina's) U.S. Patent No. 4,674,041 (the '041 patent). Because the district court erroneously relied on non-limiting language in the preamble of Claim 1, this court affirms-in-part, reverses-in-part, vacates-in-part, and remands.

I.

The '041 patent, filed on September 15, 1983, claims a selection and distribution system for discount coupons. In a preferred embodiment, the system dispenses coupons to consumers at remote, kiosk-like terminals connected to a central host computer system. When a consumer activates the terminal in a retail outlet, the terminal displays available coupons on the screen. The consumer selects a coupon and a printer connected to the terminal prints it. The terminal selectively communicates with the central computer system to acquire coupon information for display. When the number of dispensed coupons for a certain product reaches a limit specified by a coupon provider, the central computer system stops providing that particular coupon. Figure 3a depicts the terminal:

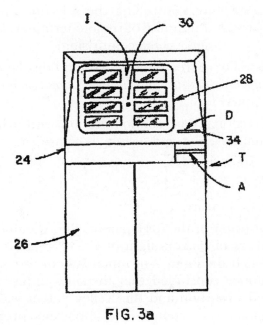

FIG. 3a

There are two independent claims at issue, namely Claims 1 and 25. [Claim 1] reads as follows:

1. A systen [sic] for controlling the selection and dispensing of product coupons at a plurality of remote terminals *located at predesignated sites such as consumer stores* wherein each terminal comprises:

activation means for activating such terminal for consumer transactions;

display means operatively connected with said activation means for displaying a plurality of coupons available for selection;

selection means operatively connected with said display means provided to permit selection of a desired displayed coupon by the consumer;

print means operatively connected with said selection means for printing and dispensing the coupon selected by the consumer; and

control means operatively connected with said display means for monitoring each consumer transaction and for controlling said display means to prevent the display of coupons having exceeded prescribed coupon limits.

'041 patent, col. 30, ll. 46–65 (emphasis added).

[Claim 25 is very similar to claim 1. In claim 25, however, the preamble was shortened slightly and an additional limitation was added after the "comprises" transition phrase. As a result, claim 25 recites (with emphasis added):

25. A system for controlling the selection and dispensing of product coupons at a plurality of remote terminals *located at predesignated sites such as consumer stores*, comprising:

a plurality of free standing coupon display terminals *located at predesignated sites such as consumer stores*, each of said terminals being adapted for

bidirectional data communication with a host central processing unit; each of said terminals comprising

activation means . . . ;

display means . . . ;

selection means. . . .]

During prosecution of the '041 patent, the examiner rejected all of the original claims as obvious in light of U.S. Patent No. 4,449,186 (the Kelley patent), which disclosed a terminal system for dispensing airline tickets. The examiner concluded that the only difference between the applicants' claimed invention and the Kelley patent was the location of the coupon terminal. In response, the applicants provided a general overview of the invention and amended the structural limitations of Claim 1 to distinguish the Kelley patent. The examiner again rejected all of the pending claims.

Responsive to the second rejection, the applicants again amended Claim 1 and submitted several declarations to bolster their assertion of nonobviousness. The applicants did not amend the claim language relating to the location of the terminals. Although stating that their invention involved terminals "located in stores" for the dispensing of coupons "on-site," the applicants also did not argue that the location of the terminals in stores distinguished the invention from the Kelley patent.

Coolsavings uses a web-based coupon system to monitor and control the distribution of coupons from its www.coolsavings.com website. After registering with the coolsavings.com website and providing demographic data, users can browse the website for available coupons. Users then select and print coupons for in-store redemption. Additionally, in some cases, users may access a coupon provider's website for on-line redemption of a coupon offer for on-line products. A centralized computer system stores coupon and user data. Users may access the Coolsavings system from any Internet-accessible computer by simply logging onto the coolsavings.com website. Coolsavings received U.S. Patent No. 5,761,648 (the '648 patent) for its web-based coupon system. Catalina's '041 patent was cited during prosecution of the '648 patent.

Catalina sued Coolsavings, alleging that Coolsavings' web-based coupon system infringed the '041 patent. The district court construed the claim language "located at predesignated sites such as consumer stores," and held that Coolsavings did not infringe, either literally or by equivalents, the construed language. After determining that Coolsavings did not infringe under the doctrine of equivalents, the district court then alternatively held that prosecution history estoppel barred Catalina from seeking equivalents on the location of the terminals.

On appeal, Catalina argues that the disputed language, which appears only in the preamble of Claim 1, is not a limitation because it merely states an intended use for the claimed system. Alternatively, Catalina contends that the district court misconstrued the "located at predesignated sites such as consumer stores" claim language. In addition, Catalina asserts that prosecution history estoppel does not bar equivalents when the applicants did not amend the disputed language or argue patentability based on that language.

II.

The district court's claim construction focused solely on the phrase "located at predesignated sites such as consumer stores." This phrase appears in the preamble of Claim 1, and in both the preamble and body of Claim 25. The district court construed this disputed phrase without discussion as to whether the phrase, which appears only in the preamble of Claim 1, was indeed a limitation of Claim 1.

Whether to treat a preamble as a limitation is a determination "resolved only on review of the entire[ ] ... patent to gain an understanding of what the inventors actually invented and intended to encompass by the claim." *Corning Glass Works v. Sumitomo Electric U.S.A., Inc.*, 868 F.2d 1251, 1257 (Fed.Cir.1989). In general, a preamble limits the invention if it recites essential structure or steps, or if it is "necessary to give life, meaning, and vitality" to the claim. *Pitney Bowes*, 182 F.3d at 1305. Conversely, a preamble is not limiting "where a patentee defines a structurally complete invention in the claim body and uses the preamble only to state a purpose or intended use for the invention." *Rowe v. Dror*, 112 F.3d 473, 478(Fed.Cir.1997).

No litmus test defines when a preamble limits claim scope. *Corning Glass*, 868 F.2d at 1257. Some guideposts, however, have emerged from various cases discussing the preamble's effect on claim scope. For example, this court has held that Jepson claiming generally indicates intent to use the preamble to define the claimed invention, thereby limiting claim scope. *Rowe*, 112 F.3d at 479. Additionally, dependence on a particular disputed preamble phrase for antecedent basis may limit claim scope because it indicates a reliance on both the preamble and claim body to define the claimed invention. *Bell Communications Research, Inc. v. Vitalink Communications Corp.*, 55 F.3d 615, 620 (Fed.Cir.1995) ("[W]hen the claim drafter chooses to use both the preamble and the body to define the subject matter of the claimed invention, the invention so defined, and not some other, is the one the patent protects."). Likewise, when the preamble is essential to understand limitations or terms in the claim body, the preamble limits claim scope. *Pitney Bowes*, 182 F.3d at 1306.

Further, when reciting additional structure or steps underscored as important by the specification, the preamble may operate as a claim limitation. *Corning Glass*, 868 F.2d at 1257. Moreover, clear reliance on the preamble during prosecution to distinguish the claimed invention from the prior art transforms the preamble into a claim limitation because such reliance indicates use of the preamble to define, in part, the claimed invention. Without such reliance, however, a preamble generally is not limiting when the claim body describes a structurally complete invention such that deletion of the preamble phrase does not affect the structure or steps of the claimed invention. Thus, preamble language merely extolling benefits or features of the claimed invention does not limit the claim scope without clear reliance on those benefits or features as patentably significant. Moreover, preambles describing the use of an invention generally do not limit the claims because the patentability of apparatus or composition claims depends on the claimed structure, not on the use or purpose of that structure. *In re Gardiner*, 36 C.C.P.A. 748, 171 F.2d 313, 315–16 (1948) ("It is trite to state that the patentability of apparatus claims must be shown in the structure claimed and not merely upon a use, function, or result thereof."). Indeed, "[t]he inventor of a machine is entitled to the benefit of all the uses to which it can be put, no matter whether he had conceived the idea of the use or not." *Roberts v. Ryer*, 91 U.S. 150, 157, 23 L.Ed. 267 (1875). More specifically, this means that a patent grants the right to exclude others from making, using, selling, offering to sale, or importing the claimed apparatus or composition for any use of that apparatus or composition, whether or not the patentee envisioned such use. *See* 35 U.S.C. § 271 (1994). Again, statements of intended use or asserted benefits in the preamble may, in rare instances, limit apparatus claims, but only if the applicant clearly and unmistakably relied on those uses or benefits to distinguish prior art. Likewise, this principle does not mean that apparatus claims necessarily prevent a subsequent inventor from obtaining a patent on a new method of using the apparatus where that new method is useful and nonobvious.

Perhaps a hypothetical best illustrates these principles: Inventor A invents a shoe polish for shining shoes (which, for the sake of example, is novel, useful, and nonobvious). Inventor A receives a patent having composition claims for shoe polish. Indeed, the preamble of these hypothetical claims recites "a composition for polishing shoes." Clearly, Inventor B could not later secure a patent with composition claims on the same composition because it would not be novel. Likewise, Inventor B could not secure claims on the method of using the composition for shining shoes because the use is not a "new use" of the composition but, rather, the same use—shining shoes.

Suppose Inventor B discovers that the polish also repels water when rubbed onto shoes. Inventor B could not likely claim a method of using the polish to repel water on shoes because repelling water is inherent in the normal use of the polish to shine shoes. In other words, Inventor B has not invented a "new" use by rubbing polish on shoes to repel water. Upon discovering, however, that the polish composition grows hair when rubbed on bare human skin, Inventor B can likely obtain method claims directed to the new use of the composition to grow hair. *See* 35 U.S.C. § 101 (1994) ("Whoever invents or discovers any new and useful process ... may obtain a patent therefor."); 35 U.S.C. § 100(b) (1994) ("The term 'process' means process, art or method, and includes a new use of a known process, machine, manufacture, composition of matter, or material."). Hence, while Inventor B may obtain a blocking patent on the use of Inventor A's composition to grow hair, this method patent does not bestow on Inventor B any right with respect to the patented composition. Even though Inventor A's claim recites "a composition for polishing shoes," Inventor B cannot invoke this use limitation to limit Inventor A's composition claim because that preamble phrase states a use or purpose of the composition and does not impose a limit on Inventor A's claim.

In this case, the claims, specification, and prosecution history of the '041 patent demonstrate that the preamble phrase "located at predesignated sites such as consumer stores" is not a limitation of Claim 1. The applicant did not rely on this phrase to define its invention nor is the phrase essential to understand limitations or terms in the claim body. Although the specification refers to terminals located at points of sale, and even once states that terminals may be placed in retail stores, the specification, in its entirety, does not make the location of the terminals an additional structure for the claimed terminals.

The applicants also did not rely on the preamble phrase to distinguish over the Kelly patent. Rather, the examiner expressly rejected the claims on the basis that the location of the terminals in stores was not patentably significant. In response, the applicants amended structural limitations in the claim body to distinguish the Kelly patent. Thus, while the applicants stated during prosecution that their invention involved terminals "located in stores" for the dispensing of coupons "on-site," such statements, without more, do not indicate a clear reliance on the preamble to distinguish the prior art, especially where the examiner's initial rejection considered terminal location insignificant for patentability.

Moreover, deletion of the disputed phrase from the preamble of Claim 1 does not affect the structural definition or operation of the terminal itself. The claim body defines a structurally complete invention. The location of the terminals in stores merely gives an intended use for the claimed terminals. As already noted, the applicants did not rely on this intended use to distinguish their invention over the prior art.

In this case, the disputed preamble language does not limit Claim 1—an apparatus claim. To hold otherwise would effectively impose a method limitation on an apparatus claim without justification. Accordingly, this court holds that the district court erroneously treated the preamble as a limitation of Claim 1.

While the phrase "located at predesignated sites such as consumer stores" appears only in the preamble of Claim 1, this language appears in both the preamble and body of Claim 25." Hence, the applicants specifically included this language in the claim not once, but twice. By virtue of its inclusion in the body of Claim 25, this phrase limits Claim 25. [The Circuit then proceeded to analyze the trial court's claim construction and determined that the claim requires location of terminals at "predesignated" locations. In the words of the Circuit, "Claim 25 requires that the physical position of the terminal be designated before placement of the terminal at a point of sale location. For Coolsavings to be liable for literal infringement Coolsavings' accused system must designate the physical position of the terminals before location of the terminals at a point of sale. Coolsavings' system, however, does not designate (or even recognize) the physical position of computers connecting to its website; thus, Coolsavings' system does not literally satisfy this limitation of Claim 25."]

Because the district court erroneously relied on non-limiting language in the preamble of Claim 1, this court vacates the district court's judgment of non-infringement of Claim 1, both literally and by equivalents, to give the district court the opportunity to construe the limitations of Claim 1. [B]ecause the accused system does not infringe literally Claim 25, as properly construed, this court affirms the holding of no literal infringement of Claim 25. This court vacates and remands the holding of no infringement of Claim 25 by equivalents because the trial court should have an opportunity to develop and assess the record under the proper claim construction.

NOTES

1. Unique Kind of Preamble. One of the special claim formats discussed later in this chapter, the Jepson claim, intentionally employs the preamble as a tool to recite important structural claim limitations. Thus, in a Jepson claim, the preamble is impliedly admitted to be prior art unless it reflects the inventor's own work. In any event, Jepson claims invoke a special rule for preambles.

2. "Dot.com" Cases. Besides explicating the rules for construing a preamble as a claim limitation, this case is also one of the early "dot.com" cases before the Federal Circuit. Does this case give an indication about the Federal Circuit's approach to the application of old technology in a new setting, namely the Internet?

§ 9.2[a][2]   THE TRANSITION

The transition phrase falls between the preamble and various defining elements in the body of the claim. This phrase performs the essential legal function of signaling that the claim is "open" or "closed" to additional elements. In practice, the drafter must choose from one of three phrases: "comprising," "consisting of," or "essentially consisting of." This choice has significant substantive effect, for these words determine that the claim is open to structures containing *at least* the recited elements (open or hybrid terminology) or is limited to structures with only those elements (closed terminology). Note that the words "the steps of" appear after the transition when the claim is directed towards a method.

The Open Transition ("comprising"): The use of the term "comprising" captures any product or process that contains each and every element described in the body of the claim. The presence of additional elements in an accused (allegedly infringing) product or process does not affect at all the coverage of the claims. The claimed invention encompasses the recited elements and may embrace more. Thus, if a claim recites elements "A" and "B," a device with "A," "B" *and others* is an infringement. *Mannesmann Demag Corp. v. Engineered Metal Products Co., Inc.*, 793 F.2d 1279 (Fed.Cir.1986). Open terminology—the broadest and most preferred transition phrase—captures elements *in addition to* the enumerated elements. For example, consider the claim:

A composition of matter which *comprises*:

    (i) element A;

    (ii) element B; and

    (iii) element C.

The term "comprises" makes the claim "open" to the inclusion of additional ingredients. This open claim includes any composition with *at least* elements $A + B + C$. Thus, the claim encompasses a product or process with elements $A + B + C$ or $A + B + C + "X"$.

The closed transition ("consisting of"): In contrast, a claim with the transition phrase "consisting of" is "closed" to additional ingredients. Infringement can occur only when the accused technology has exactly the same elements recited in the claim—no more, no less. Consider the same claim hypothetical with the new transition phrase:

A composition of matter *consisting of*:

    (i) element A;

     (ii) element B; and

     (iii) element C.

In this hypothetical, identical except for the transition phrase, sale of a composition with ingredients A+B+C+"X" is *outside* the literal scope of the claim. Infringement of this claim under the doctrine of equivalents is another matter.

Why would anyone want to employ such a limiting transitional phrase? Often, the nature of an invention lies in the elimination of certain components or process steps. "Closed" claim language allows an inventor to claim an existing technology or patented invention (minus the deleted feature or step) without running into the prior art. As one can imagine, however, claim drafters do not favor this transition because a potential infringer can easily avoid literal infringement by the mere addition of a superfluous element.

The Hybrid Transition ("Consisting Essentially of"): The open and closed transitions have legal implications parallel to the ordinary meaning of those phrases. The hybrid phrase, "consisting essentially of * * *," is unique to patent law and usage. This term of art, however, dates back to the nineteenth century, with a well-developed practice to support its application. This hybrid phrase renders the claim "open" to include additional elements that do not materially affect the basic and novel characteristics of the claimed combination. Consider again the hypothetical, this time with the hybrid transition:

A composition of matter *consisting essentially of*:

     (i) element A;

     (ii) element B; and

     (iii) element C.

If element "X" would *not* materially change the composition, then A+B+C+"X" *is* within the scope of this "consisting essentially of" claim. If "X" would materially change the properties versus A+B+C alone, then A+B+C+"X" is *not* within the scope of the claim. In appropriate situations, this form of transition can be very powerful. *See U.S. Steel Corp. v. Phillips Petroleum Co.*, 865 F.2d 1247 (Fed.Cir.1989) ("Normally solid polypropylene *consisting essentially of* recurring propylene units, having a substantial crystalline polypropylene content."). The "consisting essentially of" language is thus a hybrid. Claim drafters prefer it to the extremely restrictive closed phrase "consisting of."

§ 9.2[a][3]   THE BODY

The body of the claim recites the elements of the invention, as well as their interaction with each other either structurally or functionally. Claims ordinarily devote one clause to each of the primary elements of the invention. These clauses may be given a reference label, such as "(a)," "(b)," "(c)," to allow readers to parse its language more readily. The drafter should also indicate how that element interacts with the others to form an operative technology, employing such language as "attached to," "operated by," or "positioned above."

As this chapter repeatedly stresses, drafting claims requires knowledge that some words carry meanings affected by years of judicial gloss. Just a few of such terms are "integral," *see Advanced Cardiovascular Systems, Inc. v. Scimed Life Systems, Inc.*, 887 F.2d 1070 (Fed.Cir.1989); "extrinsic," *see Nobell, Inc. v. Sharper Image Corp.*, 950 F.2d 732 (Fed.Cir. 1991); "approximately," *see Borg–Warner Corp. v. Paragon Gear Works, Inc.*, 355 F.2d 400 (1st Cir.1965); "horizontal," *see In re Gordon*, 221 U.S.P.Q. 1125 (Fed.Cir.1984); and "solid," *see Standard Oil Co. v. Montedison S.p.A.*, 494 F.Supp. 370 (D.Del.1980). *See generally* IRWIN M. AISENBERG, ATTORNEY'S DICTIONARY OF PATENT CLAIMS (1997).

Elements of an invention are ordinarily introduced with an indefinite article, such as "a" or "an," as well as terms such as "one," "several," or "a plurality of." Reference to elements recited earlier in the claim usually requires a signaling term, such as the definite article "the" or the term "said." If a drafter places a "the" or a "said" before an element appearing for the first time in the claim, then the patent examiner may reject the claim for lack of an "antecedent basis." The following claim from U.S. Patent No. 5,632,254 employs the signaling articles correctly:

1. A combustion enhancement device, comprising:

> a housing which defines an interior chamber;

> at least one magnet disposed within said interior chamber; and

> a far infrared ray generating composition comprising SiO_2, Al_2O_3, CaO, MnO, TiO_2, and Ag or Au disposed within said interior chamber.

This claim also illustrates a peculiarity of patent law: the reluctance to claim an empty space, such as a chamber, hollow, hole, or gap, directly. Instead, drafters usually define such spaces in terms of the structures that form them. "This 'rule' may seem to make little sense, but it is another founded in antiquity like the single sentence rule. Perhaps someone thought that a hole, etc. is nothing—and that people should not claim nothing." ROBERT C. FABER, LANDIS ON MECHANICS OF PATENT CLAIM DRAFTING § 26 (4th ed. 1996).

Section 112, paragraphs 3–5 allow the use of so-called "dependent" patent claims. The statute mandates that dependent claims must recite an earlier claim and provide additional limitations. For example, following independent claim 1, dependent claim 2 might provide: "A waffle iron as recited in claim 1, further comprising...." Such claims include all of the limitations of the independent claim as well as the new limitations recited in claim 2. Patent law also permits multiple dependent claims, such as a claim which recites "A waffle iron as recited in claims 1 or 2, further comprising...." The statute instructs readers to "incorporate by reference all the limitations of the particular claim in relation to which it is being considered."

Patent applicants have attempted to interlink their trademark and patent protection by using trademarks or trade names within a patent claim. One early case rejected a claim reciting the term "Formica" because the manufacturer could change the nature of its flooring product at any time. *See Ex parte Bolton*, 42 U.S.P.Q. 40 (Pat. Off. Bd. App. 1938). Should the uncertain duration of trademark protection also influence this result? Suppose the specification first describes the nature of the product subject to the trademark before employing the trademark in a claim? *See Ex parte Canter*, 70 U.S.P.Q. 372 (Pat. Off. Bd. App. 1946); *see generally* Butler, *Rules Defining the Use of Trade Terms in Patent Applications*, 51 J. PAT. OFF. SOC'Y 339 (1969). The European Patent Office also disfavors the use of trademarks in claims "unless their use is unavoidable." GUIDELINES FOR EXAMINATION IN THE EUROPEAN PATENT OFFICE, Part C, Chapter III, Paragraph 4.5b (Dec. 1994).

U.S. cases routinely state that patent applicants may coin their own terms to define their invention. As stated in the vernacular of patent law, "a patentee is free to be his or her own lexicographer...." *Hormone Research Foundation, Inc. v. Genentech, Inc.*, 904 F.2d 1558, 1563 (Fed.Cir. 1990). However, an applicant cannot use misdescriptive terms nor banal terms like "gadget" or "widget."

§ 9.2[b]   PRODUCT-BY-PROCESS CLAIMS

In some circumstances a new product cannot be defined other than by the process of making it. In other instances inventors claim a new product by its structure and also add another backup claim defining the product by the process for making it. In either instance, the product-by-process claim specifies a product defined only by several process steps. Nonetheless the standard rule is that a product claim covers that product regardless of how it is made. Thus, although a product-by-process claim sets forth only one way of making the product, it might be construed to cover all ways of making that same product. In fact, a Federal Circuit panel concluded in 1991:

> In determining patentability we construe the product as not limited by the process stated in the claims. Since claims must be construed the same way for validity and for infringement, the correct reading of product-by-process claims is that they are not limited to product prepared by the process set forth in the claims.

Scripps Clinic & Research Fdn. v. Genentech, Inc., 927 F.2d 1565, 1583 (Fed.Cir.1991). In *Scripps Clinic*, the product was Factor VIII C, a coagulant or clotting agent. Factor VIII C was not a new product: "Before the invention..., scientists had succeeded in concentrating Factor VIII C in plasma. This concentrate had been used to replace transfusions of whole blood in the treatment of hemophilia. The process was expensive...." *Id.* at 1568. Scripps Clinic thus patented a process that separated Factor VIII C from the other complex materials in blood. This process involved straining plasma through a column packed with agarose beads. Scripps Clinic obtained both product claims and product-by-process claims. Scripps Clinic then sued Genentech, which cheaply and efficiently made pure Factor VIIIC with a recombinant DNA process. During trial, one of the primary issues was the purity of Factor VIII C produced by the Scripps' process, namely were the Scripps Clinic and Genentech products synonymous. Genentech also challenged the Scripps Clinic patents on grounds of enablement, best mode, anticipation, inequitable conduct, and infringement. In a well-reasoned opinion citing the Supreme Court cases mentioned in the *Atlantic Thermoplastics* case (which follows this note), the district court granted Genentech summary judgment of noninfringement of the product-by-process claims. Without addressing the Supreme Court precedent, the panel in *Scripps Clinic* made the statement quoted above. Less than a year later, another panel of the Federal Circuit confronted a case that directly presented the question of the coverage for product-by-process claims.

ATLANTIC THERMOPLASTICS CO. INC. v. FAYTEX CORP.

United States Court of Appeals, Federal Circuit, 1992
970 F.2d 834

Before Archer, Michel, and Rader, Circuit Judges.

RADER, J.

Atlantic Thermoplastics owns U.S. Patent No. 4,674,204 ('204 patent) entitled "Shock Absorbing Innersole and Method of Preparing Same." Atlantic sued Faytex Corporation for infringing the '204 patented process with innersoles manufactured by two separate processes. After a bench trial, the United States District Court for the District of Massachusetts held that Faytex infringed the '204 patent by selling innersoles manufactured by Surge, Inc. The court held, however, that Faytex did not infringe the '204 patent by selling innersoles manufactured by Sorbothane, Inc.

BACKGROUND

The '204 patent contains both process claims and product-by-process claims for a shock absorbing shoe Innersole. The innersole is formed in a mold having a contoured heel and arch section. Two different materials combine to make the innersole: an elastomeric material in the heel section, and a polyurethane foam. The elastomeric heel insert enhances shock absorption. The polyurethane foam forms around the heel insert and supplies the rest of the innersole.

Claim 1 of the '204 patent defines the process:

In a method of manufacturing a shock-absorbing, molded innersole for insertion in footwear, which method comprises:

(a) introducing an expandable, polyurethane into a mold; and

(b) recovering from the mold an innersole which comprises a contoured heel and arch section composed of a substantially open-celled polyurethane foam material, the improvement which comprises:

(i) placing an elastomeric insert material into the mold, the insert material having greater shock-absorbing properties and being less resilient than the molded, open-celled polyurethane foam material, and the insert material having sufficient surface tack to remain in the placed position in the mold on the introduction of the expandable polyurethane material so as to permit the expandable polyurethane material to expand about the insert material without displacement of the insert material; and

(ii) recovering a molded innersole with the insert material having a tacky surface forming a part of the exposed bottom surface of the recovered innersole.

Faytex distributes half-sole innersoles, or heel cups, with an elastomeric heel insert. Two different manufacturers—Surge Products and Sorbothane—make Faytex's innersoles. The Surge process for making innersoles differs from the Sorbothane process. Surge first manually places a solid elastomeric insert into the heel section of the innersole mold. Surge then injects polyurethane around the solid heel insert to form the innersole. Sorbothane, on the other hand, first injects a liquid elastomeric precursor into the mold, which solidifies to form the heel insert. While the heel insert is solidifying, Sorbothane injects polyurethane into the same mold to form the rest of the innersole.

The parties agree that the Surge process infringes the '204 patent. The district court concluded that the Sorbothane process did not infringe the '204 patent. The district court read the claims to require placement of a solid elastomeric insert into the mold. This reading leaves injection of liquid elastomers outside the scope of the claims. Atlantic contests this construction.

Because Faytex does not manufacture the innersoles, Atlantic cannot charge Faytex with infringement of the process claims. However, claim 24 of the '204 patent states: "The molded innersole produced by the method of claim 1." Atlantic argues that Faytex, by distributing products allegedly made by the claimed process, is liable as an infringer. Faytex cross-appeals from the award of lost profit damages for the sale of surge and Sorbothane innersoles. Faytex also appeals the district court's determination that the '204 patent is not invalid under the on-sale bar of 35 U.S.C. Section 102(b).

DISCUSSION

Atlantic argues that *Scripps Clinic & Research Foundation v. Genentech, Inc.*, 927 F.2d 1565 (Fed.Cir.1991) demands reversal of the non-infringement finding, even under the district court's present interpretation of the claims. In Scripps Clinic, this court stated:

[T]he correct reading of product-by-process claims is that they are not limited to product prepared by the process set forth in the claims.

Atlantic states that the Sorbothane process results in innersoles which are indistinguishable from innersoles made by the Surge process and claimed in the '204 patent. Therefore, according to Atlantic, the Sorbothane innersoles—though made by a different non-infringing process—also infringe. In sum, Atlantic urges this court to ignore the process claim language in its product-by-process claim.

A. Supreme Court History

To construe and apply the product-by-process claim of the '204 patent, this court must examine the history of products claimed with process terms. [*From footnote:* This court in *Scripps Clinic* ruled without reference to the Supreme Court's previous cases involving product claims with process limitations. In the absence of responsive briefing of the issues by the *Scripps Clinic* parties, this court noted that it was reviewing an "undeveloped record," and devoted one paragraph to resolving the jurisdictional issue and one paragraph to the merits. *Scripps Clinic & Research Foundation v. Genentech, Inc.*, 927 F.2d 1565, 1583–84 (Fed.Cir.1991). A decision that fails to consider Supreme Court precedent does not control if the court determines that the prior panel would have reached a different conclusion if it had considered controlling precedent. See *Tucker v. Phyfer*, 819 F.2d 1030, 1035 n. 7 (11th Cir.1987). For the reasons set forth below, we necessarily so conclude.] This inquiry begins with several century-old Supreme Court cases.

* * * *

In *Cochrane v. Badische Anilin & Soda Fabrik*, 111 U.S. 293 (1884) (BASF), the Supreme Court considered an infringement case. BASF involved alizarine, a dye. BASF obtained Reissue Patent No. 4,321 covering the product, artificial alizarine, as produced by a bromine reaction process. The claim stated:

Artificial alizarine, produced from anthracine or its derivatives by either of the methods herein described, or by any other method which will produce a like result.

Id. at 296. The Supreme Court noted, "No. 4,321 furnishes no test by which to identify the product it covers, except that such product is to be the result of the process it describes." *Id.* at 305.

Cochrane, the accused infringer, sold artificial alizarine made by a sulfuric acid reaction process. BASF sued Cochrane for infringing the 4,321 patent. The district court determined that Cochrane's product made by a sulfuric process infringed the 4,321 patent. The circuit agreed. Before the Supreme Court, BASF contended that Cochrane infringed because it made artificial alizarine "from anthracine or its derivatives by some method." Id. at 309. BASF argued that Cochrane made artificial alizarine; therefore, the process did not matter. Id. at 310. The Supreme Court disagreed.

Instead, the Supreme Court enunciated a rule for products claimed with process limitations:

> Every patent for a product or composition of matter must identify it so that it can be recognized aside from the description of the process for making it, or else nothing can be held to infringe the patent which is not made by that process.

Id. at 310. Based on this standard, the Supreme Court held the claim of the 4,321 patent not infringed because the defendants had used a different process.

After stating this rule for claim construction, the Supreme Court offered an alternative "view of the case." BASF, 111 U.S. at 311. BASF's artificial alizarine was an "old article." Id. In the words of the Supreme Court, "While a new process for producing it was patentable, the product itself could not be patented, even though it was a product made artificially for the first time." Id.; see also The Wood-Paper Patent, 90 U.S. 566, 596 (1874). In other words, a patent applicant could not obtain exclusive rights to a product in the prior art by adding a process limitation to the product claim. A new process, although eligible for a process patent, could not capture exclusive rights to a product already in the prior art. Therefore, BASF could have claimed a new process for making artificial alizarine, but it had no rights to claim the product.

Thus, in BASF, the Supreme Court addressed both infringement and validity (in terms of patentability) of product claims containing process limitations. In judging infringement, the Court treated the process terms as limitations on the patentee's exclusive rights. In assessing validity in terms of patentability, the Court forbade an applicant from claiming an old product by merely adding a new process. The infringement rule focused on the process as a limitation; the other rule focused on the product with less regard for the process limits. A decision from the Patent Office, for instance, cited BASF twice—once for an infringement rule and once for a patentability rule. Ex parte Fesenmeier, 1922 C.D. 18, 302 Off. Gaz. Pat. Office 199 (1922).

In General Electric v. Wabash Appliance, 304 U.S. 364 (1938), the Supreme Court considered a product claim for a filament in incandescent lamps.... [In considering infringement,] the Court quoted from BASF: "nothing can be held to infringe the patent which is not made by that process." Id. at 373–74.

Thus, the Supreme Court stated in a line of cases that the infringement inquiry for product claims with process limitations focuses on whether the accused product was made by the claimed process or its equivalent. Commentators have generally read this line of cases to mean that, in infringement proceedings, the process in a product-by-process claim serves as a limitation. In his treatise, Donald Chisum states:

A "product-by-process" claim is one in which the product is defined at least in part in terms of the method or process by which it is made. Most decisions hold that such a claim is infringed only by a product made through a substantially identical process. . . .

2 D. CHISUM, PATENTS § 8.05 (1991) (footnotes omitted). Lipscomb's Walker on Patents states:

A claim to a product by a specific process is not infringed by the same product made by a different process.

3 E. LIPSCOMB III, LIPSCOMB'S WALKER ON PATENTS § 11:19 (3d ed. 1985). Finally, one treatise concludes:

There is considerable case authority supporting th[e] position [that product-by-process claims cover only products made by the process specified in the claim] including a nineteenth century Supreme Court decision. [This precedent represents] a hundred years of prior law. . . .

2 MARTIN J. ADELMAN ET AL., PATENT LAW PERSPECTIVES § 2.6 [10] (2d ed. 1991). These commentators discerned a rule treating process terms as limitations on product-by-process claims in infringement actions.

B. PTO and Court of Customs and Patent Appeals (CCPA)

The CCPA consistently stated the general rule that an applicant must claim an article of manufacture by its structural characteristics, not by reference to its manufacturing process. For instance, the court stated:

This court has repeatedly held that a claim for an article capable of such definition must define the article by its structure and not by the process of making it.

Thus, the Patent and Trademark Office's Manual of Patent Examining Procedure (MPEP) still refers to product-by-process claims as "peculiar" in comparison to products "claimed in the conventional fashion." MPEP 706.03(e) (5th ed. 1983, rev. 1989). . . . Thus, where applicants could not adequately describe their inventions in terms of structural characteristics, whether due to language lagging behind innovations or existing technology lagging behind in the ability to determine those characteristics, the court permitted product-by-process claiming. As noted, however, this claim format remained an exception to the general rule.

As product-by-process claiming became more common, the CCPA moved toward accepting product-by-process without a showing of necessity. In 1969, the court reversed a Board of Appeal's decision holding a product-by-process claim improper because the applicant could claim the invention without relying on the process. *In re Pilkington*, 411 F.2d 1345 (CCPA 1969). The court instead determined that the applicant had adequately described the invention in accordance with the requirements of section 112. Id. Thus, the court shifted the emphasis away from the necessity for product-by-process claiming and toward determining whether the claim adequately defines the invention.

* * *

The CCPA, even in reviewing only for patentability, treated the claimed process as a limitation. In *Hughes*, for instance, the court clarified that the process defines and limits the scope of the claim. *Hughes*, 496 F.2d at 1218–19 (product claim was of a broader scope than product-by-process claims). In fact, if the process limitations of a product-by-process claim did not adequately define the invention, an applicant would fail to satisfy section 112. In other words, the process is a defining limit. In *Moeller*, the court stated:

> We think the rule is well established that where one has produced an article in which invention rests over prior art articles, and where it is not possible to define the characteristics which make it inventive except by referring to the process by which the article is made, he is permitted to so claim his article, but is limited in his protection to articles produced by his method referred to in the claims.

117 F.2d at 568.

* * *

The PTO and the CCPA did not reason that the process was not a defining limit of the product. To the contrary, the process was the only way to define and limit—in sum, to claim—the product. *Hughes*, 496 F.2d at 1218. Thus, in both patentability actions before the CCPA and infringement actions before the Supreme Court or the regional circuits, the courts regarded the process language in product-by-process claims as limiting the claim. Indeed by definition in most cases, the product could not be claimed in any other terms.

This court, in its initial consideration of a product-by-process claim for patentability, acknowledged that process claim limitations define the product:

> Product-by-process claims are not specifically discussed in the patent statute. The practice and governing law have developed in response to the need to enable an applicant to claim an otherwise patentable product that resists definition by other than the process by which it is made. For this reason, even though product-by-process claims are limited by and defined by the process, determination of patentability is based on the product itself.

In re Thorpe, 777 F.2d 695, 697 (Fed.Cir.1985).

The entire history of product-by-process claims suggests a ready explanation for the apparent difference of view about treatment of those claims during ex parte administrative proceedings and during litigation. This court already distinguishes treatment of claims for patentability before the PTO from treatment of claims for validity before the courts. This court permits the PTO to give claims their broadest reasonable meaning when determining patentability. During litigation determining validity or infringement, however, this approach is inapplicable. Rather the courts must consult the specification, prosecution history, prior art, and other claims to determine the proper construction of the claim language. Thus, accommodating the demands of the administrative process and recognizing the capabilities of the trial courts, this court treats claims differently for patentability as opposed to validity and infringement. The PTO's treatment of product-by-process claims as a product claim for patentability is consistent with policies giving claims their broadest reasonable interpretation. The same rule, however, does not apply in validity and infringement litigation. In any event, claims mean the same for infringement and validity.

Moreover, accepting Atlantic's invitation to ignore the process limitations in the '204 patent's product-by-process claims would require this court to disregard several other mainstay patent doctrines. For instance, Atlantic in effect invites this court to discount the significance of excluding claim limitations from infringement analysis. See, e.g., *Continental Paper Bag Co. v. Eastern Paper Bag Co.*, 210 U.S. 405, 419 (1908) ("[T]he claims measure the invention."). This court has repeatedly stated that infringement requires the presence of every claim limitation or its equivalent. An accused infringer can avoid infringement by showing that the accused device lacks even a single claim limitation. Thus, ignoring the claim limits of a product-by-process claim would clash directly with basic patent principles enunciated by the Supreme Court and this court.

In so holding, this court acknowledges that it has in effect recognized another reason to regard product-by-process claims as exceptional. This court recognizes that product-by-process claims will receive different treatment for administrative patentability determinations than for judicial infringement determinations. This difference originated with the Supreme Court's BASF rules—a difference this court endorsed as recently as 1985.

This court, therefore, rejects Atlantic's invitation to ignore the process limitations in its product-by-process claims. This court's infringement rules do not require reversal of the district court's non-infringement finding regarding the Sorbothane process. Neither does this court disturb the PTO's present practice for assessing patentability of product-by-process claims. * * *

VACATED–IN–PART, AFFIRMED–IN–PART, AND REMANDED

NOTES

1. **The Impact of *Atlantic Thermoplastics*.** The classic rule for product-by-process claiming only allowed this claim form if the applicant could not otherwise describe the invention. Using contemporary technology to discern the nature of an invention, applicants can describe almost any invention in terms of its structure or characteristics. The classic justification for product-by-

process techniques has practically disappeared. Nonetheless patent drafters often include product-by-process claims as backup claims behind product claims. What advice would you give inventors about this practice in light of *Scripps Clinic* and *Atlantic Thermoplastics*? If you were defending an obscure chemical patent that could not be defined structurally at all but only by its process, how would you present an argument to evade the *Atlantic Thermoplastics* holding? In the *Scripps Clinic* case, the Federal Circuit remanded the case to the District Court. If on remand the trial court found that Genentech produced a far more pure product far more cheaply under its process, what would you argue as counsel for Genentech to avoid infringement of the Scripps patent?

2. District Court Reaction. In *Tropix, Inc. v. Lumigen*, Inc., 825 F.Supp. 7 (D.Mass.1993), the court was squarely faced with the choice between the two lines of Federal Circuit precedent regarding product-by-process claims. There, the asserted patent included product-by-process claims covering a process for producing purified chemiluminescent, water-soluble 1,2–dioxetane derivatives. The defendant manufactured identical derivatives by a different process. The plaintiff claimed that its product-by-process claims covered the product, no matter how produced, relying on *Scripps Clinic*, while the defendant cited *Atlantic Thermoplastics Co.* for the proposition that a product-by-process patent covers only products produced via the claimed process. Noting that "the judges of the Federal Circuit Court are in open disagreement on the point," the court concluded:

> If it should be determined as a matter of fact that the purified substance is a totally novel product, then the choice between Scripps and Atlantic becomes crucial. There is much to be said as a matter of policy for Judge Newman's distinction between a process which produces a totally new substance and a novel process applied to a product which exists in the prior art, particularly in the present age of rampant biotechnology. I do not find any authority for this proposition before Scripps, however. The cases establishing the proposition that the claims are limited to the process originate from the period where product-by-process patents were allowed when the product could not be defined or distinguished from the prior art except by reference to the process. Judge Newman's assertion that there must be symmetry between the position taken by the Patent Office and the position taken by the courts in determining infringement does not appear to be supported by any authority, given the different functions of each institution. Even if symmetry were desirable, it would seem that the practice of the Patent Office should conform to the substantive rule of the courts rather than the other way around. It would appear to me, even in the confused state of the record, that a majority of the judges of the Federal Circuit would rule that Atlantic states the controlling law, and I so rule in this case.

825 F.Supp. at 10. *But see Trustees of Columbia University v. Roche Diagnostics GmbH,* 126 F.Supp.2d 16 (D.Mass.2000). The Federal Circuit noted but did not resolve the dispute in *SmithKline Beecham Corp. v. Apotex Corp.*, 439 F.3d 1312, 1317 (Fed. Cir. 2006).

3. Approaches Across the Atlantic (and Pacific). In diametric opposition to the *Atlantic Thermoplastics* panel, European patent law recognizes "product-by-process" claims to reach the product as obtained by any possible process. As noted in the Guidelines for Examination in the European Patent Office, Part C, Chapter III, Paragraph 4.7b:

> Claims for products defined in terms of processes of manufacture are admissible only if the products as such fulfill the requirements for patentability, i.e. inter alia that they are new and inventive. A product is not rendered novel merely by the fact that it is produced by means of a new process (see T 150/82, OJ 7/1984, 309). A claim defining a product in terms of a process is to be construed as a claim to the product as such and the claim should preferably take the form "Product X obtainable by process Y," or any wording equivalent thereto, rather than "Product X obtained by Process Y."

The Japanese Examination Guidelines provide for more limited use of product-by-process claims and are ambivalent about the effect of their use, EXAMINATION GUIDELINES FOR PATENT AND UTILITY MODEL IN JAPAN, PART I at 5–6 (AIPPI 1994).

4. Judicial Dilemma. The *Atlantic Thermoplastics* case went before the full court pursuant to a petition suggesting *en banc* review. The court declined to reconsider the case *en banc*, but Judge Rich wrote a colorful opinion dissenting from the denial of *en banc*. Judge Rich felt that the *Scripps Clinic* decision should bind the *Atlantic* panel: "This is not only insulting to the *Scripps* panel (Chief Judge Markey, Judge Newman and a visiting judge), it is mutiny. It is heresy. It is illegal." Do you think the *Atlantic* panel gave an adequate justification for departing from the *Scripps Clinic* statement? By confronting the conflict with *Scripps Clinic* directly, the *Atlantic* panel introduced some uncertainty into the law because subsequent cases must choose which rule to apply. On the other hand, would the *Atlantic* panel have created any less uncertainty by taking the standard judicial course of acknowledging the *Scripps Clinic* case and then distinguishing it and in effect creating an exception to the prior case?

§ 9.2[c]   FUNCTIONAL CLAIMING

Title 35 specifically authorizes inventors to claim an element in a new combination in functional terms. In fact, the section in The Patent Act that permits functional claiming is the only provision that expressly authorizes a particular claim format. 35 U.S.C § 112, ¶ 6 permits an inventor to claim an invention as a means for performing a function, commonly known as a means-plus-function claim. The United States alone amongst the world's patent systems gives special treatment to functional claims. The history of functional claiming begins long before § 112 became part of title 35 in 1952. One of the earliest and most famous patent cases in the United States involved a functional claim. In *O'Reilly v. Morse*, 56 U.S. (15 How.) 62 (1853), the famous inventor of the telegraph, Samuel Morse, claimed "use of [electricity] . . . for marking or printing intelligible characters." With this language, Morse really sought approval of a claim containing a single means clause. A single means claim is now clearly forbidden under § 112 which requires "that the enabling disclosure of the specification be commensurate in scope with the claim." *In re Hyatt*, 708 F.2d 712 (Fed.Cir.1983) (citing *O'Reilly*, 56 U.S. at 112). The Supreme Court rejected Morse's claim because its breadth encompassed far more than the telegraph machine Morse had in fact invented. *See O'Reilly*, 56 U.S. at 112.

After the famous *O'Reilly* case, however, functional claims began to appear in combination claims, as distinguished from Morse's single means claim. In fact, functional claim elements perform an important "function" in claim drafting. In a sentence, this claim form permits a drafter to list a multitude of the ways to perform a claimed function. To understand the importance of this convenience, consider a claim for an invention that for the first time attaches a flash mechanism to a camera. To simplify this hypothetical, the claim would recite a camera and a flash device. Then the claim must recite the relationship between the camera and the flash device. Of course, the flash is fastened to the camera. At this point the problem arises. How does the drafter claim the myriad ways of fastening—rivets, bolts, screws, glue, and so forth? The novelty of this invention is not the way of fastening, but the combination of a camera and an attached flash mechanism. Thus, the claim drafter wants to find a convenient way to claim all known ways of fastening that will facilitate the invention. A functional claim will accomplish that classic purpose with just a few words: "means for fastening." On their face, those words appear to capture all known ways of fastening.

In any event, in 1946, the Supreme Court again dealt with the breadth of functional claiming. At that time, the Supreme Court prohibited use of functional claims at the exact point of novelty in a combination claim. *See Halliburton Oil Well Cementing Co. v. Walker* 329 U.S. 1, 9 (1946) ("The language of the claim thus describes this most crucial element in the 'new' combination in terms of what it will do rather than in terms of its own physical characteristics. . . . We have held that a claim with such a description of a product is invalid. . . ."). The Supreme Court foresaw that functional language could embrace every conceivable way of performing a function, thus claiming more than the inventor had invented or claiming subject matter already available to the public. To prevent "the broadness, ambiguity, and overhanging threat of the functional claim," *Halliburton*, 329 U.S. at 9, the Supreme Court prohibited this particular functional claim. Read carefully, *Halliburton* does not create a problem for functional claiming, only for functional claiming at the exact point of novelty in a claim. In terms of our earlier hypothetical, if the camera and flash combination was old and the only new feature in the invention was a new connector (perhaps a plastic snap attachment which allows removal and reattachment), then a claim that recited broadly a "means for fastening" would not distinguish the novel new connector from all old fasteners. In this context, *Halliburton* makes intuitive sense and does not endanger the classic purpose of functional claiming.

Nonetheless, a few years later, as part of a major restructuring of patent law, the United States Congress undertook to protect functional claiming in the wake of the *Halliburton* case. Acknowledging the utility of the functional format to embrace conveniently a wide variety of ways to perform an element of a combination, Congress authorized means-plus-function claims by adding § 112, ¶ 6 to Title 35. The 1952 Act did not ignore the problem of breadth in functional language. In the words of the Federal Circuit: "The second clause of [§ 112, ¶ 6], however, places a limiting condition on an applicant's use of means-plus-function language. [Otherwise a] claim limitation described as a means for performing a function, if read literally, could encompass any conceivable means for performing the function." *Valmont*, 983 F.2d at 1042. This second clause confines the breadth of protection otherwise permitted by the first clause. *See id.* It requires the applicant to describe in the patent specification the various structures that the inventor expects to perform the specified function. The statute then expressly confines coverage of the functional claim language to "the corresponding structure, material, or acts described in the specification and equivalents thereof." The next two opinions explain this interpretational protocol more fully and demonstrate some pitfalls associated with claiming technique.

AL–SITE CORP. v. VSI INTERNATIONAL, INC.

United States Court of Appeals, Federal Circuit, 1999
174 F.3d 1308

Before Mayer, Chief Judge, Rich and Rader, Circuit Judges.

RADER, CIRCUIT JUDGE.

I.

Magnivision and VSI both sell non-prescription eyeglasses. Magnivision is the assignee of U.S. Patent Nos. 4,976,532 (the '532 patent), 5,144,345 (the '345 patent), 5,260,726 (the '726 patent), and 5,521,911 (the '911 patent). These patents claim technology for displaying eyeglasses on racks. The claimed inventions allow consumers to try on eyeglasses and return them to the rack without removing them from their display hangers.

The jury determined that one of VSI's products (the Version 1 hanger tag) literally infringed the '532 patent. The jury also determined that a second VSI product (the Version 2 hanger tag) did not literally infringe the '345, '726, and '911 patents, but did infringe those patents under the doctrine of equivalents.

II.

Literal Infringement of the '532 patent

The jury determined that the Version 1 hanger tag literally infringes claims 8, 9, 14, 15, and 17 of the '532 patent. Claim 8, the independent claim from which the other infringed claims depend, claims the combination of a pair of eyeglasses and a hanger means for removably mounting the eyeglasses on a cantilevered support. The claim itself gives some structural definition of the hanger means as "including a body having aperture means adapted" for suspending the hanger and eyeglasses on the cantilevered support. Additionally, the hanger means includes an extension projecting from the bottom edge portion of the hanger body. This extension encircles the nose bridge of the eyeglasses. The claim specifies that "fastening means in engagement with said extension" hold the extension in a closed loop. Figure 1 from the '532 patent illustrates these claimed features:

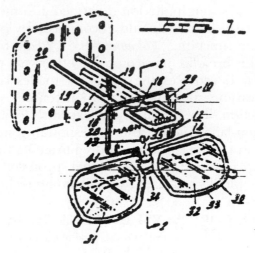

The district court determined that the "fastening means" was a means-plus-function element subject to the interpretation requirements of 35 U.S.C. § 112, ¶ 6 (1994). Consistent with that determination, the trial court instructed the jury that "the fastening means ... is either a rivet or a button and hole arrangement as shown in the '532 patent or the structural equivalents thereof." Neither party challenges this part of the district court's claim construction.

On appeal, VSI contends that its Version 1 hanger tag does not infringe because it does not include the "fastening means" required by claim 8. VSI's Version 1 hanger tag is a one-piece paper sticker having two large portions connected by a narrow extension. The entire back of the tag, including the extension, is coated with an adhesive. Backing paper covers the adhesive to prevent undesired adhesion. In use, a merchant removes the backing paper from the large portions of the tag. The extension (still covered with backing paper) then wraps around the nose bridge of the glasses. This wrapping glues the large portions together. In use, therefore, glue secures the two large portions of the tag to each other, leaving the narrow extension of the tag wrapped around the bridge of the eyeglasses.

The adhesive used by VSI is not identical to the fastening structure (namely, a rivet or button) described in the '532 patent. The jury, however, applying the rules of § 112, ¶ 6, determined that the VSI adhesive was equivalent to the structure disclosed in the specification. Accordingly, the jury returned a verdict of literal infringement of the '532 patent. VSI argues that substantial evidence does not support the jury's finding of literal infringement.

VSI first challenges the jury determination that adhesive is structurally equivalent to the mechanical fasteners disclosed in the specification of the '532 patent. Magnivision's technical expert, Mr. Anders, testified that, for one of ordinary skill in the art, it would be an insubstantial change "to substitute a rivet for a staple or for glue or for any other method that's standard in the [point of purchase] industry to maintain this loop as a closed loop." *See Chiuminatta Concrete Concepts, Inc. v. Cardinal Indus., Inc.*, 145 F.3d 1303, 1309 (Fed.Cir.1998) ("The proper test [for determining equivalence under § 112, ¶ 6] is whether the differences between the structure in the accused device and any disclosed in the specification are insubstantial.... The question of known interchangeability is ... an important factor in determining equivalence [under § 112, ¶ 6]."). Mr. Anders further testified that the use of glue "in between the two layers of the body ... is an insubstantial change from the other structure ... which was one of a rivet. People in point of purchase displays use glue or rivets or staples to accomplish the same function." *But see Chiuminatta*, 145 F.3d at 1309 ("Almost by definition, two structures that perform the same function may be substituted for one another. The question of known interchangeability is not whether both structures serve the same function, but whether it was known that one structure was an equivalent of another."). Mr. Anders additionally testified that "equivalent fastening means could be a rivet, glue or staple or some such similar [structure]." This testimony constitutes sufficient evidence to sustain the jury's verdict that persons of ordinary skill in the art consider glue an equivalent structure to those disclosed in the specification for maintaining a closed loop.

As a fallback position, VSI argues that, even if the glue is an equivalent of the rivet or button, Magnivision presented no evidence that the glue was "in engagement" with the extension as claim 8 requires. On cross examination, Mr. Anders identified the middle section of the Version 1 hanger tag as the "extension" element. Mr. Anders also identified the glue as the "fastening means" element. Because VSI leaves the backing paper on its extension (presumably to prevent the tag from adhering to the eyeglasses), VSI argues that its extension does not engage the fastening means as required by the claims of the '532 patent.

VSI's argument is unpersuasive. The claims of the '532 patent only require that the fastening means be "in engagement with" the extension. As noted above, VSI coats the extension of its Version 1 hanger tag with glue—the fastening means identified by Mr. Anders. Furthermore, Mr. Anders' testimony explains that the extension and the glued portions are one integral piece. The jury could have interpreted his testimony to mean that the extension includes more than the narrow, middle portion of the Version 1 tag. Under this interpretation, the extension would also directly engage the glue fastening means. Alternatively, the jury could have determined that the extension is only the narrow portion of the Version 1 tag, but that the fastening means includes one of the two portions of the tag body in addition to the glue. Under any of these reasonable views of the accused product, the extension of the Version 1 hanger tag is in engagement with the glue fastening means as required by the claims.

As the finder of fact, the jury receives deference for its function of weighing witness demeanor, credibility, and meaning. *See Anderson v. City of Bessemer City, North Carolina*, 470 U.S. 564, 575 (1985) (factfinder entitled to deference on credibility determinations). Substantial evidence therefore supports the jury's verdict that VSI's Version 1 hanger tag literally infringes the '532 patent.

INFRINGEMENT OF THE '345, '726, AND '911 PATENTS

The jury determined that VSI's Version 2 hanger tag and display rack did not literally infringe claims 1 and 2 of the '345 patent; claims 1 and 2 of the '726 patent; or claims 1, 2, and 3 of the '911 patent. The jury nevertheless found infringement of each of these claims under the doctrine of equivalents. Magnivision argues that the district court misconstrued these claims, and that, under the proper claim construction, VSI's products literally infringe these claims as a matter of law. VSI, on the other hand, embraces the district court's claim construction and argues that prosecution history estoppel precludes a finding of infringement under the doctrine of equivalents.

Claim 1 of the '345 patent and claim 1 of the '726 patent are similar. Both claim "[t]he combination of an eyeglass display member and an eyeglass hanger member." In each of these claims, this combination includes a "display member" with "cantilever support means" and "an eyeglass hanger member for mounting a pair of eyeglasses." Both claims further define the structure of the eyeglass hanger member. Claim 1 of the '345 patent describes the eyeglass hanger member as "made from flat sheet material," and having an "opening means formed . . . below [its] upper edge." According to claim 1 of the '726 patent, the eyeglass hanger member has "an attaching portion attachable to a portion of said frame of said pair of eyeglasses to enable the temples of the frame [to be opened and closed]." Similarly, claim 2 of the '726 patent encompasses a "method of displaying eyeglass/hanger combinations . . . the eyeglass hangers having an attaching portion attached to a portion of the frame of an associated pair of eyeglasses."

Claims 1, 2, and 3 of the '911 patent encompass a "combination of an eyeglass display member and an eyeglass contacting member." The '911 patent further describes the structure of the "eyeglass contacting member" as "having an encircling portion adapted to encircle a part of said frame of said pair of eyeglasses."

The district court construed the "eyeglass hanger member" element of the '345 patent as a means-plus-function claim element subject to § 112, ¶ 6. Accordingly, the district court instructed the jury that "[t]he 'eyeglass hanger member for mounting a pair of eyeglasses' [in claim 1 of the '345 patent] is the body of the hanger disclosed in the '345 patent and its drawings and the structural equivalents thereof." The district court similarly interpreted the "eyeglass hanger member" element of the '726 patent. The district court instructed the jury that "[t]he 'eyeglass hanger member for mounting a pair of eyeglasses' [in claim 1 of the '726 patent] is the hanger disclosed in the '726 patent and its drawings as having a body, an aperture, and an attaching portion and the structural equivalents thereof."

With respect to the '911 patent, the district court concluded that the "eyeglass contacting member" was a means-plus-function element. The district court therefore instructed the jury that the "eyeglass contacting member" is "the hanger disclosed in the '911 patent and its drawings having a body and an aperture and an 'encircling portion,' and the structural equivalents thereof."

This court reviews the district court's claim interpretation without deference. See *Cybor Corp. v. FAS Technologies, Inc.*, 138 F.3d 1448, 1454–56 (Fed.Cir.1998) (en banc). This court has delineated several rules for claim drafters to invoke the strictures of 35 U.S.C. § 112, ¶ 6. Specifically, if the word "means" appears in a claim element in combination with a function, it is presumed to be a means-plus-function element to which § 112, ¶ 6 applies. See *Sage Prods., Inc. v. Devon Indus., Inc.*, 126 F.3d 1420, 1427 (Fed.Cir.1997). Nevertheless, according to its express terms, § 112, ¶ 6 governs only claim elements that do not recite sufficient structural limitations. See 35 U.S.C. § 112, ¶ 6. Therefore, the presumption that § 112, ¶ 6 applies is overcome if the claim itself recites sufficient structure or material for performing the claimed function. See *Sage*, 126 F.3d at 1427–28 ("[W]here a claim recites a function, but then goes on to elaborate sufficient structure, material, or acts within the claim itself to perform entirely the recited function, the claim is not in means-plus-function format.").

Although use of the phrase "means for" (or "step for") is not the only way to invoke § 112, ¶ 6, that terminology typically invokes § 112, ¶ 6 while other formulations generally do not. See *Greenberg*, 91 F.3d at 1583–84. Therefore, when an element of a claim does not use the term "means," treatment as a means-plus-function claim element is generally not appropriate. See *Mas–Hamilton Group v. LaGard, Inc.*, 156 F.3d 1206, 1213–15 (Fed.Cir.1998). However, when it is apparent that the element invokes purely functional terms, without the additional recital of specific structure or material for performing that function, the claim element may be a means-plus-function element despite the lack of express means-plus-function language. See, e.g., *Cole*, 102 F.3d at 531 ("[M]erely because an element does not include the word 'means' does not automatically prevent that element from being construed as a means-plus-function element."); *Mas–Hamilton*, 156 F.3d at 1213–15 (interpreting "lever moving element" and "movable link member" under § 112, ¶ 6).

Under this established analytical framework, the "eyeglass hanger member" elements in the claims of both the '345 and the '726 patents do not invoke § 112, ¶ 6. In the first place, these elements are not in traditional means-plus-function format. The word "means" does not appear within these elements. Moreover, although these claim elements include a function, namely, "mounting a pair of eyeglasses," the claims themselves contain sufficient structural limitations for performing those functions. As noted above, claim 1 of the '345 patent describes the eyeglass hanger member as "made from flat sheet material" with an "opening means formed ... below [its] upper edge." This structure removes this claim from the purview of § 112, ¶ 6. Similarly, according to claim 1 of the '726 patent, the eyeglass hanger member has "an attaching portion attachable to a portion of said frame of said pair of eyeglasses to enable the temples of the frame [to be opened and closed]." This structure also precludes treatment as a means-plus-function claim element. The district court therefore improperly restricted the "eyeglass hanger member" in these claims to the structural embodiments in the specification and their equivalents.

The district court also erred in interpreting the "attaching portion attachable to a portion of said frame of said pair of eyeglasses" element of claim 1 of the '726 patent as a means-plus-function element. It instructed the jury that the "attachable portion" is "a mechanically fastened loop that goes around the nose bridge of the glasses as disclosed in the specification, or the structural equivalent thereof." Because this claim element is also not in traditional means-plus-function form and supplies structural, not functional, terms, the trial court erred by applying § 112, ¶ 6 to this claim element. This error caused the district court to incorporate unduly restrictive structural limitations into the claim.

For reasons similar to those discussed above with respect to the claim elements of the '345 and the '726 patents, the "eyeglass contacting member" element of the '911 patent claims is also not a means-plus-function element. Again, this claim element is not in traditional means-plus-function form. Furthermore, the claim itself recites sufficient structure for performing the recited function. Specifically, claim 1 of the '911 patent describes the "eyeglass contacting member" as "having an encircling portion adapted to encircle a part of said frame of said pair of eyeglasses to enable the temples of the frame to be selectively [opened and closed]." Similarly, claim 3 of the '911 patent describes the "eyeglass contacting member" as "having an attaching portion attachable to a portion of said frame of said eyeglasses." Therefore, the district court erred by applying § 112, ¶ 6 to these claim elements.

Magnivision also complains that the district court erred in its construction of the language "means for securing a portion of said frame of said eyeglasses to said hanger member" in claim 1 of the '345 patent. With respect to this element, the district court instructed the jury that "[t]he 'means for securing' limitation is a mechanically fastened loop that goes around the nose bridge of the glasses ... or an equivalent thereof." The district court went on, however, to instruct the jury that "[t]he means for securing can be formed from a separate extension or integral extension and includes either the rivet fastener or the button and hole fastener." Magnivision argues that the district court should have included the phrase "or equivalents thereof" after "button and hole fastener" in its instruction to the jury. Absent this and the other claimed errors in the district court's interpretation of claim 1 of the '345 patent, Magnivision argues that the jury would have found literal infringement rather than infringement under the doctrine of equivalents.

The "means for securing" claim element is in conventional means-plus-function format without specific recital of structure and therefore invokes § 112, ¶ 6. The jury's finding of infringement of claim 1 of the '345 patent under the doctrine of equivalents indicates that the jury found every element of the claim literally or equivalently present in the accused device. The question before this court, therefore, is whether the jury's finding that the accused structure was equivalent to the "means for securing" element under the doctrine of equivalents, also indicates that it is equivalent structure under § 112, ¶ 6.

This court has on several occasions explicated the distinctions between the term "equivalents" found in § 112, ¶ 6 and the doctrine of equivalents. See, e.g., *Valmont Indus., Inc. v. Reinke Mfg. Co.*, 983 F.2d 1039, 1042–44 (Fed.Cir.1993); *Chiuminatta*, 145 F.3d at 1310; *Dawn Equipment Co. v. Kentucky Farms Inc.*, 140 F.3d 1009, 1018–23 (Fed.Cir. 1998) (Plager, J., additional views) (Newman, J., additional views) (Michel, J., additional views). Indeed, the Supreme Court recently acknowledged distinctions between equivalents as used in § 112, ¶ 6 and the doctrine of equivalents. See *Warner–Jenkinson Co. v. Hilton Davis Chem. Co.*, 520 U.S. 17, 27 (1997) ("[Equivalents under § 112, ¶ 6] is an application of the doctrine of equivalents in a restrictive role, narrowing the application of broad literal claim elements. [Section 112, ¶ 6] was enacted as a targeted cure to a specific problem.. The added provision, however, is silent on the doctrine of equivalents as applied where there is no literal infringement.")

Section 112, ¶ 6 recites a mandatory procedure for interpreting the meaning of a means-or step-plus-function claim element. These claim limitations "shall be construed to cover the corresponding structure, material, or acts described in the specification and equivalents thereof." 35 U.S.C. § 112, ¶ 6. Thus, § 112, ¶ 6 procedures restrict a functional claim element's "broad literal language ... to those means that are 'equivalent' to the actual means shown in the patent specification."

Warner–Jenkinson, 117 S.Ct. at 1048. Section 112, ¶ 6 restricts the scope of a functional claim limitation as part of a literal infringement analysis. See *Pennwalt Corp. v. Durand–Wayland, Inc.*, 833 F.2d 931, 934 (Fed.Cir. 1987). Thus, an equivalent under § 112, ¶ 6 informs the claim meaning for a literal infringement analysis. The doctrine of equivalents, on the other hand, extends enforcement of claim terms beyond their literal reach in the event "there is 'equivalence' between the elements of the accused product or process and the claimed elements of the patented invention." *Warner–Jenkinson*, 117 S.Ct. at 1045.

One important difference between § 112, ¶ 6 and the doctrine of equivalents involves the timing of the separate analyses for an "insubstantial change." As this court has recently clarified, a structural equivalent under § 112 must have been available at the time of the issuance of the claim. See *Chiuminatta*, 145 F.3d at 1310. An equivalent structure or act under § 112 cannot embrace technology developed after the issuance of the patent because the literal meaning of a claim is fixed upon its issuance. An "after arising equivalent" infringes, if at all, under the doctrine of equivalents. See *Warner–Jenkinson*, 117 S.Ct. at 1052; *Hughes Aircraft Co. v. U.S.*, 140 F.3d 1470, 1475 (Fed.Cir.1998). Thus, the temporal difference between patent issuance and infringement distinguish an equivalent under § 112 from an equivalent under the doctrine of equivalents. In other words, an equivalent structure or act under § 112 for literal infringement must have been available at the time of patent issuance while an equivalent under the doctrine of equivalents may arise after patent issuance and before the time of infringement. An "after-arising" technology could thus infringe under the doctrine of equivalents without infringing literally as a § 112, ¶ 6 equivalent.[2] Furthermore, under § 112, ¶ 6, the accused device must perform the identical function as recited in the claim element while the doctrine of equivalents may be satisfied when the function performed by the accused device is only substantially the same.

Although § 112, ¶ 6 and the doctrine of equivalents are different in purpose and administration, "a finding of a lack of literal infringement for lack of equivalent structure under a means-plus-function limitation may preclude a finding of equivalence under the doctrine of equivalents." *Chiuminatta*, 145 F.3d at 1311. Both equivalence analyses, after all, apply "similar analyses of insubstantiality of the differences." Id. This confluence occurs because infringement requires, either literally or under the doctrine of equivalents, that the accused product or process

---

2. These principles, as explained in *Chiuminatta Concrete Concepts*, 145 F.3d 1303, (Fed.Cir.1998), suggest that title 35 will not produce an "equivalent of an equivalent" by applying both § 112, ¶ 6 and the doctrine of equivalents to the structure of a given claim element. A proposed equivalent must have arisen at a definite period in time, i.e., either before or after patent issuance. If before, a § 112, ¶ 6 structural equivalents analysis applies and any analysis for equivalent structure under the doctrine of equivalents collapses into the § 112, ¶ 6 analysis. If after, a non-textual infringement analysis proceeds under the doctrine of equivalents. Patent policy supports application of the doctrine of equivalents to a claim element expressed in means-plus-function form in the case of "after-arising" technology because a patent draftsman has no way to anticipate and account for later developed substitutes for a claim element. Therefore, the doctrine of equivalents appropriately allows marginally broader coverage than § 112, ¶ 6.

incorporate each limitation of the claimed invention. See *Warner–Jenkinson*, 117 S.Ct. at 1049; *Pennwalt*, 833 F.2d at 935. Therefore, if an accused product or process performs the identical function and yet avoids literal infringement for lack of a § 112, ¶ 6 structural equivalent, it may well fail to infringe the same functional element under the doctrine of equivalents. See *Chiuminatta*, 145 F.3d at 1311. This same reasoning may be applied in reverse in certain circumstances. Where, as here, there is identity of function and no after-arising technology, a means-plus-function claim element that is found to be infringed only under the doctrine of equivalents due to a jury instruction failing to instruct on § 112, ¶ 6 structural equivalents is also literally present in the accused device.

VSI's Version 2 hanger tag has a central body and two arms, with one arm extending from each side of the body. Each arm has a hole near the end for receipt of an eyeglasses temple. The body also has an aperture through which a cantilever rod can be placed so the hanger tag can be hung from a display rack. VSI's Version 2 hanger tag is the subject of U.S. Patent No. 5,141,104 (the '104 patent). Figure 4 of the '104 patent illustrates these features.

FIG. 4

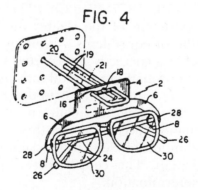

As noted above, the doctrine of equivalents and structural equivalents under § 112, ¶ 6, though different in purpose and administration, can at times render the same result. In this case, the jury found infringement under the doctrine of equivalents. This finding presupposes that the jury found an equivalent for each element of the claimed invention, including the "means for securing." The holes in the arms of VSI's Version 2 hanger tag secure a portion of the eyeglasses frame (the temples) to the hanger member and therefore perform the identical function of the claim element in question. The jury was instructed that the "means for securing" disclosed in the '345 patent "is a mechanically fastened loop that . . . can be formed from a separate extension or integral extension and includes either the rivet fastener or the button and hole fastener." Based on this instruction, the jury found that the holes in the arms of the Version 2 hanger tag were equivalent to the mechanically fastened loop of the '345 patent under the doctrine of equivalents.

The parties do not dispute that the holes in the arms of the accused device perform a function identical to the extension of the patented device. Furthermore, the holes do not constitute an after-arising technology. Because the functions are identical and the holes are not an after-arising technology, the jury's finding of infringement under the doctrine of equivalents indicates that the jury found insubstantial structural differences between the holes in the arms of the Version 2 hanger tag and the loop of the '345 patent claim element. That finding is also sufficient to support the inference that the jury considered these to be structural equivalents under § 112, ¶ 6. For these reasons, any perceived error in the district court's jury instruction regarding the "means for securing" is, at most, harmless.

In sum, the district court erred by interpreting several of the claim elements in the '345, '726 and '911 patents as means-plus-function elements subject to § 112, ¶ 6. Because, properly construed, these claims do not call for interpretation under § 112, ¶ 6, the district court's reading unnecessarily limited their scope. This court has cautioned against incorporating unwarranted functional or structural limitations from the specification into the claims. *See Transmatic, Inc. v. Gulton Indus.,* Inc., 53 F.3d 1270, 1277 (Fed.Cir.1995). Despite the district court's unwarranted restriction of the claims, the jury found infringement under the doctrine of equivalents. Although a reasonable dispute as to the application of the correctly interpreted claims to the accused structure prevents a determination of literal infringement as a matter of law, because the jury found infringement under the trial court's more restricted reading of the claims, this court need not remand for an infringement determination according to this court's broader claim interpretation. Proceeding claim element by claim element, the jury has already found infringement. This court's correction of the claim scope does not disturb that determination.

NOTES

1. **The Hypothetical Returns to Haunt.** Every patent teacher in the decades since the 1952 Act has probably taught the implications of § 112, ¶ 6 with the hypothetical "a fastening means." This case serves as warning to both teachers and students. Sometimes the banal examples of today form the crux of the ghastly litigation of tomorrow. Does this case follow the usual advice of the hypothetical? The "fastening means" described in the specification included only mechanical fasteners (rivets and buttons) yet the jury found that this means included a chemical fastener. How does the Federal Circuit reason that the jury was within its rights to include chemical fasteners within a term limited to mechanical fasteners?

2. **When *Does "After Arising"* Technology Arise?** The Federal Circuit takes considerable care to explain differences between the doctrine of equivalents and structural equivalents. Perhaps the most significant difference is the application to "after arising" technology. "[B]ecause the literal meaning of a

claim is fixed upon its issuance," the Federal Circuit reasons, structural equivalents cannot embrace technology developed after patent issuance but only technology "insubstantially different" from technology described in the specification to perform the claimed function.

Technology arising after patent issuance infringes, if at all, under the doctrine of equivalents. Is patent issuance the proper place to draw this line? Because the meaning of words are fixed in claim at the filing date, *In re Hogan*, 559 F.2d 595 (CCPA 1977), would patent filing be a better cut-off date? Does it make any difference whether technology created between patent filing and patent issuance is analyzed for infringement under the doctrine of equivalents or under the structural equivalents principles? When considering this question, recall that the patent law looks backward when considering validity, but gazes forward when assessing infringement.

3.   **Recognizing a Functional Claim.** As this case demonstrates, a means-plus-function claim invokes a very different method for interpretation. Claim language, however, can mix functional and structural elements and complicate the task of recognizing when to use § 112, ¶ 6. Although this case addresses the subject, a few more Federal Circuit cases might supply further guidance about classifying claim language as functional or structural. In interpreting a claim to a new conveyor belt technology, Chief Judge Nies wrote for the court:

> The recitation of some structure in a means plus function element does not preclude the applicability of section 112 (6). For example, in this case, the structural description in the joining means clause merely serves to further specify the function of that means. The recited structure tells only what the means-for-joining *does*, not what it *is* structurally.

Laitram Corp. v. Rexnord, Inc., 939 F.2d 1533, 1536 (Fed.Cir.1991). In another case, the Federal Circuit interpreted a claim to a liner for the bed of a pickup truck with ridges to lock a load in place:

> In determining whether to apply the statutory procedures of section 112, paragraph 6, the use of the word "means" triggers a presumption that the inventor used this term advisedly to invoke the statutory mandates for means-plus-function clauses.

* * *

> The claim language, however, does not link the term "means" to a function . . . Without an identified function, the term "means" in this claim cannot invoke 35 U.S.C. section 112 (6). Without a "means" sufficiently connected to a recited function, the presumption in use of the word "means" does not operate. In any case, the structural limits of the claim language limit its scope. Thus, this court construes this claim without reference to section 112, paragraph 6.

York Products Inc. v. Central Tractor Farm & Family Center, 99 F.3d 1568 (Fed.Cir.1996). *See also Greenberg v. Ethicon Endo–Surgery, Inc.*, 91 F.3d 1580, 1584 (Fed.Cir.1996) ("[T]he use of the term 'means' has come to be so closely associated with 'means-plus-function' claiming that it is fair to say that the use of the term 'means' (particularly as used in the phrase 'means for') generally invokes section 112 (6) . . .").

The presumption discussed in *York* and *Greenberg*, however, seems to have additional limits. In a later case, the Federal Circuit construed a claim involving disposable diapers with sides that easily tear open to facilitate removal of the soiled brief. The claim term in question read: "perforation means extending from the leg band means to the waist band means through the outer impermeable layer means for tearing the outer impermeable layer means for removing the training brief in the case of an accident by the user. . . ." The district court determined on summary judgment that a "perforation means" is merely a "perforation" and that the bonded tearable side seams on the accused briefs were not perforations. The Federal Circuit, declining to apply § 112 ¶ 6, agreed:

> The drafter of claim 1 in the '239 patent was clearly enamored of the word "means": six of seven elements in that claim include the word "means," which occurs in the claim fourteen times. We find, however, no reason to construe any of the claim language in claim 1 as reciting means-plus-function elements within the meaning of § 112, ¶ 6. For example, the "perforation means . . . for tearing" element of Cole's claim fails to satisfy the statute because it describes the structure supporting the tearing function (i.e., perforations). The claim describes not only the structure that supports the tearing function, but also its location (extending from the leg band to the waist band) and extent (extending through the impermeable layer). An element with such a detailed recitation of its structure, as opposed to its function, cannot meet the requirements of the statute.

Cole v. Kimberly–Clark Corp., 102 F.3d 524, 531 (Fed.Cir.1996). A dissent in this case, relying on *Laitram* and *York*, noted: "the word 'perforation' [does not] provide enough structure to negate the import of the very next word— 'means.'" 102 F.3d at 533. Is *Cole* consistent with *Laitram* and *York*?

Don't answer the last question too quickly. In *Laitram*, the Federal Circuit clarified that the claimed structure in that case operated primarily "to further specify the function," 939 F.2d at 1536, not to define a recognizable structure. The claimed structure informed the court of what the means "does, not what it is structurally." *Id*. Moreover the Federal Circuit did not say that the presence of structure in a claim is irrelevant to use of section 112 (6). Instead it said "some structure" would not preclude application of section 112 (6). *Id*. at 1536. In *Cole*, the court expressly noted the "detailed recitation" of structure. Moreover, can *Cole* be read to mean that definite and complete structure in the claim can overcome the presumption alluded to in *York*? In any event, *Cole* seems to raise the inevitable question, how much structure removes a claim with the word "means" from § 112 ¶ 6 treatment? How much structure is too much? What guidance would you give claim drafters about means-plus-function claiming? As a matter of policy, is the patent system better served by a rule that invariably requires structure in the specification whenever an inventor uses the words "means for"?

ARISTOCRAT TECHNOLOGIES AUSTRALIA PTY LTD.
v. INTERNATIONAL GAME TECHNOLOGY

United States Court of Appeals for the Federal Circuit, 2008
521 F.3d 1328

Before Lourie, Schall, and Bryson, Circuit Judges.

BRYSON, CIRCUIT JUDGE.

The appellants, referred to collectively as "Aristocrat," are the owner and exclusive licensee of U.S. Patent No. 6,093,102 ("the '102 patent"). The patent is directed to an electronic slot machine that allows a player to select winning combinations of symbol positions. The appellees, referred to collectively as "IGT," manufacture and sell gaming products that Aristocrat asserts infringe the '102 patent. In an infringement action brought by Aristocrat against IGT in the United States District Court for the District of Nevada, the district court held all of the claims of the '102 patent invalid for indefiniteness.

The game disclosed in the '102 patent purportedly increases player interest in slot machines by providing the player with greater control over the definition of winning opportunities. It allows the player to define the winning opportunities based on symbols displayed on the top and side of a multi-line screen representing slot machine reels. Using the invention on a 3x5 screen, for example, the player can define numerous different arrangements that will allow the player to win for some subset of the 243 possible winning combinations. The player can do so by selecting symbol positions and thereby activating winning opportunities for combinations in which the symbols are not necessarily aligned with one another. The only constraint is that the selected combination must contain at least one symbol from each column. Figure 2 from the '102 patent shows a 3x5 screen with selections, and the figure on the right shows one of the winning combinations for the selection in Figure 2.

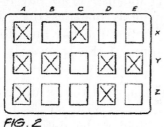

FIG. 2

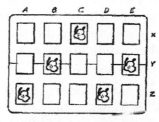

A winning combination

On summary judgment, the trial court held all of the claims of the '102 patent invalid. Aristocrat does not dispute that all of the claims rise and fall together. Like the parties, we therefore focus on independent claim 1.

Claim 1 reads as follows:

A gaming machine

having display means arranged to display a plurality of symbols in a display format having an array of n rows and m columns of symbol positions,

game control means arranged to control images displayed on the display means,

the game control means being arranged to pay a prize when a predetermined combination of symbols is displayed in a predetermined arrangement of symbol positions selected by a player, playing a game, including one and only one symbol position in each column of the array,

the gaming machine being characterized in that selection means are provided to enable the player to control a definition of one or more predetermined arrangements by selecting one or more of the symbol positions and

the control means defining a set of predetermined arrangements for a current game comprising each possible combination of the symbol positions selected by the player which have one and only one symbol position in each column of the display means,

wherein the number of said predetermined arrangements for any one game is a value which is the product $k1 \ldots X \ldots ki \ldots X \ldots km$ where ki is a number of symbol positions which have been selected by the player in an ith column of the n rows by m columns of symbol positions on the display (0 < i m and ki n).

I

The district court observed that the key question in this case is the definiteness of the claim term "game control means" or "control means" that is used several times in claim 1. The court explained that the claim describes the "game control means" as performing three functions: (1) to control images displayed on the display means; (2) to pay a prize when a predetermined combination of symbols matches the symbol positions selected by the player; and (3) to define the pay lines for the game according to each possible combination of the selected symbol positions.

The district court noted that the parties agreed the term "control means" is a means-plus-function term that invokes 35 U.S.C. § 112 ¶ 6. As such, the scope of that claim limitation had to be defined by the structure disclosed in the specification plus any equivalents of that structure; in the absence of structure disclosed in the specification to perform those functions, the claim limitation would lack specificity, rendering the claim as a whole invalid for indefiniteness under 35 U.S.C. § 112 ¶ 2. *See In re Donaldson,* 16 F.3d 1189, 1195 (Fed.Cir.1994) (en banc).

The court noted that there were slight linguistic differences in the parties' characterizations of the functions performed by the "control means," but that the differences were unimportant, because there was no adequate disclosure of structure in the specification to perform those functions, regardless of how they were defined. Although Aristocrat argued that the structure corresponding to the recited functions was a standard microprocessor-based gaming machine with "appropriate programming," the court noted that the specification contained no "guidance to determine the meaning of 'standard microprocessor' or 'appropriate programming.' " The court ruled that "[m]erely stating that a standard microprocessor is the structure without more is not sufficient." In particular, the court noted that the specification did not create any specific structure or new machine because "it does not set forth any specific algorithm" for performing the recited function.

Citing decisions of this court, the trial court explained that in a means-plus-function claim "in which the disclosed structure is a computer or a microprocessor programmed to carry out an algorithm, a corresponding structure must be a specific algorithm disclosed in the specification, rather than merely 'an algorithm executed by a computer.' " Because the specification of the '102 patent lacks "any specific algorithm" or any "step-by-step process for performing the claimed functions of controlling images on the slot machines [sic] video screen, paying a prize when a predetermined combination of symbols comes up or defining the pay lines for games," the court held the asserted structure to be insufficient to satisfy section 112 paragraph 6. In addition, the district court held that the specification did not link the asserted structure to any of the claimed functions. The court held claim 1 invalid for that reason as well.

III

Aristocrat's principal contention is that the district court was wrong to hold that the patent's disclosure of a general purpose, programmable microprocessor was not a sufficient disclosure of structure to satisfy section 112 paragraph 6. In particular, Aristocrat argues that computer-implemented means-plus-function claims do not require disclosure of a corresponding algorithm, as held by the district court. Instead, Aristocrat contends that the structure disclosed in the specification of the '102 patent, which was simply "any standard microprocessor base [sic] gaming machine [with] appropriate programming," was a sufficient disclosure of structure under this court's precedents.

In cases involving a computer-implemented invention in which the inventor has invoked means-plus-function claiming, this court has consistently required that the structure disclosed in the specification be more than simply a general purpose computer or microprocessor. The point of the requirement that the patentee disclose particular structure in the specification and that the scope of the patent claims be limited to that structure and its equivalents is to avoid pure functional claiming. As this court explained in *Medical Instrumentation & Diagnostics Corp. v. Elekta AB*, 344 F.3d 1205, 1211 (Fed.Cir.2003), "If the specification is not clear as to the structure that the patentee intends to correspond to the claimed function, then the patentee has not paid the price but is attempting to claim in functional terms unbounded by any reference to structure in the specification." *See also Biomedino, LLC v. Waters Techs. Corp.*, 490 F.3d 946, 948 (Fed.Cir.2007) ("[I]n return for generic claiming ability, the applicant must indicate in the specification what structure constitutes the means."). For a patentee to claim a means for performing a particular function and then to disclose only a general purpose computer as the structure designed to perform that function amounts to pure functional claiming. Because general purpose computers can be programmed to perform very different tasks in very different ways, simply disclosing a computer as the structure designated to perform a particular function does not limit the scope of the claim to "the corresponding structure, material, or acts" that perform the function, as required by section 112 paragraph 6.

That was the point made by this court in *WMS Gaming, Inc. v. International Game Technology,* 184 F.3d 1339 (Fed.Cir.1999). In that case, the court criticized the district court, which had determined that the structure disclosed in the specification to perform the claimed function was "an algorithm executed by a computer." The district court erred, this court held, "by failing to limit the claim to the algorithm disclosed in the specification." *Id.* at 1348. The rationale for that decision is equally applicable here: a general purpose computer programmed to carry out a particular algorithm creates a "new machine" because a general purpose computer "in effect becomes a special purpose computer once it is programmed to perform particular functions pursuant to instructions from program software." *Id., quoting In re Alappat,* 33 F.3d 1526, 1545 (Fed.Cir.1994). The instructions of the software program in effect "create a special purpose machine for carrying out the particular algorithm." *WMS Gaming,* 184 F.3d at 1348. Thus, in a means-plus-function claim "in which the disclosed structure is a computer, or microprocessor, programmed to carry out an algorithm, the disclosed structure is not the general purpose computer, but rather the special purpose computer programmed to perform the disclosed algorithm." *Id.* at 1349.

In this case, Aristocrat acknowledges that the only portion of the specification that describes the structure corresponding to the three functions performed by the "control means" is the statement that it is within the capability of a worker in the art "to introduce the methodology on any standard microprocessor base [sic] gaming machine by means of appropriate programming." '102 patent, col. 3, ll. 2–4. That description goes no farther than saying that the claimed functions are performed by a general purpose computer. The reference to "appropriate programming" imposes no limitation whatever, as any general purpose computer must be programmed. The term "appropriate programming" simply references a computer that is programmed so that it performs the function in question, which is to say that the function is performed by a computer that is capable of performing the function.

Aristocrat offers two responses to the district court's conclusion that the patent did not disclose sufficient structure. First, Aristocrat argues that the specification disclosed algorithms that were sufficient to constitute a qualifying disclosure of structure. Second, Aristocrat argues that no disclosure of specific algorithms was necessary in any event.

A

As to the first argument, Aristocrat contends that the language of claim 1 referring to "the game control means being arranged to pay a prize when a predetermined combination of symbols is displayed in a predetermined arrangement of symbol positions selected by a player" implicitly discloses an algorithm for the microprocessor. That is, when the winning combination of symbols is displayed, the program should pay a prize. But that language simply describes the function to be performed, not the algorithm by which it is performed. Aristocrat's real point is that devising an algorithm to perform that function would be within the capability of one of skill in the art, and therefore it was not necessary for the patent to designate any particular algorithm to perform the claimed function. As we have noted above, however, that argument is contrary to this court's law.

Aristocrat also points to language in claim 1 that, according to Aristocrat, "sets forth the mathematical equation that describes the result of practicing the third function." The language in question recites "defining a set of predetermined arrangements for a current game comprising each possible combination of the symbol position selected by the player which have one and only one symbol position in each column of the display means." The problem with Aristocrat's argument is underscored by Aristocrat's very characterization of the role of the equation: It describes the result of practicing the third function. That is, the equation is not an algorithm that describes how the function is performed, but is merely a mathematical expression that describes the outcome of performing the function. To be sure, as Aristocrat argues, the equation "restricts 'appropriate programming' to algorithms which result in the specified number of winning opportunities." But that argument simply concedes that the equation describes an outcome, not a means for achieving that outcome. The equation thus does not disclose the structure of the claimed device, but is only another way of describing the claimed function.

Finally, Aristocrat contends that "the written description delineates what constitutes 'appropriate programming' through the disclosed embodiments of the invention." Again, however, the description of the embodiments is simply a description of the outcome of the claimed functions, not a description of the structure, i.e., the computer programmed to execute a particular algorithm.

In making this argument, Aristocrat relies on Figure 1 and Table 1 from the patent, which provide examples of how player selections translate to possible winning combinations:

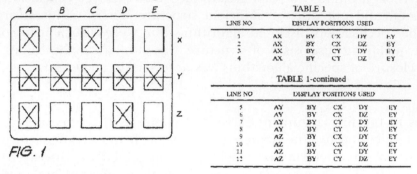

FIG. 1

TABLE 1

LINE NO	DISPLAY POSITIONS USED				
1	AX	BY	CX	DY	EY
2	AX	BY	CX	DZ	EY
3	AX	BY	CY	DY	EY
4	AX	BY	CY	DZ	EY

TABLE 1-continued

LINE NO	DISPLAY POSITIONS USED				
5	AY	BY	CX	DY	EY
6	AY	BY	CX	DZ	EY
7	AY	BY	CY	DY	EY
8	AY	BY	CY	DZ	EY
9	AZ	BY	CX	DY	EY
10	AZ	BY	CX	DZ	EY
11	AZ	BY	CY	DY	EY
12	AZ	BY	CY	DZ	EY

Two other pairs of figures and tables, Figures 3 and 4, and Tables 2 and 3, offer similar examples. The corresponding portion of the written description contains mathematical descriptions of how many winning combinations would be produced. '102 patent, col. 3, line 54, through col. 5, line 21. Aristocrat refers to these examples as "algorithms." The figures, tables, and related discussion, however, are not algorithms. They are simply examples of the results of the operation of an unspecified algorithm. Like the mathematical equation set forth in claim 1, these combinations of figures and tables are, at best, a description of the claimed function of the means-plus-function claim.

Aristocrat has elected to claim using section 112 paragraph 6 and therefore must disclose corresponding structure. It has disclosed, at most, pictorial and mathematical ways of describing the claimed function of the game control means. That is not enough to transform the disclosure of a general-purpose microprocessor into the disclosure of sufficient structure to satisfy section 112 paragraph 6.

B

In support of the contention that it is not necessary to disclose a particular algorithm in order to disclose sufficient structure for a means-plus-function limitation in a computer-implemented invention, Aristocrat relies primarily on *In re Dossel*, 115 F.3d 942 (Fed.Cir.1997). Aristocrat argues that the application in *Dossel* did not disclose a particular algorithm, and that the court held the disclosure sufficient even though the application stated, with respect to the performance of one of the claimed functions, that "[k]nown algorithms can be used for this purpose."

The means-plus-function limitation at issue in *Dossel* was a "means for reconstructing the current distribution" on the surface of an element inside a biological object, such as on the surface of a tumor inside a human brain. The application stated that the reconstruction unit would reconstruct the density of the current at various points on that surface from the values of the magnetic flux density at corresponding pixels at the same time. See U.S. Patent No. 5,885,215, col. 4, ll. 6–10 (the patent that issued from the Dossel application). The application explained that "[k]nown algorithms can be used for this purpose." *Id.*, col. 4, ll. 10–11. The application then provided the particular equation by which the relationship between the values of magnetic flux density and current density could be described in matrix form, *id.*, col. 4, ll. 12–15, and it described in great detail the components of that equation, *id.*, col. 4, ll. 16–55. Accordingly, while providing a detailed explanation of how the claimed device would perform the claimed function, the specification left the mathematical techniques used to solve the recited equations to persons of ordinary skill in the art. That is what this court referred to when it stated that the application stated "that 'known algorithms' can be used to solve standard equations which are known in the art." *Dossel*, 115 F.3d at 946.

From the context and from reviewing the application, it is clear that the *Dossel* court used the term "algorithm" in a narrow sense, referring to particular well-known mathematical operations that could be used to solve the equations disclosed in the application. Far from supporting Aristocrat's claim that a reference to a general purpose computer with "appropriate programming" discloses sufficient structure for section 112 paragraph 6, the *Dossel* case provides an example of an extremely detailed disclosure of all information necessary to perform the function, except for basic mathematical techniques that would be known to any person skilled in the pertinent art.

Aristocrat also argues that, even if there is no disclosure of an algorithm in the patent, the disclosure of a microprocessor with "appropriate programming" is a sufficient disclosure of structure for means-plus-function purposes, because the evidence showed that one of ordinary skill in the art could build the device claimed in the '102 patent based on the disclosure in the specification. That argument, however, conflates the requirement of enablement under section 112 paragraph 1 and the requirement to disclose the structure that performs the claimed function under section 112 paragraph 6.

Although the examples given in the '102 patent might enable one of ordinary skill to make and use the invention, they do not recite the particular structure that performs the function and to which the means-plus-function claim is necessarily limited.

Whether the disclosure would enable one of ordinary skill in the art to make and use the invention is not at issue here. Instead, the pertinent question in this case is whether Aristocrat's patent discloses structure that is used to perform the claimed function. Enablement of a device requires only the disclosure of sufficient information so that a person of ordinary skill in the art could make and use the device. A section 112 paragraph 6 disclosure, however, serves the very different purpose of limiting the scope of the claim to the particular structure disclosed, together with equivalents. The difference between the two is made clear by an exchange at oral argument. In response to a question from the court, Aristocrat's counsel contended that, in light of the breadth of the disclosure in the specification, any microprocessor, regardless of how it was programmed, would infringe claim 1 if it performed the claimed functions recited in the means-plus-function limitations of that claim. That response reveals that Aristocrat is in essence arguing for pure functional claiming as long as the function is performed by a general purpose computer. This court's cases flatly reject that position.

IV

Aristocrat was not required to produce a listing of source code or a highly detailed description of the algorithm to be used to achieve the claimed functions in order to satisfy 35 U.S.C. § 112 ¶ 6. It was required, however, to at least disclose the algorithm that transforms the general purpose microprocessor to a "special purpose computer programmed to perform the disclosed algorithm." *WMS Gaming*, 184 F.3d at 1349. Because the district court correctly held that was not done in this case, we uphold the judgment of the district court.

AFFIRMED.

NOTES

1. **Means–Plus–Function Claiming: A Sucker's Bet?** *Aristocrat Technologies* suggests that functional claiming is not entirely a "free lunch"—the patent drafter must be sure that the written description discloses specific structural elements that correspond to the claimed means-plus-function limitation. This requirement applies even where such structure would be well known to the art. This standard may be difficult to fulfill where the claim language evolves over time, or where (as in *Aristocrat Technologies*) the application to be filed in the United States was originally drafted overseas. Alternative claim drafting solutions may be more appropriate in these circumstances.

2. **Step–Plus–Function.** Section 112, ¶ 6 expressly permits step-plus-function claims for processes. The Federal Circuit has only rarely addressed the legal requirements of such claims, however. In the case of *Seal-Flex, Inc. v. Athletic Track and Court Construction*, 172 F.3d 836 (Fed.Cir.1999), the claims included step-plus-function language. The appellate court declined to enunciate requirements for step-plus-function claims, but a concurrence discussed the claim format at length. Judge Rader's concurrence stressed that "[t]he statute's format and language suggest a strong correlation between means and step-plus-function claim elements in both their identification and interpretation." Step-plus-function claims, however, present an additional problem, namely "[t]he difficulty of distinguishing acts from functions in step-plus-function claim elements." The concurrence offered some guidance on this question:

> This difficulty places a significant burden on the claim drafter to choose language with a definite and clear meaning. To invoke a presump-

tion of § 112, ¶ 6 application, a claim drafter must use language that expressly signals the recitation of a function as distinguished from an act.

As used in § 112, ¶ 6, "step" is the generic term for "acts" in the same sense that "means" is the generic term for "structure" and "material." The word "step," however, may introduce either an act or a function depending on context within the claim. Therefore, use of the word "step," by itself, does not invoke a presumption that § 112, ¶ 6 applies. For example, method claim elements may begin with the phrase "steps of" without invoking application of § 112, ¶ 6. The phrase "steps of" colloquially signals the introduction of specific acts, rather than functions, and should therefore not presumptively invoke application of § 112, ¶ 6.

Unlike "of," the preposition "for" colloquially signals the recitation of a function. Accordingly, the phrase "step for" generally introduces functional claim language falling under § 112, ¶ 6. Thus, the phrase "step for" in a method claim raises a presumption that § 112, ¶ 6 applies. This presumption gives legal effect to the commonly understood meanings of "of"—introducing specific materials, structure or acts—and "for"—introducing a function.

The semantic distinction between the words "step of" and "step for" seems quite small. Is Judge Rader's guidance for § 112, ¶ 6 loading that distinction with too much significance? The PTO has recently drafted guidelines for functional claiming. The PTO guidelines follow at least some of the reasoning of the concurrence by stating that use of the term "step for" invokes a presumption that the claim drafter intended § 112, ¶ 6 coverage. In any event, the Federal Circuit in *Masco Corp. v. United States*, 303 F.3d 1316 (Fed.Cir.2002), followed Judge Rader's methodology in deciding whether certain claim limitations were step-plus-function limitations.

§ 9.2[d]   JEPSON CLAIMS

A "Jepson claim" defines an invention in two parts: a preamble which recites elements or steps of the invention that are known to the art, followed by an "improvement" clause which recites what the applicant regards as his invention. The following claim, at issue in *Pharmacia & Upjohn Co. v. Mylan Pharmaceuticals, Inc.*, 170 F.3d 1373 (Fed. Cir. 1999), was drafted in Jepson format:

1. In an micronized anti-diabetic pharmaceutical composition as a unit dose, containing one or more pharmaceutically acceptable excipients, the improvement which comprises: spray-dried lactose as the preponderant excipient in said composition, being present therein at about not less than seventy percent (70%) by weight of the final composition.

Id. at 1375.

The consequences of use of this claim format are significant. Observe the transition phrase "the improvement which comprises" in the above claim. "The portion of the claim preceding this statement is the

Jepson claim format and is impliedly prior art." *In re Pfeiffer*, 243 F.3d 565 (Fed. Cir. 2000). Because the preamble of Jepson claims is presumed to qualify as prior art, such claims are favored by many PTO examiners. Their examination task is greatly simplified by the instant admission of prior art status for everything in the claim but the "improvement" clause. Consider the two following claims to the same invention, where the inventor claims a combination of elements A, B and C, with the improvement residing in new species C':

1. The combination of elements A, B and C'.

2. In the combination of elements A, B and C, the improvement which comprises use of C' as the element C.

With respect to claim 1, the examiner must show that the combination of A, B and C' would have been obvious in light of prior art. As claim 2 appears in Jepson format, however, the examiner starts the "given" that the combination A + B + C is old. The only task remaining is to show that the use of C' would have been obvious in place of C generally.

An early case from the United States Court of Appeals for the Federal Circuit, *Reading & Bates Construction Co. v. Baker Energy Resources Corp.*, 748 F.2d 645 (Fed.Cir.1984), held that the presumption of prior art status of preamble recitations may be rebutted. In a case involving the preamble's recitation of the inventor's prior invention, the court noted that no statutory basis existed for treating the preamble's recitation as prior art. "[W]here an inventor continues to improve upon his own work product, his foundational work product should not, without a statutory basis, be treated as prior art solely because he admits knowledge of *his own work*."

§ 9.2[e] MARKUSH GROUPS

"Markush" claims are common only in chemical practice. A proper Markush claim is a generic claim which defines a family of compounds by showing the common structural nucleus for all members of that family, with the variable substituent being defined by an "R" (or other letter) to represent the various alternatives. Traditionally, a Markush group is proper when it applies to products with at least one common utility. When defining a family of chemical compounds with Markush terminology, clarity within a claim often requires a vast amount of verbiage that stretches the length of the claim into an indigestible chunk. Thus, an applicant can present a generic claim that runs for pages, rather than recognizing that the critical novelty of the entire group of generic compounds is one particular shared feature. Students should also bear in mind that a document that discloses a large Markush group may later serve as prior art against a sub-genus or even one compound that a later inventor is claiming is a selection invention raising the question of when a genus invention should anticipate or render obvious a compound within the genus.

The term "Markush" has become internationally accepted as describing this sort of claim. The GUIDELINES FOR EXAMINATION IN THE EUROPEAN PATENT OFFICE, Part C, Chapter II, Paragraph 7.4a (Dec. 1994) provide:

> Where a single claim defines (chemical or non-chemical) alternatives, i.e., a so-called "Markush grouping", unity of invention should be considered to be present when the alternatives are of a similar nature.
>
> When the Markush grouping is for alternatives of chemical compounds, they should be regarded as being of a similar nature where:
>
> (i) all alternatives have a common property or activity, and
>
> (ii) a common structure is present, i.e., a significant structural element is shared by all of the alternatives, or all alternatives belong to a recognized class of chemical compounds in the art to which the invention pertains.

The Japanese Patent Office employs a similar standard. EXAMINATION GUIDELINES FOR PATENT AND UTILITY MODEL IN JAPAN, Part I at 4 (AIPPI 1994).

§ 9.3　CLAIM DEFINITENESS

Because of the importance of claims, the second paragraph of § 112 requires the patent instrument to close with claims "particularly pointing out and distinctly claiming the subject matter which the applicant regards as his invention." "Distinctly" means that the claim must give a clear definition of the scope of the invention when construed in light of the entire patent document. This requirement ensures that patentees have staked well-marked boundaries around their technological property rights. These boundaries, in turn, provide competitors notice of which technologies are proprietary and which are available for exploitation. Thus, this requirement sets a standard for claim adequacy.

ORTHOKINETICS, INC. v. SAFETY TRAVEL CHAIRS, INC.

United States Court of Appeals, Federal Circuit, 1986
806 F.2d 1565

Judges: Markey, Chief Judge, Newman, Circuit Judge, and Swygert, Senior Circuit Judge.

MARKEY, CHIEF JUDGE.

Orthokinetics, Inc. (Orthokinetics) appeals from orders granting a judgment notwithstanding the verdict (JNOV) holding that claims 1–5 of its U.S. Patent Re. 30,867 ('867 patent) are invalid under 35 U.S.C.

§ 112. We reverse and remand with instructions to reinstate the jury verdicts.

BACKGROUND

I. The Claimed Inventions

Orthokinetics manufactures products for invalids and handicapped individuals, including pediatric wheelchairs. It is the assignee of the '586 patent issued to Raymond A. Kazik (Kazik) on June 11, 1974, entitled "Orthopedic Chair With Scoliosis Pads" and of the '867 patent reissued to Edward J. Gaffney (Gaffney) on February 16, 1982, entitled "Travel Chair".

The '867 reissue patent discloses a collapsible pediatric wheelchair which facilitates the placing of wheelchair-bound persons, particularly children, in and out of an automobile. Orthokinetics asserted infringement of claims 1 through 5 by Safety. Claim 1 reads:

> 1. In a wheel chair having a seat portion, a front leg portion, and a rear wheel assembly, the improvement wherein said front leg portion is so dimensioned as to be insertable through the space between the doorframe of an automobile and one of the seats thereof whereby said front leg is placed in support relation to the automobile and will support the seat portion from the automobile in the course of subsequent movement of the wheel chair into the automobile, and the retractor means for assisting the attendant in retracting said rear wheel assembly upwardly independently of any change in the position of the front leg portion with respect to the seat portion while the front leg portion is supported on the automobile and to a position which clears the space beneath the rear end of the chair and permits the chair seat portion and retracted rear wheel assembly to be swung over and set upon said automobile seat.

II. Procedural History

Orthokinetics introduced the Travel Chair to the market in November of 1973. In 1978, Safety Travel Chairs, Inc. (STC) began to sell similar chairs manufactured by Entron, Inc. (Entron).

Opinion

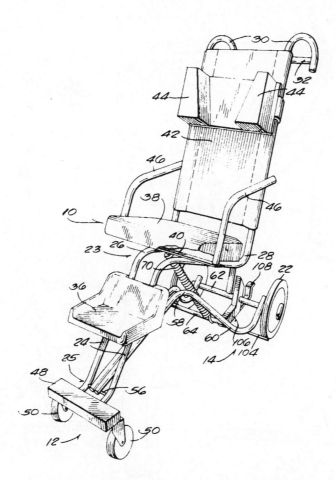

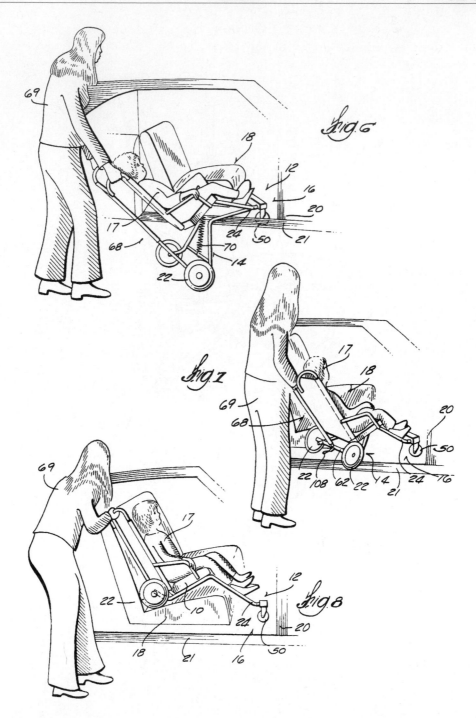

The jury found (question No. 51) that Safety failed to prove by clear and convincing evidence that the '867 patent was invalid because of claim language that does not particularly point out and distinctly claim the invention. 35 U.S.C. § 112, 2d ¶. The district court determined otherwise and granted Safety's motion for JNOV.

Claim 1, from which the rest of the claims depend, contains the limitation: "wherein said front leg portion is so dimensioned as to be insertable through the space between the doorframe of an automobile and one of the seats thereof."

Noting the testimony of Orthokinetics' expert, Mr. Hobbs, who said the dimensions of the front legs depend upon the automobile the chair is designed to suit, the district court stated:

> In response to this testimony, which clearly and convincingly establishes that claim 1 of the patent does not describe the invention in "full, clear, concise and exact terms," Orthokinetics points only to the conclusory statements of Hobbs, Gaffney and expert witness William McCoy, Jr., that the patent is, in fact definite. These conclusory statements are not an adequate basis for the jury to reject Safety's defense. The undisputed, specific testimony of Gaffney and Hobbs demonstrates that an individual desiring to build a noninfringing travel chair cannot tell whether that chair violates the ['867] patent until he constructs a model and tests the model on vehicles ranging from a Honda Civic to a Lincoln Continental to a Checker cab. Without those cars, "so dimensioned" is without meaning.

The foregoing statement employs two measures impermissible in law: (1) it requires that claim 1 "describe" the invention, which is the role of the disclosure portion of the specification, not the role of the claims; and (2) it applied the "full, clear, concise, and exact" requirement of the first paragraph of § 112 to the claim, when that paragraph applies only to the disclosure portion of the specification, not to the claims. The district court spoke, inappropriately, of indefiniteness of the "patent," and did not review the claim for indefiniteness under the second paragraph of § 112.

A decision on whether a claim is invalid under § 112, 2d para., requires a determination of whether those skilled in the art would understand what is claimed when the claim is read in light of the specification.

It is undisputed that the claims require that one desiring to build and use a travel chair must measure the space between the selected automobile's doorframe and its seat and then dimension the front legs of the travel chair so they will fit in that particular space in that particular automobile. Orthokinetics' witnesses, who were skilled in the art, testified that such a task is evident from the specification and that one of ordinary skill in the art would easily have been able to determine the appropriate dimensions. The jury had the right to credit that testimony and no reason exists for the district court to have simply discounted that testimony as "conclusory".

The claims were intended to cover the use of the invention with various types of automobiles. That a particular chair on which the claims read may fit within some automobiles and not others is of no moment.

The phrase "so dimensioned" is as accurate as the subject matter permits, automobiles being of various sizes. As long as those of ordinary skill in the art realized that the dimensions could be easily obtained, § 112, 2d ¶ requires nothing more. The patent law does not require that all possible lengths corresponding to the spaces in hundreds of different automobiles be listed in the patent, let alone that they be listed in the claims.

Compliance with the second paragraph of § 112 is generally a question of law. On the record before us, we observe no failure of compliance with the statute, and thus no basis on § 112 grounds for disturbing the jury's verdict. The district court's grant of Safety's motion for JNOV for claim indefiniteness was in error and must be reversed.

NOTES

1.   Definiteness Established by the Subject Matter. "The degree of precision necessary for adequate claims is a function of the nature of the subject matter." *Miles Laboratories, Inc. v. Shandon Inc.*, 997 F.2d 870, 875 (Fed.Cir. 1993). If a skilled artisan would find the claim language sufficiently distinct to understand its meaning, then even claim limitations such as "close proximity" will be considered "as precise as the subject matter permits." *Rosemount, Inc. v. Beckman Instruments, Inc.*, 727 F.2d 1540, 1547 (Fed.Cir.1984).

2.   Weasel Words. Perplexing issues of definiteness often arise when patent claims employ words of degree, such as "about," "approximately," "close to," "substantially equal," or "closely approximate." The Federal Circuit has noted that these terms "are ubiquitous in patent claims. Such usages, when serving reasonably to describe the claimed subject matter to those of skill in the field of the invention, and to distinguish the claimed subject matter from the prior art, have been accepted in patent examination and upheld by the courts." *Andrew Corp. v. Gabriel Electronics, Inc.*, 847 F.2d 819 (Fed.Cir.1988). According to *Seattle Box Co., Inc. v. Industrial Crating & Packing, Inc.*, 731 F.2d 818 (Fed.Cir.1984), "[w]hen a word of degree is used the district court must determine whether the patent's specification provides some standard for measuring that degree. The trial court must decide, that is, whether one of ordinary skill in the art would understand what is claimed when the claim is read in light of the specification."

Although it is fair to say that the Federal Circuit has been fairly accepting of the use of such words of approximation, in some cases the court has held that such terms violate § 112 ¶ 2. In *Amgen, Inc. v. Chugai Pharmaceutical Co., Ltd.*, 927 F.2d 1200 (Fed.Cir.1991), the court considered U.S. Patent 4,677,195, entitled "Method for the Purification of Erythropoietin and Erythropoietin Compositions." The patent claims both homogeneous EPO and compositions thereof and a method for purifying human EPO using reverse phase high performance liquid chromatography. Claim 4 of the '195 patent provided:

> 4.   Homogeneous erythropoietin characterized by a molecular weight of about 34,000 daltons on SDS PAGE, movement as a single peak on reverse phase high performance liquid chromatography and a specific

activity of at least about 160,000 IU per absorbance unit at 280 nanometers.

The district court had earlier held that "bioassays provide an imprecise form of measurement with a range of error" and that use of the term "about" 160,000 IU/AU, coupled with the range of error already inherent in the specific activity limitation, served neither to distinguish the invention over the close prior art (which described preparations of 120,000 IU/AU), nor to permit one to know what specific activity values below 160,000 might constitute infringement. On appeal, the Federal Circuit affirmed the holding of the district court that the specific activity limitation of "at least about 160,000" was indefinite, reasoning:

> The court found the "addition of the word 'about' seems to constitute an effort to recapture ... a mean activity somewhere between 120,000, which the patent examiner found was anticipated by the prior art, and [the] 160,000 IU/AU" claims which were previously allowed. Because "the term 'about' 160,000 gives no hint as to which mean value between the Miyake et al. value of 128,620 and the mean specific activity level of 160,000 constitutes infringement," the court held the "at least about" claims to be invalid for indefiniteness. This holding was further supported by the fact that nothing in the specification, prosecution history, or prior art provides any indication as to what range of specific activity is covered by the term "about," and by the fact that no expert testified as to a definite meaning for the term in the context of the prior art. In his testimony, Fritsch tried to define "about" 160,000, but he could only say that while "somewhere between 155[,000] might fit within that number," he had not "given a lot of direct considerations to that...."

The court hastened to add that: "In arriving at this conclusion, we caution that our holding that the term "about" renders indefinite [claim 4] should not be understood as ruling out any and all uses of this term in patent claims. It may be acceptable in appropriate fact situations, *e.g., W.L. Gore & Assocs., Inc. v. Garlock, Inc.,* 721 F.2d 1540, 1557 (Fed.Cir.1983) ("use of 'stretching ... at a rate exceeding about 10% per second' in the claims is not indefinite"), even though it is not here."

DATAMIZE, LLC v. PLUMTREE SOFTWARE, INC.

United States Court of Appeals, Federal Circuit, 2005
417 F.3d 1342

Before Clevenger, Bryson, and Prost, Circuit Judges.

PROST, CIRCUIT JUDGE.

Datamize, L.L.C. ("Datamize") appeals from a decision of the United States District Court for the Northern District of California holding each claim of United States Patent No. 6,014,137 ("the '137 patent") invalid as indefinite under 35 U.S.C. § 112, ¶ 2. We affirm.

BACKGROUND

A. The '137 Patent and Related Prosecution History

The '137 patent, entitled "Electronic Kiosk Authoring System," discloses a software program that allows a person to author user interfaces for electronic kiosks. "The authoring system enables the user interface for each individual kiosk to be customized quickly and easily within wide limits of variation, yet subject to constraints adhering the resulting interface to good standards of aesthetics and user friendliness." '137 patent, Abstract; *see also id.* at col. 3, ll. 28–32.

The authoring system gives the system author a limited range of pre-defined design choices for stylistic and functional elements appearing on the screens. *Id.* at col. 3, ll. 52–57. "[M]ajor aesthetic or functional design choices . . . as well as hierarchical methods of retrieving information may be built into the system [while] taking into account the considered opinions of aesthetic design specialists, database specialists, and academic studies on public access kiosk systems and user preferences and problems." *Id.* at col. 3, ll. 57–64.

Claim 1, the '137 patent's only independent claim, recites:

1. In an electronic kiosk system having a plurality of interactive electronic kiosks for displaying information provided by a plurality of information providers, a method for defining custom interface screens customized for individual kiosks of said plurality and operable to make different assortments of said information available for display at different kiosks of said plurality, said method comprising the steps of:

providing a master database of information from said plurality of information providers, said master database referencing substantially all information content from said providers to be displayed on any of said plurality of kiosks;

providing a plurality of pre-defined interface screen element types, each element type defining a form of element available for presentation on said custom interface screens, wherein each said element type permits limited variation in its on-screen characteristics in conformity with a desired uniform and *aesthetically pleasing* look and feel for said interface screens on all kiosks of said kiosk system,

> each element type having a plurality of attributes associated therewith, wherein each said element type and its associated attributes are subject to pre-defined constraints providing element characteristics in conformance with said uniform and *aesthetically pleasing* look and feel for said interface screens, and

> wherein said plurality of pre-defined element types includes at least one pre-defined window type, at least one pre-defined button type, and at least one pre-defined multimedia type;

selecting a plurality of elements to be included in a custom interface screen under construction, said plurality of elements being selected from said plurality of pre-defined elements types, said plurality of selected elements including at least one button type;

assigning values to the attributes associated with each of said selected elements consistent with said pre-defined constraints, whereby the aggregate layout of said plurality of selected elements on said interface screen under construction will be *aesthetically pleasing* and functionally operable for effective delivery of information to a kiosk user;

selecting from said master database an assortment of information content deriving from selected ones of said information providers to define kiosk information content for an individual kiosk of said kiosk system;

associating said kiosk information content with at least a portion of said selected elements for said interface screen under construction; and

linking said at least one selected button type element to an action facilitating the viewing of at least portions of said kiosk information content by a kiosk user.

At issue in this appeal is the definiteness of "aesthetically pleasing" as it is used in the context of claim 1 of the '137 patent.

B.　The District Court Proceedings

Datamize sued Plumtree Software, Inc. ("Plumtree") for infringing the '137 patent, and Plumtree responded by moving for summary judgment on the ground that the '137 patent is invalid for indefiniteness under 35 U.S.C. § 112, ¶ 2. The district court granted Plumtree's motion, concluding that the '137 patent's only independent claim is indefinite due to use of the phrase "aesthetically pleasing."

DISCUSSION

A.　Standard of Review

We review a district court's grant of summary judgment *de novo*. *High Concrete Structures, Inc. v. New Enter. Stone & Lime Co.*, 377 F.3d 1379, 1382 (Fed.Cir.2004). "A determination of claim indefiniteness is a legal conclusion that is drawn from the court's performance of its duty as the construer of patent claims." *Personalized Media Communications., L.L.C. v. Int'l Trade Comm'n*, 161 F.3d 696, 705 (Fed Cir.1998). Thus, as with claim construction, we exercise *de novo* review over the conclusion that a claim is indefinite under 35 U.S.C. § 112, ¶ 2. *Id.*

B.　The Law of Indefiniteness

Every patent's specification must "conclude with one or more claims particularly pointing out and distinctly claiming the subject matter which the applicant regards as his invention." 35 U.S.C. § 112, ¶ 2 (2000). Because the claims perform the fundamental function of delineating the scope of the invention, *Chimie v. PPG Indus., Inc.*, 402 F.3d

1371, 1379 (Fed.Cir.2005), the purpose of the definiteness requirement is to ensure that the claims delineate the scope of the invention using language that adequately notifies the public of the patentee's right to exclude, *Honeywell Int'l, Inc. v. Int'l Trade Comm'n,* 341 F.3d 1332, 1338 (Fed.Cir.2003).

According to the Supreme Court, "[t]he statutory requirement of particularity and distinctness in claims is met only when [the claims] clearly distinguish what is claimed from what went before in the art and clearly circumscribe what is foreclosed from future enterprise." *United Carbon Co. v. Binney & Smith Co.,* 317 U.S. 228, 236, 63 S.Ct. 165, 87 L.Ed. 232 (1942). The definiteness requirement, however, does not compel absolute clarity. Only claims "not amenable to construction" or "insolubly ambiguous" are indefinite. *See Novo Indus., L.P. v. Micro Molds Corp.,* 350 F.3d 1348, 1353 (Fed.Cir.2003); *Honeywell Int'l,* 341 F.3d at 1338; *Exxon Research & Eng'g Co. v. United States,* 265 F.3d 1371, 1375 (Fed.Cir.2001). Thus, the definiteness of claim terms depends on whether those terms can be given any reasonable meaning. Furthermore, a difficult issue of claim construction does not *ipso facto* result in a holding of indefiniteness. *Exxon Research & Eng'g,* 265 F.3d at 1375. "If the meaning of the claim is discernible, even though the task may be formidable and the conclusion may be one over which reasonable persons will disagree, we have held the claim sufficiently clear to avoid invalidity on indefiniteness grounds." *Id.* In this regard it is important to note that an issued patent is entitled to a statutory presumption of validity. *See* 35 U.S.C. § 282 (2000). "By finding claims indefinite only if reasonable efforts at claim construction prove futile, we accord respect to the statutory presumption of validity and we protect the inventive contribution of patentees, even when the drafting of their patents has been less than ideal." *Exxon Research & Eng'g,* 265 F.3d at 1375 (citation omitted). In this way we also follow the requirement that clear and convincing evidence be shown to invalidate a patent. *See Budde v. Harley–Davidson, Inc.,* 250 F.3d 1369, 1376 (Fed.Cir.2001).

In the face of an allegation of indefiniteness, general principles of claim construction apply. *See Oakley, Inc. v. Sunglass Hut Int'l,* 316 F.3d 1331, 1340–41 (Fed.Cir.2003) (noting that a determination of definiteness "requires a construction of the claims according to the familiar canons of claim construction"). Intrinsic evidence in the form of the patent specification and file history should guide a court toward an acceptable claim construction. *Phillips v. AWH Corp.,* 415 F.3d 1303, 1314 (Fed.Cir.2005) (en banc). And while "we have emphasized the importance of intrinsic evidence in claim construction, we have also authorized district courts to rely on extrinsic evidence," such as expert testimony. *Id.* at 1317. In construing claims, "what matters is for the court to attach the appropriate weight to be assigned to those sources in light of the statutes and policies that inform patent law." *Id.* at 1324.

C. Analysis

With these principles in mind, we proceed to the question at hand: whether the '137 patent's use of "aesthetically pleasing" meets the standards articulated in our case law concerning definiteness. We begin our analysis by noting our agreement with the district court's understanding that the ordinary meaning of "aesthetically pleasing" includes "having beauty that gives pleasure or enjoyment" or, in other words, "beautiful." We also recognize that the district court's opinion presents a reasoned and detailed analysis of both the intrinsic evidence, including the specification of the '137 patent and the prosecution history of the '040 patent, and the extrinsic evidence in the form of Datamize's expert testimony. Datamize, however, argues that the district court erred by considering the phrase "aesthetically pleasing" divorced from the context of claim 1.

Datamize is right to point out that the phrase "aesthetically pleasing" should be considered in the context of claim 1. Claim construction involves reviewing the intrinsic evidence of record, including the claim language itself. *See Chimie,* 402 F.3d at 1377; *Abbott Labs. v. Syntron Bioresearch, Inc.,* 334 F.3d 1343, 1351 (Fed.Cir.2003) (explaining that usage of disputed claim terms in the context of the claims as a whole informs the proper construction of the terms).

[I]n the context of claim 1, "aesthetically pleasing" relates to the look and feel of custom interface screens on kiosks, and the aggregate layout of elements on an interface screen is apparently one example or aspect of the interface screens that may be "aesthetically pleasing."

This context, while helpful in terms of identifying the components of the claimed invention that must be "aesthetically pleasing," does not suggest or provide any meaningful definition for the phrase "aesthetically pleasing" itself. Merely understanding that "aesthetically pleasing" relates to the look and feel of interface screens, or more specifically to the aggregate layout of elements on interface screens, fails to provide one of ordinary skill in the art with any way to determine whether an interface screen is "aesthetically pleasing."

Datamize, however, contends that when construed in the context of claim 1, the phrase "aesthetically pleasing" applies to the process of defining a "desired" result and not the actual result itself. Datamize believes a reasonable construction of "aesthetically pleasing" in the context of the claims involves the intent, purpose, wish, or goal of a person practicing the invention: that person simply must intend to create an "aesthetically pleasing" interface screen; whether that person actually succeeds is irrelevant. In other words, Datamize suggests we adopt a construction of "aesthetically pleasing" that only depends on the subjective opinion of a person selecting features to be included on an interface screen. Indeed, Datamize argues that the district court erred by requiring an objective definition for the phrase "aesthetically pleasing."

Datamize's proposed construction of "aesthetically pleasing" in the context of claim 1 is not reasonable for several reasons. First and foremost, the plain meaning of the claim language requires that the look and feel of interface screens actually be "aesthetically pleasing." The first use of "aesthetically pleasing" in claim 1 clearly sets forth two requirements for the look and feel of interface screens: the look and feel must be (1) uniform and (2) "aesthetically pleasing." That the uniform and "aesthetically pleasing" look and feel must also be "desired" does not alter that fact.

Furthermore, in *Orthokinetics* we did not conclude, as Datamize suggests, that the absence of an objective definition for a claim term does not render the phrase indefinite. In that case we concluded that the phrase "so dimensioned" in the following limitation is not indefinite: "wherein said front leg portion is *so dimensioned* as to be insertable through the space between the doorframe of an automobile and one of the seats thereof." *Orthokinetics*, 806 F.2d at 1575. We noted that based on expert testimony it was undisputed that one of ordinary skill in the art would easily have been able to determine the appropriate dimensions that the claim language required. *Id.* at 1576. One desiring to build and use the invention, a travel chair, "must measure the space between the selected automobile's doorframe and its seat and then dimension the front legs of the travel chair so they will fit in that particular space in that particular automobile." *Id.* The fact that the claims were intended to cover the use of the invention with various types of automobiles made no difference; we concluded that the phrase "so dimensioned" is as accurate as the subject matter permits since automobiles are of various sizes. *Id.* Thus, in *Orthokinetics* we recognized that an objective definition encompassed by the claim term "so dimensioned" could be applied to innumerable specific automobiles.

In stark contrast to *Orthokinetics*, here Datamize has offered no objective definition identifying a standard for determining when an interface screen is "aesthetically pleasing." In the absence of a workable objective standard, "aesthetically pleasing" does not just include a subjective element, it is completely dependent on a person's subjective opinion. To the extent Datamize argues that such a construction of "aesthetically pleasing" does not render the phrase indefinite, we disagree. The scope of claim language cannot depend solely on the unrestrained, subjective opinion of a particular individual purportedly practicing the invention. *See Application of Musgrave*, 431 F.2d 882, 893 (1970) (noting that "[a] step requiring the exercise of subjective judgment without restriction might be objectionable as rendering a claim indefinite"). Some objective standard must be provided in order to allow the public to determine the scope of the claimed invention. Even if the relevant perspective is that of the system creator, the identity of who makes aesthetic choices fails to provide any direction regarding the relevant question of how to determine whether that person succeeded in creating an "aesthetically pleasing" look and feel for interface screens. A purely subjective construction of "aesthetically pleasing" would not notify the public of the patentee's right to exclude since the meaning of the claim language would depend on the unpredictable vagaries of any one person's opinion of the aesthetics of interface screens. While beauty is in the eye of the beholder, a claim term, to be definite, requires an objective anchor. Thus, even if we adopted a completely subjective construction of "aesthetically pleasing," this would still render the '137 patent invalid.

Furthermore, "aesthetically pleasing" does not exactly compare to words of degree such as "substantially equal to," *see Seattle Box Co.*, 731 F.2d at 826, "about," *see BJ Servs. Co. v. Halliburton Energy Servs., Inc.,* 338 F.3d 1368, 1372–73 (Fed.Cir.2003), or "substantial absence," *see Exxon Research & Eng'g*, 265 F.3d at 1380–81. The language, however, invokes a similar analysis. "When a word of degree is used the district court must determine whether the patent's specification provides some standard for measuring that degree." *Seattle Box Co.,* 731 F.2d at 826. Similarly, when faced with a purely subjective phrase like "aesthetically pleasing," a court must determine whether the patent's specification supplies some standard for measuring the scope of the phrase. Thus, we next consult the written description. *See id.; see also Chimie*, 402 F.3d at 1377 (" 'When the claim language itself lacks sufficient clarity to ascertain the scope of the claims,' we look to the written description for guidance." (quoting *Deering Precision Instruments, L.L.C. v. Vector Distribution Sys., Inc.,* 347 F.3d 1314, 1324 (Fed.Cir.2003))).

The inventor describes various advantages of his invention in the "Summary of the Invention" section of the '137 patent. Most relevant to the construction of "aesthetically pleasing," the inventor states:

> The authoring system enables the user interface for each individual kiosk to be customized quickly and easily within wide limits of variation, yet subject to constraints adhering the resting [sic, resulting, *see* '137 patent, Abstract] interface to good standards of aesthetics and user friendliness.... It is a further advantage of the present authoring system that an individual using the authoring software to devise a kiosk interface screen (that individual is referred to herein as a "system author") is only given a limited range of choices for stylistic and functional elements appearing in the screen displays. In this way major aesthetic or functional design choices such as button syles [sic] and sizes, window borders, color combinations, and type fonts as well as hierarchical methods of retrieving information may he built into the system taking into account the considered opinions of aesthetic design specialists, database specialists, and academic studies on public access kiosk systems and user preferences and problems.

'137 patent, col. 3, ll. 28–32; 52–64. Furthermore, in the "Detailed Description of Illustrative Embodiments" section of the '137 patent, the inventor, discussing a particular embodiment of the invention, states:

A closer look at the structure of the screen layout of FIG. 2A is in order. The buttons 21 have a fixed predefined size, which is chosen not only to make them aesthetically pleasing in appearance, but also easy to use on a touch screen by persons generally unpracticed with touch screen operation. The button placement in FIG. 2A is generally fixed along two adjacent edges. This is an aesthetic choice, but it is a choice that is forced by the authoring software to assure that once an aesthetically and functionally acceptable button size and layout has been chosen, it will be maintained throughout all further screen layouts for all kiosks without having to expend time and effort re-creating an acceptable button layout anew for each kiosk. Other aesthetic button layouts may also be used, but once a general button layout is devised, the software makes it available for use in all kiosk interface screens. Considering that many many [sic] screen layouts will generally have to be set up and then regularly revised, limiting the system author's freedom to devise new button patterns and button styles greatly enhances the ease with which new kiosks may be brought in operation and ensures that the button pattern will be aesthetically and operationally acceptable.... The authoring system of the present invention then allows each kiosk to be customized quickly and easily while maintaining a high degree of variability in the screen layouts without sacrificing aesthetic appearance.

'137 patent, col. 5, ll. 35–56.

In general, neither these statements nor any others in the written description set forth an objective way to determine whether an interface screen is "aesthetically pleasing." The description of the advantages of the invention indicates that there are "good standards of aesthetics," which of course implies that there are also standards of aesthetics that are "not good." The inventor does not attempt to explain what distinguishes the two, except to say that experts, specialists, and academics may have views that are influential in determining what aesthetic standards are good. Some statements indicate particular aspects of the screen that might affect whether the screen is "aesthetically pleasing": button styles, sizes, and placements, window borders, color combinations, and type fonts. There is no indication, however, other than by referring to "the considered opinions of aesthetic design specialists, database specialists, and academic studies on public access kiosk systems and user preferences and problems," how to determine what button styles, sizes, and placements, for example, are "aesthetically pleasing." Moreover, whatever the considered opinions of unnamed people and studies say is altogether unclear.

And while the description of an embodiment provides examples of aesthetic features of screen displays that can be controlled by the authoring system, it does not explain what selection of these features would be "aesthetically pleasing." Major aesthetic choices apparently may include some aspect of button styles and sizes, window borders, color combinations, and type fonts. The written description, however, provides no guidance to a person making aesthetic choices such that their choices will result in an "aesthetically pleasing" look and feel of an interface screen. For example, the specification does not explain what factors a person should consider when selecting a feature to include in the authoring system. Left unanswered are questions like: which color combinations would be "aesthetically pleasing" and which would not? And more generally, how does one determine whether a color combination is "aesthetically pleasing"? Again, one skilled in the art reading the specification is left with the unhelpful direction to consult the subjective opinions of aesthetic design specialists, database specialists, and academic studies.

Simply put, the definition of "aesthetically pleasing" cannot depend on an undefined standard. *See Amgen,* 314 F.3d at 1342 (finding indefinite claim requiring comparison to moving target since the patent failed to direct those of ordinary skill in the art to a standard by which the appropriate comparison could be made). Reference to undefined standards, regardless of whose views might influence the formation of those standards, fails to provide any direction to one skilled in the art attempting to determine the scope of the claimed invention. In short, the definition of "aesthetically pleasing" cannot depend on the undefined views of unnamed persons, even if they are experts, specialists, or academics. Thus, the written description does not provide any reasonable, definite construction of "aesthetically pleasing."

[The Federal Circuit next reviewed the prosecution history and extrinsic evidence of record and concluded that these sources also did not provide any objective way to determine whether the look and feel of an interface screen were "aesthetically pleasing."]

CONCLUSION

"Aesthetically pleasing," as it is used in the only independent claim of the '137 patent, fails to "particularly point[ ] out and distinctly claim [ ] the subject matter which the patentee regards as his invention." *See* 35 U.S.C. § 112, ¶ 2. We therefore affirm the district court's grant of summary judgment of invalidity of all claims of the '137 patent.

AFFIRMED.

NOTES

1. **Other Examples.** Which of the following claim limitations strikes you as suspect in view of the definiteness requirement?

- Filaments that are "substantially completely wetted"
- Treating a catalyst for a period "sufficient to increase substantially the initial catalyst activity"
- Concrete "hardened sufficiently to allow cutting by a . . . saw while still producing an acceptable surface finish"

Would it surprise you that each of these limitations has been considered sufficiently definite to fulfill Patent Act standards? *See LNP Eng'g Plastics, Inc. v. Miller Waste Mills, Inc.*, 275 F.3d 1347 (Fed. Cir. 2001); *Exxon Research & Eng'g Co. v. United States*, 265 F.3d 1371, 1379 (Fed. Cir. 2001); *Chiuminatta Concrete Concepts, Inc. v. Cardinal Indus., Inc.*, 145 F.3d 1303, 1306 (Fed. Cir. 1998). What implications does this lenient definiteness jurisprudence hold for the public notice that patent instruments are intended to provide?

2. Whereby Clauses. A discussion earlier in this Chapter discussed the effect of the preamble upon the scope of a patent claim. Similarly perplexing is the drafter's use of "whereby" clauses, an example of which may be found in claim 1 of the United States Patent No. 4,081,879, set forth in the *Chemcast* case. 913 F.2d 923 (Fed.Cir.1990). Although the use of a "whereby" or similar clauses may appear as an admirable attempt to further delimit the claimed invention in keeping with § 112 ¶ 2, the extent to which such clauses actually limit the scope of the claimed invention often presents difficult issues. In *Texas Instruments Inc. v. United States International Trade Commission*, 988 F.2d 1165 (Fed.Cir.1993), the court considered claims directed towards a process for encapsulating electronic components in plastic through a process called transfer molding. The court discussed the asserted claims and effect of "whereby" clauses as follows:

Claim 12 concludes with a clause that states "whereby the fluid will not directly engage the device and electrical connection means at high velocity, and the conductors will be secured against appreciable displacement by the fluid." Claims 14 and 17 conclude with the clause "to preclude direct high velocity engagement between the fluid and the device and the electrical connections thereto." The Commission determined that the "whereby" clause in claim 12 and the "to preclude" clauses in claims 14 and 17 only express the necessary results of what is recited in the claims. For this reason, the Commission gave them no weight in its infringement analysis.

Respondents assert that the "whereby/to preclude" clauses of these claims establish specific further limitations to the claims relating to the velocity of the fluid inside the mold and the manner of securing the conductors which must be met in the respondents' opposite-side gating processes in order for those processes to infringe the claims of the '027 patent. We disagree. A "whereby" clause that merely states the result of the limitations in the claim adds nothing to the patentability or substance of the claim. *Israel v. Cresswell*, 166 F.2d 153, 156, 35 C.C.P.A. 890, 76 U.S.P.Q. 594, 597 (1948). The "whereby/to preclude" clauses of claims 12, 14 and 17 merely describe the result of arranging the components of the claims in the manner recited in the claims: the fluid does not directly engage the device and the electrical connection means because the gate through which the fluid enters is remote from them; the conductors are secured against appreciable displacement by the fluid because they are clamped in notches by the upper and lower halves of the mold die. Therefore, the Commission correctly determined that the "whereby/to preclude" clauses do not contain any limitations not inherent to the process found in claims 12, 14 and 17.

The use of whereby clauses is somewhat more popular in the Commonwealth, although many applications of domestic origin also employ such clauses. Why would a drafter wish to employ a "whereby" clause in lieu of: (1) putting the language in the preamble; (2) employing a means-plus-function claim under § 112–57 6; or (3) not including a particular result in the patent claim at all?

3. Claiming Requirements Abroad. Article 84 of the European Patent Convention mandates that claims "shall define the matter for which protection is sought. They shall be clear and concise and be supported by the specification." Section 35(5) of the Japanese patent statute requires that the claims contain "all matters which an applicant for a patent considers necessary in defining an invention for which a patent is sought." Section 35(6) of the Japanese statute goes on to mandate that the claims must be clear, concise, and directed towards an invention that is described in the specification.

4. Claiming Criticized. To some, claim drafting is a rigid, formalistic art that erects considerable barriers against the accurate description of technological inventions. Formalized drafting conventions, such as the single sentence rule, the limited number of claim formats, and the evolution of settled meanings of claim terms such as "integral" or "grooved" as a result of decades of judicial and administrative interpretation, render claim drafting a needlessly complex undertaking. *See* John R. Thomas, *The Question Concerning Patent Law and Pioneer Inventions*, 10 High Tech. L. J. 35, 53–55 (1995). Would you propose any changes to the current scheme of patent claiming? Alternatively, what other means of establishing boundaries to an applicant's technological properties could be established?

5. Further Reading. Additional sources on the significant body of law that surrounds patent claims include Robert C. Faber, Landis on Mechanics of Patent Claim Drafting (4th ed. 1999); Anthony W. Deller, Patent Claims (2d ed. 1971); Emerson Stringham, Patent Claim Drafting (2d ed. 1952); and Risdale Ellis, Patent Claims (1949).

CLAIM DRAFTING EXERCISES

Note

The PTO Registration Examination. The United States Patent and Trademark Office requires individuals to pass a Registration Examination for Patent Practitioners in order to practice before the PTO in patent matters. Although one need not be admitted to a state bar to sit for the Registration Examination, the PTO requires individuals to have obtained certain technical or scientific credentials. You can find the latest information on the "patent bar" examination at www.uspto.gov.

Exercise One. Your desktop is constantly cluttered with computer equipment, papers, and other office supplies. Because you often like to drink a beverage while working at your desk, you frequently place a can of soda on what is often the only free space available, your computer mouse pad. In this way, you avoid leaving water marks on your desktop. But you have found this solution less than satisfactory: condensation from the can often leaves water on the mouse pad, damaging your mouse, and the cord that connects the mouse to the computer sometimes knocks the can over.

One day, you arrive at a solution. By attaching a coaster to the mouse pad made of foam material, you find that the soda can is always readily within your grasp. Because the lower surface of the mouse pad has a high coefficient of friction, the attached coaster is far more stable than a free-standing coaster. The upper surface of the mouse pad has a relatively low coefficient of friction, allowing ready movement of the mouse. Because the coaster is so effective at preventing spills and capturing condensation, you decide to seek patent protection on your invention.

You perform a search of the prior art and discover that an earlier patent, granted to one Lee, described the concept of a child's table mat including a beverage holder. Lee's table mat is constructed of a hard plastic material, however. Further, Lee does not describe the use of a computer mouse, nor does it disclose the use of different coefficients of friction on the different surfaces of the mat.

You also decide to expand upon your invention by attaching a pencil holder to the mouse pad as well. The pencil holder consists simply of a base with four sockets. It is fashioned from a material of sturdier construction than the foam mouse pad. Each socket is sized such that inserted pencils are snugly held.

Draft three claims to the mouse pad with beverage holder. Claim 1 should be directed towards the combination of mouse pad and coaster. Claim 2 should depend from claim 1 and include the concept of differing frictional surfaces. Claim 3 should depend from claim 2 and add the pencil holder feature. When drafting the claims, attempt to use the most broad and general language that you can to describe the features of the invention, yet distinguish over the Lee reference.

Exercise Two. The invention illustrated and described below is directed towards a three ring loose-leaf album. Figure 1 shows an end view with the album in the closed position. Figure 2 depicts a view of the exterior surface of the album in the open position.

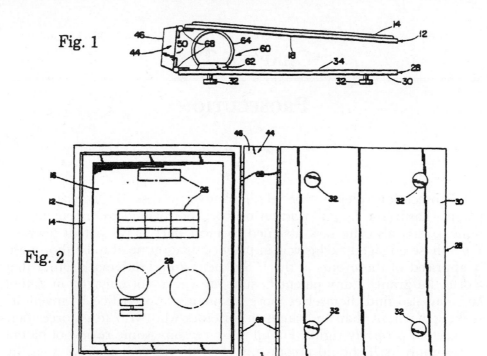

Fig. 1

Fig. 2

The album includes top 12 and bottom 38 covers; spine 44; exterior surfaces 14, 30, and 46; interior surfaces 18, 34, and 50; a ring assembly 60 including base 62 and three rings 64 equally spaced along the base; feet 32; four hinges 68; recessed exterior surface portion 16; and indicia 26.

One feature of the invention is a recessed portion 16 in the exterior surface 14 of the top cover 12 wherein personalized indicia 26 are positioned. An important feature of the invention is the presence of a hardened polymer resin which has been poured into the recess to bond the indicia in place. The hardened polymer resin is clear to permit the indicia to be visible. Another feature is the four projecting feet 32 on the back cover. Although not specifically illustrated, the feet may be decorative, e.g., ball and claw, as in the instance when the top and bottom covers and the spine are made of wood. Whether or not the feet or decorative, they permit the album to be displayed in a fashion similar to furniture.

Another important feature of the invention is the arrangement of hinges 68 so that there is a minimal external exposure of the hinges and so as not to detract from the decorative aspects of the album when cover 12 and 28 are in a closed position as shown in Figure 1. When opened, the top cover exposes a three ring loose-leaf assembly of a base 62 and three rings 64, equally spaced along the base.

Draft a single claim to a three ring loose-leaf album as described above and shown in Figures 1 and 2. Your claim must include and interrelate at least the following elements: the hardened polymer resin; top and bottom covers 12 and 28; spine 44; hinges 68; interior surfaces 18, 34, and 50; base 62 and rings 64; feet 32; exterior surfaces 14, 30, and 46; recess 16; and indicia 26.

CHAPTER TEN

PROSECUTION

■ ■ ■

Prosecution refers to the administrative process for acquisition of a patent. Easily the largest portion of work performed by patent practitioners, it is also the task assigned to most entry-level patent lawyers. Even those engaged exclusively in patent litigation need to be thoroughly apprised of the events at the U.S. Patent and Trademark Office that led to the grant of any patent in suit. Attorneys not engaged in patent law may also find themselves more frequently approached by inventors seeking a patent than by patent proprietors who wish to enforce their intellectual property rights. For all these reasons, some review of patent prosecution itself should accompany even the most basic review of the patent law.

A topic conveniently taken up alongside prosecution is that of inventorship. As we have seen, prior art under § 102 must be the work of someone other than the inventor. The identification of the appropriate individuals as inventors is thus a significant preliminary step in the acquisition of patent rights in the United States. Although the patent statute demonstrates a liberal approach towards the naming of inventors in a given application, it is insistent that they ultimately be correctly named. These issues are taken up in § 10.2 of this Chapter.

The subsequent two sections of this Chapter consider the law relating to applicant abuses of the patent acquisition system. The first of these abuses is inequitable conduct, defined as failure to disclose material information, or submission of false material information, to the PTO with an intent to deceive. Because the prosecution process is *ex parte*, the PTO relies to a great extent upon applicant observance of a duty of candor. Patent law recognizes, however, that applicants may be tempted not to disclose information that might jeopardize the patentability of an application. Thus, inequitable conduct—the intentional refusal to disclose material prior art—brings a severe penalty: courts will refuse to enforce the issued patent.

A second applicant abuse of the patent acquisition process relates to double patenting. The patent system envisions the issuance of only a single patent per invention. Otherwise, a patentee might extend the statutory period of exclusivity by filing a series of related patent applications directed towards the same invention. The need for this doctrine in light of the statutory definition of prior art, as well as the thorny problem of obviousness-type double patenting, are considered below.

Although the PTO does not ordinarily monitor the status of issued patents, the Patent Act does provide for certain post-grant proceedings that allow for the amendment or reconsideration of issued patents. The statute limits these to three different sorts of proceedings: issuing certificates of correction that fix typographical or minor mistakes, examining reissue applications to correct substantive errors, and reexamining the validity of a patent in view of additional prior art references or arguments. Section 10.5 of this Chapter considers these procedures.

The final portion of this chapter considers patent acquisition outside the United States. There is no global patent system. Inventors who seek patent rights in other nations must secure rights operative in those jurisdictions. They are assisted on this front by a modest number of international agreements that, together, establish a basic framework for multinational patent acquisition. This Chapter closes with a brief introduction to that system and its implementation in domestic law.

§ 10.1   OVERVIEW OF PATENT PROSECUTION

§ 10.1[a]   PROSECUTION IN THE UNITED STATES

As befits one of the more venerable governmental agencies in the United States, the PTO has established an elaborate administrative practice. This casebook can present only an overview of this specialized field of law. Further details on patent prosecution may be found in two primary sources: The Rules of Practice in Patent Cases, housed in Title 37 of the Code of Federal Regulations, and the Manual of Patent Examining Procedure (MPEP). The latter, an imposing volume relied upon by examiners and members of the patent bar alike, provides detailed rules and regulations on which the public can rely. The MPEP is promulgated by the PTO and therefore does not bind the courts. *See, e.g., In re Recreative Technologies, Corp.*, 83 F.3d 1394 (Fed. Cir.1996).

A threshold issue concerning patent prosecution is the identity of the individual preparing and pursuing the application. Although any inventor is free to prosecute his own application, the vast majority choose to seek the assistance of a professional representative. Patent acquisition thus ordinarily begins with a discussion between a patent attorney and the inventor, from which the attorney obtains a full description of the invention. Usually, the attorney will arrange for a search of the prior art to determine whether an existing patent or printed publication bears upon the novelty or nonobviousness of the disclosed invention. With this prior art in hand, the attorney can assist the inventor or his assignee in determining whether a patent application should be filed or not. If the decision is made to go forward, the patent attorney then initiates patent prosecution with the filing of a patent application to the Director of the United States Patent and Trademark Office. 35 U.S.C.A. § 111 offers the applicant two choices: nonprovisional applications under § 111(a), or provisional applications under § 111(b).

Provisional applications present simplified requirements in comparison with nonprovisional applications. Most noticeably, the provisional application need not include patent claims. The PTO does not examine these applications and will consider the applicant to have abandoned them after 12 months. Their primary importance lies in the entitlement of nonprovisional applications to the benefit of the filing date of earlier provisional applications to the same invention. In a sense, then, an applicant may subsequently perfect a provisional application by later filing an nonprovisional application without loss of the earlier filing date. Importantly, the pendency of a provisional application does not subtract from the twenty-year term of any subsequent nonprovisional application that matures into an issued patent.

In contrast, nonprovisional applications filed under § 111(a) will be examined as quickly as an examiner is able to turn to the task. 35 U.S.C. § 131 authorizes the Director to order the examination of an ordinary application by providing simply:

Examination of Application

> The Director shall cause an examination to be made of the application and the alleged new invention; and if on such examination it appears that the applicant is entitled to a patent under the law, the Director shall issue a patent therefor.

When the PTO receives an applicant's filing, it designates the application with a filing date and serial number. After determining that the filed papers comprise a complete patent application, it then forwards the application to the appropriate Examining Group. The application is then assigned to an examiner, who ordinarily considers applications in the order of their filing date. The examiner first considers whether the application conforms with the PTO's formal requirements. Rejection of an application can result at this early stage from an incomprehensible English translation, poorly executed drawings, and other defects.

The examiner next conducts a search of the prior art. In addition to art disclosed by the applicant, the examiner will then search domestic and foreign patents as well as various printed publications. To assist examiners in this regard, the PTO maintains a library of patents from around the world along with various technical journals and texts.

Following the search, the examiner then turns to examination of the application. This task entails ensuring that the application satisfies the disclosure requirements and warrants a patent in light of the prior art. 35 U.S.C.A. § 132(a) then provides:

Notice of Rejection; Reexamination

Whenever, on examination, any claim for a patent is rejected, or any objection or requirement made, the Director shall notify the applicant thereof, stating the reasons for such rejection, or objection or requirement, together with such information and references as may be useful in judging of the propriety of continuing the prosecution of his application; and if after receiving such notice, the applicant persists in his claim for a patent, with or without amendment, the application shall be reexamined. No amendment shall introduce new matter into the disclosure of the invention.

The examiner's notification is denominated an <u>Office Action.</u> The Office Action identifies each claim, indicates whether it has been rejected or allowed, and offers the examiner's "reasoning." The Office Action also provides a period for response by the applicant.

If a rejection has resulted, the attorney will usually respond by either asserting that the rejection was improper or by amending the claims. Under the first option, the attorney offers substantive arguments that the rejection was improper. PTO nomenclature designates these arguments a "<u>traverse.</u>" Alternatively, the attorney will amend the claims, typically augmenting the claim language in order to overcome a rejection founded on the prior art or lack of claim definiteness.

If still unconvinced, the examiner will issue a second Office Action titled a "Final Rejection." The applicant ordinarily has three options: abandon the application, file a so-called "continuing application," or seek review of the examiner's actions by filing a petition to the Director or appeal to the Board of Patent Appeals and Interferences. This chapter discusses the latter two options. Of course, the examiner may agree that the amended or explained application deserves a patent and issue a "notice of allowance." Then, upon payment of an issuance fee, the applicant receives a patent. The PTO then publishes the patent's abstract and broadest claim, along with a selected drawing, in its Official Gazette.

§ 10.1[b] CONTINUING APPLICATION PRACTICE

The Patent Act allows inventors to file "continuing applications." Stated generally, a continued application is one that has been "re-filed" at the USPTO, commonly following the rejection of some or all of its claims. Continuing patent applications allow inventors to extend the period of examination at the USPTO in order to negotiate further with a patent examiner, amend claims, submit new claims, and gain additional time to prepare evidence to be submitted to the USPTO in support of their applications, among other potential benefits. The following opinion discusses the different sorts of continuing applications in greater detail.

TRANSCO PRODUCTS INC. v. PERFORMANCE CONTRACTING, INC.

United States Court of Appeals, Federal Circuit, 1994
38 F.3d 551

An applicant may file a continuation, divisional, or continuation-in-part (CIP) application of a prior application, all of which the PTO characterizes as "continuing" applications. *See* MPEP § 201.11. In general, a continuing application is one filed during the pendency of another application which contains at least part of the disclosure of the other application and names at least one inventor in common with that application.

"Continuation" and "divisional" applications are alike in that they are both continuing applications based on the same disclosure as an earlier application. They differ, however, in what they claim. A "continuation" application claims the same invention claimed in an earlier application, although there may be some variation in the scope of the subject matter claimed. *See* MPEP § 201.07. A "divisional" application, on the other hand, is one carved out of an earlier application which disclosed and claimed more than one independent invention, the result being that the divisional application claims only one or more, but not all, of the independent inventions of the earlier application. *See* MPEP § 201.06. A "CIP" application is a continuing application containing a portion or all of the disclosure of an earlier application together with added matter not present in that earlier application. See MPEP § 201.08. The term "parent" is often used to refer to the immediately preceding application upon which a continuing application claims priority; the term "original" is used to refer to the first application in a chain of continuing applications. *See* MPEP §§ 201.04, 201.04(a).

The PTO has noted that the expressions "continuation," "divisional," and "continuation-in-part" are merely terms used for administrative convenience. *See* MPEP § 201.11.

Section 120 appeared in the statutes for the first time in the Patent Act of 1952. Prior to 1952, continuing application practice was a creature of patent office practice and case law, and section 120 merely codified the procedural rights of an applicant with respect to this practice. Before section 120 was enacted, the Supreme Court noted that a continuing application and the application on which it is based are considered part of the same transaction constituting one continuous application. The legislative history of section 120 does not indicate any congressional intent to alter the Supreme Court's interpretation of continuing application practice.

NOTES

1. **Continuation Applications.** As discussed in *Transco*, the statutory basis for continuation applications is provided in § 120, which reads:

Benefit of Earlier Filing Date in the United States

An application for patent for an invention disclosed in the manner provided by the first paragraph of section 112 of this title in an application previously filed in the United States, or as provided by section 363 of this title, which is filed by an inventor or inventors named in the previously filed application shall have the same effect, as to such invention, as though filed on the date of the prior application, if filed before the patenting or abandonment of or termination of proceedings on the first application or on an application similarly entitled to the benefit of the filing date of the first application and if it contains or is amended to contain a specific reference to the earlier application.

The parallel between this provision and § 119 should be apparent. Both parts of the Patent Act allow applicants to obtain the effect of an earlier filing date of another application. While § 119 relates to international application priority, § 120 concerns domestic application priority. Continuation applications are based upon a parent application and, compared to that application, contain no additional disclosure. The continuation application's claims are directed to the same invention as the parent, although the scope of the claims may change as the prosecution process continues.

A simple example illustrates continuing application practice. Suppose that an inventor files a patent application on January 1, 2010. After the USPTO examiner subsequently issues a "final rejection" of that application, the inventor files a continuing application (more specifically, a continuation application) on February 1, 2014. The continuation application includes the same disclosure as the 2010 application. By filing it, the inventor may continue to assert to the USPTO that a patent should issue on that invention. If the USPTO approves the continuation application, it will issue as a patent that expires on January 1, 2030—twenty years from the date of filing of the original or "parent" application.

It should be appreciated that an applicant may file a continuing application even though the "parent" application has resulted in an issued patent itself. Even in circumstances where the USPTO examiner has allowed all of the claims of a patent application to issue, the inventor may nonetheless file a continuing application. He may do so in order to obtain broader claims, to obtain claims that more closely track his competitor's products, or for any other reason. The following opinion discusses continuing applications in greater detail.

2. **Divisional Applications.** The Patent Act provides for divisional applications at § 121, which reads in part:

If two or more independent and distinct inventions are claimed in one application, the Director may require the application to be restricted to one of the inventions. If the other invention is made the subject of a divisional application which complies with the requirements of section 120 of this title it shall be entitled to the benefit of the filing date of the original application.

The restriction requirement serves several distinct purposes. Easily the most important is the maintenance of the integrity of the Patent and Trademark

Office's fee structure. Otherwise, applicants would be sorely tempted to cut their prosecution costs by claiming several different inventions in one application. The PTO also desires to limit the size of a particular patent instrument and to ensure that examiners may confine their search and examination efforts to a particular technological art.

3. Continuation-in-Part Applications. Another sort of continuing application is the so-called "continuation-in-part" or CIP. Such applications rely to some extent upon the disclosure of a parent application. However, they also contain so-called "new matter" not disclosed in the earlier application. Continuation-in-part applications thus have two or more effective filing dates. Claims in the continuation-in-part application that were present in the parent application, or were first included in the continuation-in-part application but are supported entirely by the parent application's disclosure, are entitled to the filing date of the parent application. Otherwise, they must rely upon the later filing date of the continuation-in-part application.

4. Request for Continued Examination. Finally, an applicant who is dissatisfied with an applicant's "final rejection" may file an RCE, or Request for Continued Examination. Congress established RCEs via the American Inventors Protection Act of 1999. Codified at 35 U.S.C.A. § 132(b), the RCE typically allows an applicant to obtain one additional review of an amendment by the same examiner with a minimum of delay and paperwork. It should be appreciated that an RCE is not considered an entirely new or continuation application.

5. Controversy Concerning Continuing Applications. Continued applications are widely used in modern patent practice. In 2006, about 29.4% of the applications filed at the USPTO were continued applications, as compared to approximately 18.9% in 1990 and approximately 11.4% in 1980. Furthermore, the relevant provisions of the Patent Act place no numerical limits upon the number of continued applications that may be filed. Many existing U.S. patents have relied upon a chain of four, five, or even greater number of continuations, CIPs, and RCEs.

Despite their increased use, continuing applications have been subject to criticism. Mark Lemley and Kimberly Moore, then members of the Berkeley and George Mason law school faculties respectively,* stated that continuing application practice has introduced a number of deleterious consequences into the patent law:

First, at a minimum, continuation practice introduces substantial delay and uncertainty into the lives of a patentee's competitors, who cannot know whether a patent application is pending in most circumstances. Second, the structure of the PTO suggests that continuations may well succeed in "wearing down" the examiner, so that the applicant obtains a broad patent not because he deserves one, but because the examiner has neither incentive nor will to hold out any longer. Third, continuation practice can be—and has been—used strategically to gain advantages over competitors

---

* Professor Lemley has since joined the faculty of the Stanford Law School, while Professor Moore has been appointed as a Circuit Judge of the United States Court of Appeals for the Federal Circuit.

by waiting to see what product the competitor will make, and then drafting patent claims specifically designed to cover that product. Finally, some patentees have used continuation practice to delay the issuance of their patent precisely in order to surprise a mature industry, a process known as "submarine patenting."

Mark A. Lemley & Kimberly A. Moore, *Ending Abuse of Patent Continuations*, 84 B.U. L. REV. 65 (2004).

Itself expressing concerns over perceived abuses of continuing application practice, the PTO proposed new rules that would limit the number of continuing applications that could be filed, absent a petition and showing by the patent applicant of the need for such applications. *See* Department of Commerce, Patent and Trademark Office, Final Rule *Change to Practice for Continued Examination Filings, Patent Applications Containing Patentably Indistinct Claims, and Examination of Claims in Patent Applications*, 72 FED. REG. 46,716 (Aug. 21, 2007). The USPTO rules concerning claims and continued applications proved immediately controversial. Some patent professionals expressed considerable concerns that the rules would make the process of patent acquisition more costly, impede the ability of innovators to protect their inventions adequately, and ultimately harm innovation. Some have also opined that the rules are inconsistent with the provisions of the governing patent legislation, the Patent Act of 1952. These criticisms of the USPTO rules have led to legal challenges before the U.S. District Court for the Eastern District of Virginia. The result was the decision in *Tafas v. Dudas*, 541 F.Supp.2d 805 (E.D. Va. 2008) that that enjoined the USPTO from implementing its new rules. The *Tafas v. Dudas* litigation is proceeding through the appeals process at the time of the publication of this casebook.

§ 10.1[c]　U.S. PATENT APPEAL AND PETITION PRACTICE

An impasse between examiner and applicant results in either a petition to the Director or an appeal to the Board of Patent Appeals and Interferences, 35 U.S.C.A. § 134. As explained in *In re Searles*, 422 F.2d 431, 435 (CCPA 1970):

> Decisions of the examiner directly relating to the rejection of claims are subject to appeal. These questions generally deal with the merits of the invention, involving factual determinations and the legal conclusions drawn therefrom regarding the application disclosure, the claims and the prior art. The examiner's rulings dealing with procedural matters, such as whether an affidavit or amendment is untimely, and formal requirements, such as whether a new application title will be required, are reviewable upon petition.

Prior to 1984, the PTO housed both a Board of Appeals and Board of Interferences; these entities were merged in order to streamline interference proceedings and minimize jurisdictional disputes. The Board consists of a number of experienced examiners, currently titled "Administrative Patent Judges," who ordinarily sit in panels of three. *See* 35 U.S.C.A. § 6. The Board is required to provide opinions sufficiently thorough to satisfy Rule 52(a) of the Federal Rules of Civil Procedure. *See Gechter v. Davidson*, 116 F.3d 1454 (Fed.Cir.1997). The Federal Circuit clarified the relationship between the Board and the Director as follows:

> Even though Board members serve an essential function, they are but examiner-employees of the PTO, and the ultimate authority regarding the granting of patents lies with the [Director]. For example, if the Board rejects an application, the [Director] can control the PTO's position in any appeal through the Solicitor of the PTO; the Board cannot demand that the Solicitor attempt to sustain the Board's position. Conversely, if the Board approves an application, the [Director] has the option of refusing to sign a patent; an action which would be subject to a mandamus action by the applicant. The [Director] has an obligation to refuse to grant a patent if he believes that doing so would be contrary to law. The foregoing evidences that the Board is merely the highest level of the Examining Corps, and like all other members of the Examining Corps, the Board operates subject to the [Director]'s overall ultimate authority and responsibility.

In re Alappat, 33 F.3d 1526, 1535 (Fed.Cir.1994) (*in banc*).

An unsuccessful petitioner may seek judicial review through a number of mechanisms, including the Administrative Procedure Act, 5 U.S.C.A. §§ 701–706; the All Writs Act, 28 U.S.C.A. § 1651; or a civil action against the Director under 28 U.S.C.A. § 1338(a). Such actions may be brought in any United States district court, with the Federal Circuit as the court of second instance. The choice of fora from an adverse decision of the Board is more limited: the applicant must bring a civil action against the Director in the United States District Court for the District of Columbia, 35 U.S.C.A. § 145, or file an appeal at the Court of Appeals for the Federal Circuit, 35 U.S.C.A. § 141. The primary advantage of the former route is that the applicant may submit new evidence into the record, an option unavailable at the Federal Circuit. Appeals from suits lodged in the D.C. District Court under § 145 go to the Federal Circuit as well.

§ 10.1[d] PUBLICATION OF PENDING APPLICATIONS

The U.S. PTO traditionally maintained pending patent applications in confidence. Patents were published only on the date that they issued. However, the American Inventors Protection Act changed this long-standing principle, to some degree aligning U.S. practice with global norms. One of the titles of the American Inventors Protection Act, the Domestic Publication of Foreign Filed Patent Applications Act of 1999, now requires the PTO Director to publish certain pending patent applications promptly after the expiration of 18 months from the earliest filing date to which they are entitled. Significantly, not all applications will be published prior to their issuance. If an applicant certifies that the invention disclosed in the U.S. application will not be the subject of a patent application in another country that requires publication of applications 18 months after filing, then the PTO will not publish the application. *See* 35 U.S.C. § 122(b).

Some background into international and comparative patent law will assist understanding of this provision. First, there is no global patent system. Patent rights must be applied for and secured in each jurisdiction. In a world where technology knows no borders and international trade increasingly dominates, patent protection in a single country is often insufficient to protect inventors.

In recognition of these realities, the United States has long been a signatory of the Paris Convention for the Protection of Industrial Property. This treaty attempts to ease the burdens of maintaining patent rights in many jurisdictions. Among the chief provisions of the Paris Convention is the so-called priority right. The priority right allows patent applicants to benefit from an earlier filing date in a foreign country. So long as an inventor files abroad within one year of his first filing and complies with certain formalities, his subsequent foreign filings will be treated as if they were made as of the date of his initial filing.

A second important background principle is that foreign patent offices ordinarily publish patent applications 18 months after their first effective filing date. As an example, suppose that an inventor filed an application at the U.S. PTO on June 1, 2006. Suppose further that the inventor sought patent rights in Germany, which is also a signatory to the Paris Convention. If the inventor files a German patent application by June 1, 2007, his application will be treated as having been filed on the U.S. filing date of June 1, 2006. The German Patent Office will publish the German application on December 1, 2007, 18 months after the first effective filing date to which the inventor is entitled.

In contrast to overseas regimes, the U.S. patent system for many years maintained all applications in secrecy. This regime advantaged patent applicants because it allowed them to understand the scope of any allowed claims before disclosing an invention. Thus, applicants retained the final option to issue the allowed claims or to abandon the application and retain their invention as a trade secret.

However, this secrecy regime has been perceived as imposing costs as well. Others might well engage in repetitive research efforts during the pendency of patent applications, unaware that an earlier inventor had already staked a claim to that technology. Without publication of applications, inventors could also commence litigation on the very day a patent issues, without any degree of notice to the rest of the technological community.

The Domestic Publication of Foreign Filed Patent Applications Act of 1999 attempts to strike a middle ground. U.S. patent applications will be published 18 months from the date of filing, except where the inventor represents that he will not seek patent protection abroad. In effect, the Act calls for the publication of applications domestically only when their foreign counterparts would be published prior to grant anyway. To discourage applicants from delaying their claims of foreign priority under the Paris Convention, the Act allows the PTO Director to consider the failure of the applicant to file a timely claim for priority as a waiver of such claim.

Sometimes inventors seek more robust patent protection in some countries than in others. This step may be taken for business reasons or due to differences in the patent or competition laws in varying jurisdictions. The Domestic Publication of Foreign Filed Patent Applications Act therefore contains a provision allowing applicants to "submit a redacted copy of the application filed in the Patent and Trademark Office eliminating any part or description of the invention in such application that is not also contained in any of the corresponding application filed in a foreign country." As a result, if an applicant seeks broader patent protection in the United States than in other countries, only the more limited version of the application will be published here.

This Act also creates so-called provisional rights that may attach to published patent applications. Provisional rights are equivalent to a reasonable royalty, the amount that the patentee would have charged an infringer had the two parties entered into a licensing arrangement at the time the infringement began. Persons who employ the invention as claimed in the published patent application are potentially liable for this amount. Provisional rights are subject to several qualifications. They are only effective at such time as the patent issues, apply only when the infringer had actual notice of the published patent application and the claims of the published application are "substantially identical" to those of the issued patent.

An example may clarify the workings of provisional rights. Suppose that an inventor files a U.S. patent application on February 1, 2008. Assuming the inventor does not file the appropriate certification, the PTO will publish the application 18 months later, on August 1, 2009. Suppose further that this application results in an issued patent that the PTO formally grants on June 1, 2010. Under these facts, the inventor may file a patent infringement suit on or after June 1, 2010. Assuming the statutory requirements are fulfilled, the inventor may claim provisional rights equivalent to a reasonable royalty from August 1, 2009, the date the application was published, through June 1, 2010, the date the patent was granted. Infringing acts that occur after June 1, 2010, will be subject to the full range of remedies under the Patent Act of 1952, including an injunction and damages based upon the lost profits of the patentee.

§ 10.1[e] PATENT TERM

Once the Patent and Trademark Office issues a patent, that patent enjoys an effective term established by the statute. The publication of the book finds United States patent law in a transition period regarding patent term. Formerly, patents extended for 17 years from the date the patent issued. *See generally* C. Michael White, *Why a Seventeen Year Patent,* 38 J. PAT. OFF. SOC'Y 839 (1956). As a result of the Uruguay Round Agreements Act (URAA), however, patents endure for 20 years from the date that the patent application was filed. As noted in *Merck & Co., Inc. v. Kessler,* 80 F.3d 1543, 1547–48 (Fed.Cir.1996):

> The purpose of the URAA was not to extend patent terms, although it has that effect in some cases, but to harmonize the term provision of United States patent law with that of our leading trading partners which grant a patent term of 20 years from the date of filing of the patent application. Prior to June 8, 1995, U.S. patents had an expiration date under 35 U.S.C. § 154 measured as 17 years from the date the patent issued, except where terminal disclaimers were filed. Amended section 154(a) now reads:

> > Subject to the payment of fees under this title, such grant shall be for a term beginning on the date on which the patent issues and ending 20 years from the date on which the application for the patent was filed in the United States or, if the application contains a specific reference to an earlier filed application or applications under section 120, 121, or 365(c) of this title, from the date on which the earliest such application was filed.

35 U.S.C. § 154(a)(2) (1994).

For certain patents which were issued and for pending applications which were filed prior to June 8, 1995, a transitional provision preserves a guaranteed 17–year term, if it is longer than 20 years from filing, by the following provision:

> The term of a patent that is in force on or that results from an application filed before the date that is 6 months after the date of the enactment of the Uruguay Round Agreements Act shall be the greater of the 20–year term as provided in subsection (1), or 17 years from grant, subject to any terminal disclaimers.

Id. at § 154(c)(1). Patents in the section 154(c)(1) category thus are entitled to keep or to enjoy the 17–year term from issuance of the patent or a 20–year from filing term, whichever is longer.

Although the distinction between the two regimes may not appear to loom particularly large, significant consequences flow from United States adoption of a twenty-year patent term measured from the filing date. Prior to June 8, 1995, the filing of continuing applications did not affect the length of the effective patent term. Once the patent issued, it obtained a seventeen-year term. Currently, the term of a patent is measured as twenty years from the earliest filing date. The new term scheme puts an end to so-called "submarine" patents that plagued particular industries in the United States. Submarine patents emerged from a series of concealed continuation applications, sometimes filed thirty or more years earlier, to "torpedo" industries that had developed in ignorance of the pending applications.

Several significant qualifications exist to the twenty-year rule. First, under § 154(b), patentees may obtain term extensions of up to five years due to delays caused by the declaration of an interference, the imposition of secrecy order, or the successful pursuit of an appeal to the Board of Patent Appeals and Interferences or federal court. Second, the term of a patent may also be extended under § 156, a provision of the Hatch–Waxman Act. This complex statute authorizes increased patent terms on inventions that have been subject to a lengthy pre-market approval process under the Federal Food, Drug and Cosmetic Act.

Third, enjoyment of the full patent term is subject to the payment of maintenance fees. Currently, a patent expires after four, eight, or twelve years if maintenance fees are not timely paid on each occasion. As only about 33% of the patents issued in the United States are maintained beyond their eleventh year, maintenance fees effectively dedicate a great deal of patented technology into the public domain.

Finally, the Patent Term Guarantee Act of 1999 provides certain deadlines that, if not met by the PTO, result in an automatic extension of the term of individual patents. The most significant of these deadlines appear to be fourteen months for a First Office Action and four months for a subsequent Office Action. As well, the prosecution of an original patent application must be complete within three years of the actual U.S. filing date, with exceptions granted for continuing applications and appeals. The Director is charged with calculating any patent term extensions that might result from missed PTO deadlines.

Patent term has been of considerable interest to economists, who have long pondered what the optimal patent duration should be. Because different industries are marked by varying environments of technological growth, some scholars have concluded that patent term should be adjusted on an industry-by-industry basis. A good introduction to the economic literature may be found in W. NORDHAUS, INVENTION, GROWTH AND ECONOMIC WELFARE (1969), and F.M. Scherer, *Nordhaus's Theory of Optimal Patent Life: A Geometric Reinterpretation*, 62 AM. ECON. REV. 422 (1972).

§ 10.1[f]   PATENT PROSECUTION ABROAD

In addition to understanding the basics of domestic prosecution procedures, patent attorneys are well advised to possess some grasp of the practice of other national and regional patent offices. Inventors increasingly seek protection outside the United States and often request that domestic patent counsel coordinate these efforts. Although United States practitioners ordinarily engage knowledgeable overseas associates as part of this effort, some sense of the differences among the world's patent offices will allow more efficient interaction with colleagues abroad as well as more competent client representation.

Unlike many other patent offices, the U.S. system allows for essentially unlimited prosecution—at least until twenty years passes from the filing date, when no patent rights could possibly accrue from the application. Most other patent systems are not so generous: if an impasse is reached, the proper route is to begin an appeal of the examiner's final decision, not to attempt to reinitiate dialogue by paying an additional fee and filing a continuation application.

A notable aspect of patent practice in other nations, particularly in Japan and Germany, is that the actual prior art search and examination is automatically deferred following submission of an application. Rather than examine every submitted application, certain patent offices instead merely publish the application. Applicants, and sometimes third parties, seeking an actual examination must submit additional requests for a search and then an examination. Such requests must occur within a specified time and be accompanied by the appropriate fee. Deferred examination systems may be justified in that they allow applicants to further postpone their decision to pursue patent coverage or not, but they often are adopted in order to increase patent office revenues and reduce agency backlogs. Note that the PTO does allow examination to be deferred for short periods in cases of "good and sufficient cause"; for example, where the applicant lacks funds to continue the prosecution. *See* 37 C.F.R. § 1.103.

The United States remains unique in its mandate that the actual inventor or inventors file the patent application, rather than the assignee of the inventor. The result in the United States is that most applications are filed by the inventors' assignees—usually their employer—in the name of the inventors. Foreign patent offices avoid this complexity by allowing assignee filing. Although the U.S. rule may appear strictly procedural, it sometimes leads to unusual substantive consequences, particularly with respect to the best mode requirement. It also renders the filing of applications more burdensome, with minimal perceived benefits towards upholding the individual rights of inventors. The 1992 Advisory Commission Report recommended that the United States adopt assignee filing along with certain procedural obligations designed to safeguard the interests of inventor-assignors. *See* The Advisory Commis-

SION ON PATENT LAW REFORM, A REPORT TO THE SECRETARY OF COMMERCE 179–81 (1992).

§ 10.2 INVENTORSHIP

Section 102(f) requires that the patentee be the actual inventor of the patented technology. In keeping with this substantive law, the Patent Act and judicial opinions have consistently required that patents and applications identify the true inventors of the technology set forth. *See* 35 U.S.C.A. § 111; *Kennedy v. Hazelton*, 128 U.S. 667 (1888). The following opinion not only introduces inventorship concepts, it also illustrates their extraordinary significance.

ETHICON, INC. v. UNITED STATES SURGICAL CORP.

United States Court of Appeals, Federal Circuit, 1998
135 F.3d 1456

Before Newman, Circuit Judge, Skelton, Senior Circuit Judge, and Rader, Circuit Judge.

RADER, CIRCUIT JUDGE.

In this patent infringement action, Dr. InBae Yoon (Yoon) and his exclusive licensee, Ethicon, Inc. (Ethicon), appeal from the judgment of the United States District Court for the District of Connecticut. In 1989, Yoon and Ethicon sued United States Surgical Corporation (U.S. Surgical) for infringement of U.S. Patent No. 4,535,773 (the '773 patent). In 1993, the parties stipulated to the intervention of Mr. Young Jae Choi (Choi) as defendant-intervenor. Choi claimed to be an omitted co-inventor of the '773 patent and to have granted U.S. Surgical a retroactive license under that patent. On U.S. Surgical's motion to correct inventorship of the '773 patent under 35 U.S.C. § 256, the district court ruled that Choi was an omitted co-inventor of two claims, and subsequently granted U.S. Surgical's motion to dismiss the infringement complaint. Because the district court's determination of co-inventorship was correct, and because Choi is a joint owner of the '773 patent who has not consented to suit against U.S. Surgical, this court affirms.

I. BACKGROUND

The '773 patent relates to trocars, an essential tool for endoscopic surgery. A trocar is a surgical instrument which makes small incisions in the wall of a body cavity, often the abdomen, to admit endoscopic instruments. Trocars include a shaft within an outer sleeve. One end of the shaft has a sharp blade. At the outset of surgery, the surgeon uses the blade to puncture the wall and extend the trocar into the cavity. The surgeon then removes the shaft, leaving the hollow outer sleeve, through which the surgeon may insert tiny cameras and surgical instruments for the operation.

Conventional trocars, however, pose a risk of damage to internal organs or structures. As the trocar blade punctures the cavity wall, the sudden loss of resistance can cause the blade to lunge forward and injure an internal organ. The '773 patent claims a trocar that alleviates this danger. In one embodiment, the invention equips the trocar with a blunt, spring-loaded rod. As the trocar pierces the cavity wall, the rod automatically springs forward to precede the blade and shield against injury. A second embodiment has a retractable trocar blade that springs back into a protective sheath when it passes through the cavity wall. The patent also teaches the use of an electronic sensor in the end of the blade to signal the surgeon at the moment of puncture.

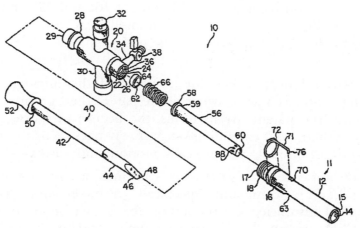

Yoon is a medical doctor and inventor of numerous patented devices for endoscopic surgery. In the late 1970s, Yoon began to conceive of a safety device to prevent accidental injury during trocar incisions. Yoon also conceived of a device to alert the surgeon when the incision was complete. In 1980, Yoon met Choi, an electronics technician, who had some college training in physics, chemistry, and electrical engineering, but no college degree. Choi had worked in the research and development of electronic devices. After Choi had demonstrated to Yoon some of the devices he had developed, Yoon asked Choi to work with him on several projects, including one for safety trocars. Choi was not paid for his work.

In 1982, after collaborating for approximately eighteen months, their relationship ended. Choi believed that Yoon found his work unsatisfactory and unlikely to produce any marketable product. For these reasons, Choi withdrew from cooperation with Yoon.

In the same year, however, Yoon filed an application for a patent disclosing various embodiments of a safety trocar. Without informing Choi, Yoon named himself as the sole inventor. In 1985, the Patent and Trademark Office issued the '773 patent to Yoon, with fifty-five claims. Yoon thereafter granted an exclusive license under this patent to Ethicon. Yoon did not inform Choi of the patent application or issuance.

In 1989, Ethicon filed suit against U.S. Surgical for infringement of claims 34 and 50 of the '773 patent. In 1992, while this suit was still pending, U.S. Surgical became aware of Choi, and contacted him regarding his involvement in Yoon's safety trocar project. When Choi confirmed his role in the safety trocar project, U.S. Surgical obtained from Choi a "retroactive license" to practice "Choi's trocar related inventions." Under the license, Choi agreed to assist U.S. Surgical in any suit regarding the '773 patent. For its part, U.S. Surgical agreed to pay Choi contingent on its ultimate ability to continue to practice and market the invention. With the license in hand, U.S. Surgical moved to correct inventorship of the '773 patent under 35 U.S.C. § 256, claiming that Choi was a co-inventor of claims 23, 33, 46, and 47. Following an extensive hearing, the district court granted U.S. Surgical's motion, finding that Choi had contributed to the subject matter of claims 33 and 47.

U.S. Surgical next moved for dismissal of the infringement suit, arguing that Choi, as a joint owner of the patent, had granted it a valid license under the patent. By its terms, the license purported to grant rights to use the patent extending retroactively back to its issuance. The district court granted U.S. Surgical's motion and dismissed the suit.

Ethicon appeals the district court's finding of co-inventorship and its dismissal of the complaint. Specifically, Ethicon contends that (1) Choi supplied insufficient corroboration for his testimony of co-invention; (2) Choi presented insufficient evidence to show co-invention of claims 33 and 47 clearly and convincingly; [and] (4) the terms of the license agreement limit it to only that part of the invention to which Choi contributed, not the entire patent.

II. CO-INVENTORSHIP

Patent issuance creates a presumption that the named inventors are the true and only inventors. *See Hess v. Advanced Cardiovascular Sys., Inc.*, 106 F.3d 976, 980 (Fed. Cir. 1997). Inventorship is a question of law, which this court reviews without deference. *See Sewall v. Walters*, 21 F.3d 411, 415 (Fed.Cir.1994). However, this court reviews the underlying findings of fact which uphold a district court's inventorship determination for clear error.

A patented invention may be the work of two or more joint inventors. *See* 35 U.S.C. § 116 (1994). Because "[c]onception is the touchstone of inventorship," each joint inventor must generally contribute to the conception of the invention. *Burroughs Wellcome Co. v. Barr Lab., Inc.*, 40 F.3d 1223, 1227–28 (Fed.Cir.1994). "Conception is the 'formation in the mind of the inventor, of a definite and permanent idea of the complete and operative invention, as it is hereafter to be applied in practice.'" *Hybritech, Inc. v. Monoclonal Antibodies, Inc.*, 802 F.2d 1367, 1376 (Fed.Cir.1986) (quoting 1 *Robinson on Patents* 532 (1890)). An idea is sufficiently "definite and permanent" when "only ordinary skill would be necessary to reduce the invention to practice, without extensive research or experimentation." *Burroughs Wellcome*, 40 F.3d at 1228.

The conceived invention must include every feature of the subject matter claimed in the patent. Nevertheless, for the conception of a joint invention, each of the joint inventors need not "make the same type or amount of contribution" to the invention. 35 U.S.C. § 116. Rather, each needs to perform only a part of the task which produces the invention. On the other hand, one does not qualify as a joint inventor by merely assisting the actual inventor after conception of the claimed invention. One who simply provides the inventor with well-known principles or explains the state of the art without ever having "a firm and definite idea" of the claimed combination as a whole does not qualify as a joint inventor. *See Hess*, 106 F.3d at 981 (citing *O'Reilly v. Morse*, 56 U.S. (15 How.) 62, 111, 14 L.Ed. 601 (1853)). Moreover, depending on the scope of a patent's claims, one of ordinary skill in the art who simply reduced the inventor's idea to practice is not necessarily a joint inventor, even if the specification discloses that embodiment to satisfy the best mode requirement.

Furthermore, a co-inventor need not make a contribution to every claim of a patent. *See* 35 U.S.C. § 116. A contribution to one claim is enough. Thus, the critical question for joint conception is who conceived, as that term is used in the patent law, the subject matter of the claims at issue.

35 U.S.C. § 256 provides that a co-inventor omitted from an issued patent may be added to the patent by a court "before which such matter is called in question." To show co-inventorship, however, the alleged co-inventor or co-inventors must prove their contribution to the conception of the claims by clear and convincing evidence. However, "an inventor's testimony respecting the facts surrounding a claim of derivation or priority of invention cannot, standing alone, rise to the level of clear and convincing proof." *Price v. Symsek*, 988 F.2d 1187, 1194 (Fed.Cir.1993). The rule is the same for an alleged co-inventor's testimony. Thus, an alleged co-inventor must supply evidence to corroborate his testimony. Whether the inventor's testimony has been sufficiently corroborated is evaluated under a "rule of reason" analysis. Under this analysis, "[a]n evaluation of *all* pertinent evidence must be made so that a sound determination of the credibility of the [alleged] inventor's story may be reached."

Corroborating evidence may take many forms. Often contemporaneous documents prepared by a putative inventor serve to corroborate an inventor's testimony. Circumstantial evidence about the inventive process may also corroborate. Additionally, oral testimony of someone other than the alleged inventor may corroborate.

A. Claim 33

The district court determined that Choi contributed to the conception of the subject matter of claim 33. Claim 33 (with emphasis to highlight relevant elements) reads:

[Margin notes: Dont have to make same contribution. But needs to be more than just assistance. Cant be well know principles or just building it for inventor. 116 - only need contribution to one claim. 256 - allows co-inventor to be added. Prove conception w/ clear and convincing evidence. Need corroborative evidence. Evidence has many forms.]

(Claim 33)

A surgical instrument for providing communication through an anatomical organ structure, comprising:

means having an abutment member and *shaft longitudinally accommodatable within an outer sleeve,* longitudinal movement of said shaft inside said sleeve being limited by contact of said abutment member with said sleeve, said shaft having a distal end with a distal blade surface tapering into a sharp distal point, *said distal blade surface being perforated along one side by an aperture,* for puncturing an anatomical organ structure when subjected to force along the longitudinal axis of said shaft;

means having a blunt distal bearing surface, slidably extending through said aperture, for reciprocating through said aperture while said abutment member is in stationary contact with said sleeve;

means positionable between said puncturing means and said reciprocating means for biasing a distal section of said reciprocating means to protrude beyond said aperture and permitting said distal section of said reciprocating means to recede into said aperture when said bearing surface is subject to force along its axis . . .; and

means connectible to the proximal end of said puncturing means *for* responding to longitudinal movement of said reciprocating means relative to said puncturing means and *creating a sensible signal* having one state upon recision of said distal section of said reciprocating means into said aperture and another state upon protrusion of said distal section of said reciprocating means from said aperture.

To determine whether Choi made a contribution to the conception of the subject matter of claim 33, this court must determine what Choi's contribution was and then whether that contribution's role appears in the claimed invention. If Choi in fact contributed to the invention defined by claim 33, he is a joint inventor of that claim.

Figures 18 and 19 of the '773 patent illustrate an embodiment of claim 33. These figures show a trocar blade with an aperture through which a blunt rod can extend. When the trocar blade penetrates the inner wall of a cavity, a spring releases the rod, which juts out past the end of the trocar blade and prevents the blade from cutting further. The embodiment also includes a structure that gives the surgeon aural and visual signals when the blade nears penetration.

Yoon conceived of blunt probe but Choi conceived of

The district court found that Yoon conceived of the use of a blunt probe. However, the court found that Choi conceived of and thereby contributed two features contained in the embodiment shown in figures 18 and 19: first, Choi conceived of locating the blunt probe in the trocar shaft and allowing it to pass through an aperture in the blade surface; second, Choi conceived of the "means . . . for . . . creating a sensible signal."

If Choi did indeed conceive of "locating the blunt probe in the shaft and allowing it to pass through an aperture in the blade surface," he contributed to the subject matter of claim 33. Claim 33 requires that the "distal blade surface" be "perforated along one side by an aperture" and requires the "shaft" to be "longitudinally accommodatable within [the] outer sleeve." Properly construed, claim 33 includes the elements that Choi contributed to the invention according to the district court's findings.

In making this finding, the district court relied extensively on Choi's testimony. Choi testified that the idea of extending the blunt probe through an aperture in the trocar blade itself was his idea. To corroborate this testimony, Choi produced a series of sketches he created while working with Yoon. One sketch shows a probe inside the shaft of a trocar blade, extending through an opening in the side of the end of the blade.

To rebut Choi's showing, Yoon presented a drawing dated July 1973, which disclosed elements of claim 33. The district court determined, however, that Dr. Yoon had altered this drawing. In fact, according to the district court, it had originally depicted a device from an entirely different patent. Due to its suspicious origins, the trial court rejected it as unreliable.

The court also discounted Yoon's testimony for lack of credibility. Indeed the record supports the trial court's conclusion that Yoon altered and backdated documents to make it appear that he had independently invented trocars, shields, and electronics. Moreover, Yoon's trial testimony clashed with his earlier deposition testimony. For instance, before learning of Choi's role in the case, Yoon falsely testified at his deposition that (1) he had worked with Choi as early as 1975 and (2) the sketches at issue in this case had been drawn completely by him. However, the two did not meet until 1980, and when later questioned about authorship of the documents, Yoon replied, "If I said [that] at that time, then maybe I was confused." The district court justifiably discounted Yoon's testimony.

In sum, after full consideration of the relevant evidence, the district court determined that Choi conceived part of the invention recited in claim 33. This court detects no cause to reverse this determination.

B. Claim 47

The district court also determined that Choi contributed to the conception of the subject matter of claim 47. Claim 47 (with emphasis to highlight relevant elements) reads:

A surgical instrument for providing communication through an anatomical organ structure, comprising:

means having an elongate shaft exhibiting a longitudinal axis and terminating in a sharp, distal end, for puncturing the cavity wall of an anatomical organ structure;

means borne by said puncturing means distal end for converting counterforce exerted by said cavity wall against said distal end into transmissible energy;

means connected to said converting means for conveying said transmissible energy toward the proximal end of said puncturing means;

means having an interior bore coaxially aligned with the longitudinal axis of said shaft for receiving said puncturing means proximal end;

means for biasing said puncturing means proximal end to withdraw into said interior bore;

means interposed between said puncturing means proximal end and said interior bore assuming a normally protruding position for detaining said puncturing means proximal end extended from said interior cavity in opposition to said biasing means.

To determine whether Choi made a contribution to the conception of the subject matter of claim 47, this court must determine what Choi's contribution was and then construe the claim language to determine if Choi's contribution found its way into the defined invention.

Figures 34, 35, and 36 illustrate the invention in claim 47. In these embodiments, a cocked spring pulls the trocar back into a protective sheath as soon as the blade has punctured the inner wall. Release of the detaining means triggers the retracting spring action. The two detaining means disclosed in the specification are (1) a detent extending radially outward from the trocar through a hole in the sheath and (2) a rod extending horizontally from the proximal end of the trocar that butts against an off-center, but slidable, bar with a hole in its center. In the case of the detent detaining means, when a sensor detects that the trocar blade has pierced the wall of a cavity, the plunger of a solenoid pushes the detent out of the hole in the sheath. In the case of the rod detaining means, the solenoid plunger positions the bar so that the hole in its center aligns with the rod.

The district court concluded that Yoon generally invented the retractable trocar, but that Choi invented both of the detaining means disclosed in the specification. In addition to oral testimony of the parties, the district court cited Choi's sketches, one of which clearly shows the rod detaining means. However, the sketch in which the district court would find the detent detaining means appears to work differently than the embodiment described in the '773 patent. Instead of a detent that extends radially outward through a hole in the sheath, the sketch illustrates the use of the solenoid plunger itself as a detent, extending radially *inward* through a hole in the sheath. Thus, the record does not show that Choi contributed to the detent detaining means. Therefore, this court affirms the district court's finding that Choi contributed the rod detaining means, but determines that the trial court clearly erred in finding that Choi contributed the detent detaining means.

In this instance, however, claim 47 recites a "means . . . for [detaining]." The use of the word "means" gives rise to "a presumption that the inventor used the term advisedly to invoke the statutory mandates for means-plus-function clauses." *York Prods., Inc. v. Central Tractor Farm & Family Ctr.*, 99 F.3d 1568, 1574 (Fed.Cir.1996). Although the presumption is not conclusive, the means language here invokes the interpretation regimens of section 112, paragraph 6. Thus applying section 112, paragraph 6 to interpret this claim, the language adopted the two structures in the specification to define the means for detaining.

Choi showed contribution to one of these alternative structures. The contributor of any disclosed means of a means-plus-function claim element is a joint inventor as to that claim, unless one asserting sole inventorship can show that the contribution of that means was simply a reduction to practice of the sole inventor's broader concept. Although the district court found that Yoon first conceived of a retractable trocar generally, Yoon did not show that Choi's contribution was simply a reduction to practice of the broader concept of using any detaining means commensurate with the scope of claim 47. Thus, Choi showed entitlement to the status of co-inventor for this claim as well.

[handwritten margin note: Choi—co-inventor here also]

C.   Corroboration

As corroboration for his testimony of co-invention, Choi proffers sketches of his work. These sketches were in Yoon's possession since their creation. The parties do not dispute, however, that Choi in fact created the sketches. Instead, Yoon contends that he first disclosed the invention to Choi, who then made the sketches to illustrate what he learned from Yoon. Absent sufficient corroboration, inventorship would turn solely on a credibility contest between Yoon and Choi. The district court, however, found sufficient corroboration.

[handwritten margin note: Choi offers sketches in Yoon's possession]

Taken together, the alleged co-inventor's testimony and the corroborating evidence must show inventorship "by clear and convincing evidence." This requirement is not to be taken lightly. Under the "rule of reason" standard for corroborating evidence, the trial court must consider corroborating evidence in context, make necessary credibility determinations, and assign appropriate probative weight to the evidence to determine whether clear and convincing evidence supports a claim of co-inventorship.

In this case, Choi's sketches show the invention. The parties agree that Choi made the sketches. The contest involves whether Choi conceived of the material in the sketches or merely drew what Yoon conceived. The district court noted many circumstantial factors further corroborating Choi's conception claim: (1) Yoon's need for a person with expertise in electronics; (2) Choi's background in electronics, (3) Yoon's proposal that he and Choi should work together to develop new

[handwritten margin note: circumstantial factors]

products, including safety trocars, (4) their informal business relationship, (5) the length of time they worked together, (6) the absence of any pay to Choi for his work, (7) the similarity between Choi's sketches and the patent figures, and (8) the letter in which Choi stated that he could no longer be a "member" of Yoon's business. Additionally, U.S. Surgical introduced expert testimony that some of the sketches dealt with sophisticated concepts that only an electrical engineer or technician would understand. Consequently, the district court found that Choi was presenting ideas to Yoon as the sketches were drawn, rather than the other way around.

On appeal, this court declines to reweigh the evidence. Instead, this court determines that the record shows that corroboration evidence in this case satisfies the "rule of reason." Thus, this court must only further assess whether the district court's factual conclusions, given the clear and convincing evidence standard, were clearly erroneous. Here, given the sketches, Choi's testimony, and the established circumstances, in contrast with Yoon's testimony, expressly found to lack credibility by the trial court, this court discerns no clear error.

In reaching this determination, this court has also considered alleged inconsistencies in Choi's testimony. In August 1992, U.S. Surgical's counsel first sent Choi a copy of the '773 patent. Choi circled figures and claims describing that which he claimed to have contributed. Choi circled some claims that he does not now assert to have had a role in inventing. He also did not circle claims he now claims to have co-invented. However, the district court could have reasonably found that a layman, untrained in the language of the patent law, may reasonably err in interpreting claim language. Moreover, Choi might well have confused the legal distinction between conception (which justifies a finding of inventorship) and reduction to practice (which does not). In any event, this court affirms the district court's holding that Choi was a co-inventor of claims 33 and 47.

IV.   SCOPE OF THE CHOI–U.S. SURGICAL LICENSE

Questions of patent ownership are distinct from questions of inventorship. In accordance with this principle, this court has nonetheless noted that "an invention presumptively belongs to its creator."

Indeed, in the context of joint inventorship, each co-inventor presumptively owns a *pro rata* undivided interest in the entire patent, no matter what their respective contributions. Several provisions of the Patent Act combine to dictate this rule. 35 U.S.C. § 116, as amended in 1984, states that a joint inventor need not make a contribution "to the subject matter of every claim of the patent." In amending section 116 as to joint inventorship, Congress did not make corresponding modifications as to joint ownership. For example, section 261 continues to provide that "patents shall have the attributes of personal property." This provision suggests that property rights, including ownership, attach to patents as a whole, not individual claims. Moreover, section 262 continues to speak of "joint owners of a patent," not joint owners of a claim. Thus, a joint inventor as to even one claim enjoys a presumption of ownership in the entire patent.

This rule presents the prospect that a co-inventor of only one claim might gain entitlement to ownership of a patent with dozens of claims. As noted, the Patent Act accounts for that occurrence: "Inventors *may* apply for a patent jointly even though ... each did not make a contribution to the subject matter of every claim." 35 U.S.C. § 116 (emphasis added). Thus, where inventors choose to cooperate in the inventive process, their joint inventions may become joint property without some express agreement to the contrary. In this case, Yoon must now effectively share with Choi ownership of all the claims, even those which he invented by himself. Thus, Choi had the power to license rights in the entire patent. [After reviewing the terms of the license between Choi and U.S. Surgical, the majority concluded that Choi had indeed licensed to U.S. Surgical all of his rights as a joint owner.]

Because Choi did not consent to an infringement suit against U.S. Surgical and indeed can no longer consent due to his grant of an exclusive license with its accompanying "right to sue," Ethicon's complaint lacks the participation of a co-owner of the patent. Accordingly, this court must order dismissal of this suit.

VI. Conclusion

Accordingly, the judgment of the United States District Court for the District of Connecticut is affirmed.

Pauline Newman, Circuit Judge, dissenting.

I respectfully dissent, for whether or not Mr. Choi made an inventive contribution to two of the fifty-five claims of the '773 patent, he is not a joint owner of the other fifty-three claims of the patent. Neither the law of joint invention nor the law of property so requires, and indeed these laws mandate otherwise.

A. The Law of Joint Invention

The purpose of the amendment of § 116 was to remedy the increasing technical problems arising in team research, for which existing law, deemed to require simultaneous conception as well as shared contribution by each named inventor to every claim, was producing pitfalls for patentees, to no public purpose. As stated in its legislative history, the amendment to 35 U.S.C. § 116 "recognizes the realities of modern team research." 130 Cong. Rec. 28,069–71 (1984) (statement of Rep. Kastenmeier).

Before 1984 precedent did not permit naming as an inventor a person who did not share in the conception of the invention and who did not contribute to all of the claims of the patent. If different persons made an inventive contribution to various parts of an invention or to different claims of a patent, the legalistic problems that arose were not readily soluble, even by the complex, expensive, and often confusing expedient of filing separate patent applications on separate claims.

The progress of technology exacerbated the inventorship problems. Patents were invalidated simply because all of the named inventors did not contribute to all the claims; and patents were also invalidated when there were contributors to some of the claims who were not named. Indeed, at the time the '773 patent application was filed in 1982, most practitioners believed that a separate application was required if it was desired to present, for example, the two claims that contain Mr. Choi's contribution.

As team research increased with the growth of technology-based industry, so did the dilemma, for the rules of joint inventorship were not readily adaptable to the development of complex inventions. It became apparent that legislative remedy was needed. The amendment of 35 U.S.C. § 116 provided a simple solution to a complex problem:

> § 116 [second sentence]. Inventors may apply for a patent jointly even though (1) they did not physically work together or at the same time, (2) each did not make the same type or amount of contribution, or (3) each did not make a contribution to the subject matter of every claim of the patent.

Pub.L. 98–622, § 104, 98 Stat. 3384, Nov. 8, 1984. The amendment identified the three major pitfalls that had arisen, and removed them.

This amendment did not also deal with the laws of patent ownership, and did not automatically convey ownership of the entire patent to everyone who could now be named as an inventor, whatever the contribution. The amendment simply permitted persons to be named on the patent document, whether as minor contributors to a subordinate embodiment, or full partners in the creation and development of the invention. The ownership relationships among the persons who, under § 116, could now be recognized as contributors to the invention, is irrelevant to the purpose of the amendment of § 116, and to its consequences. Section 116 has nothing to do with patent ownership.

B.   The Law of Joint Ownership

The pre–1984 rule of joint ownership of joint inventions can be readily understood in its historical context, for a legally cognizable "joint invention" required mutuality of interaction and a real partnership in the creation and development of the invention. On this foundation, a "joint inventor" was also, justly and legally, an equal owner of the idea and of any patent thereon.

The law of patent ownership has its roots in the common law of property—although a patent has its own peculiar character, for it deals with intangibles. Certain incidents of patent ownership have been created or clarified by statute, *see* 35 U.S.C. § 262, yet the common law provided the basic rules, as manifested in the concepts of tenancy in common and undivided interests that courts have drawn upon in patent ownership disputes.

The jurisprudence governing property interests is generally a matter of state law. Even when the property is the creation of federal statute, private rights are usually defined by state laws of property. This has long been recognized with respect to patent ownership and transfers. It is equally established that inventorship and patent ownership are separate issues.

Most of the disputes concerning patent ownership that reached the Supreme Court dealt not with joint invention, but assignments and other transfers. The oft-cited case of *Waterman v. Mackenzie*, 138 U.S. 252, 11 S.Ct. 334, 34 L.Ed. 923 (1891) dealt with a dispute among the inventor's spouse and various assignees concerning ownership of the fountain pen patent, not inventorship. Occasionally an issue of ownership of patent property arose based on whether the claimant actually shared fully in the creation of the invention. In such cases, as cited *supra,* the decision on "joint invention" also decided the issue of ownership, for a person who had fully shared in the creation of the invention was deemed to be a joint owner of the entire patent property. On this premise each joint inventor was deemed to occupy the entirety of the patented subject matter, on a legal theory of tenancy in common. *See* 7 Richard R. Powell, *Powell on Real Property* ¶ 602[5] (1997) ("undivided fractional shares held by tenants in common are usually equal and are presumed equal unless circumstances indicate otherwise"). As patent property became viewed more precisely as personal property, *see* 35 U.S.C. § 261, the concept of tenancy in common was adjusted to that of an undivided interest, although with no substantial change in legal rights.

After the major change that the 1984 amendment to § 116 made in "joint invention," by authorizing the naming of any contributor to any claim of a patent, the legal premise that each named person had made a full and equal contribution to the entire patented invention became obsolete. It is not an implementation of the common law of property, or its statutory embodiments, to treat all persons, however minor their contribution, as full owners of the entire property as a matter of law. The law had never given a contributor to a minor portion of an invention a full share in the originator's patent.

By amending § 116 in order to remove an antiquated pitfall whereby patents were being unjustly invalidated, the legislators surely did not intend to create another inequity. Apparently no one foresaw that judges might routinely transfer pre–1984 ownership concepts into the changed inventorship law. I have come upon no discussion of this anomaly in various scholarly articles on the amended § 116.

In the case at bar, the district court recognized that Dr. Yoon originated the fundamental concept and the major aspects of its implementation. The court, however, construed the law as requiring that since Mr. Choi was named as a "joint inventor" (in accordance with the retroactivity legislated for the amendment to § 116) he automatically owned an undivided interest in the entire patent, and had the unencumbered and unfettered right to alienate an interest in the entire patent. Thus Mr. Choi, who would not pass the pre–1984 test of joint inventor, was nonetheless awarded full property rights in the entire invention and patent, as if he had been a true joint inventor of all the claims.

The panel majority, confirming this error, holds that Mr. Choi's contribution to two claims means and requires that Yoon "must now effectively share with Choi ownership of all the claims, even those which he invented by himself." That is incorrect. As I have discussed, the law of shared ownership was founded on shared invention, a situation that admittedly does not here prevail. Whether or not Mr. Choi is now properly named under § 116 because of his contribution to two claims, he is not a joint owner and he does not have the right to grant a license under all fifty-five claims. No theory of the law of property supports such a distortion of ownership rights. Thus I must, respectfully, dissent from the decision of the panel majority.

NOTES

1. Legal Aspects of Inventorship. As demonstrated by *Ethicon v. United States Surgical*, the combination of the liberality of § 116 and the importance of the inventive entity under § 102 can lead to some sophisticated legal strategizing as to which claims to place within a particular patent application. Consider, for example, two inventors, Avo and Bolivar, who have assigned rights to their inventions to their common employer, Xino Ltd. Suppose that Avo files an application directed towards a technology of which he is the sole inventor. Later, Avo and Bolivar jointly develop an obvious variant on Avo's earlier claimed technology and file a patent application with both as named inventors. Still later, Avo's application matures into an issued patent.

Under these circumstances, the patent examiner could properly reject Avo and Bolivar's joint application in light of Avo's prior application, due to the combination of § 102(e) and § 103(a). Xino Ltd. might respond by eliminating all of Bolivar's technical contributions from the claims of the subsequent application. *See* 37 C.F.R. § 1.48(b). With Avo as the sole inventor in both applications, his earlier application no longer comprises a valid § 102(e) reference as it was not filed "by another"—that is, by a different inventive entity. Note that double patenting concerns might arise in such a scenario, however, as described later in this Chapter.

2. Inventorship and the Patent Instrument. Despite the significant consequences that attach to the inventive entity, at present the U.S. patent instrument simply lists all the inventors corresponding to its set of claims. Do you believe that patentees should be required to name the appropriate inventors on a claim-by-claim basis?

3. Practical Aspects of Inventorship. As inventors named in a patent often receive benefits ranging from financial rewards from their employers to recognition from the technical community, intracorporate disputes over inventorship are not uncommon. Patent attorneys must often demonstrate persistence and tact in order to ensure that the appropriate individuals are named in a given patent. They should also be aware of corporate technical disclosure forms and other documents that label a person as the "inventor"; such determinations are often made without awareness of the strictures of the Patent Act.

4. Joint Ownership. *Ethicon v. U.S. Surgical* explains that joint inventors ordinarily become joint owners of any patents resulting from their efforts. Although § 262 invites joint owners to contract their way around the statute, the grant of a patent often acts to turn technological partners into business competitors. Do you find this policy a wise one? Patent law apparently reflects such a strong desire to encourage the commercial development of patented inventions that the courts are willing to enforce mercenary attitudes among patent co-owners. On the other hand, one can readily imagine the sorts of transaction costs that the patent law bluntly sweeps away by allowing any joint owner to exploit or license a patented technology. Does society favor commercial development of inventions so greatly such that other policies, such as equity among joint owners, should play no role whatsoever? Do you see a difference between personal working and licensing of a patented technology that the United States joint ownership rule would do well to recognize? Robert P. Merges & Lawrence A. Locke, *Co–Ownership of Patents: A Comparative and Economic View*, 72 J. PAT. & TRADEMARK OFF. SOC'Y 586 (1990), offers further economic, historical, and comparative perspectives on patent co-ownership.

5. Muddy Waters. One court noted the conceptual complexities surrounding joint inventorship:

> The exact parameters of joint inventorship are quite difficult to define. It is one of the muddiest concepts in the muddy metaphysics of the patent law. On the one hand, it is reasonably clear that a person who has merely followed instructions of another in performing experiments is not a co-inventor of the object to which those experiments are directed. To claim inventorship is to claim at least some role in the final conception of that which is sought to be patented. Perhaps one need not be able to point to a specific component as one's sole idea, but one must be able to say that without his contribution to the final conception, it would have been less-less efficient, less simple, less economical, less something of benefit.

Mueller Brass Co. v. Reading Indus, 352 F.Supp. 1357, 1372 (E.D.Pa.1972), *aff'd*, 487 F.2d 1395 (3d Cir.1973).

6. Comparative Approaches. Although foreign patent systems are no less concerned with identifying the appropriate individuals to which credit as an inventor is due than is the U.S. regime, the first-to-file priority framework and more streamlined prior art definitions ordinarily found overseas often result in less emphasis upon inventorship as a recurring theme of patent acquisition and enforcement. In addition, most patent regimes allow assignees to file patent applications in their own name, rather than that of the inventor, as discussed below. An example of this lesser weight is demonstrated by Section 7(1) of the German patent statute, which provides:

> In order not to delay substantive examination of the patent application by determining the identity of the inventor, the applicant shall, for the purpose of proceedings before the Patent Office, be deemed to be entitled to request grant of the patent.

Under German law, inventorship may be readily corrected with the consent of the displaced individual. German Patent Law § 63. Alternatively, an individual may bring an action in district court claiming at least partial title to the patent. German Patent Law § 8. This suit must be instituted within two years following grant of the patent. Otherwise, the displaced inventor's only recourse is to bring a so-called nullity action, German Patent Law § 22, which if successful will result in patent invalidity, rather than transfer to the proper inventors.

§ 10.3   INEQUITABLE CONDUCT

Patent acquisition procedures are conducted *ex parte*. A consequence of this administrative setting is that the usual advantages of an adversarial system are unavailable. In addition, the Patent and Trademark Office does not operate laboratories, perform product testing, or verify submitted data attesting to commercial success through independent market research. The result is that the patent system relies to a great extent upon applicant observance of a duty of truthfulness towards the PTO. Experience teaches, however, that applicant obligations of candor may be tempered by the great incentive they possess not to disclose information that might deleteriously impact their prospective patent rights. Thus the concept of inequitable conduct: the intentional failure to disclose material information brings about the unenforceability of the resulting patent. The following materials explore the applicant's disclosure duties during prosecution and the consequences of their breach.

§ 10.3[a]   INTENT

KINGSDOWN MEDICAL CONSULTANTS, LTD. v. HOLLISTER INC.

United States Court of Appeals, Federal Circuit, 1988
863 F.2d 867

Before Markey, Chief Judge, Smith and Archer, Circuit Judges.

MARKEY, CHIEF JUDGE.

Kingsdown Medical Consultants, Ltd. and E.R. Squibb & Sons, Inc., (Kingsdown) appeal from a judgment of the United States District Court for the Northern District of Illinois, No. 84 C 6113, holding U.S. Patent No. 4,460,363 ('363) unenforceable because of inequitable conduct before the United States Patent and Trademark Office (PTO). We reverse and remand.

BACKGROUND

Kingsdown sued Hollister Incorporated (Hollister) for infringement of claims 2, 4, 5, 9, 10, 12, 13, 14, 16, 17, 18, 27, 28, and 29 of Kingsdown's '363 patent. The district court held the patent unenforceable because of Kingsdown's conduct in respect of claim 9 and reached no other issue.

The invention claimed in the '363 patent is a two-piece ostomy appliance for use by patients with openings in their abdominal walls for release of waste.

The two pieces of the appliance are a pad and a detachable pouch. The pad is secured to the patient's body encircling the abdominal wall opening. Matching coupling rings are attached to the pad and to the pouch. When engaged, the rings provide a water tight seal. Disengaging the rings allows for removal of the pouch.

A.   The Prosecution History

Kingsdown filed its original patent application in February 1978. The '363 patent issued July 17, 1984. The intervening period of more than six-and-a-half years saw a complex prosecution, involving the submission, rejection, amendment, re-numbering, etc., of 118 claims, a continuation application, an appeal, a petition to make special, and citation and discussion of 44 references.

After a series of office actions and amendments, Kingsdown submitted claim 50. With our emphasis on the language of interest here, claim 50 read:

> A coupling for an ostomy appliance comprising a pad or dressing having a generally circular aperture for passage of the stoma, said *pad or dressing aperture encircled by a coupling member* and an ostomy bag also having a generally circular aperture for passage of the stoma, *said bag aperture encircled by a second coupling member*, one of said coupling members being two opposed walls of closed looped annular channel form and the other coupling member of closed loop form having a rib or projection dimensioned to be gripped between the mutaully (sic) opposed channel walls when said coupling members are connected, said rib or projection having a thin resilient deflectable seal strip extending therefrom, which, when said rib or projection is disposed between said walls, springs away therefrom to sealingly engage one of said walls, and in which each coupling member is formed of resilient synthetic plastics material.

The examiner found that claim 50 contained allowable subject matter, but rejected the claim for indefiniteness under 35 U.S.C. § 112, second paragraph, objecting to "encircled", because the coupling ring could not, in the examiner's view, "encircle" the aperture in the pad, the ring and aperture not being "coplanar." The examiner had not in earlier actions objected to "encircled" to describe similar relationships in other claims. Nor had the examiner found the identical "encircled" language indefinite in original claims 1 and 6 which were combined to form claim 50.

To render claim 50 definite, and thereby overcome the § 112 rejection, Kingsdown amended the claim. With our emphasis on the changed language, amended claim 50 read:

> A coupling for an ostomy appliance comprising a pad or dressing having *a body contacting surface and an outer surface with* a generally circular aperture for passage of the stoma *extending through* said pad or dressing, a coupling member *extending outwardly from said outer pad or dressing surface and encircling the intersection of said aperture and said outer pad or dressing surface,* and an ostomy bag also having a generally circular aperture *in one bag wall* for passage of the stoma *with* a second coupling member *affixed to said bag wall around the periphery of said bag wall aperture and extending outwardly from said bag wall,* one of said coupling members being two opposed walls of closed looped *annular* channel form and the other coupling member of closed loop form having a rib or projection dimensioned to be gripped between the mutually opposed channel walls when said coupling members are connected, said rib or projection having a thin resilient deflectable seal strip extending therefrom, which, when said rib or projection is disposed between said walls, springs away therefrom to sealingly engage one of said walls, and in which each coupling member is formed of resilient synthetic plastic material.

To avoid the § 112 rejection, Kingsdown had thus added the pad's two surfaces, replaced "aperture encircled", first occurrence, with "encircling the intersection of said aperture and said outer pad or dressing surface", and deleted "encircled", second occurrence. In an advisory action, the examiner said the changes in claim language overcame the § 112 rejection and that amended claim 50 would be allowable.

While Kingsdown's appeal of other rejected claims was pending, Kingsdown's patent attorney saw a two-piece ostomy appliance manufactured by Hollister. Kingsdown engaged an outside counsel to file a continuation application and withdrew the appeal.

Thirty-four claims were filed with the continuation application, including new and never-before-examined claims and 22 claims indicated as corresponding to claims allowed in the parent application. In prosecuting the continuation, a total of 44 references, including 14 new references, were cited and 29 claims were substituted for the 34 earlier filed, making a total of 63 claims presented. Kingsdown submitted a two-column list, one column containing the claim numbers of 22 previously allowed claims, the other column containing the claim numbers of the 21 claims in the continuation application that corresponded to those previously allowed claims. That list indicated, incorrectly, that claim 43 in the continuation application corresponded to allowed claim 50 in the parent application. Claim 43 actually corresponded to the unamended claim 50 that had been rejected for indefiniteness under § 112. Claim 43 was renumbered as the present claim 9 in the '363 patent.

There was another claim 43. It was in the parent application and was combined with claim 55 of the parent application to form claim 61 in the continuation. Claim 55 contained the language of amended claim 50 relating to "encircled." It was allowed as submitted and was not involved in any discussion of indefiniteness. Claim 61 became claim 27 of the patent. Claim 27 reads as follows:

> An ostomy appliance comprising a pad or dressing having a body contacting surface and an outer surface with an aperture for passage of the stoma extending through said pad or dressing, *a coupling member extending outwardly from said pad or dressing and encircling the intersection of said aperture and the outer surface of said pad or dressing* and an ostomy bag also having an aperture in one bag wall for passage of the stoma with a second coupling member affixed to said bag wall around the periphery of said bag wall aperture and extending outwardly from said bag wall, said bag coupling member being two opposed walls of closed loop channel form and said pad or dressing coupling member being a closed loop form having a rib or projection dimensioned to be gripped between the opposed channel walls when said coupling members are connected, and a thin resilient seal strip extending at an angle radially inward from an inner surface of said rib or projection which engages the outer surface of said inner channel wall and wherein said rib or projection has a peripheral bead extending therefrom in a direction opposite said deflectable seal strip and said outer channel wall has a complementary bead on its inner surface, each of said two beads having an annular surface inclined to the common axis of said coupling members when connected, the arrangement being such that said two annular surfaces are in face-to-face contact when said two members are in their mutually coupled positions. (emphasis provided)

B.   The District Court

Having examined the prosecution history, the district court found that the examiner could have relied on the representation that claim 43 corresponded to allowable claim 50 and rejected Kingsdown's suggestion that the examiner must have made an independent examination of claim 43, because: (1) in the Notice of Allowance, the examiner said the claims were allowed "in view of applicant's communication of 2 July 83"; (2) there was no evidence that the examiner had compared the language of amended claim 50 with that of claim 43; and (3) the examiner could justifiably rely on the representation because of an applicant's duty of candor.

The district court stated that the narrower language of amended claim 50 gave Hollister a possible defense, i.e., that Hollister's coupling member does not encircle the intersection of the aperture and the pad surface because it has an intervening "floating flange" member. The court inferred motive to deceive the PTO because Kingsdown's patent attorney viewed the Hollister appliance after he had amended claim 50 and before the continuation application was filed. The court expressly declined to make any finding on whether the accused device would or would not infringe any claims, but stated that Kingsdown's patent attorney must have perceived that Hollister would have a defense against infringement of the amended version of claim 50 that it would not have against the unamended version.

ISSUE

Whether the district court's finding of intent to deceive was clearly erroneous, rendering its determination that inequitable conduct occurred an abuse of discretion.

OPINION

We confront a case of first impression, in which inequitable conduct has been held to reside in an incorrect inclusion in a continuation application of a claim that contained allowable subject matter, but had been rejected as indefinite in the parent application.

Inequitable conduct resides in failure to disclose material information, or submission of false material information, with an intent to deceive, and those two elements, materiality and intent, must be proven by clear and convincing evidence. *J.P. Stevens & Co., Inc. v. Lex Tex Ltd., Inc.*, 747 F.2d 1553, 1559 (Fed.Cir.1984), *cert. denied*, 474 U.S. 822, 106 S.Ct. 73, 88 L.Ed.2d 60 (1985). The findings on materiality and intent are subject to the clearly erroneous standard of Rule 52(a) FED.R.CIV.P. and are not to be disturbed unless this court has a definite and firm conviction that a mistake has been committed.

"To be guilty of inequitable conduct, one must have intended to act inequitably." *FMC Corp. v. Manitowoc Co., Inc.*, 835 F.2d 1411, 1415 (Fed.Cir.1987). Kingsdown's attorney testified that he was not aware of the error until Hollister mentioned it in March 1987, and the experts for both parties testified that they saw no evidence of deceptive intent. As above indicated, the district court's finding of Kingsdown's intent to mislead is based on the alternative grounds of: (a) gross negligence; and (b) acts indicating an intent to deceive. Neither ground, however, supports a finding of intent in this case.

a.   Negligence

The district court inferred intent based on what it perceived to be Kingsdown's gross negligence. Whether the intent element of inequitable conduct is present cannot always be inferred from a pattern of conduct that may be described as gross negligence. That conduct must be sufficient to require a finding of deceitful intent in the light of all the circumstances. We are not convinced that deceitful intent was present in

Kingsdown's negligent filing of its continuation application or, in fact, that its conduct even rises to a level that would warrant the description "gross negligence."

It is well to be reminded of what actually occurred in this case—a ministerial act involving two claims, which, because both claims contained allowable subject matter, did not result in the patenting of anything anticipated or rendered obvious by anything in the prior art and thus took nothing from the public domain. In preparing and filing the continuation application, a newly-hired counsel for Kingsdown had two versions of "claim 50" in the parent application, an unamended rejected version and an amended allowed version. As is common, counsel renumbered and transferred into the continuation all (here, 22) claims "previously allowed". In filing its claim 43, it copied the "wrong", i.e., the rejected, version of claim 50. That error led to the incorrect listing of claim 43 as corresponding to allowed claim 50 and to incorporation of claim 43 as claim 9 in the patent. In approving the continuation for filing, Kingsdown's regular attorney did not, as the district court said, "catch" the mistake.

In view of the relative ease with which others also overlooked the differences in the claims, Kingsdown's failure to notice that claim 43 did not correspond to the amended and allowed version of claim 50 is insufficient to warrant a finding of an intent to deceive the PTO. Undisputed facts indicating that relative ease are: (1) the similarity in language of the two claims; (2) the use of the same claim number, 50, for the amended and unamended claims; (3) the multiplicity of claims involved in the prosecution of both applications; (4) the examiner's failure to reject claims using "encircled" in the parent application's first and second office actions, making its presence in claim 43 something less than a glaring error; (5) the two-year interval between the rejection/amendment of claim 50 and the filing of the continuation; (6) failure of the examiner to reject claim 43 under § 112 or to notice the differences between claim 43 and amended claim 50 during what must be presumed, absent contrary evidence, to have been an examination of the continuation; and (7) the failure of Hollister to notice the lack of correspondence between claim 43 and the amended version of claim 50 during three years of discovery and until after it had carefully and critically reviewed the file history 10 to 15 times with an eye toward litigation. That Kingsdown did not notice its mistake during more than one opportunity of doing so, does not in this case, and in view of Hollister's frequent and focused opportunities, establish that Kingsdown intended to deceive the PTO.

We do not, of course, condone inattention to the duty of care owed by one preparing and filing a continuation application. Kingsdown's counsel may have been careless, but it was clearly erroneous to base a finding of intent to deceive on that fact alone.

Thus the first basis for the district court's finding of deceitful intent (what it viewed as "gross negligence") cannot stand.

b. Acts

The district court also based its finding of deceitful intent on the separate and alternative inferences it drew from Kingsdown's acts in viewing the Hollister device, in desiring to obtain a patent that would "cover" that device, and in failing to disclaim or reissue after Hollister charged it with inequitable conduct. The district court limited its analysis here to claim 9 and amended claim 50.

It should be made clear at the outset of the present discussion that there is nothing improper, illegal or inequitable in filing a patent application for the purpose of obtaining a right to exclude a known competitor's product from the market; nor is it in any manner improper to amend or insert claims intended to cover a competitor's product the applicant's attorney has learned about during the prosecution of a patent application. Any such amendment or insertion must comply with all statutes and regulations, of course, but, if it does, its genesis in the marketplace is simply irrelevant and cannot of itself evidence deceitful intent.

The district court appears to have dealt with claim 9 in isolation because of Hollister's correct statement that when inequitable conduct occurs in relation to one claim the entire patent is unenforceable. *J.P. Stevens*, 747 F.2d at 1561. But Hollister leapfrogs from that correct proposition to one that is incorrect, i.e., that courts may not look outside the involved claim in determining, in the first place, whether inequitable conduct did in fact occur at all. Claims are not born, and do not live, in isolation. Each is related to other claims, to the specification and drawings, to the prior art, to an attorney's remarks, to co-pending and continuing applications, and often, as here, to earlier or later versions of itself in light of amendments made to it. The district court accepted Hollister's argument that Kingsdown included claim 43 (unamended claim 50) in its continuing application because its chances of proving infringement of claim 43 were greater than would have been its chances of proving infringement of amended claim 50, in view of Hollister's "floating flange" argument against infringement of the latter. Neither the court nor Hollister tells us how Kingsdown could have known in July 1982 what Hollister's defense would be years later, when suit was filed.

Faced with Hollister's assertion that an experienced patent attorney would knowingly and intentionally transfer into a continuing application a claim earlier rejected for indefiniteness, without rearguing that the claim was not indefinite, the district court stated that "how an experienced patent attorney could allow such conduct to take place" gave it "the greatest difficulty." A knowing failure to disclose and knowingly false statements are always difficult to understand. However, a transfer of numerous claims en masse from a parent to a continuing application, as the district court stated, is a ministerial act. As such, it is more vulnerable to errors which by definition result from inattention, and is less likely to result from the scienter involved in the more egregious acts of omission and commission that have been seen as reflecting the deceitful intent element of inequitable conduct in our cases.

Because there has been no decision on whether any of claims 2, 4, 5, and 27 are infringed by Hollister's product, or on whether Kingsdown could have reasonably believed they are, it cannot at this stage be said that Kingsdown needed claim 9 to properly bring suit for infringement. If it did not, the district court's implication of sinister motivation and the court's inference of deceptive intent from Kingsdown's acts would collapse.

The district court, in finding intent, made a passing reference to Kingsdown's continuation of its suit after Hollister charged inequitable conduct. Hollister vigorously argues before us that Kingsdown's continuing its suit while failing to disclaim or reissue is proof of bad faith. A failure to disclaim or reissue in 1987, however, would not establish that Kingsdown acted in bad faith when it filed its continuation application in 1982. Moreover, a suggestion that patentees should abandon their suits, or disclaim or reissue, in response to every charge of inequitable conduct raised by an alleged infringer would be nothing short of ridiculous. The right of patentees to resist such charges must not be chilled to extinction by fear that a failure to disclaim or reissue will be used against them as evidence that their original intent was deceitful. Nor is there in the record any basis for expecting that any such disclaimer or reissue would cause Hollister to drop its inequitable conduct defense or refrain from reliance on such remedial action as support for that defense. Kingsdown's belief in its innocence meant that a court test of the inequitable conduct charge was inevitable and appropriate. A requirement for disclaimer or reissue to avoid adverse inferences would merely encourage the present proliferation of inequitable conduct charges.

We are forced to the definite and firm conviction that a mistake has been committed, amounting to an abuse of discretion. The district court's finding of deceitful intent was clearly erroneous.

RESOLUTION OF CONFLICTING PRECEDENT[16]

"Gross Negligence" and The Intent Element of Inequitable Conduct

Some of our opinions have suggested that a finding of gross negligence compels a finding of an intent to deceive. *In re Jerabek*, 789 F.2d 886, 891(Fed.Cir.1986); *Driscoll v. Cebalo*, 731 F.2d 878, 885 (Fed.Cir.1984). Others have indicated that gross negligence alone does not mandate a finding of intent to deceive. *FMC Corp. v. Manitowoc Co.*, 835 F.2d 1411, 1415 n. 9 (Fed.Cir.1987).

---

16. Because precedent may not be changed by a panel, *South Corp. v. United States*, 690 F.2d 1368, 1370 n. 2 (Fed.Cir.1982) *(in banc)*, this section has been considered and decided by an in banc court.

must look at circumstances

"gross negligence" alone not enough

"Gross negligence" has been used as a label for various patterns of conduct. It is definable, however, only in terms of a particular act or acts viewed in light of all the circumstances. We adopt the view that a finding that particular conduct amounts to "gross negligence" does not of itself justify an inference of intent to deceive; the involved conduct, viewed in light of all the evidence, including evidence indicative of good faith, must indicate sufficient culpability to require a finding of intent to deceive. *See Norton v. Curtiss*, 433 F.2d 779 (CCPA 1970).

Nature of Question

Question is equitable in nature

Some of our opinions have indicated that whether inequitable conduct occurred is a question of law. *In re Jerabek*, 789 F.2d at 890 (Fed.Cir.1986). In *Gardco Mfg. Inc. v. Herst Lighting Co.*, 820 F.2d 1209, 1212 (Fed.Cir.1987) (citing *Precision Instrument Mfg. Co. v. Automotive Maintenance Mach. Co.*, 324 U.S. 806, 65 S.Ct. 993, 89 L.Ed. 1381 (1945)), the court indicated that the inequitable conduct question is equitable in nature. We adopt the latter view, i.e., that the ultimate question of whether inequitable conduct occurred is equitable in nature.

Standard of Review

abuse of discretion standard.

As an equitable issue, inequitable conduct is committed to the discretion of the trial court and is reviewed by this court under an abuse of discretion standard. We, accordingly, will not simply substitute our judgment for that of the trial court in relation to inequitable conduct.

Effect of Inequitable Conduct

inequitable conduct at one claim rendered entire patent unenforceable.

When a court has finally determined that inequitable conduct occurred in relation to one or more claims during prosecution of the patent application, the entire patent is rendered unenforceable. We, in banc, reaffirm that rule as set forth in *J.P. Stevens & Co. v. Lex Tex Ltd.*, 747 F.2d 1553, 1561 (Fed.Cir.1984).

CONCLUSION

Reversed.

Having determined that the district court's finding of intent is clearly erroneous, the panel reverses the judgment based on a conclusion of inequitable conduct before the PTO and remands the case for such further proceedings as the district court may deem appropriate.

REVERSED AND REMANDED.

NOTES

1. Inequitable Conduct at the PTO. The Director of the Patent Office announced in 1988 that the "Office will no longer investigate and reject original or reissue applications under 37 C.F.R. § 1.56 and to the extent 37 C.F.R. § 1.56 now requires the Office to do so, it is hereby waived." Noting that *Kingsdown* required a high level of proof of applicant intent to mislead the examiner, the Director reasoned that the Office was not well-equipped to make such a determination. The PTO does continue to consider inequitable conduct in a few contexts, notably interference proceedings where one party asserts inequitable conduct, and in disciplinary proceedings against a patent practitioner for violation of ethical standards. Inequitable conduct has therefore become almost exclusively a matter for the judicial forum with its ability to issue subpoenas, hear live testimony, and provide for cross-examination.

What do you think of the PTO's current policy? Note that at least one Federal Circuit decision, *Paragon Podiatry Lab., Inc. v. KLM Labs., Inc.*, 984 F.2d 1182 (Fed.Cir.1993), affirmed a finding of intent to mislead the office based upon a motion for summary judgment, without the use of live testimony. Consider also the small number of issued patents that are actually subject to litigation. Why should inequitable conduct be relevant only for such a meager subset of patents?

2. **"Plague!"** The Federal Circuit opined in 1988: "[T]he habit of charging inequitable conduct in almost every major patent case has become an absolute plague." *Burlington Indus., Inc. v. Dayco Corp.*, 849 F.2d 1418, 1422 (Fed.Cir.1988). Assuming that the Federal Circuit is correct about abuse of this defense, why is it overused? What advantages does a litigant get from charging inequitable conduct? If the Federal Circuit in 1988 actually considered inequitable conduct an overused "plague," what changes might you expect in the law of inequitable conduct? Have those changes occurred?

3. **Return of the "plague?"** In the years immediately following *Kingsdown*, allegations of inequitable conduct dwindled, but the doctrine has seen a rejuvenation in more recent years. The next opinion, *Aventis Pharma SA v. Amphastar Pharmaceuticals, Inc.*, illustrates this trend. In the *Aventis* case, a supporting witness, decorated scientist Dr. Uzan, disclosed a test designed to show the half-life of a prior art composition without disclosing its dosage. The defendants asserted that disclosing the dosage would have made the composition less favorable to the patented composition than it appeared to be. Amphastar accused Dr. Uzan of deliberately concealing the dosage. On that basis, the Federal Circuit sustained the trial court's finding of inequitable conduct. Ironically, as a matter of science, the undisclosed dosage of the prior art could not have involved deception because the half-life of a compound can increase, but not decline with an increase in dosage. Therefore in general the testing of half-life at a higher dose might lead to a longer half-life measurement, but not a shorter one. To be favorable to Aventis, Aventis wanted to show a lower rather than a higher half-life for the prior art. The Federal Circuit did not comment on that point at all.

As an equitable doctrine, inequitable conduct arrives at the Federal Circuit on appeal under an "abuse of discretion" standard of review. Does that standard make it hard to reverse a finding of inequitable conduct and perhaps even give district courts a way to avoid the rigors of a patent trial? How does the Federal Circuit address this issue, if at all?

§ 10.3[b]   MATERIALITY

AVENTIS PHARMA S.A. v. AMPHASTAR PHARMACEUTICALS, INC.

United States Court of Appeals, Federal Circuit, 2008
525 F.3d 1334

Before Rader, Prost, and Moore, Circuit Judges.

PROST, CIRCUIT JUDGE.

This infringement case returns to us for the second time after remand to the district court on the issue of whether Aventis committed inequitable conduct before the United States Patent and Trademark Office (PTO). In our earlier opinion, we held that the dosage of the prior art composition used in half-life comparisons with the patented composition was information material to patentability, but we remanded to the district court to determine whether there was an intent to deceive by Aventis in failing to disclose the dosage. After a trial on the matter, the district court found that there was intent to deceive and held the patents unenforceable for inequitable conduct. Because we find no abuse of discretion by the district court in its holding of inequitable conduct, we affirm.

I

Aventis is the owner of U.S. Patent No. RE 38,743 (the '743 patent) and U.S. Patent No. 5,389,618 (the '618 patent), which was surrendered upon the issuance of the '743 Patent. The patents are directed to a composition comprising low molecular weight heparins (LMWHs). Claim 1 of the '618 patent recites:

A heterogeneous intimate admixture of sulfated heparinic polysaccharides, such sulfated polysaccharides having a weight average molecular weight less than that of heparin and said admixture consisting essentially of

from 9% to 20% of polysaccharide chains having a molecular weight less than 2,000 daltons

from 5% to 20% of polysaccharide chains having a molecular weight greater than 8,000 daltons, and

from 60–86% of polysaccharide chains having a molecular weight of between 2,000 and 8,000 daltons,

the ratio between the weight average molecular weight and the number average molecular weight thereof ranging from 1.3 to 1.6

said admixture (i) exhibiting a bioavailability and antithrombotic activity greater than heparin and (ii) having an average molecular weight of between approximately 3,500 and 5,500 daltons.

The drug is marketed as Lovenox in the United States and Clexane in Europe and is effective in preventing thromboses (blood clotting) while minimizing the possibility of hemorrhaging, especially during high-risk surgery. According to the specification, the advantage of the claimed LMWHs as compared to heparin is that they exhibit a longer half-life, excellent bioavailability, higher rate of absorption, low clearance, resistance to degradation, increased residence time, and reduced sensitivity to serum factors. '618 patent, col. 2, l. 55–col. 3, l. 26.

A

The prosecution history of the '618 patent is germane to the issue of inequitable conduct. Original claim 1 of the '618 patent application recited as follows:

> A heterogeneous intimate admixture of sulfated heparinic polysaccharides, such sulfated polysaccharides having a weight average molecular weight less that that of heparin and which comprise from 9% to 20% of polysaccharide chains having a molecular weight less than 2,000 daltons and from 5% to 20% of polysaccharide chains having a molecular weight greater than 8,000 daltons, the ratio between the weight average molecular weight and the number average molecular weight thereof ranging from 1.3 to 1.6.

In the first office action, the patent examiner rejected the claims under 35 U.S.C. §§ 102(b)/103 over several references, including European Patent 40,144 (EP '144). The examiner stated that each of the prior art references teaches sulfated heparinic admixtures within the molecular weight (MW) range of the claims and is considered to be inherently the same as the claimed admixtures. In particular, the examiner explained that

> the Patent and Trademark Office does not have facilities for testing and comparing various products, and where the prior art teaches a product which is *identical or nearly identical* to that claimed, it is incumbent upon the Applicant to convincingly demonstrate that the claimed product provides some *unexpected or unobvious property* not demonstrated by the prior art products.

(Emphases added).

In response to the office action, Aventis independently addressed the anticipation and obviousness portion of the rejection. With respect to anticipation, Aventis argued that EP '144 does not expressly state that the mixture contains two types of polysaccharides, one with a MW less than 2,000 daltons and one with a MW greater than 8,000 daltons, nor does it state the number average/weight average MW ratio. Presuming, therefore, that the examiner's anticipation rejection rested on inherency, Aventis argued that the evidence in the specification rebuts inherency. In particular, Aventis pointed to example 6 in the specification, which provides in relevant part:

> This example illustrates the increase in stability, in vivo, of the mixtures of the invention, expressed by their plasma half-life.

. . . .

(1) From the mixtures produced in Examples 3 and 4:

40 mg dose: in 75% of the cases, the half-life was longer than 4 hours, and was even longer than *4 1/2 hours in approximately 45% of the cases;*

60 mg dose: in 75% of the cases, the half-life was longer than 3.7 hours.

. . . .

(3) When the product was prepared according to the process described in European Patent *EP 40,144,* the half-life was longer than *4 1/2 hours in 17% of the cases.*

618 patent, col. 9, ll. 33–58 (emphases added). Example 6 was prepared with the assistance of Dr. André Uzan, a French chemist who was a non-inventor. Based on the example, Aventis argued that the claimed LMWHs exhibit a significantly longer half-life than formulations prepared in accordance with EP '144. Aventis went on to explain that, because it is well established that compounds are inseparable from their properties, the evidence of a difference in a property, i.e., half-life, serves as evidence of a difference in structure. With regard to the obviousness portion of the rejection, Aventis contended that, under 35 U.S.C. § 103, the prior art must suggest the modification to one of skill in the art, yet EP '144 provides absolutely no suggestion to select the particular combination of oligosaccharide chains of specified lengths as claimed.

The examiner was not convinced and issued a second (final) office action, maintaining the prior 102/103 rejection for the reasons of record in the last Office action. The examiner reiterated that the MW requirements of the claimed compounds are within the range of the compounds disclosed in EP '144 and that any properties would be inherent in the prior art compounds because they have the same structure as the claimed compounds

Thereafter, Aventis amended claim 1 to read:

A heterogeneous intimate admixture of sulfated heparinic polysaccharides, such sulfated polysaccharides having a weight average molecular weight less that that of heparin and said admixture comprising[3]

from 9% to 20% of polysaccharide chains having a molecular weight less than 2,000 daltons

from 5% to 20% of polysaccharide chains having a molecular weight greater than 8,000 daltons, and

from 60–86% of polysaccharide chains having a molecular weight of between 2,000 and 8,000 daltons,

---

3. Upon filing a continuing application comprising was changed to consisting essentially of, which is how the claim read when it issued.

the ratio between the weight average molecular weight and the number average molecular weight thereof ranging from 1.3 to 1.6,

said admixture (i) exhibiting a bioavailability and antithrombotic activity greater than heparin and (ii) having an average molecular weight of between approximately 3,500 and 5,500 daltons.

Aventis also submitted a declaration from Dr. Uzan (first Uzan declaration). In 8 of the declaration, Dr. Uzan distinguished the claimed formulations from the formulations in EP '144. First, he noted that the half-life of the claimed formulation is greater than 4 1/2 hours 45% of the time, as compared to the EP '144 formulation which achieved such a half-life only 17% of the time. He remarked, This represents an increase in 250% in the half life and is very significant because it enables the same effect to be achieved with lower dosages. Further, Dr. Uzan stated that he analyzed the EP '144 product and found that 21% of the chains had a MW lower than 2,000; 6% of the chains had a MW greater than 8,000; and 73% of the chains had a MW between 2,000 and 8,000. *Id.* Finally, he concluded that the formulations of [EP '144] are clearly outside the scope of the present invention. Aventis relied on example 6 and the first Uzan declaration to address the anticipation rejection, arguing that the compounds disclosed in EP '144 are not inherently the same as the claimed compounds because the claimed compounds have a longer half-life and because compounds prepared in accordance with EP '144 fall outside the scope of the claims. With respect to obviousness, Aventis argued that the claimed compounds are non-obvious over EP '144 because the compositions in EP '144 did not exhibit the unexpected properties of the claimed combination of MW chains.

In the third office action (first office action in the continuing application), the examiner affirmatively withdrew several 102/103 rejections over other prior art references. The examiner continued to reject the claims under 35 U.S.C. § 103 over EP '144 for the reasons of record in the second office action. According to the examiner, EP '144 teaches admixtures of sulfated heparinic polysaccharides having molecular weight ranges which are not patentably distinct from those of the instant claims. The examiner explained that the instant molecular weight requirements are highly similar to those of the prior art molecular weight ranges, and that no evidence has been presented that the claimed compounds would have any properties or activities not necessarily inherent [in] the prior art compounds. With respect to the half-life comparisons between the claimed compounds and EP '144, the examiner stated that the [a]pplicant has failed to provide evidence that the alleged difference between the half-life of the [EP '144] product and that of the [claimed] mixture is statistically significant. Further, the examiner contended that the first Uzan declaration showed that the differences in composition based on MW were minimal and there was no showing of any unexpected results. Aventis responded by submitting another declaration from Dr. Uzan (second Uzan declaration). In 3 of the declaration, Dr. Uzan referenced five tables comprising the raw data from the half-life comparisons between the claimed compound and the EP '144 compound, which tables were attached to the declaration. Dr. Uzan also provided results from a statistical analysis showing a statistically significant difference between the mean half-life for the claimed compound and that of the EP '144 compound. Specifically, Dr. Uzan reported, For the claimed compound T 1/2 was 4.36 1.07. For the compound of [EP '144], T 1/2 was 3.33 ± 0.2, and the statistical analysis showed that 4.36 and 3.33 were statistically significant. The mean half-life of 4.36 for the claimed compound was taken from Table X, which indicated the dosage to be 40 mg. The mean half-life of 3.33 for the EP '144 compound was taken from Table III, which did not mention the dosage.

Aventis argued, in its response, that EP '144 does not suggest compounds containing polysaccharides of the claimed MW in the claimed proportions and that the examiner improperly relied on inherency to reject the claimed compounds over EP '144. Referring to the second Uzan declaration, Aventis asserted that different half-lives are obtained with the claimed preparation as compared to the preparation of EP '144. Therefore, Aventis averred, the claimed compounds have been shown to differ from the compounds of EP '144 in both their structure and properties.

Thereafter, the '618 patent application was allowed.

B

Aventis sued [two generic pharmaceutical firms] for infringement of the '618 patent in the United States District Court for the Central District of California. *Aventis Pharma S.A. v. Amphastar Pharms., Inc.*, 390 F.Supp.2d 936, 938 (C.D.Cal.2005) ("*Aventis I*").

The district court determined that the representation by Aventis that the patented compound had an improved half-life as compared to the EP '144 compound was material to patentability because Aventis referred to the improved half-life at least four times during prosecution and the examiner ultimately allowed the '618 patent application after the final representation that the difference in mean half-life was statistically significant. *Id.* at 950–51. The court found a strong inference of intent to deceive because it could find no credible explanation for comparing half-lives at different doses and because comparisons at the same dose showed little difference in half-life. *Id.* at 951–52. After weighing the evidence of materiality and intent, the court found weighty uncontroverted evidence establishing inequitable conduct. *Id.* at 952. It, therefore, granted summary judgment against Aventis and held the '618 patent unenforceable.[6] *Id.*

---

6. One day prior to issuance of the district court's order, Aventis surrendered the '618 patent to the PTO pursuant to reissue proceedings in the '743 patent application. *Aventis Pharma S.A. v. Amphastar Pharms., Inc.*, 390 F.Supp.2d 952, 954 (C.D.Cal.2005). In a subsequent order, the district court granted Aventis's motion to substitute the '743 patent for the '618 patent, and amended its earlier holding of unenforceability to apply also to the '743 patent. *Id.* at 957. In so holding, the district court relied on the well-settled principle articulated in *Hoffman-La Roche Inc. v. Lemmon Co.*, 906 F.2d 684 (Fed.Cir.1990), that a reissue proceeding cannot rehabilitate a patent held to be

On appeal, Aventis argued that the district court erred in finding materiality because if the dose information were material to patentability, the examiner would have requested it because: she was presented with half-life data that enabled her to compare various doses, Dr. Uzan informed the examiner that the half-life comparison was done at different doses, those of skill in the art frequently compare half-lives at different doses, and half-life is independent of dose. *Aventis Pharma S.A. v. Amphastar Pharms., Inc.*, 176 Fed.Appx. 117, 120 (Fed.Cir.2006) ("*Aventis II*"). To support the argument that Dr. Uzan informed the examiner that the half-life comparisons were done at different doses, Aventis relied on the statement in the first Uzan declaration that [t]his represents an increase in 250% in the half life and is very significant because *it enables the same effect to be achieved with lower dosages,* and Dr. Uzan's deposition testimony stating that he believed this to mean that the comparison is a comparison between two doses of which one is lower than the other. *Id.* at 120–21 (emphasis added) (internal quotations omitted). Aventis relied on this same statement to argue that Dr. Uzan did not intend to deceive the examiner. *Id.* at 123. Aventis further argued lack of intent based on the fact that Dr. Uzan submitted half-life data for the claimed compound at 60 mg, as well as at 40 mg. *Id.*

With regard to materiality, this court held that it was not plausible to read the statement in the first Uzan declaration as indicating to the examiner that the half-life comparison was done at different doses and, therefore, there was no genuine issue of material fact that Dr. Uzan did not disclose that the comparison was made using data for the two compounds at different doses. *Id.* at 121. We also rejected Aventis's explanation for nondisclosure that using different doses in half-life comparisons was common practice in the field because, in contrast to the references cited in support of this proposition, Aventis did not disclose the actual doses. *Id.* Further, this court did not accept the explanation that the half-life data were dose independent because the evidence clearly suggested otherwise. *Id.* at 121–22. Therefore, we concluded that the withholding of the EP '144 dosage information prevented the examiner from considering information important to patentability and constituted a failure to disclose material information. *Id.* at 122.

While this court found that the dosage of the EP '144 composition was indeed information material to patentability, we held that the district court erred in finding intent to deceive on summary judgment. *Id.* In particular, we held that the reasonableness of the comparison at different doses is relevant to determining whether there was an intent to deceive in withholding the dosage of the EP '144 composition. *Id.* at 122–23. This court reasoned:

> [T]he district court ... ultimately concluded that the facts supported a strong inference of intent to deceive. The district court's

---

inference was reasonable-by failing to disclose that the EP 40,144 data was at a 60 mg dose, Aventis may have been painting the rosiest picture possible as to the half-life improvement of its claimed compounds in an attempt to deceive the examiner.... However, there is another reasonable inference-namely, as Aventis argues, if the comparison between different doses was reasonable, the failure to disclose may have been due purely to inadvertence.

Id. at 123. Accordingly, this court reversed the grant of summary judgment of unenforceability of the '618 patent and '743 patent, and remanded to the district court for determination of whether there was intent to deceive. *Id.*

Following remand, the district court held a bench trial limited to the issue of intent. *Aventis Pharma S.A. v. Amphastar Pharms., Inc.,* 475 F.Supp.2d 970, 975 (C.D.Cal.2007) ("*Aventis III*"). Thereafter, the court issued its opinion, considering the principle explanations proffered by Aventis for Dr. Uzan's failure to disclose the dose of the EP '144 composition in its half-life comparisons. These explanations were that: (1) comparison of half-lives at different doses was reasonable because it was customary to compare the half-lives of different drugs at the clinically relevant dose, i.e., the dose presenting the best efficacy-safety ratio, and the half-life comparisons were intended to show a difference in therapeutic properties, not a compositional difference; (2) comparison of half-lives at different doses was reasonable because half-lives are dose independent; and (3) the failure to disclose was due merely to inadvertence. *Id.* at 977–92.

The district court found Dr. Uzan's clinical relevance justification implausible because such a justification presumed a compositional difference between the compounds being compared, yet the issue of inherency was repeatedly raised by the examiner during prosecution. *Id.* at 977–82. The court noted that the examiner recognized that a compound's properties, e.g., half-life, are inherent in its composition and thereby rejected the claims as anticipated by the EP '144 compound under 35 U.S.C. § 102. *Id.* Therefore, the court was not persuaded that Dr. Uzan presented the half-life comparisons to show only a difference in property and not also a difference in composition. *Id.* The court was similarly unpersuaded by Aventis's dose-independence argument because the evidence did not establish that the half-lives were dose-independent, given the high intra-subject variability. *Id.* at 984–86.

Furthermore, the court rejected Dr. Uzan's clinically-relevant dose justification on the grounds that it was incredible because: (1) there was no statistical difference in half-lives when the 60 mg dose of EP '144 composition was compared to the patented composition at a 20 mg, 60 mg or 80 mg dose, i.e., there was a statistical difference only when a 40 mg dose of the patented composition was compared; (2) the '618 patent was not limited to safe and effective doses for particular therapeutic indications; (3) there were a number of preferred therapeutic doses for the patented composition; and (4) Aventis offered no corroborating evidence to support Dr. Uzan's clinically relevant dose justification. *Id.* at 986–89.

Finally, the court declined to find that Dr. Uzan's failure to disclose the difference in doses could be justified based on inadvertence because it was not credible that a scientist with Dr. Uzan's qualifications could have committed, and failed to correct during a lengthy prosecution, such an egregious error, and there was a complete absence of evidence suggesting negligence throughout prosecution. *Id.* at 989–92.

Based on the totality of the facts and circumstances, the court determined that but for Dr. Uzan's intentional omissions, the probability was high that the '618 patent would not have issued. *Id.* at 994. Accordingly, the court held the '618 patent and the '743 patent unenforceable due to inequitable conduct. *Id.*

Aventis appeals the district court's finding of intent to deceive and holding of inequitable conduct.

II

We review a district court's finding of intent to deceive for clear error. *Monsanto Co. v. Bayer Bioscience N.V.*, 514 F.3d 1229, 1233 (Fed. Cir.2008); *Cargill, Inc. v. Canbra Foods, Ltd.*, 476 F.3d 1359, 1364 (Fed.Cir.2007). A finding of intent will not be overturned in the absence of a definite and firm conviction that a mistake has been made. *Hoffmann-LaRoche, Inc. v. Promega Corp.*, 323 F.3d 1354, 1359 (Fed.Cir.2003) (quoting *Molins PLC v. Textron, Inc.*, 48 F.3d 1172, 1178 (Fed.Cir.1995)). We review the district court's ultimate holding of inequitable conduct for abuse of discretion. *Monsanto*, 514 F.3d at 1233–34; *Cargill*, 476 F.3d at 1365. We will overturn a holding of inequitable conduct only if it is based on clearly erroneous findings of fact or a misapplication or misinterpretation of relevant law or if the holding evidences a clear error of judgment. *Kingsdown Med. Consultants, Ltd. v. Hollister, Inc.*, 863 F.2d 867, 876 (Fed.Cir.1988) (en banc in relevant part). Decisions by the district court concerning the admission or exclusion of evidence are reviewed for abuse of discretion. *United States v. Curtin*, 489 F.3d 935, 943 (9th Cir.2007) (en banc); *DSU Med. Corp. v. JMS Co.*, 471 F.3d 1293, 1310 (Fed.Cir.2006).

To satisfy the intent to deceive element of inequitable conduct, the involved conduct, viewed in light of all the evidence, including evidence indicative of good faith, must indicate sufficient culpability to require a finding of intent to deceive. *Impax Labs., Inc. v. Aventis Pharms. Inc.*, 468 F.3d 1366, 1374–75 (Fed.Cir.2006) (quoting *Kingsdown*, 863 F.2d at 876). Given that direct evidence is often unavailable, intent is generally inferred from surrounding facts and circumstances. *Id.* at 1375. The district court, upon finding materiality and intent, shall balance the equities to determine whether the patentee has committed inequitable conduct that warrants holding the patent unenforceable. *Id.* (quoting

Monsanto Co. v. Bayer Bioscience N.V., 363 F.3d 1235, 1239 (Fed.Cir. 2004)). The more material the omission or misrepresentation, the less intent that must be shown to elicit a finding of inequitable conduct. *Id.*

III

A

Now, on its second time on appeal, Aventis offers a new justification for Dr. Uzan's failure to disclose the dosage information in his half-life comparisons.[7] According to Aventis, Dr. Uzan's half-life comparisons were intended to show a difference in properties in response to the obviousness rejection under 35 U.S.C. § 103, not to demonstrate a compositional difference to address the anticipation rejection under 35 U.S.C. § 102, as the district court concluded. Aventis's argument is premised on the fact that while a half-life comparison must be done using equivalent doses to establish a compositional difference, a half-life comparison may be done using different doses if the purpose is to establish a difference in property. In fact, Aventis argues, it is more appropriate to use the clinically relevant dose of each compound to demonstrate a difference in property.

As a preliminary matter, it appears that Aventis's argument would require us, at least in part, to revisit our prior holding on materiality. The essence of Aventis's argument is that the reason that Dr. Uzan did not disclose the dosage of the prior art compound in his half-life comparisons is that the comparisons were not being used to show a compositional difference and, therefore, the dosage information was not material. We have previously determined, however, that the dosage information was material to patentability. *Aventis II,* 176 Fed.Appx. at 122. Nevertheless, because materiality and intent to deceive are necessarily intertwined, *Kimberly-Clark Corp. v. Johnson & Johnson,* 745 F.2d 1437, 1455 (Fed.Cir.1984), we will consider the merits of Aventis's argument with respect to deceptive intent.

Aventis contends that the district court made two clearly erroneous findings of fact: (1) that the central question relating to patentability was compositional differences, and (2) that the purpose of Dr. Uzan's half-life comparisons was to show compositional differences. According to Aventis, coursing throughout the district court's opinion is the notion that the central question relating to patentability was compositional differences. During oral argument, Aventis emphasized that the district court referred to compositional differences nineteen times in its opinion. Oral Arg. at 3:9–3:17, *available at* http:// www. cafc. uscourts. gov/ oralarguments/ mp 3/ 2007–1280. mp 3. As an example, Aventis quoted the court:

---

7. We note that in its first appeal, Aventis argued only that Dr. Uzan did not have deceptive intent in failing to disclose the dosage information because he thought he informed the examiner that the comparisons were done at different doses, and because he did provide half-life data for the claimed compound at 60 mg as well as at 40 mg. *Aventis II,* 176 Fed.Appx. at 123.

Thus, the central question throughout the prosecution of the '618 patent was whether the [claimed] and [the] EP '144 LMWH products were compositionally different.

Id. at 10:50–11:03; *see Aventis III,* 475 F.Supp.2d at 982. Aventis thus contends that the district court erroneously concluded that anticipation was the only rejection of record, even though there was an obviousness rejection present throughout prosecution. Moreover, Aventis asserts that the district court erred in concluding that the issue of obviousness necessarily folds into, and is subsumed, by inherency. *Aventis III,* 475 F.Supp.2d at 982 n. 10.

We find nothing in the district court's opinion to suggest that it did not recognize the existence of the obviousness rejection, or that it believed the anticipation rejection to be the *only* rejection of record. Indeed, several statements in the opinion clearly indicate that the court was aware of the obviousness rejection. *Id.* at 980 (It also relied on [the claimed composition's] properties *to rebut obviousness.*), ([B]ecause the ratio identified by [the claimed] LMWH exhibited superior properties over EP '144, the inventive formulation could neither be inherent *nor obvious.*), (This signaled to Aventis that its reliance on biochemical properties held promise for overcoming both the [primary examiner's] inherency *and obviousness rejections.*) (emphases added). Although the court incorrectly suggested, in a footnote, that obviousness is subsumed by inherency, we see this as merely a recognition by the court that the notion of inherency was part and parcel of the examiner's rejections. *Id.* at 979. In other words, the properties of a compound are inherent in its composition and, therefore, a difference in property could successfully demonstrate a difference in composition. *Id.* The court understood that, based on the information available to her, the examiner viewed the patented composition and the EP '144 composition to be inherently the same, or nearly the same, and, because the Patent Office did not have the facilities to test the products, the examiner invited Aventis to provide evidence of a difference in property to show a compositional difference. *Id.* at 980; *see In re Best,* 562 F.2d 1252, 1255 (CCPA 1977). We find no clear error in the district court's ultimate conclusion.

Aventis next contends that the district court clearly erred in finding that the purpose of Dr. Uzan's half-life comparison was to show compositional differences to address the anticipation rejection under 35 U.S.C. § 102. Instead, Aventis argues, the MW distribution analysis in the first Uzan declaration, showing a difference between the claimed compounds and those disclosed in EP '144 in the proportion of chains of a given MW, was directed to the anticipation rejection; the half-life comparisons were directed to the obviousness rejection. Further, Aventis contends, Dr. Uzan's statement at the end of the declaration that the formulations of [EP '144] are outside the scope of the claimed invention, was based on the MW distribution analysis, not the half-life comparisons. According to Aventis, the district court improperly concluded that Aventis could not establish compositional differences with the MW distribution analysis, so it relied instead on the half-life comparisons to show that the compounds were not identical. In support, Aventis quotes the court's opinion:

> But Aventis could not successfully distinguish [the patented compound] merely by appealing to [its] ratio of number average and weight average molecular weights. The EP '144 patent is not limited by a specific ratio of constituents. Rather it employs open claim language comprising various proportions of particular molecular weight products. Therefore, Aventis attacked sameness based on a difference in properties.

Oral Arg. at 14:21–14:52 (quoting *Aventis III*, 475 F.Supp.2d at 980).

We cannot agree that the district court clearly erred in its determination that the half-life comparisons were, at least in part, intended to show compositional differences. Nothing in example 6 suggests that the half-life comparison was designed to show only non-obviousness and not lack of identity. The beginning of the example merely states: This example illustrates the increase in stability, in vivo, of the mixtures of the invention, expressed by their plasma half-life. '618 patent, col. 9, ll. 33–35. Moreover, the first Uzan declaration does not clearly delineate between evidence intended to address the anticipation rejection and evidence intended to address the obviousness rejection. All of the evidence directed to the EP '144 reference appears in 8 of the declaration, without distinction between the § 102 and the § 103 aspects of the rejection, and there is no basis for concluding that the final statement in 8–Thus, the formulations of [EP '144] are clearly outside the scope of the present invention-refers only to the MW distribution data and not to the half-life data. We likewise reject Aventis's contention that the court did not recognize that the half-life comparisons were, in part, intended to demonstrate nonobviousness. In fact, immediately following the portion of the opinion quoted by Aventis, the court continued: It also relied on [the claimed composition's] properties to rebut obviousness. *Aventis III*, 475 F.Supp.2d at 980. In addition, the court, in reference to a statement by the examiner in the second office action, observed, This signaled to Aventis that its reliance on biochemical properties held promise for overcoming both the [primary examiner's] inherency and obviousness rejections. *Id.* Therefore, we conclude that the district court properly found that the half-life comparisons were intended to address both the anticipation and obviousness rejections, and, to the extent that they were intended to address the anticipation rejection, the failure to disclose the dosage information evidenced intent to deceive.

Aventis further contends that, in the third office action, the examiner withdrew the § 102 rejection and maintained only the § 103 rejection over EP '144. Yet, Aventis asserts, it was not until the second Uzan declaration, which was submitted after the third office action, that Dr. Uzan provided a statistical analysis showing that the half-life differences were statistically significant. Hence, Aventis urges, the examiner clearly withdrew the § 102 rejection based on the MW distribution data, and the half-life data in the second Uzan declaration was intended only to overcome the § 103 rejection. Aventis thus avers that the district court erred in concluding that the anticipation rejection was still pending at the time of the third office action.

The court apparently came to the conclusion that the anticipation rejection was still pending because the rejection had not been expressly withdrawn. *Id.* at 982 n. 9. Although the court may have erred in concluding that the anticipation rejection was still pending in the third office action, that conclusion was not critical to the court's ultimate determination that there was intent to deceive. In fact, as explained by the court:

> Even if the Court were to accept as true Aventis'[s] unlikely contention that, by the time of Dr. Uzan's Second Declaration, the [primary examiner] had conceded that the [claimed] and EP '144 products were different, there can be no question that inherency was the central, dispositive question up to that point.

Id. at 982. Therefore, even if anticipation were not at issue at the time of the third office action, the court still concluded, based on evidence prior to the third office action, that there was deceptive intent. Any error by the court in concluding that anticipation was still at issue in the third office action does not override the evidence of intent to deceive based on the failure to disclose dosage information in the half-life comparisons in example 6 of the specification and in the first Uzan declaration, both of which were submitted prior to the third office action. We cannot agree that the court clearly erred in its factual findings prior to the third office action and in its determinations with respect to intent to deceive based thereon.

In sum, we find that the district court did not clearly err in determining that the half-life comparisons were, in part, intended to show compositional differences to address the anticipation rejection under 35 U.S.C. § 102 and, therefore, rejecting Aventis's argument that they were intended only to show differences in property, such that dosage information was immaterial.

C

Aventis advances several additional arguments focused on whether Dr. Uzan really had deceptive intent. First, Aventis argues that the court erred in not considering exculpatory testimony by Dr. Uzan indicating that he believed that he informed the examiner that he was comparing half-lives at different doses when he stated, in the first Uzan declaration: [T]his represents an increase in 250% in the half life and is very significant because it enables the same effect to be achieved with lower dosages. This court already concluded in the prior appeal, that there is no genuine issue of material fact that Dr. Uzan did not disclose in this statement that the comparison was made using data from different doses. *Aventis II*, 176 Fed.Appx. at 121. We left open the possibility, however, that Dr. Uzan may have *intended* by this statement to convey to the examiner that the half-life comparisons were done at different doses. *Id.* at 121 n. 2. The district court heard Dr. Uzan's testimony and considered it along with all other evidence relevant to deceptive intent, yet determined that it did not outweigh the cumulative evidence evincing an intent to deceive. We cannot find that the district court clearly erred in concluding that other evidence outweighed Dr. Uzan's testimony that he intended by this statement to inform the examiner that the half-life comparisons were done at different doses.

Next, Aventis avers that Dr. Uzan did not fail to disclose the dosage information for the patented compound to the examiner. In example 6, Aventis urges, Dr. Uzan provided half-life data for the patented compound at 60 mg as well as at 40 mg; and, in the second Uzan declaration, he attached the raw half-life data for the patented compound in Table XI, which showed that the half-life of the patented compound was less at a 60 mg dose than at the 40 mg dose that was used in the comparison with the EP '144 compound. Even if we acknowledge that half-life data at other doses for the patented compound were provided to the examiner, the data were provided in a very misleading way. *Paragon Podiatry Lab., Inc. v. KLM Labs., Inc.*, 984 F.2d 1182, 1191 (Fed.Cir.1993) (inference of deceptive intent may arise from misleading character of affidavit); *accord B.F. Goodrich Co. v. Aircraft Braking Sys. Corp.*, 72 F.3d 1577, 1585 (Fed.Cir.1996). In example 6, half-life data for the patented compound at the 4 1/2 hour cut-off, which could be readily compared to the 4 1/2 hour cut-off data for the EP '144 compound, were only provided at the 40 mg dose. In the first Uzan declaration, reference was made only to the half-life comparison at the 4 1/2 hour cut-off, without reference to the dosage of the patented compound. Moreover, Dr. Uzan failed to disclose, in either example 6 or the first Uzan declaration, the dosage information for the EP '144 compound. Accordingly, we cannot conclude that the district court's finding that Dr. Uzan failed to disclose the dosage information was clearly erroneous.

Lastly, Aventis contends that Dr. Uzan's failure to disclose the dosage information was purely due to inadvertence. In support, Aventis relies on other evidence of inadvertent and benign mistakes made during prosecution of the '618 patent application, suggesting that its omission of the dose of the EP '144 compound was likewise inadvertent. For example, Aventis points out that the first Uzan declaration mistakenly stated that the claimed compound had 1.5% of chains below a specified MW, whereas the remarks by Aventis in its response stated 31.5% of the chains. Here, however, in contrast to any inadvertent omissions made during prosecution, there is sufficient evidence of concealment to warrant a determination that the dose information was intentionally withheld. The fact that Aventis made other inadvertent errors during prosecution has no bearing on this material failure to disclose. Therefore, we cannot agree that the district court clearly erred by not concluding that Dr. Uzan's failure to disclose the dosage information was due to mere inadvertence.

IV

For the foregoing reasons, we affirm the district court's finding of inequitable conduct and holding of unenforceability of the '618 and '743 patents.

AFFIRMED

RADER, CIRCUIT JUDGE, dissenting.

This court today affirms the unenforceability of a patent due to inequitable conduct. To my eyes, this record does not show clear and convincing evidence of intent to deceive the United States Patent and Trademark Office (USPTO). Moreover, my reading of our case law restricts a finding of inequitable conduct to only the most extreme cases of fraud and deception.

Without doubt, candor and truthful cooperation are essential to an ex parte examination system. With burgeoning application rates, the USPTO must rely on applicant submissions to narrow the prior art search. And, of course, those submissions must be reliable. The threat of inequitable conduct, with its atomic bomb remedy of unenforceability, ensures that candor and truthfulness.

Although designed to facilitate USPTO examination, inequitable conduct has taken on a new life as a litigation tactic. The allegation of inequitable conduct opens new avenues of discovery; impugns the integrity of patentee, its counsel, and the patent itself; excludes the prosecuting attorney from trial participation (other than as a witness); and even offers the trial court a way to dispose of a case without the rigors of claim construction and other complex patent doctrines. This court has even observed a number of cases, such as this one, that arrive on appeal solely on the basis of inequitable conduct where the trial court has apparently elected to try this issue in advance of the issues of infringement and validity. *See, e.g., Frazier v. Roessel Cine Photo Tech, Inc.,* 417 F.3d 1230 (Fed.Cir.2005); *Semiconductor Energy Lab. Co. v. Samsung Elecs. Co.,* 204 F.3d 1368 (Fed.Cir.2000).

This phenomenon is not new or unprecedented. At an earlier time, the Federal Circuit also observed that inequitable conduct as a litigation strategy had become a plague. *Burlington Indus. v. Dayco Corp.,* 849 F.2d 1418, 1422 (Fed.Cir.1988). In response, this court took a case to reduce abuse of inequitable conduct. *Kingsdown Med. Consultants, Ltd. v. Hollister, Inc.,* 863 F.2d 867, 876 (Fed.Cir.1988) (en banc).

In light of the rejuvenation of the inequitable conduct tactic, this court ought to revisit occasionally its *Kingsdown* opinion. Kingsdown claimed a two-piece ostomy device. *Id.* at 869. The examiner rejected claim 50 as indefinite. *Id.* at 870. In response, Kingsdown amended claim 50. *Id.* Then, later in the prosecution, Kingsdown copied the rejected claim 50, not the amended version, into a continuation application as new claim 43. *Id.* at 870–71. The once rejected, now recopied claim 43 matured into claim 9 of U.S. Patent No. 4,460,363. *Id.* at 871. On the basis of this error that certainly called into question the integrity of the examination system, the district court found inequitable conduct. *Id.* at 871–72. This court, en banc, reversed. *Id.* at 877.

In *Kingsdown,* this court clearly conveyed that the inequitable conduct was not a remedy for every mistake, blunder, or fault in the patent procurement process. Even mistakes that struck at the heart and integrity of the process-like repeatedly recopying and acquiring rights to a rejected claim-did not amount to inequitable conduct. Instead this court required culpable conduct supported by clear and convincing evidence of intent to deceive the USPTO. *Halliburton Co. v. Schlumberger Tech. Corp.,* 925 F.2d 1435, 1443 (Fed.Cir.1991) (citing *Consol. Aluminum Corp. v. Foseco Int'l Ltd.,* 910 F.2d 804, 809 (Fed.Cir.1990)). At the same time, it is hard to imagine a more material mistake than reasserting claims to rejected subject matter. Materiality of any undisclosed or misleading information, of course, is the other prong of an inequitable conduct analysis. *Cargill, Inc. v. Canbra Foods, Ltd.,* 476 F.3d 1359, 1363 (Fed.Cir. 2007). In sum, *Kingsdown* properly made inequitable conduct a rare occurrence.

More recently, however, the judicial process has too often emphasized materiality almost to the exclusion of any analysis of the lofty intent requirement for inequitable conduct. Merging intent and materiality at levels far below the *Kingsdown* rule has revived the inequitable conduct tactic

In this case, Dr. Uzan, Associate Director of Biological Research at Aventis, assisted in the prosecution of the application that led to U.S. Patent No. 5,389,618 ('618) covering a low molecular weight heparin mixture invented by Roger Debrie (Debrie LMWH). Specifically, Dr. Uzan assembled data from various clinical studies comparing the half-lives of the Debrie LMWH to a prior art LMWH invented by Mardiguian (Mardiguian LMWH). Dr. Uzan submitted this data, from the Duchier study and the Foquet study respectively, as example 6 of the patent. In submitting the data, Dr. Uzan did not draw attention to the different doses in those studies.

Without question, Dr. Uzan should have disclosed the dosage of the Mardiguian LMWH in example 6 subsection 3. Unfortunately, the Foquet study chart that Dr. Uzan used did not show the dosage information. Dr. Uzan neglected to add the information. To make it clear, Dr. Uzan did not attempt to conceal data that were otherwise present. Rather he just submitted the study without adding to the disclosure. This omission, even if negligent, is hardly *Kingsdown*'s culpable intent to deceive. Moreover this omission strikes less at the integrity of the system than issuance of a rejected claim, which *Kingsdown* sanctioned.

Likewise, Dr. Uzan ought to have disclosed to the USPTO that he compared the 60 mg dose of the prior art Mardiguian LMWH to the 40 mg dose of the Debrie LMWH in the declaration he submitted on March 29, 1993. Dr. Uzan testified that the different dose did not come to his mind. In context, this explanation has merit. Dr. Uzan was asked to compare the superior pharmacokinetic properties of the Debrie LMWH over the Mardiguian LMWH prior art compound. Comparison of drug properties at their clinically relevant (and different) dosages is, of course, completely appropriate. Again, this oversight may have been careless, but hardly culpable. To my eyes, Dr. Uzan's negligence does not rise to the level of intent to deceive, particularly in comparison with *Kingsdown*.

Even a cursory review of example 6 shows no dosage indications. The Debrie LMWH in subsection 1 indicates two dosages. Dosage is an element in subsections 2 and 4 as well. Thus, the absence of a dosage in subsection 3 is blatantly obvious. Surely if Dr. Uzan had intended to deceive the USPTO, he would not have made this omission so conspicuous. Moreover, I find it difficult to fathom that a scientist of Dr. Uzan's caliber and reputation would engage in such deception. As the district court points out, Dr. Uzan has had a magnificent fifty year career with Aventis, has published over 350 scientific articles and has received numerous prestigious awards including the Galien Research Prize, France's highest award for drug discovery. This world-class scientist would hardly risk his reputation and tarnish his brilliant career for a single example in the prosecution of a patent for an invention in which he was not even involved.

Most important, Dr. Uzan himself revealed the error. This candor is inconsistent with deceptive intent. He submitted all of the underlying data to the patent office with his second declaration on June 9, 1994. Thus, unlike the situation in *Kingsdown,* Dr. Uzan corrected the mistake before it resulted in an issued patent. In Dr. Uzan's second declaration, he clearly articulated that the half-life data showed superior properties of the Debrie LMWH over the prior art Mardiguian LMWH. Still, with all information before the USPTO, the examiner allowed the patent. Lastly, in early 2003, before filing its infringement suit, Aventis filed a reissue application for the '618 patent. The patent reissued on June 14, 2005 with all of the original independent claims, but without example 6. The half-life data were apparently not even necessary for patentability. The USPTO determined that the Debrie LMWH was inventive over the prior art Mardiguian LMWH without relying on the controversial half-life data from example 6.

In sum, read in the context of *Kingsdown,* I would reverse the district court's determination of inequitable conduct.

NOTES

1. **Purging Inequitable Conduct.** In *Rohm & Haas Co. v. Crystal Chemical Co.*, 722 F.2d 1556 (Fed.Cir.1983), the court set forth three requirements for purging inequitable conduct:

> The first requirement to be met by an applicant, aware of misrepresentation in the prosecution of his application and desiring to overcome it, is that he expressly advised the PTO of its existence, stating specifically wherein it resides. The second requirement is that, if the misrepresentation is of one or more facts, the PTO be advised what the actual facts are, the applicant making it clear that further examination in light thereof may be required if any PTO action has been based on the misrepresentation. Finally, on the basis of the new and factually accurate record, the applicant must establish patentability of the claimed subject matter.... It does not suffice that one knowing of misrepresentation in an application or in its prosecution merely supplies the examiner with accurate facts without calling to his attention to the untrue or misleading assertions sought to be overcome, leaving him to formulate his own conclusions.

As to whether inequitable conduct can be purged in a reissue proceeding, see *Hewlett–Packard Co. v. Bausch & Lomb, Inc.*, 882 F.2d 1556, 1563 n. 7 (Fed.Cir. 1989).

2. **Immunized by Examiner's Independent Discovery?** In *Molins PLC v. Textron, Inc.*, 48 F.3d 1173, 1185 (Fed. Cir. 1995), Judge Lourie discussed the effect of nondisclosure of prior art references which the examiner later discovered on his own:

> "When a reference was before the examiner whether through the examiner's search or the applicant's disclosure, it cannot be deemed to have been withheld from the examiner." *Scripps*, 927 F.2d at 1582; *Orthopedic Equipment Co. v. All Orthopedic Appliances, Inc.*, 707 F.2d 1376 (Fed.Cir. 1983).

In a spirited dissent, Judge Nies took issue with the above statement:

> Not only is the statement relied on [from *Scripps*] overly broad dicta [footnote deleted], it conflicts with an earlier decision of this court. [Prior to our decision in *Scripps*, this court found inequitable conduct based on a failure to disclose art that eventually was independently discovered by the Examiner and made of record. *A.B. Dick Co. v. Burroughs Corp.*, 798 F.2d 1392 (Fed.Cir.1986).... Thus, prior to *Scripps*, this court concluded that a reference not disclosed to the Examiner but which is later discovered by the Examiner *can* be deemed to be withheld from the PTO, on facts similar in nature to those of the present case.]

Molins, 48 F.3d at 1189–90. Is this an instance where one panel at the Federal Circuit declined to follow a prior ruling on the same issue? Although the rule in *Newell Companies, Inc. v. Kenney Mfg. Co.*, 864 F.2d 757, 765 (Fed.Cir.1988), obligates a panel to follow an earlier ruling, what is the remedy when a panel does not follow the *Newell* rule? In any event, after *Molins*, the Federal Circuit remains unclear on whether an examiner's independent discovery of undisclosed prior art immunizes the applicant.

Which of these inconsistent positions should the Federal Circuit adopt? Consider whether you agree with the following:

> The law of "inequitable conduct" is designed to discourage certain forms of behavior. The success or failure of that behavior should be irrelevant. It is similar to the situation where one shoots someone in the head with the intent to kill. But, the intended victim has a metal plate in his head due to an old war injury which deflects the bullet harmlessly. Why should the existence of the metal plate effect the decision to punish or not to punish?

8 MARTIN J. ADELMAN, PATENT LAW PERSPECTIVES, § 17.2[1] at n.57 (2d ed. 1996).

3. Cumulative References. Suppose the applicant fails to disclose a reference that merely duplicates the teachings of cited references, but is nonetheless quite relevant to the claimed invention. Should such a reference be considered material? In *Halliburton Co. v. Schlumberger Technology Corp.*, 925 F.2d 1435 (Fed.Cir.1991), the court observed that "a patentee has no obligation to disclose an otherwise material reference if the reference is cumulative or less material than those already before the examiner." The Federal Circuit overturned the district court's holding of inequitable conduct based on the conclusion that references discovered by the examiner were more pertinent to the claimed invention than those that were not cited. Do you agree that examiner competence should provide a windfall to an otherwise unscrupulous patentee?

Another Federal Circuit opinion dealt with the problem of cumulative affidavits. In *Refac Int'l, Ltd. v. Lotus Development Corp.*, 81 F.3d 1576 (Fed.Cir. 1996), the court affirmed the holding that the asserted patent was invalid for inequitable conduct. The inventors there had submitted several affidavits attesting to the sufficiency of the patent's disclosure. One of the affidavits did not mention that the affiant had worked for the inventors' company and had helped develop the commercial embodiment of the patented software process. On appeal, the patentee argued that because the tainted affidavit was merely cumulative to others that had been submitted, it was not material as a matter of law. Acknowledging the holding in *Halliburton Co. v. Schlumberger Technology Corp.*, the court nonetheless rejected the patentee's argument:

> We decline to place submitted cumulative affidavits in the same status as unsubmitted cumulative prior art. While it is not necessary to cite cumulative prior art because it adds nothing to what is already of record (although it may be prudent to do so), one cannot excuse the submission of a misleading affidavit on the ground that it was only cumulative. Affidavits are inherently material, even if only cumulative. The affirmative act of submitting an affidavit must be construed as being intended to be relied upon. It is not comparable to omitting an unnecessary act.

4. Overemphasizing materiality? In the *Aventis* case, the dissent expressed concern that "the judicial process has too often emphasized materiality almost to the exclusion of any analysis of the lofty intent requirement for inequitable conduct." *Aventis*, 525 F.3d at 1350. What are the implications of "emphasizing materiality?" Because of the inverse relationship between materiality and intent (higher materiality can help infer intent on less evidence), does materiality become the center stage for inequitable conduct dramas?

5. Inequitable Conduct Overseas. To the surprise of many United States practitioners, inequitable conduct is generally unavailable as an infringement defense abroad. At least three reasons support this result. First, many countries allow individuals to bring a so-called "nullity action" against an issued patent throughout the life of the patent. This proceeding is typically brought before a specialized patent tribunal; given this expertise and the focus of the proceeding upon patent validity issues, the time and expense of such proceedings are far less than that of a United States patent infringement trial. Second, most countries follow the so-called "English rule" and routinely award attorney fees to the victorious litigant. Inventors and their assignees who knowingly fail to disclose pertinent prior art may find themselves bearing the entire expenses of a nullity action. Finally, no other nation has yet adopted American-style discovery, so the likelihood that an applicant's inequitable conduct might even be found out is far less than in the United States.

6. Questioning Inequitable Conduct. John F. Lynch, *An Argument for Eliminating the Defense of Patent Unenforceability Based on Inequitable Conduct*, 16 AM. INTELL. PROP. L. ASS'N Q.J. 7 (1988), offers some interesting commentary upon the inequitable conduct doctrine:

> The strategic and technical advantages that the inequitable conduct defense offers the accused infringer make it almost too attractive to ignore. In addition to the potential effect on the outcome of the litigation, injecting the inequitable conduct issue into patent litigation wreaks havoc in the patentee's camp. The inequitable conduct defense places the patentee on the defensive, subjects the motives and conduct of the patentee's personnel to intense scrutiny, and provides an avenue for discovery of attorney-client and work product documents. * * *

The author offers the following proposal in light of these perceived difficulties:

> The defense of unenforceability because of inequitable conduct in the Patent and Trademark Office (PTO) should not be available in private patent litigation to render unenforceable a patent that is otherwise valid. Under this proposal, parties opposing a patent would have available only defenses of invalidity, noninfringement and purgeable unenforceability resulting from patent misuse. Thus, if no "but for" materiality existed, an inequitable conduct defense would be unavailing. Of course, a party opposing a patent who was successful in establishing invalidity and inequitable conduct might be awarded attorney fees, or might base an unfair competition action or an antitrust claim upon that inequitable conduct under existing authority.

> It should be emphasized that we are focusing upon patents which are wholly and completely valid. Not one change in one claim would be necessary to sustain the validity of the patents that this argument seeks to preserve. The societal benefit which is derived from refusing to enforce a patent that is wholly and completely valid because of some supposed

"wrong" that occurred during the obtaining of the patent is remote, and perhaps illusory. If there should exist any right to challenge the enforceability of a patent based only upon conduct occurring in the United States Patent and Trademark Office, that right should be one reserved to the government as sovereign in a district court action initiated expressly for that purpose.

What do you make of these observations? What other mechanisms might the United States patent system effectively employ to encourage candor during prosecution?

§ 10.4   DOUBLE PATENTING

Recall that 35 U.S.C.A. § 101 provides, with emphasis added, that:

> Whoever invents or discovers any new and useful process, machine, manufacture, or composition of matter, or any new and useful improvement thereof, may obtain *a patent* therefor, subject to the conditions and requirements of this title.

The Patent Office and the courts have interpreted this language to require the issuance of only a single patent per invention. When an inventor files duplicative applications directed towards the same invention, the examiner should issue a double patenting rejection. If the examiner fails to do so, then double patenting may serve as a validity defense during infringement litigation. One policy rationale for this rejection is straightforward: otherwise, the inventor might extend the statutory period of exclusivity by filing a series of related patent applications covering the same invention.

You may be surprised to learn that no other statutory mechanism operates to achieve this effect. However, your knowledge of 35 U.S.C.A. § 102 should reinforce the need for a double patenting doctrine. Recall that many activities must be performed *by another* to be patent-defeating under § 102, including the secret prior art established by § 102(e). Only the statutory bars of § 102(b) may be the result of the inventor's own work and still deny a patent to the applicant. Thus, in the absence of other activities that disclose the invention to the public, an inventor could extend the statutory protection period through a simple policy: file an application no later than one year after an earlier, related application has matured into a patent.

Suppose that the applications do not disclose the identical invention, but instead obvious variations of each other? In such cases the patent will also be struck down under so-called "obviousness-type double patenting," a doctrine with the same policy foundation but altogether less sure statutory moorings. In contrast to a double patenting rejection based on multiple claims to the same invention, judges and patent examiners may employ prior art references in combination with the claims of the earlier application or issued patent to determine whether the invention claimed in the later application or patent is obvious to those of skill in the art.

IN RE VOGEL

United States Court of Customs and Patent Appeals, 1970
422 F.2d 438

Before Rich, Acting Chief Judge, Almond, Baldwin, Lane, Judges, and Matthews, Senior Judge, United States District Court for the District of Columbia, sitting by designation.

LANE, JUDGE.

This appeal is from the decision of the Patent Office Board of Appeals affirming the rejection of all claims (7, 10 and 11) in appellants' patent application serial No. 338,158, filed January 16, 1964, for "Process of Preparing Packaged Meat Products for Prolonged Storage."

The ground of rejection for each claim is double patenting, based upon the claims of appellants' U.S. patent 3,124,462, issued March 10, 1964, in view of a reference patent of Ellies, Re. 24,992, reissued May 30, 1961. No terminal disclaimer has been filed.

THE APPEALED CLAIMS

Claims 7 and 10 are directed to a process of packaging meat generally. Claim 10 is illustrative:

10. A method for prolonging the storage life of packaged meat products comprising the steps of: removing meat from a freshly slaughtered carcass at substantially the body bleeding temperature thereof under ambient temperature conditions; comminuting the meat during an exposure period following slaughter while the meat is at a temperature between said bleeding and ambient temperatures; sealing the comminuted meat within a flexible packaging material having an oxygen permeability ranging from 0.01 X 10–(10) to 0.1 X 10–(10) cc.mm/sec/cm(2) /cm Hg at 30 degrees C during said exposure period and before the meat has declined in temperature to the ambient temperature; and rapidly reducing the temperature of the packaged meat to a storage temperature below the ambient temperature immediately following said packaging of the meat.

The invention is based on appellants' discovery that spoilage and discoloration of meat are markedly accelerated if the meat is allowed to reach ambient temperature before packaging.

Claim 11 is directed to a similar process specifically limited to beef.

PRIOR ART

The only reference of record is Ellies. Ellies teaches the use of meat-packaging material having the oxygen permeability range recited in the claims.

THE PATENT

Appellants' patent, which is not prior art, claims a method of processing pork. Claim 1 of the patent is illustrative.

1. A method of preparing pork products, comprising the steps of: bonding a freshly slaughtered carcass while still hot into trimmings; grinding desired carcass trimmings while still warm and fluent; mixing the ground trimmings while fluent and above approximately 80 degrees F., mixing to be complete not more than approximately 3 1/2 hours after the carcass has been bled and stuffing the warm and fluent mixed trimmings into air impermeable casings.

THE BOARD

The board characterized the rejection as follows:

The sole ground of rejection is that claims 7, 10 and 11 are unpatentable over appellants' copending patented claims in Vogel et al., in view of Ellies. This is a double-patenting type rejection, whose statutory basis is 35 U.S.C. 101 . . . .

Thus the board viewed this case as involving "same invention" type double patenting. The board then discussed the differences between the appealed claims and the patent claims and found that the former did not define a "patentable advance" over the latter. It is thus clear that the board was not at all dealing with "same invention" type double patenting but with the "obvious variation" type. The board found that the appealed claims merely extended the pork process to beef, and that this was not a "patentable advance." Such language states only a conclusion, since patentability is the very issue to be determined. The board gave the following analysis to support its conclusion:

We agree with the Examiner's reasons for holding the application of the claimed method to beef to be an unpatentable adaptation. In addition, the definition of "sausage" in Webster's 3rd New International Dictionary of 1963, on page 2019 is pertinent:

"sausage—a highly seasoned finely divided meat that is usually a mixture (as of beef or pork) * * * "

The examiner's reasons as stated in his answer were that the process steps are essentially the same, and the choice of beef rather than pork "is of no patentable significance since this would appear to be a judicious choice of available meat products, well within the ordinary skill of the art, and particularly so, in the absence of any unusual or unobvious result."

The board's use of the dictionary meaning of "sausage," as above quoted, is apparently intended to show that beef and pork are equivalents. Whatever may be their equivalency in other contexts, the dictionary definition of "sausage" does not show that beef and pork are equivalents in the sense of the invention now claimed. Appellants contend that the examiner and the board used the disclosure of the patent as a basis for concluding obviousness. To the effect that consideration of the patent disclosure is improper in testing for obvious-type double patenting, appellants cite *In re Baird*, 348 F.2d 974 (1965).

OPINION

The proceedings below in this case indicate the advisability of a restatement of the law of double patenting as enunciated by this court.

The first question in the analysis is: Is the same invention being claimed twice? 35 U.S.C. § 101 prevents two patents from issuing on the same invention. As we have said many times, "invention" here means what is defined by the claims, whether new or old, obvious or unobvious; it must not be used in the ancient sense of "patentable invention," or hopeless confusion will ensue. By "same invention" we mean identical subject matter. Thus the invention defined by a claim reciting "halogen" is not the same as that defined by a claim reciting "chlorine," because the former is broader than the latter. On the other hand, claims may be differently worded and still define the same invention. Thus a claim reciting a length of "thirty-six inches" defines the same invention as a claim reciting a length of "three feet," if all other limitations are identical. In determining the meaning of a word in a claim, the specification may be examined. It must be borne in mind, however, especially in non-chemical cases, that the words in a claim are generally not limited in their meaning by what is shown in the disclosure. Occasionally the disclosure will serve as a dictionary for terms appearing in the claims, and in such instances the disclosure may be used in interpreting the coverage of the claim. *In re Baird,* supra. A good test, and probably the only objective test, for "same invention," is whether one of the claims could be literally infringed without literally infringing the other. If it could be, the claims do not define identically the same invention. This is essentially the test applied in *In re Eckel*, 393 F.2d 848 (1968). There the court rejected the idea of "colorable variation" as a comparison category and stated that inventions were either the same, or obvious variations, or unobvious variations. The court's holding in Eckel was that same invention means identically same invention.

If it is determined that the same invention is being claimed twice, 35 U.S.C. § 101 forbids the grant of the second patent, regardless of the presence or absence of a terminal disclaimer. If the same invention is not being claimed twice, a second question must be asked.

The second analysis question is: Does any claim in the application define merely an obvious variation of an invention disclosed and claimed in the patent? In considering the question, the patent disclosure may not be used as prior art. This does not mean that the disclosure may not be used at all. As pointed out above, in certain instances it may be used as a dictionary to learn the meaning of terms in a claim. It may also be used as required to answer the second analysis question above. We recognize that it is most difficult, if not meaningless, to try to say what is or is not an obvious variation of a claim. A claim is a group of words defining only the boundary of the patent monopoly. It may not describe any physical thing and indeed may encompass physical things not yet dreamed of. How can it be obvious or not obvious to modify a legal boundary? The disclosure, however, sets forth at least one tangible embodiment within the claim, and it is less difficult and more meaningful to judge whether that thing has been modified in an obvious manner. It must be noted that this use of the disclosure is not in contravention of the cases forbidding its use as prior art, nor is it applying the patent as a reference under 35 U.S.C. § 103, since only the disclosure of the invention claimed in the patent may be examined.

If the answer to the second question is no, there is no double patenting involved and no terminal disclaimer need be filed. If the answer is yes, a terminal disclaimer is required to prevent undue timewise extension of monopoly.

We now apply this analysis to the case before us.

The first question is: Is the same invention being claimed twice? The answer is no. The patent claims are limited to pork. Appealed claims 7 and 10 are limited to meat, which is not the same thing. Claims 7 and 10 could be infringed by many processes which would not infringe any of the patent claims. Claim 11 is limited to beef. Beef is not the same thing as pork.

We move to the second question: Does any appealed claim define merely an obvious variation of an invention disclosed and claimed in the patent? We must analyze the claims separately.

As to claim 11 the answer is no. This claim defines a process to be performed with beef. We must now determine how much of the patent disclosure pertains to the invention claimed in the patent, which is a process to be performed with pork, to which all the patent claims are limited. The specification begins with certain broad assertions about meat sausages. These assertions do not support the patent claims. The patent claims recite "pork" and "pork" does not read on "meat." To consider these broad assertions would be using the patent as prior art, which it is not. The specification then states how the process is to be carried out with pork. This portion of the specification supports the patent claims and may be considered. It describes in tabular form the time and temperature limits associated with the pork process. Appealed claim 11, reciting beef, does not read on the pork process disclosed and claimed in the patent. Further, we conclude that claim 11 does not define merely an obvious variation of the pork process. The specific time and temperature considerations with respect to pork might not be applicable to beef. There is nothing in the record to indicate that the spoliation characteristics of the two meats are similar. Accordingly, claim 11 does not present any kind of double patenting situation.

Appealed claim 10, supra, will now be considered. It recites a process to be performed with "meat." "Meat" reads literally on pork.

The only limitation appearing in claim 10 which is not disclosed in the available portion of the patent disclosure is the permeability range of the packaging material; but this is merely an obvious variation as shown by Ellies. The answer to the second analysis question, therefore, is yes, and the claim is not allowable in the absence of a terminal disclaimer. The correctness of this conclusion is demonstrated by observing that claim 10, by reciting "meat," includes pork. Its allowance for a full term would therefore extend the time of monopoly as to the pork process. It is further noted that viewing the inventions in reverse order, i.e. as though the broader claims issued first, does not reveal that the narrower (pork) process is in any way unobvious over the broader (meat) invention disclosed and claimed in the instant application. The same considerations and result apply to claim 7.

The decision of the board is affirmed as to claims 7 and 10 and reversed as to claim 11.

NOTES

1. Difficulties in Application. The test for double patenting is whether the claims of the two patents cover the same thing. *See Carman Indus. Inc. v. Wahl*, 724 F.2d 932, 940 (Fed. Cir. 1983). This test requires a very difficult exercise: the comparison of one set of claims to another. (Other patent doctrines compare claim language to accused devices or known prior art.) Because a claim does not describe any particular thing but only attempts to set an outer boundary of patent protection, interpreting a single set of claims can be one of the most challenging enterprises in the law. *See In re Vogel*. Yet double patenting requires interpretation of two sets of malleable words and then a comparison of the two interpretations. To the difficulties of that task, add the complexities of an obviousness determination for obviousness-type double patenting. Recognizing the mounting difficulties of this doctrine, the Federal Circuit adopted the CCPA method in *Vogel*, namely compare one claim with a disclosed tangible embodiment that falls within the scope of the other claim. *See In re Braat*, 937 F.2d 589, 592 (Fed.Cir.1991) ("We note at the outset the difficulty which arises in all obviousness-type double patenting cases of determining when a claim is or is not an obvious variation of another *claim*."). At the same time it condones this method, the Federal Circuit insists that the patent disclosure must not be used as prior art. Are you convinced? Can you see why the Federal Circuit imposes a heavy burden of proof on one seeking to prove this defense?

2. Terminal Disclaimers. The reader of *Vogel* obtains the fortunately rare privilege of learning about the making of both law and sausages. Beyond this, the court notes the possibility of a terminal disclaimer to prevent the unauthorized extension of the statutory patent term. 35 U.S.C.A. § 253 provides one tool for overcoming obviousness-style double patenting rejections by stating:

> Whenever, without any deceptive intention, a claim of a patent is invalid the remaining claims shall not thereby be rendered invalid. A patentee, whether of the whole or any sectional interest therein, may, on

payment of the fee required by law, make disclaimer of any complete claim, stating therein the extent of his interest in such patent. Such disclaimer shall be in writing and recorded in the Patent and Trademark Office; and it shall thereafter be considered as part of the original patent to the extent of the interest possessed by the disclaimant and by those claiming under him.

In like manner any patentee or applicant may disclaim or dedicate to the public the entire term, or any terminal part of the term, of the patent granted or to be granted.

By arranging for the expiration dates of all related patents to arise at the same time, the patentee overcomes the concerns of extended patent protection for a single invention. The terminal disclaimer technique allows inventors to file applications claiming obvious variants on a single inventive idea, in order to create prior art against other applicants and to obtain a tight fit for potential infringements. The usual price the applicant pays, however, is a reduction in patent term. Thus, patent applicants ordinarily dispute obviousness-type double patenting rejections by arguing that the rejected claims would not have been rendered obvious in light of the earlier application or patent, along with any other relevant prior art. Can you think of other ways to circumvent such a rejection?

Patents which issue with terminal disclaimers may be subject to abuse. Suppose that the owner of several closely related patents—all but one valid due to the filing of terminal disclaimers—sells one patent each to different, unrelated entities. Wouldn't this situation potentially subject an accused infringer to multiple infringement suits based on patents to the same invention? Such concerns led the Patent and Trademark Office to promulgate the following rule, now embodied at 37 C.F.R. § 1.321(c):

A terminal disclaimer, when filed to obviate a double patenting rejection in a patent application . . . must:

Include a provision that any patent granted on that application . . . shall be enforceable only for and during such period that said patent is commonly owned with the application or patent which formed the basis for the rejection.

This requirement was judicially approved in *In re Van Ornum*, 686 F.2d 937 (CCPA 1982).

3. The *Vogel* Trailer. Given its liberal view of double patenting, *Vogel* encourages applicants to adopt a policy of maintaining continuation applications at the PTO even where they have already obtained an issued patent on a particular disclosure. This so-called "continuation policy" allows applicants to monitor competitors and adjust claims in the continuation application without regard to the strictures of the reissue statute. In particular, applicants may avoid the two-year limitations period for a broadening reissue through this technique. Reissue and other post-grant procedures are discussed here at Chapter 13. In honor of the case that firmly opened up this possibility, the later-issued patent is sometimes termed a "*Vogel* trailer."

A leading patent jurist, Judge Avern Cohn of the Eastern District of Michigan, considered the propriety of a *"Vogel* trailer" patent in *Bott v. Four Star Corp.*, 675 F.Supp. 1069 (E.D.Mich.1987), *aff'd mem.*, 856 F.2d 202 (Fed. Cir.1988). There, the accused infringer, Four Star, asserted the defense of equitable estoppel in light of the continuation policy of Bott, the patentee. The court responded:

> Whatever the importance to the proper operation of the patent system of the public being able to determine the limits of the protection granted to a patentee by denying a patentee the right to cancel broad claims and then reassert them in a continuing chain, as argued by Four Star, the public policy is not for me to decide at this time.... The question faced by Four Star in its design-around effort was not the limits of protection afforded Bott by his issued patents but whether Bott was in a position to obtain a patent [with broadened claims]. He was. Four Star ignored this possibility even though there were "footprints in the sand." Robinson Crusoe knew of Friday's presence even though he could not see him; Four Star should have known of the likelihood of the [*Vogel* trailer] even though it was not aware of [Bott's continuation application].

675 F.Supp. at 1078. Would you have decided differently? *Cf. Symbol Technologies, Inc. v. Lemelson Medical,* 277 F.3d 1361 (Fed.Cir.2002).

4.   One-way or Two-way Street. In *Vogel,* after determining that "same invention" double patenting does not apply, the CCPA stated the obviousness prong of double patenting as follows: "Does any claim in the application define merely an obvious variation of an invention disclosed and claimed in the patent?" 422 F.2d at 441. "If the answer to [that] question is no," the court continues, "there is no double patenting involved and no terminal disclaimer need be filed." But, "[I]f the answer is yes, a terminal disclaimer is required to prevent timewise extension...." *Id.* at 442. Thus *Vogel* seems to envision a one-way street with comparison only of the application to the prior patent for assessment of obviousness. Several cases apply this same one-way street analysis. *See General Foods Corp. v. Studiengesellschaft Kohle mbH,* 972 F.2d 1272, 1280 (Fed.Cir.1992); *Quad Environmental Technologies v. Union Sanitary District,* 946 F.2d 870, 873 (Fed.Cir.1991); *In re Longi,* 759 F.2d 887, 892 (Fed.Cir.1985).

Other cases suggest that obviousness-type double patenting requires a two-way analysis—comparison of the application with the "prior art" patent and comparison of the patent with the potentially "prior art" application because delays at the PTO may have caused a patent to issue ahead of a prior-filed application. *In re Braat*, for instance, states:

> The crux of this appeal comes down to whether the Board erred in applying a "one-way" patentability determination instead of a "two-way" determination.
>
>   *   *   *   *
>
> [T]he Board erred in sustaining the double patenting rejection without making such a "two-way" determination.

* * * *

The rationale behind this proposition is that an applicant (or applicants), who files applications for basic and improvement patents should not be penalized by the rate of progress of the applications through the PTO, a matter over which the applicant does not have complete control.

937 F.2d 589, 593–94 (Fed.Cir.1991). A subsequent Federal Circuit case, however, seems to limit *In re Braat* to the facts of that case:

> In *In re Braat*, 937 F.2d 589, 593 (Fed.Cir.1991), this court required in certain circumstances, an additional inquiry to support the double patenting obviousness rejection. Under these circumstances, a double patenting obviousness rejection will only be sustained if the application claims are not patentably distinct from the prior patent claims, and the prior patent claims are also not patentably distinct from the application claims. This "two-way" analysis is necessary because a later-filed improvement patent may issue before an earlier-filed basic invention. *Id.*; see *Stanley*, 214 F.2d 151.
>
> In *Braat*, the later-filed application contained claims to a patentable combination that included a subcombination which was the subject of an independent prior application. Although the later-filed application became a patent first, this court did not reduce the term of the earlier-filed, but later-issued, patent. This court did not require a terminal disclaimer because Braat's application was held up not by the applicant, but by "the rate of progress of the application through the PTO, over which the applicant does not have complete control." *Braat*, 937 F.2d at 593. *Cf.*, *Stanley*, 214 F.2d 151 (holding that the broad genus of an earlier-filed application was patentable even though a patent issued for a species of that genus).
>
> This case requires no "two-way" analysis. Although application claims 12 and 13 form the genus containing the species of patent claim 3, PTO actions did not dictate the rate of prosecution. Rather, appellant chose to file a continuation and seek early issuance of the narrow species claims. The appellant also chose to forego an immediate appeal to this court on its broader claims when it filed a continuation application. Moreover, appellant argues that a terminal disclaimer is unwarranted.
>
> * * * *
>
> We also affirm the rejection of claims 10–13 for double patenting.

In re Goodman, 11 F.3d 1046, 1053 (Fed.Cir.1993). Is this a conflict within Federal Circuit case law or do the cases adequately define when a "two-way" analysis for obviousness-type double patenting is necessary? Should the law require a two-way analysis only when the patent owner has a strong equitable argument for obtaining the benefit of that rule?

IN RE METOPROLOL SUCCINATE PATENT LITIGATION

United States Court of Appeals, Federal Circuit, 2007

494 F.3d 1011

Before Mayer, Schall, and Gajarsa, Circuit Judges.

GAJARSA, CIRCUIT JUDGE.

This is a consolidated multidistrict patent infringement litigation. Plaintiffs AstraZeneca AB, Aktiebolaget Hässle, and AstraZeneca LP (collectively "Astra") filed multiple suits in various district courts asserting that [generic drug products intended to be marketed] by Defendants KV Pharmaceutical Co. ("KV"), Andrx Pharmaceuticals, LLC, and Andrx Corp. (collectively "Andrx"), and Eon Labs, Inc. ("Eon") . . . infringe Astra's patents. The district court found Astra's patents invalid . . . and granted Defendants' motions for summary judgment.

This court affirms the district court's invalidity holding based on double patenting.

I.

Astra manufactures and markets metoprolol succinate in "extended release" forms under the brand name Toprol–XL®. Metoprolol is a therapeutically active compound, which can form salts by reaction with acids and is used in the treatment of angina, hypertension, and congestive heart failure. Metoprolol succinate is the salt of metoprolol with succinic acid.

A. *Invention and Ownership*

In 1971, an Astra employee "named Toivo Nitenberg synthesized metoprolol succinate as well as the tartrate and sulfate salts of metoprolol" at Astra's facilities in Sweden. At the time, Astra chose to commercialize the tartrate salt product. Similarly in 1982, another Astra employee in Sweden named Lars Lilljequist synthesized a number of metoprolol salts, including metoprolol succinate. The parties submitted conflicting evidence as to whether two other Astra employees in Sweden, Curt Appelgren and Christina Eskilsson, had directed Lilljequist to synthesize metoprolol succinate.

In 1983, Appelgren and Eskilsson left Astra to join another company, Lejus Medical AB ("Lejus"). In January 1984, Lejus filed a patent application (SE 8400085) with the Swedish Patent Office, describing "delayed and extended release dosage forms of pharmaceutical compositions, including metoprolol succinate" and naming Appelgren and Eskilsson as the inventors. In January 1985, Lejus filed U.S. application Ser. No. 690,197 (the '197 Application), claiming priority from the Swedish application.

In October 1985, after noticing the publication of the Swedish application, Astra commenced a transfer of ownership action with the

Swedish Patent Office asserting that Nitenberg, not Appelgren and Eskilsson, invented metoprolol succinate. Astra and Lejus subsequently settled this ownership dispute. In the settlement agreement, Lejus agreed to divide claims to "metoprolol succinate" and to a "pharmaceutical composition, characterized in that the active substance is metoprolol succinate" from the '197 Application and to assign the divided claims to Astra. The settlement agreement listed Appelgren and Eskilsson as the inventors of the divided metoprolol succinate claims. Astra agreed that Lejus retained the rights to the '197 Application that did not include the divided claims.

B. *Astra's U.S. Patents*

In March 1988 and in accordance with the settlement agreement, Lejus filed U.S. application Ser. No. 172,897 (the '897 Application), which was a continuation-in-part of the '197 Application.

In January 1992, a continuation of the '897 Application issued as U.S. Patent No. 5,081,154 (the '154 Patent). The only claim of the '154 Patent simply reads, "Metoprolol succinate."

C. *Lejus's U.S. Patent*

During the same time period, Lejus's '197 Application issued as U.S. Patent No. 4,780,318 (the '318 Patent) in October 1988. [T]he district court invalidated Astra's '154 Patent as double patenting over Lejus's '318 Patent. Claim 6 of the '318 Patent claims an improved release oral pharmaceutical composition having (i) "a core comprising the therapeutically active compound," (ii) "a first inner layer coating on the core," and (iii) "a second outer layer coating on the inner layer." Claim 8 claims this composition,

> wherein the active compound is quinidine sulphate, quinidine bisulphate, quinidine gluconate, quinidine hydrochloride, metoprolol tartrate, *metoprolol succinate*, metoprolol fumarate, or furosemide, 5–aminosalicylic aicd [sic], propranolol or alprenolol or a pharmaceutically acceptable salt thereof, or a mixture thereof with another weak base, weak acid, or salt thereof having a pka of 1 to 8.

D. *Procedural History*

All three defendants moved for summary judgment for invalidity of '154 Patent based on double patenting . . .

In January 2006, the district court issued a summary judgment decision and accompanying judgment in favor of the defendants. . . . Astra appealed the grant of summary judgment for invalidity of the '154 Patent based on double patenting. . . .

II.

"This court reviews double patenting without deference." *Perricone v. Medicis Pharm. Corp.*, 432 F.3d 1368, 1372 (Fed.Cir.2005) (citation omitted). "De novo review is appropriate because double patenting is a matter of what is claimed, and therefore is treated like claim construction upon appellate review." *Georgia-Pacific Corp. v. U.S. Gypsum Co.*, 195 F.3d 1322, 1326 (Fed.Cir.1999); *cf. Eli Lilly & Co. v. Barr Labs., Inc.*, 251 F.3d 955, 967–72 (Fed.Cir.2001) (evaluating evidentiary submissions to determine whether claims were patentably distinct in obvious-type double patenting challenge).

We have noted that "[n]on-statutory, or 'obviousness-type,' double patenting is a judicially created doctrine adopted to prevent claims in separate applications or patents that do not recite the 'same' invention, but nonetheless claim inventions so alike that granting both exclusive rights would effectively extend the life of patent protection." *Perricone*, 432 F.3d at 1373 (citation omitted).

> Generally, an obviousness-type double patenting analysis entails two steps. First, as a matter of law, a court construes the claim in the earlier patent and the claim in the later patent and determines the differences. Second, the court determines whether the differences in subject matter between the two claims render the claims patentably distinct. A later claim that is not patentably distinct from an earlier claim in a commonly owned patent is invalid for obvious-type double patenting. A later patent claim is not patentably distinct from an earlier patent claim if the later claim is obvious over, or anticipated by, the earlier claim.

Eli Lilly, 251 F.3d at 968 (footnote and citations omitted).

In this case, under the heading "*Claim construction*," the district court construed Claim 8 of the '318 Patent as directed

> to an oral pharmaceutical composition that has (i) a core that contains metoprolol succinate (or one of several other drugs), (ii) the core is surrounded by an inner coating that allows a controlled release of metoprolol succinate, and (iii) an outer coating that resists dissolving in the stomach with the goal of releasing the *metoprolol succinate* close to or within the colon.

The only claim of the '154 Patent claims "[m]etoprolol succinate," which the district court construed to be the composition itself.

Next, under the heading "*Comparing the claims*," the district court compared the claims. Stating that Claim 8 of the '318 Patent "is directed to certain pharmaceutical compositions containing metoprolol succinate" and that the '154 Patent "broadly claims any pharmaceutical compositions containing metoprolol succinate," the district court found the '154 Patent to be a genus of the species claimed by the '318 Patent. Since the species claimed by the '318 Patent issued prior to the genus claimed by the '154 Patent, the district court concluded that the '154 Patent was "void for double patenting because it is not patentably distinct f[ro]m" Claim 8 of the '318 Patent.

The parties agree that the district court correctly construed Claim 8 of the '318 Patent and the only claim of the '154 Patent in its summary judgment decision under the heading "*Claim construction.*" This court perceives no error in the district court's claim constructions, and therefore, the only issue on appeal regarding the invalidity of the '154 Patent is whether the district court correctly found the claims not patentably distinct.

Astra asserts that the district court erred in concluding that Claim 8 of the '318 Patent and Claim 1 of the '154 Patent recited a species/genus relationship. Instead, Astra asserts that the claims define an element/combination relationship. This court has stated that such disputes "about the characterization of the relation between the two claims" in a double patenting context are irrelevant.

> Emert insists that the claims stand in a combination ('624 patent) and subcombination ('887 application) relationship. The PTO insists that the claims stand in a genus ('887 application) and species ('624 patent) relationship.... In spite of the parties' eagerness to conform the round-peg facts of the case into semantic, square holes, the critical inquiry remains whether the claims in the '887 application define an obvious variation of the invention claimed in the '624 patent.

In re Emert, 124 F.3d 1458, 1461–62 (Fed.Cir.1997). Therefore, Astra's reliance on semantic distinctions fails.

The holding of *Emert* also dictates that this court affirm the district court's finding of double patenting in this case. In *Emert,* this court held the claims of an application unpatentable for double patenting, finding that "the '887 application's claimed invention, an oil soluble dispersant comprising B1, while not anticipated by the '624 patent due to the slight modification of three claim limitations, would have been prima facie obvious in light of the claim to the combination [A and B]" because the patentee "effectively conced [ed] that the differences between B and B1 are not material and would have been obvious to a person having ordinary skill in the art." 124 F.3d at 1463. Similarly, in this case, Claim 1 of the '154 Patent claiming a compound (A1) is an obvious variation of Claim 8 of the '318 Patent claiming a composition comprised of one compound of an enumerated list (A1, A2, A3, etc.), an inner layer (B), and an outer layer (C). Specifically, it would have been an obvious variation of Claim 8 of the '318 Patent to omit the inner layer (B) and the outer layer (C). Astra offers no convincing reason why *Emert* does not apply. *See also Geneva Pharms., Inc. v. GlaxoSmithKline PLC,* 349 F.3d 1373, 1382–83 (Fed.Cir.2003) (holding that later patent claiming pharmaceutical composition was obvious variant of earlier patent claiming pharmaceutical composition with "enhanced storage stability, the closed container, [and] the packaged unit-dosages").

Instead, Astra asserts that other cases favor a finding of validity in this case. First, Astra cites three decisions of the Court of Customs and

Patent Appeals, one of the predecessors of this court, for the proposition that there is no double patenting because an earlier claim to a combination sets forth a later claimed element. The cases cited by Astra do appear to support this proposition. *See In re Walles,* 366 F.2d 786 (1966); *In re Allen,* 343 F.2d 482 (1965); *In re Heinle,* 342 F.2d 1001 (1965). Indeed, the dissent in *Allen* characterizes the decision as establishing "a new and dangerous rule" and provides a presciently appropriate hypothetical:

> Thus, as I interpret the majority opinion, an applicant would be allowed to patent a chemical combination, e.g., a wonder drug and a suitable carrier for the drug, and then later to patent the drug alone based upon an application filed after the combination application. Seventeen years after the combination of drug and carrier had been patented, the public would still not be free to use the drug with the carrier or in any other obvious manner because of the dominance of the later issued patent to the drug alone. That result is an unlawful extension of the patent. . . .

343 F.2d at 1322–23 (Almond, J., dissenting).

The decisions of the Court of Customs and Patent Appeals bind this court. *In re Stereotaxis, Inc.,* 429 F.3d 1039, 1041 (Fed.Cir.2005) (citing *South Corp. v. United States,* 690 F.2d 1368, 1371 (Fed.Cir.1982) (en banc)). Where decisions of the Court of Customs and Patent Appeals conflict, however, the later issued decision controls "because the Court of Customs and Patent Appeals always sat in banc and therefore later decisions overcome earlier inconsistent ones." *Celestaire, Inc. v. United States,* 120 F.3d 1232, 1235 (Fed.Cir.1997) (citation omitted).

Here, *In re Schneller,* 397 F.2d 350 (1968), is a later issued decision that refutes the suggestion that under the previous holdings of *Walles, Allen,* and *Heinle,* a patentee may claim an element after claiming the combination without fear of double patenting. In *Schneller,* the Court of Customs and Patent Appeals affirmed a double patenting rejection where the patentee's

> first application disclosed ABCXY and other matters. He obtained a patent claiming BCX and ABCX, but so claiming these combinations as to cover them no matter what other feature is incorporated in them, thus covering effectively ABCXY. He now, many years later, seeks more claims directed to ABCY and ABCXY. Thus, protection he already had would be extended, albeit in somewhat different form, for several years beyond the expiration of his patent, were we to reverse. . . . He was shown no justification for such extended protection. He has made no effort not to extend it.

397 F.2d at 355–56. Similarly, in this case, Lejus first obtained a patent claiming (A1, A2, A3, etc.)BC in Claim 6 of the '318 Patent, and years later, Astra obtained a patent claiming A1 in Claim 1 of the '154 Patent. Moreover, *Schneller* explicitly limited *Heinle* and *Allen* to the "particular fact situations" of those cases. *Id.* at 355 (citation omitted). Therefore,

Astra's reliance on *Walles, Allen*, and *Heinle* fails because *Schneller* controls as the later issued Court of Customs and Patent Appeals decision.

Second, citing to *General Foods Corp. v. Studiengesellschaft Kohle mbH*, 972 F.2d 1272, 1281 (Fed.Cir.1992), Astra asserts in its briefs that this court's "precedent makes clear that the *disclosure* of a patent cited in support of a double patenting rejection cannot be used as though it were prior art, *even where the disclosure is found in the claims*." This is true. The disclosure of the claims forming the basis of a double patenting rejection cannot be used as "prior art" for a rejection under 35 U.S.C. §§ 102, 103. The language of *General Foods* and of the precedents cited in the decision explain, however, that what is *claimed*, as opposed to what is *disclosed* to one skilled in the art, remains critical. *See id.* at 1281–82. Indeed, adopting Astra's argument that there can never be "double patenting simply because a later claimed element is set forth in an earlier claim to the combination," Appellant Br. 52, would require that this court eviscerate obviousness-type double patenting, thereby reducing invalidity based on double patenting to the § 101 statutory prohibition against claims of the same invention. *See Geneva*, 349 F.3d at 1377–78 (stating that "applicants can evade this [§ 101] statutory requirement by drafting claims that vary slightly from the earlier patent" and that this "court's predecessor ... recognized this problem and fashioned a doctrine of nonstatutory double patenting (also known as 'obviousness-type' double patenting) to prevent issuance of a patent on claims that are nearly identical to claims in an earlier patent" (footnote omitted)).

General Foods is also factually distinguishable. In *General Foods*, the earlier patent claimed a nine-step process for recovering caffeine. 972 F.2d at 1277. The later patent, challenged for double patenting, claimed a two-step process for decaffeinating coffee. *Id.* at 1276. Contrary to the district court's findings, *id.* at 1280, and the representations of the dissent-in-part, *post* at 1023–24, these two processes had only one step in common—"decaffeinating raw coffee with supercritical water-moist carbon dioxide," *see General Foods*, 972 F.2d at 1277–78. The other eight steps of the earlier patent related to recovering *caffeine*, while the other step of the later patent related to recovering *decaffeinated coffee*. *See id.* Therefore, the earlier patent claimed a nine-step process comprising steps ABCDEFGHJ, and the later patent claimed a two-step process comprising steps AK. Based on this construction of the claims, this court reversed the district court's holding that the later patent was an obvious variant of the earlier patent. Specifically, the district court's opinion exhibited a "distressing failure to adhere to firmly established and universally understood rules of claim interpretation" by "using nothing but the *disclosure* of clause (a) of claim 1 as though it were prior art, and in not reading claim 1 to determine what invention it *defines*—like the metes and bounds of a deed." *See id.* at 1280–81, 1283. By contrast, in this case, the composition of the earlier patent claim includes the compound of the later patent claim in its entirety. Specifically, the earlier patent not only *discloses* but also *claims* a composition comprised-in-part of metoprolol succinate. Therefore, *General Foods* does not preclude a finding that a claim on a compound (A) cannot be an obvious variant of an earlier claim on a composition comprised of compound (A), inner layer (B), and outer layer (C).

Third, Astra asserts that *In re Coleman,* 189 F.2d 976 (1951), requires that courts analyze "badges of distinctness." Astra does not dispute that it never raised this "badges of distinctness" argument with the district court. Even if Astra had preserved this argument, the defendants correctly point out that *Coleman* examined statutory "same invention" double patenting before the Court of Customs and Patent Appeals recognized the doctrine of non-statutory, obvious-type double patenting in its current form. *See id.* at 979 ("As is usual in such cases, the issue reduces itself to a determination of whether or not the appealed claims and those in the patents are directed to one and the same invention."); *General Foods,* 972 F.2d at 1280 ("[T]he development of the law came to a turning point in *In re Zickendraht,* 319 F.2d 225 (1963), particularly in the concurring opinion therein. Soon thereafter the obvious variant kind of double patenting came to be known as 'obviousness-type' double patenting."). Moreover, Astra fails to cite any controlling case that has applied the "badges of distinctness."

Lastly, Astra asserts that the district court's public policy statement that a contrary finding of validity "would defeat the public policy behind the double patenting doctrine which is to allow the public to freely use a patent upon its expiration" was erroneous. Regardless of the parties' characterization of it, the district court made this statement in a concluding paragraph after already holding that the '154 Patent was invalid for double patenting.

Therefore, based on *Emert,* this court agrees with the district court that Claim 1 of Astra's '154 Patent is invalid for obviousness-type double patenting. Astra does not appeal the district court's invalidity holdings regarding Astra's '161 Patent. Accordingly, we affirm the district court's summary judgment holding Astra's asserted patents invalid.

AFFIRMED–IN–PART.

SCHALL, CIRCUIT JUDGE, dissenting-in-part.

[B]ecause I believe that claim 1 of the '154 patent is patentably distinct from claim 8 of the '318 patent, I respectfully dissent from the court's opinion insofar as it holds that claim 1 is invalid by reason of obviousness-type double patenting.

I.

Claim 8 of the '318 patent depends from claims 6 and 7 of the patent. Claim 6 of the '318 patent claims an improved release oral pharmaceutical composition having (i) "a core comprising the therapeutically active compound," (ii) "a first inner layer coating on the core," and (iii) "a second outer layer coating on the inner layer." Claim 7 claims a pharmaceutical composition according to claim 6 wherein the

therapeutically active compound in the core has a solubility in a specified pH range. *Id.* col.5 ll.56–59. Claim 8 claims the composition of claim
7

> wherein the active compound is quinidine sulphate, quinidine bi-
> sulphate, quinidine gluconate, quinidine hydrochloride, metoprolol
> tartrate, *metoprolol succinate*, metoprolol fumarate, or furosemide, 5–
> aminosalicylic aicd [sic], propranolol or alprenolol or a pharmaceu-
> tically acceptable salt thereof, or a mixture thereof with another
> weak base, weak acid, or salt thereof having a pka of 1 to 8.

As I think the majority does, I agree with the district court that,
distilled to its essence, claim 8 of the '318 patent claims an oral
pharmaceutical composition that has (i) a core that contains one of
eleven possible active ingredients (metoprolol succinate being one of the
eleven), (ii) an inner coating surrounding the core (that allows a
controlled release of the active ingredient), and (iii) an outer coating
(that resists dissolving in the stomach, with the goal of releasing the
active ingredient close to or within the colon).

Claim 1 of the '154 patent, which is the sole claim of that patent,
claims the compound metoprolol succinate. As just seen, metoprolol
succinate is one of the possible active compounds of the composition of
claim 8 of the '318 patent.

The majority starts from the premise that claim 8 of the '318 patent
claims (i) a composition comprised of one compound of an enumerated
list of eleven compounds (one of which is metoprolol succinate); (ii) an
inner layer; and (iii) an outer layer. The majority states that "the
composition of the ['318] patent claim includes the compound of the
['154] patent claim in its entirety. Specifically, the ['318] patent not only
discloses but also *claims* a composition comprised-in-part of metoprolol
succinate." The majority reasons that "a claim on a compound (A)" is
"an obvious variant of an earlier claim on a composition comprised of
compound (A), inner layer (B), and outer layer (C)." Based upon that
reasoning, the majority concludes that claim 1 of the '154 patent is
invalid by reason of obviousness type double patenting because it is an
obvious variation of claim 8 of the '318 patent.

II.

A double patenting analysis turns on what is claimed. *General Foods
Corp. v. Studiengesellschaft Kohle mbII*, 972 F.2d 1272, 1275 (Fed.Cir.1992)
("[T]he law of double patenting is concerned *only* with what patents
claim. 'Double patenting,' therefore, involves an inquiry into what, if
anything, has been claimed twice.") To me, the critical point is that, in
this case, the compound metoprolol succinate has not "been claimed
twice." We explained in *General Foods*:

> [E]ach claim is an *entity* which must be considered *as a whole*. It
> cannot be said—though it often is, incorrectly, by the uninitiated-
> that a part of a claim is "claimed" subject matter. For example, a

claim to a process comprising the step A followed by step B followed by step C defines, as a matter of law, only the A–B–C process and one cannot properly speak of any single step as being "claimed", for it is not; all that is claimed is the process consisting of the *combination* of all three steps. Such a claim, therefore, creates no patent right or monopoly in step A, no right to prevent others from using step A apart from the combination of steps A–B–C. Step A is not "patented."

Another way of stating the legal truism is that patent claims, being definitions which must be read *as a whole,* do not "claim" or cover or protect all that their words may *disclose.* Even though the claim to the A–B–C combination of steps contains a detailed description of step A, that does not give the patentee any patent right in step A and it is legally incorrect to say that step A is "patented."

972 F.2d at 1274–75 (emphases in original).

Bearing the foregoing in mind, I believe that what is patented by claim 8 of the '318 patent is a three-element composition having (i) a core with any one of eleven possible compounds, one of them being metoprolol succinate; (ii) an inner coating; and (iii) an outer coating. Anything less than a compound with all three of these elements is not what is claimed. *See General Foods,* 972 F.2d at 1280 ("There is a claim 1 [of the '619 patent] and the *first step* of its 9 recited steps is designated '(a).' . . . [S]tep (a) is not 'claimed' in the '619 patent, nor is it 'patented' or 'covered' . . . What is patented by claim 1 of '619 is a *9–step caffeine recovery process,* nothing more and nothing less."(emphases in original)). In contrast, what is claimed by claim 1 of the '154 patent is a single compound: metoprolol succinate.

In my view, a comparison of the inventions actually patented by the two claims reveals that claim 1 of the '154 patent is patentably distinct from claim 8 of the '318 patent. Far from claiming an obvious variation on the three-element composition 2006–1254 claimed in the '318 patent, the '154 patent, I think, lacks any semblance to the second two elements in the three-element composition of claim 8. The patent does not claim any type of inner coating or outer coating whatsoever. While the first element of claim 8 of the '319 patent does disclose metoprolol succinate as one possible active ingredient, that disclosure does not equate to a claim for metoprolol succinate or render obvious the '154 patent claim to that compound. In short, the two claims involve different inventions. *See Aro Mfg. Co. v. Convertible Top Replacement Co.,* 365 U.S. 336, 344, 81 S.Ct. 599, 5 L.Ed.2d 592 (1961) (recognizing that "if anything is settled in the patent law, it is that the combination patent covers only the totality of the elements in the claim and that no element, separately viewed, is within the grant"); *Leeds & Catlin Co. v. Victor Talking Mach. Co.,* 213 U.S. 301, 318, 29 S.Ct. 495, 53 L.Ed. 805 (1909) (noting that "[a] combination is a union of elements, which may be partly old and partly new, or wholly old or wholly new. But, whether new or old, the combination is a means-an invention-distinct from them").

I believe the law is that there is no double patenting simply because a later claimed element is set forth in an earlier claim to a combination. Significantly, in *General Foods*, claims 1 and 4 of a later issued patent, the "decaffeination patent," defined a process of decaffeinating raw coffee with supercritical water-moist carbon dioxide and recovering the decaffeinated coffee. 972 F.2d at 1277–78. The district court relied on claim 1 of an earlier issued patent, the "caffeine recovery patent," to invalidate the later issued decaffeination patent claims based on double patenting. *Id.* at 1274. The earlier caffeine recovery patent defined a 9–step process of obtaining caffeine from green coffee. *Id.* at 1280. The first step recited "the essence of the very same process claimed in the [later issued] patent in suit." *Id.* at 1280. The district court determined that the first step of the earlier caffeine recovery patent anticipated, or at least rendered obvious, claims 1 and 4 of the later decaffeination patent because every step of claims 1 and 4 were set forth in the first step of the caffeine recovery patent. On appeal, this court concluded that the district court had erroneously used the disclosure in the first step of the caffeine recovery patent as though it was prior art. *Id.* at 1281. After describing the claimed inventions, this court stated: "It should be amply clear by now that the decaffeination *invention* and the caffeine recovery *invention* are separate and distinct inventions, directed to different objectives, and *patentably distinguishable* one from the other." *Id.* at 1277 (emphases in original). In sum, *General Foods* held that a later patent claim to step A is patentably distinct from an earlier patent claim to steps A–B–C–D. To me, it follows that, in this case, a later patent claim to compound A is patentably distinct from an earlier patent claim to composition A–B–C. *See also In re Walles*, 366 F.2d 786 (1966) (finding that patent claims to a hair setting composition, in which the resin of the appealed claims provided one component, were not a bar per se to the application claims to the resin itself); *In re Allen*, 343 F.2d 482 (1965) (holding no double patenting between the claims on appeal, directed to a whaler bracket per se, and patent claims directed to a combination of walls, headed tie rods having spacing washers and positioning means, and a whaler bracket); *In re Heinle*, 342 F.2d 1001 (1965) (reversing Patent Office Board of Appeals double patenting rejection of claims to a single element E based on a patent claim to a combination of A, B, C, D, and E).

While the majority recognizes *General Foods* and *Walles, Allen,* and *Heinle*, it states that the former is distinguishable from this case, while the authority of the latter three was undermined by the decision of the Court of Customs and Patent Appeals in *In re Schneller*, 397 F.2d 350 (1968). I am unable to agree with the majority on either point.

The facts of *General Foods* are set forth above. As far as I can tell, the only difference between *General Foods* and this case is that *General Foods* dealt with method claims, while this case involves product claims. That seems to me to be a distinction without a difference. Neither am I able to agree that *In re Schneller* overruled *Walles, Allen*, and *Heinle*. Briefly, in *Schneller*, the court upheld the rejection of application claims to the combination ABCY as double patenting in light of earlier patent claims to the combination ABCX. The court noted that the patented claims to ABCX covered the preferred embodiment of ABCXY that was disclosed in the patent because the claims were "comprising-type" claims, and that the later application claims to ABCY would also cover the preferred embodiment of ABCXY that was disclosed in the application because they were also "comprising-type" claims. *In re Schneller*, 397 F.2d at 354. Thus, the court stated, "anyone undertaking to utilize what [the inventor] disclosed in the patent . . . in the preferred and only form in which he described the invention, would run afoul of" the application claims. Accordingly, the court held that this timewise extension of protection was impermissible. *Id.* at 356. In this case, however, the '318 patent does not identify one single preferred embodiment that would be impaired by the later application claim to metoprolol succinate. Metoprolol succinate is only one of eleven possible active ingredients identified for the core of the composition claimed in claim 8 of the '318 patent. Moreover, that *Schneller* did not overrule the *Walles, Allen, Heinle*, line of cases is made clear, I believe, by the following paragraph in *Schneller* distinguishing *Heinle:*

> *In re Heinle* is clearly distinguishable. The issued patent claimed a mechanical combination for holding a toilet paper roll. The application claimed a separately usable and salable element of that combination, a particular core for the roll. A combination claim does not 'cover' or read on a single element. The protection of the combination afforded by the single *Heinle* patent claim would not have been extended by the application claims directed to the element. We refer to our opinions therein and in *In re Allen*, 343 F.2d 482, 52 C.C.P.A. 1315, decided the same day, for further elucidation of our thinking on the subject and for the several earlier precedents permitting patenting of a patentable element after the patenting of a combination containing it, in the absence of a terminal disclaimer.

In re Schneller, 397 F.2d at 355.

III.

In affirming the district court's holding of double patenting with respect to claim 1 of the '154 patent, the majority relies on *In re Emert*, 124 F.3d 1458 (Fed.Cir.1997). In *Emert*, we upheld a double patenting rejection of a claim in a patent application, which we characterized as a claim to "An oil soluble dispersant mixture useful as an additive comprising: [B1]." *Id.* at 1460 (quoting U.S. Application No. 07/250,887) (alteration in original). The rejection was based on an earlier patent claim that we characterized as a claim to "An oil soluble dispersant mixture useful as an additive comprising: [A and B]." *Id.* at 1459 (quoting U.S. Patent No. 5,8763,624) (alteration in original). I do not believe that *Emert* controls this case. In *Emert*, both the patent claim and the application claim were to an oil soluble dispersant and the inquiry focused on whether the content of one claimed dispersant was patentably distinct from the content of the later claimed dispersant. In contrast, here we have an earlier claim to a three-element composition and a later claim to a single compound. In my view, for this reason, *Emert* is not controlling in this case.

IV.

The district court stated that "[i]f the '161 and '154 patents were valid, they would prevent the public from using the earlier issued invention of claim 8 of the '318 patent upon its expiration because they completely encompass claim 8 as to metoprolol succinate," and that "[s]uch a result would defeat the public policy behind the double patenting doctrine which is to allow the public to freely use a patent upon its expiration." "The basic concept of double patenting is that the *same* invention cannot be patented more than once, which, if it happened, would result in a second patent which would expire some time after the original patent and extend the protection timewise." *General Foods*, 972 F.2d at 1279–80. Allowance of claim 1 of the '154 patent to metoprolol succinate will not result in the improper extension of the patent for the invention claimed in the '318 patent. That is because in this case, each patent is capable of being practiced by itself, without infringing the other. The public can practice the invention in claim 8 of the '318 patent when it expires by using any of the ten active ingredients recited in the claim other than metoprolol succinate. While some may find it desirable to use metoprolol succinate as the active ingredient in claim 8 of the '318 patent, and those individuals will be unable to do so until the '154 patent expires, that does not result in the "extension" of claim 8 in the '318 patent, or in any recognized form of double patenting.

For the foregoing reasons, I respectfully dissent from the court's opinion insofar as it holds that claim 1 of the '154 patent is invalid by reason of obviousness-type double patenting. I would reverse the decision of the district court on that issue.

NOTE

1. **What is the Test?** Should the test for impermissible double patenting be whether a single product must necessarily infringe both claims? Or should double patenting be judged to occur merely when one product or process could somehow be configured to infringe both claims? The majority and dissent in *Metoprolol* appear to have some differences of view on this point. It is possible that their perspectives were influenced by their views toward a phenomenon termed "evergreening" by some observers and "life-cycle management" by others. This technique calls for multiple patents to cover different aspects of a particular product. With respect to pharmaceuticals, properties eligible for

patenting include uses, formulations, mechanisms of action, biological targets, dosing regimes, delivery profiles, intermediates, and combinations with other products. Critics say that this "patent stockpile" delays the outset of competition as firms must wait until for numerous, overlapping patents to expire. The U.S. Patent Act contains no express statutory mechanism against addressing these strategies, leaving double patenting as the primary response to abusive evergreening/life-cycle management techniques.

2. Double Patenting at the Patent Office. Suppose a patent examiner encounters two pending applications by the same inventive entity claiming the same invention. Because the examiner is as yet unsure whether these application will mature into patents, what result should follow? In such cases, the Patent and Trademark Office ordinarily issues a provisional rejection on the duplicative application. When all other prosecution issues are resolved with respect to the application, the examiner will allow the initial application to issue as a patent. At that time, the provisional rejection of any conflicting claims in subsequent applications is then converted into an actual double patenting rejection. *See* MANUAL FOR PATENT EXAMINING PROCEDURE § 804.n.

3. Still Needed? The double patenting doctrine arose when U.S. law awarded patents a 17–year term, measured from the date of grant, and called for pending patent applications to be maintained in secrecy prior to the award of a patent. Today, of course, the patent term is set to 20 years from the date of filing, and most (but not all) pending applications are published approximately 18 months after they are filed. Do these changes to U.S. law eliminate, or at least reduce, the need for the double patenting doctrine?

§ 10.5   POST–GRANT PROCEDURES

The Patent and Trademark Office's involvement in the U.S. patent system does not necessarily end when it formally grants a patent. The law has long recognized the numerous possibilities for mistakes, ranging from insignificant typesetting errors to substantive flaws that render the patent invalid or unenforceable, to creep into the patent instrument. The patent statute thus provides the PTO with several different mechanisms for correcting the inevitable. The magnitude of the mistake largely determines which procedure will be employed.

The least onerous and most frequently used of these procedures is a *certificate of correction*, as set forth at 35 U.S.C.A. §§ 254 and 255. A certificate of correction is ordinarily used to address minor typographical errors and may be obtained by filing a simple petition. Mistakes incurred through the fault of the PTO may be corrected free of charge; otherwise, the petitioner must submit a fee along with proof that the error occurred in good faith. Use of a certificate of correction is ordinarily uncontroversial and will not be further reviewed here.

A second, more significant correction technique comprises the *reissue* proceeding, governed by 35 U.S.C.A. §§ 251 and 252. Reissue allows applicants to correct more significant errors affecting the validity and enforceability of an issued patent. It presents the most versatile possibility for correction and is often used to prepare a patent for enforcement litigation.

The third sort of correction mechanism, *reexamination*, is more limited than a reissue. As codified at 35 U.S.C.A. § 302–307, the statutory reexamination proceeding allows applicants or third parties to request that the PTO reconsider the validity of a patent. As traditionally structured, reexamination proceedings were largely *ex parte* in nature. The American Inventors Protection Act of 1999 added a new form of reexamination, termed *inter partes* reexamination, that provides a more significant role for the party challenging the patent.

§ 10.5[a] REISSUE

The need for reissue proceedings is made clear by the following example. Suppose that an inventor procures a patent, but subsequently discovers prior art might render the claimed invention anticipated or obvious. Because the patent has already issued and administrative proceedings with the PTO have been closed, the inventor cannot simply telephone the PTO and request a new set of claims. The inventor may wish to file a reissue application, however, in order to add further language of restriction to her patent's claims. The inventor may be able to distinguish successfully his invention from the prior art and turn an invalid patent into a valid, albeit more circumscribed one.

Before describing reissue proceedings further, this casebook addresses a preliminary issue: When is the reissue proceeding available to an applicant? The next decision discusses this point, with reference to the reissue "oath." As set forth in 37 C.F.R. § 1.175(a), the reissue oath, or declaration filed by the patentee, must provide in part that:

> (1) The applicant believes the original patent to be wholly or partly inoperative or invalid by reason of a defective specification or drawing, or by reason of the patentee claiming more or less than the patentee had the right to claim in the patent, stating at least one error being relied upon as the basis for reissue; and

> (2) All errors being corrected in the reissue application up to the time of filing of the oath or declaration under this paragraph arose without any deceptive intention on the part of the applicant.

HEWLETT–PACKARD CO. v. BAUSCH & LOMB INC.

United States Court of Appeals, Federal Circuit, 1989
882 F.2d 1556

Before Nies and Bissell, Circuit Judges, and Baldwin, Senior Circuit Judge.

NIES, CIRCUIT JUDGE.

Bausch and Lomb Incorporated (B & L) appeals from a final judgment, in favor of Hewlett–Packard Company (HP), entered by the

United States District Court for the Northern District of California in a patent infringement suit. Hewlett–Packard Co. v. Bausch & Lomb Inc., 692 F.Supp. 1118 (N.D.Cal.1988). The judgment is based on the district court's holdings that B & L's United States Patent No. Re. 31,684 ('684) is unenforceable and partially invalid. We affirm-in-part, vacate-in-part, and remand.

The court held claims 10–12, which were added during reissue, invalid because B & L filed blatantly inaccurate affidavits to support reissue. Absent the affidavits, the court held, B & L failed to comply with the requirements of the oath specified in 35 U.S.C. § 251 (1982) and 37 C.F.R. § 1.175 (1988).

We affirm the court's holding that claims 10–12, but not claims 1–9, are invalid because the reissue application was defective. We vacate that part of the judgment [concerning inequitable conduct] and remand for reconsideration.

I

ISSUES

Is a failure to include narrower or dependent claims in a patent sufficient in itself to establish error warranting reissue under 35 U.S.C. § 251?

II

BACKGROUND

John Yeiser invented an "X–Y Plotter," described in United States Patent No. 3,761,950 ('950), in which chart paper moves under a marking pen. Yeiser's patent issued in 1973 with nine claims. Following a series of assignments, the Milton Roy Company (MRC) acquired the '950 patent. The invention claimed in that patent was commercialized only briefly. MRC had been out of the plotter business for some time when, in late 1980 or early 1981, HP introduced its first moving-paper X–Y plotter, with great success.

B & L, a competitor of HP, discovered the '950 patent during an investigation of HP's patent protection on its plotter. In 1982, B & L bought the '950 patent from MRC for $30,000, admittedly for the purpose of gaining leverage in negotiations—hoping to obtain a cross license from HP—and possible litigation. The record indicates that B & L was concerned, however, that claim 1, which arguably covers HP's plotter and is the only independent claim asserted, was overly broad. To obtain narrower claims which would incorporate details of the HP plotter specifically, B & L filed a reissue application containing three new claims, 10–12. The original nine claims of the '950 patent were included in the reissue application without substantive change.

The PTO rejected the application, inter alia, on the grounds that B & L failed to specify either an error warranting reissue or how the error occurred. B & L successfully overcame the PTO rejections by supplementing the initial declaration with two affidavits signed by the patent agent, Lawrence Fleming, who had prosecuted the original patent. The facts surrounding those affidavits and the effect they had on the reissue will be discussed below in detail in connection with addressing the issues of the validity and enforceability of the '684 patent, which are the central issues of this appeal.

With issuance of the '684 patent imminent, B & L charged HP with infringement. HP countered with a petition for reexamination of claims 1, 2, and 10–12 over certain prior art. The PTO found that HP's petition raised a substantial new question of patentability, but ultimately upheld the validity of all claims. HP then filed a declaratory judgment action in October 1984, asserting invalidity of all claims of the '684 patent under 35 U.S.C. §§ 102, 103, 112, and 251 (1982), and later added an allegation of unenforceability for inequitable conduct in B & L's prosecution of the reissue application. B & L counterclaimed, charging HP with infringement of claims 1 and 2, which were original claims, and claims 10–12 added by reissue.

On a summary judgment motion, the district court held claims 10–12, but not claims 1–9, invalid. More specifically, the court found that the oath (declaration) in the application for reissue was defective. B & L contends that, as a matter of law, the oath was not defective. On the other hand, HP urges that, because the oath was defective, the district court should have held original claims 1–9 also invalid.

III

FACTS CONCERNING THE REISSUE AFFIDAVITS

The facts surrounding the two Fleming affidavits submitted by B & L to support the reissue application are central to the issues of validity and enforceability. Accordingly, those facts must be set forth in detail.

Upon acquisition of the '950 patent, B & L immediately began steps to secure its reissue. The matter was handled by Bernard Bogdon, B & L's in-house counsel, and William Hyer, outside patent counsel. Hyer delegated the task to an associate of his firm, Jonathan Jobe. It was Jobe's first experience with drafting a reissue application.

Working from the '950 patent file and the specifics Hyer gave him on the HP plotter, Jobe drafted the reissue application, adding three dependent claims to Claim 1 to cover specific features of the HP plotter. Jobe drafted the declaration, later signed by B & L's vice president, George More, to state that the '950 patent was "partly or wholly inoperative ... by reason of the patentee claiming less than he had a right to claim in that he had a right to claim [his invention] more specifically," and that the omission of the dependent claims was caused "because of oversight and without deceptive intent on the part of said John O. Yeiser or his attorney." No one had at that time consulted with Lawrence Fleming, the patent agent (by then retired) who had prosecuted the '950 patent.

Although he signed the declaration, More knew nothing about the alleged "error," either personally or based on others' investigations. Indeed, he was told that he was better off not asking any questions. Jobe testified that he included the reference to an "oversight" because "it is required by the statute" and because he could not "imagine any deceptive reason for not including those claims."

Filed in due course, the reissue application was rejected on the ground:

> The declaration is insufficient because it does not specify an error. The addition of narrower claims, by itself, is not an error. Note that there is no allegation that base claim 1 is inoperative or invalid. Why are claims of narrower scope necessary? The declaration is further insufficient because it does not specify how the error arose or occurred. The statement that the alleged errors occurred or arose because of oversight on the part of the inventor or his attorney does not specify in detail how and why such an oversight occurred. A declaration from the original attorney may be in order.

Following the examiner's rejection, Jobe made his first contact with Fleming, by telephone, informing him generally of the nature of the reissue application and of the PTO rejection and asking how Fleming's alleged "oversight" occurred. In essence, per the district court, Jobe asked Fleming how he could have made the "tremendous blunder" of omitting claims specifically encompassing features of the pinch roller assembly. Hewlett–Packard, 692 F.Supp. at 1140, 8 U.S.P.Q.2d at 1198. Fleming attempted to justify his action with the explanation, later confirmed by letter, that he was unable to get much information from Yeiser.

Jobe then prepared an affidavit for Fleming, which was submitted to the PTO. Essentially, Fleming averred that he had only limited contacts and ability to communicate with the inventor; that no one at the company where Fleming was employed, or its predecessor, provided any substantive help or guidance during prosecution of the patent application; that Yeiser sent him a single, brief memorandum to guide him on what to claim; and that claims which further define and distinguish the invention from the prior art could have been drafted and allowed had further communications and guidance been received. Although Fleming had made references to his "old file" in discussing matters with Jobe, Jobe never asked for documentation or otherwise sought confirmation of Fleming's averments.

The PTO maintained its rejection of B & L's reissue application despite the first Fleming affidavit, reiterating the same grounds as in its initial rejection. Specifically, the PTO found that the More declaration and the Fleming affidavit failed to specify an error or how, when, and why the alleged error arose. Particularly addressing Fleming's affidavit, the examiner stated:

The Fleming affidavit states that the contacts and ability to communicate with the inventor by the agent who prepared the application were significantly limited. It is acceptable on this point. It is not acceptable however as to how and by whom the scope of the subject matter claimed was determined and why.

At this point, house counsel Howard Robbins took over prosecution of the reissue. After speaking with Fleming, Robbins drafted the second Fleming affidavit. In that affidavit, Fleming averred that he had been given a "crude model of the invention" to review on only one occasion for about two hours; that the scope of the claims was determined solely by him based on this brief disclosure; that he had no discussions with Yeiser concerning the scope of the claims; and that Yeiser had sold his plotter business and was not focusing on such matters. Robbins' accompanying argument to the PTO reiterated these "facts" and that Fleming's action was "without full cognizance of what was significant in view of the art." The PTO reconsidered the original declaration, together with the two Fleming affidavits, and found them sufficient under 37 C.F.R. § 1.175. Accordingly, the PTO allowed claims 1–12 in reissue patent '684.

V

VALIDITY

A. Reissue Claims 10–12 Are Invalid

Even before specific provisions were included in the patent statute for correcting defective patents, Chief Justice Marshall, in *Grant v. Raymond*, 31 U.S. (6 Pet.) 218, 244, 8 L.Ed. 376 (1832), articulated the principle that a defective patent was an inadequate exchange for the patentee's disclosure of an invention and that a new patent should be issued, in appropriate circumstances, which secures to the patentee the benefits which the law intended. The circumstances under which reissue is permissible are now set forth in 35 U.S.C. § 251, which provides in pertinent part:

> Whenever any patent is, through error without any deceptive intention, deemed wholly or partly inoperative or invalid, by reason of a defective specification or drawing, or by reason of the patentee claiming more or less than he had a right to claim in the patent, the Director shall, on the surrender of such patent and the payment of the fee required by law, reissue the patent for the invention disclosed in the original patent, and in accordance with a new and amended application, for the unexpired part of the term of the original patent. No new matter shall be introduced into the application for reissue.

B & L argues that an "error" is present, within the meaning of section 251, if it can be discerned from the patent specification, claims, and prosecution history that the patentee could have included a narrower claim, unless there is evidence that such "omission" was intentional.

The omission of narrower claims 10–12, per B & L, also falls within the statutory language that the patentee claimed "less than he had a right to claim."

The district court found that the facts in the Fleming affidavits were essential to reissue and that without those facts, which turned out to be "grossly inaccurate," there was no error warranting reissue. Conversely, B & L asserts that More's original declaration established "reissuable error" and that the Fleming affidavits were both unnecessary and wrong only in immaterial details. Our precedent rejects B & L's simplistic interpretation of the reissue statute with respect to what constitutes error under section 251.

As explained in *In re Wilder*, 736 F.2d 1516 (Fed.Cir.1984):

> There are two distinct statutory requirements that a reissue oath or declaration must satisfy. First, it must state that the patent is defective or partly inoperative or invalid because of defects in the specification or drawing, or because the patentee has claimed more or less than he is entitled to. Second, the applicant must allege that the defective, inoperative, or invalid patent arose through error without deceptive intent.

In sum, the statutorily required "error" of section 251 has two parts: (1) error in the patent, and (2) error in conduct.

On the first part, the precedent of this court is that the expression "less than he had a right to claim" generally refers to the scope of a claim. Thus, that provision covers the situation where the claims in the patent are narrower than the prior art would have required the patentee to claim and the patentee seeks broader claims. Conversely, the alternative that the patentee claimed "more . . . than he had a right to claim" comes into play where a claim is too broad in scope in view of the prior art or the specification and the patentee seeks narrower claims.

In this case, B & L averred that the inventor claimed "less" than he had a right to claim, which ordinarily would mean that B & L sought broader claims by reissue. But B & L did not seek broader claims; instead, B & L sought to add several dependent claims in hopes that it could assert the patent should independent claim 1 be held invalid. Otherwise, the dependent claims add nothing to the patent's protection against infringements. Any device that infringes new claims 10–12 ipso facto infringes carry-over claim 1, which B & L maintains is valid. Thus, in fact, B & L is not asserting that the claims in the '684 patent are inoperative (i.e., ineffective to protect the invention) by reason of the patentee claiming either too much or too little in scope, but because he included, in a sense, too few claims.

Although neither "more" nor "less" in the sense of scope of the claims, the practice of allowing reissue for the purpose of including narrower claims as a hedge against the possible invalidation of a broad claim has been tacitly approved, at least in dicta, in our precedent. For purposes of this case, we will assume that that practice is in accordance with the remedial purpose of the statute, although B & L clearly did not allege an "error" in the patent which meets the literal language of the statute. We need not decide here whether omission of narrow claims which more specifically cover a broadly claimed invention meets the first prong of the requirement for error, that is, error in the patent, because B & L clearly did not establish the second prong, namely, inadvertent error in conduct. Contrary to B & L's position, a reissue applicant does not make a prima facie case of error in conduct merely by submitting a sworn statement which parrots the statutory language.

The language of the current statute, "error without deceptive intent," replaced, but did not substantively change, the language of the prior statute, section 4916 of the Revised Statutes, 35 U.S.C. § 64 (1946), "error ... by inadvertence, accident, or mistake, and without fraudulent or deceptive intent." The term "error" encompasses "inadvertence, accident or mistake," and those words were eliminated as redundant. As explained in *Ball Corp. v. United States*, 729 F.2d 1429, 1435 & n. 9 (Fed.Cir.1984):

> The 1952 revision of the patent laws made no substantive change in the definition of error under section 251.... "Error" is interpreted in the same manner as under section 64 of the old law, i.e., accident, inadvertence, or mistake.

The statutory provision has been implemented and expanded by the PTO regulations of 37 C.F.R. § 1.175.

B & L asserts the theory that, whenever it is apparent that narrower claims could have been obtained, error warranting reissue exists. Under B & L's theory, the dual error inquiry collapses into one because the omission of additional narrow claims not only makes the patent "defective," but also gives rise to an inference of "oversight". Were that theory correct, it is difficult to conceive of any extant patent for which a right of reissue would not exist, a view which this court has unequivocally and repeatedly rejected. For example, as explained in *In re Weiler*, 790 F.2d 1576 (Fed.Cir.1986), reissue is not intended to give the patentee simply a second chance to prosecute the patent application:

> The reissue statute was not enacted as a panacea for all patent prosecution problems, nor as a grant to the patentee of a second opportunity to prosecute de novo his original application.

Id. at 1582. *Weiler* further advises:

> [T]he grant of reissues [is not required] on anything and everything mentioned in a disclosure.... [Section] 251 does not authorize a patentee to re-present his application. Insight resulting from hindsight on the part of new counsel does not, in every case, establish error.

Id. at 1583 n. 4.

B & L seeks to avoid the admonitions of Weiler with an argument, in effect, that an error in conduct must be presumed, absent affirmative evidence that the defect in the patent which is asserted in the reissue application was intentional. For this premise, B & L relies on language in Ball stating that reissue was there appropriate because "there is no evidence that the [patentee] intentionally omitted or abandoned the claimed subject matter". 729 F.2d at 1435–36. In Ball, that analysis was apropos; it is not germane here. The patentee in Ball was seeking broader claims and an abandonment inquiry was necessary under the facts presented. B & L does not suggest circumstances which would constitute abandonment of the subject matter of the dependent claims while not, at the same time, abandoning the subject matter of the independent claim. Thus, B & L's proposed restriction on reissue where narrower claims are sought is, in truth, no restriction at all.

Returning to the district court's holdings, we discern no legal error in its conclusion that the original More declaration in itself was inadequate to establish error and that the supplemental Fleming affidavits were necessary. The Fleming affidavits were critical to provide the required explanation of what his error was and how and why it occurred.

The evidence of record establishes beyond doubt that Fleming's affidavits, in explaining why narrow claims were not included, were factually untrue. We need not repeat those errors, which are set out above and are substantially undisputed. B & L argues that the misstatements were innocent and should be ignored. Assuming that they were due only to Fleming's faulty memory, the misstatements are not thereby corrected to provide a valid assertion of error. Accordingly, the district court properly held that the factual inaccuracy of the affidavits eliminated the basis for reissue and rendered the '684 patent invalid, albeit only as to claims 10–12.

B. "Carry–Over" Claims 1–9 Remain Valid

Only claims 10–12 were added by B & L during prosecution of the reissue application. Aside from correction of a typographical error in claim 3, the original claims 1–9 of the '950 patent remained identical. HP contends that the effect of the court's holding that B & L failed to submit a valid reissue application is to render the '684 patent invalid in its entirety, that is, all claims must be held invalid. The district court noted that there was some illogic in invalidating the reissue patent and, at the same time, upholding the carry-over claims therein. The carry-over claims cannot be asserted based on the original patent, because the patent owner must surrender the original patent upon reissuance. 35 U.S.C. § 252 (1982). Logically, it would follow that B & L has no claims to enforce. Indeed, some precedent exists to support invalidation of all claims when the reissue declaration is found wanting. We agree with the district court, however, that such a result is neither compelled by the patent statute nor by the circumstances here.

There is no disagreement with the long-standing proposition that invalidation of a new claim (added during reissue) on prior art does not invalidate the other claims. Nor could there be any disagreement, for the patent statute provides: "Whenever, without any deceptive intention, a claim of a patent is invalid the remaining claims shall not thereby be rendered invalid." 35 U.S.C. § 253 (1982). That proposition offers little guidance, however, because the invalidity resulting from a defective reissue application may be viewed as affecting the entire patent and not merely any particular claim.

We find support for upholding carry-over claims in *Gage v. Herring*, 107 U.S. 640, 27 L.Ed. 601 (1883). There, the Supreme Court expressed its view that the inadequacy of the ground for reissuing a patent did not "impair the validity of the original claim which is repeated and separately stated in the reissued patent." *Gage* is especially on point because the invalidity of the reissue claim did not turn on prior art but on the negation of a right to reissue. The patentee repeated one claim from his original patent and attempted to add a second claim by reissue, arguing that the original claim was "too much restricted." The Supreme Court held the added claim invalid because that claim was one the patentee "did not make, or suggest the possibility of, in the original patent." Nevertheless, the Court upheld the validity of the original claim.

We see no reason to reach a contrary result under the circumstances here. Accordingly, we affirm the district court's ruling that the lack of error warranting reissue invalidates only new claims 10–12, and not original claims 1–9.

NOTES

1. Can the Decision not to Include Narrower Claims in a Patent Ever Be Deceptive? Do you agree with the following comment respecting *Hewlett–Packard*?

> In the United States, in contrast to some foreign systems, the PTO does not examine narrower claims once it allows a broad claim or set of claim. The fees and legal expenses for such claims, at least when written in dependent form, are small and it is probably malpractice not to put a reasonable set into an application. Thus the court went astray when it disregarded the remedial nature of the reissue statute in *Hewlett-Packard*. The patent law uses dependent claims to cope with the principle that limitations from the specification cannot be read into claims to save them from invalidity. Bausch & Lomb was merely dealing with a possible future problem in its reissue application, a problem that could only be the result of error rather than any strategic calculation during the prosecution of the original patent.

> Further, the court's decision is not consistent with the fundamental philosophy of reissue law. Essentially the only reason for placing limits on what can be corrected during reissue is because if actions taken or omissions made during the prosecution of the original patent are correctable there is less incentive for the original applicant to get it right in the

first place. Thus, the best approach to reissue law would carefully balance these two considerations, how far to permit remedial action with the inevitable lessening of pressure to get it correct in the first place, in deciding "error without any deceptive intention" questions.

6 MARTIN J. ADELMAN, PATENT LAW PERSPECTIVES, § 10.2[2] at n.38 (2d ed. 1990).

2. Erroneous Policy? Given the uncertainties surrounding the sorts of mistakes that suffice to file a reissue application, should the concept of "error" as a requirement for reissue simply be abolished? The 1992 Advisory Commission thought so. It stated:

> The statutory requirement of an "error" unduly limits the basis for reissue and generates a great deal of uncertainty. The courts have been inconsistent in their interpretation of "error" as it appears in 35 U.S.C.A. § 251. *Compare, e.g., In re Byers*, 230 F.2d 451, 454 (CCPA 1956), *with In re Wesseler*, 367 F.2d 838, 839 (CCPA 1966), *and with In re Wadlinger*, 496 F.2d 1200, 1207 (CCPA 1974). What mistakes constitute error for purposes of reissue are also subject to differing opinions. *Compare In re Wilder*, 736 F.2d 1516, 1519 (Fed.Cir.1984), and *In re Richman*, 424 F.2d 1388, 1391–92 (CCPA 1970), *with Hewlett–Packard, supra, and In re Weiler*, 790 F.2d 1576, 1582–83 (Fed.Cir.1986). The public's need for certainty is not helped by the uncertain limits on the right to a reissue. There is no public policy reason for limiting reissue to "errors" except in the case of deceptive intent. Absent the latter, and subject to time limits on broader claims, a patentee should be entitled to obtain by reissue any valid claim to which he or she would have been entitled during the original prosecution.

THE ADVISORY COMMISSION ON PATENT LAW REFORM, A REPORT TO THE SECRETARY OF COMMERCE 129 (1992).

3. Effect of Reissue Application. When the Patent Office accepts a reissue application, it essentially starts prosecution *ab initio*. The PTO requests that reissue applicants include the originally issued patent instrument (the so-called "ribboned copy") along with the other paperwork. This requirement is in keeping with the statute's mandate that the patentee surrender the original patent in order to obtain a reissued patent. Although a patentee may ultimately abandon a reissue proceeding and receive her patent back, she should be reluctant to do so: the cloud this abandoned application would cast upon the abandoned application will be duly noted by courts and competitors.

The usual sequence of Office Actions and responses applies, and applicants may also file continuation and divisional applications as necessary. *See In re Graff*, 111 F.3d 874 (Fed.Cir.1997). Note that continuation-in-part applications are not allowed during reissue proceedings: this step would involve the introduction of new matter, which is prohibited by § 251, first paragraph. The second paragraph of § 251 also allows several patents to issue from a single reissue application.

Reissue proceedings are open to the public. To this end, the Patent and Trademark Office Official Gazette announces the filing of reissue applications each week. PTO regulations then mandate that the reissue proceeding not commence for at least two months, in order to allow third parties to submit evidence and arguments relating to the patentability of the reissue application.

Reissue proceedings therefore expose the patentee to some risk. Although he may have carefully calculated the steps he needs to take to move through the reissue proceeding, these plans may be thrown off by interested parties. Competitors and licensors in particular may vigorously contest the reissue of the patent by submitting additional prior art or arguments against patentability. If the patent reissues, however, the patentee has likely strengthened his patent for use in licensing negotiations or during litigation.

4. Broadening Reissues. When a patentee seeks to expand the scope of its claims, thereby increasing the technologies that constitute an infringement, she is said to have applied for a "broadening reissue." The fourth paragraph of § 251 sets forth a two-year statute of limitations for seeking a reissue that enlarges the scope of the claims. Meeting this deadline has proved a somewhat subtle affair, as suggested by two cases, *In re Doll*, 419 F.2d 925 (CCPA 1970), and *In re Graff*, 111 F.3d 874 (Fed.Cir.1997).

In *Doll*, the patentee filed a reissue application containing broadened claims within the two-year statutory period. The claims were further broadened during the course of prosecution after the two-year period had expired, prompting a rejection by the examiner under the § 251, fourth paragraph. The Court of Customs and Patent Appeals reversed in a tersely drafting opinion, holding that the reissue oath was proper.

Graff involved an applicant who filed a reissue application approximately twenty-two months after the issuance date. The initial reissue application was solely directed towards an erroneous drawing and contained no changes to the claims whatsoever. During the course of prosecution and following the expiration of the two-year period, however, Griff introduced broadened claims. The examiner rejected these claims as untimely under § 251, fourth paragraph. On appeal, the Federal Circuit affirmed. The court characterized the holding in *Doll* as recognizing that "the public was placed on notice of the patentee's intention to enlarge the claims by the filing of a broadening reissue application within the two year statutory period." According to the Federal Circuit, because the public lacked notice that Graff sought a broadening reissue within the statutory period, any enlarged claims were properly rejected.

5. The Recapture Rule. Along with the two-year statute of limitations, the courts have developed another significant restriction on broadening reissues. The recapture rule prevents a patentee from acquiring through reissue claims of the same or broader scope that those canceled from the original application. *See Ball Corp. v. United States*, 729 F.2d 1429 (Fed.Cir.1984). This doctrine typically arises when an examiner rejected the original application based upon the prior art. If the patentee opted to narrow its claims to avoid a prior art reference, then he cannot use the reissue proceeding to recapture the abandoned subject matter.

The Federal Circuit opinion in *Mentor Corp. v. Coloplast, Inc.*, 998 F.2d 992 (Fed.Cir.1993), demonstrates the recapture rule. Mentor had obtained a patent claiming a condom catheter that transferred an adhesive from its outer to its inner surfaces upon unrolling. A review of the prosecution history indicated that Mentor had inserted this limitation into the claims following the examiner's prior art rejection. Mentor later learned of Coloplast's competing product, a catheter with adhesive applied directly to its inner surface. Aware that its patent claims did not read directly on the Coloplast product, Mentor initiated a reissue proceeding at the PTO. After Mentor submitted detailed evidence of commercial success, the examiner reissued the patent. Notably absent from the reissued claims were limitations calling for adhesive transfer.

Mentor then sued Coloplast for infringement of both the original and reissue patents. Coloplast denied infringement of the original patent claims because its catheters did not transfer adhesive from the outer to the inner surface. Coloplast admitted infringement of the reissue patent but asserted that Mentor had improperly invoked the reissue statute by recapturing what it had deliberately surrendered during the original prosecution in response to a prior art rejection. The jury disagreed, and the trial judge denied Coloplast's motion for judgment as a matter of law after the adverse verdict.

On appeal, the Federal Circuit reversed. The court concluded that Mentor could not use the reissue proceeding to modify its deliberate actions during the original prosecution. Because Mentor had deliberately added claim language requiring adhesive transfer following the examiner's prior art rejection, the court reasoned, Mentor should not be allowed to recapture that subject matter by deleting these claim limitations during reissue. In so doing, the court justified the recapture rule both upon the requirement of error as well as concerns for the reliance interests of third parties. The Federal Circuit did not consider Mentor's deliberate decision to narrow its claims, instead of filing a continuation application or appealing to the Board, to be the sort of error comprehended by the reissue statute. Additionally, the court sympathized with a hypothetical third party that might have reviewed the prosecution history and made commercial decisions based upon Mentor's express surrender of claimed subject matter.

6. Uncorrectable Errors. Some errors in a patent are simply too grave to be corrected through the use of a reissue proceeding. These include a specification that does not fulfill the requirements of § 112; when the applicant has engaged in inequitable conduct during the original prosecution; and when the invention has been entirely anticipated under § 102. What other options does the patentee possess in such instances?

7. Intervening Rights. Congress recognized that third parties may have made commercial decisions based upon the precise wording of the claims of an issued patent. If that patent is later reissued with different claims, this reliance interest could be frustrated. In order to protect individuals who may have relied upon the scope of the claims of the original patent, the second paragraph of section 251 provides for so-called intervening rights. There are two sorts of intervening rights: absolute and equitable.

Absolute intervening rights are set forth in the first sentence of the second paragraph of section 251. According to that provision, no reissued patent shall prevent one from employing a "specific thing" covered by the reissue patent, so long as that individual made use of that thing prior to the grant of the reissue. Absolute intervening rights are limited to the sale or continued use of individual machines, manufactures, or products covered by the reissue patent. There is one significant exception: if the infringed claim of the reissue patent was also within the original patent, then no absolute intervening right arises.

The second sentence of the second paragraph of section 251 provides for equitable intervening rights. This statute allows a court to authorize the continued practice of an invention claimed in a reissue patent "to the extent and under such terms as the court deems equitable for the protection of investments made or business commenced before the grant of the reissue." To qualify for equitable intervening rights, an infringer must have made at least substantial preparations to practice the patented invention. As with the absolute intervening right, equitable intervening rights apply only when a valid, infringed claim appears solely in the reissue patent.

That intervening rights may apply to broadening reissues should be apparent. Less intuitive is that intervening rights may also arise when the claims are narrowed during reissue. However, even prior to a narrowing reissue, a defendant may have believed the original, broader claims to be invalid. Such grounds as anticipation, nonobviousness, indefiniteness, or lack of an enabling disclosure may apply to the claims of the original patents but not to those that were reissued. The better view is that intervening rights may apply during any reissue, not just a broadening one.

A paucity of case law considers either sort of intervening right. This absence is likely due to artful reissue practice on behalf of patentees. Wise to the wording of the reissue statute, most patentees transfer as many claims from the original patent to the reissued patent as possible without amendment. Of course, if the defendant infringes a claim that appears in both the original and reissued patents, then no intervening rights are possible.

§ 10.5[b]   REEXAMINATION

Reexamination proceedings were introduced into the U.S. patent law in 1980. The American Inventors Protection Act of 1999 renamed the traditional sort of reexamination as an "*ex parte* reexamination" and also introduced the possibility of an "*inter partes* reexamination." The principal purpose of either sort of reexamination is to provide third parties with an avenue for resolving validity disputes more quickly and less expensively than litigation.

Under the *ex parte* reexamination procedure, any individual, including the patentee, a licensee, and even the Director of the United States Patent and Trademark Office himself, may cite a patent or printed publication to the PTO and request that a reexamination occur. The chief limitation upon reexamination is that the cited grounds for invalidity must constitute a patent or printed publication. 35 U.S.C.A. § 302. Other grounds for patent invalidity, such as the on-sale bar of § 102(b), may not be considered during reexamination. If the PTO determines that this art raises "a substantial new question of patentability," 35 U.S.C.A. § 303(a), then it will essentially reinitiate examination of the patent, ordinarily opening with a rejection of some of the patent's claims over the prior art.

Ex parte reexamination actually may have a short-lived *inter partes* initial phase. If the *ex parte* reexamination requestor is other than the patentee, the patentee is initially allowed to file a preliminary statement "including any amendment to his patent and new claim or claims he may wish to propose, for consideration in the reexamination." 35 U.S.C.A. § 304. If the patentee submits such a statement, the requestor "may file and have considered in the reexamination a reply to any statement filed by the patent owner." *Id.* Because patentees are ordinarily loath to allow the input of an opponent of a patent before the PTO, however, they usually observe silence at this early stage, foregoing any opportunity of the *ex parte* reexamination requestor to provide further objections to the claims of the patent.

Following this preliminary period, the PTO will essentially reinitiate examination of the patent. Because the PTO has determined that a substantial new question of patentability exists, ordinarily the First Office Action includes a rejection of at least one of the claims. As the PTO's determination of whether a substantial new question of patentability must be based upon a patent or printed publication, this rejection will ordinarily be based upon anticipation, obviousness or double patenting. To the extent that the owner of the reexamined patent adds new claims or otherwise amends the application, then the examiner may also raise issues pertaining to § 112.

Prosecution then continues following the usual rules for examination of applications. However, several special rules apply to reexaminations. First, the PTO conducts reexaminations with special dispatch. 35 U.S.C. § 305. Examiners must give priority to patents under reexamination, and will set aside their work on other patent applications in favor of the reexamination proceeding. To further ensure their timely resolution, patentees may not file a continuation application in connection with a reexamination. Second, no new matter may be introduced into the patent during reexamination. *Id.*

If the reexamined claims are upheld in original or amended form, the PTO will issue a certificate of conformation. Once this certificate has issued, the reexamined patent once more enjoys the statutory presumption of validity. 35 U.S.C. § 307(a). The doctrine of intervening rights, introduced with respect to reissued patents, also applies to claims that survive reexamination. 35 U.S.C.A. § 307(b). If the PTO judges the claims to be unpatentable over the cited reference, then it will issue a certificate of cancellation. 35 U.S.C.A. § 307(a). Patentees adversely affected by a reexamination may appeal to the Board or to the courts as necessary. 35 U.S.C.A. § 306.

In lieu of provoking a reexamination, individuals may simply cite patents or printed publications to the Patent and Trademark Office under 35 U.S.C.A. § 301. If accompanied by a written explanation of the relevance of the cited prior art to the patent, this submission will be included in the patent's official record. Section 301 allows competitors to place prior art on the record, ensuring that it will be considered if a reexamination is declared. Of course, particularly pertinent prior art will undoubtedly hamper the patentee's enforcement or licensing efforts, and may even encourage another party to file a reexamination itself.

As traditionally structured, the *ex parte* reexamination statute encountered criticism. As the name of these proceedings suggests, the role of the reexamination requestor is very limited. Only the patentee may participate in the dialogue with the examiner, and only the patentee may appeal the matter to the Board or to the courts if the PTO reaches an unsatisfactory conclusion. Many third parties did not believe the limited role provided for them offered a viable alternative to validity challenges in court. As a result, the ability of *ex parte* reexamination to provide an expert forum as a faster, less expensive alternative to litigation of patent validity was compromised. Data supported these observations, for far fewer *ex parte* reexaminations were requested than had been originally anticipated. *See* Mark D. Janis, *Rethinking Reexamination: Toward a Viable Administrative Revocation System for U.S. Patent Law*, 11 HARV. J. L. & TECH. 1 (1997).

The Optional Inter Partes Reexamination Procedure Act of 1999 responded to these concerns by providing third party requesters with an additional option. *See* 35 U.S.C. §§ 311–318. They may employ the traditional reexamination system, which has been renamed an *ex parte* reexamination. Or, they may opt for a considerable degree of participation in the newly minted *inter partes* reexamination. Under this legislation, third party requesters may opt to submit written comments to accompany patentee responses to the PTO. The requester may also appeal PTO determinations that a reexamined patent is not invalid to the Board and the courts. To discourage abuse of *inter partes* reexamination proceedings, the statute provides that third party participants are estopped from raising issues that they raised or could have raised during reexamination during subsequent litigation. Unsuccessful challengers are also *not* allowed to appeal to the Federal Circuit.

Up through an amendment of the *inter partes* reexamination law on November 2, 2002, there had been virtually no use at all of *inter partes* reexamination. The PTO had received a mere handful of requests for *inter partes* reexamination. The new 2002 law, however, permits third parties a right of appeal an *inter partes* reexamination to the Board of Patent Appeals and Interferences and all the way to the Federal Circuit. This advantage for third parties is unique to the *inter partes* reexamination proceeding and not shared by the *ex parte* reexamination requester.

The difference between a reexamination and a reissue may appear elusive, but the following points should illuminate the distinctions between the two post-grant proceedings:

- A request for reexamination may be filed by "any person," while a reissue must be filed with the approval of the patentee.

- A request for reexamination need not point out "error" without deceptive intent, while a reissue application must do so. Thus, the patentee may use reexamination to add narrower claims to the patent without having to file affidavits explaining why they were not included in the original patent.

- A reexamination is directed towards prior art patents and printed publications, while a reissue is directed towards any issue that may be considered in an original application. Where the patentee amends matter in the patent, however, ancillary issues concerning compliance with § 112 and other statutes may arise in a reexamination as well.

- A reexamination cannot be employed to broaden the patent's claims. An applicant may employ a reissue to provide broadened claims if the reissue application is filed within two years from the date of the patent grant, and may also choose to abandon the reissue and the return of its original patent from the PTO. A reexamination cannot be abandoned once initiated by the PTO.

- Claims may be copied from a reissue application in order to place the application into an interference. Reexaminations do not give rise to interferences.

§ 10.6 INTERNATIONAL PROSECUTION

To be effective in an increasingly global economy, inventors often must secure patent rights within many different jurisdictions. So in addition to prosecuting patent applications before their own national or regional patent office, patent attorneys are often called upon to coordinate patent acquisition efforts before many different administrative agencies overseas. Despite the existence of international agreements like the Paris Convention, the Patent Cooperation Treaty (PCT), and the TRIPS Agreement, this effort frequently requires attorneys to address multiple substantive patent laws, granting procedures, and languages. Further, the coordinating attorney must ensure that prosecution efforts in one country do not imperil patentability elsewhere, for example, by invoking one of the several statutory bars under § 102.

The foundational patent law treaty, the Paris Convention, takes some steps to ease this onerous task. As noted in Chapter 1, the Paris Convention, in essence, allows an applicant to obtain a priority date by filing an initial application, typically in the inventor's home country. The applicant may then file a patent application in any country bound by the Convention within twelve months and maintain the earlier priority date.

This basic scheme includes some significant details, which require a more thorough examination of Article 4 of the Paris Convention and its implementing provision, § 119 of the United States Patent Act.

PARIS CONVENTION FOR THE PROTECTION OF INDUSTRIAL PROPERTY

July 14, 1967
21 U.S.T. 1583, T.I.A.S. 6295, 828 U.N.T.S. 305

ARTICLE 4, SECTION A

1. Any person who has duly filed an application for a patent, or for the registration of a utility model, or of an industrial design, or of a trademark, in one of the countries of the Union, or his successor in title, shall enjoy, for the purpose of filing in the other countries, a right of priority during the periods hereinafter fixed.

2. Any filing that is equivalent to a regular national filing under the domestic legislation of any country of the Union or under bilateral or multilateral treaties concluded between countries of the Union shall be recognized as giving rise to the right of priority.

3. By a regular national filing is meant any filing that is adequate to establish the date on which the application was filed in the country concerned, whatever may be the subsequent fate of the application.

ARTICLE 4, SECTION B

Consequently, any subsequent filing in any of the other countries of the Union before the expiration of the periods referred to above shall not be invalidated by reason of any acts accomplished in the interval, in particular, another filing, the publication or exploitation of the invention, the putting on sales of copies of the design, or the use of the mark, and such acts cannot give rise to any third-party right or any right of personal possession. Rights acquired by third parties before the date of the first application that serves as the basis for the right of priority are reserved in accordance with the domestic legislation of each country of the Union.

ARTICLE 4, SECTION C

(1) The periods of priority referred to above shall be twelve months for patents and utility models, and six months for industrial designs and trademarks.

(2) These periods shall start from the date of filing of the first application; the day of filing shall not be included in the period. . . .

ARTICLE 4, SECTION H

Priority may not be refused on the ground that certain elements of the invention for which priority is claimed do not appear among the claims formulated in the application in the country of origin, provided that the application documents as a whole specifically disclose such elements.

NOTES

1. **The Significance of the Paris Convention.** The Paris Convention is the starting point for a consideration of any intellectual property rights in virtually every part of the world. The original Paris treaty from 1883 has been revised several times and today stands in the form of its 1967 Stockholm Revision. Intermediate revisions were completed in Brussels (1900), Washington, D.C. (1911), The Hague (1925), London (1934), and Lisbon (1958). While this casebook focuses upon patents, the treaty is equally important for trademarks and designs. For more information on the Paris Convention, *see* Friedrich–Karl Beier, *One Hundred Years of International Cooperation—The Role of the Paris Convention in the Past, Present and Future*, 15 INT'L REV. INDUS. PROP. & COPYRIGHT L. 1 (1984).

The most fundamental, practical right under Paris is the offensive priority right: By filing in the United States (or in any union country), the clock stands still for one year. Article 4, Section B thus creates a bar against actions leading to patent invalidity based on activities that occurred after the filing in the first union state, but before the filing in any second union state within that one-year period. Thus for this purpose only, one can talk about dating the application in the second union state back to the original union state filing. Of course, the applicant must make a timely claim for priority and meet other formalities. For example, some signatory states require that a priority claim be made simultaneously with the filing of the second application, while others require the filing of a ribboned, certified copy of the priority filing document along with the national application.

2. **Implementation of Article 4 of the Paris Convention in § 119(a).** Section 119(a) lays out the following requirements for ensuring a claim to priority based upon a foreign application.

Both applications must be filed by the same applicant, legal representative or assigns.

Both applications must be for the same invention.

The foreign application must be for a patent. As with § 102, consider the meaning of the term "patent" in light of different schemes.

The first filing must be in an appropriate foreign country. The recognition of the right of priority is not limited to Paris Convention signatories, but to those foreign countries "which afford similar privileges in the case of applications filed in the United States or to citizens of the United States." Note that, in particular, Article 2 of the TRIPS Agreement requires that WTO members comply with Articles 1–12 and 19 of the Paris Convention. The United States is also a party to the scantly invoked Inter–American Convention on Inventions, Patents, Designs, and Industrial Models, 38 Stat. 1811 (1910), which provides for a comparable priority right to that of the Paris Convention.

The United States application must be filed within twelve months of the foreign filing.

A one-year grace period must be respected. Section 119(a) closes with the admonition that "no patent shall be granted on any application for patent for an invention which had been patented or described in a printed publication in any country more than one year before the date of the actual filing of the application in this country, or which had been in public use or on sale in this country more than one year prior to such filing." Is this statute consistent with the Paris Convention? Can you create a fact pattern where this restatement of § 102(b) invalidates a patent that was based on a Paris Convention filing?

3. Importance of the Filing Date. The Paris Convention is concerned only with the initial filing date, without regard to whether that filing actually matures into a granted patent. Thus, the application could be rejected over the prior art or abandoned, yet the filing would remain valid for preserving the right of priority in subsequent filings abroad. However, suppose an inventor files an application claiming a pharmaceutical compound in a country where such inventions are not patent-eligible. Should such an application give rise to a priority right as well?

4. Notice of Priority Filing. The applicant must declare he is relying upon the priority right for it to be effective under Article 4, Section D of the Paris Convention, under § 119(b). This provision also allows each national patent system to set "the latest date on which such declaration must be made." In particular, the Japanese system has imposed strict requirements. TETSU TANABE & HAROLD WEGNER, JAPANESE PATENT PRACTICE 133 (1986). In the United States, failure to claim the benefit of the priority right may be corrected through a reissue proceeding, considered in this casebook at Chapter 13.

5. Patent Office Priority Practice. The U.S. Patent and Trademark Office instructs examiners to make use of claimed priority applications during patent acquisition proceedings only as need requires. "The only times during *ex parte* prosecution that the examiner considers the merits of an applicant's claim or priority is when a reference is found with an effective date of the foreign filing and the date of filing and the United States and when an interference situation is under consideration." MANUAL OF PATENT EXAMINING PROCEDURE § 201.15 (8th ed. 2001). Priority is determined on a claim-by-claim basis, so some claims of a single patent may be entitled to priority from an earlier application, and others may not. Further, an applicant may rely upon two or more foreign applications and may be entitled to the filing date of one of them with regard to certain claims, and to another application with regard to other claims.

6. Resetting the Clock. Article 4(C)(4) permits an applicant to reset his priority date by effectively cancelling the first application:

A subsequent application * * * in the same country * * * shall be considered as the first application [for purposes of starting the priority year] if, at the time of filing the subsequent application, the said previous application has been withdrawn, abandoned, or refused, without having been laid open to public inspection and without leaving any rights outstanding, and if it has not yet served as a basis for claiming a right of priority. The previous application may not thereafter serve as a basis for claiming a right of priority.

The one-year period of priority does not apply for design patents, which are awarded only a six-month period.

7. Provisional Applications. Could an inventor file a provisional application in the United States, as provided in § 111(b) and considered here at Chapter 12, and then claim a right of priority based upon the application when filing abroad? If so, is the filing of a provisional application always the first union application? Alternatively, could an inventor who filed first overseas subsequently file a provisional application in the United States, claiming the priority right? *See* 35 U.S.C.A. § 111(b)(7).

8. Supremacy of Paris over other Treaties. The PCT, EPC, and any other treaties are "sub-treaties" under Paris. They are specifically tolerated through Article 19 of the Paris Convention, which allows signatories to "reserve the right to make separately between themselves special agreements for the protection of industrial property, in so far as these agreements do not contravene the provisions of this Convention."

The recent Trade Related Aspects of Intellectual Property of the World Trade Organization (WTO) is now in force for developed countries and is to be fully implemented even in developing countries by 2005. The TRIPS Agreement sets minimum standards that are complementary to Paris.

9. Disclosure Requirements. Under Paris Convention Article 4H, the invention claimed in subsequent Convention applications must be one in which "the [priority] application documents as a whole specifically discloses [the claimed] elements." The following opinion explores this requirement in further detail.

IN RE GOSTELI

United States Court of Appeals, Federal Circuit, 1989
872 F.2d 1008

Before Bissell and Archer, Circuit Judges, and Re, Chief Judge.

BISSELL, CIRCUIT JUDGE.

DECISION

The decision of the United States Patent and Trademark Office (PTO) Board of Patent Appeals and Interferences (Board), affirming the examiner's final rejection of claims 48–51 in the patent application, Serial No. 423,348, of Jacques Gosteli, Ivan Ernest and Robert B. Woodward [hereinafter Gosteli or Applicants], under 35 U.S.C. § 102(e) (1982), is affirmed.

BACKGROUND

Gosteli's patent application discloses bicyclic thia-aza compounds containing a beta-lactam ring unsubstituted in the beta-position and having antibiotic properties. The claimed compounds are chemical intermediates used in the preparation of antibiotics known as 2–penems. Claims 48 and 49 are Markush-type genus claims, and dependent claims 50 and 51 are subgenus claims, each consisting of 21 specific chemical species. The examiner rejected claims 48–51 under section 102(e) as being anticipated by United States Patent No. 4,155,912 (Menard). Menard discloses, but does not claim, a first species that is within the scope of claims 48 and 50, and a second species, that is within the scope of claims 49 and 51.

Attempting to antedate Menard, Gosteli claimed the benefit, under 35 U.S.C. § 119 (1982), of their Luxembourg patent application's foreign priority date. The disclosure of the Luxembourg application is not as complete as that of Gosteli's United States application. The Luxembourg application discloses a subgenus of the genus claimed in the United States application and specifically describes the two chemical species disclosed by Menard. Menard's effective date is December 14, 1977, seven months after the May 9, 1977, filing date of Gosteli's Luxembourg application, but five months before Gosteli's May 4, 1978, United States filing date. Thus, Menard is not an effective reference under section 102(e) if Applicants are entitled to their Luxembourg priority date.

The Board denied Gosteli the benefit of their Luxembourg priority date reasoning that:

> [Gosteli's] problem in attempting to antedate the Menard reference is that their Luxembourg priority application does not disclose the "same invention" in a manner that complies with the first paragraph of 35 USC 112 as is claimed in the claims on appeal (48–51). In other words claims 48–51 contain considerable subject matter which is not specifically disclosed in the Luxembourg application. . . . Since [Gosteli's] Luxembourg application does not provide a written description of the entire subject matter set forth in the appealed claims 48–51, as required by the first paragraph of 35 USC 112, we have concluded that claims 48–51 have an effective filing date as of the May 4, 1978 filing date of [Gosteli's] grandparent application Serial No. 902,639, and not as of the Luxembourg filing date. Accordingly, [Applicants have] not antedated the Menard reference.

Alternatively, Gosteli attempted to swear behind Menard by using declarations submitted under 37 C.F.R. § 1.131 (1988) (Rule 131). The Board rejected the use of Rule 131, because "the declaration does not . . . contain 'facts showing a completion of the invention in this country before the filing date of' Menard." Gosteli appeals from the Board's decision.

ISSUES

1. Whether claims 48–51 are entitled, under section 119, to the benefit of a foreign priority date.

2. Whether Rule 131 allows Gosteli to swear behind the two chemical species disclosed in Menard by establishing a constructive reduction to practice in this country based on Gosteli's foreign priority date of those two species.

3. Whether Gosteli's Luxembourg priority application provides a written description sufficient to support the entire subject matter of claims 48–51, as required by 35 U.S.C. § 112, ¶ 1 (1982).

OPINION

I. Section 119

Claims 48–51 of Gosteli's application stand rejected under section 102(e) as anticipated by Menard. The two chemical species disclosed by Gosteli's Luxembourg priority application are disclosed by Menard and also fall within the scope of the claims on appeal. Section 102(e) bars the issuance of a patent if its generic claims are anticipated by prior art disclosing individual chemical species. *See, e.g., In re Slayter*, 276 F.2d 408, 411 (CCPA 1960) (stating that species anticipate a generic claim). The parties agree that Menard is an effective anticipatory prior art reference unless Applicants are entitled to their Luxembourg priority date.

Generally, an applicant may antedate prior art by relying on the benefit of a previously filed foreign application to establish an effective date earlier than that of the reference. See 35 U.S.C. § 119; *In re Wertheim*, 541 F.2d 257, 261 (CCPA 1976); Rollins, *35 USC 119— Description and Enablement Requirements*, 67 J.PAT.OFF.SOC'Y 386, 386 (1985). Under section 119, the claims set forth in a United States application are entitled to the benefit of a foreign priority date if the corresponding foreign application supports the claims in the manner required by section 112, ¶ 1. *Wertheim*, 541 F.2d at 261–62; *Kawai v. Metlesics*, 480 F.2d 880, 887–89 (CCPA 1973).

Gosteli contends that their rights under section 119 are determined by focusing on (1) what is the subject matter disclosed in the Luxembourg priority application, and (2) whether that subject matter removes Menard. We disagree with Gosteli's reading of section 119. The statute provides, in pertinent part: An application for patent for an invention filed in this country by any person who has ... previously regularly filed an application for a patent for the same invention in a foreign country ... shall have the same effect as the same application would have if filed in this country on the date on which the application for patent for the same invention was first filed in such foreign country.... 35 U.S.C. § 119. The reference to the "invention" in section 119 clearly refers to what the claims define, not what is disclosed in the foreign application. Cf. *In re Scheiber*, 587 F.2d 59, 61 (CCPA 1978) (stating that "invention" as used in 35 U.S.C. § 120 (Supp. IV 1986), refers to what is claimed). Section 119 provides that a foreign application "shall have the same effect" as if it had been filed in the United States. 35 U.S.C.

§ 119. Accordingly, if the effective filing date of what is claimed in a United States application is at issue, to preserve symmetry of treatment between sections 120 and 119, the foreign priority application must be examined to ascertain if it supports, within the meaning of section 112, ¶ 1, what is claimed in the United States application. Compare *Kawai*, 480 F.2d at 886 (construing the section 112, ¶ 1 requirements of section 119) with *Scheiber*, 587 F.2d at 62 (construing the section 112, ¶ 1 requirements of section 120).

At oral argument, the government conceded that if Gosteli claims the species disclosed in the Luxembourg application they would be entitled to the foreign priority date with regard to those claims. Thus, Menard would be ineffective as a reference against those claimed species, or any other claim properly supported by the Luxembourg disclosure as required by section 112, ¶ 1. We conclude, therefore, that claims 48–51 are entitled to the benefit of their foreign priority date under section 119 only if the foreign priority application properly supports them as required by section 112, ¶ 1. An application relying on the benefit of an earlier filing date in the United States would receive the same treatment under 35 U.S.C. § 120. See *Kawai*, 480 F.2d at 886.

II. Rule 131

As an alternative position, Gosteli contends that they can swear behind Menard, under Rule 131, by establishing a constructive reduction to practice in this country based on their foreign priority date of the two species disclosed by Menard. They reason that the use of a foreign priority date to establish the reduction to practice component for a Rule 131(b) showing is authorized by *In re Mulder*, 716 F.2d 1542, 1544–46 (Fed.Cir.1983), and therefore, showing priority with respect only to as much of the invention as Menard discloses is needed. Gosteli cites the rationale in *In re Stempel*, 241 F.2d 755, 760 (CCPA 1957), in support of their reasoning. We disagree.

Rule 131 requirements are quite specific. To antedate a prior art reference, the applicant submits an oath or declaration alleging acts that establish a completion of the invention in this country before the effective date of the prior art. 37 C.F.R. § 1.131(a).

The requirements and operation of section 119 differ from those of Rule 131. Rule 131 provides a mechanism for removing specific prior art references, whereas section 119 is concerned only with an applicant's effective filing date. Because section 119, unlike Rule 131, operates independently of the prior art, it is appropriate that the showing required under section 119 differs from that required under Rule 131.

This case is distinguishable from *Mulder*. Gosteli's declarations make no mention of acts in this country. Gosteli relies on their Luxembourg application for a constructive reduction to practice date for the two chemical species at issue. That reliance is misplaced. *Mulder* is not purely a section 119 case. In *Mulder*, the conception date was based on activity in the United States, a date earlier than the prior art. Mulder was permitted to establish a constructive reduction to practice date based on his foreign filing. However, the constructive reduction to practice date was after the prior art. Rule 131 permitted Mulder to swear behind the reference, from the constructive reduction to practice date back to his conception date. The use of a foreign filing date in such circumstances is not inconsistent with our decisions. In *Mulder*, there was no dispute about compliance with the section 112 requirements subsumed in section 119. See *Mulder*, 716 F.2d at 1543, 219 USPQ at 191 (stating that "[t]here is no question that applicants complied with all the formalities required by § 119 and related PTO rules").

Gosteli does not point to any activity inside the United States. Furthermore, Gosteli would not need activity in this country if section 119 gave them the benefit of an effective foreign filing date prior to Menard. Under these circumstances, Rule 131 is irrelevant. Thus, we affirm the Board; Gosteli cannot use the Rule 131 declarations filed to swear behind Menard.

III. Written Description Requirement

The Board found that Gosteli's Luxembourg application did not provide a sufficient written description of the entire subject matter of claims 48–51, as required by the first paragraph of section 112, and, accordingly, section 119 was not effective to antedate Menard. Although Gosteli does not have to describe exactly the subject matter claimed, *In re Lukach*, 442 F.2d 967, 969 (CCPA 1971), the description must clearly allow persons of ordinary skill in the art to recognize that Gosteli invented what is claimed. *Wertheim*, 541 F.2d at 262. We review this factual inquiry under the clearly erroneous standard. See id.

"[T]he PTO has the initial burden of presenting evidence or reasons why persons skilled in the art would not recognize in the disclosure a description of the invention defined by the claims." Id. at 263, 191 USPQ at 97. In this case, the PTO has met that burden by pointing out a number of differences between what is disclosed in the Luxembourg priority application and what is claimed in Gosteli's United States application. Gosteli does not dispute that additional subject matter is present in the United States application. Accordingly, the Board's findings are not clearly erroneous.

The Board's decision is

AFFIRMED.

NOTES

1. The Impact of *Gosteli*. After filing a Paris Convention application, inventors will often make further advances in the claimed technology. The inventors want to include those advances in their later-filed applications at the end of the Paris Convention year. These later advances, however, are not supported by earlier-filed applications from which the inventor hopes to obtain priority. The Federal Circuit's insistence that Gosteli's priority document literally describe the expanded chemical genus, or Markush group, recited in claims 48–51 suggests a strict stance towards these circumstances. Although *Gosteli* involved a chemical technology, its holding might reach other sorts of inventions as well. Consider, for example, a priority document that contains a specific pH, temperature, or voltage, followed by a later United States filing that claims a range of such characteristics.

   2. **Responding to *Gosteli*.** In light of *Gosteli*, applicants should be certain to include some claims in a later-filed application which correspond precisely to the disclosure in the priority document. This step will allow at least some patent protection and allow the patent instrument itself to indicate the priority document, a step the United States Patent and Trademark Office takes even where only one claim is entitled to priority. Note that if the later-filed United States patent has issued and the applicant becomes aware of an intervening reference, the applicant may be able to take advantage of reissue proceedings in order to obtain claims that match the disclosure of the priority document. For other strategies on complying with *Gosteli*, see Donald G. Daus, *Paris Convention Priority*, 77 J. PAT. & TRADEMARK OFF. SOC'Y 138, 149 (1995).

   3. **Impact of Changes to § 104.** The Federal Circuit handed down *Gosteli* prior to United States adherence to the TRIPS Agreement. Among other things, the TRIPS Agreement caused the United States to amend 35 U.S.C.A. § 104, thereby allowing individuals to submit evidence of inventive activity that took place abroad. Does this change in the statute weaken Judge Bissel's reasoning in Part III of her opinion?

   4. **The Defensive, Patent–Defeating Right.** Many interpret the "third-party right" language of Paris Convention Article 4B as providing a patent-defeating right to the patentee as to whatever is claimed in his patent, retroactive to his priority date. Commentators sometimes refer to this entitlement as the "senior right." Most patent systems will reject an applicant's claim in an application filed after another individual's priority date. Consider the following sequence of applications, each claiming the identical invention:

	Files		Files	
Inventor A	Country X		Country Z	>
	Jan. 24, 1957		Jan. 23, 1958	

	Files		Files	
Inventor B	Country Y		Country Z	>
	July 31, 1957		July 25, 1958	

Under these circumstances, the officials of the Country Z Patent Office will reject Inventor B's application due to the priority of the Country X application of Inventor A.

   Under this view of the Paris Convention only a "prior claim" approach would be required. This would give a patent owner a patent-defeating right retroactive to the priority date for what is claimed in the patent. The Swiss continue to employ this narrow minimum scope definition of the patent-defeating right.

Most other countries go further and provide a broader patent-defeating right. They employ a "whole contents" patent-defeating effect that covers everything disclosed in the priority document that is carried forward into the patent application. Furthermore, the patent-defeating effect exists not when the patent issues, but at the publication date of 18 months after the priority date. For a general discussion of these issues, see Richard Wieczorek, *Convention Application as Patent–Defeating Rights*, 6 INT'L REV. INDUS. PROP. & COPYRIGHT L. 135 (1975).

Exceptionally, the United States law does not provide for any patent-defeating effect based on a Paris Convention filing. This rule was established in the infamous *Hilmer* opinions set forth below. As set forth in these decisions, the facts are as in the diagram above, with A as Habicht, B as Hilmer, Country X as Switzerland, Country Y as Germany, and Country Z as the United States.

IN RE HILMER

United States Court of Customs and Patent Appeals, 1966
359 F.2d 859

Before Worley, Chief Judge, and Rich, Martin, Smith and Almond, Judges.

RICH JUDGE.

The sole issue is whether a majority of the Patent Office Board of Appeals erred in overturning a consistent administrative practice and interpretation of the law of nearly forty years standing by giving a United States patent effect as prior art as of a foreign filing date to which the patentee of the reference was entitled under 35 U.S.C. 119.

Because it held that a U.S. patent, cited as a prior art reference under 35 U.S.C. 102(e) and 103, is effective as of its foreign "convention" filing date, relying on 35 U.S.C. 119, the board affirmed the rejection of claims 10, 16, and 17 of application serial No. 750,887, filed July 25, 1958, for certain sulfonyl ureas.

This opinion develops the issue, considers the precedents, and explains why, on the basis of legislative history, we hold that section 119 does not modify the express provision of section 102(e) that a reference patent is effective as of the date the application for it was "filed in the United States."

The two "references" relied on are:

Habicht 2,962,530 Nov. 29, 1960 (filed in the United States January 23, 1958, found to be entitled to priority as of the date of filing in Switzerland on January 24, 1957)

Wagner et al. 2,975,212 March 14, 1961 (filed in the United States May 1, 1957)

The rejection here is the aftermath of an interference (No. 90,218) between appellants and Habicht, a priority dispute in which Habicht was the winning party on a single count. He won because appellants conceded priority of the invention of the count to him. The earliest date asserted by appellants for their invention is their German filing date, July 31, 1957, which, we note, is a few months later than Habicht's priority date of January 24, 1957.

After termination of the interference and the return of this application to the examiner for further ex parte prosecution, the examiner rejected the appealed claims on Habicht, as a primary reference, in view of Wagner et al., as a secondary reference, holding the claimed compounds to be "unpatentable over the primary reference in view of the secondary reference which renders them obvious to one of ordinary skill in the art."

Appellants appealed to the board contending, inter alia, that "The Habicht disclosure cannot be utilized as anticipatory art." They said, "The rejection has utilized * * * the disclosure of the winning party as a basis for the rejection. The appellants insist that this is contrary to the patent statutes." Explaining this they said:

> * * * the appellants' German application was filed subsequent to the Swiss filing date (of Habicht) *but prior to the U.S. filing date of the Habicht application.* The appellants now maintain that the Habicht disclosure cannot be utilized as anticipatory in view of 35 U.S.C. 119 which is entitled "Benefit of Earlier Filing Date in Foreign Countries: Right of Priority." This section defines the rights of foreign applicants and more specifically defines those rights with respect to dates to which they are entitled if this same privilege is awarded to citizens of the United States. There is no question (but) that Section 119 only deals with "right of priority." The section does not provide for the use of a U.S. patent as an anticipatory reference as of its foreign filing date. This interpretation of Section 119 is also set forth in the Manual of Patent Examining Procedure (Section 715.01). The Manual refers to *Viviani v. Taylor v. Herzog*, 72 USPQ 448, wherein Commissioner Coe clarified the question of priority rights with respect to foreign and domestic filing.

Appellants further pointed out that:

> "The interference only decided the priority of the interference issue (i.e. the count); there was no decision made nor was there any attempt to decide who was the inventor of the disclosure. The appellants readily admit the priority of Habicht as to the interference issue, but there is no admission as far as the remaining subject matter is concerned."

The board, one member dissenting with an opinion, affirmed the rejection.

The board's statement of the issue is that "the reference patent is found to be entitled to the date of a prior foreign application under 35 USC 119 * * *." To some degree this loads the question. There is in it an implicit assumption that if the patent is "entitled to the date of a prior foreign application," it is *entitled* to it, and that is that. But one must examine closely into what is meant by the word "entitled." In essence, that is the problem in this appeal and we wish to point to it at the outset to dispel any mistaken assumptions. A patent may be "entitled" to a foreign filing date for some purposes and not for others, just as a patent may be "used" in two ways. A patent owner uses his patent as a legal right to exclude others, granted to him under 35 U.S.C. 154. Others, wholly unrelated to the patentee, use a patent, not as a legal right, but simply as evidence of prior invention or prior art, i.e., as a "reference." This is not an exercise of the patent right. This is how the Patent Office is "using" the Habicht patent. These are totally different things, governed by different law, founded on different theories, and developed through different histories.

We have seen that 35 U.S.C. 119 is involved with respect to the so-called "priority date" of the Habicht reference patent. The other statutory provision involved in this case, applicable to both of the references, is 35 U.S.C. 102(e). Section 102 has been aptly described (Meyer article, infra) as containing "patent defeating provisions." They fall into two classes, events prior to an applicant's date of invention and events prior to filing his U.S. application, related respectively to the requirement of novelty and to provisions for loss of right through delay in filing after certain events have made the invention public. Subsection (e) is one of the novelty provisions, one of the "conditions for patentability," and if the facts of an applicant's case bring him within it, his right to a patent is defeated.

Thus, though both references here were patents copending with appellants' application, issuing after it was filed, 102(e) makes then available as of their U.S. filing dates which are earlier than appellants' U.S. filing date. However, since 102(e) refers to the applicant's date of invention, not to his filing date, he is entitled to an opportunity to establish his date of invention to show that his invention possessed statutory novelty when he made it. In this case appellants did this by showing that they filed a German application earlier than the U.S. filing dates of the references, specified in 102(e), and that they were entitled to its date for "priority" under section 119. This right is not in question. The board ruled:

> Appellants have overcome the U.S. filing date of Habicht by claiming the benefit under 35 USC 119 of an application filed in Germany on July 31, 1957. The specification of this German application has been examined and is found to contain a full disclosure of the subject matter of the claims, and the U.S. filing date of Habicht is considered overcome.

We can now summarize the issue and simultaneously state the board's decision. Continuing the above quotation, the board said:

> The Examiner insists, however, that the effective date of the Habicht patent is January 24, 1957, the date of an application filed in Switzerland which is claimed by Habicht under 35 USC 119.

Appellants have not overcome this earlier date of Habicht. The issue is hence presented of whether the foreign priority date of a United States patent can be used as the effective filing date of the patent when it is used as a reference. (And this is the second statement of the issue by the board.) Our conclusion is that the priority date governs * * *.

This is the decision alleged to be in error. We think it was error.

OPINION

The board's construction is based on the idea that the language of [§ 119] is plain, that it means what it says, and that what it says is that the application filed abroad is to have the same effect as though it were filed here—for all purposes. We can reverse the statement to say that the actual U.S. application is to have the same effect as though it were filed in the U.S. on the day when the foreign application was filed, the whole thing being a question of effective date. We take it either way because it makes no difference here.

Before getting into history, we note first that there is in the very words of the statute a refutation of this literalism. It says "shall have the same effect" and it then says "but" for several situations it shall not have the same effect, namely, it does not enjoy the foreign date with respect to any of the patent-defeating provisions based on publication or patenting anywhere in the world or public use or being on sale in this country more than one year before the date of actual filing in this country.

As to the other statute involved, we point out that the words of section 102(e), which the board "simply" reads together with section 119, also seem plain. Perhaps they mean precisely what they say in specifying, as an express patent-defeating provision, an application by another describing the invention but only as of the date it is "filed in the United States."

The great logical flaw we see in the board's reasoning is in its premise (or is it an a priori conclusion?) that "these two provisions must be read together." Doing so, it says 119 in effect destroys the plain meaning of 102(e) but the board will not indulge the reverse construction in which the plain words of 102(e) limit the apparent meaning of 119. We see no reason for reading these two provisions together and the board has stated none. We believe, with the dissenting board member, that 119 and 102(e) deal with unrelated concepts and further that the historical origins of the two sections show neither was intended to affect the other, wherefore they should not be read together in violation of the most basic rule of statutory construction, the "master rule," of carrying out the legislative intent. Additionally, we have a long and consistent administrative practice in applying an interpretation contrary to the new view of the board, confirmed by legislation ratification in 1952. We will consider these matters separately.

Section 119

We shall now take up the history and purpose of section 119. The board opinion devotes the equivalent of four pages in the printed record to a scholarly and detailed review of the history of section 119 with all of which we agree, except for the interwoven conclusions as to its meaning as it bears on the effective date of a U.S. patent used as a reference.

The board shows that the predecessor statute (R.S. 4887), containing the words "shall have the same force and effect," was enacted March 3, 1903 (32 Stat. 1225). Theodore Roosevelt signed it into law. The bill was drafted and proposed by a Commission created by Act of Congress in 1898 (30 Stat. 431) to study the effect of the Convention of Paris for the Protection of Industrial Property of 20th March 1883, which was under revision at Brussels even as the Commission deliberated, the revision being adopted at Brussels on 14th December 1900. (It was last revised at Lisbon on 31st October 1958.) The Commission made a report November 27, 1900, printed in 1902, entitled "Report of the Commissioners Appointed to Revise the Laws Relating to Patents, Trademarks, and Trade Names, with Reference to Existing Conventions and Treaties," which is fairly descriptive of its purpose. The section entitled "The Revision of the Patent Law," which we have read, extends from page 6 to page 39. It begins by saying (p. 6):

We have found it desirable in considering the question of revision of the patent law to first consider what changes in the law are needed to give full force and effect to the treaty obligations which the United States has undertaken touching the protection of inventions made by the subjects or citizens of certain foreign countries.

Under the heading "Priority Under the Convention," it says (p. 12):

The second provision of the Convention to be noticed, and one which may be of very great advantage to those of our citizens who desire to secure patents in foreign countries for their inventions, is that contained in article 4, and relates to the so called "delay of priority," or "period of priority."

It then explained that in most countries no valid patent can be obtained if *before the application is filed*, the invention has been described in a printed publication, either in the country of application or even, as in the case of France and six other countries, in any country; that the same was true as to public use of the invention; and that the convention gives applicants in member countries a period (then 7 months, soon extended to 12) in which they can file applications in other countries after the filing in their own country and obtain valid patents notwithstanding publication or use in the interval and before the filing of the foreign application. This, it explained, is the "delay of priority." In plain English, it was the right of an applicant to have the foreign application treated at law as prior to the intervening publication or public use, though in fact it was not, by giving a right to that applicant to delay filing in the foreign country, instead of filing simultaneously with the home application, yet have it treated as though filed on the date of the home application. This is what today we call simply "Convention priority," or just "priority." The foreign filing date is the "convention date" or the "priority date."

This priority right was a protection to one who was trying to obtain patents in foreign countries, the protection being against patent-defeating provisions of national laws based on events intervening between the time of filing at home and filing abroad. Under the heading "Recapitulation of Advantages Secured by the Convention," the Commission said, so far as relevant here (pp. 14–15):

> The advantages to our citizens in the matter of patents directly afforded by the convention may be thus recapitulated.

> First. The enjoyment in foreign countries of equal rights with subjects or citizens of those countries.

> Second. The "delay of priority" of seven months within which to file applications abroad after filing in this country.

> Third. The privilege of introducing articles embodying the invention manufactured in this country into foreign countries to a certain extent without thereby causing the forfeiture of the patents taken out there.

Note the emphasis repeatedly placed in the Commission Report on advantages to United States citizens. It was felt we should do what was necessary to comply with the reciprocity provisions to enjoy the benefits of the convention for our own citizens. It was also believed that by reason of Opinions of Attorneys General, Vol. 19, 273, "the International Convention, in so far as the agreements therein contained are not in accordance with the present laws of the United States, is without force and effect; that it is not self-executing, but requires legislation to render it effective * * * and * * * it is our opinion that such legislation should be adopted * * *." (Report p. 19.)

Specific to the question here, the Commission Report says (p. 24):

> We are, therefore, of the opinion that an amendment to the law should be made, providing that the foreign application shall have, in case an application is filed in this country by the applicant abroad within the specified period, the same effect as if filed here on the day it was filed abroad.

The board thinks this "shows the intention of the Commissioners" to create "a status of (an application) having been filed in the U.S. for all purposes * * *." In the contest of this case, that means for the purpose of using a U.S. patent, obtained with a claim of priority, as a prior art patent to defeat the right of a third party to a patent on subject matter which does not patentably distinguish from anything that happens to be disclosed in such patent—or at least from anything disclosed "relevant to the (there) claimed invention," depending on which recent board opinion one looks at. We have read every word of the Commission Report looking for any suggestion of such a concept and have found none. All the board found was the above quotation. We deem it wholly inadequate as a basis for finding an intent to create a "status" for an application—to say nothing of the patent granted thereon—"for all purposes." There are other factors to consider which negative any such legislative intent.

There is another sentence in the Commission Report we should consider on page 26. It called attention to the fact that in most foreign countries the patent is granted to the first to apply and said:

> The Convention has created an exception to the rule and made an application in any State of the Union for the Protection of Industrial Property of the same effect as an application in the country where an application is subsequently made within the time specified as a period of priority.

This couples very nicely with the wording of the first recommendation for a change in U.S. laws on page 27 where it was said:

> First. The application for a patent filed within seven months of the filing of an application for a patent for the same invention in any foreign country which is a party to the International Convention should be given the same force as regards the question of priority that it would have if filed on the date on which the foreign application was filed.

The Commission, page 36, recommended proposed legislation, which is, in substance, the amendment to R.S. 4887 which was passed and is, with no change in substance, what we have today in section 119. The proposed bill in the Commission Report was entitled "A BILL to give effect to treaty stipulations relating to letters patent for inventions." The Act passed was entitled "An Act To effectuate the provisions of the additional act of the international convention for the protection of industrial property." Throughout, the same phrase has always appeared, "shall have the same force and effect," until it was simplified in the 1952 codification to "shall have the same effect." This change was mere modernization in legislative drafting. The Revisers Note to the section says: "The first paragraph is the same as the present law with changes in language." The Federico Commentary on the 1952 Act, 35 U.S.C.A., says (p. 29):

> This so-called right of priority was provided for in the second paragraph of R.S. 4887 which is the basis for the first paragraph of section 119 of this title. * * * (he here states the 4 conditions for obtaining the right) * * * The new statute made no changes in these conditions of the corresponding part of the old statute except to revise the language slightly * * *.

We need not guess what Congress has since believed to be the meaning of the disputed words in section 119, for it has spoken clearly. World wars interfere with normal commerce in industrial property. The one-year period of priority being too short for people in "enemy" countries, we had after World War I a Nolan Act (41 Stat. 1313, Mar. 3, 1921) and after World War II a Boykin Act. Foreign countries had reciprocal acts. One purpose was to extend the period of priority. House Report No. 1498, January 28, 1946, by Mr. Boykin, accompanied H.R. 5223 which became Public Law 690 of the 79th Cong., 2d Sess., Aug. 8, 1946, 60 Stat. 940. Section 1 of the bill, the report says, was to extend "the so-called period of priority," which then existed under R.S. 4887. On p. 3 the report says:

> In this connection, it may be observed that the portion of the statute which provides that the filing of a foreign application—shall have the same force and effect as the same application would have if filed in this country on the date on which the application for patent for the same invention, discovery, or design was first filed in such foreign country—is intended to mean "shall have the same force and effect," etc., insofar as applicant's right to a patent is concerned. This statutory provision has no bearing upon the right of another party to a patent except in the case of an interference where the two parties are claiming the same patentable invention. U.S. Code Congressional Service 1946, p. 1493.

We emphasize none of those words because we wish to emphasize them all. We cannot readily imagine a clearer, more definitive statement as to the legislature's own view of the words "same effect," which now appear in section 119. This statement flatly contradicts the board's views. The board does not mention it. * * *

For the foregoing reasons, we are clearly of the opinion that section 119 is not to be read as anything more than it was originally intended to be by its drafters, the Commission appointed under the 1898 Act of Congress, namely, a revision of our statutes to provide for a right of priority in conformity with the International Convention, for the benefit of United States citizens, by creating the necessary reciprocity with foreign members of the then Paris Union.

The board has mentioned that it was not limited in its terms to that treaty, which is true, so that it also functions relative to other treaties and reciprocal laws. We are unable to deduce from this any intent to affect the date as of which U.S. reference patents are effective. Nor can we do so by reason of another "deviation" from the Convention the board finds in section 4887 (now 119) as to the protection of third parties.

Section 102(e)

We have quoted this section above and pointed out that it is a patent-defeating section, by contrast with section 119 which gives affirmative "priority" rights to applicants notwithstanding it is drafted in terms of "An application." The priority right is to save the applicant (or his application if one prefers to say it that way) from patent-defeating provisions such as 102(e); and of course it has the same effect in guarding the validity of the patent when issued.

Section 102(e), on the other hand, is one of the provisions which defeats applicants and invalidates patents and is closely related in fact and in history to the requirement of section 102(a) which prohibits a patent if

> (a) the invention was known or used by others in this country, or patented or described in a printed publication in this or a foreign country, before the invention thereof by the applicant for patent, * * *.

In fact, section 102(e) springs straight from 102(a)'s predecessor, R.S. 4886, by decision of the United States Supreme Court in 1926. It was pure case law until 1952 when, having become firmly established, that law was codified by incorporating it in the statute.

We will not undertake to trace the ancestry of 102(e) back of its immediate parentage but clearly it had ancestors or it would never have come to the Supreme Court. We will regard its actual birth as the case of *Alexander Milburn Co. v. Davis–Bournonville* Co., 270 U.S. 390, 46 S.Ct. 324, 70 L.Ed. 651 (March 8, 1926), which we shall call *Milburn*. . . .

We need not go into the reasoning of the *Milburn* case, which has its weaknesses, because all that matters is the rule of law it established: That a complete description of an invention in a U.S. patent application, filed before the date of invention of another, if it matures into a patent, may be used to show that that other was not the first inventor. This was a patent-defeating, judge-made rule and now is section 102(e). The rule has been expanded somewhat subsequent to 1926 so that the reference patent may be used as of its U.S. filing date as a general prior art reference, as shown by *In re Harry*, 333 F.2d 920, 51 CCPA 1541 (1964), and the December 8, 1965 Supreme Court decision in *Hazeltine Research, Inc. v. Brenner*, 382 U.S. 252, 86 S.Ct. 335, 15 L.Ed.2d 304.

What has always been pointed out in attacks on the *Milburn* rule, or in attempts to limit it, is that it uses, as prior knowledge, information which was secret at the time as of which it is used—the contents of U.S. patent applications which are preserved in secrecy, generally speaking, 35 U.S.C. 122. This is true, and we think there is some validity to the argument that that which is secret should be in a different category from knowledge which is public. Nevertheless we have the rule. However, we are not disposed to extend that rule, which applies to the date of filing applications in the United States, the actual filing date when the disclosure is on deposit in the U.S. Patent Office and on its way, in due course, to publication in an issued patent.

The board's new view, as expressed in this case and in the Zemla and Rapala decisions, the latter sustained in Lilly, has the practical potential effect of pushing back the date of the unpublished, secret disclosures, which ultimately have effect as prior art references in the form of U.S. patents, by the full one-year priority period of section 119.

We think the *Milburn* rule, as codified in section 102(e), goes far enough in that direction. We see no valid reason to go further, certainly no compelling reason.

We have seen that section 119 originated in 1903 and that its purpose was to grant protective priority rights so that the United States might be a participating member in the International Convention by giving reciprocal priority rights to foreign applicants with respect to the obtaining of patents. We have also seen that section 102(e) was the codification of a court-developed patent-defeating rule based on a statutory requirement that an applicant's invention must not have been previously known by others in this country. We see no such relation between these two rules of law as requires them to be read together and it is our view that section 119 should not be so read with 102(e) as to modify the express limitation of the latter to applications "filed in the United States."

Section 104

It seems clear to us that the prohibitions of 104, the limitations in sections 102(a) and 102(g) to "in this country," and the specifying in 102(e) of an application filed "in the United States" clearly demonstrates a policy in our patent statutes to the effect that knowledge and acts in a foreign country are not to defeat the rights of applicants for patents, except as applicants may become involved in priority disputes. We think it follows that section 119 must be interpreted as giving only a positive right or benefit to an applicant who has first filed abroad to protect him against possible intervening patent-defeating events in obtaining a patent. Heretofore it has always been so interpreted with the minor exceptions, of little value as precedents, hereinafter discussed. So construed, it has no effect on the effective date of a U.S. patent as a reference under section 102(e).

Section 120

At oral argument the Patent Office Solicitor argued by "analogy" from 35 U.S.C. 120 (a section which he said gives one U.S. application the benefit of an earlier U.S. application under specified circumstances for all purposes) that section 119 should similarly give to a patent, used as a reference under section 102(e), effect as of an earlier foreign filing date.

* * * One aspect of it is that sections 119 and 120 contain the "same phrase," namely "shall have the same effect."

We find no substance in this argument because: (1) as above pointed out, out statute law makes a clear distinction between acts abroad and acts here except for patents and printed publications. Section 120, following policy in sections 102(a), (e) and (g) and 104, contains the limitation to applications "filed in the United States," excluding foreign applications from its scope. (2) Use of the same expression is mere happenstance and no reason to transfer the meaning and effect of section 120 as to U.S. filing dates to section 119 with respect to foreign filing dates. Section 120 was not drafted until 49 years after the predecessor of section 119 was in the statute.

* * * The decision of the board is reversed and the case is remanded for further proceedings consistent herewith.

Reversed and remanded.

NOTES

1.   The Effect of *Hilmer*. Does the *Hilmer* rule result in more granted United States patents or fewer? In terms of nationality, who most often stands to benefit from the *Hilmer* Rule? Do strong policy reasons support the granting of more than one valid patent towards inventions that are not patentably distinct?

2.   *Hilmer II*. Another opinion, *In re Hilmer*, 424 F.2d 1108 (CCPA 1970) ("*Hilmer II*"), involved the same dispute and effectively served as a sequel to its well-known predecessor. There the PTO asserted a different ground for rejection of Hilmer's application: It tried to combine section 119 with section 102(g) to establish Habicht as disqualifying prior art. Stated differently, the PTO argued that the Habicht reference should be deemed to have been invented at the latest as of its filing date in Switzerland (January 24, 1957)—which is an earlier date of invention that Hilmer could demonstrate via his German filing date (July 31, 1957). As a result, the PTO reasoned this second time around, Habicht could serve as prior art against Hilmer under section 102(g). Predictably, the CCPA once more reversed. The court once again concluded that Habicht was not prior art because it deemed section 119 to serve a defensive priority-preserver, not an offensive patent-defeater—whether the provision defining prior art was section 102(e) or section 102(g).

3.   Bypassing *Hilmer*. One way to avoid the *Hilmer* holdings is to file an application in the United States as quickly as possible after the foreign filing. A ready means of doing this is by filing a provisional patent application under § 111(b), given its diminished formal requirements as compared to an ordinary application. See Chapter 12 of this casebook for more details. An impediment against this approach may be a particular national patent system's requirement for a foreign patent filing license, analogous to § 181 of the United States Patent Act. Another way is to file a PCT application and then have it published in English. For more information on this method see the PCT materials, *infra*.

4.   Further Reading. The *Hilmer* rule finds a defender in Kate H. Murashige, *The* Hilmer *Doctrine, Self–Collision, Novelty and the Definition of Prior Art*, 26 J. MARSHALL L. REV. 549 (1993). Kevin L. Leffel, Comment, Hilmer *Doctrine and Patent System Harmonization: What Does A Foreign Inventor Have At Stake?*, 26 AKRON L. REV. 355 (1992) describes the origin of the *Hilmer* doctrine and proposes legislative reforms.

5.   The Patent Cooperation Treaty. Open to any Paris Convention signatory, the PCT complements that treaty by providing for the filing of a patent application than can have an effect in many countries. Within the one-year

Paris Convention deadline for foreign filing, one may file a PCT application in his home country patent office that *designates* the states for which protection is desired. This step serves as an alternative to filing in numerous foreign patent offices, deferring the huge costs of foreign filings that often include expensive translations.

The PCT application is processed in the home patent office that operates as a PCT "Receiving Office." The application is automatically published eighteen months from the priority date. Officials from a PCT office also conduct a prior art search. Within nineteen months from priority date, an optional fee may be paid with a request for an international preliminary examination.

An international preliminary examination is a most abbreviated affair, creating a non-binding opinion on the patentability of the invention. Within thirty months from the priority date, the patent applicant must convert the PCT application into a series of parallel foreign applications as part of the "national stage." Failure to convert to the national stage constitutes a forfeiture of the patent application for such states.

The PCT filing is important today as a time and cost shifting mechanism. Global rights can be put on hold, at the Paris Convention deadline, for a moderate fee of several thousand dollars—putting off the several tens of thousands of dollars in fees that will be required thirty months from the priority date when the "national stage" is to be entered. Often, the money for the PCT application can be raised simply through giving a right to negotiate or an option on foreign rights. The patent applicant then has a precious, additional eighteen months until the thirty month national stage deadline to evaluate the invention and raise funding for the large foreign filing costs that will kick in at the thirty month national stage deadline. Or, the application can be abandoned in good conscience when no takers appear after a diligent effort.

6. The European Patent Convention. Under the European Patent Convention, applicants file a single European application instead of in some or all of the member states of the treaty. After conclusion of this single prosecution, a single opposition period occurs for the granted European patent. Thereafter, the European rights are split into a country-by-country situation of patent validity and claim interpretation, with rights being enforced and defended individually.

Prosecution Exercises

1. Norton, Shottky, and Thevenin each work for the Consolidated Technology Corporation. Norton, a technical manager, directs research engineer Shottky to develop an improved snowboard boot. Shottky studies the various products available on the market and conceives of the concept of a removable stiffening stay housed in a pocket on the upper portion of the boot. He then instructs Thevenin, a laboratory technician, to construct such a boot with a stiffening stay. Thevenin constructed the boot following Shottky's instructions and ran standardized tests that demonstrated its improved quality. Norton subsequently directs that a patent application be filed relating to an adjustably

stiffenable boot for use with snowboarding. *Which individuals should be named as inventors?*

2. Rosenberg filed a nonprovisional utility patent application on May 3, 2004, in the United States claiming an apparatus and method for cryogenically cleaning surfaces. Rosenberg also filed an application in Belgium on April 2, 2005, directed to the identical apparatus and method. The Belgian application was patented and published on May 1, 2006.

As of July 8, 2008, Rosenberg had abandoned the application he had filed on May 3, 1994. Previously, on July 2, 2007, Rosenberg filed a continuation of the original application, making specific reference to the original application. The continuation matured into a patent claiming only the method of cryogenically cleaning surfaces on February 14, 2008. On February 10, 1998, Rosenberg filed a third application, claiming the apparatus, which specifically referred to and was properly labeled a division of the application filed July 2, 2007. However, this third application did not mention the original application Rosenberg had filed May 3, 2004.

The Examiner rejects the claims of the third application as being anticipated by the Belgian patent. *Is the Examiner's rejection proper? What steps might Rosenberg take to overcome the rejection?*

3. Landau obtained a patent containing one claim to a pencil sharpener on January 19, 2005. On November 17, 2004, Landau had on file a second application containing two claims. Claim 1 is drawn to a pencil sharpener having the same scope as the pencil sharpener covered by the Landau patent, but uses somewhat different descriptive language. Claim 2 is drawn to a pencil sharpener with a support bracket. In view of the Landau patent and another reference, a prior art article written by Mowery, the subject matter of claim 2 would have been obvious.

During prosecution of the second application, the Examiner rejects claims 1 and 2 on the ground of double patenting. In response to the rejection, Landau's patent attorney files an appropriate terminal disclaimer and argues that the double patenting rejection should be withdrawn. The Examiner nonetheless makes the rejection final. *Did the Examiner act appropriately?*

4. Lattimore, while an employee of the ABC Company, filed a first application in the PTO on August 17, 2007, and assigned it to ABC. On December 15, 2007, she left the ABC Company and started work at the XYZ Company. On June 19, 2008, as part of her duties at XYZ Company, Lattimore devised an improvement over the invention claimed in the first application. A second application was filed in the PTO and assigned to the XYZ Company. The XYZ Company subsequently receives an Office Action in which the claims of the second application have been rejected over the claims of the first on the ground of obviousness-type double patenting. As representative of the XYZ Company, you have copies of both of Lattimore's applications and do not believe that the improvement would have been obvious. *What steps should you take in response to the Office Action?*

5. Anthony and Carter are employed by the Retro Bowling Company. Working together, they developed a vacuum vice for holding bowling balls

during drilling operations. Anthony and Carter turned over their laboratory notebooks describing their invention to their supervisor, Dalzell. Dalzell thoroughly reviewed the invention and later instructed Schenkel, a patent attorney, to prepare a patent application directed towards a vice.

On September 1, 2007, Schenkel filed the application at the PTO naming Anthony and Carter as the inventors. On December 1, 2007, Dalzell discovered some sales literature that was published by a competitor on January 10, 1995, and brought these documents to the attention of Schenkel. Dalzell and Schenkel agreed that the sales literature would plainly anticipate some of the claims in the pending patent application. *Under Rule 56, which individuals are obliged to bring the sales literature to the attention of the PTO?*

6. The '777 patent contains one independent and two dependent claims. The owner of the '777 patent, Johnson, files a reissue application fourteen months following the patent's issue date. As requested, the PTO reissues claim 1 as in the original patent, but broadens the scope of claims 2 and 3. Later, Johnson sues Boswell for patent infringement. Boswell admits infringement of all claims of the reissued patent and that the claims are valid. May Boswell successfully raise the defense of intervening rights?

7. The '888 patent relates to an exhaust hood assembly useful for placement above a stove or other cooking apparatus. It issued to MacDaniel on January 5, 2007, with a single claim defining elements A, B, and C. Element B consisted of "a fan with five blades." On July 1, 2009, MacDaniel filed a reissue application, again with a single claim. That claim comprised elements A, B, C, D, and E, where element B consisted of "a fan with a plurality of blades." Did MacDaniel file a proper reissue application?

8. Which of the following may *not* be corrected via reissue?

(A) One of the actual inventors is not named on the patent.

(B) Foreign priority was not claimed under § 119.

(C) The applicant failed to disclose an extremely pertinent prior art reference of which he had knowledge.

(D) The applicant knew, but did not disclose, a particular mode that was determined only after the time of filing to be the superior method of practicing the invention; he did disclose what he in good faith considered to be the best mode.

9. On January 4, 2008, Lestrade, a registered patent attorney, filed in the United States Patent Office a patent application on behalf of inventor Moriarity. The application is directed towards an O-ring seal useful with various chemical processing techniques. The patent ultimately issued on December 13, 2009.

On April 1, 2009, Moriarity begins selling O-rings that were fully disclosed in his application. On September 4, 2010, Moriarity realized that his patent does not claim the precise elements that comprise the O-ring he is actually selling. Moriarity tells Lestrade, "I would like to file a reissue application to seek broadened claims to cover the O-rings I have been selling. However, I'm worried about an on-sale bar under section 102(b). What is the last possible date on which I can file—or should have filed—a reissue application?"

What is the last possible date that a broadening reissue may be filed with respect to the Moriarity patent?

10. A United States patent issued to Nimmer on September 1, 2007. The Nimmer patent describes and claims a coffee grinding machine. Nimmer's chief competitor, Goldstein, wishes to file a third party request for reexamination. He is aware of the following possibilities for filing the request:

(A) Goldstein's own patent application filed on August 12, 2005. The application disclosed, but did not claim, the identical coffee grinding machine in Nimmer's patent. However, Goldstein ultimately abandoned the application on May 1, 2007, and no patent ever arose out of that application.

(B) Evidence that Nimmer sold the claimed invention to the Brown & Denicola Company of Boston, Massachusetts, on January 5, 2006.

(C) Evidence that a third party, the Litman Coffee Company, publicly used the same coffee grinder in Ann Arbor, Michigan, from March through June, 2006.

(D) A British patent, issued to Dworkin, which describes and claims the invention. The British patent issued on November 6, 2001, based upon an application filed in the United Kingdom on January 28, 2000.

May Goldstein file a request for reexamination with any chance of success? On what ground, if any?

11. Okimoto files a patent application at the Japanese Patent Office on March 12, 2005. Its specification describes a toothbrush with bristles fabricated from a novel artificial fiber which supposedly is particularly effective at removing plaque. The specification also describes a specially-shaped handle which is easy to grip. The sole claim of the patent claims the artificial fiber for use as a toothbrush bristle material.

Is Okimoto able to obtain priority in the United States based upon the Japanese application in the following circumstances? Unless otherwise noted, all subsequent applications are precise translations of the Japanese original.

a. Okimoto files a United States application on March 12, 2006.

b. Okimoto notifies the Japanese Patent Office that he will abandon his application on April 2, 2000. He then files a United States application on January 25, 2006.

c. Okimoto files a German application on September 1, 2005. He then files a United States application on May 1, 2006.

d. Okimoto files a United States application on December 1, 2005, with a single claim directed to a particular shape of a toothbrush handle.

CHAPTER ELEVEN

INFRINGEMENT

■ ■ ■

    With few words, the patent statute addresses infringement at section 271:

> Except as otherwise provided in this title, whoever without authority makes, uses, offers to sell, or sells any patented invention, within the United States or imports into the United States any patented invention during the term of the patent therefor, infringes the patent.

This modest provision carries much of the weight of the Patent Act. For instance, § 271(a) twice uses the term "patented invention"—a deceptively simple phrase. The words "patented invention" determine the scope of the infringement inquiry. If the accused infringer appropriated the patented invention without authority, he has infringed and must "face the music." Before any determination of infringement or remedies, however, § 271(a) demands a definition of the "patented invention." As the preceding chapters have shown, the one task in patent law that may rival the difficulty of drafting claims is discerning what these claims mean. The following magisterial dicta serve as a fine prelude to this thorny issue.

AUTOGIRO CO. OF AMERICA v. UNITED STATES

United States Court of Claims, 1967
384 F.2d 391

I

* * *

    The claims of the patent provide the concise formal definition of the invention. They are the numbered paragraphs which "particularly (point) out and distinctly (claim) the subject matter which the applicant regards as his invention." 35 U.S.C. § 112. It is to these wordings that one must look to determine whether there has been infringement. Courts can neither broaden nor narrow the claims to give the patentee something different than what he has set forth. No matter how great the temptations of fairness or policy making, courts do not rework claims. They only interpret them. Although courts are confined by the language of the claims, they are not, however, confined to the language of the claims in interpreting their meaning.

Courts occasionally have confined themselves to the language of the claims. When claims have been found clear and unambiguous, courts have not gone beyond them to determine their content. Courts have also held that the fact that claims are free from ambiguity is no reason for limiting the material which may be inspected for the purpose of better understanding the meaning of claims.

We find both approaches to be hypothetical. Claims cannot be clear and unambiguous on their face. A comparison must exist. The lucidity of a claim is determined in light of what ideas it is trying to convey. Only by knowing the idea, can one decide how much shadow encumbers the reality.

The very nature of words would make a clear and unambiguous claim a rare occurrence. Writing on statutory interpretation, Justice Frankfurter commented on the inexactitude of words:

> They are symbols of meaning. But unlike mathematical symbols, the phrasing of a document, especially a complicated enactment, seldom attains more than approximate precision. If individual words are inexact symbols, with shifting variables, their configuration can hardly achieve invariant meaning or assured definiteness.

Frankfurter, *Some Reflections on the Reading of Statutes*, 47 COL.L.REV. 527, 528 (1947). *See, also, A Re–Evaluation of the Use of Legislative History in the Federal Courts*, 52 COL.L.REV. 125 (1952).

The inability of words to achieve precision is none the less extant with patent claims than it is with statutes. The problem is likely more acute with claims. Statutes by definition are the reduction of ideas to print. Since the ability to verbalize is crucial in statutory enactment, legislators develop a facility with words not equally developed in inventors. An invention exists most importantly as a tangible structure or a series of drawings. A verbal portrayal is usually an afterthought written to satisfy the requirements of patent law. This conversion of machine to words allows for unintended idea gaps which cannot be satisfactorily filled. Often the invention is novel and words do not exist to describe it. The dictionary does not always keep abreast of the inventor. It cannot. Things are not made for the sake of words, but words for things. To overcome this lag, patent law allows the inventor to be his own lexicographer.

Allowing the patentee verbal license only augments the difficulty of understanding the claims. The sanction of new words or hybrids from old ones not only leaves one unsure what a rose is, but also unsure whether a rose is a rose. Thus we find that a claim cannot be interpreted without going beyond the claim itself. No matter how clear a claim appears to be, lurking in the background are documents that may completely disrupt initial views on its meaning.

The necessity for a sensible and systematic approach to claim interpretation is axiomatic. The Alice-in-Wonderland view that something means whatever one chooses it to mean makes for enjoyable reading, but bad law. Claims are best construed in connection with the other parts of the patent instrument and with the circumstances surrounding the inception of the patent application. In utilizing all the patent documents, one should not sacrifice the value of these references by the 'unimaginative adherence to well-worn professional phrases.' Frankfurter, *supra*, at 529. Patent law is replete with major canons of construction of minor value which have seldom provided useful guidance in the unraveling of complex claims. Instead, these canons have only added confusion to the problem of claim interpretation.

II

In deriving the meaning of a claim, we inspect all useful documents and reach what Justice Holmes called the "felt meaning" of the claim. In seeking this goal, we make use of three parts of the patent: the specification, the drawings, and the file wrapper.

Specification.—Section 112 of the 1952 Patent Act requires the specification to describe the manner and process of making and using the patent so that any person skilled in the patent's art may utilize it. In serving its statutory purpose, the specification aids in ascertaining the scope and meaning of the language employed in the claims inasmuch as words must be used in the same way in both the claims and the specification. The use of the specification as a concordance for the claim is accepted by almost every court, and is a basic concept of patent law. Most courts have simply stated that the specification is to be used to explain the claims; others have stated the proposition in different terms, but with the same effect.

Drawings.—The patent may contain drawings. In those instances where a visual representation can flesh out words, drawings may be used in the same manner and with the same limitations as the specification.

File wrapper.—The file wrapper contains the entire record of the proceedings in the Patent Office from the first application papers to the issued patent. Since all express representations of the patent applicant made to induce a patent grant are in the file wrapper, this material provides an accurate charting of the patent's pre-issuance history. One use of the file wrapper is file wrapper estoppel, which is the application of familiar estoppel principles to Patent Office prosecution and patent infringement litigation. The patent applicant must convince the patent examiner that his invention meets the statutory requirements; otherwise, a patent will not be issued. When the application is rejected, the applicant will insert limitations and restrictions for the purpose of inducing the Patent Office to grant his patent. When the patent is issued, the patentee cannot disclaim these alterations and seek an interpretation that would ignore them. He cannot construe the claims narrowly before the Patent Office and later broadly before the courts. File wrapper estoppel serves two functions in claim interpretation; the applicant's statements not only define terms, but also set the barriers within which the claim's meaning must be kept. These results arise when the file wrapper discloses either what the claim covers or what it does not cover.

The file wrapper also has a broader and more general use. This is its utilization, like the specification and drawings, to determine the scope of claims. For example, the prior art cited in the file wrapper is used in this manner. In file wrapper estoppel, it is not the prior art that provides the guidelines, but the applicant's acquiescence with regard to the prior art. In its broader use as source material, the prior art cited in the file wrapper gives clues as to what the claims do not cover.

NOTES

1. **The Hermeneutics of *Autogiro*.** This wandering dicta from the Court of Claims remains among the leading attempts to set forth broadly applicable norms of that fundamental task of the patent bar, claim interpretation. Because the patent law first and foremost transforms technology into text, patent lawyers share much in common with practitioners of the disciplines of linguistic philosophy, philology, hermeneutics, and, more recently, the "law and literature" movement. Yet few jurists turn to the teaching of these authorities, perhaps with good reason; why should one read patent claims differently from, say, a historical narrative or a work of fiction? What holistic comments can you offer about these technological aphorisms, such as the grammar, internal consistency, physical embodiment, or intent of the drafter regarding a particular claim? Should any of these factors even bear relevance to the ontological task of the reader? As you will see in the pages that follow, the search for a serviceable lodestar of patent claim interpretation has been an elusive one.

2. **Interpretation vs. Construction.** As seen in the *Markman* opinion which follows, most courts and commentators employ the terms "interpretation" and "construction" interchangeably to refer to the process of understanding the meaning of a patent claim. However, at one point, the United States Patent and Trademark Office contended that a substantive difference existed between these terms. More specifically, according to the PTO, courts were the only entities which "construed" claims, while the PTO performed the task of "interpretation." The PTO pointed to language in opinions such as *Burlington Industries v. Quigg*, 822 F.2d 1581, 1583 (Fed.Cir.1987), which provided that "[i]ssues of judicial claim construction such as arise after patent issuance, for example during infringement litigation, have no place in prosecution of pending claims before the PTO...." Should the use of the term "construed" in § 112 ¶ 6 influence this decision?

The Federal Circuit has recognized one significant difference that does arise between claim interpretation at the PTO versus claim interpretation during infringement litigation. As stated in *In re Zletz*, 893 F.2d 319 (Fed.Cir. 1989):

The Board erred in its interpretation of claims 13 and 14, the error apparently flowing from the Board's choice of inapplicable legal premise. The Board applied the mode of claim interpretation that is used by the courts in litigation, when interpreting the claims of issued patents in connection with determinations of infringement or validity. *See, e.g., Tandon Corp. v. United States Int'l Trade Comm'n,* 831 F.2d 1017, 1021 (Fed.Cir. 1987) (meaning of claims of issued patent interpreted in light of specification, prosecution history, prior art, and other claims). That is not the mode of claim interpretation that is applicable during prosecution of a pending application before the PTO.

During patent examination the pending claims must be interpreted as broadly as their terms reasonably allow. When the applicant states the meaning that the claim terms are intended to have, the claims are examined with that meaning, in order to achieve a complete exploration of the applicant's invention and its relation to the prior art. The reason is simply that during patent prosecution when claims can be amended, ambiguities should be recognized, scope and breadth of language explored, and clarification imposed. An essential purpose of patent examination is to fashion claims that are precise, clear, correct, and unambiguous. Only in this way can uncertainties of claim scope be removed, as much as possible, during the administrative process.

893 F.2d at 321–22.

3. Copyright Contrast. Note that unlike copyright law, patent law does not require that infringers copy the protected subject matter. A competitor who independently creates the claimed invention is still an infringer. Why do you think the protection offered by a patent is so much stronger? Is this simply a matter for legal historians, or does such a telling difference exist between patentable inventions and works of authorship that justifies the dissimilarities between these intellectual property schemes?

In considering this question, imagine what you would advise corporate engineers who are working on a new technology. Would you instruct them not to read anything for fear that anything they learn from reading will lead to liability? Would you demand clean-room conditions? *See* Martin J. Adelman, *Property Rights Theory and Patent–Antitrust: The Role of Compulsory Licensing,* 52 N.Y.U. L. REV. 977, 983–84 (1977).

4. Trademark Contrast. The essential test of trademark infringement stands markedly close to one of the chief aims of trademark law itself: prevention of consumer confusion. As will be seen throughout this chapter, patent infringement law has not achieved this transparency. How could standards of patent infringement law be better tuned towards the constitutionally mandated aspiration of promoting the useful arts? For some suggestions, see JAMES BOYLE, SHAMANS, SOFTWARE AND SPLEENS 172 (1996) ("Patents should be voidable at the instance of any party who can prove that an adequate return would have been provided merely by being first to market, with the state paying the legal fees for successful suits."); Robert P. Merges & Richard R. Nelson, *On the Complex Economics of Patent Scope,* 90 COL. L. REV. 839 (1990) (advocating use of the reverse doctrine of equivalents and other mechanisms governing claim breadth in order to optimize the promotion of technological development).

No intent needed for Infringement & quasi in rem

5. Patent Infringement and Intent. Similarly, a defendant's intent is irrelevant to the outcome of an infringement inquiry. Even an individual who has never previously known of the asserted patent or even of the entire patent system may be found to be an infringer. Infringement analyses thus have a *quasi in rem* flavor; they are entirely based upon a comparison of the patent's claim to a physical technology. Note, however, that an infringer's intent may be relevant to indirect infringement, discussed later in this Chapter; as well as when a remedy is fashioned, as considered in Chapter 17. Further, some judges would bring an equitable flavor into infringement inquiries under the Doctrine of Equivalents, which could introduce intent elements there as well.

offers to sell and imports are acts of infringement

6. Infringing Acts. Before 1996, § 271(a) and its predecessor statutes defined as infringements only the acts of making, using, or selling the patented invention. Domestic legislation implementing the TRIPS Agreement augmented this definition by including the acts of making "offers to sell" and introducing "imports into the United States" as well. Under § 271(i), an offer to sell only infringes where the sale will occur before expiration of the patent.

§ 11.1 LITERAL INFRINGEMENT

Before the Federal Circuit, jury trials in patent cases were somewhat rare. No doubt the difficulty of defending the patent against validity challenges contributed to that rarity. Nonetheless the advent of the Federal Circuit invigorated the practice of patent law and the frequency of jury trials. More jury trials also prompted serious questions about a lay jury's ability to comprehend and resolve complex scientific and legal issues. Claim interpretation, of course, was particularly difficult for juries. At length, the Federal Circuit resolved to settle *en banc* the question of whether claim interpretation is an issue within the ambit of the Seventh Amendment. This *en banc* opinion became perhaps the most important patent opinion of the 1990s because it defines the modern approach to claim interpretation.

MARKMAN v. WESTVIEW INSTRUMENTS, INC.

United States Supreme Court, 1996
517 U.S. 370

JUSTICE SOUTER delivered the opinion of the Court.

The question here is whether the interpretation of a so-called patent claim, the portion of the patent document that defines the scope of the patentee's rights, is a matter of law reserved entirely for the court, or subject to a Seventh Amendment guarantee that a jury will determine the meaning of any disputed term of art about which expert testimony is offered. We hold that the construction of a patent, including terms of art within its claim, is exclusively within the province of the court.

I

The Constitution empowers Congress "[t]o promote the Progress of Science and useful Arts, by securing for limited Times to Authors and Inventors the exclusive Right to their respective Writings and Discoveries." Art. I, § 8, cl. 8. Congress first exercised this authority in 1790, when it provided for the issuance of "letters patent," Act of Apr. 10, 1790, ch. 7, § 1, 1 Stat. 109, which, like their modern counterparts, granted inventors "the right to exclude others from making, using, offering for sale, selling, or importing the patented invention," in exchange for full disclosure of an invention, H. SCHWARTZ, PATENT LAW AND PRACTICE 1, 33 (2d ed.1995). It has long been understood that a patent must describe the exact scope of an invention and its manufacture to "secure to [the patentee] all to which he is entitled, [and] to apprise the public of what is still open to them." *McClain v. Ortmayer*, 141 U.S. 419, 424, 12 S.Ct. 76, 77, 35 L.Ed. 800 (1891). Under the modern American system, these objectives are served by two distinct elements of a patent document. First, it contains a specification describing the invention "in such full, clear, concise, and exact terms as to enable any person skilled in the art ... to make and use the same." 35 U.S.C. § 112; see also 3 E. LIPSCOMB, WALKER ON PATENTS § 10:1, pp. 183–184 (3d ed. 1985) (LIPSCOMB) (listing the requirements for a specification). Second, a patent includes one or more "claims," which "particularly poin[t] out and distinctly clai[m] the subject matter which the applicant regards as his invention." 35 U.S.C. § 112. "A claim covers and secures a process, a machine, a manufacture, a composition of matter, or a design, but never the function or result of either, nor the scientific explanation of their operation." 6 LIPSCOMB § 21:17, at 315–316. The claim "define[s] the scope of a patent grant," 3 id., § 11:1, at 280, and functions to forbid not only exact copies of an invention, but products that go to "the heart of an invention but avoids the literal language of the claim by making a noncritical change," SCHWARTZ, *supra*, at 82.[1] In this opinion, the word "claim" is used only in this sense peculiar to patent law.

Characteristically, patent lawsuits charge what is known as infringement, Schwartz, supra, at 75, and rest on allegations that the defendant "without authority ma[de], use[d] or [sold the] patented invention, within the United States during the term of the patent therefor...." 35 U.S.C. § 271(a). Victory in an infringement suit requires a finding that the patent claim "covers the alleged infringer's product or process," which in turn necessitates a determination of "what the words in the claim mean." SCHWARTZ, *supra*, at 80; *see also* 3 LIPSCOMB § 11:2, at 288–290.

---

1. Thus, for example, a claim for a ceiling fan with three blades attached to a solid rod connected to a motor would not only cover fans that take precisely this form, but would also cover a similar fan that includes some additional feature, e.g., such a fan with a cord or switch for turning it on and off, and may cover a product deviating from the core design in some noncritical way, e.g., a three-bladed ceiling fan with blades attached to a hollow rod connected to a motor. H. SCHWARTZ, PATENT LAW AND PRACTICE 81–82 (2d ed.1995).

Petitioner in this infringement suit, Markman, owns United States Reissue Patent No. 33,054 for his "Inventory Control and Reporting System for Drycleaning Stores." The patent describes a system that can monitor and report the status, location, and movement of clothing in a dry-cleaning establishment. The Markman system consists of a keyboard and data processor to generate written records for each transaction, including a bar code readable by optical detectors operated by employees, who log the progress of clothing through the dry-cleaning process. Respondent Westview's product also includes a keyboard and processor, and it lists charges for the dry-cleaning services on bar-coded tickets that can be read by portable optical detectors.

Markman brought an infringement suit against Westview and Althon Enterprises, an operator of dry-cleaning establishments using Westview's products (collectively, Westview). Westview responded that Markman's patent is not infringed by its system because the latter functions merely to record an inventory of receivables by tracking invoices and transaction totals, rather than to record and track an inventory of articles of clothing. Part of the dispute hinged upon the meaning of the word "inventory," a term found in Markman's independent claim 1, which states that Markman's product can "maintain an inventory total" and "detect and localize spurious additions to inventory." The case was tried before a jury, which heard, among others, a witness produced by Markman who testified about the meaning of the claim language.

After the jury compared the patent to Westview's device, it found an infringement of Markman's independent claim 1[2] and dependent claim 10. The District Court nevertheless granted Westview's deferred motion for judgment as a matter of law, one of its reasons being that the

---

2.   1.   The inventory control and reporting system, comprising:

a data input device for manual operation by an attendant, the input device having switch means operable to encode information relating to sequential transactions, each of the transactions having articles associated therewith, said information including transaction identity and descriptions of each of said articles associated with the transactions;

a data processor including memory operable to record said information and means to maintain an inventory total, said data processor having means to associate sequential transactions with unique sequential indicia and to generate at least one report of said total and said transactions, the unique sequential indicia and the descriptions of articles in the sequential transactions being reconcilable against one another;

a dot matrix printer operable under control of the data processor to generate a written record of the indicia associated with sequential transactions, the written record including optically-detectable bar codes having a series of contrasting spaced bands, the bar codes being printed only in coincidence with each said transaction and at least part of the written record bearing a portion to be attached to said articles; and,

at least one optical scanner connected to the data processor and operable to detect said bar codes on all articles passing a predetermined station,

whereby said system can detect and localize spurious additions to inventory as well as spurious deletions therefrom.

term "inventory" in Markman's patent encompasses "both cash inventory and the actual physical inventory of articles of clothing." 772 F.Supp. 1535, 1537–1538 (E.D.Pa.1991). Under the trial court's construction of the patent, the production, sale, or use of a tracking system for dry cleaners would not infringe Markman's patent unless the product was capable of tracking articles of clothing throughout the cleaning process and generating reports about their status and location. Since Westview's system cannot do these things, the District Court directed a verdict on the ground that Westview's device does not have the "means to maintain an inventory total" and thus cannot " 'detect and localize spurious additions to inventory as well as spurious deletions therefrom,' " as required by claim 1. *Id.,* at 1537.

Markman appealed, arguing it was error for the District Court to substitute its construction of the disputed claim term 'inventory' for the construction the jury had presumably given it. The United States Court of Appeals for the Federal Circuit affirmed, holding the interpretation of claim terms to be the exclusive province of the court and the Seventh Amendment to be consistent with that conclusion. 52 F.3d 967 (1995). Markman sought our review on each point, and we granted certiorari. 515 U.S. 1192, 116 S.Ct. 40, 132 L.Ed.2d 921 (1995). We now affirm.

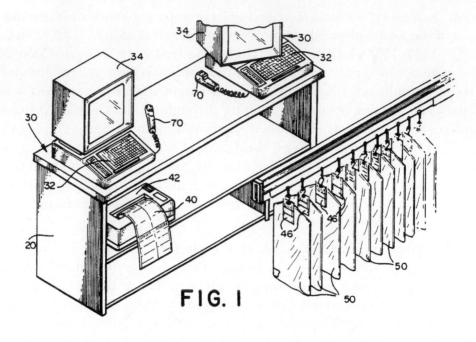

FIG. I

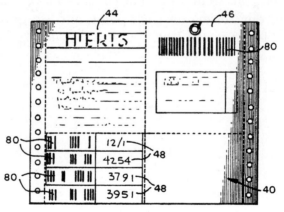

FIG. 2

II

The Seventh Amendment provides that "[i]n Suits at common law, where the value in controversy shall exceed twenty dollars, the right of trial by jury shall be preserved...." U.S. Const., Amdt. 7. Since Justice Story's day, *United States v. Wonson*, 28 F. Cas. 745, 750 (No. 16,750) (CC Mass. 1812), we have understood that "[t]he right of trial by jury thus preserved is the right which existed under the English common law when the Amendment was adopted." *Baltimore & Carolina Line, Inc. v. Redman*, 295 U.S. 654, 657, 55 S.Ct. 890, 891, 79 L.Ed. 1636 (1935). In keeping with our longstanding adherence to this "historical test," Wolfram, *The Constitutional History of the Seventh Amendment*, 57 MINN. L.REV. 639, 640–643 (1973), we ask, first, whether we are dealing with a cause of action that either was tried at law at the time of the founding or is at least analogous to one that was, *see, e.g., Tull v. United States*, 481 U.S. 412, 417, 107 S.Ct. 1831, 1835, 95 L.Ed.2d 365 (1987). If the action in question belongs in the law category, we then ask whether the particular trial decision must fall to the jury in order to preserve the substance of the common-law right as it existed in 1791. *See infra*, at 1389–1390.

A

As to the first issue, going to the character of the cause of action, "[t]he form of our analysis is familiar. 'First we compare the statutory action to 18th-century actions brought in the courts of England prior to the merger of the courts of law and equity.'" *Granfinanciera, S.A. v. Nordberg*, 492 U.S. 33, 42, 109 S.Ct. 2782, 2790, 106 L.Ed.2d 26 (1989) (citation omitted). Equally familiar is the descent of today's patent infringement action from the infringement actions tried at law in the 18th century, and there is no dispute that infringement cases today must be tried to a jury, as their predecessors were more than two centuries ago. *See, e.g., Bramah v. Hardcastle*, 1 Carp. P.C. 168 (K.B.1789).

B

This conclusion raises the second question, whether a particular issue occurring within a jury trial (here the construction of a patent claim) is itself necessarily a jury issue, the guarantee being essential to preserve the right to a jury's resolution of the ultimate dispute. In some instances the answer to this second question may be easy because of clear historical evidence that the very subsidiary question was so regarded under the English practice of leaving the issue for a jury. But when, as here, the old practice provides no clear answer, see infra, at 1390–1391, we are forced to make a judgment about the scope of the Seventh Amendment guarantee without the benefit of any foolproof test.

The Court has repeatedly said that the answer to the second question "must depend on whether the jury must shoulder this responsibility as necessary to preserve the 'substance of the common-law right of trial by jury.'" *Tull v. United States, supra*, at 426 (emphasis added) (quoting *Colgrove v. Battin*, 413 U.S. 149, 156, 93 S.Ct. 2448, 2452, 37 L.Ed.2d 522 (1973)); see also *Baltimore & Carolina Line, supra*, at 657, 55 S.Ct., at 891. "'"Only those incidents which are regarded as fundamental, as inherent in and of the essence of the system of trial by jury, are placed beyond the reach of the legislature."'" *Tull v. United States, supra*, at 426 (citations omitted).

The "substance of the common-law right" is, however, a pretty blunt instrument for drawing distinctions. We have tried to sharpen it, to be sure, by reference to the distinction between substance and procedure. [citations omitted] We have also spoken of the line as one between issues of fact and law. [citations omitted].

But the sounder course, when available, is to classify a mongrel practice (like construing a term of art following receipt of evidence) by using the historical method, much as we do in characterizing the suits and actions within which they arise. Where there is no exact antecedent, the best hope lies in comparing the modern practice to earlier ones whose allocation to court or jury we do know, seeking the best analogy we can draw between an old and the new, *see Tull v. United States, supra*, at 420–421, 107 S.Ct., at 1836–1837 (we must search the English common law for "appropriate analogies" rather than a "precisely analogous common-law cause of action").

C

"Prior to 1790 nothing in the nature of a claim had appeared either in British patent practice or in that of the American states," Lutz, *Evolution of the Claims of U.S. Patents*, 20 J. Pat. Off. Soc. 134 (1938), and we have accordingly found no direct antecedent of modern claim construction in the historical sources. Claim practice did not achieve statutory recognition until the passage of the Act of July 4, 1836, ch. 357, § 6, 5 Stat. 119, and inclusion of a claim did not become a statutory requirement until 1870, Act of July 8, 1870, ch. 230, § 26, 16 Stat. 201; see 1 A. Deller, Patent Claims § 4, p. 9 (2d ed.1971). Although, as one historian has observed, as early as 1850 "judges were . . . beginning to express more frequently the idea that in seeking to ascertain the invention 'claimed' in a patent the inquiry should be limited to interpreting the summary, or 'claim,' " Lutz, *supra*, at 145, "[t]he idea that the claim is just as important if not more important than the description and drawings did not develop until the Act of 1870 or thereabouts." Deller, *supra*, § 4, at 9.

At the time relevant for Seventh Amendment analogies, in contrast, it was the specification, itself a relatively new development, H. Dutton, The Patent System and Inventive Activity During the Industrial Revolution, 1750–1852, pp. 75–76 (1984), that represented the key to the patent. Thus, patent litigation in that early period was typified by so-called novelty actions, testing whether "any essential part of [the patent had been] disclosed to the public before," *Huddart v. Grimshaw*, Dav. Pat. Cas. 265, 298 (K.B.1803), and "enablement" cases, in which juries were asked to determine whether the specification described the invention well enough to allow members of the appropriate trade to reproduce it, *see, e.g., Arkwright v. Nightingale*, Dav. Pat. Cas. 37, 60 (C.P. 1785).

The closest 18th-century analogue of modern claim construction seems, then, to have been the construction of specifications, and as to that function the mere smattering of patent cases that we have from this period shows no established jury practice sufficient to support an argument by analogy that today's construction of a claim should be a guaranteed jury issue. . . .

[A]s soon as the English reports did begin to describe the construction of patent documents, they show the judges construing the terms of the specifications. *See Bovill v. Moore*, Dav. Pat. Cas. 361, 399, 404 (C.P. 1816) (judge submits question of novelty to the jury only after explaining some of the language and "stat[ing] in what terms the specification runs"); *cf. Russell v. Cowley & Dixon*, Webs. Pat. Cas. 457, 467–470 (Exch.1834) (construing the terms of the specification in reviewing a verdict); *Haworth v. Hardcastle*, Webs. Pat. Cas. 480, 484–485 (1834) (same). This evidence is in fact buttressed by cases from this Court; when they first reveal actual practice, the practice revealed is of the judge construing the patent. *See, e.g., Winans v. New York & Erie R. Co.*, 21 How. 88, 100, 16 L.Ed. 68 (1859); *Winans v. Denmead*, 15 How. 330, 338, 14 L.Ed. 717 (1854); *Hogg v. Emerson*, 6 How. 437, 484, 12 L.Ed. 505 (1848); *cf. Parker v. Hulme*, 18 F. Cas. 1138 (No. 10,740) (CC ED Pa. 1849). These indications of our patent practice are the more impressive for being all of a piece with what we know about the analogous contemporary practice of interpreting terms within a land patent, where it fell to the judge, not the jury, to construe the words.

D

Losing, then, on the contention that juries generally had interpretive responsibilities during the 18th century, Markman seeks a different anchor for analogy in the more modest contention that even if judges were charged with construing most terms in the patent, the art of defining terms of art employed in a specification fell within the province of the jury. Again, however, Markman has no authority from the period in question, but relies instead on the later case of *Neilson v. Harford*, Webs. Pat. Cas. 328 (Exch.1841). There, an exchange between the judge and the lawyers indicated that although the construction of a patent was ordinarily for the court, id., at 349 (Alderson, B.), judges should "leav[e] the question of words of art to the jury," id., at 350 (Alderson, B.); see also id., at 370 (judgment of the court); *Hill v. Evans*, 4 De. G.F. & J. 288, 293–294, 45 Eng. Rep. 1195, 1197 (Ch. 1862). Without, however, in any way disparaging the weight to which Baron Alderson's view is entitled, the most we can say is that an English report more than 70 years after the time that concerns us indicates an exception to what probably had been occurring earlier. In place of Markman's inference that this exceptional practice existed in 1791 there is at best only a possibility that it did, and for anything more than a possibility we have found no scholarly authority.

III

Since evidence of common-law practice at the time of the framing does not entail application of the Seventh Amendment's jury guarantee to the construction of the claim document, we must look elsewhere to characterize this determination of meaning in order to allocate it as between court or jury. We accordingly consult existing precedent and consider both the relative interpretive skills of judges and juries and the statutory policies that ought to be furthered by the allocation.

A

The two elements of a simple patent case, construing the patent and determining whether infringement occurred, were characterized by the former patent practitioner, Justice Curtis. "The first is a question of law, to be determined by the court, construing the letters-patent, and the description of the invention and specification of claim annexed to them. The second is a question of fact, to be submitted to a jury." *Winans v. Denmead, supra,* at 338.

In arguing for a different allocation of responsibility for the first question, Markman relies primarily on two cases, *Bischoff v. Wethered*, 9 Wall. 812, 19 L.Ed. 829 (1870), and *Tucker v. Spalding*, 13 Wall. 453, 20 L.Ed. 515 (1871). These are said to show that evidence of the meaning of patent terms was offered to 19th-century juries, and thus to imply that the meaning of a documentary term was a jury issue whenever it was subject to evidentiary proof. That is not what Markman's cases show, however. . . .

Bischoff does not, as Markman contends, hold that the use of expert testimony about the meaning of terms of art requires the judge to submit the question of their construction to the jury. It is instead a case in which the Court drew a line between issues of document interpretation and product identification, and held that expert testimony was properly presented to the jury on the latter, ultimate issue, whether the physical objects produced by the patent were identical. The Court did not see the decision as bearing upon the appropriate treatment of disputed terms. As the opinion emphasized, the Court's "view of the case is not intended to, and does not, trench upon the doctrine that the construction of written instruments is the province of the court alone. It is not the construction of the instrument, but the character of the thing invented, which is sought in questions of identity and diversity of inventions." *Id.,* at 816. *Tucker,* the second case proffered by Markman, is to the same effect. . . . . Its reasoning rested expressly on *Bischoff,* and it just as clearly noted that in addressing the ultimate issue of mixed fact and law, it was for the court to "lay down to the jury the law which should govern them." *Tucker, supra*, at 455.

If the line drawn in these two opinions is a fine one, it is one that the Court has drawn repeatedly in explaining the respective roles of the jury and judge in patent cases, and one understood by commentators writing in the aftermath of the cases Markman cites. Walker, for example, read *Bischoff* as holding that the question of novelty is not decided by a construction of the prior patent, "but depends rather upon the outward embodiment of the terms contained in the [prior patent]; and that such outward embodiment is to be properly sought, like the explanation of latent ambiguities arising from the description of external things, by evidence in pais." A. WALKER, PATENT LAWS § 75, p. 68 (3d ed. 1895). He also emphasized in the same treatise that matters of claim construction, even those aided by expert testimony, are questions for the court:

Virtually the same description of the court's use of evidence in its interpretive role was set out in another contemporary treatise:

"The duty of interpreting letters-patent has been committed to the courts. A patent is a legal instrument, to be construed, like other legal instruments, according to its tenor. . . . Where technical terms are used, or where the qualities of substances or operations mentioned or any similar data necessary to the comprehension of the language of the patent are unknown to the judge, the testimony of witnesses may be received upon these subjects, and any other means of information be employed. But in the actual interpretation of the patent the court proceeds upon its own responsibility, as an arbiter of the law, giving to the patent its true and final character and force."

2 W. Robinson, Law of Patents § 732, pp. 481–483 (1890) (emphasis added; footnotes omitted). In sum, neither *Bischoff* nor *Tucker* indicates that juries resolved the meaning of terms of art in construing a patent, and neither case undercuts Justice Curtis's authority.

B

Where history and precedent provide no clear answers, functional considerations also play their part in the choice between judge and jury to define terms of art. We said in *Miller v. Fenton*, 474 U.S. 104, 114, 106 S.Ct. 445, 451, 88 L.Ed.2d 405 (1985), that when an issue "falls somewhere between a pristine legal standard and a simple historical fact, the fact/law distinction at times has turned on a determination that, as a matter of the sound administration of justice, one judicial actor is better positioned than another to decide the issue in question." So it turns out here, for judges, not juries, are the better suited to find the acquired meaning of patent terms.

The construction of written instruments is one of those things that judges often do and are likely to do better than jurors unburdened by training in exegesis. Patent construction in particular "is a special occupation, requiring, like all others, special training and practice. The judge, from his training and discipline, is more likely to give a proper interpretation to such instruments than a jury; and he is, therefore, more likely to be right, in performing such a duty, than a jury can be expected to be." *Parker v. Hulme*, 18 F. Cas., at 1140. Such was the understanding nearly a century and a half ago, and there is no reason to weigh the respective strengths of judge and jury differently in relation to the modern claim; quite the contrary, for "the claims of patents have become highly technical in many respects as the result of special doctrines relating to the proper form and scope of claims that have been developed by the courts and the Patent Office." Woodward, *Definiteness and Particularity in Patent Claims*, 46 Mich. L.Rev. 755, 765 (1948).

Markman would trump these considerations with his argument that a jury should decide a question of meaning peculiar to a trade or profession simply because the question is a subject of testimony requiring credibility determinations, which are the jury's forte. It is, of course, true that credibility judgments have to be made about the experts who testify in patent cases, and in theory there could be a case in which a simple credibility judgment would suffice to choose between experts whose testimony was equally consistent with a patent's internal logic. But our own experience with document construction leaves us doubtful that trial courts will run into many cases like that. In the main, we expect, any credibility determinations will be subsumed within the necessarily sophisticated analysis of the whole document, required by the standard construction rule that a term can be defined only in a way that comports with the instrument as a whole. See *Bates v. Coe*, 98 U.S. 31, 38, 25 L.Ed. 68 (1878); 6 LIPSCOMB § 21:40, at 393; 2 ROBINSON, *supra*, § 734, at 484. Thus, in these cases a jury's capabilities to evaluate demeanor, *cf.* MILLER, *supra*, at 114, 117, 106 S.Ct., at 451, 453, to sense the "mainsprings of human conduct," *Commissioner v. Duberstein*, 363 U.S. 278, 289, 80 S.Ct. 1190, 1198, 4 L.Ed.2d 1218 (1960), or to reflect community standards, *United States v. McConney*, 728 F.2d 1195, 1204 (C.A.9 1984) (en banc), are much less significant than a trained ability to evaluate the testimony in relation to the overall structure of the patent. The decision-maker vested with the task of construing the patent is in the better position to ascertain whether an expert's proposed definition fully comports with the specification and claims and so will preserve the patent's internal coherence. We accordingly think there is sufficient reason to treat construction of terms of art like many other responsibilities that we cede to a judge in the normal course of trial, notwithstanding its evidentiary underpinnings.

C

Finally, we see the importance of uniformity in the treatment of a given patent as an independent reason to allocate all issues of construction to the court. As we noted in *General Elec. Co. v. Wabash Appliance Corp.*, 304 U.S. 364, 369 (1938), "[t]he limits of a patent must be known for the protection of the patentee, the encouragement of the inventive genius of others and the assurance that the subject of the patent will be dedicated ultimately to the public." Otherwise, a "zone of uncertainty which enterprise and experimentation may enter only at the risk of infringement claims would discourage invention only a little less than unequivocal foreclosure of the field," *United Carbon Co. v. Binney & Smith Co.*, 317 U.S. 228, 236, 63 S.Ct. 165, 170, 87 L.Ed. 232 (1942), and "[t]he public [would] be deprived of rights supposed to belong to it, without being clearly told what it is that limits these rights." *Merrill v. Yeomans*, 94 U.S. 568, 573, 24 L.Ed. 235 (1877). It was just for the sake of such desirable uniformity that Congress created the Court of Appeals for the Federal Circuit as an exclusive appellate court for patent cases, H.R.Rep. No. 97–312, pp. 20–23 (1981), observing that increased uniformity would "strengthen the United States patent system in such a way as to foster technological growth and industrial innovation." *Id.*, at 20.

Uniformity would, however, be ill served by submitting issues of document construction to juries. Making them jury issues would not, to be sure, necessarily leave evidentiary questions of meaning wide open in every new court in which a patent might be litigated, for principles of issue preclusion would ordinarily foster uniformity. Cf. *Blonder–Tongue Laboratories, Inc. v. University of Ill. Foundation*, 402 U.S. 313 (1971). But whereas issue preclusion could not be asserted against new and independent infringement defendants even within a given jurisdiction, treating interpretive issues as purely legal will promote (though it will not guarantee) intrajurisdictional certainty through the application of stare decisis on those questions not yet subject to interjurisdictional uniformity under the authority of the single appeals court.

* * *

Accordingly, we hold that the interpretation of the word "inventory" in this case is an issue for the judge, not the jury, and affirm the decision of the Court of Appeals for the Federal Circuit.

NOTE

The Federal Circuit had reasoned differently to reach its result in *Markman*. Specifically, the Federal Circuit reasoned: "we conclude that the interpretation and construction of patent claims, which define the scope of the patentee's rights under the patent, is a matter of law exclusively for the court." 52 F.3d at 970 (Fed. Cir. 1995). The Supreme Court did not adopt the Federal Circuit's reasoning that claim interpretation is a question of law, calling it instead a "mongrel" mixture of law and fact. In fact, the Supreme Court made a practical determination that judges will handle claim construction better than juries more than a determination that claim construction is a pure question of law. The difference in reasoning led to another *en banc* case at the Federal Circuit a few years later.

CYBOR CORP. v. FAS TECHNOLOGIES, INC.

United States Court of Appeals, Federal Circuit, 1998
138 F.3d 1448

Opinion for the court filed by Senior Circuit Judge Archer, in which Circuit Judges Rich, Michel, Plager, Lourie, Clevenger, Schall, Bryson, and Gajarsa join; Circuit Judge Rader joins as to part IV. Concurring opinions filed by Circuit Judges Plager and Bryson. Opinions concurring in the judgment filed by Chief Judge Mayer, which Circuit Judge Newman joins, and Circuit Judge Rader. Additional views filed by Circuit Judge Newman, which Chief Judge Mayer joins.

ARCHER, SENIOR CIRCUIT JUDGE.

[Cybor Corporation (Cybor) appealed a judgment of the United States District Court for the Northern District of California that its pump infringes the claims of U.S. Patent No. 5,167,837 (the '837 patent) which was owned by FAStar, Ltd. (FAS). Cybor argued on appeal that the district court erred in construing the claims.]

We affirm the district court's judgment in its entirety. In so doing, we conclude that the Supreme Court's unanimous affirmance in *Markman v. Westview Instruments, Inc.*, 517 U.S. 370, 116 S.Ct. 1384, 134 L.Ed.2d 577 (1996) (Markman II), of our in banc judgment in that case fully supports our conclusion that claim construction, as a purely legal issue, is subject to de novo review on appeal. *See Markman v. Westview Instruments, Inc.*, 52 F.3d 967, 979 (Fed.Cir.1995) (in banc) (*Markman I*).

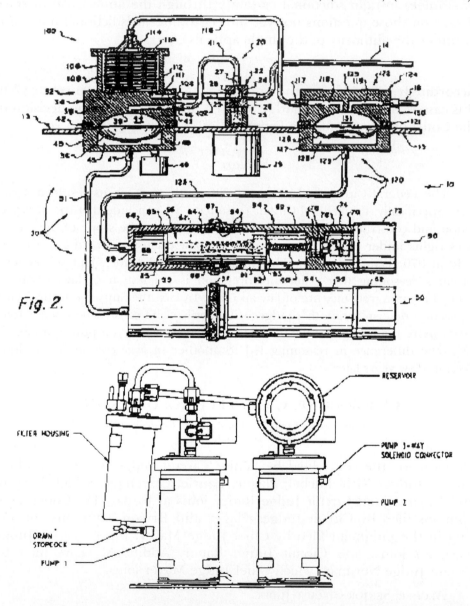

Fig. 2.

An infringement analysis involves two steps. First, the court determines the scope and meaning of the patent claims asserted, *see Markman*

II, 517 U.S. at 371–73, 116 S.Ct. at 1387–88, and then the properly construed claims are compared to the allegedly infringing device. Although the law is clear that the judge, and not the jury, is to construe the claims, this case presents the issue of the proper role of this court in reviewing the district court's claim construction.

After the Supreme Court's decision in *Markman II*, panels of this court have generally followed the review standard of *Markman I*. In some cases, however, a clearly erroneous standard has been applied to findings considered to be factual in nature that are incident to the judge's construction of patent claims. *See Eastman Kodak Co. v. Goodyear Tire & Rubber Co.*, 114 F.3d 1547, 1555–56 (Fed.Cir.1997)....

The Supreme Court framed the question before it in *Markman II* in the alternative: "whether the interpretation of a so-called patent claim . . . is a matter of law reserved entirely for the court, or subject to a Seventh Amendment guarantee that a jury will determine the meaning of any disputed term of art about which expert testimony is offered." *Markman II*, 517 U.S. at 372 (emphasis added). When it answered that question by stating that "[w]e hold that the construction of a patent, including terms of art within its claim, is exclusively within the province of the court," id., the Court held that the totality of claim construction is a legal question to be decided by the judge. Nothing in the Supreme Court's opinion supports the view that the Court endorsed a silent, third option—that claim construction may involve subsidiary or underlying questions of fact. To the contrary, the Court expressly stated that "treating interpretive issues as purely legal will promote (though not guarantee) intrajurisdictional certainty through the application of stare decisis on those questions not yet subject to interjurisdictional uniformity under the authority of the single appeals court." *Id.* at 391, 116 S.Ct. at 1396 (emphasis added); *see also id.* at 387, 116 S.Ct. at 1394 (" 'Questions of construction are questions of law for the judge, not questions of fact for the jury' " (quoting A. WALKER, PATENT LAWS § 75 at 173 (3d ed. 1895))). Indeed, the sentence demonstrates that the Supreme Court endorsed this court's role in providing national uniformity to the construction of a patent claim, a role that would be impeded if we were bound to give deference to a trial judge's asserted factual determinations incident to claim construction.

The opinions in some of our cases suggesting that there should be deference to what are asserted to be factual underpinnings of claim construction assert support from the language in *Markman II* stating that "construing a term of art after receipt of evidence" is a "mongrel practice," id. at 378, 116 S.Ct. at 1390, and that the issue may " 'fall[ ] somewhere between a pristine legal standard and a simple historical fact,' " *id.* at 388, 116 S.Ct. at 1395 (*quoting Miller v. Fenton*, 474 U.S. 104, 114 (1985)). These characterizations, however, are only prefatory comments demonstrating the Supreme Court's recognition that the determination of whether patent claim construction is a question of law or fact is not simple or clear cut; they do not support the view that the

Court held that while construction is a legal question for the judge, there may also be underlying fact questions. To the contrary, the court noted that

> when an issue "falls somewhere between a pristine legal standard and a simple historical fact, the fact/law distinction at times has turned on a determination that, as a matter of sound administration of justice, one judicial actor is better positioned than another to decide the issue in question."

Id. (*quoting Miller v. Fenton*, 474 U.S. 104, 114 (1985)) (emphasis added). Thus, the Supreme Court was addressing under which category, fact or law, claim construction should fall and not whether it should be classified as having two components, fact and law.

Further supporting the conclusion that claim construction is a pure issue of law is the Supreme Court's analysis of the role of expert testimony in claim construction. Generally, the Court has recognized the important role played by juries in evaluating the credibility of a witness, a key consideration in determining the appropriate judicial actor to decide an issue. *See Miller*, 474 U.S. at 114. In the context of claim construction, however, the Court reasoned that, while credibility determinations theoretically could play a role in claim construction, the chance of such an occurrence is "doubtful" and that "any credibility determinations will be subsumed within the necessarily sophisticated analysis of the whole document, required by the standard construction rule that a term can be defined only in a way that comports with the instrument as a whole." *Markman II*, 517 U.S. at 389; *see also id.* at 388, 116 S.Ct. at 1394–95 ("'[T]he testimony of witnesses may be received.... But in the actual interpretation of the patent the court proceeds upon its own responsibility, as an arbiter of the law, giving to the patent its true and final character and force.'" (*quoting* 2 W. ROBINSON, LAW OF PATENTS § 732 at 481–83 (1890))). Such a conclusion is consistent with the view that claim construction, as a form of "document construction," *id.* at 388–90, is solely a question of law subject to de novo review, as noted above....

Thus, we conclude that the standard of review in *Markman I*, as discussed above, was not changed by the Supreme Court's decision in *Markman II*, and we therefore reaffirm that, as a purely legal question, we review claim construction de novo on appeal including any allegedly fact-based questions relating to claim construction. Accordingly, we today disavow any language in previous opinions of this court that holds, purports to hold, states, or suggests anything to the contrary.

[The Federal Circuit then examined and affirmed the trial court's claim construction.]

AFFIRMED.

BRYSON, CIRCUIT JUDGE, concurring.

While I join the opinion of the court without reservation, I think it important to note that our adoption of the rule that claim construction is an issue of law does not mean that we intend to disregard the work done by district courts in claim construction or that we will give no weight to a district court's conclusion as to claim construction, no matter how the court may have reached that conclusion. Simply because a particular issue is denominated a question of law does not mean that the reviewing court will attach no weight to the conclusion reached by the tribunal it reviews. In fact, reviewing courts often acknowledge that as to particular legal issues lower tribunals have special competence and their judgments on those legal issues should be accorded significant weight.... [W]e approach the legal issue of claim construction recognizing that with respect to certain aspects of the task, the district court may be better situated than we are, and that as to those aspects we should be cautious about substituting our judgment for that of the district court.

RADER, CIRCUIT JUDGE, dissenting from the pronouncements on claim interpretation in the en banc opinion, concurring in the judgment, and joining part IV of the en banc opinion.

To evade the strictures of the Seventh Amendment, *Markman I* necessarily reasoned that claim construction is purely a matter of law.... [T]he Supreme Court [on the other hand] repeatedly intimated that claim construction was not a purely legal matter. *See, e.g., Markman II*, 517 U.S. at 377–79 (the construction of a term of art is a "mongrel practice"); *id.* at 388 (claim interpretation "falls somewhere between a pristine legal standard and a single historical fact"); *id.* at 390 ("notwithstanding [claim construction's] evidentiary underpinnings").... Nonetheless this court relies on its earlier en banc decision, *Markman I*, 52 F.3d at 979, to make claim construction purely a question of law, subject to independent appellate review without deference to or encumbrance by the trial process. To my eyes, this rejection of the trial process as the "main event" will undermine, if not destroy, the values of certainty and predictability sought by *Markman I*.

The question of the proper standard of review seems an esoteric legal topic of interest only to law professors and appellate judges. In most cases, however, the review standard influences greatly both the trial judges who preside over the trial process and patent practitioners who must advise clients to accommodate their business plans to an uncertain legal regime.

From the vantage point of trial judges, *Markman I* dictates many deviations from the normal procedural course for litigation.[3] Perhaps

---

3. The following is an incomplete list of procedural deviations required by *Markman I*:

1. Multiple trials, problem I: If hearings are necessary to interpret complex claims, the trial court must set aside time in its crowded docket for one proceeding to interpret claims and a second (potentially with a jury) to determine infringement and other issues.

2. Claim interpretation, problem I: Fearing that it may not receive the opportunity to supplement expert reports or reopen discovery after the judge's interpretation, a party often argues

the central deviation, however, affects the trial court's discretion to use expert testimony. When confronted with sophisticated technology, district court judges often seek testimony from experts to help them understand and interpret the claim. Under the guise of setting standards for claim construction, this court instructs experienced trial judges that they may use experts to understand, but not to interpret, the claim terms. As a matter of logic, this instruction is difficult to grasp. What is the distinction between a trial judge's understanding of the claims and a trial judge's interpretation of the claims to the jury? Don't judges instruct the jury in accordance with their understanding of the claims? In practice, how does this court's lofty appellate logic work? As this court acknowledges, a trial court must often resort to experts to learn complex new technologies. *See, e.g., Markman I,* 52 F.3d at 986. What happens when that learning influences a trial judge's interpretation of the claim terms? Are trial judges supposed to disguise the real reasons for their interpretation? How will this perverse incentive to "hide the ball" improve appellate review?...

From the patent practitioner's standpoint, this court's enthusiastic assertion of its unfettered review authority has the potential to undercut the benefits of *Markman I. Markman I* potentially promised to supply early certainty about the meaning of a patent claim. This certainty, in turn, would prompt early settlement of many, if not most, patent suits. Once the parties know the meaning of the claims, they can predict with some reliability the likelihood of a favorable judgment, factor in the

---

alternative claim construction theories from the outset of litigation. This extends the time and expense of the claim interpretation proceedings.

3. Bias toward summary judgments: In practical terms, *Markman I* directs the proceedings toward summary judgment on the central issue of the litigation at a potentially premature stage of issue development. Prematurely addressing issues, even at the appellate level, can result in expensive repetition of effort.

4. Claim interpretation, problem II: As soon as the trial court issues a claim interpretation, both sides often seek to shift their original claim interpretations to accommodate the judge's views. Thus, the parties seek to revise expert reports or reopen discovery to account for the judge's interpretation. This maneuvering leads to procedural battles over surprise and motions for additional time to prepare for trial. *See Loral Fairchild Corp. v. Victor Co.,* 906 F.Supp. 798 (E.D.N.Y.1995) (interpreting claims); *Loral Fairchild Corp. v. Victor Co.,* 911 F.Supp. 76, 80–81 (E.D.N.Y.1996) (preventing plaintiff from changing theory of infringement in response to claim interpretation).

5. The new evidence dilemma: As a result of the new and perhaps somewhat unexpected interpretation, the parties scramble to create and acquire new evidence for their infringement arguments.

6. The learning curve problem: Like all human endeavors, claim interpretation is a learning process. The trial judge makes every effort to state the precise scope of the claims at the close of the initial proceeding, but often, with the additional learning during the infringement trial, realizes that the initial interpretation was too broad or too narrow in some respects. The judge then faces the dilemma of changing the rules in the middle of the game.

7. The judge as a trial issue: With the judge's claim interpretation central to the issues of infringement, trial counsel will try to exploit the judge's stature with the jury to show that the court is on their side.

8. Multiple trials, problem II: In the words of United States District Court Judge Roderick McKelvie: "[I]n spite of a trial judge's ruling on the meaning of disputed words in a claim, should a three-judge panel of the Federal Circuit disagree, the entire case could be remanded for retrial on [a] different [claim interpretation]." *Elf Atochem North Am., Inc. v. Libbey–Owens–Ford Co.,* 894 F.Supp. 844, 857 (D.Del.1995).

Trial judges can often address each of the above with careful case management, but at the cost of expending scarce trial court resources.

economics of the infringement, and arrive at a settlement to save the costs of litigation. *Markman I* promised to provide this benefit early in the trial court process. To provide fairness under the *Markman I* regime, trial judges would provide claim interpretations before the expense of trial. Patent practitioners would then be armed with knowledge of the probable outcome of the litigation and could facilitate settlement.

The problem with this plan was in its implementation because as a question of law, claim interpretation is subject to free review by the appellate court. The Federal Circuit, according to its own official 1997 statistics, reversed in whole or in part 53% of the cases from district courts (27% fully reversed; 26% reversed-in-part). Granted this figure deals with all issues in cases with many issues. Nonetheless, one study shows that the plenary standard of review has produced reversal, in whole or in part, of almost 40% of all claim constructions since *Markman I*.[4] A reversal rate in this range reverses more than the work of numerous trial courts; it also reverses the benefits of *Markman I*. In fact, this reversal rate, hovering near 50%, is the worst possible. Even a rate that was much higher would provide greater certainty.

Instead, the current *Markman I* regime means that the trial court's early claim interpretation provides no early certainty at all, but only opens the bidding. The meaning of a claim is not certain (and the parties are not prepared to settle) until nearly the last step in the process-decision by the Court of Appeals for the Federal Circuit. . . . In implementation, a de novo review of claim interpretations has post-poned the point of certainty to the end of the litigation process, at which point, of course, every outcome is certain anyway.

In practical terms, this implementation record has other perverse effects. Trial attorneys must devote much of their trial strategy to positioning themselves for the "endgame"—claim construction on appeal. As the focus shifts from litigating for the correct claim construction to preserving ways to compel reversal on appeal, the uncertainty, cost, and duration of patent litigation only increase. Thus, the en banc court's de novo regime belies the purpose and promise of *Markman I*. . . .

Because patent trial practitioners understand the distinct prospect of overturning trial court results on appeal, the trial arena loses some of its luster as the center stage of the dispute resolution drama. Instead the trial court becomes a ticket to the real center stage, the Court of Appeals for the Federal Circuit. Taking a cue from the Supreme Court, this court would more wisely take a functional approach to setting a standard of review for claim construction.

---

4. This figure is based on a survey of every patent decision rendered by the Court of Appeals for the Federal Circuit between 5 April 1995 (the date Markman I was decided) and 24 November 1997. A total of 246 patent cases, originating in the Board of Patent Appeals and Interferences (BPAI), the district courts, and the Court of Federal Claims, were evaluated. Of the 246 cases, 141 cases expressly reviewed claim construction issues. Among these 141 decisions, this court reversed, in whole or in part, 54 or 38.3% of all claim constructions. With respect to the district court and Court of Federal Claims cases, the rate of reversal of claim constructions is 47 out of 126 or 37.3%.

In *Markman II*, the Supreme Court noted that neither history nor precedent provided "clear answers" about the role of the jury and the factual or legal nature of claim construction. 517 U.S. at 388–90. Therefore, the Court pursued a functional inquiry to determine whether the judge or jury could best balance the complexities of claim construction. A similar functional inquiry might best clarify the roles of the trial and appellate benches during claim interpretation.

Applying this general counsel, the trial judge enjoys a potentially superior position to engage in claim interpretation. For the complex case where the claim language and specification do not summarily dispose of claim construction issues, the trial court has tools to acquire and evaluate evidence that this court lacks. Trial judges can spend hundreds of hours reading and rereading all kinds of source material, receiving tutorials on technology from leading scientists, formally questioning technical experts and testing their understanding against that of various experts, examining on site the operation of the principles of the claimed invention, and deliberating over the meaning of the claim language. If district judges are not satisfied with the proofs proffered by the parties, they are not bound to a prepared record but may compel additional presentations or even employ their own court-appointed expert.

An appellate court has none of these advantages. It cannot depart from the record of the trial proceedings. To properly marshal its resources, the appellate bench must enforce strict time and page limits in oral and written presentations. Moreover a sterile written record can never convey all the nuances and intangibles of the decisional process. Indeed a careful consideration of the institutional advantages of the district court would counsel deference. This court's categorical response that claim interpretation involves no factual assessments does not advance a functional analysis of trial and appellate roles in claim construction. As a matter of fact (so to speak), claim construction requires assessment of custom and usage in the relevant art, assessment of events during prosecution, assessment of the level of ordinary skill in the art, assessment of the understanding of skilled artisans at the time of invention—to name just a few factual components of the complex process of claim interpretation. A careful functional analysis counsels deference for district court claim interpretations.

NOTES

1. **Practical Implications: Statistical Inquiry.** In the dissent by Judge Rader, he referred to statistical evidence about the rate of reversal of district court claim constructions at the Federal Circuit. These references led to considerable statistical debate over the Federal Circuit's rate of reversing trial courts. Two studies in 2001 fueled the debate. *See* Christian Chu, *Empirical Analysis of the Federal Circuit's Claim Construction Trends*, 16 BERK TECH. L. J. 1075 (2001) (giving a reversal rate of 44%); Kimberly Moore, *Are District Court Judges*

Equipped to Resolve Patent Cases?, 15 HARV. J.L. TECH. 1 (2001) (giving a reversal rate of 33%). The discrepancy between the Moore and Chu findings derives from two factors. The two studies cover slightly different time frames. More important, Moore includes within her population of cases the non-controversial matters resolved by Rule 36 summary affirmance at the Federal Circuit. When Chu factored into his statistical base the summary affirmances, he found a reversal rate of 36.6%.

2. **The Markman hearing.** Judge Rader's footnote details "procedural deviations" that will complicate patent trials after *Markman.* Many of those deviations are the result of the need for a Markman hearing to construe the claims before a trial. With years of experience, the Markman hearing process has become an established practice in patent adjudication. Do you suppose district judges have adjusted to the different procedure for patent trials? Does the difference in patent trials make it easier or harder to obtain time on a crowded district court docket for patent cases?

3. **Is *Cybor* secure?** Nearly a decade later, in 2006, the Federal Circuit revisited the issue of deference to trial courts in claim construction. *Amgen Inc. v. Hoechst Marion Roussel, Inc.*, 469 F.3d 1039 (2006). In declining to reconsider *Amgen en banc*, four Federal Circuit judges (Chief Judge Michel and Judges Newman, Rader, and Moore) expressed a desire to overturn *Cybor*. Three other Federal Circuit judges (Gajarsa, Linn, and Dyk) said, "we would be willing to reconsider limited aspects of the *Cybor* decision . . . [such as when] the district court found it necessary to resolve conflicting expert evidence to interpret particular claim terms." *Id.* at 1045. With seven out of twelve judges willing to revisit *Cybor* to some degree, the Federal Circuit may yet reconsider its relationship to district courts in relation to claim construction.

4. **Terminology.** Even though courts and commentators commonly refer to "patent infringement," infringement analyses are actually based upon a particular claim of a patent. A claim is also said to "read on" an accused product or process in the event of literal infringement occurs. *Baxter Healthcare Corp. v. Spectramed, Inc.*, 49 F.3d 1575 (Fed.Cir. 1995).

5. **Additions and Omissions.** To literally infringe, an accused product or process must include each and every limitation of a claim. Therefore, the *omission* of any limitation is fatal to literal infringement. As noted in *Lantech, Inc. v. Keip Machine Co.*, 32 F.3d 542 (Fed.Cir.1994), "[f]or literal infringement, each limitation of the claim must be met by the accused device exactly, any deviation from the claim precluding a finding of infringement." The *addition* of elements beyond those recited in a claim, however, has different implications. Additions beyond the claimed elements have different effects on literal infringement depending on the particular transition phrase in the claim.

6. **The Patentee's Commercial Embodiment.** Section 271 (a) states clearly that the infringement inquiry compares the accused product or process to the "patented invention," or in other words, to the claims. Thus, the patentee's commercial products are not relevant to the infringement inquiry. The Federal Circuit has made this point clear: "As we have repeatedly said, it is error for a court to compare in its infringement analysis the accused product or process

with the patentee's commercial embodiment or other version of the product or process; the only proper comparison is with the claims of the patent." *Zenith Labs. v. Bristol–Myers Squibb Co.*, 19 F.3d 1418 (Fed.Cir.1994).

7. Claim Interpretation after *Markman* and *Cybor*. With the jury no longer part of the claim construction process, judges sought clarification on the legal standards for construing claims. After years of experience, claim construction still resembles statutory construction. In both cases, a variety of factors often influence the process. No single method or theory of construction seems to capture all the nuances of the complex enterprise. With rising complaints over indeterminate standards and high reversal rates, the Federal Circuit decided to attempt to again bring more certainty to claim construction.

PHILLIPS v. AWH CORPORATION

United States Court of Appeals, Federal Circuit, 2005
415 F.3d 1303

Opinion for the court filed by Circuit Judge Bryson, in which Chief Judge Michel and Circuit Judges Clevenger, Rader, Schall, Gajarsa, Linn, Dyk, and Prost join; and in which Circuit Judge Lourie joins with respect to parts I, II, III, V, and VI; and in which Circuit Judge Pauline Newman joins with respect to parts I, II, III, and V. Opinion concurring in part and dissenting in part filed by Circuit Judge Lourie, in which Circuit Judge Pauline Newman joins. Dissenting opinion filed by Circuit Judge Mayer, in which Circuit Judge Pauline Newman joins.

BRYSON, CIRCUIT JUDGE.

Edward H. Phillips invented modular, steel-shell panels that can be welded together to form vandalism-resistant walls. The panels are especially useful in building prisons because they are load-bearing and impact-resistant, while also insulating against fire and noise. Mr. Phillips obtained a patent on the invention, U.S. Patent No. 4,677,798 ("the '798 patent")....

In February 1997, Mr. Phillips brought suit in the United States District Court for the District of Colorado charging AWH with ... infringement of claims 1, 21, 22, 24, 25, and 26 of the '798 patent.

With regard to the patent infringement issue, the district court focused on the language of claim 1, which recites "further means disposed inside the shell for increasing its load bearing capacity comprising internal steel baffles extending inwardly from the steel shell walls." The court interpreted that language as "a means ... for performing a specified function," subject to 35 U.S.C. § 112, paragraph 6, which provides that such a claim "shall be construed to cover the corresponding structure, material, or acts described in the specification and equivalents thereof." Looking to the specification of the '798 patent, the court noted that "every textual reference in the Specification and its diagrams show baffle deployment at an angle other than 90 to the wall faces" and that "placement of the baffles at such angles creates an intermediate interlocking, but not solid, internal barrier." The district court therefore ruled that, for purposes of the '798 patent, a baffle must "extend inward from the steel shell walls at an oblique or acute angle to the wall face" and must form part of an interlocking barrier in the interior of the wall module. Because Mr. Phillips could not prove infringement under that claim construction, the district court granted summary judgment of noninfringement.

Mr. Phillips appealed ... [and a split] panel of this court affirmed. *Phillips v. AWH Corp.*, 363 F.3d 1207 (Fed.Cir.2004). The majority sustained the district court's summary judgment of noninfringement, although on different grounds. The dissenting judge would have reversed the summary judgment of noninfringement....

We now ... reverse.

I

Claim 1 of the '798 patent is representative of the asserted claims with respect to the use of the term "baffles." It recites:

Building modules adapted to fit together for construction of fire, sound and impact resistant security barriers and rooms for use in securing records and persons, comprising in combination, an outer shell ..., sealant means ... and further means disposed inside the shell for increasing its load bearing capacity comprising internal steel baffles extending inwardly from the steel shell walls.

As a preliminary matter, we agree with the panel that the term "baffles" is not means-plus-function language that invokes 35 U.S.C. § 112, paragraph 6. To be sure, the claim refers to "means disposed inside the shell for increasing its load bearing capacity," a formulation that would ordinarily be regarded as invoking the means-plus-function claim format. However, the claim specifically identifies "internal steel baffles" as structure that performs the recited function of increasing the shell's load-bearing capacity. In contrast to the "load bearing means" limitation, the reference to "baffles" does not use the word "means," and we have held that the absence of that term creates a rebuttable presumption that section 112, paragraph 6, does not apply.

Means-plus-function claiming applies only to purely functional limitations that do not provide the structure that performs the recited function. While the baffles in the '798 patent are clearly intended to perform several functions, the term "baffles" is nonetheless structural; it is not a purely functional placeholder in which structure is filled in by the specification. The claims and the specification unmistakably establish that the "steel baffles" refer to particular physical apparatus. The claim characterizes the baffles as "extend [ing] inwardly" from the steel shell walls, which plainly implies that the baffles are structures. The specification likewise makes clear that the term "steel baffles" refers to particular internal wall structures and is not simply a general description of any structure that will perform a particular function. *See, e.g.*, '798 patent, col. 4, ll. 25–26 ("the load bearing baffles 16 are optionally used with longer panels"); *id.*, col. 4, ll. 49–50 (opposing panels are "compressed between the flange 35 and the baffle 26"). Because the term "baffles" is not subject to section 112, paragraph 6, we agree with the panel that the district court erred by limiting the term to corresponding structures disclosed in the specification and their equivalents. Accordingly, we must determine the correct construction of the structural term "baffles," as used in the '798 patent.

II

The first paragraph of section 112 of the Patent Act, 35 U.S.C. § 112, states that the specification

> shall contain a written description of the invention, and of the manner and process of making and using it, in such full, clear, concise, and exact terms as to enable any person skilled in the art to which it pertains . . . to make and use the same. . . .

The second paragraph of section 112 provides that the specification

> shall conclude with one or more claims particularly pointing out and distinctly claiming the subject matter which the applicant regards as his invention.

Those two paragraphs of section 112 frame the issue of claim interpretation for us. The second paragraph requires us to look to the language of the claims to determine what "the applicant regards as his invention." On the other hand, the first paragraph requires that the specification describe the invention set forth in the claims. The principal question that this case presents to us is the extent to which we should resort to and rely on a patent's specification in seeking to ascertain the proper scope of its claims.

This is hardly a new question. The role of the specification in claim construction has been an issue in patent law decisions in this country for nearly two centuries. We addressed the relationship between the specification and the claims at some length in our en banc opinion in *Markman v. Westview Instruments, Inc.*, 52 F.3d 967, 979–81 (Fed.Cir.1995) (*en banc*), *aff'd*, 517 U.S. 370 (1996). We again summarized the applicable principles in *Vitronics Corp. v. Conceptronic, Inc.*, 90 F.3d 1576 (Fed.Cir. 1996), and more recently in *Innova/Pure Water, Inc. v. Safari Water Filtration Systems, Inc.*, 381 F.3d 1111 (Fed.Cir.2004). What we said in those cases bears restating, for the basic principles of claim construction outlined there are still applicable, and we reaffirm them today. We have also previously considered the use of dictionaries in claim construction. What we have said in that regard requires clarification.

A

It is a "bedrock principle" of patent law that "the claims of a patent define the invention to which the patentee is entitled the right to exclude." *Innova*, 381 F.3d at 1115. That principle has been recognized since at least 1836, when Congress first required that the specification include a portion in which the inventor "shall particularly specify and point out the part, improvement, or combination, which he claims as his own invention or discovery." Act of July 4, 1836, ch. 357, § 6, 5 Stat. 117, 119. In the following years, the Supreme Court made clear that the claims are "of primary importance, in the effort to ascertain precisely what it is that is patented." *Merrill v. Yeomans*, 94 U.S. 568, 570 (1876). Because the patentee is required to "define precisely what his invention is," the Court explained, it is "unjust to the public, as well as an evasion of the law, to construe it in a manner different from the plain import of its terms." *White v. Dunbar*, 119 U.S. 47, 52 (1886).

We have frequently stated that the words of a claim "are generally given their ordinary and customary meaning." *Vitronics*, 90 F.3d at 1582. We have made clear, moreover, that the ordinary and customary meaning of a claim term is the meaning that the term would have to a person of ordinary skill in the art in question at the time of the invention, i.e., as of the effective filing date of the patent application.

The inquiry into how a person of ordinary skill in the art understands a claim term provides an objective baseline from which to begin claim interpretation. That starting point is based on the well-settled understanding that inventors are typically persons skilled in the field of the invention and that patents are addressed to and intended to be read by others of skill in the pertinent art.

Importantly, the person of ordinary skill in the art is deemed to read the claim term not only in the context of the particular claim in which the disputed term appears, but in the context of the entire patent, including the specification. This court explained that point well in *Multiform Desiccants, Inc. v. Medzam, Ltd.*, 133 F.3d 1473, 1477 (Fed.Cir. 1998):

> It is the person of ordinary skill in the field of the invention through whose eyes the claims are construed. Such person is deemed to read the words used in the patent documents with an understanding of their meaning in the field, and to have knowledge of any special meaning and usage in the field. The inventor's words that are used to describe the invention—the inventor's lexicography—must be understood and interpreted by the court as they would be understood and interpreted by a person in that field of technology. Thus the court starts the decisionmaking process by reviewing the same resources as would that person, viz., the patent specification and the prosecution history.

B

In some cases, the ordinary meaning of claim language as understood by a person of skill in the art may be readily apparent even to lay judges, and claim construction in such cases involves little more than the application of the widely accepted meaning of commonly understood words. In such circumstances, general purpose dictionaries may be helpful. In many cases that give rise to litigation, however, determining the ordinary and customary meaning of the claim requires examination of terms that have a particular meaning in a field of art. Because the meaning of a claim term as understood by persons of skill in the art is often not immediately apparent, and because patentees frequently use terms idiosyncratically, the court looks to "those sources available to the public that show what a person of skill in the art would have understood disputed claim language to mean." *Innova*, 381 F.3d at 1116. Those sources include "the words of the claims themselves, the remainder of the specification, the prosecution history, and extrinsic evidence concerning relevant scientific principles, the meaning of technical terms, and the state of the art." *Id.*

1

Quite apart from the written description and the prosecution history, the claims themselves provide substantial guidance as to the meaning of particular claim terms. To begin with, the context in which a term is used in the asserted claim can be highly instructive. To take a simple example, the claim in this case refers to "steel baffles," which strongly implies that the term "baffles" does not inherently mean objects made of steel.

Other claims of the patent in question, both asserted and unasserted, can also be valuable sources of enlightenment as to the meaning of a claim term. Because claim terms are normally used consistently throughout the patent, the usage of a term in one claim can often illuminate the meaning of the same term in other claims. Differences among claims can also be a useful guide in understanding the meaning of particular claim terms. For example, the presence of a dependent claim that adds a particular limitation gives rise to a presumption that the limitation in question is not present in the independent claim.

2

The claims, of course, do not stand alone. Rather, they are part of "a fully integrated written instrument," *Markman*, 52 F.3d at 978, consisting principally of a specification that concludes with the claims. For that reason, claims "must be read in view of the specification, of which they are a part." *Id.* at 979. As we stated in *Vitronics*, the specification "is always highly relevant to the claim construction analysis. Usually, it is dispositive; it is the single best guide to the meaning of a disputed term." 90 F.3d at 1582.

This court and its predecessors have long emphasized the importance of the specification in claim construction. In *Autogiro Co. of America v. United States*, 384 F.2d 391, 397–98 (1967), the Court of Claims characterized the specification as "a concordance for the claims," based on the statutory requirement that the specification "describe the manner and process of making and using" the patented invention....

That principle has a long pedigree in Supreme Court decisions as well. [Many citations deleted.]

The importance of the specification in claim construction derives from its statutory role. The close kinship between the written description and the claims is enforced by the statutory requirement that the specification describe the claimed invention in "full, clear, concise, and exact terms." 35 U.S.C. § 112, para. 1. In light of the statutory directive that the inventor provide a "full" and "exact" description of the claimed invention, the specification necessarily informs the proper construction of the claims. . . .

[handwritten margin notes: specs very important; 112 requires]

Consistent with that general principle, our cases recognize that the specification may reveal a special definition given to a claim term by the patentee that differs from the meaning it would otherwise possess. In such cases, the inventor's lexicography governs. In other cases, the specification may reveal an intentional disclaimer, or disavowal, of claim scope by the inventor. In that instance as well, the inventor has dictated the correct claim scope, and the inventor's intention, as expressed in the specification, is regarded as dispositive.

[handwritten margin notes: specs set meaning of words if included]

The pertinence of the specification to claim construction is reinforced by the manner in which a patent is issued. The Patent and Trademark Office ("PTO") determines the scope of claims in patent applications not solely on the basis of the claim language, but upon giving claims their broadest reasonable construction "in light of the specification as it would be interpreted by one of ordinary skill in the art." *In re Am. Acad. of Sci. Tech. Ctr.*, 367 F.3d 1359, 1364 (Fed.Cir. 2004). Indeed, the rules of the PTO require that application claims must "conform to the invention as set forth in the remainder of the specification and the terms and phrases used in the claims must find clear support or antecedent basis in the description so that the meaning of the terms in the claims may be ascertainable by reference to the description." 37 C.F.R. § 1.75(d)(1). It is therefore entirely appropriate for a court, when conducting claim construction, to rely heavily on the written description for guidance as to the meaning of the claims.

[handwritten margin notes: PTO grants patents based on claims in light of the specs; can rely heavy on written description]

3

In addition to consulting the specification, we have held that a court "should also consider the patent's prosecution history, if it is in evidence." *Markman*, 52 F.3d at 980; *see also Graham v. John Deere Co.*, 383 U.S. 1, 33, 86 S.Ct. 684 (1966) ("[A]n invention is construed not only in the light of the claims, but also with reference to the file wrapper or prosecution history in the Patent Office."). The prosecution history, which we have designated as part of the "intrinsic evidence," consists of the complete record of the proceedings before the PTO and includes the prior art cited during the examination of the patent. *Autogiro*, 384 F.2d at 399. Like the specification, the prosecution history provides evidence of how the PTO and the inventor understood the patent. Furthermore, like the specification, the prosecution history was created

[handwritten margin notes: prosecution history important — provides evidence to how PTO and inventor understood claims to mean]

by the patentee in attempting to explain and obtain the patent. Yet because the prosecution history represents an ongoing negotiation between the PTO and the applicant, rather than the final product of that negotiation, it often lacks the clarity of the specification and thus is less useful for claim construction purposes.

C

Although we have emphasized the importance of intrinsic evidence in claim construction, we have also authorized district courts to rely on extrinsic evidence, which "consists of all evidence external to the patent and prosecution history, including expert and inventor testimony, dictionaries, and learned treatises." *Markman*, 52 F.3d at 980. However, while extrinsic evidence "can shed useful light on the relevant art," we have explained that it is "less significant than the intrinsic record in determining 'the legally operative meaning of claim language.'" *C.R. Bard, Inc. v. U.S. Surgical Corp.*, 388 F.3d 858, 862 (Fed.Cir.2004).

Within the class of extrinsic evidence, the court has observed that dictionaries and treatises can be useful in claim construction. We have especially noted the help that technical dictionaries may provide to a court "to better understand the underlying technology" and the way in which one of skill in the art might use the claim terms. *Vitronics*, 90 F.3d at 1584 n. 6. . . .

We have also held that extrinsic evidence in the form of expert testimony can be useful to a court for a variety of purposes, such as to provide background on the technology at issue, to explain how an invention works, to ensure that the court's understanding of the technical aspects of the patent is consistent with that of a person of skill in the art, or to establish that a particular term in the patent or the prior art has a particular meaning in the pertinent field. However, conclusory, unsupported assertions by experts as to the definition of a claim term are not useful to a court. Similarly, a court should discount any expert testimony "that is clearly at odds with the claim construction mandated by the claims themselves, the written description, and the prosecution history, in other words, with the written record of the patent." [*Key Pharms. v. Hercon Labs. Corp.*, 161 F.3d 709, 716 (Fed. Cir. 1998)].

We have viewed extrinsic evidence in general as less reliable than the patent and its prosecution history in determining how to read claim terms, for several reasons. First, extrinsic evidence by definition is not part of the patent and does not have the specification's virtue of being created at the time of patent prosecution for the purpose of explaining the patent's scope and meaning. Second, while claims are construed as they would be understood by a hypothetical person of skill in the art, extrinsic publications may not be written by or for skilled artisans and therefore may not reflect the understanding of a skilled artisan in the field of the patent. Third, extrinsic evidence consisting of expert reports and testimony is generated at the time of and for the purpose of litigation and thus can suffer from bias that is not present in intrinsic evidence.... Fourth, there is a virtually unbounded universe of potential extrinsic evidence of some marginal relevance that could be brought to bear on any claim construction question. In the course of litigation, each party will naturally choose the pieces of extrinsic evidence most favorable to its cause, leaving the court with the considerable task of filtering the useful extrinsic evidence from the fluff.

In sum, extrinsic evidence may be useful to the court, but it is unlikely to result in a reliable interpretation of patent claim scope unless considered in the context of the intrinsic evidence. Nonetheless, because extrinsic evidence can help educate the court regarding the field of the invention and can help the court determine what a person of ordinary skill in the art would understand claim terms to mean, it is permissible for the district court in its sound discretion to admit and use such evidence. In exercising that discretion, and in weighing all the evidence bearing on claim construction, the court should keep in mind the flaws inherent in each type of evidence and assess that evidence accordingly.

III

Although the principles outlined above have been articulated on numerous occasions, some of this court's cases have suggested a somewhat different approach to claim construction, in which the court has given greater emphasis to dictionary definitions of claim terms and has assigned a less prominent role to the specification and the prosecution history. The leading case in this line is *Texas Digital Systems, Inc. v. Telegenix, Inc.*, 308 F.3d 1193 (Fed.Cir.2002).

A

In *Texas Digital,* the court noted that "dictionaries, encyclopedias and treatises are particularly useful resources to assist the court in determining the ordinary and customary meanings of claim terms." 308 F.3d at 1202. Those texts, the court explained, are "objective resources that serve as reliable sources of information on the established meanings that would have been attributed to the terms of the claims by those of skill in the art," and they "deserve no less fealty in the context of claim construction" than in any other area of law. *Id.* at 1203.... The *Texas Digital* court further explained that the patent's specification and prosecution history must be consulted to determine if the patentee has used "the words [of the claim] in a manner clearly inconsistent with the ordinary meaning reflected, for example, in a dictionary definition." 308 F.3d at 1204.

The *Texas Digital* court explained that it advanced the methodology set forth in that opinion in an effort to combat what this court has termed "one of the cardinal sins of patent law—reading a limitation from the written description into the claims," [*SciMed Life Sys., Inc. v. Advanced Cardiovas. Sys., Inc.*, 242 F.3d 1337, 1340 (Fed. Cir. 2001)]. The court concluded that it is improper to consult "the written description and prosecution history as a threshold step in the claim construction process, before any effort is made to discern the ordinary and customary meanings attributed to the words themselves." *Texas Digital*, 308 F.3d at 1204. To do so, the court reasoned, "invites a violation of our precedent counseling against importing limitations into the claims." *Id.*

B

Although the concern expressed by the court in *Texas Digital* was valid, the methodology it adopted placed too much reliance on extrinsic sources such as dictionaries, treatises, and encyclopedias and too little on intrinsic sources, in particular the specification and prosecution history. While the court noted that the specification must be consulted in every case, it suggested a methodology for claim interpretation in which the specification should be consulted only after a determination is made, whether based on a dictionary, treatise, or other source, as to the ordinary meaning or meanings of the claim term in dispute. Even then, recourse to the specification is limited to determining whether the specification excludes one of the meanings derived from the dictionary, whether the presumption in favor of the dictionary definition of the claim term has been overcome by "an explicit definition of the term different from its ordinary meaning," or whether the inventor "has disavowed or disclaimed scope of coverage, by using words or expressions of manifest exclusion or restriction, representing a clear disavowal of claim scope." 308 F.3d at 1204. In effect, the *Texas Digital* approach limits the role of the specification in claim construction to serving as a check on the dictionary meaning of a claim term if the specification requires the court to conclude that fewer than all the dictionary definitions apply, or if the specification contains a sufficiently specific alternative definition or disavowal. That approach, in our view, improperly restricts the role of the specification in claim construction.

Assigning such a limited role to the specification, and in particular requiring that any definition of claim language in the specification be express, is inconsistent with our rulings that the specification is "the single best guide to the meaning of a disputed term," and that the specification "acts as a dictionary when it expressly defines terms used in the claims or when it defines terms by implication." *Vitronics*, 90 F.3d at 1582.

The main problem with elevating the dictionary to such prominence is that it focuses the inquiry on the abstract meaning of words rather than on the meaning of claim terms within the context of the patent. Properly viewed, the "ordinary meaning" of a claim term is its meaning to the ordinary artisan after reading the entire patent. Yet heavy reliance on the dictionary divorced from the intrinsic evidence risks transforming the meaning of the claim term to the artisan into the meaning of the term in the abstract, out of its particular context, which is the specification.... Thus, there may be a disconnect between the patentee's responsibility to describe and claim his invention, and the dictionary editors' objective of aggregating all possible definitions for particular words. . . .

Dictionaries, by their nature, provide an expansive array of definitions. General dictionaries, in particular, strive to collect all uses of particular words, from the common to the obscure. By design, general dictionaries collect the definitions of a term as used not only in a particular art field, but in many different settings. In such circumstances, it is inevitable that the multiple dictionary definitions for a term will extend beyond the "construction of the patent [that] is confirmed by the avowed understanding of the patentee, expressed by him, or on his behalf, when his application for the original patent was pending." *Goodyear Dental Vulcanite Co. v. Davis*, 102 U.S. 222, 227, 26 L.Ed. 149 (1880). . . . Even technical dictionaries or treatises, under certain circumstances, may suffer from some of these deficiencies. There is no guarantee that a term is used in the same way in a treatise as it would be by the patentee. . . . Moreover, different dictionaries may contain somewhat different sets of definitions for the same words. A claim should not rise or fall based upon the preferences of a particular dictionary editor, or the court's independent decision, uninformed by the specification, to rely on one dictionary rather than another.

As we have noted above, however, we do not intend to preclude the appropriate use of dictionaries. Dictionaries or comparable sources are often useful to assist in understanding the commonly understood meaning of words and have been used both by our court and the Supreme Court in claim interpretation. *See Exhibit Supply Co. v. Ace Patents Corp.*, 315 U.S. 126, 134, 62 S.Ct. 513, 86 L.Ed. 736 (1942).

We also acknowledge that the purpose underlying the Texas Digital line of cases—to avoid the danger of reading limitations from the specification into the claim—is sound. Moreover, we recognize that the distinction between using the specification to interpret the meaning of a claim and importing limitations from the specification into the claim can be a difficult one to apply in practice. However, the line between construing terms and importing limitations can be discerned with reasonable certainty and predictability if the court's focus remains on understanding how a person of ordinary skill in the art would understand the claim terms. For instance, although the specification often describes very specific embodiments of the invention, we have repeatedly warned against confining the claims to those embodiments. In particular, we have expressly rejected the contention that if a patent describes only a single embodiment, the claims of the patent must be construed as being limited to that embodiment. That is not just because section 112 of the Patent Act requires that the claims themselves set forth the limits of the patent grant, but also because persons of ordinary skill in the art rarely would confine their definitions of terms to the exact representations depicted in the embodiments.

To avoid importing limitations from the specification into the claims, it is important to keep in mind that the purposes of the specification are to teach and enable those of skill in the art to make and use the invention and to provide a best mode for doing so. One of the best ways to teach a person of ordinary skill in the art how to make and use the invention is to provide an example of how to practice the invention in a particular case. Much of the time, upon reading the specification in that context, it will become clear whether the patentee is setting out specific examples of the invention to accomplish those goals, or whether the patentee instead intends for the claims and the embodiments in the specification to be strictly coextensive. *See SciMed Life Sys.*, 242 F.3d at 1341. The manner in which the patentee uses a term within the specification and claims usually will make the distinction apparent.

In the end, there will still remain some cases in which it will be hard to determine whether a person of skill in the art would understand the embodiments to define the outer limits of the claim term or merely to be exemplary in nature. While that task may present difficulties in some cases, we nonetheless believe that attempting to resolve that problem in the context of the particular patent is likely to capture the scope of the actual invention more accurately than either strictly limiting the scope of the claims to the embodiments disclosed in the specification or divorcing the claim language from the specification.

In *Vitronics*, this court grappled with the same problem and set forth guidelines for reaching the correct claim construction and not imposing improper limitations on claims. 90 F.3d at 1582. The underlying goal of our decision in *Vitronics* was to increase the likelihood that a court will comprehend how a person of ordinary skill in the art would understand the claim terms. See id. at 1584. In that process, we recognized that there is no magic formula or catechism for conducting claim construction. Nor is the court barred from considering any particular sources or required to analyze sources in any specific sequence, as long as those sources are not used to contradict claim meaning that is unambiguous in light of the intrinsic evidence.... In *Vitronics*, we did not attempt to provide a rigid algorithm for claim construction, but simply attempted to explain why, in general, certain types of evidence are more valuable than others. Today, we adhere to that approach and reaffirm the approach to claim construction outlined in that case, in *Markman*, and in *Innova*. We now turn to the application of those principles to the case at bar.

IV

A

The critical language of claim 1 of the '798 patent—"further means disposed inside the shell for increasing its load bearing capacity comprising internal steel baffles extending inwardly from the steel shell walls"— imposes three clear requirements with respect to the baffles. First, the baffles must be made of steel. Second, they must be part of the load-bearing means for the wall section. Third, they must be pointed inward from the walls. Both parties, stipulating to a dictionary definition, also conceded that the term "baffles" refers to objects that check, impede, or obstruct the flow of something. The intrinsic evidence confirms that a person of skill in the art would understand that the term "baffles," as used in the '798 patent, would have that generic meaning.

The other claims of the '798 patent specify particular functions to be served by the baffles. For example, dependent claim 2 states that the baffles may be "oriented with the panel sections disposed at angles for deflecting projectiles such as bullets able to penetrate the steel plates." The inclusion of such a specific limitation on the term "baffles" in claim 2 makes it likely that the patentee did not contemplate that the term "baffles" already contained that limitation. *See Dow Chem. Co. v. United States*, 226 F.3d 1334, 1341–42 (Fed.Cir.2000) (concluding that an independent claim should be given broader scope than a dependent claim to avoid rendering the dependent claim redundant). Independent claim 17 further supports that proposition. It states that baffles are placed "projecting inwardly from the outer shell at angles tending to deflect projectiles that penetrate the outer shell." That limitation would be unnecessary if persons of skill in the art understood that the baffles inherently served such a function. Dependent claim 6 provides an additional requirement for the baffles, stating that "the internal baffles of both outer panel sections overlap and interlock at angles providing deflector panels extending from one end of the module to the other." If the baffles recited in claim 1 were inherently placed at specific angles, or interlocked to form an intermediate barrier, claim 6 would be redundant.

The specification further supports the conclusion that persons of ordinary skill in the art would understand the baffles recited in the '798 patent to be load-bearing objects that serve to check, impede, or obstruct flow. At several points, the specification discusses positioning the baffles so as to deflect projectiles. *See* '798 patent, col. 2, II. 13–15; id., col. 5, II. 17–19. The patent states that one advantage of the invention over the prior art is that "[t]here have not been effective ways of dealing with these powerful impact weapons with inexpensive housing." Id., col. 3, II. 28–30. While that statement makes clear the invention envisions baffles that serve that function, it does not imply that in order to qualify as baffles within the meaning of the claims, the internal support structures must serve the projectile-deflecting function in all the embodiments of all the claims. The specification must teach and enable all the claims, and the section of the written description discussing the use of baffles to deflect projectiles serves that purpose for claims 2, 6, 17, and 23, which specifically claim baffles that deflect projectiles. *See In re Wright*, 999 F.2d 1557, 1561 (Fed.Cir.1993).

The specification discusses several other purposes served by the baffles. For example, the baffles are described as providing structural support. The patent states that one way to increase load-bearing capacity is to use "at least in part inwardly directed steel baffles 15, 16." '798 patent, col. 4, II. 14–15. The baffle 16 is described as a "strengthening triangular baffle." *Id.*, col. 4, line 37. Importantly, Figures 4 and 6 do not show the baffles as part of an "intermediate interlocking, but not solid, internal barrier." In those figures, the baffle 16 simply provides structural support for one of the walls, as depicted below:

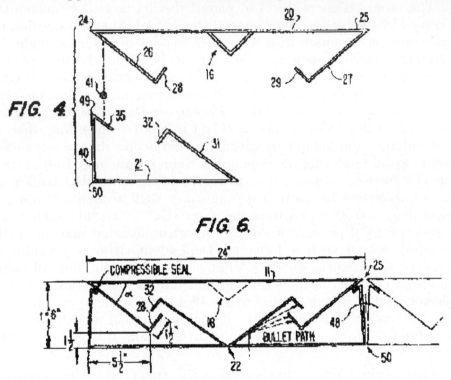

Other uses for the baffles are listed in the specification as well. In Figure 7, the overlapping flanges "provide for overlapping and interlocking the baffles to produce substantially an intermediate barrier wall between the opposite [wall] faces":

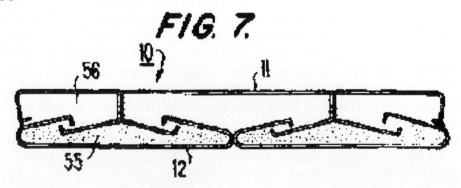

'798 patent, col. 5, II. 26–29. Those baffles thus create small compartments that can be filled with either sound and thermal insulation or rock and gravel to stop projectiles. *Id.*, col. 5, II. 29–34. By separating the interwall area into compartments (see, e.g., compartment 55 in Figure 7), the user of the modules can choose different types of material for each compartment, so that the module can be "easily custom tailored for the specific needs of each installation." *Id.*, col. 5, II. 36–37. When material is placed into the wall during installation, the baffles obstruct the flow of material from one compartment to another so that this "custom tailoring" is possible.

The fact that the written description of the '798 patent sets forth multiple objectives to be served by the baffles recited in the claims confirms that the term "baffles" should not be read restrictively to require that the baffles in each case serve all of the recited functions. We have held that "[t]he fact that a patent asserts that an invention achieves several objectives does not require that each of the claims be construed as limited to structures that are capable of achieving all of the objectives." Although deflecting projectiles is one of the advantages of the baffles of the '798 patent, the patent does not require that the inward extending structures always be capable of performing that function. Accordingly, we conclude that a person of skill in the art would not interpret the disclosure and claims of the '798 patent to mean that a structure extending inward from one of the wall faces is a "baffle" if it is at an acute or obtuse angle, but is not a "baffle" if it is disposed at a right angle.

B

Invoking the principle that "claims should be so construed, if possible, as to sustain their validity," *Rhine v. Casio, Inc.*, 183 F.3d 1342, 1345 (Fed.Cir.1999), AWH argues that the term "baffles" should be given a restrictive meaning because if the term is not construed restrictively, the asserted claims would be invalid.

AWH's argument

While we have acknowledged the maxim that claims should be construed to preserve their validity, we have not applied that principle broadly, and we have certainly not endorsed a regime in which validity analysis is a regular component of claim construction. [*See Nazomi Communications, Inc. v. Arm Holdings, PLC*, 403 F.3d 1364, 1368–69 (Fed. Cir. 2005).] Instead, we have limited the maxim to cases in which "the court concludes, after applying all the available tools of claim construction, that the claim is still ambiguous." In such cases, we have looked to whether it is reasonable to infer that the PTO would not have issued an invalid patent, and that the ambiguity in the claim language should therefore be resolved in a manner that would preserve the patent's validity.

In this case, . . . the claim term at issue is not ambiguous. Thus, it can be construed without the need to consider whether one possible construction would render the claim invalid while the other would not. The doctrine of construing claims to preserve their validity, a doctrine of limited utility in any event, therefore has no applicability here.

In sum, we reject AWH's arguments in favor of a restrictive definition of the term "baffles." Because we disagree with the district court's claim construction, we reverse the summary judgment of noninfringement. In light of our decision on claim construction, it is necessary to remand the infringement claims to the district court for further proceedings.

Remanded.

NOTES

1. **The "ordinary and customary meaning" principle: The court will not "recook" the claims.** The ordinary meaning principle carries a warning. The claim language governs even over common sense. In *Chef America v. Lamb–Weston, Inc.*, 358 F.3d 1371 (Fed. Cir. 2004), the patent claimed a process for making a pre-cooked biscuit dough that could be quickly ready by warming in a microwave. The claim language recited, "heating the ... dough *to* a temperature in the range of about 400°F to 850°F." *Id.* at 1372. At those temperatures, of course, the dough would become an unusable charcoal briquet, not an edible biscuit. No doubt the claims drafter meant to heat the dough in an oven *at* a temperature of 400–850° for a brief time. The claim used the wrong preposition. The Federal Circuit declined to redraft the claim to correct the obvious error: "Even a nonsensical result does not require the court to redraft the claims ... Where, as here, the claim is susceptible to only one reasonable construction, ... we must construe the claims [as the applicant] drafted it." *Id.* at 1374.

2. **The role of the Specification in Claim Construction.** In *Phillips*, the Federal Circuit reiterated the standard doctrine that "[c]laims must be read in view of the specification, of which they are part." *Phillips* also repeated the standard caution against "one of the cardinal sins of patent law—reading a limitation from the written description into the claims." Indeed *Phillips* had a primary purpose of correcting *Texas Digital*'s overreliance on dictionaries as an effort to prevent this cardinal sin. The distinction between "reading claim terms in light of the specification" and the prohibited practice of "importing limitations from the specification into the claims," *see SRI Intern'l v. Matsushita Elec. Corp.*, 775 F.2d 1107 (Fed.Cir.1985), is not easy to draw. The *Phillips* court expresses confidence that it can discern "the line between construing terms and importing limitations ... if the ... focus remains on understanding how a person of ordinary skill in the art could understand claim terms." Maybe the Federal Circuit with its expertise in handling patent law and technical subject matter can discern that line confidently. Do district judges who handle patent cases only intermittently have the same ability to discern that line? Can you articulate a neutral standard for distinguishing the permitted from the prohibited uses of the specification?

3. The Meaning of "A." In a Federal Circuit case featuring a meningitis vaccine, the inventor discovered that linking a protein along the polysaccharide chain of the vaccine enhances the immune response. The claim specified linking a protein to *"a terminal portion* of the polysaccharide." The accused vaccine linked a protein to both terminal ends of the polysaccharide, not just to one terminal end. The Federal Circuit determined that the accused vaccine did not infringe because the linkage was limited to *a* terminal portion:

> While it is generally accepted in patent parlance that "a" can mean one or more, *see*, ROBERT C. FABER, LANDIS ON MECHANICS OF PATENT CLAIM DRAFTING 531 (3d ed. 1990) ("In a claim, the indefinite article A or AN connotes 'one or more'.") there is no indication in the specification that the inventors here intended it to have other than its normal singular meaning.

North American Vaccine v. American Cyanamid Co., 7 F.3d 1571, 1575–76 (Fed.Cir. 1993). This single sentence is astounding in its inconsistency. It acknowledges the general rule that "a" means "one or more," but then abandons the rule because the specification did not contain anything against a singular reading. The rule was already against a singular reading. Why then would an inventor need to include anything in a specification to invoke this normal patent usage? This reliance on what the specification did not say to vary from a normal construction rule may be a high point for improper use of the specification in claim construction. By the way, even if the accused vaccine did attach a protein at both terminal ends or multiple terminal ends, why doesn't the claim language still read on the accused composition?

In any event, the Federal Circuit now says that "a" means "one or more." In *KCJ Corp. v. Kinetic Concepts, Inc.*, 223 F.3d 1351, the Federal Circuit said: "This court has encountered "a" or "an" in patent claims on several occasions. This court has uniformly applied the general rule for indefinite articles.... [S]tanding alone, a disclosure of a preferred or exemplary embodiment encompassing a singular element does not disclaim a plural embodiment." *Electro Med. Sys., S.A. v. Cooper Life Sciences, Inc.*, 34 F.3d 1048, 1054 (Fed.Cir.1994).

4. Experts and Claim Interpretation. The role of the expert has always been a controversial part of the claim meaning process. In the late 1990's, the Federal Circuit in *Vitronics Corp. v. Conceptronic, Inc.*, 90 F.3d 1576 (Fed.Cir. 1996), created a rift with trial judges by opining that expert testimony on the proper construction of a disputed claim term should "rarely, if ever, occur." Id. at 1585. This commentary caused concern amongst trial judges and in the patent bar because it appeared to discredit experts as a source of technical information essential to understanding and interpreting the claims. Later, in *Pitney Bowes, Inc. v. Hewlett–Packard Co.*, 182 F.3d 1298 (Fed.Cir.1999), the Federal Circuit backed off of its language to allow experts to offer relevant evidence as long as it did not contradict the intrinsic record. An unusual two-judge concurrence in the *Pitney Bowes* cases gave additional reasons to credit reliable expert testimony in the court's claim construction process:

> This appellate court, however, should refrain from dictating a claim interpretation process that excludes reliable expert testimony. The process of claim construction at the trial court level will often benefit from expert

testimony which may (1) supply a proper technological context to understand the claims (words often have meaning only in context), (2) explain the meaning of claim terms as understood by one of skill in the art (the ultimate standard for claim meaning, see *Markman v. Westview Instruments Inc.*, 52 F.3d 967, 986 (1996)), and (3) help the trial court understand the patent process itself (complex prosecution histories—not to mention specifications—are not familiar to most trial courts).

182 F.3d at 1314. *Phillips* also bristles with skepticism about expert testimony "generated at the time of and for the purpose of litigation." 415 F.3d at 1318. Underlying this commentary is a concern over "battles of the experts." Those "battles" indeed can mislead and confuse juries. Are the considerations in favor of protecting the trial process against "hired guns" as prominent when district judges construe claims on their own?

5. Prosecution history as a claim construction device: U.S. divergence. The U.S. patent system alone gives broad reliance to the administrative record of patent acquisition in the claim construction process. *Phillips* explained the U.S. rule. The following case illustrates its application.

COMPUTER DOCKING STATION CORP. v. DELL, INC.

United States Court of Appeals, Federal Circuit, 2008
519 F.3d 1366

RADER, CIRCUIT JUDGE.

On summary judgment, the United States District Court for the Western District of Wisconsin determined that Dell, Inc., Gateway, Inc., Toshiba America, Inc., and Toshiba America Information Systems, Inc. (collectively Defendants) did not infringe claims 17–20, 22, 24, and 26–28 of Computer Docking Station Corporation's (CDSC's) United States Patent No. 5,187,645 ('645 patent). Because the patentee disavowed an interpretation of "portable computer" that would encompass a computer with a built-in display or keyboard, this court affirms the district court's holding of no infringement.

I

The '645 patent claims a portable microprocessor system with sufficient processing power, memory, and network compatibility for business applications. '645 patent col.3 II.18–20. Figure 1 below depicts this system with the microprocessor contained in the main housing under the label 10. The specification teaches that the main housing's size and weight account in part for the system's portability. Id. col.1 II.29–36, 56–62; col.3 II.44–45. The main housing "resembles a brick" about eleven inches high, eight inches wide, and three inches thick. It weighs approximately eight pounds. As illustrated in Figure 2, the main housing may fit in one half of an attaché case. *Id.* col.3 II.33–45.

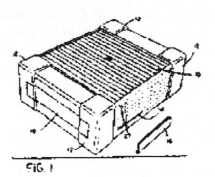

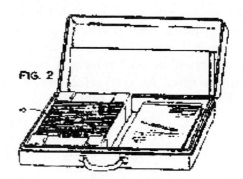

The system also includes the capability to connect to peripheral devices, such as a keyboard or mouse. The parties agree that the term "peripheral device" means "an external device that is capable of connecting to, and is capable of being controlled by, a computer." The main housing connects to these peripheral devices either through individual connectors (one connector per peripheral device), or through a docking connector, which "allows all peripheral connections to be realized through a single connector." '645 patent col.1 ll.24–31; col.2 ll.23–34. The docking connector simplifies coupling and decoupling of the main housing with peripheral devices. *Id.* col.1 ll.29–36; col.3 ll.64–66 ("[O]nly one connection is necessary to disconnect the system or connect the system."). Figure 6 illustrates individual connections between the main housing and each peripheral device; Figure 3 illustrates a connection between the main housing and docking connector. *Id.* col.7 ll.23–26; col.2 ll.42–43.

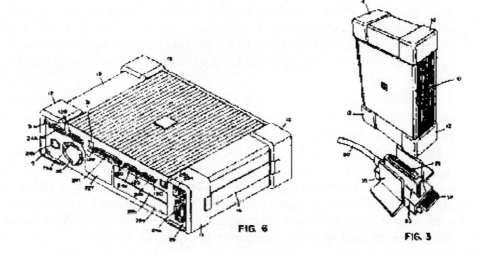

The specification explains that a keyboard and visual display are "options available with the system." *Id.* col.2 ll.8–11. Figures 13–15 illustrate these options. Figure 13 shows that a keyboard 60 and display 58 "may be coupled with the microcomputer system." *Id.* col.7 ll.23–24.

The keyboard connects to the housing using connector 24b, shown on the left-hand side of the rear bezel in Figure 6. *Id*. col.5 II.30–31. As shown in Figure 14, display 58 is also external to the housing, but may be attached to and removed from it using individual connectors and thumbscrews. *Id*. col.7 II.28–42. Figure 15 shows the housing as it fits with the display and keyboard.

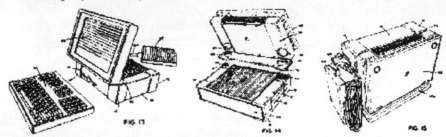

Each of the asserted claims requires a "portable computer" or "portable computer microprocessing system" (the "portable computer limitation") and a "single connector for making all connections from the microprocessor to said specific computer peripheral devices" (the "all connections limitation"). Claim 28 is representative of the three asserted independent claims:

28.   A **portable computer** comprising:

a) a microprocessor for processing instructions;

b) a housing containing the microprocessor;

c) a plurality of computer-peripheral-device-specific connectors in electrical communication with the microprocessor such that each of said plurality of computer-peripheral-device specific connectors provides a computer-peripheral-device specific data link to said microprocessors, said connectors for connecting the microprocessor to specific computer peripheral devices and being mounted on the housing; and

d) another single connector on the housing, said single connector comprising a set of pins, said set further comprising a plurality of subsets of computer-peripheral-device-specific pins being in electrical communication with said microprocessor such that one of each of said subsets of computer-peripheral-device-specific pins provides the same computer-peripheral-device-specific data link as said each of said plurality of computer-peripheral-device-specific connectors, **said single connector for making all connections from the microprocessor to said specific computer peripheral devices.**

Id. col. 12 II.11–34 (emphases added).

During prosecution, the examiner rejected several claims as anticipated and obvious in view of U.S. Patent No. 5,030,128 to Herron et al. ('128 patent or Herron). Herron discloses a laptop computer and a docking module that facilitates operation on a desktop. Herron connects each peripheral to the docking module. '128 patent col.2 II.3–38. Attempting to distinguish Herron, the applicants expressly defined their invention in different terms. In addition, the applicants amended the claims. After an interview, the examiner found that the amended "claims directed to redundant connectors (one set plural & one a single connector) would be allowable." The '645 patent issued in February 1993 and was later assigned to CDSC.

Defendants produce various computer devices, including laptops and docking stations. In its amended complaint, CDSC identified a number of defendants' laptop computers and docking stations as infringing. The record shows that each accused laptop computer has a built-in display or keyboard.

The district court construed "portable computer" and "portable computer microprocessing system" in the preambles of the asserted claims to mean "a computer without a built-in display or keyboard that is capable of being moved or carried about." The trial court determined that the prosecution history and the specification distinguished the claimed invention from a laptop computer. In particular, the district court found that the applicants had emphasized the differences between their invention and laptop computers to overcome the examiner's rejections based on Herron. Because the district court held that the statements in the prosecution history amounted to a clear and unmistakable disavowal, it construed the terms "portable computer" and "portable computer microprocessing system" to exclude computers with built-in displays or keyboards. The district court also construed the phrase "said single connector for making all connections from the microprocessor to said computer peripheral devices" to require "that all individual peripheral device connections on the housing that connect to the microprocessor also pass through the single connector."

II

The words of the claims define the scope of the patented invention. *Vitronics Corp. v. Conceptronic, Inc.*, 90 F.3d 1576, 1582 (Fed.Cir.1996). "It is well-settled that, in interpreting an asserted claim, the court should look first to the intrinsic evidence of record, i.e., the patent itself, including the claims, the specification and, if in evidence, the prosecution history." Id. Claim terms are generally given their ordinary and customary meaning, which is "the meaning that the term would have to a person of ordinary skill in the art in question at the time of the invention." *Phillips v. AWH Corp.*, 415 F.3d 1303, 1313 (Fed.Cir.2005) (en banc). However, the person of ordinary skill is deemed to read the claim terms in the context of the entire patent, including the specification and prosecution history. Id.

Occasionally specification explanations may lead one of ordinary skill to interpret a claim term more narrowly than its plain meaning suggests. Nonetheless, this court will not countenance the importation of claim limitations from a few specification statements or figures into the claims, particularly if those specification extracts describe only embodiments of a broader claimed invention. By the same token, "the specification 'is always highly relevant to the claim construction analysis. Usually, it is dispositive; it is the single best guide to the meaning of a disputed term.'" *Phillips*, 415 F.3d at 1315. The specification may show that "the patentee has disclaimed subject matter or has otherwise limited the scope of the claims." For example, repeated and definitive remarks in the written description could restrict a claim limitation to a particular structure.

Statements made during prosecution may also affect the scope of the claims. Specifically, "a patentee may limit the meaning of a claim term by making a clear and unmistakable disavowal of scope during prosecution." *Purdue Pharma L.P. v. Endo Pharms., Inc.*, 438 F.3d 1123, 1136 (Fed.Cir.2006). A patentee could do so, for example, by clearly characterizing the invention in a way to try to overcome rejections based on prior art. The doctrine of prosecution disclaimer "protects the public's reliance on definitive statements made during prosecution" by "precluding patentees from recapturing through claim interpretation specific meanings [clearly and unmistakably] disclaimed during prosecution." Claims should not be construed "one way in order to obtain their allowance and in a different way against accused infringers."

Prosecution disclaimer does not apply to an ambiguous disavowal. Prosecution disclaimer does not apply, for example, if the applicant simply describes features of the prior art and does not distinguish the claimed invention based on those features.

As a threshold matter, neither party disputes that the terms "portable computer" and "portable computer microprocessing system," as used in the preambles of the asserted claims, limit their scope.... The district court construed the portable computer limitation to require "a computer without a built-in display or keyboard that is capable of being moved or carried about." The parties do not dispute that the limitation requires a computer "that is capable of being moved or carried about." This appeal focuses on the "a built-in display or keyboard" component of the district court's construction.

During prosecution, in a Response dated June 15, 1992, the applicants sought to distinguish their invention from Herron. The applicants' statements clearly and unambiguously disavowed computers with built-in displays and keyboards-that is, laptops. At the outset of those statements, the applicants distinguished their invention, a portable microprocessing system, from its peripheral devices.... [Indeed] [t]he applicants expressly listed a keyboard and display as peripheral devices. They also explained that the interface connectors for the keyboard and display are located on the rear bezel of the housing. If the keyboard and display were built-in or attached to the housing like a laptop, these peripheral connections would not be necessary.

In the same Response, the applicants also contrasted the advantages of their invention with the limitations of the Herron laptop:

> Rather than requiring a portable display and keyboard, the present invention concentrates on portability of an exceptionally large memory capacity in hard disk drive.... For the same sized unit as a conventional lap-top computer, the invention does require that peripherals be made available at each location, a requirement that would lead one away from the present invention. However, even that requirement can be an advantage over laptop computers in that higher quality peripherals will more likely be used since they need not be transported. Thus, lap-top machines make concessions in memory, display and other areas in favor of portability. The Applicants' system, on the other hand, is a portable full service microprocessing system which concedes portability of peripherals.

Id. at 14–15. (emphases added). In this statement, the applicants clearly distinguished their invention from computers with a built-in display or keyboard.... In fact, the applicants explained that the invention requires these peripherals at each location of use. In contrast, the applicants emphasized that laptops sacrificed the power of the claimed full-service microprocessing system in favor of built-in peripherals. The applicants also stated that the built-in display and keyboard of a laptop would be inferior in quality to the peripherals stored permanently at each location and used with the claimed invention.

Moreover, the applicants further distinguished their system from the Herron "laptop computer with its own flat panel display and keyboard," arguing that laptops did not have the memory capacity, utilities and functionalities of their system:

> This lap-top computer does not possess utilities and functionalities comparable to those of the Applicants' system.

Id. at 17.

The applicants also distinguished their invention from laptops based on how the devices connect to the docking station. Because the keyboard and display are not built into the claimed microprocessing system, the applicants described the system as able to fit vertically in the docking station. Because of its built-in keyboard and display, a laptop could not fit vertically. Specifically, the applicants stated: "The Herron reference discloses a docking module which is latched to the rear of a lap-top computer. The computer and docking module rest on a desk top." *Id.* at 16. "[T]he computer in Herron is not oriented vertically as in the Applicants' system. It would make no sense to do so with the Herron lap-top with its attached keyboard and display. Therefore, Herron does not have the Applicants' reduced footprint size." *Id.* at 17.

A careful reading of the prosecution history leaves little doubt that the distinctions between the invention and Herron are more extensive than only the single connector limitation. This court observes that the applicants distinguished their invention from the prior art in multiple ways. Nonetheless a disavowal, if clear and unambiguous, can lie in a single distinction among many. Of course, a multitude of distinctions may serve to make any single distinction in the group less clear and unmistakable as the point of distinction over prior art and as a critical defining point for the invention as a whole.

Moreover, the prosecution history must always receive consideration in context. In this case, the specification of the '645 patent does not provide an express definition of "portable computer" that would override or make the distinctions in the prosecution history ambiguous.

As noted, the specification in this case does not create any ambiguity. The ... specification contrasts the microcomputer system with a laptop computer. Furthermore, the specification repeatedly describes the invention as a microcomputer. *See, e.g., id.*, Abstract ("A microcomputer system includes a microprocessor and a housing for holding the microprocessor."); col.3 ll.14–16 ("In accordance with the present invention a microcomputer works equally well for business applications as it does for personal applications."); col.3 ll.21–22 ("Fig. 1 depicts the main housing 10 of the microcomputer of the present invention.") In contrast, the specification never identifies the invention as a laptop.

As noted above, the "totality of the prosecution history" informs the disavowal inquiry. *Rheox, Inc. v. Entact, Inc.*, 276 F.3d 1319, 1326 (Fed.Cir.2002). Here the sum of the patentees' statements during prosecution would lead a competitor to believe that the patentee had disavowed coverage of laptops. CDSC cannot recapture claim scope disavowed during prosecution to prove infringement. The trial court correctly determined that the portable computer limitation requires "a computer without a built-in display or keyboard that is capable of being moved or carried about."

This court affirms the district court's grant of summary judgment of non-infringement of the portable computer limitation.

AFFIRMED

NOTES

Burn the File Wrapper! Professor Thomas has been a vigorous opponent of the use of prosecution history as a tool of claim interpretation. He concludes that the patent bar ought to renew its focus upon the claims as ultimately granted, rather than on preparatory texts of uncertain relationship to the proprietary right ultimately granted. What do you make of the following points urged by Professor Thomas?

- Because patent applications may be held in secret by the PTO, and patentees not infrequently launch infringement actions on the day such a patent issues, notice is a poor justification for the use of prosecution histories in claim interpretation.

- Aware that a court may review each stage of their work product, PTO examiners tend to rely upon the prosecution history to define the patented invention, rather than requiring the applicant to spell out limitations within the claims themselves. Use of the prosecution history to interpret claims also disrupts the integrity of prosecution by encouraging formulaic applicant responses rather than more forthcoming, unhindered dialogue.

- To the extent that the patent community encourages the use of prosecution histories, it promotes a cyclical search for meaning that requires a transcoding from one text to another. Prosecution histories too must be interpreted, and resort to them increases our burdens rather than lessens them.

- An essential element of the traditional estoppel doctrine is reliance, a consideration that is wholly absent from prosecution history estoppel decisions. At a minimum, the courts should determine whether the accused infringer actually relied upon the prosecution history in its technical decision making, rather than turning to the file wrapper only after the patentee filed its infringement suit.

- Thanks to the *Wilson Sporting Goods* line of cases, considered in this casebook immediately below, the courts already possess techniques for accounting for the prior art in claim interpretation. The use of prosecution histories serves as an inferior proxy for this established, objective mechanism for restraining the scope of equivalency.

- If unforeseeability is the post-*Festo* gatekeeper to equivalency, then why look at the prosecution history at all? Nothing within the file wrapper could possibly illuminate what was unknown to the applicant.

See John R. Thomas, *On Preparatory Texts and Proprietary Technologies: The Place of Prosecution Histories in Patent Claim Interpretation*, 47 UCLA L. REV. 183 (1999).

§ 11.2   THE DOCTRINE OF EQUIVALENTS OR NON–TEXTUAL INFRINGEMENT

In a statement of law that holds up remarkably well in the United States, the House of Lords provided in *C. Van der Lely N.V. v. Bamfords Ltd.*, [1963] RPC 61 (H.L. 1962) that:

> Copying an invention by taking its "pith and marrow" without textual infringement of the patent is an old and familiar abuse which the law has never been powerless to prevent. It may be that in doing so there is some illogicality, but our law has always preferred good sense to strict logic. The illogicality arises in this way. On the one hand the patentee is tied strictly to the invention which he claims and the mode of effecting an improvement which he says is his invention. Logically it would seem to follow that if another person is ingenious enough to effect that improvement by a slightly different method he will not infringe. But it has long been recognised that there "may be an essence or substance of the

invention underlying the mere accident of form; and that invention, like every other invention, may be pirated by a theft in a disguised or mutilated form, and it will be in every case a question of fact whether the alleged piracy is the same in substance and effect, or is a substantially new or different combination." (Per James, L.J., in *Clark v. Adie* (1873) L.R. 10 Ch. 667.)

Every modern non-textual infringement case traces its roots to the following United States Supreme Court decision. A case over fifty years old would hardly seem to warrant consideration in light of the Supreme Court's more recent pronouncements in 1997 and 2002. Nonetheless, the Supreme Court itself invoked its fifty-year-old case as a foundation for its newer explanations. As the Federal Circuit explains in *Johnson & Johnston*, another case in this section, this case features a unique fact situation. Specifically, one of the Jones patent's claims literally described the accused product. That claim, however, had been invalidated for describing one or two inoperative embodiments (a now-antiquated doctrine). Despite the unique facts, the language of this opinion reappears repeatedly even five decades later.

GRAVER TANK v. LINDE AIR PRODUCTS CO.

United States Supreme Court, 1950
339 U.S. 605

MR. JUSTICE JACKSON delivered the opinion of the Court.

* * *

In determining whether an accused device or composition infringes a valid patent, resort must be had in the first instance to the words of the claim. If accused matter falls clearly within the claim, infringement is made out and that is the end of it.

But courts have also recognized that to permit imitation of a patented invention which does not copy every literal detail would be to convert the protection of the patent grant into a hollow and useless thing. Such a limitation would leave room for—indeed encourage—the unscrupulous copyist to make unimportant and insubstantial changes and substitutions in the patent which, though adding nothing, would be enough to take the copied matter outside the claim, and hence outside the reach of law. One who seeks to pirate an invention, like one who seeks to pirate a copyrighted book or play, may be expected to introduce minor variations to conceal and shelter the piracy. Outright and forthright duplication is a dull and very rare type of infringement. To prohibit no other would place the inventor at the mercy of verbalism and would be subordinating substance to form. It would deprive him of the benefit of his invention and would foster concealment rather than disclosure of inventions, which is one of the primary purposes of the patent system.

The doctrine of equivalents evolved in response to this experience. The essence of the doctrine is that one may not practice a fraud on a patent. Originating almost a century ago in the case of *Winans v. Denmead*, 15 How. 330, 14 L.Ed. 717, it has been consistently applied by this Court and the lower federal courts, and continues today ready and available for utilization when the proper circumstances for its application arise. "To temper unsparing logic and prevent an infringer from stealing the benefit of the invention" a patentee may invoke this doctrine to proceed against the producer of a device "if it performs substantially the same function in substantially the same way to obtain the same result." *Sanitary Refrigerator Co. v. Winters*, 280 U.S. 30, 42, 50 S.Ct. 9, 13, 74 L.Ed. 147. The theory on which it is founded is that "if two devices do the same work in substantially the same way, and accomplish substantially the same result, they are the same, even though they differ in name, form or shape." *Union Paper–Bag Machine Co. v. Murphy*, 97 U.S. 120, 125, 24 L.Ed. 935. The doctrine operates not only in favor of the patentee of a pioneer or primary invention, but also for the patentee of a secondary invention consisting of a combination of old ingredients which produce new and useful results, *Imhaeuser v. Buerk*, 101 U.S. 647, 655, 25 L.Ed. 945, although the area of equivalence may vary under the circumstances. . . .

What constitutes equivalency must be determined against the context of the patent, the prior art, and the particular circumstances of the case. Equivalence, in the patent law, is not the prisoner of a formula and is not an absolute to be considered in a vacuum. It does not require complete identity for every purpose and in every respect. In determining equivalents, things equal to the same thing may not be equal to each other and, by the same token, things for most purposes different may sometimes be equivalents. Consideration must be given to the purpose for which an ingredient is used in a patent, the qualities it has when combined with the other ingredients, and the function which it is intended to perform. An important factor is whether persons reasonably skilled in the art would have known of the interchangeability of an ingredient not contained in the patent with one that was.

A finding of equivalence is a determination of fact. Proof can be made in any form: through testimony of experts or others versed in the technology; by documents, including texts and treatises; and, of course, by the disclosures of the prior art. Like any other issue of fact, final determination requires a balancing of credibility, persuasiveness and weight of evidence. It is to be decided by the trial court and that court's decision, under general principles of appellate review, should not be disturbed unless clearly erroneous. Particularly is this so in a field where so much depends upon familiarity with specific scientific problems and principles not usually contained in the general storehouse of knowledge and experience.

In the case before us, we have two electric welding compositions or fluxes: the patented composition, Unionmelt Grade 20, and the accused composition, Lincolnweld 660. The patent . . . claims essentially a combination of alkaline earth metal silicate and calcium fluoride; Unionmelt actually contains, however, silicates of calcium and magnesium, two alkaline earth metal silicates. Lincolnweld's composition is similar to Unionmelt's, except that it substitutes silicates of calcium and manganese—the latter not an alkaline earth metal—for silicates of calcium and magnesium. In all other respects, the two compositions are alike.

The question which thus emerges is whether the substitution of the manganese which is not an alkaline earth metal for the magnesium which is, under the circumstances of this case, and in view of the technology and the prior art, is a change of such substance as to make the doctrine of equivalents inapplicable; or conversely, whether under the circumstances the change was so insubstantial that the trial court's invocation of the doctrine of equivalents was justified.

Without attempting to be all-inclusive, we note the following evidence in the record: Chemists familiar with the two fluxes testified that manganese and magnesium were similar in many of their reactions. There is testimony by a metallurgist that alkaline earth metals are often found in manganese ores in their natural state and that they serve the same purpose in the fluxes; and a chemist testified that "in the sense of the patent" manganese could be included as an alkaline earth metal.

* * *

The trial judge found on the evidence before him that the Lincolnweld flux and the composition of the patent in suit are substantially identical in operation and in result. He found also that Lincolnweld is in all respects equivalent to Unionmelt for welding purposes. And he concluded that "for all practical purposes, manganese silicate can be efficiently and effectively substituted for calcium and magnesium silicates as the major constituent of the welding composition." These conclusions are adequately supported by the record; certainly they are not clearly erroneous.

It is difficult to conceive of a case more appropriate for application of the doctrine of equivalents. The disclosures of the prior art made clear that manganese silicate was a useful ingredient in welding compositions. Specialists familiar with the problems of welding compositions understood that manganese was equivalent to and could be substituted for magnesium in the composition of the patented flux and their observations were confirmed by the literature of chemistry. Without some explanation or indication that Lincolnweld was developed by independent research, the trial court could properly infer that the accused flux is the result of imitation rather than experimentation or invention. Though infringement was not literal, the changes which avoid literal infringement are colorable only. We conclude that the trial court's judgment of infringement respecting the four flux claims was proper, and we adhere to our prior decision on this aspect of the case.

Affirmed.

MR. JUSTICE BLACK, with whom MR. JUSTICE DOUGLAS concurs, dissenting.

Dissent

I heartily agree with the Court that "fraud" is bad, "piracy" is evil, and "stealing" is reprehensible. But in this case, where petitioners are not charged with any such malevolence, these lofty principles do not justify the Court's sterilization of the Acts of Congress.

NOTES

1. **Criticizing *Graver Tank*.** Is *Graver Tank* right as a matter of chemistry? One commentator notes that "[m]anganese and magnesium are both metals and start with an 'm' and have at least three syllables, but otherwise are so different structurally that they are in different categories on the periodic table of elements." Harold C. Wegner, *Equitable Equivalents: Weighing the Equities to Determine Patent Infringement in Biotechnology and Other Emerging Technologies*, 18 RUTGERS COMPUTER & TECH. L.J. 1, 28–29 n.100 (1992).

2. **Should the Doctrine of Equivalents Be Available as a Vehicle for Correcting Applicant Errors?** In Martin J. Adelman & Gary L. Francione, *The Doctrine of Equivalents in Patent Law: Questions that Pennwalt Did Not Answer*, 137 U. PA. L. REV. 673 (1989) the authors argue that the most frequent use of the doctrine of equivalents in cases decided by the Federal Circuit is to correct errors made by applicants. Further, they argue that *Graver Tank* was unusual in that it was not a case where the use of the doctrine of equivalents was used to correct error. The PTO had passed on the patentability of the accused flux and the public had been notified that the accused flux was within the scope of the patent as issued by the PTO.

The Federal Circuit had occasion to muse on this theme in *Sage Products, Inc. v. Devon Industries, Inc.*, 126 F.3d 1420 (Fed.Cir.1997). There, the patentee Sage accused a competitor of infringing a narrowly drafted claim with a number of structural limitations. The Federal Circuit rejected the attempt to apply the doctrine of equivalents to correct a claiming error:

No application of doctrine of equivalents to correct a claiming error.

> The claim at issue defines a relatively simple structural device. A skilled patent drafter would foresee the limiting potential of [a narrowly drawn structural] limitation. No subtlety of language or complexity of the technology, nor any subsequent change in the state of the art, such as later-developed technology, obfuscated the significance of this limitation at the time of its incorporation into the claim. If Sage desired broad patent protection ., it could have sought claims with fewer structural encumbrances. . . . However, as between the patentee who had a clear opportunity to negotiate broader claims but did not do so, and the public at large, it is the patentee who must bear the cost of its failure to seek protection for this foreseeable alteration of its claimed structure.

> This court recognizes that such reasoning places a premium on forethought in patent drafting. Indeed this premium may lead to higher costs of patent prosecution. However, the alternative rule—allowing broad play for the doctrine of equivalents to encompass foreseeable variations,

not just of a claim element, but of a patent claim—also leads to higher costs. Society at large would bear these latter costs in the form of virtual foreclosure of competitive activity within the penumbra of each issued patent claim.

126 F.3d at 1425.

3. Further Reading. Paul M. Janicke, *Heat of Passion: What Really Happened in* Graver Tank, 24 AM. INTELL. PROP. L. ASS'N Q.J. 1 (1996), presents a detailed historical account of the circumstances leading to the Supreme Court's opinion in *Graver Tank.*

WARNER–JENKINSON COMPANY v. HILTON DAVIS CHEMICAL CO.

United States Supreme Court, 1997
520 U.S. 17

Thomas, J., delivered the opinion for unanimous Court. Ginsburg, J., filed a concurring opinion, in which Kennedy, J., joined.

JUSTICE THOMAS delivered the opinion of the Court.

Nearly 50 years ago, this Court in *Graver Tank & Mfg. Co. v. Linde Air Products Co.*, 339 U.S. 605 (1950), set out the modern contours of what is known in patent law as the "doctrine of equivalents." Under this doctrine, a product or process that does not literally infringe upon the express terms of a patent claim may nonetheless be found to infringe if there is "equivalence" between the elements of the accused product or process and the claimed elements of the patented invention. Id., at 609. Petitioner, which was found to have infringed upon respondent's patent under the doctrine of equivalents, invites us to speak the death of that doctrine. We decline that invitation. The significant disagreement within the Court of Appeals for the Federal Circuit concerning the application of Graver Tank suggests, however, that the doctrine is not free from confusion. We therefore will endeavor to clarify the proper scope of the doctrine.

I

The essential facts of this case are few. Petitioner Warner–Jenkinson Co. and respondent Hilton Davis Chemical Co. manufacture dyes. Impurities in those dyes must be removed. Hilton Davis holds United States Patent No. 4,560,746 ('746 patent), which discloses an improved purification process involving "ultrafiltration." The '746 process filters impure dye through a porous membrane at certain pressures and pH levels, resulting in a high purity dye product.

The '746 patent issued in 1985. As relevant to this case, the patent claims as its invention an improvement in the ultrafiltration process as follows:

"In a process for the purification of a dye . . . the improvement which comprises: subjecting an aqueous solution . . . to ultrafiltration through a membrane having a nominal pore diameter of 5–15 Angstroms under a hydrostatic pressure of approximately 200 to 400 p.s.i.g., at a pH from approximately 6.0 to 9.0, to thereby cause separation of said impurities from said dye...."

The inventors added the phrase "at a pH from approximately 6.0 to 9.0" during patent prosecution. At a minimum, this phrase was added to distinguish a previous patent (the "Booth" patent) that disclosed an ultrafiltration process operating at a pH above 9.0. The parties disagree as to why the low-end pH limit of 6.0 was included as part of the claim.[1]

In 1986, Warner–Jenkinson developed an ultrafiltration process that operated with membrane pore diameters assumed to be 5–15 Angstroms, at pressures of 200 to nearly 500 p.s.i.g., and at a pH of 5.0. Warner–Jenkinson did not learn of the '746 patent until after it had begun commercial use of its ultrafiltration process. Hilton Davis eventually learned of Warner–Jenkinson's use of ultrafiltration and, in 1991, sued Warner–Jenkinson for patent infringement.

As trial approached, Hilton Davis conceded that there was no literal infringement, and relied solely on the doctrine of equivalents. Over Warner–Jenkinson's objection that the doctrine of equivalents was an equitable doctrine to be applied by the court, the issue of equivalence was included among those sent to the jury. The jury found that the '746 patent was not invalid and that Warner–Jenkinson infringed upon the patent under the doctrine of equivalents. The jury also found, however, that Warner–Jenkinson had not intentionally infringed, and therefore awarded only 20% of the damages sought by Hilton Davis. The District Court denied Warner–Jenkinson's post-trial motions, and entered a permanent injunction prohibiting Warner–Jenkinson from practicing ultrafiltration below 500 p.s.i.g. and below 9.01 pH. A fractured *en banc* Court of Appeals for the Federal Circuit affirmed. 62 F. 3d 1512 (C.A.Fed.1995).

The majority below held that the doctrine of equivalents continues to exist and that its touchstone is whether substantial differences exist between the accused process and the patented process. The court also held that the question of equivalence is for the jury to decide and that the jury in this case had substantial evidence from which it could conclude that the Warner–Jenkinson process was not substantially different from the ultrafiltration process disclosed in the '746 patent.

There were three separate dissents, commanding a total of 5 of 12 judges. Four of the five dissenting judges viewed the doctrine of equivalents as allowing an improper expansion of claim scope, contrary to this Court's numerous holdings that it is the claim that defines the

---

1. Petitioner contends that the lower limit was added because below a pH of 6.0 the patented process created "foaming" problems in the plant and because the process was not shown to work below that pH level. Brief for Petitioner 4, n. 5, 37, n. 28. Respondent counters that the process was successfully tested to pH levels as low as 2.2 with no effect on the process because of foaming, but offers no particular explanation as to why the lower level of 6.0 pH was selected. Brief for Respondent 34, n. 34.

invention and gives notice to the public of the limits of the patent monopoly. The fifth dissenter, the late Judge Nies, was able to reconcile the prohibition against enlarging the scope of claims and the doctrine of equivalents by applying the doctrine to each element of a claim, rather than to the accused product or process "overall." As she explained it, "[t]he 'scope' is not enlarged if courts do not go beyond the substitution of equivalent elements." All of the dissenters, however, would have found that a much narrowed doctrine of equivalents may be applied in whole or in part by the court.

We granted certiorari and now reverse and remand.

II

In *Graver Tank* we considered the application of the doctrine of equivalents to an accused chemical composition for use in welding that differed from the patented welding material by the substitution of one chemical element. The substituted element did not fall within the literal terms of the patent claim, but the Court nonetheless .. concluded that the trial court's judgment of infringement under the doctrine of equivalents was proper.

A

Petitioner's primary argument in this Court is that the doctrine of equivalents, as set out in *Graver Tank* in 1950, did not survive the 1952 revision of the Patent Act, 35 U.S.C. § 100 et seq., because it is inconsistent with several aspects of that Act. In particular, petitioner argues: (1) the doctrine of equivalents is inconsistent with the statutory requirement that a patentee specifically "claim" the invention covered by a patent, 35 U.S.C. § 112; (2) the doctrine circumvents the patent reissue process—designed to correct mistakes in drafting or the like—and avoids the express limitations on that process, 35 U.S.C. §§ 251–252; (3) the doctrine is inconsistent with the primacy of the Patent and Trademark Office (PTO) in setting the scope of a patent through the patent prosecution process; and (4) the doctrine was implicitly rejected as a general matter by Congress' specific and limited inclusion of the doctrine in one section regarding "means" claiming, 35 U.S.C. § 112, ¶ 6. All but one of these arguments were made in *Graver Tank* in the context of the 1870 Patent Act, and failed to command a majority.

The 1952 Patent Act is not materially different from the 1870 Act with regard to claiming, reissue, and the role of the PTO. In the context of infringement, we have already held that pre–1952 precedent survived the passage of the 1952 Act. *See Aro Mfg. Co. v. Convertible Top Replacement Co.*, 365 U.S. 336, 342 (1961). We see no reason to reach a different result here.

Petitioner's fourth argument for an implied congressional negation of the doctrine of equivalents turns on the reference to "equivalents" in the "means" claiming provision of the 1952 Act. Section 112, ¶ 6, a provision not contained in the 1870 Act, states:

"An element in a claim for a combination may be expressed as a means or step for performing a specified function without the recital of structure, material, or acts in support thereof, and such claim shall be construed to cover the corresponding structure, material, or acts described in the specification and equivalents thereof."

Thus, under this new provision, an applicant can describe an element of his invention by the result accomplished or the function served, rather than describing the item or element to be used (e.g., "a means of connecting Part A to Part B," rather than "a two-penny nail"). Congress enacted § 112, ¶ 6 in response to *Halliburton Oil Well Cementing Co. v. Walker*, which rejected claims that "do not describe the invention but use 'conveniently functional language at the exact point of novelty,'" 329 U.S. 1, 8 (1946) (citation omitted). *See In re Donaldson Co.*, 16 F. 3d 1189, 1194 (C.A.Fed.1994) (Congress enacted predecessor of § 112, ¶ 6 in response to *Halliburton*). Section 112, ¶ 6 now expressly allows so-called "means" claims, with the proviso that application of the broad literal language of such claims must be limited to only those means that are "equivalent" to the actual means shown in the patent specification. This is an application of the doctrine of equivalents in a restrictive role, narrowing the application of broad literal claim elements. We recognized this type of role for the doctrine of equivalents in *Graver Tank* itself. The added provision, however, is silent on the doctrine of equivalents as applied where there is no literal infringement.

Because § 112, ¶ 6 was enacted as a targeted cure to a specific problem, and because the reference in that provision to "equivalents" appears to be no more than a prophylactic against potential side effects of that cure, such limited congressional action should not be overread for negative implications. Congress in 1952 could easily have responded to *Graver Tank* as it did to the *Halliburton* decision. But it did not. Absent something more compelling than the dubious negative inference offered by petitioner, the lengthy history of the doctrine of equivalents strongly supports adherence to our refusal in *Graver Tank* to find that the Patent Act conflicts with that doctrine. Congress can legislate the doctrine of equivalents out of existence any time it chooses. The various policy arguments now made by both sides are thus best addressed to Congress, not this Court.

B

We do, however, share the concern of the dissenters below that the doctrine of equivalents, as it has come to be applied since *Graver Tank*, has taken on a life of its own, unbounded by the patent claims. There can be no denying that the doctrine of equivalents, when applied broadly, conflicts with the definitional and public-notice functions of the statutory claiming requirement. Judge Nies identified one means of avoiding this conflict:

scope not enlarged if court does not go beyond substitution of equivalent elements

"[A] distinction can be drawn that is not too esoteric between substitution of an equivalent for a component in an invention and enlarging the metes and bounds of the invention beyond what is claimed."

. . .

"Where a claim to an invention is expressed as a combination of elements, as here, 'equivalents' in the sobriquet 'Doctrine of Equivalents' refers to the equivalency of an element or part of the invention with one that is substituted in the accused product or process."

. . .

"This view that the accused device or process must be more than 'equivalent' overall reconciles the Supreme Court's position on infringement by equivalents with its concurrent statements that 'the courts have no right to enlarge a patent beyond the scope of its claims as allowed by the Patent Office.' [Citations omitted.] The 'scope' is not enlarged if courts do not go beyond the substitution of equivalent elements."

doc of equ only apply to individual claims not invention as a whole

We concur with this apt reconciliation of our two lines of precedent. Each element contained in a patent claim is deemed material to defining the scope of the patented invention, and thus the doctrine of equivalents must be applied to individual elements of the claim, not to the invention as a whole. It is important to ensure that the application of the doctrine, even as to an individual element, is not allowed such broad play as to effectively eliminate that element in its entirety. So long as the doctrine of equivalents does not encroach beyond the limits just described, or beyond related limits to be discussed infra, we are confident that the doctrine will not vitiate the central functions of the patent claims themselves.

III

Should doc be stricter?

Understandably reluctant to assume this Court would overrule *Graver Tank*, petitioner has offered alternative arguments in favor of a more restricted doctrine of equivalents than it feels was applied in this case. We address each in turn.

A

A claims any limiting during prosecution must be upheld

limited process to PH between 6-9

Petitioner first argues that *Graver Tank* never purported to supersede a well-established limit on non-literal infringement, known variously as "prosecution history estoppel" and "file wrapper estoppel." According to petitioner, any surrender of subject matter during patent prosecution, regardless of the reason for such surrender, precludes recapturing any part of that subject matter, even if it is equivalent to the matter expressly claimed. Because, during patent prosecution, respondent limited the pH element of its claim to pH levels between 6.0 and 9.0, petitioner would have those limits form bright lines beyond which no equivalents may be claimed. Any inquiry into the reasons for a surrender, petitioner claims, would undermine the public's right to clear notice of the scope of the patent as embodied in the patent file.

We can readily agree with petitioner that *Graver Tank* did not dispose of prosecution history estoppel as a legal limitation on the doctrine of equivalents. But petitioner reaches too far in arguing that the reason for an amendment during patent prosecution is irrelevant to any subsequent estoppel. In each of our cases cited by petitioner and by the dissent below, prosecution history estoppel was tied to amendments made to avoid the prior art, or otherwise to address a specific concern—such as obviousness—that arguably would have rendered the claimed subject matter unpatentable. Thus, in *Exhibit Supply Co. v. Ace Patents Corp.*, Chief Justice Stone distinguished inclusion of a limiting phrase in an original patent claim from the "very different" situation in which "the applicant, in order to meet objections in the Patent Office, based on references to the prior art, adopted the phrase as a substitute for the broader one" previously used. 315 U.S. 126, 136 (1942). Similarly, in *Keystone Driller Co. v. Northwest Engineering Corp.*, 294 U.S. 42 (1935), estoppel was applied where the initial claims were "rejected on the prior art," and where the allegedly infringing equivalent element was outside of the revised claims and within the prior art that formed the basis for the rejection of the earlier claims.

It is telling that in each case this Court probed the reasoning behind the Patent Office's insistence upon a change in the claims. In each instance, a change was demanded because the claim as otherwise written was viewed as not describing a patentable invention at all—typically because what it described was encompassed within the prior art. But, as the United States informs us, there are a variety of other reasons why the PTO may request a change in claim language. And if the PTO has been requesting changes in claim language without the intent to limit equivalents or, indeed, with the expectation that language it required would in many cases allow for a range of equivalents, we should be extremely reluctant to upset the basic assumptions of the PTO without substantial reason for doing so. Our prior cases have consistently applied prosecution history estoppel only where claims have been amended for a limited set of reasons, and we see no substantial cause for requiring a more rigid rule invoking an estoppel regardless of the reasons for a change.

In this case, the patent examiner objected to the patent claim due to a perceived overlap with the Booth patent, which revealed an ultrafiltration process operating at a pH above 9.0. In response to this objection, the phrase "at a pH from approximately 6.0 to 9.0" was added to the claim. While it is undisputed that the upper limit of 9.0 was added in order to distinguish the Booth patent, the reason for adding the lower limit of 6.0 is unclear. The lower limit certainly did not serve to distinguish the Booth patent, which said nothing about pH levels below 6.0. Thus, while a lower limit of 6.0, by its mere inclusion, became a material element of the claim, that did not necessarily preclude the application of the doctrine of equivalents as to that element. *See Hubbell v. United States*, 179 U.S. 77, 82 (1900) (" '[A]ll [specified elements] must be regarded as material,' " though it remains an open "question whether an omitted part is supplied by an equivalent device or instrumentality" (citation omitted)). Where the reason for the change was not related to avoiding the prior art, the change may introduce a new element, but it does not necessarily preclude infringement by equivalents of that element.

We are left with the problem, however, of what to do in a case like the one at bar, where the record seems not to reveal the reason for including the lower pH limit of 6.0. In our view, holding that certain reasons for a claim amendment may avoid the application of prosecution history estoppel is not tantamount to holding that the absence of a reason for an amendment may similarly avoid such an estoppel. Mindful that claims do indeed serve both a definitional and a notice function, we think the better rule is to place the burden on the patent-holder to establish the reason for an amendment required during patent prosecution. The court then would decide whether that reason is sufficient to overcome prosecution history estoppel as a bar to application of the doctrine of equivalents to the element added by that amendment. Where no explanation is established, however, the court should presume that the PTO had a substantial reason related to patentability for including the limiting element added by amendment. In those circumstances, prosecution history estoppel would bar the application of the doctrine equivalents as to that element. The presumption we have described, one subject to rebuttal if an appropriate reason for a required amendment is established, gives proper deference to the role of claims in defining an invention and providing public notice, and to the primacy of the PTO in ensuring that the claims allowed cover only subject matter that is properly patentable in a proffered patent application. Applied in this fashion, prosecution history estoppel places reasonable limits on the doctrine of equivalents, and further insulates the doctrine from any feared conflict with the Patent Act.

Because respondent has not proffered in this Court a reason for the addition of a lower pH limit, it is impossible to tell whether the reason for that addition could properly avoid an estoppel. Whether a reason in fact exists, but simply was not adequately developed, we cannot say. On remand, the Federal Circuit can consider whether reasons for that portion of the amendment were offered or not and whether further opportunity to establish such reasons would be proper.

B

Petitioner next argues that even if *Graver Tank* remains good law, the case held only that the absence of substantial differences was a necessary element for infringement under the doctrine of equivalents, not that it was sufficient for such a result. Relying on *Graver Tank*'s references to the problem of an "unscrupulous copyist" and "piracy," 339 U. S., at 607, petitioner would require judicial exploration of the equities of a case before allowing application of the doctrine of equivalents. To be sure, *Graver Tank* refers to the prevention of copying and piracy when describing the benefits of the doctrine of equivalents. That the doctrine produces such benefits, however, does not mean that its application is limited only to cases where those particular benefits are obtained.

Elsewhere in *Graver Tank* the doctrine is described in more neutral terms. And the history of the doctrine as relied upon by *Graver Tank* reflects a basis for the doctrine not so limited as petitioner would have it. In *Winans v. Denmead*, 15 How. 330, 343 (1854), we described the doctrine of equivalents as growing out of a legally implied term in each patent claim that "the claim extends to the thing patented, however its form or proportions may be varied." Under that view, application of the doctrine of equivalents involves determining whether a particular accused product or process infringes upon the patent claim, where the claim takes the form—half express, half implied—of "X and its equivalents." *Machine Co. v. Murphy*, 97 U.S. 120, 125 (1878), on which *Graver Tank* also relied, offers a similarly intent-neutral view of the doctrine of equivalents. Application of the doctrine of equivalents, therefore, is akin to determining literal infringement, and neither requires proof of intent. . . .

Although *Graver Tank* certainly leaves room for petitioner's suggested inclusion of intent-based elements in the doctrine of equivalents, we do not read it as requiring them. The better view, and the one consistent with *Graver Tank*'s predecessors and the objective approach to infringement, is that intent plays no role in the application of the doctrine of equivalents.

C

Finally, petitioner proposes that in order to minimize conflict with the notice function of patent claims, the doctrine of equivalents should be limited to equivalents that are disclosed within the patent itself. A milder version of this argument, which found favor with the dissenters below, is that the doctrine should be limited to equivalents that were known at the time the patent was issued, and should not extend to after-arising equivalents.

As we have noted, with regard to the objective nature of the doctrine, a skilled practitioner's knowledge of the interchangeability between claimed and accused elements is not relevant for its own sake, but rather for what it tells the fact-finder about the similarities or differences between those elements. Much as the perspective of the hypothetical "reasonable person" gives content to concepts such as "negligent" behavior, the perspective of a skilled practitioner provides content to, and limits on, the concept of "equivalence." Insofar as the question under the doctrine of equivalents is whether an accused element is equivalent to a claimed element, the proper time for evaluating equivalency—and thus knowledge of interchangeability between elements—is at the time of infringement, not at the time the patent was issued. And rejecting the milder version of petitioner's argument necessarily rejects the more severe proposition that equivalents must not only be known, but must also be actually disclosed in the patent in order for such equivalents to infringe upon the patent.

IV

The various opinions below, respondents, and amici devote considerable attention to whether application of the doctrine of equivalents is a task for the judge or for the jury. However, despite petitioner's argument below that the doctrine should be applied by the judge, in this Court petitioner makes only passing reference to this issue. . . .

The Federal Circuit held that it was for the jury to decide whether the accused process was equivalent to the claimed process. There was ample support in our prior cases for that holding. *See, e.g., Winans v. Denmead,* 15 How., at 344 ("[It] is a question for the jury" whether the accused device was "the same in kind, and effected by the employment of [the patentee's] mode of operation in substance"). Nothing in our recent *Markman* decision necessitates a different result than that reached by the Federal Circuit. Indeed, *Markman* cites with considerable favor, when discussing the role of judge and jury, the seminal *Winans* decision. *Markman v. Westview Instruments, Inc.,* 517 U.S. 370, 384–85 (1996). Whether, if the issue were squarely presented to us, we would reach a different conclusion than did the Federal Circuit is not a question we need decide today.[5]

V

All that remains is to address the debate regarding the linguistic framework under which "equivalence" is determined. Both the parties and the Federal Circuit spend considerable time arguing whether the so-called "triple identity" test—focusing on the function served by a particular claim element, the way that element serves that function, and the result thus obtained by that element—is a suitable method for

---

5. With regard to the concern over unreviewability due to black-box jury verdicts, we offer only guidance, not a specific mandate. Where the evidence is such that no reasonable jury could determine two elements to be equivalent, district courts are obliged to grant partial or complete summary judgment. *See* FED. RULE CIV. PROC. 56; *Celotex Corp. v. Catrett,* 477 U.S. 317, 322–323 (1986). If there has been a reluctance to do so by some courts due to unfamiliarity with the subject matter, we are confident that the Federal Circuit can remedy the problem. Of course, the various legal limitations on the application of the doctrine of equivalents are to be determined by the court, either on a pretrial motion for partial summary judgment or on a motion for judgment as a matter of law at the close of the evidence and after the jury verdict. FED. RULE CIV. PROC. 56; FED. RULE CIV. PROC. 50. Thus, under the particular facts of a case, if prosecution history estoppel would apply or if a theory of equivalence would entirely vitiate a particular claim element, partial or complete judgment should be rendered by the court, as there would be no further material issue for the jury to resolve. Finally, in cases that reach the jury, a special verdict and/or interrogatories on each claim element could be very useful in facilitating review, uniformity, and possibly postverdict judgments as a matter of law. *See* FED. RULE CIV. PROC. 49; FED. RULE CIV. PROC. 50. We leave it to the Federal Circuit how best to implement procedural improvements to promote certainty, consistency, and reviewability to this area of the law.

determining equivalence, or whether an "insubstantial differences" approach is better. There seems to be substantial agreement that, while the triple identity test may be suitable for analyzing mechanical devices, it often provides a poor framework for analyzing other products or processes. On the other hand, the insubstantial differences test offers little additional guidance as to what might render any given difference "insubstantial."

[margin: or insubstantial differences approach should be used.]

In our view, the particular linguistic framework used is less important than whether the test is probative of the essential inquiry: Does the accused product or process contain elements identical or equivalent to each claimed element of the patented invention? Different linguistic frameworks may be more suitable to different cases, depending on their particular facts. A focus on individual elements and a special vigilance against allowing the concept of equivalence to eliminate completely any such elements should reduce considerably the imprecision of whatever language is used. An analysis of the role played by each element in the context of the specific patent claim will thus inform the inquiry as to whether a substitute element matches the function, way, and result of the claimed element, or whether the substitute element plays a role substantially different from the claimed element. With these limiting principles as a backdrop, we see no purpose in going further and micromanaging the Federal Circuit's particular word-choice for analyzing equivalence. We expect that the Federal Circuit will refine the formulation of the test for equivalence in the orderly course of case-by-case determinations, and we leave such refinement to that court's sound judgment in this area of its special expertise.

[margin: main test ↓ actually "wording" of Fed Cir. not important.]

VI

Today we adhere to the doctrine of equivalents. The determination of equivalence should be applied as an objective inquiry on an element-by-element basis. Prosecution history estoppel continues to be available as a defense to infringement, but if the patent-holder demonstrates that an amendment required during prosecution had a purpose unrelated to patentability, a court must consider that purpose in order to decide whether an estoppel is precluded. Where the patent-holder is unable to establish such a purpose, a court should presume that the purpose behind the required amendment is such that prosecution history estoppel would apply. Because the Court of Appeals for the Federal Circuit did not consider all of the requirements as described by us today, particularly as related to prosecution history estoppel and the preservation of some meaning for each element in a claim, we reverse and remand for further proceedings consistent with this opinion.

[margin: objective element by element basis. History of prosecution important. ↓ reverse and remanded]

It is so ordered.

NOTES

1. Return to the Federal Circuit. On remand, the Federal Circuit re-stated its holding that a pH of 5.0 was equivalent to the claimed pH of "approximately 6.0" under the circumstances of the case, reasoning:

> We have reconsidered the pH equivalence issue in light of the Su-preme Court's guidance and hold that there is substantial record evidence to support the jury's verdict of equivalence. The '746 patent claim recites a pH range "from approximately 6.0 to 9.0." Warner–Jenkinson performed the process using a pH of 5.0. Although there is nothing in the written description part of the specification to indicate that the invention extends beyond the specific range given in the claim, there is substantial record evidence to prove that one of ordinary skill in the art would know that performing ultrafiltration at a pH of 5.0 will allow the membrane to perform substantially the same function in substantially the same way to reach substantially the same result as performing ultrafiltration at 6.0. In this regard, Dr. Cook, one of the inventors, testified that the process would work to separate the dye from the impurities at pH values as low as 2.0 (albeit with foaming). Moreover, Warner–Jenkinson's expert testified that the Hilton Davis process would operate at a pH of 5.0. The jury's finding that the accused process with a pH of 5.0 is equivalent to the claimed process with a lower limit of approximately 6.0 does not therefore vitiate the claim limitation. Accordingly, assuming prosecution history estoppel does not preclude such a finding, we reaffirm our prior decision that a pH of 5.0 is equivalent to a pH of "approximately 6.0" in the context of the claimed process.

Hilton Davis Chem. Co. v. Warner–Jenkinson Co., 114 F.3d 1161, 1164 (Fed.Cir. 1997).

The Federal Circuit also provided the Supreme Court with a chemistry tutorial. In its first footnote in *Warner–Jenkinson,* the Supreme Court had noted: "Although measurement of pH is on a logarithmic scale, with each whole number difference representing a ten-fold difference in acidity, the practical significance of any such difference will often depend on the context." Apparent-ly impressed by a ten-fold difference *in acidity*, the Supreme Court asked the Federal Circuit to consider whether application of the doctrine of equivalents to permit a ten-fold difference did not allow "such broad play as to effectively eliminate that element in its entirety." 520 U.S. at 29. In a footnote, the Federal Circuit supplied its tutorial to explain its summary disposition: "We observe, however, that the pH number is derived from hydrogen ion concentration, and a one unit change in pH states a ten-fold difference in hydrogen ion concentra-tion, rather than literally indicating a ten-fold difference in 'acidity.'" The Circuit also noted that the record showed that the process would work at pH values as low as 2.0.

Perhaps this footnote was the Federal Circuit's subtle way of noting that it had not overlooked the question of preserving the meaning of each claim element at all in its original opinion. To the contrary, the Circuit seems to say, it had in fact considered and summarily dismissed that issue on a correct understanding that the ten-fold difference was a difference in hydrogen ion concentration. The Supreme Court, in reliance on a Federal Circuit dissent, had perhaps stated too much when it remanded "[b]ecause the Federal Circuit did not consider all of the requirements as described by us today . . ." 520 U.S. at 41.

The Federal Circuit further remanded the case to the district court on the issue of prosecution history estoppel, leaving "the district court to conduct an inquiry to ascertain whether Hilton Davis can rebut the presumption by showing the reason for the amendment of the claim to place a lower pH limit of approximately 6.0 on the ultrafiltration process and whether that reason is sufficient to overcome the estoppel bar to the application of the doctrine of equivalents." 114 F.3d at 1163.

  2. Can 47.8% be the equivalent of a majority? *Moore U.S.A., Inc. v. Standard Register Co.,* 229 F.3d 1091 (Fed.Cir.2000), featured a patent claiming a mailer-type business form. The patent's claims called for longitudinal strips of adhesive that extended "the majority" of the lengths of the form. The accused product featured adhesive strips running 47.8% of the form's length. The Federal Circuit upheld the district court's *summary judgment* of noninfringement, concluding that "it would defy logic to conclude that a minority—the very antithesis of a majority—could be insubstantially different from a claim limitation requiring a majority, and no reasonable juror could find otherwise." 229 F.3d at 1106. Besides demonstrating the current tenor of equivalency law at the Federal Circuit, *Moore* again invokes the implicit negation principle to find an effective elimination of a claimed element. Is there any number less than 50.1% that could be an equivalent under this approach?

  3. Elemental Equivalents. Did *Warner–Jenkinson* present a good opportunity for the Supreme Court to discuss the all elements rule? Was this a case about an absent claim limitation or simply one that was not literally met? Ironically, the Supreme Court sealed the All Elements Rule into equivalents law just at a time that the Federal Circuit was realizing that it embodies an internal and irresolvable inconsistency. Upon reflection, the inconsistency is quite easy to grasp. On the one hand, the doctrine of equivalents applies to find infringement when the claim does not literally cover the accused product or process, i.e., when a claim limitation is literally missing. On the other hand, the all-elements limitation precludes application of the doctrine when a claim limitation is literally missing. After years of experience, the Federal Circuit was unable to articulate a standard that decides when a missing limitation compels infringement under the doctrine of equivalents or precludes infringement under the All Elements Rule. *See, e.g., Dolly, Inc. v. Spalding & Evenflow,* 16 F.3d 394 (Fed. Cir. 1994); *Athletic Alternatives, Inc. v. Prince Manf.,* 73 F.3d 1573 (Fed. Cir. 1996). As a matter of practice, the All Elements Rule really just turns on a repeat assessment of the substantiality of the differences between the claims and the accused products or processes. If the missing element creates a "substantial" difference, the All Elements rule precludes infringement. If the missing element does not create a "substantial" difference, the doctrine of equivalents will operate to find infringement.

The All Elements Rule, however, does add one feature of significant import. The rule converts equivalency (a matter of fact for the jury) into a question of law (easily resolved by the Federal Circuit on appeal without deference). The next case, *Corning Glass*, illustrates the difficulty of deciding when a missing limitation invokes the equivalents doctrine or precludes the equivalents doctrine.

4. Federal Circuit Supervisory Authority. Compare the last footnote of the Supreme Court's opinion with the statement from *Petersen Manufacturing Co. v. Central Purchasing, Inc.*, 740 F.2d 1541 (Fed.Cir.1984) that: "Unlike other Circuit Courts of Appeal, (see e.g., *Cord v. Smith*, 338 F.2d 516, 526 (9th Cir.1964)), we have no direct supervisory authority over district courts. *C.P.C. v. Nosco Plastics, Inc.*, 719 F.2d 400 (Fed.Cir.1983)." Absent an e*n banc* change to this line of precedent, how will the Federal Circuit be able to implement the Supreme Court's advice in its footnote?

§ 11.3 LIMITATIONS ON THE DOCTRINE OF EQUIVALENTS

As noted in the decisions previously presented here, four legal tenets restrain the reach of non-textual infringement. The first of these is the "all elements" rule: the requirement that the doctrine of equivalents can only apply to an accused product or process that contains each limitation of a claim, either literally or equivalently. Non-textual infringement, unlike obviousness or other patent doctrines, is not oriented to a patent claim as a whole, but instead applies element-by-element within a claim. In *Warner–Jenkinson,* the Supreme Court endorsed this rule: "It is important to ensure that the application of the doctrine, even as to an individual element, is not allowed such broad play as to effectively eliminate that element in its entirety." Another limitation on non-textual infringement is prosecution history estoppel, a doctrine that precludes recapture under the doctrine of equivalents of subject matter surrendered during the patent application process. The third restraint on the doctrine of equivalents springs from the scope of the prior art for an invention. Sound patent policy dictates that patentees should not be able to extend their exclusive rights to cover technologies that prior art would have rendered unpatentable. Finally, the fourth restraint prevents a patentee from using the doctrine of equivalents to cover an embodiment that its specification discloses but does not claim. Under those circumstances, the patentee has dedicated the disclosed but unclaimed subject matter to the public. The following cases explore these limitations.

§ 11.3[a] THE "ALL ELEMENTS" RULE

The Supreme Court embraced the "all elements" rule in its *Warner–Jenkinson* opinion. Of course, the Federal Circuit had articulated and applied this rule for years before *Warner–Jenkinson*. In 1987, the Federal

Circuit, sitting *en banc*, defined this limitation on the doctrine of equivalents. *Pennwalt Corp. v. Durand–Wayland, Inc.*, 833 F.2d 931 (Fed.Cir. 1987). In the *Pennwalt* case, the Federal Circuit, citing its own earlier opinions, affirmed:

> [I]n applying the doctrine of equivalents, each limitation must be viewed in the context of the entire claim.... "It is ... well settled that each element of a claim is material and essential, and that in order for a court to find infringement, the plaintiff must show the presence of every element or its substantial equivalent in the accused device." *Lemelson v. United States*, 752 F.2d 1538, 1551 (Fed.Cir.1985).

Pennwalt, 833 F.2d at 935. *Pennwalt*, although featuring an internal inconsistency, became a centerpiece of *Warner–Jenkinson*, as already noted. Another Federal Circuit case reflects the difficulties of applying the *Pennwalt* limitation.

CORNING GLASS WORKS v. SUMITOMO ELECTRIC USA, INC.

United States Court of Appeals, Federal Circuit, 1989
868 F.2d 1251

Before Rich, Nies and Bissell, Circuit Judges.

NIES, CIRCUIT JUDGE.

Sumitomo Electric U.S.A., Inc.... appeal[s] from the judgment of the United States District Court for the Southern District of New York holding Sumitomo liable for infringement of claims 1 and 2 of United States Patent No. 3,659,915 ('915) and claim 1 of United States Patent No. 3,884,550 ('550), all directed to the structure of optical waveguide fibers. On appeal, Sumitomo challenges the validity of both patents and the finding of infringement of the '915 patent by one of its accused products. We affirm the judgment in all respects.

I

BACKGROUND

A.   General Technology

The inventions involved in this case relate to optical waveguide fibers of the type now widely used for telecommunications, such as long-distance telephone transmissions. Such fibers were developed as a medium for guiding the coherent light of a laser a distance suitable for optical communications.

It had long been known that light could be guided through a transparent medium that was surrounded by another medium having a lower refractive index (RI). A glass fiber surrounded by air, for example, will function as a conduit for light waves, because air has a lower RI than glass. To prevent scratches, imperfections, or foreign materials on the fiber surface from scattering light away from the fiber, glass fibers were cladded with a glass layer having a lower RI. Before 1970, however, these glass-clad, glass-core fibers, referred to generally as "fiber optics," were capable of transmitting light of practical intensity only for very short distances due to high attenuation of the glass fibers then available. While suitable for illumination or for imaging systems, as in endoscopic probes, they could not be used for optical communications.

Upon entering a fiber core, the light modes travel to the cladding and then back into the core, thus "bouncing" back and forth in a zig-zag path along the length of the fiber. The shallower the angle at which the modes enter the core, the less they will "bounce" and the sooner they will reach the receiving end of the fiber. When the number of modes are restricted, intelligibility of the information transmitted increases. The optimum restriction is achieved when only a single mode is transmitted, and by limiting the core diameter, that purpose is accomplished. By the mid–1960's, worldwide efforts were ongoing to develop long-distance lightwave transmission capability.

B.   The '915 Invention

Corning's work on optical waveguides began in 1966, when it was contacted by the British Post Office. Drs. Robert D. Maurer and Peter C. Schultz, working at Corning, developed the world's first 20 db/km optical waveguide fiber by early 1970. That achievement was due, in part, to the development of a fiber with a pure fused silica cladding and a fused silica core containing approximately three percent by weight of titania as the dopant in the core. It was also due to the careful selection of the core diameter and the RI differential between the core and the cladding.

Bell Laboratories confirmed the attenuation measurements of Corning's fibers and considered Corning's achievement an important breakthrough. . . . That announcement created enormous interest and was the subject of many articles in both technical and general publications. The inventors' advancement in technology won them accolades from various societies and institutes, for which they were presented with many prestigious awards and honors.

In addition, the invention of the '915 patent has achieved impressive commercial success on a worldwide basis. The district court determined that "[t]he 915 patent clearly covers a basic, pioneering invention." 671 F.Supp. at 1377.

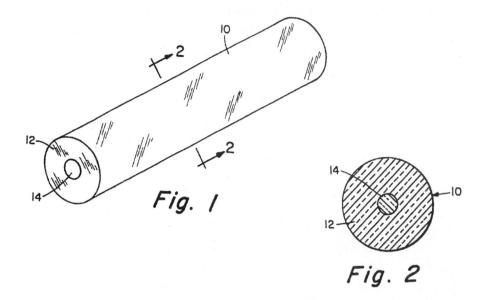

Fig. 1

Fig. 2

The '915 patent discloses a fused silica optical waveguide fiber capable of limiting the transmitted light to preselected modes for use in optical communication systems. Specifically, such a fiber is disclosed as having a doped fused silica core and a fused silica cladding (doping optional), wherein the RI of the core is greater than that of the cladding. Prior to the filing date of the application for the '915 patent, the inventors had experimented with dopants which increased the RI of fused silica, e.g. titania, and the '915 specification mentions only such positive dopant materials. At the time the application was filed, the inventors did not know of specific dopants that would decrease the RI of fused silica, although it had been known in the art since 1954 that the introduction of fluorine decreases the RI of certain multicomponent glasses.

[Claim 1 of the '915 patent provides:

An optical waveguide comprising

(a) a cladding layer formed of a material selected from the group consisting of pure fused silica and fused silica to which a dopant material on at least an elemental basis has been added, and

(b) a core formed of fused silica to which a dopant material on at least an elemental basis has been added to a degree in excess of that of the cladding layer so that the index of refraction thereof is of a value greater than the index of refraction of said cladding layer, said core being formed of at least 85 percent by weight of fused silica and an effective amount up to 15 percent by weight of said dopant material.] . . . .

[handwritten annotations in right margin:] 915 disclosed fused silica waveguide. ↓ before patent inventors experiment w/ many dopants to increase RI only positive dopants disclosed

Claim 1

E. District Court

The trial court held, inter alia, that claims 1 and 2 of the '915 patent ... were not invalid and were infringed by Sumitomo....

II

INFRINGEMENT OF CLAIMS 1 AND 2 OF '915 PATENT

The infringement issue on appeal involves only Sumitomo's S–3 fibers which were found to infringe under the doctrine of equivalents. * * * The district court found that th[e] test for infringement was met, stating:

> Although fiber S–3 is not within the literal language of either claim 1 or 2 of the '915 patent, it performs substantially the same function in substantially the same way to obtain the same result as the optical waveguide fiber described in those claims of the '915 patent.

Corning Glass Works v. Sumitomo Elec. U.S.A., Inc., 671 F.Supp. 1369, 1387 (S.D.N.Y.1987).

In the instant case, there is no dispute that the accused S–3 fiber performs substantially the same overall function to obtain the same overall result as the claimed invention. The question then is whether it does so in "substantially the same way."

The accused S–3 fibers are optical waveguides as defined in the claims at issue in that the fibers have the differential in RI between core and cladding ... Corning concedes, however, that all of the limitations of paragraph (b) do not literally read on the accused fibers. Although each claim limitation may not literally be found in the accused structure, the "substantially the same way" prong of the Graver Tank test is met if an equivalent of a recited limitation has been substituted in the accused device.

Applying these principles, the district court found that the accused S–3 fibers infringed the '915 claims. In so ruling, the district court recognized that the claim limitation calling for addition of a dopant to the core was not literally met in the accused S–3 fibers. 671 F.Supp. at 1387. Nevertheless, the court found that the substitution of "fluorine ... dopant which negatively alters the index of refraction of fused silica[ ] in the cladding" equivalently met the limitation requiring the addition to the core of "a dopant which positively alters the index of refraction of fused silica." *Id.* at 1386–87.

Sumitomo alleges clear error in the court's finding of equivalency. The premise on which Sumitomo relies, known as the "All Elements" rule correctly states the law of this circuit adopted *in banc* in *Pennwalt*. *See Pennwalt Corp.*, 833 F.2d at 935. However, we do not agree that an "element" of the claim is entirely "missing" from the S–3 fibers.

Sumitomo's analysis is faulty in that it would require equivalency in components, that is, the substitution of something in the core for the absent dopant. However, the determination of equivalency is not subject to such a rigid formula. An equivalent must be found for every limitation of the claim somewhere in an accused device, but not necessarily in a corresponding component, although that is generally the case.

[handwritten margin note: equivalents dont have to be found in the corresponding components]

Corning urges that the question of equivalency here is a narrow one: Is the substitution of a negative dopant in the cladding equivalent to a positive dopant in the core? When the limitations of paragraph (b) are analyzed individually, the accused S–3 fibers literally meet the limitation that the fiber be composed of a core of fused silica as well as the limitation that "the index of refraction [of the core] is of a value greater than the index of refraction of said cladding layer." The question of equivalency then does center on the part of the claim following the word "core," namely, "to which a dopant material . . . has been added to a degree in excess of that of the cladding layer." If those limiting words are met equivalently, no "element," i.e., limitation, of the claim is missing.

[handwritten margin note: Sub itoms just used a neg dopant in cladding instead of positive one in the core.]

This court has not set out in its precedent a definitive formula for determining equivalency between a required limitation or combination of limitations and what has been allegedly substituted therefor in the accused device. Nor do we propose to adopt one here.

[handwritten margin note: While not same components the switch is still equivalent and produces same result]

The district court's "function/way/result" equivalency analysis with respect to a claim limitation appears to be a helpful way to approach the problem and entirely in accord with the analysis actually made in *Graver Tank*, 339 U.S. at 609–10. . . .

In sum, we are unpersuaded of error either in the district court's understanding of the law; in its finding that adding negative dopant to the cladding is equivalent to adding positive dopant to the core in the context of the claimed invention; or in its finding that the S–3 fiber is an infringement of the inventions of claims 1 and 2 of the '915 patent.

AFFIRMED.

NOTES

1. *Pennwalt* and Claim Drafting. Should the scope of patent protection for a claim depend upon how a claim drafter has chosen to organize a description of an invention? Consider the following simplified claims:

1. A fork comprising a cylindrical handle; and four tines attached to said handle.

2. A fork comprising a cylindrical handle; a first tine attached to said handle; a second tine attached to said handle; a third tine attached to said handle; and a fourth tine attached to said handle.

These claims appear to provide the same scope of protection in terms of literal infringement. Yet, suppose a competitor markets a fork with three tines. Can you imagine any differences between the outcome of an equivalents analysis for these two claims under the all elements rule? This example illustrates again the problems with application of the All Elements Rule.

2. ***Corning Glass* and Claim Drafting.** Does the observation that the All Elements Rule renders concise claim drafting advisable hold true following *Corning Glass*? What about the statement in *Corning Glass* that: " 'Element' may be used to mean a single limitation, but it has also been used to mean a series of limitations which, taken together, make up a component of the claimed invention"? Consider a process that performs four steps. Steps A, B, and C consist of novel and nonobviousness technology, while step D is one that is well known to the art. Would the patentee be better off claiming A+B+C or A+B+C+D?

Before you answer too quickly, consider an accused process that performs A'+B'+C'+D. In the accused process, step A' presents substantial differences from A, step B' presents substantial differences from B, and step C' presents substantial differences from C. However, when the three steps are considered as a whole, the differences between A+B+C and A'+B'+C' are insubstantial. Step D is common to both processes. Wouldn't the addition of step D in a claim take the patentee away from the holistic approach rejected in *Pennwalt* and allow application of the rule of *Corning Glass*? If these two cases do not necessarily teach that streamlined claims are preferable, what do they tell us about claim drafting?

3. ***Corning Glass*, Past and Future.** However important the All Elements Rule might appear to be, as a practical matter, it stands for nothing more than the principle that a claim for a combination invention cannot be infringed by a sub-combination. This became abundantly clear from the original panel decision in *Festo Corp. v. Shoketsu Kinzoku Kogyo Kabushiki Co. Ltd.*, 172 F.3d 1361 (Fed.Cir.1999). On that point, the panel decision survived both the Federal Circuit *en banc* and the Supreme Court. The vacated *Festo* panel opinion explained that *Warner–Jenkinson* teaches that it is appropriate to inquire into the "role" of the pair of sealing rings, and to compare that role with the role of the substituted two-way sealing ring.... (considering the role of each element in the context of the claim). Applying this principle, the court observed that the pair of sealing rings, as stated in the claim, effect a fluid-tight seal with the cylinder. The accused SMC devices preserve this role in the two-way sealing ring. The accused device fully performed the claimed function with the two-way sealing ring. Thus, the court reasoned: "The claimed pair of sealing rings has not been eliminated in its entirety, but has been substituted with a single two-way sealing ring that fully preserves the function stated in the claim. We therefore again affirm the district court's ruling that the all-elements rule is met by the sealing ring structure in the SMC devices, and that consideration of equivalency *vel non* of this limitation is not barred." *Id*. Thus, as always, the important question is the application of the Court's admonition that "[i]t is important to ensure that the application of the doctrine, even as to an individual element, is not allowed such broad play as to effectively eliminate that element in its entirety."

§ 11.3[b]   PROSECUTION HISTORY ESTOPPEL

Prosecution history estoppel is a very useful doctrine for a defendant because it <u>enables an accused infringer to win on summary judgment.</u> A defendant may prevail by simply introducing the prosecution history. The Supreme Court invoked this doctrine in *Warner–Jenkinson*. At one point in its discussion, the Supreme Court explained: "Where no explanation is established [explaining the reason for a narrowing amendment], however, the court should presume that the PTO had a substantial reason related to patentability for including the limiting element added by amendment. In those circumstances, prosecution history estoppel would bar the application of the doctrine of equivalents as to that element." This reference to a "bar" on non-textual infringement caused a split in the Federal Circuit that was resolved by *en banc* action. When the Federal Circuit's *en banc* ruling prompted many requests, including that of the Solicitor General of the United States, for further review, the Supreme Court agreed to revisit prosecution history estoppel and non-textual infringement.

FESTO CORP. v. SHOKETSU KINZOKU KOGYO KABUSHIKI CO., LTD.

United States Supreme Court, 2002
535 U.S. 722

MR. JUSTICE KENNEDY delivered the opinion of the Court.

This case requires us to address once again the relation between two patent law concepts, the doctrine of equivalents and the rule of prosecution history estoppel. The Court considered the same concepts in *Warner–Jenkinson Co. v. Hilton Davis Chemical Co.*, 520 U.S. 17, 117 S.Ct. 1040, 137 L.Ed.2d 146 (1997), and reaffirmed that a patent protects its holder against efforts of copyists to evade liability for infringement by making only insubstantial changes to a patented invention. At the same time, we appreciated that by extending protection beyond the literal terms in a patent the doctrine of equivalents can create substantial uncertainty about where the patent monopoly ends. *Id.*, at 29, 117 S.Ct. 1040. If the range of equivalents is unclear, competitors may be unable to determine what is a permitted alternative to a patented invention and what is an infringing equivalent.

To reduce the uncertainty, *Warner–Jenkinson* acknowledged that <u>competitors may rely on the prosecution history, the public record of the patent proceedings.</u> In some cases the Patent and Trademark Office (PTO) may have rejected an earlier version of the patent application on the ground that a claim does not meet a statutory requirement for patentability. 35 U.S.C. § 132 (1994 ed., Supp. V). When the patentee responds to the rejection by <u>narrowing his claims</u>, this prosecution history estops him from later arguing that the subject matter covered by the original, broader claim was nothing more than an equivalent.

Competitors may rely on the estoppel to ensure that their own devices will not be found to infringe by equivalence.

In the decision now under review the Court of Appeals for the Federal Circuit held that by narrowing a claim to obtain a patent, the patentee surrenders all equivalents to the amended claim element. Petitioner asserts this holding departs from past precedent in two respects. First, it applies estoppel to every amendment made to satisfy the requirements of the Patent Act and not just to amendments made to avoid pre-emption by an earlier invention, *i.e.*, the prior art. Second, it holds that when estoppel arises, it bars suit against every equivalent to the amended claim element. The Court of Appeals acknowledged that this holding departed from its own cases, which applied a flexible bar when considering what claims of equivalence were estopped by the prosecution history. Petitioner argues that by replacing the flexible bar with a complete bar the Court of Appeals cast doubt on many existing patents that were amended during the application process when the law, as it then stood, did not apply so rigorous a standard.

We granted certiorari to consider these questions.

I

Petitioner Festo Corporation owns two patents for an improved magnetic rodless cylinder, a piston-driven device that relies on magnets to move objects in a conveying system. The device has many industrial uses and has been employed in machinery as diverse as sewing equipment and the Thunder Mountain ride at Disney World. Although the precise details of the cylinder's operation are not essential here, the prosecution history must be considered.

Petitioner's patent applications, as often occurs, were amended during the prosecution proceedings. The application for the first patent, the Stoll Patent (U.S. Patent No. 4,354,125), was amended after the patent examiner rejected the initial application because the exact method of operation was unclear and some claims were made in an impermissible way. (They were multiply dependent.) 35 U.S.C. § 112 (1994 ed.). The inventor, Dr. Stoll, submitted a new application designed to meet the examiner's objections and also added certain references to prior art. 37 CFR § 1.56 (2000). The second patent, the Carroll Patent (U.S. Patent No. 3,779,401), was also amended during a reexamination proceeding. The prior art references were added to this amended application as well. Both amended patents added a new limitation—that the inventions contain a pair of sealing rings, each having a lip on one side, which would prevent impurities from getting on the piston assembly. The amended Stoll Patent added the further limitation that the outer shell of the device, the sleeve, be made of a magnetizable material.

After Festo began selling its rodless cylinder, respondents (whom we refer to as SMC) entered the market with a device similar, but not identical, to the ones disclosed by Festo's patents. SMC's cylinder, rather than using two one-way sealing rings, employs a single sealing ring with a two-way lip. Furthermore, SMC's sleeve is made of a nonmagnetizable alloy. SMC's device does not fall within the literal claims of either patent, but petitioner contends that it is so similar that it infringes under the doctrine of equivalents.

SMC contends that Festo is estopped from making this argument because of the prosecution history of its patents. The sealing rings and the magnetized alloy in the Festo product were both disclosed for the first time in the amended applications. In SMC's view, these amendments narrowed the earlier applications, surrendering alternatives that are the very points of difference in the competing devices—the sealing rings and the type of alloy used to make the sleeve. As Festo narrowed its claims in these ways in order to obtain the patents, says SMC, Festo is now estopped from saying that these features are immaterial and that SMC's device is an equivalent of its own.

The United States District Court for the District of Massachusetts disagreed. It held that Festo's amendments were not made to avoid prior art, and therefore the amendments were not the kind that give rise to estoppel. A panel of the Court of Appeals for the Federal Circuit affirmed. 72 F.3d 857 (1995). We granted certiorari, vacated, and remanded in light of our intervening decision in *Warner–Jenkinson v. Hilton Davis Chemical Co.*, 520 U.S. 17, 117 S.Ct. 1040, 137 L.Ed.2d 146 (1997). After a decision by the original panel on remand, 172 F.3d 1361 (1999), the Court of Appeals ordered rehearing en banc to address questions that had divided its judges since our decision in *Warner–Jenkinson*, 187 F.3d 1381 (1999).

The en banc court reversed, holding that prosecution history estoppel barred Festo from asserting that the accused device infringed its patents under the doctrine of equivalents. 234 F.3d 558 (2000). The court held, with only one judge dissenting, that estoppel arises from any amendment that narrows a claim to comply with the Patent Act, not only from amendments made to avoid prior art. *Id.*, at 566. More controversial in the Court of Appeals was its further holding: When estoppel applies, it stands as a complete bar against any claim of equivalence for the element that was amended. *Id.*, at 574–575. The court acknowledged that its own prior case law did not go so far. Previous decisions had held that prosecution history estoppel constituted a flexible bar, foreclosing some, but not all, claims of equivalence, depending on the purpose of the amendment and the alterations in the text. The court concluded, however, that its precedents applying the flexible-bar rule should be overruled because this case-by-case approach has proved unworkable. In the court's view a complete-bar rule, under which estoppel bars all claims of equivalence to the narrowed element, would promote certainty in the determination of infringement cases.

Four judges dissented from the decision to adopt a complete bar. *Id.*, at 562. In four separate opinions, the dissenters argued that the majority's decision to overrule precedent was contrary to *Warner–Jenkinson* and would unsettle the expectations of many existing patentees, Judge Michel, in his dissent, described in detail how the complete bar required the Court of Appeals to disregard 8 older decisions of this Court, as well as more than 50 of its own cases. 234 F.3d, at 601–616.

II

The patent laws "promote the Progress of Science and useful Arts" by rewarding innovation with a temporary monopoly. U.S. Const., Art. I, § 8, cl. 8. The monopoly is a property right; and like any property right, its boundaries should be clear. This clarity is essential to promote progress, because it enables efficient investment in innovation. A patent holder should know what he owns, and the public should know what he does not. For this reason, the patent laws require inventors to describe their work in "full, clear, concise, and exact terms," 35 U.S.C. § 112, as part of the delicate balance the law attempts to maintain between inventors, who rely on the promise of the law to bring the invention forth, and the public, which should be encouraged to pursue innovations, creations, and new ideas beyond the inventor's exclusive rights.

Unfortunately, the nature of language makes it impossible to capture the essence of a thing in a patent application. The inventor who chooses to patent an invention and disclose it to the public, rather than exploit it in secret, bears the risk that others will devote their efforts toward exploiting the limits of the patent's language. . . . The language in the patent claims may not capture every nuance of the invention or describe with complete precision the range of its novelty. If patents were always interpreted by their literal terms, their value would be greatly diminished. Unimportant and insubstantial substitutes for certain elements could defeat the patent, and its value to inventors could be destroyed by simple acts of copying. For this reason, the clearest rule of patent interpretation, literalism, may conserve judicial resources but is not necessarily the most efficient rule. The scope of a patent is not limited to its literal terms but instead embraces all equivalents to the claims described. *See Winans v. Denmead*, 56 U.S. (15 How.) 330, 347.

It is true that the doctrine of equivalents renders the scope of patents less certain. It may be difficult to determine what is, or is not, an equivalent to a particular element of an invention. If competitors cannot be certain about a patent's extent, they may be deterred from engaging in legitimate manufactures outside its limits, or they may invest by mistake in competing products that the patent secures. In addition the uncertainty may lead to wasteful litigation between competitors, suits that a rule of literalism might avoid. These concerns with the doctrine of equivalents, however, are not new. Each time the Court has considered the doctrine, it has acknowledged this uncertainty as the price of ensuring the appropriate incentives for innovation, and it has affirmed the doctrine over dissents that urged a more certain rule. . . .

Most recently, in *Warner–Jenkinson*, the Court reaffirmed that equivalents remain a firmly entrenched part of the settled rights protected by the patent. A unanimous opinion concluded that if the doctrine is to be discarded, it is Congress and not the Court that should do so. 520 U.S., at 28.

III

Prosecution history estoppel requires that the claims of a patent be interpreted in light of the proceedings in the PTO during the application process. Estoppel is a "rule of patent construction" that ensures that claims are interpreted by reference to those "that have been cancelled or rejected." *Schriber–Schroth Co. v. Cleveland Trust Co.*, 311 U.S. 211, 220–221 (1940). The doctrine of equivalents allows the patentee to claim those insubstantial alterations that were not captured in drafting the original patent claim but which could be created through trivial changes. When, however, the patentee originally claimed the subject matter alleged to infringe but then narrowed the claim in response to a rejection, he may not argue that the surrendered territory comprised unforeseen subject matter that should be deemed equivalent to the literal claims of the issued patent. On the contrary, "[b]y the amendment [the patentee] recognized and emphasized the difference between the two phrases[,] ... and [t]he difference which [the patentee] thus disclaimed must be regarded as material." *Exhibit Supply Co. v. Ace Patents Corp.*, 315 U.S. 126, 136–137 (1942).

A rejection indicates that the patent examiner does not believe the original claim could be patented. While the patentee has the right to appeal, his decision to forgo an appeal and submit an amended claim is taken as a concession that the invention as patented does not reach as far as the original claim. Were it otherwise, the inventor might avoid the PTO's gatekeeping role and seek to recapture in an infringement action the very subject matter surrendered as a condition of receiving the patent.

Prosecution history estoppel ensures that the doctrine of equivalents remains tied to its underlying purpose. Where the original application once embraced the purported equivalent but the patentee narrowed his claims to obtain the patent or to protect its validity, the patentee cannot assert that he lacked the words to describe the subject matter in question. The doctrine of equivalents is premised on language's inability to capture the essence of innovation, but a prior application describing the precise element at issue undercuts that premise. In that instance the prosecution history has established that the inventor turned his attention to the subject matter in question, knew the words for both the broader and narrower claim, and affirmatively chose the latter.

A

The first question in this case concerns the kinds of amendments that may give rise to estoppel. Petitioner argues that estoppel should arise when amendments are intended to narrow the subject matter of the patented invention, for instance, amendments to avoid prior art, but not when the amendments are made to comply with requirements concerning the form of the patent application. In *Warner–Jenkinson* we recognized that prosecution history estoppel does not arise in every instance when a patent application is amended. Our "prior cases have consistently applied prosecution history estoppel only where claims have been amended for a limited set of reasons," such as "to avoid the prior art, or otherwise to address a specific concern—such as obviousness—that arguably would have rendered the claimed subject matter unpatentable." While we made clear that estoppel applies to amendments made for a "substantial reason related to patentability," we did not purport to define that term or to catalog every reason that might raise an estoppel. Indeed, we stated that even if the amendment's purpose were unrelated to patentability, the court might consider whether it was the kind of reason that nonetheless might require resort to the estoppel doctrine. *Id.*, at 40–41.

Petitioner is correct that estoppel has been discussed most often in the context of amendments made to avoid the prior art. See *Exhibit Supply Co., supra,* at 137. Amendment to accommodate prior art was the emphasis, too, of our decision in *Warner–Jenkinson, supra,* at 30, 117 S.Ct. 1040. It does not follow, however, that amendments for other purposes will not give rise to estoppel. Prosecution history may rebut the inference that a thing not described was indescribable. That rationale does not cease simply because the narrowing amendment, submitted to secure a patent, was for some purpose other than avoiding prior art.

We agree with the Court of Appeals that a narrowing amendment made to satisfy any requirement of the Patent Act may give rise to an estoppel. As that court explained, a number of statutory requirements must be satisfied before a patent can issue. The claimed subject matter must be useful, novel, and not obvious. 35 U.S.C. §§ 101–103 (1994 ed. and Supp. V). In addition, the patent application must describe, enable, and set forth the best mode of carrying out the invention. § 112 (1994 ed.). . . .

Petitioner contends that amendments made to comply with § 112 concern the form of the application and not the subject matter of the invention. The PTO might require the applicant to clarify an ambiguous term, to improve the translation of a foreign word, or to rewrite a dependent claim as an independent one. In these cases, petitioner argues, the applicant has no intention of surrendering subject matter and should not be estopped from challenging equivalent devices. While this may be true in some cases, petitioner's argument conflates the patentee's reason for making the amendment with the impact the amendment has on the subject matter.

Estoppel arises when an amendment is made to secure the patent and the amendment narrows the patent's scope. If a § 112 amendment is truly cosmetic, then it would not narrow the patent's scope or raise an estoppel. On the other hand, if a § 112 amendment is necessary and narrows the patent's scope—even if only for the purpose of better description—estoppel may apply. A patentee who narrows a claim as a condition for obtaining a patent disavows his claim to the broader subject matter, whether the amendment was made to avoid the prior art or to comply with § 112. We must regard the patentee as having conceded an inability to claim the broader subject matter or at least as having abandoned his right to appeal a rejection. In either case estoppel may apply.

B

Petitioner concedes that the limitations at issue—the sealing rings and the composition of the sleeve—were made for reasons related to § 112, if not also to avoid the prior art. Our conclusion that prosecution history estoppel arises when a claim is narrowed to comply with § 112 gives rise to the second question presented: Does the estoppel bar the inventor from asserting infringement against any equivalent to the narrowed element or might some equivalents still infringe? The Court of Appeals held that prosecution history estoppel is a complete bar, and so the narrowed element must be limited to its strict literal terms. Based upon its experience the Court of Appeals decided that the flexible-bar rule is unworkable because it leads to excessive uncertainty and burdens legitimate innovation. For the reasons that follow, we disagree with the decision to adopt the complete bar.

Though prosecution history estoppel can bar challenges to a wide range of equivalents, its reach requires an examination of the subject matter surrendered by the narrowing amendment. The complete bar avoids this inquiry by establishing a *per se* rule; but that approach is inconsistent with the purpose of applying the estoppel in the first place—to hold the inventor to the representations made during the application process and to the inferences that may reasonably be drawn from the amendment. By amending the application, the inventor is deemed to concede that the patent does not extend as far as the original claim. It does not follow, however, that the amended claim becomes so perfect in its description that no one could devise an equivalent. After amendment, as before, language remains an imperfect fit for invention. The narrowing amendment may demonstrate what the claim is not; but it may still fail to capture precisely what the claim is. There is no reason why a narrowing amendment should be deemed to relinquish equivalents unforeseeable at the time of the amendment and beyond a fair interpretation of what was surrendered. Nor is there any call to foreclose claims of equivalence for aspects of the invention that have only a peripheral relation to the reason the amendment was submitted. The amendment does not show that the inventor suddenly had more foresight in the drafting of claims than an inventor whose application was granted without amendments having been submitted. It shows only that he was familiar with the broader text and with the difference between the two. As a result, there is no more reason for holding the patentee to the literal terms of an amended claim than there is for abolishing the doctrine of equivalents altogether and holding every patentee to the literal terms of the patent. . . .

The Court of Appeals ignored the guidance of *Warner–Jenkinson,* which instructed that courts must be cautious before adopting changes that disrupt the settled expectations of the inventing community. See 520 U.S., at 28. In that case we made it clear that the doctrine of equivalents and the rule of prosecution history estoppel are settled law. The responsibility for changing them rests with Congress. *Ibid.* Fundamental alterations in these rules risk destroying the legitimate expectations of inventors in their property. The petitioner in *Warner–Jenkinson* requested another bright-line rule that would have provided more certainty in determining when estoppel applies but at the cost of disrupting the expectations of countless existing patent holders. We rejected that approach: "To change so substantially the rules of the game now could very well subvert the various balances the PTO sought to strike when issuing the numerous patents which have not yet expired and which would be affected by our decision." *Id.,* at 32 As *Warner–Jenkinson* recognized, patent prosecution occurs in the light of our case law. Inventors who amended their claims under the previous regime had no reason to believe they were conceding all equivalents. If they had known, they might have appealed the rejection instead. There is no justification for applying a new and more robust estoppel to those who relied on prior doctrine.

In *Warner–Jenkinson* we struck the appropriate balance by placing the burden on the patentee to show that an amendment was not for purposes of patentability. When the patentee is unable to explain the reason for amendment, estoppel not only applies but also "bar[s] the application of the doctrine of equivalents as to that element." *Ibid.* These words do not mandate a complete bar; they are limited to the circumstance where "no explanation is established." They do provide, however, that when the court is unable to determine the purpose underlying a narrowing amendment—and hence a rationale for limiting the estoppel to the surrender of particular equivalents—the court should presume that the patentee surrendered all subject matter between the broader and the narrower language.

Just as *Warner–Jenkinson* held that the patentee bears the burden of proving that an amendment was not made for a reason that would give rise to estoppel, we hold here that the patentee should bear the burden of showing that the amendment does not surrender the particular equivalent in question. This is the approach advocated by the United States, see Brief for United States as *Amicus Curiae* 22–28, and we regard it to be sound. The patentee, as the author of the claim language, may be expected to draft claims encompassing readily known equivalents. A patentee's decision to narrow his claims through amendment may be presumed to be a general disclaimer of the territory between the original claim and the amended claim. There are some cases, however, where the amendment cannot reasonably be viewed as surrendering a particular equivalent. The equivalent may have been unforeseeable at the time of the application; the rationale underlying the amendment may bear no more than a tangential relation to the equivalent in question; or there may be some other reason suggesting that the patentee could not reasonably be expected to have described the insubstantial substitute in question. In those cases the patentee can overcome the presumption that prosecution history estoppel bars a finding of equivalence.

This presumption is not, then, just the complete bar by another name. Rather, it reflects the fact that the interpretation of the patent must begin with its literal claims, and the prosecution history is relevant to construing those claims. When the patentee has chosen to narrow a claim, courts may presume the amended text was composed with awareness of this rule and that the territory surrendered is not an equivalent of the territory claimed. In those instances, however, the patentee still might rebut the presumption that estoppel bars a claim of equivalence. The patentee must show that at the time of the amendment one skilled in the art could not reasonably be expected to have drafted a claim that would have literally encompassed the alleged equivalent.

IV

On the record before us, we cannot say petitioner has rebutted the presumptions that estoppel applies and that the equivalents at issue have been surrendered. Petitioner concedes that the limitations at issue—the sealing rings and the composition of the sleeve—were made in response to a rejection for reasons under § 112, if not also because of the prior art references. As the amendments were made for a reason relating to patentability, the question is not whether estoppel applies but what territory the amendments surrendered. While estoppel does not effect a complete bar, the question remains whether petitioner can demonstrate that the narrowing amendments did not surrender the particular equivalents at issue. On these questions, respondents may well prevail, for the sealing rings and the composition of the sleeve both were noted expressly in the prosecution history. These matters, however, should be determined in the first instance by further proceedings in the Court of Appeals or the District Court.

The judgment of the Federal Circuit is vacated, and the case is remanded for further proceedings consistent with this opinion.

It is so ordered.

NOTES

1.   Prosecution History Estoppel Without a Claim Amendment. Often during prosecution a claim element is narrowed by arguments that narrow the meaning of a pending claim element so that the claim literally covers less than it would cover in the absence of the prosecution history. Indeed the Federal Circuit's *en banc* version of *Festo* explained: "Arguments made voluntarily during prosecution may give rise to prosecution history estoppel if they evidence a surrender of subject matter." 234 F.3d at 569. In most instances, the Federal Circuit requires the explanations during prosecution to show a "clear and unmistakable surrender" of subject matter. *KCJ Corp. v. Kinetic Concepts, Inc.*, 223 F.3d 1351, 1359–60 (Fed.Cir.2000). Nothing in the Supreme Court opinion alters this established principle that prosecution history estoppel does not require an amendment. These principles complicate the acquisition of a patent considerably. An applicant must realize that amending claims relinquishes both literal scope and the doctrine of equivalents, but arguing to avoid amendment can have the same implications. What might an applicant do to avoid either amending or arguing against amendment?

2. **Was the Supreme Court Case a Victory for Festo?** The *Festo* case was widely perceived to be the most important commercial case of the Court's 2002–03 term. The high-profile nature of the case was established by Festo's retention of the celebrated former circuit judge Robert Bork to argue its case. However, after this result, Festo had few other causes to rejoice. On remand, the Federal Circuit ruled that Festo's proposed equivalents did not meet the tangentiality or "some other reason" exceptions to prosecution history estoppel. 344 F.3d at 1371–72. The Circuit then remanded for a determination of foreseeability. In 2007, the *Festo* case was back at the Federal Circuit where the court finally put an end to the dispute by upholding the district court's decision that neither the use of an aluminum alloy sleeve nor the use of one sealing ring was unforeseeable at the time of the 1981 amendment: "[A]n equivalent is foreseeable if one skilled in the art would have known that the alternative existed in the field of art as defined by the original claim scope, even if the suitability of the alternative for the particular purposes defined by the amended claim scope were unknown." *Festo*, 493 F.3d at 1382.

3. **Still another explanation about the exception (foreseeability) to the exception (prosecution history estoppel) to the exception (the doctrine of equivalents itself).** In *Honeywell Intern. v. Hamilton Sunstrand Corp.*, 370 F.3d 1131 (Fed. Cir. 2004) (*en banc*), the Federal Circuit explained that an applicant would have trouble avoiding prosecution history estoppel by simply canceling claims. In that case, the applicant rewrote dependent claims into independent form and then cancelled the original broader independent claim. The Federal Circuit saw this action as a narrowing amendment. *Id.* at 1134. Then, like the *Festo* case itself, the Federal Circuit in 2008 affirmed a district court's decision to bar Honeywell from invoking the doctrine of equivalents because its proposed equivalent was foreseeable at the time of the narrowing amendment: "The principle of foreseeability ties patent enforcement appropriately to patent acquisition. In making this connection, foreseeability reconciles the preeminent notice function of patent claims with the protective function of the doctrine of equivalents. Thus, foreseeability in this context ensures that the doctrine does not capture subject matter that the patent drafter could have foreseen during prosecution and included in the claims. The goal of the principle is to ensure

that the claims continue to define patent scope in all foreseeable circumstances, while protecting patent owners against insubstantial variations from a claimed element in unforeseeable circumstances. The foreseeability principle thus relegates the doctrine of equivalents to its appropriate exceptional place in patent enforcement." *Honeywell*, 523 F.3d at 1313.

4.   The origin of the foreseeability principle. Foreseeability as a limitation on the doctrine of equivalents first gained prominence in 1997 when the Federal Circuit employed a foreseeability bar:

> The claim at issue defines a relatively simple structural device. A skilled patent drafter would foresee the limiting potential of the "over said slot" limitation. No subtlety of language or complexity of the technology, nor any subsequent change in the state of the art, such as later-developed technology, obfuscated the significance of this limitation at the time of its incorporation into the claim.... However, as between the patentee who had a clear opportunity to negotiate broader claims but did not do so, and the public at large, it is the patentee who must bear the cost of its failure to seek protection for this foreseeable alteration of its claimed structure.

Sage Prods., Inc. v. Devon Indus., Inc., 126 F.3d 1420 (Fed.Cir.1997). This principle undoubtedly came to the Supreme Court's attention via the following case which created the Federal Circuit's fourth limitation on the doctrine of equivalents.

§ 11.3[c]   THE DEDICATION DOCTRINE

The Federal Circuit decided the following case setting forth the dedication doctrine limitation on the doctrine of equivalents during the time the Supreme Court was drafting its *Festo* decision.

JOHNSON & JOHNSTON ASSOCIATES INC., v. R.E. SERVICE CO., INC.

United States Court of Appeals, Federal Circuit, 2002
285 F.3d 1046

Before Mayer, Chief Judge, Newman, Circuit Judge, Archer, Senior Circuit Judge, Michel, Lourie, Clevenger, Rader, Schall, Bryson, Gajarsa, Linn, Dyk and Prost, Circuit Judges.

PER CURIAM.

Johnson and Johnston Associates (Johnston) asserted United States Patent No. 5,153,050 (the '050 patent) against R.E. Service Co. and Mark Frater (collectively RES). A jury found that RES willfully infringed claims 1 and 2 of the patent under the doctrine of equivalents and awarded Johnston $1,138,764 in damages. Upon entry of judgment, the United States District Court for the Northern District of California further granted Johnston enhanced damages, attorney fees, and expenses. After a hearing before a three-judge panel on December 7, 1999, this court ordered *en banc* rehearing of the doctrine of equivalents issue which occurred on October 3, 2001. Because this court concludes that RES, as a matter of law, could not have infringed the '050 patent under the doctrine of equivalents, this court reverses the district court's judgment of infringement under the doctrine of equivalents.

I.

The '050 patent, which issued October 6, 1992, relates to the manufacture of printed circuit boards. Printed circuit boards are composed of extremely thin sheets of conductive copper foil joined to sheets of a dielectric (nonconductive) resin-impregnated material called "prepreg." The process for making multi-layered printed circuit boards stacks sheets of copper foil and prepreg in a press, heats them to melt the resin in the prepreg, and thereby bonds the layers.

In creating these circuit boards, workers manually handle the thin sheets of copper foil during the layering process. Without the invention claimed in the '050 patent, stacking by hand can damage or contaminate the fragile foil, causing discontinuities in the etched copper circuits. The '050 patent claims an assembly that prevents most damage during manual handling. The invention adheres the fragile copper foil to a stiffer substrate sheet of aluminum. With the aluminum substrate for protection, workers can handle the assembly without damaging the fragile copper foil. After the pressing and heating steps, workers can remove and even recycle the aluminum substrate. Figure 5 of the '050 patent shows the foil-substrate combination, with the foil layer peeled back at one corner for illustration:

Surface Ci is the protected inner surface of the copper foil; Ai is the inner surface of the aluminum substrate. A band of flexible adhesive 40 joins the substrate and the foil at the edges, creating a protected central zone CZ. The specification explains:

> Because the frail, thin copper foil C was adhesively secured to its aluminum substrate A, the [laminate] is stiffer and more readily handled resulting in far fewer spoils due to damaged copper foil. The use of the adhered substrate A, regardless of what material it is made of, makes the consumer's (manufacturer's) objective of using thinner and thinner foils and ultimately automating the procedure more realistic since the foil, by use of the invention, is no longer without the much needed physical support.

'050 patent, col. 8, ll. 21–30. The specification further describes the composition of the substrate sheet:

> While aluminum is currently the preferred material for the substrate, other metals, such as stainless steel or nickel alloys, may be used. In some instances . . . polypropelene [sic] can be used.

'050 patent, col. 5, ll. 5–8.

As noted, the jury found infringement of claims 1 and 2:

Claim 1. A component for use in manufacturing articles such as printed circuit boards comprising:

a laminate constructed of a sheet of copper foil which, in a finished printed circuit board, constitutes a functional element and a sheet of *aluminum* which constitutes a discardable element;

one surface of each of the copper sheet and the *aluminum* sheet being essentially uncontaminated and engageable with each other at an interface,

a band of flexible adhesive joining the uncontaminated surfaces of the sheets together at their borders and defining a substantially uncontaminated central zone inwardly of the edges of the sheets and unjoined at the interface.

'050 patent, Claim 1, col. 8, ll. 47–60 (emphasis supplied). Claim 2 defines a similar laminate having sheets of copper foil adhered to both sides of the aluminum sheet.

* * *

In 1997, RES began making new laminates for manufacture of printed circuit boards. The RES products, designated "SC2" and "SC3," joined copper foil to a sheet of steel as the substrate instead of a sheet of aluminum. Johnston filed a suit for infringement.... The jury found RES liable for willful infringement under the doctrine of equivalents and awarded Johnston $1,138,764 in damages....

II.

On appeal, RES does not challenge the jury's factual finding of equivalency between the copper-steel and copper-aluminum laminates. Instead, citing [*Maxwell v. J. Baker, Inc.*, 86 F.3d 1098 (Fed. Cir. 1996)], RES argues that Johnston did not claim steel substrates, but limited its patent scope to aluminum substrates, thus dedicating to the public this unclaimed subject matter. On this ground, RES challenges the district court's denial of its motion for summary judgment that RES's copper-steel laminates are not equivalent, as a matter of law, to the claimed copper-aluminum laminates. Johnston responds that the steel substrates are not dedicated to the public, citing [*YBM Magnex, Inc. v. International Trade Commission*, 145 F.3d 1317 (Fed. Cir. 1998)]. In other words, the two parties dispute whether *Maxwell* or *YBM Magnex* applies in this case with regard to infringement under the doctrine of equivalents.

In *Maxwell*, the patent claimed a system for attaching together a mated pair of shoes. 86 F.3d at 1101–02. Maxwell claimed fastening tabs between the inner and outer soles of the attached shoes. Maxwell disclosed in the specification, but did not claim, fastening tabs that could be "stitched into a lining seam of the shoes." U.S. Patent No. 4,624,060, col. 2, l. 42. Based on the "well-established rule that 'subject matter disclosed but not claimed in a patent application is dedicated to the public,'" this court held that Baker could not, as a matter of law, infringe under the doctrine of equivalents by using the disclosed but unclaimed shoe attachment system. *Maxwell,* 86 F.3d at 1106. This court stated further:

> By [Maxwell's failure] to claim these alternatives, the Patent and Trademark Office was deprived of the opportunity to consider whether these alternatives were patentable. A person of ordinary skill in the shoe industry, reading the specification and prosecution history, and interpreting the claims, would conclude that Maxwell, by failing to claim the alternate shoe attachment systems in which the tabs were attached to the inside shoe lining, dedicated the use of such systems to the public.

Maxwell, 86 F.3d at 1108.

In *YBM Magnex,* the patent claimed a permanent magnet alloy comprising certain elements, including "6,000 to 35,000 ppm oxygen." U.S. Patent No. 4,588,439 (the '439 patent), col. 3, l. 12. The accused infringer used similar magnet alloys with an oxygen content between 5,450 and 6,000 ppm (parts per million), which was allegedly disclosed but not claimed in the '439 patent. In *YBM Magnex,* this court stated that *Maxwell* did not create a new rule of law that doctrine of equivalents could never encompass subject matter disclosed in the specification but not claimed. 145 F.3d at 1321. Distinguishing *Maxwell,* this court noted:

> Maxwell avoided examination of the unclaimed alternative, which was distinct from the claimed alternative. In view of the distinctness of the two embodiments, both of which were fully described in the specification, the Federal Circuit denied Maxwell the opportunity to enforce the unclaimed embodiment as an equivalent of the one that was claimed.

Id. at 1320. In other words, this court in *YBM Magnex* purported to limit *Maxwell* to situations where a patent discloses an unclaimed alternative distinct from the claimed invention. Thus, this court must decide whether a patentee can apply the doctrine of equivalents to cover unclaimed subject matter disclosed in the specification.

III.

Both the Supreme Court and this court have adhered to the fundamental principle that claims define the scope of patent protection. *See, e.g., Aro Mfg. v. Convertible Top Replacement Co.,* 365 U.S. 336, 339 (1961) The claims give notice both to the examiner at the U.S. Patent and Trademark Office during prosecution, and to the public at large, including potential competitors, after the patent has issued.

Consistent with its scope definition and notice functions, the claim requirement presupposes that a patent applicant defines his invention in the claims, not in the specification. After all, the claims, not the specification, provide the measure of the patentee's right to exclude. *Milcor Steel Co. v. George A. Fuller Co.,* 316 U.S. 143, 146 (1942). Moreover, the law of infringement compares the accused product with the claims as construed by the court. Infringement, either literally or under the *accused product compared to claims* doctrine of equivalents, does not arise by comparing the accused product "with a preferred embodiment described in the specification, or with a commercialized embodiment of the patentee." *SRI Int'l,* 775 F.2d at 1121....

The doctrine of equivalents extends the right to exclude beyond the literal scope of the claims. The Supreme Court first applied the modern doctrine of equivalents in *Graver Tank & Mfg. Co. v. Linde Air Prods. Co.* (*Graver II*). *Graver* In that case, the Court explained: "equivalency must be determined against the context of the patent, the prior art, and the particular circumstances of the case." 339 U.S. 605, 609, 70 S.Ct. 854, 94 L.Ed. 1097 (1950). In *Graver I,* a predecessor case addressing the validity of the claims at issue, the Court held invalid composition claims 24 and 26 comprising "silicates" and "metallic silicates." *Graver Tank & Mfg. v. Linde Air Prods. Co.,* 336 U.S. 271, 276–77, 69 S.Ct. 535, 93 L.Ed. 672 (1949) (*Graver I*). Specifically, the Court found those claims too broad because they encompassed some inoperative silicates along with the nine operative metallic silicates in the specification. *Id.* at 276, 69 S.Ct. 535. The Court did not hold invalid narrower claims comprising "alkaline earth metals."

Thus, in the infringement action of *Graver II,* the Supreme Court addressed only the narrower claims comprising "alkaline earth metals." The alleged infringing compositions in *Graver II* are similar to the compositions of the narrower claims, except that they substitute silicate of manganese—a metallic silicate such as in the earlier invalidated claims—for silicates of "alkaline earth metals" (e.g., magnesium or calcium) claimed in the narrower claims. Because the Court determined *in Graver unclaimed subject matter not given to public* that "under the circumstances the change was so insubstantial," and because the accused compositions "perform[ed] substantially the same function in substantially the same way to obtain the same result," the Court upheld the finding of infringement under the doctrine of equivalents. *Graver II,* 339 U.S. at 608–10, 70 S.Ct. 854 (quoting *Sanitary Refrigerator Co. v. Winters,* 280 U.S. 30, 42, 50 S.Ct. 9, 74 L.Ed. 147 (1929)). The Court's holding and the history of *Graver II* show that the patentee had not dedicated unclaimed subject matter to the public. In fact, the patentee had claimed the "equivalent" subject matter, even if the Court eventually held the relevant claims too broad.

In 1997, less than a year after this court decided *Maxwell,* the Supreme Court addressed the doctrine of equivalents again in *Warner–* *Warner case no dedication of subject matter* *Jenkinson Co. v. Hilton Davis Chem. Co.,* 520 U.S. 17, 117 S.Ct. 1040.... The patent at issue in *Warner–Jenkinson* did not disclose or suggest an ultrafiltration process where the pH of the reaction mixture was 5.0. *Hilton Davis Chem. Co. v. Warner–Jenkinson Co.,* 114 F.3d 1161, 1164 (Fed.Cir.1997). In fact, the specification practically repeated the claim language: "it is preferred to adjust the *pH to approximately 6.0 to 8.0* before passage through the ultrafiltration membrane." U.S. Patent No. 4,560,746, col. 7, ll. 59–61 (emphasis added). Thus, *Warner–Jenkinson* did not present an instance of the patentee dedicating subject matter to the public in its specification. In 1998, less than a year later, this court decided *YBM Magnex.*

V.

As stated in *Maxwell,* when a patent drafter discloses but declines to claim subject matter, as in this case, this action dedicates that unclaimed subject matter to the public. Application of the doctrine of equivalents to recapture subject matter deliberately left unclaimed would "conflict with the primacy of the claims in defining the scope of the patentee's exclusive right." *Sage Prods. Inc. v. Devon Indus., Inc.,* 126 F.3d 1420, 1424 (Fed.Cir.1997). . . . Moreover, a patentee cannot narrowly claim an invention to avoid prosecution scrutiny by the PTO, and then, after patent issuance, use the doctrine of equivalents to establish infringement because the specification discloses equivalents. "Such a result would merely encourage a patent applicant to present a broad disclosure in the specification of the application and file narrow claims, avoiding examination of broader claims that the applicant could have filed consistent with the specification." *Maxwell,* 86 F.3d at 1107. By enforcing the *Maxwell* rule, the courts avoid the problem of extending the coverage of an exclusive right to encompass more than that properly examined by the PTO. *Keystone Bridge Co. v. Phoenix Iron Co.,* 95 U.S. 274, 278 (1877) ("[T]he courts have no right to enlarge a patent beyond the scope of its claim as allowed by the Patent Office, or the appellate tribunal to which contested applications are referred.").

IV.

In this case, Johnston's '050 patent specifically limited the claims to "a sheet of aluminum" and "the aluminum sheet." The specification of the '050 patent, however, reads: "While aluminum is currently the preferred material for the substrate, other metals, such as stainless steel or nickel alloys may be used." Col. 5, ll. 5–10. Having disclosed without claiming the steel substrates, Johnston cannot now invoke the doctrine of equivalents to extend its aluminum limitation to encompass steel. Thus, Johnston cannot assert the doctrine of equivalents to cover the disclosed but unclaimed steel substrate. To the extent that *YBM Magnex* conflicts with this holding, this *en banc* court now overrules that case.

A patentee who inadvertently fails to claim disclosed subject matter, however, is not left without remedy. Within two years from the grant of the original patent, a patentee may file a reissue application and attempt to enlarge the scope of the original claims to include the disclosed but previously unclaimed subject matter. 35 U.S.C. § 251 (2000). In addition, a patentee can file a separate application claiming the disclosed subject matter under 35 U.S.C. § 120 (2000) (allowing filing as a continuation application if filed before all applications in the chain issue). Notably, Johnston took advantage of the latter of the two options by filing two continuation applications that literally claim the relevant subject matter.

REVERSED.

RADER, CIRCUIT JUDGE, with whom MAYER, CHIEF JUDGE, joins, concurring.

While endorsing the results and reasoning of the court, I would offer an alternative reasoning. This alternative would also help reconcile the preeminent notice function of patent claims with the protective function of the doctrine of equivalents. This reconciling principle is simple: the doctrine of equivalents does not capture subject matter that the patent drafter reasonably could have foreseen during the application process and included in the claims. This principle enhances the notice function of claims by making them the sole definition of invention scope in all foreseeable circumstances. This principle also protects patentees against copyists who employ insubstantial variations to expropriate the claimed invention in some unforeseeable circumstances.

Few problems have vexed this court more than articulating discernible standards for non-textual infringement. On the one hand, the Supreme Court has recognized that the doctrine of equivalents provides essential protection for inventions: "[T]o permit imitation of a patented invention which does not copy every literal detail would be to convert the protection of the patent grant into a hollow and useless thing ... leav[ing] room for indeed encourag[ing] the unscrupulous copyist to make unimportant and insubstantial changes." *Graver Tank & Mfg. Co. v. Linde Air Prods. Co.*, 339 U.S. 605, 607, 70 S.Ct. 854, 94 L.Ed. 1097 (1950). The protective function of non-textual infringement, however, has a price. Recently, the Supreme Court acknowledged that a broad doctrine of equivalents can threaten the notice function of claims: "There can be no denying that the doctrine of equivalents, when applied broadly, conflicts with the definitional and public-notice functions of the statutory claiming requirement." *Warner–Jenkinson Co. v. Hilton Davis Chem. Co.*, 520 U.S. 17, 29, 117 S.Ct. 1040, 137 L.Ed.2d 146 (1997). These competing policies make it difficult to set a standard that protects the patentee against insubstantial changes while simultaneously providing the public with adequate notice of potentially infringing behavior.

In general, the Supreme Court and this court have attempted to deal with these competing principles by placing limits on non-textual infringement. Thus, in furtherance of the notice objective, *Pennwalt* and *Warner–Jenkinson* require an equivalent for each and every element of a claim. Similarly, to enhance notice, *Festo* and *Warner–Jenkinson* propose to bar patentees from expanding their claim to embrace subject matter surrendered during the patent acquisition process. Finally, *Wilson Sporting Goods* prevents the doctrine of equivalents from expanding claim scope to embrace prior art. *Wilson Sporting Goods Co. v. David Geoffrey & Assocs.*, 904 F.2d 677, 683 (Fed.Cir.1990).

Perhaps more than each of these other restraints on non-textual infringement, a foreseeability bar would concurrently serve both the predominant notice function of the claims and the protective function of the doctrine of equivalents. When one of ordinary skill in the relevant art would foresee coverage of an invention, a patent drafter has an obligation to claim those foreseeable limits. This rule enhances the notice function of claims by making them the sole definition of invention scope in all foreseeable circumstances. When the skilled artisan cannot have foreseen a variation that copyists employ to evade the literal text of the claims, the rule permits the patentee to attempt to prove that an "insubstantial variation" warrants a finding of non-textual infringement. In either event, the claims themselves and the prior art erect a foreseeability bar that circumscribes the protective function of non-textual infringement. Thus, foreseeability sets an objective standard for assessing when to apply the doctrine of equivalents.

A foreseeability bar thus places a premium on claim drafting and enhances the notice function of claims . . . . . In other words, the patentee has an obligation to draft claims that capture all reasonably foreseeable ways to practice the invention. The doctrine of equivalents would not rescue a claim drafter who does not provide such notice. Foreseeability thus places a premium on notice while reserving a limited role for the protective function of the doctrine of equivalents.

This court actually already has articulated this foreseeability principle in the context of the doctrine of equivalents. . . . [In] *Sage Prods., Inc. v. Devon Indus., Inc.*, 126 F.3d 1420 (Fed.Cir.1997), [the Federal Circuit applied foreseeability as a bar.] *Sage* is not the only case to acknowledge the value of a foreseeability limit on non-textual infringement. [Citing many cases.] In one of those cases, *Kinzenbaw v. Deere & Co.*, this court concluded that the "doctrine of equivalents is designed to protect inventors from unscrupulous copyists . . . and *unanticipated equivalents*." 741 F.2d at 389 (emphasis added). Referencing a case involving after-arising technology, the Federal Circuit did not require the patent applicant to claim "all future developments which enable the practice of [each limitation of] his invention in substantially the same way." *Id.* In other words, the court acknowledged the role of foreseeability in enforcing the doctrine of equivalents.

In this case, Johnston's '050 patent claimed only a "sheet of aluminum" and "the aluminum sheet" twice specifying the aluminum limitation. The patent specification then expressly mentioned other potential substrate metals, including stainless steel. col. 5, ll. 5–10. Johnston's patent disclosure expressly admits that it foresaw other metals serving as substrates. Yet the patent did not claim anything beyond aluminum. Foreseeability bars Johnston from recapturing as an equivalent subject matter not claimed but disclosed.

Foreseeability relegates non-textual infringement to its appropriate exceptional place in patent policy. The doctrine of equivalents should not rescue claim drafters who fail to give accurate notice of an invention's scope in the claims.... Implicit in the protective function of the doctrine of equivalents is the notion that the patentees could not have protected themselves with reasonable care and foresight. Enforcing this *Sage* principle more aggressively will help achieve a better balance between the notice function of claims and the protective function of non-textual infringement.

handwritten margin note: doctrine of equivalents shouldn't rescue poorly written claims

NOTES

1. Is There Language in *Festo* that Would Suggest the Supreme Court Should Reverse *Johnston*'s Dedication Doctrine? In the *Johnston* case, one of the claim limitations at issue recited "a sheet of aluminum." That limitation was not amended in the PTO, and yet it did not receive the benefit of equivalents. Therefore, if *Festo* decided that unamended claim elements cover whatever they literally describe and equivalents, then *Johnston* seems to conflict with *Festo*. Would you be willing to argue that the Court should reverse *Johnston*?

2. Does *Johnston* Penalize Disclosure? Suppose that, contrary to the facts of *Johnston*, the '050 patent disclosed only an aluminum sheet. Further suppose that considerable evidence showed that skilled artisans were fully aware that a steel sheet could be substituted for an aluminum sheet. If an equivalent is foreseeable, but not claimed and not disclosed in the specification (and thus not dedicated to the public), why should that equivalent be treated differently from situations where the equivalent actually was disclosed in the specification? Has *Johnston* penalized disclosure? The *Johnston* court did not address this question. Can you justify *Johnston* if indeed foreseeable, unclaimed, and undisclosed technology is permitted equivalents coverage?

3. A Less Sanguine View of Foreseeability. In a concurring opinion in *Johnston*, Judge Lourie stated that "I am not convinced that introducing the concept of foreseeability is the answer to the equivalence dilemma." He further explained:

> I do not agree that the concept of foreseeability would simplify equivalence issues and make them more amenable to summary judgment. In fact, it would raise new factual issues. Determining what is foreseeable would often require expert testimony as to what one skilled in the art would have foreseen. How would a trial judge know whether to grant summary judgment other than to make factual findings? What is foreseeable is quite different from what is disclosed in the patent, as in our case here, which is readily determinable. Foreseeability is not solely a question of law.

385 F.3d at 1046, 1063. Of course, the Supreme Court opinion in *Festo*, issued shortly after the *Johnston* decision from the *en banc* Federal Circuit, seems to make foreseeability part of the question under the doctrine of equivalents. Do you think Judge Lourie is correct that trial courts will need to hold "*Festo* hearings" to ascertain facts before applying non-textual infringement or will the question turn on a simple examination of the prior art?

§ 11.3[d] PRIOR ART LIMITATIONS

The third limitation on the doctrine of equivalents relates to the coverage of prior art. Obviously no system of patent law can permit an exclusive right to encompass a product or process already in the prior art. That principle may include as well subject matter that is obvious in light of the prior art. The case that follows adopts this approach. Later cases have adopted a more stringent standard.

WILSON SPORTING GOODS CO. v. DAVID GEOFFREY & ASSOCIATES

United States Court of Appeals, Federal Circuit, 1990
904 F.2d 677

Before MARKEY, Chief Judge, RICH, Circuit Judge, and COWEN, Senior Circuit Judge.

RICH, CIRCUIT JUDGE.

[Wilson sued Dunlop and DGA for patent infringement in the United States District Court for the District of South Carolina for infringement of a patent on a "longer" golf ball. Wilson's '168 patent claims a certain configuration of dimples on a golf ball cover. The shape and width of the dimples in the '168 create a more symmetrical distribution of dimples. The patent divides the ball's surface into 80 imaginary spherical triangles and six great circles. All of the claims of the '168 patent require that dimples must be arranged on the surface of the ball so that no dimple intersects any great circle.

The accused Dunlop balls have 432 to 480 dimples, 60 of which intersect great circles in amounts from 4 to 9 thousandths of an inch. Because the dimples on the accused ball only slightly intersected the great circles, the jury found infringement under the doctrine of equivalents.

Uniroyal sold a golf ball that qualified as prior art to the '168 patent. An analysis of that ball disclosed that its dimples intersected the hypothetical great circles at a rate with no "principled difference" from the intersection rate of the accused Dunlop ball.]

OPINION

The only theory of liability presented to the jury by Wilson was infringement under the doctrine of equivalents. Dunlop's argument for reversal is straightforward. It contends that there is no principled difference between the balls which the jury found to infringe and the prior art Uniroyal ball; thus to allow the patent to reach Dunlop's balls under the doctrine of equivalents would improperly ensnare the prior art Uniroyal ball as well.

Infringement may be found under the doctrine of equivalents if an accused product "performs substantially the same overall function or work, in substantially the same way, to obtain substantially the same overall result as the claimed invention." *Pennwalt Corp. v. Durand–Wayland, Inc.*, 833 F.2d 931, 934 (1987). Even if this test is met, however, there can be no infringement if the asserted scope of equivalency of what is literally claimed would encompass the prior art. *Id.*

The answer is that a patentee should not be able to obtain, under the doctrine of equivalents, coverage which he could not lawfully have obtained from the PTO by literal claims. The doctrine of equivalents exists to prevent a fraud on a patent, not to give a patentee something which he could not lawfully have obtained from the PTO had he tried. Thus, since prior art always limits what an inventor could have claimed, it limits the range of permissible equivalents of a claim.

Accordingly, Wilson's claim 1 cannot be given a range of equivalents broad enough to encompass the accused Dunlop balls.

[Judgment of infringement reversed.]

NOTES

1. **The Progeny of *Wilson Sporting Goods*.** This abbreviated version of *Wilson Sporting Goods* did not detail some of the case's complicated reasoning. To ensure that Wilson's proposed equivalent encompassed prior art, the court proposed a hypothetical claim that encompassed the full proposed range of equivalents. Then it proposed a further analysis to see if that hypothetical claim would be valid in light of prior art. Trial practitioners within the patent bar widely criticized the opinion because it placed on patentees the burden of both concocting, and proving the validity of, a hypothetical claim as part of their case in chief. *See* Henrik D. Parker, *Doctrine of Equivalents Analysis after Wilson Sporting Goods: The Hypothetical Claim Hydra*, 18 AM. INTELL. PROP. L. ASS'N Q. J. 262 (1990). At first, the Federal Circuit stepped back somewhat from the *Wilson Sporting Goods*:

> While not obligatory in every doctrine of equivalents determination, the hypothetical claim rationale of *Wilson Sporting Goods* helps define the limits imposed by prior art on the range of equivalents. The *Wilson* hypothetical claim analysis does not envision application of a full-blown patentability analysis to a hypothetical claim. *Wilson* simply acknowledges that prior art limits the coverage available under the doctrine of equivalents. A range of equivalents may not embrace inventions already disclosed by prior art.

Key Manufacturing Group, Inc. v. Microdot, Inc., 925 F.2d 1444, 1449 (Fed. Cir. 1991); *see also International Visual Corp. v. Crown Metal Mfg. Co.*, 991 F.2d 768 (Fed.Cir.1993).

2. **Is the Hypothetical Claim Approach Now Mandatory?** However, in *Streamfeeder, LLC v. Sure–Feed Systems, Inc.*, 175 F.3d 974 (Fed.Cir.1999), Streamfeeder's hypothetical claim may well have been non-obvious because of the narrowing of certain limitations. These narrowed limitations may have provided a basis for patentability. The Federal Circuit appeared to concede that the

Sure–Feed feeder may have been patentable over the prior art. Therefore, the Federal Circuit did not find the Sure–Feed device obvious over the prior art, but instead set out a key restriction on the drafting of a hypothetical claim, *i.e.*, that the limitations can be expanded, but not narrowed so as to read on the disclosure and on the accused product or process, but not on the prior art. Do you approve of this hypothetical claim requirement over the simple rule that the alleged infringing device cannot be obvious from the prior art? For a detailed discussion of the added restrain put on the doctrine of equivalents by *Streamfeeder*, *see* 3 MARTIN J. ADELMAN, PATENT LAW PERSPECTIVES, § 3.4[1] n.373 (2d ed. 1999). As a practical matter, this prior art limitation rarely appears in doctrine of equivalents cases because it only applies in a crowded field where the slight expansion of the exclusive right under the doctrine of equivalents will actually ensnare literally and in every aspect another piece of prior art.

§ 11.4   INDIRECT INFRINGEMENT

The patent statute provides the patentee with two additional exclusive rights conveniently discussed together. 35 U.S.C.A. § 271(b) tersely provides for inducement of infringement as follows:

> Whoever actively induces infringement of a patent shall be liable as an infringer.

35 U.S.C.A. § 271(c) next sets forth the standard for "contributory infringement":

> Whoever offers to sell or sells within the United States or imports into the United States a component of a patented machine, manufacture, combination or composition, or a material or apparatus for use in practicing a patented process, constituting a material part of the invention, knowing the same to be especially made or especially adapted for use in an infringement of said patent, and not a staple article or commodity of commerce suitable for substantial noninfringing use, shall be liable as a contributory infringer.

These provisions, addressing two species of "indirect infringement," allow patentees to reach those entities whose acts facilitate a direct infringement by others. The next decision explores the elements of contributory infringement and inducement of infringement.

DSU MEDICAL CORPORATION v. JMS COMPANY, LTD.

United States Court of Appeals, Federal Circuit, 2006
471 F.3d 1293

Before Rader, Schall, and Linn, Circuit Judges.

Opinion for the court filed by Circuit Judge Rader.

RADER, CIRCUIT JUDGE.

DSU Medical Corporation and Medisystems Corporation (collectively DSU) sued JMS Company, Limited and JMS North America (collectively JMS) and ITL Corporation Pty, Limited for patent infringement, inducement to infringe, and contributory infringement of United States Patent Nos. 5,112,311 ('311) and 5,266,072 ('072). After a six-week jury trial produced a unanimous verdict, the United States District Court for the Northern District of California entered a final judgment.... The jury awarded total damages of $5,055,211 for infringement against JMS and JMS North America, and the trial court entered a final judgment holding both jointly and severally liable for the award. Finding no reversible error, this court affirms.

I.

The '311 and '072 patents claim a guarded, winged-needle assembly. The invention reduces the risk of accidental needle-stick injuries. Needle puncture wounds can transmit blood-borne diseases such as Hepatitis B and AIDS. The '311 and '072 patented inventions effectively guard standard winged-needle-sets to prevent needle-stick injuries.

The '311 patent claims a "slotted, locking guard for shielding a needle, and a winged needle assembly including a needle, a winged needle hub, and a slotted, locking guard." '311, col.1, l. 8–11. This invention includes both "[a] slotted guard for locking a needle in a shielded position as the needle is removed from the patient", and "a guarded winged needle assembly ... slidably mounted within the guard." Id., abstract. Figures 5–6 illustrate one embodiment of the patented invention:

Figure 5 is a side view of a needle, winged needle hub (3), and slotted needle guard (1).'311 patent, col. 3, ll. 4–6. In this depiction, the needle (5) remains retracted within the needle guard (1). Id. Figure 6 shows the same needle from above. '311 patent, col. 3, ll. 7–10.

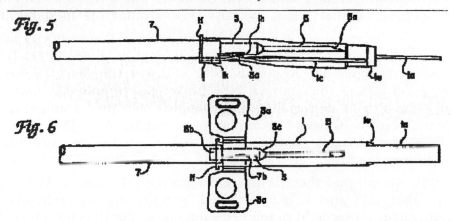

The alleged infringing device, made by ITL (an Australian company) sells under the name Platypus TM Needle Guard (Platypus). ITL manufactures the Platypus in Malaysia and Singapore. The Platypus needle guard is a "stand-alone" product: a small configured piece of plastic. This plastic guard structure is not attached to any other device. In other words, the Platypus does not include a needle, but only a sheathing structure. Some claims of the '311 patent recite both a slotted guard and a guarded winged needle assembly. Before use, the Platypus resembles an open clamshell (open-shell configuration). During use, the halves of the clam shell close to form the needle guard (closed-shell configuration). The following illustration shows the Platypus in open- and closed-shell configuration:

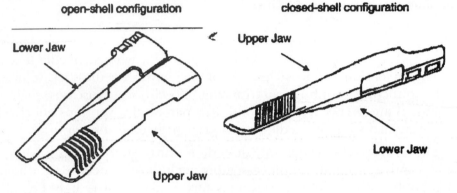

The Platypus has an upper and a lower "jaw." When closed, the upper jaw extends around and overlaps the inner, lower jaw. During use, a medical technician closes the Platypus and locks it around tubing connected to the winged needle assembly. When the technician removes the needle from a patient, the worker slides the guard down the tube until the needle assembly's wings meet and pry the jaws apart. The wings and their attached needle assembly slide into and through the guard, forcing the jaws ever wider as the wings make their way into a notched opening at the guard's back. Ultimately the wings slide into the rear opening. At that point, the jaws close around the used needle.

JMS is a large Japanese medical supply business that competes with MDS in the United States market. Beginning in June 1999, JMS purchased Platypus needle guards from ITL, entering into an agreement to distribute the Platypus worldwide (the Supply Agreement). Under the Supply Agreement, JMS bought open-shell configuration Platypus guard units from ITL in Singapore and Malaysia. JMS generally closed the Platypus guards around needle sets before distributing them to customers.

DSU alleges that the Platypus infringes the '311 patent. DSU also alleges that JMS and ITL contributed to and induced each other's infringement. JMS sought to sell ITL's infringing Platypus until it could produce its substitute non-infringing product, the WingEater. ITL offered to supply its infringing Platypus. DSU additionally seeks damages from JMS because it "stole" MDS's ability to renew a MasterGuard exclusive license with a former customer, Fresenius USA Manufacturing, Inc. (Fresenius).

II.

The trial court construed "slidably enclosing" in claim 1 of the '311 patent:

> 1. A guard slidably enclosing a sliding assembly comprising a needle and a winged needle hub. . . .

'311 patent, col. 15, ll. 46–47 (emphasis added). The trial court concluded that this term in claim 1 "requires that the guard substantially contain the needle-assembly at all times." Because the Platypus is a "stand-alone guard" without a needle, the trial court granted summary judgment of non-infringement to the defendants on multiple claims.

In the first place, claim 1 expressly recites the presence of a needle as part of the sliding assembly. Thus, the claimed "assembly" would not be complete without a needle. The claim also uses the term "enclosing." In the context of an invention "for locking a needle in a shielded position as the needle is removed from a patient," that language suggests constant shielding or covering of the sharp. '311 patent, col. 2, ll. 8–9. The specification reinforces that suggestion:

> [T]he guard is folded about its hinge position and locked . . . into a generally cylindrical, folded configuration. Alternatively, the guard may be molded . . . to enclose a sliding hub/needle assembly that has been positioned between the two pieces.

'311 patent, col. 2, ll. 53–58. By emphasizing that the guard is locked in a protective configuration, or molded to enclose the needle assembly, the specification conveys the concept of a permanent cover for the needle. Indeed, the figures in the specification show a completely enclosed, and thus guarded, needle. Figures 15–19 also show the needle hub as permanently housed in the guard. '311 patent, figures 15–19. The trial court also methodically considered and rejected each of DSU's arguments that the term means only generally surrounding the needle and hub. This court concurs in the district court's analysis.

The court also construed "slot," as used in claims 1, 46, and 52. The relevant portion of claim 46 is:

> 46. A guard for slidably enclosing a sliding assembly . . . said guard comprising . . .
>
> a hollow member proportioned for receiving said needle and winged needle hub, said hollow member defining at least one longitudinal *slot* proportioned to receive a wing of said needle hub projecting outwardly through the slot when the needle hub resides within the hollow member in sliding relation thereto, and means, associated with the hollow member, for engaging said wing projecting through said *slot* when the needle and hub are in a slidingly retracted position in which the needle is enclosed by the hollow member for locking said needle hub and needle in said retracted position.

'311 patent, col. 20, ll. 20–39 (emphases added).... The trial court held that the term did not require "a defined width." Later the district court, at the request of defendants, clarified that " '[s]lot' shall mean 'an opening in the guard capable of receiving a wing that projects through the opening and having both an upper edge and a lower edge that are defined by the sidewall of the guard.' " In claim 46, because "proportioned to receive" modifies "slot," the trial court explained that "slot" "shall mean 'sized relative to the wing so that the wing extends through the slot when the hub is within the hollow member and so said slot can accommodate the wing's movement as it translates the length of the slot.' "

The trial court identified the crux of the dispute over "slot" as "whether ... the slots for the wings should have defined widths closely approximating the wings' thickness." If "slot" limits the size of the opening to accommodate the "minor" thickness of the '311 patent's wings, the Platypus would not infringe because its jaws accommodate any thickness. On the other hand, if "slot" contains no thickness limitation, the Platypus would infringe because it opens to receive a wing of any size.

The claim language recites only "slot." Thus, the claim itself does not incorporate any thickness limitation. Moreover, the specification provided no size limitation on the opening. In a tribute to its complete analysis, the trial court went beyond those primary sources to also consult the prosecution history. Phillips, 415 F.3d at 1317 (a court "should also consider the patent's prosecution history, if it is in evidence"). The record before the Patent Office shows that the patentees amended the claims of Application Serial Number 252,564, which is the application from which the '311 patent (and '072 patent) derived, to avoid U.S. Patent No. 4,840,619 (Hughes Patent).

In amending the claims to avoid the Hughes Patent, however, the applicant did not limit the size of the slot, as argued by JMS and ITL. The amendments concerned only the orientation of the needle wings that moved back and forth through the slot. To distinguish the Hughes Patent, the patentee did not have to, and did not actually, limit the width of the slot. Thus, the trial court correctly construed "slot" as not requiring a defined width, as long as it was capable of receiving a wing.

Under this claim construction, the trial court found that "as a matter of law, every reasonable jury would find that there is a slot in the [Platypus] closed-shell configuration." Therefore, the trial court held that when sold in the United States in its "closed-shell" configuration, the Platypus literally infringed claims 46–47, 49, and 52–53 of '311 patent, when closed over the tubing of a needle-set.

This court holds that the trial court correctly concluded that the closed-shell configuration of the Platypus does have a slot. As applied to the Platypus, its slot is an opening in a needle guard capable of receiving a wing that projects through the opening. Further, the slot has both an upper edge and a lower edge defined by the sidewall of the guard. The Platypus's slot is also sized relative to the wing and can accommodate the needle wing as it moves through the length of the slot. Furthermore, the Platypus contains the other limitations of claims 46–47, 49, and 52–53 of the '311 patent. Therefore, in its closed-shell configuration, the Platypus does infringe claims 46–47, 49, and 52–53 of the '311 patent. [DSU's damages were based on this literal infringement.]

III.

The jury found that JMS North America and JMS directly and contributorily infringed, and that JMS additionally induced JMS North America to infringe. However, the jury returned a verdict of non-infringement in favor of ITL. Id., at 453–54. The jury entered a verdict finding that ITL did not engage in contributory infringement or inducement to infringe. Id., at 453. The trial court denied DSU's motion for new trial on the jury's verdict that ITL did not contributorily infringe or induce infringement.

A.

On appeal, DSU argues that ITL committed contributory infringement. According to DSU, the Platypus, which ITL sold to JMS, had no substantial noninfringing use. Therefore, DSU argues, ITL committed contributory infringement as a matter of law. ITL responds that it made and sold "most Platypus guards" outside of the United States. ITL also contends that the record contains no evidence that the Platypus was used in an infringing manner in the United States.

The Platypus sets that came into the United States fall within three categories:

(1) JMS imported into the United States approximately 30 million Platypus guards that, prior to importation into the United States, it had already assembled into the closed-shell configuration, combined with needle sets. These units accounted for the vast majority of Platypus sales in the United States.

(2) Fresenius purchased approximately 3.5 million Platypus guards, in the open-shell configuration without needle sets. ITL billed JMS for the shipments and shipped them to Fresenius in the United States at JMS's request. Fresenius ultimately decided that guards without needle sets did not meet FDA regulations, and it returned about 3 million.

(3) ITL sent approximately 15,000 Platypus in the open-shell configuration to JMS in San Francisco. DSU introduced no evidence that those units were ever put into the closed-shell configuration in the United States.

Additionally, the record contained evidence that when instructed to do so by JMS, ITL would ship Platypus guard units F.O.B. into the United

States. The record also shows, however, that ITL only sold the Platypus in its open-shell configuration.

In discussing 35 U.S.C. § 271(c), the Supreme Court stated:

> One who makes and sells articles which are only adapted to be used in a patented combination will be presumed to intend the natural consequences of his acts; he will be presumed to intend that they shall be used in the combination of the patent.

Metro–Goldwyn–Mayer Studios, Inc. v. Grokster, Ltd., 545 U.S. 913 (2005). In addition, the patentee always has the burden to show direct infringement for each instance of indirect infringement. *Joy Techs., Inc. v. Flakt, Inc.*, 6 F.3d 770, 774 (Fed.Cir.1993) ("Liability for either active inducement of infringement or contributory infringement is dependent upon the existence of direct infringement."). Thus, to prevail on contributory infringement, DSU must have shown that ITL made and sold the Platypus, that the Platypus has no substantial non-infringing uses in its closed-shell configuration, that ITL engaged in conduct (made sales) within the United States that contributed to another's direct infringement, and that JMS engaged in an act of direct infringement on those sales that ITL made in the United States.

The trial court properly applied these legal principles. The trial court determined that the record showed that ITL supplied the Platypus, that the Platypus had no substantial non-infringing uses in its closed-shell configuration, and that ITL intended to make the Platypus that resulted in the potential for contributory infringement as a product designed for use in the patented combination. In fact, even beyond the minimal intent requirement for contributory infringement, ITL acted with the knowledge of the '311 patent and knowledge that the component was especially made or adapted for use in an infringing manner. *Id.*, slip op. at 22–24. However, the district court denied the motion for a new trial because the record does not show that "the alleged contributory act ha[d] a direct nexus to a specific act of direct infringement." In denying the new trial, the court stated:

> And while it is true that Plaintiffs introduced evidence that "ITL sold and shipped millions of 'stand alone' guards directly to United States customers, including JMS [North America] and end-users like Fresenius," there was no direct evidence at trial establishing that these guards were actually closed and used as an act of direct infringement in the United States.

Id., slip op. at 26.

Upon review of the record, this court perceives, as well, an absence of evidence of direct infringement to which ITL contributed in the United States. Under the terms of the '311 patent, the Platypus only infringes in the closed-shell configuration. When open, the Platypus, for instance, lacks a "slot" as well as other claimed features. ITL only contributed to placing the Platypus into the closed-shell configuration in Malaysia (category 1, above); not in the United States. Section 271(c) has a territorial limitation requiring contributory acts to occur in the United States. Furthermore, this court cannot reverse a jury verdict of non-infringement on mere inferences that the Platypus guard units sold in the United States (i.e., the open-shell configuration in categories 2 and 3, above) were put into the infringing closed-shell configuration. The record does not show that the Platypus guards ITL shipped into the United States in the open-shell configuration were ever put into an infringing configuration, i.e., closed-shell. On categories 2 and 3, above, the record contains no evidence of direct infringement, i.e., that the open-shell Platypus guards imported by ITL were sold or used in their closed-shell configuration. As a result, the trial court did not abuse its discretion in denying DSU's motion for new trial on ITL's contributory infringement.

On the issue of induced infringement, DSU argues that ITL induced infringement by inducing JMS to sell the closed-shell configuration in the United States. The district court denied DSU's motion for a new trial on the ground that, although JMS directly infringed, ITL did not intend JMS to infringe.

B.

RESOLUTION OF CONFLICTING PRECEDENT

Opinion for the court filed by Circuit Judge Rader, with Newman, Lourie, Schall, Bryson, Gajarsa, Linn, Dyk, Prost, and Moore, Circuit Judges, join. Concurring opinion filed by Michel, Chief Judge, and Mayer, Circuit Judge.

This court addresses Part III. B., of this opinion en banc. This section addresses, in the context of induced infringement, "the required intent . . . to induce the specific acts of [infringement] or additionally to cause an infringement." This section clarifies that intent requirement by holding en banc that, as was stated in *Manville Sales Corp. v. Paramount Systems, Inc.*, 917 F.2d 544, 554 (Fed.Cir.1990), "[t]he plaintiff has the burden of showing that the alleged infringer's actions induced infringing acts and that he knew or should have known his actions would induce actual infringements." The requirement that the alleged infringer knew or should have known his actions would induce actual infringement necessarily includes the requirement that he or she knew of the patent.

DSU claims the district court improperly instructed the jury on the state of mind necessary to prove inducement to infringe under 35 U.S.C. § 271(b). . . . Under section 271(b), "[w]hoever actively induces infringement of a patent shall be liable as an infringer." 35 U.S.C. § 271(b). To establish liability under section 271(b), a patent holder must prove that once the defendants knew of the patent, they "actively and knowingly aid[ed] and abett[ed] another's direct infringement." *Water Technologies Corp. v. Calco, Ltd.*, 850 F.2d 660, 668 (Fed.Cir.1988) (emphasis in original). However, "knowledge of the acts alleged to constitute infringement" is not enough. The "mere knowledge of possible infringement by others does not amount to inducement; specific intent and action to induce infringement must be proven."

DSU asked the court to instruct the jury, purportedly in accordance with *Hewlett–Packard Co. v. Bausch & Lomb, Inc.*, 909 F.2d 1464 (Fed.Cir. 1990), that to induce infringement, the inducer need only intend to cause the acts of the third party that constitute direct infringement. The trial court gave the following instruction to the jury:

> The defendant must have intended to cause the acts that constitute the direct infringement and must have known or should have known than[sic] its action would cause the direct infringement. Unlike direct infringement, which must take place within the United States, induced infringement does not require any activity by the indirect infringer in this country, as long as the direct infringement occurs here.

Thus, the court charged the jury in accordance with *Manville*. The statute does not define whether the purported infringer must intend to induce the infringement or whether the purported infringer must merely intend to engage in the acts that induce the infringement regardless of whether it knows it is causing another to infringe. DSU complains that the instruction is incorrect because it requires that the inducer possess specific intent to encourage another's infringement, and not merely that the inducer had knowledge of the acts alleged to constitute infringement.

In *Grokster*, which was a copyright case, the Supreme Court cited with approval this court's decision in Water Technologies when it discussed inducement of infringement, stating:

> The rule on inducement of infringement as developed in the early cases is no different today. Evidence of "active steps ... taken to encourage direct infringement," such as advertising an infringing use or instructing how to engage in an infringing use, show an affirmative intent that the product be used to infringe, and a showing that infringement was encouraged overcomes the law's reluctance to find liability when a defendant merely sells a commercial product suitable for some lawful use.

Grokster, 125 S.Ct. at 2779 (citation and footnote omitted). As a result, if an entity offers a product with the object of promoting its use to infringe, as shown by clear expression or other affirmative steps taken to foster infringement, it is then liable for the resulting acts of infringement by third parties. *Id*. at 2780. "The inducement rule ... premises liability on purposeful, culpable expression and conduct...." *Id*.

Grokster, thus, validates this court's articulation of the state of mind requirement for inducement. *See Manville*, 917 F.2d at 544. In *Manville*, this court held that the "alleged infringer must be shown ... to have knowingly induced infringement," 917 F.2d at 553, not merely knowingly induced the acts that constitute direct infringement. This court explained its "knowing" requirement:

It must be established that the defendant possessed specific intent to encourage another's infringement and not merely that the defendant had knowledge of the acts alleged to constitute inducement. The plaintiff has the burden of showing that the alleged infringer's actions induced infringing acts and that he knew or should have known his actions would induce actual infringements.

Id. at 553. In *Water Technologies*, also cited with approval by the Supreme Court, 125 S.Ct. at 2779, this court clarified: "While proof of intent is necessary, direct evidence is not required; rather, circumstantial evidence may suffice." 850 F.2d at 668. Although this court stated "that proof of actual intent to cause the acts which constitute the infringement is a necessary prerequisite to finding active inducement," *Hewlett–Packard*, 909 F.2d at 1469, *Grokster* has clarified that the intent requirement for inducement requires more than just intent to cause the acts that produce direct infringement. Beyond that threshold knowledge, the inducer must have an affirmative intent to cause direct infringement. In the words of a recent decision, inducement requires " 'that the alleged infringer knowingly induced infringement and possessed specific intent to encourage another's infringement.' " *MEMC Elec.*, 420 F.3d at 1378 (Fed.Cir.2005). Accordingly, inducement requires evidence of culpable conduct, directed to encouraging another's infringement, not merely that the inducer had knowledge of the direct infringer's activities. *Grokster*, 125 S.Ct. at 2780. Accordingly, the district court correctly instructed the jury in this case.

C.

In denying the motion for new trial, the trial court stated:

> Although Plaintiffs introduced circumstantial evidence which permitted inferences of ITL's intentions, it is up to the Jury to decide whether or not to draw any inference and to consider the weight of any such evidence. Assessing competing evidence is what the law asks juries to do, and the Court declines to take over this fundamental role of the Jury.

The jury heard evidence about the commercial transactions between ITL and JMS, including JMS's intention to sell ITL's Platypus to Fresenius until JMS could get its own WingEater approved by the Food and Drug Administration (FDA) and ready for market. The jury also heard evidence that Mr. Utterberg's lawyer informed ITL in January 1997 that the Platypus infringed the '311 patent. Additionally, the jury learned that ITL contacted an Australian attorney, who concluded that its Platypus would not infringe. JMS and ITL then also obtained letters from U.S. patent counsel advising that the Platypus did not infringe. Mr. William Mobbs, one of the owners of ITL who had participated in the design of the Platypus, testified that ITL had no intent to infringe the '311 patent.

Thus, on this record, the jury was well within the law to conclude that ITL did not induce JMS to infringe by purposefully and culpably encouraging JMS's infringement. To the contrary, the record contains evidence that ITL did not believe its Platypus infringed. Therefore, it had no intent to infringe. Accordingly, the record supports the jury's verdict based on the evidence showing a lack of the necessary specific intent. The trial court certainly did not abuse its discretion.

AFFIRMED

NOTES

1. **Distinguishing § 271(b) and § 271(c).** Students who attempt to determine the distinction between § 271(b) and (c) by looking only at these two statutory paragraphs will find the exercise bewildering indeed. In fact, all conduct which falls under § 271(c) could also fall under § 271(b). Section 271(b) is drawn towards situations where the technology has multiple uses, only one of which infringes. Section 271(c) addresses situations where only a single substantial infringing use exists. Because mere promotion of technology could by itself constitute an inducement where the only substantial use of that technology infringes, all conduct falling under § 271(c) would also be addressed by § 271(b).

Why, then, does § 271 house these two paragraphs? A review of § 271(d) reveals the elusive answer: Congress had declared that conduct falling under § 271(c) does not constitute misuse of the patent.

2. **Dependent Infringement.** The Federal Circuit sometimes groups the concepts of induced and contributory infringement under the rubric of "dependent infringement." *See Joy Technologies, Inc. v. Flakt, Inc.*, 6 F.3d 770 (Fed.Cir.1993).

3. **Liability of Officers and Directors.** Section 271(b) has also served as a font of personal liability for officers and directors of corporations under the traditional theory of "piercing the corporate veil." *See Orthokinetics, Inc. v. Safety Travel Chairs, Inc.*, 806 F.2d 1565 (Fed.Cir.1986). Thus, "[t]he tort of 'inducement' under 35 U.S.C.A. Section 271(b), when applied to invoke personal liability, is premised on a concept of tortfeasance whereby persons in authority and control may in appropriate circumstances be deemed liable for wrongdoing, when inducing direct infringement by another." *Sensonics, Inc. v. Aerosonic Corp.*, 81 F.3d 1566 (Fed.Cir.1996). *Hoover Group Inc. v. Custom Metalcraft Inc.*, 84 F.3d 1408 (Fed.Cir.1996), discusses what these "appropriate circumstances" might be:

> [A]cts of a corporate officer that are within the scope of the officer's responsibility are not always sufficient grounds for penetrating the corporate protection and imposing personal liability. The policy considerations that underlie the corporate structure yield to personal liability for corporate acts only in limited circumstances.

> In general, a corporate officer is personally liable for his tortious acts, just as any individual may be liable for a civil wrong. This general rule "does not

depend on the same grounds as 'piercing the corporate veil,' that is, inadequate capitalization, use of the corporate form for fraudulent purposes, or failure to comply with the formalities of corporate organization." *Crigler v. Salac*, 438 So.2d 1375, 1380 (Ala.1983). When personal wrongdoing is not supported by legitimate corporate activity, the courts have assigned personal liability for wrongful actions even when taken on behalf of the corporation. However, this liability has been qualified, in extensive jurisprudence, by the distinction between commercial torts committed in the course of the officer's employment, and negligent and other culpable wrongful acts.

Thus when a person in a control position causes the corporation to commit a civil wrong, imposition of personal liability requires consideration of the nature of the wrong, the culpability of the act, and whether the person acted in his/her personal interest or that of the corporation. *See* 3A WILLIAM MEADE FLETCHER, FLETCHER CYCLOPEDIA OF THE LAW OF PRIVATE CORPORATIONS §§ 1134–1166 (1994 Revised Volume) (XXIX "Liability of Officers and Directors to Third Persons for Torts"). The decisions have not always distinguished among the various legal premises, i.e. (1) justification for piercing the corporate veil based on such criteria as absence of corporate assets or use of the corporate form for illegal purposes; (2) corporate commitment of a commercial tort (such as interference with contract or business advantage, or patent infringement) caused by the officer acting as agent of the corporation; (3) actions similar to (2) but exacerbated by culpable intent or bad faith on the part of the officer; or (4) personal commitment of a fraudulent or grossly negligent act.

For example, corporate officers have been held personally liable when they participated in conversion, breach of fiduciary duty, fraud, and malicious prosecution; and have been held not to be personally liable for commercial torts such as interference with contractual relations if they were acting in the corporation's interest. The fact-dependency of such issues is apparent in decisions relating to patent infringement.

For an example of the latter point, compare *Sensonics*, affirming an award of officer liability under § 271(b), with *Hoover Group*, which reversed a similar judgment.

4. The *Aro* Decisions and the Implied Right to Repair. A pair of Supreme Court cases resulting from the same patent litigation, *Aro Manufacturing Co. v. Convertible Top Replacement Co.*, 365 U.S. 336 (1961) ("*Aro I*") and *Aro Manufacturing Co. v. Convertible Top Replacement Co.*, 377 U.S. 476 (1964) ("*Aro II*"), are the leading authorities on contributory infringement and the implied right to repair. This principle essentially holds that a purchaser of patented goods obtains an implied license to repair a patented good; thus, those who sell replacement parts to the patentee's customers cannot be held to have committed contributory infringement.

The patent at issue in the *Aro* cases was directed towards the combination of various mechanical parts and a cloth top for a convertible automobile. Certain car manufacturers employed the claimed invention, including General Motors, which took a license under the patent, and Ford Motor, which did not. When the patentee brought suit against a manufacturer of replacement cloth tops, the Supreme Court held that General Motors customers possessed the right to repair their cars by replacing the tops. Because no direct infringement had occurred, neither could the defendant be found a contributory infringer. However, because Ford Motor customers had no right to employ the claimed invention, the defendant was liable for contributory infringement with respect to those cars.

A more contemporary decision is set forth below.

JAZZ PHOTO CORP. v. INTERNATIONAL TRADE COMM.

United States Court of Appeals, Federal Circuit, 2001
264 F.3d 1094

Before NEWMAN, MICHEL, and GAJARSA, Circuit Judges.

PAULINE NEWMAN, CIRCUIT JUDGE.

In an action brought under section 337 of the Tariff Act of 1930 as amended, 19 U.S.C. § 1337, Fuji Photo Film Co. charged twenty-seven respondents, including the appellants Jazz Photo Corporation, Dynatec International, Inc., and Opticolor, Inc., with infringement of fifteen patents owned by Fuji. The charge was based on the respondents' importation of used "single-use" cameras called "lens-fitted film packages" (LFFP's), which had been refurbished for reuse in various overseas facilities. Section 337 makes unlawful "[t]he importation into the United States ... of articles that ... infringe a valid and enforceable United States patent ... [or that] are made, produced, processed, ... under, or by means of, a process covered by the claims of a valid and enforceable United States patent." 19 U.S.C. § 1337(a)(1)(B). Eight respondents did not respond to the Commission's complaint, ten more failed to appear before the Commission, and one was dismissed. Eight respondents participated in the hearing, and three have taken this appeal.

The Commission determined that twenty-six respondents, including the appellants, had infringed all or most of the claims in suit of fourteen Fuji United States patents, and issued a General Exclusion Order and Order to Cease and Desist. *In the Matter of Certain Lens–Fitted Film Packages,* Inv. No. 337–TA–406 (Int'l Trade Comm'n June 28, 1999). This court stayed the Commission's orders during this appeal. *Dynatec Int'l, Inc. v. Int'l Trade Comm'n,* No. 99–1504 (Fed.Cir. Sept. 24, 1999) (unpublished).

The Commission's decision rests on its ruling that the refurbishment of the used cameras is prohibited "reconstruction," as opposed to permissible "repair." On review of the law and its application, we conclude that precedent does not support the Commission's application of the law to the facts that were found. We conclude that for used cameras whose first sale was in the United States with the patentee's authorization, and for which the respondents permitted verification of their representations that their activities were limited to the steps of (1) removing the cardboard cover, (2) cutting open the plastic casing, (3) inserting new film and a container to receive the film, (4) replacing the winding wheel for certain cameras, (5) replacing the battery for flash cameras, (6) resetting the counter, (7) resealing the outer case, and (8) adding a new cardboard cover, the totality of these procedures does not satisfy the standards required by precedent for prohibited reconstruction; precedent requires, as we shall discuss, that the described activities be deemed to be permissible repair.

[handwritten marginalia: only repair allowed]

For those cameras that meet the criteria outlined above, the Commission's ruling of patent infringement is reversed and the Commission's exclusion and cease and desist orders are vacated. For all other cameras, the Commission's orders are affirmed.

[handwritten marginalia: Commissioners ruling overturned]

DISCUSSION

* * *

The Patented Inventions

The LFFP is a relatively simple camera, whose major elements are an outer plastic casing that holds a shutter, a shutter release button, a lens, a viewfinder, a film advance mechanism, a film counting display, and for some models a flash assembly and battery. The casing also contains a holder for a roll of film, and a container into which the exposed film is wound. At the factory a roll of film is loaded into the camera. The casing is then sealed by ultrasonic welding or light-tight latching, and a cardboard cover is applied to encase the camera.

[handwritten marginalia: Simple single use camera]

LFFPs are intended by the patentee to be used only once. After the film is exposed the photo-processor removes the film container by breaking open a pre-weakened portion of the plastic casing which is accessed by removal of the cardboard cover. Discarded LFFPs, subsequently purchased and refurbished by the respondents, are the subject of this action.

The parts of an LFFP are illustrated in Figure 8 of the '087 patent:

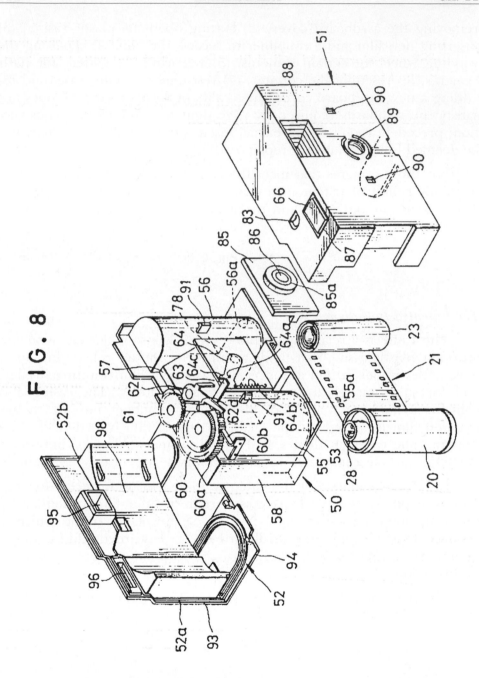

FIG. 8

Claim 1 of the '087 patent is representative of claims directed to the entire LFFP:

1. A lens-fitted photographic film package having an externally operable member for effecting an exposure, comprising:

a light-tight film casing which must be destroyed to open the same, having an opening through which said exposure is made when said externally operable member is operated;

an unexposed rolled film disposed on one side of said opening in said light-tight casing;

a removable light-tight film container having a film winding spool therein disposed on the opposite side of said opening in said light-tight casing from said rolled film, one end of said rolled film being attached to said film winding spool;

means for winding said rolled film into said light-tight film container and around said film winding spool;

and winding control means responsive to operation of said externally operable member for allowing said film winding spool to rotate so as to enable said rolled film to be advanced by only one frame after every exposure; said winding control means including: a sprocket wheel driven by movement of said rolled film;

and a frame counter driven by said sprocket wheel, said frame counter being provided with indications designating a series of frame numbers and means for disabling said winding control means responsive to said frame counter indicating there remains on said unexposed film no film frame capable of being exposed.

Other patents are directed to various components of the LFFP. The '857 patent is directed to a specific film winding mechanism. The '495 patent is directed to a mechanism whereby the film in the LFFP is advanced smoothly without being scratched or gouged, and which prevents the film roll from becoming loose. The '774 patent is directed to the film chambers and film path. The '364 patent claims the LFFP with a flash unit comprising a circuit board, a capacitor, a discharge (flash) tube, and a battery. The '111 patent is directed to the pushbutton that trips the shutter and has a protective structure that prevents the pushbutton from accidentally being depressed. The '200 patent is directed to the shutter mechanism, including the shutter mount, shutter opening, and shutter blade. The '288 patent claims an LFFP in which the winding wheel and film cassette are positively linked through a gear and shaft mechanism requiring the two to rotate relative to each other, avoiding the loss of usable film. The '685 patent is directed to an LFFP assembly that allows easier recycling of used plastic and metal, in which the plastic casing including the film path and film chambers is easily separable from the photo-taking unit containing metal parts including the shutter mechanism and the winding and stop mechanisms.

FIG. 1

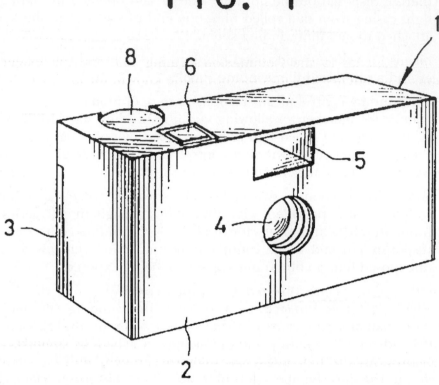

[handwritten margin notes: not in dispute / refurbished camera is the same / most refused discovery / steps taken]

It is not disputed that the imported refurbished cameras contain all of the elements of all or most of the claims in suit.

The Accused Activities

The appellants import used LFFPs that have been refurbished by various overseas entities (called "remanufacturers" in the ITC proceeding). Some of the remanufacturers refused discovery entirely or in part, and some presented evidence that the ALJ found incomplete or not credible. The Commission explains: "Since so little was known about the accused infringing processes, the ALJ considered the common steps that each participating respondent admitted during the hearing were part of their processes." ITC Brief at 15–16. The ALJ summarized these common steps as follows:

removing the cardboard cover;

opening the LFFP body (usually by cutting at least one weld);

replacing the winding wheel or modifying the film cartridge to be inserted;

resetting the film counter;

replacing the battery in flash LFFPs;

winding new film out of a canister onto a spool or into a roll;

resealing the LFFP body using tape and/or glue;

applying a new cardboard cover.

Initial Determination at 108–109. The Commission held that these activities constitute prohibited reconstruction. In view of this holding, it was not material to the Commission's ruling that the full extent of various respondents' activities was not made known, for in all events the importation would be infringing and unlawful.

The appellants argue that they are not building new LFFPs, but simply replacing the film in used cameras. They argue that the LFFPs have a useful life longer than the single use proposed by Fuji, that the patent right has been exhausted as to these articles, and that the patentee can not restrict their right to refit the cameras with new film by the procedures necessary to insert the film and reset the mechanism. Unless these activities are deemed to be permissible, infringement of at least some of the patents in suit is conceded.

* * *

The Law of Permissible Repair and Prohibited Reconstruction

The distinction between permitted and prohibited activities, with respect to patented items after they have been placed in commerce by the patentee, has been distilled into the terms "repair" and "reconstruction." The purchaser of a patented article has the rights of any owner of personal property, including the right to use it, repair it, modify it, discard it, or resell it, subject only to overriding conditions of the sale. Thus patented articles when sold "become the private individual property of the purchasers, and are no longer specifically protected by the patent laws." *Mitchell v. Hawley*, 83 U.S. (16 Wall.) 544, 548, 21 L.Ed. 322 (1872). The fact that an article is patented gives the purchaser neither more nor less rights of use and disposition. However, the rights of ownership do not include the right to construct an essentially new article on the template of the original, for the right to make the article remains with the patentee.

While the ownership of a patented article does not include the right to make a substantially new article, it does include the right to preserve the useful life of the original article. It is readily apparent that there is a continuum between these concepts; precedent demonstrates that litigated cases rarely reside at the poles wherein "repair" is readily distinguished from "reconstruction." Thus the law has developed in the body of precedent, illustrating the policy underlying the law as it has been applied in diverse factual contexts. *Cf. Goodyear Shoe Mach. Co. v. Jackson*, 112 F. 146, 150 (1st Cir.1901) ("It is impracticable, as well as unwise, to attempt to lay down any rule on this subject, owing to the number and infinite variety of patented inventions.")

The principle of the distinction between permissible and prohibited activities was explained in *Wilson v. Simpson*, 50 U.S. (9 How.) 109, 13

L.Ed. 66 (1850), where the Court distinguished the right of a purchaser of a patented planing machine to replace the machine's cutting-knives when they became dull or broken, from the patentee's sole right to make or renew the entire machine. The Court observed that the knives had to be replaced every 60–90 days whereas the machines would last for several years, explaining, "what harm is done to the patentee in the use of his right of invention, when the repair and replacement of a partial injury are confined to the machine which the purchaser has bought?" *Id.* at 123.

This principle underlies the application of the law. It was elaborated by the Court in *Aro Manufacturing Co. v. Convertible Top Replacement Co.,* 365 U.S. 336, 81 S.Ct. 599, 5 L.Ed.2d 592 (1961), where the patented combination was a fabric convertible top and the associated metal support structure. The Court explained that replacement of the worn fabric top constituted permissible repair of the patented combination, and could not be controlled by the patentee. The Court restated the principles that govern the inquiry as applied to replacement of unpatented parts of a patented article:

> The decisions of this Court require the conclusion that reconstruction of a patented entity, comprised of unpatented elements, is limited to such a true reconstruction of the entity as to "in fact make a new article," *United States v. Aluminum Co. of America,* [148 F.2d 416, 425 (2d Cir.1945)], after the entity, viewed as a whole, has become spent. In order to call the monopoly, conferred by the patent grant, into play for a second time, it must, indeed, be a second creation of the patented entity, as, for example, in *American Cotton–Tie Co. v. Simmons,* [106 U.S. 89, 1 S.Ct. 52 (1882)]. Mere replacement of individual unpatented parts, one at a time, whether of the same part repeatedly or different parts successively, is no more than the lawful right of the owner to repair his property. 365 U.S. at 346, 81 S.Ct. 599.

This right of repair, provided that the activity does not "in fact make a new article," accompanies the article to succeeding owners. In *Wilbur–Ellis Co. v. Kuther,* 377 U.S. 422, 84 S.Ct. 1561, 12 L.Ed.2d 419 (1964), the Court dealt with the refurbishing of patented fish-canning machines by a purchaser of used machines. The Court held that the fairly extensive refurbishment by the new owner, including modification and resizing of six separate parts of the machine, although more than customary repair of spent or broken components, was more like repair then reconstruction, for it extended the useful life of the original machine. *See id.* at 425 ("Petitioners in adapting the old machines to a related use were doing more than repair in the customary sense; but what they did was kin to repair for it bore on the useful capacity of the old combination, on which the royalty had been paid.").

Precedent has classified as repair the disassembly and cleaning of patented articles accompanied by replacement of unpatented parts that had become worn or spent, in order to preserve the utility for which the article was originally intended. In *General Electric Co. v. United States*, 215 Ct.Cl. 636, 572 F.2d 745 (1978), the court held that the Navy's large-scale "overhauling" of patented gun mounts, including disassembly into their component parts and replacement of parts that could not be repaired with parts from other gun mounts or new parts, was permissible repair of the original gun mounts. The court explained that the assembly-line method of reassembly, without regard to where each component had originated, was simply a matter of efficiency and economy, with the same effect as if each gun mount had been refurbished individually by disassembly and reassembly of its original components with replacement of a minor amount of worn elements. *Id.* at 780–86, 198 USPQ at 95–100.

Similarly, in *Dana Corp. v. American Precision Co.*, 827 F.2d 755 (Fed.Cir.1987), the court held that the "rebuilding" of worn truck clutches, although done on a commercial scale, was permissible repair. The defendants in *Dana Corp.* acquired worn clutches that had been discarded by their original owners, disassembled them, cleaned and sorted the individual parts, replaced worn or defective parts with new or salvaged parts, and reassembled the clutches. Although the patentee stressed that some new parts were used and that the rebuilding was a large scale commercial operation, the activity was held to be repair. *Id.* at 759, 827 F.2d 755. The court also observed that in general the new parts were purchased from Dana, the original manufacturer of the patented clutches, and that repair of used clutches was contemplated by the patentee. The court rejected the argument that the complete disassembly and production-line reassembly of the clutches constituted a voluntary destruction followed by a "second creation of the patented entity," invoking the phrase of *Aro Manufacturing*, 365 U.S. at 346, 81 S.Ct. 599.

"Reconstruction," precedent shows, requires a more extensive rebuilding of the patented entity than is exemplified in *Aro Manufacturing*, *Wilbur–Ellis*, *General Electric*, and *Dana Corp. See also, e.g., Bottom Line Mgmt., Inc. v. Pan Man, Inc.*, 228 F.3d 1352 (Fed.Cir.2000) (repair of cooking device by reapplying non-stick coating); *Hewlett–Packard Co. v. Repeat–O–Type Stencil Mfg. Corp.*, 123 F.3d 1445 (Fed.Cir.1997) (modifying unused printer cartridges akin to repair); *Kendall Co. v. Progressive Med. Tech., Inc.*, 85 F.3d 1570 (Fed.Cir.1996) (replacement of used pressure sleeve in medical device is repair); *Sage Prods., Inc. v. Devon Indus., Inc.*, 45 F.3d 1575 (Fed.Cir.1995) (replacement of inner container for medical waste is repair); *FMC Corp. v. Up–Right, Inc.*, 21 F.3d 1073 (Fed.Cir.1994) (replacing worn unpatented picking heads of harvester is repair); *Everpure, Inc. v. Cuno, Inc.*, 875 F.2d 300 (Fed.Cir.1989) (replacement of entire cartridge containing spent filter is repair); *Porter v. Farmers Supply Serv., Inc.*, 790 F.2d 882 (Fed.Cir.1986) (replacement of disks in tomato harvester head is repair). In contrast, in *Sandvik Aktiebolag v. E.J. Co.*, 121 F.3d 669 (Fed.Cir.1997), reconstruction was held to apply when a patented drill bit was "recreated" by construction of an entirely new cutting tip after the existing cutting tip could no longer be resharpened and reused. The court explained that it was not dispositive that the cutting tip was the "novel feature" of the invention, but that prohibited reconstruction occurred because a "new article" was made after the patented article, "viewed as a whole, has become spent." *See also Lummus Indus., Inc. v. D.M. & E. Corp.*, 862 F.2d 267 (Fed.Cir.1988) (jury verdict of reconstruction for cutter wheels that were material part of patented invention).

Underlying the repair/reconstruction dichotomy is the principle of exhaustion of the patent right. The unrestricted sale of a patented article, by or with the authority of the patentee, "exhausts" the patentee's right to control further sale and use of that article by enforcing the patent under which it was first sold. In *United States v. Masonite Corp.*, 316 U.S. 265, 278, 62 S.Ct. 1070, 86 L.Ed. 1461 (1942), the Court explained that exhaustion of the patent right depends on "whether or not there has been such a disposition of the article that it may fairly be said that the patentee has received his reward for the use of the article." *See, e.g., Intel Corp. v. ULSI Sys. Tech., Inc.*, 995 F.2d 1566, 1568 (Fed.Cir.1993) ("The law is well settled that an authorized sale of a patented product places that product beyond the reach of the patent."). Thus when a patented device has been lawfully sold in the United States, subsequent purchasers inherit the same immunity under the doctrine of patent exhaustion. However, the prohibition that the product may not be the vehicle for a "second creation of the patented entity" continues to apply, for such re-creation exceeds the rights that accompanied the initial sale.

Fuji states that some of the imported LFFP cameras originated and were sold only overseas, but are included in the refurbished importations by some of the respondents. The record supports this statement, which does not appear to be disputed. United States patent rights are not exhausted by products of foreign provenance. To invoke the protection of the first sale doctrine, the authorized first sale must have occurred under the United States patent. *See Boesch v. Graff*, 133 U.S. 697, 701–703, 10 S.Ct. 378, 33 L.Ed. 787 (1890) (a lawful foreign purchase does not obviate the need for license from the United States patentee before importation into and sale in the United States). Our decision applies only to LFFPs for which the United States patent right has been exhausted by first sale in the United States. Imported LFFPs of solely foreign provenance are not immunized from infringement of United States patents by the nature of their refurbishment.

Application of the Law

In the Commission's Initial Determination the administrative judge, applying the four factors discussed in *Sandvik Aktiebolag*, 121 F.3d at 673, held that the remanufacturers had made a new LFFP after the useful life of the original LFFP had been spent. Thus, the ALJ ruled that the remanufacturers were engaged in prohibited reconstruction. The Commission adopted the ALJ's findings and conclusions that the remanufacturers were not simply repairing an article for which either the producer or the purchaser expected a longer useful life, pointing out that the purchaser discarded the camera after use. The Commission ruled that the respondents were not simply repairing the LFFP in order to achieve its intended life span, but created a new single use camera that would again be discarded by its purchaser after use.

Although the Commission's conclusion is supported by its reasoning and reflects concern for the public interest, for there was evidence of imperfections and failures of some refurbished cameras, precedent requires that these cameras be viewed as repaired, not reconstructed. In *Dana Corp.*, for example, the truck clutches had lived their intended lives as originally produced, yet the court ruled that the "rebuilding" of the used clutches was more akin to repair than to reconstruction. The activities of disassembly and rebuilding of the gun mounts of *General Electric* were similarly extensive, yet were deemed to be repair. *Aro Manufacturing* and the other Supreme Court decisions which underlie precedent require that infringing reconstruction be a "second creation" of the patented article. Although the Commission deemed this requirement met by the "remanufactured" LFFPs, precedent places the acts of inserting new film and film container, resetting the film counter, and resealing the broken case—the principal steps performed by the remanufacturers—as more akin to repair.

The Court has cautioned against reliance on any specific set of "factors" in distinguishing permissible from prohibited activities, stating in *Aro Manufacturing* that "While there is language in some lower court opinions indicating that 'repair' or 'reconstruction' depends on a number of factors, it is significant that each of the three cases of this Court, cited for that proposition, holds that a license to use a patented combination includes the right 'to preserve its fitness for use....'" 365 U.S. at 345, 81 S.Ct. 599. Indeed, this criterion is the common thread in precedent, requiring consideration of the remaining useful capacity of the article, and the nature and role of the replaced parts in achieving that useful capacity. The appellants stress that all of the original components of the LFFP except the film and battery have a useful remaining life, and are reused. The appellants state that but for the exposed roll of film and its container, any portion of the case that was broken by the photo processor, and the winding wheel in certain cameras, the refurbished LFFP is substantially the original camera, for which the patent right has been exhausted.

The Commission placed weight on Fuji's intention that the LFFP not be reused. The '087 patent specification states that forming an opening in the film package makes it impossible to reuse the film package. Therefore, it will be impossible to refill a new film into the used film package in order to reclaim a film package for reuse.

'087 patent, col. 6, lines 14–18. However, the patentee's unilateral intent, without more, does not bar reuse of the patented article, or convert repair into reconstruction. *See Hewlett–Packard,* 123 F.3d at 1453 ("a seller's intent, unless embodied in an enforceable contract, does not create a limitation on the right of a purchaser to use, sell, or modify a patented product so long as a reconstruction of the patented combination is avoided").

Claim 7 of the '087 patent is representative of those claims that specifically recite the film container and unexposed film roll, elements that are replaced by the remanufacturers:

7.   A lens-fitted photographic film package comprising:

a light-tight film casing which must be destroyed to open the same, having an opening through which an exposure is made;

a light-tight film container having a film winding spool therein disposed on one side of said opening in said light-tight film casing;

a rotatable spool disposed on the opposite side of said opening in said light-tight film casing from said light-tight film container;

one end of said spool being exposed outside said light-tight film casing;

a film roll of unexposed film of which one end is attached to said film winding spool in said light-tight film container and which is rolled around said rotatable spool.

The appellants state that the film and its removable container are commercial items, and that their replacement in a camera can not be deemed to be reconstruction. As discussed in *Aro Manufacturing,* the replacement of unpatented parts, having a shorter life than is available from the combination as a whole, is characteristic of repair, not reconstruction. On the totality of the circumstances, the changes made by the remanufacturers all relate to the replacement of the film, the LFFP otherwise remaining as originally sold.

Several of the Fuji patents in suit are directed to specific components of LFFPs, including the '495 (film path), '774 (film chambers and film path), '111 (pushbutton), '200 (shutter mechanism), '685 (recyclable LFFP body), and RE '168 (LFFP body) patents. For example, claim 1 of the '111 patent is directed to a LFFP having a pushbutton designed to avoid inadvertent activation during handling of the camera:

1.   A lens-fitted photographic film unit containing a photographic film and being adapted to take photographs, comprising:

at least one plastic pushbutton formed integrally with a wall of said film unit, only a portion of said pushbutton being separated from said wall by a slit which surrounds most but not all of said pushbutton, said pushbutton being connected to said film unit by an integral bridge, said pushbutton being adapted to be depressed inwardly of the wall from an initial position and to move back outwardly to said initial position when released;

and a barrier formed on an outer surface of said wall surrounding said pushbutton only partially, said barrier projecting outwardly relative to an actuating surface of said pushbutton when said pushbutton is in said initial position, said barrier terminating in two ends disposed on opposite sides of said bridge.

The ruling of reconstruction as to these patents is incorrect, because the remanufacturing processes simply reuse the original components, such that there is no issue of replacing parts that were separately patented. If the claimed component is not replaced, but simply is reused, this component is neither repaired nor reconstructed.

[handwritten margin note: Components are only reused not replaced]

* * *

CONCLUSION

The judgment of patent infringement is reversed with respect to LFFPs for which the patent right was exhausted by first sale in the United States, and that were permissibly repaired. Permissible repair is limited, as discussed herein, to the steps of removing the cardboard cover, cutting open the casing, inserting new film and film container, resetting the film counter, resealing the casing, and placing the device in a new cardboard cover. Included in permissible repair is replacement of the battery in flash cameras and the winding wheel in the cameras that so require. For these products the Commission's orders are vacated.

[handwritten margin note: Permissible Repair]

* * *

AFFIRMED IN PART, REVERSED IN PART, AND REMANDED; STAY LIFTED.

NOTE

1. Reconstruction at the Federal Circuit. The great majority of Federal Circuit cases addressing the distinction between repair and reconstruction find that the defendant's activities constituted the former, and therefore were noninfringing. One of the few exceptions is *Sandvik Aktiebolag v. E.J. Co.*, 121 F.3d 669 (Fed.Cir.1997). That case involved Sandvik's patented drill and a drill repair service operated by E.J. E.J. claimed that by retipping Sandvik drills, it was merely repairing them. Sandvik instead asserted that these activities amounted to an infringing reconstruction. The court sided with Sandvik, reasoning:

The drill tip was not manufactured to be a replaceable part, although it could be resharpened a number of times to extend its life. It was not intended or expected to have a life of temporary duration in comparison to the drill shank. And finally, the tip was not attached to the shank in a manner to be easily detachable. . . .

Finally, there was no intent evidenced by the patentee that would support E.J.'s argument that replacement of tips was a repair. . . . The evidence shows that Sandvik never intended its drills to be retipped. It did not manufacture or sell replacement drill tips. It did not publish instructions on how to retip its patented drills or suggest that drills could or should be retipped. Sandvik was aware that the drill tip would need occasional resharpening and instructed its customer on how to resharpen the tip. There is, therefore, no objective evidence that Sandvik's drill tip was intended to be a replaceable part. Although the repair or reconstruction issue does not turn on the intention of the patentee alone, the fact that no replacement drill tips have ever been made or sold by the patentee is consistent with the conclusion that replacement of the carbide tip is not a permissible repair.

How would you harmonize the holdings of *Jazz Photo* with *Sandvik*?

2. A [T]axing Inquiry. The distinction between repair and reconstruction can be a vexing one. In this context one court was reminded of "the apocryphal axe, of which the owner brags: 'This is my great-grandfather's original axe, although the handle has been replaced five times, and the head twice.'" *FMC Corp. v. Up–Right, Inc.*, 816 F.Supp. 1455, 1464 n. 15 (N.D.Cal.1993), *aff'd*, 21 F.3d 1073 (Fed.Cir.1994). "So what does it take to 'make' a new axe?", Professor Mark Janis asks, concluding the courts would do better to focus on the implied license between patentee and purchaser, rather than on whether the original product is sufficiently "spent." *See* Mark D. Janis, *A Tale of the Apocryphal Axe: Repair, Reconstruction and the Implied License In Intellectual Property Law*, 58 MD. L. REV. 423 (1999).

3. Exportation of Components under § 271(f). Prior to 1984 amendments to the Patent Act, the manufacture and exportation of the unassembled components of a patented article was not considered an infringing act. Exemplifying this rule was *Deepsouth Packing Co. v. Laitram Corp.*, 406 U.S. 518 (1972). Here, the defendant manufactured all the components of a patented shrimp peeler and shipped them in an unassembled state to clients abroad. The Supreme Court held that no infringement occurred because the defendant had not made or sold the combination of mechanical features that fulfilled the conditions of the asserted claims.

Congress reacted to the *Deepsouth* decision by enacting § 271(f). This provision was intended to prevent copiers from avoiding U.S. patents by supplying components of a patented product in this country so that the assembly of the components may be completed abroad. The clear parallel between § 271(f)(1) and § 271(b), as well as § 271(f)(2) and § 271(c), is discussed in *T.D. Williamson Inc. v. Laymon*, 723 F.Supp. 587 (N.D.Okla.1989), *aff'd*, 923 F.2d 871 (Fed.Cir.1990).

§ 11.5 INFRINGEMENT ANALYSES OVERSEAS

§ 11.5[a] EUROPE

Claim construction issues as well as questions of equivalence often arise in litigation involving patents issued by foreign governments. In member countries of the European Patent Convention patent claims are construed in accordance with article 69 of the convention. Perhaps the most famous claim construction cases in Europe are the quintet of cases issued in 2002 by the highest appellate court for patents in Germany, the 10th Senate of the German Federal Court (Bundesgerichtshof) and the *Kirin–Amgen* case from the British House of Lords. The later case extensively discusses the German cases as well as the availability of equivalents in Europe. Lord Hoffmann, the drafter of the principal speech in *Kirin–Amgen*, is one of the most famous patent jurists in the world.

Turning first to *Kirin–Amgen*, it involved one of the most famous inventions of the biotech era, the identification of the gene coding for human erythropoietin. Amgen built one of the largest biotechnology companies in the world largely based on this invention. The key to the Amgen invention was that Amgen was able to isolate the gene coding for human erythropoietin. Once Amgen had the gene then it was routine, but not easy, to insert the gene into Chinese hamster ovary (CHO) cells and get those cells to make human erythropoietin. This invention, made in the early 1980s, was held not to be obvious by the Federal Circuit in 1991, *Amgen Inc. v. Chugai Pharmaceutical Co.*, 927 F.2d 1200 (Fed. Cir. 1991). At the time of the invention, the only known method of using an isolated gene to make its corresponding protein was to insert the isolated gene into a cell. The cell might well be termed a "host cell" for the gene came from outside the cell. A few years later a new technology initiated the era of gene activation. Instead of inserting a gene into a cell, this technology activates human cells to make erythropoietin on their own. After all, every human cell already contains the gene that codes for the desired protein. Once modern technology can locate the erythropoietin gene within the genome of the cell, then the new gene activation technique can insert a promoter that causes the cell to make more of its own erythropoietin. With the advent of this new gene activation technology, the courts in Europe encountered the issue of whether the cell that receives a promoter to make its own human erythropoietin may be called a "host cell." After all that cell did not receive the human erythropoietin gene isolated by Amgen.

The court of first instance, the High Court (Patents Court) in London found that the "host cell" limitation was satisfied, but the Court of Appeal felt that it was not. The House of Lords then agreed with the Court of Appeal.

KIRIN–AMGEN INC AND OTHERS v. HOECHST MARION ROUSSEL LIMITED AND OTHERS

[2004] UKHL 46 Session 2003–04, [2002] EWCA Civ 1096
Thursday 21st October, 2004

HOUSE OF LORDS

Before: Lord Hoffmann, Lord Hope of Craighead, Lord Rodger of Earlsferry, Lord Walker of Gestingthorpe, Lord Brown of Eaton–Under–Heywood

JUDGMENT

LORD HOFFMANN

My Lords,

The proceedings

Extent of protection: the statutory provisions

18. Until the Patents Act 1977, which gave effect to the European Patent Convention ("EPC") there was nothing in any UK statute about the extent of protection conferred by a patent. It was governed by the common law, the terms of the royal grant and general principles of construction. It was these principles which Lord Diplock expounded in the leading case of *Catnic Components Ltd v Hill & Smith Ltd [1982] RPC 183*, which concerned a patent granted before 1977. But the EPC and the Act deal expressly with the matter in some detail. Article 84 specifies the role of the claims in an application to the European Patent Office for a European patent:

"The claims shall define the matter for which protection is sought. They shall be clear and concise and be supported by the description."

19. For present purposes, the most important provision is article 69 of the EPC, which applies to infringement proceedings in the domestic courts of all Contracting States:

"The extent of the protection conferred by a European patent or a European patent application shall be determined by the terms of the claims. Nevertheless, the description and drawings shall be used to interpret the claims."

20. In stating unequivocally that the extent of protection shall be "determined" (in German, "bestimmt") by the "terms of the claims" (den Inhalt der Patentansprüche) the Convention followed what had long been the law in the United Kingdom. During the course of the 18th and 19th centuries, practice and common law had come to distinguish between the part of the specification in which the patentee discharged his duty to disclose the best way of performing the invention and the section which delimited the scope of the monopoly which he claimed. The best-known statement of the status of the claims in UK law is by Lord Russell of Killowen in *Electric and Musical Industries Ltd v Lissen Ltd (1938) 56 RPC 23, 39*:

"The function of the claims is to define clearly and with precision the monopoly claimed, so that others may know the exact boundary of the area within which they will be trespassers. Their primary object is to limit and not to extend the monopoly. What is not claimed is disclaimed. The claims must undoubtedly be read as part of the entire document and not as a separate document; but the forbidden field must be found in the language of the claims and not elsewhere."

21.   The need to set clear limits upon the monopoly is not only, as Lord Russell emphasised, in the interests of others who need to know the area "within which they will be trespassers" but also in the interests of the patentee, who needs to be able to make it clear that he lays no claim to prior art or insufficiently enabled products or processes which would invalidate the patent.

22.   In Germany, however, the practice before 1977 in infringement proceedings (validity is determined by a different court) was commonly to treat the claims as a point of departure ("Ausgangspunkt") in determining the extent of protection, for which the criterion was the inventive achievement ("erfinderische Leistung") disclosed by the specification as a whole. Likewise in the Netherlands, Professor Jan Brinkhof, former Vice–President of the Hague Court of Appeals, has written that the role of the claims before 1977 was "extremely modest." What mattered was the "essence of the invention" or what we would call the inventive concept.

The Protocol

23.   Although the EPC thus adopted the United Kingdom principle of using the claims to determine the extent of protection, the Contracting States were unwilling to accept what were understood to be the principles of construction which United Kingdom courts applied in deciding what the claims meant. These principles, which I shall explain in greater detail in a moment, were perceived as having sometimes resulted in claims being given an unduly narrow and literal construction. The Contracting Parties wanted to make it clear that legal technicalities of this kind should be rejected. On the other hand, it was accepted that countries which had previously looked to the "essence of the invention" rather than the actual terms of the claims should not carry on exactly as before under the guise of giving the claims a generous interpretation.

24.   This compromise was given effect by the "Protocol on the Interpretation of Article 69":

"Article 69 should not be interpreted in the sense that the extent of the protection conferred by a European patent is to be understood as that defined by the strict, literal meaning of the wording used in the claims, the description and drawings being employed only for the purpose of resolving an ambiguity found in the claims. Neither should it be interpreted in the sense that the claims serve only as a guideline and that the actual protection conferred may extend to what, from a consideration of the description and drawings by a person skilled in the art, the patentee has contemplated. On the contrary, it is to be interpreted as defining a position between these extremes which combines a fair protection for the patentee with a reasonable degree of certainty for third parties."

25. It is often said, on the basis of the words "a position between these extremes", that the Protocol represents a compromise between two different approaches to the interpretation of claims. But that is not quite accurate. It is a protocol on the interpretation of article 69, not a protocol on the interpretation of claims. The first sentence does deal with interpretation of the claims and, to understand it, one needs to know something about the rules which English courts used to apply, or impose on themselves, when construing not merely patents but documents in general. The second sentence does not deal with the interpretation of claims. Instead, it makes it clear that one cannot go beyond the claims to what, on the basis of the specification as a whole, it appears that "the patentee has contemplated". But the last sentence indicates that, in determining the extent of protection according to the content of the claims but avoiding literalism, the courts of the Contracting States should combine "a fair protection for the patentee with a reasonable degree of certainty for third parties."

26. Both article 69 and the Protocol are given effect in United Kingdom law, in relation to infringement, by sections 60 and 125 of the Act. . . .

The English rules of construction

27. As I indicated a moment ago, it is impossible to understand what the first sentence of the Protocol was intending to prohibit without knowing what used to be the principles applied (at any rate in theory) by an English court construing a legal document. These required the words and grammar of a sentence to be given their "natural and ordinary meaning", that is to say, the meanings assigned to the words by a dictionary and to the syntax by a grammar. This meaning was to be adopted regardless of the context or background against which the words were used, unless they were "ambiguous", that is to say, capable of having more than one meaning. As Lord Porter said in *Electric & Musical Industries Ltd v Lissen Ltd* (1938) 56 RPC 23, 57:

> "If the Claims have a plain meaning in themselves [emphasis supplied], then advantage cannot be taken of the language used in the body of the Specification to make them mean something different."

28. On the other hand, if the language of the claim "in itself" was ambiguous, capable of having more than one meaning, the court could have regard to the context provided by the specification and drawings. If that was insufficient to resolve the ambiguity, the court could have regard to the background, or what was called the "extrinsic evidence" of facts which an intended reader would reasonably have expected to have been within the knowledge of the author when he wrote the document.

29.   These rules, if remorselessly applied, meant that unless the court could find some ambiguity in the language, it might be obliged to construe the document in a sense which a reasonable reader, aware of its context and background, would not have thought the author intended. Such a rule, adopted in the interests of certainty at an early stage in the development of English law, was capable of causing considerable injustice and occasionally did so. The fact that it did not do so more often was because judges were generally astute to find the necessary "ambiguity" which enabled them to interpret the document in its proper context. Indeed, the attempt to treat the words of the claim as having meanings "in themselves" and without regard to the context in which or the purpose for which they were used was always a highly artificial exercise.

30.   It seems to me clear that the Protocol, with its reference to "resolving an ambiguity", was intended to reject these artificial English rules for the construction of patent claims. As it happens, though, by the time the Protocol was signed, the English courts had already begun to abandon them, not only for patent claims, but for commercial documents generally. The speeches of Lord Wilberforce in *Prenn v Simmonds [1971] 1 WLR 1381* and *Reardon Smith Line Ltd. v Yngvar Hansen–Tangen [1976] 1 WLR 989* are milestones along this road. It came to be recognised that the author of a document such as a contract or patent specification is using language to make a communication for a practical purpose and that a rule of construction which gives his language a meaning different from the way it would have been understood by the people to whom it was actually addressed is liable to defeat his intentions. It is against that background that one must read the well known passage in the speech of Lord Diplock in *Catnic Components Ltd v Hill & Smith Ltd [1982] RPC 183, 243* when he said that the new approach should also be applied to the construction of patent claims:

"A patent specification should be given a purposive construction rather than a purely literal one derived from applying to it the kind of meticulous verbal analysis in which lawyers are too often tempted by their training to indulge."

31.   This was all of a piece with Lord Diplock's approach a few years later in *The Antaios [1985] AC 191, 201* to the construction of a charterparty:

"I take this opportunity of re-stating that if detailed semantic and syntactical analysis of words in a commercial contract is going to lead to a conclusion that flouts business commonsense, it must be made to yield to business commonsense."

32.   Construction, whether of a patent or any other document, is of course not directly concerned with what the author meant to say. There is no window into the mind of the patentee or the author of any other document. Construction is objective in the sense that it is concerned with what a reasonable person to whom the utterance was addressed

would have understood the author to be using the words to mean. Notice, however, that it is not, as is sometimes said, "the meaning of the words the author used", but rather what the notional addressee would have understood the author to mean by using those words. The meaning of words is a matter of convention, governed by rules, which can be found in dictionaries and grammars. What the author would have been understood to mean by using those words is not simply a matter of rules. It is highly sensitive to the context of and background to the particular utterance. It depends not only upon the words the author has chosen but also upon the identity of the audience he is taken to have been addressing and the knowledge and assumptions which one attributes to that audience.

33.   In the case of a patent specification, the notional addressee is the person skilled in the art. He (or, I say once and for all, she) comes to a reading of the specification with common general knowledge of the art. And he reads the specification on the assumption that its purpose is to both to describe and to demarcate an invention—a practical idea which the patentee has had for a new product or process—and not to be a textbook in mathematics or chemistry or a shopping list of chemicals or hardware. It is this insight which lies at the heart of "purposive construction". If Lord Diplock did not invent the expression, he certainly gave it wide currency in the law. But there is, I think, a tendency to regard it as a vague description of some kind of divination which mysteriously penetrates beneath the language of the specification. Lord Diplock was in my opinion being much more specific and his intention was to point out that a person may be taken to mean something different when he uses words for one purpose from what he would be taken to mean if he was using them for another.... The purpose of a patent specification, as I have said, is no more nor less than to communicate the idea of an invention. An appreciation of that purpose is part of the material which one uses to ascertain the meaning. But purpose and meaning are different. If, when speaking of the widest purpose, Jacob LJ meant the widest meaning, I would respectfully disagree. There is no presumption about the width of the claims. A patent may, for one reason or another, claim less than it teaches or enables.

34.   "Purposive construction" does not mean that one is extending or going beyond the definition of the technical matter for which the patentee seeks protection in the claims. The question is always what the person skilled in the art would have understood the patentee to be using the language of the claim to mean. And for this purpose, the language he has chosen is usually of critical importance. The conventions of word meaning and syntax enable us to express our meanings with great accuracy and subtlety and the skilled man will ordinarily assume that the patentee has chosen his language accordingly. As a number of judges have pointed out, the specification is a unilateral document in words of the patentee's own choosing. Furthermore, the words will usually have been chosen upon skilled advice. The specifica-

tion is not a document inter rusticos for which broad allowances must be made. On the other hand, it must be recognised that the patentee is trying to describe something which, at any rate in his opinion, is new; which has not existed before and of which there may be no generally accepted definition. There will be occasions upon which it will be obvious to the skilled man that the patentee must in some respect have departed from conventional use of language or included in his description of the invention some element which he did not mean to be essential. But one would not expect that to happen very often.

35.   One of the reasons why it will be unusual for the notional skilled man to conclude, after construing the claim purposively in the context of the specification and drawings, that the patentee must nevertheless have meant something different from what he appears to have meant, is that there are necessarily gaps in our knowledge of the background which led him to express himself in that particular way. The courts of the United Kingdom, the Netherlands and Germany certainly discourage, if they do not actually prohibit, use of the patent office file in aid of construction. There are good reasons: the meaning of the patent should not change according to whether or not the person skilled in the art has access to the file and in any case life is too short for the limited assistance which it can provide. It is however frequently impossible to know without access, not merely to the file but to the private thoughts of the patentee and his advisors as well, what the reason was for some apparently inexplicable limitation in the extent of the monopoly claimed. One possible explanation is that it does not represent what the patentee really meant to say. But another is that he did mean it, for reasons of his own; such as wanting to avoid arguments with the examiners over enablement or prior art and have his patent granted as soon as possible. This feature of the practical life of a patent agent reduces the scope for a conclusion that the patentee could not have meant what the words appear to be saying. It has been suggested that in the absence of any explanation for a restriction in the extent of protection claimed, it should be presumed that there was some good reason between the patentee and the patent office. I do not think that it is sensible to have presumptions about what people must be taken to have meant but a conclusion that they have departed from conventional usage obviously needs some rational basis.

The doctrine of equivalents

36.   At the time when the rules about natural and ordinary meanings were more or less rigidly applied, the United Kingdom and American courts showed understandable anxiety about applying a construction which allowed someone to avoid infringement by making an "immaterial variation" in the invention as described in the claims. In England, this led to the development of a doctrine of infringement by use of the "pith and marrow" of the invention (a phrase invented by Lord Cairns in *Clark v Adie (1877) 2 App Cas 315, 320*) as opposed to a "textual infringement". The pith and marrow doctrine was always a bit vague

("necessary to prevent sharp practice" said Lord Reid in C *Van Der Lely NV v Bamfords Ltd [1963] RPC 61, 77*) and it was unclear whether the courts regarded it as a principle of construction or an extension of protection outside the claims.

37.   In the United States, where a similar principle is called the "doctrine of equivalents", it is frankly acknowledged that it allows the patentee to extend his monopoly beyond the claims. In the leading case of *Graver Tank & Manufacturing Co Inc v Linde Air Products Company* 339 US 605, 607 (1950), Jackson J said that the American courts had recognised

"that to permit imitation of a patented invention which does not copy every literal detail would be to convert the protection of the patent grant into a hollow and useless thing. Such a limitation would leave room for—indeed encourage—the unscrupulous copyist to make unimportant and insubstantial changes and substitutions in the patent which, though adding nothing, would be enough to take the copied matter outside the claim, and hence outside the reach of law."

38.   In similar vein, Learned Hand J (a great patent lawyer) said that the purpose of the doctrine of equivalents was "to temper unsparing logic and prevent an infringer from stealing the benefit of the invention": *Royal Typewriter Co v Remington Rand Inc (CA2nd Conn)* 168 F2nd 691, 692. The effect of the doctrine is thus to extend protection to something outside the claims which performs substantially the same function in substantially the same way to obtain the same result.

39.   However, once the monopoly had been allowed to escape from the terms of the claims, it is not easy to know where its limits should be drawn. In *Warner–Jenkinson Co v Hilton Davis Chemical Co* 520 US 17, 28–29 (1997) the United States Supreme Court expressed some anxiety that the doctrine of equivalents had "taken on a life of its own, unbounded by the patent claims." It seems to me, however, that once the doctrine is allowed to go beyond the claims, a life of its own is exactly what it is bound to have. The American courts have restricted the scope of the doctrine by what is called prosecution history or file wrapper estoppel, by which equivalence cannot be claimed for integers restricting the monopoly which have been included by amendment during the prosecution of the application in the patent office. The patentee is estopped against the world (who need not have known of or relied upon the amendment) from denying that he intended to surrender that part of the monopoly. File wrapper estoppel means that the true scope of patent protection often cannot be established without an expensive investigation of the patent office file. Furthermore, the difficulties involved in deciding exactly what part of the claim should be taken to have been withdrawn by an amendment drove the Federal Court of Appeals in *Festo Corporation v Shoketsu Kinzoku Kogyo Kabushiki Co Ltd* 234 F3rd 558 (2000) to declare that the law was arbitrary and unworkable.

40.   In order to restore some certainty, the Court of Appeals laid down a rule that any amendment for reasons of patent validity was an absolute bar to any extension of the monopoly outside the literal meaning of the amended text. But the Supreme Court reversed this retreat to literalism on the ground that the cure was worse than the disease: see *Festo Corporation v Shoketsu Kinzoku Kogyo Kabushiki Co Ltd* (28 May 2002) US Supreme Court.

41.   There is often discussion about whether we have a European doctrine of equivalents and, if not, whether we should. It seems to me that both the doctrine of equivalents in the United States and the pith and marrow doctrine in the United Kingdom were born of despair. The courts felt unable to escape from interpretations which "unsparing logic" appeared to require and which prevented them from according the patentee the full extent of the monopoly which the person skilled in the art would reasonably have thought he was claiming. The background was the tendency to literalism which then characterised the approach of the courts to the interpretation of documents generally and the fact that patents are likely to attract the skills of lawyers seeking to exploit literalism to find loopholes in the monopoly they create. (Similar skills are devoted to revenue statutes).

42.   If literalism stands in the way of construing patent claims so as to give fair protection to the patentee, there are two things that you can do. One is to adhere to literalism in construing the claims and evolve a doctrine which supplements the claims by extending protection to equivalents. That is what the Americans have done. The other is to abandon literalism. That is what the House of Lords did in the *Catnic* case, where Lord Diplock said at [1982] RPC 183, 242:

> "Both parties to this appeal have tended to treat 'textual infringement' and infringement of the 'pith and marrow' of an invention as if they were separate causes of action, the existence of the former to be determined as a matter of construction only and of the latter upon some broader principle of colourable evasion. There is, in my view, no such dichotomy; there is but a single cause of action and to treat it otherwise . . . is liable to lead to confusion."

43.   The solution, said Lord Diplock, was to adopt a principle of construction which actually gave effect to what the person skilled in the art would have understood the patentee to be claiming.

44.   Since the *Catnic* case we have article 69 which, as it seems to me, firmly shuts the door on any doctrine which extends protection outside the claims. I cannot say that I am sorry because the *Festo* litigation suggests, with all respect to the courts of the United States, that American patent litigants pay dearly for results which are no more just or predictable than could be achieved by simply reading the claims.

Is *Catnic* consistent with the Protocol?

45.   In *Improver Corp v Remington Consumer Products Ltd* [1989] RPC 69 the Court of Appeal said that Lord Diplock's speech in *Catnic* advocated

the same approach to construction as is required by the Protocol. But in *PLG Research Ltd v Ardon International Ltd [1995] RPC 287*, 309 Millett LJ said:

"Lord Diplock was expounding the common law approach to the construction of a patent. This has been replaced by the approach laid down by the Protocol. If the two approaches are the same, reference to Lord Diplock's formulation is unnecessary, while if they are different it is dangerous."

46.   This echoes, perhaps consciously, the famous justification said to have been given by the Caliph Omar for burning the library of Alexandria: "If these writings of the Greeks agree with the Book of God, they are useless and need not be preserved: if they disagree, they are pernicious and ought to be destroyed"—a story which Gibbon dismissed as Christian propaganda. But I think that the Protocol can suffer no harm from a little explanation and I entirely agree with the masterly judgment of Aldous J in *Assidoman Multipack Ltd v The Mead Corporation [1995] RPC 321*, in which he explains why the *Catnic* approach accords with the Protocol.

47.   The Protocol, as I have said, is a Protocol for the construction of article 69 and does not expressly lay down any principle for the construction of claims. It does say what principle should not be followed, namely the old English literalism, but otherwise it says only that one should not go outside the claims. It does however say that the object is to combine a fair protection for the patentee with a reasonable degree of certainty for third parties. How is this to be achieved? The claims must be construed in a way which attempts, so far as is possible in an imperfect world, not to disappoint the reasonable expectations of either side. What principle of interpretation would give fair protection to the patentee? Surely, a principle which would give him the full extent of the monopoly which the person skilled in the art would think he was intending to claim. And what principle would provide a reasonable degree of protection for third parties? Surely again, a principle which would not give the patentee more than the full extent of the monopoly which the person skilled in the art would think that he was intending to claim. Indeed, any other principle would also be unfair to the patentee, because it would unreasonably expose the patent to claims of invalidity on grounds of anticipation or insufficiency.

48.   The *Catnic* principle of construction is therefore in my opinion precisely in accordance with the Protocol. It is intended to give the patentee the full extent, but not more than the full extent, of the monopoly which a reasonable person skilled in the art, reading the claims in context, would think he was intending to claim. . . .

Equivalents as a guide to construction

49.   Although article 69 prevents equivalence from extending protection outside the claims, there is no reason why it cannot be an important part of the background of facts known to the skilled man which would

affect what he understood the claims to mean. That is no more than common sense. It is also expressly provided by the new article 2 added to the Protocol by the Munich Act revising the EPC, dated 29 November 2000 (but which has not yet come into force):

"For the purpose of determining the extent of protection conferred by a European patent, due account shall be taken of any element which is equivalent to an element specified in the claims."

50.   In the *Catnic case [1982] RPC 183*, 243 Lord Diplock offered some observations on the relevance of equivalence to the question of construction:

"The question in each case is: whether persons with practical knowledge and experience of the kind of work in which the invention was intended to be used, would understand that strict compliance with a particular descriptive word or phrase appearing in a claim was intended by the patentee to be an essential requirement of the invention so that any variant would fall outside the monopoly claimed, even though it could have no material effect upon the way the invention worked.

The question, of course, does not arise where the variant would in fact have a material effect upon the way the invention worked. Nor does it arise unless at the date of publication of the specification it would be obvious to the informed reader that this was so. Where it is not obvious, in the light of then-existing knowledge, the reader is entitled to assume that the patentee thought at the time of the specification that he had good reason for limiting his monopoly so strictly and had intended to do so, even though subsequent work by him or others in the field of the invention might show the limitation to have been unnecessary. It is to be answered in the negative only when it would be apparent to any reader skilled in the art that a particular descriptive word or phrase used in a claim cannot have been intended by a patentee, who was also skilled in the art, to exclude minor variants which, to the knowledge of both him and the readers to whom the patent was addressed, could have no material effect upon the way in which the invention worked."

51.   In *Improver Corporation v Remington Consumer Products Ltd [1990] FSR 181*, 189 I tried to summarise this guidance:

"If the issue was whether a feature embodied in an alleged infringement which fell outside the primary, literal or acontextual meaning of a descriptive word or phrase in the claim ("a variant") was nevertheless within its language as properly interpreted, the court should ask itself the following three questions:

(1) Does the variant have a material effect upon the way the invention works? If yes, the variant is outside the claim. If no?

(2) Would this (ie that the variant had no material effect) have been obvious at the date of publication of the patent to a reader skilled in the art? If no, the variant is outside the claim. If yes?

(3) Would the reader skilled in the art nevertheless have understood from the language of the claim that the patentee intended that strict compliance with the primary meaning was an essential requirement of the invention? If yes, the variant is outside the claim.

On the other hand, a negative answer to the last question would lead to the conclusion that the patentee was intending the word or phrase to have not a literal but a figurative meaning (the figure being a form of synecdoche or metonymy) denoting a class of things which include the variant and the literal meaning, the latter being perhaps the most perfect, best-known or striking example of the class."

52. These questions, which the Court of Appeal in *Wheatly v Drillsafe Ltd* [2001] RPC 133, 142 dubbed "the Protocol questions" have been used by English courts for the past fifteen years as a framework for deciding whether equivalents fall within the scope of the claims. On the whole, the judges appear to have been comfortable with the results, although some of the cases have exposed the limitations of the method. When speaking of the "*Catnic* principle" it is important to distinguish between, on the one hand, the principle of purposive construction which I have said gives effect to the requirements of the Protocol, and on the other hand, the guidelines for applying that principle to equivalents, which are encapsulated in the Protocol questions. The former is the bedrock of patent construction, universally applicable. The latter are only guidelines, more useful in some cases than in others. I am bound to say that the cases show a tendency for counsel to treat the Protocol questions as legal rules rather than guides which will in appropriate cases help to decide what the skilled man would have understood the patentee to mean. The limits to the value of the guidelines are perhaps most clearly illustrated by the present case and therefore, instead of discussing the principles in the abstract as I have been doing so far, I shall make my comments by reference to the facts of the case.

The judge's construction of the claims

53. It will be recalled that claim 1 is to a DNA sequence, selected from the sequences set out in Table VI or related sequences, for securing the expression of EPO in a "host cell". The chief question of construction is whether the person skilled in the art would understand "host cell" to mean a cell which is host to the DNA sequence which coded for EPO. The alternative, put forward by Amgen, is that it can include a sequence which is endogenous to the cell, like the human EPO gene which expresses GA–EPO, as long as the cell is host to some exogenous DNA. In the TKT process, it is host to the control sequence and other machinery introduced by homologous recombination.

54. On this question, the judge had the advantage of hearing the evidence of a number of witnesses who were highly skilled in the art. They all said that they would have understood claim 1 to be referring to a DNA sequence coding for EPO which had been isolated or synthesised and was suitable for expression in a host cell. In other words, the claim

was to a sequence coding for EPO which was exogenous to the cell in which expression took place. The judge summed up his conclusions in paragraph 215:

"I am of the view that a cell is not a 'host cell' unless it is host to exogenous DNA encoding for EPO or its analogue. Such a conclusion is based in part on the teaching of the [patent in suit]. The terms 'host' and 'host cell' are used consistently to describe cells which have been transfected with exogenous or foreign DNA (ie DNA from outside that particular cell) which encodes EPO, with a view to securing expression of EPO in those host cells. That was accepted by [Amgen's expert] Dr Brenner. The examples contained in the [patent in suit] are all concerned with EPO-encoding DNA which has been isolated outside the cell and inserted into the cell to which it is foreign. Indeed, at the relevant time, the routine method of production of a recombinant protein was by cloning the gene encoding the protein and the introduction of that clone into a self-replicating organism by transfection or transformation. There was no knowledge of the technique of 'switching on' an endogenous encoding sequence by transfecting the cell with exogenous DNA sequences as including an artificial promoter."

55. Besides these general considerations, the judge relied upon other indications in the language of the specification. The words "for use in securing expression ... of a polypeptide" suggested the DNA which coded for that polypeptide rather than a control sequence which promoted expression of endogenous DNA. That was supported by paragraph (b) of claim 1, which extended the claim to sequences which were not in Table VI but which hybridised under stringent conditions to "the protein coding regions" of Table VI.

56. Furthermore, the specification appears anxious to point out that the invention covers the use of mammalian cells which already have an EPO gene of their own:

"It will be understood that expression of, e.g., monkey origin DNA in monkey host cells in culture and human host cells in culture, actually constitute instances of 'exogenous' DNA expression inasmuch as the EPO DNA whose high level expression is sought would not have its origins in the genome of the host."

57. That certainly suggests that the patentee regarded it as essential to his invention that the DNA of which high level expression was sought should not have its origin in the genome of the host cell. That would clearly exclude the DNA sequence which expresses GA–EPO, which forms part of the genome of the host cell.

58. For these reasons, which I find entirely convincing, the judge came to the conclusion that the person skilled in the art would not regard the endogenous coding sequence which expressed GA–EPO as falling within claim 1. It followed that GA–EPO was not the expression of a DNA sequence within claim 1 and therefore did not infringe claim 26. And by the same process of reasoning, the judge concluded that the person

skilled in the art would not regard GA–EPO as "the product of . . . expression of an exogenous DNA sequence" within claim 19. At this point in the judgment, TKT might have concluded that they had won. I shall return in a moment to consider why the judge nevertheless held claim 26 to have been infringed. . . .

The judge's application of the Protocol questions

63.   Having thus construed the claims, the judge described his construction as "literal" and moved on to the Protocol questions. In what sense could the construction have been literal? The first difficulty about the application of the Protocol questions is to decide what is meant by a "primary, literal or acontextual meaning". The judge's construction could not possibly be described as acontextual. It was entirely dependent on context and reflected the evidence of how the claim would have been understood by men skilled in the art.

64.   No one has ever made an acontextual statement. There is always some context to any utterance, however meagre. "Acontextual meaning" can refer only to the conventional rules for the use of language, such as one finds in a dictionary or grammar. But then, to compare acontextual meaning in that sense with contextual meaning is to compare apples with pears. The one refers to a general rule about how words or syntax should be used and the other to the fact of what on a specific occasion the language was used to mean. So, to make any sense of the terms "primary, literal or acontextual meaning" in the Protocol questions, it must be taken to mean a construction which assumes that the author used words strictly in accordance with their conventional meanings.

65.   The notion of strict compliance with the conventional meanings of words or phrases sits most comfortably with the use of figures, measurements, angles and the like, when the question is whether they allow for some degree of tolerance or approximation. That was the case in *Catnic* and it is significant that the "quintet" of cases in which the German Bundesgerichtshof referred to *Catnic* and said that its approach accorded with that of the House of Lords were all concerned with figures and measurements. In such cases, the contrast with strict compliance is approximation and not the rather pretentious figures of speech mentioned in the Protocol questions.

66.   No doubt there are other cases, not involving figures or measurements, in which the question is whether a word or phrase was used in a strictly conventional or some looser sense. But the present case illustrates the difficulty of applying the Protocol questions when no such question arises. No one suggests that "an exogenous DNA sequence coding for EPO" can have some looser meaning which includes "an endogenous DNA sequence coding for EPO". The question is rather whether the person skilled in the art would understand the invention as operating at a level of generality which makes it irrelevant whether the DNA which codes for EPO is exogenous or not. That is a difficult question to put through the mangle of the Protocol questions because

the answer depends entirely upon what you think the invention is. Once you have decided that question, the Protocol questions answer themselves.

67.   The judge thought that the invention was the discovery of the sequence of the EPO gene and the associated information. It followed that any method of making EPO which used that information, whether by the expression of exogenous or endogenous DNA, would operate in the same way and that this would be obvious to the person skilled in the art. Furthermore, there was no reason why the patentee should have wished to insist upon any particular method of using the information to obtain the expression of EPO.

68.   The Court of Appeal, on the other hand, thought that the invention was a way of making EPO. The information about the sequence of the gene was necessary to enable the invention to be performed but was not and could not be the invention itself. It followed that a different way of making EPO worked in a different way from that described in the invention and that this would have been obvious to a person skilled in the art. The Court of Appeal added that if they had answered the first two Protocol questions in favour of Amgen they would also have answered the third in its favour. That is a somewhat unreal hypothesis and seems only to mean that if upon the true construction of the claims the invention was broad enough to include any method of making EPO, they would not have understood the patentee to be insisting on any particular method.

69.   I shall say in a moment why I agree with the Court of Appeal, but I want first to emphasise a point I have already made about the use of the Protocol questions. The determination of the extent of protection conferred by a European patent is an examination in which there is only one compulsory question, namely that set by article 69 and its Protocol: what would a person skilled in the art have understood the patentee to have used the language of the claim to mean? Everything else, including the Protocol questions, is only guidance to a judge trying to answer that question. But there is no point in going through the motions of answering the Protocol questions when you cannot sensibly do so until you have construed the claim. In such a case—and the present is in my opinion such a case—they simply provide a formal justification for a conclusion which has already been reached on other grounds.

70.   I agree with the Court of Appeal that the invention should normally be taken as having been claimed at the same level of generality as that at which it is defined in the claims. . . .

72.   This is perhaps an appropriate point at which to mention what may appear to be a difference between the German, United Kingdom and Netherlands approach to these questions. It used to be thought that despite article 69 and the Protocol, there remained serious differences between the approaches to construction of the United Kingdom on the one hand and Germany and the Netherlands on the other. And it is true

that in the early years of the EPC, there was a view in the German and Netherlands courts that the Convention had made no difference and that the Protocol entitled the courts of Contracting States to go on deciding the extent of protection exactly as before. The position in the Netherlands is described by Professor Brinkhof in the article *Is there a European Doctrine of Equivalence?* (2002) IIC 911 to which I have already referred.

73.   But I do not think that this is any longer true. The highest courts in both Germany (see Batteriekastenschnur [1989] GRUR 903, 904) and the Netherlands (see Ciba–Geigy/Oté Optics (1995) Nederlandse Jurisprudentie 39) have said that the effect of article 69 is to give the claims what the European Patent Office has called a "central role": see BAYER/Plant growth regulating agent [1990] EPOR 257, 261. The Bundesgerichtshof said in the Batteriekastenschnur case that the claims are no longer merely a point of departure but the decisive basis for determining the extent of protection.

74.   In addressing the 10th Symposium of European Patent Judges in Luxembourg in 2000, the distinguished German patent lawyer Dr Rüdiger Rogge (then presiding judge of the 10th (intellectual property) Senate of the Bundesgerichtshof) said that he regarded the decisions of other countries on the extent of protection afforded by article 69 as important contributions to the jurisprudence of his own country. The same is true of the judges of the United Kingdom.

75.   The German courts have their own guidelines for dealing with equivalents, which have some resemblance to the Protocol questions. In the "quintet" of cases before the Bundesgerichtshof (see, for example, Kunstoffrohrteil [2002] GRUR 511 and Schneidemesser 1 [2003] ENPR 12 309) which concerned questions of whether figures or measurements in a claim allow some degree of approximation (and, if so, what degree), the court expressly said that its approach was similar to that adopted in Catnic. But there are differences from the Protocol questions which are lucidly explained by Dr Peter Meier–Beck (currently a judge of the 10th Senate) in a paper to be published in the International Review of Intellectual Property and Competition Law (IIC). For example, German judges do not ask whether a variant "works in the same way" but whether it solves the problem underlying the invention by means which have the same technical effect. That may be a better way of putting the question because it avoids the ambiguity illustrated by *American Home Products Corporation v Novartis Pharmaceuticals UK Ltd [2001] RPC 159* over whether "works in the same way" involves an assumption that it works at all. On the other hand, as is illustrated by the present case, everything will depend upon what you regard as "the problem underlying the invention." It seems to me, however, that the German courts are also approaching the question of equivalents with a view to answering the same ultimate question as that which I have suggested is raised by Article 69, namely what a person skilled in the art would have thought the patentee was using the language of the claim to mean.

The decision of the Court of Appeal

76.   I agree with the Court of Appeal on construction for a number of reasons. First, I think that the judge's construction pays no attention to the claims. It does not even use them as "guidelines" but goes straight to Table VI and declares that to be the invention. Secondly, I think that the Court of Appeal was right in saying that Table VI could not have been the invention. Standing alone, it was a "discovery ... as such" within the meaning of section 1(2) of the Act. . . .

77.   In such a case, while it may be true to say, as the Court of Appeal did ([2003] RPC 31, 62) that Table VI lay "at the heart of the invention", it was not the invention. . . .

New technology

78.   The effect of the construction for which Amgen contends is that claim 1 should be read as including any DNA sequence, whether exogenous or endogenous, which expresses EPO in consequence of the application to the cell of any form of DNA recombinant technology. It would have been easy to draft such a claim. Whether the specification would have been sufficient to support it, in the sense of enabling expression by any form of DNA recombinant technology, is another matter to which I shall return when I deal with validity. But the person skilled in the art (who must, in my opinion, be assumed to know the basic principles of patentability) might well have thought that the claims were restricted to existing technology because of doubts about sufficiency rather than lack of foresight about possible developments. Amgen would have been well aware in 1983 that recombinant technology was developing rapidly and that artificial homologous recombination had been achieved in bacterial and yeast cells and that its use in mammalian cells was regarded as a desirable goal.

79.   Amgen submit that although homologous recombination was a known phenomenon in 1983, its use to achieve "gene activation" was unknown. The method of manufacture by DNA recombinant technology referred to in the claim was the only one known at the priority date. At the time, it was in practice equivalent to a general claim for manufacture by recombinant DNA technology. It should therefore be construed as such. Amgen say that if the claims cannot be construed in terms sufficiently general to include methods unknown at the priority date, the value of a patent would be destroyed as soon as some new technology for achieving the same result was invented.

80.   I do not dispute that a claim may, upon its proper construction, cover products or processes which involve the use of technology unknown at the time the claim was drafted. The question is whether the person skilled in the art would understand the description in a way which was sufficiently general to include the new technology. There is no difficulty in principle about construing general terms to include embodiments which were unknown at the time the document was written. One frequently does that in construing legislation, for example,

by construing "carriage" in a 19th century statute to include a motor car. In such cases it is particularly important not to be too literal. It may be clear from the language, context and background that the patentee intended to refer in general terms to, for example, every way of achieving a certain result, even though he has used language which is in some respects inappropriate in relation to a new way of achieving that result. In the present case, however, I agree with the Court of Appeal (and with the judge, before he came to apply the Protocol questions) that the man skilled in the art would not have understood the claim as sufficiently general to include gene activation. He would have understood it to be limited to the expression of an exogenous DNA sequence which coded for EPO. . . .

85.　For these reasons I would hold that TKT did not infringe any of the claims and dismiss Amgen's appeal.

NOTES

1. The German Quintet on claim construction and equivalents: *P T GmbH v. G A G* ("Cutting Knife 1"), *Schneidmesser 1*, (Case X ZR 168/00) Bundesgerichtshof (X. Zivilsenat) (Federal Court of Justice (Xth Civil Division)) and *V SpA v. WBV* ("Plastic Pipe Part") ("Kunststoffrohteil") (Case X ZR 43/01) Bundesgerichtshof (X. Zivilsenat) (Federal Court of Justice (Xth Civil Division)) are two key cases of the Quintet decided on March 12, 2002, and extensively discussed by Lord Hoffmann. These cases contain the approach of Germany's highest patent court to claim construction and equivalents. English translations are available in the Westlaw database European National Patent Reports (ENP–RPTS).

2. "Host Cell" hypothetical: Would Lord Hoffman's conception of purposive claim construction (without any equivalents) protect an invention that is infringed by after-arising technology? Consider how Lord Hoffmann would have handled the infringement issue before him if the alleged infringer had inserted a human erythropoietin gene into a protein machine which produces proteins corresponding to the gene that is inserted into it. Assume that this protein making machine was invented around 1995 and is itself the subject of many patents. Would Lord Hoffmann have decided that the protein machine included a "host cell?"

3. Japan's Doctrine of Equivalents. No country's patent system has received more criticism than that of Japan. For years among the chief complaints was that the courts gave patent claims an extremely narrow scope and that equivalents were not recognized. This all changed in 1998.

TSUBAKIMOTO SEIKO CO. LTD. v. THK K.K.

Supreme Court of Japan, 1998
Case No. 1994 (*o*) 1083

1.　The present case is a suit seeking damages for patent infringement. The Tokyo High Court found the following facts:

(1) The patent in suit is Japanese Patent No. 999139. The filing date of the patent is April 26, 1971. Its publication date is July 7, 1978 and its registration date is May 30, 1980. Its claim reads as follows:

An endlessly sliding ball spline shaft bearing comprising:

an outer cylinder having torque transmitting load bearing ball-guiding grooves with a U-shaped cross-section and torque transmitting non-load bearing ball-guiding grooves with a U-shaped cross-section being slightly deeper than that of the load bearing ball-guiding grooves, the load bearing ball-guiding groove and the non-load bearing ball-guiding groove extending alternately in the axial direction within the cylindrical inner wall, the outer cylinder having an annular circumferentially directed groove at each end with the same depth as that of the deeper groove;

a thin wall portion and a thick wall portion formed respectively in conformity with the torque transmitting load bearing ball-guiding groove and the torque transmitting non-load bearing ball-guiding groove formed in the axial direction within the inner wall of the outer cylinder;

a joint portion between the thin wall portion and the thick wall portion having a through-hole;

a retainer with an endless track groove for allowing balls to smoothly slide into the non-load ball-guiding groove formed in the thick wall portion; and

a spline shaft provided with a plurality of ribs extending in the axial direction thereof, said ribs being shaped to conform with a plurality of recessed spaces formed by the balls incorporated between the retainer and said outer cylinder for engaging the spline shaft with the outer cylinder.

The accused product was manufactured and sold from January, 1983 to October, 1988 and has a step of about 50 microns in height between the non-load ball-guiding groove and the cylindrical portion. The Tokyo High Court found that it literally met all limitations except for the "outer cylinder" limitation and the "thin wall portion" limitation. As to the "outer cylinder" limitation it found there are elements such as "U-shaped cross-section" and "annular circumferentially directed grooves". Whereas, with respect to the accused product, the corresponding portions of these elements are "semi-circular cross-section" and "cylindrical portion", and hence differ from the claimed features.

With respect to the "thin wall portion limitation", the retainer is an integral structure providing the functions of guiding balls to move in endless circulation, retaining balls when the spline shaft is withdrawn, and forming a recessed portions for guiding the rib portions of the spline shaft. Whereas, the accused product has cooperative action of three members, i.e. the upper edge portions of the ribs formed between the load bearing ball-guiding grooves of the outer cylinder, a plate-like member and a return cap. Nevertheless the Tokyo High Court found that the accused product is substantially the same as that shown in the patent with respect to the solution for the technical problem, the basic technical idea, and the effects obtained. . . .

However, the decision of the Tokyo High Court cannot be affirmed for the following reasons:

In determining whether an accused product or method falls within the technical scope of a patented invention, the technical scope of the invention must be determined with respect to the claim (see Patent Law Section 70 (1). If there are elements that differ between the claim and the accused product, the accused product and the like cannot be said to fall within the technical scope of the patented invention. On the other hand, even if there are elements in the claim that differ from the corresponding product and the like, the corresponding product and the like may be equivalent and may appropriately be said to fall within the technical scope of the patented invention if the following conditions are satisfied: (1) the differing elements are not the essential elements in the patented invention; (2) even if the differing elements are interchanged by elements of the accused product and the like, the object of the patented invention can be achieved and the same effects can be obtained; (3) by interchanging as above, a person of ordinary skill in the art to which the invention pertains (hereinafter referred to as an artisan) could have easily arrived at the accused product and the like at the time of manufacture; (4) the accused product and the like are not the same as the known art at the time of application for patent or could not have been easily conceived by an artisan at the time of application for patent; and (5) there is not any special circumstances such that the accused product and the like are intentionally excluded from the scope of the claim during patent prosecution).

The above results from the fact that it is very difficult to describe claims to cover all possible infringing embodiments of the patented invention. If a competitor can escape from patent enforcement including injunction etc. by simply replacing some claimed elements with a material or technical means etc that are developed after the patent application, incentive for innovation is significantly reduced, which conflicts with the goal of patent system to contribute the industrial developments through the protection and encouragement of inventions. Further, such an interpretation of law to allow competitors to escape from the charge of infringement would be unfair to the sense of justice in the society and conflict with the concept of fairness. In considering these points, the substantial value of a patented invention extends to a structure which would have been readily conceived by a third party from the structure recited in the claim as being substantially identical to a patented invention. It is proper to assume that a third party must expect such extension of the patent protection. On the other hand, the technical scope of a patent cannot include an accused product which is part of the state of art as of the application time of the patented invention, or would have been readily conceived by one skilled from the state of art because no one could have obtained a patent on such accused product (Patent Law, Article 29). Additionally, under the rule of estoppel, a patentee is prevented from claiming a patent rights on an accused product which was intentionally removed by an applicant from the claim scope during the patent prosecution where the applicant admitted that the accused product does not fall within the technical scope of the patented invention or the applicant's behavior indicates such removal of the accused product from the claim scope.

[The Japanese Supreme Court ultimately remanded the matter for further determination of whether the accused product would have been obvious in view of the prior art.]

NOTES

1. **Which Elements are Essential?** It is widely believed that the House of Lords in *Catnic* adopted purposive construction to avoid the necessity of determining whether an element was essential. Why do you think the Japanese Supreme Court adopted this requirement in 1998? Is an amended claim element by definition an essential element? If so, did the Japanese Supreme Court adopt the absolute bar rule adopted by the Federal Circuit in *Festo*.

2. **Is the Obviousness Test of (3) the One Adopted by Improver Court?** When thinking about this question remember that the Supreme Court specifically said that equivalency is judged as of the time of manufacture of the accused product.

3. **In Addition to Adopting a Theory of Prosecution History Estoppel, does (5) include Improver Question 3?** Improver Question 3 relates to the teaching of the specification itself and asks whether it effectively disclaimed equivalents. If you were writing the law for a country such as Japan, would you adopt a doctrine of prosecution history estoppel; Improver Question 3; or neither?

4. **Further Reading.** With regard to infringement law, TOSHIKO TAKENAKA, INTERPRETING PATENT CLAIMS: THE UNITED STATES, GERMANY AND JAPAN (1995) presents a painstakingly researched comparative analysis with particular strengths in Japanese law. With regard to European patent infringement law an excellent compilation of articles covering the leading European patent systems is found in JOCHEN PAGENBERG AND WILLIAM R. CORNISH, INTERPRETATION OF PATENTS IN EUROPE (Carl Heymanns Verlag 2006). This superb work is partially available as a Google book at http://books.google.com.

Infringement Exercise

You are employed as a patent attorney in Alexandria, Virginia. On September 2, 2001, Mr. Vance Varnish, president of Varnish, Inc., comes to your office seeking advice. "Our primary client, Massive Motors, has just been sued for patent infringement!" he exclaims.

After Mr. Varnish has relaxed somewhat, he shows you a copy of United States Patent No. 9,999,999. The '999 patent was filed on June 15, 1996, issued on February 1, 1998, and has been assigned to the Primer Products Corporation. The patent bears the title "Method for Coating Metal," and has only a single claim, Claim 1. According to the patent specification, the disclosed method for coating metal results in a painted surface that is particularly long-lasting and corrosion resistant. Claim 1 of the '999 patent provides:

Claim 1. A method for coating a metal surface with paint, comprising the steps of:

spraying said metal surface with urea;

heating said metal surface to approximately 300E C;

spraying said metal surface with said paint; and

drying said metal surface.

Mr. Varnish explains that Varnish, Inc. sells painting supplies to various automobile manufacturers, primarily the Massive Motors Company. Varnish, Inc. works closely with Massive Motors in designing new paints, as well as ways to apply these paints to automobile surfaces. "This entire affair began on April 1, 2000," Mr. Varnish says. "That's when Primer Products Corporation sent our chief customer, Massive Motors, a letter." Mr. Varnish shows you the letter, which provides in part:

April 1, 2000

To the Massive Motors Company:

We are pleased to call to your attention United States Patent No. 9,999,-999, directed towards a "Method for Coating Metal." We ask you to review your product line to ensure that you are not infringing claim 1 of the '999 patent. We will be in touch shortly to inquire as to the results of your infringement study.

Sincerely yours,

Paul Primer

President, Primer Products Corporation

"After reading the '999 patent, I asked a chemist to see if the results obtained by the patented process were as good as the patent stated," Mr. Varnish continues. "It was true—the experimental results he reached were far superior to our existing painting techniques! I decided that this kind of finishing was the wave of the future, but that Varnish, Inc. shouldn't risk infringing the '999 patent. After spending almost four months and about $500,000 in company funds, we came up with the following technique." Mr. Varnish then hands you a piece of paper which reads:

VARNISH INC.'S PROPRIETARY PAINTING PROCESS

Top Secret!

1. Spray the metal surface with paint.

2.　*Spray the metal surface with melamine resin.*

3.　*Heat the metal surface to 365E C.*

"Look, I'm a business person, not a chemist. But see how different our technique is!" Mr. Varnish exclaims. "Not only do we employ melamine resin, not urea, the order of the process steps is crucial. It's like making a piece of toast with strawberry jam. If you spread strawberry jam on a piece of bread before putting the bread in the toaster, you would burn the jam and not reach the desired result."

You then ask Mr. Varnish whether, once the metal surface has been heated, Massive Motors dries the metal surface or not. "Oh, Primer Products Corporation just wants to ensure that the paint is fully dry," Mr. Varnish explains. "But because the metal surface is quite hot at this point, we've learned that the paint dries in a matter of two or three minutes even without additional work. So Massive Motors doesn't bother to do anything after heating the surface—it just waits a few moments and then moves the part down the assembly line."

"Anyway, we had no further contact with Primer Products Corporation until yesterday, September 1, 2001," Mr. Varnish continues, "when Primer Products Corporation filed suit for patent infringement against Massive Motors. Not only am I worried about Massive Motors being found liable for patent infringement, I've heard that Varnish, Inc. could be sued itself. We sell the paint and the melamine resin to Massive Motors, which actually performs our method in its factory. While both the paint and melamine resin are available on the market generally, we sell these products in appropriate amounts for use in automobile assembly. With each sale, we also include a set of instructions on how to use these materials in accordance with our own coating method."

Promising you will call Mr. Varnish back tomorrow, you escort him to his automobile—a late-model Massive Motors brand, of course. Upon consulting a chemical encyclopedia, you are able to construct the following chart comparing melamine and urea:

Trait	Urea	Melamine
Formula	H_2N-CO-NH_2	$(NéC\text{-}NH_2)_3$
Formula Weight	60.6	126.12
Appearance	Colorless crystalline solid	White solid
Melting Point	132.7° C	355° C
Specific Gravity	1.335	1.56

Confused and lacking technical knowledge in this area, you call a noted chemistry professor, Dr. Cheryl Shellac, and describe the patented and accused coating techniques. She explains: "Although urea and melamine seem fairly distinct, in fact the only practical way to make melamine is to synthesize it from urea. First, urea is thermally decomposed into a gas mixture of cyanic acid and NH_3; second, cyanic gas is thermally decomposed into a melamine-CO_2 vapor. This simple two-step endothermic reaction is extremely well-known to the art. Indeed, you can think of melamine as a straightforward derivative of urea."

Professor Shellac continues: "Melamine resins are well known to possess outstanding resistance to heat, water and various chemicals. However, until early 1995, it was extremely expensive to make these resins on a large scale. Advances in chemical processing technologies that occurred in late 1998 and early 1999 have made melamine resins quite cheap to synthesize. At that time, they became sufficiently inexpensive and practical enough to employ in everyday manufacturing."

Professor Shellac goes on to explain: "Regarding the order of the steps, all that the patented process does is mix the paint together with a reactant, urea, at a high temperature. The order in which the paint and reactant are applied to the metal surface is immaterial. So long as they both occupy the same heated metal surface at the same time, the melamine resin almost instantly polymerizes and the result is a superior, long-lasting coating."

You thank Professor Shellac and next conduct some research on an on-line database. You discover an article in an industry journal, *The Thinner Times*, written by a Primer Products Corporation researcher. The researcher describes how he invented the patented process after three years of painstaking research, at a total cost of nearly five million dollars.

As you are signing off the database, a courier arrives from Varnish, Inc., with a copy of the '999 patent's prosecution history in hand. You carefully examine the prosecution history. You note that the examiner offered a Notice of Allowance with regard to the '999 patent on his First Office Action. The only comment offered in the Reasons for Allowance was: "The claims patentably distinguish over the prior art."

Last, you order a prior art search. The searcher finds only one pertinent reference: an article written by one Ulrich Undercoat, published on November 1, 1995, in a trade journal entitled *The Pigment Pages*. Undercoat discloses a process for coating the surfaces of certain steel machine parts in order to increase their working life. According to Undercoat, superior results are obtained when the surface of the machine parts is heated to 380 degrees C; paint is subsequently applied to the heated surface; and the surface is then immediately sprayed with melamine resin.

How would you advise Mr. Varnish as to the prospects of Primer Products Corporation's possible charges of infringement against the Massive Motors Company and Varnish, Inc.?

CHAPTER TWELVE

ADDITIONAL DEFENSES

■ ■ ■

In addition to such doctrines as inequitable conduct and double patenting, reviewed here at Chapter 10, U.S. patent law includes a number of other defenses that may ultimately bar the patentee from relief in an infringement action. Chief among them are the experimental use exemption, misuse, laches, estoppel, the implied license termed a "shop right," and the first inventor defense. These doctrines relate not to the validity of a patent but to its enforceability against another. If successfully invoked, they provide the defendant with a limited license to practice the patented technology.

In contrast to the "fair use" privilege codified in the Copyright Act of 1976, 17 U.S.C. § 107, the Patent Act of 1952 nowhere identifies an "experimental use" defense. The courts have nonetheless developed a "common law" experimental use privilege using their judicial powers. As will be seen, the patent law defense as been appropriately described as "crabbed," "narrowly construed," and "rarely sustained." *See* James Boyle, *Foreword: The Opposite of Property*, 66–SPG LAW & CONT. PROBLEMS 27 (Winter/Spring 2003); Kevin Sandstrom, *How Much Do We Value Research and Development: Broadening the Experimental use Privilege in Light of* Integra Lifesciences I v. Merck KGaA, 30 WILL. MITCH. L. REV. 1067 (2004); Rebecca S. Eisenberg, *Proprietary Rights and the Norms of Science in Biotechnology Research*, 97 YALE L.J. 177, 220 (1987). Congress complemented the limited common law experimental use defense with a statutory "safe harbor" that applies to patents covering pharmaceuticals, medical devices, and certain other products regulated by the Food and Drug Administration. This provision, found at § 271(e)(1) of the Patent Act, is taken up further in Chapter 13 of this text.

Another important defense, one that is intimately involved with antitrust law, is the equitable doctrine of patent misuse. The detailed relationship between antitrust law and patent law is beyond the scope of this casebook. However, a violation of the antitrust laws by the patentee may constitute a defense to a suit for patent infringement under the rubric of patent misuse, at least until the adverse effects of the misuse are purged by the patentee. The patent misuse doctrine is not easy to understand because it provides a specific remedy for a litigant who brings a substantive misuse violation to the attention of the court during infringement litigation. These substantive misuse activities frequently are, but need not be antitrust violations.

The doctrinal development of substantive patent misuse began with a series of cases where the patent owner brought suit for contributory infringement against a manufacturer who was selling unpatented supplies, used by licensees of patented machines in violation of their license. The manufacturer defended on the ground that the patent owner was trying to monopolize an unpatented product. Hence, the court should not enforce the patent against it. The classic case was the decision of the Sixth Circuit written by Judge Taft (later President Taft and then Chief Justice Taft) in *Heaton–Peninsular Button–Fastener Co. v. Eureka Specialty Co.*, 77 F. 288 (6th Cir.1896). This opinion manifests a sophisticated approach to the economics of tying practices. The opinion recognized that permitting a patentee to control the supplies used in the operation of its patented machines merely measured the intensity of use of the patented machine and did not constitute improper monopolization of an unpatented product. However, this approach did not survive the passage of the Clayton Act for in 1917 the Supreme Court, while it did not rely on the Clayton Act, refused to enforce a patent against a contributory infringer who was selling movies used in connection with licensed patented projectors, *Motion Picture Patents Co. v. Universal Film Mfg. Co.*, 243 U.S. 502 (1917).

Motion Picture Patents was followed by a series of cases involving the refusal of courts to enforce patents against contributory infringers who were selling unpatented components that were either used with or were part of, but not the complete, patented combination or process. Then in 1942 the Supreme Court decided *Morton Salt Co. v. G.S. Suppiger Co.*, 314 U.S. 488 (1942). It held that a direct infringer could successfully assert an equitable defense that the patentee practiced a business strategy with the patent which it considered to be a substantive misuse of the patent. Remarkably the alleged infringer also used the same marketing technique which was condemned by the Court when practiced by the patentee. The door thus opened permitting any defendant to try to defend against a good claim for patent infringement by asserting that somehow the patentee was misusing his patent even if the alleged misuse did not impact the defendant in any manner.

§ 12.1   EXPERIMENTAL USE

ROCHE PRODUCTS, INC. v. BOLAR PHARMACEUTICAL CO., INC.

United States Court of Appeals for the Federal Circuit, 1984
733 F.2d 858

Before Markey, Chief Judge, Nichols, Senior Circuit Judge, and Kashiwa, Circuit Judge.

NICHOLS, SENIOR CIRCUIT JUDGE.

This is an appeal from a judgment entered on October 14, 1983, in which the United States District Court 572 F.Supp. 255 for the Eastern

District of New York held United States Patent No. 3,299,053 not infringed and denied relief. We reverse and remand.

reversed and remanded

I

At stake in this case is the length of time a pharmaceutical company which has a patent on the active ingredient in a drug can have exclusive access to the American market for that drug. Plaintiff-appellant Roche Products, Inc. (Roche), a large research-oriented pharmaceutical company, wanted the United States district court to enjoin Bolar Pharmaceutical Co., Inc. (Bolar), a manufacturer of generic drugs, from taking, during the life of a patent, the statutory and regulatory steps necessary to market, after the patent expired, a drug equivalent to a patented brand name drug. Roche argued that the use of a patented drug for federally mandated premarketing tests is a use in violation of the patent laws.

Roche wants to enjoin Bolar from doing prep steps while patent still good to get approval to sell when patent expires

Roche was the assignee of the rights in U.S. Patent No. 3,299,053 (the '053 patent), which expired on January 17, 1984. The '053 patent, which issued on January 17, 1967, is entitled "Novel 1 and/or 4–substituted alkyl 5–aromatic–3H–1,4–benzodiazepines and benzodiazepine–2–ones." One of the chemical compounds claimed in the '053 patent is flurazepam hydrochloride (flurazepam hcl), the active ingredient in Roche's successful brand name prescription sleeping pill "Dalmane."

expires Jan 17 1984
issued Jan 17 1967
—sleeping pill "Dalmane"

In early 1983, Bolar became interested in marketing, after the '053 patent expired, a generic drug equivalent to Dalmane. Because a generic drug's commercial success is related to how quickly it is brought on the market after a patent expires, and because approval for an equivalent of an established drug can take more than 2 years, Bolar, not waiting for the '053 patent to expire, immediately began its effort to obtain federal approval to market its generic version of Dalmane. In mid–1983, Bolar obtained from a foreign manufacturer 5 kilograms of flurazepam hcl to form into "dosage form capsules, to obtain stability data, dissolution rates, bioequivalence studies, and blood serum studies" necessary for a New Drug Application to the United States Food and Drug Administration (FDA).

1983 Bolar obtained patented drug from overseas and started all necessary tests to pass approval by the FDA

On July 28, 1983, Roche filed a complaint in the United States District Court for the District of New Jersey against three parties: Bolar, Bolar's principal officer, and the importer of the infringing flurazepam hcl. Only Bolar remains a party defendant. Roche sought to enjoin Bolar from using flurazepam hcl for any purpose whatsoever during the life of the '053 patent. When Bolar stated during discovery, on August 30, 1983, that it intended immediately to begin testing its generic drug for FDA approval, Roche moved for and was granted a Temporary Restraining Order, on September 2, 1983.

July 28 1983 filed in NJ court against Bolar, Bolar's officer and the importer. only Bolar left in suit. Roche wants enjoinment on any use.
Got temp Restraining Order

On September 26, 1983, Bolar was granted a change of venue and the case was transferred to the United States District Court for the Eastern District of New York. That court consolidated Roche's motion for a preliminary injunction with the trial on the merits pursuant to Fed.R.Civ.P. 65(a)(2) (both parties had stipulated to all the pertinent facts so no testimony was necessary) and on October 11, 1983, issued a Memorandum and Order denying Roche's application for a permanent injunction. The court held that Bolar's use of the patented compound for federally mandated testing was not infringement of the patent in suit because Bolar's use was de minimis and experimental. The court entered judgment for Bolar on October 14, 1983, and Roche filed its notice of appeal that same day.

II

The district court correctly recognized that the issue in this case is narrow: does the limited use of a patented drug for testing and investigation strictly related to FDA drug approval requirements during the last 6 months of the term of the patent constitute a use which, unless licensed, the patent statute makes actionable? The district court held that it does not. This was an error of law.

III

A

Bolar argues that its intended use of flurazepam hcl is excepted from the use prohibition. It claims two grounds for exception: the first ground is based on a liberal interpretation of the traditional experimental use exception; the second ground is that public policy favors generic drugs and thus mandates the creation of a new exception in order to allow FDA required drug testing. We discuss these arguments seriatim.

B

The so-called experimental use defense to liability for infringement generally is recognized as originating in an opinion written by Supreme Court Justice Story while on circuit in Massachusetts. In *Whittemore v. Cutter*, 29 Fed.Cas. 1120, 1121, (C.C.D.Mass.1813) (No. 17,600), Justice Story sought to justify a trial judge's instruction to a jury that an infringer must have an intent to use a patented invention for profit, stating:

> [I]t could never have been the intention of the legislature to punish a man who constructed such a machine merely for philosophical experiments, or for the purpose of ascertaining the sufficiency of the machine to produce its described effects.

Despite skepticism, *see, e.g., Byam v. Bullard*, 4 Fed.Cas. 934 (C.C.D.Mass. 1852) (No. 2,262) (opinion by Justice Curtis), Justice Story's seminal statement evolved until, by 1861, the law was "well-settled that an experiment with a patented article for the sole purpose of gratifying a philosophical taste, or curiosity, or for mere amusement is not an infringement of the rights of the patentee." *Peppenhausen v. Falke*, 19 Fed.Cas. 1048, 1049 (C.C.S.D.N.Y.1861) (No. 11,279).

The Court of Claims, whose precedents bind us, on several occasions has considered the defense of experimental use. *See Ordnance Engineering Corp. v. United States*, 84 Ct.Cl. 1, (1936); *Chesterfield v. United States*, 159 F.Supp. 371 (1958); *Douglas v. United States*, 181 USPQ 170 (Ct.Cl.Tr.Div.1974), *aff'd*, 510 F.2d 364 (Ct. Cl. 1975); *Pitcairn v. United States*, 547 F.2d 1106 (Ct. Cl.1976). Bolar concedes, as it must, that its intended use of flurazepam hcl does not fall within the "traditional limits" of the experimental use exception as established in these cases or those of other circuits. Its concession here is fatal. Despite Bolar's argument that its tests are "true scientific inquiries" to which a literal interpretation of the experimental use exception logically should extend, we hold the experimental use exception to be truly narrow, and we will not expand it under the present circumstances. Bolar's argument that the experimental use rule deserves a broad construction is not justified.

Pitcairn, the most persuasive of the Court of Claims cases concerning the experimental use defense, sets forth the law which must control the disposition of this case: "[t]ests, demonstrations, and experiments * * * [which] are in keeping with the legitimate business of the * * * [alleged infringer]" are infringements for which "[e]xperimental use is not a defense." 547 F.2d at 1125–1126. We have carefully reviewed each of the other Court of Claims cases, and although they contain some loose language on which Bolar relies, they are unpersuasive. The *Ordnance Engineering* case provides no guidance concerning the boundaries of an appropriately applied experimental use rule other than flatly stating that a device must have been "built for experimental purposes." In *Chesterfield*, the court's flat declaration that "experimental use does not infringe" is pure obiter dictum. *Douglas* has no precedential value here since the Court of Claims never affirmed the part of the trial judge's opinion dealing with experimental use; moreover, Trial Judge Cooper's well-reasoned analysis of the experimental use rule concluded that no case had permitted a pattern of systematic exploitation of a patented invention for the purpose of furthering the legitimate business interests of the infringer. The authority of Trial Judge Cooper's views rests on his reputation as a fine patent lawyer, and on their own intrinsic persuasiveness.

Bolar's intended "experimental" use is solely for business reasons and not for amusement, to satisfy idle curiosity, or for strictly philosophical inquiry. Bolar's intended use of flurazepam hcl to derive FDA required test data is thus an infringement of the '053 patent. Bolar may intend to perform "experiments," but unlicensed experiments conducted with a view to the adaption of the patented invention to the experimentor's business is a violation of the rights of the patentee to exclude others from using his patented invention. It is obvious here that it is a misnomer to call the intended use *de minimis*. It is no trifle in its economic effect on the parties even if the quantity used is small. It is no dilettante affair such as Justice Story envisioned. We cannot construe the experimental use rule so broadly as to allow a violation of the patent laws in the guise of "scientific inquiry," when that inquiry has definite, cognizable, and not insubstantial commercial purposes.

C

Bolar argues that even if no established doctrine exists with which it can escape liability for patent infringement, public policy requires that we create a new exception to the use prohibition. Parties and amici seem to think, in particular, that we must resolve a conflict between the Federal Food, Drug, and Cosmetic Act (FDCA), 21 U.S.C. §§ 301–392 (1982), and the Patent Act of 1952, or at least the Acts' respective policies and purposes. We decline the opportunity here, however, to engage in legislative activity proper only for the Congress.

The new drug approval procedure which existed between 1938 and 1962 was relatively innocuous and had little impact on the development of pioneer prescription new drugs. Section 505 of the FDCA, ch. 675, 52 Stat. 1052 (1938), required the manufacturer of a pioneer new drug to submit to the FDA a New Drug Application (NDA) containing information concerning the safety of the drug. If the FDA did not disapprove the new drug within 60 days after it received the NDA, marketing could begin.

The provisions of the Drug Amendments of 1962, Pub.L. No. 87–781, 76 Stat. 780, caused a substantial increase in the time required for development and approval of a pioneer new drug. Beginning in 1962, the amended Section 505 (codified at 21 U.S.C. § 355 (1982)) required an NDA to contain proof of efficacy (effectiveness) as well as safety, and required the FDA affirmatively to approve the NDA rather than just to permit marketing by inaction. A recent study indicated that it now can take on average from 7 to 10 years for a pharmaceutical company to satisfy the current regulatory requirements. National Academy of Engineering, The Competitive Status of the U.S. Pharmaceutical Industry 79–80 (1983).

Because most FDA-required testing is done after a patent issues, the remaining effective life of patent protection assertedly may be as low as 7 years. Id., citing Statement of William M. Wardell to the Subcommittee on Investigations and Oversight of the Committee on Science and Technology, U.S. House of Representatives, Feb. 14, 1982, at 14. Litigation such as this is one example of how research-oriented pharmaceutical companies have sought to regain some of the earning time lost to regulatory entanglements. They gain for themselves, it is asserted, a de facto monopoly of upwards of 2 years by enjoining FDA-required testing of a generic drug until the patent on the drug's active ingredient expires.

Bolar argues that the patent laws are intended to grant to inventors only a limited 17–year property right to their inventions so that the public can enjoy the benefits of competition as soon as possible, consistent with the need to encourage invention. The FDCA, Bolar contends, was only intended to assure safe and effective drugs for the public, and not to extend a pharmaceutical company's monopoly for an indefinite and substantial period of time while the FDA considers whether to grant a pre-marketing clearance. Because the FDCA affected prevailing law, namely the Patent Act, Bolar argues that we should apply the patent laws to drugs differently.

Simply because a later enacted statute affects in some way an earlier enacted statute is poor reason to ask us to rewrite the earlier statute. Repeals by implication are not favored. *See, e.g., Mercantile National Bank v. Langdeau*, 371 U.S. 555, 565, 83 S.Ct. 520, 525, 9 L.Ed.2d 523 (1963). Thus, "courts are not at liberty to pick and choose among congressional enactments, and when two statutes are capable of co-existence, it is the duty of the courts, absent a clearly expressed congressional intention to the contrary, to regard each as effective." *Morton v. Mancari*, 417 U.S. 535, 551, 94 S.Ct. 2474, 2483, 41 L.Ed.2d 290 (1974). There is no affirmative obligation on Congress to explain why it deems a particular enactment wise or necessary, or to demonstrate that it is aware of the consequences of its action. See *Harrison v. PPG Industries, Inc.*, 446 U.S. 578, 592, 100 S.Ct. 1889, 1897, 64 L.Ed.2d 525 (1980). Rather, because "laws are presumed to be passed with deliberation, and with full knowledge of all existing ones on the same subject," T. SEDGWICK, THE INTERPRETATION AND CONSTRUCTION OF STATUTORY AND CONSTITUTIONAL LAW 106 (2d ed. 1874), we must presume Congress was aware that the FDCA would affect the earning potentiality of a drug patent, and chose to permit it. Although arguably Title 21 and Title 35 are not laws on the "same subject," we note that during Congress' deliberations on the 1962 amendments to the FDCA, it considered the relationship and interaction of the patent laws with the drug laws. *See* S.Rep. No. 1744, 87th Cong., 2d Sess., reprinted in 1962 U.S.Code Cong. & Ad.News 2884, 2911–2915.

It is the role of Congress to maximize public welfare through legislation. Congress is well aware of the economic and societal problems which the parties debate here, and has before it legislation with respect to these issues. *See* H.R. 3605, 98th Cong., 1st Sess. (1983) ("Drug Price Competition Act of 1983") (amending 21 U.S.C. § 355(b) to allow faster marketing of new generic drugs equivalent to approved new drugs); S. 1306, 98th Cong., 1st Sess. (1983) ("Patent Term Restoration Act of 1983") (amending 35 U.S.C. § 155 to add to the patent grant a period of time equivalent to that lost due to regulatory delay), Cong.Rec.S. 6863 (daily ed. May 17, 1983), 26 Pat. Trademark & Copyright J. (BNA) 87–88 (May 26, 1983). No matter how persuasive the policy arguments are for or against these proposed bills, this court is not the proper forum in which to debate them. Where Congress has the clear power to

Only apply laws on the books, not write new ones.

enact legislation, our role is only to interpret and apply that legislation. "[I]t is not our job to apply laws that have not yet been written." *Sony Corp. of America v. Universal City Studios, Inc.*, 464 U.S. 417, 456, 104 S.Ct. 774, 796, 78 L.Ed.2d 574 (1984). We will not rewrite the patent laws here.

V

CONCLUSION

The decision of the district court holding the '053 patent not infringed is reversed. The case is remanded with instructions to fashion an appropriate remedy. Each party to bear its own costs.

REVERSED AND REMANDED

NOTES

1. **The Significance of *Roche v. Bolar*.** *Roche v. Bolar* could quite credibly be ranked as one the most important opinions ever issued by the Federal Circuit, both in terms of its domestic impact and its consequences for patent regimes overseas. The congressional response to *Roche v. Bolar* was the Drug Price Competition and Patent Term Restoration Act of 1984, Pub.L. No. 84–417, 98 Stat. 1585 (1984), popularly known as the Hatch–Waxman Act. Not only did the Hatch–Waxman Act effectively establish a robust generic drug industry in the United States, it deeply impacted pharmaceutical research and development by innovative pharmaceutical firms around the world. The Hatch–Waxman Act is taken up at further length in this text at Chapter 14.

2. **Competing Views on Experimental Use**. Some commentators believe that a broad experimental use privilege is inappropriate as a matter of technology policy. Under this view, a liberal experimental allowance would greatly ease the ability of competitors to "design around" the invention or develop competing technologies. Patent owners in turn would be less able to appropriate the returns of their investments in research and development, this account continues, and would therefore be discouraged from making future investments in research and development. As one observer concludes: "Rather than spurring increased innovative activity, a broad experimental use exception would have just the opposite effect." Jordan P. Karp, *Experimental Use as Patent Infringement: The Impropriety of a Broad Exception*, 100 YALE L.J. 2169 (1991).

In contrast, others believe that the common law experimental use privilege is overly narrow. They assert that the current scope of this doctrine too greatly restricts the ability of innovators to "tinker" with the developments of others. Under this view, research may be chilled if scientists cannot experiment upon state-of-the-art technology free from charges of patent infringement. By limiting the tools with which researchers can work, these commentators say, the patent system could ultimately depress, rather than promote innovation. *See generally* Maureen A. O'Rourke, *Toward a Doctrine of Fair Use in Patent Law*, 100 COL. L. REV. 1177 (2000).

Finally, a third set of commentators remain agnostic about the propriety of an experimental use privilege, but believe that this issue is not of great importance for practical reasons. Patent infringement litigation is widely regarded as costly, time-consuming, and complex. There may be insufficient economic justification to commence litigation against individuals who are not making commercially important uses of patented inventions. As a result, patent infringement suits may only rarely be brought against hobbyists, philosophers, and noncommercial defendants, regardless of how narrowly or broadly the experimental use privilege is defined. *See* Andrew J. Caruso, *The Experimental Use Exception: An Experimentalist's View*, 14 ALBANY J.L., SCI. & TECH. 217 (2003).

3. Don't Forget Exhaustion! It is also important to remember that the patent law may, in certain circumstances, provide researchers with the ability to use products even though they have been patented by others. One of these principles, discussed in this text in Chapter 11, is known as the "exhaustion" or "first sale" doctrine. Under this legal rule, once a patent owner has sold a patented product, he cannot control the use of that particular product. Any patent rights in that specific physical item are said to have been "exhausted" by this initial sale.

For example, suppose that a chemical manufacturing firm wished to analyze a chemical compound manufactured by one of its competitors. If the firm is able simply to purchase the patented product on the open market, then no issues of patent infringement will ordinarily arise. Any patent on the compound is exhausted once the drug has been sold, allowing the purchasing firm to use the compound as it wishes. The scope of the experimental use privilege is irrelevant in this scenario.

On the other hand, suppose that a patented compound is not available for purchase within the market. In order to experiment with that compound, a competing firm must synthesize it within its own laboratories. This step would be an act of patent infringement, however, because the right to make a patented invention is exclusive to the patent proprietor. In this case the experimental use privilege would, at least theoretically, come into play as a possible defense to patent infringement. *See generally* Edward T. Lentz, *Pharmaceutical and Biotechnology Research After* Integra *and* Madey, 23 BIOTECH. L. REP. 265 (2004).

MADEY v. DUKE UNIVERSITY

Court of Appeals for the Federal Circuit, 2002
307 F.3d 1351

Before Bryson, Gajarsa, and Linn, Circuit Judges.

GAJARSA, CIRCUIT JUDGE.

Dr. John M.J. Madey ("Madey") appeals from a judgment of the United States District Court for the Middle District of North Carolina. Madey sued Duke University ("Duke"), bringing claims of patent infringement.... After discovery, the district court granted summary judgment in favor of Duke.... [The district court in part] held that the experimental use defense applied to Duke's use of Madey's patented laser technology.... The district court ... erred in applying the experimental use defense.... Accordingly, we reverse-in-part ... and remand.

BACKGROUND

In the mid–1980s Madey was a tenured research professor at Stanford University. At Stanford, he had an innovative laser research program, which was highly regarded in the scientific community. An opportunity arose for Madey to consider leaving Stanford and take a tenured position at Duke. Duke recruited Madey, and in 1988 he left Stanford for a position in Duke's physics department. In 1989 Madey moved his free electron laser ("FEL") research lab from Stanford to Duke. The FEL lab contained substantial equipment, requiring Duke to build an addition to its physics building to house the lab. In addition, during his time at Stanford, Madey had obtained sole ownership of two patents practiced by some of the equipment in the FEL lab.

At Duke, Madey served for almost a decade as director of the FEL lab. During that time the lab continued to achieve success in both research funding and scientific breakthroughs. However, a dispute arose between Madey and Duke. Duke contends that, despite his scientific prowess, Madey ineffectively managed the lab. Madey contends that Duke sought to use the lab's equipment for research areas outside the allocated scope of certain government funding, and that when he objected, Duke sought to remove him as lab director. Duke eventually did remove Madey as director of the lab in 1997. The removal is not at issue in this appeal, however, it is the genesis of this unique patent infringement case. As a result of the removal, Madey resigned from Duke in 1998. Duke, however, continued to operate some of the equipment in the lab. Madey then sued Duke for patent infringement of his two patents, and brought a variety of other claims.

The Patent Motion and the Experimental Use Defense

The district court acknowledged a common law "exception" for patent infringement liability for uses that, in the district court's words, are "solely for research, academic or experimental purposes." Summary Judgment Opinion at 9 (citing *Deuterium Corp. v. United States*, 19 Cl.Ct. 624, 631 (1990); *Whittemore v. Cutter*, 29 F. Cas. 1120 (C.C.D.Mass.1813) (No. 17,600); and citing two commentators[2]). The district court recognized the debate over the scope of the experimental use defense, but cited this court's opinion in *Embrex, Inc. v. Service Engineering Corp.*, 216 F.3d 1343, 1349 (Fed.Cir.2000) to hold that the defense was viable for experimental, non-profit purposes. Summary Judgment Opinion at 9 (citing *Embrex*, 216 F.3d at 1349 (noting that courts should not "construe

---

2. Janice M. Mueller, *No "Dilettante Affair": Rethinking the Experimental Use Exception to Patent Infringement for Biomedical Research Tools*, 76 WASH. L.REV. 1, 17 (2001); 5 CHISUM ON PATENTS § 16.03[1] (2000).

the experimental use rule so broadly as to allow a violation of the patent laws in the guise of 'scientific inquiry,' when that inquiry has definite, cognizable, and not insubstantial commercial purposes" (quoting *Roche Prods., Inc. v. Bolar Pharm. Co.*, 733 F.2d 858, 863 (Fed.Cir.1984))[3])).

After having recognized the experimental use defense, the district court then fashioned the defense for application to Madey in the passage set forth below.

> Given this standard [for experimental use], for [Madey] to over-come his burden of establishing actionable infringement in this case, he must establish that [Duke] has not used the equipment at issue "solely for an experimental or other non-profit purpose." 5 DONALD S. CHISUM, CHISUM ON PATENTS § 16.03[1] (2000). More specifically, [Madey] must sufficiently establish that [Duke's] use of the patent had "definite, cognizable, and not insubstantial commercial pur-poses." *Roche Prods., Inc. v. Bolar Pharm. Co.*, 733 F.2d 858, 863 (Fed.Cir.1984).

On appeal, Madey attacks this passage as improperly shifting the burden to the plaintiff to allege and prove that the defendant's use was not experimental.

Before the district court, Madey argued that Duke's research in its FEL lab was commercial in character and intent. Madey relied on *Pitcairn v. United States*, 547 F.2d 1106 (Ct. Cl. 1976), where the government used patented rotor structures and control systems for a helicopter to test the "lifting ability" and other attributes of the patented technology. *Pitcairn*, 547 F.2d at 1125–26. The *Pitcairn* court held that the helicopters were not built solely for experimental purposes because they were also built to benefit the government in its legitimate business. Id. Based on language in Duke's patent policy, Madey argues that Duke is in the business of "obtaining grants and developing possible commer-cial applications for the fruits of its 'academic research.'"

The district court rejected Madey's argument, relying on another statement in the preamble of the Duke patent policy which stated that Duke was "dedicated to teaching, research, and the expansion of knowledge ... [and] does not undertake research or development work principally for the purpose of developing patents and commercial applications." The district court reasoned that these statements from the patent policy refute any contention that Duke is "in the business" of developing technology for commercial applications. According to the district court, Madey's "evidence" was mere speculation,[4] and thus

---

3. The accused infringer in *Roche* sought to assert the experimental use defense to allow early development of a generic drug. After the *Roche* decision, however, Congress changed the law, overruling *Roche* in part, but without impacting the experimental use doctrine. Congress provided limited ability for a company to practice a patent in furtherance of a drug approval application.

4. Madey also argued that Duke's acceptance of funding from the government and private foundations was evidence of developing patented devices with commercial intent. The district court also rejected this proposition. Summary Judgment Opinion at 13 (citing *Ruth v. Stearns–Roger Mfg. Co.*, 13 F.Supp. 697, 713 (D.Colo.1935) (concluding that the experimental use defense applies when a university uses a patented device in furtherance of its educational purpose); Ronald D. Hartman,

Madey did not meet his burden of proof to create a genuine issue of material fact.[5] The court went on to state that "[w]ithout more concrete evidence to rebut [Duke's] stated purpose with respect to its research in the FEL lab, Plaintiff has failed to meet its burden of establishing patent infringement by a preponderance of the evidence."

C. The District Court's Application of Experimental Use

On appeal, Madey asserts three primary errors related to experimental use. First, Madey claims that the district court improperly shifted the burden to Madey to prove that Duke's use was not experimental. Second, Madey argues that the district court applied an overly broad version of the very narrow experimental use defense inconsistent with our precedent. Third, Madey attacks the supporting evidence relied on by the district court as overly general and not indicative of the specific propositions and findings required by the experimental use defense, and further argues that there is no support in the record before us to allow any court to apply the very narrow experimental use defense to Duke's ongoing FEL lab operation. We substantially agree with Madey on all three points. In addition, Madey makes a threshold argument concerning the continued existence of the experimental use doctrine in any form, which we turn to first. Our precedent, to which we are bound, continues to recognize the judicially created experimental use defense, however, in a very limited form.

The Experimental Use Defense

Citing the concurring opinion in Embrex, Madey contends that the Supreme Court's opinion in *Warner–Jenkinson Co. v. Hilton Davis Chem. Co.*, 520 U.S. 17, 117 S.Ct. 1040, 137 L.Ed.2d 146 (1997) eliminates the experimental use defense. *Embrex,* 216 F.3d at 1352–53 (Rader, J., concurring). The Supreme Court held in *Warner–Jenkinson* that intent plays no role in the application of the doctrine of equivalents. *Warner–Jenkinson,* 520 U.S. at 36, 117 S.Ct. 1040. Madey implicitly argues that the experimental use defense necessarily incorporates an intent inquiry, and thus is inconsistent with *Warner–Jenkinson*. Like the majority in *Embrex,* we do not view such an inconsistency as inescapable, and conclude the experimental use defense persists albeit in the very narrow form articulated by this court in *Embrex,* 216 F.3d at 1349, and in *Roche,* 733 F.2d at 863.

The District Court Improperly Shifted the Burden to Madey

As a precursor to the burden-shifting issue, Madey argues that the experimental use defense is an affirmative defense that Duke must plead or lose. We disagree. Madey points to no source of authority for its

Experimental Use as an Exception to Patent Infringement, 67 J. Pat. Off. Soc'y 617, 633 (1985) (concluding that Ruth supports application of the experimental use defense to a university's operations in furtherance of its educational function)).

5. The district court discussed and dismissed in a footnote other evidence suggested by Madey, including the fact that Duke had established (but not yet applied) an hourly fee for industrial users wishing to use the FEL lab's resources, and statements from Duke's website for the FEL lab indicating an interest in corporate partnerships.

assertion that experimental use is an affirmative defense. Indeed, we have referred to the defense in a variety of ways. *See Roche,* 733 F.2d at 862 (referring to experimental use as both an exception and a defense). Given this lack of precise treatment in the precedent, Madey has no basis to support its affirmative defense argument. The district court and the parties in the present case joined the issue during the summary judgment briefing. We see no mandate from our precedent, nor any compelling reason from other considerations, why the opportunity to raise the defense if not raised in the responsive pleading should not also be available at the later stages of a case, within the procedural discretion typically afforded the trial court judge.

The district court held that in order for Madey to overcome his burden to establish actionable infringement, he must establish that Duke did not use the patent-covered free electron laser equipment solely for experimental or other non-profit purposes. Madey argues that this improperly shifts the burden to the patentee and conflates the experimental use defense with the initial infringement inquiry.

We agree with Madey that the district court improperly shifted the burden to him. The district court folded the experimental use defense into the baseline assessment as to whether Duke infringed the patents. Duke characterizes the district court's holding as expressing the following sequence: first, the court recognized that Madey carried his burden of proof on infringement; second, the court held that Duke carried its burden of proof on the experimental use defense; and third, the court held that Madey was unable to marshal sufficient evidence to rebut Duke's shifting of the burden. We disagree with Duke's reading of the district court's opinion. The district court explicitly contradicts Duke's argument by stating that Madey failed to "meet its burden to establish patent infringement by a preponderance of the evidence." This statement is an assessment of whether Madey supported his initial infringement claim. It is not an assessment of which party carried or shifted the burden of evidence related to the experimental use defense. Thus, the district court did not conclude that Madey failed to rebut Duke's assertion of the experimental use defense. Instead, it erroneously required Madey to show as a part of his initial claim that Duke's use was not experimental. The defense, if available at all, must be established by Duke.

The District Court's Overly Broad Conception of Experimental Use

Madey argues, and we agree, that the district court had an overly broad conception of the very narrow and strictly limited experimental use defense. The district court stated that the experimental use defense inoculated uses that "were solely for research, academic, or experimental purposes," and that the defense covered use that "is made for experimental, non-profit purposes only." Both formulations are too broad and stand in sharp contrast to our admonitions in *Embrex* and *Roche* that the experimental use defense is very narrow and strictly limited. In *Embrex*, we followed the teachings of *Roche* and *Pitcairn* to hold that the defense was very narrow and limited to actions performed "for amusement, to satisfy idle curiosity, or for strictly philosophical inquiry." *Embrex*, 216 F.3d at 1349, 55 USPQ2d at 1163. Further, use does not qualify for the experimental use defense when it is undertaken in the "guise of scientific inquiry" but has "definite, cognizable, and not insubstantial commercial purposes." *Id.* (quoting *Roche*, 733 F.2d at 863). The concurring opinion in *Embrex* expresses a similar view: use is disqualified from the defense if it has the "slightest commercial implication." *Id.* at 1353, 216 F.3d 1343. Moreover, use in keeping with the legitimate business of the alleged infringer does not qualify for the experimental use defense. *See Pitcairn*, 547 F.2d at 1125–26. The district court supported its conclusion with a citation to *Ruth v. Stearns–Roger Mfg. Co.*, 13 F.Supp. 697, 713 (D.Colo.1935), a case that is not binding precedent for this court.

The *Ruth* case represents the conceptual dilemma that may have led the district court astray. Cases evaluating the experimental use defense are few, and those involving non-profit, educational alleged infringers are even fewer. In *Ruth*, the court concluded that a manufacturer of equipment covered by patents was not liable for contributory infringement because the end-user purchaser was the Colorado School of Mines, which used the equipment in furtherance of its educational purpose. Thus, the combination of apparent lack of commerciality, with the non-profit status of an educational institution, prompted the court in *Ruth*, without any detailed analysis of the character, nature and effect of the use, to hold that the experimental use defense applied. This is not consistent with the binding precedent of our case law postulated by *Embrex, Roche* and *Pitcairn*.

Our precedent clearly does not immunize use that is in any way commercial in nature. Similarly, our precedent does not immunize any conduct that is in keeping with the alleged infringer's legitimate business, regardless of commercial implications. For example, major research universities, such as Duke, often sanction and fund research projects with arguably no commercial application whatsoever. However, these projects unmistakably further the institution's legitimate business objectives, including educating and enlightening students and faculty participating in these projects. These projects also serve, for example, to increase the status of the institution and lure lucrative research grants, students and faculty.

In short, regardless of whether a particular institution or entity is engaged in an endeavor for commercial gain, so long as the act is in furtherance of the alleged infringer's legitimate business and is not solely for amusement, to satisfy idle curiosity, or for strictly philosophical inquiry, the act does not qualify for the very narrow and strictly limited experimental use defense. Moreover, the profit or non-profit status of the user is not determinative.

In the present case, the district court attached too great a weight to the non-profit, educational status of Duke, effectively suppressing the fact that Duke's acts appear to be in accordance with any reasonable interpretation of Duke's legitimate business objectives.[7] On remand, the district court will have to significantly narrow and limit its conception of the experimental use defense. The correct focus should not be on the non-profit status of Duke but on the legitimate business Duke is involved in and whether or not the use was solely for amusement, to satisfy idle curiosity, or for strictly philosophical inquiry.

III.   Conclusion

The district court erred in its application of the common law experimental use defense, and, consequently, incorrectly found that there was no genuine issue of material fact upon which Madey could prevail. Accordingly, we … reverse-in-part the district court's decision and remand for additional proceedings consistent with this opinion.

Notes

1. The Impact of *Madey v. Duke*. Many patent law experts agree that following the *Madey v. Duke University* case, colleges, universities, and other academic institutions are unlikely to be able to rely upon the common law experimental use privilege as a defense to a charge of patent infringement. Lawrence Sung and Claire M. Maisano explain that the "decision in *Madey* leaves grave doubt that the common law exemption to patent infringement liability can act as a safe harbor for any academic research effort." Lawrence M. Sung & Claire M. Maisano, *Piercing the Academic Veil: Disaffecting the Common Law Exception to Patent Infringement Liability and the Future of a Bona Fide Research Use Exemption After* Madey v. Duke University, 9 J. Health Care L. & Pol'y 256 (2003). Commentator Michelle Cai further opines that "practically any project conducted by a research university, even one without any commercial implications, would be in keeping with the university's legitimate business interests and hence would not qualify for the experimental use defense." Michelle Cai, "Madey v. Duke University: *Shattering the Myth of Universities' Experimental Use Defense*," 19 Berkeley Tech. L.J. 175, 175 (2004).

Observers generally agree that *Madey v. Duke University* either retains, or perhaps restricts to an even greater degree, the quite limited nature of the common law experimental use privilege as it might be applied outside of academic settings. Attorneys Paul Devinksy and Mark G. Davis concluded that the opinion is consistent with previous judicial interpretations of the common law experimental use privilege. As a result the privilege "lives on as a narrow defense to a claim of infringement." Paul Devinksy & Mark G. Davis, *2003 Patent Law Decisions of the Federal Circuit*," 53 Am. U. L.Rev. 773, 883 (2004).

---

7. Duke's patent and licensing policy may support its primary function as an educational institution. See Duke University Policy on Inventions, Patents, and Technology Transfer (1996), available at http:// www.ors.duke.edu/policies/patpol.htm (last visited Oct. 3, 2002). Duke, however, like other major research institutions of higher learning, is not shy in pursuing an aggressive patent licensing program from which it derives a not insubstantial revenue stream.

Other observers would go further. Cathryn Campbell and R.V. Lupo explain that after *Madey* "the Experimental Use Exception would appear to provide little, if any protection in today's world." Cathryn Campbell & R.V. Lupo, *Exemption to Patent Infringement Under 35 U.S.C. Section 271(e)(1): Safe Harbor or Storm A–Brewing?*, 5 SEDONA CONF. J. 29 (2004).

2. Pro–*Madey*. For some observers, a broad experimental use privilege is inappropriate even when research takes place within an academic research setting. In the modern world, university research is often not isolated from the private sector, but instead may have significant commercial implications. As stated by two patent experts who were then senior officers of the PTO, the *Madey v. Duke University* decision "recognized a basic economic truth underlying research performed by large universities—it is a business, and universities derive substantial commercial value from that research." Stephen G. Kunin & Linda S. Therkorn, *Workship on Future Public Policy and Ethical Issues Facing the Biotechnology Industry*, 86 J. PAT. & TRADEMARK OFF. SOC'Y 503 (2004).

Indeed, some commentators believe that university research is increasingly likely to have commercial implications. This shift is believed to be due in part to federal legislation commonly known as the Bayh–Dole Act. Act of Dec. 12, 1980, Pub. L. No. 96–517, 94 Stat. 3015. The Bayh–Dole Act aims to encourage the commercialization of basic research by allowing universities and small businesses to procure patents on inventions that result from federally funded research. Since the passage of the Bayh–Dole Act, many research universities have developed patent portfolios and garnered significant royalties from intellectual property licensing. Because academic institutions have increasingly benefited from the patent system, some observers reason, they should also be held accountable when they infringe the patents of others. *See* Traci Dreher Quigley, *Commercialization of the State University: Why the Intellectual Property Restoration Act of 2003 Is Necessary*, 152 U. PENN. L.REV. 2001 (2004).

3. Anti–*Madey*. Other observers believe that limiting the experimental use privilege with respect to universities and nonprofit institutes could impede academic research. Some university-based scientists believe that, unlike some of their counterparts in the private sector, academic researchers have all but ignored the patent system. John P. Walsh et al., *Working Through the Patent Problem*, 299 SCI. 1021, 1021 (2003) ("[Research universities] have largely ignored the growing number of patents covering technology that their scientists use without license and without apology."). In order to avoid patent infringement, universities may have to devote scarce resources to perform costly patent searches and engage in licensing negotiations with patent holders. To a greater extent than profit-seeking firms, educational institutions may find that these obligations weigh heavily on their frequently tight budgets. *See* Jennifer Miller, *Sealing the Coffin on Experimental Use*, 2003 DUKE L. & TECH. REV. 12.

4. Experimental Use Overseas. Article 69(1) of the Japanese Patent Act provides that "[t]he effects of the patent right shall not extend to the working of the patent right for the purposes of experiment or research." On April 16, 1999, the Supreme Court of Japan in *Ono Pharmaceutical Co. Ltd. v. Kyoto Pharmaceutical Co. Ltd.* decided that activities designed to obtain marketing approval in order to begin commercial activities after the expiration of the patent are for experiment and research under Section 69(1). The court gave the following as its reasons:

(a) The patent system encourages creation of inventions by rewarding persons who disclose inventions to the public with an exclusive right for a limited time, and contributes to the development of industry by giving third parties opportunities to exploit the disclosed invention. One of the fundamental purposes of the patent system is to benefit society as a whole by allowing persons to freely exploit an invention once its patent term expires.

(b) The Drug Regulation Act requires, as a means of ensuring drug safety, approval from the Ministry of Health prior to manufacturing a new drug. The statute requires an applicant to conduct several types of clinical testing and attach resulting data to its application. With respect to a generic drug, the application requirements are the same as for a new drug in that an applicant must conduct the specified testing over a significant period of time. In conducting the testing, an applicant must produce and use a chemical compound or pharmaceutical product that falls within the technical scope of the patentee's patented invention. If the Court were to find that said testing is not an "experiment" under Article 69, Paragraph 1 of the Patent Act, thereby preventing an applicant from engaging in said production and use, third parties would not be able to freely exploit the invention for a significant time after the expiration of a patent. This result conflicts with the fundamental purpose of the patent system stated in the above paragraph.

(c) On the other hand, if a third party exploits the invention beyond the scope required to apply for approval under the Drug Regulation Act, and produces a patented generic drug or produces and uses a patented chemical compound with intent to assign them after the expiration of the patent, such exploitation constitutes an infringement and is not permissible. This interpretation guarantees patentees exclusive exploitation of their patented invention during the protection term. If, on the other hand, patentees are given the right to prevent third parties from engaging in said production and use of the patented invention for testing necessary to apply for manufacturing approval, this would result in a significant extension of the patent protection term. This result exceeds the benefit to patentees intended under the Patent Act.

Similarly, the European Community Patent Convention indicates that "acts done for experimental purposes relating to the subject-matter of the patented invention" are exempted from infringement. CPC Article 31. Although the CPC is not yet in force in Europe, the laws of many member states already reflect this principle. Jochen Pagenberg, *Clinical Tests ("Klinische Versuche")*, 28 INT'L REV. INDUS. PROP. & COPYRIGHT L. 103 (1997), presents an English translation and commentary regarding a controversial decision of the German Federal Supreme Court (*"Bundesgerichtshof"*). Another English translation is found at [1997] R.P.C. 623. Shortly thereafter came *Klinische Versuche II* from the same court, [1998] R.P.C. 423. These cases hold that one who seeks to discover new knowledge relating to the subject-matter of the patent is not infringing the patent even if the purpose for obtaining such knowledge is to obtain marketing approval. However, use of a patented research tool for its intended purpose may still infringe. An extensive comparative study may be found in DAVID GILAT, EXPERIMENTAL USE AND PATENTS (1995) (Studies in Industrial Property and Copyright Law Vol. 16).

In 2004 the European Commission acted to harmonize for the countries of the Union a Bolar exemption for the patent laws of the member states of the Union, Article 10(6) of Directive 2004/27/EC. In addition, the relationship between the TRIPS Agreement and Bolar exemptions in the patent laws of WTO members is reviewed in *WTO, Report of the Panel, Canada—Patent Protection of Pharmaceutical Products*, WT/DS114/R, 2000 WL 301021 (Mar. 17, 2000).

§ 12.2   MISUSE

USM CORP. v. SPS TECHNOLOGIES, INC.

United States Court of Appeals, Seventh Circuit, 1982
694 F.2d 505

Before Pell, Circuit Judge, Stewart, Associate Justice (Retired), and Posner, Circuit Judge.

POSNER, CIRCUIT JUDGE.

SPS, a manufacturer of industrial fasteners, owned a patent, issued in 1963, on a patch-type self-locking industrial fastener. In 1969 it sued USM, a competing manufacturer of fasteners, for infringement. After a trial on the issue whether USM had a valid license under the patent by virtue of a grant-back clause in a licensing agreement between the parties, the district court held that USM did not have a valid license. *Standard Pressed Steel Co. v. Coral Corp.*, 168 U.S.P.Q. 741 (N.D.Ill.1971). The parties then settled the case by entry of a consent judgment in which USM acknowledged that the patent was valid and had been infringed. As part of the settlement SPS granted USM a license which allowed USM to continue using the patent but required it to pay royalties to SPS.

In 1974, three years after SPS's suit had been settled, USM brought the present suit, seeking to invalidate SPS's patent and get back the royalties it had paid since the settlement. . . . USM's suit not only challenges the validity of the patent but also alleges that certain terms that first appeared in the license agreement entered into at the termination of the first suit constitute patent misuse. * * * The remaining issue is whether SPS committed patent misuse by including a differential royalty schedule in the license agreement entered into as part of the settlement of the earlier suit. The agreement requires USM to remit to SPS 25 percent of any royalties it obtains by sublicensing SPS's patent, except that if USM should happen to sublicense any of four companies that SPS had previously licensed directly USM must remit 75 percent of the royalties obtained from the sublicensee(s).

The doctrine of patent misuse has been described as an equitable concept designed to prevent a patent owner from using the patent in a manner contrary to public policy. *Morton Salt Co. v. G.S. Suppiger Co.*, 314 U.S. 488 (1942). This is too vague a formulation to be useful; taken seriously it would put all patent rights at hazard; and in application the doctrine has largely been confined to a handful of specific practices by which the patentee seemed to be trying to "extend" his patent grant beyond its statutory limits. An early example was fixing the price at which the purchaser of the patented item could resell it. *See Bauer & Cie. v. O'Donnell*, 229 U.S. 1 (1913). The courts reasoned (in rather a circular fashion, one must admit) that once the patent owner had given up title to the patented item his patent rights were at an end, and any further restriction on the purchaser would extend the patent beyond its statutory bounds. Similar thinking lies behind the most common application of the doctrine, which is to prevent the patent owner from requiring his licensees to buy an unpatented staple item used with the patented device—for example, ink with a mimeograph machine. See generally *Dawson Chem. Co. v. Rohm & Haas Co.*, 448 U.S. 176, 188–93 (1980).

Both examples—resale price maintenance and tying—suggest an overlap between misuse and antitrust principles. But although resale price maintenance by patentees was condemned as misuse shortly after *Dr. Miles Medical Co. v. John D. Park & Sons Co.*, 220 U.S. 373 (1911), held that the Sherman Act forbade resale price maintenance in nonpatent cases, see Bauer & Cie. v. O'Donnell, supra, and patent tie-ins were condemned as misuse shortly after the enactment of the tying provision (section 3) of the Clayton Act, 15 U.S.C. § 14, in 1914, see *Motion Picture Patents Co. v. Universal Film Mfg. Co.*, 243 U.S. 502, 517–18 (1917), in both instances the condemnation of the patentee's conduct was based on the doctrine of patent misuse rather than on antitrust law. More recently the doctrine has been used to forbid the patentee to require his licensees to pay royalties beyond the expiration of the patent, *Brulotte v. Thys Co.*, 379 U.S. 29 (1964), or to measure royalties by the sales of unpatented end products containing the patented item, *Zenith Radio Corp. v. Hazeltine Research, Inc.*, 395 U.S. 100, 133–40 (1969), or to require licensees not to make any items competing with the patented item, *Stewart v. Motrim, Inc.*, 192 U.S.P.Q. 410 (S.D.Ohio 1975).

As an original matter one might question whether any of these practices really "extends" the patent. The patentee who insists on limiting the freedom of his purchaser or licensee—whether to price, to use complementary inputs of the purchaser's choice, or to make competing items—will have to compensate the purchaser for the restriction by charging a lower price for the use of the patent. If, for example, the patent owner requires the licensee to agree to continue paying royalties after the patent expires, he will not be able to get him to agree to pay as big a royalty before the patent expires.

In all of these cases the patentee's total income may be higher—why else would he impose the restriction? But there is nothing wrong with trying to make as much money as you can from a patent. True, a tie-in can be a method of price discrimination. It enables the patent owner to vary the amount he charges for the use of the patent by the intensity of each user's demand for the patent (e.g., the mimeograph), as measured by the user's consumption of the tied product (e.g., the ink). *Heaton–Peninsular Button–Fastener Co. v. Eureka Specialty Co.*, 77 F. 288, 296 (6th Cir.1896); STIGLER, THE THEORY OF PRICE 210–11 (3d ed. 1966); BOWMAN, PATENT AND ANTITRUST LAW 55, 116–19 (1973). But since, as we shall see, there is no principle that patent owners may not engage in price discrimination, it is unclear why one form of discrimination, the tie-in, alone is forbidden.

But whether decided rightly or wrongly these are all cases where the license purports to enlarge the licensee's obligations beyond the limits of the patent grant. There is nothing of that sort here. But we must also consider whether the patent-misuse doctrine goes beyond these specific practices and constitutes a general code of patent licensing distinct from antitrust law.

The doctrine arose before there was any significant body of federal antitrust law, and reached maturity long before that law (a product very largely of free interpretation of unclear statutory language) attained its present broad scope. Since the antitrust laws as currently interpreted reach every practice that could impair competition substantially, it is not easy to define a separate role for a doctrine also designed to prevent an anticompetitive practice—the abuse of a patent monopoly. One possibility is that the doctrine of patent misuse, unlike antitrust law, condemns any patent licensing practice that is even trivially anticompetitive, at least if it has no socially beneficial effects. This might seem to explain cases such as *Duplan Corp. v. Deering Milliken, Inc.*, 444 F.Supp. 648, 697 (D.S.C.1977), *aff'd in relevant part*, 594 F.2d 979 (4th Cir.1979), which held that a patent tie-in agreement is misuse per se unless the patentee shows that he had some nonmonopolistic reason for the tie-in, such as protection of goodwill. To prove a tie-in prima facie unlawful under the antitrust laws all you have to show is that the defendant has some economic power in the market for the tying product, *United States Steel Corp. v. Fortner Enterprises, Inc.*, 429 U.S. 610 (1977), and *Duplan* eliminates this requirement in misuse cases. But if a patentee has no market power (and, of course, not every patent confers market power, *SCM Corp. v. Xerox Corp.*, 645 F.2d 1195, 1203 (2d Cir.1981)) he cannot use a tie-in to practice price discrimination, which presupposes market power. STIGLER, *supra*, at 211. Much less can he lever his way into a dominant position in the market for the tied product. The logical presumption in such a case is that the tie-in promotes efficiency—and there is no lack of hypotheses as to how it might do that. See BORK, THE ANTITRUST PARADOX 375–81 (1978). It is hard to understand why in these circumstances, where if any presumption is warranted it is that the tie-in promotes efficiency rather than reduces competition, the burden of proof on the issue of misuse should be shifted to the patentee.

But probably cases like *Duplan*—which was, like *Motion Picture Patents Co., supra,* a tie-in case—are best understood simply as applications of the patent-misuse doctrine within its conventional, rather stereotyped boundaries. Outside those boundaries there is increasing convergence of patent-misuse analysis with standard antitrust analysis. See, e.g., *Carter–Wallace, Inc. v. United States,* 449 F.2d 1374, 1378–82 (Ct.Cl. 1971); *Congoleum Indus., Inc. v. Armstrong Cork Co.,* 366 F.Supp. 220, 227–32 (E.D.Pa.1973), *aff'd,* 510 F.2d 334 (3d Cir.1975); *SCM Corp. v. Xerox Corp.,* 463 F.Supp. 983, 997–98 (D.Conn.1978) (the lengthy subsequent history of this case is irrelevant). One still finds plenty of statements in judicial opinions that less evidence of anticompetitive effect is required in a misuse case than in an antitrust case. See, e.g., *Transitron Electronic Corp. v. Hughes Aircraft Co.,* 487 F.Supp. 885, 892–93 (D.Mass. 1980), aff'd, 649 F.2d 871 (1st Cir.1981). But apart from the conventional applications of the doctrine we have found no cases where standards different from those of antitrust law were actually applied to yield different results. For example, the issue in *Transitron* was whether patent misuse is a tort; the court held it was not.

If misuse claims are not tested by conventional antitrust principles, by what principles shall they be tested? Our law is not rich in alternative concepts of monopolistic abuse; and it is rather late in the day to try to develop one without in the process subjecting the rights of patent holders to debilitating uncertainty.

We come at last to the particulars of USM's charge of patent misuse, which the district court dismissed on summary judgment and which for the reasons just explained we think must be evaluated under antitrust principles. The basic charge is simply that SPS has set a discriminatory royalty schedule. But no general principle of antitrust law forbids charging different prices to different customers, what is often but loosely called "price discrimination." (The technical economic definition of price discrimination is disparity of price-cost ratios rather than of prices alone. Stigler, *supra,* at 209.) It is not illegal per se, even under section 2(a) of the Clayton Act as amended by the Robinson–Patman Act, 15 U.S.C. § 13(a). *O. Hommel Co. v. Ferro Corp.,* 659 F.2d 340, 346 (3d Cir.1981); *American Oil Co. v. FTC,* 325 F.2d 101, 106 (7th Cir 1963). It might in a particular case be condemned as an attempt to monopolize or as an act of monopolization under section 2 of the Sherman Act, 15 U.S.C. § 2, or as a violation of the Rule of Reason under section 1 of that Act, but USM has made no effort to prove the elements of any of these offenses.

Specifically, there is no antitrust prohibition against a patent owner's using price discrimination to maximize his income from the patent. *Bela Seating Co. v. Poloron Prods., Inc.,* 438 F.2d 733, 738 (7th Cir.1971). The furthest the courts have gone in condemning patent price discrimination under antitrust principles is in a series of cases involving a patented process for machine peeling of shrimp. *See La Peyre v. FTC*, 366 F.2d 117 (5th Cir.1966); *Laitram Corp. v. King Crab, Inc.*, 244 F.Supp. 9, *modified*, 245 F.Supp. 1019 (D.Alaska 1965); *Peelers Co. v. Wendt*, 260 F.Supp. 193 (W.D.Wash.1966). The patentee leased the machines at twice the price to Pacific Northwest shrimp processors as to Gulf Coast processors, because hand peeling the smaller Pacific Northwest shrimp required twice as much labor. This was price discrimination in its economic sense. The lease rate varied according to the different intensities of the buyers' demands for the patented process (greater in the Pacific Northwest because of higher labor costs replaced by the patented process), rather than according to any difference in the patentee's costs of dealing with the two regions. But the focus of concern of the Federal Trade Commission and the courts was not on the evils of price discrimination in any abstract sense but on the effect of the discrimination in limiting the competition that the Pacific Northwest industry would have been able to offer the Gulf Coast industry if equal lease rates had been charged—an effect that seemed all the more sinister because the patentee had an interest in a Gulf Coast processor.

The decisions have been criticized. *See* BOWMAN, *supra*, at 105–10; Baxter, *Legal Restrictions on Exploitation of the Patent Monopoly: An Economic Analysis*, 76 YALE L.J. 267, 280–99 (1966). They require a patentee to establish a pricing schedule that will increase competition in the industries that use the invention—as if the function of antitrust law were to compel firms to maximize competition (between customers, no less), rather than to prevent them from restricting it. There is a difference between positive and negative duties, and the antitrust laws, like other legal doctrines sounding in tort, have generally been understood to impose only the latter. The pricing schedule did not harm the Pacific Northwest industry, but merely left it in the same position relative to the Gulf Coast industry that it had occupied before the patented process was invented.

But whether they were decided correctly or incorrectly, the shrimp peeler cases are distinguishable from the present case; no competitive effects in the market of the patentee's customers have been shown here. *See Bela Seating Co. v. Poloron Prods., Inc.*, *supra*, 438 F.2d 733 at 738–39. USM has made no offer to prove that competition in the manufacture or sale of the products made by SPS's licensees and sublicensees (corresponding to the shrimp peelers) would be greater but for the royalty differential; and it is unlikely that it would be. The main differential is in the amount of royalties retained by USM rather than in the amount paid by the sublicensees. True, there potentially is some differential in that amount. While the usual royalty rate is 4 percent, of which USM retains 3 percent and SPS gets 1 percent, if USM sublicenses the four companies already licensed by SPS and those companies do not drop their SPS licenses, the royalty rate rises to 5 percent, with USM retaining 1 percent and SPS getting the other 4 percent. But a one percent cost difference is too small to give rise to an inference of significant competitive effect.

Conceivably the much larger difference between the amount of royalties retained by USM and the amount retained by SPS could affect competition not among the sublicensees but between these two firms. USM presented evidence that its technology embodying SPS's patent was superior to SPS's own technology and that SPS had imposed the royalty retention differential because it knew that without it USM would outcompete SPS to license the four companies. Even if this were true, it would not get USM very far in making out an antitrust case; as the district court pointed out, the essence of the patent grant is to allow the patentee to exclude competition in the use of the patented invention or, within broad limits not apparently exceeded here, to license competitors only on such terms as he sees fit. In any event, USM made no effort to present evidence of actual or probable anticompetitive effect in a relevant market, as is required in every Rule of Reason antitrust case in the Seventh Circuit. *Dos Santos v. Columbus–Cuneo–Cabrini Medical Center*, 684 F.2d 1346, 1352 (7th Cir.1982). There is no argument that the royalty differential is unlawful per se. Patent licensing agreements between competitors are sometimes struck down under antitrust law, of course, but only upon proof of an anticompetitive effect beyond that implicit in the grant of the patent.

Moreover, the licensing agreement entitles the four companies licensed directly by SPS to obtain a sublicense from USM on the same terms as USM's other sublicensees. If USM's technology really were better than SPS's—enough better at any rate to make it worth their while to pay an additional one percent royalty to be able to use it—the four companies would have taken up their right to get sublicenses from USM. That USM would have been worse off if they had done so than it would have been had it negotiated a different licensing agreement with SPS in settlement of the earlier litigation is not in itself a basis for finding a violation of the antitrust laws. Those laws are solicitous not of the individual firm but of the competitive process. When, four years into the case (it was filed in 1974, and summary judgment on the misuse issue was granted in 1978), USM had presented no evidence of actual or probable anticompetitive effect, the dismissal of its misuse claim on a motion for summary judgment was proper.

The fact that the four direct licensees of SPS had the right at little or no additional cost to demand sublicenses from USM casts doubt, moreover, on USM's explanation of why SPS imposed the royalty retention differential. An alternative explanation is supplied in a deposition submitted by SPS in support of its motion for summary judgment, though not referred to by the district court. The deposition suggests that the royalty retention differential was an effort to overcome a "free rider" problem. SPS rather than USM had licensed the four companies in question and wanted a fair return on its efforts in doing so. There are costs to lining up licensees, as USM itself has emphasized in contending that 1 percent is too little to compensate it for sublicensing SPS's four direct licensees. Otherwise SPS would not allow USM to keep 75 percent of the royalties on sublicenses obtained by USM. That is compensation for USM's efforts in arranging for the use of the patent. It is overcompensation if the efforts are SPS's, as apparently was the case with the four companies in question; if, in other words, USM wants to reap where SPS has sown. In these circumstances the royalty differential would not even be "discriminatory" in any interesting sense. And antitrust law increasingly is tolerant of contractual arrangements that reduce free-rider problems and thereby increase competition (here, competition to line up patent users).

Admittedly there is irony in our recitation of the reasons that the challenged features of the licensing agreement may actually be procompetitive and in any event are not anticompetitive, when the district court found, in findings that we have not reviewed, that the patent was procured by fraud and was therefore invalid. If the patent really is invalid, and well it may be, the licensing agreement may be altogether more sinister than our discussion implies; USM and SPS are, after all, competitors. But unless we are to overrule Wikomi, which we have no mind to do, we must approach the misuse issue on the assumption that the patent is valid, for the defense of res judicata prevents USM from showing the contrary. Of course nothing we say in this opinion is intended to prejudge any other challenge that may be brought against SPS's patent; and, in any event, the patent has now expired, and can no longer restrain trade.

To sum up, we vacate the order of the district court holding SPS's patent invalid and granting USM other relief, and otherwise we affirm the orders appealed from, with costs in this court to SPS.

NOTES

1. How Should the Federal Circuit Deal With Misuse Cases? The Federal Circuit does not have exclusive jurisdiction over patent-antitrust cases. They can be heard in any of the regional circuits. However, since misuse is an equitable defense to a charge of patent infringement, what constitutes substantive misuse is ordinarily a matter within the control of the Federal Circuit. Should the Federal Circuit adopt the policy that no conduct will be labeled a misuse unless there is Supreme Court authority squarely holding that the challenged conduct is a misuse, or alternatively, that the conduct is anticompetitive and therefore violates the antitrust laws? Beyond the *Mallinckrodt* decision, the Federal Circuit may have adopted this view in *Windsurfing International, Inc. v. AMF Inc.*, 782 F.2d 995 (Fed.Cir.1986). However, in *Senza–Gel Corp. v. Seiffhart*, 803 F.2d 661 (Fed.Cir.1986) the court appears to have stepped away from it. For an analysis of these cases as well as the views of the Justice Department on the need for anticompetitive conduct in misuse cases see 8 MARTIN J. ADELMAN, PATENT LAW PERSPECTIVES, § 18.6[2.–3–2] at nn.21 and 22 (2d ed. 1989).

2. Misuse misused? Misuse releases one wrongdoer (the infringer) from responsibility because the victim (the patentee) may have also wronged third parties (the anticompetitive activity) in ways unrelated to the specifics of this infringement action. Does this observation explain the limited role given to patent misuse outside of genuine antitrust violations?

§ 12.3   LACHES AND ESTOPPEL

In its watershed *Auckerman* decision, the *in banc* Federal Circuit refined and in some aspects redefined the defenses of laches and estoppel in patent cases.

A.C. AUKERMAN CO. v. R.L. CHAIDES CONSTRUCTION CO.

United States Court of Appeals, Federal Circuit, 1992
960 F.2d 1020

Before Nies, Chief Judge, Rich, Newman, Archer, Mayer, Michel, Plager, Lourie, Clevenger, and Rader, Circuit Judges.

Nies, Chief Judge.

This court reheard Appeal No. 90–1137 in banc to reconsider the principles of laches and equitable estoppel applicable in a patent infringement suit. A.C. Aukerman Co. sued R.L. Chaides Construction Co. in the United States District Court for the Northern District of California for infringement of Aukerman's patents, U.S. Patent Nos. 3,793,133 ('133) and 4,014,633 ('633). The district court held on summary judgment that Aukerman was barred under principles of laches and equitable estoppel from maintaining the suit and Aukerman appeals. We conclude that the correct standards, which we have clarified herein, were not applied in the district court's grant of summary judgment. Moreover, upon application of the correct law, genuine issues of material fact arise with respect to the issues of laches and equitable estoppel. Accordingly, we reverse the court's ruling on the motion for summary judgment and remand for proceedings consistent with this opinion.

I.

BACKGROUND

The following facts are not disputed. Aukerman is the assignee of the '133 and '633 patents, relating to, respectively, a method and device for forming concrete highway barriers capable of separating highway surfaces of different elevations. The device allows a contractor to slip-form an asymmetrical barrier as the mold is moved down the highway, i.e., to pour the barriers directly onto the highway without having to construct a mold. In settlement of litigation with Gomaco Corporation, a manufacturer of slip-forms which may be used to form regular or variable height barriers, Aukerman entered into an agreement in 1977 which made Gomaco a licensee under the patents and required Gomaco to notify Aukerman of all those who purchased Gomaco's adjustable slip-forms.

Upon notification that Chaides had purchased a slip-form from Gomaco, counsel for Aukerman advised Chaides by letter dated February 13, 1979, that use of the device raised "a question of infringement with respect to one or more of [Aukerman's patents-in-suit]," and offered Chaides a license. Follow-on letters were sent by Aukerman's counsel to Chaides on March 16 and April 12, 1979. Chaides replied by telephone on April 17, 1979 but was unable to speak with counsel for Aukerman. By letter of April 24, 1979, Aukerman's counsel advised Chaides that Aukerman was seeking to enforce its patents against all infringers and that, even though Chaides might be among the smaller contractors, it had the same need for a license as larger firms. He advised further that Aukerman would waive liability for past infringement and infringement under existing contracts if Chaides took a license by June 1, 1979. Chaides responded in late April with a note handwritten on Aukerman's last letter stating that he felt any responsibility was Gomaco's and that, if Aukerman wished to sue Chaides "for $200–$300 a year," Aukerman should do so. There was no further correspondence or contact between the parties for more than eight years. In the interim, Chaides increased its business of forming asymmetrical highway barrier walls. Sometime in the mid–80's, Chaides made a second adjustable mold for pouring step wall which Aukerman alleges is an infringement.

Apparently in 1987, one of Aukerman's licensees, Baumgartner, Inc., advised Aukerman that Chaides was a substantial competitor for pouring asymmetrical wall in California. This advice prompted Aukerman's new counsel to send a letter to Chaides on October 22, 1987, referencing the earlier correspondence, advising that litigation against another company had been resolved, and threatening litigation unless Chaides executed the licenses previously sent within two weeks. Another period of silence followed. On August 2, 1988, Aukerman's counsel again wrote Chaides explaining more fully Aukerman's licensing proposal. When no reply was received, on October 26, 1988, Aukerman filed suit charging Chaides with infringing its '133 and '633 patents.

The district court granted summary judgment in favor of Chaides, holding that the doctrines of laches and estoppel barred Aukerman's claims for relief.

II.

SUMMARY

The court has taken this case in banc to clarify and apply principles of laches and equitable estoppel which have been raised as defenses in this patent infringement suit. In summary, for reasons to be more fully discussed, we hold with respect to laches:

1. Laches is cognizable under 35 U.S.C. § 282 (1988) as an equitable defense to a claim for patent infringement. 2. Where the

defense of laches is established, the patentee's claim for damages prior to suit may be barred. 3. Two elements underlie the defense of laches: (a) the patentee's delay in bringing suit was unreasonable and inexcusable, and (b) the alleged infringer suffered material prejudice attributable to the delay. The district court should consider these factors and all of the evidence and other circumstances to determine whether equity should intercede to bar pre-filing damages. 4. A presumption of laches arises where a patentee delays bringing suit for more than six years after the date the patentee knew or should have known of the alleged infringer's activity. 5. A presumption has the effect of shifting the burden of going forward with evidence, not the burden of persuasion.

With respect to equitable estoppel against a patent infringement claim, we hold that: 1. Equitable estoppel is cognizable under 35 U.S.C. § 282 as an equitable defense to a claim for patent infringement. 2. Where an alleged infringer establishes the defense of equitable estoppel, the patentee's claim may be entirely barred. 3. Three elements must be established to bar a patentee's suit by reason of equitable estoppel: a. The patentee, through misleading conduct, leads the alleged infringer to reasonably infer that the patentee does not intend to enforce its patent against the alleged infringer. "Conduct" may include specific statements, action, inaction, or silence where there was an obligation to speak. b. The alleged infringer relies on that conduct. c. Due to its reliance, the alleged infringer will be materially prejudiced if the patentee is allowed to proceed with its claim. 4. No presumption is applicable to the defense of equitable estoppel.

As equitable defenses, laches and equitable estoppel are matters committed to the sound discretion of the trial judge and the trial judge's decision is reviewed by this court under the abuse of discretion standard. We appreciate that the district court, in deciding the instant case, did not have the benefit of these statements of legal principles which differ in some respects from our precedent. We have no alternative, however, but to rule that, when these principles are applied to the record before us, the district court erred in granting summary judgment in favor of Chaides.

III.

LACHES

It is ... well settled that, to invoke the laches defense, a defendant has the burden to prove two factors: 1. the plaintiff delayed filing suit for an unreasonable and inexcusable length of time from the time the plaintiff knew or reasonably should have known of its claim against the defendant, and 2. the delay operated to the prejudice or injury of the defendant.

The length of time which may be deemed unreasonable has no fixed boundaries but rather depends on the circumstances. The period of delay is measured from the time the plaintiff knew or reasonably should have known of the defendant's alleged infringing activities to the date of suit. However, the period does not begin prior to issuance of the patent.

Material prejudice to adverse parties resulting from the plaintiff's delay is essential to the laches defense. Such prejudice may be either economic or evidentiary. Evidentiary, or "defense" prejudice, may arise by reason of a defendant's inability to present a full and fair defense on the merits due to the loss of records, the death of a witness, or the unreliability of memories of long past events, thereby undermining the court's ability to judge the facts.

Economic prejudice may arise where a defendant and possibly others will suffer the loss of monetary investments or incur damages which likely would have been prevented by earlier suit. Such damages or monetary losses are not merely those attributable to a finding of liability for infringement. Economic prejudice would then arise in every suit. The courts must look for a change in the economic position of the alleged infringer during the period of delay. On the other hand, this does not mean that a patentee may intentionally lie silently in wait watching damages escalate, particularly where an infringer, if he had had notice, could have switched to a noninfringing product. Indeed, economic prejudice is not a simple concept but rather is likely to be a slippery issue to resolve.

A court must also consider and weigh any justification offered by the plaintiff for its delay. Excuses which have been recognized in some instances, and we do not mean this list to be exhaustive, include: other litigation; negotiations with the accused; possibly poverty and illness under limited circumstances; wartime conditions; extent of infringement; and dispute over ownership of the patent. The equities may or may not require that the plaintiff communicate its reasons for delay to the defendant.

A patentee may also defeat a laches defense if the infringer "has engaged in particularly egregious conduct which would change the equities significantly in plaintiff's favor." Conscious copying may be such a factor weighing against the defendant, whereas ignorance or a good faith belief in the merits of a defense may tilt matters in its favor.

In the simplest or purest form of laches, there need be no direct contact between the plaintiff and the defendant from the time the plaintiff becomes aware of its claim until the suit. In other instances, the plaintiff may make an objection to the defendant and then do nothing more for years. Where there has been contact or a relationship between the parties during the delay period which may give rise to an inference that the plaintiff has abandoned its claim against the defendant, the facts may lend themselves to analysis under principles of equitable estoppel, as well as laches. However, the two defenses are not the same. As we have indicated, laches focuses on the reasonableness of the plaintiff's delay in suit. As will become evident, equitable estoppel focuses on what the defendant has been led to reasonably believe from the plaintiff's conduct. Thus, for laches, the length of delay, the seriousness of prejudice, the reasonableness of excuses, and the defendant's conduct or culpability must be weighed to determine whether the patentee dealt unfairly with the alleged infringer by not promptly bringing suit. In sum, a district court must weigh all pertinent facts and equities in making a decision on the laches defense. [The court concluded that:] Upon the record before us, summary judgment of laches was improperly granted. The issue of laches must be tried.

EFFECT OF LACHES DEFENSE

The district court ruled that laches can bar relief in a patent suit only for infringement prior to suit. The general rule is that laches may bar partial or entire relief. A question was raised in the original panel opinion concerning this difference in the effect of a laches defense. Inasmuch as this case will be remanded, it is appropriate to address this issue for the guidance of the district court.

Probably no better statement of reasons for limiting a laches defense in patent cases to past acts can be found than in *George J. Meyer Mfg. v. Miller Mfg.*, 24 F.2d 505, 507 (7th Cir.1928):

> There are peculiar and special reasons why the holder of a patent should not be barred from enforcing his right under the patent because of his failure to promptly sue infringers. Frequently the position of the patentee (financial and otherwise) prevents the institution of suits. The patent litigation is often prolonged and expensive. Moreover from the very nature of the thing he cannot be fully cognizant of all infringements that occur throughout the length and breadth of this country. His information may be largely hearsay. Then, also, the validity of his patent and the infringement thereof may be, as here, disputed. These defenses present mixed questions of fact and law concerning which there is necessarily some doubt and uncertainty. In many cases, if not in most cases, the doubts are serious ones. For an infringer naturally avoids making [an exact] copy of the patent. In a doubtful case the commercial success of the patented art is at times determinative of the issue of validity. This factor cannot be shown save as time establishes it. Moreover, common experience proves that inventions which appear to be revolutionary are often not accepted by the public and never become a commercial success. A patentee is therefore justified in waiting to ascertain whether realizations equal expectations. We think, therefore, that there is justification in patent suits for withholding damages for infringements committed prior to the commencement of the suit when laches is established, notwithstanding injunctional relief be granted. But, when it can be shown that the holder of the patent in addition to being guilty of laches has, by his conduct, estopped himself from asserting his rights under the patent, all relief should be denied and the bill dismissed.

As an additional reason, we do not believe future relief should be barred as a result of the presumption afforded to a patent defendant in the usual laches situation.

Finally, the general rule had to be broadly stated to cover a single wrong as well as a series of continuing wrongful acts. All relief would generally be denied by a finding of laches if there is only a single wrong. Relief from liability for past wrongs, but not future wrongs, is viewed as only a partial defense. No conflict between the rule stated in our precedent and the general rule necessarily exists.

In any event, we will continue to hold, as a matter of policy, that laches bars relief on a patentee's claim only with respect to damages accrued prior to suit. At least on the facts presented in this case, we have no reason to revisit this accepted principle.

IV.

EQUITABLE ESTOPPEL

A. General Principles

Equitable estoppel to assert a claim is another defense addressed to the sound discretion of the trial court. Where equitable estoppel is established, all relief on a claim may be barred. Like laches, equitable estoppel is not limited to a particular factual situation nor subject to resolution by simple or hard and fast rules. At most, courts have provided general guidelines based on fact patterns which have been litigated, albeit attempting to provide a unifying set of principles.

The following statement of the underlying factual elements of equitable estoppel which generally are deemed significant reflects a reasonable and fairly complete distillation from the case law:

> An [equitable] estoppel case ... has three important elements. [1] The actor, who usually must have knowledge of the true facts, communicates something in a misleading way, either by words, conduct or silence. [2] The other relies upon that communication. [3] And the other would be harmed materially if the actor is later permitted to assert any claim inconsistent with his earlier conduct.

[D.B. DOBBS, HANDBOOK ON THE LAW OF REMEDIES] § 2.3, at 42. In other authorities, elements [2] and [3] are frequently combined into a single "detrimental reliance" requirement. However, the statement of reliance and detriment as separate factors adds some clarity in this confusing area of the law.

Unlike laches, equitable estoppel does not require the passage of an unreasonable period of time in filing suit. However, the patent cases which have come before this court involving the issue of a patentee's inequitable delay in suing have almost invariably raised the defense not only of laches but also of equitable estoppel. In [*Jamesbury Corp. v. Litton Indus. Prods.*, 839 F.2d 1544 (Fed.Cir.1988),] which was such a case, we stated that equitable estoppel requires: (1) unreasonable and inexcusable dclay in filing suit, (2) prejudice to the infringer, (3) affirmative conduct by the patentee inducing the belief that it abandoned its claims against the alleged infringer, [later defined to include silence] and (4) detrimental reliance by the infringer. This listing of factors followed earlier case law in our sister circuits.

The test set out in *Jamesbury* confusingly intertwines the elements of laches and equitable estoppel and is expressly overruled. Delay in filing suit may be evidence which influences the assessment of whether the patentee's conduct is misleading but it is not a requirement of equitable estoppel. Even where such delay is present, the concepts of equitable estoppel and laches are distinct from one another.

The first element of equitable estoppel concerns the statements or conduct of the patentee which must "communicate something in a misleading way." The "something" with which this case, as well as the vast majority of equitable estoppel cases in the patent field is concerned, is that the accused infringer will not be disturbed by the plaintiff patentee in the activities in which the former is currently engaged. The patentee's conduct must have supported an inference that the patentee did not intend to press an infringement claim against the alleged infringer. It is clear, thus, that for equitable estoppel the alleged infringer cannot be unaware—as is possible under laches—of the patentee and/or its patent. The alleged infringer also must know or reasonably be able to infer that the patentee has known of the former's activities for some time. In the most common situation, the patentee specifically objects to the activities currently asserted as infringement in the suit and then does not follow up for years. However, plaintiff's inaction must be combined with other facts respecting the relationship or contacts between the parties to give rise to the necessary inference that the claim against the defendant is abandoned.

The second element, reliance, is not a requirement of laches but is essential to equitable estoppel. The accused infringer must show that, in fact, it substantially relied on the misleading conduct of the patentee in connection with taking some action. Reliance is not the same as prejudice or harm, although frequently confused. An infringer can build a plant being entirely unaware of the patent. As a result of infringement, the infringer may be unable to use the facility. Although harmed, the infringer could not show reliance on the patentee's conduct. To show reliance, the infringer must have had a relationship or communication with the plaintiff which lulls the infringer into a sense of security in going ahead with building the plant.

Finally, the accused infringer must establish that it would be materially prejudiced if the patentee is now permitted to proceed. As with laches, the prejudice may be a change of economic position or loss of evidence.

Another significant difference from laches is that no presumption adheres to an equitable estoppel defense. Despite a six-year delay in suit being filed, a defendant must prove all of the factual elements of estoppel on which the discretionary power of the court rests. The reasons for this are two-fold. First, the presumed laches factors, that is, unreasonable and inexcusable delay and prejudice resulting therefrom are not elements of estoppel. Second, the relief granted in estoppel is broader than in laches. Because the whole suit may be barred, we conclude that the defendant should carry a burden to establish the defense based on proof, not a presumption.

Finally, the trial court must, even where the three elements of equitable estoppel are established, take into consideration any other evidence and facts respecting the equities of the parties in exercising its discretion and deciding whether to allow the defense of equitable estoppel to bar the suit.

B.   Application of Equitable Estoppel Against Aukerman

While equitable estoppel may be determined on summary judgment, we conclude that the district court improperly granted summary judgment in this case.

The district court concluded that Aukerman's conduct led Chaides to believe Aukerman had abandoned its claim, that Chaides had relied on Aukerman's conduct to its detriment, and that Chaides was not guilty of unclean hands which would bar Chaides from assertion of an equitable defense. We conclude that the elements supporting equitable estoppel were in genuine dispute, that the evidence was not perceived in the light most favorable to Aukerman, that inferences of fact were drawn against Aukerman and that the entire issue must, in any event, be tried in light of the principles adopted here.

The initial dispute is whether the patentee's conduct was misleading in that Chaides reasonably inferred from Aukerman's conduct that it would be unmolested in using Aukerman's invention. Chaides argued that this factor was shown by the last letter from Aukerman in 1979 setting a deadline for taking a license followed by nine plus years of silence. Aukerman argued that Chaides had to prove intentionally misleading silence. The district court properly rejected Aukerman's argument respecting the need to prove intent to mislead on the basis of Hottel. How one characterizes a patentee's silence is immaterial. Properly focused, the issue here is whether Aukerman's course of conduct reasonably gave rise to an inference in Chaides that Aukerman was not going to enforce the '133 and '633 patents against Chaides. Moreover, silence alone will not create an estoppel unless there was a clear duty to speak, or somehow the patentee's continued silence reenforces the defendant's inference from the plaintiff's known acquiescence that the defendant will be unmolested. Finally, on summary judgment, such inference must be the only possible inference from the evidence.

In view of the Aukerman/Chaides correspondence, Chaides was in a position to infer, following Chaides' reply stating any infringement problem was Gomaco's, that by remaining silent Aukerman abandoned its claim against Chaides. The length of the delay also favors drawing the inference because the longer the delay, the stronger the inference becomes. Aukerman argues that the delay is excused by reason of litigation against others, even though Chaides was not informed of the litigation. However, that argument is off the mark. A party must generally notify an accused infringer about other litigation for it to impact the defense of equitable estoppel. This "requirement" is a matter of logic. Other litigation can not logically enter into whether Chaides reasonably drew an inference that it would not be sued if such facts are not known to Chaides.

[handwritten margin note: if fighting other litigation must tell infringer]

While the above factors favor the nonenforcement inference, Chaides' further statement that Aukerman would only recover $200–$300 a year could lead one in Chaides' position to infer that Aukerman did not sue because the amount in issue was de minimis, not that Aukerman was abandoning its claim against Chaides for all time regardless of quantum. At most Aukerman could merely have been waiving an infringement claim for $300.00 per year.

[handwritten margin note: nonenforcement over $200]

In view of the different inferences which could be drawn from the exchange of correspondence, it is clear that the court drew an unfavorable inference against Aukerman. That is impermissible on summary judgment.

[handwritten margin note: different inferences not good for summary judgment]

We conclude that summary judgment, holding that Aukerman was equitably estopped from assertion of infringement against Chaides, was improperly granted and is reversed. The issue is remanded for trial.

NOTES

1. *De Minimus* **Infringement and Estoppel.** Do you agree that Auckerman should not have been equitably estopped—at least for purposes of summary judgment—based on the response Chaides provided to Auckerman's assertion of patent infringement? This decision suggests that responses to an infringement charge should be carefully considered. If, as here, a competitor dissuades the patentee from suing based upon the minimal nature of its infringement, it may be left without an equitable estoppel defense if its use of the patented technology increases.

2. **The Significance of *Aukerman*.** The *Aukerman* decision was generally seen as weakening the effectiveness of the laches defense in patent litigation, particularly when employed in a summary judgment motion. As noted in the excerpt from the *Aukerman* opinion above, and as discussed in greater detail in a portion of the opinion not reprinted here, the presumption of laches only shifts the burden of going forward with this evidence, not the burden of persuasion. The accused infringer always maintains the burden or proof with regard to laches and estoppel—matters that may be more readily demonstrated or disproved by evidence within the possession of the patentee. Some observers believe that, in practice, patentees are too readily able to present reasons

excusing their delay for filing suit. Further, in the event the trier of fact cannot decide whether the patentee's delay was reasonable or unreasonable, the patentee would still prevail. *See* Evan Finkel, *What Remains of the Laches and Estoppel Defenses After* Aukerman?, 9 SANTA CLARA COMPUTER & HIGH TECH. L.J. 1 (1993); Jerry R. Selinger, Aukerman *and Equitable Defenses: Evolution or Revolution?*, 1 TEX. INTELL. PROP. L.J. 87 (1993); Russell D. Slifer, Comment, *En Banc Ruling Bursts More Than Bubbles in Patent Litigation:* A.C. Aukerman Co. v. R.L. Chaides Construction Co. *and Its Impact*, 13 N. ILL. U. L. REV. 335 (1993).

Aukerman is thus of considerable importance in an era where patent litigation has become an increasingly lucrative endeavor. Patentees have demonstrated a renewed willingness to review their portfolios in order to consider whether any claims are being infringed. Sometimes this effort results in the "dusting off" of patents that are near expiration or have in fact expired, and infringement suits filed regarding infringements that began years before. If *Aukerman* indeed limits the availability of laches as a defense, then accused infringers possess a decreased opportunity to defend against such suits. Does this opinion present sound patent policy?

3. Other Letters. Beyond working an estoppel, patentee letters to suspected infringers invoke two other principal concerns. First, the letter may serve as the basis for a declaratory judgment action brought by the addressee against the patent owner. Declaratory judgment jurisdiction is briefly discussed here at Chapter 13. Second, such a letter may serve as sufficient notice to allow the patentee to recover damages, as set forth in § 287. This text addresses the concepts of notice and marking in Chapter 14.

§ 12.4   SHOP RIGHTS

McELMURRY v. ARKANSAS POWER & LIGHT CO.

United States Court of Appeals, Federal Circuit, 1993
995 F.2d 1576

Before Nies, Chief Judge, Rich, and Mayer, Circuit Judges.

RICH, CIRCUIT JUDGE.

Max C. McElmurry and White River Technologies, Inc. (WRT) appeal the February 10, 1992 Judgment of the U.S. District Court for the Eastern District of Arkansas, Northern Division, granting a motion for summary judgment filed by Arkansas Power & Light Company (AP & L) and Entergy Corporation. The district court held that there were no relevant or material factual disputes precluding a finding that AP & L holds "shop rights" to certain subject matter claimed in U.S. Patent No. 4,527,714, titled "Pressure Responsive Hopper Level Detector System" (Bowman patent), and thus, as a matter of law, AP & L had not infringed any claim of the Bowman patent. For the reasons set forth below, we affirm.

A. BACKGROUND

AP & L hired Harold L. Bowman, the patentee, as a consultant on October 24, 1980, to assist in the installation, maintenance and operation of electrostatic precipitators at AP & L's White Bluff Steam Electric Station (White Bluff) located near Redfield, Arkansas. An electronic precipitator is a device which removes granular ash particles (fly ash) from the gasses emitted by coal-fired boilers used to generate steam. As fly ash is removed, it is collected in hoppers referred to as precipitator hoppers. Prior to April of 1982, the precipitator hoppers at White Bluff employed a level detector system using a nuclear power source (K-ray system) to detect the level of fly ash in the hoppers.

AP & L was not satisfied with the K-ray system. As a result, in the early part of 1982, Bowman discussed with a Mr. Richard L. Roberts, an AP & L employee, replacing the K-ray system with a new level detector, an initial design of which they drew on a napkin. In the proposed level detector, a vacuum gauge was connected to a pipe inserted and welded into the wall of a precipitator hopper. If the level of the fly ash collected in the hopper extended above the point where the pipe was inserted into the hopper, the vacuum gauge would no longer indicate that a vacuum existed, as it would if the level of the fly ash were below that point. Thus, by monitoring the vacuum gauge, one could determine whether the fly ash exceeded a certain level in the hopper.

AP & L considered the proposed level detector and, during a power outage in March of 1982, ordered its installation on one hopper at White Bluff for testing purposes. When it proved successful, AP & L ordered that the level detector be installed on a total of sixteen (16) precipitator hoppers at White Bluff. In each case, level detectors were installed both near the bottom and top of the hopper, thus allowing for the detection of the fly ash at two different levels in the hopper. When this system proved successful, AP & L ordered that the level detectors be installed on the remaining one hundred and twelve (112) precipitator hoppers at White Bluff. All costs associated with the installation and testing of the level detector on the one hundred and twenty eight (128) hoppers at White Bluff, including materials and working drawings, were paid by AP & L.

On October 24, 1982, Bowman moved from White Bluff to AP & L's Independence Steam Electric Station (ISES) located near Newark, Arkansas, to assist in the start-up, maintenance and operation of electronic precipitators at that facility. In November of 1982, Bowman formed White Rivers Technology, Inc. with McElmurry and a Mr. Johnny Mitchum, to market certain inventions on which Bowman held patents or was planning to seek patent protection. Bowman filed a patent application on the level detector on February 18, 1983, and the patent-in-suit issued on July 9, 1985. At some point prior to its issuance, Bowman assigned his patent rights to WRT.

While at ISES, Bowman assisted another AP & L engineer, a Mr. Will Morgan, in installing the level detector on precipitator hoppers at that facility. AP & L requested bids for the project and ultimately contracted with WRT to install the level detector on sixty four (64) of the hoppers at that location. An outside contractor other than WRT installed the level detector on the remaining sixty four (64) hoppers. AP & L did contract with WRT, however, to install certain electronic components of the level detectors installed by the outside contractor. The level detectors had been installed and were in operation on all one hundred and twenty eight (128) precipitator hoppers by the end of 1984, prior to the issuance of the Bowman patent. Bowman's contract with ISES ended, however, in October of 1983 before completion of the project. All costs associated with the installation and testing of the level detectors at ISES, including materials and working drawings, were paid by AP & L even though some of the work was contracted out.

In 1985, based upon the success of the level detector on the precipitator hoppers at White Bluff and ISES, another AP & L engineer, a Mr. John Harvey, implemented a plan to install the level detector on fourteen (14) hydroveyer hoppers at ISES. Harvey informed Bowman of the plan to install the level detector on the hydroveyer hoppers, and Bowman indicated that he thought it was a good idea. Bowman also indicated that WRT would be interested in bidding on the project. AP & L ultimately awarded the contract, however, to another contractor because WRT was not the low bidder. In soliciting bids on the hydroveyer project, AP & L provided the contractors with specifications prepared by AP & L showing the work to be performed. The installation of the level detectors on the hydroveyer hoppers at ISES was completed in 1985, and all costs associated with their installation were paid by AP & L.

B.   District Court Litigation

On April 25, 1990, WRT brought suit against AP & L for patent infringement based on AP & L's solicitation of and contracting with a party other than WRT to install Bowman's patented level detector on the hydroveyer hoppers at ISES. The district court granted summary judgment in favor of AP & L on the basis that AP & L had acquired a "shop right" in the level detector claimed in the Bowman patent. AP & L argued and the court agreed that, as a matter of law, Bowman's development of the patented level detector at AP & L's facilities at AP & L's expense entitled AP & L, under the "shop rights" rule, to reproduce and use the level detector in its business. WRT then appealed to this court.

C.   Analysis

A "shop right" is generally accepted as being a right that is created at common law when the circumstances demand it, under principles of equity and fairness, entitling an employer to use without charge an invention patented by one or more of its employees without liability for infringement. However, as recognized by several commentators, the immense body of case law addressing the issue of "shop rights" suggests that not all courts agree as to the doctrinal basis for "shop rights," and, consequently, not all courts agree as to the particular et of circumstances necessary to create a "shop right."

For example, many courts characterize a "shop right" as being a type of implied license, and thus the focus is often on whether the employee engaged in any activities, e.g., developing the invention on the employer's time at the employer's expense, which demand a finding that he impliedly granted a license to his employer to use the invention. Other courts characterize a "shop right" as a form of equitable estoppel, and thus the focus is often on whether the employee's actions, e.g., consent or acquiescence to his employer's use of the invention, demand a finding that he is estopped from asserting a patent right against his employer. Neither characterization appears to be inherently better than the other, and the end result under either is often the same, given that the underlying analysis in each case is driven by principles of equity and fairness, and given that the courts often analyze a "shop right" as being a combination of the two even though they may characterize it in name as one or the other.

It is thus not surprising that many courts adopt neither characterization specifically, instead choosing to characterize a "shop right" more broadly as simply being a common law "right" that inures to an employer when the circumstances demand it under principles of equity and fairness. These courts often look to both the circumstances surrounding the development of the invention and the facts regarding the employee's activities respecting that invention, once developed, to determine whether it would be fair and equitable to allow an employee to preclude his employer from making use of that invention. This is essentially the analysis that most courts undertake regardless of how they characterize "shop rights."

In view of the foregoing, we believe that the proper methodology for determining whether an employer has acquired a "shop right" in a patented invention is to look to the totality of the circumstances on a case by case basis and determine whether the facts of a particular case demand, under principles of equity and fairness, a finding that a "shop right" exists. In such an analysis, one should look to such factors as the circumstances surrounding the development of the patented invention and the inventor's activities respecting that invention, once developed, to determine whether equity and fairness demand that the employer be allowed to use that invention in his business. A factually driven analysis such as this ensures that the principles of equity and fairness underlying the "shop rights" rule are considered. Because this is exactly the type of analysis that the district court used to reach its decision, we see no error in the district court's analysis justifying reversal.

To reach its decision, the district court looked to the discussion of "shop rights" set forth in the often-cited *Dubilier* case, in which the Court said:

where a servant, during his hours of employment, working with his master's materials and appliances, conceives and perfects an invention for which he obtains a patent, he must accord his master a nonexclusive right to practice the invention. [citation omitted] This is an application of equitable principles. Since the servant uses his master's time, facilities and materials to attain a concrete result, the latter is in equity entitled to use that which embodies his own property and to duplicate it as often as he may find occasion to employ similar appliances in his business.

[*United States v. Dubilier Condenser Corp.*, 289 U.S. 178, 188–89 (1933).] The district court also accepted a discussion of "shop rights" set forth in one of WRT's briefs filed in the district court action as correctly summarizing several factors that may be considered in analyzing a "shop rights" case. At pages 9–10 of its opinion, the district court included the following excerpt from pages 6–8 of WRT's Memorandum Brief in Support of Response to Motion for Summary Judgment:

Because broad equitable principles are involved in determining whether shop rights in [an] invention arise, "[t]he full nature of the parties' relationship must be examined to determine whether a shop right exists." ROSENBERG, PATENT LAW FUNDAMENTALS, § 11.04, 11–20 (1991). The following factors have been considered: the contractual nature of the relationship between employer and employee, whether the employee consented to the employer's use of the invention, and whether the employee induced, acquiesced in, or assisted the employer in the use of the invention.... [footnote omitted]

An employer will have shop rights in an invention in situations where the employer has financed an employee's invention by providing wages, materials, tools and a work place. Other factors creating shop rights include an employee's consent, acquiescence, inducement, or assistance to the employer in using the invention without demanding compensation or other notice of restriction.

Applying *Dubilier* and the summary of the law set forth in WRT's own brief to the facts of this case, the district court properly found that AP & L had acquired a "shop right" in Bowman's patented level detector which entitled AP & L to duplicate the level detector for use in its business.

Bowman developed the patented level detector while working at AP & L and suggested it to AP & L as an alternative to the K-ray system. AP & L installed the level detector on one hundred and twenty eight (128) precipitator hoppers at White Bluff with Bowman's consent and participation. Bowman also consented to, and participated at least in part in, the installation of the level detector on one hundred and twenty eight (128) precipitator hoppers at ISES. In addition, the level detectors on half of the hoppers at ISES were installed by a contractor other than WRT, with Bowman's and WRT's knowledge and consent. All costs and expenses associated with the testing and implementation of the level detector on the hoppers at White Bluff and ISES were paid by AP & L.

Furthermore, Bowman never asserted that AP & L was precluded from using the level detector without his permission or that AP & L was required to compensate him for its use. Indeed, the record suggests that Bowman believed quite the opposite. As recognized by the district court:

> Bowman admitted in a deposition that he believed all along that AP & L would have shop rights. His patent attorney had informed him of that possibility and he subsequently shared the attorney's opinion with his partners in WRT.

WRT argues that Bowman's consent or acquiescence after he had assigned his rights in the Bowman application to WRT is irrelevant. Even if this were true, Bowman's actions at White Bluff prior to this assignment justify the district court's finding that a "shop right" was created. Nevertheless, WRT, of which Bowman was a part owner during the relevant time period, acquiesced both to AP & L's continued use of the level detector at White Bluff and ISES and to the installation of the level detector by outside contractors at ISES. This lends further support to the district court's decision.

WRT also argues that, even if AP & L had acquired a "shop right" to use the patented level detector, AP & L somehow exceeded the scope of that right when it allegedly "carelessly and casually disseminated the design and specifications of the patented device to private contractors." WRT argues that, by putting information of this nature on the open market, AP & L rendered the patent "worthless" and robbed Bowman of the "fruit of his labor." We find these arguments unpersuasive for two reasons.

First, WRT has failed to explain how AP & L's mere dissemination of specifications of the patented level detector constituted patent infringement. Clearly, it did not. The owner of a patent right may exclude others from making, using or selling the subject matter of a claimed invention. AP & L's dissemination of information obviously does not fall into any of these categories. Even so, it is also unclear how disseminating specifications of the level detector after it was patented rendered the Bowman patent "worthless." The owner of the Bowman patent still retained the right to exclude all others than AP & L from practicing the claimed invention.

Second, we find no error in the district court's holding that AP & L's "shop right" entitled it to duplicate the level detector and to continue to use it in its business. Furthermore, AP & L's "shop right" was not limited to AP & L's use of level detectors that AP & L itself had manufactured and installed. Quite to the contrary, we find that AP & L's "shop right" entitled it to procure the level detector from outside contractors.

AFFIRMED.

NOTES

1. **Comparative Approaches to Employed Inventors.** The *Arbeitnehmerer-finderrecht*, or German Employed Inventor's Rights Law, provides far greater mandatory compensation for employed inventors than does the United States law. The German Act distinguishes between so-called "tied" and "free" inventions; the employer obtains rights in only the former, which must result from the employee's tasks or are based upon the activities of the employer. In the case of a tied invention, the inventor obtains the right to demand reasonable compensation from the employer. The Act forbids employees from waiving their rights to compensation by prior agreement with the employer. For a fine English-language discussion of the German law on employee inventions, see Dr. Matthias Brandi–Dohrn & Peter Chrocziel, *Federal Republic of Germany: Patent Law* § 2G, in WORLD INTELLECTUAL PROPERTY GUIDEBOOK: FEDERAL REPUBLIC OF GERMANY, AUSTRIA, SWITZERLAND (Dr. Bernd Rüster, ed., 1991).

2. **Reform for the Employed Inventor.** A considerable body of literature is critical of the current United States regime, under which employers almost universally obtain rights to their employees' inventions through contractual mechanisms. Proposed solutions include the creation of a "reverse shop right" for the inventor; the establishment of government guidelines for determining compensation to the employed inventor, backed up by a Patent Office arbitration board; and the voiding of contractual provisions whereby the employee-inventor assigns his entire interest in any invention to the inventor, particularly where such clauses concern periods following the termination of the employment relationship. *See, e.g.*, Marc B. Hershovitz, Note, *Unhitching the Trailer Clause: The Rights of Inventive Employees and their Employers*, 3 J. INTELL. PROP. L. 187 (1995); Henrik D. Parker, Note, *Reform for Rights of Employed Inventors*, 57 S. CAL. L. REV. 603 (1984); William P. Hovell, Note, *Patent Ownership: An Employer's Rights to his Employee's Invention*, 58 NOTRE DAME L. REV. 863 (1983); Jay Dratler, Jr. *Incentives for People: The Forgotten Purpose of the Patent System*, 16 HARV. J. LEGIS. 129 (1979).

3. **Other Implied Licenses.** Recall that the United States patent law provides for other sorts of implied licenses beyond shop rights. Most commonly, this license arises when the patentee sells a patented good; in such circumstances the patentee is said to "exhaust" his right to future remuneration from the public.

§ 12.5 THE FIRST INVENTOR DEFENSE

One of the titles of the American Inventors Protection Act of 1999, the First Inventor Defense Act, created an infringement defense for an earlier inventor of a method of doing or conducting business that was later patented by another. *See* 35 U.S.C.A. § 273. The defendant must have reduced the infringing subject matter to practice one year before the effective filing date of the patent and made commercial use of that subject matter in the United States before the effective filing date.

The impetus for this provision lies in the rather complex relationship between the law of trade secrets and the patent system. As discussed in Chapter One of this casebook, trade secrecy protects individuals from misappropriation of valuable information that is useful in commerce. One reason an inventor might maintain the invention as a trade secret rather than seek patent protection is that the subject matter of the invention may not be regarded as patentable. Such inventions as customer lists or data compilations have traditionally been regarded as amenable to trade secret protection but not to patenting. Inventors might also maintain trade secret protection due to ignorance of the patent system or because they believe they can keep their invention secret longer than the period of exclusivity granted through the patent system.

It is important to note from the outset that the patent system has not favored trade secret holders. Well-established patent law establishes that an inventor who makes a secret, commercial use of an invention for more than one year prior to filing a patent application at the PTO forfeits his own right to a patent. *See W.L. Gore & Associates v. Garlock, Inc.*, 721 F.2d 1540 (Fed.Cir.1983) (discussed in this casebook in Chapter Five). This policy is principally based upon the desire to maintain the integrity of the patent term. The Patent Act grants patents a term of twenty years commencing from the date a patent application is filed. 35 U.S.C. § 154(a)(2). If the trade secret holder could make commercial use of an invention for many years before choosing to file a patent application, he could disrupt this regime by delaying the expiration date of his patent.

On the other hand, settled patent law principles established that prior secret uses would not defeat the patents of later inventors. *See Gore v. Garlock, supra.* If an earlier inventor made secret commercial use of an invention, and another person independently invented the same technology later and obtained patent protection, then the trade secret holder could face liability for patent infringement. This policy was based upon the reasoning that issued, published patent instruments fully inform the public about the invention, while trade secrets do not. As between a subsequent inventor who patented the invention, and had disclosed the invention to the public, and an earlier trade secret holder who did not, the law favored the patent holder.

Legal developments in the late 1990's concerning methods of doing business focused attention upon the relationship between patents and trade secrets. Inventors of methods of doing business traditionally relied upon trade secret protection because such inventions had long been regarded as unpatentable subject matter. As a result, inventors of innovative business methods obtained legal advice not to file applications at the PTO. This advice was sound under the patent law as it then stood.

The 1998 Federal Circuit opinion in *State Street Bank & Trust Co. v. Signature Financial Group, Inc.*, 149 F.3d 1368 (Fed.Cir.1998) (discussed in this casebook in Chapter Two), altered this traditional principle. In the *State Street Bank* opinion, the Federal Circuit explained that no bar prevented the issuance of patents on methods of doing business. As a consequence, inventors in such sectors as finance, insurance, and services have sought proprietary interests in their inventions through the patent system.

The change in this background principle was perceived as dealing a harsh blow to individuals that have invented business methods prior to the issuance of the *State Street Bank* opinion. Many of these inventors had maintained their innovative business methods as trade secrets for many years. As a result, they were unable belatedly to obtain patent protection on their business methods. As well, because trade secrets did not constitute prior art against the patent applications of others, a subsequent inventor would be able to obtain patent protection. Under these circumstances, a trade secret holder could find himself an adjudicated infringer of a patented business method that he actually invented first.

The First Inventor Defense Act reconciles these principles by providing an infringement defense for an earlier inventor of a method of doing business that was later patented by another. This infringement defense is subject to several qualifications. First, the defendant must have reduced the infringing subject matter to practice at least one year before the effective filing date of the patent application. Second, the defendant must have commercially used the infringing subject matter prior to the effective filing date of the patent. Finally, any reduction to practice or use must have been made in good faith, without derivation from the patentee or persons in privity with the patentee.

The first inventor defense has yet to be the subject of a reported judicial opinion. When such case arises, it will be interesting to learn the court's interpretation of the phrase "method of doing or conducting business," a term Congress opted not to define. Looking further forward, it would seem a rather straightforward matter to alter the first inventor defense to embrace a more expansive range of patentable subject matter. In this regard the first inventor defense could prove quite similar to those prevailing in other countries. These statutes are commonly referred to as creating "prior user rights." Unlike the more limited regime created by the First Inventor Defense Act, prior user rights abroad are not limited to methods of doing business. They instead apply to any sort of invention. Experience with the First Inventor Defense Act might suggest whether the Congress should consider a more full-fledged prior user rights regime, or maintain the current system as a limited cure of a specific problem.

Additional Defenses Exercise

Lawson, who was incarcerated in a Federal Correctional Institution, volunteered to work as an unskilled laborer in a special government manufacturing program. The program produced helmets for use by the military. The helmets were made in part of a synthetic fiber that was known by its trademark, Kevlar. Lawson quickly learned that Kevlar was an exceptionally difficult material to cut. His cutting device frequently failed during production, damaging the helmet he was attempting to manufacture. Other program workers shared his difficulties.

An experienced machinist, Lawson thought that he could develop an improved technique for cutting Kevlar. He took some scrap materials to his cell and worked on the invention during his free time. By November 15, 2000, he had developed an effective cutting device for use with Kevlar. Lawson demonstrated his device to prison guards on December 1, 2000. Impressed with the technology, program officials adopted Lawson's invention for general use on December 20, 2000. The device was enormously successful, allowing the program to double the number of manufactured helmets each year from 2000 through 2009.

Upon his release from the Federal Correctional Institution on January 10, 2001, Lawson immediately contacted a patent attorney. An application was filed on August 1, 2001, directed towards an improved Kevlar cutting device. The application ultimately matured into the '999 patent on February 10, 2002.

While reading an industry newsletter on October 1, 2002, Lawson noticed an advertisement placed by the HeadsUp Equipment Company. The advertisement described a Kevlar cutting device which appeared to infringe the '999 patent. Lawson directed correspondence to the Heads-Up Equipment Company on October 5, 2002, which included the following language he had taken from a legal form book:

> I believe you are selling Kevlar cutting devices of a type covered by one or more of the claims of the '999 patent. I am willing to consider granting you a license under the patent on reasonable terms. If, however, you should continue your infringing activities without a license, I am prepared to take whatever action is necessary to enforce my patent rights.

> Please let me know promptly if you are interested in a license under the patent. I am docketing this matter for further attention two weeks from the date of this letter in the event I do not receive a satisfactory response from you.

Lawson received no response to his letter. Busy working on another invention, Lawson subsequently took no immediate action regarding the '999 patent. Lawson then filed suit against the United States government in the Court of Federal Claims on July 15, 2008, and against the HeadsUp Equipment Company in the District Court for the Eastern District of Virginia on July 22, 2008.

Address the following issues:

(1) Does the U.S. government possess a shop right in Lawson's patented invention?

(2) Is Lawson barred by laches or estoppel from pursuing his claims against either the United States government or the HeadsUp Equipment Company?

CHAPTER THIRTEEN

REMEDIES

■ ■ ■

Once a court has determined that a patent claim is not invalid and infringed, it must then shape the remedy due to the patentee. This effort primarily involves the following provisions of U.S. Code Title 35:

§ 283.   Injunctive Relief.

The several courts having jurisdiction of cases under this title may grant injunctions in accordance with the principles of equity to prevent the violation of any right secured by patent, on such terms as the court deems reasonable.

§ 284.   Damages.

at least reasonable royalty

Upon finding for the claimant the court shall award the claimant damages adequate to compensate for the infringement, but in no event less than a reasonable royalty for the use made of the invention by the infringer, together with interest and costs as fixed by the court.

A right to exclude necessarily implies injunctive relief. In most instances, the most attractive remedy for a patent owner is an injunction to exclude infringers from making, using, and selling the invention. Until recent years, courts routinely awarded prevailing patent proprietors a permanent injunction against the adjudicated infringer. As we will see, the watershed Supreme Court opinion in *eBay, Inc. v. MercExchange, L.L.C.* has left the award of a permanent injunction a more nuanced determination.

In one sense, damages are an indication of the value of the invention. Beyond compensating a patent owner for infringement, however, damages theories also significantly influence substantive patent law. The availability and amount of damages informs an applicant's claiming techniques and even the administrative practices of the U.S. Patent and Trademark Office. Remedies also demark the borders between patent law and other, related regimes, particularly the law of antitrust and unfair competition. In short, the remedial aspects of U.S. patent law hold more significance than may be apparent at first blush, and are well worthy of careful study.

§ 13.1   INJUNCTIONS

Early in its history, the Federal Circuit remarked upon the importance of injunctive relief to patent holders:

> The very nature of the patent right is the right to exclude others. Once the patentee's patents have been held to be valid and infringed, he should be entitled to the full enjoyment and protection of his patent rights. The infringer should not be allowed to continue his infringement in the face of such a holding. A court should not be reluctant to use its equity powers once a party has so clearly established his patent rights.

Smith Int'l, Inc. v. Hughes Tool Co., 718 F.2d 1573 (Fed.Cir.1983). The Court of Appeals maintained this line of thinking for most of its history. Although the prospect of declining to award a permanent injunction following a successful patent enforcement effort was mentioned in dicta, the Federal Circuit not once chose affirmatively to employ this option. That situation has changed, however, following the following paradigm-shifting opinion from the Supreme Court.

eBAY INC. v. MercEXCHANGE, L.L.C.

United States Supreme Court, 2006
547 U.S. 388

JUSTICE THOMAS delivered the opinion of the Court.

Ordinarily, a federal court considering whether to award permanent injunctive relief to a prevailing plaintiff applies the four-factor test historically employed by courts of equity. Petitioners eBay Inc. and Half.com, Inc., argue that this traditional test applies to disputes arising under the Patent Act. We agree and, accordingly, vacate the judgment of the Court of Appeals.

I

Petitioner eBay operates a popular Internet Web site that allows private sellers to list goods they wish to sell, either through an auction or at a fixed price. Petitioner Half.com, now a wholly owned subsidiary of eBay, operates a similar Web site. Respondent MercExchange, L.L.C., holds a number of patents, including a business method patent for an electronic market designed to facilitate the sale of goods between private individuals by establishing a central authority to promote trust among participants. See U.S. Patent No. 5,845,265. MercExchange sought to license its patent to eBay and Half.com, as it had previously done with other companies, but the parties failed to reach an agreement. MercExchange subsequently filed a patent infringement suit against eBay and Half.com in the United States District Court for the Eastern District of Virginia. A jury found that MercExchange's patent was valid, that eBay and Half.com had infringed that patent, and that an award of damages was appropriate.

[margin notes: D.C. - denied injunction / Appeals overturned / S.Ct. / 4 factor test. / ① irreparable injury / ② law remedies inadequate / ③ consider hardships of each. / ④ public interest / Abuse of discretion standard / Apply to disputes in Patent Act. / Patents are property have right to exclude / but must follow equity principles]

Following the jury verdict, the District Court denied MercExchange's motion for permanent injunctive relief. 275 F.Supp.2d 695 (2003). The Court of Appeals for the Federal Circuit reversed, applying its "general rule that courts will issue permanent injunctions against patent infringement absent exceptional circumstances." 401 F.3d 1323, 1339 (2005). We granted certiorari to determine the appropriateness of this general rule.

II

According to well-established principles of equity, a plaintiff seeking a permanent injunction must satisfy a four-factor test before a court may grant such relief. A plaintiff must demonstrate: (1) that it has suffered an irreparable injury; (2) that remedies available at law, such as monetary damages, are inadequate to compensate for that injury; (3) that, considering the balance of hardships between the plaintiff and defendant, a remedy in equity is warranted; and (4) that the public interest would not be disserved by a permanent injunction. *See, e.g., Weinberger v. Romero–Barcelo*, 456 U.S. 305, 311–313, 102 S.Ct. 1798, 72 L.Ed.2d 91 (1982); *Amoco Production Co. v. Gambell*, 480 U.S. 531, 542, 107 S.Ct. 1396, 94 L.Ed.2d 542 (1987). The decision to grant or deny permanent injunctive relief is an act of equitable discretion by the district court, reviewable on appeal for abuse of discretion. *See, e.g., Romero–Barcelo*, 456 U.S., at 320, 102 S.Ct. 1798.

These familiar principles apply with equal force to disputes arising under the Patent Act. As this Court has long recognized, "a major departure from the long tradition of equity practice should not be lightly implied." *Ibid.; see also Amoco,supra*, at 542, 107 S.Ct. 1396. Nothing in the Patent Act indicates that Congress intended such a departure. To the contrary, the Patent Act expressly provides that injunctions "may" issue "in accordance with the principles of equity." 35 U.S.C. § 283.

To be sure, the Patent Act also declares that "patents shall have the attributes of personal property," § 261, including "the right to exclude others from making, using, offering for sale, or selling the invention," § 154(a)(1). According to the Court of Appeals, this statutory right to exclude alone justifies its general rule in favor of permanent injunctive relief. 401 F.3d, at 1338. But the creation of a right is distinct from the provision of remedies for violations of that right. Indeed, the Patent Act itself indicates that patents shall have the attributes of personal property "[s]ubject to the provisions of this title," 35 U.S.C. § 261, including, presumably, the provision that injunctive relief "may" issue only "in accordance with the principles of equity," § 283.

This approach is consistent with our treatment of injunctions under the Copyright Act. Like a patent owner, a copyright holder possesses "the right to exclude others from using his property." *Fox Film Corp. v. Doyal*, 286 U.S. 123, 127, 52 S.Ct. 546, 76 L.Ed. 1010 (1932); *see also id.*, at 127–128, 52 S.Ct. 546 ("A copyright, like a patent, is at once the equivalent given by the public for benefits bestowed by the genius and meditations and skill of individuals, and the incentive to further efforts for the same important objects" (internal quotation marks omitted)). Like the Patent Act, the Copyright Act provides that courts "may" grant injunctive relief "on such terms as it may deem reasonable to prevent or restrain infringement of a copyright." 17 U.S.C. § 502(a). And as in our decision today, this Court has consistently rejected invitations to replace traditional equitable considerations with a rule that an injunction automatically follows a determination that a copyright has been infringed. *See, e.g., New York Times Co. v. Tasini,* 533 U.S. 483, 505, 121 S.Ct. 2381, 150 L.Ed.2d 500 (2001).

Neither the District Court nor the Court of Appeals below fairly applied these traditional equitable principles in deciding respondent's motion for a permanent injunction. Although the District Court recited the traditional four-factor test, 275 F.Supp.2d, at 711, it appeared to adopt certain expansive principles suggesting that injunctive relief could not issue in a broad swath of cases. Most notably, it concluded that a "plaintiff's willingness to license its patents" and "its lack of commercial activity in practicing the patents" would be sufficient to establish that the patent holder would not suffer irreparable harm if an injunction did not issue. *Id.,* at 712. But traditional equitable principles do not permit such broad classifications. For example, some patent holders, such as university researchers or self-made inventors, might reasonably prefer to license their patents, rather than undertake efforts to secure the financing necessary to bring their works to market themselves. Such patent holders may be able to satisfy the traditional four-factor test, and we see no basis for categorically denying them the opportunity to do so. To the extent that the District Court adopted such a categorical rule, then, its analysis cannot be squared with the principles of equity adopted by Congress. The court's categorical rule is also in tension with *Continental Paper Bag Co. v. Eastern Paper Bag Co.,* 210 U.S. 405, 422–430, 28 S.Ct. 748, 52 L.Ed. 1122 (1908), which rejected the contention that a court of equity has no jurisdiction to grant injunctive relief to a patent holder who has unreasonably declined to use the patent.

In reversing the District Court, the Court of Appeals departed in the opposite direction from the four-factor test. The court articulated a "general rule," unique to patent disputes, "that a permanent injunction will issue once infringement and validity have been adjudged." 401 F.3d, at 1338. The court further indicated that injunctions should be denied only in the "unusual" case, under "exceptional circumstances" and " 'in rare instances . . . to protect the public interest.' " *Id.,* at 1338–1339. Just as the District Court erred in its categorical denial of injunctive relief, the Court of Appeals erred in its categorical grant of such relief. *Cf. Roche Products v. Bolar Pharmaceutical Co.,* 733 F.2d 858, 865 (C.A.Fed.1984) (recognizing the "considerable discretion" district courts have "in determining whether the facts of a situation require it to issue an injunction").

Because we conclude that neither court below correctly applied the traditional four-factor framework that governs the award of injunctive relief, we vacate the judgment of the Court of Appeals, so that the District Court may apply that framework in the first instance. In doing so, we take no position on whether permanent injunctive relief should or should not issue in this particular case, or indeed in any number of other disputes arising under the Patent Act. We hold only that the decision whether to grant or deny injunctive relief rests within the equitable discretion of the district courts, and that such discretion must be exercised consistent with traditional principles of equity, in patent disputes no less than in other cases governed by such standards.

Accordingly, we vacate the judgment of the Court of Appeals, and remand for further proceedings consistent with this opinion.

It is so ordered.

CHIEF JUSTICE ROBERTS, with whom JUSTICE SCALIA and JUSTICE GINSBURG join, concurring.

I agree with the Court's holding that "the decision whether to grant or deny injunctive relief rests within the equitable discretion of the district courts, and that such discretion must be exercised consistent with traditional principles of equity, in patent disputes no less than in other cases governed by such standards," and I join the opinion of the Court. That opinion rightly rests on the proposition that "a major departure from the long tradition of equity practice should not be lightly implied." *Weinberger v. Romero–Barcelo,* 456 U.S. 305, 320, 102 S.Ct. 1798, 72 L.Ed.2d 91 (1982).

From at least the early 19th century, courts have granted injunctive relief upon a finding of infringement in the vast majority of patent cases. This "long tradition of equity practice" is not surprising, given the difficulty of protecting a right to *exclude* through monetary remedies that allow an infringer to *use* an invention against the patentee's wishes—a difficulty that often implicates the first two factors of the traditional four-factor test. This historical practice, as the Court holds, does not *entitle* a patentee to a permanent injunction or justify a *general rule* that such injunctions should issue. The Federal Circuit itself so recognized in *Roche Products, Inc. v. Bolar Pharmaceutical Co.,* 733 F.2d 858, 865–867 (1984). At the same time, there is a difference between exercising equitable discretion pursuant to the established four-factor test and writing on an entirely clean slate. "Discretion is not whim, and limiting discretion according to legal standards helps promote the basic principle of justice that like cases should be decided alike." *Martin v. Franklin Capital Corp.,* 546 U.S. 132, 139, 126 S.Ct. 704, 710, 163 L.Ed.2d 547 (2005). When it comes to discerning and applying those standards, in this area as others, "a page of history is worth a volume of logic." *New York Trust Co. v. Eisner,* 256 U.S. 345, 349, 41 S.Ct. 506, 65 L.Ed. 963 (1921) (opinion for the Court by Holmes, J.).

JUSTICE KENNEDY, with whom JUSTICE STEVENS, JUSTICE SOUTER, and JUSTICE BREYER join, concurring.

The Court is correct, in my view, to hold that courts should apply the well-established, four-factor test—without resort to categorical rules—in deciding whether to grant injunctive relief in patent cases. THE CHIEF JUSTICE is also correct that history may be instructive in applying this test. The traditional practice of issuing injunctions against patent infringers, however, does not seem to rest on "the difficulty of protecting a right to *exclude* through monetary remedies that allow an infringer to *use* an invention against the patentee's wishes." Both the terms of the Patent Act and the traditional view of injunctive relief accept that the existence of a right to exclude does not dictate the remedy for a violation of that right. To the extent earlier cases establish a pattern of granting an injunction against patent infringers almost as a matter of course, this pattern simply illustrates the result of the four-factor test in the contexts then prevalent. The lesson of the historical practice, therefore, is most helpful and instructive when the circumstances of a case bear substantial parallels to litigation the courts have confronted before.

In cases now arising trial courts should bear in mind that in many instances the nature of the patent being enforced and the economic function of the patent holder present considerations quite unlike earlier cases. An industry has developed in which firms use patents not as a basis for producing and selling goods but, instead, primarily for obtaining licensing fees. *See* FTC, *To Promote Innovation: The Proper Balance of Competition and Patent Law and Policy*, ch. 3, pp. 38–39 (Oct.2003), available at http://www.ftc.gov/os/2003/ 10/innovationrpt.pdf (as visited May 11, 2006, and available in Clerk of Court's case file). For these firms, an injunction, and the potentially serious sanctions arising from its violation, can be employed as a bargaining tool to charge exorbitant fees to companies that seek to buy licenses to practice the patent. *See ibid.* When the patented invention is but a small component of the product the companies seek to produce and the threat of an injunction is employed simply for undue leverage in negotiations, legal damages may well be sufficient to compensate for the infringement and an injunction may not serve the public interest. In addition injunctive relief may have different consequences for the burgeoning number of patents over business methods, which were not of much economic and legal significance in earlier times. The potential vagueness and suspect validity of some of these patents may affect the calculus under the four-factor test.

The equitable discretion over injunctions, granted by the Patent Act, is well suited to allow courts to adapt to the rapid technological and legal developments in the patent system. For these reasons it should be recognized that district courts must determine whether past practice fits the circumstances of the cases before them. With these observations, I join the opinion of the Court.

NOTES

1. **The Impact of *eBay*.** The three opinions here seem to provide something for everyone, with virtually any patent litigant apparently able to point to a favorable passage somewhere. The bottom line impact of this opinion was therefore difficult to predict at the time it was granted. Through December 31, 2007, Professor Joseph Scott Miller counted 10 instances where a district court had denied a permanent injunction and 28 instances where they were granted. (Professor Miller reports his results on his blog, *The Fire of Genius*.) As this litigation continues to advance the Federal Circuit, we will be better able to identify the most relevant factors that influence judicial thought on the decision to enjoin a patent infringer or not.

2. **Property Rules versus Liability Rules**. Those familiar with the literature regarding "property rules" and "liability rules" may view the *eBay* opinion as another episode in this long-running dialogue. As described in Guide Calabresi & A. Douglas Melamed, *Property Rules, Liability Rules and Inalienability: One View of the Cathedral*, 85 HARV. L. REV. 1089 (1972), two different means of protecting entitlements consist of property rules, where the permission of the owner is required in order to trespass, and liability rules, which confer a lesser degree of protection that is akin to tort law: the right to collect damages caused by another's intrusion. Property rules are more likely to be found where the transaction costs of private bargaining about the rights are low, while liability rules tend to involve circumstances with high transaction costs. As Calabresi and Melamed explained, "[i]f we were to give a property entitlement not to be accidentally injured we would have to require all who engage in activities that may injure individuals to negotiate with them before an accident"—an unduly expensive and inefficient proposition. *Id.* at 1108.

Prior to the *eBay* ruling, the patent right appeared to most appropriately be deemed a property rule. Some might question this remedial alignment in due of the notorious difficulty in evaluating the worth of individual patents, and therefore coming to a private agreement about their use. The large number of issued patents that particular technologies employ also creates apparent difficulties for manufacturers. A laptop computer may employ tens of thousands of patent inventions subject to a fragmented ownership, for example. To what extent does *eBay* make the patent right more difficult to classify as a property or liability rule?

3. **Business Method Patents.** Justice Kennedy's concurrence speaks to the "potential vagueness and suspect validity" of business method patents. Recall that at this stage of the litigation, the successfully asserted patent has survived any potential challenge for failing to include definite claims, as well as any other patentability criteria. Are vagueness and invalidity appropriately considered at the moment a court decides whether to issue a permanent injunction or not?

4. **Patent Trolling.** In the view of some observers, the pre-*eBay* rule that prevailing patentees were awarded injunctions virtually automatically encouraged strategic behavior by speculators. These entrepreneurs do not themselves market goods or services, and thus do not acquire patents in order to protect

their own markets. Rather, as suggested in Justice Kennedy's concurrence, they are said to use patents to threaten manufacturers and service providers. Because such speculators may legitimately threaten to halt use of the patented invention entirely, accused infringers may enter into a license on even a dubious patent in the face of losing the company business. This practice is sometimes termed "trolling," after creatures from folklore that would emerge from under a bridge in order to exact a fee for passage from travelers.

Patent enforcement suits brought by patent speculators appear to present special concerns for manufacturers and service providers. If one manufacturer or service provider commences litigation against another, the defendant can often assert its own claims of patent infringement against the plaintiff. Because patent speculators do not otherwise participate in the marketplace, however, the defendant is unable to counter with its own patent infringement charges. This asymmetry in litigation position reportedly reduces the bargaining power of manufacturers and service providers, potentially exposing them to harassment. Particularly where the patented invention forms just one part of a larger whole, the possibility of reaping windfall patent profits through holdup of the marketed product or service has disturbed some commentators.

Observers hasten to note, however, that not every patent proprietor who does not commercialize the patented invention should properly be considered an opportunistic "troll." A nonmanufacturing patentee may lack the expertise or resources to produce a patented product, prefer to commit itself to further innovation, or otherwise have legitimate reasons for its behavior. Universities and small biotechnology companies often fit into this category. Further, whether classified as a "troll" or not, each patent owner has presumptively fulfilled all of the relevant statutory requirements. Among these obligations is a thorough disclosure of a novel, nonobvious invention to the public.

How does *eBay* impact the phenomenon of patent trolling? Does the requirement of additional proof to obtain a permanent injunction change the calculus of negotiations for a royalty before litigation?

5. Compulsory Licenses? The concept of a "compulsory license" used to be (and probably still is) anathema to many patent attorneys. The United States Trade Representative also has spent considerable efforts attempting to limit the availability of compulsory licenses in foreign patent statutes. In the post-*eBay* era, however, the Federal Circuit routinely employs this phrase when it discusses the availability of a permanent injunction. *See, e.g., Finisar Corp. v. DirecTV Group, Inc.*, 523 F.3d 1323, 1339 (Fed. Cir 2008); *Innogenetics, N.V. v. Abbott Laboratories*, 512 F.3d 1363, 1381 (Fed. Cir. 2008). On the other hand, one panel of the Federal Circuit sought to distinguish the denial of a permanent injunction from a compulsory license:

> We use the term ongoing royalty to distinguish this equitable remedy from a compulsory license. The term "compulsory license" implies that *anyone* who meets certain criteria has congressional authority to use that which is licensed. *See, e.g.,* 17 U.S.C. § 115 ("When phonorecords of a nondramatic musical work have been distributed . . . under the authority of the copyright owner, *any other person* . . . may, by complying with the provisions of

this section, obtain a compulsory license to make and distribute phonorec-ords of the work." (emphasis added)). By contrast, the ongoing-royalty order at issue here is limited to one particular set of defendants; there is no implied authority in the court's order for any other auto manufacturer to follow in Toyota's footsteps and use the patented invention with the court's imprimatur.

Paice LLC v. Toyota Motor Corp., 504 F.3d 1293, 1313 (Fed. Cir. 2007). Are you persuaded by this distinction? A concurring judge was not convinced: "[C]alling a compulsory license an 'ongoing royalty' does not make it any less a compulso-ry license." *Id.* at 1316 (Rader, J. concurring). The concurring judge would have required a remand to the trial court to obtain the permission of both parties before setting an "ongoing royalty." Would this just give the patentee a "second bite" at proving an applicable royalty rate? Is that "second bite" justified? In *Paice*, the Federal Circuit remanded for a recalculation of damages. Do you think the injunction outcome affected the Circuit's damages judgment?

6. "Ongoing royalties"—ongoing litigation? When the district court de-clines to enter a permanent injunction, it must impose a royalty to account for the ongoing infringement. What happens when economic conditions a few years downstream from the judgment make the court-imposed royalty either much too high or much too low? Of course, even a negotiated license can face the same problem, but a negotiated license can take account of changed circumstances. How does a court-imposed royalty avoid giving one of the parties an unintended windfall? If circumstances change enough, can a party bring a new action to reconsider the amount of the ongoing royalty?

7. Additional Contexts for Injunctions. In addition to being awarded alongside a final judgment, injunctive relief is also available preliminary to adjudication. It is also subject to enforcement via contempt proceedings. The following opinion takes up the topic of preliminary injunctions in patent law in the wake of *eBay*.

SANOFI–SYNTHELABO v. APOTEX, INC.

United States Court of Appeals for the Federal Circuit, 2006
470 F.3d 1368

Before Lourie and Bryson, Circuit Judges, Clevenger, Senior Cir-cuit Judge.

LOURIE, CIRCUIT JUDGE.

Apotex, Inc. and Apotex Corp. (collectively referred to as "Apotex") appeal from the decision of the United States District Court for the Southern District of New York granting a preliminary injunction in favor of Sanofi–Synthelabo, Sanofi–Synthelabo, Inc., and Bristol–Myers Squibb ("BMS") Sanofi Pharmaceuticals Holding Partnership (collective-ly referred to as "Sanofi"). Because we conclude that the district court did not abuse its discretion in granting the preliminary injunction, we affirm.

BACKGROUND

Sanofi markets Plavix®, a platelet aggregation inhibiting agent used to reduce thrombotic events such as heart attacks and strokes. The active ingredient in Plavix® is clopidogrel bisulfate, which is covered by Sanofi's patent, U.S. Patent 4,847,265 ("the '265 patent"), which will expire on November 17, 2011.

In November 2001, Apotex filed an Abbreviated New Drug Application ("ANDA") pursuant to the Hatch–Waxman Act seeking U.S. Food and Drug Administration ("FDA") approval to manufacture and sell a generic version of clopidogrel bisulfate. Apotex filed a Paragraph IV certification with its ANDA, pursuant to 21 U.S.C. § 355(j)(2)(A)(vii)(IV), asserting that the '265 patent is invalid. In response, Sanofi sued Apotex on March 21, 2002, claiming that the filing of the ANDA infringed the '265 patent. Apotex counterclaimed, asserting that the patent is invalid and unenforceable. A thirty-month stay of FDA approval for the ANDA was triggered when the suit was filed in the district court, pursuant to 21 U.S.C. § 355(j)(5)(B)(iii). The stay expired May 17, 2005, and on January 20, 2006, the FDA approved the ANDA.

Apotex launched its generic clopidogrel bisulfate product on August 8, 2006. Sanofi filed its motion for a preliminary injunction on August 15, 2006, and requested a recall of Apotex's products that were already distributed. After a two-day evidentiary hearing, the district court granted the motion for injunctive relief on August 31, 2006, but denied the request for recall. During the period between the generic launch and the entry of the preliminary injunction, Apotex shipped a six-month supply of its product to distributors in the United States.

In reaching its decision, the district court applied the established four-factor test for preliminary injunctive relief, and found that the factors weighed in favor of an injunction. Regarding the likelihood of success on the merits, the court noted that Apotex conceded that its accused products infringe claim 3 of the '265 patent. The court then found that Apotex failed to establish a likelihood of proving invalidity at trial-rejecting its anticipation, obviousness, and obviousness-type double patenting invalidity defenses. The court also determined that Apotex failed to raise a substantial question as to whether the '265 patent is unenforceable due to inequitable conduct. Additionally, the court found that the remaining three factors of the test favored issuance of a preliminary injunction. The court set bond in the amount of $400 million. Trial is scheduled to commence on January 22, 2007.

Apotex moved for a stay of the injunction, which we denied on September 21, 2006, and it filed its appeal from the district court's grant of the preliminary injunction. An expedited briefing schedule was set, and oral argument was heard on October 31, 2006. We have jurisdiction pursuant to 28 U.S.C. § 1292(c) in view of §§ 1292(a) and 1295(a)(1).

DISCUSSION

A decision to grant or deny a preliminary injunction pursuant to 35 U.S.C. § 283 is within the sound discretion of the district court, and we review such a decision for an abuse of discretion. *Amazon.com, Inc. v. Barnesandnoble.com, Inc.,* 239 F.3d 1343, 1350 (Fed.Cir.2001). Thus, a decision granting a preliminary injunction will be overturned on appeal only if it is established "that the court made a clear error of judgment in weighing relevant factors or exercised its discretion based upon an error of law or clearly erroneous factual findings." *Genentech, Inc. v. Novo Nordisk A/S,* 108 F.3d 1361, 1364 (Fed.Cir.1997). To the extent the court's decision is based upon an issue of law, we review that issue de novo. *Tate Access Floors, Inc. v. Interface Architectural Res., Inc.,* 279 F.3d 1357, 1364 (Fed.Cir.2002).

Sanofi, as the moving party, may be entitled to a preliminary injunction if it establishes four factors: "(1) a reasonable likelihood of its success on the merits; (2) irreparable harm if an injunction is not granted; (3) a balance of hardships tipping in its favor; and (4) the injunction's . . . impact on the public interest." *Amazon.com,* 239 F.3d at 1350.

A. *Likelihood of Success on the Merits*

In order to satisfy the first element of the test, Sanofi must demonstrate that, "in light of the presumptions and burdens that will inhere at trial on the merits," *Amazon.com,* 239 F.3d at 1350, Sanofi will likely prove that Apotex's product infringes the '265 patent and that it will withstand Apotex's challenges to the validity and enforceability of the '265 patent. Because Apotex stipulated to infringement, only the second inquiry is at issue in this case. Thus, the first element was properly found satisfied if Apotex failed to raise a "substantial question" with regard to the validity or enforceability of the '265 patent—or, if it succeeded in doing so, Sanofi demonstrated that those defenses "lack substantial merit." *Genentech,* 108 F.3d at 1364. On appeal, Apotex challenges the district court's rulings with respect to anticipation, obviousness, obviousness-type double patenting, and enforceability.

[The Court of Appeals concluded that the district court had not clearly erred in finding no substantial merit to Apotex's invalidity and unenforceability assertions.]

B. *Other Preliminary Injunction Factors*

We next consider the remaining elements of the preliminary injunction test. The district court applied a presumption of irreparable harm in light of its conclusion that Sanofi established a likelihood of success on the merits. The court also found that Sanofi proffered substantial evidence establishing other forms of irreparable harm, including irreversible price erosion, loss of good will, potential lay-offs of Sanofi employees, and the discontinuance of clinical trials that are devoted to other medical uses for Plavix®.

Apotex argues that the district court clearly erred in concluding that Sanofi would suffer irreparable harm in the absence of an injunction. Additionally, Apotex challenges the court's findings with regard to the other kinds of irreparable harm established by Sanofi.

In response, Sanofi ... asserts that the court did not clearly err by crediting the evidence it proffered establishing the additional kinds of irreparable harm it would suffer if Apotex were allowed to continue selling its generic product.

We conclude that the district court did not clearly err in finding that Sanofi satisfied this factor.

[W]e reject Apotex's assertion that the district court abused its discretion in concluding that Sanofi would suffer irreversible price erosion if an injunction were not entered. Based on the evidence Sanofi adduced, including the testimony of its economics expert, Professor Hausman, and a declaration from a Sanofi executive, Hugh O'Neill, the court found that Sanofi would suffer irreversible price erosion in light of a complex pricing scheme that is directly affected by the presence of the generic product in the market. In particular, the court found that since Apotex's generic product entered the market, Sanofi has been forced to offer discounted rates and price concessions to third-party payors, such as health maintenance organizations, in order to keep Plavix® on a favorable pricing tier, which governs what consumers pay for that drug. The court found that the availability of a generic product encourages third party payors to place Plavix® on a less favorable tier, thereby requiring consumers to pay a higher co-pay, and perhaps deterring them from purchasing Plavix®. The court identified additional consequences of unfavorable tier placement, including a decrease in demand for Plavix®. According to Sanofi, it is nearly impossible to restore Plavix® to its pre-launch price since the generic product entered the market.

Apotex does not argue that price erosion is not a valid ground for finding irreparable harm, but rather challenges the district court's findings as to price erosion. We conclude that the district court did not clearly err in its evaluation of the evidence relating to price erosion. While Apotex asserts that price erosion had already occurred, and thus an injunction is not necessary because it cannot ameliorate Sanofi's position, Apotex fails to identify clear errors in the district court's analysis, and fails to proffer evidence of its own sufficient to rebut the court's findings. Apotex also fails to demonstrate that the court clearly erred in its findings with respect to the additional factors that established irreparable harm, including loss of good will, the potential reduction in work force, and the discontinuation of clinical trials. Accordingly, we conclude that the district court did not clearly err in finding irreparable harm.[9]

_____

9. Apotex also argues that the district court erred by applying a presumption of irreparable harm because Sanofi established a likelihood of success on the merits. Apotex contends that

As to the third factor of the test, Apotex argues that the court erred in balancing the hardships because it ignored the harm Apotex would face if an injunction were granted.... Sanofi responds that the court did not abuse its discretion in finding that that factor favored Sanofi, particularly because it was Apotex's own decision to engage in an at-risk launch that would trigger its 180–day exclusivity period before reaching the merits of the case. Based on the record on appeal, we conclude that the court did not clearly err in finding that Apotex's harms were "almost entirely preventable" and were the result of its own calculated risk to launch its product pre-judgment. Accordingly, the court did not abuse its discretion in finding that the balance of hardships tipped in Sanofi's favor.

The fourth factor we consider is the public interest, which the court found tips in favor of Sanofi, albeit slightly. Apotex, as well as amici, argue that the district court erred in failing to consider certain public harms that would result if an injunction issues. Apotex, in particular, contends that if the generic products were removed from the market, consumers would be inclined not to purchase their medication because of the accompanying price increase for the brand name drug, leading to possible deaths. Apotex further argues that significant consumer confusion may ensue because of the six-month supply that was shipped to the American market, which was not equally distributed among vendors. Sanofi responds that the court did not clearly err in finding that the interest in encouraging pharmaceutical research and development outweighed the public interest advanced by Apotex.

We agree with Sanofi. While Apotex raises legitimate concerns, the district court did not abuse its discretion in concluding that those concerns were outweighed by the public interests identified by Sanofi. We have long acknowledged the importance of the patent system in encouraging innovation. Indeed, the "encouragement of investment-based risk is the fundamental purpose of the patent grant, and is based directly on the right to exclude." *Patlex Corp. v. Mossinghoff*, 758 F.2d 594, 599 (Fed.Cir.1985). The district court relied on the testimony of Dr. Hausman in finding that the average cost of developing a blockbuster drug is $800 million. Importantly, the patent system provides incentive to the innovative drug companies to continue costly development efforts. We therefore find that the court did not clearly err in concluding that the significant "public interest in encouraging investment in drug development and protecting the exclusionary rights conveyed in valid pharmaceutical patents" tips the scales in favor of Sanofi.

---

applying such a presumption is in direct contravention of the Supreme Court's decision in *eBay Inc. v. MercExchange, L.L.C.*, 547 U.S. 388, 126 S.Ct. 1837, 164 L.Ed.2d 641 (2006). Because we conclude that the district court did not clearly err in finding that Sanofi established several kinds of irreparable harm, including irreversible price erosion, we need not address this contention.

D. *Bond*

Lastly, Apotex challenges the court's decision to set bond in the amount of $400 million, which it asserts fails to provide sufficient security because it represents only 10% of the annual market and ignores Apotex's loss of market share. Sanofi responds that the amount far exceeds any damage Apotex may face, particularly in light of the fact that there was no recall of Apotex's generic product after it launched its product on August 8, 2006.

The posting of a bond is governed by Federal Rule of Civil Procedure 65(c) which provides that:

> No restraining order or preliminary injunction shall issue except upon the giving of security by the applicant, in such sum as the court deems proper, for the payment of such costs and damages as may be incurred or suffered by any party who is found to have been wrongfully enjoined or restrained.

FED.R.CIV.P. 65(C). The amount of a bond is a determination that rests within the sound discretion of a trial court. *Doctor's Assocs., Inc. v. Distajo*, 107 F.3d 126, 136 (2d Cir.1997) (noting that a district court has wide discretion under Rule 65(c) in setting the amount of a bond). The court based its determination on evidence presented before the court that concerned Apotex's "potential lost profits, lost market share and associated costs of relaunch" in the event of wrongful enjoinment. We find no basis for disturbing the court's assessment of the facts, and thus conclude that the court did not abuse its discretion in setting the bond amount.

CONCLUSION

We have considered Apotex's remaining arguments with respect to the myriad of issues it has raised on appeal and find them unpersuasive. We therefore conclude that the district court did not abuse its discretion in granting preliminary injunctive relief. Accordingly, for the foregoing reasons, we affirm the district court's grant of the preliminary injunction. We wish to note that, while we have carefully considered all of the arguments presented to us in reviewing the district court's grant of the preliminary injunction, we have done so in the context of the standard of review applicable to grant of preliminary injunctions, and that the district court is not bound to its earlier conclusions on full trial on the merits. We leave to that court the conduct of any further proceedings. *AFFIRMED*.

NOTES

1. **One Size Fits All?** Prior to the issuance of the *eBay* opinion, Congress had considered amendments to the Patent Act that would have stressed the equitable and discretionary nature of injunctive relief. This proposed amendment exposed a growing political rift between the pharmaceutical industry, on one hand, and the "high tech" industries such as electronics manufacturers and software houses.

To a large extent, the patent statute subjects all inventions to the same standards, regardless of the field in which those inventions arose. Whether the invention is an automobile engine, semiconductor, or a pharmaceutical, it is for the most part subject to the same patentability requirements, scope of rights, and term of protection. Both experience and economic research suggest that distinct industries experience the patent system in different ways, however.

Although broad generalizations should be drawn with care, two industries widely perceived as viewing the patent system in different ways are the pharmaceutical and electronics sectors. Within the pharmaceutical industry, individual patents are perceived as critical to a business model that provides life-saving and life-enhancing medical innovations, but eventually allows members of the public access to medicines at low cost. In particular, often only a handful, and sometimes only one or two patents cover a particular drug product. Patents are also judged to be crucial to the pharmaceutical sector because of the relative ease of replicating the finished product. For example, while it is expensive, complicated, and time consuming to duplicate an airplane, it is relatively simple to perform a chemical analysis of a pill and reproduce it.

In contrast to the pharmaceutical field, innovations in the electronics field are typically cumulative and new products often embody numerous patentable inventions. It is not uncommon for thousands of different patents (relating to hardware and software) to be embodied in one single computer, for example. In addition, ownership of these patents may well be fractured among hundreds or thousands of different individuals and firms. No wonder, then, that a perceived "automatic injunction" rule was not viewed favorably by actors in this industry.

To what extent do Federal Circuit opinions *Sanofi–Synthelabo v. Apotex, Inc.* bring a measure of relief to pharmaceutical innovators in the post-*eBay* era? To what extent is the opinion consistent with *eBay*?

2. Contempt Proceedings. As with other sorts of cases, injunctions in patent cases are typically enforced via contempt proceedings. A typical fact pattern involves an enjoined infringer's attempt to modify the adjudicated infringement in order to fall without the scope of patent coverage and hence the injunction. Patent proprietors not uncommonly judge the enjoined infringer's efforts insufficient and bring charges of contempt of court. The Federal Circuit has fashioned the analysis to be undertaken as follows:

> [W]e have held that before entering a judgment of contempt of an injunction in a patent infringement case, a district court must address two separate questions. First, the district court must address whether a contempt hearing is an appropriate forum for adjudging whether an allegedly redesigned product is infringing. In doing so, the district court must compare the accused product with the original infringing product. If there is "more than a colorable difference" between the accused product and the adjudged infringing product such that "substantial open issues with respect to infringement to be tried" exist, contempt proceedings are not appropriate. We review the district court's decision to entertain a contempt proceeding for an abuse of discretion, applying Federal Circuit law. *Id.* "An

abuse of discretion may be established under Federal Circuit law by showing that the court made a clear error of judgment in weighing the relevant factors or exercised its discretion based on an error of law or clearly erroneous fact finding." *Laboratory Corp. of Am. Holdings v. Chiron Corp.*, 384 F.3d 1326, 1331 (Fed. Cir. 2004).

Second, if contempt proceedings are appropriate, the district court must address whether the accused product infringes the claims of the asserted patent. To show infringement, the patentee "must prove by clear and convincing evidence that 'the modified device falls within the admitted or adjudicated scope of the claims.' "

Abbott Labs. v. TorPharm, Inc., 503 F.3d 1372, 1379–81 (Fed. Cir. 2007) (selected citations omitted).

3. Preliminary Measures Available Abroad. Legal regimes based overseas feature a variety of preliminary measures available to patent holders. Some, such as Italian precautionary measures and Austrian interim injunctions, are roughly analogous to United States preliminary injunctions. *See* Paul Traxler, *Interim Measures in Patent Infringement Proceedings Under Austrian Law*, 24 INT'L REV. INDUS. PROP. & COPYRIGHT L. 751 (1993); Massimo Scuffi, *European Patents and Interlocutory Injunctions for Acts of Patent Infringement Under Italian Law*, 22 INT'L REV. INDUS. PROP. & COPYRIGHT L. 1009 (1991). Also of note are various ex parte orders, including the British "Anton Piller" order and the French saisie-contrefaçon. Such orders do not aim to allow patentees to confiscate infringing technologies, but are in a sense are a form of discovery, allowing patentees to establish the origin and extent of the infringement. *See Anton Piller v. Manufacturing Processes*, [1976] R.P.C. 719; André Bertrand, *Seizures to Acquire Evidence Under French Patent Law*, 26 INT'L REV. INDUS. PROP. & COPYRIGHT L. 175 (1995).

§ 13.2   DAMAGES

§ 13.2[a]   BASIC PRINCIPLES

PANDUIT CORP. v. STAHLIN BROS. FIBRE WORKS, INC.

United States Court of Appeals, Sixth Circuit, 1978
575 F.2d 1152

Before Phillips, Chief Circuit Judge, Celebrezze, Circuit Judge, and Markey, Chief Judge of the Court of Customs and Patent Appeals.

MARKEY, CHIEF JUDGE.

Appeal from a judgment of the district court, adopting, with an unpublished opinion, the report of the special master awarding plaintiff, as damages for patent infringement, a reasonable royalty of 2 1/2%. We reverse and remand.

LITIGATION BACKGROUND

In 1964 plaintiff Panduit Corp. (Panduit) sued defendant Stahlin Bros. Fibre Works, Inc. (Stahlin) for infringement of Panduit's Walch patent No. 3,024,301, covering duct for wiring of electrical control systems. In 1969, the district court found claim 5 valid and infringed by the "Lok–slot" and "Web–slot" ducts made and sold by Stahlin, enjoined Stahlin from further infringement, and ordered an accounting. That judgment was affirmed on appeal.

Thereafter, the district court adjudged Stahlin in contempt of the court's injunction, because of Stahlin's making and selling the "Tear Drop" duct, a colorable imitation of the infringing "Lok–slot." That judgment was also affirmed on appeal.

In 1971, the district court appointed a master to determine Panduit's damages pursuant to 35 U.S.C. § 284, to take evidence, and render a report on the issues of treble damages, interest, costs, and attorney fees. The district court, in adopting in toto the master's report, considered the master's findings of fact not clearly erroneous, and stated that "the Master had correctly applied the law to the circumstances of this case." The report recommended $44,709.60 in damages, based on a royalty of 2½% of gross sales price, the percentage being calculated on Stahlin's testimony that its normal profit on all of its products was 4.04% and the concept that a "reasonable royalty" entailed some level of profit to the "licensee".

FACT BACKGROUND

The duct manufactured by Panduit was invented by its president, Jack Caveney. Panduit began to make and sell the duct in 1955, and Caveney applied for a patent in 1956. In an interference proceeding in the Patent Office, it was determined that Walch, an employee of General Electric, was the first inventor of the duct. A patent issued to General Electric, as Walch's assignee, on March 6, 1962. Panduit then acquired the Walch patent from General Electric and established a firm policy of exercising its right to that patent property, i.e., of the right to exclude others from making and selling the patented duct.

Stahlin began to manufacture and sell the "Lok–slot" and "Web–slot" ducts in 1957, and continued to do so after issuance of the Walch patent and its sale to Panduit in 1962. On January 1, 1963, Stahlin introduced a price cut of approximately 30% on its "Lok–slot" and "Web–slot" ducts.

Panduit seeks $808,003 as damages for lost profits on lost sales over the period March 6, 1962, the date of first infringement, to August 7, 1970, the effective date of the initial injunction; or, alternatively, a 35% reasonable royalty rate yielding $625,940. In addition, Panduit seeks $4,069,000 in profits lost on Panduit's own sales because of Stahlin's price cut.

ISSUE

The dispositive issue is whether the master's determination of a reasonable royalty was in error.

OPINION

The statute, 35 U.S.C. § 284, requires that the patent owner receive from the infringer "damages adequate to compensate for the infringement." In *Aro Mfg. Co. v. Convertible Top Replacement Co.*, 377 U.S. 476 at 507, 84 S.Ct. 1526, 1543, 12 L.Ed.2d 457(1964), the Supreme Court stated:

> But the present statutory rule is that only "damages" may be recovered. These have been defined by this Court as "compensation for the pecuniary loss he (the patentee) has suffered from the infringement, without regard to the question whether the defendant has gained or lost by his unlawful acts." *Coupe v. Royer*, 155 U.S. 565, 582, 15 S.Ct. 199, 39 L.Ed. 263. They have been said to constitute "the difference between his pecuniary condition after the infringement, and what his condition would have been if the infringement had not occurred." *Yale Lock Mfg. Co. v. Sargent*, 117 U.S. 536, 552, 6 S.Ct. 934, 29 L.Ed. 954. The question to be asked in determining damages is "how much had the Patent Holder and Licensee suffered by the infringement. And that question (is) primarily: had the Infringer not infringed, what would Patent Holder–Licensee have made?"

Panduit argues that the district court erred (1) in denying Panduit its lost profits due to lost sales, or, in the alternative, a 35% reasonable royalty; and (2) in denying Panduit its lost profits from its own actual sales due to Stahlin's price cut.

LOST PROFITS DUE TO LOST SALES

To obtain as damages the profits on sales he would have made absent the infringement, i.e., the sales made by the infringer, a patent owner must prove: (1) demand for the patented product, (2) absence of acceptable noninfringing substitutes, (3) his manufacturing and marketing capability to exploit the demand, and (4) the amount of the profit he would have made. 3 R. WHITE, PATENT LITIGATION: PROCEDURE AND TACTICS § 9.03(2).

It is not disputed that Panduit established elements (1) and (3). Regarding (2), the master found that: "The evidence clearly shows the existence of acceptable non-infringing substitute ducts which would have permitted the defendant to retain its customers." That finding, as discussed below, was in error. However, Panduit is not entitled to its lost profits on lost sales in this case because of its failure to establish element (4).

The district court upheld as not clearly erroneous the master's finding that "there was insufficient evidence from which a fair determination could be made as to the amount of profit plaintiff would have made on such sales."

Panduit's Achilles heel on element (4) is a lack of evidence on its fixed costs. Panduit alleges that its omission is overcome by other evidence. . . .

In the present case, Stahlin did dispute Panduit's accounting theory, presenting its own expert witnesses to contradict it. [T]he accuracy of the patent owner's accounting method is "a matter to be decided on the basis of testimony in the hearing before the Master." The master here found, on the basis of the evidence before him, and the district court agreed, that Panduit's accounting theory was deficient.

On the issue of Panduit's lost profits on lost sales, we affirm the district court.

REASONABLE ROYALTY

When actual damages, *e.g.*, lost profits, cannot be proved, the patent owner is entitled to a reasonable royalty. 35 U.S.C. § 284. A reasonable royalty is an amount "which a person, desiring to manufacture and sell a patented article, as a business proposition, would be willing to pay as a royalty and yet be able to make and sell the patented article, in the market, at a reasonable profit." *Goodyear Tire and Rubber Co. v. Overman Cushion Tire Co.*, 95 F.2d 978 at 984 (6th Cir.1937).

The key element in setting a reasonable royalty after determination of validity and infringement is the necessity for return to the date when the infringement began. In the present case, that date is March 6, 1962. On that date, Panduit possessed the particular property right found to have been infringed by Stahlin. At that point Stahlin chose to continue the making and selling of the patented product.

As a result of Stahlin's election to infringe its property right, Panduit has suffered substantially. *See United States Frumentum Co. v. Lauhoff*, 216 F. 610 (6th Cir.1914). Though unable to prove the actual amount of lost profits or to establish a damage figure resulting from Stahlin's price cut, Panduit was clearly damaged by having been forced, against its will, to share sales of the patented product with Stahlin. Further, Panduit has been forced into thirteen years of expensive litigation, involving $400,000 in attorney fees, a trial, a contempt proceeding to enforce the court's injunction, a hearing on damages, and three appeals. For all this, the "damages adequate to compensate for the infringement," 35 U.S.C. § 284, have thus far been found to total $44,709.60.

Having elected to continue the manufacture and sale of the patented duct after the patent issued, and having elected to manufacture and sell a second infringing product in the face of the court's injunction, Stahlin was able to make infringing sales, as found by the master, totalling $1,788,384.

The setting of a reasonable royalty after infringement cannot be treated, as it was here, as the equivalent of ordinary royalty negotiations among truly "willing" patent owners and licensees. That view would constitute a pretense that the infringement never happened. It would also make an election to infringe a handy means for competitors to impose a "compulsory license" policy upon every patent owner.

Except for the limited risk that the patent owner, over years of litigation, might meet the heavy burden of proving the four elements required for recovery of lost profits, the infringer would have nothing to lose, and everything to gain if he could count on paying only the normal, routine royalty non-infringers might have paid. As said by this court in another context, the infringer would be in a "heads-I-win, tails-you-lose" position.

Determination of a "reasonable royalty" after infringement, like many devices in the law, rests on a legal fiction. Created in an effort to "compensate" when profits are not provable, the "reasonable royalty" device conjures a "willing" licensor and licensee, who like Ghosts of Christmas Past, are dimly seen as "negotiating" a "license." There is, of course, no actual willingness on either side, and no license to do anything, the infringer being normally enjoined, as is Stahlin, from further manufacture, use, or sale of the patented product.

In determining that a reasonable royalty rate here was 2 1/2%, the master found: (1) there were present in the market on the date of first infringement acceptable noninfringing substitutes and competing duct producers, (2) Panduit could not have maintained a high price differential in the face of competition from the substitute ducts, (3) on the hypothetical negotiation date, both Panduit and Stahlin would have been aware of the competitive state of the market, and of the probability of future price cuts, including Stahlin's. We disagree.

In the present case, the master's finding that Panduit had competitors was not erroneous, but the implication drawn therefrom was. At the time the patent issued, there were four competitors, but they were recognized as making and selling not substitutes but infringing ducts. Competition between those selling infringing ducts was admittedly fierce. Infringer Stahlin, however, cannot expect to pay a lesser royalty, as compensation for its infringement, on the ground that it was not the only infringer.

Illustrative of the absence of acceptable substitutes is Stahlin's inability to avoid infringement, even if it had ever wanted to. Having begun manufacture of the duct in 1957, Stahlin continued after the patent issued in 1962, after Panduit instituted its infringement suit in 1964, and after the district court's injunction in 1969.

At the time of the first injunction, virtually all of Stahlin's sales of electrical duct were of the infringing type. Stahlin's early-but-grudging recognition of the unique advantages of Panduit's patented duct was evidenced by an intra-company memo. Dated June 21, 1957, it was issued in the earliest stages of Stahlin's manufacture of the "Lok–Slot:"

> It seems that some of our customers have preferred a full-slotted channel; one that permits slipping the wire in place rather

than threading the end through an opening. It's advantages are questionable but we always try to give our customers even more than they want. Thus, we have developed the Lok–Slot construction.

... and Lok–Slot is the best design approach yet to this form of channel.

Proof of the absence of noninfringing substitutes:

(I)nvolves some of the same evidence as that which was introduced in support of the validity of the patent. The patent owner who had proved a long-felt need for a particular invention has a lighter burden in establishing that his customers, as well as the infringer's customers, were in fact seeking to obtain the patented solution to such need or problem. The other side of the coin involves a strong showing by the infringer that although the patent may have embodied some trifling improvement which was patentable to a narrow extent, such improvement did not create any preference for the patented product rather than a noninfringing substitute....

3 R. WHITE, § 9.03(2). The prior district and appellate court opinions leave no doubt that the patented product filled a waiting need and met with commercial success due to its merits. Stahlin's own intra-company memo (PX 58), and its $1,788,384 sales of infringing ducts during the period when allegedly acceptable noninfringing substitutes are now said to have been available, leave no doubt that the patented improvement created a substantial customer preference. A product lacking the advantages of that patented can hardly be termed a substitute "acceptable" to the customer who wants those advantages. The post-hoc circumstance that Stahlin, when finally forced to obey the court's injunction, was successful in "switching" customers to a noninfringing product, does not destroy the advantage-recognition attributable to the patent over the prior 15 years. Those preferred advantages were recognized by Stahlin itself, by other infringers, by customers, by the district court, and by this court.

Hence, the 2½% royalty rate recommended by the master and adopted by the district court is clearly erroneous on its face, the master's recommendation having been based in large part on erroneous finding (1), that there were "acceptable" noninfringing substitutes during the relevant period.

CONCLUSION

Elements necessary to the determination of a reasonable royalty in the present case Panduit's actual profit margin in March 1962, and the customary profit allowed licensees in the electrical duct industry, were not determined by the master in his report and cannot be discerned from the record. They therefore must be determined on remand. On remand, the following factors must also be considered: (1) the lack of acceptable noninfringing substitutes, (2) Panduit's unvarying policy of not licensing the Walch patent, (3) the future business and attendant profit Panduit would expect to lose by licensing a competitor, and (4) that the infringed patent gave the entire marketable value to the infringed duct.

For the reasons stated, we reverse the district court's determination of a reasonable royalty, and remand the case for further proceedings consistent herewith.

NOTES

1. The Nonexclusive Standard. Many Federal Circuit cases follow the four-part test of *Panduit*, which Professor Roberta Morris has conveniently summarized as the DAMP test. Although the court just as frequently states that the *Panduit* test is not the exclusive standard for proving lost profits, *see BIC Leisure*, reprinted below, it has been less forthcoming with other approved methodologies for doing so. The Federal Circuit has held that an award of lost profits may be based upon an inference of lost revenue is proper in markets where only two suppliers exist: the patentee and the adjudicated infringer. *See Kaufman Co. v. Lantech, Inc.*, 926 F.2d 1136 (Fed.Cir.1991); *Lam, Inc. v. Johns–Manville Corp.*, 718 F.2d 1056 (Fed.Cir.1983).

2. A True Coin Flip? Is it true that an infringer has nothing to lose if it can count on paying a reasonable royalty? Has the Sixth Circuit forgotten that an infringer might also be preliminarily enjoined, and almost certainly will be permanently enjoined, during the course of the infringement litigation? Unless the infringer can cheaply switch to a noninfringing alternative, then it would ordinarily be in far worse shape than if it had never started to infringe.

Consider also whether these statements from *Panduit* are sound patent policy. Society should encourage fair challenges to patents in order that courts may strike down invalid patents. To some degree, then, the law should support the socially useful activity some accused infringers will perform. Yet, because the *Panduit* methodology puts infringers in a worse position than they would have been had they paid royalties to the patentee, competitors are actually discouraged from challenging patents they may believe are invalid. For an alternative approach from the House of Lords, see *General Tire and Rubber Co. v. Firestone Tyre and Rubber Co. Ltd.*, [1975] 2 All E. R. 173.

3. Lost Profits vs. Reasonable Royalty. Patent holders typically seek lost profits damages under the *Panduit* test, otherwise hoping for a reasonable royalty as a lesser alternative. Does this relationship always hold? Can you construct a situation where the deal struck at a hypothetical negotiation would ultimately exceed the profits the patentee would have realized? Consider a market where demand is very elastic (a small price change produces a big shift in the quantity sold) and the infringer actually is more efficient and has a distinct cost advantage over the patentee's production. In that circumstance, the infringer can sell greater quantities, due to efficiencies, at a lower price. The patentee in that circumstance may actually profit more by taking a royalty.

4. **Deterrence vs. Compensation as a Damages Model.** *Panduit* follows a deterrence model for damages. The language of *Panduit* evinces a primary desire to punish infringement and protect property owners. The following opinion, the leading Federal Circuit opinion on monetary relief for patent infringement, shifts the emphasis for monetary recovery towards a compensation model.

RITE–HITE CORP. v. KELLEY CO.

United States Court of Appeals, Federal Circuit, 1995
56 F.3d 1538

Before Archer, Chief Judge, Rich, Circuit Judge, Smith, Senior Circuit Judge and Nies, Newman, Mayer, Michel, Plager, Lourie, Clevenger, Rader, and Schall, Circuit Judges.

LOURIE, CIRCUIT JUDGE.

Kelley Company appeals from a decision of the United States District Court for the Eastern District of Wisconsin, awarding damages for the infringement of U.S. Patent 4,373,847, owned by Rite–Hite Corporation. *Rite–Hite Corp. v. Kelley Co.*, 774 F.Supp. 1514 (E.D.Wis. 1991). The district court determined, inter alia, that Rite–Hite was entitled to lost profits for lost sales of its devices that were in direct competition with the infringing devices, but which themselves were not covered by the patent in suit. The appeal has been taken in banc to determine whether such damages are legally compensable under 35 U.S.C. § 284. We affirm in part, vacate in part, and remand.

BACKGROUND

On March 22, 1983, Rite–Hite sued Kelley, alleging that Kelley's "Truk Stop" vehicle restraint infringed Rite–Hite's U.S. Patent 4,373,-847 ("the '847 patent"). The '847 patent, issued February 15, 1983, is directed to a device for securing a vehicle to a loading dock to prevent the vehicle from separating from the dock during loading or unloading. Any such separation would create a gap between the vehicle and dock and create a danger for a forklift operator.

Rite–Hite distributed all its products through its wholly-owned and operated sales organizations and through independent sales organizations (ISOs). During the period of infringement, the Rite–Hite sales organizations accounted for approximately 30 percent of the retail dollar sales of Rite–Hite products, and the ISOs accounted for the remaining 70 percent. Rite–Hite sued for its lost profits at the wholesale level and for the lost retail profits of its own sales organizations.

The district court bifurcated the liability and damage phases of the trial and, on March 5, 1986, held the '847 patent to be not invalid and to be infringed by the manufacture, use, and sale of Kelley's Truk Stop device. The court enjoined further infringement. The judgment of liability was affirmed by this court.

On remand, the damage issues were tried to the court. Rite–Hite sought damages calculated as lost profits for two types of vehicle restraints that it made and sold: the "Manual Dok–Lok" model 55 (MDL–55), which incorporated the invention covered by the '847 patent, and the "Automatic Dok–Lok" model 100 (ADL–100), which was not covered by the patent in suit. The ADL–100 was the first vehicle restraint Rite–Hite put on the market and it was covered by one or more patents other than the patent in suit. The Kelley Truk Stop restraint was designed to compete primarily with Rite–Hite's ADL—100. Both employed an electric motor and functioned automatically, and each sold for $1,000–$1,500 at the wholesale level, in contrast to the MDL–55, which sold for one-third to one-half the price of the motorized devices. Rite–Hite does not assert that Kelley's Truk Stop restraint infringed the patents covering the ADL–100.

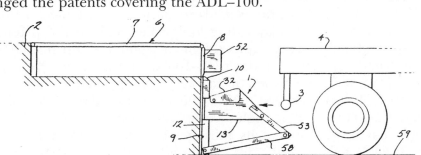

Of the 3,825 infringing Truk Stop devices sold by Kelley, the district court found that, "but for" Kelley's infringement, Rite–Hite would have made 80 more sales of its MDL–55; 3,243 more sales of its ADL–100; and 1,692 more sales of dock levelers, a bridging platform sold with the restraints and used to bridge the edges of a vehicle and dock. The court awarded Rite–Hite as a manufacturer the wholesale profits that it lost on lost sales of the ADL–100 restraints, MDL–55 restraints, and restraint-leveler packages. It also awarded to Rite–Hite as a retailer ... reasonable royalty damages on lost ADL–100, MDL–55, and restraint-leveler sales caused by Kelley's infringing sales. Finally, prejudgment interest, calculated without compounding, was awarded. Kelley's infringement was found to be not willful.

On appeal, Kelley contends that the district court erred as a matter of law in its determination of damages. Kelley does not contest the award of damages for lost sales of the MDL–55 restraints; however, Kelley argues that the patent statute does not provide for damages based on Rite–Hite's lost profits on ADL–100 restraints because the ADL–100s are not covered by the patent in suit; lost profits on unpatented dock levelers are not attributable to demand for the '847 invention and, therefore, are not recoverable losses; and the court erred in calculating a reasonable royalty based as a percentage of ADL–100 and dock leveler profits. Rite–Hite and the ISOs challenge the district court's refusal to award lost retail profits and its award of prejudgment interest at a simple, rather than a compound, rate.

We affirm the damage award with respect to Rite–Hite's lost profits as a manufacturer on its ADL–100 restraint sales, affirm the court's computation of a reasonable royalty rate, [and] vacate the damage award based on the dock levelers.

DISCUSSION

I. Lost Profits on the ADL–100 Restraints

The district court's decision to award lost profits damages pursuant to 35 U.S.C. § 284 turned primarily upon the quality of Rite–Hite's proof of actual lost profits. The court found that, "but for" Kelley's infringing Truk Stop competition, Rite–Hite would have sold 3,243 additional ADL–100 restraints and 80 additional MDL–55 restraints. The court reasoned that awarding lost profits fulfilled the patent statute's goal of affording complete compensation for infringement and compensated Rite–Hite for the ADL–100 sales that Kelley "anticipated taking from Rite–Hite when it marketed the Truk Stop against the ADL–100." The court stated, "[t]he rule applied here therefore does not extend Rite–Hite's patent rights excessively, because Kelley could reasonably have foreseen that its infringement of the '847 patent would make it liable for lost ADL–100 sales in addition to lost MDL–55 sales." The court further reasoned that its decision would avoid what it referred to as the "whip-saw" problem, whereby an infringer could avoid paying lost profits damages altogether by developing a device using a first patented technology to compete with a device that uses a second patented technology and developing a device using the second patented technology to compete with a device that uses the first patented technology.

Kelley maintains that Rite–Hite's lost sales of the ADL–100 restraints do not constitute an injury that is legally compensable by means of lost profits. It has uniformly been the law, Kelley argues, that to recover damages in the form of lost profits a patentee must prove that, "but for" the infringement, it would have sold a product covered by the patent in suit to the customers who bought from the infringer. Under the circumstances of this case, in Kelley's view, the patent statute provides only for damages calculated as a reasonable royalty. Rite–Hite, on the other hand, argues that the only restriction on an award of actual lost profits damages for patent infringement is proof of causation-in-fact. A patentee, in its view, is entitled to all the profits it would have made on any of its products "but for" the infringement. Each party argues that a judgment in favor of the other would frustrate the purposes of the patent statute. Whether the lost profits at issue are legally compensable is a question of law, which we review de novo.

Our analysis of this question necessarily begins with the patent statute. *See General Motors Corp. v. Devex Corp.*, 461 U.S. 648, 653–54

(1983). Implementing the constitutional power under Article I, section 8, to secure to inventors the exclusive right to their discoveries, Congress has provided in 35 U.S.C. § 284 as follows: Upon finding for the claimant the court shall award the claimant damages adequate to compensate for the infringement, but in no event less than a reasonable royalty for the use made of the invention by the infringer, together with interest and costs as fixed by the court. 35 U.S.C. § 284 (1988). The statute thus mandates that a claimant receive damages "adequate" to compensate for infringement. Section 284 further instructs that a damage award shall be "in no event less than a reasonable royalty"; the purpose of this alternative is not to direct the form of compensation, but to set a floor below which damage awards may not fall. Thus, the language of the statute is expansive rather than limiting. It affirmatively states that damages must be adequate, while providing only a lower limit and no other limitation.

The Supreme Court spoke to the question of patent damages in *General Motors*, stating that, in enacting § 284, Congress sought to "ensure that the patent owner would in fact receive full compensation for 'any damages' [the patentee] suffered as a result of the infringement." *General Motors*, 461 U.S. at 654; *see also* H.R.Rep. No. 1587, 79th Cong., 2d Sess., 1 (1946) (the Bill was intended to allow recovery of "any damages the complainant can prove"); S.Rep. No. 1503, 79th Cong., 2d Sess., 2 (1946), (same). Thus, while the statutory text states tersely that the patentee receive "adequate" damages, the Supreme Court has interpreted this to mean that "adequate" damages should approximate those damages that will fully compensate the patentee for infringement. Further, the Court has cautioned against imposing limitations on patent infringement damages, stating: "When Congress wished to limit an element of recovery in a patent infringement action, it said so explicitly." *General Motors*, 461 U.S. at 653.

In *Aro Mfg. Co. v. Convertible Top Replacement Co.*, 377 U.S. 476 (1964), the Court discussed the statutory standard for measuring patent infringement damages, explaining: The question to be asked in determining damages is "how much had the Patent Holder and Licensee suffered by the infringement. And that question [is] primarily: had the Infringer not infringed, what would the Patentee Holder–Licensee have made?" 377 U.S. at 507. This surely states a "but for" test. In accordance with the Court's guidance, we have held that the general rule for determining actual damages to a patentee that is itself producing the patented item is to determine the sales and profits lost to the patentee because of the infringement. To recover lost profits damages, the patentee must show a reasonable probability that, "but for" the infringement, it would have made the sales that were made by the infringer.

Panduit Corp. v. Stahlin Bros. Fibre Works, Inc., 575 F.2d 1152 (6th Cir.1978), articulated a four-factor test that has since been accepted as a useful, but non-exclusive, way for a patentee to prove entitlement to lost profits damages. The *Panduit* test requires that a patentee establish: (1)

demand for the patented product; (2) absence of acceptable non-infringing substitutes; (3) manufacturing and marketing capability to exploit the demand; and (4) the amount of the profit it would have made. A showing under *Panduit* permits a court to reasonably infer that the lost profits claimed were in fact caused by the infringing sales, thus establishing a patentee's prima facie case with respect to "but for" causation. A patentee need not negate every possibility that the purchaser might not have purchased a product other than its own, absent the infringement. The patentee need only show that there was a reasonable probability that the sales would have been made "but for" the infringement. When the patentee establishes the reasonableness of this inference, *e.g.*, by satisfying the *Panduit* test, it has sustained the burden of proving entitlement to lost profits due to the infringing sales. The burden then shifts to the infringer to show that the inference is unreasonable for some or all of the lost sales.

Applying *Panduit*, the district court found that Rite–Hite had established "but for" causation. In the court's view, this was sufficient to prove entitlement to lost profits damages on the ADL–100. Kelley does not challenge that Rite–Hite meets the *Panduit* test and therefore has proven "but for" causation; rather, Kelley argues that damages for the ADL–100, even if in fact caused by the infringement, are not legally compensable because the ADL–100 is not covered by the patent in suit.

Preliminarily, we wish to affirm that the "test" for compensability of damages under § 284 is not solely a "but for" test in the sense that an infringer must compensate a patentee for any and all damages that proceed from the act of patent infringement. Notwithstanding the broad language of § 284, judicial relief cannot redress every conceivable harm that can be traced to an alleged wrongdoing. For example, remote consequences, such as a heart attack of the inventor or loss in value of shares of common stock of a patentee corporation caused indirectly by infringement are not compensable. Thus, along with establishing that a particular injury suffered by a patentee is a "but for" consequence of infringement, there may also be a background question whether the asserted injury is of the type for which the patentee may be compensated.

Judicial limitations on damages, either for certain classes of plaintiffs or for certain types of injuries have been imposed in terms of "proximate cause" or "foreseeability." Such labels have been judicial tools used to limit legal responsibility for the consequences of one's conduct that are too remote to justify compensation. The general principles expressed in the common law tell us that the question of legal compensability is one "to be determined on the facts of each case upon mixed considerations of logic, common sense, justice, policy and precedent."

We believe that under § 284 of the patent statute, the balance between full compensation, which is the meaning that the Supreme

Court has attributed to the statute, and the reasonable limits of liability encompassed by general principles of law can best be viewed in terms of reasonable, objective foreseeability. If a particular injury was or should have been reasonably foreseeable by an infringing competitor in the relevant market, broadly defined, that injury is generally compensable absent a persuasive reason to the contrary. Here, the court determined that Rite–Hite's lost sales of the ADL–100, a product that directly competed with the infringing product, were reasonably foreseeable. We agree with that conclusion. Being responsible for lost sales of a competitive product is surely foreseeable; such losses constitute the full compensation set forth by Congress, as interpreted by the Supreme Court, while staying well within the traditional meaning of proximate cause. Such lost sales should therefore clearly be compensable.

Recovery for lost sales of a device not covered by the patent in suit is not of course expressly provided for by the patent statute. Express language is not required, however. Statutes speak in general terms rather than specifically expressing every detail. Under the patent statute, damages should be awarded "where necessary to afford the plaintiff full compensation for the infringement." *General Motors*, 461 U.S. at 654. Thus, to refuse to award reasonably foreseeable damages necessary to make Rite–Hite whole would be inconsistent with the meaning of § 284.

Kelley asserts that to allow recovery for the ADL–100 would contravene the policy reason for which patents are granted: "[T]o promote the progress of . . . the useful arts." U.S. CONST., art. I, § 8, cl. 8. Because an inventor is only entitled to exclusivity to the extent he or she has invented and disclosed a novel, nonobvious, and useful device, Kelley argues, a patent may never be used to restrict competition in the sale of products not covered by the patent in suit. In support, Kelley cites antitrust case law condemning the use of a patent as a means to obtain a "monopoly" on unpatented material.

These cases are inapposite to the issue raised here. The present case does not involve expanding the limits of the patent grant in violation of the antitrust laws; it simply asks, once infringement of a valid patent is found, what compensable injuries result from that infringement, i.e., how may the patentee be made whole. Rite–Hite is not attempting to exclude its competitors from making, using, or selling a product not within the scope of its patent. The Truk Stop restraint was found to infringe the '847 patent, and Rite–Hite is simply seeking adequate compensation for that infringement; this is not an antitrust issue. Allowing compensation for such damage will "promote the Progress of . . . the useful Arts" by providing a stimulus to the development of new products and industries.

Kelley further asserts that, as a policy matter, inventors should be encouraged by the law to practice their inventions. This is not a meaningful or persuasive argument, at least in this context. A patent is granted in exchange for a patentee's disclosure of an invention, not for the patentee's use of the invention. There is no requirement in this country that a patentee make, use, or sell its patented invention. If a patentee's failure to practice a patented invention frustrates an important public need for the invention, a court need not enjoin infringement of the patent. Accordingly, courts have in rare instances exercised their discretion to deny injunctive relief in order to protect the public interest. Whether a patentee sells its patented invention is not crucial in determining lost profits damages. Normally, if the patentee is not selling a product, by definition there can be no lost profits. However, in this case, Rite–Hite did sell its own patented products, the MDL–55 and the ADL–100 restraints.

Kelley next argues that to award lost profits damages on Rite–Hite's ADL–100s would be contrary to precedent. Citing *Panduit,* Kelley argues that case law regarding lost profits uniformly requires that "the intrinsic value of the patent in suit is the only proper basis for a lost profits award." Kelley argues that each prong of the *Panduit* test focuses on the patented invention; thus, Kelley asserts, Rite–Hite cannot obtain damages consisting of lost profits on a product that is not the patented invention.

Generally, the *Panduit* test has been applied when a patentee is seeking lost profits for a device covered by the patent in suit. However, *Panduit* is not the sine qua non for proving "but for" causation. If there are other ways to show that the infringement in fact caused the patentee's lost profits, there is no reason why another test should not be acceptable. Moreover, other fact situations may require different means of evaluation, and failure to meet the *Panduit* test does not *ipso facto* disqualify a loss from being compensable.

In any event, the only *Panduit* factor that arguably was not met in the present fact situation is the second one, absence of acceptable non-infringing substitutes. Establishment of this factor tends to prove that the patentee would not have lost the sales to a non-infringing third party rather than to the infringer. That, however, goes only to the question of proof. Here, the only substitute for the patented device was the ADL–100, another of the patentee's devices. Such a substitute was not an "acceptable, non-infringing substitute" within the meaning of *Panduit* because, being patented by Rite–Hite, it was not available to customers except from Rite–Hite. Rite–Hite therefore would not have lost the sales to a third party. The second Panduit factor thus has been met. If, on the other hand, the ADL–100 had not been patented and was found to be an acceptable substitute, that would have been a different story, and Rite–Hite would have had to prove that its customers would not have obtained the ADL–100 from a third party in order to prove the second factor of *Panduit*.

Kelley's conclusion that the lost sales must be of the patented invention thus is not supported. Kelley's concern that lost profits must relate to the "intrinsic value of the patent" is subsumed in the "but for" analysis; if the patent infringement had nothing to do with the lost sales, "but for" causation would not have been proven. However, "but for" causation is conceded here. The motive, or motivation, for the infringement is irrelevant if it is proved that the infringement in fact caused the loss. We see no basis for Kelley's conclusion that the lost sales must be of products covered by the infringed patent.

Kelley has thus not provided, nor do we find, any justification in the statute, precedent, policy, or logic to limit the compensability of lost sales of a patentee's device that directly competes with the infringing device if it is proven that those lost sales were caused in fact by the infringement. Such lost sales are reasonably foreseeable and the award of damages is necessary to provide adequate compensation for infringement under 35 U.S.C. § 284. Thus, Rite–Hite's ADL–100 lost sales are legally compensable and we affirm the award of lost profits on the 3,283 sales lost to Rite–Hite's wholesale business in ADL–100 restraints.

II. Damages on the Dock Levelers

Based on the "entire market value rule," the district court awarded lost profits on 1,692 dock levelers that it found Rite–Hite would have sold with the ADL–100 and MDL–55 restraints. Kelley argues that this award must be set aside because Rite–Hite failed to establish that the dock levelers were eligible to be included in the damage computation under the entire market value rule. We agree.

When a patentee seeks damages on unpatented components sold with a patented apparatus, courts have applied a formulation known as the "entire market value rule" to determine whether such components should be included in the damage computation, whether for reasonable royalty purposes, or for lost profits purposes. Early cases invoking the entire market value rule required that for a patentee owning an "improvement patent" to recover damages calculated on sales of a larger machine incorporating that improvement, the patentee was required to show that the entire value of the whole machine, as a marketable article, was "properly and legally attributable" to the patented feature. Subsequently, our predecessor court held that damages for component parts used with a patented apparatus were recoverable under the entire market value rule if the patented apparatus "was of such paramount importance that it substantially created the value of the component parts." We have held that the entire market value rule permits recovery of damages based on the value of a patentee's entire apparatus containing several features when the patent-related feature is the "basis for customer demand."

The entire market value rule has typically been applied to include in the compensation base unpatented components of a device when the unpatented and patented components are physically part of the same machine. The rule has been extended to allow inclusion of physically separate unpatented components normally sold with the patented components. However, in such cases, the unpatented and patented components together were considered to be components of a single assembly or parts of a complete machine, or they together constituted a functional unit.

In [*Paper Converting Machine Co. v. Magna–Graphics Corp.*, 745 F.2d 11 (Fed.Cir.1984)], this court articulated the entire market value rule in terms of the objectively reasonable probability that a patentee would have made the relevant sales. Furthermore, we may have appeared to expand the rule when we emphasized the financial and marketing dependence of the unpatented component on the patented component. In Paper Converting, however, the rule was applied to allow recovery of profits on the unpatented components only because all the components together were considered to be parts of a single assembly. The references to "financial and marketing dependence" and "reasonable probability" were made in the context of the facts of the case and did not separate the rule from its traditional moorings.

Specifically, recovery was sought for the lost profits on sales of an entire machine for the high speed manufacture of paper rolls comprising several physically separate components, only one of which incorporated the invention. The machine was comprised of the patented "rewinder" component and several auxiliary components, including an "unwind stand" that supported a large roll of supply paper to the rewinder, a "core loader" that supplied paperboard cores to the rewinder, an "embosser" that embossed the paper and provided a special textured surface, and a "tail sealer" that sealed the paper's trailing end to the finished roll. Although we noted that the auxiliary components had "separate usage" in that they each separately performed a part of an entire rewinding operation, the components together constituted one functional unit, including the patented component, to produce rolls of paper. The auxiliary components derived their market value from the patented rewinder because they had no useful purpose independent of the patented rewinder. Similarly, our subsequent cases have applied the entire market value rule only in situations in which the patented and unpatented components were analogous to a single functioning unit.

Thus, the facts of past cases clearly imply a limitation on damages, when recovery is sought on sales of unpatented components sold with patented components, to the effect that the unpatented components must function together with the patented component in some manner so as to produce a desired end product or result. All the components together must be analogous to components of a single assembly or be parts of a complete machine, or they must constitute a functional unit. Our precedent has not extended liability to include items that have essentially no functional relationship to the patented invention and that may have been sold with an infringing device only as a matter of convenience or business advantage. We are not persuaded that we should extend that liability. Damages on such items would constitute more than what is "adequate to compensate for the infringement."

The facts of this case do not meet this requirement. The dock levelers operated to bridge the gap between a loading dock and a truck. The patented vehicle restraint operated to secure the rear of the truck to the loading dock. Although the two devices may have been used together, they did not function together to achieve one result and each could effectively have been used independently of each other. The parties had established positions in marketing dock levelers long prior to developing the vehicle restraints. Rite–Hite and Kelley were pioneers in that industry and for many years were primary competitors. Although following Rite–Hite's introduction of its restraints onto the market, customers frequently solicited package bids for the simultaneous installation of restraints and dock levelers, they did so because such bids facilitated contracting and construction scheduling, and because both Rite–Hite and Kelley encouraged this linkage by offering combination discounts. The dock levelers were thus sold by Kelley with the restraints only for marketing reasons, not because they essentially functioned together. We distinguish our conclusion to permit damages based on lost sales of the unpatented (not covered by the patent in suit) ADL–100 devices, but not on lost sales of the unpatented dock levelers, by emphasizing that the Kelley Truk Stops were devices competitive with the ADL–100s, whereas the dock levelers were merely items sold together with the restraints for convenience and business advantage. It is a clear purpose of the patent law to redress competitive damages resulting from infringement of the patent, but there is no basis for extending that recovery to include damages for items that are neither competitive with nor function with the patented invention. Promotion of the useful arts, see U.S. Const., art. I, § 8, cl. 8, requires one, but not the other. These facts do not establish the functional relationship necessary to justify recovery under the entire market value rule. Therefore, the district court erred as a matter of law in including them within the compensation base. Accordingly, we vacate the court's award of damages based on the dock leveler sales.

Nies, Circuit Judge, with whom Archer, Chief Judge, Smith, Senior Circuit Judge, and Mayer, Circuit Judge join, dissenting-in-part.

The majority uses the provision in 35 U.S.C. § 284 for "damages" as a tool to expand the property rights granted by a patent. I dissent.

No one disputes that Rite–Hite is entitled to "full compensation for any damages suffered as a result of the infringement." *General Motors Corp. v. Devex Corp.*, 461 U.S. 648, 653–54, 103 S.Ct. 2058, 2062, 76 L.Ed.2d 211 (1983). "Damages," however, is a word of art. "Damages in a legal sense means the compensation which the law will award for an injury done." Recovery in Patent Infringement Suits: Hearings on H.R. 5231 [later H.R. 5311] Before the Committee on Patents, 79th Cong., 2nd Sess. 9 (1946) (statement of Conder C. Henry, Asst. Comm'r of Patents) (hereinafter "House Hearings"). Thus, the question is, "What are the injuries for which full compensation must be paid?".

The majority divorces "actual damages" from injury to patent rights. The majority holds that a patentee is entitled to recover its lost profits caused by the infringer's competition with the patentee's business in ADL-restraints, products not incorporating the invention of the patent in suit but assertedly protected by other unlitigated patents. Indeed, the majority states a broader rule for the award of lost profits on any goods of the patentee with which the infringing device competes, even products in the public domain.

I would hold that the diversion of ADL–100 sales is not an injury to patentee's property rights granted by the '847 patent. To constitute legal injury for which lost profits may be awarded, the infringer must interfere with the patentee's property right to an exclusive market in goods embodying the invention of the patent in suit. The patentee's property rights do not extend to its market in other goods unprotected by the litigated patent. Rite–Hite was compensated for the lost profits for 80 sales associated with the MDL–55, the only product it sells embodying the '847 invention. That is the totality of any possible entitlement to lost profits. Under 35 U.S.C. § 284, therefore, Rite–Hite is entitled to "damages" calculated as a reasonable royalty on the remainder of Kelley's infringing restraints.

PAULINE NEWMAN, CIRCUIT JUDGE, with whom CIRCUIT JUDGE RADER joins, concurring in part and dissenting in part.

The court today takes an important step toward preserving damages as an effective remedy for patent infringement. Patent infringement is a commercial tort, and the remedy should compensate for the actual financial injury that was caused by the tort. Thus I concur in the majority's result with respect to entitlement to damages for lost sales of the ADL–100.

Yet the court draws a new bright line, adverse to patentees and the businesses built on patents, declining to make the injured claimants whole. The majority now restricts en banc the patentee's previously existing, already limited right to prove damages for lost sales of collateral items—the so-called "convoyed" sales. Such remedy is now eliminated entirely unless the convoyed item is "functionally" inseparable from the patented item. The court thus propounds a legally ambivalent and economically unsound policy, authorizing damages for the lost sales of the ADL–100 but not those dock levelers that were required to be bid and sold as a package with the MDL–55 and the ADL–100.

The district court, in contrast, took a straightforward approach to the damages determination. The district court awarded compensatory damages for (1) Rite–Hite's lost sales of the MDL–55 and the ADL–100 models of truck restraint, recognizing the commercial and competitive relationships of these models and the infringing device; [and] (2) Rite–Hite's lost sales of 1,692 dock levelers that were bid and sold in packages with the truck restraints, recognizing that the dock leveler business was a significant factor in Kelley's infringing activity.

The majority affirms only the first of these areas of pecuniary injury ... I know of no law or policy served by eliminating recovery of actual damages when patents are involved. In holding that those injured by the infringement shall not be made whole, the value of the patent property is diminished. The majority's half-a-loaf award, wherein the patentee and the other plaintiffs are denied recovery of a significant portion or all of their proven damages, is an important policy decision.

award should match D.C.

NOTES

1. **The Dissenters.** The complete dissenting opinions of Judges Nies and Newman, omitted here due to space limitations, are well worth reading in full. The opinion of Judge Nies was primarily directed towards the award of lost profits due to trade in goods not embodying the infringed patent. According to Judge Nies, the majority erred because "[p]atent 'damages' are limited to legal injury to property rights created by the patent, not merely causation in fact." 56 F.3d at 1557. In addition to mustering considerable case law supporting this position, Judge Nies offered the following policy argument, 56 F.3d at 1575:

> It cannot be disputed that Congress intended that the patent grant provide an incentive to make investments in patented products during the patent term. If a patentee is rewarded with lost profits on its established products, the incentive is dulled if not destroyed. Why make the investment to produce and market a new drug if the patent on the new discovery not only protects the *status quo* in the market but also provides lost profits for the old?

In contrast, Judge Newman's dissenting opinion largely considered the issue of convoyed sales. In measuring lost profits, the *Rite–Hite* majority sought proof of damages "reasonably foreseeable ... in the relevant market." Yet when it considered convoyed sales, the majority abandoned the "reasonable foreseeability" test and adopted a test based on whether "unpatented components must function together with the patented components." Judge Newman advocated a consistent approach. Thus, under her view, foreseeable damage in the relevant market ought to have applied uniformly to the convoyed sales question as well. The United Kingdom has followed the approach advocated by Judge Newman. *Gerber Garment Tech. v. Lectra Sys.*, [1995] R.P.C. 383 (Pat. Ct.), aff'd [1997] R.P.C. 443 (CA).

2. ***Rite–Hite* versus *Panduit*.** Does *Rite–Hite* remain true to the *Panduit* test regarding acceptable noninfringing substitutes? After all, wouldn't the ADL–100 serve as an acceptable noninfringing substitute to the Truk'stop sales?

3. **Competing Patents.** Professor Adelman offered the following observation on *Rite–Hite*:

> Essentially, in *Rite–Hite*, we may view the fact pattern as one where Rite–Hite owns two competing patents. Thus, the value of each of them is dependent on the fact that the other is also owned by Rite–Hite. Had one been owned by a third party, the value of each patent would be substantially less. Indeed, each patent could be essentially valueless as Rite–Hite and

the owner of the other patent could compete away their total value. As the '847 patent is more valuable than it otherwise would be because it is owned by Rite–Hite, and as Rite–Hite is suppressing its use in the automatic truck stop field, there is a strong patent policy argument against awarding Rite–Hite the profits lost to it owing to sales of a product using the '847 invention in the automatic truck stop area, an area where Rite–Hite deliberately chose not to exploit.

4 MARTIN J. ADELMAN, PATENT LAW PERSPECTIVES § 5.2[2] at n. 119 (2d ed. 1995). Do you agree? Other criticism of the decision may be found in Lisa C. Childs, Note, 27 LOY. U. CHI. L.J. 665 (1996); Robert J. Cox, *But How Far?* Rite–Hite Corp. v. Kelley Co.'*s Expansion of the Scope of Patent Damages*, 3 J. INTELL. PROP. L. 327 (1996).

4. A Companion Case. In *King Instruments Corp. v. Perego*, 65 F.3d 941 (Fed.Cir.1995), a Federal Circuit panel expanded upon the reasoning in *Rite–Hite*. This case involved two competitors in the market for automated cassette-loading machines. King, the plaintiff in an infringement action, did not commercialize its patented splicing technology. Tapematic, the adjudicated infringer, did, although the device it marketed was otherwise quite different from King's commercial embodiment. The court affirmed the award of lost profits damages based upon forty-nine sales completed by Tapematic. Of course, unlike King Instruments, Inc., the Rite–Hite Corporation did embody its patent, in that case in the MDL–100 restraint. Further, given the small role of the infringing technology in the marketed machine, the standard of "but for" causation seemed rather lower here than in *Rite–Hite*. Another Federal Circuit applying the reasoning of *King Instruments* is *Hebert v. Lisle Corp.*, 99 F.3d 1109 (Fed.Cir.1996).

King Instruments is also notable for its discussion of two other significant points in favor of Judge Lourie's holding on the award of profits based on lost trade in competitive goods. First, the panel suggested that a contrary rule would require a patentee to prove that it embodied its own invention in order to obtain lost profits damages. According to the *King Instruments* panel, the creation of a new category of "reverse infringement" would create needless complexity in patent infringement proceedings. Second, the panel indicated that a commercialization requirement "would force patent owners to accept a reasonable royalty in cases where a reasonable royalty is inadequate compensation. Infringers would in effect receive the windfall of a retroactive compulsory license from the patent owner." 65 F.3d at 951. Persuasive as the first point may be, does a reasonable royalty truly amount to a compulsory license given the availability of equitable relief? For more on the contrast between *Rite–Hite* and *King Instruments, see* Brent Rabowsky, Note, 70 S. CAL. L. REV. 281, 318–31 (1996).

§ 13.2[b]　THE MARKET SHARE RULE

BIC LEISURE PRODUCTS, INC. v. WINDSURFING INTERNATIONAL, INC.

United States Court of Appeals, Federal Circuit, 1993
1 F.3d 1214

Before NIES, Chief Judge, SMITH, Senior Circuit Judge, and RADER, Circuit Judge.

RADER, CIRCUIT JUDGE.

The United States District Court for the Southern District of New York awarded Windsurfing International, Inc. lost profits for BIC Leisure Products, Inc.'s infringement of U.S. Reissue Patent No. 31,167. The court refused to award lost profits for alleged price erosion.

Assuming BIC had not been in the market, Windsurfing did not show that BIC's customers would have purchased sailboards from Windsurfing and other manufacturers in proportion to their market shares. Therefore, this court reverses the award of lost profits based upon Windsurfing's market share. Otherwise, this court affirms.

BACKGROUND

BIC infringed Windsurfing's Reissue Patent No. 31,167, which covers sailboards. Windsurfing seeks damages from BIC for the period from March 8, 1983 (the reissue date of Windsurfing's patent) to September 30, 1985 (the date the district court enjoined BIC from further infringement).

Windsurfing primarily manufactured and marketed sailboards embodying its patented invention for the "One–Design Class." The One–Design Class refers to a uniform competition class as defined by a sailboarding association. A sailboarding association sponsors regattas in which sailboarders compete against each other on boards of uniform weight and shape. Most of Windsurfing's sailboards fit within the weight and shape requirements for the One–Design competition class.

One–Design sailboards lost favor with most sailboarders, however, with the advent of faster, more maneuverable, and more versatile "funboards" and "wave boards." These newer boards had a lighter hull design. Despite the rising popularity of these newer boards in the early 1980s, Windsurfing decided to continue to concentrate on its One–Design boards.

Windsurfing licensed its patented technology extensively. Windsurfing licensed at least twelve companies in Europe. At least one of the European licensees granted sublicenses to other European manufacturers. Windsurfing also granted licenses in the United States. Eventually, Windsurfing licensed twelve companies in the United States. With few exceptions, Windsurfing charged 7.5% of net sales for the U.S. licenses.

All of the U.S. licensees, as well as some of the European licensees, competed against Windsurfing in the United States.

Windsurfing manufactured its boards using a rotomolding process. During the early 1980s, many of Windsurfing's competitors reduced their production costs with a new blowmolding process. Instead of switching to the more efficient blowmolding process, Windsurfing invested one million dollars in an unsuccessful attempt to improve its rotomolding process. Windsurfing controlled 29.2% of the sailboard market in 1983, 25.6% in 1984, and 13.6% in 1985.

BIC began selling sailboards in 1981. BIC manufactured with the more efficient blowmolding process. BIC did not sell sailboards with the One Design hull form. Rather, BIC's sailboards differed from Windsurfing's products. BIC instead sold boards at the lower end of the market's price spectrum, reflecting its decision to target the entry level segment of the sailboard market.

In comparison, Windsurfing priced its sailboards at the upper end of the sailboard price spectrum. During the years covered by the damages period, U.S. sailboard dealers charged the following average prices:

1983		1984		1985	
Marker	837	Brockhaus	753	Mistral	804
Brockhaus	753	Mistral	741	Marker	774
Mistral	750	Marker	674	Brockhaus	750
Windsurfing	670	SAN/Romney	623	SAN	623
SAN/Romney	643	Windsurfing	589	Schutz	575
Alpha	574	Schutz	575	Windsurfing	571
Wayler	550	HiFly	527	HiFly	570
HiFly	518	Wayler	500	Wayler	500
SAN/Schaeffer	441	Alpha	450	O'Brien	477
O'Brien	436	O'Brien	412	Alpha	450
BIC	407	SAN/Schaeffer	388	AMF Inc.	380
AMF Inc.	377	AMF Inc.	384	BIC	312
Ten Cate	366	BIC	335	Ten Cate	253
AMF Mares	244	Ten Cate	299	AMF Mares	244
		AMF Mares	234		

The Patent and Trademark Office reissued Windsurfing's patent on March 8, 1983. On that date, BIC had 5,245 sailboards in its inventory and another 5,625 on order. BIC confirmed its purchase of the boards on order with a February 10, 1983 telex.

The district court applied the Panduit test to determine whether Windsurfing lost profits. The district court required Windsurfing to show (1) a demand for the patented product, (2) the absence of acceptable noninfringing substitutes, (3) its capacity to exploit the demand, and (4) the profits lost due to the infringement. The district court modified the Panduit test by presuming that Windsurfing would have captured a share of BIC's sales in proportion to Windsurfing's share of the sailboard market. Relying on *State Industries, Inc. v. Mor–Flo Indus-*

tries, Inc., 883 F.2d 1573 (Fed.Cir.1989), the district court awarded Windsurfing lost profits based upon its pro rata percentage of BIC's sales for each year of the damages period. In addition, the district court awarded Windsurfing lost royalties for the boards its licensees would have sold absent BIC's infringement. The court calculated the amount of lost royalties based upon a weighted average price of the boards sold by the licensees.

DISCUSSION

Lost Profits

The finding of the amount of damages for patent infringement is a question of fact on which the patent owner bears the burden of proof. Where the district court fixes the amount of damages, this court reviews that finding under the clearly erroneous standard of Federal Rule of Civil Procedure 52(a).

To recover lost profits as opposed to royalties, a patent owner must prove a causal relation between the infringement and its loss of profits. The patent owner must show that "but for" the infringement, it would have made the infringer's sales. An award of lost profits may not be speculative. Rather the patent owner must show a reasonable probability that, absent the infringement, it would have made the infringer's sales.

The district court clearly erred by failing to apply the "but for" test before awarding lost profits. The record in this case does not evince a reasonable probability that Windsurfing would have made its pro rata share of BIC's sales had BIC not been in the market. During the period in question, at least fourteen competitors vied for sales in the sailboard market with prices ranging from $234 to $837. BIC's boards sold for $312 to $407; Windsurfing's boards sold for $571 to $670—a difference of over $250 or about 60–80% above BIC's selling range. Because Windsurfing concentrated on the One Design class hull form and BIC did not, Windsurfing's boards differed fundamentally from BIC's boards.

The record contains uncontradicted evidence that demand for sailboards is relatively elastic. The record further contains uncontradicted evidence that the sailboard market's entry level, in which BIC competed, is particularly sensitive to price disparity. By purchasing BIC sailboards, BIC's customers demonstrated a preference for sailboards priced around $350, rather than One–Design boards priced around $600. Therefore, without BIC in the market, BIC's customers would have likely sought boards in the same price range.

Several manufacturers offered sailboards at prices much closer to BIC than to Windsurfing. At least two of Windsurfing's licensees, O'Brien and HiFly, sold boards resembling BIC's in the same distribution channels as BIC. On this record, Windsurfing did not show with reasonable probability that BIC's customers would have purchased from Windsurfing in proportion with Windsurfing's market share. The record shows rather that the vast majority of BIC's customers would have purchased boards from O'Brien or HiFly if BIC's boards had not been available. The district court erred in assuming that, without BIC in the market, its customers would have redistributed their purchases among all the remaining sailboards, including Windsurfing's One Design boards at a price $200 to $300 more than BIC's.

Moreover, Windsurfing's sales continued to decline after the district court enjoined BIC's infringement. This aspect of the record shows as well that Windsurfing did not capture its market share of the sales replacing BIC's market sales. According to the record, the principal beneficiary of BIC's exit appears to be O'Brien.

The district court applied the *Panduit* test for lost profits. Properly applied, the *Panduit* test is an acceptable, though not an exclusive, test for determining "but for" causation. The *Panduit* test, however, operates under an inherent assumption, not appropriate in this case, that the patent owner and the infringer sell products sufficiently similar to compete against each other in the same market segment. If the patentee's and the infringer's products are not substitutes in a competitive market, *Panduit*'s first two factors do not meet the "but for" test—a prerequisite for lost profits.

The first *Panduit* factor—demand for the patented product—presupposes that demand for the infringer's and patent owner's products is interchangeable. Under this assumption, evidence of sales of the infringing product may suffice to show *Panduit*'s first factor, "demand for the patented product." This analysis assumes that the patent owner and the infringer sell substantially the same product. In [*Gyromat Corp. v. Champion Spark Plug Co.*, 735 F.2d 549 (Fed.Cir.1984)], for instance, the patent owner's and the infringer's products were similar in price and product characteristics. If the products are not sufficiently similar to compete in the same market for the same customers, the infringer's customers would not necessarily transfer their demand to the patent owner's product in the absence of the infringer's product. In such circumstances, as in this case, the first *Panduit* factor does not operate to satisfy the elemental "but for" test.

Similarly, the second *Panduit* factor—absence of acceptable, noninfringing alternatives—presupposes that the patentee and the infringer sell substantially similar products in the same market. To be acceptable to the infringer's customers in an elastic market, the alleged alternative "must not have a disparately higher price than or possess characteristics significantly different from the patented product." *Kaufman Co. v. Lantech, Inc.*, 926 F.2d 1136, 1142 (Fed.Cir.1991) (citing *Gyromat*, 735 F.2d at 553). In *Kaufman*, for instance, the patent owner and the infringer sold substantially the same product. Thus Panduit's second factor, properly applied, ensures that any proffered alternative competes in the same market for the same customers as the infringer's product. *See Yarway Corp. v. Eur–Control USA, Inc.*, 775 F.2d 268, 276 (Fed.Cir.1985) (alternative products did not possess features of the patent owner's and the infringer's products, nor compete in the same " 'special niche' or mini-market").

This court has held that a patent owner may satisfy the second *Panduit* element by substituting proof of its market share for proof of the absence of acceptable substitutes. This market share approach allows a patentee to recover lost profits, despite the presence of acceptable, noninfringing substitutes, because it nevertheless can prove with reasonable probability sales it would have made "but for" the infringement. Like *Panduit*'s second prong, however, this market share test also assumes that the patent owner and the infringer compete in the same market. In *State Industries*, for instance, the patent owner, infringer, and the other manufacturers sold substantially similar products. This similarity of products is necessary in order for market share proof to show correctly satisfaction of Panduit's second factor.

The assumption underlying *Panduit*, *Gyromat*, and *State Industries* is not appropriate in this case. Instead, the record reveals that during the damages period the sailboard market was not a unitary market in which every competitor sold substantially the same product. Windsurfing and BIC sold different types of sailboards at different prices to different customers. As noted, their sailboards differed significantly in terms of price, product characteristics, and marketing channels. On the facts of this case, Windsurfing did not show "but for" causation under a correct application of Panduit or otherwise. The district court erred in awarding lost profits.

Moreover, Windsurfing itself set the value of its patent rights by licensing its technology to nearly every company supplying sailboards in the United States without competing itself in most sailboard submarkets. Windsurfing valued its patent in terms of licensing royalties, not in terms of profits it could make by excluding others from the market. *See Seymour v. McCormick*, 57 U.S. (How.) 480, 490, 14 L.Ed. 1024 (1854). Without evidence to support Windsurfing's claim to lost profits, this court reverses the district court's award.

With regard to royalties, Windsurfing is entitled to receive lost royalties (on amounts Windsurfing's licensees would have paid "but for" the infringement) and reasonable royalties (on amounts of any other BIC use, if any, of the patented invention). BIC challenges the methodology of the district court in calculating lost royalties per board, but this court concludes that the chosen methodology was within the court's discretion. On remand, the trial court may award damages based upon the lost royalties per board calculation.

Price Erosion

The district court evaluated the documentary and testimonial evidence on price erosion and found it too speculative to support an award of price erosion lost profits. This court finds nothing clearly erroneous in the district court's finding.

The record shows that other market forces, not BIC, forced Windsurfing to lower its prices. The record is replete with evidence that funboards, wave boards, and other designs replaced One Design boards as the sailboard of choice for many practitioners. Besides reducing the demand for One Design boards, consumer choices also caused many companies to discount their stock of One Design boards to make room for the newer boards.

Furthermore, Windsurfing licensed many competitors who produced boards at less cost. The more efficient blowmolding process allowed Windsurfing's competitors to cut prices. Windsurfing's own licensing policies exacerbated this problem. When the European market peaked in the early 1980s, Windsurfing's European licensees sold their excess inventory in the United States. The influx of European boards increased the supply of sailboards and further reduced prices. In light of these facts, the district court correctly found that Windsurfing failed to meet its burden of proof. Simply put, Windsurfing did not prove that it could have sold its boards at higher prices "but for" BIC's infringement.

NOTES

1. BIC's "Market Share" of Future Federal Circuit Cases. In *Crystal Semiconductor Corp. v. TriTech Microelec. Int'l, Inc.*, 246 F.3d 1336 (Fed.Cir.2001), the Federal Circuit explained:

> In *BIC Leisure*, this court required proper identification of the actual market affected by the infringement. This court explained: "[T]he patent owner and the infringer [must] sell products sufficiently similar to compete against each other in the same market segment." 1 F.3d at 1218. In other words, for lost profits based on the infringer's sales, a patentee must show that the infringing units do "not have a disparately higher price than or possess characteristics significantly different from the patented product." *Id.* at 1219. Similarly, to determine a patentee's market share, the record must accurately identify the market. This requires an analysis which excludes alternatives to the patented product with disparately different prices or significantly different characteristics.

With this introduction, the Federal Circuit then segmented the market and placed audio chips of a different quality in a different market category for assessment of lost profits. Is price always a reliable measure of a different market segment? Can't infringers always offer a lower price because their price does not include R & D expenses?

2. Price Erosion. As early as 1886, the Supreme Court opened the door for price erosion damages: "Reduction of prices, and consequent loss of profits, enforced by infringing competition, is a proper ground for awarding of damages. The only question is as to the character and sufficiency of the evidence in the particular case." *Yale Lock Mfg. Co. v. Sargent*, 117 U.S. 536, 551

(1886). Price erosion thus assumes that, without infringing competition, the patentee could have sustained a higher price and allows damages to compensate for the lower prices necessitated by the illicit competition. The Supreme Court, however, emphasizes "the character and sufficiency of the evidence." In the modern era of compensatory damages following *Rite–Hite*, these evidentiary considerations take on a distinctly economic flavor. The Federal Circuit explained:

> Moreover, in a credible economic analysis, the patentee cannot show entitlement to a higher price divorced from the effect of that higher price on demand for the product. In other words, the patentee must also present evidence of the (presumably reduced) amount of product the patentee would have sold at the higher price ... "[B]ut for" infringement, Crystal would have tried to charge at least 89¢ more per CODEC.

> Most of the CODECs Crystal sold were priced at under $10 per unit. A minimum 89price increase would have translated to an approximate 10% increase in selling price. Because Crystal was competing in a competitive market, a 10% price increase would have likely caused customers to substitute the CODECs of other manufacturers for Crystal's CODECs. Crystal, however, presented no evidence of the elasticity of demand of the PC sound card CODEC market. Nor did Crystal make any estimates as to the number of sales it would have lost or kept had it increased its prices by 89¢ per unit. Thus, Crystal did not make a showing of "but for" causation of price erosion.

> Without economic evidence of the resulting market for higher priced CODECs, Crystal cannot have both lost profits and price erosion damages on each of those lost sales. The district court correctly denied Crystal's price erosion damages for lack of adequate record support.

Crystal Semiconductor Corp. v. TriTech Microelec. Int'l Inc., 246 F.3d 1336 (Fed.Cir. 2001). Does this type of economic reasoning place a premium on economic experts in the damage phase of a trial?

3. Availability of Non-infringing Substitutes In *Panduit*, the U.S. Court of Appeals for the Sixth Circuit reasoned: "A product lacking the advantages of that patented can hardly be termed a substitute 'acceptable' to the customer who wants those advantages." This phrase emphasizes that the claimed invention will rarely have substitutes unless they encompass all the same advantages. In other words, the test for non-infringing substitutes is quite strict.

The marketplace, on the other hand, very often supplies several substitutes for every product—each with its own advantages and trade-offs. Thus, as the emphasis in damages law has shifted towards a compensation model, the requirements for "non-infringing substitutes" have reflected economic reasoning. *Grain Processing Corp. v. American Maize–Prods.*, Co., 185 F.3d 1341 (Fed. Cir. 1999). In *Grain Processing* the Court of Appeals explained:

> By the same token, a fair and accurate reconstruction of the "but for" market also must take into account, where relevant, alternative actions the infringer foreseeably would have undertaken had he not infringed. Without the infringing product, a rational would-be infringer is likely to offer

an acceptable noninfringing alternative, if available, to compete with the patent owner rather than leave the market altogether. The competitor in the "but for" marketplace is hardly likely to surrender its complete market share when faced with a patent, if it can compete in some other lawful manner. Moreover, only by comparing the patented invention to its next-best available alternative(s)—regardless of whether the alternative(s) were actually produced and sold during the infringement—can the court discern the market value of the patent owner's exclusive right, and therefore his expected profit or reward, had the infringer's activities not prevented him from taking full economic advantage of this right. Thus, an accurate reconstruction of the hypothetical "but for" market takes into account any alternatives available to the infringer. *See Aro*, 377 U.S. at 507; MARTIN J. ADELMAN, PATENT LAW PERSPECTIVES § 5.2[2] (2d Ed.1998) ("[w]here an infringer demonstrates that it could have chosen to market a noninfringing alternative and that it would have done so had it known that it was infringing . . . the sales that it made of the infringing products were not sales that the patentee would otherwise have made. . . .").

Assume for a moment that *Grain Processing* will have a wide application, meaning that nearly every marketplace will feature some market alternatives that the infringer might have used "but for" infringement. With that assumption, *Grain Processing* has considerably reduced the risk of costly lost profits awards. Does this development in damages law thus give competitors an incentive to test the boundaries of a patent? Does this testing, in turn, both reduce the practical value of patent protection and provide a formula for increased litigation?

§ 13.2[c] REASONABLE ROYALTIES

In *Panduit*, Chief Judge Markey examined the standards for deriving a correct reasonable royalty, including the hypothetical negotiation test. The hypothetical negotiation test often obtains a very logical result by reference to an actual established royalty in the marketplace. Even if the patentee has not licensed the patented invention, a court may consider royalties on comparable patents or products in the market. *Mahurkar v. C.R. Bard, Inc.*, 79 F.3d 1572 (Fed.Cir.1996). Nonetheless a reasonable royalty may exceed an established royalty when, for instance, the record shows that widespread infringement artificially depressed the value of the license. *Nickson Indus. Inc. v. Rol Mfg. Co., Ltd.*, 847 F.2d 795 (Fed.Cir.1988).

GEORGIA–PACIFIC CORP. v. UNITED STATES PLYWOOD CORP.

United States District Court, S.D. New York, 1970
318 F.Supp. 1116, *modified*, 446 F.2d 295

TENNEY, DISTRICT JUDGE.

A comprehensive list of evidentiary facts relevant, in general, to the determination of the amount of a reasonable royalty for a patent license may be drawn from a conspectus of the leading cases. The following are some of the factors mutatis mutandis seemingly more pertinent to the issue herein:

1. The royalties received by the patentee for the licensing of the patent in suit, proving or tending to prove an established royalty.

2. The rates paid by the licensee for the use of other patents comparable to the patent in suit.

3. The nature and scope of the license, as exclusive or non-exclusive; or as restricted or non-restricted in terms of territory or with respect to whom the manufactured product may be sold.

4. The licensor's established policy and marketing program to maintain his patent monopoly by not licensing others to use the invention or by granting licenses under special conditions designed to preserve that monopoly.

5. The commercial relationship between the licensor and licensee, such as, whether they are competitors in the same territory in the same line of business; or whether they are inventor and promoter.

6. The effect of selling the patented specialty in promoting sales of other products of the licensee; that existing value of the invention to the licensor as a generator of sales of his non-patented items; and the extent of such derivative or convoyed sales.

7. The duration of the patent and the term of the license.

8. The established profitability of the product made under the patent; its commercial success; and its current popularity.

9. The utility and advantages of the patent property over the old modes or devices, if any, that had been used for working out similar results.

10. The nature of the patented invention; the character of the commercial embodiment of it as owned and produced by the licensor; and the benefits to those who have used the invention.

11. The extent to which the infringer has made use of the invention; and any evidence probative of the value of that use.

12. The portion of the profit or of the selling price that may be customary in the particular business or in comparable businesses to allow for the use of the invention or analogous inventions.

13. The portion of the realizable profit that should be credited to the invention as distinguished from non-patented elements, the manufacturing process, business risks, or significant features or improvements added by the infringer.

14. The opinion testimony of qualified experts.

15. The amount that a licensor (such as the patentee) and a licensee (such as the infringer) would have agreed upon (at the time the infringement began) if both had been reasonably and voluntarily trying

to reach an agreement; that is, the amount which a prudent licensee—who desired, as a business proposition, to obtain a license to manufacture and sell a particular article embodying the patented invention—would have been willing to pay as a royalty and yet be able to make a reasonable profit and which amount would have been acceptable by a prudent patentee who was willing to grant a license.

The drawing of proper conclusions from conflicting evidence concerning the amount of a reasonable royalty has been said to call "for the exercise of judicial discretion by the District Court." *General Motors Corp. v. Dailey*, 93 F.2d 938, 942 (6th Cir.1937).

NOTES

1. **Federal Circuit Recognition.** The *Georgia–Pacific* laundry list of appropriate factors is often used in reasonable royalty cases. *E.g. Unisplay, S.A. v. American Electronic Sign Co.*, 69 F.3d 512, 517 n. 7 (Fed.Cir.1995); *SmithKline Diagnostics, Inc. v. Helena Laboratories Corp.*, 926 F.2d 1161, 1168 (Fed.Cir.1991); *Sun Studs, Inc. v. ATA Equip. Leasing, Inc.*, 872 F.2d 978, 993 (Fed.Cir.1989).

2. **Reasonable Royalty Methodology.** In *Fromson v. Western Litho Plate & Supply Co.*, 853 F.2d 1568 (Fed.Cir.1988), the court mused on the "hypothetical negotiation" standard as follows:

> Like all methodologies based on a hypothetical, there will be an element of uncertainty; yet, a court is not at liberty, in conducting the methodology, to abandon entirely the statutory standard of damages "adequate to compensate" for the infringement. The royalty arrived at must be "reasonable" under all the circumstances; i.e., it must be at least a close approximation of what would be "adequate to compensate" for the "use made of the invention by the infringer." The methodology encompasses fantasy and flexibility; fantasy because it requires a court to imagine what warring parties would have agreed to as willing negotiators; flexibility because it speaks of negotiations as of the time infringement began, yet permits and often requires a court to look to events and facts that occurred thereafter and that could not have been known to or predicted by the hypothesized negotiators.

As has been said by the Supreme Court:

> At times the only evidence available may be that supplied by testimony of experts as to the state of the art, the character of the improvement, and the probable increase of efficiency or savings of expense.... This will generally be the case if the trial follows quickly after the issue of the patent. But a different situation is presented if years have gone by before the evidence is offered. Experience is then available to correct uncertain prophecy. Here is a book of wisdom that courts may not neglect. We find no rule of law that sets a clasp upon its pages, and forbids us to look within....

Sinclair Ref. Co. v. Jenkins Petroleum Process Co., 289 U.S. 689, 698–99 (1933) (citations omitted).

Forced to erect a hypothetical, it is easy to forget a basic reality—a license is fundamentally an agreement by the patent owner not to sue the licensee. In a normal negotiation, the potential licensee has three basic choices: forego all use of the invention; pay an agreed royalty; infringe the patent and risk litigation. The methodology presumes that the licensee has made the second choice, when in fact it made the third. Thus Western must be viewed as negotiating for the right to exclude competitors or to compete only with licensed competitors, a landscape far different from that created, post May 1965, by the infringement of Western and others.

Whatever royalty may result from employment of the methodology, the law is not without means for recognizing that an infringer is unlike a true "willing" licensee; nor is the law without means for placing the injured patentee "in the situation he would have occupied if the wrong had not been committed."

853 F.2d at 1575–76.

3. A *Panduit* "Kicker?" In 1996, a United States District Court attempted to enhance a reasonable royalty award apparently to compensate the patent owner for the expenses of defending the patent. The Federal Circuit sustained the district court's reasonable royalty of 25.88%. To this amount, the district court added 9%. The Federal Circuit stated:

To this reasonable royalty, however, the trial court added an additional 9%. It labeled this addition a "Panduit kicker," citing *Panduit Corp. v. Stahlin Bros. Fibre Works, Inc.*, 575 F.2d 1152, 197 U.S.P.Q. 726 (6th Cir.1978).

Although one method for proving damages, the *Panduit* methodology does not include a "kicker" to account for litigation expenses or for any other expenses. In *Panduit*, the Sixth Circuit noted that the patentee had incurred more than $400,000 in litigation expenses battling with the infringer for over thirteen years.

More important, *Panduit* does not authorize additional damages or a "kicker" on top of a reasonable royalty because of heavy litigation or other expenses. In sections 284 and 285, the Patent Act sets forth statutory requirements for awards of enhanced damages and attorney fees. The statute bases these awards on clear and convincing proof of willfulness and exceptionality. *Panduit* at no point suggested enhancement of a compensatory damage award as a substitute for the strict requirements for these statutory provisions. The district court's "kicker," on the other hand, enhances a damages award, apparently to compensate for litigation expenses, without meeting the statutory standards for enhancement and fees. Therefore, the district court abused its discretion in awarding a 9% "*Panduit* kicker."

Mahurkar v. C.R. Bard, Inc., 79 F.3d 1572, 1580–81 (Fed.Cir.1996). How then is a litigant to get full compensation in a reasonable royalty case for the expenses of litigation?

Shortly after the court's decision in *Mahurkar* the court may have reintroduced the idea of a "kicker" in *Maxwell v. J. Baker, Inc.*, 86 F.3d 1098 (Fed.Cir.1996), where the trial court instructed the jury to determine whether Maxwell was damaged in an amount in excess of the amount of the reasonable royalty and if so, by how much. The jury did so and the Federal Circuit affirmed. Should the law encourage such challenges to patents? For an argument that good faith challenges to patents perform an important function in properly regulating a patent system *see* Martin J. Adelman, *Property Rights Theory and Patent–Antitrust: The Role of Compulsory Licensing*, 52 N.Y.U. L. REV. 977 (1977) and 4 MARTIN J. ADELMAN, PATENT LAW PERSPECTIVES, § 5.2[3] at nn.135 and 152 (2d ed. 1995 & 1996).

§ 13.2[d]   FOREIGN APPROACHES

U.S. intellectual property lawyers have often criticized foreign courts as being overly conservative when awarding damages in patent cases. Recent trends in damages awards overseas may blunt some of these criticisms. Many foreign courts have become more generous in their damages awards, now attempting to approximate the financial situation the patentee would have enjoyed "but for" the infringement. The leading British decision of *Gerber Garment Technology v. Lectra Systems*, [1995] RPC 383, is exemplary of this approach.

The most notable changes have occurred in Japan. The Japanese patent system has traditionally been subject to severe criticism for the limited equitable and monetary relief available to patentees. Damages awards were often viewed as limited to the payment of minimal royalties. *See* Scott K. Dinwiddie, *A Shifting Barrier? Difficulties in Obtaining Patent Infringement Damages in Japan*, 70 WASH. L. REV. 833 (1995). Legislative and judicial developments have recently transformed this aspect of Japanese patent law. Reforms adopted by the Diet resulted in 1998 legislation clarifying that damages may be awarded based upon the patentee's lost profits, not just upon a conservative royalty amount. The October 12, 1998, judgment of the Tokyo District Court in *Smithkline & Beecham French Lab. Ltd. v. Fujimoto Seiyaku* resulted in a damages award based upon lost profits of $23.5 million. Given that acceptable noninfringing substitutes were probably available in the Japanese market during the period of infringement, the Tokyo District Court's award may have been greater than the amount available under U.S. patent law. Adjudicated infringers of Japanese patents can now expect to be subjected to increased liability in comparison to previous years.

Although German courts traditionally awarded patent claims a capacious scope, and even after the advent of the European Patent Convention are considered friendly to the patentee, the level of damage awards was formerly quite low. Several principles leads to this result: damages could only be awarded against infringers acting "with fault," a three-year statute of limitations applied, and limited discovery procedures indicated that the extent of the infringement was difficult to prove. More recent German Supreme Court cases have liberalized these strictures to some extent, allowing damages to be claimed under more generous unfair competition principles. *See generally* Jochen Pagenberg, *Assessment of Damages for Patent Infringement*, 14 INT'L REV. INDUS. PROP. & COPYRIGHT L. 85 (1983).

Those interested in European patent damages law should consider the work of a leading international intellectual property scholar, Professor Gunnar Karnell. His article, *Computation of Damages for Patent Infringement In Particular as Related to Extensions Outside the Scope of Patented Matter: A Comparative Law Overview*, appears in the first issue of INTERNATIONAL PATENT QUARTERLY.

Jurisdictions vary on the remedies available to applicants between the publication of their applications and the time of the patent grant. In particular, Article 67 of the European Patent Convention allows its contracting states considerable flexibility in the level of protection conferred. One implementation of Article 67 is Section 33 of the German patent statute, which provides:

Section 33—Rights Conferred by a Patent Application After Publication

(1) As from the publication [of the patent application], the applicant may request from any person who has used the subject of the application, although he knew or should have known that the invention used by him was the subject of the application, compensation reasonable under the circumstances; the claiming of further remedies shall not be permitted.

(2) The request for compensation shall not be admissible if the subject of the application is obviously unpatentable.

In *Open–End Spinning Machine (Offenend-spinnmaschine)*, Case No. X ZR 26/87 (1989) (English translation available at 21 INT'L REV. INDUS. PROP. & COPYRIGHT L. 241 (1990)), the German Federal Supreme Court set forth the following principles regarding Section 33:

a) It is not illegal to use the subject matter of a non-examined patent application that is merely laid open for public inspection.

b) A right to compensation can be demanded from the direct beneficiary and not, in addition, from the party who (as the legal representative or employee in charge) merely implements the use.

c) The method of the license analogy offers a suitable means for calculating the amount of reasonable compensation. It is not admissible to request an award of damages for actual losses nor surrender of user profits.

d) The right to demand disclosure—which is granted for the purpose of calculating the amount of compensation for use of the invention—does not, as a matter of principle, extend to disclosure of actual production and marketing costs.

See Wilfred Neuhaus, *The Claim for Compensation Under Section 33 of the German Patent Law in Practice*, 21 INT'L REV. INDUS. PROP. & COPYRIGHT L. 526 (1990). Article 32(1) of the dormant Community Patent Convention appears to follow German law, providing:

> Compensation reasonable in the circumstances may be claimed from a third party who, in the period between the date of publication of a European patent application in which the Contracting States are designated and the date of publication of the mention of the grant of the European patent, has made any use of the invention which, after that period would be prohibited by virtue of the Community patent.

Some patent statutes are far more generous when providing protection following publication of their patent applications, however. Consider, for example, section 57(1) of the Australian Patents Act 1990:

> After a complete specification relating to an application for a standard patent grant has become open to public inspection and until a patent is granted on an application, the applicant has the same rights as he or she would have had if a patent for the invention had been granted on the day when the specification become open to public inspection.

The Australian statute goes on to provide that applicants may not start infringement proceedings until the patent is granted, and that accused infringers possess a defense regarding acts performed between publication and grant where "a patent could not validly have been granted to the applicant in respect of the claim (as framed when the act was done) that is alleged to have been infringed by the doing of the act." Australian Patents Act 1990 at § 57(3). What is your view of the appropriate level of protection for patentees following publication of the application, but prior to the grant of a patent?

§ 13.3   ENHANCED DAMAGES AND ATTORNEY FEES

The patent statute permits augmented damage awards in remarkably terse language, as follows:

§ 284.   Damages

[T]he court may increase the damages up to three times the amount found or assessed.

§ 285.   Attorney Fees

The court in exceptional cases may award reasonable attorney fees to the prevailing party.

The Federal Circuit explains that these provisions apply in instances of bad faith litigation and, more usually, in cases were the defendant has engaged in "willful infringement." *Beatrice Foods Co. v. New England*

Printing and Lithographing Co., 930 F.2d 1572 (Fed. Cir. 1991). No matter the size of the compensatory award and no matter whether the patentee establishes it by lost profits, a reasonable royalty, or a combination of both, the statute allows a court to enhance the damages as well as award attorney fees to the prevailing party. Enhanced damages are authorized by § 284:

> [T]he court may increase the damages up to three times the amount found or assessed.

Attorney fees are authorized by § 285:

> The court in exceptional cases may award reasonable attorney fees to the prevailing party.

Under these sections, the court has discretion to treble the damages and to award attorney fees in cases of "willful infringement." Under § 285, the court has additional discretion to award attorney fees in cases of bad faith litigation or inequitable conduct. Nevertheless, willful infringement forms a substantial portion of the case law on enhanced damages.

Much like a reasonable royalty, willfulness requires an assessment of the totality of the circumstances surrounding the infringement. These factors traditionally include:

1. Whether the infringer deliberately copied the ideas or design of another.

2. Whether the infringer, when he knew of the other's patent protection, investigated the scope of the patent and formed a good-faith belief that it was invalid or that it was not infringed.

3. The infringer's behavior as a party to the litigation.

4. The infringer's size and financial condition.

5 The closeness of the case.

6. The duration of the defendant's misconduct.

7. Remedial action by the defendant.

8. The defendant's motivation for harm.

9. Whether the defendant attempted to conceal its misconduct.

See Read Corp. v. Portec, Inc., 970 F.2d 816 (Fed. Cir. 1992). Because willful infringement depends on the totality of the circumstances—a fact-based inquiry—the factfinder will determine whether the infringer willfully infringed the patent. But even if the jury concludes that the infringer acted willfully, the court retains the discretion to decline to award enhanced damages or attorney fees.

In practical terms, the *Read* factors compelled putative infringers to obtain opinion letters to satisfy the duty to avoid infringing another's patent rights. Although providing a steady source of employment, that compulsion became problematic during a trial on infringement. For example, the opinion letter might provide opposing counsel insight into the infringer's litigation strategy, might make the opinion drafter a witness (thus disqualifying her and possibly her firm), might force waiver of the attorney-client privilege, might compel disclosure of the putative infringer's trade secrets, and most importantly might impair the opinion drafter's ability to provide an alleged infringer with a full and frank assessment of the chances of avoiding liability. To resolve some of these concerns, the Federal Circuit took up the issue of willful infringement generally in *Knorr–Bremse Systeme fuer Nutzfahrzeuge Gmbh v. Dana Corp.,* 383 F.3d 1337 (Fed. Cir. 2004). To prevent some of the friction between the attorney-client privilege and the necessity of opinion letters to avoid willfulness, the court decided that the trial court shall not draw any adverse inference when a party invokes the attorney-client or work product privilege to shield an opinion letter. Nevertheless, the court maintained that "there continues to be an affirmative duty of due care to avoid infringement of the known patent rights of others." *Id.* at 1345 (citation omitted). This last holding, however, led to another *en banc* examination of the willfulness rules.

IN RE SEAGATE TECHNOLOGY, LLC

United States Court of Appeals, Federal Circuit, 2007
497 F.3d 1360

Opinion for the court filed by Circuit Judge Mayer, in which Circuit Judges Newman, Lourie, Rader, Schall, Bryson, Gajarsa, Linn, Dyk, and Prost join. Concurring opinion filed by Circuit Judge Gajarsa, in which Circuit Judge Newman joins. Concurring opinion filed by Circuit Judge Newman.

MAYER, CIRCUIT JUDGE.

Seagate Technology, LLC ("Seagate") petitions for a writ of mandamus directing the United States District Court for the Southern District of New York to vacate its orders compelling disclosure of materials and testimony that Seagate claims is covered by the attorney-client privilege and work product protection. We ordered en banc review, and now grant the petition. We overrule *Underwater Devices Inc. v. Morrison–Knudsen Co.,* 717 F.2d 1380 (1983), and we clarify the scope of the waiver of attorney-client privilege and work product protection that results when an accused patent infringer asserts an advice of counsel defense to a charge of willful infringement.

BACKGROUND

Convolve, Inc. and the Massachusetts Institute of Technology (collectively "Convolve") sued Seagate on July 13, 2000, alleging infringement of U.S. Patent Nos. 4,916,635 ("the '635 patent") and 5,638,267 ("the '267 patent"). Subsequently, U.S. Patent No. 6,314,473 ("the '473 patent") issued on November 6, 2001, and Convolve amended its complaint on January 25, 2002, to assert infringement of the '473 patent. Convolve also alleged that Seagate willfully infringed the patents.

Prior to the lawsuit, Seagate retained Gerald Sekimura to provide an opinion concerning Convolve's patents, and he ultimately prepared three written opinions. Seagate received the first opinion on July 24, 2000, shortly after the complaint was filed. This opinion analyzed the '635 and '267 patents and concluded that many claims were invalid and that Seagate's products did not infringe. The opinion also considered Convolve's pending International Application WO 99/45535 ("the '535 application"), which recited technology similar to that disclosed in the yet-to-be-issued '473 patent. On December 29, 2000, Sekimura provided an updated opinion to Seagate. In addition to his previous conclusions, this opinion concluded that the '267 patent was possibly unenforceable. Both opinions noted that not all of the patent claims had been reviewed, and that the '535 application required further analysis, which Sekimura recommended postponing until a U.S. patent issued. On February 21, 2003, Seagate received a third opinion concerning the validity and infringement of the by-then-issued '473 patent. There is no dispute that Seagate's opinion counsel operated separately and independently of trial counsel at all times.

In early 2003, pursuant to the trial court's scheduling order, Seagate notified Convolve of its intent to rely on Sekimura's three opinion letters in defending against willful infringement, and it disclosed all of his work product and made him available for deposition. Convolve then moved to compel discovery of any communications and work product of Seagate's other counsel, including its trial counsel. On May 28, 2004, the trial court concluded that Seagate waived the attorney-client privilege for all communications between it and any counsel, including its trial attorneys and in-house counsel, concerning the subject matter of Sekimura's opinions, i.e., infringement, invalidity, and enforceability. It further determined that the waiver began when Seagate first gained knowledge of the patents and would last until the alleged infringement ceased. Accordingly, the court ordered production of any requested documents and testimony concerning the subject matter of Sekimura's opinions. It provided for *in camera* review of documents relating to trial strategy, but said that any advice from trial counsel that undermined the reasonableness of relying on Sekimura's opinions would warrant disclosure. The court also determined that protection of work product communicated to Seagate was waived.

Based on these rulings, Convolve sought production of trial counsel opinions relating to infringement, invalidity, and enforceability of the patents, and also noticed depositions of Seagate's trial counsel. After the trial court denied Seagate's motion for a stay and certification of an interlocutory appeal, Seagate petitioned for a writ of mandamus. We stayed the discovery orders and, recognizing the functional relationship between our willfulness jurisprudence and the practical dilemmas faced in the areas of attorney-client privilege and work product protection, sua sponte ordered en banc review of the petition. The en banc order set out the following questions:

1. Should a party's assertion of the advice of counsel defense to willful infringement extend waiver of the attorney-client privilege to communications with that party's trial counsel? *See In re EchoStar Commc'ns Corp.*, 448 F.3d 1294 (Fed.Cir.2006).

2. What is the effect of any such waiver on work-product immunity?

3. Given the impact of the statutory duty of care standard announced in *Underwater Devices, Inc. v. Morrison–Knudsen Co.*, 717 F.2d 1380 (Fed.Cir.1983), on the issue of waiver of attorney-client privilege, should this court reconsider the decision in *Underwater Devices* and the duty of care standard itself?

In re Seagate Tech., LLC, 214 Fed.Appx. 997 (Fed.Cir.2007).

MANDAMUS

A party seeking a writ of mandamus bears the burden of proving that it has no other means of attaining the relief desired, *Mallard v. U.S. Dist. Court for the S. Dist. of Iowa*, 490 U.S. 296, 309 (1989), and that the right to issuance of the writ is "clear and indisputable," *Allied Chem. Corp. v. Daiflon, Inc.*, 449 U.S. 33, 35 (1980). In appropriate cases, a writ of mandamus may issue "to prevent the wrongful exposure of privileged communications." *In re Regents of the Univ. of Cal.*, 101 F.3d 1386, 1387 (Fed.Cir.1996). Specifically, "mandamus review may be granted of discovery orders that turn on claims of privilege when (1) there is raised an important issue of first impression, (2) the privilege would be lost if review were denied until final judgment, and (3) immediate resolution would avoid the development of doctrine that would undermine the privilege." *Id.* at 1388. This case meets these criteria.

We review the trial court's determination of the scope of waiver for an abuse of discretion. *In re EchoStar Commc'ns. Corp.*, 448 F.3d 1294, 1300 (Fed.Cir.2006); *In re Pioneer Hi–Bred Int'l, Inc.*, 238 F.3d 1370, 1373 n. 2 (Fed. Cir. 2001). Because willful infringement and the scope of waiver accompanying the advice of counsel defense invoke substantive patent law, we apply the law of this circuit. *EchoStar*, 448 F.3d at 1298.

DISCUSSION

Because patent infringement is a strict liability offense, the nature of the offense is only relevant in determining whether enhanced damages are warranted. Although a trial court's discretion in awarding enhanced damages has a long lineage in patent law, the current statute, similar to its predecessors, is devoid of any standard for awarding them. Absent a statutory guide, we have held that an award of enhanced damages requires a showing of willful infringement. *Beatrice Foods Co. v. New England Printing & Lithographing Co.*, 923 F.2d 1576, 1578 (Fed.Cir. 1991); *see also Jurgens v. CBK, Ltd.*, 80 F.3d 1566, 1570 (Fed.Cir.1996) (holding that bad faith infringement, which is a type of willful infringement, is required for enhanced damages). This well-established standard accords with Supreme Court precedent. *See Aro Mfg. Co. v. Convertible Top Replacement Co.*, 377 U.S. 476, 508, 84 S.Ct. 1526, 12 L.Ed.2d 457 (1964) (enhanced damages were available for willful or bad faith infringement); *see also Dowling v. United States*, 473 U.S. 207, 227 n. 19 (1985)(enhanced damages are available for "willful infringement"); *Seymour v. McCormick*, 57 U.S. 480, 489, 16 How. 480, 14 L.Ed. 1024 (1853) ("wanton or malicious" injury could result in exemplary damages). But, a finding of willfulness does not require an award of enhanced damages; it merely permits it. *See* 35 U.S.C. § 284; *Odetics, Inc. v. Storage Tech. Corp.*, 185 F.3d 1259, 1274 (Fed.Cir.1999); *Jurgens*, 80 F.3d at 1570.

This court fashioned a standard for evaluating willful infringement in *Underwater Devices Inc. v. Morrison–Knudsen Co.*, 717 F.2d 1380, 1389–90 (Fed.Cir.1983): "Where . . . a potential infringer has actual notice of another's patent rights, he has an affirmative duty to exercise due care to determine whether or not he is infringing. Such an affirmative duty includes, *inter alia*, the duty to seek and obtain competent legal advice from counsel *before* the initiation of any possible infringing activity." (citations omitted). This standard was announced shortly after the creation of the court, and at a time "when widespread disregard of patent rights was undermining the national innovation incentive." *Knorr–Bremse Systeme Fuer Nutzfahrzeuge GmbH v. Dana Corp.*, 383 F.3d 1337, 1343 (Fed.Cir.2004) (en banc) (citing Advisory Committee on Industrial Innovation Final Report, Dep't of Commerce (Sep. 1979)). Indeed, in *Underwater Devices*, an attorney had advised the infringer that "[c]ourts, in recent years, have—in patent infringement cases—found [asserted patents] invalid in approximately 80% of the cases," and on that basis the attorney concluded that the patentee would not likely sue for infringement. 717 F.2d at 1385. Over time, our cases evolved to evaluate willfulness and its duty of due care under the totality of the circumstances, and we enumerated factors informing the inquiry.

In light of the duty of due care, accused willful infringers commonly assert an advice of counsel defense. Under this defense, an accused willful infringer aims to establish that due to reasonable reliance on advice from counsel, its continued accused activities were done in good faith. Typically, counsel's opinion concludes that the patent is invalid, unenforceable, and/or not infringed. Although an infringer's reliance on favorable advice of counsel, or conversely his failure to proffer any favorable advice, is not dispositive of the willfulness inquiry, it is crucial to the analysis. *E.g.*, *Electro Med. Sys., S.A. v. Cooper Life Scis., Inc.*, 34 F.3d 1048, 1056 (Fed.Cir.1994) ("Possession of a favorable opinion of counsel is not essential to avoid a willfulness determination; it is only one factor to be considered, albeit an important one.").

Since *Underwater Devices*, we have recognized the practical concerns stemming from our willfulness doctrine, particularly as related to the attorney-client privilege and work product doctrine. For instance, *Quantum Corp. v. Tandon Corp.*, 940 F.2d 642, 643 (Fed. Cir. 1991), observed that "[p]roper resolution of the dilemma of an accused infringer who must choose between the lawful assertion of the attorney-client privilege and avoidance of a willfulness finding if infringement is found, is of great importance not only to the parties but to the fundamental values sought to be preserved by the attorney-client privilege." We cautioned there that an accused infringer "should not, without the trial court's careful consideration, be forced to choose between waiving the privilege in order to protect itself from a willfulness finding, in which case it may risk prejudicing itself on the question of liability, and maintaining the privilege, in which case it may risk being found to be a willful infringer if liability is found." *Id.* at 643–44. We advised that *in camera* review and bifurcating trials in appropriate cases would alleviate these concerns. *Id.* However, such procedures are often considered too onerous to be regularly employed.

Recently, in *Knorr–Bremse,* we addressed another outgrowth of our willfulness doctrine. Over the years, we had held that an accused infringer's failure to produce advice from counsel "would warrant the conclusion that it either obtained no advice of counsel or did so and was advised that its [activities] would be an infringement of valid U.S. Patents." *Knorr–Bremse,* 383 F.3d at 1343. Recognizing that this inference imposed "inappropriate burdens on the attorney-client relationship," we held that invoking the attorney-client privilege or work product protection does not give rise to an adverse inference. We further held that an accused infringer's failure to obtain legal advice does not give rise to an adverse inference with respect to willfulness.

More recently, in *EchoStar* we addressed the scope of waiver resulting from the advice of counsel defense. First, we concluded that relying on in-house counsel's advice to refute a charge of willfulness triggers waiver of the attorney-client privilege. Second, we held that asserting the advice of counsel defense waives work product protection and the attorney-client privilege for all communications on the same subject matter, as well as any documents memorializing attorney-client communications. However, we held that waiver did not extend to work product that was not communicated to an accused infringer. *EchoStar* did not consider waiver of the advice of counsel defense as it relates to trial counsel.

In this case, we confront the willfulness scheme and its functional relationship to the attorney-client privilege and work product protection. In light of Supreme Court opinions since *Underwater Devices* and the practical concerns facing litigants under the current regime, we take this opportunity to revisit our willfulness doctrine and to address whether waiver resulting from advice of counsel and work product defenses extend to trial counsel.

I. Willful Infringement

The term willful is not unique to patent law, and it has a well-established meaning in the civil context. For instance, our sister circuits have employed a recklessness standard for enhancing statutory damages

shouldn't have to chose between giving up privilege and risk liability

In camera review and bifurcation not good ways to fix

No inferences of willfulness if privilege envoked or didn't seek legal advice

relying on inhouse counsel triggers waiver

waives all comm on same subject matter

does this extend to trial counsel?

for copyright infringement. Under the Copyright Act, a copyright owner can elect to receive statutory damages, and trial courts have discretion to enhance the damages, up to a statutory maximum, for willful infringement. 17 U.S.C. § 504(c). Although the statute does not define willful, it has consistently been defined as including reckless behavior. *See, e.g., Yurman Design, Inc. v. PAJ, Inc.*, 262 F.3d 101, 112 (2d Cir.2001) ("Willfulness in [the context of statutory damages for copyright infringement] means that the defendant 'recklessly disregarded' the possibility that 'its conduct represented infringement.' ") (quoting *Hamil Am., Inc. v. GFI, Inc.*, 193 F.3d 92, 97 (2d Cir.1999) (additional citations omitted)); *Wildlife Express Corp. v. Carol Wright Sales*, 18 F.3d 502, 511–12 (7th Cir.1994) (same); *RCA/Ariola Int'l, Inc. v. Thomas & Grayston Co.*, 845 F.2d 773, 779 (8th Cir.1988) (same); *see also eBay Inc. v. MercExchange, L.L.C.*, 547 U.S. 388 (2006) (noting with approval that its resolution of the permanent injunction standard in the patent context created harmony with copyright law).

Just recently, the Supreme Court addressed the meaning of willfulness as a statutory condition of civil liability for punitive damages. *Safeco Ins. Co. of Am. v. Burr*, ___ U.S. ___, 127 S.Ct. 2201, 167 L.Ed.2d 1045 (2007). *Safeco* involved the Fair Credit Reporting Act ("FCRA"), which imposes civil liability for failure to comply with its requirements. Whereas an affected consumer can recover actual damages for negligent violations of the FCRA, 15 U.S.C. § 1681 o(a), he can also recover punitive damages for willful ones, 15 U.S.C. § 1681 n(a). Addressing the willfulness requirement in this context, the Court concluded that the "standard civil usage" of "willful" includes reckless behavior. *Id.* at 2209; *accord McLaughlin v. Richland Shoe Co.*, 486 U.S. 128, 132–33 (1988) (concluding that willful violations of the Fair Labor Standards Act include reckless violations); *Trans World Airlines, Inc. v. Thurston*, 469 U.S. 111, 128 (1985). Significantly, the Court said that this definition comports with the common law usage, "which treated actions in 'reckless disregard' of the law as 'willful' violations." *Id.* at 2209 (citing W. Keeton, D. Dobbs, R. Keeton, & D. Owen, *Prosser and Keeton on Law of Torts* § 34, p. 212 (5th ed. 1984)).

In contrast, the duty of care announced in *Underwater Devices* sets a lower threshold for willful infringement that is more akin to negligence. This standard fails to comport with the general understanding of willfulness in the civil context, *Richland Shoe Co.*, 486 U.S. at 133, 108 S.Ct. 1677 ("The word 'willful' ... is generally understood to refer to conduct that is not merely negligent."), and it allows for punitive damages in a manner inconsistent with Supreme Court precedent, *see, e.g., Safeco*, 127 S.Ct. at 2209, 2214–15, 2216 n.20; *Smith v. Wade*, 461 U.S. 30, 39–49 (1983). Accordingly, we overrule the standard set out in *Underwater Devices* and hold that proof of willful infringement permitting enhanced damages requires at least a showing of objective recklessness. Because we abandon the affirmative duty of due care, we also reemphasize that there is no affirmative obligation to obtain opinion of counsel.

reckless
defined

willful
infringement
defined

state of mind
not needed

objective
standard

scope of
discovery
dispute in
case

We fully recognize that "the term [reckless] is not self-defining." *Farmer v. Brennan*, 511 U.S. 825, 836 (1994). However, "[t]he civil law generally calls a person reckless who acts ... in the face of an unjustifiably high risk of harm that is either known or so obvious that it should be known." *Id.* (citing Prosser and Keeton § 34, pp. 213–14; *Restatement (Second) of Torts* § 500 (1965)). Accordingly, to establish willful infringement, a patentee must show by clear and convincing evidence that the infringer acted despite an objectively high likelihood that its actions constituted infringement of a valid patent. *See Safeco,* 127 S.Ct. at 2215 ("It is [a] high risk of harm, objectively assessed, that is the essence of recklessness at common law."). The state of mind of the accused infringer is not relevant to this objective inquiry. If this threshold objective standard is satisfied, the patentee must also demonstrate that this objectively-defined risk (determined by the record developed in the infringement proceeding) was either known or so obvious that it should have been known to the accused infringer. We leave it to future cases to further develop the application of this standard.

Finally, we reject the argument that revisiting our willfulness doctrine is either improper or imprudent, as Convolve contends. The ultimate dispute in this case is the proper scope of discovery. While it is true that the issue of willful infringement, or even infringement for that matter, has not been decided by the trial court, it is indisputable that the proper legal standard for willful infringement informs the relevance of evidence relating to that issue and, more importantly here, the proper scope of discovery. *See United States Nat'l Bank of Or. v. Indep. Ins. Agents of Am., Inc.,* 508 U.S. 439, 447 (1993) ("[A] court may consider an issue 'antecedent to ... and ultimately dispositive of' the dispute before it, even an issue the parties fail to identify and brief."(quoting *Arcadia v. Ohio Power Co.,* 498 U.S. 73, 77 (1990))); *see also* Fed. R. Civ. Pro. R. 26(b) (limiting discovery to relevant, not necessarily admissible, information); *accord Singleton v. Wulff,* 428 U.S. 106, 121 (1976) ("The matter of what questions may be taken up and resolved for the first time on appeal is one left primarily to the discretion of the courts of appeals, to be exercised on the facts of individual cases."); *Forshey v. Principi,* 284 F.3d 1335, 1355–59 (Fed. Cir. 2002) (*en banc*). Accordingly, addressing willfulness is neither hypothetical nor advisory.

II. *Attorney–Client Privilege*

attorney
client
privilege

We turn now to the appropriate scope of waiver of the attorney-client privilege resulting from an advice of counsel defense asserted in response to a charge of willful infringement. Recognizing that it is "the oldest of the privileges for confidential communications known to the common law," we are guided by its purpose "to encourage full and frank communication between attorneys and their clients and thereby promote broader public interests in the observance of law and administration of justice." *Upjohn Co. v. United States,* 449 U.S. 383, 389 (1981). The privilege also "recognizes that sound legal advice or advocacy serves public ends and that such advice or advocacy depends upon the lawyer's being fully informed by the client." *Id.*

The attorney-client privilege belongs to the client, who alone may waive it. *E.g., Knorr–Bremse,* 383 F.3d at 1345; *Am. Standard, Inc. v. Pfizer, Inc.,* 828 F.2d 734, 745 (Fed.Cir.1987). "The widely applied standard for determining the scope of a waiver ... is that the waiver applies to all other communications relating to the same subject matter." *Fort James Corp. v. Solo Cup Co.,* 412 F.3d 1340, 1349 (Fed.Cir.2005). This broad scope is grounded in principles of fairness and serves to prevent a party from simultaneously using the privilege as both a sword and a shield; that is, it prevents the inequitable result of a party disclosing favorable communications while asserting the privilege as to less favorable ones. *EchoStar,* 448 F.3d at 1301; *Fort James,* 412 F.3d at 1349. Ultimately, however, "[t]here is no bright line test for determining what constitutes the subject matter of a waiver, rather courts weigh the circumstances of the disclosure, the nature of the legal advice sought and the prejudice to the parties of permitting or prohibiting further disclosures." *Fort James,* 412 F.3d at 1349–50.

In considering the scope of waiver resulting from the advice of counsel defense, district courts have reached varying results with respect to trial counsel. Some decisions have extended waiver to trial counsel, *e.g., Informatica Corp. v. Bus. Objects Data Integration, Inc.,* 454 F.Supp.2d 957 (N.D.Cal.2006), whereas others have declined to do so, *e.g., Collaboration Props., Inc. v. Polycom, Inc.,* 224 F.R.D. 473, 476 (N.D.Cal.2004); *Ampex Corp. v. Eastman Kodak Co.,* 2006 WL 1995140, 2006 U.S. Dist. LEXIS 48702 (D.Del. July 17, 2006). Still others have taken a middle ground and extended waiver to trial counsel only for communications contradicting or casting doubt on the opinions asserted. *E.g., Intex Recreation Corp. v. Team Worldwide Corp.,* 439 F.Supp.2d 46 (D.D.C.2006); *Beneficial Franchise Co., Inc. v. Bank One, N.A.,* 205 F.R.D. 212 (N.D.Ill. 2001); *Micron Separations, Inc. v. Pall Corp.,* 159 F.R.D. 361 (D.Mass. 1995).

Recognizing the value of a common approach and in light of the new willfulness analysis set out above, we conclude that the significantly different functions of trial counsel and opinion counsel advise against extending waiver to trial counsel. Whereas opinion counsel serves to provide an objective assessment for making informed business decisions, trial counsel focuses on litigation strategy and evaluates the most successful manner of presenting a case to a judicial decision maker. And trial counsel is engaged in an adversarial process. We previously recognized this distinction with respect to our prior willfulness standard in *Crystal Semiconductor Corp. v. TriTech Microelectronics International, Inc.,* 246 F.3d 1336, 1352 (Fed.Cir.2001), which concluded that "defenses prepared [by litigation counsel] for a trial are not equivalent to the competent legal opinion of non-infringement or invalidity which qualify as 'due care' before undertaking any potentially infringing activity." Because of the fundamental difference between these types of legal advice, this situation does not present the classic "sword and shield" concerns typically mandating broad subject matter waiver. Therefore, fairness counsels against disclosing trial counsel's communications on an entire subject matter in response to an accused infringer's reliance on opinion counsel's opinion to refute a willfulness allegation.

Moreover, the interests weighing against extending waiver to trial counsel are compelling. The Supreme Court recognized the need to protect trial counsel's thoughts in *Hickman v. Taylor*, 329 U.S. 495, 510–11 (1947):

> [I]t is essential that a lawyer work with a certain degree of privacy, free from unnecessary intrusion by opposing parties and their counsel. Proper preparation of a client's case demands that he assemble information, sift what he considers to be the relevant from the irrelevant facts, prepare his legal theories and plan his strategy without undue and needless interference. That is the historical and the necessary way in which lawyers act within the framework of our system of jurisprudence to promote justice and to protect their clients' interests.

The Court saw that allowing discovery of an attorney's thoughts would result in "[i]nefficiency, unfairness and sharp practices," that "[t]he effect on the legal profession would be demoralizing" and thus "the interests of the clients and the cause of justice would be poorly served." *Id.* at 511. Although *Hickman* concerned work product protection, the attorney-client privilege maintained with trial counsel raises the same concerns in patent litigation. In most cases, the demands of our adversarial system of justice will far outweigh any benefits of extending waiver to trial counsel. *See Jaffee v. Redmond*, 518 U.S. 1, 9 (1996) ("Exceptions from the general rule disfavoring testimonial privileges may be justified, however, by a 'public good transcending the normally predominant principle of utilizing all rational means for ascertaining the truth.'") (quoting *Trammel v. United States*, 445 U.S. 40, 50 (1980) (quoting *Elkins v. United States*, 364 U.S. 206 (1960) (Frankfurter, J., dissenting))) (additional internal quotation marks omitted).

Further outweighing any benefit of extending waiver to trial counsel is the realization that in ordinary circumstances, willfulness will depend on an infringer's prelitigation conduct. It is certainly true that patent infringement is an ongoing offense that can continue after litigation has commenced. However, when a complaint is filed, a patentee must have a good faith basis for alleging willful infringement. Fed. R. Civ. Pro. 8, 11(b). So a willfulness claim asserted in the original complaint must necessarily be grounded exclusively in the accused infringer's pre-filing conduct. By contrast, when an accused infringer's post-filing conduct is reckless, a patentee can move for a preliminary injunction, which generally provides an adequate remedy for combating post-filing willful infringement. *See* 35 U.S.C. § 283; *Amazon.com, Inc. v. Barnesandnoble.com, Inc.*, 239 F.3d 1343, 1350 (Fed. Cir. 2001). A patentee who does not attempt to stop an accused infringer's activities in this manner should not be allowed to accrue enhanced damages based solely on the infringer's post-filing conduct. Similarly, if a patentee attempts to secure injunctive relief but fails, it is likely the infringement did not rise to the level of recklessness.

We fully recognize that an accused infringer may avoid a preliminary injunction by showing only a substantial question as to invalidity, as opposed to the higher clear and convincing standard required to prevail on the merits. *Amazon.com*, 239 F.3d at 1359 ("Vulnerability is the issue at the preliminary injunction stage, while validity is the issue at trial. The showing of a substantial question as to invalidity thus requires less proof than the clear and convincing showing necessary to establish invalidity itself."). However, this lessened showing simply accords with the requirement that recklessness must be shown to recover enhanced damages. A substantial question about invalidity or infringement is likely sufficient not only to avoid a preliminary injunction, but also a charge of willfulness based on post-filing conduct.

We also recognize that in some cases a patentee may be denied a preliminary injunction despite establishing a likelihood of success on the merits, such as when the remaining factors are considered and balanced. In that event, whether a willfulness claim based on conduct occurring solely after litigation began is sustainable will depend on the facts of each case.

Because willful infringement in the main must find its basis in prelitigation conduct, communications of trial counsel have little, if any, relevance warranting their disclosure, and this further supports generally shielding trial counsel from the waiver stemming from an advice of counsel defense to willfulness. Here, the opinions of Seagate's opinion counsel, received after suit was commenced, appear to be of similarly marginal value. Although the reasoning contained in those opinions ultimately may preclude Seagate's conduct from being considered reckless if infringement is found, reliance on the opinions after litigation was commenced will likely be of little significance.

In sum, we hold, as a general proposition, that asserting the advice of counsel defense and disclosing opinions of opinion counsel do not constitute waiver of the attorney-client privilege for communications with trial counsel. We do not purport to set out an absolute rule. Instead, trial courts remain free to exercise their discretion in unique circumstances to extend waiver to trial counsel, such as if a party or counsel engages in chicanery. We believe this view comports with Supreme Court precedent, which has made clear that rules concerning privileges are subject to review and revision, when necessary. *See Jaffee*, 518 U.S. at 9 (noting that federal courts are "to 'continue the evolutionary development of testimonial privileges.' ").

III. Work Product Protection

An advice of counsel defense asserted to refute a charge of willful infringement may also implicate waiver of work product protection.

Again, we are here confronted with whether this waiver extends to trial counsel's work product. We hold that it does not, absent exceptional circumstances.

The work product doctrine is "designed to balance the needs of the adversary system: promotion of an attorney's preparation in representing a client versus society's general interest in revealing all true and material facts to the resolution of a dispute." *In re Martin Marietta Corp.,* 856 F.2d 619, 624 (4th Cir.1988). Unlike the attorney-client privilege, which provides absolute protection from disclosure, work product protection is qualified and may be overcome by need and undue hardship. Fed. R. Civ. Pro. 26(b)(3). However, the level of need and hardship required for discovery depends on whether the work product is factual, or the result of mental processes such as plans, strategies, tactics, and impressions, whether memorialized in writing or not. Whereas factual work product can be discovered solely upon a showing of substantial need and undue hardship, mental process work product is afforded even greater, nearly absolute, protection.

Like the attorney-client privilege, however, work product protection may be waived. *United States v. Nobles,* 422 U.S. 225, 239 (1975). Here, the same rationale generally limiting waiver of the attorney-client privilege with trial counsel applies with even greater force to so limiting work product waiver because of the nature of the work product doctrine. Protecting lawyers from broad subject matter of work product disclosure "strengthens the adversary process, and ... may ultimately and ideally further the search for the truth." *Martin Marietta,* 856 F.2d at 626; *accord EchoStar,* 448 F.3d at 1301 ("[W]ork-product immunity ... promotes a fair and efficient adversarial system...."); *Coastal States Gas Corp. v. Dep't of Energy,* 617 F.2d 854, 864 (D.C.Cir.1980) ("The purpose of the privilege, however, is not to protect any interest of the attorney ... but to protect the adversary trial process itself. It is believed that the integrity of our system would suffer if adversaries were entitled to probe each other's thoughts and plans concerning the case."). In addition, trial counsel's mental processes, which fall within Convolve's discovery requests, enjoy the utmost protection from disclosure; a scope of waiver commensurate with the nature of such heightened protection is appropriate.

The Supreme Court has approved of narrowly restricting the scope of work product waiver. In *United States v. Nobles,* a criminal case, an accused armed robber presented the testimony of an investigator in an attempt to discredit the two eyewitnesses. When they testified for the prosecution, the defense attorney relied on the investigator's report in cross-examining the eyewitnesses. 422 U.S. at 227. After the prosecution rested, the defense attempted to call the investigator to testify. The trial court, however, ruled that if the investigator testified, his affirmative testimony would mandate disclosure of the portions of his report relating to his testimony. *Id.* at 229. The Supreme Court agreed that the investigator's affirmative testimony waived work product protection, but it approvingly noted the "quite limited" scope of waiver imposed by the trial court and its refusal to allow a general "fishing expedition" into the defense files or even the investigator's report. *Id.* at 239–40. Similarly, Convolve has been granted access to the materials relating to Seagate's opinion counsel's opinion, and he was made available for deposition. The extent of this waiver accords with the principles and spirit of *Nobles*.

Accordingly, we hold that, as a general proposition, relying on opinion counsel's work product does not waive work product immunity with respect to trial counsel. Again, we leave open the possibility that situations may arise in which waiver may be extended to trial counsel, such as if a party or his counsel engages in chicanery. And, of course, the general principles of work product protection remain in force, so that a party may obtain discovery of work product absent waiver upon a sufficient showing of need and hardship, bearing in mind that a higher burden must be met to obtain that pertaining to mental processes. *See* Fed. R. Civ. Pro. 26(b)(3).

[handwritten margin note: using opinion counsel's work doesn't waive trial lawyers work]

Finally, the work product doctrine was partially codified in Rule 26(b)(3) of the Federal Rules of Civil Procedure, which applies work product protection to "documents and tangible things." Courts continue to apply *Hickman v. Taylor,* 329 U.S. 495, 67 S.Ct. 385, 91 L.Ed. 451, to "nontangible" work product. This is relevant here because Convolve sought to depose Seagate's trial counsel. We agree that work product protection remains available to "nontangible" work product under *Hickman*. Otherwise, attorneys' files would be protected from discovery, but attorneys themselves would have no work product objection to depositions.

CONCLUSION

Accordingly, Seagate's petition for a writ of mandamus is granted, and the district court will reconsider its discovery orders in light of this opinion.

[handwritten margin note: writ granted]

NOTES

1. Willfulness at Sea? *Seagate's* holdings holds many implications. For example, without a duty of due care, defendants may often succeed in disposing of willfulness charges in a preliminary summary judgment decision. Patentees, on the other hand, may have an incentive to provide more information about the patent to the marketplace at an earlier time to build a case for reckless disregard of infringement warnings. Of course, a patentee who undertakes these pre-suit communications also increases the risk of a declaratory judgment action that allows the defendant to choose the district court for adjudication. In addition, potential defendants no longer need to obtain an opinion of counsel. Nonetheless these opinions will still yield important advantages at and before trial. Indeed, those opinions will undoubtedly contain more candid assessments of infringement and validity because they are no longer the linchpin of a willfulness defense. Finally, and perhaps most important, major manufacturers and researchers can actually consult patents in their design work (particularly during efforts to design around protected technology) without fearing that mere knowledge of the patent will trigger charges of willfulness. The objective standard enunciated in *Seagate* thus encourages prompt, frank communications regarding potential infringement issues and minimizes incentives to fashion a record with an eye to potential future litigation.

2. Willful Infringement Doctrine? Why should a court ever award enhanced damages for willful infringement where that infringement occurs only under the Doctrine of Equivalents? Should Congress amend § 284 to limit judicial increases of damages awards to cases of literal infringement?

3. The "Exceptional" Requirement for Attorney Fees. In *Interspiro USA, Inc. v. Figgie International, Inc.*, 18 F.3d 927 (Fed.Cir.1994), the court further discussed the award of attorney fees under § 285:

> When considering a request for an award of attorney fees under 35 U.S.C.A. § 285, the trial judge undertakes a two-step inquiry: he or she must determine whether there is clear and convincing evidence that the case is "exceptional," and if so, whether an award of attorney fees to the prevailing party is warranted.

18 F.3d at 933–34. "Bad faith litigation, willful infringement, or inequitable conduct are among the circumstances which may make a case exceptional." *Mahurkar v. C.R. Bard, Inc.*, 79 F.3d 1572 (Fed.Cir.1996). Other sources of attorney fee awards include Federal Rule of Civil Procedure 11, *see Cambridge Prods., Ltd. v. Penn Nutrients, Inc.*, 962 F.2d 1048 (Fed.Cir.1992), the inherent power of the court, *see L.E.A. Dynatech, Inc. v. Allina*, 49 F.3d 1527 (Fed.Cir. 1995), and, on appeal, Federal Rule of Appellate Procedure Rule 38, *see Finch v. Hughes Aircraft Co.*, 926 F.2d 1574 (Fed.Cir.1991).

§ 13.4 MARKING

The Patent Act provides a significant incentive for patentees to give notice of their intellectual property rights on the patented device or its packaging. As set forth in 35 U.S.C. § 287:

> Patentees, and persons making or selling any patented article for or under them, may give notice to the public that the same is patented, either by fixing thereon the word "patent" or the abbreviation "pat.", together with the number of the patent, or when, from the character of the article, this can not be done, by fixing to it, or to the package wherein one or more of them is contained, a label containing a like notice. In the event of failure so to mark, no damages shall be recovered by the patentee in any action for infringement, except on proof that the infringer was notified of the infringement and continued to infringe thereafter, in which event damages may be recovered only for infringement occurring after such notice. Filing of an action for infringement shall constitute such notice.

The details of patent marking, as well as the consequences of failing to do so, are reviewed in the following opinion.

AMSTED INDUSTRIES INC. v. BUCKEYE STEEL CASTINGS CO.

United States Court of Appeals, Federal Circuit, 1994
24 F.3d 178

Before Plager, Lourie, and Rader, Circuit Judges.

LOURIE, CIRCUIT JUDGE.

The '269 patent, which issued in the name of Stanley H. Fillion as inventor on May 23, 1972 and was assigned to Dresser Industries, is entitled "Combined Body Bolster Center Filler and Center Plate for Railway Cars" and claims a particular center plate in combination with several other components to form a railroad car underframe structure. The center plate component is the basis of the present dispute. Dresser made and sold the component center plate under the name "Low Profile" until 1985, at which time it sold the '269 patent and the Low Profile trademark to Amsted. Amsted thereafter began making and selling the Low Profile plate to rail car builders for assembly into the patented combination.

MARKING/NOTICE REQUIREMENT OF 35 U.S.C. § 287

1. Amsted's Cross–Appeal

Amsted cross-appeals from the district court's ruling that, because the patented articles were not marked, Amsted's recovery of damages was limited to the period after which it notified Buckeye of its infringement pursuant to 35 U.S.C. § 287.

The district court held that section 287 limited Amsted's recovery of damages because Amsted's customers, to whom Amsted sold one element of the patented combination with the expectation that they would use that element to make and sell the patented invention, were implied licensees who were "making or selling [the] patented article for or under [Amsted]" within the meaning of section 287. The court reasoned that "[t]he distribution or manufacturing arrangement of a patentee, unilaterally chosen by the patentee, cannot be allowed to relieve the patentee of its duty to mark under Section 287."

Amsted argues that section 287(a) does not so limit its damages. Amsted emphasizes that it never made the patented article and that its customers, who did make and sell the patented articles, did not do so "for or under" Amsted within the meaning of section 287(a). Amsted thus asserts that its recovery of damages should not have been predicated on marking or notice under section 287(a) and that it was entitled to damages from the beginning of Buckeye's infringement.

The question before us is the scope to be accorded the "for or under" language of section 287(a). This is an issue of statutory construction which we review for correctness as a matter of law. A licensee who makes or sells a patented article does so "for or under" the patentee, thereby limiting the patentee's damage recovery when the patented article is not marked. In view of the purpose of section 287, "to encourage the patentee to give notice to the public of the patent," there is no reason why section 287 should only apply to express licensees and not to implied licensees.

There is no dispute that Amsted impliedly authorized its customers to make, use, and sell the patented article. The record reveals that Amsted manufactured and sold its center plates for use in the patented combination, and that Amsted provided its customers with installation drawings which instruct how to assemble the center plate, along with other components, according to the teachings of the patent. Amsted argues that had it marked its center plate it would have violated 35 U.S.C. § 292 which prohibits the marking of an unpatented article. This is not persuasive. A marking such as "for use under U.S. X,XXX,XXX" would have sufficed. Moreover, Amsted could have sold its plates with a requirement that its purchaser-licensees mark the patented products "licensed under U.S. X,XXX,XXX." Such marking by either Amsted or its purchasers would have fulfilled the policy goal of notifying the public concerning the patent status of items in commerce. Thus, we conclude that Amsted's right to recover damages prior to actual notification is dependent upon compliance with the marking or notice requirements of section 287(a). Since there is no dispute that the patented articles sold by Amsted's customers were never marked, Amsted is precluded from recovering damages prior to the date that Buckeye, the accused infringer, "was notified of the infringement." Accordingly, the next issue before us is the date on which effective notice occurred.

2. Proper Notice Under Section 287

The parties dispute which of two letters written by Amsted to Buckeye, one dated January 10, 1986 and the other January 27, 1989, constituted effective statutory notice. The contents of these letters are not disputed. The 1986 letter stated in pertinent part:

This is to advise you that Amsted . . . has acquired a number of properties [from Dresser] . . . including [the '269 patent]. . . .

It is our understanding that Dresser Industries actively sought to enforce its patent . . . and those rights have been heretofore respected in the industry. AMSTED–ASF expects to continue to enforce those rights which it has acquired and similarly expects our industry to respect its patents.

Accordingly, you should acquaint yourself with the ['269 patent] and refrain from supplying or offering to supply component parts which would infringe or contribute to the infringement of the patent[ ]. You should not offer to supply items which are copies of or designed to replace our LOW PROFILE center plate.

This letter was broadcast to a number of other companies, not only to Buckeye. It did not explicitly charge Buckeye with infringement of Amsted's '269 patent.

Amsted's 1989 letter stated in pertinent part:

> On January 10, 1986 I wrote to you and advised of AMSTED Industries' ownership and enforcement policy respecting the ['269 patent]. . . .

> In our view [your center plate, a photocopy of which is attached,] or the intended application thereof to a freight car infringes the ['269 patent]. Accordingly we demand that you immediately cease and desist from any further unauthorized production and sales of such castings that . . . include features covered by our patents. . . .

> We expect to . . . enforce our patent rights against your company should the matter remain unresolved.

Both parties agree that the 1989 was proper notice; the dispute is whether the 1986 letter so qualifies.

The jury found that the 1986 letter constituted statutory notice. In denying Buckeye's motion for JMOL on this issue, the court held that the notice requirement of section 287 does not require a specific charge of infringement and that, "[g]iven all the circumstances, the jury permissibly concluded that the 1986 letter notified Buckeye of [its] infringement." The court specifically pointed to evidence that Buckeye knew that it was infringing at the time it received Amsted's letter and evidence evincing Buckeye's "understanding" that the 1986 letter was a notice of infringement. Buckeye argues that the district court erred in denying its motion for JMOL on this issue because the 1986 letter did not constitute a notice of infringement under section 287 as a matter of law. Buckeye asserts that the statute requires a patentee to specifically charge an infringer with infringement and that a general communication which merely gives notice of the patent and the patentee's intention to enforce it is insufficient. Buckeye maintains that it was not notified of its infringement by Amsted until it received the 1989 letter and that Amsted was thus precluded from recovering damages under section 287 prior to that date.

Amsted argues that the notice provision does not require the patentee to identify an accused device, but only to inform the defendant of the type of product that would infringe. Amsted asks us to hold that the 1986 letter was sufficient notice in the context of what Buckeye knew at the time it received that letter and what Buckeye understood the letter to mean. Amsted emphasizes that Buckeye had known about the '269 patent for ten years and ultimately decided to copy it after numerous unsuccessful attempts to design around it. Amsted asserts that when Buckeye received the 1986 letter it knew it was infringing.

The question before us, the proper interpretation of the statutory language "notified of the infringement," is one which we review for correctness as a matter of law. Section 287(a) provides that absent marking, a patentee may not recover damages without proof that "the infringer was notified of the infringement." The Supreme Court in *Dunlap v. Schofield*, 152 U.S. 244, 14 S.Ct. 576, 38 L.Ed. 426 (1894), held that the "clear meaning" of this section is that a patentee cannot recover damages absent marking or notice to the "particular defendants by informing them of his patent and of their infringement of it." 152 U.S. at 247–48, 14 S.Ct. at 577. The Court further stated that notice "is an affirmative act, and something to be done by him." Because the plaintiffs in *Dunlap* offered no proof in support of their allegation that they had notified the defendants of the patent and of their infringement, the Court held that they could not recover damages. 152 U.S. at 248, 14 S.Ct. at 577. *Dunlap* thus established that notice must be an affirmative act on the part of the patentee which informs the defendant of his infringement. We regard *Dunlap* as highly persuasive, if not controlling, on the meaning of the notice requirement of section 287.

For purposes of section 287(a), notice must be of "the infringement," not merely notice of the patent's existence or ownership. Actual notice requires the affirmative communication of a specific charge of infringement by a specific accused product or device. The 1986 letter does not meet this standard. It is irrelevant, contrary to the district court's conclusion, whether the defendant knew of the patent or knew of his own infringement. The correct approach to determining notice under section 287 must focus on the action of the patentee, not the knowledge or understanding of the infringer. The 1986 letter was merely informational, of the kind that companies often send to others without intending to charge infringement. Just as such letters tend not to be threats sufficient to justify a declaratory judgment action, they also are not charges of infringement for "notice" purposes.

We thus conclude as a matter of law that the 1986 letter, which notified the whole industry, including Buckeye, only of Amsted's ownership of the patent and generally advised companies not to infringe, was not notice within the meaning of section 287. Amsted accordingly did not give Buckeye notice for purposes of section 287 until its 1989 letter, which specifically charged Buckeye with infringement and specified an infringing device. The district court thus erred as a matter of law in denying Buckeye's motion for JMOL on this issue. Amsted may recover damages only after it notified Buckeye of its infringement with the 1989 letter. We thus vacate the jury's damage award and remand for a recalculation of damages from the date of the 1989 letter.

NOTES

1. **False Marking.** 35 U.S.C.A. § 292 provides the unusual remedy of a *qui tam* action against entities that mark an article with a patent number "with

the intent of counterfeiting or imitating the mark of the patentee, or of deceiving the public." Anyone may bring suit, and the fine of up to $500 per falsely marked article is split between the plaintiff and the United States Treasury. Courts have strictly construed the intent element of false marking, such that no violation occurs if the mismarking occurred in good faith, *Brose v. Sears, Roebuck and Co.*, 455 F.2d 763 (5th Cir.1972), or due to a mistake.

Another concern that may arise out of false marking is the threat of charges of an antitrust violation. A safe harbor of sorts appears to exist if the article is marked with a notice to the effect that the article is "[p]rotected by one or more of the following patents." At least one court has held that this sort of notice does not comprise a restraint on competition even if only one of the listed patents covers the product. *United States v. General Electric Co.*, 82 F.Supp. 753 (D.N.J.1949). Given that many products are subject to protection to patents that may expire at different times, and that products are frequently redesigned, are you sympathetic to this holding? Or is it simply a convenient loophole?

2. Patent Marking Estoppel. Several courts have held "that placing a patent number on a product will estop a manufacturer from denying that his product embodies the patent for purposes of liability for both patent infringement damages and patent license royalties." *Boyd v. Schildkraut Giftware Corp.*, 936 F.2d 76, 79 (2d Cir.1991) (citations omitted). The Federal Circuit has yet to discuss this equitable doctrine in a published opinion. At least one district court has declared that the doctrine is no longer extant, but on appeal the Federal Circuit expressly declined to address this holding one way or the other. *High Frequency Products, Inc. v. Wynn's Climate Systems, Inc.*, 91 F.3d 167 (Fed.Cir.1996) (nonprecedential).

3. Patents with both product and process claims. The Federal Circuit stated the rule in *Devices for Medicine* again in *American Medical Sys., Inc. v. Medical Eng'g Corp.*, 6 F.3d 1523 (Fed.Cir.1993):

> The purpose behind the marking statute is to encourage the patentee to give notice to the public of the patent. The reason that the marking statute does not apply to method claims is that, ordinarily, where the patent claims are directed to only a method or process there is nothing to mark. Where the patent contains both apparatus and method claims, however, to the extent that there is a tangible item to mark by which notice of the asserted method claims can be given, a party is obliged to do so if it intends to avail itself of the constructive notice provisions of section 287(a).

6 F.3d at 1538–39. Does this statement square with the holding in *Hanson v. Alpine Valley Ski Area, Inc.*, 718 F.2d 1075 (Fed.Cir.1983)? In *Hanson*, the patent covered a method and apparatus for making artificial snow. The infringer, Alpine, sought to avoid damages because Hanson's licensee had not marked the patented snow-making machines. The Federal Circuit did not apply § 287:

> Alpine states that the Hanson patent also includes apparatus claims. The only claims that were found infringed in this case, however, were claims 1, 2, and 6 of the Hanson patent, which are drawn to "[t]he method of forming, distributing and depositing snow upon a surface . . . ." It is

"settled in the case law that the notice requirement of this statute does not apply where the patent is directed to a process or method."

718 F.2d at 1083. Similarly, in *Crystal Semiconductor Corp. v. TriTech Microelec. Int'l, Inc.*, 246 F.3d 1336 (Fed.Cir.2001), the Federal Circuit sustained damages on an unmarked process when the patentee could have marked an apparatus that operated the process. How can you reconcile *Hanson/Crystal Semiconductor* and *American Medical Systems*? If you reconcile them on the basis that the patentee in *Hanson* did not assert apparatus claims, only method claims, does this strict pleading rule accurately reflect the reasoning in *American Medical Systems* that concentrates on the need to supply notice whenever a tangible item presents the opportunity? Moreover in *Crystal Semiconductor* the patentee asserted both product and process claims.

4. **Marking Abroad.** The United States occupies a middle ground in its attitude towards the marking of patented articles. Most jurisdictions do not impose a marking requirement. Others appear to provide for marking as an affirmative right afforded by the patent grant, as indicated by Article 15 of the Patent Law of the People's Republic of China:

> The patentee has the right to affix a patent marking and to indicate the number of the patent on the patented product or on the packing of that product.

Still other regimes require marking. As indicated by Article 20 of the Chilean patent statute, failure to mark essentially renders the patent unenforceable:

> To have a right to the protection afforded by the law to industrial property, every product patented in the country must be clearly marked with the number and date of the patent, either on the article itself or its wrapper.

> The only exceptions to be made to this rule are the methods or processes that from their nature cannot possibly comply with it.

> On the expiry of the period of the monopoly the aforesaid marks must be suppressed. . . .

Given such varying requirements, multinational actors must be wary when embodying their patented inventions in different states.

Remedies Exercise

You work as an attorney in Detroit, Michigan. On November 15, 2008, you are contacted by Bob Battel, President of the Battel Toy Company and proprietor of U.S. Patent No. 9,876,543. The '543 patent is directed towards a miniature track and car system. Its embodiment, the Battel "Tot Wheels," is one of the most commercially successful toys in history. You know that Battel successfully enforced the '543 patent against a leading competitor, Angler–Preis Toys Unlimited, in a decision that was recently affirmed by the Federal Circuit. According to a newspaper article, Battel and Angler–Preis then settled the dispute for an undisclosed amount.

"Besides Battel and Angler–Preis," begins Mr. Battel, "there is only one other competitor in the car-and-track market, the Hasbeen Toy Company. Hasbeen sells a product called the 'Matchbook Racer Set.' Hasbeen's 'Matchbook Racer Set' is just like the one produced by Angler–Preis, so I am certain that Hasbeen also infringes the '543 patent. Before we bring suit against Hasbeen, I want to know what kind of remedies we can expect to obtain if we are ultimately successful.

"The '543 patent issued on January 1, 2002," Mr. Battel explains. "We began marketing 'Tot Wheels' the year before, on January 1, 2001. Since January 1, 2001, we have made annual sales of about 200,000 'Tot Wheels' units. We make a profit of about five dollars per unit. Further, we could have sold 'Tot Wheels' for another two dollars per unit, but competition from Hasbeen and Angler–Preis caused us to lower our price. Of course, that additional amount would have been pure profit for us. I understand that Hasbeen has sold approximately 150,000 'Matchbook Racer Sets' per year. I also suspect that they make a profit of about six dollars per unit on their sales.

"Within six months after we started marketing 'Tot Wheels'," Mr. Battel continues, "Hasbeen had came out with its 'Matchbook Racer Sets,' which was a total knock-off of our product. The day after the '543 patent issued, we sent Hasbeen a letter warning it about the patent and our intention to enforce it against the 'Matchbook Racer Set.' Hasbeen replied that it was studying the '543 patent. Later, on May 15, 2002, Hasbeen wrote and stated that it obtained an opinion from a patent attorney from the Washington, D.C. law firm of Beatum & Cheatum. According to this attorney, the '543 patent would have been obvious over a reference that hadn't been before the examiner, the Spielzeug patent.

"Fortunately for us, Angler–Preis also raised that defense," Mr. Battel concludes with glee. "But the Federal Circuit just said that the Spielzeug patent comprised nonanalogous art! We're really ready to sock it to Hasbeen. However, we decided to take on Angler–Preis first, and wrote Hasbeen a letter on June 1, 2002, saying that we would sue them once we were done with Angler–Preis. Hasbeen never altered its 'Matchbook Racer Set' despite our correspondence."

"I should also tell you that in addition to selling the basic 'Tot Wheels' set, which comes with a track and two cars," Mr. Battel notes, "we sell sets of additional cars, four to a pack. These sets come in different styles, like Formula One racers or funny cars, and are extremely popular. Our cars are especially designed to fit in the grooves of the 'Tot Wheels' track, although one can also just roll them along any surface. We sell about 100,000 sets of these additional cars each year, and guess that 80% of them are used in conjunction with the 'Tot Wheels' unit. We make a profit of two dollars per set on the additional cars. Hasbeen also maintains annual sales of about 25,000 additional sets of cars. None of our 'Tot Wheels' cars works with Hasbeen's 'Matchbook Racer Set', or vice versa."

You ask Mr. Battel about his manufacturing capabilities. "Well, our plant is currently capable of making about 300,000 'Tot Wheels' a year," Mr. Battel replies. "However, had our competitors respected our patent from the beginning, then we could have assuredly scaled up production to at least 500,000 units annually as early as 2005. We can easily make as many additional cars as you like-perhaps as many as five million a year."

Next, you inquire as to Battel's licensing policies. "Nobody ever approached us about licensing the '543 patent," Mr. Battel explains, "but we have licensed other patents in the toy industry. Our going rate varies from 10–15% of profits. You see, the toy industry is a real gold mine?profits here average around 20% of the sales price or so."

"We make nearly 70% of our annual sales during the holiday shopping season; that is, between Thanksgiving and December 31st," Mr. Battel notes in conclusion. "I realize that I have given you short notice, but do we have any options to protect our most profitable sales period? We want to stay on track for our shareholders this year, and not get beaten down the stretch by Hasbeen!"

What advice would you give to Mr. Battel regarding possible remedies against Hasbeen?

CHAPTER FOURTEEN

THE HATCH–WAXMAN ACT

■ ■ ■

Nowhere is the social impact of intellectual property more keenly felt than in the discipline of pharmaceutical patents. When we confront both glaring inequities in the global health care system, and the list of loathsome diseases for which no treatment is available at any price, the patent system appropriately stands at the center of the discussion. For the pharmaceutical industry may be the sole market segment where traditional accounts of the patent system hold true. Pharmaceutical patents almost invariably support a single supplier for the innovative drug company for the full length of their term. And for many drugs, the very day relevant patents expire is the moment generic competition begins. This commonplace reality provides strong testimony to the significance of patents to the drug industry.

Yet nowhere in the world, it seems, are pharmaceuticals subject to a garden variety patent law. Jurisdictions have modified the everyday patent law regime in different ways when it comes to drugs. Many countries include detailed statutes allowing compulsory licenses that, although generally worded, are effectively specific to pharmaceuticals. *See* Brittany Whobrey, *International Patent Law and Public Health: Analyzing TRIPS' Effect on Access to Pharmaceutical in Developing Countries*, 45 BRANDEIS L.J. 623 (2007). Other patent statutes enumerate provisions establishing precise standards of inventive step that will govern the granting of pharmaceutical patents. *See* Janice M. Mueller, *Taking TRIPS to India–Novartis, Patent Law, and Access to Medicines*, 365 NEW ENG. J. MED. no. 6 at 541 (Feb. 8, 2007). Still others supplement patent rights with new forms of intellectual property, data protection and marketing exclusivities, that effectively time the commencement of patent litigation. *See* Rebecca S. Eisenberg, *The Role of the FDA in Innovation Policy*, 13 MICH. TELECOMM. & TECH. L. REV. 345, 359–64 (2007).

In the United States, this level of specificity has perhaps gone the furthest of any patent-granting state. Immediately following the 1984 Federal Circuit opinion in *Roche Products, Inc. v. Bolar Pharmaceutical Co., Inc.*, 733 F.2d 858 (Fed. Cir. 1984), Congress responded by enacting the Drug Price Competition and Patent Term Restoration Act of 1984, Pub.L. No. 84–417, 98 Stat. 1585 (1984). Popularly known as the Hatch–Waxman Act, this statute features, among other provisions, the grant of quasi-patents to non-innovators, a government-sponsored patent clearinghouse, and a pharmaceutical patent enforcement regime that is both unique and elaborate. Not only did the Hatch–Waxman Act effectively establish a robust generic drug industry in the United States, it deeply impacted pharmaceutical research and development by innovative pharmaceutical firms. Subsequent statutes and regulations, built upon the framework of the Hatch–Waxman Act, have resulted in one of the most complex disciplines in the entirety of legal practice.

This chapter is intended to introduce entry-level patent students to the Hatch–Waxman Act. Section 14.1 explains the so-called "*Bolar* exemption," the statutory safe harbor that shields generic drug companies and other actors from charges of patent infringement in certain circumstances. Section 14.2 then sets forth the dispute resolution regime that the statute applies to patents on pharmaceuticals, medical devices, and other products regulated by the Food and Drug Administration (FDA). In Section 14.3, this chapter goes into greater detail about the FDA publication *Approved Drug Products With Therapeutic Equivalence Evaluations,* more commonly known as the "Orange Book."

The remainder of the chapter considers advanced issues with respect to the Hatch–Waxman regime. Section 14.4 involves the potential ability of innovative firms to opt out of the Hatch–Waxman dispute resolution system, a debate that has involved the concept of declaratory judgment jurisdiction. Finally, in section 14.5, this chapter considers the concept of "authorized generics"—brand-name drugs that are sold under a generic name—and their potential ability to defeat the incentives established by the Hatch–Waxman Act.

If you have not yet read *Roche v. Bolar*, 733 F.2d 858 (Fed. Cir. 1984), presented here in Chapter 12, you should start with that opinion and then return here. And as you continue through the chapter, you may wish to consider whether this lengthy experiment in patent specialization has proved productive. By many measures the Hatch–Waxman Act has been a resounding success: The number of generic prescriptions has increased dramatically since 1984, a period of time in which innovation in pharmaceuticals and medical devices has flourished. Yet these materials remind us that the patent system in general, and this statute in particular, rely upon individual actors to promote both innovation and competition. Within the Hatch–Waxman regime, even elaborately worded legislation has not always aligned private incentives with public goals. Ever-changing innovation environments and public health needs may suggest either future refinements to this legislation, or perhaps a fundamental revisiting of what is arguably the most important intellectual property right of them all, the pharmaceutical patent.

§ 14.1 THE *BOLAR* EXEMPTION

Recall that in *Roche v. Bolar*, the Federal Circuit held that generic drug companies could not rely upon the "experimental use" exception to patent infringement during their development of their own versions of patented drugs. This ruling, in combination with the requirement of marketing approval for new drugs under the Federal Food, Drug and Cosmetic Act, was broadly perceived as leading to two distortions of the statutory patent term. First, the patent term clock would run whether or not the FDA had approved the claimed pharmaceutical for marketing. As a result, the period of time that the proprietor of a patent claiming a regulated drug actually could enjoy exclusive rights could be quite significantly reduced. In effect, each day of delay associated with the FDA approval process amounted to a lost day of patent term.

Second, under *Roche v. Bolar*, generic competitors that commenced activities necessary for regulatory approval before a patent had expired could be enjoined as patent infringers. This possibility was seen as a *de facto* period of market exclusivity that the patent proprietor enjoyed beyond the statutory patent term.

Although brand-name and generic drug firms had engaged in congressionally-sponsored negotiations prior to the issuance of *Roche v. Bolar*, the Federal Circuit's holding hastened the pace of discussion. The outcome of these negotiations was the Drug Price Competition and Patent Term Restoration Act of 1984. Pub. L. No. 84–417, 98 Stat. 1585 (1984). Signed into law on September 24, 1984, that law has come to be known as the Hatch–Waxman Act. The new law was subsequently codified in Titles 15, 21, 28 and 35 of the United States Code.

Although the Hatch–Waxman Act is a complex statute, observers have frequently noted that it presents a fundamental trade-off. Generic firms obtained a narrow reversal of *Roche v. Bolar* in the form of 35 U.S.C. § 271(e)(1), a statute that set out a "safe harbor" for certain experimental activities conducted with an eye towards FDA approval. In exchange, brand-name firms received a period of patent term extension that as set forth in 35 U.S.C. § 156. The Supreme Court's *Merck v. Integra* case, set forth below, provides a definitive view of the former provision, while the notes following the opinion describe the patent term extension regime.

MERCK KGAA v. INTEGRA LIFESCIENCES I, LTD.

United States Supreme Court, 2005
545 U.S. 193

JUSTICE SCALIA delivered the opinion of the Court.

This case presents the question whether uses of patented inventions in preclinical research, the results of which are not ultimately included in a submission to the Food and Drug Administration (FDA), are exempted from infringement by 35 U.S.C. § 271(e)(1).

I

It is generally an act of patent infringement to "mak[e], us[e], offe[r] to sell, or sel[l] any patented invention . . . during the term of the patent therefor." § 271(a). In 1984, Congress enacted an exemption to this general rule, see Drug Price Competition and Patent Term Restoration Act of 1984, § 202, 98 Stat. 1585, as amended, 35 U.S.C. § 271(e)(1), which provides:

> "It shall not be an act of infringement to make, use, offer to sell, or sell within the United States or import into the United States a patented invention (other than a new animal drug or veterinary biological product (as those terms are used in the Federal Food, Drug, and Cosmetic Act and the Act of March 4, 1913) . . .) solely for uses reasonably related to the development and submission of information under a Federal law which regulates the manufacture, use, or sale of drugs. . . ."

The Federal Food, Drug, and Cosmetic Act (FDCA), ch. 675, 52 Stat. 1040, as amended, 21 U.S.C. § 301 et seq., is "a Federal law which regulates the manufacture, use, or sale of drugs." See § 355(a); *Eli Lilly & Co. v. Medtronic, Inc.*, 496 U.S. 661, 665–666, 674, 110 S.Ct. 2683, 110 L.Ed.2d 605 (1990). Under the FDCA, a drugmaker must submit research data to the FDA at two general stages of new-drug development.[1] First, a drugmaker must gain authorization to conduct clinical trials (tests on humans) by submitting an investigational new drug application (IND). See 21 U.S.C. § 355(i); 21 CFR § 312.1 et seq. (2005).[2] The IND must describe "preclinical tests (including tests on animals) of [the] drug adequate to justify the proposed clinical testing." 21 U.S.C. § 355(i)(1)(A); see 21 CFR §§ 312.23(a)(5) and (a)(8) (specifying necessary information from preclinical tests). Second, to obtain authorization to market a new drug, a drugmaker must submit a new drug application (NDA), containing "full reports of investigations which have been made to show whether or not [the] drug is safe for use and whether [the] drug is effective in use." 21 U.S.C. § 355(b)(1). Pursuant to FDA regulations, the NDA must include all clinical studies, as well as preclinical studies related to a drug's efficacy, toxicity, and pharmacological properties. See 21 CFR §§ 314.50(d)(2) (preclinical studies) and (d)(5) (clinical studies).

II

A

Respondents, Integra Lifesciences I, Ltd., and the Burnham Institute, own five patents related to the tripeptide sequence Arg–Gly–Asp, known in single-letter notation as the "RGD peptide." U.S. Patent Nos.

---

1. Drugmakers that desire to market a generic drug (a drug containing the same active ingredients as a drug already approved for the market) may file an abbreviated new drug application (ANDA) with the FDA. See 21 U.S.C. § 355(j). The sponsor of a generic drug does not have to make an independent showing that the drug is safe and effective, either in preclinical or clinical studies. See § 355(j)(2)(A). It need only show that the drug includes the same active ingredients as, and is bioequivalent to, the drug that it is mimicking. See §§ 355(j)(2)(A)(ii) and (iv); § 355(j)(8)(B).

2. We cite the current versions of federal statutes and regulations. The provisions cited are materially unchanged since the period of petitioner's alleged infringement.

4,988,621, 4,792,525, 5,695,997, 4,879,237, and 4,789,734, Supp.App. SA11–SA19. The RGD peptide promotes cell adhesion by attaching to $<\alpha>V<\beta>3$ integrins, receptors commonly located on the outer surface of certain endothelial cells. 331 F.3d 860, 862–863 (C.A.Fed.2003).

Beginning in 1988, petitioner Merck KGaA provided funding for angiogenesis research conducted by Dr. David Cheresh at the Scripps Research Institute (Scripps). Angiogenesis is the process by which new blood vessels sprout from existing vessels; it plays a critical role in many diseases, including solid tumorcancers, diabetic retinopathy, and rheumatoid arthritis. In the course of his research, Dr. Cheresh discovered that it was possible to inhibit angiogenesis by blocking the $<\alpha>V<\beta>3$ integrins on proliferating endothelial cells. In 1994, Dr. Cheresh succeeded in reversing tumor growth in chicken embryos, first using a monoclonal antibody (LM609) he developed himself and later using a cyclic RGD peptide (EMD 66203) provided by petitioner.[3] Dr. Cheresh's discoveries were announced in leading medical journals and received attention in the general media.

With petitioner's agreement to fund research at Scripps due to expire in July 1995, Dr. Cheresh submitted a detailed proposal for expanded collaboration between Scripps and petitioner on February 1, 1995. The proposal set forth a 3–year timetable in which to develop "integrin antagonists as angiogenesis inhibitors," beginning with *in vitro* and *in vivo* testing of RGD peptides at Scripps in year one and culminating with the submission of an IND to the FDA in year three. Petitioner agreed to the material terms of the proposal on February 20, 1995, and on April 13, 1995, pledged $6 million over three years to fund research at Scripps. Petitioner's April 13 letter specified that Scripps would be responsible for testing RGD peptides produced by petitioner as potential drug candidates but that, once a primary candidate for clinical testing was in "the pipeline," petitioner would perform the toxicology tests necessary for FDA approval to proceed to clinical trials. *See* 21 CFR § 312.23(a)(8)(iii) (2005) (requirement that "nonclinical laboratory study" include a certification that it was performed under good laboratory practices); see also § 58.3(d) (2004) (defining "[n]onclinical laboratory study"). Scripps and petitioner concluded an agreement of continued collaboration in September 1995.

Pursuant to the agreement, Dr. Cheresh directed in vitro and in vivo experiments on RGD peptides provided by petitioner from 1995 to 1998. These experiments focused on EMD 66203 and two closely related derivatives, EMD 85189 and EMD 121974, and were designed to evaluate the suitability of each of the peptides as potential drug candidates. 331 F.3d, at 863. Accordingly, the tests measured the efficacy, specificity, and toxicity of the particular peptides as angiogenesis inhibitors, and evaluated their mechanism of action and pharmacokinetics in

---

3. In the proceedings below, the Court of Appeals held that respondents' patents covered the cyclic RGD peptides developed by petitioner. 331 F.3d 860, 869 (C.A.Fed.2003). Petitioner does not contest that ruling here.

animals. *Ibid.* Based on the test results, Scripps decided in 1997 that EMD 121974 was the most promising candidate for testing in humans. Ibid. Over the same period, Scripps performed similar tests on LM609, a monoclonal antibody developed by Dr. Cheresh.[4] Scripps also conducted more basic research on organic mimetics designed to block $<\lceil>V<\beta>3$ integrins in a manner similar to the RGD peptides, it appears that Scripps used the RGD peptides in these tests as "positive controls" against which to measure the efficacy of the mimetics.

In November 1996, petitioner initiated a formal project to guide one of its RGD peptides through the regulatory approval process in the United States and Europe. *Id.*, at 129a. Petitioner originally directed its efforts at EMD 85189, but switched focus in April 1997 to EMD 121974. Petitioner subsequently discussed EMD 121974 with officials at the FDA. In October 1998, petitioner shared its research on RGD peptides with the National Cancer Institute (NCI), which agreed to sponsor clinical trials. Although the fact was excluded from evidence at trial, the lower court's opinion reflects that NCI filed an IND for EMD 121974 in 1998. 331 F.3d, at 874 (Newman, J., dissenting).

B

On July 18, 1996, respondents filed a patent-infringement suit against petitioner, Scripps, and Dr. Cheresh in the District Court for the Southern District of California. Respondents' complaint alleged that petitioner willfully infringed and induced others to infringe respondents' patents by supplying the RGD peptide to Scripps, and that Dr. Cheresh and Scripps infringed the same patents by using the RGD peptide in experiments related to angiogenesis. Respondents sought damages from petitioner and a declaratory judgment against Dr. Cheresh and Scripps. Id., at 863. Petitioner answered that its actions involving the RGD peptides did not infringe respondents' patents, and that in any event they were protected by the common-law research exemption and 35 U.S.C. § 271(e)(1).

At the conclusion of trial, the District Court held that, with one exception, petitioner's pre–1995 actions related to the RGD peptides were protected by the common-law research exemption, but that a question of fact remained as to whether petitioner's use of the RGD peptides after 1995 fell within the § 271(e)(1) safe harbor. With the consent of the parties, the District Court gave the following instruction regarding the § 271(e)(1) exemption:

> "To prevail on this defense, [petitioner] must prove by a preponderance of the evidence that it would be objectively reason-

---

4. Scripps licensed the patent for the monoclonal antibody to Ixsys, a California biotechnology company. Based on research conducted at Scripps and at Ixsys in consultation with Dr. Cheresh, an IND application for a humanized version of the antibody called Vitaxin was filed with the FDA on December 30, 1996. In addition to toxicology tests, the application included information from Dr. Cheresh's in vitro and in vivo experiments related to the antibody's mechanism of action and efficacy as an inhibitor of angiogenesis. Ixsys began clinical testing of the antibody as an angiogenesis inhibitor in February 1997.

able for a party in [petitioner's] and Scripps' situation to believe that there was a decent prospect that the accused activities would contribute, relatively directly, to the generation of the kinds of information that are likely to be relevant in the processes by which the FDA would decide whether to approve the product in question.

"Each of the accused activities must be evaluated separately to determine whether the exemption applies.

"[Petitioner] does not need to show that the information gathered from a particular activity was actually submitted to the FDA." The jury found that petitioner, Dr. Cheresh, and Scripps infringed respondents' patents and that petitioner had failed to show that its activities were protected by § 271(e)(1). It awarded damages of $15 million.

In response to post-trial motions, the District Court dismissed respondents' suit against Dr. Cheresh and Scripps, but affirmed the jury's damages award as supported by substantial evidence, and denied petitioner's motion for judgment as a matter of law. With respect to the last, the District Court explained that the evidence was sufficient to show that "any connection between the infringing Scripps experiments and FDA review was insufficiently direct to qualify for the [§ 271(e)(1) exemption]."

A divided panel of the Court of Appeals for the Federal Circuit affirmed in part and reversed in part. The panel majority affirmed the denial of judgment as a matter of law to petitioner, on the ground that § 271(e)(1)'s safe harbor did not apply because "the Scripps work sponsored by [petitioner] was not clinical testing to supply information to the FDA, but only general biomedical research to identify new pharmaceutical compounds." 331 F.3d, at 866. It reversed the District Court's refusal to modify the damages award and remanded for further proceedings. Judge Newman dissented on both points. The panel unanimously affirmed the District Court's ruling that respondents' patents covered the cyclic RGD peptides developed by petitioner. We granted certiorari to review the Court of Appeals' construction of § 271(e)(1).

III

As described earlier, 35 U.S.C. § 271(e)(1) provides that "[i]t shall not be an act of infringement to ... use ... or import into the United States a patented invention ... solely for uses reasonably related to the development and submission of information under a Federal law which regulates the ... use ... of drugs." Though the contours of this provision are not exact in every respect, the statutory text makes clear that it provides a wide berth for the use of patented drugs in activities related to the federal regulatory process.

As an initial matter, we think it apparent from the statutory text that § 271(e)(1)'s exemption from infringement extends to all uses of patented inventions that are reasonably related to the development and submission of any information under the FDCA. *Cf. Eli Lilly*, 496 U.S., at 665–669, 110 S.Ct. 2683 (declining to limit § 271(e)(1)'s exemption from infringement to submissions under particular statutory provisions that regulate drugs). This necessarily includes preclinical studies of patented compounds that are appropriate for submission to the FDA in the regulatory process. There is simply no room in the statute for excluding certain information from the exemption on the basis of the phase of research in which it is developed or the particular submission in which it could be included.[6]

Respondents concede the breadth of § 271(e)(1) in this regard, but argue that the only preclinical data of interest to the FDA is that which pertains to the safety of the drug in humans. In respondents' view, preclinical studies related to a drug's efficacy, mechanism of action, pharmacokinetics, and pharmacology are not reasonably included in an IND or an NDA, and are therefore outside the scope of the exemption. We do not understand the FDA's interest in information gathered in preclinical studies to be so constrained. To be sure, its regulations provide that the agency's "primary objectives in reviewing an IND are . . . to assure the safety and rights of subjects," 21 CFR § 312.22(a) (2005), but it does not follow that the FDA is not interested in reviewing information related to other characteristics of a drug. To the contrary, the FDA requires that applicants include in an IND summaries of the pharmacological, toxicological, pharmacokinetic, and biological qualities of the drug in animals. *See* § 312.23(a)(5); U.S. Dept. of Health and Human Services, *Guidance for Industry, Good Clinical Practice: Consolidated Guidance* 45 (Apr.1996) ("The results of all relevant nonclinical pharmacology, toxicology, pharmacokinetic, and investigational product metabolism studies should be provided in summary form. This summary should address the methodology used, the results, and a discussion of the relevance of the findings to the investigated therapeutic and the possible unfavorable and unintended effects in humans"). The primary (and, in some cases, only) way in which a drugmaker may obtain such information is through preclinical in vitro and in vivo studies.

Moreover, the FDA does not evaluate the safety of proposed clinical experiments in a vacuum; rather, as the statute and regulations reflect, it asks whether the proposed clinical trial poses an "unreasonable risk." 21 U.S.C. § 355(i)(3)(B)(i); *see also* 21 CFR § 312.23(a)(8) (2005) (requiring applicants to include pharmacological and toxicological studies that serve as the basis of their conclusion that clinical testing would be "reasonably safe"); § 56.111(a)(2) (2004) (providing that the Institutional Review Boards that oversee clinical trials must consider whether the

---

6. Although the Court of Appeals' opinion suggests in places that § 271(e)(1)'s exemption from infringement is limited to research conducted in clinical trials, *see* 331 F.3d, at 866, we do not understand it to have adopted that position. The Court of Appeals recognized that information included in an IND would come within § 271(e)(1)'s safe harbor. *Ibid.* Because an IND must be filed before clinical trials may begin, such information would necessarily be developed in preclinical studies.

"[r]isks to subjects are reasonable in relation to anticipated benefits"). This assessment involves a comparison of the risks and the benefits associated with the proposed clinical trials. As the Government's brief, filed on behalf of the FDA, explains, the "FDA might allow clinical testing of a drug that posed significant safety concerns if the drug had a sufficiently positive potential to address a serious disease, although the agency would not accept similar risks for a drug that was less likely to succeed or that would treat a less serious medical condition." Brief for United States as Amicus Curiae 10. Accordingly, the FDA directs that an IND must provide sufficient information for the investigator to "make his/her own unbiased risk-benefit assessment of the appropriateness of the proposed trial." Guidance for Industry, *supra*, at 43. Such information necessarily includes preclinical studies of a drug's efficacy in achieving particular results.

Respondents contend that, even accepting that the FDA is interested in preclinical research concerning drug characteristics other than safety, the experiments in question here are necessarily disqualified because they were not conducted in conformity with the FDA's good laboratory practices regulations. This argument fails for at least two reasons. First, the FDA's requirement that preclinical studies be conducted under "good laboratory practices" applies only to experiments on drugs "to determine their safety," 21 CFR § 58.3(d) (2004). *See* § 58.1(a); § 312.23(a)(8)(iii) (2005) (only "nonclinical laboratory study subject to the good laboratory practice regulations under part 58" must certify compliance with good laboratory practice regulations). The good laboratory practice regulations do not apply to preclinical studies of a drug's efficacy, mechanism of action, pharmacology, or pharmacokinetics. Second, FDA regulations do not provide that even safety-related experiments not conducted in compliance with good laboratory practices regulations are not suitable for submission in an IND. Rather, such studies must include "a brief statement of the reason for the noncompliance." *Ibid*.

The Court of Appeals' conclusion that § 271(e)(1) did not protect petitioner's provision of the patented RGD peptides for research at Scripps appeared to rest on two somewhat related propositions. First, the court credited the fact that the "Scripps–Merck experiments did not supply information for submission to the [FDA], but instead identified the best drug candidate to subject to future clinical testing under the FDA processes." 331 F.3d, at 865; *see also id.*, at 866 (similar). The court explained:

> "The FDA has no interest in the hunt for drugs that may or may not later undergo clinical testing for FDA approval. For instance, the FDA does not require information about drugs other than the compound featured in an [IND] application. Thus, the Scripps work sponsored by [petitioner] was not 'solely for uses reasonably related' to clinical testing for FDA." *Ibid*.

Second, the court concluded that the exemption "does not globally embrace all experimental activity that at some point, however attenuated, may lead to an FDA approval process." *Id.,* at 867.[7]

We do not quibble with the latter statement. Basic scientific research on a particular compound, performed without the intent to develop a particular drug or a reasonable belief that the compound will cause the sort of physiological effect the researcher intends to induce, is surely not "reasonably related to the development and submission of information" to the FDA. It does not follow from this, however, that § 271(e)(1)'s exemption from infringement categorically excludes either (1) experimentation on drugs that are not ultimately the subject of an FDA submission or (2) use of patented compounds in experiments that are not ultimately submitted to the FDA. Under certain conditions, we think the exemption is sufficiently broad to protect the use of patented compounds in both situations.

As to the first proposition, it disregards the reality that, even at late stages in the development of a new drug, scientific testing is a process of trial and error. In the vast majority of cases, neither the drugmaker nor its scientists have any way of knowing whether an initially promising candidate will prove successful over a battery of experiments. That is the reason they conduct the experiments. Thus, to construe § 271(e)(1), as the Court of Appeals did, not to protect research conducted on patented compounds for which an IND is not ultimately filed is effectively to limit assurance of exemption to the activities necessary to seek approval of a generic drug: One can know at the outset that a particular compound will be the subject of an eventual application to the FDA only if the active ingredient in the drug being tested is identical to that in a drug that has already been approved.

The statutory text does not require such a result. Congress did not limit § 271(e)(1)'s safe harbor to the development of information for inclusion in a submission to the FDA; nor did it create an exemption applicable only to the research relevant to filing an ANDA for approval of a generic drug. Rather, it exempted from infringement all uses of patented compounds "reasonably related" to the process of developing information for submission under any federal law regulating the manufacture, use, or distribution of drugs. *See Eli Lilly,* 496 U.S., at 674, 110 S.Ct. 2683. We decline to read the "reasonable relation" requirement so narrowly as to render § 271(e)(1)'s stated protection of activities leading to FDA approval for all drugs illusory. Properly construed, § 271(e)(1) leaves adequate space for experimentation and failure on the road to regulatory approval: At least where a drugmaker has a reasonable basis

---

7. The Court of Appeals also suggested that a limited construction of § 271(e)(1) is necessary to avoid depriving so-called "research tools" of the complete value of their patents. Respondents have never argued the RGD peptides were used at Scripps as research tools, and it is apparent from the record that they were not. *See* 331 F.3d, at 878 (Newman, J., dissenting) ("Use of an existing tool in one's research is quite different from study of the tool itself"). We therefore need not—and do not—express a view about whether, or to what extent, § 271(e)(1) exempts from infringement the use of "research tools" in the development of information for the regulatory process.

for believing that a patented compound may work, through a particular biological process, to produce a particular physiological effect, and uses the compound in research that, if successful, would be appropriate to include in a submission to the FDA, that use is "reasonably related" to the "development and submission of information under ... Federal law." § 271(e)(1).

For similar reasons, the use of a patented compound in experiments that are not themselves included in a "submission of information" to the FDA does not, standing alone, render the use infringing. The relationship of the use of a patented compound in a particular experiment to the "development and submission of information" to the FDA does not become more attenuated (or less reasonable) simply because the data from that experiment are left out of the submission that is ultimately passed along to the FDA. Moreover, many of the uncertainties that exist with respect to the selection of a specific drug exist as well with respect to the decision of what research to include in an IND or NDA. As a District Court has observed, "[I]t will not always be clear to parties setting out to seek FDA approval for their new product exactly which kinds of information, and in what quantities, it will take to win that agency's approval." *Intermedics, Inc. v. Ventritex, Inc.*, 775 F.Supp. 1269, 1280 (N.D.Cal.1991), *aff'd*, 991 F.2d 808 (C.A.Fed.1993). This is especially true at the preclinical stage of drug approval. FDA regulations provide only that "[t]he amount of information on a particular drug that must be submitted in an IND ... depends upon such factors as the novelty of the drug, the extent to which it has been studied previously, the known or suspected risks, and the developmental phase of the drug." 21 CFR § 312.22(b). We thus agree with the Government that the use of patented compounds in preclinical studies is protected under § 271(e)(1) as long as there is a reasonable basis for believing that the experiments will produce "the types of information that are relevant to an IND or NDA." Brief for United States as Amicus Curiae 23 (emphasis deleted).

* * *

Before the Court of Appeals, petitioner challenged the sufficiency of the evidence supporting the jury's finding that it failed to show that "all of the accused activities are covered by [§ 271(e)(1)]." That court rejected the challenge on the basis of a construction of § 271(c)(1) that was not consistent with the text of that provision or the relevant jury instruction.[8] Thus, the evidence presented at trial has yet to be reviewed under the standards set forth in the jury instruction, which we believe to be consistent with, if less detailed than, the construction of § 271(e)(1)

---

8. The relevant jury instruction provided only that there must be a "decent prospect that the accused activities would contribute, relatively directly, to the generation of the kinds of information that are likely to be relevant in the processes by which the FDA would decide whether to approve the product in question." It did not say that, to fall within § 271(e)(1)'s exemption from infringement, the patented compound used in experimentation must be the subject of an eventual application to the FDA. And it expressly rejected the notion that the exemption only included experiments that produced information included in an IND or NDA.

that we adopt today. We decline to undertake a review of the sufficiency of the evidence under a proper construction of § 271(e)(1) for the first time here. Accordingly, we vacate the judgment of the Court of Appeals and remand the case for proceedings consistent with this opinion.

NOTE

1. **On Remand.** The saga of *Merck v. Integra* appeared to come to a close in 2007 with the return of that litigation to the Federal Circuit. 496 F.3d 1134 (Fed. Cir. 2007). On remand, the Court of Appeals crisply summarized the Supreme Court's interpretation of the 35 U.S.C. § 271(e)(1) safe harbor as encompassing "uses in research that are conducted after the biological mechanism and physiological effect of a candidate drug have been recognized, such that if the research is successful it would appropriately be included in a submission to the FDA." *Id.* at 1339. Applying this standard, the Federal Circuit concluded that each of Merck's uses of Integra's patented RGD peptides was exempted under 35 U.S.C. § 271(e)(1).

In particular, the Merck experiments that Integra had asserted were infringements that fell into 16 categories:

- $\alpha_v\beta_3$ receptor binding assay (efficacy);

- angiogenesis chick chorioallantoic membrane (CAM) assay (efficacy, mechanism of action, and pharmacokinetics);

- angio-matrigel tests (efficacy and mechanism of action);

- cell adhesion assay (efficacy);

- chemotaxis assay (efficacy and mechanism of action);

- chick embryo pharmacokinetics assay (pharmacokinetics);

- fluorescence-activated cell sorting (FACS) analysis (mechanism of action and efficacy);

- rabbit pharmacokinetics assay (pharmacokinetics);

- tumor growth in severe combined immunodeficiency (SCID) mouse (efficacy, mechanism of action, pharmacology);

- tumor growth nude mouse assay (efficacy, pharmacology, pharmacokinetics, and mechanism of action);

- mice retina vasculo assay (efficacy, mechanism, pharmacology, and pharmacokinetics);

- rabbit cornea assay (pharmacokinetics and efficacy);

- mouse retina IF vasculogenesis assays (pharmacokinetics);

- rabbit arthritis experiments (efficacy, pharmacology, pharmacokinetics, safety, and mechanism of action);

- mice arthritis experiments (efficacy);

- chick CAM tumor growth with melanoma cells (efficacy and mechanism of action).

Id. at 1342–43. As to the first part of the test, the Federal Circuit observed that the evidence of record demonstrated "that all of the experiments here at issue were conducted after it had been discovered that a RGD peptide shrank tumors in an animal model." *Id.* at 1345. The second part of the test was satisfied, Judge Newman reasoned, because "the accused experiments yielded data relating to efficacy, mechanism of action, pharmacology, or pharmacokinetics," information that must be included in an Investigational New Drug Application (IND). *Id.* at 1341 (citing 21 C.F.R. § 312.23(a)(8)(i)). As a result, the experimental use privilege of 35 U.S.C. § 271(e)(1) shielded each of Merck's experiments.

In reaching this conclusion, the Federal Circuit rejected Integra's argument that the experimental use privilege was reserved for experiments that worked a "discovery," as compared to being entirely "routine." The Supreme Court's discussion of 35 U.S.C. § 271(e)(1) did not allow for such a distinction, Judge Newman reasoned, as the Court had "recognized that experiments are run in order to learn information, whatever the stage of the research." *Id.* at 1347.

    2. Research Tools. On remand, Judge Rader issued a dissenting opinion that voiced concern that the majority "cast[] a large shadow over patent protection by its overly expansive interpretation of the 35 U.S.C. § 271(e)(1) exemption. In particular, this court today expands the exemption beyond the Supreme Court's limits on the provision to eliminate protection for research tool inventions." *Id.* at 1348. Judge Rader further explained:

> Sadly this court does not even examine the patents at issue in this case. This court, noted for its emphasis on claims as definers of patent scope, ironically does not recite or analyze the claims of these patents in the slightest. Moreover this court speaks in broad terms about the experiments and results without specifying which patented compound or method was in use in the experiments. A careful examination of the patents shows that two of them have no application at all outside of a laboratory. If the patents in this case are not research tools, then of course this court could quickly construe the claims and show that they claim drugs or other products likely to undergo FDA clearance, not simply laboratory methods. Unfortunately even a cursory analysis of the patents (undertaken in this dissent) shows that two of them have no application outside the laboratory.

Id. at 1348–49. Judge Rader's dissent ensures that the "research tools" issue remains a live one with respect to the Hatch–Waxman Act, however. Argument in future cases involving the 35 U.S.C. § 271(e)(1) experimental use privilege may well center upon whether a patent claims a "research tool" or not.

    3. Research Tools—the sequel. In *Proveris Scientific Corp. v. Innovasystems, Inc.*, 536 F.3d 1256 (Fed. Cir. 2008), the Federal Circuit considered a patent on a system and apparatus for ensuring that aerosol sprays (often nasal spray pumps and inhalers) deliver a calibrated dose to a patient. Of course, the device is used to measure aerosol sprays in FDA regulatory submissions. Innova claimed that its unauthorized sale of the patented measuring device fell within the 35 U.S.C. § 271(e)(1) exemption. In upholding the trial court's judgment that Innova's conduct did not fall within the safe harbor, the Federal Circuit noted:

> Innova's OSA device is not subject to FDA pre-market approval. Rather, FDA pre-market approval is required only in the case of the aerosol drug delivery product whose spray plume characteristics the OSA measures. In short, Innova is not a party seeking FDA approval for a product in order to enter the market to compete with patentees. Because the OSA device is not subject to FDA pre-market approval, and therefore faces no regulatory barriers to market entry upon patent expiration, Innova is not a party who, prior to enactment of the Hatch–Waxman Act, could be said to have been adversely affected. . . . . For this reason, we do not think Congress could have intended that the safe harbor of section 271(e)(1) apply to it.

§ 14.2   ANDA LITIGATION

With the enactment of section 271(e)(1) of the Patent Act, generic drug companies and other actors were granted a statutory safe harbor from acts of patent infringement under specified circumstances. This provision leads one to wonder: When exactly does the patent system come into play? That question is answered by section 271(e)(2), a provision that has come to represent an increasing percentage of the Federal Circuit's workload. These appeals involve cases where no marketed product has been accused of infringement. What is at stake is instead a proposed product described in an FDA filing called an "Abbreviated New Drug Application," or ANDA. The following opinion lays out the Hatch–Waxman Act's patent dispute resolution framework and, as described by the Supreme Court, the "somewhat artificial" form of infringement that it causes to occur. *Eli Lilly & Co. v. Medtronic, Inc.*, 496 U.S. 661, 676 (1990).

MYLAN PHARMACEUTICALS, INC. v. THOMPSON
United States Court of Appeals for the Federal Circuit, 2001
268 F.3d 1323

Before Mayer, Chief Judge, Newman and Michel, Circuit Judges.

MAYER, CHIEF JUDGE.

Under the Federal Food, Drug, and Cosmetic Act ("FFDCA"), a pharmaceutical company seeking to manufacture a new drug is required to file a New Drug Application ("NDA") for consideration by the FDA. 21 U.S.C. § 355(a) (1994). Preparing an NDA is frequently a time-intensive and costly process, because among other things, it must contain detailed clinical studies of the drug's safety and efficacy. *See id.* § 355(b)(1) (Supp. V 1999). The NDA must also include a list of patents which claim the drug:

> The applicant shall file with the application the patent number and the expiration date of any patent which claims the drug for which the applicant submitted the application or which claims a method of

using such drug and with respect to which a claim of patent infringement could reasonably be asserted if a person not licensed by the owner engaged in the manufacture, use, or sale of the drug.... Upon approval of the application, the Secretary shall publish information submitted under [this section].

Id.

If the FDA approves the NDA, it publishes a listing of the drug and patents on the drug's approved aspects in *Approved Drug Products with Therapeutic Equivalence Evaluations,* otherwise known as the "Orange Book." *Id.* § 355(j)(7)(A)(iii) (1994); *id.* § 355(b)(1); *see also* 21 C.F.R. § 314.53(c)(2) (2001). Because an applicant may not receive original approval for all aspects of the drug as described in the original NDA submission, once the NDA is approved, the applicant must amend the patent submission to list only the patents that meet the listing criteria for the approved drug product. 21 C.F.R. § 314.53(c)(2)(ii) (2001).

Under the Drug Price Competition and Patent Term Restoration Act of 1984, Pub.L. No. 98–417, 98 Stat. 1585 (1984), *codified at* 21 U.S.C. §§ 355, 360cc, and 35 U.S.C. §§ 156, 271, 282 (the "Hatch–Waxman Amendments" to the FFDCA and to Title 35 of the U.S. Code relating to patents), a pharmaceutical manufacturer seeking approval to market a generic version of a previously approved drug may submit an abbreviated new drug application ("ANDA") to the FDA. 21 U.S.C. § 355(j) (1994). An ANDA offers an expedited approval process for generic drug manufacturers. Instead of filing a full NDA with new safety and efficacy studies, in an ANDA a generic manufacturer may rely in part on the pioneer manufacturer's work by submitting data demonstrating the generic product's bioequivalence with the previously approved drug. *See id.* § 355(j)(2)(A) (Supp. V 1999). These provisions of the Hatch–Waxman Amendments "emerged from Congress' efforts to balance two conflicting policy objectives: to induce name brand pharmaceutical firms to make the investments necessary to research and develop new drug products, while simultaneously enabling competitors to bring cheaper, generic copies of those drugs to market." *Abbott Labs. v. Young,* 920 F.2d 984, 991 (D.C.Cir.1990) (Edwards, J., dissenting on other grounds). Thus, Title I of the Act was intended to "make available more low cost generic drugs by establishing a generic drug approval procedure for pioneer drugs first approved after 1962." H.R.Rep. No. 98–857, pt. 1 at 14 (1984), *reprinted in* 1984 U.S.C.C.A.N. 2647, 2647. Title II, on the other side of the scale, was intended to benefit pioneer drug manufacturers by "restor[ing] ... some of the time lost on patent life while the product is awaiting pre-market approval." H.R.Rep. No. 98–857, pt. 1 at 15, 1984 U.S.C.C.A.N. at 2648.

The Hatch–Waxman provisions concerning patent infringement are part of this balance. Under 35 U.S.C. § 271(e)(1), it is not infringement to conduct otherwise infringing acts necessary to prepare an ANDA. 35 U.S.C. § 271(e)(1) (Supp. V 1999) ("It shall not be an act of infringement to make, use, offer to sell, or sell ... a patented invention ... solely for uses reasonably related to the development and submission of information under a Federal law which regulates the manufacture, use, or sale of drugs."). Under section 271(e)(2), however, a generic drug manufacturer infringes by filing an ANDA to obtain FDA approval for the purpose of marketing a generic drug product claimed in a patent before the patent expires. 35 U.S.C. § 271(e)(2) (1994) ("It shall be an act of infringement to submit ... [an ANDA] ... if the purpose of such submission is to obtain [FDA] approval ... to engage in the *commercial* manufacture, use, or sale of a drug ... claimed in a patent before the expiration of such patent.") (emphasis added). Despite this provision, not all ANDA applicants can be sued immediately for infringement; moreover, they cannot sue immediately for declaratory judgment with respect to the patent, as further discussed below.

As part of the ANDA process, an applicant seeking to market a generic version of a listed drug must make a certification as to each patent listed in the Orange Book which "claims the listed drug ... or which claims a use for such listed drug for which the applicant is seeking approval." 21 U.S.C. § 355(j)(2)(A)(vii) (1994).

[T]he applicant must certify either that: (I) no such patent information has been submitted to the FDA; (II) the patent has expired; (III) the patent is set to expire on a certain date; or (IV) such patent is invalid or will not be infringed by the manufacture, use, or sale of the new generic drug for which the ANDA is submitted. 21 U.S.C. § 355(j)(2)(A)(vii)(I–IV) (1994). These are commonly referred to as Paragraph I, II, III, and IV certifications. Further, if one of the listed patents is a method-of-use patent which does not claim a use for which the applicant is seeking approval, the applicant must make a statement to that effect (a "Section viii Statement"). *Id.* § 355(j)(2)(A)(viii).

An ANDA containing a Paragraph I or II certification may be approved without additional delay. *See* 21 U.S.C. § 355(j)(5)(B)(i) (Supp. V 1999). An ANDA containing a Paragraph III certification indicates that the applicant does not intend to market the drug until after the expiration of the patent, and the approval of the ANDA cannot be made final until the patent expires. *Id.* § 355(j)(5)(B)(ii).

When an ANDA contains a Paragraph IV certification, the ANDA applicant must give notice to the patentee and must provide detailed bases for its belief that the patent is invalid, unenforceable, or not infringed. *Id.* § 355(j)(2)(B)(i); 21 C.F.R. § 314.95(c)(6) (2001). The patentee is then given forty-five days to sue the ANDA applicant for infringement. 21 U.S.C. § 355(j)(5)(B)(iii) (Supp. V 1999). If the patentee does not file suit, the application may be approved. If the patentee files suit within that period, the FDA may not approve the ANDA until the expiration of the patent, judicial resolution of the infringement suit, a judicial determination that the patent is invalid or unenforceable, or thirty months from the patentee's receipt of notice, whichever is earliest.

Id.; 21 C.F.R. § 314.107(b)(1)(iv) (2001). The court in which the suit is pending may order a shorter or longer stay on the approval time if "either party to the action fail[s] to reasonably cooperate in expediting the action." 21 U.S.C. § 355(j)(5)(B)(iii) (Supp. V 1999). Moreover, the availability of declaratory judgment actions is limited: "Until the expiration of forty-five days from the date the notice made under paragraph (2)(B)(i) is received, no action may be brought under section 2201 of Title 28, for a declaratory judgment with respect to the patent." *Id.* These provisions give the pioneer manufacturer the first opportunity to file suit against the ANDA applicant for infringement, and may substantially delay the ANDA approval during the pendency of the litigation.

NOTES

1. New Chemical Entity Exclusivity. In addition to the essential patent dispute resolution system described by Judge Mayer in *Mylan v. Thompson*, a few additional points should be appreciated. The Hatch–Waxman Act also established new forms of intellectual property rights that are collectively termed "marketing exclusivities" or, sometimes, "data protection." The FDA administers these provisions by issuing approval to sell a pharmaceutical to only a single entity. As a result, generic drug companies may not be able to file an ANDA, or have it approved by the FDA, immediately upon approval of the innovator's NDA. Rather, they must wait a period of time.

In brief, the length and scope of a marketing exclusivity is contingent on whether or not the drug is considered a "new chemical entity" (NCE). The Hatch–Waxman Act defines an NCE drug as an approved drug that consists of active ingredients, including the ester or salt of an active ingredient, none of which has been approved in any other full NDA. 21 U.S.C. § 355(j)(4)(D)(i), (ii) (2006). If the approved drug is not an NCE, then the FDA may not approve an ANDA for a generic version of the approved drug until three years after the approval date of the pioneer NDA. 21 U.S.C. § 355(j)(4)(D)(iii) (2006). In contrast, if the approved drug is an NCE, then a would-be generic manufacturer cannot submit an ANDA until five years after the date of the approval of the pioneer NDA. The effect of this provision is to restrict a potential generic manufacturer from bringing a product to market for five years plus the length of the FDA review of the ANDA 21 U.S.C. § 355(c)(3)(d)(ii) (2006).

The Hatch–Waxman calls for a diminution of the term of the NCE exclusivity in one circumstance. The NCE exclusivity is reduced to four years if the ANDA application includes a paragraph IV certification. 21 U.S.C. § 355(j)(5)(F)(ii) (2006). In the event that a paragraph IV ANDA application is filed in the one-year period commencing on the fourth year following the approval of the NDA, the Hatch–Waxman Act requires the thirty-month stay to be "extended by such amount of time (if any) which is required for seven and one-half years to have elapsed from the date of approval" of the NDA. 21 U.S.C. § 355(j)(5)(F)(ii) (2006). Stated differently, the thirty-month stay may actually extend for up to 42 months in the event that a paragraph IV generic application is filed as soon as the Hatch–Waxman Act allows.

2. New Clinical Study Exclusivity. If a drug does not quality as an NCE, it may instead be awarded a three-year new clinical study exclusivity period. NCS exclusivity may be awarded with respect to either an NDA that contains reports of new clinical studies conducted by the sponsor that are essential to FDA approval of that application. 21 U.S.C. § 355(j)(5)(F)(iii) (2006). The FDA has granted NCS exclusivity for such changes as new dosage forms, new indications, or for a switch from prescription to over-the-counter status for the drug.

The most important requirement to obtain NCS exclusivity is that the study must be "essential to the approval" of the application or supplement. The FDA has defined the term "essential to approval" as meaning "that there are no other data available that could support approval of the application." *See* 21 C.F.R. § 314.108(a) (2008). A study that is interesting and provides useful background information, but not essential to approving the change in the drug, does not provide sufficient basis for an FDA award of new clinical study exclusivity. *See Upjohn Co. v. Kessler*, 938 F.Supp. 439 (W.D. Mich. 1996).

New clinical study exclusivity only applies to the use of the product that was supported by the new clinical study. If, for example, the new studies support a new indication or dosage form of the previously approved ingredient, then the three-year exclusivity applies only to that particular use or dosage form. The FDA is not barred from approving a generic drugs for other indications or dosage forms. Because three-year exclusivities are more easily avoided than five-year NCE exclusivities, they are also generally of less value in the marketplace.

A drug product may be subject both to NCE exclusivity and new clinical study exclusivity during the life of that product. Commonly, a new drug will initially enjoy a five-year NCE exclusivity. Later in the life of that product, the sponsor of the drug may perform additional clinical trials to qualify the drug for additional three-year exclusivities.

3. Generic Exclusivity. The Hatch–Waxman Act also established a marketing exclusivity that operates in favor of generic firms. Prospective manufacturers of generic pharmaceuticals are afforded an exclusivity in the event they challenge a patent associated with an approved pharmaceutical. The reward consists of a 180–day generic drug exclusivity period awarded to the first ANDA applicant that challenges the validity or scope of a patent. During this 180–day period, the FDA may not approve of another patent-challenging ANDA with respect to the same drug. 21 U.S.C. § 355(j)(5)(B)(iv) (2004).

Congress established this proprietary right in order to ameliorate collective action problems that may arise with regard to pharmaceutical patent challenges. A generic firm that challenges a patent must bear the expensive, up-front cost of litigation. If the generic firm is successful, however, the challenged patent is declared invalid with regard to all the world. Any firm—not just the one who challenged the patent—could then introduce a competing product to the marketplace. Understandably, this forced sharing may undermine the incentives any one generic firm would possess to challenge a brand-name firm's patent. The award of 180 days of generic exclusivity is therefore intended to allow a successful patent challenger to capture an individual benefit for its effort, in turn encouraging such challenges in the first instance. In essence, this provision uses litigation as a public policy tool to encourage challenges to patent validity. Is a period of exclusivity necessary to encourage challenges to weak patents?

4. **Pediatric Exclusivity.** Congress established the final marketing exclusivity in 1997 in order to promote the availability of medicines for children. Food and Drug Administration Modernization Act of 1997, Pub. L. No. 105–115, 111 Stat. 2296, at § 11 (1997) (codified at 21 U.S.C. § 355a). This exclusivity reflects concerns that many marketed drugs had not yet been clinically tested upon children. Investigations upon a pediatric population raise complex issues of informed consent and the inability of children to describe the effect of a medication accurately. As a result, most drugs are tested solely upon adults. By establishing a pediatric marketing exclusivity, Congress hoped to encourage additional pediatric testing, which in turn could allow medications to be labeled for use by children. Under this system, the FDA issues written requests to NDA applicants and holders to perform pediatric studies with respect to the drug. Response to this written request is wholly voluntary. If the innovative drug company submits a report to the satisfaction of the FDA, however, then it will be awarded the six-month pediatric marketing exclusivity that is added to the term of any existing patent or marketing exclusivity associated with the drug.

5. **Section 505(b) Applications.** Besides the ANDA, the Hatch–Waxman Act also authorizes another sort of application that generic firms may file with the FDA. A § 505 (b)(2) application is one for which one or more of the investigations relied upon by the applicant for approval "were not conducted by or for the applicant and for which the applicant has not obtained a right of reference or use from the person by or for whom the investigations were conducted. . . ." The name of this application refers to its section number in the Hatch–Waxman Act itself. This provision has been codified at 21 U.S.C. § 355(b)(2), where it may be more conveniently located.

A § 505(b)(2) application differs from an ANDA in that it includes full reports of investigations of the safety and effectiveness of the proposed product. However, a § 505(b)(2) application is distinct from an NDA in that the § 505(b)(2) application relies upon data that the applicant did not develop itself—for example, data published in the scientific literature. If the applicant obtains rights to refer to the data underlying that study, it may file a full NDA rather than a § 505(b)(2) application. U.S. Department of Health and Human Services, Food and Drug Administration, Center for Drug Evaluation and Research (CDER), *Guidance for Industry: Applications Covered by Section 505(b)(2)* at 2–3 (Oct. 1999).

An important ramification of filing a § 505(b)(2) application, as compared to an NDA under § 505(b)(1) of the Hatch–Waxman Act, is that a § 505(b)(2) application may be delayed due to patent or exclusivity provisions covering an approved product. Unlike an NDA, a § 505(b)(2) application must include patent certifications, and the § 505(b)(2) applicant must provide notice of these certifications to the NDA holder and the patent proprietor.

6.   Patent Term Extension. Although the generic drug industry achieved many gains from the Hatch–Waxman Act, innovative pharmaceutical firms also obtained a significant benefit: Patent term extension intended to compensate for some of the delays associated with FDA regulatory approval. Codified at 35 U.S.C. § 156, the patent term extension provision of the Hatch–Waxman Act stands among the most unwieldy statutes in the federal code. In a nutshell, a patent proprietor who wishes to obtain the term extension offered by the Hatch–Waxman Act must submit an application to the PTO. 35 U.S.C. § 156(d)(1) (2006). That application must be filed prior to the expiration of that patent, 35 U.S.C. § 156(a)(1) (2006), and within sixty days of receiving FDA marketing approval. 35 U.S.C. § 156(d)(1) (2006). Only one patent can be extended based upon an approval for commercial marketing use. In the event multiple patents cover that product, the proprietor must select one. 35 U.S.C. § 156(c)(4) (2006).The period of extension is set to one-half of the testing phase (IND to NDA filing), less any period during which the applicant did not act with due diligence, plus the entirety of the FDA review period. However, the maximum extension period is capped at a five-year extension period, or a total effective patent term after the extension of not more than fourteen years. 35 U.S.C. § 156(b) (2006). The scope of rights during the period of extension is generally limited to the use approved for the product that subjected it to regulatory delay. 35 U.S.C. § 156(b)(1) (2006).

§ 14.3   THE ORANGE BOOK

The FDA publishes a list of all drugs approved for marketing in the United States under the title *Approved Drug Products with Therapeutic Equivalence Evaluations*. The FDA today maintains this list in electronic format, where it can be readily accessed via the Internet. *See* U.S. Department of Health and Human Services, Food and Drug Administration, Electronic Orange Book, Center for Drug Evaluation and Research, *Approved Drug Products with Therapeutic Evaluations* (available at http://www.fda.gov/cder/ob/). Because its print version featured an orange cover, however, this list is universally known as the "Orange Book."

Among pharmacists, the Orange Book is perhaps best known for providing therapeutic equivalence evaluations for multi-source prescription drug products. In this capacity, the Orange Book uses a two-letter coding system. The first letter is set to A if the product is believed to be therapeutically equivalent; otherwise the product receives a B. The second letter relates to the dosage form. The code "AA," for example, indicates that the product contains active ingredients and dosage forms that are not regarded as presenting either actual or potential bioequivalence problems, drug quality concerns, or standards issues.

Under the Hatch–Waxman Act, the Orange Book also plays a significant role in the resolution of pharmaceutical patent disputes. In particular, NDA applicants are required to identify "any patent which claims the drug for which the applicant submitted the application or which claims a method of using such drug and with respect to which a claim of patent infringement could reasonably be asserted." 21 U.S.C. § 355(b)(1) (2006). Although this statutory language has been subject to conflicting interpretations, regulations promulgated by the FDA in 2003 attempted to clarify those patents that are appropriate for listing in the Orange Book. Department of Health and Human Services, Food and Drug Administration, *Applications for FDA Approval to Market a New Drug: Patent Submission and Listing Requirements and Application of 30–Month Stays on Approval of Abbreviated New Drug Applications Certifying That a Patent Claiming a Drug Is Invalid or Will Not Be Infringed*, 65 FED. REG. 36676 (June 18, 2003).

The patent functions of the Orange Book have proven controversial. Persistent questions have arisen over the eligibility of patents that may be listed in the Orange Book, the timing of patent listings, and the availability of a mechanism for resolving disputes over Orange Book listings in the courts. The next opinion describes some of the controversy and the role of the FDA in maintaining the Orange Book.

AAIPHARMA INC. v. THOMPSON

United States Court of Appeals for the Fourth Circuit, 2002
296 F.3d 227

Before Michael, Circuit Judge, Jackson, United States District Judge for the Eastern District of Virginia, sitting by designation, and Friedman, United States District Judge for the Eastern District of Virginia, sitting by designation.

OPINION

MICHAEL, CIRCUIT JUDGE.

The Federal Food, Drug, and Cosmetic Act (FFDCA) requires the manufacturer of a brand name drug approved by the Food and Drug Administration (FDA) to provide the FDA with a listing of all patents that claim the approved drug or a method of using the drug. *See* 21 U.S.C. § 355(b)(1), (c)(2). The FDA publishes these listings in its *Approved Drug Products With Therapeutic Equivalence Evaluations,* a publication commonly known as the Orange Book. The plaintiff, aaiPharma Inc., has sued the FDA, contending that the agency has a duty to ensure the accuracy of Orange Book listings and that the agency's refusal to do so violates the Administrative Procedure Act (APA). The district court rejected aaiPharma's APA challenge, concluding that the FFDCA assigns the FDA a purely ministerial role regarding Orange Book listings. We affirm.

I.

Orange Book listings play an important role in the statutory and regulatory framework created by the Drug Price Competition and

Patent Term Restoration Act of 1984, Pub.L. No. 98–417, 98 Stat. 1585 (codified at 21 U.S.C. §§ 355, 360cc and 35 U.S.C. §§ 156, 271, 282), commonly known as the Hatch–Waxman Act (Hatch–Waxman or the Act). Hatch–Waxman amended both the FFDCA and the patent laws in an effort to strike a balance between "two conflicting policy objectives: to induce name-brand pharmaceutical firms to make the investments necessary to research and develop new drug products, while simultaneously enabling competitors to bring cheaper, generic copies of those drugs to market." *Abbott Labs. v. Young*, 920 F.2d 984, 991 (D.C.Cir.1990) (Edwards, J., dissenting on other grounds).

Prior to Hatch–Waxman's passage in 1984, both pioneer (brand name) and generic drug manufacturers who wished to bring a drug to market were required to file a New Drug Application (NDA) with the FDA. This requirement posed a formidable barrier to market entry for generic drug companies because preparation of an NDA requires expensive clinical studies demonstrating the proposed drug's safety and effectiveness. In addition, a generic manufacturer could not begin the necessary research and clinical studies until any patents on the brand name drug it sought to copy had expired because its research efforts would have infringed the patents held by the pioneer drug company. This meant that a pioneer drug company's monopoly on its brand name drug was effectively extended to include not only the terms of any patents on the brand name drug, but also the time it took generic competitors to complete the NDA process after these patents had expired. Hatch–Waxman addressed these problems by creating a streamlined procedure for FDA approval of generic drugs. A drug company that wishes to market a generic version of a brand name drug may now submit an Abbreviated New Drug Application (ANDA) to the FDA. *See* 21 U.S.C. § 355(j). By filing an ANDA, a generic manufacturer can rely on the clinical studies performed by the pioneer drug manufacturer and is not required to prove the safety and effectiveness of its generic drug from scratch. Instead, the generic manufacturer must prove only that its drug is bioequivalent to the brand name drug it wants to copy. *See id.* § 355(j)(2)(A). In addition, Hatch–Waxman amended the patent laws so that a generic drug manufacturer no longer infringes the patents on a brand name drug by performing acts necessary to prepare an ANDA. *See* 35 U.S.C. § 271(e)(1).

Hatch–Waxman also contains a complex set of provisions designed to protect the intellectual property rights of pioneer drug companies and others holding patents on brand name drugs. The Act requires each drug company filing an NDA to include in its application a list of all the patents that "claim [ ] the drug for which the applicant submitted the application or which claim [ ] a method of using such drug and with respect to which a claim of patent infringement could reasonably be asserted if a person not licensed by the owner engaged in the manufacture, use, or sale of the drug." 21 U.S.C. § 355(b)(1). If the FDA approves the application, the agency is required to publish this list in the

Orange Book.[1] An NDA applicant must also amend its application to include information about any new patents claiming its drug that issue while the NDA is pending. *Id.* In addition, the holder of an approved NDA is required to submit to the FDA for Orange Book listing any new patents that claim the approved drug within thirty days of their issuance. *Id.* § 355(c)(2). With respect to each patent listed in the Orange Book for a pioneer drug, an ANDA applicant seeking to copy that drug must make one of the following four certifications in its initial application for FDA approval: (I) that no patent information for the pioneer drug has been submitted to the FDA (a "paragraph I certification"), (II) that the patent has expired (a "paragraph II certification"), (III) that the patent will expire on a specific date (a "paragraph III certification"), or (IV) that the patent "is invalid or will not be infringed by the manufacture, use, or sale of the new drug" for which the ANDA applicant seeks approval (a "paragraph IV certification"). *Id.* § 355(j)(2)(A)(vii)(I)–(IV). An ANDA applicant must also make an additional certification as to any new patent listed in the Orange Book while its application is pending, so long as the NDA holder submits the new patent to the FDA for listing no more than thirty days after the patent's issuance. 21 C.F.R. § 314.94(a)(12)(vi). The certification made by the ANDA applicant determines the date on which FDA approval of the application can become effective. ANDAs containing paragraph I or II certifications may be approved immediately if the FDA finds that all the relevant scientific and regulatory requirements have been met. 21 U.S.C. § 355(j)(5)(B)(i). An ANDA that contains a paragraph III certification becomes effective on the patent's expiration date, assuming that other FDA requirements have been satisfied. *Id.* § 355(j)(5)(B)(ii). Thus, certifications under paragraphs I, II, and III tell the FDA that it need not worry about the patent law implications of the generic drug because the drug will not enter the market until any relevant patents have expired. In contrast, an ANDA applicant making a paragraph IV certification intends to market its product before the relevant patents have expired. The effective date for an ANDA containing a paragraph IV certification is determined by the outcome of the following sequence of events.

An ANDA applicant making a paragraph IV certification with respect to a patent must give notice of this certification to both the NDA holder and the patent holder (often, but not always, these will be the same party) and must explain in detail why it believes that the patent is invalid or will not be infringed by the generic drug for which it seeks approval. *Id.* § 355(j)(2)(B). Hatch–Waxman provides that the act of filing a paragraph IV certification with respect to a patent creates a cause of action for patent infringement in the patent holder. *See* 35 U.S.C. § 271(e)(2)(A) ("It shall be an act of infringement to submit . . . [an ANDA] . . . if the purpose of such submission is to obtain [FDA]

---

1. For ease of reference, we will refer to those patents that meet the statutory criteria for Orange Book listing with respect to a given drug as patents that claim the drug. We need not explain the statutory criteria in any detail, but the general idea is that a patent claims a drug under 21 U.S.C. § 355(b)(1) if the patent might be infringed by a generic version of that drug.

approval ... to engage in the commercial manufacture, use, or sale of a drug ... claimed in a patent ... before the expiration of such patent."). Once the patent holder receives notice of the certification, it has forty-five days in which to file a suit for patent infringement. Failure to file within this forty-five day period means that the FDA may approve the ANDA without delay. 21 U.S.C. § 355(j)(5)(B)(iii). But if the patent holder files suit, FDA approval of the ANDA is automatically stayed for up to thirty months.[2] Together, these provisions protect the holder of a patent that claims a brand name drug by giving the patent holder a chance to vindicate its intellectual property rights before the FDA approves a generic version of the drug. *See Bristol–Myers Squibb Co. v. Royce Labs., Inc.,* 69 F.3d 1130, 1135 (Fed.Cir.1995). Orange Book listing of a patent is important because it is the trigger for this protection. If a patent is not listed in the Orange Book, ANDA applicants do not have to file a paragraph IV certification, and the patent holder is unable to take advantage of the thirty-month stay.

II.

On July 10, 2001, aaiPharma received a patent (the '853 patent) on a polymorphic variant of the active ingredient in Prozac, a widely prescribed antidepressant drug manufactured by Eli Lilly & Company (Lilly). U.S. Patent No. 6,258,853. Lilly's claim of exclusivity for Prozac under the patent laws was scheduled to expire on August 2, 2001. Several generic drug manufacturers (including intervenors Barr Laboratories, Inc. and Par Pharmaceuticals, Inc.) were set to begin marketing generic versions of Prozac the next day. aaiPharma was concerned that its new patent might be infringed by these generic drugs, and the company therefore sought to have its '853 patent included in the Orange Book listing for Prozac. As explained above, Orange Book listing of the '853 patent would confer significant benefits on aaiPharma. An ANDA applicant seeking to market a generic version of Prozac before the expiration of the '853 patent would be required to make a paragraph IV certification regarding the patent. aaiPharma would then have the ability to trigger the thirty-month stay (and so delay FDA approval of the ANDA applicant's generic version of Prozac) by filing a patent infringement suit against the applicant.

Because only the NDA holder can submit patents claiming its approved drug for listing in the Orange Book, aaiPharma asked Lilly to submit the '853 patent to the FDA. Lilly refused. aaiPharma then sent a letter to the FDA asking the agency to "contact Lilly to confirm the correctness of Lilly's omission of information about the '853 patent from the list of Prozac-related patents in the Orange Book." aaiPharma suggested that if Lilly persisted in its refusal to list the '853 patent, the

---

2. More precisely, the stay continues until the earliest of (1) the expiration of the patent, (2) judicial resolution of the patent infringement suit, or (3) thirty months from the patent holder's receipt of notice. 21 U.S.C. § 355(j)(5)(B)(iii). In addition, a court in which a patent suit is pending may order a shorter or longer stay if "either party to the action fail[s] to reasonably cooperate in expediting the action." *Id.*

FDA had an obligation to intervene. The FDA, however, has determined that it will not become an arbiter of the correctness of Orange Book listings. Its regulations implementing the Hatch–Waxman Act provide only a very limited mechanism for resolving disputes regarding those listings. *See* 21 C.F.R. § 314.53(f). Consistent with its regulation, the FDA responded to aaiPharma's request by sending a letter to Lilly requesting that Lilly confirm the correctness of its Orange Book listing for Prozac. The letter explained that the FDA would make no change to the listing unless Lilly asked it to do so. The record does not indicate whether Lilly has responded to this letter.

Having failed in its efforts to secure Orange Book listing for the '853 patent by contacting Lilly and the FDA, aaiPharma brought this lawsuit under the Administrative Procedure Act in the Eastern District of North Carolina on August 2, 2001, only hours before the FDA was set to approve the marketing of several generic versions of Prozac. [The district court denied relief, resulting in an appeal by aaiPharma.]

IV.

Because Lilly's NDA for Prozac was approved long before aaiPharma obtained the '853 patent, 21 U.S.C. § 355(c)(2) determines Lilly's obligations with respect to that patent. It provides that for patents issued after the approval of an NDA, the NDA holder

> shall file with the [FDA] the patent number and the expiration date of any patent which claims the drug for which the application was submitted or which claims a method of using such drug and with respect to which a claim of patent infringement could reasonably be asserted if a person not licensed by the owner engaged in the manufacture, use, or sale of the drug.... [I]f the [NDA holder] could not file [the required patent information as part of its application] because no patent had been issued when an application was filed or approved, the holder shall file [the required information regarding the new patent] not later than thirty days after the date the patent involved is issued. Upon the submission of patent information under this subsection, the [FDA] shall publish it.

21 U.S.C. § 355(c)(2). It is clear, then, that if (as aaiPharma asserts) the '853 patent "claims" Prozac in the sense provided in § 355(c)(2), Lilly is obligated to submit the '853 patent for listing in the Orange Book, and the FDA is required to publish the submitted listing. It is unclear, however, whether there is any effective way to enforce an NDA holder's obligation to submit for Orange Book listing every patent that claims its approved drug (or its corresponding obligation not to submit patents that do not claim its approved drug).

The question is important because, as we explained earlier, listing of a patent in the Orange Book triggers the availability of the thirty-month stay. If there is no enforcement mechanism to ensure that an NDA holder complies with its statutory obligations, an NDA holder can abuse the Orange Book listing process in such a way that (1) the NDA holder enjoys the protection of the thirty-month stay when it is not entitled to do so, or (2) a third party patentee (a person or entity other than the pioneer drug company that holds a patent claiming a pioneer drug) fails to receive the protection of the stay even though it is entitled to receive that protection. The first (and more serious) problem arises when an NDA holder wrongly lists a patent in the Orange Book that does not actually claim its approved drug under the standard set forth in § 355(c)(2). Once the patent is listed, the NDA holder can delay an ANDA applicant's entry into the marketplace for up to thirty months (and extend its monopoly power) simply by filing a patent infringement suit. The NDA holder receives this benefit regardless of whether the patent meets the statutory criteria for Orange Book listing. Thus, the absence of any mechanism for ensuring the accuracy of Orange Book listings means that "the patentee/NDA holder [can receive] almost automatic injunctive relief for even marginal infringement claims." Terry G. Mahn, *Patenting Drug Products: Anticipating Hatch–Waxman Issues During the Claims Drafting Process*, 54 FOOD DRUG COSM. L.J. 245, 250 (1999). The harm to generic drug manufacturers, and ultimately to the consuming public, is obvious. The second problem arises when an NDA holder refuses to submit an eligible third-party patent for listing in the Orange Book. This is the wrong complained of by aaiPharma. Although an improper refusal to list a patent in the Orange Book is less obviously threatening to the public interest than an improper listing of a patent, we agree with aaiPharma that third-party holders of patents claiming an approved drug are also entitled to the thirty-month stay. Accordingly, aaiPharma has a legitimate grievance if Lilly has wrongfully refused to list the '853 patent in the Orange Book.

We are not the first court to consider whether parties aggrieved by an NDA holder's Orange Book listings have any remedy. Generic drug manufacturers have brought suits against NDA holders to compel them to delist certain patents on the ground that the patents did not claim the approved drug under the statutory criteria in §§ 355(b)(1) and (c)(2). It is now well established, however, that "a generic drug manufacturer cannot bring a declaratory judgment action or an injunctive action against a NDA holder under either the FFDCA or the patent laws requiring it to take steps to 'delist' a patent from the Orange Book." *Andrx Pharm., Inc. v. Biovail Corp.*, 276 F.3d 1368, 1373–74 (Fed.Cir. 2002). If a generic manufacturer cannot sue an NDA holder to compel delisting of a patent, it follows that a third-party patentee cannot sue an NDA holder to compel listing of a patent. This is why aaiPharma has brought suit against the FDA rather than against Lilly. The Federal Circuit, however, has acknowledged that a party aggrieved by an NDA holder's Orange Book listing could properly bring a lawsuit under the APA raising a challenge to the FDA's practice of "refusing to inquire into the correctness of [an Orange Book] listing." *Id*. at 1379 n. 8. This is that case.

The FDA's policy regarding Orange Book listing disputes is codified in § 314.53(f) of the regulations implementing Hatch Waxman:

> *Correction of patent information errors.* If any person disputes the accuracy or relevance of patent information submitted to the agency under this section and published by the FDA in the list [the Orange Book], or believes that an applicant has failed to submit required patent information, that person must first notify the agency in writing stating the grounds for disagreement.... The agency will then request of the applicable new drug application holder that the correctness of the patent information or omission of patent information be confirmed. *Unless the application holder withdraws or amends its patent information in response to FDA's request, the agency will not change the patent information in the list.*

21 C.F.R. § 314.53(f) (emphasis added). The regulation goes on to say that ANDA applicants must make a proper certification regarding each patent listed in the Orange Book "despite any disagreement as to the correctness of the patent information." *Id.* In short, the FDA's position is that if the NDA holder stands on its Orange Book listing, aggrieved parties are out of luck. The FDA defends this purely ministerial conception of its role in the Orange Book listing process by explaining that it lacks both the resources and the expertise to police the correctness of Orange Book listings. aaiPharma acknowledges that the FDA has no responsibility to independently evaluate the correctness of every patent listing submitted by an NDA holder. It simply argues that if a party alerts the FDA to concerns that an NDA holder has incorrectly failed to list a patent, the FDA must do more than simply ask the NDA holder to look into the matter and accept whatever it says. Specifically, aaiPharma contends that upon learning of a dispute about the correctness of an Orange Book listing, "the FDA is required to make a substantive determination about eligibility and to take remedial measures against the NDA holder if it determines that the patent should be listed." According to aaiPharma, the FDA's refusal to inquire into the correctness of Orange Book listings improperly delegates the FDA's statutory duties to NDA holders.

In evaluating the FDA's interpretation of its governing statute, we employ the familiar two-step analysis established by the Supreme Court in *Chevron U.S.A., Inc. v. Natural Res. Def. Council, Inc.,* 467 U.S. 837, 842–45, 104 S.Ct. 2778, 81 L.Ed.2d 694 (1984). In step one of the *Chevron* analysis, we ask whether "Congress has directly spoken to the precise question at issue." Here, that question is whether the FDA has an obligation to police the correctness of an NDA holder's Orange Book listings. "If the intent of Congress is clear, that is the end of the matter; for the court, as well as the agency, must give effect to the unambiguously expressed intent of Congress." *Id.* at 842–43, 104 S.Ct. 2778. If, on the other hand, we find that "the statute is silent or ambiguous with respect to the specific issue, the question ... is whether the agency's answer is based on a permissible construction of the statute." *Id.* at 843, 104 S.Ct. 2778.

Both aaiPharma and the FDA claim that this case can be resolved at step one of the *Chevron* analysis because Congress has clearly expressed its intentions about the proper role of the FDA in Orange Book listing disputes. The FDA relies on the language of 21 U.S.C. § 355(c)(2), which says:

> [I]f the holder of an approved [new drug] application could not file patent information [for a patent claiming the new drug] because . . . no patent had been issued when an application was filed or approved, the holder shall file such information . . . not later than thirty days after the date the patent involved is issued. Upon the submission of patent information under this subsection, the [FDA] shall publish it.

According to the FDA, this statute clearly indicates that the NDA holder bears the sole responsibility for filing the required information on all the patents that claim its approved drug and that the FDA's role in the process is completely passive. aaiPharma relies on two different provisions, 21 U.S.C. §§ 355(d)(6) and (e)(4), to claim that Congress clearly intended for the FDA to play some role in ensuring that all eligible patents are listed in the Orange Book. Subsection (d) outlines the various grounds on which the FDA may refuse to approve an NDA. It states, among other things, that if, after notice and an opportunity for hearing, the FDA finds that "(6) the application failed to contain the patent information prescribed by subsection (b) of this section [a list of the patents claiming the drug] . . . [it] shall issue an order refusing to approve the application." 21 U.S.C. § 355(d). Similarly, § 355(e) says that, after notice and opportunity for hearing, the FDA "shall . . . withdraw approval of an application" if it finds that "(4) the patent information prescribed by subsection (c) of this section was not filed within thirty days after the receipt of written notice from the [FDA] specifying the failure to file such information." *Id.* § 355(e). According to aaiPharma, these provisions indicate that the FDA has a duty to ensure that a pioneer drug company has submitted all the patents eligible for inclusion in the Orange Book.

Considered in isolation, the provisions cited by the FDA and aaiPharma could arguably qualify as clear expressions of congressional intent about the proper role of the FDA in Orange Book listing disputes. Step one of *Chevron,* however, requires us to look to the statute as a whole to determine whether Congress has unambiguously expressed its intent. *See Mova Pharm. Corp. v. Shalala,* 140 F.3d 1060, 1067–68 (D.C.Cir.1998). Because subsection (c)(2) appears to conflict with subsections (d)(6) and (e)(4), we conclude that Congress has failed to express clearly its intent about the FDA's role in the Orange Book listing process. Accordingly, we proceed to step two of *Chevron* and ask whether the FDA's interpretation of its role as purely ministerial rests on a permissible construction of § 355.

There can be no question that the FDA's reading of subsection (c)(2) is reasonable. Indeed, that provision's requirement that the FDA "shall file" the patent information submitted by NDA holders is most naturally read to suggest that Congress intended for the FDA to play a purely ministerial role. The harder question is whether the apparent reasonableness of the FDA's position is undermined by the language of subsections (d)(6) and (e)(4).

Subsection (d)(6) requires the FDA to refuse to approve an NDA that fails to contain the patent information required by § 355(b)(1), namely, a listing of the patents that claim the drug for which the application was submitted. According to aaiPharma, this provision obligates the FDA to independently determine whether the NDA applicant has listed all the patents that meet the statutory criteria for Orange Book listing. We conclude, however, that the statute can reasonably be read to impose only a much more limited duty on the FDA. This is because an NDA's "failure to contain the patent information prescribed by subsection (b)" can be understood in two different ways. On the reading proposed by aaiPharma, an NDA applicant fails to file the required patent information whenever its submissions for Orange Book listing fail to properly identify those patents that meet the statutory criteria. In other words, aaiPharma reads subsection (d)(6) to say that an NDA must be denied whenever the NDA applicant's patent law judgments are incorrect. There is, however, a far more modest interpretation of subsection (d)(6). On this more modest reading, an NDA applicant fails to file the required patent information only when it completely fails to submit a list of patents or a declaration that its drug is not claimed by any current patents. *See* 21 C.F.R. § 314.53(c)(3). In other words, the FDA's duty is not to ensure the correctness of the list of patents submitted for Orange Book listing, but simply to ensure that either a patent list has been filed or a declaration has been made that there are no patents to be listed. This second reading of subsection (d)(6) is at least as reasonable as the first. Further, aaiPharma's reading of subsection (d)(6) leads to an implausibly broad account of the FDA's duties under Hatch–Waxman. aaiPharma concedes that the Act does not require the FDA to assess the correctness of every determination by an NDA applicant that a patent claims or fails to claim its drug. Instead, aaiPharma contends that the FDA must make its own determination about whether a patent is eligible for listing only if a dispute is brought to the FDA's attention. We find it difficult, however, to read subsection (d)(6) as imposing only this relatively limited enforcement obligation on the FDA. If the statute requires the FDA to police the correctness of Orange Book listings at all, the obligation is far broader than aaiPharma is prepared to acknowledge. Subsection (c)(1)(A) requires the FDA to "approve [an NDA] if [it] . . . finds that none of the grounds for denying approval specified in subsection (d) of this section applies." This means that the FDA has an obligation to evaluate *every* NDA for compliance with the standards in subsection (d), including the requirement in subsection (d)(6) that the application "contain the patent information prescribed in subsection (b) of this section." If as aaiPharma contends, subsection (d)(6) commands the FDA to second guess the NDA applicant's judgments about which patents claim its drug, that command is not limited to cases in which a third party has questioned the correctness of those judgments. In short, aaiPharma's reading of subsection (d)(6) must be wrong because it would require the FDA to "screen the universe of patents to determine which ones should be listed" a result aaiPharma explicitly disclaims. Reply Brief for Appellant at 9. We conclude that on the better reading of subsection (d)(6), the FDA is required only to ensure that each NDA applicant has submitted either a list of patents claiming its drug or a declaration that there are no patents to be listed.

Section 355(e)(4) says that the FDA shall withdraw approval of an NDA if "the patent information prescribed by subsection (c) of this section [a list of patents claiming the approved drug] was not filed within thirty days after the receipt of written notice from the [FDA] specifying the failure to file such information." According to aaiPharma, this provision allows the FDA to make a written demand that an NDA holder submit a patent for listing and to enforce compliance with that demand by threatening to withdraw approval of an NDA. The company argues that the FDA must necessarily have made a prior determination that a patent is eligible for listing before making such a written demand. This means, aaiPharma says, that the FDA has a duty to ensure that all eligible patents are listed in the Orange Book. The argument is somewhat more persuasive than aaiPharma's argument regarding subsection (d)(6). It sounds plausible to say that because subsection (e)(4) concerns the withdrawal of a previously approved NDA, its reference to an NDA holder's failure to file the patent information prescribed by subsection (c) must mean that the NDA holder has failed to list some specific patent that is eligible for listing. The conclusion appears to follow because an NDA that failed to contain a list of patents (or a declaration that there were no patents to be listed) would never have been approved in the first place. We note, however, that subsection (c)(2) requires the submission of patent information by holders of approved NDAs in two different situations. The situation emphasized by aaiPharma occurs when a new patent claiming a pioneer drug is issued after the NDA for that drug has been approved. In this situation, the NDA holder is obligated to submit the new patent for Orange Book listing no later than thirty days after the patent is issued. However, subsection (c)(2) also addresses the situation of drug companies whose NDAs were approved before the passage of the Hatch–Waxman Act. Such companies had never submitted information about patents claiming their drugs to the FDA because they were not required to do so. Subsection (c)(2) required these NDA holders to submit patents for listing in the Orange Book no later than thirty days after September 24, 1984, the date of Hatch–Waxman's enactment. We think it likely that in drafting subsection (e)(4), Congress intended to provide the FDA with a means to ensure that holders of NDAs approved prior to the Act's passage would comply with the new patent listing requirements. Accordingly, we conclude that, just as in subsection (d)(6), the "failure to file the required patent information" discussed in subsection (e)(4) can reasonably be read to mean that the pioneer drug company has failed to submit a list of patents claiming the drug or a declaration that there are no patents to be listed. It follows that subsection (e)(4) does not undermine the reasonableness of the FDA's reading of 21 U.S.C. § 355.

[T]he FDA's reading of the statute is reasonable in light of the division of intellectual labor established by the Hatch–Waxman Act. The FDA points out that the whole point of the Act's paragraph IV certification scheme is to let private parties sort out their respective intellectual property rights through patent infringement suits while the FDA focuses on its primary task of ensuring that drugs are safe and effective. This division of labor is appropriate because the FDA has no expertise in making patent law judgments. It seems unlikely, then, that Congress intended to require the FDA to take on the responsibilities urged upon it by aaiPharma. For all these reasons, we conclude that the FDA's conception of its role in Orange Book listings as purely ministerial rests on a permissible construction of § 355.

None of this is to say that we are unsympathetic to aaiPharma's concerns. We agree with aaiPharma that Hatch Waxman protects the intellectual property rights of third-party patentees and that, if the '853 patent claims Prozac, aaiPharma is entitled to enjoy the benefits of the thirty-month stay. Ultimately, aaiPharma's argument boils down to the plausible claim that if NDA holders have a statutory obligation to submit the correct list of patents for publication in the Orange Book and the failure to comply with that obligation deprives third parties of benefits conferred by Congress, there must be some mechanism to enforce this obligation. Because the FFDCA clearly does not allow private enforcement of an NDA holder's listing obligations, aaiPharma concludes that enforcement responsibility must fall on the FDA and that the agency's refusal to accept that responsibility is arbitrary and capricious. Although we find some force in this argument, we cannot accept the proposition that an agency's failure to fill an enforcement gap created by a statute is necessarily arbitrary and capricious. We conclude that until Congress takes further action to address the enforcement gap in Hatch Waxman's patent listing provisions, the FDA may persist in its purely ministerial approach to the Orange Book listing process.

V.

For the foregoing reasons, the district court's order rejecting aaiPharma's APA challenge is affirmed.

NOTES

1. **Chaos in the Orange Book!** In previous years, considerable concern had been expressed about the integrity of the Orange Book. As a leading commentator observed in 1999:

> A cursory inspection of the FDA Orange Book's patent and exclusivity listings will reveal that most approved products have more than one listed patent. Sometimes, there are five or six patents listed for a single product. Some of these patents claim unapproved uses, special crystalline forms of the active ingredient, specific formulations, tablet shape or other subject matter which can easily be circumvented while still producing an equivalent generic version of an approved drug. These patents nonetheless prevent competition for at least thirty months.

Alfred B. Engelberg, *Special Patent Provisions for Pharmaceuticals: Have They Outlived Their Usefulness?*, 35 IDEA: J. L. & TECH. 389, 415 (1999). *See also* Elizabeth Dickinson, *FDA's Role in Making Exclusivity Determinations*, 54 FOOD & DRUG L.J. 195 (1999) ("FDA has had patents listed for scoring patterns and for bottles or drug containers."). Although judicial opinions like *aaiPharma v. Thompson* did little to relieve the controversy, some relief was in sight with both regulatory and legislative reactions.

2. **The FDA Regulations.** In view of perceived abuses of the Orange Book, the FDA issued regulations that define appropriate patents for Orange Book listing more precisely. Dept. of Health and Human Services, Food and Drug Admin., *Applications for FDA Approval to Market a New Drug: Patent Submission and Listing Requirements and Application of 30–Month Stays on Approval of Abbreviated New Drug Applications Certifying That a Patent Claiming a Drug Is Invalid or Will Not Be Infringed*, 68 FED. REG. 36676 (June 18, 2003) According to the latest thinking of the FDA, patents on drug substances (active ingredients), drug products (formulations and compositions), and method-of-use patents must be listed in the Orange Book. 21 C.F.R. § 314.53(b)(1) (2004). However, patents pertaining to processes, packaging, metabolites, and intermediates must not be submitted to the FDA. *Id.* Although this regulation may assist in cleaning up the Orange Book, what consequences does it hold for the Orange Book's role as a patent clearinghouse?

3. **The 2003 Amendments.** In addition, Congress amended the Hatch–Waxman Act as part of the Medicare Prescription Drug, Improvement, and Modernization Act of 2003. Pub. L. No. 108–173; 117 Stat. 2066. This legislation made two significant changes that put to rest some of the more egregious Orange Book listing practices. First, the 2003 amendments were intended to put an end to the practice, known as "late listing," where the NDA holder would obtain and list additional patents on a particular drug following the filing of an ANDA. Such an approach allowed the NDA holder to obtain an additional 30–month stay for each subsequent patent. See Federal Trade Comm'n, *Generic Drug Entry Prior to Patent Expiration: An FTC Study* (July 2002). The 2003 amendments stipulated that only one 30–month stay is possible even where patents are subsequently obtained from the PTO and brought to the attention

of the FDA. *See* 21 U.S.C. § 355 (j)(5)(B)(iii) (2006). Because fewer consequences flow from an Orange Book listing, there are diminished incentives to list patents that do not meet the statutory criteria.

Second, the 2003 amendments stipulated that a generic applicant that is sued for patent infringement may bring a counterclaim to an infringement action that requests de-listing a patent from the Orange Book. More specifically, the Hatch–Waxman Act now provides:

(ii) Counterclaim to infringement action

(I) In general

If an owner of the patent or the holder of the [NDA] for the drug that is claimed by the patent or a use of which is claimed by the patent brings a patent infringement action against the applicant, the applicant may assert a counterclaim seeking an order requiring the holder to correct or delete the patent information submitted by the holder under subsection (b) or (c) of this section on the ground that the patent does not claim either—

(aa) the drug for which the application was approved; or

(bb) an approved method of using the drug.

(II) No independent cause of action

Subclause (I) does not authorize the assertion of a claim described in subclause (I) in any civil action or proceeding other than a counterclaim described in subclause (I).

21 U.S.C. § 355(j)(5)(C)(ii); 21 U.S.C. § 355(c)(3)(D)(ii).

§ 14.4 DECLARATORY JUDGMENT JURISDICTION

The Hatch–Waxman framework establishes a system in which patent disputes between innovative and generic firms may be resolved as soon as possible. No law or norm ordinarily obligates patent proprietors to enforce their rights, however, a reality that may raise special concerns in the pharmaceutical field. Suppose that a patent holder opts not to pursue litigation at this time upon receiving notice of a generic applicant's paragraph IV certification. Assuming the generic applicant's filings are in order, the FDA could in theory grant final marketing approval as soon as 45 days have passed (although in practice the generic drug approval process usually consumes some months). The possibility of avoiding an expensive and time-consuming patent trial may seem to be a positive development for the ANDA applicant. Yet generic firms are usually displeased with this scenario. At a minimum, they may not wish to commit further investments towards the manufacturing and distribution of their products in view of unresolved patent issues.

Under these circumstances, the generic applicant may wish to pursue a declaratory judgment action against the patent proprietor. The lower courts were relatively skeptical that declaratory judgment jurisdiction existed under prevailing law, however. For example, in *Teva Pharmaceuticals USA, Inc. v. Pfizer, Inc.*, 395 F.3d 1324 (Fed. Cir. 2005), the Court of Appeals concluded that declaratory judgment jurisdiction did not exist to support a claim by a paragraph IV ANDA applicant against a passive patent proprietor under the facts of that case. As the materials below suggest, a subsequent Supreme Court ruling and congressional amendment may have altered the landscape with respect to declaratory judgment jurisdiction, both within the Hatch–Waxman framework and the patent field more generally.

MEDIMMUNE, INC. v. GENENTECH, INC.
United States Supreme Court, 2007
549 U.S. 118

JUSTICE SCALIA delivered the opinion of the Court.

We must decide whether Article III's limitation of federal courts' jurisdiction to "Cases" and "Controversies," reflected in the "actual controversy" requirement of the Declaratory Judgment Act, 28 U.S.C. § 2201(a), requires a patent licensee to terminate or be in breach of its license agreement before it can seek a declaratory judgment that the underlying patent is invalid, unenforceable, or not infringed.

I

Petitioner MedImmune, Inc., manufactures Synagis, a drug used to prevent respiratory tract disease in infants and young children. In 1997, petitioner entered into a patent license agreement with respondent Genentech, Inc. (which acted on behalf of itself as patent assignee and on behalf of the coassignee, respondent City of Hope). The license covered an existing patent relating to the production of "chimeric antibodies" and a then-pending patent application relating to "the coexpression of immunoglobulin chains in recombinant host cells." Petitioner agreed to pay royalties on sales of "Licensed Products," and respondents granted petitioner the right to make, use, and sell them. The agreement defined "Licensed Products" as a specified antibody, "the manufacture, use or sale of which . . . would, if not licensed under th[e] Agreement, infringe one or more claims of either or both of [the covered patents,] which have neither expired nor been held invalid by a court or other body of competent jurisdiction from which no appeal has been or may be taken." The license agreement gave petitioner the right to terminate upon six months' written notice.

In December 2001, the "coexpression" application covered by the 1997 license agreement matured into the "Cabilly II" patent. Soon thereafter, respondent Genentech delivered petitioner a letter expressing its belief that Synagis was covered by the Cabilly II patent and its expectation that petitioner would pay royalties beginning March 1, 2002. Petitioner did not think royalties were owing, believing that the

Cabilly II patent was invalid and unenforceable, and that its claims were in any event not infringed by Synagis. Nevertheless, petitioner considered the letter to be a clear threat to enforce the Cabilly II patent, terminate the 1997 license agreement, and sue for patent infringement if petitioner did not make royalty payments as demanded. If respondents were to prevail in a patent infringement action, petitioner could be ordered to pay treble damages and attorney's fees, and could be enjoined from selling Synagis, a product that has accounted for more than 80 percent of its revenue from sales since 1999. Unwilling to risk such serious consequences, petitioner paid the demanded royalties "under protest and with reservation of all of [its] rights." This declaratory-judgment action followed.

Petitioner sought the declaratory relief discussed in detail in Part II below. Petitioner also requested damages and an injunction with respect to other federal and state claims not relevant here. The District Court granted respondents' motion to dismiss the declaratory-judgment claims for lack of subject-matter jurisdiction, relying on the decision of the United States Court of Appeals for the Federal Circuit in *Gen–Probe Inc. v. Vysis, Inc.,* 359 F.3d 1376 (2004). Gen–Probe had held that a patent licensee in good standing cannot establish an Article III case or controversy with regard to validity, enforceability, or scope of the patent because the license agreement "obliterate[s] any reasonable apprehension" that the licensee will be sued for infringement. *Id.,* at 1381. The Federal Circuit affirmed the District Court, also relying on Gen–Probe. 427 F.3d 958 (2005). We granted certiorari.

III

The Declaratory Judgment Act provides that, "[i]n a case of actual controversy within its jurisdiction ... any court of the United States ... may declare the rights and other legal relations of any interested party seeking such declaration, whether or not further relief is or could be sought." 28 U.S.C. § 2201(a). There was a time when this Court harbored doubts about the compatibility of declaratory-judgment actions with Article III's case-or-controversy requirement. *See Willing v. Chicago Auditorium Assn.,* 277 U.S. 274, 289, 48 S.Ct. 507, 72 L.Ed. 880 (1928); *Liberty Warehouse Co. v. Grannis,* 273 U.S. 70, 47 S.Ct. 282, 71 L.Ed. 541 (1927); *see also Gordon v. United States,* 117 U.S. Appx. 697, 702 (1864) (the last opinion of Taney, C. J., published posthumously) ("The award of execution is ... an essential part of every judgment passed by a court exercising judicial power"). We dispelled those doubts, however, in *Nashville, C. & St. L.R. Co. v. Wallace,* 288 U.S. 249, 53 S.Ct. 345, 77 L.Ed. 730 (1933), holding (in a case involving a declaratory judgment rendered in state court) that an appropriate action for declaratory relief can be a case or controversy under Article III. The federal Declaratory Judgment Act was signed into law the following year, and we upheld its constitutionality in *Aetna Life Ins. Co. v. Haworth,* 300 U.S. 227, 57 S.Ct. 461, 81 L.Ed. 617 (1937). Our opinion explained that the phrase "case of actual controversy" in the Act refers to the type of "Cases" and "Controversies" that are justiciable under Article III. Id., at 240, 57 S.Ct. 461.

Aetna and the cases following it do not draw the brightest of lines between those declaratory-judgment actions that satisfy the case-or-controversy requirement and those that do not. Our decisions have required that the dispute be "definite and concrete, touching the legal relations of parties having adverse legal interests"; and that it be "real and substantial" and "admi[t] of specific relief through a decree of a conclusive character, as distinguished from an opinion advising what the law would be upon a hypothetical state of facts." Id., at 240–241, 57 S.Ct. 461. In Maryland Casualty Co. v. Pacific Coal & Oil Co., 312 U.S. 270, 273, 61 S.Ct. 510, 85 L.Ed. 826 (1941), we summarized as follows: "Basically, the question in each case is whether the facts alleged, under all the circumstances, show that there is a substantial controversy, between parties having adverse legal interests, of sufficient immediacy and reality to warrant the issuance of a declaratory judgment."

There is no dispute that these standards would have been satisfied if petitioner had taken the final step of refusing to make royalty payments under the 1997 license agreement. Respondents claim a right to royalties under the licensing agreement. Petitioner asserts that no royalties are owing because the Cabilly II patent is invalid and not infringed; and alleges (without contradiction) a threat by respondents to enjoin sales if royalties are not forthcoming. The factual and legal dimensions of the dispute are well defined and, but for petitioner's continuing to make royalty payments, nothing about the dispute would render it unfit for judicial resolution. Assuming (without deciding) that respondents here could not claim an anticipatory breach and repudiate the license, the continuation of royalty payments makes what would otherwise be an imminent threat at least remote, if not nonexistent. As long as those payments are made, there is no risk that respondents will seek to enjoin petitioner's sales. Petitioner's own acts, in other words, eliminate the imminent threat of harm.[8] The question before us is whether this causes the dispute no longer to be a case or controversy within the meaning of Article III.

Our analysis must begin with the recognition that, where threatened action by government is concerned, we do not require a plaintiff to expose himself to liability before bringing suit to challenge the basis for the threat-for example, the constitutionality of a law threatened to be enforced. The plaintiff's own action (or inaction) in failing to violate the

---

8. The justiciability problem that arises, when the party seeking declaratory relief is himself preventing the complained-of injury from occurring, can be described in terms of standing (whether plaintiff is threatened with "imminent" injury in fact "'fairly ... trace[able] to the challenged action of the defendant,'" Lujan v. Defenders of Wildlife, 504 U.S. 555, 560, 112 S.Ct. 2130, 119 L.Ed.2d 351 (1992)), or in terms of ripeness (whether there is sufficient "hardship to the parties [in] withholding court consideration" until there is enforcement action, Abbott Laboratories v. Gardner, 387 U.S. 136, 149, 87 S.Ct. 1507, 18 L.Ed.2d 681 (1967)). As respondents acknowledge, standing and ripeness boil down to the same question in this case. Brief for Respondent Genentech 24; Brief for Respondent City of Hope 30–31.

law eliminates the imminent threat of prosecution, but nonetheless does not eliminate Article III jurisdiction. For example, in *Terrace v. Thompson*, 263 U.S. 197, 44 S.Ct. 15, 68 L.Ed. 255 (1923), the State threatened the plaintiff with forfeiture of his farm, fines, and penalties if he entered into a lease with an alien in violation of the State's anti-alien land law. Given this genuine threat of enforcement, we did not require, as a prerequisite to testing the validity of the law in a suit for injunction, that the plaintiff bet the farm, so to speak, by taking the violative action. *Id.*, at 216, 44 S.Ct. 15. *See also, e.g., Village of Euclid v. Ambler Realty Co.*, 272 U.S. 365, 47 S.Ct. 114, 71 L.Ed. 303 (1926); *Ex parte Young*, 209 U.S. 123, 28 S.Ct. 441, 52 L.Ed. 714 (1908). Likewise, in *Steffel v. Thompson*, 415 U.S. 452, 94 S.Ct. 1209, 39 L.Ed.2d 505 (1974), we did not require the plaintiff to proceed to distribute handbills and risk actual prosecution before he could seek a declaratory judgment regarding the constitutionality of a state statute prohibiting such distribution. *Id.*, at 458–460, 94 S.Ct. 1209. As then–Justice Rehnquist put it in his concurrence, "the declaratory judgment procedure is an alternative to pursuit of the arguably illegal activity." *Id.*, at 480, 94 S.Ct. 1209. In each of these cases, the plaintiff had eliminated the imminent threat of harm by simply not doing what he claimed the right to do (enter into a lease, or distribute handbills at the shopping center). That did not preclude subject-matter jurisdiction because the threat-eliminating behavior was effectively coerced. *See Terrace, supra,* at 215–216, 44 S.Ct. 15; *Steffel, supra,* at 459, 94 S.Ct. 1209. The dilemma posed by that coercion— putting the challenger to the choice between abandoning his rights or risking prosecution—is "a dilemma that it was the very purpose of the Declaratory Judgment Act to ameliorate." *Abbott Laboratories v. Gardner*, 387 U.S. 136, 152, 87 S.Ct. 1507, 18 L.Ed.2d 681 (1967).

Supreme Court jurisprudence is more rare regarding application of the Declaratory Judgment Act to situations in which the plaintiff's self-avoidance of imminent injury is coerced by threatened enforcement action of a private party rather than the government. Lower federal courts, however (and state courts interpreting declaratory judgment Acts requiring "actual controversy"), have long accepted jurisdiction in such cases [citations omitted].

The only Supreme Court decision in point is, fortuitously, close on its facts to the case before us. *Altvater v. Freeman*, 319 U.S. 359, 63 S.Ct 1115, 87 L.Ed. 1450 (1943), held that a licensee's failure to cease its payment of royalties did not render nonjusticiable a dispute over the validity of the patent. In that litigation, several patentees had sued their licensees to enforce territorial restrictions in the license. The licensees filed a counterclaim for declaratory judgment that the underlying patents were invalid, in the meantime paying "under protest" royalties required by an injunction the patentees had obtained in an earlier case. The patentees argued that "so long as [licensees] continue to pay royalties, there is only an academic, not a real controversy, between the parties." *Id.*, at 364, 63 S.Ct. 1115. We rejected that argument and held that the declaratory-judgment claim presented a justiciable case or controversy: "The fact that royalties were being paid did not make this a 'difference or dispute of a hypothetical or abstract character.'" *Ibid.* (*quoting Aetna,* 300 U.S., at 240, 57 S.Ct. 461). The royalties "were being paid under protest and under the compulsion of an injunction decree," and "[u]nless the injunction decree were modified, the only other course [of action] was to defy it, and to risk not only actual but treble damages in infringement suits." 319 U.S., at 365, 63 S.Ct. 1115. We concluded that "the requirements of [a] case or controversy are met where payment of a claim is demanded as of right and where payment is made, but where the involuntary or coercive nature of the exaction preserves the right to recover the sums paid or to challenge the legality of the claim." *Ibid.*

The Federal Circuit's *Gen–Probe* decision distinguished *Altvater* on the ground that it involved the compulsion of an injunction. But *Altvater* cannot be so readily dismissed. Never mind that the injunction had been privately obtained and was ultimately within the control of the patentees, who could permit its modification. More fundamentally, and contrary to the Federal Circuit's conclusion, *Altvater* did not say that the coercion dispositive of the case was governmental, but suggested just the opposite. The opinion acknowledged that the licensees had the option of stopping payments in defiance of the injunction, but explained that the consequence of doing so would be to risk "actual [and] treble damages in infringement suits" by the patentees. 319 U.S., at 365, 63 S.Ct. 1115. It significantly did not mention the threat of prosecution for contempt, or any other sort of governmental sanction. Moreover, it cited approvingly a treatise which said that an "actual or threatened serious injury to business or employment" by a private party can be as coercive as other forms of coercion supporting restitution actions at common law; and that "[t]o imperil a man's livelihood, his business enterprises, or his solvency, [was] ordinarily quite as coercive" as, for example, "detaining his property." F. WOODWARD, THE LAW OF QUASI CONTRACTS § 218 (1913), cited in *Altvater, supra,* at 365, 63 S.Ct. 1115.[11]

Jurisdiction over the present case is not contradicted by *Willing v. Chicago Auditorium Association,* 277 U.S. 274, 48 S.Ct. 507, 72 L.Ed. 880. There a ground lessee wanted to demolish an antiquated auditorium

---

11. Even if *Altvater* could be distinguished as an "injunction" case, it would still contradict the Federal Circuit's "reasonable apprehension of suit" test (or, in its evolved form, the "reasonable apprehension of imminent suit" test, *Teva Pharm. USA, Inc. v. Pfizer, Inc.,* 395 F.3d 1324, 1333 (2005)). A licensee who pays royalties under compulsion of an injunction has no more apprehension of imminent harm than a licensee who pays royalties for fear of treble damages and an injunction fatal to his business. The reasonable-apprehension-of-suit test also conflicts with our decisions in *Maryland Casualty Co. v. Pacific Coal & Oil Co.,* 312 U.S. 270, 273, 61 S.Ct. 510, 85 L.Ed. 826 (1941), where jurisdiction obtained even though the collision-victim defendant could not have sued the declaratory-judgment plaintiff-insurer without first obtaining a judgment against the insured; and *Aetna Life Ins. Co. v. Haworth,* 300 U.S. 227, 239, 57 S.Ct. 461, 81 L.Ed. 617 (1937), where jurisdiction obtained even though the very reason the insurer sought declaratory relief was that the insured had given no indication that he would file suit. It is also in tension with *Cardinal Chemical Co. v. Morton Int'l, Inc.,* 508 U.S. 83, 98, 113 S.Ct. 1967, 124 L.Ed.2d 1 (1993), which held that appellate affirmance of a judgment of noninfringement, eliminating any apprehension of suit, does not moot a declaratory judgment counterclaim of patent invalidity.

and replace it with a modern commercial building. The lessee believed it had the right to do this without the lessors' consent, but was unwilling to drop the wrecking ball first and test its belief later. Because there was no declaratory judgment act at the time under federal or applicable state law, the lessee filed an action to remove a "cloud" on its lease. This Court held that an Article III case or controversy had not arisen because "[n]o defendant ha[d] wronged the plaintiff or ha[d] threatened to do so." *Id.*, at 288, 290, 48 S.Ct. 507. It was true that one of the colessors had disagreed with the lessee's interpretation of the lease, but that happened in an "informal, friendly, private conversation," *id.*, at 286, 48 S.Ct. 507, a year before the lawsuit was filed; and the lessee never even bothered to approach the other co-lessors. The Court went on to remark that "[w]hat the plaintiff seeks is simply a declaratory judgment," and "[t]o grant that relief is beyond the power conferred upon the federal judiciary." Id., at 289, 48 S.Ct. 507. Had *Willing* been decided after the enactment (and our upholding) of the Declaratory Judgment Act, and had the legal disagreement between the parties been as lively as this one, we are confident a different result would have obtained. The rule that a plaintiff must destroy a large building, bet the farm, or (as here) risk treble damages and the loss of 80 percent of its business, before seeking a declaration of its actively contested legal rights finds no support in Article III.

Respondents assert that the parties in effect settled this dispute when they entered into the 1997 license agreement. When a licensee enters such an agreement, they contend, it essentially purchases an insurance policy, immunizing it from suits for infringement so long as it continues to pay royalties and does not challenge the covered patents. Permitting it to challenge the validity of the patent without terminating or breaking the agreement alters the deal, allowing the licensee to continue enjoying its immunity while bringing a suit, the elimination of which was part of the patentee's quid pro quo. Of course even if it were valid, this argument would have no force with regard to petitioner's claim that the agreement does not call for royalties because their product does not infringe the patent. But even as to the patent invalidity claim, the point seems to us mistaken. To begin with, it is not clear where the prohibition against challenging the validity of the patents is to be found. It can hardly be implied from the mere promise to pay royalties on patents "which have neither expired nor been held invalid by a court or other body of competent jurisdiction from which no appeal has been or may be taken." Promising to pay royalties on patents that have not been held invalid does not amount to a promise not to seek a holding of their invalidity.

Respondents appeal to the common-law rule that a party to a contract cannot at one and the same time challenge its validity and continue to reap its benefits, citing *Commodity Credit Corp. v. Rosenberg Bros. & Co.*, 243 F.2d 504, 512 (C.A.9 1957), and *Kingman & Co. v. Stoddard*, 85 F. 740, 745 (C.A.7 1898). *Lear*, they contend, did not suspend that rule for patent licensing agreements, since the plaintiff in that case had already repudiated the contract. Even if *Lear*'s repudiation of the doctrine of licensee estoppel was so limited (a point on which, as we have said earlier, we do not opine), it is hard to see how the common-law rule has any application here. Petitioner is not repudiating or impugning the contract while continuing to reap its benefits. Rather, it is asserting that the contract, properly interpreted, does not prevent it from challenging the patents, and does not require the payment of royalties because the patents do not cover its products and are invalid. Of course even if respondents were correct that the licensing agreement or the common-law rule precludes this suit, the consequence would be that respondents win this case on the merits—not that the very genuine contract dispute disappears, so that Article III jurisdiction is somehow defeated. In short, Article III jurisdiction has nothing to do with this "insurance-policy" contention.

Lastly, respondents urge us to affirm the dismissal of the declaratory-judgment claims on discretionary grounds. The Declaratory Judgment Act provides that a court "may declare the rights and other legal relations of any interested party," 28 U.S.C. § 2201(a) (emphasis added), not that it must do so. This text has long been understood "to confer on federal courts unique and substantial discretion in deciding whether to declare the rights of litigants." *Wilton v. Seven Falls Co.*, 515 U.S. 277, 286, 115 S.Ct. 2137, 132 L.Ed.2d 214 (1995). . We have found it "more consistent with the statute," however, "to vest district courts with discretion in the first instance, because facts bearing on the usefulness of the declaratory judgment remedy, and the fitness of the case for resolution, are peculiarly within their grasp." *Wilton, supra,* at 289, 115 S.Ct. 2137. The District Court here gave no consideration to discretionary dismissal, since, despite its "serious misgivings" about the Federal Circuit's rule, it considered itself bound to dismiss by Gen–Probe. Discretionary dismissal was irrelevant to the Federal Circuit for the same reason. Respondents have raised the issue for the first time before this Court, exchanging competing accusations of inequitable conduct with petitioner. Under these circumstances, it would be imprudent for us to decide whether the District Court should, or must, decline to issue the requested declaratory relief. We leave the equitable, prudential, and policy arguments in favor of such a discretionary dismissal for the lower courts' consideration on remand. Similarly available for consideration on remand are any merits-based arguments for denial of declaratory relief.

* * *

We hold that petitioner was not required, insofar as Article III is concerned, to break or terminate its 1997 license agreement before seeking a declaratory judgment in federal court that the underlying patent is invalid, unenforceable, or not infringed. The Court of Appeals erred in affirming the dismissal of this action for lack of subject-matter jurisdiction.

The judgment of the Court of Appeals is reversed, and the cause is remanded for proceedings consistent with this opinion.

NOTES

1. The Impact of *MedImmune*. In a notable Federal Circuit opinion issued in the wake of *MedImmune, SanDisk Corp. v. STMicroelectronics, Inc.*, 480 F.3d 1372, 1381 (Fed. Cir. 2007), the Court of Appeals explained that "where a patentee asserts rights under a patent based on certain identified ongoing or planned activity of another party, and where the party contends that it has the right to engage in the accused activity without license, an Article III case or controversy will arise." Of course, almost any suggestion to enter into a patent license implies a charge of infringement—leaving the potential licensee with significant ability to commence a declaratory judgment action in a forum of its choosing. As Judge Bryson noted in his concurring opinion in *SanDisk*, "under the court's standard virtually any invitation to take a paid license relating to the prospective licensee's activities would give rise to an Article III case or controversy." *Id.* at 1384. Such a standard places the patent proprietor at a significant risk of having to defend its rights in federal court. For further discussion of this point, see Paul J. LaVanway, Jr., *Patent Licensing and Discretion: Reevaluating the Discretionary Prong of Declaratory Judgment Jurisdiction After* MedImmune, 92 MINN. L. REV. 1966 (2008).

2. Licensing After *MedImmune*. Supreme Court rulings have contributed to the notion of a patent license as an option contract, where the licensee pays but retains the option of challenging the patent. Patent licensing experts have been hard at work attempting to ameliorate the impact of these holdings, although whether courts will enforce the provisions they have proposed in light of patent and antitrust principles in some cases remains to be seen. Consider the following provisions proposed in Ronald A. Bleeker & Michael V. O'Shaughnessy, *One Year After MedImmune—The Impact on Patent Licensing & Negotiation*, 17 FED. Cir. B.J. 401, 433 (2008):

1. licensor can terminate the agreement if licensee challenges the licensed patent;

2. licensee must give advance notice to licensor of a challenge, and must also identify the prior art (if any) on which it intends to rely;

3. licensee must bring its challenge in a particular court or other forum;

4. licensee must pay licensor's costs, and counsel fees, during a challenge; [and]

5. if licensee loses the challenge, licensee must resume payments at an increased royalty rate.

Which of these clauses do you believe are enforceable following *MedImmune*?

3. Betting the Pharma? Although *MedImmune* is not a Hatch–Waxman Act case, it was broadly seen as impacting uncertainties in pharmaceutical patent litigation that could arise under that statute. The next opinion, issued shortly after *MedImmune*, considered this issue.

TEVA PHARMACEUTICALS USA, INC. v. NOVARTIS PHARMACEUTICALS CORP.

United States Court of Appeals for the Federal Circuit, 2007
482 F.3d 1330

Before Mayer, Circuit Judge, Friedman, Senior Circuit Judge, and Gajarsa, Circuit Judge.

GAJARSA, CIRCUIT JUDGE.

Teva Pharmaceuticals ("Teva") appeals from the dismissal of its declaratory judgment action by the United States District Court for the District of New Jersey. The district court, relying on our two-part declaratory judgment test for patent non-infringement as modified by our recent decision in *Teva Pharmaceuticals USA, Inc., v. Pfizer, Inc.*, 395 F.3d 1324 (2005) ("*Pfizer*"), found that Teva failed to establish a reasonable apprehension of imminent suit and that it therefore lacked jurisdiction over the declaratory judgment action. In light of the Supreme Court's recent decision in *MedImmune, Inc. v. Genentech, Inc.*, 549 U.S. 118, 127 S.Ct. 764, 166 L.Ed.2d 604 (2007), which finds that our declaratory judgment test for non-infringement or invalidity "conflicts" with its precedent, we reverse.

I. BACKGROUND

Novartis holds a New Drug Application ("NDA") for three strengths of the drug Famvir®. Upon filing its Famvir® NDA, Novartis listed five patents in the Food and Drug Administration's ("FDA") Orange Book, each of which covers and is directed to various aspects of Famvir®, including U.S Patent Nos: 5,246,937 ("'937 patent"); 5,840,763 ("'763 patent"); 5,866,581 ("'581 patent"); 5,916,893 ("'893 patent"); and 6,124,304 ("'304 patent"). The '937 patent is directed to the active ingredient in Famvir®, famciclovir, while the remaining Orange Book patents are directed to methods of therapeutic use ("method patents") of Famvir®. The '937 patent expires in 2010, but the related therapeutic use patents do not expire until 2014–15.

In 2004, Teva filed an Abbreviated New Drug Application ("ANDA") with the FDA for generic famciclovir tablets in which Teva certified under paragraph IV of 21 U.S.C. § 355(j)(2)(A)(vii) that its drug did not infringe any of the five Novartis Famvir® Orange Book patents or that the patents were invalid. Teva's paragraph IV certifications constitute technical infringement under 35 U.S.C. § 271(e)(1). Accordingly, Novartis had 45 days to sue on these patents in order to invoke a statutorily mandated 30–month stay to delay immediate FDA approval of Teva's famciclovir ANDA. *See* 21 U.S.C. § 355(j)(5)(B)(iii).

Novartis brought an infringement suit against Teva on the '937 patent alone and did not include in the action the related therapeutic use patents. The infringement suit is pending in the United States

District Court for the District of New Jersey. *Novartis Pharm. Corp. v. Teva Pharm. USA, Inc.*, No. 05–1887, 2005 WL 3664014 (D.N.J.2005).

After Novartis filed suit, Teva brought this declaratory judgment action on the four remaining method patents under 21 U.S.C. § 355(j)(5)(C) and 35 U.S.C. § 271(e)(5) to establish "patent certainty." Title 21 U.S.C. § 355(j)(5)(C) is a 2003 amendment to the ANDA statute entitled "civil action to obtain patent certainty." Under this provision, if the patentee or NDA holder does not bring an infringement suit within 45 days after receiving notice of a paragraph IV certification, the ANDA applicant may bring a civil action for a declaratory judgment that the patent at issue is invalid or will not be infringed by the drug for which the ANDA was submitted. *Id.* Title 35 U.S.C. § 271(e)(5) is a 2003 amendment to the patent statute that works in conjunction with the 2003 amendment to the ANDA statute to provide that in a civil action to obtain patent certainty, federal courts "shall, to the extent consistent with the Constitution, have subject matter jurisdiction in any action brought . . . under § 2201 of title 28 for a declaratory judgment that such patent is invalid or not infringed." Teva argues that by bringing suit on the '937 patent alone in the first instance, "Novartis has sought to put Teva to the hard choice of either launching at risk of massive liability for patent infringement when the '937 patent expires or Teva prevails in the pending infringement action, or foregoing that opportunity and thereby effectively extending the term of the '937 patent." Appellant Br. 9 (footnotes omitted).

Novartis moved to dismiss for lack of subject matter jurisdiction, arguing that Teva had no reasonable apprehension that it would be sued by Novartis for infringing the four method patents. In response, Teva argued that: (1) Novartis had already sued Teva on the underlying composition patent; (2) listing patents in the Orange Book established infringement as a matter of law; (3) Novartis had a history of aggressively suing generic drug companies; and (4) Novartis had declined to give Teva a covenant not to sue.

The district court dismissed Teva's declaratory judgment action requesting "patent certainty" on the four method patents. *Teva Pharm., USA, Inc., v. Novartis Pharm. Corp.*, No. 05–2881, slip op. at 10, 2005 WL 3619389 (D.N.J. Dec. 12, 2005). In so doing, the district court applied our two prong "reasonable-apprehension-of-imminent-suit" test from *Pfizer*.[1] 395 F.3d at 1332. After comparing the facts of this case to those in *Pfizer*, the district court found that Teva had failed to establish a reasonable apprehension of imminent suit and that the district court therefore lacked jurisdiction over the declaratory judgment action. *Teva*, slip op. at 10. Teva timely appealed to this court. We have jurisdiction under 28 U.S.C. § 1295(a)(1).

---

1.   Under this two prong test, the ANDA declaratory judgment plaintiff must show both: (1) a "reasonable apprehension" of "imminent" suit by the patentee; and (2) activity constituting infringement or the intent to infringe. *See Pfizer*, 395 F.3d at 1332.

The district court's dismissal of Teva's declaratory judgment action for lack of jurisdiction presents a question of law that we review without deference. *See Pfizer*, 395 F.3d at 1332 (citing *Gen–Probe Inc. v. Vysis, Inc.*, 359 F.3d 1376, 1379 (Fed.Cir.2004)). The determination of whether an actual controversy exists under the Declaratory Judgment Act in a patent case is a question of law that we review *de novo*. *BP Chems. Ltd. v. Union Carbide Corp.*, 4 F.3d 975, 978 (Fed.Cir.1993). The district court's factual findings supporting its determination are reviewed for clear error. *Id.*

II. ANALYSIS

A.

Our starting point in analyzing Teva's appeal is the Declaratory Judgment Act, 28 U.S.C. § 2201(a) under which Teva filed this suit. The relevant text of the Act reads:

> In a case of actual controversy within its jurisdiction ... any court of the United States, upon the filing of an appropriate pleading, may declare the rights and other legal relations of any interested party seeking such declaration, whether or not further relief is or could be sought.

28 U.S.C. § 2201(a).

In the ANDA context, Congress explicitly extended federal court declaratory judgment jurisdiction under 28 U.S.C. § 2201 to ANDA paragraph IV disputes such as Teva's and did so "to the extent consistent with the Constitution." 35 U.S.C. § 271(e)(5).[2]

The Supreme Court recently re-affirmed that the Act's "actual controversy" requirement "refers to the type of 'Cases' and 'Controversies' that are justiciable under Article III." *MedImmune*, 127 S.Ct. at 771 ("[T]he phrase 'case of actual controversy' in the Act refers to the type of 'Cases' and 'Controversies' that are justiciable under Article III.") (citing *Aetna Life Ins. Co. v. Haworth*, 300 U.S. 227, 240, 57 S.Ct. 461, 81 L.Ed. 617 (1937)).

In *MedImmune*, the Court found that its precedent "did not draw the brightest of lines between those declaratory-judgment actions that satisfy the case-or-controversy requirement and those that do not." *Id.* Instead of applying a bright line, the Court stated that its decisions required:

---

2. The Declaratory Judgment Act and 35 U.S.C. § 271(e)(5) "serve [ ] the policies underlying the patent laws by enabling a test of the validity and infringement of patents that are ... being used only as ... 'scarecrows.'" *Arrowhead Indus. Water, Inc. v. Ecolochem*, 846 F.2d 731, 735 (1988) (quoting Judge Learned Hand in *Bresnick v. U.S. Vitamin Corp.*, 139 F.2d 239 (2d Cir.1943)). Before the declaratory judgment provisions, competitors were "victimized" by patent owners who engaged in "extrajudicial patent enforcement with scare-the-customer-and-run tactics that infect[ed] the competitive environment of the business community with uncertainty and insecurity" and that rendered competitors "helpless and immobile so long as the patent owner refused to ... sue." *Id.* at 735 (quoting *Japan Gas Lighter Ass'n v. Ronson Corp.*, 257 F.Supp. 219, 237 (D.N.J.1966)). After enactment of these provisions, competitors "were no longer restricted to [the hard] choice between incurrence of a growing potential liability for patent infringement and abandonment of their enterprises; they could clear the air by suing for a [declaratory] judgment." *Id.*

that the dispute be "definite and concrete, touching the legal relations of the parties having adverse legal interests"; and that it be "real and substantial" and "admi[t] of specific relief through a decree of a conclusive character, as distinguished from an opinion advising what the law would be upon a hypothetical state of facts." *Id.* (citing *Aetna Life Ins. Co.,* 300 U.S. at 240–41, 57 S.Ct. 461).

Previously, the Court held that "the difference between an abstract question and a 'controversy' contemplated by the Declaratory Judgment Act is necessarily one of degree, and it would be difficult, if it would be possible, to fashion a precise test for determining in every case whether there is such a controversy." *Md. Cas. Co. v. Pac. Coal & Oil Co.,* 312 U.S. 270, 273, 61 S.Ct. 510, 85 L.Ed. 826 (1941). In *MedImmune,* the Court re-affirmed the correct standard for determining a justiciable declaratory judgment action: "Basically, the question in each case is whether the facts alleged, under all the circumstances, show that there is a substantial controversy, between the parties having adverse legal interests, of sufficient immediacy and reality to warrant the issuance of a declaratory judgment." *Id.* (citing *Md. Cas. Co.,* 312 U.S. at 273, 61 S.Ct. 510).

Thus, *MedImmune* teaches that in a declaratory judgment action, "all the circumstances" must demonstrate that a justiciable Article III "controversy" exists. A justiciable Article III controversy requires the party instituting the action to have standing and the issue presented to the court to be ripe. *Lujan v. Defenders of Wildlife,* 504 U.S. 555, 560, 112 S.Ct. 2130, 119 L.Ed.2d 351 (1992).

Article III standing requires "[a] plaintiff [to] allege personal injury fairly traceable to the defendant's allegedly unlawful conduct and likely to be redressed by the requested relief." *Allen v. Wright,* 468 U.S. 737, 751, 104 S.Ct. 3315, 82 L.Ed.2d 556 (1984). Of the three standing requirements, injury-in-fact is the most determinative: "[W]hatever else the 'case or controversy' requirement embodie[s], its essence is a requirement of 'injury in fact.'" *Schlesinger v. Reservists Comm. to Stop the War,* 418 U.S. 208, 218, 94 S.Ct. 2925, 41 L.Ed.2d 706 (1974) (citing *Ass'n of Data Processing Serv. Org., Inc. v. Camp,* 397 U.S. 150, 152, 90 S.Ct. 827, 25 L.Ed.2d 184 (1970)). An injury-in-fact must be "personal," "concrete and particularized," and "actual or imminent." *Lujan,* 504 U.S. at 560, 112 S.Ct. 2130; *Warth v. Seldin,* 422 U.S. 490, 501, 95 S.Ct. 2197, 45 L.Ed.2d 343 (1975)

Under the declaratory judgment standard, "all the circumstances" must demonstrate the Article III justiciability requirement that the case be ripe for judicial review. *Abbott Labs. v. Gardner,* 387 U.S. 136, 87 S.Ct. 1507, 18 L.Ed.2d 681 (1967). The doctrine of ripeness focuses on the conduct of the defendant to determine whether the defendants actions have harmed, are harming, or are about to harm the plaintiff. Ripeness can be an issue in obtaining anticipatory relief like declaratory judgments. *Id.* at 149, 87 S.Ct. 1507. A "controversy" is "ripe" if the question presented is "fit for judicial review," meaning it is entirely or substantially a question of law and postponing a decision would work a substantial hardship on the challenging party. *Id.* at 149–50, 87 S.Ct. 1507 (applying the test and holding that a regulation requiring drug manufacturers to change labeling was ripe for review before it was enforced because the regulation had an immediate and expensive impact on the plaintiffs' operations and plaintiffs risked a substantial sanction for non-compliance).

Similar to the ripeness doctrine and based on the same constitutional "controversy" requirement is the Court's prohibition against advisory opinions. Under this doctrine, federal courts are to decide only "actual controversies by judgment which can be carried into effect, and not to give opinions upon moot questions or abstract propositions, or to declare principles or rules of law which cannot affect the matter in the case before it." *Local No. 8–6, Oil, Chem. & Atomic Workers Int'l Union v. Missouri,* 361 U.S. 363, 367, 80 S.Ct. 391, 4 L.Ed.2d 373 (1960). Although there can be a fine line between declaratory judgments and advisory opinions, the Supreme Court maintains the necessity of avoiding issuing advisory opinions based upon hypothetical facts. *Elec. Bond & Share Co. v. Sec. & Exch. Comm'n,* 303 U.S. 419, 58 S.Ct. 678, 82 L.Ed. 936 (1938).

Notwithstanding the Court's justiciability precedent, it is well established that Congress by legislation "may expand standing to the full extent permitted by [A]rticle [III] of [the] Constitution, thus permitting litigation by one who otherwise would be barred." *Gladstone Realtors v. Vill. of Bellwood,* 441 U.S. 91, 100, 99 S.Ct. 1601, 60 L.Ed.2d 66 (1979). Congress, however, cannot expand standing beyond the Article III jurisdiction of federal courts. *Id.* Thus, as long as Congress remains within constitutional limits, it may "enact statutes creating legal rights, the invasion of which creates standing, even though no injury would exist without the statute." *Linda R.S. v. Richard D.,* 410 U.S. 614, 617 n. 4, 93 S.Ct. 1146, 35 L.Ed.2d 536 (1973) (citing *Trafficante v. Metro. Life Ins. Co.,* 409 U.S. 205, 212, 93 S.Ct. 364, 34 L.Ed.2d 415 (1972) (White, J., concurring)).

The Declaratory Judgment Act and 35 U.S.C. § 271(e)(5) are examples of legislation that expand standing to constitutional limits and provide a way for plaintiffs to bring actions in federal court when they might otherwise be barred. The sole requirement for federal court jurisdiction under both provisions is an "actual controversy," 28 U.S.C. § 2201(a), which is the same as an Article III case or controversy. *See Aetna Life Ins.,* 300 U.S. at 239–41, 57 S.Ct. 461. This means that under both provisions, a declaratory judgment plaintiff is only required to satisfy Article III, which includes standing and ripeness, by showing under "all the circumstances" an actual or imminent injury caused by the defendant that can be redressed by judicial relief and that is of "sufficient immediacy and reality to warrant the issuance of a declaratory judgment." *MedImmune*, 127 S.Ct. at 771 (internal citations omitted).[3]

In the instant case, we follow the Court's analysis in *MedImmune* in determining whether Teva has a justiciable controversy within the meaning of Article III. *Id.* By following *MedImmune*, we recognize that we are not relying on our two-part reasonable-apprehension-of-suit test. *See, e.g., Pfizer*, 395 F.3d at 1332–33. This court respects the principle of stare decisis and follows its own precedential decisions unless the decisions are "overruled by the court en banc, or by other controlling authority such as an intervening . . . Supreme Court decision." *Tex. Am. Oil Co. v. U.S. Dep't of Energy*, 44 F.3d 1557, 1561 (Fed.Cir.1995) (en banc).

Under our patent jurisprudence, we developed a two-part test to determine if an "actual controversy" exists in a general declaratory judgment action for patent non-infringement or invalidity. *See, e.g., Pfizer*, 395 F.3d at 1332–33. This test requires both (1) an explicit threat or other action by the patentee, which creates a reasonable apprehension on the part of the declaratory plaintiff that it will face an infringement suit and (2) present activity which could constitute infringement or concrete steps taken with the intent to conduct such an activity. *See, e.g., id.*

In *MedImmune*, the Supreme Court in a detailed footnote stated that our two-prong "reasonable apprehension of suit" test "conflicts" and would "contradict" several cases in which the Supreme Court found that a declaratory judgment plaintiff had a justiciable controversy. 127 S.Ct. at 774 n. 11. In *MedImmune*, the Court disagreed with our "reasonable apprehension of imminent suit" test and re-affirmed that the "actual controversy" requirement in the Declaratory Judgment Act is the same as the "Cases" and "Controversies" requirement in Article III. *Id.* at 771. The Court further re-affirmed that an "actual controversy" requires only that a dispute be " 'definite and concrete, touching the legal relations of parties having adverse legal interests'; and that it be 'real and substantial' and 'admi[t] of specific relief through a decree of a conclusive character, as distinguished from an opinion advising what the law would be upon a hypothetical set of facts.' " *Id.* (quoting *Aetna Life Ins. Co.*, 300 U.S. at 240–41, 57 S.Ct. 461). The Court summarized the declaratory judgment "actual controversy" requirement by quoting the "all the circumstances" test from *Maryland Casualty Id.* Thus, because the Supreme Court in *MedImmune* cautioned that our declaratory judgment "reasonable-apprehension-of-suit" test "contradict[s]" and "conflicts" with its precedent, these Federal Circuit tests have been "overruled by . . . an intervening . . . Supreme Court decision." *Tex. Am. Oil*

---

3. However, unlike non-declaratory judgment actions, even if there is an actual controversy, the district court is not required to exercise jurisdiction to address the merits of the action, as it retains discretion under the Act to decline declaratory judgment jurisdiction. *Public Serv. Comm'n v. Wycoff Co.*, 344 U.S. 237, 241, 73 S.Ct. 236, 97 L.Ed. 291 (1952); *Spectronics Corp. v. H.B. Fuller Co.*, 940 F.2d 631, 634 (Fed.Cir.1991) ("When there is no actual controversy, the court has no [jurisdiction and no] discretion to decide the case. When there is an actual controversy and thus jurisdiction, the exercise of that jurisdiction is discretionary.").

Co., 44 F.3d at 1561; *see also, Sandisk v. STMicroelectronics,* 480 F.3d 1372 (Fed.Cir.2007). Therefore, we follow *MedImmune's* teaching to look at "all the circumstances" under *Maryland Casualty* to determine whether Teva has a justiciable Article III controversy.

B.

The district court was bound by our precedent in *Pfizer* to apply the "reasonable-apprehension-of-imminent-suit" test to Teva's declaratory judgment action. *Teva,* slip op. at 9, 2005 WL 3619389. In applying this test, the district court considered Teva's standing and concluded that Teva had failed to establish the type of injury-in-fact that we required in *Pfizer* because Teva could not show a reasonable apprehension of imminent suit. *Teva,* slip op. at 9, 2005 WL 3619389; *see Pfizer,* 395 F.3d at 1333 (requiring a showing of "*imminent* suit"). The district court found that because Teva could not establish an Article III controversy under our precedent, it did not have jurisdiction and dismissed Teva's declaratory judgment action.

We hold that *MedImmune* applies to Teva's declaratory judgment action and takes precedence over the district court's application of *Pfizer,* which required Teva to show a single type of Article III injury-in-fact, "a reasonable apprehension of imminent suit." 395 F.3d at 1333. The question in this case is whether Teva has a justiciable controversy within Article III, which is the only limitation on our jurisdiction under the Declaratory Judgment Act. *See* 28 U.S.C § 2201. An Article III controversy is found where a plaintiff has demonstrated an injury-in-fact caused by the defendant that can be redressed by the court. *See Steel Co.,* 523 U.S. at 83, 118 S.Ct. 1003. In the present case, only the concrete injury-in-fact requirement under Article III is in dispute.

We hold that under "all the circumstances" as found in this case, Teva has an injury-in-fact and therefore has a justiciable Article III controversy. Here, Novartis argues that there is no actual controversy between it and Teva on the four method patents in spite of Teva's paragraph IV certifications of the four method patents because Novartis has not filed suit nor threatened to sue Teva on the method patents. Moreover, Novartis contends that the suit on the '937 patent is an entirely different controversy. Novartis is incorrect. There is no question that Novartis has already filed suit based on Teva's act of infringement in submitting the ANDA. Under 35 U.S.C. § 271(e)(2)(A), submitting an ANDA, regardless of how many paragraph IV certifications it may contain, is a single act of infringement: "It shall be *an act* of infringement to submit-an [ANDA] application ... for a drug claimed in a patent or for the use of which is claimed in a patent." (Emphasis added). While it is true that the suit on the '937 patent is a different "case" than Teva's declaratory judgment action, Novartis created a present and actual "controversy" by choosing to sue under 35 U.S.C. § 271(e)(2)(A) on Teva's single act of infringement, thereby placing into actual dispute the soundness of Teva's ANDA and Teva's ability to secure approval of the ANDA. Thus, while Teva's declaratory judgment action and the pending '937 suit are different "cases," they arise from the same controversy created when Novartis listed its Famvir® patents in the Orange Book, Teva submitted its ANDA certifying all five Famvir® patents under paragraph IV, and Novartis sued Teva challenging the submission of Teva's ANDA.[5]

Novartis' conduct raises the questions of if and how 35 U.S.C. § 271(e)(2) applies to multiple suits between the same parties on the submission of a single ANDA with more than one paragraph IV certification. It is clear from the statutory language that recovering damages for a 35 U.S.C. § 271(e)(2)(A) infringement action is only time barred by the statutory six-year statute of limitations. *See* 35 U.S.C. § 286 ("[N]o recovery shall be had for any infringement committed more than six years prior to the filing of the complaint or counterclaim for infringement in the action."); *see also, A.C. Aukerman Co. v. R.L. Chaides Const. Co.,* 960 F.2d 1020, 1030 (Fed.Cir.1992) (explaining that § 286 is "not a statute of limitations in the sense of barring a suit for infringement" ... but rather a "limit to recovery to damages for infringing acts committed within six years of the date of the filing of the infringement action."). Thus, Novartis has the right of an immediate action against Teva under 35 U.S.C. § 271(e)(2)(A) on any or all of the remaining Famvir® Orange Book patents. These actions could be brought at any time until the patents expire and damages would be limited only by the six-year limitations period. While it is unclear whether Novartis would be prohibited from suing under the doctrine of claim preclusion, Teva remains under the threat of an infringement suit because the 45–day statutory window does not preclude Novartis from pursuing additional infringement suits under 35 U.S.C. § 271(e)(2)(A). In light of Novartis' pending suit on the same ANDA, this threat of litigation is a present injury creating a justiciable controversy. Moreover, Novartis retains the right to sue Teva under the Famvir® patents pursuant to 35 U.S.C. § 271(a). Therefore, Novartis has numerous opportunities to bring an

---

5. In analyzing Novartis' election not to sue on the four method patents, it appears from the greater part of the district court's analysis that the district court may have erred in explaining the purpose of the 45–day statutory "window" in 21 U.S.C. § 355(j)(5)(B)(iii). The provision provides an automatic 30–month stay of approval of an ANDA if an infringement action is brought by a patent holder within 45 days against the ANDA filer on a patent it has certified under paragraph IV; if no suit is brought the ANDA is immediately approved. *Id.* The district court seemed to incorrectly interpret this provision as a waiver, finding that Novartis had only a 45–day window in which to sue Teva on all the paragraph IV patents in Teva's ANDA, and because Novartis had allowed this window to expire, it could not bring suit on the four remaining method patents. *Teva,* slip op. at 7, 9–10, 2005 WL 3619389. This is not what the statute provides. Novartis' selective action against Teva is an attempt by Novartis to limit the impact of Teva's ANDA under the Hatch–Waxman Act, while at the same time using it to forestall a challenge on all the remaining four method patents. By suing solely on the '937 patent, Novartis has not only invoked the 30–month stay, preventing Teva's entire ANDA from immediate approval, but Novartis is also selectively suing on the patent with the earliest expiration date leaving the remaining four method patents overhanging Teva for future litigation. This conduct prevents Teva's generic from entering the market until the expiration of the last patent and is directly contrary to the purpose of the 30–month stay. The stay is explicitly offered to patent holders who "reasonably cooperate in expediting[ ] action[s]" challenging their patents. 21 U.S.C. § 355(j)(5)(B)(iii).

action at any time for patent infringement and is not precluded by the 45–day window.

The district court erred in finding that *Teva* did not demonstrate an Article III controversy. A justiciable controversy can arise from either an actual or an imminent injury. While it is true that several of Teva's grounds alleging an "actual controversy" when standing alone might not be sufficient, if taken as a whole these circumstances establish a justiciable controversy with Novartis that can be resolved by allowing Teva to bring a declaratory judgment.

First, Novartis listed its Famvir® patents in the Orange Book. By so doing, Novartis represents that "a claim of patent infringement could reasonably be asserted if a person not licensed by the owner engaged in the manufacture, use or sale" of generic famciclovir covered by the claims of its listed Famvir® patents. 21 U.S.C. § 355(b)(1); *see Pfizer*, 395 F.3d at 1341 (Mayer, J., dissenting). While this conduct on its own may not be sufficient to establish an Article III controversy, it is a circumstance to be considered in determining whether a justiciable controversy exists under the totality of the circumstances.

A second circumstance that supports Teva's claim of a justiciable controversy is Teva's submission of its ANDA certifying that it did not infringe Novartis' Famvir® Orange Book patents or that the patents were invalid. The very act of submitting an ANDA is an act of infringement. 35 U.S.C. § 271(e)(2); *see Eli Lilly & Co. v. Medtronic, Inc.*, 496 U.S. 661, 678, 110 S.Ct. 2683, 110 L.Ed.2d 605 (1990) (holding that the statute creates an "act of infringement that consists of submitting an ANDA ... containing the fourth type of certification"). There is no question that under 35 U.S.C. § 271(e)(2), Novartis would have an immediate justiciable controversy against Teva as soon as Teva submitted the ANDA; indeed, that is exactly what occurred in this case. It logically follows that if such an action creates a justiciable controversy for one party, the same action should create a justiciable declaratory judgment controversy for the opposing party. In fact, the Supreme Court has stated: "It is immaterial that frequently, in the declaratory judgment suit, the positions of the parties in the conventional suit are reversed; the inquiry is the same in either case." *Md. Cas. Co.*, 312 U.S. at 273, 61 S.Ct. 510. This conclusion is supported in the legislative history of the 2003 "civil action to obtain patent certainty" amendment to the Hatch–Waxman Act:

> [T]he Hatch–Waxman Act has always provided that patent owners and brand drug companies can bring patent infringement suits against a generic applicant immediately upon receiving notice that the generic applicant is challenging a patent [by filing an ANDA]. The [ANDA] declaratory judgment provisions ... simply level the playing field by making it clear that the generic applicant can also seek a prompt resolution of these patent issues by bringing a declaratory judgment action if [it is not sued] ... within 45 days.

149 Cong. Rec. S15885 (Nov. 25, 2003) (remarks of Sen. Kennedy, ranking member of the Senate HELP committee).

A third circumstance we find relevant in determining whether Teva has established an actual controversy is the combination of three statutory provisions: 1) the "civil action to obtain patent certainty" under 21 U.S.C. § 355(j)(5)(C); 2) the ANDA declaratory judgment provision under 35 U.S.C § 271(e)(5); and 3) the purpose of the Hatch–Waxman Act. The "civil action to obtain patent certainty," which was enacted in 2003 is designed to prevent patentees from "gaming" the Hatch–Waxman Act. *See* 21 U.S.C. § 355(j)(5)(C). This amendment specifically permits an ANDA applicant to file a declaratory judgment action under 28 U.S.C. § 2201 against the patent owner or the brand-name drug company "for a declaratory judgment that the patent [listed in the Orange Book] is invalid or will not be infringed by the drug" covered by the ANDA if the patentee has not brought an infringement action within 45 days. *Id.* By virtue of 35 U.S.C § 271(e)(5), Congress extended federal court jurisdiction over these ANDA declaratory judgment actions "to the extent consistent with the Constitution." 35 U.S.C. § 271(e)(5).

By filing a lawsuit on only one its five patents certified under paragraph IV in Teva's ANDA, Novartis has tried to simultaneously leverage the benefits provided to a patentee under the Hatch–Waxman Act and avoid the patentee's accompanying responsibilities. Novartis' '937 patent suit against Teva has invoked the statutory automatic 30–month stay and is concurrently insulating the four method patents from a validity challenge. In the statute, Congress explicitly required that in exchange for the 30–month stay, patentees were to "reasonably cooperate in expediting the action" of whether the paragraph IV patents were invalid or not infringed. 21 U.S.C. § 355(j)(5)(B)(iii). Novartis' action insulates it from any judicial determination of the metes and bounds of the scope of the claims of its four Famvir® method patents in relation to design-around, a determination that is central to the proper function of our patent system and is a central purpose of the Hatch–Waxman Act. *Teva Pharm. USA, Inc. v. Pfizer Inc.*, 405 F.3d 990, 992 (Fed.Cir.2005) (rehearing en banc denied) (Gajarsa, J., dissenting).

It is clear from the legislative history that Congress intended this "civil action" to adjudicate the very controversy that Novartis has created here:

> The provision [a "civil action to obtain patent certainty"] . . . is intended to clarify that Federal district courts are to entertain such suits for declaratory judgments so long as there is a "case or controversy" under Article III of the Constitution. We fully expect that, in almost all situations where a generic applicant has challenged a patent [by filing an ANDA with a paragraph IV certification] and not been sued for patent infringement, a claim by the generic applicant seeking declaratory judgment on the patent will give rise to a justiciable "case or controversy" under the Constitu-

tion. We believe that the only circumstance in which a case or controversy might not exist would arise in the rare circumstance in which the patent owner and brand drug company have given the generic applicant a covenant not to sue, or otherwise formally acknowledge that the generic applicant's drug does not infringe.

The mere fact that neither the patent owner nor the brand drug company has brought a patent infringement suit within 45 days against a generic applicant does not mean there is no "case or controversy." The sole purpose of requiring the passage of 45 days is to provide the patent owner and brand-name drug company the first opportunity to begin patent litigation. Inaction within the 45–day period proves nothing, as there are tactical reasons why a patent owner or brand drug company might refrain from bringing suit on a patent within 45 days.

For example, the brand drug company might have several patents listed in the Food and Drug Administration's Orange Book with respect to a particular drug. It could be in the company's interest to bring suit within 45 days on one patent and to hold the others in reserve. The suit on one patent would automatically stay approval of the generic application until the lawsuit is resolved or the 30 months elapses. Holding the other patents in reserve would introduce uncertainty that could discourage generic companies from devoting resources to bring the generic drug to market and that would give the brand drug company a second opportunity to delay generic competition by suing the generic company for infringement of the reserved patents after the resolution of the initial infringement suit.

In each of these and in other circumstances, generic applicants must be able to seek a resolution of disputes involving all patents listed in the Orange Book with respect to the drug immediately upon the expiration of the 45–day period. We believe there can be a case or controversy sufficient for courts to hear these cases merely because the patents at issue have been listed in the FDA Orange Book, and because the statutory scheme of the Hatch–Waxman Act relies on early resolution of patent disputes. The declaratory judgment provisions in this bill are intended to encourage such early resolution of patent disputes.

149 Cong. Rec. S15885 (Nov. 25, 2003) (remarks of Sen. Kennedy, ranking member of Senate HELP committee) (emphasis added). A central purpose of the Hatch–Waxman Act and the subsequent ANDA declaratory judgment amendment to that Act is "to enable competitors to bring cheaper, generic . . . drugs to market as quickly as possible." *Id.* Novartis' actions frustrate this purpose and create a basis for finding a justiciable controversy.

A fourth circumstance contributing to Teva's justiciable controversy is Novartis' pending infringement litigation. As stated previously, Novartis' suit against Teva on Teva's submitted ANDA is an Article III controversy. A justiciable declaratory judgment controversy arises for an ANDA filer when a patentee lists patents in the Orange Book, the ANDA applicant files its ANDA certifying the listed patents under paragraph IV, and the patentee brings an action against the submitted ANDA on one or more of the patents. The combination of these three circumstances is dispositive in establishing an actual declaratory judgment controversy as to all the paragraph IV certified patents, whether the patentee has sued on all or only some of the paragraph IV certified patents. Our conclusion supports what we have already established in non-ANDA cases—that related litigation involving the same technology and the same parties is relevant in determining whether a justiciable declaratory judgment controversy exists on other related patents. *See Vanguard Research, Inc. v. PEAT, Inc.*, 304 F.3d 1249, 1255 (Fed.Cir. 2002) (following *Goodyear* and finding a justiciable declaratory judgment controversy where the defendant had sued the declaratory judgment plaintiff for misappropriation of trade secrets thereby demonstrating "a willingness to protect [its] technology."); *Goodyear Tire & Rubber Co. v. Releasomers, Inc.*, 824 F.2d 953, 955 (Fed.Cir.1987) (finding a justiciable declaratory judgment controversy in a patent non-infringement and invalidity action where the defendant had sued the declaratory judgment plaintiff in state court for misappropriation of trade secrets involving the same technology, thereby engaging in "a course of conduct that shows a willingness to protect that technology.").

Novartis' selective '937 suit creates uncertainty as to Teva's legal rights under its ANDA. Ordinarily, a potential competitor in other fields is legally free to market its product in the face of an adversely-held patent. In contrast, under the Hatch–Waxman Act an ANDA filer in Teva's situation is not legally free to enter the market because federal statutes prohibit it. *See* 21 U.S.C § 355(j)(5)(B)(iii). Hence, Teva suffers a direct legal injury from the actions that Novartis has already taken-Novartis' listing of the five Famvir® patents in the Orange Book and Novartis' suit against Teva challenging the validity of Teva's ANDA-which requires judicial relief. It is this exact type of uncertainty of legal rights that the ANDA declaratory judgment action was enacted to prevent. *See id.* § 355(j)(5)(C). Congress clearly has authority to give standing and create justiciable injuries through legislation for parties that might otherwise have no recourse as long as Congress does not exceed the limitations of Article III. *Gladstone*, 441 U.S. at 100, 99 S.Ct. 1601 ("Congress may, by legislation, expand standing to the full extent permitted by Art. III, thus permitting litigation by one 'who otherwise would be barred....'" (internal citations omitted)). Congress created the ANDA declaratory judgment action for generic drug companies specifically to avoid the type of legal uncertainty that Novartis has created. The legislative history of the ANDA declaratory judgment amendment explicitly states that the "uncertainty" caused by a brand-name company when it chooses to sue on only selective patents submitted in a single ANDA is an injury sufficient to support a justiciable controversy. *See* 149 Cong. Rec. S15885 (Nov. 25, 2003). The type of legal uncertainty as to the legal status of Teva's ANDA that Novartis has created by suing on only one of the five paragraph IV certified Famvir® patents listed in the Orange Book is a present injury sufficient for a justiciable controversy.

Finally, the possibility of future litigation that Novartis created by electing to challenge Teva's ANDA on only one of the five Orange Book listed Famvir® patents is a fifth circumstance contributing to finding that Teva has a justiciable declaratory judgment controversy. Novartis' suit on the '937 patent alone leaves open the possibility of future litigation regardless of whether Teva wins or loses the '937 infringement suit. The possibility that an ANDA filer will be subject to multiple infringement suits from the same patentee based on the submission of a single ANDA containing several paragraph IV certifications is an injury relevant to finding a justiciable controversy. If Teva is successful in defending the pending '937 infringement suit, it remains subject to four additional infringement actions by Novartis under 35 U.S.C. § 271(e)(2) on the remaining Famvir® Orange Book patents certified in Teva's ANDA under paragraph IV. By its action, Novartis is insulating its Famvir® Orange Book patents from any challenge of invalidity or non-infringement until all the patents expire. This threat of protracted litigation creates a present and real harm that is a relevant circumstance in finding whether a justiciable controversy exists.

III. CONCLUSION

The Court re-affirmed in *MedImmune* the "all circumstances" analysis as the correct standard to use in determining whether a justiciable Article III controversy exists in a declaratory judgment action. Under this standard, we find that Teva has an injury-in-fact and a justiciable controversy that can be fully resolved by a declaratory judgment. Allowing Teva's declaratory judgment action is consistent with the "controversy" requirement in Article III and the Declaratory Judgment Act because the suit will achieve a final determination that resolves the entire dispute between Teva and Novartis. Teva has experienced real and actual injury. Consequently, Teva's injuries are traceable to Novartis' conduct and those injuries can be redressed by a favorable judicial decision. Therefore, Teva has established standing and an actual controversy sufficient to confer jurisdiction under the Declaratory Judgment Act.

For these reasons we reverse the district court's decision dismissing Teva's declaratory judgment action.

REVERSED

FRIEDMAN, SENIOR CIRCUIT JUDGE, concurring in the judgment.

I agree with the court that the appellant Teva Pharmaceuticals USA, Inc. ("Teva") has shown an "actual controversy" under the Declaratory Judgment Act, 28 U.S.C. § 2201(a), and that the district court's judgment dismissing Teva's declaratory judgment action for lack of jurisdiction should be reversed. I write separately because I take a somewhat different, and shorter, path than the court does in reaching that conclusion.

In *MedImmune, Inc., v. Genentech, Inc.*, 549 U.S. 118, 127 S.Ct. 764, 166 L.Ed.2d 604 (2007), the Supreme Court rejected this court's settled view that a patent licensee must "terminate or be in breach of its license agreement before it can seek a declaratory judgment that the underlying patent is invalid, unenforceable, or not infringed." *Id.*, 127 S.Ct. at 767; *see Gen–Probe Inc. v. Vysis*, 359 F.3d 1376 (Fed.Cir.2004). The Supreme Court ruled that the jurisdiction of the district court did not turn on whether the declaratory judgment plaintiff had stopped paying royalties under or otherwise terminated the license, but on the general broader principles governing declaratory judgment jurisdiction, namely, whether the dispute between the parties is " 'definite and concrete, touching the legal relations of parties having adverse legal interests'; and that it be 'real and substantial' and 'admi[t] of specific relief through a decree of a conclusive character, as distinguished from an opinion advising what the law would be upon a hypothetical state of facts.... Basically, the question in each case is whether the facts alleged, under all the circumstances, show that there is a substantial controversy, between parties having adverse legal interests, of sufficient immediacy and reality to warrant the issuance of a declaratory judgment.' " *MedImmune*, 127 S.Ct. at 771–72 (citation and footnote omitted).

In a somewhat detailed footnote, the Supreme Court stated that this court's " 'reasonable apprehension of *imminent* suit' test" for determining declaratory judgment jurisdiction in patent cases (*see Teva Pharms. USA, Inc. v. Pfizer*, 395 F.3d 1324, 1333 (2005)) "would still contradict" a prior Supreme Court case and also "conflict[ ]" with another Supreme Court case, both of which that Court had relied on in its license breach ruling. *Id.*, 127 S.Ct. at 775 n. 11. Although these footnote statements were dicta, the Court apparently was telling us that it rejected our "reasonable apprehension of *imminent* suit" test for determining declaratory judgment jurisdiction in patent cases, and that the broader general rules governing declaratory judgment jurisdiction also govern patent cases.

In these unusual circumstances, where the Supreme Court went out of its way to state its disagreement with our "reasonable apprehension of *imminent* suit" test, which was not an issue in the case before it, it appears incumbent on us to stop using that test and hereafter to apply the general declaratory judgment standards that the Supreme Court applied in *MedImmune*.

I agree with the court that under these general standards there was an "actual controversy" between Teva and Novartis about the infringement and validity of the four patents relating to the Famvir® technology. All five of Novartis' Famvir® patents are closely related. As this court here recognizes, by listing those five patents in the Orange Book, "Novartis represent[ed] that a 'claim of patent infringement could reasonably be asserted if a person not licensed by the owner engaged in the manufacture, use or sale' of generic famciclovir covered by the claims of its listed Famvir® patents." In its Abbreviated New Drug Application filed with the Food and Drug Administration, Teva certified under paragraph IV of 21 U.S.C. § 355(j)(2)(A)(vii) that "its drug did not infringe" any of the five Novartis Famvir® Orange Book patents or that the patents were invalid. There thus is an existing controversy between the parties over whether Teva's generic version of Famvir® would infringe the four other Famvir® patents listed in the Orange Book, and whether these patents are valid. Novartis' filing of the suit charging that Teva has infringed one of those five patents and Teva's filing a declaratory judgment suit relating to the other four patents confirms that the controversy between the parties is continuing.

NOTES

1. **The Distinction Between Majority and Dissent**. Does *Teva v. Novartis* entirely put an end to the passive (or at least delayed) patent enforcement of pharmaceutical patents? Perhaps not. In this respect the distinction in approaches between the majority and dissent is significant. Suppose that the patent proprietor opts not to bring any charges of infringement under § 271(e)(2) at all. In this scenario, Judge Friedman would conclude that the requirements for declaratory judgment jurisdiction were satisfied. In contrast, the majority would look to additional facts and circumstances to see if a justiciable case or controversy existed. Such factors as the patent proprietor's infringement charges against other generic applicants, with respect to the product in dispute and perhaps other products; the history of litigation between the declaratory judgment plaintiff and the patent proprietor; and possibly a more general appreciation of the economics and marketplace realities of ANDA litigation would appear to be relevant in such cases. What advice would you give to brand-name drug companies following *Teva v. Novartis*?

2. **The Laches Defense.** Chapter 12 of this casebook introduced the concept of laches—the unreasonable delay in pursuing charges of patent infringement that may prejudice the rights of the patent holder. Under the *en banc* ruling in *A.C. Aukerman Co. v. R.L. Chaides Construction Co.*, 960 F.2d 1020 (Fed. Cir. 1992), a presumption of laches arises only where the patent proprietor delays bringing suit for more than six years after the date it knew or should have known of the alleged infringer's activity. Is this lengthy period of delay appropriate in the context of the Hatch–Waxman Act? Is one alternative—presuming laches after the expiration of the brief 45–day delay period set out in 21 U.S.C. § 355(j)(5)(B)(iii)—simply too short and unfair to NDA holders? In any event, the equitable defense of laches may yet come to play a rule in policing pharmaceutical patent owners who waive their § 271(e)(2) causes of action and await the rise of a cause of action under § 271(a).

§ 14.5 AUTHORIZED GENERICS

An "authorized" or "flanking" generic is a pharmaceutical that was originally approved via an NDA. The NDA holder then relabels and markets the product under a generic name, either under its own auspices or via a license to a generic firm. This "authorized copy" is ordinarily sold at an amount that is less than the brand-name drug, typically in competition with "true generics" also on the marketplace.

Perhaps the most common reason for launching an authorized generic is simply to maximize profits. This strategy allows the innovative firm to participate in both brand-name and generic markets once generic competition begins. An innovative firm may also wish to launch an authorized generic with the assistance of a generic partner in order to settle patent litigation with that firm, or to take advantage of additional manufacturing capabilities.

Authorized generics appear to be pro-consumer in that they increase competition and lower prices. Notably, firms in other industries have also availed themselves of this strategy. Companies outside of the pharmaceutical field often sell products under both their own "private label" and a "store brand," for example, allowing them to preserve the integrity of their trademark yet sell goods at lower prices.

This practice has nonetheless proven controversial. The reason is that an authorized generic potentially diminishes the value of the 180–day generic exclusivity. A generic firm that had just completed a costly patent challenge would face marketplace competition not just from its courtroom opponent, but also from another generic competitor that had simply obtained authorization from the innovative drug company. The authorized generic could take away market share and drive down prices, leaving the patent challenger with a diminished financial reward for its efforts. This possibility could in turn discourage generic firms from including paragraph IV certifications in their ANDAs.

Predictably, debate over authorized generics practice has spilled into courtrooms. The following opinion from the Fourth Circuit assesses the legality of authorized generics within the Hatch–Waxman framework.

MYLAN PHARMACEUTICALS, INC. v. U.S. FOOD AND DRUG ADMINISTRATION

United States Court of Appeals for the Fourth Circuit, 2006
454 F.3d 270

Before Michael, Motz, and Shedd, Circuit Judges.

MICHAEL, CIRCUIT JUDGE.

The Food and Drug Administration (FDA) approved Mylan Pharmaceuticals, Inc.'s application to sell a generic version of a drug that Procter & Gamble Pharmaceuticals, Inc. sold under the brand name

Macrobid. Just as Mylan began selling its generic drug, a third party under license from Procter & Gamble started selling a competing generic version. Sales of the generic authorized by Procter & Gamble crimped revenues from Mylan's version. Mylan petitioned the FDA for a ruling that under a provision of the Federal Food, Drug, and Cosmetic Act (FFDCA or Act) the authorized generic could not be sold until Mylan's drug had been on the market for 180 days. *See* 21 U.S.C. § 355(j)(5)(B)(iv). After the FDA denied the petition, Mylan commenced this action against the agency under the Administrative Procedure Act. 5 U.S.C. § 706(2)(A). The district court dismissed the case. We affirm the dismissal, concluding that the statute does not grant the FDA the power to prohibit the marketing of authorized generics during the 180–day exclusivity period afforded to a drug company in Mylan's position.

I.

A.

Drugs fall into two broad categories: pioneer drugs sold under brand names and generics. *United States v. Generix Drug Corp.*, 460 U.S. 453, 454–55, 103 S.Ct. 1298, 75 L.Ed.2d 198 (1983). Pioneer and generic drugs are regulated under the FFDCA, 21 U.S.C. § 301 *et seq.*, which Congress amended extensively in 1984. *See* Drug Price Competition and Patent Term Restoration Act of 1984, Pub.L. No. 98–417, 98 Stat. 1585 (commonly known as the Hatch–Waxman Act). The Hatch–Waxman Act made it easier to obtain FDA approval of generic drugs. The legislation aimed to "strike a balance between two conflicting policy objectives: to induce name-brand pharmaceutical firms to make the investments necessary to research and develop new drug products, while simultaneously enabling competitors to bring cheaper, generic copies of those drugs to market." *aaiPharma Inc. v. Thompson*, 296 F.3d 227, 230 (4th Cir.2002) (punctuation omitted).

The Hatch–Waxman scheme distinguishes between New Drug Applications (NDAs) and Abbreviated New Drug Applications (ANDAs). To seek FDA approval for a pioneer drug, the manufacturer must file a complete NDA. Such a filing must "provide the FDA with a listing of all patents that claim the approved drug or a method of using the drug." *aaiPharma Inc.*, 296 F.3d at 230. The NDA must also set forth data establishing that the drug is safe and effective. *See* 21 U.S.C. § 355(b). Later, a company that makes a generic drug that is biologically equivalent to the pioneer drug may seek FDA approval for the drug by filing an ANDA. The ANDA relies on the pioneer drug's safety and effectiveness studies. *See* 21 U.S.C. § 355(j); *aaiPharma Inc.*, 296 F.3d at 231.

The ANDA must contain a certification as to whether the proposed generic drug would infringe the patent protecting the pioneer drug, and if not, why not. Pertinent here is the fourth of the statute's four certification options (the paragraph IV option), allowing the ANDA applicant to certify that the pioneer drug's patent is "invalid or will not be infringed by the manufacture, use, or sale of the new drug for which the application is submitted." 21 U.S.C. § 355(j)(2)(A)(vii)(IV). Thus, "an ANDA applicant making a paragraph IV certification intends to market its product before the relevant patents have expired." *aaiPharma Inc.*, 296 F.3d at 232. The patent holder and the NDA holder (which usually are the same company, the pioneer drug maker) are entitled to notice that a paragraph IV ANDA has been filed. If, upon receiving such notice, the patent holder sues the applicant for patent infringement within 45 days, the FDA must stay a decision on whether to approve the ANDA for 30 months (unless the patent expires or a court holds that it is invalid or not infringed during that time). 21 U.S.C. § 355(j)(5)(B)(iii).

The first applicant to file a paragraph IV ANDA enjoys a unique advantage. For 180 days it may sell its drug without competition from later ANDA applicants. The 180–day period starts to run on the earlier of two dates: (1) the date the FDA receives notice "of the first commercial marketing of the drug under the previous application" (the commercial marketing trigger) or (2) the date a court decides that the patent is either invalid or not infringed (the patent litigation trigger). *See* 21 U.S.C. § 355(j)(5)(B)(iv) (preventing the FDA from making effective a later paragraph IV ANDA earlier than 180 days after one of these two triggering events)*

The 180–day exclusivity period created in § 355(j)(5)(B)(iv) is a significant boon to the recipient. As the Federal Trade Commission put it, the period "increases the economic incentives for a generic company to be the first to file, because the generic applicant has the potential to reap the reward of marketing the only generic product (and, thus, to charge a higher price until more generic products enter [the market])." Federal Trade Commission, *To Promote Innovation: The Proper Balance of Competition and Patent Law and Policy,* Ch. 3, at 12 (Oct.2003), *available at* http://www.ftc.gov/os/2003/10/innovationrpt.pdf. This benefit motivates "generic manufacturers to challenge the validity of listed patents and to 'design around' patents to find alternative, noninfringing forms of patented drugs" so that they can be the first to file paragraph IV ANDAs. *Teva Pharms. USA, Inc. v. Pfizer, Inc.*, 395 F.3d 1324, 1328 (Fed.Cir.2005).

The pioneer drug maker who holds the approved NDA wants to stave off possible competition from the ANDA applicants (the generic makers). One strategy for the NDA holder is to grant a third party a license to sell a generic version of the drug described in the approved NDA. The economic benefits of this practice are clear. Such an authorized generic appeals to patients because it is sold at a lower price than

---

* Throughout this opinion we refer to the statute as worded in January 2003, when Mylan filed the paragraph IV ANDA at issue here. In December 2003 Congress amended the Act. *See* Medicare Prescription Drug, Improvement, and Modernization Act of 2003, Pub.L. No. 108–173, 117 Stat.2066. As the FDA noted, the amendments "altered the eligibility requirements and triggering events for 180–day exclusivity and established circumstances under which forfeiture of exclusivity can occur." J.A. 368 n.1. But the FDA determined, and the parties agree, that the amendments do not change the analysis here because they did not "substantively alter" § 355(j)(5)(B)(iv), the provision in dispute. *Id.*

the branded pioneer drug. It also appeals to the pioneer drug maker, who benefits from sales of the authorized generic even after the patent protecting the pioneer drug has expired. By selling an authorized generic during the exclusivity period enjoyed by the first paragraph IV ANDA applicant, the pioneer drug maker prevents that applicant from winning all of the customers who want to switch from the branded drug to a cheaper generic form. "[T]he additional competition [for the applicant] from an authorized generic may result in significantly less profit during the period of 180–day exclusivity than if" the applicant "had no authorized-generic competition during that time." Federal Trade Commission Information Collection Notice, 71 FED.REG. 16,779, 16,780 (Apr. 4, 2006). The question before us is whether § 355(j)(5)(B)(iv) empowers the FDA to prohibit sale of authorized generics during the exclusivity period.

B.

This dispute began when Mylan filed a paragraph IV ANDA seeking authorization to produce nitrofurantoin, a generic version of a drug to treat urinary tract infections. Procter & Gamble held the approved NDA for the drug and sold it under the brand name Macrobid. The FDA approved Mylan's application on March 22, 2004. Mylan began commercial marketing of nitrofurantoin on March 23, the same day that Watson Pharmaceuticals began selling the authorized generic version of Macrobid under a license from Procter & Gamble. Mylan lost sales worth "tens of millions" of dollars as a result of this competition.

Anticipating Procter & Gamble's move, Mylan had filed a citizen petition in February 2004 requesting that the FDA "prohibit the marketing and distribution of 'authorized generic' versions of brand name drugs until the expiration of the first generic applicant's 180–day exclusivity period." Teva Pharmaceuticals USA, Inc., another generic drug maker, submitted a petition in June 2004 seeking a similar ruling. The FDA denied these two petitions in a letter dated July 2, 2004. The agency concluded in part that the Act did not "prohibit an ANDA or NDA holder's use of alternative marketing practices for its own approved new drug (so long as any related manufacturing changes do not pose safety or effectiveness concerns . . .)." J.A. 373. The agency also rejected the argument that the FDA's position in *Mylan Pharmaceuticals, Inc. v. Thompson,* 207 F.Supp.2d 476 (N.D.W.Va.2001), a case concerning the hypertension and angina medicine nifedipine, obligated the agency to treat authorized generics "as the legal and functional equivalents of ANDA generics" for exclusivity period purposes. J.A. 377.

In August 2004 Teva and Mylan each sued the FDA, contending that the agency's denial of the petitions was "arbitrary, capricious . . . or otherwise not in accordance with law" under the Administrative Procedure Act. 5 U.S.C. § 706(2)(A). Teva sued in the district court for the District of Columbia while Mylan sued in the district court for the Northern District of West Virginia. Mylan sought a preliminary injunction, but voluntarily dismissed its complaint on August 30, 2004, the same day the district court had been expected to decide on the request for preliminary relief. In November 2004 Mylan again filed its case against the FDA in the Northern District of West Virginia. The district court for the District of Columbia ruled against Teva in December 2004. Teva appealed to the D.C. Circuit, and Mylan filed an amicus brief in support of Teva. (The West Virginia district court granted Mylan's request to stay its case while the appeal in the D.C. Circuit was pending.) The D.C. Circuit affirmed in June 2005. *Teva Pharms. Indus. Ltd. v. Crawford,* 410 F.3d 51 (D.C.Cir.2005). That court held that 21 U.S.C. § 355(j)(5)(B)(iv) did not by its terms prohibit the holder of an approved NDA from marketing an authorized generic during the exclusivity period. Rather, the court held that the statute's limits expressly apply only to later-filed ANDAs. *Id.* at 53–55.

Mylan's suit thereafter resumed and the FDA moved to dismiss. *See* Fed.R.Civ.P. 12(b)(6). In September 2005 the district court dismissed Mylan's complaint for failure to state a claim upon which relief could be granted, and Mylan appealed. Our review is de novo.

II.

Mylan's claim that the FDA's denial of its petition was "arbitrary, capricious . . . or otherwise not in accordance with law" boils down to a challenge to the agency's interpretation of 21 U.S.C. § 355(j)(5)(B)(iv). Specifically, Mylan argues that the FDA impermissibly ignored two considerations in construing the statute: legislative intent and the agency's prior interpretation.

To evaluate the FDA's interpretation of the statute, we must determine at the first step "whether Congress has directly spoken to the precise question at issue." *Chevron U.S.A. Inc. v. Natural Res. Def. Council, Inc.,* 467 U.S. 837, 842, 104 S.Ct. 2778, 81 L.Ed.2d 694 (1984). "If so, courts, as well as the agency, 'must give effect to the unambiguously expressed intent of Congress.'" *Household Credit Servs., Inc. v. Pfennig,* 541 U.S. 232, 239, 124 S.Ct. 1741, 158 L.Ed.2d 450 (2004) (quoting *Chevron,* 467 U.S. at 842–843, 104 S.Ct. 2778). At the second step, "whenever Congress has 'explicitly left a gap for the agency to fill,' the agency's regulation is 'given controlling weight unless [it is] arbitrary, capricious, or manifestly contrary to the statute.'" *Id.* (quoting *Chevron,* 467 U.S. at 843–844, 104 S.Ct. 2778). At the first step a court focuses purely on statutory construction without according any weight to the agency's position because "[t]he traditional deference courts pay to agency interpretation is not to be applied to alter the clearly expressed intent of Congress." *Board of Governors, FRS v. Dimension Fin. Corp.,* 474 U.S. 361, 368, 106 S.Ct. 681, 88 L.Ed.2d 691 (1986). And although "[s]tatutory construction is a holistic endeavor," *Koons Buick Pontiac GMC, Inc. v. Nigh,* 543 U.S. 50, 60, 125 S.Ct. 460, 160 L.Ed.2d 389 (2004) (punctuation omitted), "[i]t is well established that when the statute's language is plain, the sole function of the courts—at least where the disposition required by the text is not absurd—is to enforce it according to its terms," *Lamie v. United States Trustee,* 540 U.S. 526, 534, 124 S.Ct. 1023, 157 L.Ed.2d 1024 (2004) (punctuation omitted).

Mylan concedes that the language of § 355(j)(5)(B)(iv) is plain. The provision makes no mention of drugs under approved NDAs. It speaks only about the rights of the paragraph IV ANDA applicant who files first as against all subsequent paragraph IV ANDA applicants. Indeed, the statute describes the 180–day exclusivity period entirely from the point of view of a later-filing paragraph IV ANDA applicant. *See* 21 U.S.C. § 355(j)(5)(B)(iv) (an application containing a paragraph IV certification "shall be made effective not earlier than one hundred and eighty days after (I) the date the Secretary receives notice from the applicant under the previous application of the first commercial marketing of the drug under the previous application, or (II) the date of [a court decision on patent infringement] . . ., whichever is earlier."). Because the exclusivity is described from the perspective of the later-filing paragraph IV ANDA applicant, the FDA could only read the statute to cover drugs under approved NDAs by completely redefining the language describing paragraph IV ANDAs to also include NDAs. Interpretation of this kind would amount to rewriting rather than reading. It would dramatically depart from the statute's language and would be tantamount to an agency effort to exercise authority never delegated by Congress.

Mylan would have us set aside the statutory language and instead give determinative weight to its asserted understanding of the congressional intent behind the statute. Mylan contends that authorized generics may not be sold during the 180–day exclusivity period because Congress sought to give the first-filing paragraph IV ANDA applicant the sole right to sell a generic during that period. For three reasons Mylan's legal arguments cannot prevail. First, Mylan points to no textual ambiguity of the sort that would ordinarily lead us to consult materials outside the statute's four corners. "Given the straightforward statutory command, there is no reason to resort to legislative history." *United States v. Gonzales,* 520 U.S. 1, 6, 117 S.Ct. 1032, 137 L.Ed.2d 132 (1997); *see also Black & Decker Corp. v. United States,* 436 F.3d 431, 436 (4th Cir.2006). The statute's tolerance of the sale of authorized generics during the exclusivity period is not an outcome that "shock [s] the general moral or common sense," and therefore it does not count as the sort of "absurd" result that courts seek to avoid in construing statutes. *RCI Tech. Corp. v. Sunterra Corp. (In re Sunterra Corp.),* 361 F.3d 257, 265 (4th Cir.2004). Second, Mylan relies heavily on public criticism of authorized generics by some members of Congress in October and November 2004. These comments came some 20 years after the 1984 enactment of the Hatch–Waxman Act, and we give "little weight" to such post-enactment statements by legislators. Third, Mylan's characterization of Congress as having been solely concerned with making generic drugs available more speedily fails to recognize a countervailing interest that Congress sought to protect, namely, the intellectual property rights of pioneer drug companies. *See aaiPharma Inc.*, 296 F.3d at 230. Nothing in the statute restricts the established right of such companies to make ordinary licensing agreements with third parties. As the D.C. Circuit recognized, companies were free to license generic versions of their pioneer drugs at any time before the passage of the Hatch–Waxman Act, and Hatch–Waxman did not purport to restrain that freedom. *Teva*, 410 F.3d at 53.

Mylan fares no better with its argument that the FDA's interpretation of the statute here is fatally inconsistent with the agency's position in the nifedipine case. The Supreme Court has observed that "[u]nexplained inconsistency is, at most, a reason for holding an interpretation to be an arbitrary and capricious change from agency practice under the Administrative Procedure Act." *Nat'l Cable & Telecomms. Ass'n v. Brand X Internet Servs.*, 545 U.S. 967, 125 S.Ct. 2688, 2699, 162 L.Ed.2d 820 (2005). That principle has no application here. Prior agency interpretation (whether or not it supports Mylan's reading) is irrelevant because the statute unambiguously forecloses that reading.

Mylan's inconsistency argument would fail even if we were to entertain it. The nifedipine case simply did not pose the same question that this case does. In the previous case Mylan filed the earliest paragraph IV ANDA seeking authorization to make nifiedipine, a generic form of Procardia XL, a pioneer drug for which Pfizer, Inc. held the approved NDA. *Mylan*, 207 F.Supp.2d at 481. Pfizer sued Mylan for patent infringement but later settled and granted Mylan a license to make the authorized generic form of Procardia XL. *Id.* When Mylan's competitor Teva subsequently sought an FDA ruling that Mylan's 180–day exclusivity period had expired, the FDA determined that the period began to run on the date that Mylan first sold the authorized generic form of Procardia XL. *Id.* at 482–83. In the FDA's view, sale of that authorized generic constituted the "first commercial marketing of the drug under the [earliest paragraph IV ANDA]," § 355(j)(5)(B)(iv)(I), which started the clock on the exclusivity period. The agency rejected Mylan's argument that the exclusivity period could not have begun until Mylan started selling the generic form of nifedipine described in its ANDA. For purposes of the commercial marketing trigger the agency thus refused to distinguish between Mylan's authorized generic form of Procardia XL on the one hand and Mylan's paragraph IV ANDA generic on the other hand. In short, that case was about the proper scope of the commercial marketing trigger. The FDA did *not* decide that generic drugs made under approved NDAs and those made under paragraph IV ANDAs are "functional equivalents" for all statutory purposes. Rather, the FDA determined that a paragraph IV ANDA applicant's marketing of an authorized generic activates the commercial marketing trigger. The agency's prior position was not inconsistent with its action here.

III.

Although the introduction of an authorized generic may reduce the economic benefit of the 180 days of exclusivity awarded to the first paragraph IV ANDA applicant, § 355(j)(5)(B)(iv) gives no legal basis for the FDA to prohibit the encroachment of authorized generics on that exclusivity. The denial of Mylan's petition therefore was not "arbitrary, capricious . . . or otherwise not in accordance with law," and the district court correctly dismissed the case. The judgment of the district court is therefore affirmed.

NOTES

1. What happened to exclusivity? At several points the Hatch–Waxman Act describes the 180–day timeframe as an "exclusivity period." *See* 21 U.S.C. § 355(j)(5)(B)(iv) (2004) (repetitively using the term "180–day exclusivity period"). Does the Fourth Circuit's ruling render this phrasing a curious drafting choice? Do you believe Congress intended this result?

2. Broader Currents. Notably, whether the 180–day exclusivity period strikes an appropriate balance between encouraging patent challenges and ensuring prompt access to generic medications is itself a contested proposition within the pharmaceutical industry. Requiring patients to compensate generic drug companies for correcting the PTO's mistakes is for many observers a poor intellectual property policy choice. Others are more disturbed by the prospect of one industry competitor being able unilaterally to deny another with what is essentially a mini-patent. For further discussion of authorized generics, see Thomas Chen, *Authorized Generics: A Prescription for Hatch–Waxman Reform*, 93 VA. L. REV. 438 (2007).

§ 14.6 EXERCISES

1. Which sorts of patents may be listed in the Orange Book?
   a. active ingredient
   b. formulation
   c. method of making
   d. method of medical treatment
2. In patent infringement litigation under the Hatch–Waxman Act, the asserted patent is compared to what accused infringement?
   a. the product sold by the generic firm
   b. a generic drug is presumed to infringe, so the only litigated issues concern the enforceability and validity of the patent
   c. the proposed product described by the ANDA
   d. samples of the generic drug taken from the accused infringer's manufacturing facilities
3. Authorized generics are said to defeat which incentive provided under the Hatch–Waxman Act?
   a. 180–day period of generic exclusivity
   b. 30–month stay of FDA marketing approval
   c. 6–month period of pediatric exclusivity
   d. 5–year period of New Chemical Entity data exclusivity

4. Two generic firms file paragraph IV ANDAs with the FDA on the earliest possible date allowed by the Hatch–Waxman Act. Which is considered to be a "first filer" eligible for the 180–day generic exclusivity period?
   a. neither one
   b. both
   c. the firm that was the earlier to submit its application on that date, considering the exact time of day
   d. the first filer is determined randomly

5. What is the maximum period of term extension provided by the Hatch–Waxman Act?
   a. 3 years
   b. 5 years
   c. 14 years
   d. 15 years

*

INDEX

References are to Pages

971

†